ALASKA
& THE PACIFIC NORTHWEST
INCLUDING WESTERN CANADA
2003

BENJAMIN G. WELLS EDITOR

ROBERT J. DUBBIN ASSOCIATE EDITOR

RESEARCHER-WRITERS
POSY BUSBY
CARLETON GOOLD
CATHERINE GOWL
SARAH MURPHY
JAMES PINTO
GREG SCHMELLER

ABIGAIL BURGER MANAGING EDITOR
NATHANIEL R. BROOKS MAP EDITOR
CALEB S. EPPS TYPESETTER

MACMILLAN

HELPING LET'S GO If you want to share your discoveries, suggestions, or corrections, please drop us a line. We read every piece of correspondence, whether a postcard, a 10-page email, or a coconut. Please note that mail received after May 2003 may be too late for the 2004 book, but will be kept for future editions. **Address mail to:**

> **Let's Go: Alaska & The Pacific Northwest**
> **67 Mount Auburn Street**
> **Cambridge, MA 02138**
> **USA**

Visit Let's Go at **http://www.letsgo.com,** or send email to:

> **feedback@letsgo.com**
> **Subject: "Let's Go: Alaska & The Pacific Northwest"**

In addition to the invaluable travel advice our readers share with us, many are kind enough to offer their services as researchers or editors. Unfortunately, our charter enables us to employ only currently enrolled Harvard students.

Published in Great Britain 2003 by Macmillan, an imprint of Pan Macmillan Ltd.
20 New Wharf Road, London N1 9RR
Basingstoke and Oxford
Associated companies throughout the world
www.panmacmillan.com

Maps by David Lindroth copyright © 2003 by St. Martin's Press.

Published in the United States of America by St. Martin's Press.

ISBN: 1-4050-0052 X
First edition
10 9 8 7 6 5 4 3 2 1

Let's Go: Alaska & The Pacific Northwest is written by Let's Go Publications, 67 Mount Auburn Street, Cambridge, MA 02138, USA.

Let's Go® and the LG logo are trademarks of Let's Go, Inc.
Printed in the USA on recycled paper with soy ink.

HOW TO USE THIS BOOK

ORGANIZATION. The first three chapters of the book are designed to familiarize you with the Pacific Northwest and prepare you to visit. After that, we begin in **Oregon,** traveling up the **US Pacific Coast** until we reach **Washington.** From there, our coverage enters **Canada** via **British Columbia,** making a detour to visit **Alberta** before taking a deep breath and heading into the **Yukon Territory.** All that's left to cover is **Alaska,** which we do in two parts; first, you'll see the **Alaskan Panhandle,** and then we'll finish up in **Central Alaska.**

PRICE RANGES AND RANKINGS. Our researchers list establishments in order of value from best to worst. Our absolute favorites are denoted by the Let's Go thumbs-up (🖐). Since the best value does not always mean the cheapest price, we have incorporated a system of price ranges in the guide. The table below lists how prices fall within each bracket.

PACIFIC NW	❶	❷	❸	❹	❺
ACCOMMODATIONS	$1-15	$16-30	$31-50	$51-80	$81+
FOOD	$1-5	$6-10	$11-15	$16-20	$21+

PHONE CODES. Area codes for each region appear opposite the name of the region and are denoted by the ☎ icon.

WHEN TO USE IT

TWO MONTHS BEFORE. The first chapter, **Discover Alaska and the Pacific Northwest,** contains highlights of the region; it includes Suggested Itineraries (p. 6) that can help you plan your trip, whether you want to hike the Canadian Rockies or stick to a single Oregon beach. The **Essentials** (p. 21) section contains practical information about traveling in the US and Canada, and can help you create a budget, make reservations, rent a car, renew your passport, and more.

ONE MONTH BEFORE. Take care of insurance and write down a list of emergency numbers and hotlines. Make a list of packing essentials (see **Packing,** p. 33) and shop for anything you are missing, such as camping gear or weather-appropriate clothing. Read through the coverage and make sure you understand the logistics of your itinerary (mileage, catching trains and buses, etc.). Make any reservations for camping, hostels, hotels, and B&Bs, along with any required bus, plane, boat or car reservations.

2 WEEKS BEFORE. Leave an itinerary and list of contact phone numbers with someone at home. Take some time to peruse the **unauthorized, uncensored story** of Alaska and the Pacific Northwest (see p. 10), which has info on history, culture, flora and fauna, recent political events, the entertainment industry, and more.

A NOTE TO OUR READERS

The information for this book was gathered by *Let's Go* researchers from May through August of 2002. Each listing is based on one researcher's opinion, formed during his or her visit at a particular time. Those traveling at other times may have different experiences since prices, dates, hours, and conditions are always subject to change. You are urged to check the facts presented in this book beforehand to avoid inconvenience and surprises.

CONTENTS

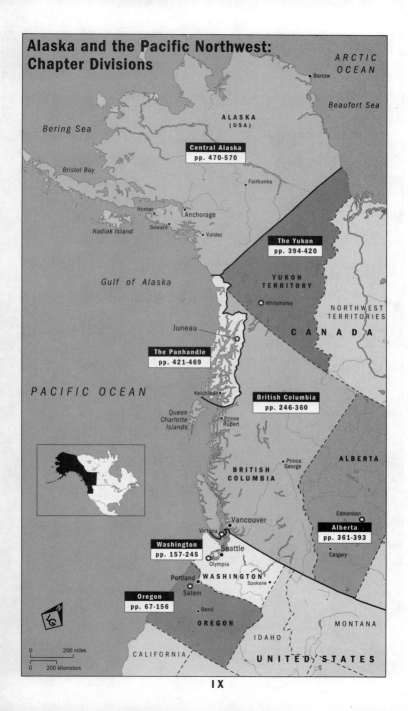

Alaska and the Pacific Northwest: Chapter Divisions

ARCTIC OCEAN

Barrow

Beaufort Sea

ALASKA (USA)

Central Alaska
pp. 470-570

Bering Sea

Bristol Bay

Fairbanks

Homer

Anchorage

Kodiak Island

Seward

Valdez

The Yukon
pp. 394-420

YUKON TERRITORY

Gulf of Alaska

Whitehorse

NORTHWEST TERRITORIES

C A N A D A

Juneau

The Panhandle
pp. 421-469

PACIFIC OCEAN

Ketchikan

British Columbia
pp. 246-360

Queen Charlotte Islands

Prince Rupert

Prince George

ALBERTA

BRITISH COLUMBIA

Vancouver

Victoria

Seattle

Edmonton

Alberta
pp. 361-393

Washington
pp. 157-245

Olympia

WASHINGTON

Spokane

Calgary

Portland

Salem

Oregon
pp. 67-156

Bend

OREGON

IDAHO

MONTANA

0   200 miles

0   200 kilometers

CALIFORNIA

UNITED STATES

X

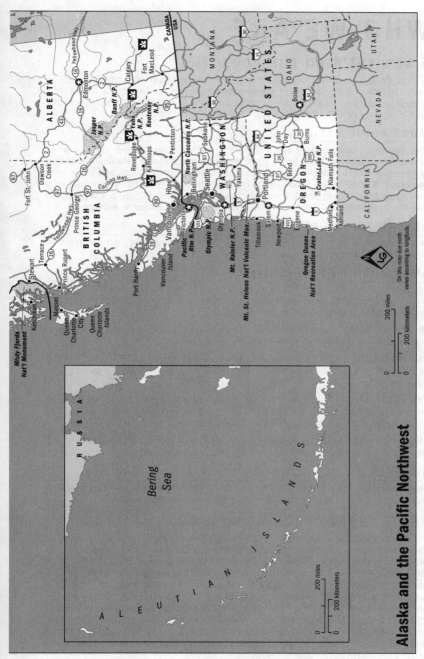

Alaska and the Pacific Northwest

XI

WHO WE ARE

A NEW LET'S GO FOR 2003

With a sleeker look and innovative new content, we have revamped the entire series to reflect more than ever the needs and interests of the independent traveler. Here are just some of the improvements you will notice when traveling with the new *Let's Go.*

MORE PRICE OPTIONS

Still the best resource for budget travelers, *Let's Go* recognizes that everyone needs the occassional indulgence. Our "Big Splurges" indicate establishments that are actually worth those extra pennies (pulas, pesos, or pounds), and price-level symbols (❶ ❷ ❸ ❹ ❺) allow you to quickly determine whether an accommodation or restaurant will break the bank. We may have diversified, but we'll never lose our budget focus—"Hidden Deals" reveal the best-kept travel secrets.

BEYOND THE TOURIST EXPERIENCE

Our Alternatives to Tourism chapter offers ideas on immersing yourself in a new community through study, work, or volunteering.

AN INSIDER'S PERSPECTIVE

As always, every item is written and researched by our on-site writers. This year we have highlighted more viewpoints to help you gain an even more thorough understanding of the places you are visiting.

IN RECENT NEWS. *Let's Go* correspondents around the globe report back on current regional issues that may affect you as a traveler.

CONTRIBUTING WRITERS. Respected scholars and former *Let's Go* writers discuss topics on society and culture, going into greater depth than the usual guidebook summary.

THE LOCAL STORY. From the Parisian monk toting a cell phone to the Russian *babushka* confronting capitalism, *Let's Go* shares its revealing conversations with local personalities—a unique glimpse of what matters to real people.

FROM THE ROAD. Always helpful and sometimes downright hilarious, our researchers share useful insights on the typical (and atypical) travel experience.

SLIMMER SIZE

Don't be fooled by our new, smaller size. *Let's Go* is still packed with invaluable travel advice, but now it's easier to carry with a more compact design.

FORTY-THREE YEARS OF WISDOM

For over four decades *Let's Go* has provided the most up-to-date information on the hippest cafes, the most pristine beaches, and the best routes from border to border. It all started in 1960 when a few well-traveled students at Harvard University handed out a 20-page mimeographed pamphlet of their tips on budget travel to passengers on student charter flights to Europe. From humble beginnings, *Let's Go* has grown to cover six continents and *Let's Go: Europe* still reigns as the world's best-selling travel guide. This year we've beefed up our coverage of Latin America with *Let's Go: Costa Rica* and *Let's Go: Chile;* on the other side of the globe, we've added *Let's Go: Thailand* and *Let's Go: Hawaii.* Our new guides bring the total number of titles to 61, each infused with the spirit of adventure that travelers around the world have come to count on.

RESEARCHER-WRITERS

Posy Busby   *Washington, British Columbia*

An avid hiker, biker, and outdoorswoman, Posy brought the discerning eye of an Environmental Science and Public Policy major to Washington and BC. Moving from the biggest of cities to the remotest of forests, Posy handled everything Seattle, the North Cascades, and the rest her route threw at her with cheery aplomb, using her inside knowledge as an Oregon native to send back polished, insightful copybatches.

Carleton Goold   *Oregon, Washington*

A two-time member of the US Junior National Whitewater Slalom Kayaking team and a former extreme kayak racer, Carleton brought considerable experience to bear in the mountains and on the rivers of Oregon and Washington. Not even a horrible case of poison oak could keep him from pursuing his research with a tenacity unlikely to be matched at *Let's Go* for years to come. Carleton truly made Oregon his own.

Catherine Gowl   *The Alaska Panhandle*

From the moment Catherine set foot in Alaska, everything was looking up. She revamped coverage of the Panhandle, gaining a knowledge and love of the state as comprehensive as any native's. She made it all the way from Juneau to Prudhoe without a hitch, all the while sending back copy clearly written with the passion of a History and Literature major—pages of notes and plenty of great stories to keep everyone entertained.

Sarah Murphy   *Central Alaska*

Equally comfortable fishing for salmon on the Kenai River and braving changing weather conditions around Denali, Sarah never found an outdoor activity she couldn't handle. That stands to reason; a true-blue sourdough, she's lived in Alaska her entire life, and her perspective as a native helped us enrich this book immeasurably and helped her survive a close encounter with a Kodiak brown bear.

James Pinto   *Washington, British Columbia, Alberta*

Fresh off his cross-country journey to the Pacific Northwest, James immediately took to the backcountry and got the most out of every park he visited. An expert at finding both little-known hiking routes and gorgeous (and free) places to camp, James used his extensive wilderness experience to focus on what he considered the true allure of the Pacific Northwest, and the result is expanded insider coverage in several major areas.

Greg Schmeller   *British Columbia, the Yukon Territory*

A native of Oregon, Greg drove his trusty steed to the farthest reaches of the Yukon and back, shrugging off engine failures, flat tires, and dead batteries along the way with extreme competence. His series of morality plays became the stuff of office legend, and did indeed inspire us to "secure him monies." Not even a charging moose could stop Greg, who was the definition of hard core during his 7-week odyssey.

CONTRIBUTING WRITERS

Mandy Davis was a Researcher-Writer for *Let's Go: Ireland 2001*. She lived in Ketchikan, Alaska for 18 years, and has written for the Ketchikan Daily News. She now works in Seattle in a Japanese print gallery.

Nathaniel Brooks, a native of Homer, Alaska, is the Map Editor for this book. He was a Researcher-Writer for *Let's Go: Peru, Ecuador, and Bolivia 2002,* and has traveled extensively throughout Alaska and the Pacific Northwest and Europe.

ACKNOWLEDGMENTS

THE TEAM THANKS Abi for catching our many mistkaes, all of our proofers, Nitin and Ariel, Nathaniel for not letting us forget about maps, and Trader Joe's for their high quality standards. We'd also like to thank Neil Diamond and Robert Goulet, for reasons they're well aware of.

WELLS THANKS the best team of researchers in the series—you guys made our job infinitely easier. Many thanks to Abi, our amazing ME, for saving our book by catching every time we messed up, and Dubbin for saving me from technological hell—not to mention making me laugh like the idiot that I am. Nathaniel, for improving our maps 1000 times and being a great guy. Team California, team Southwest, and team USA—the best group of people I could think of working with. You guys kept me (relatively) sane this summer. Thanks to 4A Hingham St. for not evicting me when I was never around, and LG for keeping an eye on me and at least trying to make sure I ate, slept, and left the basement occasionally. 44 JFK for always giving me somewhere to go and people to hang out with when I actually left the office. Digamma. Mom, Dad, John, and Dan, for putting up with me all summer and for the past 20 years—you guys always help me keep things in perspective. And Shilla, for giving me all the love and support I could ask for and then some—you made this the best summer of my life. I love you.

ROB THANKS his group of wicked awesome researchers. Sarah, James, Carleton, Catherine, Greg and Posy: I know it's hard to put 3 months of travel into guide form, but I'll be impressed forever by the job you guys did. Innumerable thanks go to Abi for her care and meticulousness, to Than for his candor and mappiness, to Nitin and Ariel for their willingness to let me throw things at them (selflessness), Eli for somethingorother, Mrs. Wells for her thoughtfulness, and Larry Coker. Special hugs and kisses for my friends at the Harvard Lampoon. This book would never have been finished without Joe Hickey. Thanks to Shilla for making Ben sound funny when he answered the phone, and to Ben for being a heap and half of fun to work with, not to mention the greatest technological computer genius who has ever walked the earth. Up high To Brian, Marty, Ari, and especially Frank: sorry this book kept me in debtor's prison at the end of things. Nicole, I need to take you to some of these places... maybe (see p. 103), or (see p. 404), or (see p. 484). You're the only person I can think of who would make them more beautiful than they already are. Mom, Dad, Jeff, Andy, and Emmit: I missed you this summer—to the extent that I can dedicate anything, this book is for you guys. Tonight's winning lotto numbers are: ❸❾❷❶❸❹

NATHANIEL THANKS: My superstar RWs, who took cartography in stride and went right on redefining the term hard-core. J-Dawg for keeping me ramen-free. N-Dawg for the occasional loan his letter and, last but not least, the doughty duo who helmed A&P to greatness: Wells and Dubbin, collectively the man.

Editor
Benjamin G. Wells
Associate Editor
Robert J. Dubbin
Managing Editor
Abigail Burger
Map Editor
Nathaniel R. Brooks
Morality Playwright
Greg Schmeller

LET'S GO

Publishing Director
Matthew Gibson
Editor-in-Chief
Brian R. Walsh
Production Manager
C. Winslow Clayton
Cartography Manager
Julie Stephens
Design Manager
Amy Cain
Editorial Managers
Christopher Blazejewski,
Abigail Burger, D. Cody Dydek,
Harriett Green, Angela Mi Young Hur,
Marla Kaplan, Celeste Ng
Financial Manager
Noah Askin
Marketing & Publicity Managers
Michelle Bowman, Adam M. Grant
New Media Managers
Jesse Tov, Kevin Yip
Online Manager
Amélie Cherlin
Personnel Managers
Alex Leichtman, Owen Robinson
Production Associates
Caleb Epps, David Muehlke
Network Administrators
Steven Aponte, Eduardo Montoya
Design Associate
Juice Fong
Financial Assistant
Suzanne Siu
Office Coordinators
Alex Ewing, Adam Kline,
Efrat Kussell

Director of Advertising Sales
Erik Patton
Senior Advertising Associates
Patrick Donovan, Barbara Eghan,
Fernanda Winthrop
Advertising Artwork Editor
Leif Holtzman
Cover Photo Research
Laura Wyss

President
Bradley J. Olson
General Manager
Robert B. Rombauer
Assistant General Manager
Anne E. Chisholm

PDAs & Travel

DISCOVER ALASKA & THE PACIFIC NORTHWEST

From the dense, misty rainforests of Oregon to the last desolate, treeless island in the Aleutian chain, North America's northwest coast is a land of staggering natural beauty. Along the coast, sharp young peaks soar skyward from the water's edge, spilling pieces of glacier into the ocean at their bases. Human settlements of varying sizes and degrees of polish mark the spots where rivers meet the coast, pointing the way to the country's interior. There, peaks give way to sometimes arable land, desert, tundra, and more mountains, peppered with more cities and towns.

For thousands of years, human settlement in the region has relied on natural resources. In the last two hundred years, human activities have significantly impacted the land—enthusiastic logging, mining, and fishing proved the land isn't inexhaustible—but the birth of the environmental spirit in the late 20th century is revitalizing the region's natural charm. That spirit (visible in the adoption of sustainable practices by resource-based industries) and the explosive growth of tourism (dependent on the beauty of the region's forests) have helped modern governments see old-growth forests as something more than raw lumber.

While you are assured of seeing many visitors wherever you go, with a minimum of effort you are just as able to lose the crowds. For example, while Banff National Park, in the Rockies, welcomes five million visitors a year, the right dayhike—or a visit to one of the park's lesser-known neighbors—is all it takes to find solitude. For those overwhelmed by the boundless backcountry, welcoming hostels, quirky communities, and laid-back cities anchor the wilderness.

Winter visits promise hundreds of miles of skiing, snowboarding, snowshoeing, and snowmachining out of snow-bound cities. Farther south along the coast, winter is more wet than white, and the litany of snow sports is restricted to higher elevations.

However audacious it is to cram this many miles of coast and this deep an interior into a single book, the present attempt is culled from what our researchers insisted they would do again if they could turn around and do their trips over. The sample itineraries that follow are intended to help you picture what your own trip might look like. For practical trip-planning resources, including campground reservation numbers, road reports, climate charts, Internet resources, and preferred outdoor publishing companies, see the **Essentials** (p. 21) chapter, and begin thumbing through the rest of *Let's Go: Alaska and the Pacific Northwest 2003*.

WHEN TO GO

In general, tourist season in the US and Canada runs from late May to early September. In Canada, the beginning is marked by the Victoria Day long weekend; in the US, the Memorial Day long weekend. Summer ends with the Labour/Labor Day long weekend at the beginning of September. In the off season, accommodations may be cheaper and less crowded, but sights you traveled so far to see may also be closed, and camping is not nearly as pleasant. On national holidays, many sights and all banks and government offices will be closed, and transportation may run on restricted schedules. The coastal cities are justly famous for rain, which pours down 10 months of the year, and the same ocean that produces all that precipitation keeps coastal temperatures moderate year-round. In Portland and Vancouver, a few snow days a year are the norm, but the white stuff doesn't stick around for long. To the east of the coastal mountains, expect less precipitation, warmer summers, and colder winters. The same variation is experienced up north, only on a shifted scale—winters in the interior of the Yukon and Alaska are bitterly cold, while summers are decidedly cool. As in the south, things are more even on the coast, with plenty of rain (liquid sunshine, as some coastal residents call it).

NATIONAL HOLIDAYS

USA	
Date in 2003	**Holiday**
January 1	New Year's Day
January 20	Martin Luther King, Jr. Day
February 17	Presidents' Day
May 26	Memorial Day
July 4	Independence Day
September 1	Labor Day
October 13	Columbus Day
November 11	Veterans Day
November 27	Thanksgiving
December 25	Christmas Day

CANADA	
Date in 2003	**Holiday**
January 1	New Year's Day
April 20	Easter Sunday
April 21	Easter Monday
May 19	Victoria Day
July 1	Canada Day
September 1	Labour Day
October 13	Thanksgiving
November 11	Remembrance Day
December 25	Christmas Day
December 26	Boxing Day

MEET YOUR TERRITORY: AN INTRODUCTION IN FACTS AND FIGURES

OREGON: FOR THE YOUNG AND THE "SPIRITED."

Best place to feel the spirit: Portland, the city with more microbreweries than any other.

Deepest lake in the US: Crater Lake.

Deepest river gorge in North America: Hell's Canyon.

WASHINGTON: BETTER THAN CALIFORNIA, DARNIT.

Number of wineries in 1981: 19. Number of wineries in 2001: 160.

Though (grrr) second in premium wine production in the US, Washington boasts more awards and competitions proportional to its production than any other wine region in the world. And they have sunlight 2hr. longer per day than California. And they receive more rain than California.

BRITISH COLUMBIA: THERE ARE BEARS HERE.

British Columbia's rank among the film and TV production centers in the world: 3.

Number of films shot in British Columbia in year 2000: 192.

Total area in square kilometers of California: 400,000.

Total area in square kilometers of British Columbia: 950,000. Booyah!

ALBERTA: "STRONG AND FREE." AND HITTING ITS GROOVE.

Number 1 export: oil. Number 2 export: marijuana. Number 3 export: Do you really need anything else? Number 1 import: Fritos.

Km of road: 180,000. Km of paved roads: 31,000. Km of pipelines for oil: 184,000.

YUKON: YES, YUKON.

Lowest temperature ever recorded in Canada: -62.8°C (northwest of Kluane Lake).

Most famous resident: Jack London.

Close runners-up: Klondike Kate and the Yukon Dancehall Girls (Diamond Tooth Gertie, Mollie Fewclothes, Nellie the Pig, Ethel the Moose, and Snake-hips Lulu).

ALASKA: LAND OF THE BIG AND HARD CORE.

17 of the 20 highest peaks in the US are in Alaska, and the longest river in North America is the 2000-mile Yukon River. Alaska has more active glaciers and icefields than any other place in the inhabited world, including the Malespina glacier, which spans 850 sq. mi. Come, all ye adventurers, and she will give you risks, and maybe frostbite too.

THINGS TO DO

ON FOOT

The vast scenic lands in Alaska and the Pacific Northwest provide hikers with limitless opportunities. Known for its natural beauty, impressive landscape, and sparkling clean waters, this region is arguably the most desirable place in North America to hit the trails. The national, provincial, and state parks provide some of the best and most varied hiking anywhere and are well-staffed, well-maintained, and well worth it. Reading the **Outdoor Activities** sections of a few parks should give a sense of the possibilities. Popular destinations often limit the number of visitors, campsites may be hard to secure, and crowds will surely be on hand, one need not be in a designated park to enjoy the outdoors in the Northwest. Trails through virgin lands more beautiful than you can imagine abound. Contact the visitors center in your specific area for more info on how to break fresh ground. Experienced hikers may wish to consider the following multi-day (month) hikes:

CHILKOOT TRAIL. This three- to five-day (33 mi./53km) hike starts in Skagway, AK, and passes through a range of dramatic climates, terrain, and vegetation, both above and below treeline, on its way through the interior. Originally a trade route protected by the Tagish and Tlingit people, the trail was the route to the Interior during the Yukon gold rush of the 1890s. For more info, see p. 404.

PACIFIC CREST TRAIL. This 2650 mi./4260km trail stretches from California's border with Mexico to Washington's border with Canada. First explored in the 1930s, the system of trails is now a federally protected Scenic Trail that takes five to six months to hike. Pick up the trail in any of the national parks along the range or in the Columbia River Gorge (see p. 89). The Pacific Crest Trail Association (PCTA) maintains the trail and sells comprehensive trail guides, videos, and PCTA mouse pads on its website. (☎916-349-2109; www.pcta.org. Call 888-728-7245 for free info pack or trail condition report.)

WEST COAST TRAIL. This spectacular trail winds through 48 mi./77km (five to seven days) of coastal forest and beach along the Pacific Ocean in the Pacific Rim National Park on the west coast of Vancouver Island. Reservations are necessary to hike the trail. (See p. 278 for info.)

ON WATER

Rivers, lakes, and ocean throughout the Northwest provide kayakers, canoeists, surfers, and plenty of rafters with more than enough opportunity to exercise their paddling urges.

Rafting is the most accessible water sport to novices, and is wildly popular in both the US and Canada. Most of Oregon's commercial trips float on the beautiful **Rogue** (see Grants Pass, p. 128) and **Deschutes** (see Bend, p. 143) rivers. Interior BC offers adrenaline rush runs on **Adam's River** (p. 300), in the Shuswap. In Jasper, two rivers present prime rafting: the **Athabasca** and the faster **Sunwapta** (p. 386). Expect professionalism from a rafting outfit. If the rafts have patches, the life jacket supply is sparse, or the paddles are different shapes and sizes, you may want to take your business elsewhere.

Kayaking in Alaska's rivers and oceans couldn't be finer (unless the water were a little warmer). The small boat allows almost unlimited access to the coastline, and is perfect for investigating small coves and inlets and losing the cruise ship crowd. The West Coast of Vancouver Island, particularly **The Broken Islands,** (p. 280), is another popular place to explore by kayak.

Alaska doesn't jump to mind for water sports that entail being *in* the water, but **Cordova** (p. 497) and **Yakutat** (p. 467) are places that both should. Both offer **surfers** incredible breaks, with Yakutat giving a bit bigger ride on a stunning black beach. **Long Beach** and **Cox Beach,** in Pacific Rim National Park, (p. 277), offer sweet rides in BC. Seward, AK offers the ultimate in cold-water fun. In the third weekend in January, the **Polar Bear Jump** (p. 501), brings bravado to the fore when residents plunge into the ice waters to raise funds for cancer research; don't lose face by using a wet-suit. The best medicine for the icy Pacific is to bear inland to the many **hot springs.** An ideal place to warm up or to soothe aching muscles, this natural phenomenon is a favorite pastime. For a start, try **Cougar Hot Springs** in Eugene, OR (p. 121), **Canyon Hot Springs,** in Revelstoke, BC (p. 331), or **Hot Springs Cove** in the Pacific Rim National Park in BC (p. 277).

Nothing makes a better combination in the Northwest than water and wind. The gods smiled fondly on **Columbia River Gorge** (p. 89), blessing it with a river, gracing it with steep canyons, and consecrating it with a howling wind. Out of this, the **windsurfing** cult arose. Although the Gorge is eminent in the minds of windsurfers, other sites abound, by virtue of good breeze off the Pacific and moderate weather.

ON SNOW

The skiing and riding (snowboarding) in the northern Rockies, the Cascades, and Coast range are some of North America's best. The biggest and best mega-resort is **Whistler-Blackcomb,** p. 265, a 1½hr. drive north of Vancouver, BC, which draws nearly two million international visitors per year. Most remarkable about the skiing, though, is that many great areas are only minutes from urban centers. Hostels in Washington, Oregon, Alberta, and BC all offer ski-and-stay packages. **Fernie Alpine Resort,** (p. 313), is working to gain the title of megalith; with its new expansion, the resort now covers more than 2500 acres. The sleeper resort to watch is **Powder Springs Resort** (p. 331), in Revelstoke. With the largest vertical drop in North America and the interest of an Austrian family that already owns 36 resorts in Europe, it may only be a matter of time until Powder Springs becomes another Whistler. Much to the joy of snowboarders across North America, ski hills have finally accepted that riders are here to stay. Valdez, AK hosts the **King and Queen of the Hill Snowboard Competition** (p. 491) to pay homage to the sport. The **World Extreme Skiing Championship** also takes place in Valdez. **Cross-country skiing** tends to get overshadowed by its vertical counterparts in the Northwest, but dump tons of snow on beautiful hiking trails, and what do you get but miles and miles of pristine skiing trails.

ON CRACK

In the past decade, outdoor sports have battled to top the thrill that plain old Mother Nature provides. Pain often seems to be a requisite for the rating of extreme. The **Chad Ogden Ultramarathon** (p. 516) is a 43 mi. race from Chiniak to Kodiak, AK that truly tests the mettle of racers. The **Ski to Sea Race** (p. 192) in Bellingham, WA, on Memorial Day weekend, is the mother of all relays with skiing, running, canoeing, and kayaking stages covering the terrain from Mt. Baker to Bellingham Bay. Golf is taken to extremes at the **Mt. Fairweather** (p. 455) course in Gustavus, AK. A measly nine holes gains its reputation as hard-core because it is open year-round. Defy gravity in Nanaimo, BC at the **Bungy Zone** (p. 284), and defy it again at the **Skaha Bluffs, BC** (p. 305), with phenomenal rock climbing. Firefighters train to sky-dive into forest fires at the **Smoke Jumpers Base** (p. 241), between Winthrop and Twisp, WA. You can off-road on the **Sand Dunes** (p. 109), along the coast of Oregon or **ski *sans* snow** (p. 327), in August on the sandy bluffs of the Nechako Cutbanks, in Prince George, BC.

⚑ LET'S GO PICKS

BEST SPORTING EVENTS: Catch a **baseball game** under the midnight sun on the solstice itself in Fairbanks, AK. The **Mountain Marathon,** in Seward, AK (p. 501), cuts to the chase, ascending 3000 ft. in 45min., while the **Equinox Marathon** in Fairbanks (p. 547) is considered one of the five hardest marathons in the country for gaining 3500 ft. over 26.2 mi.

BEST (NON-FOOT) RACES: The **Chuckwagon Derby** and the **bathtub** race highlight tests of brawn and skill during Klondike Days in Edmonton, AB (p. 366).

BEST BICYCLE RIDE: Through breathtaking glaciers from Jasper to Banff along the **Icefields Parkway** (p. 385).

BEST BOOKSTORE: Cavernous **Powell's City of Books** swallows patrons in hallowed book-lined walls (p. 79).

BEST WAY TO GET HIGH: Scale the infamous **Denali** (p. 534).

SECOND BEST WAY TO GET HIGH: Matanuska Valley Thunderfuck is incredibly potent, although *Let's Go* does not endorse using illegal substances for relaxation (p. 479).

BEST ANIMAL ENCOUNTERS: Get intimate with buffalo skeletons at **Head-Smashed-in Buffalo Jump,** AB (p. 373) to learn how a native tribe could destroy a herd of buffalo in an afternoon. In the land of winter, what would replace the earthworm, but the **iceworm?** Rangers in Portage dispel myths about the wee beasties who call glaciers home (p. 482). Cordova honors them with an annual Ice Worm Festival in February (p. 497).

BEST WAY TO RUB ELBOWS WITH STAR ATHLETES: As deadweight in his sled, you can be part of the training for Mitch Seavey's dogs as they get in shape for the famous **Iditarod** (p. 506).

BEST ILLEGAL FISHING: When the **Childs Glacier** calves, waves are sent up into the surrounding forest, stranding fish in the trees. Look but don't touch—it's illegal to harvest these beauties (p. 497).

BEST PLACE TO FIND ALLIGATOR SKIN BOOTS: Undoubtedly, **The Stampede** in Calgary, where locals celebrate their rough-and-tumble heritage (p. 372).

NATIVE CULTURE

The Northwest is home to some of the finest exhibits of Native American and First Nation (the preferred terms for the indigenous people of the US and Canada, respectively) culture on the continent, and is the birthplace of some of their most popular traditions, such as potlatch, cedar carving, and long houses. While native cultures in the Northwest have not entirely escaped the persecution that have encountered throughout North America, many tribes and customs still thrive. Major museums in the region are the **Royal British Columbia Museum** in Victoria, BC (p. 268); the **Museum of Anthropology** in Vancouver, BC (p. 260); and the **Museum at Warm Springs,** OR (p. 3). Unfortunately, museums often give a sterile feeling to native cultures. For a livelier experience, watch a performance by the **Alutiiq Dancers** (p. 516), wander mist-shrouded **totem poles** in Ketchikan, AK (p. 421), or visit the **petroglyphs** on the beach in Wrangell, AK (p. 434). For more options, the Alaska Native Brotherhood halls are good resources for events and demonstrations.

BREWERIES AND VINEYARDS

Up and down the coast of Washington and Oregon, small companies turn out unique beverages that have won more awards per liter of output than any state in the Union. The wine counter-culture is on the upswing—wine bars are cropping up and wine tastings are becoming an institution. In Washington, **Spokane** (p. 241),

Salem (p. 117), and **Lopez Island** (p. 202), have more than their fair share of vintners. In the fertile crescent of Interior BC, **Kelowna** (p. 301), and **Penticton** (p. 305), harbor prize-winning vintages. Stop by Kelowna for the **Okanagan Wine Festival** in October. A must-see for true connoisseurs is the **Shallon winery** in Astoria, p. 94, to sample rarities such as lemon meringue pie wine.

Beer rules the roost in Alaska. Fairbanks (p. 547), hosts the Alaskan Microbrew Festival, celebrating the finer craft of small-scale production. Haines hosts its own homage to hops at the Craft Beer and Home Brew Festival (p. 457). Small breweries are open for tours: try the Skagway Brewing Co., in Skagway (p. 462). In the lower 48 visit the Oregon Brewers Guild (p. 69), in Portland (the city with the most microbreweries in the US) and the Rogue Ale Brewery (p. 107), in Newport.

SUGGESTED ITINERARIES

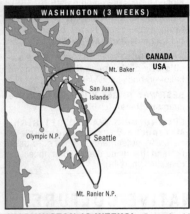

OREGON (2 WEEKS). Any journey through Oregon should begin and end in **Portland** (4 days, p. 69). Visitors could wile away weeks in this phenomenal city that combines cosmopolitan flare, crunchy outdoors, and youthful money. After satisfying the city dweller in you, embark on the open road to venture into the **Columbia River Gorge** (2 days, p. 89), where you can trade the car in for a surfboard and let loose on windsurfing heaven. Venture into the hot interior, visiting the **John Day Fossil Beds** (1 day, p. 155), where fossilized remains of tropical rainforests defy the naked eye. The unusual landscape continues at **Klamath Falls**, where **Crater Lake** plunges to a depth of 1932 feet (1 day, p. 143). Unfortunately it's forbidden to swim in the lake. Withdrawing from the rugged outdoors, stop into **Ashland** (2 days, p. 130) to sample some of the country's best Shakespeare. Gradually meander back up the coast to Portland on US 101, with stops to play in the sand and surf (2 days), making sure to ride the waves of land in **Oregon Dunes**, a mecca for sand-surfing.

WASHINGTON (3 WEEKS). Seattle (1 week, p. 157) creates its own small cosmos revolving and pulsing to the beat of the city. Head south to **Mt. Rainier National Park** (4 days, pg. 214), home to the most technical climb in the continental US and a multitude of fantastic views and dayhikes. Jump on a ferry with a small bag to spend several days hopping between the **San Juan Islands** (5 days, p. 194) and their beautiful beaches. This archipelago is perfect for kayaking. Touch base in Seattle to provision for a journey to **Mt. Baker** (3 days, p. 193). A mecca for skiing in the winter, it provides gorgeous vistas, challenging hikes, and breathtaking drives for summer visitors. A final must-see stop is the **Olympic National Park** (5 days, p. 203), an outdoor-lover's playground; true solace can be found within its rugged boundaries.

BRITISH COLUMBIA AND ALBERTA
(4 WEEKS)

DESOLATION (2-3 WEEKS)

BRITISH COLUMBIA AND ALBERTA (4 WEEKS).

When discovering western Canada, there is no better starting point than British Columbia's biggest metropolis, **Vancouver** (5 days, p. 246), which features a variety of sights and exciting nightlife. After you've had enough of the big city, trek out to **Whistler** (4 days, p. 265); don't forget to pack the skis. Together with Blackcomb, these sister mountains provide some of North America's best downhill runs. Start the National Parks escapade in **Revelstoke** (2 days, p. 331), a favorite with hikers and bikers, before heading to **Banff** (3 days, p. 376) and **Jasper National Parks** (3 days, p. 386). The **Icefields Pkwy.** accesses major portions of both parks. While hiking is the premier activity, climbing, kayaking, and rafting also keep the outdoor-lover satisfied. Strike west on the Yellowhead Hwy. to **Bella Coola**. Stay overnight here before hopping on a ferry to **Port Hardy** (2 days), on the northern tip of Vancouver Island. Meander to the southern tip, and visit the **Pacific Rim National Park** (3 days, p. 277). Perched on the sea, this park has an entirely different landscape than the inland parks. Meander down Hwy. 19, stopping in towns such as **Campbell River** and **Nanaimo** (2 days). Finally, allow at least four days for **Victoria**, at the southern tip of the island. In the most British-feeling city in British Columbia, you'll definitely want to experience high tea.

DESOLATION (2-3 WEEKS, DEPENDING ON YOUR PACE).

The Northwest is inundated with tourists for the summer. All it takes to get away is a car and the backroads. Fly into **Edmonton** (p. 361) to overstep Calgary's mobs, and go north. Cut across the AB/BC border and sojourn in **Dawson Creek** (p. 356). Get onboard the **Alaska Hwy.** (p. 356) to get the scenic overhaul of northern BC. Stop in towns like **Fort Nelson** (p. 359) for eats and shut-eye only: the drive *is* the attraction. **Whitehorse** (p. 400) is the biggest town you'll see after leaving Edmonton. Make a final stop in **Dawson City** (p. 410) to provision for the drive up the **Dempster** (p. 416). The 12hr. drive on brutal gravel is bound to torment tires. At the end of the road is **Inuvik** (p. 419), where you can stop and dip your toes into the Beaufort Sea. Flightseeing to **Tuktoyaktuk** brings you within sight of the polar caps.

CENTRAL ALASKA AND THE NORTHERN YUKON (3 WEEKS).

Anchorage (3 days, p. 471) is the hub of the largest state in the US. While not a metropolis by "continental" US standards, Anchorage has a couple of great museums, entertainment options, and jaw-dropping views. Outside

CENTRAL ALASKA AND THE
NORTHERN YUKON (3 WEEKS)

THE PANHANDLE (2 WEEKS)

Anchorage is **Denali National Park** (3 days, p. 534), home to the largest peak in North America, Mt. McKinley. Arguably the world's most amazing sight, Denali (as locals call it) alone will make your trip worthwhile. After glimpsing the giant, drive north to **Fairbanks** (4 days, p. 547), North America's northernmost hub, where there is a remarkable amount going on in and around town. It can be a base for rugged adventures to Arctic places such as **Barrow** and **Prudoe Bay.** From Fairbanks, gear up to take in small-town Alaska and experience the "Alaska effect"—things on the map are farther than they appear. Travel southeast on Rte. 2, and across the Canadian border to Kluane National Park, which is part of one of the world's largest protected wilderness areas. Be prepared for Dall sheep, bald eagles, large glaciers, and untouched landscape (1 week). Finish your trip in nearby **Whitehorse** (4 days, p. 400), the Yukon's largest city.

THE PANHANDLE (2 WEEKS). The Panhandle is best enjoyed afloat. Fly into **Seattle,** and bus up to **Bellingham** (p. 190). Get on board the **Alaska Marine Hwy.** for the trip to **Juneau** (3 days). In Juneau, set up base camp (3 days, p. 447). The plethora of ferries and prop planes connect the inlets, islands, and coves of the Panhandle. Visit **Glacier Bay National Park** for beautiful kayaking (3 days, p. 455). **Ketchikan** (2 days, p. 421) has priceless totem poles and a long house waiting to be explored. The **Misty Fjords** (1 day, p. 431) is another national park begging for your attention. Fly to **Prince Rupert** and from there embark on the ferry to the **Queen Charlotte Islands** (4 days, p. 338), affectionately dubbed the 'Canadian Galapagos.' There you can visit one of the most vibrant native communities in Canada. The **Gwaii Haanas National Park Reserve** and portions of Moresby have been declared a World Heritage Site by UNESCO, and will give you a flavor of the Northwest before Europeans arrived.

DISCOVER

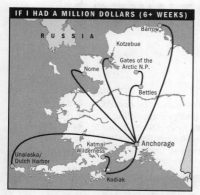

IF I HAD A MILLION DOLLARS (6+ WEEKS)

one of the finest routes in the state. **The Aleutian Islands** (p. 521) stretch into nothing but dark water and storms. The islands support fewer than twenty trees, and the velvety green ridgelines of the volcanoes billowing out of the North Pacific are truly one of the most remarkable features of the Alaskan landscape.

IF I HAD A MILLION DOLLARS (6+ WEEKS). The farthest reaches of Alaska hold a tenuous position in a budget travel guide. Very few places on earth, however, can give the sense of solitude, loneliness, and insignificance that the Arctic does. To see the wildest that Alaska has to offer, base yourself in **Anchorage** (p. 471). Trips require much preparation to ensure that you are ready to tangle with Mother Nature at her wildest. The highlights of this trip are the great outdoors—cultural events are isolated up north. Hop on a plane to **Barrow** (p. 563) to visit the northernmost point of the US and to dip your toes into the **Arctic Ocean.** A trip out to **Nome** (p. 563) will put you in position to witness the Iditarod dogsledding race, which starts or finishes here on alternating years. The **Gates of the Arctic National Park** is accessible by plane from **Bettles** (p. 563). Spend some downtime in Anchorage to enjoy the city before heading out to **Kotzebue** (p. 566). For the northern native communities this serves as a trading post, but for the traveler it is also a gateway to parks well above the Arctic Circle. Flying to **Kodiak** (p. 516) brings you to a rugged town that was the first Russian capital in Alaska. Mother Nature unleashes earthquakes and tsunamis on Kodiak with frightening regularity, but mountains abound on the island, harkening to altitude junkies. **The Katmai Wilderness** (p. 513) and its Valley of 10,000 Smokes will have you reconsidering what beautiful is about in the landscape left by one of the 20th century's most cataclysmic events: the eruption of Novarupta. With a week and a kayaking or canoe partner, the **Savanoski Loop** is

PACIFIC NORTHWEST

For years different groups have fought one another for control over the resources of the Pacific Northwest, lured by the vision of sparkling waters, lush forests, unconquered mountains, and virgin wilderness. Mesmerized by its wild beauty, these groups have resorted to any means necessary for this land. The history of the Pacific Northwest is a history of these groups struggling to claim it. Meet the players in the story:

PLAYER	MOTIVATION	WEAPONS/ASSETS
Indigenous Nations	Sense of kinship with and deep respect for the land which supports them	First dibs
Settlers/Industrialists	Money (exploitation)	Big guns, little mercy
Conservationists	True love	1) Lobbyists and legislation 2) Willingness to chain selves to trees and engage in life-endangering demonstrations for cause
Tourists (You)	A few (unbelievably awesome) thrills	*Let's Go: Alaska and the Pacific Northwest*

This is not to say that each player experienced a single motivation—many who rushed to the Pacific Northwest for gold, fur, or farmland subsequently discovered and were overwhelmed by the beauty of the land—but these are their motivations distilled for the purposes of comparison, an incomplete portrait of their identities and desires. Who, then, *are* the groups and what did they really want? And who has won the battle for the Pacific Northwest? Read on, fair reader, for the exciting, tragic, and twisted story of these groups and their relationships with Alaska and the Pacific Northwest.

HISTORY

THE INDIGENOUS PEOPLE

Once upon a time, between 12,000 and 16,000 years ago, a group of nomadic hunters bravely traipsed across the (frozen) Bering Strait from Siberia into present-day Alaska and eventually moved farther south into the Pacific Northwest. True to popular imagination, many did live in igloos, use dogsleds for transport (commemorated in the **Iditarod,** see p. 477), and sustain themselves by hunting whales and other sealife. They depended on the land, but some sign of reverence for the land or other reciprocal gesture almost always accompanied these people's use of it. For example, in the Yupik tribe, the first time a young man caught a seal he freed it to secure good luck in catching more seals in the future.

The different communities—including the Aleutians, Yuits, Inuits, and Eskimos—were distinguished from one another both by their mythologies and by their languages. Some of the most common words and phrases in Inuit, the language most common among them, include:

WHAT IS THIS POTLATCH FESTIVAL? Potlatch festivals were an opportunity for villagers to exchange and display wealth, to celebrate important transitions such as adoptions or aging, and to enact stories and history. Derived from a Chinook word meaning "gift" or "giving," the potlatch was a feast marking an important event in a person's life and required that the host lavishly give of himself, even if he had no resources for daily living. The amount one gave increased the respect he garnered from the community. At intertribal potlatches, rival chiefs might destroy hundreds of blankets and canoes just to demonstrate the excesses of their wealth. Banned for some time by both US and Canadian governments as part of a policy of integration, potlatch festivals are now starting to come back.

The languages may have defined the differences among the groups, but the land created their commonalities. The rich supply of salmon and halibut sustained these communities, and daily life centered around fishing. The economy of coastal groups focused around three main subsystems, all related to fish: fishing, construction of plank houses for smoking and drying fish, and later transportation, which provided access to the fish. Almost all native groups adjusted their lifestyles according to the season, moving between different settlements that favored the harvesting of available game, fish, and living materials. The coastal culture, prevalent throughout much of the Northwest, was one of waterside villages of cedar plank houses, wooden sculptures, massive dugout canoes, and **potlatch festivals.**

ENGLISH	INUIT	ENGLISH	INUIT
How are you?	Qanuipit?	I am hungry	Kaaktunga
I am fine.	Qanuingittunga	What is it?	Una suna?
What is your name?	Kinauvit?	I am sick	Aaniajunga
I want to take your picture.	Ajjiliurumajagit	I have to use the washroom	Quisuktunga
Thank you.	Qujannamiik	Where am I?	Namiippunga?
You are welcome.	Llaali	I want to go fishing	Iqalliarumajunga

Although large-scale potlatch festivals no longer occur, another remnant of the native culture remains a defining aspect of the Pacific Northwest: the totem pole. Particularly noticeable in British Columbia, the totem pole peppers parks, sites, and tourist shops (see "Five Things You Never Should Have Learned About Totem Poles," p. 15). In their images, these poles tell the stories of families, clans, and individuals, reflecting the family-oriented organization of the tribes. These were the indigenous cultures that the Europeans encountered when they arrived.

THE EUROPEANS ARRIVE

The indigenous tribes and the land of the Pacific Northwest enjoyed an amiable relationship that was upset by the arrival of the Europeans. Instead of arriving all at once, though, the Europeans first came in the form of a few celebrated figures:

Early Russian explorers eagerly recognized the value of trading with the skilled Aleut hunters they encountered. The Aleuts eagerly parted with their otter pelts for beads that, while common to the Russians, the Aleuts saw as portals for spirits. A short while after Britain increased its trading activity in the south, a permanent Russian settlement was established on Kodiak Island. By the time of Vancouver's voyage, the Russians had gained control of the Arctic seal hunt, eliminating the need to trade with the Native Alaskans; already, a small population of Aleuts had been relocated from the Pribilof Islands, a rich seal breeding ground. In 1799 the

Russian-American Company was established in Sitka (see p. 441), and its broker-age clout was felt as far south as California. The Russians' aggressive imposition upon the Native Alaskans incited the Tlingit, a powerful coastal nation, to raze the Russians' settlement and massacre nearly every inhabitant in 1802. Two years later, the Russians returned to bombard the Tlingit fort. The Tlingit withdrew from the area after 10 days' fighting exhausted their ammunition. Prior to this intense conflict, the Europeans considered the indigenous nations autonomous and profit-able trading partners. But the coast had become a lucrative asset for a number of well-armed and well-organized outsiders. During the coming decades, it would be bargained for among England, Russia, and the US, while indigenous nations would be forced out of their role as partners in the coastal economy.

EXPLORER	YEAR	NATIONALITY	CLAIM TO FAME
Francis Drake	16th century	English	Circumnavigated the globe; claimed Oregon for the English and affectionately described the coast as wrapped in "vile, thicke, and stinking fogges."
Vitus Bering	1741	Danish, working for Russia	Led the Russians to the Aleutian Islands.
Aleksei Chirko	mid-18th century	Russian	Explored Alaska; brought reports of seals and skilled hunters to Russia, which catalyzed an interest in the fur trade.
Juan Perez and Bruno Heceta	1774-75	Spanish	Claimed Nootka Sound for Spain and re-initi-ated European interest in the Pacific North-west.
James Cook	1778	English	Searched for a polar trade route; voyaged from Oregon to Alaska's westernmost tip.
George Vancouver	1792	English	Cartographer who accompanied Cook and mapped out the Pacific Northwest; got an island and The Major City in BC named after him (see p. 246 and p. 268).
Alexander Mackenzie	1793	English	Completed an overland exploration of the Pacific Northwest.

THE EUROPEANS START TO TURN

Trade, according to most Europeans, was mutually beneficial: Europeans took valuable furs and pelts, and natives received weapons with which they could defend themselves and their property. The Europeans also brought less welcome gifts with them: smallpox, venereal infections, and other contagious diseases. Ulti-mately, this trade crippled the indigenous people's power.

CROWDING LEADS TO CONFLICT

As more people streamed into western Washington and Oregon in the middle of the 19th century, Europeans and natives had to compete not only against one another, but also against the United States. As Thomas Jefferson sensed the Brit-ish beginning to take hold of the region, he organized the first US overland explo-ration of the West, headed by **Meriwether Lewis and William Clark.** Jefferson sent the Lewis and Clark expedition west in 1804 with political, scientific, and com-mercial goals. He believed the nation that controlled the fabled Northwest Pas-sage would control the continent's destiny. Jefferson outlined many tasks, including announcing American sovereignty in the uncharted region. The team traveled from St. Louis to the Pacific Ocean and back, returning in 1806 with information about plants, animals, rivers, mountains, and native cultures. While the team did not find a northwest passage, its safe return and promising discover-ies encouraged many families to migrate west.

EIGHT THINGS THAT YOU DIDN'T KNOW ABOUT THE OREGON TRAIL:

1. One in ten people died traveling it.

2. Oxen or mules rather than horses were the animals of choice for the wagons.

3. Because their wagons were already too full, the emigrants could not sit inside them and be pulled along by the oxen. Most of them walked. Barefoot.

4. The biggest killer on the trail was cholera.

5. As trees and fuel for the fire became scarce around 1849 when the trail got crowded, travelers resorted to using buffalo dung to get their fires going.

6. Some travelers had to wait for up to two hours for a buffalo stampede to pass.

7. Most people began their journeys by loading their wagons with over a ton of cargo, but within one day of their journey, the precious possessions would be thrown out.

8. Two hundred would-be travelers signed up to ride in the wind-wagon, a forerunner of the airplane, but the contraption never got off the ground.

Hundreds departed for the West along the famed **Oregon Trail.** The trail extended from Independence, Missouri to the mouth of the Columbia River and took four to six months to travel. While the Trail offered settlers the opportunity to stake claims in unexplored lands, it also posed great risks. The journey was often filled with the hardships of poor equipment, illness, and attacks from natives. To provide for families on the frontier and the establishment of communities, the **1862 Homestead Act** made 160 acres of land available for free to any married man who would live on and cultivate the land for five years. The same act barred the ownership of land by non-whites. The argument by natives that this was their land, and therefore not the US government's to give away, failed to sway those in power. Settlers created a provisional government in 1843, lobbied for territorial status in 1848, and joined the Union as Oregon 11 years later.

HOW THE WEST WAS DOMESTICATED

Gold and oil discoveries along the West Coast in the late 19th century also supported settlement in the Northwest. These finds not only encouraged the development of cities surrounding the gold and oil but also helped supplying towns grow. For example, gold in the Klondike in 1895 drew thousands to the interior of what would be staked out as the Yukon Territory (see p. 394) three years later. Seattle (see p. 157) and Skagway (see p. 462) proudly lay claim to their roles as the Klondike's outfitters. The San Francisco gold rush precipitated the building of Portland (see p. 69), which was well positioned to supply the California town with timber and wheat. Only one territorial acquisition of the period was considered unsound. When Russia offered the sale of Alaska to the US in 1867, the icy expanse was considered a depleted resource, as evidenced by the Russians' lackluster seal trade. It was not until years later that US Secretary of State William Seward was celebrated for purchasing the vast oil field for a piddling $0.02 per acre.

By the end of the 19th century, the indigenous culture was dying rapidly. The number of newcomers flooding the land and governmental intervention forced the native peoples onto small reservations. The indigenous nations were devastated by disease, enslavement, murder, and the strain of relocation. They had begun to develop new economic patterns more dependent upon white American and British manufactured goods. Traditional means for fishing using canoes and spears were replaced by gasoline engines, power gears, and navigation with tables, compasses, and charts. Even the aggressive warrior tribes of Northwest Coast Indians never mounted a major war against the Europeans. Intimidated by the vulnerability of their coastal villages to naval gunfire, the Native Alaskans had no choice but to share the land. Unfortunately, there peaceful response was not reciprocated, and the situation turned uglier for the indigenous people.

POLICY TOWARD THE NATIVE PEOPLE

While tribes farther east were exiled from their traditional land, the indigenous people of the Pacific Northwest seem to have retained their home court advantage. While not victims of the **Kill and Banish the Indians** policy of the 16th, 17th, 18th, and early 19th centuries, they couldn't escape the **Destroy the Indians' Culture** policy of Canada and the **Take the Indians' Land** policy of the US.

From the birth of the United States until 1924, when Congress granted Native Americans citizenship, US policy consisted of a series of broken promises of land. Laws such as the **Indian Removal Act** left little doubt of the government's intentions and led to the Cherokee's forced relocation—known as the **Trail of Tears.** Conditions improved slightly with President Roosevelt's 1934 **Indian Reorganization Act,** by which indigenous communities were recognized as tribes and directed to create their own constitutions. The effect of this policy was mitigated by a subsequent reversal of policy in **Operation Relocation** (1952), in which large groups of Native Americans were relocated from reservations into cities. The gesture had an unexpected effect as, for the first time in generations, Native Americans who lived off reservations began to recognize themselves as an ethnic group against the backdrop of mainstream society. This was the beginning of the modern native revival.

The Canadian policy toward the First Nations was not any more just or kind. The **1876 Indian Act** gave the government complete control over every person that it declared to be Indian. Children were separated from their families, forbidden to speak with their siblings, and even prohibited from speaking their native language. Those who refused to submit to this policy were severely punished, and many children were physically and sexually abused. Adults were taught methods of farming untenable in many of the regions where they were attempted, and traditions of community life were disallowed. A few rights were granted after World War II, and in 1969, presaging the trend toward euphemism, the government ended the policy of **assimilation** in favor of a new policy of **integration.** By the time residential schools were closed, some as late as the 1970s, an entire generation had been raised in isolation from their land and weakened by alcoholism, poverty, and the neglect of their traditions.

Since the 1970s, tribes in both countries have been making slow gains as the descendents of their conquerors grant them more autonomy. Much of their culture is gone forever, as are most native tongues, but for many tribes in the Pacific Northwest, now is a time of renewal.

RISING AGAIN: THE INDIGENOUS PEOPLE TODAY

Native Americans make up roughly 16% of the Alaskan population, and have recently begun to assert their rights more forcefully.

NEGOTIATING WITH THE GOVERNMENT. First Nations (the indigenous people of Canada) and Native American (the indigenous people of the United States) tribes have once again begun to flourish as independent communities. Some indigenous people live on reservations within sight of cities; others have settled land claim negotiations and are living on their traditional territory and resurrecting their customs. Most indigenous communities that are federally recognized reservation tribes in the US, or administered under the Indian Act in Canada, are allowed hunting and fishing

TOP FIVE THINGS YOU NEVER SHOULD HAVE LEARNED ABOUT TOTEM POLES
because they are wrong:

1. The totems in the Pacific Northwest are thousands of years old.
The oldest date from 1835, and most are under 100 years old.

2. Totem pole carving is a disappearing art form.
After a bout in the earlier half of the 20th century in which authentic totem building virtually vanished, totem carving experienced a renaissance in the latter half.

3. Totems were built to be worshiped.
Totems tell stories and stand for particular values, people, and ideas, but they are not objects of worship.

4. The totem poles in Stanley Park (see p. 260) are fake.
They are actually authentic and among the most valuable totems in the world.

5. Totem poles were used to ward off evil spirits.
A popular myth, but a myth nonetheless.

(see p. 260)

CULTURE

rights, as well as the right to use specified lands for ceremonial purposes. Some communities seek first and foremost to preserve the cultural heritage of their traditional lands. In British Columbia, for example, Haida tribesmen oversaw the use of ancient village sites in the disputed territory of the Queen Charlotte Islands and lobbied heavily for its preservation from logging. After the federal government purchased the land, the Haida's role in the stewardship of the spectacular **Gwaii Haanas National Park Reserve** became officially recognized. The indigenous people have been working with the government to re-assert their presence and reclaim their love: the land.

THE 1960S. Throughout the 1960s, Native Alaskans watched with increasing frustration as the federal and state governments divvied up vast tracts of land that the Inuit, Aleut, Tlingit, Haida, and Athabasca had claims upon. After the discovery in 1968 of immense oil deposits in the Beaufort Sea on Alaska's northern coast, Native Alaskans increased the pressure to settle the claims that had been so long ignored and sought a share in the anticipated economic boom.

1971. The US government finally made some degree of peace with Native Alaskans, state and federal courts, and environmental groups by passing the **Alaska Native Claims Settlement Act.** Sixty thousand Native Alaskans received a total of one billion dollars and 40 million acres of land.

1993. Yukon First Nations negotiated a settlement for self-government and land claims under a general framework known as the Umbrella Final Agreement.

1997. In the **Delgamuukw** decision of 1997, the Supreme Court of Canada allowed the Wet'suwet'en and Gitksan to cite ceremony and oral tradition to prove that their use of disputed lands preceded the arrival of Europeans.

1998. Negotiations continue over issues of self-government and the right to self-determination. In August of 1998, after years of talks between government officials and the **Nisga'a** band of northern British Columbia, representatives signed a controversial landmark treaty granting the Nisga'a a form of self-government and control over natural resources in 1940 sq. km of their traditional lands.

1999. The Supreme Court of Canada instructed the government to revise the Indian Act so that communities, and not the government, have the power to allow non-residents to vote in elections. It also passed Bill C-49, or the **First Nations Land Management Act,** which created a framework for First Nations to develop their own land-use laws. Most dramatically, on April 1, 1999, the Canadian government split the Northwest Territories in half and granted the densely Inuit-populated eastern portion, **Nunavut** ("Our Land"), self-government.

2001. On April 21, an association of tribes signed an agreement with the state of Alaska which would lay the ground rules for future dialogue between the groups. The agreement said little that was earth-shattering, but it did affirm the right of the tribes to form their own governments and conduct their own affairs.

CONTEMPORARY CULTURE
CONSERVATION AND HARVEST

Political entities in the Northwest strive to compete and to protect their independent interests within the framework of federal legislation. Inevitably, negotiations don't go smoothly. The central political tensions are between conservation and harvest, where **harvest** is synonymous with jobs, and **conservation** is synonymous with tradition. These are particularly difficult to balance in Oregon, Washington, and Alaska, home to the most federally- and state-protected land in the United States. The outright challenge of co-managing renewable resources is exacerbated in British Columbia and the Yukon by the involvement of vast quantities of land in territorial disputes with First Nations. The work of co-managing the resources that these states and provinces share—like the Pacific salmon fishery—has been the most dramatic and drawn-out subject of reconciliation.

Policies of environmental stewardship emerged in response to a variety of pressures, from civic consciousness to political activism. Oregon has led the pack in reform, beginning in 1967, when the **Oregon coast** was preserved for free and uninterrupted use by the public. Moreover, Oregon's 1971 **Bottle Bill** was the first recycling refund program in the US.

On the animal front, Washington and Oregon's **spotted owl** has remained a symbol of conflict between conservationists and industrialists after vast tracts of the bird's old-growth forest habitat were protected. A vociferous battle has also been fought over the gray whale, an interesting case in which the government waited until 1937 to ban commercial harvesting of these creatures. In many cases indigenous communities lead conservation efforts, suspending their hunting and trapping before sluggish government wheels begin to roll toward curbing industries. On Vancouver Island residents rallied to save the **endangered marmot;** efforts culminated with a "Marmot-aid" benefit concert.

> ## THE MAKAH WHALE CONTROVERSY was not a
> traditional conflict between industrialists and conservationists but one between conservationists and Native Americans. In the 1990s, when the endangered gray whales had rebounded to a viable population, the Makah applied to the International Whaling Commission, with US support, for a cultural exemption to the continuing ban. The five-whale allowance granted to the Makah enraged conservationists. Regardless, Makah returned to the ceremonial and subsistence hunt in 1999 among protest and publicity.

THE WILD THINGS

The wildlife in Alaska and the Pacific Northwest is one of the region's biggest draws. Some of the critters running around the area include:

BROWN BEARS. Alaska has about 30,000 brown bears, which is more than 98% of the United States' brown bear population. **Kodiak Island** (see p. 521) is renowned for the size of its bears, and is also one of the best (and safest) places to observe them. Though bears generally prefer solitude and tend to avoid tourists if they can help it, hikers are advised to purchase bear spray before venturing out into the backcountry. For more on bear safety, see p. 38.

CARIBOU. Better known in the popular imagination as reindeer, the caribou were made to travel over land. These animals cover more ground each year (3000 mi.) than any other mammal, and they can get up to speeds of over 50 mph, making them faster than any car on the Dempster highway (see p. 416).

MOUNTAIN GOATS. Unlike the fast-moving caribou, mountain goats move at a more deliberate pace. This can cause problems in the **Canadian Rockies** (see p. 375), where traffic stands still every time a tour bus sights one. Male goats ("billies") crawl on their bellies when they are pursuing a female goat ("nannies").

GRAY WOLVES. If the billies spent less time on their bellies, they might have better luck evading the gray wolves, who are their natural predators (see p. 211). To catch a glimpse of these elusive and cunning creatures, check out **Wolf Haven International** in Olympia (see p. 186).

BLACK BEARS. Though mother black bears will jealously guard their cubs, adult male and female bears are never together except to breed. In fact, as soon as breeding is over, the male bear leaves the female to raise the cubs. One of the best places to see black bears in the Pacific Northwest is in **Banff National Park** (see p. 376), where rangers keep a running tally of sightings in the area.

BALD EAGLES. The emblem of the United States, this majestic bird is unique to North America. Though the population once dwindled due to hunting and pesticides, the bald eagle has staged a promising comeback; in some parts of **Central Alaska**, it is ubiquitous enough that some hostels guarantee you'll see one during your stay (see p. 531).

FOOD & DRINK

The Pacific Northwest has tastes that vary drastically from one region to another, but in all cases, cities and cultures cling tenaciously to their distinctive flavors. Here are some of the foods and drinks you'll find in your travels:

SOURDOUGH IN ALASKA. Alaskans have such pride in their sourdough that they name entire campgrounds (see p. 558) after it. A type of bread with a distinct tangy flavor, it can be consumed at every meal with everything from moose sausage to soup. Some of the best can be found at the **Bake Shop** in Girdwood (see p. 481).

BANNOCK IN BRITISH COLUMBIA. Though there's no single traditional recipe, bannock generally takes the form of a biscuit-like cake made from flour, lard, and honey. Some varieties (see p. 300) incorporate local delicacies such as salmon. Invariably, everyone who makes it considers theirs the best.

HALIBUT AND SALMON. In close proximity to the arctic waters these fish frequent, many cities in the Pacific Northwest are known for superior seafood. Halibut and salmon are in everything, from fish fries (see p. 495) to tacos (see p. 504).

MICROBREWS IN OREGON. Portland is the microbrewery capital of North America (see p. 84), and has the beer to prove it. One establishment in Seaside tries to cram as much alcohol as they can into the largest possible beer (see p. 108).

CULTURE

CULTURE & THE ARTS

Years ago, cities like Vancouver were middle-class port towns with burgeoning counter-cultures. In the years since, their popularity has exploded and the entire Pacific Rim seems to have breached its humdrum roots: tourists have poured in, technological industries have expanded, and resource-driven industries are grinding to a halt under environmental pressures. Yet none of the communities of the Northwest stray far from their origins—port towns remain port towns, and the festivals that first brought communities together continue to do so. The laid-back lifestyle of the Northwest results from this seamless blending, and residents' love for the land is expressed in its aggressive defense.

MUSIC AND THEATER

Music lovers wouldn't hesitate to say that **Seattle** stole the show from California at the close of the millennium. As the birthplace of **Jimi Hendrix** and the cradle of grunge, it's undeniable that rock's greatest influences emanate from the Northwest. Artists who hit it big in the 90s included **Pearl Jam, Nirvana, Alice in Chains,** and **Soundgarden,** who pioneered the **grunge** sound and look. Today, rock still reigns supreme in Seattle at the **Experience Music Project,** which opened in June, 2000 (see p. 171). Although prowling record executives signing garage bands to contracts have departed Seattle, the Northwest has been identified as a breeding ground for **riot-grrrl** rock and **guitar-timbre** bands. Seattle also has a **repertory theater** community third in size only to those of Chicago and New York, and its **opera** is internationally renowned for its Wagner productions. Several major Hollywood films have used the magnificent scenery of the Pacific Northwest as a backdrop:

MOVIE	ACTORS	YEAR	LOCATION
Dr. Dolittle 2	Eddie Murphy	2001	Wrangell, AK (p. 434)
Mystery Alaska	Russell Crowe, Hank Azaria	1999	Banff National Park, BC (p. 376)
Independence Day	Will Smith, Bill Pullman, Jeff Goldblum	1996	Grants Pass, OR (p. 128)
Maverick	Mel Gibson, Jodie Foster, James Garner	1994	Columbia River Gorge, OR (p. 89)
Free Willy	Jason James Richter	1993	Astoria and Portland, OR (Cannon Beach, p. 100)
The Goonies	Sean Astin, Josh Brolin	1985	Astoria, OR (p. 93)
Indiana Jones and the Temple of Doom	Harrison Ford, Kate Capshaw	1984	Grand Coulee Dam, WA (p. 239)
The Shining	Jack Nicholson	1980	Timberline Lodge, OR (p. 86)
One Flew Over the Cuckoo's Nest	Jack Nicholson	1975	Salem, OR (p. 117)
Call of the Wild	Clark Gable, Loretta Young	1935	Mt. Baker Lodge, WA (p. 193)

VISUAL ARTS

Some of the continent's oldest art forms can be found in the Pacific Northwest, and the cedar **masks, totems,** and **longhouses** of indigenous coastal nations have long been recognized as some of the world's most notable artistic achievements. Native carving is a versatile art that entwines religious and cultural heritage. **Bill Reid** (1920-1998), a Haida carver and Vancouver native, was one of many artists celebrated for revitalizing communities through carving, dance, song, and potlatch, all art forms suppressed by law during the last hundred years.

Government support reflects the public's commitment to the arts. Portland and Seattle, for example, funnel a 1% tax on capital improvements into the acquisition and creation of public art. While government cutbacks have compromised the

THE FRUIT OF THE EARTH
Alaska's Natural Bounty

Southeast Alaskans never go hungry. Though there may be only bland oranges and imported melons at the grocery store, the wilds of Alaska are bursting with naturally tasty morsels. Alaskan forests are loaded with berries of all kinds, most of which are edible and delicious (to both humans and animals). Near the shore, tasty seaweed and sea creatures attract hungry travelers and natives alike. While Alaska's wild foods pass under the radar of most tourists, with a little dedication and help from this handy guide to feasting in the wilderness, you can harvest salmonberries and limpets like a native.

Salmonberries and thimbleberries are both members of the Rubus family (as are raspberries and blackberries), and grow on large bushes, favoring clear-cuts and ditches. The leaves of the thimbleberry bush are furry, thornless, and larger than those of the salmonberry bush. The salmonberry, named for the bright orange drupelets resembling salmon roe that make up the berry, grows on a plant with glossy leaves and thorny stems. Bears favor the subtle-tasting salmonberry over the tart, bright-red thimbleberry. Dwarf raspberries, also in the Rubus family, are difficult to find—they trail along the ground, usually in marshy areas, and have tiny berries made up of one to five drupelets.

Southeast Alaska's beaches are filled with foods that are little known outside of the region. Beach asparagus ("sea beans") is steadily gaining in popularity among non-Alaskans, showing up on the tables of fine restaurants in the Pacific Northwest and occasionally available in grocery stores in the Seattle area. Beach asparagus is found on sheltered beaches at the high tide line. It looks like miniature asparagus, grows four to five inches tall and a few millimeters in diameter, and can be harvested in early July. Try it fresh, sautéed in butter (or bacon fat if you really want to indulge), or canned and eaten in salads or as a substitute for green beans.

Most seaweed in Southeast Alaska is also edible and tasty. Bull kelp gets eaten the most—it is often made into relish or pickles, which taste similar to watermelon rind pickles. Though long stalks of bull kelp often wash up along the beaches, only eat fresh kelp. You'll need to go a few feet offshore in a boat to a kelp forest (you'll see the fronds swirling gently at the surface) and pull up kelp from the bottom. Rockweed is the most common and noticeable Alaskan seaweed, growing along the rocky intertidal zone. The taste may put you off at first (it can best be described as "acquired"), but rockweed is an easy snack food for kayakers and shore-hikers.

By the ocean, the intertidal zone holds a cornucopia of easily-acquired and delicious sea creatures including limpets, gumboots, and sea cucumbers. Limpets, also known as china-hats, can be removed from their rocks with a quick twisting motion of the shell. Sauté limpets in butter or try steaming them—either way, you'll end up with a gourmet meal (they taste similar to snails) with help from Mother Nature. Gumboots (also known as chitons) offer much more meat per creature than limpets, but some muscle is needed to remove them from their rocks. Gumboots are oblong and are often found in the same area as limpets, firmly stuck to the underside of rocks. They can be steamed lightly, ground and made into patties, or put into chowder. Sea cucumbers, purple-red creatures that resemble large slugs, have the endearing habit of spewing their internal organs at predators as a defense. They are nevertheless one of the most delicious natural delicacies. They are found in the low tidal zone among rocks and seaweed. To enjoy them, split the cucumber with a knife and remove the long, white strips of meat. Head to the stove and sauté them with butter, or try sea cucumbers fried, ground, or in soups.

Alaskan grocery stores might hold slim pickings in fresh foods, but don't let that discourage you. Get your shoes wet and use some imagination, and you'll find yourself a multi-course meal to rival the best restaurants around.

Mandy Davis was a Researcher-Writer for Let's Go: Ireland 2001. She lived in Ketchikan, Alaska for 18 years, and has written for the Ketchikan Daily News. She now works in Seattle in a Japanese print gallery.

health of famed centers for arts in Western Canada, artist communities and colonies are alive and thriving among the San Juan and Gulf Islands of Washington and British Columbia and in small towns like Atlin, BC, and Homer, AK (p. 508). Where government comes up short, philanthropists step in: in 1998-9, the Patrons of Northwest Civic, Cultural, and Charitable Organizations, **PONCHO,** had its best year yet, dispensing $2 million in Puget Sound; since 1962, the group has poured $21 million into the region's arts organizations.

FESTIVALS (2003)

DATE	NAME & LOCATION	DESCRIPTION
Beginning March 1	**Iditarod** AK: Anchorage to Nome	The bravest of the brave hitch up a team of hardy huskies and mush over tundra and mountains across 1150 mi. of Alaska.
July 1	**Canada Day** Anywhere in Canada	Typically quiet Canada struggles with an irresistible urge to whoop it up for the anniversary of Confederation.
July 4	**Independence Day** Anywhere in the US	Fireworks, fireworks, beer, fireworks, beer, beer, fireworks, hot dogs and hamburgers on the grill, and some fireworks.
July 11-13	**Oregon Country Fair** Eugene, OR	Craft booth concessionaires and earnest crystal-worshippers converge on Eugene to eat, play, discuss sustainable energy, and hug.
July 4-13	**Stampede** Calgary, AB	One of the biggest rodeos in the world; international contestants, hundreds of thousands of visitors, and many cows.
July 18-20	**Folk Music Festival** Vancouver, BC	A modern-day Woodstock of the West, Vancouver attracts folk musicians from around the world to don their Birkenstocks and jam.
July 18-20	**Rhythm & Blues Festival** Winthrop, WA	Just what its name says. Ample rhythm and plentiful blues invade a self-proclaimed wild Western town.
September 6-8	**Bumbershoot** Seattle, WA	Seattle's block party for the arts draws hundreds of thousands of groovesters to watch every sort of big-name act, from Sir Mix-A-Lot to the Indigo Girls to Sky Cries Mary.
Mid-February to October	**Shakespeare Festival** Ashland, OR	Dude, that's a lot of drama. Enough that accommodations fill up a year in advance, and tickets are often sold for more than three times face value. Reserve your place early.

ESSENTIALS

FACTS FOR THE TRAVELER

ENTRANCE REQUIREMENTS

Passport (p. 23). Required for all visitors to the US and Canada.

Visa (p. 23). Generally required for all visitors to the US and Canada, but requirement can be waived.

Work Permit (p. 24). Required for all foreigners planning to work in the US or Canada.

Driving Permit (p. 52). Required for all those planning to drive.

EMBASSIES & CONSULATES

CONSULAR SERVICES ABROAD

Contact the nearest embassy or consulate to obtain information regarding the visas and permits necessary to travel to the United States. Listings of foreign embassies within the US as well as US embassies abroad can be found at www.embassy-world.com. A US **State Department** web site provides contact info for key officers at US overseas stations: www.state.gov/www/about_state/contacts/keyofficer_index.html. The Canadian Ministry of Foreign Affairs is at www.dfait-maeci.gc.ca/dfait/missions/menu-e.asp.

AMERICAN CONSULATES AND EMBASSIES

Australia, Moonah Pl., **Yarralumla** (Canberra), ACT 2600 (☎02 6214 5600; fax 6273 3191, www.usembassy-australia.state.gov). **Other Consulates:** MLC Centre, Level 59, 19-29 Martin Pl., **Sydney,** NSW 2000 (☎02 9373 9200; fax 9373 9184); 553 St. Kilda Rd., P.O. Box 6722, **Melbourne,** VIC 3004 (☎03 9526 5900; fax 9525 0769); 16 St. George's Terr., 13th fl., **Perth,** WA 6000 (☎08 9202 1224; fax 9231 9444).

Canada, 490 Sussex Dr., **Ottawa,** ON K1N 1G8 (☎613-238-5335; fax 688-3101; www.usembassycanada.gov). **Other Consulates:** 615 Macleod Trail SE, Room 1000, **Calgary,** AB T2G 4T8 (☎403-266-8962; fax 264-6630); 1969 Upper Water St., Purdy's Wharf Tower II, suite 904, **Halifax,** NS B3J 3R7 (☎902-429-2480; fax 423-6861); 1155 St. Alexandre St., **Montréal,** QC H3B 3Z1 (mailing address: P.O. Box 65, Postal Station Desjardins, **Montréal,** QC H5B 1G1. ☎514-398-9695; fax 398-0702); 2 Place Terrasse Dufferin, B.P. 939, **Québec City,** QC G1R 4T9 (☎418-692-2095; fax 692-4640); 360 University Ave., **Toronto,** ON M5G 1S4 (☎416-595-1700; fax 595-0051); 1095 West Pender St., 21st fl., **Vancouver,** BC V6E 2M6 (☎604-685-4311)

Ireland, 42 Elgin Rd., **Ballsbridge,** Dublin 4 (☎01 668 8777 or 668 7122; fax 668 9946; www.usembassy.ie).

New Zealand, 29 Fitzherbert Terr., **Thorndon,** Wellington (☎04 462 6000; fax 478 1701; http://usembassy.org.nz). **Other Consulate:** 23 Customs St., Citibank Building, 3rd fl., **Auckland.**

South Africa, P.O. Box 9536, Pretoria 0001, 877 Pretorius St., **Pretoria** (☎27 12 342-1048; fax 342-2244; http://usembassy.state.gov/pretoria). **Other Consulates:** Broadway Industries Center, **Heerengracht,** Foreshore (mailing address: P.O. Box 6773, Roggebaai, 8012), **Cape Town** (☎021 421-4280; fax 425-3014); 303 West Street, Old Mutual Building, 31st fl., **Durban** (☎031 305-7600; fax 305-7691); No. 1 River St., Killarney (mailing address: P.O. Box 1762, Houghton, 2041), **Johannesburg** (☎011 644-8000; fax 646-6916).

UK, 24 Grosvenor Sq., **London** W1A 1AE (☎0207 499 9000; fax 495 5012; www.usembassy.org.uk). **Other Consulates:** Queen's House, 14 Queen St., **Belfast,** N. Ireland BT1 6EQ (☎01232 328 239; fax 01232 248 482); 3 Regent Terr., **Edinburgh,** Scotland EH7 5BW (☎0131 556 8315; fax 557 6023).

CANADIAN CONSULATES AND EMBASSIES

Australia, Commonwealth Ave., **Canberra** ACT 2600 (☎02 6270 4000; www.dfait-maeci.gc.ca/australia); 111 Harrington St., Level 5, **Sydney** NSW 2000 (☎02 9364 3000); 123 Camberwell Rd., Hawthorn East, **Melbourne** VIC 3123 (☎03 9811 9999); 267 St. George's Terr., **Perth** WA 6000 (☎08 9322 7930).

Ireland, 65 St. Stephen's Green, **Dublin** 2 (☎01 478 1988).

New Zealand, 61 Molesworth St., 3rd fl., **Thorndon,** Wellington (☎04 473 9577).

South Africa, Reserve Bank Bldg., St. George's Mall St., 19th fl., **Cape Town** 8001 (☎021 423 5240); 1103 Arcadia St., **Hatfield,** Pretoria 0083 (☎012 42 3000).

UK, 30 Lothian Rd., **Edinburgh,** Scotland EH2 2XZ (☎0131 220 4333); Canada House, Trafalgar Square, **London,** SW1Y 5BJ (☎0207 258 6600).

US, 1251 Ave. of the Americas, **New York,** NY 10020 (☎212-596-1658); 550 S. Hope St. 9th fl., **Los Angeles,** CA 90071 (☎213-346-2700); 2 Prudential Plaza, 180 N. Stetson, Ave., Ste. 2400, **Chicago,** IL 60601 (☎312-616-1860); 501 Pennsylvania Ave. NW, **Washington,** D.C. 20001 (☎202-682-1740).

CONSULAR SERVICES IN THE US AND CANADA

IN WASHINGTON, D.C. (US)

Australia, 1601 Mass. Ave. NW, 20036 (☎202-797-3000; www.austemb.org).

Canada, 501 Penn. Ave., 20001 (☎202-682-1740; www.canadianembassy.org).

Ireland, 2234 Mass. Ave. NW, 20008 (☎202-462-3939; www.irelandemb.org).

New Zealand, 37 Observatory Circle, 20008 (☎202-328-4800; www.nzemb.org).

UK, 3100 Mass. Ave., 20008 (☎202-588-6500; www.britainusa.com/consular/embassy/embassy.asp).

South Africa, 3051 Mass. Ave., 20008 (☎202-232-4400; usaembassy.southafrica.net).

IN OTTAWA, ONTARIO (CANADA)

Australia, 50 O'Connor St. #710, K1P 6L2 (☎613-236-0841; www.ahc-ottawa.org).

Ireland, 130 Albert St. #700, K1P 5G4 (☎613-233-6281).

New Zealand, 99 Bank St. #727, K1P 6G3 (☎613-238-5991; www.nzhcottawa.org).

UK, 310 Summerset St., K2P 0J9 (☎613-230-2961; www.britain-in-canada.org).

US, 490 Sussex Dr., K1P 1M8 (☎613-238-5335; www.usembassycanada.gov).

South Africa, 15 Sussex Dr., K1M 1M8 (☎613-744-0330; www.docuweb.ca/SouthAfrica/).

DOCUMENTS & FORMALITIES

PASSPORTS

REQUIREMENTS. All non-Canadian and non-American citizens need valid passports to enter the US and Canada and to re-enter their countries. Returning home with an expired passport is illegal and may result in a fine. US citizens can enter Canada (and vice versa) with proof of citizenship and a photo ID—a driver's license and birth certificate should suffice.

NEW PASSPORTS. Citizens of Australia, Canada, Ireland, New Zealand, the United Kingdom, and the United States can apply for a passport at any post office, passport office, or court of law. Citizens of South Africa can apply for a passport at any Home Affairs office. Any new passport or renewal applications must be filed well in advance of the departure date, although most passport offices offer rush services for a very steep fee.

PASSPORT MAINTENANCE. Be sure to photocopy the page of your passport with your photo, as well as your visas, traveler's check serial numbers and any other important documents. Carry one set of copies in a safe place, apart from the originals, and leave another set at home. Consulates also recommend that you carry an expired passport or an official copy of your birth certificate in a part of your baggage separate from other documents.

If you lose your passport, immediately notify the local police and the nearest embassy or consulate of your home government. To expedite its replacement, you will need to know all information previously recorded and show ID and proof of citizenship. In some cases, a replacement may take weeks to process, and it may be valid only for a few months. Any visas stamped in your old passport will be irretrievably lost. In an emergency, ask for immediate temporary traveling papers that will permit you to re-enter your home country.

VISAS, INVITATIONS, & WORK PERMITS

VISAS. Citizens of some non-English speaking countries and South Africa need a visa—a stamp, sticker, or insert in your passport specifying the purpose of your travel and the permitted duration of your stay—in addition to a valid passport for entrance to the US. Canadian citizens do not need to obtain a visa for admission to the US; citizens of Australia, New Zealand, and most European countries (including the UK and Ireland) can waive US visas through the **Visa Waiver Program.** Visitors qualify if they are traveling only for business or pleasure (*not* work or study), are staying for fewer than **90 days,** have proof of intent to leave (e.g. a return plane ticket), possess an I-94W form (arrival/departure certificate attached to their visa upon arrival), and are traveling on particular air or sea carriers. See http://travel.state.gov/vwp.html for more information. For stays of longer than 90 days in the US, all travelers (except Canadians) must obtain a visa.

In Canada, citizens of some non-English speaking countries and South Africa also need a visitor's visa if they're not traveling with a valid green card. Citizens of Australia, Ireland, New Zealand, the United Kingdom, and the United States do not need a visa. All visitors to Canada must possess a valid passport in order to enter the country. Visas cost US$50, CDN$75, and can be purchased from the **Canadian Embassy** in Washington, DC Monday to Friday between 9am and noon. US citizens can take advantage of the **Center for International Business and Travel (CIBT);** which secures visas to almost all countries for a varying service charge (☎ 800-925-2428).

ESSENTIALS

WORK PERMITS. Admission as a visitor does not include the right to work; to obtain employment, one needs a work permit. Entering the US or Canada to study requires a special visa. For more information, see **Alternatives to Tourism** (p. 62).

IDENTIFICATION

Travelers should always have two or more forms of identification with them, including at least one photo ID; a passport and a driver's license or birth certificate is usually adequate. Never carry all your forms of ID together; split them up in case of theft or loss, and keep photocopies of them in your luggage and at home.

TEACHER, STUDENT & YOUTH IDENTIFICATION. The **International Student Identity Card (ISIC),** the most widely accepted form of student ID, provides discounts on sights, accommodations, food, and transport; access to a 24hr. emergency help line (in North America call ☎ 877-370-ISIC; elsewhere call US collect 715-345-0505); and insurance benefits for US cardholders (see **Insurance,** p. 32). The ISIC is preferable to an institution-specific card (such as a university ID) because it is more likely to be recognized and honored abroad. Applicants must be degree-seeking students of a secondary or post-secondary school and must be at least 12 years old. Because of the proliferation of fake ISICs, some services (particularly airlines) require additional proof of student identity, such as a school ID or a letter signed by your registrar and stamped with your school seal.

The **International Teacher Identity Card (ITIC)** offers teachers the same insurance coverage as well as similar but limited discounts. For travelers who are 25 years old or under but are not students, the **International Youth Travel Card (IYTC;** formerly the **GO 25** Card) also offers many of the same benefits as the ISIC.

Each of these identity cards costs US$22 or the equivalent. ISIC and ITIC cards are valid for roughly one and a half academic years; IYTC cards are valid for one year from the date of issue. Many student travel agencies (see p. 46) issue the cards, including STA Travel in Australia and New Zealand, Travel CUTS in Canada, usit in the Republic of Ireland and Northern Ireland, SASTS in South Africa, Campus Travel and STA Travel in the UK, and Council Travel and STA Travel in the US. For a listing of issuing agencies, or for more information, contact the **International Student Travel Confederation (ISTC),** Herengracht 479, 1017 BS Amsterdam, Netherlands (☎ +31 20 421 28 00; fax 421 28 10; istcinfo@istc.org; www.istc.org).

CUSTOMS

Upon entering the US or Canada, you must declare certain items from abroad and pay a duty on the value of those articles if they exceed the allowance established by the US or Canada's customs service. Note that goods and gifts purchased at **duty-free** shops abroad are not exempt from customs duties; "duty-free" merely means that you need not pay a sales tax in the country of purchase. Upon returning home, you must similarly declare all articles acquired abroad and pay a duty on the value of articles in excess of your home country's allowance. In order to expedite your return, make a list of any valuables brought from home and register them with customs before traveling abroad, and be sure to keep receipts.

MONEY

CURRENCY & EXCHANGE

The currency chart below is based on August 2002 exchange rates between local currency and Australian dollars (AUS$), Canadian dollars (CDN$), Irish pounds (IR£), New Zealand dollars (NZ$), South African Rand (ZAR), British pounds

AMERICAN AND CANADIAN CUSTOMS DECLARATIONS

Entering the **US** as a non-resident, you are allowed to claim US$100 of gifts and merchandise if you will be in the country for 72hr. *Residents* may claim $400 worth of goods. If 21, you may bring in 1L of wine, beer, or liquor. 200 cigarettes, 50 cigars (steer clear of Cubans), or 2kg of smoking tobacco are also permitted. Entering **Canada,** visitors may bring in gifts, each of which may not exceed CDN$60 in value. Residents who have been out of the country for 24hr. may claim CDN$50 exemption. After 48hr. they may claim CDN$200, and after 7 days CDN$750. If you are of the legal drinking age in the province, and have been out of the country for 48hr. or more, you may bring in 1.5L of wine, 1.14L of liquor, or 24 355mL bottles of beer or ale. You may also bring in 200 cigarettes, 50 cigars, 200 tobacco sticks, or 200g of manufactured tobacco.

(UK£), US dollars (US$), and European Union euros (EUR€). Check the currency converter on financial websites such as www.bloomberg.com and www.xe.com.

As a general rule, it's cheaper to convert money in the US or Canada than at home. While currency exchange will probably be available in your arrival airport, it's wise to bring enough foreign currency to last for the first 24 to 72 hours of a trip.

If you use traveler's checks or bills, carry some in small denominations (US$50 or less) for times when you are forced to exchange money at disadvantageous rates, but bring a range of denominations since charges may be levied per check cashed. Store your money in a variety of forms; ideally, at any given time you will be carrying some cash, some traveler's checks, and an ATM and/or credit card.

US DOLLARS		CANADIAN DOLLARS	
CDN$1 = US$0.63	US$1 = CDN$1.58	US$1 = CDN$1.58	CDN$1 = US$0.63
UK£1 = US$1.53	US$1 = UK£0.65	UK£1 = CDN$2.42	CDN$1 = UK£0.41
EUR€1 = US$0.97	US$1 = EUR€1.03	EUR€1 = CDN$1.53	CDN$1 = EUR€0.66
AUS$1 = US$0.53	US$1= AUS$1.87	AUS$1 = CDN$0.84	CDN$1= AUS$1.19
NZ$1 = US$0.45	US$1 = NZ$2.20	NZ$1 = CDN$0.72	CDN$1 = NZ$1.39
ZAR1 = US$0.10	US$1 = ZAR10.40	ZAR1 = CDN$0.15	CDN$1 = ZAR6.58

TRAVELER'S CHECKS

Traveler's checks are one of the safest and least troublesome means of carrying funds. American Express and Visa are the most widely recognized brands. Many banks and agencies sell them for a small commission. Check issuers provide refunds if the checks are lost or stolen, and many provide additional services, such as toll-free refund hotlines abroad, emergency message services, and stolen credit card assistance. They are readily accepted throughout the Pacific Northwest. Ask about toll-free refund hotlines and the location of refund centers when purchasing checks, and always carry emergency cash.

American Express: Checks available with commission at select banks and all AmEx offices. US residents can also purchase checks by phone (☎888-887-8986) or online (www.aexp.com). AAA (see p. 53) offers commission-free checks to its members. Checks available in US, Australian, British, Canadian, Japanese, and euro currencies. Cheques for Two can be signed by either of 2 people traveling together. For purchase locations or more information contact AmEx's service centers: in the US and Canada ☎800-221-7282; in the UK ☎0800 521 313; in Australia ☎800 251 902; in New Zealand ☎0800 441 068; elsewhere US collect ☎801-964-6665.

Visa: Checks available (generally with commission) at banks worldwide. For the location of the nearest office, call Visa's service centers: in the US ☎ 800-227-6811; in the UK 0800 89 50 78; elsewhere UK collect 020 7937 8091. Checks available in US, British, Canadian, Japanese, and euro currencies.

Travelex/Thomas Cook: In the US and Canada call ☎ 800-287-7362; in the UK call 0800 62 21 01; elsewhere call UK collect 1733 31 89 50.

CREDIT, DEBIT, AND ATM CARDS

Where they are accepted, credit cards often offer superior exchange rates—up to 5% better than the retail rate used by banks and other currency exchange establishments. Credit cards may also offer services such as insurance or emergency help, and are sometimes required to reserve hotel rooms or rental cars. Credit cards are generally accepted in all but the smallest businesses in the US and Canada. **MasterCard** and **Visa** are the most welcomed; **American Express** cards work at some ATMs and at AmEx offices and major airports.

ATM cards are widespread in the US and Canada. Depending on the system that your home bank uses, you can most likely access your personal bank account from abroad. ATMs get the same wholesale exchange rate as credit cards, but there is often a limit on the amount of money you can withdraw per day (around US$500), and unfortunately computer networks sometimes fail. There is typically also a surcharge of US$1-5 per withdrawal.

Debit cards are a relatively new form of purchasing power that are as convenient as credit cards but have a more immediate impact on your funds. A debit card can be used wherever its associated credit card company (usually Mastercard or Visa) is accepted, but the money is withdrawn directly from the holder's checking account. Debit cards often also function as ATM cards and can be used to withdraw cash from associated banks and ATMs throughout the US and Canada. Ask your local bank about obtaining one.

The two major international money networks are **Cirrus** (to locate ATMs in the US, call ☎ 800-424-7787 or check www.mastercard.com) and **Visa/PLUS** (to locate ATMs in the US call ☎ 800-843-7587 or check www.visa.com). Most ATMs charge a transaction fee that is paid to the bank that owns the ATM.

GETTING MONEY FROM HOME

If you run out of money while traveling, the easiest and cheapest solution is to have someone back home make a deposit to your home bank account. Failing that, consider one of the following options.

WIRING MONEY. It is possible to arrange a **bank money transfer,** asking a bank back home to wire money to a bank in the US or Canada. This is the cheapest way to transfer cash, but it's also the slowest, usually taking several days or more. Note that some banks may only release your funds in local currency, potentially sticking you with a poor exchange rate; inquire about this in advance. Money transfer services like **Western Union** are faster and more convenient than bank transfers, but also much pricier. Western Union has many locations worldwide. To find one, visit www.westernunion.com, or call in the US ☎ 800-325-6000, in Canada ☎ 800-235-0000, in the UK ☎ 0800 83 38 33, in Australia ☎ 800 501 500, in New Zealand ☎ 800 270 000, or in South Africa ☎ 0860 100031. To wire money within the US by credit card (Visa, MasterCard, Discover), call ☎ 800-225-5227. Money transfer services are also available at **American Express** and **Thomas Cook** offices.

US STATE DEPARTMENT (US CITIZENS ONLY). In dire emergencies only, the US State Department will forward money within hours to the nearest consular office, which will then disburse it according to instructions for a US$15 fee. If you wish to use this service, you must contact the Overseas Citizens Service division of the US State Department (☎ 202-647-5225; nights, Sundays, and holidays ☎ 202-647-4000).

COSTS

Factoring in the high costs of gas (ranging from US$1 to US$2 depending on the region) is a must. Before you go, spend some time calculating a reasonable per-day **budget** that will meet your needs.

STAYING ON A BUDGET. A bare-bones day in Alaska and the Pacific Northwest (camping or sleeping in hostels/guesthouses, buying food at supermarkets) would cost about US$30-40; a slightly more comfortable day (sleeping in hostels/guesthouses, eating one meal a day at a restaurant, going out at night) would run US$ 50-70. For a luxurious day, the sky's the limit. Also, don't forget to factor in emergency reserve funds (at least US$200) when planning how much money to bring.

TIPS FOR SAVING MONEY. Some simpler ways include searching out opportunities for free entertainment, splitting accommodation and food costs with other trustworthy fellow travelers, and buying food in supermarkets rather than eating out. If you plan on staying in hostels, you may want to bring a sleepsack to save on sheet charges, and do your **laundry** in the sink (unless you're explicitly prohibited from doing so).

TIPPING & BARGAINING

In the US and Canada, it is customary to tip waitstaff and cab drivers 15-20%, but do so at your discretion. Tips are usually not included in restaurant bills. At the airport and in hotels, porters expect a tip of at least $1 per bag to carry your baggage. Except in extremely rural regions where native culture may permit it, bargaining is generally frowned upon and fruitless in Alaska and the Pacific Northwest.

SAFETY & SECURITY

PERSONAL SAFETY

EXPLORING. What crime there is in Alaska and the Pacific Northwest is concentrated in urban areas. To avoid unwanted attention, try to blend in as much as possible. Familiarize yourself with your surroundings before setting out, and carry yourself with confidence; if you must check a map on the street, duck into a shop or restaurant. If you are traveling alone, be sure someone at home knows your itinerary, and never admit that you're traveling alone.

SELF DEFENSE. There is no sure-fire way to avoid all the threatening situations you might encounter when you travel, but a good self-defense course will give you concrete ways to react to unwanted advances. **Impact, Prepare, and Model Mugging** can refer you to local self-defense courses in the US (☎ 800-345-5425). Visit the website at www.impactsafety.org for a list of nearby chapters. Workshops (2-3hr.) start at US$50; full courses run US$350-500.

 EMERGENCY = 911. For emergencies in the US and Canada, dial **911.** This number is toll-free from all phones, including coin phones. In a very few remote communities, 911 may not work. If it does not, dial 0 for the operator and request to be connected with the appropriate emergency service. In national parks, it is usually best to call the **park warden** in case of emergency. *Let's Go* always lists emergency contact numbers.

TRAVEL ADVISORIES. The following government offices provide travel information and advisories by telephone, by fax, and on the web:

Australian Department of Foreign Affairs and Trade: ☎ 13 0055 5135; faxback service 02 6261 1299; www.dfat.gov.au.

Canadian Department of Foreign Affairs and International Trade (DFAIT): In Canada and the US call ☎800-267-6788, elsewhere call 613-944-6788; www.dfait-maeci.gc.ca. Call for their free booklet, *Bon Voyage...But.*

New Zealand Ministry of Foreign Affairs: ☎04 494 8500; fax 494 8506; www.mft.govt.nz/trav.html.

United Kingdom Foreign and Commonwealth Office: ☎0207 008 0232; fax 7008 0155; www.fco.gov.uk.

US Department of State: ☎202-647-5225, faxback service 202-647-3000; http://travel.state.gov. For *A Safe Trip Abroad,* call 202-512-1800.

DRIVING. If you are using a **car,** learn local driving signals. Children under 40 lb. should ride only in a specially-designed carseat, available for a small fee from most car rental agencies. Study route maps before you hit the road, and if you plan on spending a lot of time driving, you may want to bring spare parts. If your car breaks down, wait for the police to assist you. For long drives in desolate areas, get a cellular phone and a roadside assistance program (see p. 53). Be sure to park your vehicle in a garage or well-traveled area, and use a steering wheel locking device in larger cities. **Sleeping in your car** is one of the most dangerous (and often illegal) ways to get your rest. For info on the perils of **hitchhiking,** see p. 56.

TERRORISM. In light of the September 11th, 2001 terrorist attacks, there is an elevated threat of further attacks throughout the US and Canada. A terrorist attack would likely target a popular landmark; however, the threat is neither specific enough nor of great enough magnitude to warrant avoiding tourist attractions or certain regions. Monitor developments in the news and stay on top of any local, state, or federal terrorist warnings. In addition, prepare yourself for additional security checks in airports and avoid packing any sharp or dangerous objects in your carry on luggage—they will be confiscated faster than you can blink.

FINANCIAL SECURITY

PROTECTING YOUR VALUABLES. There are a few steps you can take to minimize the financial risk associated with traveling. First, **bring as few belongings with you as possible.** Second, buy a few combination **padlocks** to secure your belongings either in your pack or in a hostel or train station locker. Third, **carry as little cash as possible.** Keep your traveler's checks and ATM/credit cards in a **money belt**—not a "fanny pack," which will make you look like a huge, robbable doofus—along with your passport and ID cards. Fourth, **keep a small cash reserve separate from your primary stash.** This should be about US$50 sewn into or stored in the depths of your pack, along with your traveler's check numbers and important photocopies.

CON ARTISTS & PICKPOCKETS. In large cities **con artists** often work in groups, and children are among the most effective. Beware of certain classics: sob stories that require money, rolls of bills "found" on the street, mustard spilled (or saliva spit) onto your shoulder to distract you while they snatch your bag. **Don't ever let your passport or bags out of your sight.** Beware of **pickpockets** in city crowds, especially on public transportation. Also, be alert in public telephone booths: If you must say your calling card number, do so very quietly; if you punch it in, make sure no one can look over your shoulder.

ACCOMMODATIONS & TRANSPORTATION. Never leave your belongings unattended; crime *can* occur in hostels and hotels. Bring your own **padlock** for hostel lockers, and don't ever store valuables in any locker.

Be particularly careful on **buses** and **trains;** horror stories abound about determined thieves who wait for travelers to fall asleep. Carry your backpack in front of you where you can see it. When traveling with others, sleep in alternate shifts. When alone, use good judgment in selecting a train compartment: never stay in an empty one, and use a lock to secure your pack to the luggage rack. Try to sleep on top bunks with your luggage stored above you (if not in bed with you), and keep important documents and other valuables on your person. If traveling by **car,** don't leave valuables (such as radios or luggage) in it while you are away.

DRUGS & ALCOHOL

If you carry **prescription drugs** while traveling, it is vital to have a copy of the prescriptions to present at US and Canadian borders. The importation of **illegal substances** into the Canada or the US is highly risky, and a punishable offense. Border guards of both countries have unlimited rights to search your baggage, your person, and your vehicle. They will seize vehicles on the spot that are found to be involved in smuggling even small quantities of illegal substances. US border guards can also ban you on the spot from re-entering the country for years. If you are not a US citizen, you may have no right to appeal such decisions. Away from borders, police attitudes vary widely, but the old standards—marijuana, LSD, heroin, cocaine—are illegal in every province and state.

In the US, the drinking age is 21; in Canada it is 19, except in Alberta, Manitoba, and Québec, where it is 18. Drinking restrictions are strict; the youthful should expect to be asked to show government-issued identification when purchasing any alcoholic beverage. Drinking and driving is prohibited everywhere, not to mention dangerous and idiotic. Open beverage containers in your car will incur heavy fines; a failed breathalyzer test will mean fines, a suspended license, and possibly imprisonment. Most localities restrict where and when alcohol can be sold under restrictions known as "blue laws." Sales usually stop at a certain time at night and are often prohibited entirely on Sundays.

HEALTH

Common sense is the simplest prescription for good health while you travel. Fortunately, both the US and Canada have excellent health care systems, although medical facilities may be sparse in remote areas.

BEFORE YOU GO

In your **passport,** write the names of any people you wish to be contacted in case of a medical emergency, and list any allergies or medical conditions. Matching a prescription to a foreign equivalent is not always easy, safe, or possible, so carry up-to-date, legible prescriptions or a statement from your doctor stating the medication's trade name, manufacturer, chemical name, and dosage. While traveling, be sure to keep all medication with you in your carry-on luggage. For tips on packing a basic **first-aid kit** and other health essentials, see p. 33.

IMMUNIZATIONS & PRECAUTIONS

Travelers over two years old should make sure that the following vaccines are up to date: MMR (for measles, mumps, and rubella); DTaP or Td (for diphtheria, tetanus, and pertussis); OPV (for polio); HbCV (for haemophilus influenza B); and HBV (for hepatitis B).

ESSENTIALS

USEFUL ORGANIZATIONS & PUBLICATIONS

The US **Centers for Disease Control and Prevention** (**CDC**; ☎877-FYI-TRIP; toll-free fax 888-232-3299; www.cdc.gov/travel) maintains an international travelers' hotline and an informative website. The CDC's comprehensive booklet *Health Information for International Travel*, an annual rundown of disease, immunization, and general health advice, is free online or US$25 from the Public Health Foundation (☎877-252-1200). Consult the appropriate government agency of your home country for consular information sheets on health, entry requirements, and other issues for various countries (see the listings in the box on **Travel Advisories,** p. 28). For information on medical evacuation services and travel insurance firms, see the US government's website at http://travel.state.gov/medical.html or the **British Foreign and Commonwealth Office** (www.fco.gov.uk).

For detailed information on travel health, including a country-by-country overview of diseases (and a list of travel clinics in the USA), try the **International Travel Health Guide,** by Stuart Rose, MD (US$19.95; www.travmed.com). For general health info, contact the **American Red Cross** (☎800-564-1234; www.redcross.org).

MEDICAL ASSISTANCE ON THE ROAD

Medical care in both the US and Canada is world-class and widespread. In more remote regions, finding doctors can be difficult and expensive. If you are concerned about obtaining medical assistance while traveling, you may wish to employ special support services. The *MedPass* from **GlobalCare, Inc.,** 6875 Shiloh Rd. East, Alpharetta, GA, 30005-8372. (☎800-860-1111; fax 678-341-1800; www.globalems.com), provides 24hr. international medical assistance and medical evacuation resources. If your regular **insurance** policy does not cover travel abroad, you may wish to purchase additional coverage (see p. 32).

Those with medical conditions (such as diabetes, allergies to antibiotics, epilepsy, heart conditions) may want to obtain a **Medic Alert** membership (first year US$35, annually thereafter US$20), which includes a stainless steel ID tag, among other benefits, such as a 24hr. collect-call number. Contact the Medic Alert Foundation, 2323 Colorado Ave, Turlock, CA 95382, USA (☎888-633-4298; outside US ☎209-668-3333; www.medicalert.org).

ONCE IN ALASKA AND THE PACIFIC NORTHWEST

ENVIRONMENTAL HAZARDS

Heat exhaustion and dehydration: Heat exhaustion can lead to fatigue, headaches, and wooziness. Avoid it by drinking plenty of fluids, eating salty foods (e.g. crackers), and avoiding dehydrating beverages (e.g. alcohol and caffeinated beverages). Continuous heat stress can eventually lead to heatstroke, characterized by a rising temperature, severe headache, and cessation of sweating. Victims should be cooled off with wet towels and taken to a doctor.

Sunburn: If you are planning on spending time near water or in the snow (which might be unavoidable), you are at a higher risk of getting burned, even through clouds. If you get sunburned, drink more fluids than usual and apply an aloe-based lotion.

Hypothermia and frostbite: A rapid drop in body temperature is the clearest sign of overexposure to cold. Victims may also shiver, feel exhausted, have poor coordination or slurred speech, hallucinate, or suffer amnesia. **Do not let hypothermia victims fall asleep.** To avoid hypothermia, keep dry, wear layers, and stay out of the wind. When the temperature is below freezing, watch out for frostbite. If skin turns white, waxy, and cold, do not rub the area. Drink warm beverages, get dry, and slowly warm the area with dry fabric or steady body contact until a doctor can be found. While the entire region gets extremely cold in the winter, Northern Canada and Alaska are especially frigid.

High altitude: Allow your body a couple of days to adjust to less oxygen before exerting yourself. Note that alcohol is more potent and UV rays are stronger at high elevations.

INSECT-BORNE DISEASES

Many diseases are transmitted by insects—mainly mosquitoes, fleas, ticks, and lice. Be aware of insects in wet or forested areas, especially while hiking and camping; wear long pants and long sleeves, tuck your pants into your socks, and buy a mosquito net. Use insect repellents and soak or spray your gear with permethrin (licensed in the US for use on clothing). **Lyme disease** is a bacterial infection carried by ticks and marked by a circular bull's-eye rash of 2 in. or more. Later symptoms include fever, headache, fatigue, and aches and pains. Antibiotics are effective if administered early. Left untreated, Lyme can cause problems in joints, the heart, and the nervous system. **Ticks**—responsible for Lyme and other diseases—can be particularly dangerous in rural and forested regions. Be on the lookout for them while camping or hiking in any part of Alaska and the Pacific Northwest. If you find a tick attached to your skin, grasp the head with tweezers as close to your skin as possible and apply slow, steady traction. Removing a tick within 24hr. greatly reduces the risk of infection. Do not try to remove ticks by burning them or coating them with nail polish remover or petroleum jelly.

FOOD- & WATER-BORNE DISEASES

Prevention is the best cure: be sure that your food is properly cooked and the water you drink is clean. When camping, purify your water by using a water filtration system, bringing it to a rolling boil, or treating it with **iodine tablets;** note however that some parasites such as *giardia* have exteriors that resist iodine treatment, so boiling is more reliable. Always wash your hands before eating or bring a quick-drying purifying liquid hand cleaner.

Traveler's diarrhea: Results from drinking untreated water or eating uncooked foods. Symptoms include nausea and bloating. Try quick-energy, non-sugary foods with protein and carbohydrates to keep your strength up. Over-the-counter anti-diarrheals (e.g. Imodium) may counteract the problems. The most dangerous side effect is dehydration; drink 8 oz. of water with ½ tsp. of sugar or honey and a pinch of salt, try uncaffeinated soft drinks, or eat salted crackers. If you develop a fever or your symptoms don't go away after 4-5 days, consult a doctor. Consult a doctor immediately for treatment of diarrhea in children.

Parasites: Microbes, tapeworms, etc. that hide in unsafe water and food. **Giardiasis,** for example, is acquired by drinking untreated water from streams or lakes. Symptoms include swollen glands or lymph nodes, fever, rashes or itchiness, and digestive problems. Boil water, wear shoes, and eat only cooked food.

OTHER INFECTIOUS DISEASES

Rabies: Transmitted through the saliva of infected animals; fatal if untreated. By the time symptoms (thirst and muscle spasms) appear, the disease is in its terminal stage. If you are bitten, wash the wound thoroughly, seek immediate medical care, and try to have the animal located. A rabies vaccine, which consists of 3 shots given over a 21-day period, is available but is only semi-effective.

Hepatitis B: A viral infection of the liver transmitted via bodily fluids or needle-sharing. Symptoms may not surface until years after infection. A 3-shot vaccination sequence is recommended for sexually-active travelers, and anyone planning to seek medical treatment abroad; it must begin 6 months before traveling.

ESSENTIALS

Hepatitis C: Like Hepatitis B, but the mode of transmission differs. IV drug users, those with occupational exposure to blood, hemodialysis patients, and recipients of blood transfusions are at the highest risk, but the disease can also be spread through sexual contact or sharing items like razors that may have traces of blood on them.

AIDS, HIV, & STIS

For detailed information on **Acquired Immune Deficiency Syndrome (AIDS)** in Alaska and the Pacific Northwest, call the **US Centers for Disease Control**'s 24hr. hotline at ☎ 800-342-2437, or the **Joint United Nations Programme on HIV/AIDS (UNAIDS)**, 20, ave. Appia, CH-1211 Geneva 27, Switzerland (☎ 22 791 3666; fax 22 791 4187).

Sexually transmitted infections (STIs) such as gonorrhea, chlamydia, genital warts, syphilis, and herpes are easier to catch than HIV and can be just as deadly. **Hepatitis B** and **C** can also be transmitted sexually (see above). Though condoms may protect you from some STIs, oral or even tactile contact can lead to transmission. If you think you may have contracted an STI, see a doctor immediately.

INSURANCE

Travel insurance generally covers four basic areas: medical/health problems, property loss, trip cancellation/interruption, and emergency evacuation. Although your regular insurance policies may well extend to travel-related accidents, you may consider purchasing travel insurance if the cost of potential trip cancellation/interruption or emergency medical evacuation is greater than you can absorb. Prices for travel insurance purchased separately generally run about US$50 per week for full coverage, while trip cancellation/interruption may be purchased separately at a rate of about US$5.50 per US$100 of coverage.

Medical insurance (especially university policies) often covers costs incurred abroad; check with your provider. **Canadians** are protected by their home province's health insurance plan for up to 90 days after leaving the country; check with the provincial Ministry of Health or Health Plan Headquarters for details. **Homeowners' insurance** (or your family's coverage) often covers theft during travel and loss of travel documents (passport, plane ticket, railpass, etc.) up to US$500.

ISIC and **ITIC** (see p. 24) provide basic insurance benefits, including US$100 per day of in-hospital sickness for up to 60 days, US$3000 of accident-related medical reimbursement, and US$25,000 for emergency medical transport. Cardholders have access to a toll-free 24hr. helpline (run by the insurance provider **TravelGuard**) for medical, legal, and financial emergencies overseas (US and Canada ☎ 877-370-4742, elsewhere call US collect ☎ +1 715-345-0505). **American Express** (US ☎ 800-528-4800) grants most cardholders automatic car rental insurance (collision and theft, but not liability) and ground travel accident coverage of US$100,000 on flight purchases made with the card.

INSURANCE PROVIDERS. Council and **STA** (see p. 46) offer a range of plans that can supplement your basic coverage. Other private insurance providers in the US and Canada include: **Access America** (☎ 800-284-8300); **Berkely Group/Carefree Travel Insurance** (☎ 800-323-3149; www.berkely.com); **Globalcare Travel Insurance** (☎ 800-821-2488; www.globalcare-cocco.com); and **Travel Assistance International** (☎ 800-821-2828; www.europ-assistance.com). Providers in the **UK** include **Columbus Direct** (☎ 020 7375 0011). In **Australia**, try **AFTA** (☎ 02 9375 4955).

PACKING

Pack lightly: lay out only what you absolutely need, then take half the clothes and twice the money. If you plan to do a lot of hiking, also see the section on **Camping & the Outdoors,** p. 36.

LUGGAGE. If you plan to cover most of your itinerary by foot, a sturdy **frame backpack** is unbeatable. (For the basics on buying a pack, see p. 39.) Toting a **suitcase** or **trunk** is fine if you plan to live in one or two cities and explore from there, but a very bad idea if you're going to be moving around a lot. In addition to your main piece of luggage, a **daypack** (a small backpack or courier bag) is a must.

CLOTHING. Dressing in layers is the best way to handle the variable climate in Alaska and the Pacific Northwest. No matter when you're traveling, it's always a good idea to bring a **warm jacket** or wool sweater, a **rain jacket** (Gore-Tex® is both waterproof and breathable), sturdy shoes or **hiking boots,** and **thick socks. Flip-flops** or waterproof sandals are must-haves for grubby hostel showers. You may also want to add one outfit beyond the jeans and t-shirt uniform, and maybe a nicer pair of shoes if you have the room. If you plan to visit any religious or cultural sites, remember that you'll need something besides tank tops and shorts to be respectful.

CONVERTERS & ADAPTERS. In the US and Canada, electricity is 220 volts AC, which is incompatible with the 220/240V appliances found in most other countries. Appliances from anywhere outside North America will need to be used with an **adapter** (which changes the shape of the plug, price varies) and a **converter** (which changes the voltage, $20).

TOILETRIES. Toothbrushes, cold-water soap, talcum powder (to keep feet dry), deodorant, razors, tampons, and condoms are all readily available in the US and Canada. If you wear **contact lenses,** bring an extra pair as well as back-up glasses. Also bring a copy of your prescription in case you need emergency replacements.

FIRST-AID KIT. For a basic first-aid kit, pack bandages, pain reliever, antibiotic cream, a thermometer, a Swiss Army knife, tweezers, moleskin, decongestant, motion-sickness remedy, diarrhea or upset-stomach medication (Pepto Bismol or Imodium), an antihistamine, sunscreen, insect repellent, burn ointment, and a syringe for emergencies (get an explanatory letter from your doctor).

FILM. Camera stores are common in Alaska and the Pacific Northwest, and supplies should be available. Less serious photographers may want to bring a **disposable camera** or two rather than an expensive permanent one. Always pack film in your carry-on luggage, since higher-intensity X-rays are used on checked luggage.

OTHER USEFUL ITEMS. For safety purposes, you should bring a **money belt** and small **padlock.** Basic **outdoors equipment** (plastic water bottle, compass, waterproof matches, pocketknife, sunglasses, sunscreen, hat) may also prove useful. **Quick repairs** of torn garments can be done on the road with a needle and thread; also consider bringing electrical tape for patching tears. If you want to do laundry by hand, bring detergent, a small rubber ball to stop up the sink, and string for a makeshift clothes line. Other things you're liable to forget include an umbrella, sealable **plastic bags** (for damp clothes, food, shampoo, and other spillables), an **alarm clock,** safety pins, rubber bands, a flashlight, earplugs, garbage bags, and a small **calculator.**

IMPORTANT DOCUMENTS. Don't forget your passport, traveler's checks, ATM and/or credit cards, and adequate ID (see p. 24). Also check that you have any of the following that might apply to you: a hosteling membership card (see p. 34), driver's license (see p. 24), travel insurance forms, or rail or bus pass (see p. 48).

ESSENTIALS

ACCOMMODATIONS

HOSTELS

Hostels are generally laid out dorm-style, often with large single-sex rooms and bunk beds, although some offer private rooms for families and couples. They sometimes have kitchens and utensils for your use, bike or moped rentals, storage areas, and laundry facilities. There can be drawbacks: some hostels close during certain daytime "lockout" hours, have a curfew, don't accept reservations, impose a maximum stay, or, less frequently, require that you do chores. In Alaska and the Pacific Northwest, a bed in a hostel will average around US$15-20.

HOSTELLING INTERNATIONAL

Joining the youth hostel association in your own country (listed below) automatically grants you membership privileges in **Hostelling International-American Youth Hostels (HI-AYH)**, a federation of national hosteling associations. HI hostels are scattered throughout Alaska and the Pacific Northwest, and are typically less expensive than private hostels. Many accept reservations via the **International Booking Network** (Australia ☎ 02 9261 1111; Canada ☎ 800-663-5777; England and Wales ☎ 1629 58 14 18; Northern Ireland ☎ 1232 32 47 33; Republic of Ireland ☎ 01 830 1766; NZ ☎ 03 379 9808; Scotland ☎ 8701 55 32 55; US ☎ 800-909-4776; www.hostelbooking.com). HI's umbrella organization's web page (www.iyhf.org), which lists the web addresses and phone numbers of all national associations, can be a great place to begin researching hosteling in a specific region.

Most HI hostels also honor **guest memberships**—you'll get a blank card with space for six validation stamps. Each night you'll pay a nonmember supplement (one-sixth the membership fee) and earn one guest stamp; get six stamps, and you're a member. Most student travel agencies (see p. 46) sell HI cards, as do all of the national hosteling organizations listed below. All prices listed below are valid for **one-year memberships** unless otherwise noted.

Australian Youth Hostels Association (AYHA), Level 3, 10 Mallett St., Camperdown NSW 2050 (☎02 9565 1699; fax 9565 1325; www.yha.org.au). AUS$52, under 18 AUS$16.

Hostelling International-Canada (HI-C), 400-205 Catherine St., Ottawa, ON K2P 1C3 (☎800-663-5777 or 613-237-7884; fax 237-7868; info@hostellingintl.ca; www.hostellingintl.ca). CDN$35, under 18 free.

An Óige (Irish Youth Hostel Association), 61 Mountjoy St., Dublin 7 (☎830 4555; fax 830 5808; anoige@iol.ie; www.irelandyha.org). EUR€15, under 18 EUR€5.

Youth Hostels Association of New Zealand (YHANZ), P.O. Box 436, 193 Cashel St., 3rd Floor Union House, Christchurch 1 (☎03 379 9970; fax 365 4476; info@yha.org.nz; www.yha.org.nz). NZ$40, under 17 free.

Hostels Association of South Africa, 3rd fl. 73 St. George's St. Mall, P.O. Box 4402, Cape Town 8000 (☎021 424 2511; fax 424 4119; info@hisa.org.za; www.hisa.org.za). ZAR45.

Scottish Youth Hostels Association (SYHA), 7 Glebe Crescent, Stirling FK8 2JA (☎01786 89 14 00; fax 89 13 33; www.syha.org.uk). UK£6.

Youth Hostels Association (England and Wales) Ltd., Trevelyan House, 8 St. Stephen's Hill, St. Albans, Hertfordshire AL1 2DY, UK (☎0870 870 8808; fax 01727 84 41 26; www.yha.org.uk). UK£12.50, under 18 UK£6.25, families UK£25.

Hostelling International Northern Ireland (HINI), 22-32 Donegall Rd., Belfast BT12 5JN, Northern Ireland (☎02890 31 54 35; fax 43 96 99; info@hini.org.uk; www.hini.org.uk). UK£10, under 18 UK£6.

Hostelling International-American Youth Hostels (HI-AYH), 733 15th St. NW, #840, Washington, D.C. 20005 (☎202-783-6161; fax 783-6171; hiayhserv@hiayh.org; www.hiayh.org). US$25, under 18 free.

REGIONAL HOSTEL INFORMATION IN WESTERN CANADA

HI British Columbia Region: #402-134 Abbott St., Vancouver, BC V6B 2K4 (☎800-661-0020 or in BC 800-663-5777 or 604-684-7111; fax 604-684-7181; www.hihostels.bc.ca) web site offers online reservations.

HI Southern Alberta Region: 1414 Kensington Rd. NW #203, Calgary, AB T2N 3P9 (☎403-283-5551; www.hostellingintl.ca/Alberta). Online reservations and info on ski-and-stay packages at ski areas in the Rockies.

HI Northern Alberta Region: 10926-88 Avenue Edmonton, AB T6G 021 (☎780-432-7798; www.hostellingintl.ca/Alberta). Online reservations and info on northern Alberta.

OTHER TYPES OF ACCOMMODATIONS

HOTELS, GUESTHOUSES, & PENSIONS

Hotel singles in Alaska and the Pacific Northwest cost about US$45-70 per night, doubles US$65-95. You'll typically have a private bathroom and shower with hot water, although some cheaper places may offer shared restrooms. If you make reservations in writing, indicate your night of arrival and the number of nights you plan to stay. Not all hotels take reservations, and few accept traveler's checks in a foreign currency.

BED & BREAKFASTS (B&BS)

For a cozy alternative to impersonal hotel rooms, B&Bs (private homes with rooms available to travelers) range from the acceptable to the sublime. Rooms in B&Bs generally cost US$40-70 for a single and US$60-90 for a double in Alaska and the Pacific Northwest. For more info on B&Bs, see **Bed & Breakfast Inns Online**, P.O. Box 829, Madison, TN 37116 (☎615-868-1946; info@bbonline.com; www.bbonline.com), **InnFinder**, 6200 Gisholt Dr. #100, Madison, WI 53713 (☎608-285-6600; fax 285-6601; www.inncrawler.com), or **InnSite** (www.innsite.com).

CAMPING & THE OUTDOORS

For those with the proper equipment, camping is one of the least expensive and most enjoyable ways to travel through Alaska and the Pacific Northwest. Camping opportunities in this predominantly rural region are boundless, and many are accessible to inexperienced travelers. Generally, private campgrounds have sites for a small fee and offer even the most inexperienced campers safety and security. Campsites in national parks and other scenic areas vary widely in price (some are free, others as much as private campgrounds) but require more experience than camping at a campground, since there are rarely as many people around. An excellent general resource for travelers planning on camping or spending time in the outdoors is the **Great Outdoor Recreation Pages** (www.gorp.com).

USEFUL PUBLICATIONS & RESOURCES

A variety of publishing companies offer hiking guidebooks to meet the educational needs of novice or expert. For information about camping, hiking, and biking, write or call the publishers listed below to receive a free catalog.

The Milepost, 619 E Ship Creek Ave., Anchorage, AK 99501 (☎800-726-4707 or 706-722-6060; www.themilepost.com). An annual trip planning publication—essential for a trip to Alaska, but also useful for British Columbia, Alberta, and the Yukon.

Sierra Club Books, 85 Second St., 2nd fl., San Francisco, CA 94105, USA (☎415-977-5500; www.sierraclub.org/books). Publishes general resource books on hiking, camping, and provides advice for women traveling in the outdoors, as well as books on hiking in Alaska, British Columbia, The Pacific, and The Rockies.

The Mountaineers Books, 1001 SW Klickitat Way, #201, Seattle, WA 98134, USA (☎800-553-4453 or 206-223-6303; fax 223-6306; www.mountaineersbooks.org). Over 400 titles on hiking, biking, mountaineering, natural history, and conservation.

Wilderness Press, 1200 Fifth St., Berkeley, CA 94710, USA (☎800-443-7227 or 510-558-1666; fax 558-1696; www.wildernesspress.com). Over 100 hiking guides/maps, with dozens of Alaska and the Pacific Northwest.

Woodall Publications Corporation, 2575 Vista Del Mar Dr., Ventura, CA 93001, USA (☎800-323-9076 or 805-667-4100; www.woodalls.com). Woodall publishes the annually updated *Woodall's Campground Directory* (US$22).

NATIONAL PARKS

National parks protect some of the US and Canada's most precious wildlife and spectacular scenery. The parks also offer activities such as hiking, skiing, and snowshoe expeditions. Most have backcountry camping and developed campgrounds; others welcome RVs, and a few offer opulent living in grand lodges.

Entry fees vary from park to park. In US parks pedestrian and cyclist entry fees tend to range from US$2-10, while vehicles cost US$5-20. National parks in the US offer a number of passes. The **National Parks Pass** (US$50 a year) admits the bearer and accompanying passengers in a vehicle (or family members where access is not

CAMPING RESERVATION NUMBERS. Reservations Northwest (☎888-755-6900 or 206-935-1055; www.reservationsnorthwest.com) books campsites at many Oregon and Washington state parks (no reservation fee). The Oregon state parks info line (☎800-452-5687; www.prd.state.or.us) and its Washington equivalent (☎800-233-0321; www.parks.wa.gov) provide info on all state parks, including those not listed with the reservations center, and can refer callers to the agencies responsible for all other campsites in the state. The National Recreation Reservation service partners with the **US Forest Service (USFS)** to offer a reservations line (☎877-444-6777; www.reserveUSA.com) for selected campgrounds in national forests in Washington, Oregon, Alaska, and USFS cabins in southeast Alaska. For info on USFS campgrounds, cabins, and fire lookouts in Washington and Oregon not listed with the nationwide network, contact **Nature of the Northwest,** 800 NE Oregon St. #177, Portland, OR (☎503-872-2750; www.naturenw.org). **BC Discover Camping** (☎800-689-9025 or 604-689-9025) reserves sites at many of the BC provincial parks (CDN$12-20 per night; reservation fee CDN$6.42 per night for first 3 nights). For info on other, non-reservable provincial park campsites, call ☎250-387-4550. **Supernatural British Columbia** (☎800-663-6000; www.hellobc.com) can refer you to private campgrounds throughout BC. State campgrounds in Alaska are all first come, first serve, and cost about US$10.

by vehicle) entry into most US parks. For an additional $15, the Parks Service will affix a **Golden Eagle Pass** hologram to your card which will allow you access to sites managed by the US Fish and Wildlife Service, the US Forest Service, and the Bureau of Land Management. The **Golden Age Passport** ($10 one time fee), available to those 62 or older, and the **Golden Access Passport,** free to travelers who are blind or permanently disabled, allow access to US national parks and 50% off camping and other park fees. Passes are available at park entrances.

The **Western Canada Annual Pass,** available for both individuals and groups, offers a similar deal at Canadian national parks in the four western provinces (CDN$35, seniors over 64 CDN$27, ages 6-16 CDN$18, groups of up to seven adults CDN$70, groups of up to seven which include at least one senior $53).

Let's Go lists fees for individual parks and contact information for park visitors centers (check the index for a complete listing). Every national park in the US and Canada has a web page, accessible from www.nps.gov or http://parkscan-ada.pch.gc.ca, which list contact info, fees, and reservation policies.

US Forest Service, Outdoor Recreation Information Center, 222 Yale Ave. N, Seattle, WA 98109 (☎206-470-4060; www.fs.fed.us).

Parks Canada, 220 4th Ave. SE Room #550, Calgary, AB T2G 4X3 (☎800-748-7275; fax 292-4408; www.parkscanada.pch.gc.ca).

Alaska Public Lands Information Center, 605 W. 4th Ave. #105, Anchorage, AK 99501 (☎907-271-2737, in Fairbanks 456-0527; fax 907-456-0532; www.dnr.state.ak.us).

STATE AND PROVINCIAL PARKS

In contrast to national parks, the primary function of state and provincial parks is usually recreation. Prices for camping at public sites are usually better than those at private campgrounds. Don't let swarming visitors dissuade you from seeing the larger parks—these places can be huge, and even at their most crowded they offer opportunities for quiet and solitude. Most campgrounds are first come, first serve, so arrive early. Some limit your stay and/or the number of people in a group. For general information, contact:

ESSENTIALS

Alaska Department of Natural Resources Public Information, 550 W. 7th Ave. #1260, Anchorage, AK 99501 (☎907-269-8400; fax 269-8901; www.dnr.state.ak.us/parks).

Alberta Park and Protected Areas, 9820 106 St., 2nd fl., Edmonton, AB T5K 2J6 (☎780-427-7009; fax 427-5980; www.gov.ab.ca/env/parks.html).

British Columbia Ministry of Environment, Lands, and Parks, P.O. Box 9338, Stn. Prov. Govt., Victoria, BC V8W 9M1 (☎250-387-1161; www.elp.gov.bc.ca/bcparks).

Oregon State Parks and Recreation Department, 1115 Commercial St. NE, Suite 1, Portland, OR 97301 (☎800-551-6949 or 503-378-6305; fax 503-378-5002; www.prd.state.or.us).

Washington State Parks and Recreation Commission, 7150 Cleanwater Lane, P.O. Box 42650, Olympia, WA 98504, info ☎800-233-0321; www.parks.wa.gov).

Yukon Parks and Outdoor Recreation, Box 2703, Whitehorse, YT Y1A 2C6 (☎867-667-5648; fax 393-6223).

US NATIONAL FORESTS

If national park campgrounds are too developed for your tastes, **national forests** provide a purist's alternative. While some have recreation facilities, most are equipped only for primitive camping; pit toilets and no running water are the norm. (See **Camping Reservation Numbers** p. 37, for reservations.) For general information, including maps, contact the **US Forest Service, Outdoor Recreation Information Center,** 222 Yale Ave. N, Seattle, WA 98109 (☎206-470-4060; www.fs.fed.us).

Backpackers can enjoy specially designated **wilderness areas,** which are even less accessible due to regulations barring vehicles (including mountain bikes). **Wilderness permits** (generally free) are required for backcountry hiking.

In Alaska, the Forest Service oversees more than 200 scenic and well-maintained **wilderness cabins** for public use, scattered throughout the southern and central regions of the state. Reservations and user permits are required along with a fee of $25-65 per party per night. Steep fines are levied for neglecting to obtain these. Three major agencies, along with several smaller agencies, are in charge of the cabins. The best way to find out information about all the cabins is by calling the **Alaska Public Lands Information Center** (☎907-269-8400; www.nps.gov/aplic). They can answer further questions, redirect your inquiries, or mail out maps and brochures.

Many trailhead parking lots in Oregon and Washington National Forests require a Trail Park Pass ($3 per day per vehicle; annual pass for two vehicles $25). Passes are available at area outfitters and convenience stores, but not at trailheads.

The US Department of the Interior's **Bureau of Land Management (BLM)** offers a variety of outdoor recreation opportunities on the 270 million acres it oversees in ten western states and Alaska, including camping, hiking, mountain biking, rock climbing, river rafting, and wildlife viewing. Unless otherwise posted, all public lands are open for recreational use. Write the Alaska State office (☎907-269-8400) in Anchorage at 222 W 7th Ave. #13, Anchorage, AK 99513, or the Washington/Oregon office (☎503-952-6002) at 1515 SW 5th Ave., P.O. Box 2965, Portland, OR 92208 for a guide to BLM campgrounds, many of which are free.

WILDERNESS SAFETY

THE GREAT OUTDOORS

Stay warm, stay dry, and stay hydrated. The vast majority of life-threatening wilderness situations can be avoided by following this simple advice. Prepare yourself for an emergency, however, by always packing raingear, a hat and mittens, a first-aid kit, a reflector, a whistle, high energy food, and extra water for any hike.

Dress in wool or warm layers of synthetic materials designed for the outdoors; never rely on cotton for warmth, as it is useless when wet.

Check **weather forecasts** and pay attention to the skies when hiking, since weather patterns can change suddenly. Whenever possible, let someone know when and where you are going hiking—either a friend, a hostel owner, a park ranger, or a local hiking organization. Do not attempt a hike beyond your ability—you may be endangering your life. See **Health**, p. 29, for information about outdoor ailments and basic medical concerns.

BEARS WILL EAT YOU

If you are hiking in an area which might be frequented by bears, ask local rangers for information on bear behavior before entering any park or wilderness area, and obey posted warnings. No matter how irresistibly cute a bear appears, don't be fooled—they're powerful and unpredictable animals that are not intimidated by humans. If you're close enough for a bear to be observing you, you're too close. If you see a bear at a distance, calmly walk (don't run) in the other direction. If it seems interested, back away slowly while speaking to the bear in firm, low tones and head in the opposite direction or toward a settled area. If you are attacked by a bear, get in a fetal position to protect yourself, put your arms over the back of your neck, and play dead. In all situations, remain calm, as loud noises and sudden movements can trigger an attack.

Don't leave food or other scented items (trash, toiletries, the clothes that you cooked in) near your tent. Bear-bagging—hanging edibles and other good-smelling objects from a tree out of reach of hungry paws—is the best way to keep your toothpaste from becoming a condiment. Bears are also attracted to any perfume, as are bugs, so cologne, scented soap, deodorant, and hairspray should stay at home. For more information, consult *How to Stay Alive in the Woods*, by Bradford Angier (Macmillan Press, US$8).

CAMPING AND HIKING EQUIPMENT

WHAT TO BUY...

Good camping equipment is both sturdy and light. Camping equipment is generally more expensive in Australia, New Zealand, and the UK than in North America.

Sleeping Bag: Most sleeping bags are rated by season ("summer" means 30-40°F at night; "four-season" or "winter" often means below 0°F). They are made either of **down** (warmer and lighter, but more expensive, and miserable when wet) or of **synthetic** material (heavier, more durable, and warmer when wet). Prices range US$80-210 for a summer synthetic to US$250-300 for a good down winter bag. **Sleeping bag pads** include foam pads (US$10-20), air mattresses (US$15-50), and Therm-A-Rest self-inflating pads (US$45-80). Bring a **stuff sack** to store your bag and keep it dry.

Tent: The best tents are free-standing (with their own frames and suspension systems), set up quickly, and only require staking in high winds. Low-profile dome tents are the best all-around. Good 2-person tents start at US$90, 4-person at US$300. Seal the seams of your tent with waterproofer, and make sure it has a rain fly. Other tent accessories include a **battery-operated lantern,** a **plastic groundcloth,** and a **nylon tarp.**

Backpack: Internal-frame packs mold better to your back, keep a lower center of gravity, and flex adequately to allow you to hike difficult trails. **External-frame packs** are more comfortable for long hikes over even terrain, as they keep weight higher and distribute it more evenly. Make sure your pack has a strong, padded hip-belt to transfer weight to your legs. Any serious backpacking requires a pack of at least 4000 in^3 (16,000cc), plus 500 in^3 for sleeping bags in internal-frame packs. Sturdy backpacks cost anywhere from US$125-420—and this is one area in which it doesn't pay to economize. Fill up any pack with something

ESSENTIALS

heavy and walk around the store with it to get a sense of how it distributes weight before buying it. Either buy a **waterproof backpack cover,** or store all of your belongings in plastic bags inside your pack.

Boots: Be sure to wear hiking boots with good **ankle support.** They should fit snugly and comfortably over 1-2 pairs of wool socks and thin liner socks. Break in boots over several weeks first in order to spare yourself painful and debilitating blisters.

Other Necessities: Synthetic layers, like those made of polypropylene, and a **pile jacket** will keep you warm even when wet. A **"space blanket"** will help you to retain your body heat and doubles as a groundcloth (US$5-15). Plastic **water bottles** are virtually shatter- and leak-proof. Bring **water-purification tablets** for when you can't boil water. Although most campgrounds provide campfire sites, you may want to bring a small **metal grate** or **grill** of your own. For those places that forbid fires or the gathering of firewood, you'll need a **camp stove** (the classic Coleman starts at US$40) and a propane-filled **fuel bottle** to operate it. Also don't forget a **first-aid kit, pocketknife, insect repellent, calamine lotion,** and **waterproof matches** or a **lighter.**

...AND WHERE TO BUY IT

The mail-order/online companies listed below offer lower prices than many retail stores, but a visit to a local camping or outdoors store will give you a good sense of the look and weight of certain items.

Campmor, 28 Parkway, P.O. Box 700, Upper Saddle River, NJ 07458, USA (US ☎888-226-7667; elsewhere US ☎+1 201-825-8300; www.campmor.com).

Discount Camping, 880 Main North Rd., Pooraka, South Australia 5095, Australia (☎08 8262 3399; fax 8260 6240; www.discountcamping.com.au).

Eastern Mountain Sports (EMS), 1 Vose Farm Rd., Peterborough, NH 03458, USA (☎888-463-6367 or 603-924-7231; www.shopems.com).

L.L. Bean, Freeport, ME 04033 (US and Canada ☎800-441-5713; UK ☎0800 891 297; elsewhere, call US ☎+1 207-552-3028; www.llbean.com).

Mountain Designs, 51 Bishop St., Kelvin Grove, Queensland 4059, Australia (☎07 3856 2344; fax 3856 0366; info@mountaindesigns.com; www.mountaindesigns.com).

Recreational Equipment, Inc. (REI), Sumner, WA 98352, USA (☎800 426-4840 or 253-891-2500; www.rei.com).

YHA Adventure Shop, 14 Southampton St., Covent Garden, London, WC2E 7HA, UK (☎020 7836 8541; www.yhaadventure.com). The main branch of one of Britain's largest outdoor equipment suppliers.

CAMPERS AND RVS

Renting an RV will always be more expensive than tenting or hosteling, but it's cheaper than staying in hotels and renting a car (see **Rental Cars,** p. 52), and the convenience of bringing along your own bedroom, bathroom, and kitchen makes it an attractive option, especially for older travelers and families with children.

Rates vary widely by region, season (July and August are the most expensive months), and type of RV. Rental prices for a standard RV are around US$1000-1400 per week. It always pays to contact several different companies to compare vehicles and prices.

ENVIRONMENTALLY RESPONSIBLE TOURISM

The idea behind responsible tourism is to leave no trace of human presence behind. A campstove is the safer (and most efficient) way to cook. If you must make a fire, keep it small and use only dead branches or brush rather than cutting vegetation. Make sure your campsite is at least 150 ft. (50m) from water supplies or bodies of water. If there are no toilet facilities, bury human waste (but not paper) at least four inches (10cm) deep, but not more than eight inches (20cm), and 150 ft. or more from any water supplies and campsites. Always pack your trash in a plastic bag and carry it with you until you reach the next trash receptacle. For more information on these issues, contact one of the organizations listed below.

Earthwatch, 3 Clock Tower Place #100, Box 75, Maynard, MA 01754, USA (☎800-776-0188 or 978-461-0081; info@earthwatch.org; www.earthwatch.org).

Ecotourism Society, P.O. Box 668, Burlington, VT 05402, USA (☎802-651-9818; ecomail@ecotourism.org; www.ecotourism.org).

National Audobon Society, Nature Odysseys, 700 Broadway, New York, NY 10003 (☎212-979-3066; travel@audobon.org; www.audobon.org).

Tourism Concern, Stapleton House, 277-281 Holloway Rd., London N7 8HN, UK (☎020 7753 3330; www.tourismconcern.org.uk).

ORGANIZED ADVENTURE TRIPS

Organized adventure tours offer another way of exploring the wild. Activities include hiking, biking, skiing, canoeing, kayaking, rafting, climbing, and going on photo safaris and archaeological digs.

Specialty Travel Index, 305 San Anselmo Ave., #313, San Anselmo, CA 94960, USA (☎800-442-4922 or 415-459-4900; fax 415-459-9474; info@specialtytravel.com; www.specialtytravel.com). Tours worldwide.

AmeriCan Adventures & Roadrunner, P.O. Box 1155, Gardena, CA 90249, USA (☎800-TREK-USA or 310-324-3447; fax 310-324-3562; UK ☎01295 756 2000; www.americanadventures.com). Organizes group adventure camping and hostelling trips (with transportation and camping costs included) in the US and Canada.

KEEPING IN TOUCH

BY MAIL

DOMESTIC RATES

In the **United States,** first-class letters sent and received within the US take 1-3 days and cost $0.37; **Priority Mail** packages up to 1 lb. generally take two days and cost $3.85, up to 5 lb. $7.70. **All days specified denote business days.** For more details, see www.usps.com. Letters sent and received within **Canada** take two to four days and cost CDN$0.48; Xpresspost packages take less time and rates for this service can be calculated at http://www.canadapost.ca/personal/tools/rc/res/bin/rcres_ultrawide-e.shtm. For additional information, see www.canadapost.ca.

SENDING MAIL HOME FROM THE US AND CANADA

Airmail is the best way to send mail home from the US and Canada. **Aerogrammes,** printed sheets that fold into envelopes and travel via airmail, are available at post offices. Write "par avion" or "air mail" on the front. Most post offices will charge exorbitant fees or simply refuse to send aerogrammes with enclosures. **Surface mail** is by far the cheapest and slowest way to send mail. It takes one to three months to cross the Atlantic and two to four to cross the Pacific—good for items you won't need to see for a while, such as souvenirs or other articles you've acquired along the way that are weighing down your pack. Check with the closest post office to find out about postage rates to your home country.

SENDING MAIL TO THE US AND CANADA

Mark envelopes "air mail" or "par avion," or your letter or postcard will never arrive. In addition to the standard postage system whose rates are listed below, **Federal Express** (Australia ☎ 13 26 10; US and Canada ☎ 800-247-4747; New Zealand ☎ 0800 73 33 39; UK ☎ 0800 12 38 00; www.fedex.com) handles express mail services from most home countries to the US, as well as within the country; for example, they can get a letter from New York to Los Angeles in 2 days for $9.95, and from London to New York in two days for UK£25.80.

RECEIVING MAIL IN THE US AND CANADA

There are several ways to arrange pick-up of letters sent to you by friends and relatives while you are abroad. Mail can be sent via General Delivery to almost any city or town in the US or Canada that has a post office. Address General Delivery letters as in the following example:

> Butch EMMIT
> General Delivery
> Portland, OR 97204 USA

The mail will go to a special desk in the central post office, unless you specify a post office by street address or postal code. Bring your passport or other photo ID for pick-up. If the clerks insist that there is nothing for you, have them check under your first name as well. *Let's Go* lists post offices in the Practical Information section for each city and most towns.

American Express's travel offices throughout the world offer a free Client Letter Service (mail held up to 30 days and forwarded upon request) for cardholders who contact them in advance. Address the letter in the same way shown above. Some offices will offer these services to non-cardholders (especially AmEx Travelers Cheque holders), but call ahead to make sure. Let's Go lists AmEx office locations for most large cities in Practical Information sections; for a complete, free list, call ☎ 800-528-4800.

BY TELEPHONE

CALLING HOME FROM THE US AND CANADA

A **calling card** is probably your cheapest bet. Calls are billed collect or to your account. You can frequently call collect without even possessing a company's calling card just by calling their access number and following the instructions. *Let's Go* has recently partnered with ekit.com to provide a calling card that offers a number of services, including email and voice messaging. Before purchasing any calling card, always be sure to compare rates with other cards, and to make sure it serves your needs (a local phonecard is generally better for local calls, for instance). For more information, visit www.letsgo.ekit.com.

You can often also make **direct international calls** from pay phones, but if you aren't using a calling card, you may need to drop your coins as quickly as your words. Where available, prepaid phone cards (see below) and occasionally major credit cards can be used for direct international calls, but they are still less cost-effective. (See the box on **Placing International Calls** (p. 43) for directions on how to place a direct international call.)

PLACING INTERNATIONAL CALLS. To call the US or Canada from home or to call home from the US or Canada, dial:

1. The **international dialing prefix.** To dial out of out of **Canada** or the **US,** 011; **Australia,** dial 0011; the **Republic of Ireland, New Zealand,** or the **UK,** 00; **South Africa,** 09.
2. The **country code** of the country you want to call. To call **Canada** or the **US,** 1; **Australia,** dial 61; the **Republic of Ireland,** 353; **New Zealand,** 64; **South Africa,** 27; the **UK,** 44.
3. The **city/area code.** Let's Go lists the city/area codes for cities and towns in the US and Canada opposite the city or town name, next to a ☎. If the first digit is a zero (e.g., 020 for London), omit the zero when calling from abroad (e.g., dial 20 from Canada to reach London).
4. The **local number.**

CALLING WITHIN THE US AND CANADA

The simplest way to call within the country is to use a coin-operated phone; local calls cost US $0.35 in the United States and CDN$0.25 in Canada. **Prepaid phone cards,** which carry a certain amount of phone time depending on the card's denomination, usually save time and money in the long run, although they often require a US$0.25 surcharge from pay phones. These cards can be used to make both international and domestic calls.

TIME DIFFERENCES

Alaska and the Pacific Northwest covers several time zones, anywhere from 7 to 9 hours ahead of **Greenwich Mean Time (GMT).** Both the US and Canada observe daylight savings time, so clocks are set forward one hour in the spring and backward one hour in the fall.

3AM	4AM	5AM	7AM	NOON	1PM	10PM
Vancouver	Edmonton	Toronto	London	Cape Town	Sydney
Seattle	Calgary	Ottawa	(GMT)		Canberra
San Francisco	Jasper	New York			Melbourne
Los Angeles		Boston			

BY EMAIL AND INTERNET

Though in some places it's possible to forge a remote link with your home server, in most cases this is a much slower (and thus more expensive) option than taking advantage of free **web-based email accounts** (e.g., www.hotmail.com and www.yahoo.com). Travelers with laptops can call an Internet service provider via a **modem.** Long-distance phone cards specifically intended for such calls can defray normally high phone charges; check with your long-distance phone provider to see if it offers this option. **Internet cafes** and the occasional free Internet terminal at a public library or university are listed in the **Practical Information** sections of major cities. **Internet Cafés Alaska** features a large database of access points (http://www.netcafeguide.com/countries/USAAK.htm).

GETTING TO ALASKA AND THE PACIFIC NORTHWEST

BY PLANE

When it comes to airfare, a little effort can save you a bundle. If your plans are flexible enough to deal with the restrictions, courier fares are the cheapest. Tickets bought from consolidators and standby seating are also good deals, but last-minute specials, airfare wars, and charter flights often beat these fares. The key is to hunt around, to be flexible, and to ask persistently about discounts. Students, seniors, and those under 26 should never pay full price for a ticket.

COMMERCIAL AIRLINES

Airfares to the US and Canada peak over the summer; in addition, during national holidays (see p. 2), it becomes especially expensive and difficult to travel. Otherwise, flight prices remain steady throughout the year. Midweek (M-Th morning) round-trip flights run US$40-50 cheaper than weekend flights, but they are generally more crowded and less likely to permit frequent-flier upgrades. Not fixing a return date ("open return") or arriving in and departing from different cities ("open-jaw") can be pricier than round-trip flights. Patching one-way flights together is the most expensive way to travel. Flights between capitals or regional hubs in Alaska and the Pacific Northwest—such as Portland, Seattle, Calgary, and Anchorage—will tend to be cheaper.

If the Pacific Northwest is only one stop on a more extensive globe-hop, consider a round-the-world (RTW) ticket. Tickets usually include at least five stops and are valid for about a year; prices range from US$1200-5000. Try **Northwest Airlines/KLM** (US ☎ 800-447-4747; www.nwa.com) or **Star Alliance**, a consortium of 22 airlines including United Airlines (US ☎ 800-241-6522; www.star-alliance.com).

The commercial airlines' lowest regular offer is the **APEX** (Advance Purchase Excursion) fare, which provides confirmed reservations and allows "open-jaw" tickets. Generally, reservations must be made seven to 21 days ahead of departure, with seven- to 14-day minimum-stay and up to 90-day maximum-stay restrictions. These fares carry hefty cancellation and change penalties (fees rise in summer). Book summer APEX fares early; by May you will have a hard time getting your desired departure date. Use **Microsoft Expedia** (msn.expedia.com) or **Travelocity** (www.travelocity.com) to get an idea of the lowest published fares, and then use the resources outlined here to try and beat those fares.

The following chart shows a range of sample round-trip fares between various destinations and some major airport hubs in Alaska and the Pacific Northwest, with origins listed on the left and destinations listed on top. Be forewarned that airline prices change frequently; these are just guidelines.

ALL PRICES IN $US	PORTLAND	SEATTLE	CALGARY	ANCHORAGE
Most North American Locations	$250-650	$250-650	$300-750	$300-750
UK and Ireland	$600-1000	$550-950	$650-1100	$750-1150
Sydney, Australia	$1100-1500	$1000-1400	$1300-1700	$1150-1500
Auckland, New Zealand	$1250-1600	$1200-1600	$1300-1700	$1550-1950
Cape Town/Johannesburg	$800-1200	$750-1150	$650-1050	$850-1250

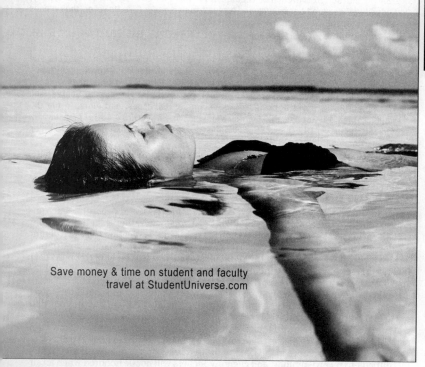

BUDGET & STUDENT TRAVEL AGENCIES

While knowledgeable agents specializing in flights to Alaska and the Pacific Northwest can make your life easy and help you save, they may not spend the time to find you the lowest possible fare—they get paid on commission. Travelers holding **ISIC and IYTC cards** (see p. 24) qualify for big discounts from student travel agencies. Most flights from budget agencies are on major airlines, but in peak season some may sell seats on less reliable chartered aircraft.

usit world (www.usitworld.com). Over 50 **usit campus** branches in the UK, including 52 Grosvenor Gardens, **London** SW1W 0AG (☎0870 240 1010); **Manchester** (☎0161 273 1880); and **Edinburgh** (☎0131 668 3303). Nearly 20 **usit NOW** offices in Ireland, including 19-21 Aston Quay, O'Connell Bridge, **Dublin** 2 (☎01 602 1600; www.usit-now.ie), and **Belfast** (☎02 890 327 111; www.usitnow.com). Offices also in Athens, Auckland, Brussels, Frankfurt, Johannesburg, Lisbon, Luxembourg, Madrid, Paris, Sofia, and Warsaw.

Council Travel (www.counciltravel.com). Countless US offices, including branches in Atlanta, Boston, Chicago, L.A., New York, San Francisco, Seattle, and Washington, D.C. Check the website or call ☎800-226-8624 for the office nearest you. Also an office at 28A Poland St. (Oxford Circus), **London,** W1V 3DB (☎0207 437 7767). *As of May, Council had declared bankruptcy and was subsumed under STA. However, their offices are still in existence and transacting business.*

CTS Travel, 44 Goodge St., **London** W1T 2AD, UK (☎0207 636 0031; fax 637 5328; ctsinfo@ctstravel.co.uk).

STA Travel, 7890 S. Hardy Dr., Ste. 110, Tempe AZ 85284, USA (24hr. reservations and info ☎800-781-4040; www.sta-travel.com). A student and youth travel organization with over 150 offices worldwide (check their website for a listing of all their offices), including US offices in Boston, Chicago, L.A., New York, San Francisco, Seattle, and Washington, D.C. Ticket booking, travel insurance, railpasses, and more. In the UK, walk-in office 11 Goodge St., **London** W1T 2PF or call ☎0207 436 7779. In New Zealand, Shop 2B, 182 Queen St., **Auckland** (☎09 309 0458). In Australia, 366 Lygon St., **Carlton** Vic 3053 (☎03 9349 4344).

Travel CUTS (Canadian Universities Travel Services Limited), 187 College St., **Toronto,** ON M5T 1P7 (☎416-979-2406; fax 979-8167; www.travelcuts.com). 60 offices across Canada. Also in the UK, 295-A Regent St., **London** W1R 7YA (☎0207 255 1944).

STANDBY FLIGHTS

Traveling standby requires considerable flexibility in arrival and departure dates and cities. Companies dealing in standby flights sell vouchers rather than tickets, along with the promise to get you to your destination (or near your destination) within a certain window of time (typically 1-5 days). You call in before your specific window of time to hear your flight options and the probability that you will be able to board each flight. You can then decide which flights you want to try to make, show up at the appropriate airport at the appropriate time, present your voucher, and board if space is available. Vouchers can usually be bought for both one-way and round-trip travel. You may receive a monetary refund only if every available flight within your date range is full; if you opt not to take an available (but perhaps less convenient) flight, you can only get credit toward future travel. Carefully read agreements with any company offering standby flights as tricky fine print can leave you in a lurch. To check on a company's service record in the US, call the **Better Business Bureau** (☎212-533-6200). It is difficult to receive refunds, and clients' vouchers will not be honored when an airline fails to receive payment in time. One established standby company in the US is **Whole Earth Travel,** 325 W. 38th St., New York, NY 10018, USA (☎800-326-2009; fax 212-864-5489; www.4standby.com) and Los Angeles, CA (☎888-247-4482), which offers intracontinental connecting flights within the US or Europe that cost US$79-139.

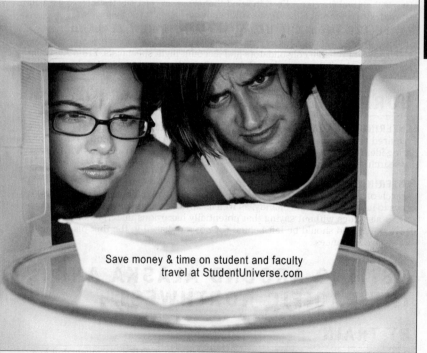

TICKET CONSOLIDATORS

Ticket consolidators, or **"bucket shops,"** buy unsold tickets in bulk from commercial airlines and sell them at discounted rates. The best place to look is in the Sunday travel section of any major newspaper, where many bucket shops place tiny ads. Call quickly, as availability is typically extremely limited. Not all bucket shops are reliable, so insist on a receipt that gives full details of restrictions, refunds, and tickets, and pay by credit card (in spite of the 2-5% fee) so you can stop payment if you never receive your tickets. For more info, see www.travel-library.com/air-travel/consolidators.html.

TRAVELING FROM THE US & CANADA

Travel Avenue (☎ 800-333-3335; www.travelavenue.com) searches for best available published fares and then uses several consolidators to attempt to beat that fare. Some consolidators worth trying are **Interworld** (☎ 305-443-4929; fax 443-0351); **Pennsylvania Travel** (☎ 800-331-0947); **Rebel** (☎ 800-227-3235; travel@rebeltours.com; www.rebeltours.com); **Cheap Tickets** (☎ 800-377-1000; www.cheaptickets.com); and **Travac** (☎ 800-872-8800; fax 212-714-9063; www.travac.com). Yet more consolidators on the web include the **Internet Travel Network** (www.itn.com); **Travel Information Services** (www.tiss.com); **TravelHUB** (www.travelhub.com); and **The Travel Site** (www.thetravelsite.com). Keep in mind that these are just suggestions to get you started with research; *Let's Go* does not endorse any of these agencies.

TRAVELING FROM THE UK, AUSTRALIA, & NEW ZEALAND

In London, the **Air Travel Advisory Bureau** (☎ 0207 636 5000; www.atab.co.uk) can provide names of reliable consolidators and discount flight specialists. From Australia and New Zealand, look for consolidator ads in the travel section of the *Sydney Morning Herald* and other papers.

BORDER CROSSINGS

ENTERING CANADA FROM THE US. Though a passport is not specifically required to cross the Canadian border, proof of citizenship is, and so it pays to bring identification to avoid annoying delays. Don't be surprised if authorities ask to search your car.

ENTERING THE US FROM CANADA. In the wake of September 11, count on a search of your car and a thorough examination of your identification papers. It pays to have your passport handy, as well as any other identification you can muster. It also goes without saying that potentially hazardous materials or items you have purchased should be left behind (or not purchased in the first place) under these circumstances.

GETTING AROUND ALASKA AND THE PACIFIC NORTHWEST

BY TRAIN

By locomotive is one of the most scenic ways to tour the US and Canada, but keep in mind that air travel is much faster, and often much cheaper, than train travel. As with airlines, you can save money by purchasing your tickets as far in advance as possible, so plan ahead and make reservations early. It is essential to travel light on trains; not all stations will check your baggage.

ESSENTIALS

GET CARD.

TRAVEL HARD.

SCENIC DRIVE
FOOD + GAS
LOOKOUT

There's only one way to max out your travel experience and make the most of your time on the road: The International Student Identity Card.

Packed with travel discounts, benefits and services, this card will keep your travel days and your wallet full. Get it before you hit it!

Visit **ISICUS.com** to get the full story on the benefits of carrying the ISIC.

90 minutes, wash & dry (one sock missing).
5 minutes to book online (Detroit to Mom's).

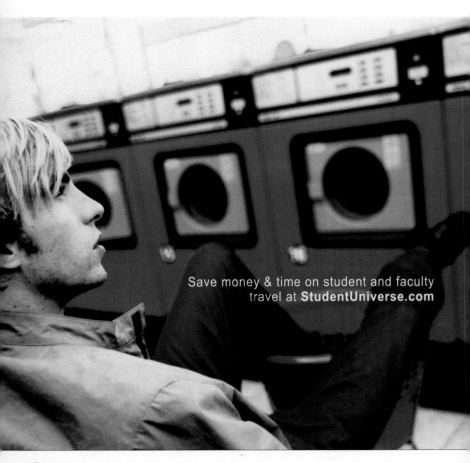

Save money & time on student and faculty
travel at **StudentUniverse.com**

AMTRAK. (☎800-872-7245; www.amtrak.com.) The only provider of intercity passenger train service in most of the US. Their informative web page lists schedules, fares, arrival and departure info, and takes reservations. Discounts on full rail fares are given to: senior citizens (15% off), students with a Student Advantage card (15% off; call 877-2JOINSA to purchase the $20 card; www.studentadvantage.com), travelers with disabilities (15% off), children ages 2-15 accompanied by an adult (50% off up to two children), children under two (free for one child), and US veterans (10% off with a VeteransAdvantage membership card). "Rail SALE" offers online discounts of up to 90%; visit the Amtrak web site for details and reservations.

VIA RAIL. (☎888-842-7245; www.viarail.ca.) Amtrak's Canadian equivalent offers **discounts** on full fares: students 18-24 with ISIC card (35% off full fare); youth 12-17 (35% off full fare); seniors 60 and over (10% off); ages 11 and under, accompanied by an adult (free). Reservations are required for first-class seats and sleep car accommodations. "Supersaver" fares offer discounts between 25-35%. The **Canrail Pass** allows unlimited travel on 12 days within a 30-day period on VIA trains. Between early June and mid-October, a 12-day pass costs CDN$658 (seniors and youths CDN $592). Off-season passes cost CDN$411 (seniors and youths CDN$370). Add CDN$33-$56 for additional days of travel. Call for information on seasonal promotions such as discounts on Grayline Sightseeing Tours.

ALASKA RAILROAD CORPORATION (ARRC). (☎800-544-0552; 907-265-2300; fax 907-265-2323; www.akrr.com). AARC covers 470 mi. of track once per day in each direction from mid-May to mid-September. It connects Seward and Whittier in the south with Anchorage, Denali National Park, and Fairbanks. Children aged 2-11 travel for 50% less. See specific locations for fares, details, and rail options.

BY BUS

Buses generally offer the most frequent and complete service between the cities and towns of the US and Canada. Often a bus is the only way to reach smaller locales without a car. *Russell's Official National Motor Coach Guide* ($17.30 including postage) is an invaluable tool for constructing an itinerary. Updated each month, *Russell's Guide* has schedules of every bus route (including Greyhound) between any two towns in the US and Canada. Russell's also publishes two semiannual supplements that are free when ordered with the May and December issues; a *Directory of Bus Lines and Bus Stations*, and a series of route maps (both $8.40 if ordered separately). To order any of the above, write Russell's Guides, Inc., P.O. Box 278, Cedar Rapids, IA 52406 (☎319-364-6138; fax 365-8728). For those who want someone else to do the itinerary planning for them, **Contiki Travel** (☎1-888-CONTIKI; www.contiki.com) runs comprehensive 8-9 day bus tours starting at $825. Tours include accommodations, transportation and some meals.

GREYHOUND

Greyhound (☎800-231-2222; www.greyhound.com) operates the most routes in the US, but does not serve Alaska. Schedule information is available at any Greyhound terminal or agency, on their web page, or by calling them toll-free.

Advance purchase fares: Reserving space far ahead of time ensures a lower fare, but expect a smaller discount during the busy summer months. For tickets purchased more than 14 days in advance, fares anywhere in the US will be no more than $109 one-way. Fares are often reduced even more for 21-day advance purchases on many popular routes; call for up to the date pricing or consult their web page.

Discounts on full fares: Senior citizens (10% off); children ages 2-11 (50% off); students with a Student Advantage card (up to 15% off); travelers with disabilities and special needs and their companions ride together for the price of one. Active and retired US military personnel and National Guard Reserves (10% off with valid ID) and their spouses and dependents may take a round-trip between any 2 points in the US for $179. With a ticket purchased 3 or more days in advance during the spring and summer months, a friend can travel along for free (some exceptions).

Ameripass: Call ☎888-454-7277. Allows adults unlimited travel through the US for 7 days ($209 for adults, $188.10 senior citizens and students with valid ID); 10 days ($259, $233); 15 days ($319, $287); 21 days ($369, $232); 30 days ($429, $368); 45 days ($469, $422); or 60 days ($599, $539). Passes that allow travel through the US and Canada are for 15 days ($399, $359 student and senior); 21 days ($439, $395); 30 days ($499, $449); 45 days ($569, $512); 60 days ($639, 575). For travel exclusively through western US and Canada, there is a 15 day pass ($299, $269) and a 30 day pass ($399, $359). Children's passes are half the price of adult passes. The pass takes effect the 1st day used.

International Ameripass: For travelers from outside the US. A 4-day pass to travel through the US is $135; a 7-day pass ($185, $166 students with a valid ID and senior citizens); a 10-day pass ($239, $215); 15-day pass ($285, $257); 30-day pass ($385, $347); 45-day pass ($419, $377); 60-day pass ($509, $458). Travel through the US and Canada for 15 days runs ($339, $305); 21 days ($389, $350); 30 days ($449, $404); 45 days ($499, $449); 60 days ($559, $503). The western US and Canada pass is available for 15 days ($299, $269); or 30 days ($399, $359). Call ☎888-454-7277 for info. International Ameripasses are not available at the terminal; they can be purchased in foreign countries at Greyhound-affiliated agencies. Telephone numbers vary by country and are listed on the web page. Passes can also be ordered at the web page, or purchased in Greyhound's International Office, in Port Authority Bus Station, 625 Eighth Ave., New York, NY 10018 (☎800-246-8572 or 212-971-0492; intlameripass@greyhound.com).

GREYHOUND CANADA TRANSPORTATION

Greyhound Canada Transportation, 877 Greyhound Way, Calgary, AB T3C 3V8 (☎800-661-8747; www.greyhound.ca) is Canada's main intercity bus company. The web page has full schedule info.

Discounts: Seniors (10% off); students (25% off with an ISIC; 10% off with other student cards); a companion of a disabled person free; ages 5-11, 50%; under 4 free. If reservations are made at least 7 days in advance, a friend travels half off. A child under 15 rides free with an adult.

Canada Pass: Offers 7, 10, 15, 21, 30, 45, and 60 day unlimited travel from the western border of Canada to Montreal on all routes for North American residents, including limited links to northern US cities. 7 day advance purchase required. 7-day pass (CDN$249, $224 for students); 10-day pass (CDN$319, CDN$287); 15-day pass (CDN$379, CDN$341); 21-day pass (CDN$419, CDN$377); 30-day pass (CDN$449, CDN$404.10); 45-day pass (CDN$535, $482); 60-day pass (CDN$599, CDN$539). The Canada Plus Pass includes coast to coast travel and is slightly more expensive.

GREEN TORTOISE

Green Tortoise, 494 Broadway, San Francisco, CA 94133 (☎800-867-8647 or 415-956-7500; www.greentortoise.com; tortoise@greentortoise.com), offers a more slow-paced, whimsical alternative to straightforward transportation. Green Tortoise's communal "hostels on wheels"—remodeled diesel buses done up for living and eating on the road—traverse the US on aptly named Adventure Tours.

Prices include transportation, sleeping space on the bus, and tours of the regions through which you pass, often including such treats as hot springs and farm stays. Meals are prepared communally and incur an additional food charge. Cross-country trips run February to October between Boston or New York City and San Francisco, Los Angeles, or Seattle (14 days; $429, plus $131). The Grand Alaska Extravaganza takes 30 days to work up from San Francisco to Alaska, and several shorter tours will begin in Alaska itself (call for prices). Prepare for an earthy trip; buses have no toilets and little privacy. Reserve one to two months in advance; deposits ($100 or $500 for Alaska) are generally required. Many trips have space available at departure. Reservations can be made over the phone or through the web.

BY CAR

Carry emergency **food and water** if there's a chance you may be stranded in a remote area. A cell phone is the perfect companion on a road trip, but beware of spotty coverage in rural areas. Always have plenty of **gas** and check road conditions ahead of time (see **Road Conditions**, below), particularly during winter. The huge travel distances of North America will require more gas than you might at first expect. To burn less fuel, make sure your tires have enough air.

> **ROAD CONDITIONS.** Both **Oregon** (☎800-977-6368 or 503-588-2941; www.tripcheck.com) and **Washington** (☎800-695-7623 or 206-368-4499; www.smarttrek.org) have comprehensive web sites with live traffic cameras and up-to-date reports on construction and snow conditions in mountain passes. In **British Columbia,** check the web site www.th.gov.bc.ca/th. The site has links to road conditions in **Alberta** and the **Yukon** as well.

Be sure to **buckle up**—seat belts are required by law in almost every region of the US and Canada. The **speed limit in the US** varies considerably from region to region and road to road. Most urban highways have a limit of 55 mph (88km per hr.), while the limit on rural routes ranges from 60-80 mph (97-128km per hr.). The **speed limit in Canada** is generally 50km per hr. in cities and towns, and 80-110km per hr. (50-68 mph) on highways.

DRIVING PERMITS

If you do not have a license issued by a US state or Canadian province or territory, you might want an **International Driving Permit (IDP).** While the US allows you to drive with a foreign license for up to a year and Canada allows it for six months, the IDP may facilitate things with police if your license is not in English. You must carry your home license with your IDP at all times. It is valid for a year and must be issued in the country of your license, and you must be 18 to obtain one.

Australia: Contact your local Royal Automobile Club (RAC) or the National Royal Motorist Association (NRMA) if in NSW or the ACT (☎08 9421 4444; www.rac.com.au/travel). Permits AUS$15.

Ireland: Contact the nearest Automobile Association (AA) office or write to the UK address below. Permits EUR€5. The Irish Automobile Association, 23 Suffolk St., Rockhill, Blackrock, Co. Dublin (☎01 677 9481), honors most foreign automobile club memberships (24hr. breakdown and road service ☎800 667 788; toll-free in Ireland).

New Zealand: Contact your local Automobile Association (AA) or their main office at Auckland Central, 99 Albert St. (☎ 9 377 4660; www.nzaa.co.nz). Permits NZ$10.

South Africa: Contact the Travel Services Department of the Automobile Association of South Africa at P.O. Box 596, 2000 Johannesburg (☎11 799 1400; fax 799 1410; http://aasa.co.za). Permits ZAR28.50.

UK: To visit your local AA Shop, contact the **AA Headquarters** (☎0870 600 0371), or write to: The Automobile Association, International Documents, Fanum House, Erskine, Renfrewshire PA8 6BW. For more info, see www.theaa.co.uk. Permits UK£4.

AUTO CLUBS

Membership in an auto club, which provides free emergency road-side assistance 24 hours per day, is an important investment for anyone planning to drive on their vacation. AAA and CAA have reciprocal agreements, so a membership in either is good for road service in Canada and America.

American Automobile Association (AAA). (Emergency road service ☎800-222-4357) Offers free trip-planning services, road maps, guidebooks, 24hr. emergency road service anywhere in the US, limited free towing, commission-free traveler's checks from American Express with over 1,000 offices scattered across the country. Discounts on Hertz car rental (5-20%), Amtrak tickets (10%), and various motel chains and theme parks. AAA has reciprocal agreements with auto associations of many other countries, which often provide you with full benefits while in the US. Membership hovers between $50-60 for the first year and less for renewals and additional family members; call ☎800-564-6222 to sign up.

Canadian Automobile Association (CAA). (Emergency road service ☎800-222-4357) 1145 Hunt Club Rd. #200, Ottawa, ON K1V 0Y3. Affiliated with AAA, the CAA provides nearly identical membership benefits. Basic membership is CDN$63 and CDN$32 for associates; call ☎800-564-6222 to sign up.

Mobil Auto Club. (Information ☎800-621-5581; emergency service ☎800-323-5880) 200 N. Martingale Rd., Schaumbourg, IL 60174. Benefits include locksmith reimbursement, towing, roadside service, and car-rental discounts. $7 per month covers you and another driver.

RENTING

Car rental agencies fall into two categories: national companies with hundreds of branches, and local agencies that serve only one city or region. National chains usually allow you to pick up a car in one city and drop it off in another (for a hefty charge, sometimes in excess of $1000), and by calling their toll-free numbers, you can reserve a reliable car anywhere in the country. Generally, airport branches have more expensive rates. All branches except Hertz charge those aged 21-24 an additional fee, but policies and prices vary from agency to agency. If you're 21 or older and have a major credit card in your name, you may be able to rent where the minimum age would otherwise rule you out.

Alamo (☎800-462-52663; www.alamo.com.)

Enterprise (☎800-736-8222; www.enterprise.com.)

Dollar (☎800-800-4000; www.dollar.com.)

Thrifty (☎800-367-2277; www.thrifty.com.)

Budget (☎800-527-0700; www.budget.com.)

Hertz (☎800-654-3131; www.hertz.com.)

Most rental packages offer unlimited mileage, although some allow you a certain number of miles free before the charge of $0.25-0.40 per mile takes effect. Quoted rates do not include gas or tax, so ask for the total cost before handing over the credit card; many large firms have added airport surcharges not covered by the designated fare. Return the car with a full tank unless you sign up for a fuel

> **DRIVING PRECAUTIONS.** When traveling in the summer, bring substantial amounts of **water** (a suggested 5L of water per person per day) for drinking. If radiator fluid is steaming, turn off the car for 30min.—never pour water over the engine to cool it. If you plan to drive in snow, you should also carry a **shovel, traction mats** (burlap sacks or car floor mats make a good substitute in a bind), and **sand** or **kitty litter.** For long drives to unpopulated areas, register with police before beginning the trek, and again upon arrival at the destination. Check with the local automobile club for details. When traveling for long distances, make sure tires are in good repair and have enough air, and get good maps. A **compass** and a **car manual** can also be very useful. You should always carry a **spare tire** and **jack, jumper cables, extra oil, flares, a torch (flashlight),** and **heavy blankets** (in case your car breaks down at night or in the winter). If you don't know how to **change a tire,** learn before heading out, especially if you are planning on traveling in deserted areas. Blowouts on dirt roads are exceedingly common. If you do have a breakdown, **stay with your car;** if you wander off, there's less likelihood trackers will find you. **Sleeping in a vehicle parked on the highway or in the city is extremely dangerous**—even the most dedicated budget traveler should not consider it an option.

option plan that stipulates otherwise. And when dealing with any car rental company, be sure to ask whether the price includes insurance against theft and collision. There may be an additional charge for a **collision and damage waiver (CDW),** which usually comes to about $12-15 per day. Major credit cards (including MasterCard and American Express) will sometimes cover the CDW if you use their card to rent a car; call your credit card company for specifics.

Bolder travelers to Alaska and the Pacific Northwest will want to access some areas that are simply not accessible without a four-wheel drive (4WD) vehicle. If you plan on off-roading it, make sure the vehicle you rent can handle the strain; don't endanger yourself in the interest of saving a few bucks. Cheaper cars tend to be less reliable and harder to handle on difficult terrain, and less expensive 4WD vehicles in particular tend to be more top heavy, making them more dangerous when navigating particularly bumpy roads.

CAR INSURANCE

Some credit cards cover standard insurance. If you rent, lease, or borrow a car, and you are not from the US or Canada, you will need a **green card,** or **International Insurance Certificate,** to certify that you have liability insurance and that it applies abroad. Green cards can be obtained at car rental agencies, car dealerships (for those leasing cars), some travel agents, and some border crossings.

BY BICYCLE

Before you rush onto the bike paths of the Pacific Northwest, remember to make a few preparations. **Bike helmets** are required by law in most of the region and are essential safety gear. A good helmet will cost about $40 to buy; get help to ensure a correct fit. A white headlight and red taillight (and not just reflectors) are likewise both required and indispensable. **Anybody's Bike Book** ($12) provides vital info on repair and maintenance during long-term rides.

Bikeways Local Network (www.bikeways.com/maps2/mapsframe.htm). A compilation of road and cycling maps in British Columbia. Key in route planning.

The Bicycling Visitor's Guide to Seattle (www.cascade.org/visitors_guide.html). Bike routes and information on cycling in and around Seattle.

Oregon Department of Transportation (☎503-986-3556; www.odot.state.or.us/tech-serv/bikewalk). *Oregon Bicycling Guide* and *Oregon Coast Bike Route Map* outline bike routes and campgrounds. (Free; order phone.)

Adventure Cycling Association, P.O. Box 8308-P, Missoula, MT 59807 (☎800-755-2453 or 406-721-1776; fax 721-8754; www.adv-cycling.org). A national, nonprofit organization that maps long-distance routes and organizes bike tours for members. Membership $30 in the US, CDN$35 in Canada, US$45 overseas.

The Canadian Cycling Association, 702-2197 Riverside Drive, Ottawa, ON K1H 7X3 (☎613-248-1353; www.canadian-cycling.com). Sells maps, books, and guides to regions of Canada, Alaska, and the Pacific Coast. Pick up *The Canadian Cycling Association's Complete Guide to Bicycle Touring in Canada* (CDN$24).

BY FERRY

Along the Pacific Coast, ferries are an exhilarating and often unavoidable way to travel. Only a small portion of the Panhandle is accessible by road; most of this area can be reached only by the **Alaska Marine Highway.** Beyond providing basic transportation, the ferries give travelers the chance to enjoy the beauty of the coast. Ferry travel can become quite expensive, however, if you bring a car along. The web site www.ferrytravel.com provides schedules for **Washington State Ferries, Alaska Ferries, BC Ferries,** and seven independent companies.

ALASKA MARINE HIGHWAY

The **Alaska Marine Highway,** Homer Ferry Terminal, 4667 Homer Spit Rd., Suite #1, Juneau, AK 99603 (☎800-382-9229; TDD 800-764-3779; www.akmhs.com) connects the Northwest Coast from Washington to Alaska. The **southeast,** or **Inside Passage,** system runs from Bellingham, WA and Prince Rupert, BC up the coast to Skagway, AK, stopping in Juneau, Ketchikan, Haines, and other towns in southeast Alaska. All southeast ferries have free showers, cafes, and a heated top-deck "solarium" where cabinless passengers can sleep comfortably in sleeping bags; some boats offer lectures on history and ecology. The **southcentral** network serves such destinations as Kodiak Island, Seward, Homer, and Prince William Sound. These two systems are connected by a once-a-month boat going from Juneau to Valdez and Seward. The **southwest** network runs from Kodiak to the Aleutian Islands. There is a slight additional charge for stopovers, which should be reserved at the same time as the rest of your trip. A free printed schedule may be ordered from their web site or by calling or writing.

The **AlaskaPass,** P.O. Box 351, Vashon, WA 98070 (North America ☎800-248-7598 or international 206-463-6550; www.alaskapass.com), offers unlimited access to most of Alaska's railroads, ferries, and buses. A 15-day pass goes for $689 (ages 2-11 $345), and a 22-day pass for $799 (ages 2-11 $400). A flex-pass allows travel on eight non-consecutive days over a 12-day period costs $589 (ages 2-11 $295); one good for 12 out of 21 days goes for $699 ($350). It is valid on most buses, trains, and ferries. Plan carefully for your trip. Short ferry hops in the Panhandle cost as little as $18, and a bus from Anchorage to Fairbanks costs $55. A lot of mileage is required to make the pass worthwhile.

OTHER FERRIES

Information about fares, reservations, vehicles, and schedules often varies with the season. Consult each ferry company when constructing your itinerary in order to clear up any additional questions before finalizing your plans.

BC Ferries (☎888-223-3779 in BC, 250-386-3431 outside BC; fax 381-5452; www.bcferries.bc.ca/ferries). Passenger and vehicle ferry service throughout coastal BC. Service is frequent and reservations are recommended on the longer routes through the **Inside Passage** and **Discovery Coast Passage,** and to the **Queen Charlotte Islands.** Heavy traffic on weekends, particularly in the summer.

Black Ball Transport, Inc. (in Victoria ☎250-386-2202, fax 386-2207; in Port Angeles ☎360-457-4491, fax 457-4493; www.northolympic.com/coho). 2-4 ferries daily between **Port Angeles** and **Victoria.** 90min. $7.50 each way, car and driver $29.50, motorcycle and driver $17.50. Bicycles $3.50 extra. Reservations not accepted.

Victoria Clipper, 2701 Alaskan Way, Pier 69, Seattle, WA 98121 (☎800-888-2535, in Seattle 206-448-5000, in Victoria 250-382-8100; www.victoriaclipper.com). Daily passenger service between **Seattle, WA** and **Victoria, BC.** 2-3hr. $66 one-way, round-trip $79-109 (order 14 days in advance for best prices); bike $10 each way.

Washington State Ferries, 801 Alaskan Way, Seattle, WA 98104 (in Seattle ☎206-464-6400 or in Victoria 250-381-1554; www.wsdot.wa.gov/ferries). Ferries to **Sidney, BC,** and throughout **Puget Sound.** No reservations, except for travel to the **San Juan Islands** or **British Columbia.** Service is frequent, but traffic is heavy—especially in summer, when waits of over an hour to board a ferry are not uncommon. Fares fluctuate but stay reasonable. Bikes $10.

BY THUMB

Let's Go urges you to consider the risks and disadvantages of hitchhiking before thumbing it. Hitching means entrusting your life to a stranger who happens to stop beside you on the road. While this may be comparatively safe in some areas of Europe and Australia, it is **NOT** in most of North America. We do **NOT** recommend it. Don't put yourself in a situation where hitching is the only option.

That said, if you decide to hitchhike, there are precautions you should take. **Women traveling alone should never hitch in the United States.** Refuse a ride if you feel in any way uncomfortable with the driver. If at all threatened or intimidated, ask to be let out no matter how uncompromising the road looks. Have a **back-up plan** in case you get stranded or face an emergency. Carrying a cellular phone for emergency use is a good idea, although coverage is spotty in some isolated areas. In rural areas, hitching is reportedly less risky than in urban areas. Many people hitchhike in the North, but it is not unusual to get stranded on a sparsely traveled route. A wait of a day or two between rides is not uncommon on certain stretches of the Alaska Highway. Alaska state law prohibits moving vehicles from not picking up stranded motorists, as the extreme weather conditions can be life-threatening. However, hitchhikers may only legally thumb for rides on the on-and-off ramps of highways—not on the highways themselves. In fact, all states prohibit hitchhiking while standing on the roadway itself or behind a freeway entrance sign; hitchers more commonly find rides near intersections where many cars converge and well-lit areas where drivers can see their prospective rider and stop safely. Hitchers riding across the **USA-Canada border** should be prepared for a series of queries about citizenship, insurance, contraband, and finances, and for an auto inspection. Walking across the border avoids the hassle.

SPECIFIC CONCERNS

WOMEN TRAVELERS

Women exploring on their own inevitably face some additional safety concerns, but it's easy to be adventurous without taking undue risks. If you are concerned, consider staying in hostels which offer single rooms that lock from the inside or in religious organizations with rooms for women only. Stick to centrally located accommodations and avoid solitary late-night treks or metro rides.

Always carry extra money for a phone call, bus, or taxi. We can't repeat it enough: **Hitchhiking** is never safe for lone women, or even for two women traveling together. When on overnight or long train rides, if there is no women-only compartment, choose one occupied by women or couples. Look as if you know where you're going and approach older women or couples for directions if you're lost or uncomfortable. Generally, the less you look like a tourist, the better off you'll be. Dress conservatively, especially in rural areas. Trying to fit in can be effective, but dressing to the style of an obviously different culture may cause you to be ill at ease and a conspicuous target. Wearing a conspicuous **wedding band** may help prevent unwanted overtures. Your best answer to verbal harassment is no answer at all; feigning deafness, sitting motionless, and staring straight ahead at nothing in particular will do a world of good that reactions usually don't achieve.

For general information about being a female traveler, contact the National Organization for Women (NOW), 733 15th St. NW, Fl. 2, Washington, DC 20005 (☎202-628-8669; www.now.org), which has branches across the US.

TRAVELING ALONE

There are many benefits to traveling alone, including independence and greater interaction with locals. On the other hand, any solo traveler is a more vulnerable target of harassment and street theft. As a lone traveler, try not to stand out as a tourist, look confident, and be especially careful in deserted or very crowded areas. If questioned, never admit that you are traveling alone. Maintain regular contact with someone at home who knows your itinerary. For more tips, pick up *Traveling Solo* by Eleanor Berman (Globe Pequot Press, US$17) or subscribe to **Connecting: Solo Travel Network,** 689 Park Road, Unit 6, Gibsons, BC V0N 1V7, Canada (☎604-886-9099; www.cstn.org; membership US$35). **Travel Companion Exchange,** P.O. Box 833, Amityville, NY 11701, USA (☎631-454-0880, or in the US 800-392-1256; www.whytravelalone.com; US$48), will link solo travelers with companions with similar travel habits and interests.

OLDER TRAVELERS

Senior citizens are eligible for a wide range of discounts on transportation, museums, movies, theaters, concerts, restaurants, and accommodations. If you don't see a senior citizen price listed, ask, and you may be delightfully surprised. The books *No Problem! Worldwise Tips for Mature Adventurers,* by Janice Kenyon (Orca Book Publishers; US$16) and *Unbelievably Good Deals and Great Adventures That You Absolutely Can't Get Unless You're Over 50,* by Joan Rattner Heilman (NTC/Contemporary Publishing; US$13) are both excellent resources. For more information, contact one of the following organizations:

ElderTreks, 597 Markham St., Toronto, ON M6G 2L7 (☎800-741-7956; www.eldertreks.com). Adventure travel programs for the 50+ traveler.

ESSENTIALS

Elderhostel, 11 Ave. de Lafayette, Boston, MA 02111 (☎877-426-8056; www.elderhostel.org). Organizes 1- to 4-week "educational adventures."

The Mature Traveler, P.O. Box 15791, Sacramento, CA 95852 (☎800-460-6676). Deals, discounts, and travel packages for the 50+ traveler. Subscription$30.

Walking the World, P.O. Box 1186, Fort Collins, CO 80522 (☎800-340-9255; www.walkingtheworld.com). Organizes trips for 50+ travelers.

BISEXUAL, GAY, & LESBIAN TRAVELERS

American cities are generally accepting of all sexualities, and thriving gay and lesbian communities can be found in most cosmopolitan areas. Most college towns are gay-friendly as well. However, homophobia can still be encountered almost anywhere. The more rural you get, the more rampant it is likely to be. Listed below are contact organizations, mail-order bookstores, and publishers that offer materials addressing some specific concerns. **Out and About** (www.planetout.com) offers a bi-weekly newsletter addressing travel concerns and a comprehensive site addressing gay travel concerns.

Gay's the Word, 66 Marchmont St., London WC1N 1AB, UK (☎20 7278 7654; www.gaystheword.co.uk). The largest gay and lesbian bookshop in the UK, with both fiction and non-fiction titles. Mail-order service available.

Giovanni's Room, 1145 Pine St., Philadelphia, PA 19107, USA (☎215-923-2960; www.queerbooks.com). An international lesbian/feminist and gay bookstore with mail-order service (carries many of the publications listed below).

International Lesbian and Gay Association (ILGA), 81 rue Marché-au-Charbon, B-1000 Brussels, Belgium (☎+32 2 502 2471; www.ilga.org). Provides political information, such as homosexuality laws of individual countries.

TRAVELERS WITH DISABILITIES

US federal law dictates that all public buildings must be handicapped-accessible, and recent laws governing building codes have made disabled access more the norm than the exception. Businesses, transportation companies, national parks, and public services must assist the disabled in using their facilities. However, traveling with a disability still requires planning and flexibility.

Those with disabilities should inform airlines and hotels of their disabilities when making reservations; some time may be needed to prepare special accommodations. Call ahead to restaurants, museums, and other facilities to find out if they are handicapped-accessible. **Guide dog owners** should inquire as to the quarantine policies of each destination country.

FURTHER READING: BISEXUAL, GAY, & LESBIAN.
Spartacus International Gay Guide 2002-2003. Bruno Gmunder Verlag (US$33).
Damron Men's Guide, Damron Road Atlas, Damron's Accommodations, and *The Women's Traveller.* Damron Travel Guides (US$14-19). For more info, call ☎800-462-6654 or visit www.damron.com.
Ferrari Guides' Gay Travel A to Z, Ferrari Guides' Men's Travel in Your Pocket, and *Ferrari Guides' Inn Places.* Ferrari Publications (US$16-20). Purchase the guides online at www.ferrariguides.com.
Gayellow Pages USA/Canada, Frances Green. Gayellow pages (US$16). They also publish smaller regional editions. Visit Gayellow pages online at www.gayellowpages.com.

In the US, both Amtrak and major airlines will accommodate disabled passengers if notified at least 72 hours in advance. Amtrak offers a 15% discount to physically disabled travelers (☎800-872-7245,TDD/TTY 800-523-6590).

If you are planning to visit a national park or attraction in the US run by the National Park Service, obtain a free **Golden Access Passport,** which is available at all park entrances and from federal offices whose functions relate to land, forests, or wildlife. The Passport entitles disabled travelers and their families to free park admission and provides a 50% discount on all campsite and parking fees.

USEFUL ORGANIZATIONS

Mobility International USA (MIUSA), P.O. Box 10767, Eugene, OR 97440, USA (☎541-343-1284, voice and TDD; www.miusa.org). Sells *A World of Options: A Guide to International Educational Exchange, Community Service, and Travel for Persons with Disabilities* (US$35).

Society for the Advancement of Travel for the Handicapped (SATH), 347 Fifth Ave., #610, New York, NY 10016, USA (☎212-447-7284; www.sath.org). An advocacy group that publishes free travel information and the travel magazine *OPEN WORLD* (US$18, free for members). Annual membership US$45, students and seniors US$30.

TOUR AGENCIES

Directions Unlimited, 123 Green Ln., Bedford Hills, NY 10507, USA (☎800-533-5343). Books individual and group vacations for the physically disabled; not an info service.

The Guided Tour Inc., 7900 Old York Rd., #114B, Elkins Park, PA 19027, USA (☎800-783-5841; www.guidedtour.com). Organizes travel programs for persons with developmental and physical challenges in the US and Canada.

MINORITY TRAVELERS

Racial and ethnic minorities sometimes face blatant and, more often, subtle discrimination and/or harassment, although regions in the US and Canada differ drastically in their general attitudes toward race relations. Verbal harassment is now less common than unfair pricing, false information on accommodations, or inexcusably slow or unfriendly service at restaurants. The best way to deal with such encounters is to remain calm and report individuals to a supervisor, and establishments to the Better Business Bureau for the region (the operator will provide local listings). Contact the police in extreme situations. *Let's Go* always welcomes reader input regarding discriminating establishments.

In larger cities, African-Americans can usually consult chapters of the Urban League and the **National Association for the Advancement of Colored People (NAACP)** (www.naacp.org) for info on events of interest to African-Americans.

TRAVELERS WITH CHILDREN

Family vacations often require that you slow your pace, and always require that you plan ahead. If you rent a car, make sure the rental company provides a car seat for younger children. **Be sure that your child carries some sort of ID** in case of an emergency or in case he or she gets lost. Finding a private place for **breast feeding** is often a problem while traveling, so plan accordingly.

Museums, tourist attractions, accommodations, and restaurants often offer discounts for children. Children under two generally fly for 10% of the adult airfare on international flights (this does not necessarily include a seat). International fares are usually discounted 25% for children from two to 11.

For more information about traveling with children of all ages, consult one of the following books:

Backpacking with Babies and Small Children, Goldie Silverman. Wilderness Press (US$10).

How to take Great Trips with Your Kids, Sanford and Jane Portnoy. Harvard Common Press (US $10).

Have Kid, Will Travel: 101 Survival Strategies for Vacationing With Babies and Young Children, Claire and Lucille Tristram. Andrews McMeel Publishing (US$9).

Kidding Around Portland. Deborah Cuyle (US$8).

Adventuring with Children: An Inspirational Guide to World Travel and the Outdoors, Nan Jeffrey. Avalon House Publishing (US$15).

Trouble Free Travel with Children, Vicki Lansky. Book Peddlers (US$9).

DIETARY CONCERNS

Vegetarians should have no problems getting by in Alaska and the Pacific Northwest. *Let's Go* consistently tries to list vegetarian-friendly establishments and grocery stores. The North American Vegetarian Society, P.O. Box 72, Dolgeville, NY 13329 (☎518-568-7970; www.navs-online.org), publishes information about vegetarian travel, including *Transformative Adventures, a Guide to Vacations and Retreats* (US$15), and the *Vegetarian Journal's Guide to Natural Food Restaurants in the US and Canada* (US$12). For more information, visit your local bookstore or health food store, and consult *The Vegetarian Traveler: Where to Stay if You're Vegetarian,* by Jed and Susan Civic (Larson Publications; US$16).

Travelers who keep kosher should contact synagogues in larger cities for information on kosher restaurants. Your own synagogue or college Hillel should have access to lists of Jewish institutions across the nation. If you are strict in your observance, you may have to prepare your own food on the road, especially as the towns you visit become more remote. A good resource is the *Jewish Travel Guide,* by Michael Zaidner (Vallentine Mitchell; US$17).

OTHER RESOURCES

Listed below are books and web sites that can serve as jumping off points for your own research beyond what *Let's Go* can offer.

TRAVEL PUBLISHERS & BOOKSTORES

Hippocrene Books, Inc., 171 Madison Ave., New York, NY 10016, USA (☎718-454-2366; www.hippocrenebooks.com). Publishes foreign language dictionaries and language learning guides.

Hunter Publishing, 470 W. Broadway, Fl. 2, South Boston, MA 02127, USA (☎617-269-0700; www.hunterpublishing.com). Has an extensive catalog of travel guides and diving and adventure travel books.

Rand McNally, P.O. Box 7600, Chicago, IL 60680, USA (☎847-329-8100; www.randmcnally.com), publishes road atlases.

Adventurous Traveler Bookstore, P.O. Box 2221, Williston, VT 05495, USA (☎800-282-3963; www.adventuroustraveler.com).

Bon Voyage!, 2069 W. Bullard Ave., Fresno, CA 93711, USA (☎800-995-9716, from abroad 559-447-8441; www.bon-voyage-travel.com). They specialize in Europe but have titles pertaining to other regions as well. Free newsletter.

Travel Books & Language Center, Inc., 4437 Wisconsin Ave. NW, Washington, D.C. 20016, USA (☎800-220-2665; www.bookweb.org/bookstore/travelbks/). Over 60,000 titles from around the world.

WORLD WIDE WEB

Almost every aspect of budget travel is accessible via the web. Within 10 minutes at the keyboard, you can make a reservation at a hostel, get advice on travel hotspots from other travelers who have just returned from Alaska and the Pacific Northwest, or find out exactly how much a train from Portland to Seattle costs.

Listed here are some budget travel sites to start off your surfing; other relevant web sites are listed throughout the book. Because website turnover is high, use search engines (such as www.google.com) to strike out on your own.

THE ART OF BUDGET TRAVEL

How to See the World, www.artoftravel.com. A compendium of great travel tips, on everything from cheap flights to self defense to interacting with local culture.

Travel Library, www.travel-library.com. A fantastic set of links for general information and personal travelogues.

Lycos, cityguide.lycos.com. General introductions to cities and regions throughout the US and Canada, with by links to applicable histories, news, and local tourism sites.

 WWW.LETSGO.COM Our newly designed website now features the full online content of all of our guides. In addition, trial versions of all nine City Guides are available for download on Palm OS™ PDAs. Our website also contains our newsletter, links for photos and streaming video, online ordering of our titles, info about our books, and a travel forum buzzing with stories and tips.

INFORMATION ON ALASKA AND THE PACIFIC NORTHWEST

CIA World Factbook, www.odci.gov/cia/publications/factbook/index.html. Tons of vital statistics on the geography, government, economy, and people of the US and Canada.

MyTravelGuide, www.mytravelguide.com. Country overviews, with everything from history to transportation to live web cam coverage of the US and Canada.

Geographia, www.geographia.com. Highlights and culture of the US and Canada.

Atevo Travel, www.atevo.com/guides/destinations. Detailed introductions, travel tips, and suggested itineraries.

World Travel Guide, www.travel-guides.com/navigate/world.asp. Helpful practical info.

PlanetRider, www.planetrider.com. For the US and Canada, this website has a subjective list of links to the "best" websites covering regional culture and tourist attractions.

ALTERNATIVES TO TOURISM

Traveling from place to place around the world may be a memorable experience. But if you are looking for a more rewarding and complete way to see the world, you may want to consider alternatives to tourism. Working, volunteering, or studying for an extended period of time can be a better way to understand life in Alaska and the Pacific Northwest. This chapter outlines some of the ways to get to know a new place, whether you want to pay your way through, or just get the personal satisfaction that comes from studying and volunteering. In most cases, you will feel that you partook in a more meaningful and educational experience—something that the average budget traveler often misses out on. In addition to their jaw-dropping beauty, the national parks and wildlife reserves of Alaska and the Pacific Northwest can offer substantial work opportunities. The bustling tourism industries of American and Canadian cities and attractions also draw students and travelers who want more than temporary fulfillment from their destinations.

VISA INFORMATION
Both the United States and Canada require special work permits before a visitor can get paid work opportunities. For information on how to obtain the proper permissions, see **"Visas, Invitations, & Work Permits,"** p. 23.

STUDYING ABROAD

If you are currently studying as an undergraduate and would like to get credit for schoolwork completed abroad, check with universities in your home country to see if they offer exchanges with particular North American schools. The website at www.studyabroad.com lists term-time and summer study opportunities around the world. Citizens of Australia, New Zealand, the UK, and Ireland can contact their local member organization of the **Experiment in International Living,** P.O. Box 676 Brattleboro, VT 05302, USA (☎802-257-7751; fax 258-3428; www.experiment.org), also known as the **School for International Training (SIT)** and **World Learning.** They can help arrange homestays, academic study abroad, study at language schools, and volunteer work.

Thanks to government subsidies, tuition at Canadian schools is generally affordable. Although foreign students pay more than Canadian citizens, the total cost can be less than half of American schools.

Foreign students who wish to study in the US or Canada must apply to schools first, be admitted, and then begin the application for the appropriate visa. Studying in the US requires either an M-1 visa (vocational studies) or an F-1 visa (for full-time students enrolled in an academic or language program). Studying in Canada requires a student authorization (IMM 1208) in addition to the appropriate tourist visa. Students must prove sufficient financial support, and be in good health (see **Entrance Requirements,** p. 21).

Most American undergraduates enroll in programs sponsored by US universities. Those relatively fluent in English may find it cheaper to enroll directly in a local university (although getting credit may be more difficult). Some schools that offer study abroad programs as well as organizations that can facilitate study abroad opportunities are listed below.

Association of Commonwealth Universities (ACU), John Foster House, 36 Gordon Sq., London WC1H OPF (☎+44 020 7380 6700; www.acu.ac.uk). Publishes information about Commonwealth institutions including the University of British Columbia, University of Alberta, and Athabasca University, among others.

International Association for the Exchange of Students for Technical Experience (IAESTE), 10400 Little Patuxent Pkwy. Suite 250, Columbia, MD 21044-3519, USA (☎410-997-2200, www.aipt.org). 8- to 12-week programs in Canada for college students who have completed 2 years of technical study. US$25 application fee.

University of Alaska, Anchorage. Summer Sessions, 3211 Providence Dr., Anchorage, AK 99508, USA (☎907-786-6740, http://www.uaa.alaska.edu).

University of Alberta Faculty of Graduate Students and Research (FGSR), Edmonton, Alberta, Canada (see website for phone contact information and correct street address, which varies with department. http://gradfile.fgsro.ualberta.ca/international.)

University of Oregon Office of International Programs (OIP), 5209 University of Oregon. Room 330 Oregon Hall, Eugene, OR 97403-5209, USA (☎541-346-3206, http://oip.oregon.edu). International students with F-1 or J-1 visas can enroll in one of the many programs offered by the university. Check the website for details and admissions information.

University of Washington, 1410 NE Campus Parkway, Box 355852, Seattle, Washington 98195-5852, USA. (☎206-543-9686; http://www.washington.edu/students/uga/in). Website offers a ton of information for international students seeking to apply. Open M-F 8am-5pm.

LANGUAGE SCHOOLS

Unlike American universities, language schools are frequently independently-run organizations or divisions of foreign universities that rarely offer college credit. Language schools are a good alternative to university study if you're looking to focus on a language or want a less rigorous courseload. These programs are also good for younger high school students that might not feel comfortable with older students in a college academic environment. Some good programs include:

Oregon State University English Language Institute (ELI), 301 Snell Hall, Corvallis, OR 97331-1632, USA (☎541-737-2464; http://www.orst.edu/dept/eli). Specifically addresses the needs of both teens and adults. US$75 application fee.

University of British Columbia English Language Institute (ELI), 2121 West Mall, Vancouver, BC, Canada V6T 1Z4 (☎604-822-1555; http://www.eli.ubc.ca). Services include both long- and short-term programs; ELI can also set visiting students up with accommodations.

University of Washington International and English Language Programs, 5001 25th Ave. NE, Seattle, WA 98105, USA (☎206-543-2320; http://www.esl.washington.edu/international). Offers certificate programs for international students with the proper visa credentials. Not all classes are for credit, see website for details.

WORKING

Some travelers want long-term jobs that allow them to get to know another part of the world in depth (e.g. teaching English, working in the tourism industry). Other travelers seek out short-term jobs to finance their travel. They usually seek work opportunities in the service sector or in agriculture, working for a few weeks at a time to finance the next leg of their journey. This section discusses both short-term and long-term opportunities for working in Alaska and the Pacific Northwest. Make sure you understand the **visa requirements** for working abroad in the US and Canada. See the box on p. 62 for more information.

LONG-TERM WORK

If you're planning on spending a substantial amount of time (more than three months) working in Alaska or the Pacific Northwest, search for a job well in advance. International placement agencies are often the easiest way to find work opportunities abroad, especially for teaching English. Internships, usually for college students, are a good way to segue into working abroad, although they are often unpaid or poorly paid (many say the experience, however, is well worth it). Be wary of advertisements or companies that claim the ability to get you a job abroad for a fee—often the same listings are available online or in newspapers.

AU PAIR WORK

Au-pairs are typically women, aged 18-27, who work as live-in nannies, caring for children and doing light housework in foreign countries in exchange for room, board, and a small spending allowance or stipend. Most former au-pairs speak favorably of their experience, and of how it allowed them to get to know the country without the high expenses of traveling. Drawbacks, however, often include long hours and the usually mediocre pay. In the United States, weekly salaries typically fall well below $200, with at least 45 hours of work expected. Much of the au pair experience really does depend on the family you're placed with. The agencies below are a good starting point for looking for work opportunities as an au pair.

Accord Cultural Exchange, 750 La Playa, San Francisco, CA 94121, USA (☎415-386-6203; www.cognitext.com/accord).

InterExchange, 161 Sixth Ave., New York, NY 10013, USA (☎212-924-0446; fax 924-0575; www.interexchange.org).

SHORT-TERM WORK

Traveling for long periods of time can get expensive; therefore, many travelers try their hand at odd jobs for a few weeks at a time to make some extra cash to carry them through another month or two of touring around. In Alaska, many college students work in **fish canneries** to earn money. While it's possible to earn a lot in a brief period of time, you must be willing to put in long, hard hours (upward of 80 per week) at menial and unrewarding tasks. As the Alaska Employment Service eloquently states, "Most seafood processing jobs are smelly, bloody, slimy, cold, wet, and tiring because of manual work and standing for many hours. The aroma of fish lingers with workers throughout the season. Most get used to it. Those who can't generally leave." If you're interested, the Alaska Department of Labor lists available jobs online (www.labor.state.ak.us) and through an info line (☎907-465-8900). Be sure you understand whether your potential employer will provide housing, food, and transportation costs. **Planting trees** is the Canadian equivalent of work in the canneries—the smell is better, but hours are long and hard, and the bugs can be horrific. Planters are usually paid between $0.10 and $0.30 per tree; an experienced planter can plunk enough trees in the ground to earn more than CDN$200 a day. Most treeplanters are university students who work from late spring to mid-summer at remote camps. The companies that hire them range from well-run, professional organizations to exploitative rip-off operations. The web site at http://web.radiant.net/harihari contains lists and reviews of companies, straight-up and detailed discussion of the work, and advice from veterans on everything from spotting good and bad companies to customizing your shovel.

The Canadian government provides a number of resources to young people looking to work in the country through the Federal Work Experience program. For outdoors-oriented jobs, check out http://parkscanada.pch.gc.ca/Employment/jobs/english/students_e.htm#fswep.

Tourist industries throughout Alaska and the Pacific Northwest provide jobs to the money-hungry traveler. Working in tourism can get repetitive, but the hours are short and the money can be good. One bountiful resource for the unemployed traveler is the Banff/Lake Louise area, where thousands of tourists flock every summer. Check out http://jb-ge.hrdc-drhc.gc.ca/Search_en.asp?ProvId=09 for a database search of jobs throughout western Canada, or http://jobresourcecentre.com/canjob/bowvalley.html for listings in the Bow Valley.

Another popular option is to work several hours a day at a hostel in exchange for free or discounted room and/or board. Most often, these short-term jobs are found by word of mouth, or simply by talking to the owner of a hostel or restaurant. *Let's Go* tries to list temporary jobs like these whenever possible; check the practical information sections in larger cities.

VOLUNTEERING

Volunteering can be an extraordinary and fulfilling experience, especially when combined with the wonder of travel in a foreign land. Many volunteer services charge you a fee to work in their various programs. These fees can be surprisingly hefty (although they frequently cover airfare and most, if not all, living expenses). Still, you can sometimes avoid high application fees by contacting individual workcamps directly, and some volunteer institutions will even provide room and board in exchange for labor. Try to do research on a program before committing—talk to people who have previously participated and find out exactly what you're getting into, as living and working conditions can vary greatly. Different programs are geared toward different ages and levels of experience, so be sure to make sure that you are not taking on too much or too little. The more informed you are and the more realistic expectations you have, the more enjoyable the program will be.

Most people choose to go through a parent organization that takes care of logistical details, and frequently provides a group environment and support system. There are two main types of organizations—religious (often Catholic), and non-sectarian—although there are rarely restrictions on participation for either.

COMMUNITY SERVICE

Action Without Borders, 79 Fifth Ave. 17th Fl., New York, NY 10003 USA (☎212-843-3973; www.idealist.org), maintains a website which lists volunteer opportunities at 18,000 nonprofits in 130 countries including the US and Canada, and has links to organizations that help arrange international volunteering stints.

Americorps, 1201 New York Ave. NW, Washington, D.C. 20525 (☎202-606-5000, www.cns.gov/americorps). The domestic equivalent to America's Peace Corps, Americorps places US citizens in community development programs throughout the US, usually for a 1-year term.

Earthwatch, 3 Clocktower Pl., P.O. Box 75, Maynard, MA 01754 (☎800-776-0188 or 978-461-0081; www.earthwatch.org). Arranges 1- to 3-week programs to promote conservation of natural resources. Programs average US$1600.

Habitat for Humanity International, 121 Habitat St., Americus, GA 31709, USA (☎800-422-4828; www.habitat.org). Offers international opportunities to live with and build houses in a host community. Costs range US$1200-3500.

Volunteers for Peace, 1034 Tiffany Rd., Belmont., VT 05730, USA (☎802-259-2759; www.vfp.org). Arranges placement in Canadian work sites. Membership required for registration. Annual *International Workcamp Directory* US$20. Programs average US$200-500 for 2-3 weeks.

OUTDOORS

Student Conservation Association (SCA), Box 550 Charlestown, NH 03603 (☎603-543-1700; www.sca-inc.org). A clearinghouse for volunteer positions and internships in US National Parks and on other public lands lasting from 4 weeks to 12 months. Some positions are part of the Americorps program (see above). A free 4- to 5-week program for high school students provides food and lodging on month-long trail maintenance

> ### FOR FURTHER READING ON ALTERNATIVES TO TOURISM
> *Alternatives to the Peace Corps: A Directory of Third World and U.S. Volunteer Opportunities,* by Joan Powell. Food First Books, 2000 (US$10).
>
> *How to Get a Job in Europe,* by Sanborn and Matherly. Surrey Books, 1999 ($US22).
>
> *How to Live Your Dream of Volunteering Oversees,* by Collins, DeZerega, and Heckscher. Penguin Books, 2002 (US$17).
>
> *International Directory of Voluntary Work,* by Whetter and Pybus. Peterson's Guides and Vacation Work, 2000 (US$16).
>
> *International Jobs,* by Kocher and Segal. Perseus Books, 1999 (US$18).
>
> *Overseas Summer Jobs 2002,* by Collier and Woodworth. Peterson's Guides and Vacation Work, 2002 (US$18).
>
> *Work Abroad: The Complete Guide to Finding a Job Overseas,* by Hubbs, Griffith, and Nolting. Transitions Abroad Publishing, 2000 ($16).
>
> *Work Your Way Around the World,* by Susan Griffith. Worldview Publishing Services, 2001 (US$18).

gigs. The **SCA Northwest Office** is at 1265 S. Main St. Suite 210, Seattle, WA 98144 (☎206-324-4649; fax 324-4998).

Parks Canada National Volunteer Program (☎888-773-8888; www.parkscanada.pch.gc.ca) suggests potential volunteer opportunities to Canadians and foreign nationals who email (via the website) or write (Coordinator, Parks Canada National Volunteer Program, 25 Eddy St., 4th Fl., Hull, QC K1A 0M5) with their qualifications and dates for which they seek placement. The deadline for summer placements is Dec. 1; for winter and spring placements June 30. Candidates may also contact individual parks; addresses are listed on the website.

Yoho National Park, Box 99, Field, British Columbia, Canada V0A IG0 (☎604-343-6324; http://www.worldweb.com/ParksCanada-Yoho). One of Canada's many aforementioned individual parks, Yoho offers a variety of outdoors volunteer projects. Call for information on program availability and participation fees.

OREGON

> **OREGON'S...** **Capital:** Salem. **Population:** 3,082,000. **Area:** 97,060 sq. mi.
> **Motto:** "She flies with her own wings." **Animal:** Beaver. **Nickname:** Beaver State.
> **Fish:** Chinook salmon. **Rock:** Thunderegg. **Dance:** Square Dance.

"Discovered" by Lewis and Clark on their overland expedition to the Pacific Ocean, Oregon soon became a hotbed of exploration and exploitation. Lured by plentiful forests and promises of gold and riches, entire families liquidated their possessions and sank their life savings into covered wagons, corn meal, and oxen, high-tailing it to Oregon in search of prosperity and a new way of life. This population of outdoors-enthusiasts and fledgling townspeople joined the Union in 1859, and has ever since become an eclectic mix of treehuggers and suave big-city types. Today, Oregon remains as popular a destination as ever for backpackers, cyclists, anglers, beachcrawlers, and families alike.

The wealth of space and natural resources that supported the prospectors and farmers of old continues to provide the backbone of Oregon today: four out of ten Oregonians are involved in some way in the most diversified agricultural center in the US. More than half of Oregon's forests lie on federally owned land, hopefully preserving them for future generations of outdoor explorers, but 80,000 workers depend on an timber industry that is threatened by over-logging, by the Endangered Species Act, and by disputes over ownership of the remaining land and rights. Nevertheless, Oregon deserves its environmentalist reputation, having created the country's first recycling refund program and spearheaded wide-scale preservation of coastline for public use.

The caves and cliffs of the coastline remain a siren call to Oregon's most precious non-natural resource: tourists. For those in search of big city life, Portland's laid-back and idiosyncratic personality—its name was determined by a coin toss (the flip side would have christened it "Boston, Oregon")—draws the microchip, mocha, and music crowds, while the college town of Eugene embraces hippies and Deadheads from around the West. From excellent microbrews to snow-capped peaks, a visit to Oregon is still worth crossing the Continental Divide.

■ OREGON'S HIGHLIGHTS

CRATER LAKE NATIONAL PARK (see p. 143) protects a placid, azure pool in the maw of an ancient and enormous volcano.

THE HIGH DESERT MUSEUM in Bend (see p. 137) bolsters appreciation for nature.

THE COLUMBIA RIVER GORGE (see p. 89) cuts a stunning chasm.

ASHLAND'S SHAKESPEARE would make Will proud (see p. 134).

CANNON BEACH'S (see p. 100) silky soft stretch of sand is the ultimate getaway.

DUNE BUGGIES gear it up in **Oregon Dunes National Recreation Area** (see p. 109).

PERUSE Portland's **Rose Garden** to see why it's dubbed the City of Roses (see p. 81).

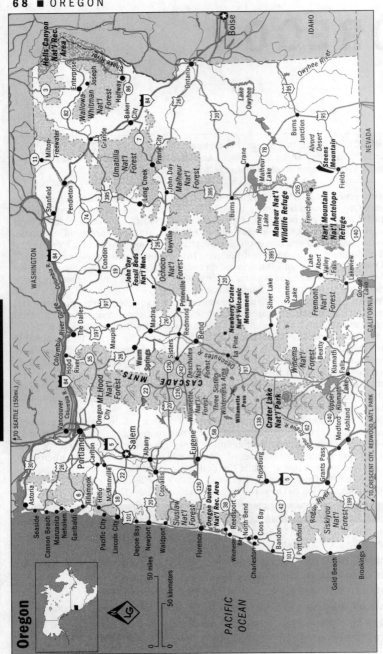

Oregon

PORTLAND ☎ 503

As a recent spate of "Best Places to Live" awards attests, Portland is no longer the secret it once was. With over 200 parks, the pristine Willamette River, and snow-capped Mt. Hood in the background, the City of Roses basks in natural beauty. An award-winning transit system and pedestrian-friendly streets make it feel more like a pleasantly overgrown town than any traffic-jammed, dirty metropolis. Yet with nearly two million residents, a respectable set of skyscrapers downtown, and industry giants Nike and Intel, Portland is a thriving component of the West Coast economy. Nor does the city lack anything in big-city cultural diversity: hippies, hipsters, the body-pierced and the tattooed, indie rockers, college kids, and yuppies all make Portland their home.

When the rain and clouds clear—and they do, in summer—outdoors lovers reap the visual and recreational rewards of the nearby Oregon Coast and Cascades. Ample delight for the eyes also awaits those who walk the flower-lined neighborhoods, and a brief ride by car or light rail to Washington Park totally immerses the traveler in natural beauty. If it's the plastic arts and not snow-capped peaks that quicken your heart, rest assured of satisfaction in the Pearl District's galleries, the public art all across downtown, and the numerous restaurant displays.

The culinary arts are not neglected here, nor is their enjoyment exclusive to the rich. The city's venerable orchestra, the oldest in the United States, maintains the traditional side of Portland's cultural scene. In the rainy season, Portlanders flood pubs and clubs, where musicians often strum, sing, or spin for cheap or free. Improvisational theaters are in constant production, and the talented and/or brave can chime in at open-mic night, in vogue all over town. And throughout it all, America's best beer pours from the taps in the microbrewery capital of the U.S.

■ INTERCITY TRANSPORTATION

Flights: Portland International Airport (☎460-4234) is served by almost every major airline. The airport is connected to the city center by the **MAX Red Line,** an efficient light rail system. (38min.; every 15min. daily 5am-11:30pm; $1.55) Taxis are also available, with flat rates to downtown (see Local Transportation, below).

Trains: Amtrak, 800 NW 6th Ave. (☎273-4866; reservations ☎800-872-7245 or through www.amtrak.com), at Irving St. in historic Union Station, built in 1896. Ticket counter open daily 7:45am-9pm. Ticket prices frequently change based on dates of departure and arrival, so be sure to check their website. To **Eugene** (2½hr.; 5 per day; $16-20 one-way, $38-45 round-trip); **San Francisco** (19hr.; 1 per day; $81-92 one-way, $150-160 round-trip, sleeper $280-330); **Seattle** (4hr.; 4 per day; $23-36 one-way, $56-65 round-trip). Student Advantage (15%), senior (15%), and military (15%) discounts.

Buses: Greyhound, 550 NW 6th Ave. (☎243-2310 or 800-231-2222), at NW Glisan by Union Station. Ticket counter open 5am-1am. To **Eugene** (2½-3½hr., 9 per day, $14); **Seattle** (3-4½hr., 9 per day, $21); **Spokane, WA** (7½-11½hr., 4 per day, $40.50). Student Advantage (15%), senior (10%), and military (10%) discounts. Lockers $5 per day.

▐ LOCAL TRANSPORTATION

The award-winning **Tri-Met bus system** is one of the most logically organized and rider-friendly public transit systems in America. The downtown **transit mall,** closed to all traffic but pedestrians and buses, lies between SW 5th and 6th Ave., where over 30 covered passenger shelters serve as stops and info centers. Southbound buses stop along SW 5th Ave., northbound along SW 6th Ave. Bus routes are colored according to their **service areas**, each with its own whimsical insignia: red salmon, orange deer, yellow rose, green leaf, blue snow, purple rain, and brown beaver. Most of downtown is in the **Fareless Square**, where all public transportation is free. (Anywhere north or east of 405, west of the river, and south of Irving St.) For directions and fares outside this zone, see **Public Transportation,** below.

Most downtown streets are **one-way.** The city's **Smart Parks** are common and well marked. (Near Pioneer Sq. $0.95 per hr., $3 per hr. after 4hr., $2 after 6pm, max. $12; weekends $5 per day.) Parking is cheaper farther from city center. **Tri-Met** is the best bet for day-long excursions downtown.

Public Transportation: Tri-Met, 701 SW 6th Ave. (☎238-7433; www.tri-met.org), in Pioneer Courthouse Sq. Open M-F 7:30am-5:30pm. Several information lines available: **Call-A-Bus** info system ☎231-3199; fare info ☎231-3198; TDD info ☎238-5811. Buses generally run 5am-midnight with reduced schedules on weekends. All buses and bus stops are marked with 1 of 7 symbols and offer public bike racks. Fare $1.25-1.55, ages 7-18 $0.95, over 65 or disabled $0.60, free downtown. All-day pass $4; 10 fares for $10.50. **MAX** (☎228-7246), based at the Customer Service Center, is Tri-Met's light-rail train running between downtown, Hillsboro in the west, and Gresham in the east. Clean and convenient, the MAX keeps pace with technology—electronic signs tell when the next train's coming at many stops. A new line serves the airport from the main line's "Gateway" stop (see above). Transfers from buses can be used to ride MAX. Runs M-F about 4:30am-1:30am, Sa 5am-12:30am, Su 5am-11:30pm.

Taxis: Radio Cab (☎227-1212), $2.50 base, $1.80 per mi. **Broadway Cab** (☎227-1234), $2.50 base, $1.80 per mi. Airport to downtown $25-30.

Car Rental: ■ **Crown Rent-A-Car,** 1315 NE Sandy Blvd. (☎230-1103). Although it has a limited selection, Crown is by far the cheapest option for anyone under 25. 18-21 must have credit card and proof of insurance. 22-25 must have credit card. Transport from airport available upon request. Open M-Sa 9am-5pm or by appointment. From $20-60 per day, $110-275 per week. **Rent-a-Wreck,** 1800 SE M.L. King Blvd. (☎233-2492 or 888-499-9111). Older cars. Will occasionally rent to under-25. Open M-F 7:30am-5pm, weekends by appointment only. From $20-30 per day, $110-150 per week, with 100-150 free mi. per day. **Dollar Rent-a-Car** (☎800-800-4000), at airport. Must be 25 with credit card, or be 21 with proof of insurance and pay a $20 per day surcharge. Open 24hr. From $20 per day, $140 per week, unlimited mileage. Extra 15% airport fee.

AAA: 600 SW Market St. (☎222-6777 or 800-222-4357), between Broadway and 6th Ave., near the Portland State University campus. Open M-F 8:30am-5pm.

⚡ ORIENTATION

Portland lies in the northwest corner of Oregon, near the confluence of the Willamette (wih-LAM-it) and Columbia Rivers. **I-5** connects Portland to San Francisco (659 mi., 11-14hr.) and Seattle (179 mi.; 3-3½hr.), while **I-84** follows the route of the Oregon Trail through the Columbia River Gorge, heading along the Oregon-Washington border toward Boise, Idaho. West of Portland, **US 30** follows the Columbia downstream to Astoria, but **US 26** is the fastest way to the coast. **I-405** makes the west side of a loop around Portland with I-5, and links the loop to US 30 and 26.

Every street name in Portland carries one of five prefixes: **N, NE, NW, SE,** or **SW,** indicating in which part of the city the address is to be found. East and west are separated by the Willamette River, and **Burnside St.** divides north from south. **Williams Ave.** marks off plain ol' north from northeast. The roads are organized as a grid: in general, numbered *avenues* run north-south, and named *streets* go east-west. The first one or two digits of an address on an east-west street generally reflect its position relative to numbered streets: 3813 Killingsworth St. will be near 38th Ave.

The principal unit of urban measurement in Portland is the neighborhood, so here are a few of the major ones. Close to the city center, **Northwest** Portland is home to **Chinatown** and most of **Old Town,** which holds the highest concentration of Portland's nightclubs and bars. **Nob Hill** and **Pearl District,** the recently revitalized homes to most of Portland's beautiful people as well as many of the chic-est shops in the city, are found further north, while **Washington Park** is found further west. **Forest Park** is a huge wooded area that stretches along the river. **Southwest** Portland includes downtown, the southern end of Old Town, and a slice of the wealthier **West Hills** area. **Portland State University** fills a large space south of the city center. **Southeast** Portland contains parks, factories, local businesses, residential areas of several socioeconomic brackets, and a rich array of cafes, stores, theaters, and restaurants, particularly around **Hawthorne Blvd.** east of SE 33rd St. **Reed College,** with its wide green quadrangles and brick halls, lies deep within the southeast district at the end of **Woodstock Ave.** (some might say appropriately), which has a distinct culture of its own. **Northeast** Portland is highly residential, but has pockets of activity; areas around **Killingsworth** and **Alberta St.** east of 99 East are currently undergoing gentrification as "hipsters" and restaurants flock to a once seedy area. The Northeast does not have any accommodations, so venturing out is a little more difficult. Some of the northeast's biggest draws are near the river, and include the Lloyd Center Shopping Mall and the Oregon Convention Center. The north of Portland is mostly residential, and receives next to no tourist traffic.

Portland Overview

OREGON

OREGON

Downtown Portland

▲ ACCOMMODATIONS
Clyde Hotel, **12**
Downtown Value Inn, **23**
Mark Spencer Hotel, **11**
Northwest Portland International
  Hostel (HI), **3**
Portland International Hostel (HI), **24**

● FOOD
Dog's Dig, **6**
Little Wing Cafe, **2**
Montage, **20**
Muu-Muu's Big World Diner, **1**
Nicholas's Restaurant, **15**
The Roxy, **9**
Western Culinary Institute:
  Chef's Corner Deli & Diner, **19**
International Bistro, **17**
Restaurant, **22**

▼ THEATERS
Artist's Repertory Theater, **10**
Oregon Ballet Theater, **18**
Portland Center Stage, **21**

■ NIGHTLIFE
Brig, The Nightclub Fez, Red Cap
  Garage, Boxxes **13**
Embers, **7**
Jimmy Mak's, **4**
Kells Irish Pub, **14**
Ohm, **8**
Satyricon, **5**
Sweetwater's Jam House, **17**

Bus Route
MAX *Streetcar*
Fareless Square

◢ PRACTICAL INFORMATION

TOURIST AND FINANCIAL SERVICES

Visitor Information: Portland Oregon Visitors Association (POVA), 701 SW Morrison St. (☎275-9750; www.travelportland.com). Located in Pioneer Courthouse Sq. Walk between the fountains through the crowds of screaming kids and more distinctive characters to enter. All the pamphlets you could want, plus a 12min. interpretive movie. Free *Portland Book* has maps and comprehensive info on local attractions. Open M-F 8:30am-5:30pm, Sa-Su 10am-4pm. Also houses a **Tri-Met Service Counter** (M-F 8:30am-5:30pm) and **Ticket Central Portland**, a counter that sells tickets to sporting events and almost any show in town, plus day-of-show half-price tickets. They only serve walk-in customers, but offer a number to call for half-price ticket availability (☎275-8358). Open M-F 9:30am-6pm, Sa 10am-2pm.

Outdoor Information: Portland Parks and Recreation, 1120 SW 5th Ave. #1302 (☎823-2223; www.parks.ci.portland.or.us), in the Portland Building between Main and Madison St. Offers a wealth of information including maps and pamphlets on Portland's parks. Open M-F 8am-5pm. **Nature of Northwest**, 800 NE Oregon St. #117 (☎872-2750; www.naturenw.org), 2 blocks east of the Convention Center on NE 7th Ave. A multitude of hiking maps, guidebooks, and raw information are on tap at this U.S. Forest Service-run shop. Pick up a Northwest Forest Pass here, required for parking in most National Forests in Washington and Oregon ($5 per day, $30 annually). Open M-F 9am-5pm. Closed holidays.

Currency Exchange: A **Thomas Cook's** can be found inside of Powell's Travel (see below) for any money-changing needs. Open M-F 9am-5:30pm, Sa 10:30am-2pm.

LOCAL SERVICES

Bookstore: See **Powell's City of Books**, p. 79. **Powell's Travel Store** (☎228-1108). Adjacent to the **Tourist information** in Pioneer Courthouse Sq. Has a vast array of road maps, hiking maps, guidebooks, and travel literature. Open M-F 9am-7pm, Sa 10am-6pm, Su 10am-5pm.

Outdoors Equipment: U.S. Outdoor Store, 219 SW Broadway (☎223-5937). Found between Pine and Ankeny Streets, this store has a huge selection of gear for almost any outdoor activity, summer or winter. Open M-F 9am-8pm, Sa 10am-6pm, Su noon-5pm.

Gay and Lesbian Info: Portland's best resource for queer info is the biweekly newspaper **Just-Out** (☎236-1252), available free around the city.

Tickets: Ticketmaster (☎224-4400). Surcharge $1.50-7.75. **Fastixx** (☎224-8499) Surcharge $2-3 per order plus an additional $1 per ticket ordered. Also try **Ticket Central Portland** (see **Tourist Services**, above).

Laundromat: Springtime Thrifty Cleaners and Laundry, 2942 SE Hawthorne Blvd. (☎232-4353). 150 ft. from the Hawthorne hostel. Open M-F 7:30am-9pm, Sa-Su 8am-8pm. Wash $1.25, dry 25¢ per 10min.

Public Pool: Call 823-5130 for a list of 14 public pools. Admission $2.50; under 17 swim for $1.50.

EMERGENCY AND COMMUNICATION

Emergency: ☎911.

Police: 1111 SW 2nd Ave. (non-emergency response ☎823-3333; info ☎823-4636; lost and found ☎823-2179), between Madison St. and Main St.

Crisis and Suicide Hotline: ☎655-8401. **Women's Crisis Line:** ☎235-5333. 24hr.

Late-Night Pharmacy: Walgreens (☎238-6053), intersection of 39th St. and Belmont St. Open 24hr.

Hospital: Legacy Good Samaritan, 1015 NW 22nd St. (☎413-8090; emergency 413-7260), between Lovejoy and Marshall. **Adventist Medical Center,** 10123 SE Market St. (☎257-2500).

Internet Access: Found at the elegant and distinguished **library,** 801 SW 10th Ave., between Yamhill and Taylor. 1hr. free access. Open Tu-Th 9am-9pm, F-Sa 9am-6pm, Su 1-5pm. **Internet Arena,** 1016 SW Taylor St. (☎224-2718), across the street from the main library. $6 per hr., minimum $2. Open M-F 11am-8pm.

Post Office: 715 NW Hoyt St. (☎800-275-8777). Open M-F 7am-6:30pm, Sa 8:30am-5pm. **Postal Code:** 97208.

⚑ ACCOMMODATIONS

Although Marriott-esque hotels dominate downtown and smaller motels are steadily raising their prices, Portland still welcomes the budget traveler. Two Hostelling International locations provide quality housing in happening areas. Prices tend to drop as you leave the city center, and inexpensive motels can be found on SE Powell Blvd. and the southern end of SW 4th Ave. All accommodations in Portland fill up during the summer months, especially during the Rose Festival, so make your reservations early.

HOSTELS AND MOTELS

▨ **Portland International Hostel (HI),** 3031 SE Hawthorne Blvd. (☎236-3380), at 31st Ave. across from Artichoke Music. Take bus #14 to SE 30th Ave. Lively common space and a huge porch define this laid-back hostel. Kitchen, laundry. Recently-installed wireless Internet access for those with laptops is free; "conventional" Internet is $1 per 10min. The $1 all-you-can-eat pancakes are a big bonus. Fills early in summer. Reception daily 8am-10pm. Check-out 11am. 34 beds and a tent yard for overflow. Dorms $15, nonmembers $18. Private rooms $41-46. ❶

Northwest Portland International Hostel (HI), 1818 NW Glisan St. (☎241-2783) at 18th Ave. Centrally located between Nob Hill and the Pearl District. Take bus #17 down Glisan to corner of 19th Ave. This snug Victorian building has a kitchen, lockers, laundry, and a small espresso bar. 34 dorm beds (co-ed available). Reception 8am-11pm. $14-16 plus tax, with a $3 fee for nonmembers. Two private doubles, $40-50. ❶

McMenamins Edgefield, 2126 SW Halsey St. (☎669-8610 or 800-669-8610), in Troutdale. Take MAX east to the Gateway Station, then Tri-Met bus #24 (Halsey) east to the main entrance. This beautiful 38-acre former farm is a posh escape that keeps two hostel rooms. On-site brewery and vineyards, plus 18-hole golf course ($8-9, $1 club rental), and several restaurants and pubs. Offers many activities, including 2-day rafting trips ($140). Lockers included. Call ahead during summer (but no reservations for the hostel). Reception 24hr. 2 single-sex dorm-style rooms with 12 beds each ($20 plus tax) are the budget option. Singles $50 with breakfast, 2 queen double $95-$105. ❷

The Clyde Hotel, 1022 SW Stark St. (☎517-5231; www.clydehotel.com), west of 10th Ave. Take MAX to SW 10th Avenue, walk towards Burnside St. Built in 1912, the charming and historic Clyde has kept all its furniture in the original style, from Victorian tubs to bureau-sized radios. Continental breakfast included. Reception 10am-9pm, front desk open 24 hr. Reservations recommended. Rooms (double or queen) $60-110, two-room suites $110-190 (for 2-4 people). Off-season rates about $10 less. ❷

The Mark Spencer, 409 SW 11th Ave., (☎800-548-3934; www.markspencer.com). Since 1907, self-proclaimed "Portland's Boutique Art Hotel" has housed the *Phantom of the Opera* cast and many other groups on tour. Continental breakfast included, plus free tea and cookies 4:30pm-7pm daily. Coin-op and valet laundry, cable TV, kitchens in every room, phones with data ports. Check-in 4 pm. Check-out noon. Summer reservations recommended one month in advance. Queens $90 summer, $80 off-season. ❸

Downtown Value Inn, 415 SW Montgomery St. (☎226-4751), at 4th Ave. Take bus #12 or #19 to the corner of 5th Ave., or follow signs to the city center and Montgomery. An inexpensive option with clean, recently remodeled rooms. Pizza hangout/pub downstairs. Phones, cable TV, laundry; microwaves in some rooms. Reception 24hr. Checkout 11am. Reservations recommended. Singles from $50; doubles from $60; rooms with jacuzzi $70. ❷

▣ FOOD

Portland ranks high nationwide in restaurants per capita, and dining experiences are seldom dull. Downtown and the NW districts tend to be expensive, but restaurants and quirky cafes in the NE and SE quadrants offer great food at reasonable prices. For some reason (perhaps a cosmic one) depictions of The Last Supper seem to be a seal of approval for some of the best restaurants in Portland: be on the look-out for Christ and His apostles.

PEARL DISTRICT AND NOB HILL

Trendy eateries line NW 21st and 23rd St. **Food Front,** 2375 NW Thurman St., a small cooperative grocery, has a superb deli and a wonderland of natural foods, fruit, and baked goods. (☎222-5658. Open daily 8am-9pm; winter 9am-9pm.)

▨ **Muu-Muu's Big World Diner,** 612 NW 21st Ave. (☎223-8169), at Hoyt St. Bus #17. Where high and low culture smash together. Artful goofiness—the name of the restaurant was drawn from a hat—amidst red velvet curtains and gold upholstery. Brutus salad, "the one that kills a caesar" $6, 'shroom-wich $7.50. Open M-F 11:30am-1am, Sa-Su 10am-2am. ❷

Little Wing Cafe, 529 NW 13th Ave. (☎228-3101), off Glisan. Bus #17. The food is arranged nearly as well as the gallery of beautiful ceramic art on the walls. Sandwiches include the Eggplant Supreme ($6). Dinner entrees run about $12. Open M-Th 11:30am-4pm and 5:30-9pm; F-Sa 11:30am-4pm and 5:30-10pm. ❸

DOWNTOWN AND OLD TOWN

The center of town and tourism, Southwest Portland can get expensive. Street carts offer an array of portable food and bento boxes (lunches of meat or vegetables on a bed of rice), making it easy to grab a quick, healthy meal. Ethnic restaurants also peddle cheap eats on Morrison St. between 10th and 11th Ave. A 24hr. **Safeway** supermarket is behind the PAM (see **Sights,** p. 77), 1025 SW Jefferson St.

▨ **Western Culinary Institute** (☎223-2245) would leave the Frugal Gourmet speechless. The ratio of cooks to patrons in these restaurants is extraordinarily high, with the culinary students rotating between restaurants and duties. WCI has 4 eateries, each catering to a different budget niche, all of them reasonable. **Chef's Diner ❶,** 1239 SW Jefferson, opens mornings to let cheerful students serve, taste, and discuss sandwiches, the breakfast special, or the occasional all-you-can-eat buffet ($5). Open Tu-F 7am-noon. **Chef's Corner Deli ❶,** 1239 SW Jefferson, is good for a quick meal on-the-go. Enormous sandwiches go for $1.25. Open Tu-F 8am-6:30pm. Moving up the price scale, the elegant **Restaurant ❹,** 1316 SW 13th Ave., serves a classy 5-course lunch ($10) rivaled only by its superb 6-course dinner (Tu, W, and F, $20). Reservations recommended. Open Tu-F 11:30am-1pm; dinner 6-8pm. **International Bistro ❸,** 1701 SW Jefferson, serves cuisine from a different region of the world every week, at prices that range just below those at Restaurant.

OREGON

■ **The Roxy,** 1121 SW Stark St. (☎223-9160). Giant crucified Jesus with neon halo, pierced wait staff, and quirky menu. The owner's collection of signed celebrity photos graces the booths; Slash (from Guns N' Roses) and other celebs have been known to stop by. Visiting the Dysha Starr Imperial Toilet seems like an important thing to do, if only because of its name. Quentin Tarantuna Melt $6.25, coffees and chai about $1-3. An ideal post-movie or after-bar stop. Open Tu-Su 24hr. ❷

Dogs Dig Vegetarian Deli, 212 NW Davis St. (☎223-3362). Vegetarian and vegan sandwiches and soups in a tiny storefront adorned with bad jokes and snapshots of every dog in Portland. Soup and sandwich $5, burrito $2.50. Open M-F 9am-5pm. ❶

SOUTHEAST PORTLAND

Anchored at happening Hawthorne Blvd., Southeast Portland is a great place to people-watch and tummy-fill. Eclectic eateries with exotic decor and economical menus hide in residential and industrial neighborhoods. **Safeway** is at 2800 SE Hawthorne, at 28th Ave. (☎232-5539; open daily 6am-midnight). Bring cash to SE Portland restaurants, since many of the best do not accept credit cards.

■ **Nicholas's Restaurant,** 318 SE Grand Ave. (☎235-5123), between Oak and Pine opposite Miller Paint. Bus #6 to the Andy and Bax stop. Phenomenal Mediterranean food in an authentic atmosphere. The meat, vegetarian, or vegan mezzas ($7.75) are fantastic deals for both quality and quantity (might feed two). Sandwiches $5-6. Open M-Sa 10am-9pm, Su noon-9pm. ❶

■ **Montage,** 301 SE Morrison St. (☎234-1324). Take bus #15 to the East end of the Morrison Bridge and walk under it. Where straight-laced, mainstream Portlanders enter a beautifully surreal land of dining. While seated Last-Supper style underneath a macaroni-framed mural of that famous meal, try oyster shooters ($1.75) and huge portions of jambalaya ($10.50 chicken, $14.50 gator). The popular mac and cheese is a cheaper option ($5). Open M-Th 11:30am-2pm and 6pm-2am, F 11:30am-2pm and 6pm-4am, Sa 6pm-4am, Su 6pm-2am. ❷

Delta Cafe, 4607 SE Woodstock Blvd. (☎771-3101). The decor is typical Portland: pastoral paintings in one room, voodoo dolls and a lone, framed Chewbacca (the wookie) portrait in the other. 40 oz. Pabst Blue Ribbon comes in champagne bucket, $3. Po' Boy Samwiches, $4-7. Open M-F 5pm-10pm, Sa-Su noon-10pm. ❶

Cafe Lena, 2239 SE Hawthorne Blvd. (☎238-7087). Bus #14. A fixture of the breakfast scene. Open Tu 8am-midnight, W-Th 8am-9:30pm, F-Sa 8am-10pm, Su 8am-3pm. ❷

Barley Mill Pub, 1629 SE Hawthorne Blvd. (☎231-1492). Bus #14. A smoky temple to Jerry Garcia. The hearty burgers are upbeat, yet mellow, like the man himself. McMenamins beer and 20 other kinds on tap ($3-4). Happy Hour M-F 4-6pm. Open M-Sa 11am-1am, Su noon-midnight. ❷

Cup and Saucer, 3566 SE Hawthorne Blvd. (☎236-6001). Ask Chef Karen to cook you a famous garden scramble any time of day. Ani DiFranco has been spotted here, and the staff promises that you'll at least hear her on their stereo. Open daily 7am-9pm. ❷

NORTHEAST PORTLAND

The northeast is distant from any hostel, but the food is worth a short trip. Places to eat line Broadway and Alberta east of the river, and other pockets of commerce produce good eats for Portland's most residential area.

Vita Cafe, 3024 NE Alberta St. (☎335-8233). Huge portions of "comfort food," with an emphasis on vegetarian and vegan fare, but carnivores can find sustenance as well. American, Asian, Mediterranean, and "Mexican Fiesta." M-F 11am-10pm, Sa 8am-10pm, Su 8am-3pm. ❷

Chez What? 2203 NE Alberta St. (☎281-1717). A strange fascination with poodles, especially pink ones, is the visual theme. Good hearty eating is the gustatory one. The dreadlocked staff create a mellow scene (but a peppier environment waits just next door at **Whatever?!** lounge). Curly Tom's Hippy Eggs, $7. M 8am-3pm, T-Sa 8am-1am, Su 9am-3pm. ❷

CAFES

Although locals sometimes complain that cafes are where trendy Portlanders try excessively hard to be cool, the decor, delicious food, and caffeine of these establishments still make them great places to make an appearance.

Palio Dessert & Espresso House, 1996 SE Ladd St. (☎232-9214), on Ladd Circle. Bus #10 stops right in front of the cafe, or walk south 3 blocks on SE 16th Ave. from Hawthorne. This tranquil cafe offers Mexican mochas ($2.50) and espresso mousse ($4). Bring a book and enjoy the outside seating, or mosey over to the park next door. Open M-F 8am-11pm, Sa-Su 10am-11pm. ❶

Pied Cow Coffeehouse, 3244 SE Belmont St. (☎230-4866). Bus #15. Sink into velvety cushions in this quirky and friendly Victorian parlor, or puff a hookah in the garden outside. Espresso drinks $1-3, cakes about $4. Open M-F 4pm-1am, Sa-Su noon-1am. ❶

Coffee Time, 712 NW 21st Ave. (☎497-1090). Sip a cup of chai ($2-3) while watching locals play chess. The intelligentsia mingle on the couches; bohemians chill to music in the parlor. Lattes $2-3. Coffee time is nearly all the time (Open daily, 6am-3am). ❶

Rimsky Korsakoffeehouse, 707 SE 12th Ave. (☎232-2640), at Alder St. Bus #15 to 12th St., then walk 2 blocks north. Unmarked and low-key, this red Victorian house is a hidden gem with a frenzy of desserts. Ask for a "mystery table." Live classical music nightly. Open Su-Th 7pm-midnight, F-Sa 7pm-1am. ❶

SIGHTS

Parks, gardens, open-air markets, innumerable museums, and galleries bedeck Portland. For $1.25, Bus #63 delivers passengers to at least 13 attractions. Catch the best of Portland's dizzying art scene on the first Thursday of each month, when the Portland Art Museum and small galleries in the Southwest and Northwest stay open until 8pm. For more info, contact the **Regional Arts and Culture Council,** 620 SW Main St. #420 (☎823-5111), across from the Portland Centre for the Performing Arts, or grab the *Art Gallery Guide* at the Visitor's Center.

DOWNTOWN

Portland's downtown centers on the pedestrian and bus mall, which runs north-south on 5th and 6th Ave. between W Burnside Blvd. on the north end and SW Clay St. on the south. On the **South Park Blocks,** a cool and shaded park snakes down the middle of Park Ave., bordered on the west by **Portland State University (PSU).** The area is accessible by any bus from the Transit Mall; once there, set out on foot.

PORTLAND ART MUSEUM (PAM). PAM sets itself apart from the rest of Portland's burgeoning arts scene on the strength of its collections, especially in Asian and Native American art. The Northwest Film Center (see Cinema, p. 83) shares space with the museum, and shows classics, documentaries, and off-beat flicks almost every day. *(1219 SW Park, at Jefferson St. on the west side of the South Block Park. Bus #6, 58, 63. ☎226-2811. Dial ext. 4245 for info on new exhibits. Open Tu-Sa 10am-5pm, Su noon-5pm, and until 8pm for Th and Fri in summer. $10, seniors 55+ and students $9, under 19 $6, under 5 free; special exhibits may be more.)*

NO ROOM FOR MUGGERS In 1948, a hole was cut through the sidewalk at the corner of SW Taylor St. and SW Naito Pkwy. (Front St.). It was expected to accommodate a mere lamp post, but greatness was thrust upon it. The streetlamp was never installed, and the 24-inch circle of earth was left empty until noticed by Dick Fagan, a columnist for the *Oregon Journal*. Fagan used his column, "Mill Ends," to publicize the patch of dirt, pointing out that it would make an excellent park. After years of such logic-heavy lobbying, the park was added to the city's roster in 1976. At 452.16 square inches, Mill Ends Park is officially the world's smallest. Locals have enthusiastically embraced it, planting flowers and hosting a hotly contested snail race on St. Patrick's Day.

PIONEER COURTHOUSE SQUARE. The still-operational **Pioneer Courthouse**, at 5th Ave. and Morrison St., is the centerpiece of the **Square**. Since opening in 1983 it has become "Portland's Living Room." Tourists and urbanites of every ilk hang out in the brick quadrangle. During late July and most of August, **High Noon Tunes** (p. 82) draws music lovers in droves. *(701 SW 6th Ave. Along the Vintage Trolley line and the MAX light-rail. Events hotline ☎ 223-1613. Music W noon-1pm.)*

5TH AVENUE ARCHITECTURE. The most controversial structure downtown is Michael Graves's **Portland Building**, 1120 SW 5th Ave., on the mall. This assemblage of pastel tile and concrete, the first major work of postmodern architecture built in the US, has been both praised as PoMo genius and condemned as nothing more than an overgrown jukebox. Walking underneath, look out for the giant pitchfork-wielding woman, *Portlandia*, reaching down from above: she's the second largest hammered copper statue in the U.S. Nearby, the **Standard Insurance Center**, 900 SW 5th Ave., between Salmon and Taylor, strokes the libido with **The Quest**, a sensual white marble sculpture commonly known as "Five Groins in the Fountain."

OLD TOWN AND CHINATOWN

The section of downtown above SW Stark running along the Willamette River comprises **Old Town**. Although not the safest part of Portland (avoid walking alone here at night), Old Town has been revitalized in recent years by storefront restoration, and new shops, restaurants, and nightclubs. On weekends, **Saturday Market** draws all of Portland for food, crafts, hackey-sacks, and live entertainment. Just west of Old Town the arched **China Gates** at NW 4th Ave. and Burnside provide an entrance to a Chinatown that, apart from a few restaurants and shops, seems more about business than Asian culture.

SHANGHAI TUNNELS. Downtown's waterfront district is laced with a complex web of underground passages known as the **Shanghai tunnels**. Urban lore has it that seamen would get folks drunk, drag them down to the tunnels, and store them there until their ship sailed. Forced aboard and taken out to sea, these hapless Portlanders would provide a free crew ("Behave or I'll make you a galley slave" is a common parental threat in Portland). Unfortunately, all entrances to the tunnels are in private businesses; fortunately, **Portland Underground Tours** guides trips through the historic passageways. *(☎ 622-4798. Adults $11, children under 12 $6.)*

CLASSICAL CHINESE GARDENS. The newest addition to Portland's long list of gardens, this city block makes up the largest Ming-style garden outside of China. The large pond, winding paths, and ornate decorations invite a relaxing, meditative stay. Ignore the skyscrapers and warehouses looming over the garden's walls, and you'll think you were back in a simpler time when relaxation was done properly. A tea house also offers a chance to experience authentic Chinese tea for $4-5.

(NW 3rd and Everett; ☎ 228-8131. Open Apr.-Oct. 9am-6pm., Nov.-Mar. 10am-5pm. $6; seniors, students, and children 6-18 $5; under 6 free.)

THE PEARL DISTRICT

Opposite the North Park Blocks, between NW 8th and Park Ave., the Pearl District buzzes. Stretching north from Burnside to I-405 along the river, this former industrial zone is packed with galleries, loft apartments, and warehouses-turned-office buildings. Stores and cafes make the area welcoming despite its boxy architecture.

▓ POWELL'S CITY OF BOOKS. The largest independent bookstore in the world, Powell's is a must-see for anyone who gets excited about the written word. If you like to dawdle in bookshops, bring a sleeping bag and rations. Nine color-coded rooms house books on everything from criminology to cooking. The atmosphere is more like a department store than a bookstore, but the sheer volume of books, poetry and fiction readings, and an extensive travel section on the Pacific Northwest make Powell's a worthy stop. *(1005 W Burnside St. on the edge of Northwest district. Bus #20. ☎ 228-4651 or 800-878-7323; www.powells.com. Open daily 9am-11pm.)* For alternative books and 'zines, nearby **Reading Frenzy** carries literature like "The Zapatista Reader." *(921 Oak St. Open M-Sa 11am-7pm, Su noon-6pm.)* Two shops over is **Counter Media** which leans much further from mainstream, carrying—you have been warned!—a highly unusual collection of erotica, comics, and graphic novels. *(927 Oak St. ☎ 226-8141. 18+ only. Same hours as Reading Frenzy.)*

GALLERIES. *First Thursday* (free at PAM) is a guide to local galleries and goings-on. For a nice selection, walk north on NW 9th Ave., turn left on NW Glisan and right on NW 12th Ave. On the way you'll pass some of the area's most engaging spaces, including the **Mark Woolley Gallery,** 120 NW 9th Ave., and the visiting artists' exhibition space at the **Pacific Northwest College of Art,** 1241 NW Johnson. **Quintana Galleries,** 501 SW Broadway, displays work by contemporary Native American artists working in traditional styles.

NORTH AND NORTHEAST PORTLAND

Nicknamed "Munich on the Willamette," Portland is the uncontested **microbrewery** capital of the US, and residents are proud of their beer. The visitors center has a list of 26 metro area breweries, most of which happily give tours if you call ahead.

BREWERIES. Widmer Bros. Brewing Co., half a mile north of the Rose Garden, offers free tours that include a video, a viewing of the facilities, and complimentary samples. *(929 N Russell. ☎ 281-2437. Tours F 3pm, Sa 1pm and 2pm.)* Many beer factories are brew pubs, sometimes offering live music with their beers. Try the **Lucky Labrador Brew Pub,** where dogs rule the loading dock for Miser Monday pints. *(915 SE Hawthorne Blvd. ☎ 236-3555. Pints $3.25. Open M-Sa 11am-midnight, Su noon-10pm.)* Also try the **Bridgeport Brewing Co.** (see **Nightlife**). Visit the **Oregon Brewers Guild** to learn how these alchemists work magic on water and hops grain. *(510 NW 3rd Ave. ☎ 295-1862 or 800-440-2537; www.oregonbeer.org. Open M-F 10am-4pm.)*

THE GROTTO. Minutes from downtown on Sandy Blvd., a 62-acre Catholic sanctuary houses magnificent religious sculptures and shrines, as well as running streams and gardens. At the heart of the grounds is "Our Lady's Grotto," a cave carved into a 110-foot cliff, and a replica of Michelangelo's *Pietà*. An elevator ($3, ages 6-11 and 65+ $2.50) ascends from the Meditation Chapel for a serene view that takes in a life-size bronze of St. Francis of Assisi. *(US 30, at NE 85th. ☎ 254-7371. Open daily May-Oct. 9am-8:30pm, Nov.-Apr. 9am-5pm. Exact closing time can vary.)*

OREGON

SOUTHEAST PORTLAND

OREGON MUSEUM OF SCIENCE AND INDUSTRY (OMSI). Flocks of kids are mesmerized by the Paleontology Lab where staff work on real dinosaur bones. The motion simulator ($3.50) spruces up the immobile exhibits and the Omnimax Theater provides an experience like no other. The Murdock Planetarium presents astronomy matinees and moonlights with rockin' laser shows—the Pink Floyd show is highly recommended. While at OMSI, visit the Navy's last diesel submarine, the U.S.S. Blueback. She never failed a mission, starred in the 1990 film *The Hunt for Red October*, and gets fantastic mileage. *(1945 SE Water Ave., 2 blocks south of Hawthorne Blvd. Right next to the river. Bus #63. ☎ 797-4000; www.omsi.edu. Open daily June 15th to Labor Day 9:30am-7pm; otherwise Tu-Sa 9:30am-5:30pm. Museum and Omnimax admission each cost $7, ages 3-13 and seniors $5. Omnimax ☎ 797-4640. Shows start on the hr. Su-Tu 11am-4pm, and W-Sa 11am-7pm. Th 2-for-1 tickets after 7pm. Planetarium ☎ 797-4646. Matinees daily $4; laser shows W-Su evenings $6.50. U.S.S. Blueback ☎ 797-4624. Open Tu-Su 10am-5pm. 40min. tour $4. OMSI offers a package, as well: admission to the museum, an Omnimax film and either the planetarium or the sub, $16, kids and seniors $12.)*

CRYSTAL SPRINGS RHODODENDRON GARDEN. Over 2500 rhododendrons of countless varieties and colors surround a lake and border an 18-hole public golf course. Take a mellow stroll through bloom-strewn paths, past cascading waterfalls and 90-year old rhodies. The flowers are in full bloom from March to May. *(SE 28th Ave., near Woodstock. Just west of Reed College. Bus #63, or take #19 Woodstock to 28th and Woodstock, and walk up 28th. Open daily Mar. 1 to Labor Day dawn-dusk; Oct.-Feb. 8am-7pm. Tu and W free, Th-M $3, under 12 free.)*

WASHINGTON PARK

Ever wonder where Nike's craze for trail running shoes came from? Once you visit Washington Park, with its miles of beautiful trails, lofty trees, and serene gardens, you won't ask again. If possible, schedule in a day to enjoy the park to its fullest. Holding some of Portland's premier (and least expensive) attractions, the park is shaped like a large "V." Take the MAX to "Washington Park," and you will be rocketed via elevator to the base of the V, where the **Zoo** and **World Forestry Center** are found. The Washington Park Shuttle (10am-8pm), free with valid MAX ticket, stops in the Zoo parking lot, at the **Rose Garden** and **Japanese Garden,** runs through a posh neighborhood, then to the **Hoyt Arboretum's** visitors center. From there the bus completes its circuit with another 5min. ride back to the MAX and zoo. Though the tall trees and moss-covered paths seem to beckon camping, it's not allowed, and there are police horse patrols at night.

JAPANESE GARDENS. Just across from the Rose Garden, these grounds complete the 1-2 punch of what is one of Portland's best destinations. Planned and planted in the early 60s, the gardens shift gracefully between various styles of landscape design. The Dry Landscape Garden *(Karsansui)* is an amazing example of Zen simplicity and beauty, and the mossy paths and rushing streams are sure to help you achieve that state. *(611 SW Kingston Ave. ☎ 223-1321. Open Apr.-Sept. Tu-Su 10am-7pm, M noon-7pm; Oct.-Mar. Tu-Su 10am-4pm, M noon-4pm. Tours daily at 10:45am and 2:30pm. $6, seniors 62+ $5, students $3.50, under 6 free.)*

HOYT ARBORETUM. Forming the wooded backdrop for the rest of Washington Park's sights, Hoyt features 183 acres of trees and 12 mi. of trails with tree-themed names, including the charming, wheelchair-accessible **Overlook** and **Bristlecone Pine Trails.** All this in an area that 100 years ago was clear-cut. The 26 mi. **Wildwood Trail** winds through Washington and Forest Parks, connecting the Arboretum to the Zoo and Japanese Garden. *Let's Go* recommends picking up a free map at the World Forestry Center, as trails are sometimes poorly marked. *(4000 SW Fairview Blvd. ☎ 228-8733. Visitors center open daily 9am-4pm.)*

A ROSE EAT ROSE WORLD An eminent source of Portland pride, during the summer the International Rose Test Garden is a sea of blooms and floral fragrance, arresting the eye and confirming Portland's title as the City of Roses. The garden serves as a botanical version of the pharmaceutical clinical trial. Experimental roses (hybrids usually, but some are genetically engineered) undergo rigorous two-year evaluations here and at 18 other test gardens: those that pass muster at a sufficient number of sites become commercial. At this point they need a name, which you can pick for a mere $50,000. Those that fail their tests, alas, are destroyed (and you thought school exams were stressful). Though these pre-grad roses might lead stressful lives, a walk in the garden is sure to lighten any heart. Peak blooms occur at 5-6 week intervals beginning around Memorial Day and lasting until September. Blooms reach their highest peak in June. *(400 SW Kingston Ave. ☎823-3636. Open daily 5am-10pm. Free, but donations appreciated.)*

FOREST PARK. Just north of Washington Park stretches a 5000-acre tract of wilderness. Washington Park provides access by car or foot to this sprawling sea of green, the largest park completely enclosed within a US city. A web of trails leads into lush forest, past scenic overlooks, and through idyllic picnic areas. The **Pittock Mansion,** within Forest Park, was built by Henry L. Pittock, founder of the daily *Oregonian.* Enjoy a striking panorama of the city from the lawn of this 85-year-old, 16,000 sq. ft. monument to the French Renaissance.

OREGON ZOO. The zoo has gained fame for its successful efforts at elephant breeding. Exhibits include a Cascade Mountains-like goat habitat and a marine pool as part of the zoo's "Great Northwest: A Crest to Coast Adventure" program. The zoo also features weekend educational talks and a **children's petting zoo.** For over 22 years, from late June to August, nationally touring artists have performed at the **Rhythm and Zoo Concerts** on the concert lawn. *(☎234-9694. W-Th 7pm; free with zoo admission.)* **Zoobeat Concerts** feature artists in blues, bluegrass, pop, and world beat on selected summer weekend evenings. *(4001 SW Canyon Rd. ☎226-1561. Open 9am-6pm in summer, hours vary by season. $7.50, seniors $6, ages 3-11 $4.50; 2nd Tu of each month free after 1pm.)*

🎵 ENTERTAINMENT

Prepare for culture. Upon request, the Visitor's Association (see **Practical Information,** p. 73) will fork over a thick packet outlining the month's events. Outdoor festivals are a way of life in Portland; the city's major daily newspaper, the **Oregonian,** lists upcoming events in its Friday edition. The city's favorite free cultural reader, the Wednesday **Willamette Week,** is a reliable guide to local music, plays, and art. Drop boxes are all over town, and the paper's office is right across from the library. **The Rocket** (bimonthly, free) provides comprehensive coverage of alternative and punk music for the whole Northwest. **Mercury** (weekly, free) gives a salty, humorous take on Portland life and lists current events in a section titled "My, what a busy week!" Yuppies find their interests represented weekly in **Outtown,** which lists downtown goings-on. Also call the *Oregonian's* **Inside Line** (☎225-5555) for up-to-date information on happenings in the area.

MUSIC

Although first-rate traveling shows never miss Portland, and many have bargain tickets available, some of the greatest shows are free and outdoors. Live music venues are listed under **Nightlife,** below.

THE LOCAL STORY

A HIRSUTE PURSUIT

Hidden among factories and behind one of the least pretentious facades of any brewery around, ◧ *Hair of the Dog Brewing Company produces what might just be the best beer in a city known for its microbreweries. Let's Go took a tour of the small-scale brewery from co-owner Alan Sprints and got the skinny on the brewing process. For all lovers of beer: these brews are superlative, and the experience is an essential notch on the microbrew belt. Call for the complicated directions. (4509 SE 23rd Ave.* ☎232-6585. Tours by appointment, during weekdays. 12 oz. bottles are $3 each, 1.5L "magnums" are $10.)

Q: Do your beers ferment in the bottle?

A: They do ferment in the bottles, but it's a very small refermention, just enough to get bubbles... if you do any more than that the bottles will explode.

Q: But they mature in the bottle like wine?

A: Yeah.

Q: And what's the reason for that?

A: Higher alcohol content, more hops, and also the bottle conditioning process... it's more like champagne, where the product is naturally fermented. That's a better environment for the product to age.

Q: Does that prevent contamination?

A: Refermention scavenges oxygen out of the liquid, and that helps stop failing and off-flavors that might occur in beer if it ages.

Oregon Symphony Orchestra, 923 SW Washington St. (☎228-1353 or 800-228-7343). Box office open M-F 9am-5pm; during Symphony Season Sa 9am-5pm, as well. Classical and pop Sept.-June $15-60. Students and seniors can purchase tickets half-price 1hr. before show time. "Symphony Sunday" afternoon concerts ($10-15). "Monday Madness" offers $5 student tickets 1 week before showtime. Call for park performance info. Wheelchair accessible. Infrared listening devices available.

High Noon Tunes (☎223-1613), at Pioneer Courthouse Sq. Jammed concerts mid-July-Aug. W noon-1pm. A potpourri of rock, jazz, folk, and world music.

Sack Lunch Concerts, 1422 SW 11th Ave. (☎222-2031; www.oldchurch.org), at Clay St. and the Old Church. Classical and jazz music W at noon (usually 1hr.).

Chamber Music Northwest, 522 SW 5th Ave. #725 (☎294-6400). Performs late June-July M, Th, and Sa at Reed College Kaul Auditorium; Tu and F at Catlin Gabel School. Call for directions. Shows at 8pm. Additional shows occur periodically throughout the year. $17-33, ages 7-14 and students with ID $5.

THEATER

Theater in Portland meets all tastes, ages, and budgets. The **Portland Center for the Performing Arts (PCPA)** is the fourth-largest arts center in the US. Free **backstage tours** begin in the lobby of the Newmark Theater, at SW Main and Broadway. (☎248-4335; www.pcpa.com. Tours every 30min. W and Sa 11am-1pm. Any bus to the Transit Mall; walk from there.) **Friends of the Performing Arts Center** (☎274-6555) stages the monthly **Brown Bag Lunch Series,** a glimpse of free professional productions on weekdays around noon. The *Oregonian* has details.

Portland Center Stage (☎274-6588), in Newmark Theater of PCPA at SW Broadway and SW Main. Classics, modern adaptations, and world premiers run late Sept.-Apr. Tu-Th and Su $21-38, F-Sa $21-44. $10 youth matinee seats sometimes available (25 and under). Half-price student rush tickets sometimes available 1hr. before curtain.

Oregon Ballet Theater, 1120 SW 10th Ave. (☎227-0977 or 888-922-5538). One of the best companies on the West Coast. Six productions Oct.-June. $5-80; half-price student rush often available 1hr. before curtain; check tourist office for discount tickets.

Artists' Repertory Theater, 1516 SW Alder St. (☎241-1278). Recruits local talent for top-notch, low-budget, and experimental productions. T-Th and Su matinees $24, seniors $18; F-Sa $28. Students always $15.

CINEMA

Portland is a haven for cinema lovers. With the help of the *Oregonian*, a full-price ticket to just about any screen can be scrupulously avoided, and McMenamins' theater-pubs are one of a kind.

Mission Theater and Pub, 1624 NW Glisan (☎288-3286 or 888-249-3983), serves home-brewed ales and sandwiches ($6-7). Watch second-run flicks while lounging on couches or in the old-time balcony. Shows begin 5:30, 8, and 10pm. $2-3. 21+.

Baghdad Theater and Pub, 3702 SE Hawthorne Blvd. (☎288-3286). Bus #14. This cine-pub is housed in a former vaudeville theater, with a separate pub in front. 21+. First show is at 5:30pm, and 2 others follow at approximately 2hr. intervals. Pub open M-Sa 11am-1am, Su noon-midnight. $2-3.

Cinema 21, 616 NW 21st St. (☎223-4515), part of Nob Hill's bustling strip. Mean, clean, and pistachio green. Mostly documentary, independent, and foreign films. $6, students $5, under 12 and seniors $3; Sa-Su first matinee $3.

Northwest Film Center, 1219 SW Park Ave. (☎221-1156; www.NWfilm.org), screens documentary, foreign, classic, experimental, and independent films at the historic **Guild Theatre,** 829 SW 9th Ave., 2 blocks north of PAM, as well as in the museum's auditorium. Every Feb. the center also hosts the **Portland International Film Festival,** with 100 films from 30 nations. Screenings begin sometime between 7pm and 9pm. Box office opens 30min. before each show. $6.50, students and seniors $5.50.

SPORTS

When Bill Walton led the **Trailblazers** (☎321-3211, tickets $15-65) to the 1979 NBA Championship, Portland went berserk—landing an NBA team in the first place was a substantial accomplishment for a city of Portland's size. The closest the Blazers have come to a title repeat came in 2000, when they lost to the Los Angeles Lakers in the Western Conference Championships. The Blazers play November to May in the sparkling new **Rose Garden Arena** by the Steel Bridge in Northeast Portland, with its own stop on MAX. Portland is also home to the Portland **Fire** of the WNBA professional women's basketball league. The **Winter Hawks** of the Western Hockey League (☎238-6366; tickets $12-20) play from September to March in the Rose Garden Arena and at the **Coliseum.** Take bus #9 or MAX. **PGE** (Portland General Electric) **Park,** 1844 SW Morrison St., on the other side of town, is home to the **Beavers,** Portland's AAA-league baseball team.

Q: Are you more interested in the consistency of your product, or do you prefer experimenting with different brews?

A: I enjoy when people like using our beer for celebrating special events and special occasions... it makes me feel good. If it wasn't for people that enjoyed the beer, brewing it wouldn't be so much fun.

Q: What about [the name of] Hair the Dog?

A: Originally, the term literally referred to using the hair of a dog that bit you to help heal the bite. They'd chase a dog down, cut off some of its hair, [then] wrap it around the wound. And that helped chase away the evil spirit.

Q: And that's also for a hangover...?

A: Yes, the term later became used in reference to curing a hangover—drinking some of the "hair of the dog" you had the night before (more beer).

Q: Do these beers, having a higher alcohol content, give stronger hangovers?

A: All I know is we've generated a few hangovers.

Q: Oh yeah? [Feels head and eyes empty glass.]

A: Whether they're worse or not I don't know. It depends on what you're used to drinking. We only use quality ingredients, so you should have a quality hangover.

The San Diego Padres also have an A-league affiliated team in Portland. (☎223-2837. June-Sept. Gen. admission $3.)

FESTIVALS

Rose Festival, 5603 SW Hood Ave. (☎227-2681). Begins on May 30, 2003. Like Alpacas? Then check out the Alpaca show. Portland's premier summer event offers concerts, celebrities, auto racing, an air show, and the largest children's parade in the world. Larger events require tickets, but smaller ones are free.

Waterfront Blues Festival (☎282-0555 or 973-3378), early July. Outrageously good entertainment featuring blues, folk, and other artists on 3 stages with open air seating. Suggested donation is $3-5 and 2 cans of food to benefit the Oregon Food Bank.

Oregon Brewers Festival (☎778-5917; www.oregonbrewfest.com), on the last full weekend in July. The continent's largest gathering of independent brewers (72 breweries) parties at Waterfront Park. $1 per taste, $3 per mug. Under 21 must be with parent.

Mt. Hood Festival of Jazz (☎219-9833, www.mthoodjazz.com), on the first weekend in Aug. at Mt. Hood Community College in Gresham. Take I-84 to Wood Village-Gresham exit and follow the signs, or ride MAX to the end of the line. The PNW's premier jazz festival. Wynton Marsalis and the late Stan Getz have been regulars. Tickets from $29 per night, more through Ticketmaster. 3-day passes $70-130. Reserve well in advance.

🎵 NIGHTLIFE

Once an uncouth and rowdy frontier town, always an uncouth and rowdy frontier town. Portland's nightclubs cater to everyone from the iron pumping college athlete to the nipple-pierced neo-goth aesthete. Bigger, flashier clubs rule **Old Town** and central **Downtown,** where mainstream, punk, jazz and gay joints all come alive on weekends. In the **Pearl District** and **Nob Hill,** yuppies and college kids kick back together in spacious bars. In the **Southeast,** cramped quarters make for instant friends over great music and drinks. Hidden in the Northeastern suburb of **Laurelhurst,** locals gather in intimate clubs to listen to the best of the city's folk and rock. The plentiful neighborhood pubs often have the most character and the best music. Mischievous minors be warned: the drinking age is strictly enforced.

DOWNTOWN AND OLD TOWN

Ohm, 31 NW 1st Ave. (☎223-9919; www.clubohm.com), at Couch under the Burnside Bridge. A venue dedicated to electronic music and unclassifiable beats. Achieve oneness dancing in the cool brick interior, or give your ears and feet a break and mingle outside. Tu brings Dhalia, W Breakbeat and Trance, Th Spoken word, and weekends often bring big-name live DJs. 21+. Cover $3-15. Open M-W 9pm-2:30am, Th-F 9pm-3:30am, Sa 9pm-4am, Su 9pm-3am. After-hours for some shows and special events stretch past 6am. Kitchen service until 2am.

Brig, The Nightclub Fez, Red Cap Garage, Panorama and **Boxxes,** 341 SW 10th St. (☎221-7262; www.boxxes.com), form a network of clubs along Stark St. between 10th and 11th. On weekdays the clubs are connected, but on weekends they are often sealed off—check at the door to see what is happening where. The 23-screen video and karaoke bar is where magic happens. On weekends, the crowds are mixed everywhere except Boxxes (which is always gay); on weekdays, all the clubs are predominantly gay. Cover $2-5. Open M-Su 9pm-2:30am; Panorama stays open until 4 or 4:30am F-Sa.

Satyricon, 125 NW 6th Ave. (☎243-2380), on the bus mall. A venue perfectly suited for punk and alternative, this intimate space hosted the Northwest's best long before grunge rock was the new kid on the block. Won't open unless a show is booked, so call ahead. 21+. Nightly cover $4-10, bigger draws $10-15. Open daily 10pm-2:30am.

Kells Irish Pub, 112 SW 2nd Ave. (☎227-4057). With a cigar bar and wood and brass interior, Kells caters to a more upscale crowd, but a great space and live Irish music every night of the week make sure that crowd is always buzzing. 21+. Happy Hour M-F 4-7pm and 11pm-1am. Open Su-W 11:30am-1am, Th-Sa 11:30am-2am.

Embers, 110 NW Broadway (☎222-3082), at Couch St. Follow rainbows to the dance floor, or watch fish swim in the bar counter. Retro and house music. The crowd is mostly gay on weekdays, but predominately straight on weekends. Happy hour until 7pm. Special events on Thurs. Open daily 11:30am-2:30am.

SOUTHEAST AND HAWTHORNE

Produce Row Cafe, 204 SE Oak St. (☎232-8355). Bus #6 to SE Oak and SE Grand; walk west along Oak toward the river. A huge deck, hip staff, and enough beers to give a German a headache. 30 beers on tap and over 150 in bottles. Rotating line-up of bands (jazz, rock, bluegrass) and open-mic. Domestic bottles $2, pints $3. Open M-Th 11am-midnight, F-Sa noon-1am, Su noon-11pm.

Dots Cafe, 2521 SE Clinton St. (☎235-0203). Listen to Black Sabbath, electronica, jazz, and everything else in the company of Portland's young hipsters. The usual excellent microbrews, $6 pitchers of Pabst Blue Ribbon, and a regal assemblage of kitsch memorabilia accompany Victorian paintings. Rent a pool table for $0.25 per game. Cheese fries $3.50. Open daily noon-2am.

Sweetwater's Jam House, 3350 SE Morrison St. (☎233-0333). Rasta decor features life-sized swordfish and an authentic ganja sack, mon. Reggae music nightly. Affordable ($5-7) drinks; an extensive rum list includes "Joe vs. the Volcano," which arrives on fire. Food is excellent, but pricey. Open M-Th 5pm-1am, F-Sa 12pm-2am, Su 12pm-11pm.

LAURELHURST

The Laurel Thirst Public House, 2958 NE Glisan St. (☎232-1504), at 30th Ave. Bus #19. Local talent makes a name for itself in 2 intimate rooms of groovin', boozin', and schmoozin'. Burgers and sandwiches $5-8. Free pool Su-Th before 7pm. Cover $3-6 after 8pm. Open Su, Tu-Th 9am-1:30am, M noon-1:30AM, F-Sa 9am-2am.

Beulahland, 118 NE 28th Ave. (☎235-2794), at Couch opposite the Coca-Cola bottling plant. Bus #19. A small venue with local art on the walls and huge, inflatable toys hanging from the ceiling. DJs on F, often spinning Ska; live music Sa. No cover. Happy hour 4-7pm. Open Su-Th 7am-midnight, F-Sa 7am-2:30am.

PEARL AND NOB HILL DISTRICTS

Jimmy Mak's, 300 NW 10th Ave. (☎295-6542), 3 blocks from Powell's Books at Flanders. Jam to Portland's renowned jazz artists. Shows 9:30pm-1am. Cover $3-6. Vegetarian-friendly Greek and Middle Eastern dinners ($8-17). Open Tu-Sa 11am-2am.

Bridgeport Brewing Co., 1313 NW Marshall (☎241-3612; www.bridgeportbrew.com), at 13th St. This old wood-beamed rope factory is the zenith of beer and pizza joints, with tables cut from old bowling alleys and sheltered outdoor eating. The on-site microbrewery produces a range of British-style ales. Open M-Th 11:30am-11pm, F-Sa 11:30am-midnight, Su 1-10pm. Also at 3632 SE Hawthorne (☎233-6540).

OREGON

⚡ DAYTRIP FROM PORTLAND: SAUVIE ISLAND

From I-405, Vaughn or Yeon Ave., take US 30 W (dir.: "Mount St. Helens"). After about 20min. watch for Sauvie Island signs to the right; one can also take bus #17 (St. Helens Rd.) from SW 6th and Salmon (40-50min.).

Peaceful Sauvie Island, found just northwest of downtown Portland at the confluence of the Columbia and Willamette Rivers, is part farming community and part nature preserve. A bridge connects Sauvie to the mainland at its southern tip, where produce-growing farms dominate, broken up only by pick-your-own berry stands and farmers markets. Most Portlanders head to Sauvie for its **beaches**, located on the northeast side of the island, which, along the rest of the northern half of the island, form the bird-laden **Sauvie Island State Wildlife Preserve.** Parking in the preserve requires a permit, and is efficiently enforced (daily permit $3.50, yearly $11). To get one, stop at **Sam's Cracker Barrel Grocery,** and grab a 10¢ map of the island while you're there. Sam's is located just over the bridge, about 50 yd. north on Sauvie Island Rd. (☎ 621-3960. Open daily 7am-8pm.) Plan ahead; Sam's is several miles from the beaches and is the most convenient place on the island to buy a permit. To get to the beaches head east and north from Sam's along Gillihan Loop Rd., and after 5 mi. bear right onto Reeder Road. Go another 4 mi. on Reeder and the beaches will be to your right. The local park office should know if there are any current advisories against dipping. The **Fish and Wildlife Office** (☎ 621-3488) is on the western side of the island, just north of where Reeder Rd. and Sauvie Island Rd. meet; they'll also be able to recommend nice routes for a short hike around the preserve (the preserve is closed to hikers from late Sept. to mid-April). Sauvie is short on roofed accommodations, but camping is available at **Sauvie Cove RV Park,** 31421 NW Reeder Rd., just south of the beaches. (☎ 621-9881. Sites with water and fire pits $17. RV sites also available for short and long-term stays.)

NEAR PORTLAND

MOUNT HOOD ☎ 503/541

You can't miss it—a magnet for the eyes, Mt. Hood is by far the most prominent feature on Northwest Oregon's horizon. Fumaroles and steam vents near the top mark this as a (relatively) recently active volcano, but that's no deterrent for thousands of outdoors enthusiasts. Home to many ski resorts—one is the only resort in the lower 48 open year-round—the mountain satisfies Portland's skiing needs. The surrounding ridgelines and mountains are relatively mellow compared to the other mega-volcanoes to the north, Mt. Adams and Rainier, allowing for decent, non-technical hiking, albeit with less spectacular views. The mountain gets its fair share of climbers to a 11,235 ft. summit.

⚡⚡ ORIENTATION AND PRACTICAL INFORMATION

Mt. Hood stands near the junction of US 26 and Hwy. 35, 1½hr. east of Portland via US 26. For a more scenic drive, take I-84 along the Columbia River Gorge to Exit 64 and approach the mountain from Hood River (see p. 89) on Hwy. 35. **Government Camp,** 50 mi. east of Portland, has food, accommodations, and gear rental.

Greyhound buses (☎ 800-231-2222) leave from the **Huckleberry Inn** (☎ 503-272-3325) in Government Camp to Portland (2hr., 1 per day, $8) and Bend (3hr., 1 per day, $17). Call ☎ 911 in an **emergency;** the nearest **hospitals** are in Portland and Hood River. The **post office** is at 88331 E Govt. Camp Loop Rd., in Government Camp.

(☎800-275-8777. Open M-F 8:30am-5pm.) **Postal Code:** 97028. **Area code:** 503 to the west and south of Mt. Hood; 541 for Hood River and the northeast.

Hood River Ranger District Station, 6780 Hwy. 35, is 11 mi. south of Hood River and 25 mi. north of the US 26 and Hwy. 35 junction. It has more specialized info on the three ranger districts in the vicinity, as well as a variety of trail maps ranging from free to $5. (☎541-352-6002. Open Memorial Day-Labor Day daily 8am-4:30pm; Labor Day-Memorial Day closed Sa-Su.) **The Mt. Hood Info Center,** 65000 E US 26, 16 mi. west of the junction of US 26 and Hwy. 35 and 30 mi. east of Gresham at the entrance to the Mt. Hood village, has topo maps and info on ranger districts. The friendly staff will also direct you to the best trails. (☎503-622-7674 or 888-622-4822; www.mthood.org. Open June-Oct. daily 8am-6pm; Nov.-May 8am-4:30pm.)

🏠 🏕 ACCOMMODATIONS AND CAMPING

Most campgrounds in **Mt. Hood National Forest** cluster near the junction of US 26 and Hwy. 35, although they can be found along the length of both highways on the way to Portland or Hood River. To get to a **free camping** spot near the mountain, take the sign towards Trillium Lake (a few miles east of Govt. Camp on Hwy. 26), then take a dirt road to the right ½ mi. from the entrance with sign "2650 13," go 200 yards, and make a left towards "Old Airstrip." Campsites with fire rings line the abandoned runway. For a far more expensive, less outdoorsy experience, stay in a hotel in **Government Camp** or on the mountain itself. (☎877-444-6777. Sites $9.)

Lost Lake Resort (☎541-386-6366; www.lostlakeresort.org). From Hwy. 35, turn east onto Woodworth Dr., right onto Dee Hwy., and then left on Lost Lake Rd. (Forest Service Rd. 13). Offers sites with water and toilets. A 3 mi. hike around the lake provides views of Mt. Hood. Rent a canoe ($8 per hr., $40 per day), or fish in the trout-stocked lake for free. 121 sites, $15; RV sites without electricity, $18; cabins, $45-100. Showers. ●

Trillium Lake, 2 mi. east of the Timberline turn-off on US 26. Trails surround the crystal-clear lake. Water and toilets, lots of RVs. Paved, secluded sites, $12; lakeside, $14. ●

Still Creek, 1 mi. west of Trillium Lake off US 26, offers sites that are unpaved and have a quieter, woodsy feel. Potable water, toilets, few RVs. $12-14. ●

Sherwood, 14 mi. north of US 26 and just off Hwy. 35, beside a rambling creek. Potable water, pit toilets. Sites $10. No showers. ●

Huckleberry Inn, 88611 Hwy. 26 Business Loop, (☎227-2335). TVs in rooms. Coin-op laundry. In summer 6 people for $85. In winter 4 people for $85. ●

🍴 FOOD

Cafeteria food at the ski resorts is extraordinarily overpriced; bring a bag lunch. Food in Government Camp is more reasonable.

Mt. Hood Brewing Co., 87304 E. Government Camp Loop (☎272-3724; www.mthood-brewing.com). An angler-friendly interior with good burgers ($7-8.50) and plenty of on-site brewed beers. Open Su-W noon-10pm, Th-Sa noon-11pm. ●

Huckleberry Inn, 88611 Hwy. 26 Business Loop (☎272-3325), Government Camp. A bit overpriced, but the portions are large. Omelettes $7.25. Open 24 hr. ●

👁 SIGHTS

Six miles up a road just east of Government Camp stands the historic **Timberline Lodge** (☎622-7979), built by hand in 1937 under the New Deal's Works Progress Administration. On the Timberline grounds is the **Wy'East Day Lodge,** which offers complimentary ski storage in the wintertime. Timberline's **Magic Mile** express lift carries passengers above the clouds for spectacular views of the mountains and ridges north, though if it's sunny extra elevation doesn't improve on the view from the Timberline lodge road. ($8, ages 7-12 $6, under 7 free.)

In the summer, Mount Hood Ski Bowl opens its **Action Park,** which features Indy Kart racing ($5 per 5min.), horseback riding ($25 per hr.), mini-golf ($5), batting cages ($1 for 10 pitches), helicopter rides ($20), bungee jumping ($25), and an alpine slide for $5. (☎ 222-2695. Open M-Th 11am-6pm, F 11am-7pm, Sa-Su 10am-7pm.) The Ski Bowl maintains 40 mi. of bike trails ($5 trail permit), and **Hurricane Racing** rents mountain bikes from mid-June to October ($10 per hr.; half-day $25, full-day $32; trail permit included). The Mt. Hood Visitors Center also lists hiking trails on which mountain biking is **free.**

⛏ HIKING

Hiking trails encircle Mt. Hood; simple maps are posted around **Government Camp.** The free *Day Hikes* booklet describes 34 trails in the area and is available from the Mt. Hood Information Center (see **Orientation and Practical Information,** p. 86). A Northwest Forest parking pass is required at several trailheads. ($5 per day or $30 per year; available at the Mt. Hood Info Center.) Mt. Hood is also a respectable technical alpine climb. **Timberline Mountain Guides,** based out of Timberline Lodge, guides summit climbs for $375. (☎ 541-312-9242; www.timberlinemtguides.com.) **Mountain Tracks Ski and Snowboard Ski Shop,** in the Huckleberry Inn, has details on more ski trails. (☎ 503-272-3380. Closed summers.)

Mirror Lake Trail (6 mi. loop, several hours). Trailhead at a parking lot off US 26, 1 mi. west of Government Camp. A very popular dayhike, this trail winds its way to the beautiful Mirror Lake through the forest. Easy to moderate hiking.

Timberline Trail (41 mi., overnight). Trailhead at **Timberline Lodge** (see **Downhill Skiing,** below) was constructed by the New Deal Civilian Conservation Corps in the 1930s and circles the mountain, offering incomparable views of the Cascades. Strenuous.

Old Salmon River Trail (5 mi. round-trip, 2-3hr.). Take Hwy. 26 to Welches. 1 mi. east of the signal, turn onto Salmon River Rd., and go for 2½ mi. Winds up gentle grades through the forests and meadows, and has creek-crossings in spring. Moderate.

Trillium Lake Loop (4½ mi. loop, 1-2hr.). Trailhead in the day-use area of the Trillium Lake campground. A lakeside trail offering wildlife-viewing and alpine wetlands that becomes a challenging cross-country ski course in winter. Easy to moderate.

⛷ SKIING

Two resorts on the mountain itself and one on nearby **Tom Dick Peak** rank best among the many ski areas around Mt. Hood. All offer **night skiing** and **terrain parks.** Mt. Hood Meadows is considered the best during the winter for its breadth of terrain and decent snow, but when the temperature drops and the rain changes over to powder, Mt. Hood Ski Bowl has the biggest vertical drops and steepest terrain. Timberline isn't anything special by wintertime standards, but skiers and riders swarm to the slopes in summertime, as do thousands of Monarch butterflies.

Mount Hood Meadows (☎ 337-2222; snow report 503-227-7669 or 541-386-7547). 9 mi. east of Government Camp on Hwy. 35. The volcanic terrain is a highlight, offering all kinds of interesting features from a natural half-pipe (it's off the Cascade Express lift, below the trail with the huge ridge/cornice) to the stark and steep Heather Canyon. Huge volumes of snow, it's not always the driest, but there's plenty of it. Mt. Hood Meadows has

$25 lift tickets through participating hotels, including the **Bingen School Hostel** (see p. 90). Open Nov. to May daily 8am-4pm. Lift tickets $41, ages 7-12 $21. Night skiing Dec.-Mar. W-Su 4-10pm, $17. Ski rental package $22, ages 7-12 $15; snowboard package $28, ages 7-12 $21. Beginner package with lift ticket, lesson, and rental $50.

Mount Hood Ski Bowl, 87000 E US 26 (☎503-222-2695 or 800-754-2695), in Government Camp 2 mi. west of Hwy. 35. Just a little guy, with a vertical drop of 1500 ft. The season is shorter (Nov.-Apr.) because of its lower elevation; however, with 34 lit trails, they offer the most night skiing in America and have a great terrain park. Open M-Tu 3:30-10pm, W-Th 9am-10pm, F 9am-11pm, Sa 8:30am-11pm, Su 8:30am-10pm. Lift tickets $26-30, under 12 $18; $16 per night. Ski rental package $19, $12; snowboard package $27 per day, $21 per night.

Timberline (☎622-0717; snow report ☎503-222-2211). Off US 26 at Government Camp. Timberline becomes a hub for hucking, jibbing and general new-school craziness in the summer—other than Whistler, it's the only resort open. Though a large portion of the resort gets cordoned off to those paying top dollar for summer ski or riding camps, a few lanes of the snowfield stay open. **Beware solar devastation:** you'll wish you were never born if you don't bring goggles or sunglasses and **plenty** of sunscreen. Also, unless you never fall, it's advisable to wear long-sleeved tops and bottoms, since the snow is soft but granule-like and gives a nasty "Palmer burn" if slid on. Slopes are intermediate to advanced. Open winter daily 9am-4pm; spring and fall 8:30am-2:30pm; summer 7am-1:30pm. Night skiing Jan.-Feb. W-F 4-9pm, Sa-Su 4-10pm. Lift tickets $38. Ski rental package $21; snowboard package $33.

COLUMBIA RIVER GORGE ☎541/509

Stretching 75 stunning miles east from Portland, the Columbia River Gorge carries the river to the Pacific Ocean through woodlands, waterfalls, and canyons. Heading inland along the gorge, heavily forested peaks give way to broad, bronze cliffs and golden hills covered with tall pines. Mt. Hood and Mt. Adams loom nearby, and breathtaking waterfalls plunge over steep cliffs into the river. The river widens out and the wind picks up at the town of Hood River, providing some of the world's best windsurfing. Once fast and full of rapids, the Columbia is more placid now, as dams now channel the water's fury for hydroelectric power.

OREGON

▐ TRANSPORTATION

To follow the gorge, which divides Oregon and Washington, take **I-84** east from Portland to Exit 22. Continue east uphill on the **Historic Columbia River Hwy. (US 30),** which follows the crest of the Gorge and affords unforgettable views. Or stay on I-84, which follows the Columbia River; **Hwy. 14** runs the length of the Washington side of the river. **Hood River, OR,** at the junction of I-84 and **Hwy. 35,** is the hub of activity in the Gorge. It gives access to the larger city of **Dalles, OR** to the east and **Mt. Hood** (see p. 86) to the south. **Bingen, WA** (BIN-jin), across the Hood River Bridge ($0.75 toll), gives access to the forests of **Mt. Adams** (see p. 229). **Maryhill, WA** is 33 mi. west of Bingen on Hwy. 14.

Trains: Amtrak (☎800-872-7245) disgorges passengers at foot of Walnut St. in **Bingen, WA,** across from Monterey Bay Fiberglass in the Burlington-Northern Santa Fe terminal. 1 train leaves per day for **Portland** (2hr., $10-18) and **Spokane** (6hr., $30-63).

Buses: Greyhound, 600 E Marina Way (☎541-386-1212), in the Hood River DMV building. Off I-84 at Exit 64, take a left at the intersection before the toll bridge and follow the signs to the DMV, the 2nd building on the right. Open M-F 8:30-11:30am and 1:30-4:30pm. To **Portland** (1¼hr., 4 per day, $12).

Public Transportation: Columbia Area Transit (CAT; ☎386-4202) provides door-to-door service within the Hood River area for $1.25; call for pick-up. Also provides weekend shuttle to Meadows during ski season ($3). Open daily 8am-4:30pm.

7 PRACTICAL INFORMATION

Visitors Information: Hood River County Chamber of Commerce, 405 Portway Ave. (☎541-386-2000 or 800-366-3530; www.hoodriver.org), in the Expo Center north off Exit 63. Helpful information on events in the region complements a plentiful collection of maps. Open Apr.-Oct. M-F 9am-5pm, Sa-Su 10am-5pm; Nov.-Mar. M-F 9am-5pm. Many other visitors centers also line the gorge.

Outdoor Information: Columbia Gorge National Scenic Area Headquarters, 902 Wasco St. #200 (☎541-386-2333; www.fs.fed.us/r6/columbia), in Sprint's Waucoma Center Building, Hood River. Forest Service camping map ($4). Open M-F 7:30am-4:30pm.

Internet Access: Hood River Library, 601 State St. (☎541-386-2535), Hood River, up the hill near Wy'East Whole Foods. 2 computers with 30min. Internet access for free; sign up well in advance. Open M-Th 8:30am-8:30pm, F-Sa 8:30am-5pm.

Weather: ☎541-386-3300.

Emergency: ☎911.

Hood River Police: 211 2nd St. (non-emergency ☎541-386-3942).

Hospital: Hood River Memorial, 13th and May St. (☎541-386-3911). 24hr. emergency.

Post Office: 408 Cascade Ave. (☎800-275-8777), Hood River. Open M-F 8:30am-5pm. **Postal Code:** 97031.

ACCOMMODATIONS

Hotel rooms in Hood River typically start around $50 and spiral upward from there. Cheaper motels line the west end of Westcliffe Dr., north off I-84 Exit 62, although they're usually full on the weekends. Camping in state parks along the river is generally affordable. **Ainsworth State Park** is also readily accessible (see **Portland: Accommodations and Campgrounds,** p. 73). For a full list of camping facilities, contact the visitors center.

Bingen School Inn Hostel/Columbia Gorge Outdoor Center (☎509-493-3363; www.bsi-cgoc.com). Take the third left after the yellow blinking light onto Cedar St.; from there it's 1 block up the hill on Humbolt St. An outdoorsy converted schoolhouse with airy rooms, 2 dorm-style and 7 private. In the summer, **windsurfing lessons** ($65 per 3hr., beginner to advanced) and **rentals** ($30 per day, $185 per week) are available. Kitchen, laundry, climbing wall, volleyball net, outdoor grill, TV/VCR, school lockers, and linen are available. Winter guests score $20 Hood Meadows lift tickets. Dorms $15; 5 large private rooms $35 for 2 people, $10 per additional person. ❶

Beacon Rock State Park (☎509-427-8265), 7 mi. west of the Bridge of the Gods on Washington's Hwy. 14. Easy access to hiking, mountain biking, fishing, and rock climbing. 28 secluded, woodsy sites $16. Coin showers. ❶

Viento State Park (☎541-374-8811 or 800-452-5678). 8 mi. west of Hood River off I-84. Offers a noisy but pleasant experience, and easy access to river hiking. Showers and toilets. 13 tent sites $14, 61 RV sites $16. Handicap facilities available. ❶

Lone Pine Motel 2429 Cascade St., Hood River (☎541-387-8882), just west of Safeway, rents comfortable hostel-style rooms with fridges, microwaves, and TV for almost nothing, but rarely has openings. Rooms $25-60, or $125 for week. ❷

OREGON

🔲 🔳 FOOD AND NIGHTLIFE

Safeway, 2249 W Cascade St., has groceries. (☎541-386-1841. Open daily 6am-1am.)
Wy'East Whole Food Market, 110 5th St., off Oak St. in Hood River, complements its
natural food selection with handmade sandwiches ($4-5) and a java, smoothie, and
juice bar. (☎541-386-6181. Open M-F 7:30am-6:30pm, Sa 9am-6pm, Su 10am-5pm.)

River City Saloon, 207 Cascade Ave. (☎541-387-2583), hosts bluegrass and rock
musicians. A chicken parmesan sandwich is $9. Happy Hour 4:30-6:30pm, with $2.50
microbrews. Also offers **Internet access,** at $1 per 15min. Open daily 4:30pm-2am. ❷

Full Sail Brewing Company and Pub, 506 Columbia Ave. (☎541-386-2247; www.full-
sailbrewing.com). Take 5th St. 2 blocks toward the river from Oak St. Relax on the deck
with a view of the river. Grill food $6-12. Open daily noon-9pm. ❷

Sage's Cafe, 202 Cascade Ave. (☎541-386-9404). Cheap, hearty breakfasts ($3-6)
and lunchtime options including quiche or a sandwich ($2.50 and $4.50). Open M-F
7am-6pm, Sa 8am-6pm, Su 8am-5pm. ❶

🔘 SIGHTS

MARYHILL MUSEUM OF ART. This elegant museum sits high above the river on
the Washington side. Built in the 1920s by Sam Hill, a great benefactor of the area
and instigator of the historic preservation of the Columbia Gorge. Hill was a friend
of Queen Marie of Romania, whose coronation garb is displayed along with Rodin
plasters. (*35 Maryhill Museum Dr. Hwy. 14 from Bingen or I-84 to Biggs, Exit 104; cross Sam
Hill Bridge, then turn left onto Hwy. 14 for 3 mi. ☎509-773-3733. Open daily mid-Mar. to mid-
Nov. 9am-5pm. $7, seniors $6, ages 6-16 $2.*)

STONEHENGE. Sam Hill built this full-scale replica of the English monument out
of concrete as a memorial to the men of Klickitat County killed in WWI. Thinking
that the original monument was used in sacrificial rituals before its astronomical
properties became known, Hill hoped to express that "humanity still is being sac-
rificed to the god of war on fields of battle." People gather here for patriotic holidays and pagan celebrations alike. (*3 mi. farther east along Hwy. 14.*)

🔺 OUTDOOR ACTIVITIES

OUTDOOR GAMES

Hood River hosts the **Subaru Gorge Games** (☎866-467-4301; www.gorge-
games.com) on the third weekend of July in 2003. World-class athletes gather to
compete in one of the most highly regarded outdoor adventure competitions,
with events including kayaking, windsurfing, kiteboarding, climbing, paragliding,
and a 24hr. mountain bike race.

A string of waterfalls adorns the Historic Columbia River Hwy. (US 30) east of
Crown Point; pick up a waterfall map at the visitors center in Hood River. A short
paved path leads to the base of **Latourell Falls,** 2½ mi. east of Crown Point. East
another 5½ mi., **Wahkeena Falls,** beautiful and visible from the road, splashes 242 ft.
down a narrow gorge. The base of the falls is less than half a mile farther east on
Historic Columbia River Hwy. From I-84 Exit 31, take the underpass to the lodge.
On a platform, you can watch the falls crash into a tiny pool. For a more strenuous
hike, follow the **Larch Mountain Trail** to the top of the falls. Multnomah Falls visitors
center in the lodge has free trail maps. (☎504-695-2372. Open daily July-Aug. 9am-
8pm; June and Sept. 9am-7pm; Oct.-May 9am-5pm.)

OREGON

WINDSURFING

Frequent 30mph winds make Hood River a windsurfing paradise. Considered one of the best sites in the world for freestyle sailboarding (the professional term for the sport), Hood River attracts some of the best windsurfers around, making watching as interesting as participating. The venerated **Rhonda Smith Windsurfing Center,** in the Port Marina Sailpark, Exit 64 off I-84, under the bridge and left after the blinking red light, offers classes. (☎541-386-9463. $140 for two 3hr. classes. Includes free evening practice.) Lessons are also available from the **Bingen School Inn** (see **Accommodations**). **Big Winds,** 207 Front St., has cheap beginner rentals, plenty of helpful advice, and a wealth of equipment. (☎541-386-6086. $25 per 2hr.) Watch surfers in action at **The Hook,** a shallow, sandy cove off I-84 Exit 63. Here, beginners learn the basic techniques of starting, handling, and jibing before moving out to the deep water of the river. **Spring Creek Fish Hatchery, a.k.a. "The Hatch,"** is on Hwy. 14 west from Bingen. This is where to see best in the business; there is plenty of parking, and the shore offers a view of the most popular stretch of water.

MOUNTAIN BIKING

The Gorge also has excellent mountain biking, with a wide variety of trails for bikers of all skill levels. **Discover Bicycles,** 205 Oak St., rents mountain bikes ($8-10 per hr., $50-60 per day), suggests routes, and sells maps for $2-5. (☎541-386-4820; www.discoverbicycles.com. Open M-Sa 9am-7pm, Su 9am-5pm.)

Seven Streams Canyon Loop (8 mi. loop, 1-2hr.). To get to the trailhead, take Oak St. from Hood River past where it merges with W Cascade, and then turn left on Country Club Rd. After 1½ mi., take a right on Post Canyon Rd. and park on the right where the road becomes gravel. The trail offers great views as it winds through canyons. Moderate.

Mosier Twin Tunnels (4½ mi., 1hr.). A segment of the Historic Columbia River Hwy. that is too narrow for cars, located between Hood River and Mosier. Parking is available at both the east and west end of the tunnels for $3. Offers mainly an on-road ride, with views of the river and the tunnels. Easy to moderate.

Surveyor's Ridge Trail (22 mi. round-trip, several hours). To get to the trailhead, take Rte. 35 south from Hood River for 11 mi. to Pinemont Dr. (Rd. 17), and go east for 6 mi. Turn right onto the dirt road at the "Surveyors Ridge" sign and park in the area by the power lines. Trail mainly follows the ridgeline and offers spectacular views of the Hood River Valley, Mt. Hood, and Mt. Adams. Open June-Oct. Moderate to strenuous.

HIKING

Mazama Trail (7½ mi., several hours). Take Hwy. 35 for 13 mi. to Woodworth Rd., then go 3 mi. to Dee Hwy. (281). Turn right and go 5 mi. before turning and following the signs to Lost Lake for 7 mi. on Rd. 18, then turn left onto Rd. 1810. Take 1810 to 1811, and drive 3 mi. to the trailhead. This trail begins in the forest, with Mt. Hood acting as a magnificent backdrop, then climbs up a steep ridge and through a dense forest to flowered glades and amazing vistas. Open June-Oct. $3 permit required. Strenuous.

Catherine Creek Trail (1¼ mi. round-trip, less than 1hr.). From Bingen, go east on Hwy. 14 and turn left on County Rd. 1230 at Rowland Lake. After about 1½ mi., park at the Catherine Creek lot. Goes along a paved path on the Washington side through wildflowers with dramatic views of the Columbia River and Mt. Hood. Easy.

Mt. Hamilton Trail (4½ mi. round-trip, several hours). Follow the directions in **Accommodations,** above, to **Beacon Rock State Park,** and park in the lot east of Beacon Rock, the 848 ft. neck of an old volcano. Climbing 2250 ft. up Mt. Hamilton on the Washington side of the river, the trail leads hikers up switchbacks to find the summit bursting with wildflowers in June and July. Moderate to difficult.

THE COAST: US 101

If not for the renowned US 101, Oregon's sandy beaches and dramatic seaside vistas might be only a beautiful rumor to those on the interior. Wherever the windy, bustling two lanes of US 101 part from the coast, a narrower road sticks to the stretches of unspoiled coast. The coast's famous beaches complement the already scenic drive (see **US 101 Scenic Drives**, p. 97), and a chain of state parks ensures that no outdoors activity will be unavailable.

There are 17 major state parks along the coast, many of which offer **campgrounds** with electricity and showers. While most of the traffic seems to be tourists in RVs, some savvy travelers choose to experience the coast by **bicycle**. In summer, prevailing winds blow southward, keeping at the backs of cyclists and easing their journey. Cyclists can contact virtually any visitors center or chamber of commerce on the coast for a free copy of the Oregon Coast Bike Route Map, which provides invaluable info for the ride. **Buses** run up and down the coast, stopping in most sizeable towns. Many local lines are affiliates of Greyhound and make connections to major urban centers like Seattle, Portland, and Eugene. The fastest way to experience the coast, however, is by car.

ASTORIA   ☎ 503

Established in 1811 by John Jacob Astor's trading party, Astoria is the oldest US city west of the Rocky Mountains. Originally built as a fort to guard the mouth of the Columbia, it quickly became a port city for ships heading to Portland and Longview, WA. A much more pleasant and less expensive destination than the overrun resort cities to the south, Astoria offers the same beautiful views of the Pacific Ocean from nearby **Fort Stevens State Park.** Its Victorian homes, bustling waterfront, rolling hills, and persistent fog suggest a smaller-scale San Francisco. Differentiating it from that metropolis is a microclimate with wicked winter storms; hurricane-force winds aren't uncommon, and many come to watch storms roll into the Columbia river outlet.

▐▀ TRANSPORTATION

From Astoria, US 30 runs 96 mi. to Portland. Astoria, a convenient link between Washington and the Oregon coast, can also be reached from Portland on US 26 and US 101 via **Seaside** (see p. 98). Two bridges run from the city: the **Youngs Bay Bridge** leads southwest where Marine Dr. becomes US 101, and the **Astoria Bridge** spans the Columbia River into Washington. All streets parallel to the water are named in alphabetical order, except for the first one.

> **Buses: Pierce Pacific Stages** (☎692-4437). A Greyhound affiliate. Pickup at Video City, 95 W Marine Dr., opposite the Chamber of Commerce. To **Portland** (3hr., $22). **Sunset Empire Transit,** 465 NE Skipanon Dr., Warrenton (☎861-7433 or 800-766-6406). Pickup at Duane and 9th St. To **Seaside** (7 per day; $2.25; seniors, students, and disabled $1.75). **Astoria Transit System** (contact Sunset Empire for info, above). Local bus service M-Sa 7am-7pm. ($0.75; seniors, students, and disabled $0.50.)
>
> **Taxis: Yellow Cab** (☎325-3131 or 861-2626). Runs 6am-10pm. Base $2, $1.80 per mi.

▟▛▟ ORIENTATION AND PRACTICAL INFORMATION

Astoria is a peninsula that extends into the Columbia River and is located approximately 7 mi. from the ocean beaches in both Fort Stevens and nearby Washington.

WINE AND CHEESE, TOGETHER AT LAST

One block up from the Maritime Museum is the Shallon Winery, 1598 Duane St., where owner Paul van der Veldt presides over a kingdom of fantastic wines. A self-proclaimed connoisseur of fine food, he insists that visitors call him at any time of day or night before considering a meal at any restaurant within 50 mi. Samplers taste wines made from local berries and the world's only commercially produced whey wines (from the cheese factories in Tillamook). Approach the cranberry-and-whey wine with caution; the fruity taste belies its high alcohol content. Sampling lemon meringue pie wine is likely to be the highlight, and Paul's chocolate orange wine is quite the decadent liqueur. (☎325-5978; www.shallon.com. Must be 21 to drink. Open almost every afternoon. Gratuities and purchases appreciated.)

Tourist Information: 111 W Marine Dr. (☎325-6311), just east of Astoria Bridge. Loads of info on Astoria and its surrounding attractions. Open June-Sept. M-F 8am-6pm, Sa 9am-6pm, Su 9am-5pm; Oct.-May M-F 8am-5pm, Sa-Su 11am-4pm.

Equipment Rental: Bikes and Beyond, 1089 Marine Dr. (☎325-2961), rents bikes ($15 per half-day, $25 per day) and boats.

Laundromat: Maytag Self-Service Laundry, 127 W Bond St. (☎325-7815), 1 block away from Marine Dr. Wash $1, dry $0.25 per 10min. or $0.50 per 40min., detergent $0.75. Open daily 8am-9pm, last wash load at 7:45pm.

Emergency: ☎911.

Crisis Line: ☎800-562-6025.

Police: 555 30th St. (☎325-4411).

Hospital: Columbia Memorial, 2111 Exchange St. (☎325-4321). 24hr.

Internet Access: Astoria Library, 450 10th St. (☎325-7323). For 1hr. of free Internet access sign up a day in advance, or get 15min. walk-up (ID required). Open Tu-Th 10am-7pm, F-Sa 10am-5pm. **Gunderson's Sunnyside Cybercafe,** at the foot of 6th St. (☎325-8642), has 2 computers and is open Tu-F 7:30am-5pm, Sa-Su 8am-5pm.

Post Office: 748 Commercial St. (☎800-275-8777). Open M-F 8:30am-5pm.

Postal Code: 97103.

ACCOMMODATIONS AND CAMPING

Motel rooms can be expensive and elusive during summer. US 101, both north and south of Astoria, is littered with clean and scenic campgrounds.

Fort Stevens State Park (☎861-1671; reservations 800-452-5687), over Youngs Bay Bridge on US 101 S, 10 mi. west of Astoria. Rugged, empty beaches and hiking and bike trails surround the campground. Toilets, water. Reservations ($6) recommended. Wheelchair accessible. 600 sites, $18; full RV sites $21; hiker/biker sites $4.25 per person; yurts $29. Showers included. ❷

Grandview B&B, 1574 Grand Ave. (☎325-0000 or 325-5555). Intimate, cheery, and luxurious rooms. Includes delicious breakfast. Rooms with shared bath from $45, private bath from $71. Off-season 2nd night is $36. ❸

Lamplighter Motel, 131 W Marine Dr. (☎325-4051 or 800-845-8847), between the Pig 'n' Pancake diner and the visitors center. Spotlessly clean, well-lit rooms with cable TV and phones. Large bathrooms, refrigerators. Coffee is available in the lobby all day. Rooms $49-55, less in winter. Senior discount in winter. ❸

OREGON

▶ FOOD

Safeway, 1153 Duane St., provides groceries. (☎325-4662. Open daily 6am-midnight.) A small but growing **farmer's market** convenes each summer Sunday downtown at 12th St.

▨ **Columbian Cafe,** 1114 Marine Dr. (☎325-2233). Local banter, wines by the glass, and fantastic pasta and seafood ($10-15, lunches $5-8) make it worthwhile. Try "Seafood" or "Vegetarian Mercy"—name the heat your mouth can stand and the chef will create you a meal ($8-9). Open lunch M-F 8am-2pm, Sa-Su 9am-2pm; dinner W-Sa 5-9pm. ❷

▨ **Home Spirit Bakery and Cafe,** 1585 Exchange St. (☎325-6846). Eat a tasty, inexpensive meal in a restored Victorian home just a block away from the Shallon Winery. Call ahead. Open Tu-Sa; lunch 11am-2pm, dinner Th-Sa 5:30-8pm. ❷

Someplace Else, 965 Commercial St. (☎325-3500). Complementing the delicious Italian fare is the nightly special ($5-14), a popular dish from a different country every night. Open W-Su 11:30am-2pm and 4-9pm. ❷

Urban Cafe, 1119 Commercial St. (☎338-5133). No two square meters of the restaurant are alike, as part of a chaotic but endearing decoration scheme. Very satisfying dinner quesadillas $7; lunches around $7. Open M-Th 9am-9pm, F-Sa 9am-10pm. ❶

◉ SIGHTS

On the rare clear day, ▨**Astoria Column** grants its climbers a stupendous view of Astoria cradled between **Saddle Mountain** to the south and the **Columbia River Estuary** to the north. You can get there by following signs from 16th Ave. and Commercial St. Completed in 1926, the column on Coxcomb Hill Rd. encloses a dizzying 164 steps past newly repainted friezes depicting local history; picture something like an exceptionally well-decorated barber's pole jutting into the sky, albeit one that (luckily) doesn't spin. (Open dawn-10pm, parking $1.) The cavernous, wave-shaped **Columbia River Maritime Museum,** 1792 Marine Dr. on the waterfront, is packed with marine lore, including displays on the salmon fisheries that once dominated Astoria. Among the model boats is the 1792 vessel that Robert Grey first steered into the mouth of the Columbia River. (☎325-2323. Open daily 9:30am-5pm. $5, seniors $4, ages 6-17 $2, under 6 free.) The **Astoria-Warrenton Crab and Seafood Festival** is a misnomer for a large assembly of Oregon winemakers, brewers, and restaurants. In 2003, it takes place April 25-27. ($5 general admission. Call the chamber of commerce, ☎800-875-6807, for more info.)

◤ NIGHTLIFE

With the recent addition of the Voodoo Room, the nightlife in Astoria has begun to come into its own. Locals say the **Soundbank,** when it opens, might also be worth checking out. Ask around for details.

▨ **Voodoo Room,** adjacent to Columbian Cafe (☎325-2233). The new hot venue for live music, known by many as the artists' hang. Egyptian sarcophagi complete the scene. Drinks about $4. F-Sa funk, jazz, and every other kind of music; cover $3-5. Su bluegrass, no cover. Open daily 5-10pm or later.

Wet Dog Cafe and Pacific Rim Brewing Co., 144 11th St. (☎325-6975). Youthful crowds pack in every weekend for hip-hop and top-40 music. Burgers go for $5.50-8, microbrews $3.25. Occasional live music. Game room. DJ Th-F. 21+ after 9pm. Opens daily at 11am, closes Su-W 10pm, Th 1am, and F-Sa 1:30am. Dinner until 9pm.

US 101
Scenic Drive
(North)

TIME: 7hr. end-to-end
DISTANCE: 320 mi.
SEASON: Year-round

From the Long Beach peninsula and Astoria in the north to Brookings in the south, US 101 hugs the shoreline along the Oregon Coast, linking a string of touristy resorts, small, unspoiled fishing villages, and pristine state parks. Oregon's beaches are some of the largest and most beautiful you will ever see; miles of untouched sand will keep the most picky beach comber content, and those brave enough to face the cold will enjoy the ocean waves. Touristy but gorgeous resort towns like Canon Beach and small communities like Bandon that line the Pacific Ocean make the Oregon Coast a worthy destination.

US 101 NORTH

1 SOUTH JETTY. Located in Ft. Stevens State Park, the jetty has great board- and kayak-surfing opportunities off the coast (p. 98).

2 WRECK OF THE PETER IREDALE. Surfers flock to this popular Ft. Stevens area. The wreck has a peculiar effect on the waves as they come in (p. 98).

3 THE COVE. Catch a wave at this spot, a beach near Seaside that few people know about. A great place to avoid the crowds (p. 100).

4 SADDLE MOUNTAIN. This is the highest peak in the coastal range. From the summit, you can see the Pacific Ocean and the Cascades (p. 102).

5 ECOLA STATE PARK. Ecola, with its many ascending trails, is the best place to see Cannon Beach's distinctive volcanic coastline (p. 102).

6 CANNON BEACH. One of most desirable locations on the coast, with white sand and great weather. (p. 100).

7 HUG POINT. Make sure you visit here at low tide; it's the only time you can access the incredible network of tidal caves (p. 103).

8 OSWALD WEST STATE PARK. Visit this surprising headland rainforest, enjoying the shelter of spruce and cedar trees (p. 103).

9 TILLAMOOK. There are great hiking and biking routes in the nearby mountains, but Tillamook is most known for having some of the best cheese in the country (p. 103).

US 101 SCENIC DRIVES: NORTH AND SOUTH

10 SALMON FISHING. This hidden estuary has some of the best salmon runs in the continental US (p. 104).

11 THE THREE CAPES LOOP. This network of three state parks, Cape Meares, Cape Lookout, and Cape Kiwanda, is one of the coast's principal attractions (p. 104).

12 OTTER CREST LOOP. A detour from US 101, this 4 mi. stretch of road has spectacular views of the ocean (p. 106).

US 101 SOUTH

1 OREGON DUNES NATIONAL RECREATION AREA. These shifting dunes offer opportunities for multiple outdoors activities, including everything from dune buggy rides to sandboarding (p. 109).

2 REEDSPORT. A popular stopover by the dunes, Reedsport has excellent camping and is a great place to rest between runs on the sand (p. 109).

3 WINCHESTER BAY. This coastal city, close to Reedsport, houses an excellent surf spot on the coast. Rent crab traps to try and capture the elusive creatures; even if you can't get one, cheap meal options abound here (p. 112).

4 UMPQUA DUNES TRAIL. Solitary and beautiful, this several-hour hike places you right in the middle of dunes as far as the eye can see. Free from the noise of ATVers and highway motorists, it's just you and the sand all the way (p. 111).

5 SHARKS! The ocean around Bandon and Coos Bay is filled with Great Whites. Ask any surfer who looks like a veteran, and odds are someone they know will have had a close encounter. Surf shops will have info on when it's safe to go out, and when it's best to stay away from the beach (p. 116).

6 HUNTER'S COVE. A beautiful spot on the coast and a major destination for windsurfing. Ask locals for information on how to find it, where to rent windsurfing equipment, and where to get lessons.

7 SAMUEL H. BOARDMAN STATE PARKS. Explore 15 mi. of countless trails, some leading to beaches covered in volcanic rocks. Don't be surprised if an exploratory hike unexpectedly ends at an intimate seaside cove (p. 116).

🅵 DAYTRIPS FROM ASTORIA

FORT CLATSOP NATIONAL MEMORIAL. Reconstructs Lewis and Clark's winter headquarters from journal descriptions. The fort has been completely restored and contains exhibits about the explorers' quest for the Pacific Ocean. In summer, rangers robed in feathers and buckskin demonstrate quill writing, moccasin sewing, and musket firing. *(5 mi. southwest of town on US 101, south from Astoria to Alt. Rte. US 101; follow signs 3 mi. to park. ☎861-2471. Open mid-June to Labor Day daily 8am-6pm; winter 8am-5pm. $2, under 17 free, families $4 per car.)*

FORT STEVENS STATE PARK. Fort Stevens was constructed in 1863 to prevent attack by Confederate naval raiders and was significantly upgraded in 1897 with the addition of 8 concrete artillery batteries. Several of these remaining batteries are the focus of a self-guided walking tour (about 2hr.) that begins up the road from the campground area. *(Located off US 101 on a narrow peninsula 10 mi. west of Astoria. ☎861-2000. Day-use pass costs $3. Get a map and pass from the camp registration.)*

SOUTH JETTY. Great places to board- or kayak-surf near Astoria are at the South Jetty, the northern tip of the peninsula in Fort Stevens state park. Waves get big when the wave refraction off the jetty kicks in. Everyone loves catching a wave in front of the **Wreck of the Peter Iredale** that sticks out of the sand, even though the breaks are nothing special. Both beaches are easy to find within Fort Stevens State Park; look for parking lot A or B for the South Jetty; the main road goes straight to the wreck of the Peter Iredale. No shop specializes in surfboards in Astoria, but **Pacific Wave** in Warrenton, immediately across the Youngs Bay Bridge in the mall on the right, embraces the growing kayak-surfing movement and offers lessons. They'll also have the latest wave forecasts and other surf info.

SEASIDE ☎503

In the winter of 1805-1806, explorers Lewis and Clark made their westernmost camp near Seaside. While the amenities were few and far between at the time, after the development of a resort in 1870 the situation improved and visitors began to pour in. The tourism industry, replete with indoor mini-golf and barrels of salt-water taffy, has transformed Seaside from a remote coastal outpost to a bustling beachfront. For those uninterested in video arcades, Seaside still has merit as a base for exploring the beautiful Oregon coast. Seaside is also less expensive than nearby Cannon Beach, and its hostel is one of the best in the Northwest.

🅜 🅸 ORIENTATION AND PRACTICAL INFORMATION

Seaside lies 17 mi. south of Astoria and 8 mi. north of Cannon Beach along **US 101**. The most direct route between Seaside and Portland is **US 26**, which intersects US 101 just south of Seaside near Saddle Mountain State Park. The Necanicum River runs north-south through Seaside, two blocks from the coastline. In town, US 101 becomes **Roosevelt Dr.**, and another major road, **Holladay Dr.**, splits off from it. **Broadway** runs perpendicular to the two, and is the town's main street and a tourist-dollar black hole. Streets north of Broadway are numbered, and those south of Broadway are lettered. The **Promenade** (or "Prom") is a paved foot-path that hugs the beach for the length of town.

Buses: Pierce Pacific Stages (☎692-4437; call Greyhound at 800-231-2222 for schedules and fares), a Greyhound affiliate, departs the hostel at 3pm for **Portland** (3¼hr., $24) and **Seattle, WA** (5½hr., $37, via **Kelso, WA**). **Sunset Empire Transit** (☎861-7433 or 800-776-6406) runs between Astoria and Cannon Beach 7 times per day M-Sa, stopping at the hostel in addition to the bus stops. Tickets available from drivers. Round-trip $4.50; seniors, disabled, students, and ages 6-12 $3.50; under 6 free.

Taxis: Yellow Cab (☎738-5252). $1.75 base, $1.50 per mi.

Tourist Information: Chamber of Commerce, 7 N Roosevelt Dr. (☎738-6391 or 800-444-6740), on US 101 and Broadway. The **Seaside Visitor Bureau** (☎738-3097 or 888-306-2326; www.seasideor.com) is in the same building. Open June-Aug. daily 8am-5pm; Oct.-May M-F 9am-5pm, Sa-Su 10am-4pm.

Equipment Rental: Prom Bike Shop, 622 12th Ave. (☎738-8251), at 12th and Holladay, rents bikes, in-line skates, beach tricycles, and surreys. Excellent repair work. Must be 18+ to sign for rental. Open daily 10am-6pm. Bikes $6 per hr., $25-30 per day.

Laundry: Clean Services, 1223 S Roosevelt Dr. (☎738-9513). Open daily 8am-10pm. Wash $1.25, dry $0.25 per 5-8min. Detergent $0.75.

Emergency: ☎911.

Police: 1091 S Holladay Dr. (☎738-6311).

Coast Guard: 2185 SE Airport Rd. (☎861-6140), in Warrenton.

Hospital: Providence Seaside Hospital, 725 S Wahanna Rd. (☎717-7000).

Internet Access: Seaside Library: 60 N Roosevelt Dr. (☎738-6742). Free 20min. of Internet access. Open Tu-Th 9am-8pm, F-Sa 9am-5pm, Su 1-5pm.

Post Office: 300 Ave. A, off Columbia Ave. (☎800-275-8777). Open M-F 8:30am-5pm, Sa 8:30-10:30am. **Postal Code:** 97138.

▌ ACCOMMODATIONS AND CAMPING

Seaside's expensive motels are hardly an issue for the budget traveler thanks to the large hostel on the south side of town. Motel prices are directly proportional to their proximity to the beach and start at $50 (less during the off-season). The closest state parks are **Fort Stevens ❶** (☎861-1671; see p. 98), 21 mi. north, and **Saddle Mountain ❶** (☎800-551-6949), 10 mi. east, off US 26 after it splits with US 101. Drive 8 mi. northeast of Necanicum Junction then another 7 mi. up a winding road to the base camp. (Drinking water. 10 sites. Oct.-Apr. $7; May-Sept. $10.) Sleeping on the beach in Seaside is illegal, as it is in all of Oregon.

▨ **Seaside International Hostel (HI),** 930 N Holladay Dr. (☎738-7911). Free nightly movies, a well-equipped kitchen, an espresso bar, and a grassy yard along the river make this lively hostel live up to its reputation. Office open 8am-11pm. Kayak and canoe rental ($9-10 per 2hr.). Call well ahead for weekends. 34 large bunks. $16, nonmembers $19; private rooms with bath and cable TV $36-42, nonmembers $39-65. $2 off for touring cyclists. ❷

Colonial Motor Inn, 1120 N Holladay Dr. (☎738-6295 or 800-221-3804). With colonial furniture, free snacks, and clean, quiet rooms, this little motel is a standout for the price. Free Internet in office. Singles $50; doubles $70. $15-20 less in winter. ❸

Riverside Inn, 430 S Holladay Dr. (☎738-8254 or 800-826-6151). Cozy bedrooms, a deck overlooking the river, and skylights. This B&B is a quiet respite from the Seaside motel madness. Rooms have private bath and TV. Homemade breakfast. Doubles from $70; Oct.-Apr. from $65; singles $5 less. ❸

▌ FOOD

Prices on Broadway, especially toward the beach, are outrageous. **Safeway,** 401 S Roosevelt Dr., stocks the basics. (☎738-7122. Open daily 6am-midnight.)

Morning Star Cafe, 280 S Roosevelt Dr. (☎717-8188), across from Safeway. Comfy beat-up couches and aging board games will remind you of your old basement rec room. Breakfast panini $3.50. Enjoy a sandwich ($3-4) or quiche ($3.50) with a mocha ($3). Open daily 7am-7pm. ❶

The Stand, 101 N Holladay Dr. (☎738-6592), serves the cheapest Mexican meals around to a local crowd. Burritos $2.25-4. Open daily 11am-8pm. ❶

Harrison's Bakery, 608 Broadway (☎738-5331). Seaside's famous beach bread and a font of frosted treats, made every day at low tide. Hosteling discounts and plate-sized donuts. Open W-M 7am-4pm. ❶

👁 SIGHTS AND ENTERTAINMENT

Seaside's tourist population (which often outnumbers that of true locals) swarms around **Broadway,** a garish strip of arcades and shops running the half mile from Roosevelt (US 101) to the beach. "The Arcade," as it is called, is the focal point of downtown and attracts a youthful crowd. Bumper cars, basketball games, and other methods of fleecing visitors abound. The turnaround at the end of Broadway signals the end of the **Lewis and Clark Trail.**

The Seaside Aquarium, 200 N Prom, is smaller than its companion in Newport, but makes up for its small size by giving visitors the chance to feed playful harbor seals. (☎738-6211. Open Mar.-June daily 9am-5pm; July-Dec. open Su-Th 9am-6pm, F-Sa 9am-8pm; winter open W-Su 9am-5pm but days open may change, so call ahead. $6, seniors $4.75, ages 6-13 $3, 5 and under free, families as large as 6 $19. Seal feeding $0.75.)

Perhaps the US's premier recreational road race, the **Hood to Coast Relay** is the ultimate team running event. Held annually at the end of August, runners tear up the trails between Mt. Hood and Seaside (195 mi.) to the cheers of 50,000 spectators. About 750 12-person teams run three 5 mi. shifts in this 1-2 day relay race. For info, call ☎292-2626 or 800-444-6749.

🏃 OUTDOOR ACTIVITIES

Seaside's beachfront is sometimes crowded despite bone-chilling water and strong undertows that more or less preclude swimming. For a slightly quieter beach, head to **Gearhart,** 2 mi. north of downtown off US 101, where long stretches of dunes await exploration. The local surfers know that one of Northern Oregon's **finest breaks** is south of town in **The Cove,** but don't tell anyone that *Let's Go* told you. To get there, take Ave. U towards the beach of Hwy. 101 and then make a left on Edgewood. **Cleanline Surf,** 719 1st Ave., rents surfing gear. (☎738-7888, or 888-546-6176. Open summer daily 10am-8pm; winter M-Sa 10am-6pm, Su 10am-5pm.)

CANNON BEACH   ☎503

Many moons ago, a rusty cannon from a shipwrecked schooner washed ashore at Arch Cape, giving this town its name. Today, home to a veritable army of boutiques, bakeries, and galleries, Cannon Beach is a more refined alternative to Seaside's crass commercialism. Arguably the most desirable location on the entire Oregon Coast because of its amazing ocean views and interesting shops, Cannon Beach is always crowded with Portlanders and other tourists. If you're just driving down US 101, it's well worth the small detour to take an exit down Hemlock street and take in the view.

◢ 🛈 ORIENTATION AND PRACTICAL INFORMATION

Cannon Beach lies 8 mi. south of Seaside, 42 mi. north of Tillamook on US 101, and 79 mi. from Portland via US 26. Lovely **Ecola and Oswald State Parks** lie just to the north and a few miles south of the town, respectively. The four exits into town from US 101 all lead to Hemlock St., which is lined with galleries and restaurants.

Buses: Sunset Transit System (☎800-776-6406). To **Seaside** ($0.75) and **Astoria** ($2.25). **Cannon Beach Shuttle** traverses downtown; to board, just signal to the driver. Runs daily 9am-6pm. $0.75 donation requested.

Tourist Information: Cannon Beach Chamber of Commerce and Visitor Info, 207 N Spruce St. (☎436-2623), at 2nd St. Open M-F 9:30am-5pm. Visitor Info open M-Sa 10am-5pm, Su 11am-4pm.

Equipment Rental: Mike's Bike Shop, 248 N Spruce St. (☎436-1266 or 800-492-1266). Mountain bikes $6-8 per hr., $20-30 per day. Beach tricycles $8 per 1½hr., electric bikes $12 per hr. Open daily 10am-5pm. **Cleanline Surf,** 171 Sunset Blvd. (☎436-9726; www.cleanlinesurf.com). Surfboards and boogieboards $15 per day, wetsuits $20 per day, the complete package $35. Open summer M-F 10am-6pm, Sa 9am-7pm, Su 10am-6pm; winter daily 10am-5pm. **Surf Lessons** are through Tony Gardner (☎738-6448), $55 for 2hr., 2 students for $80.

Emergency: ☎911.

Police: 163 Gower St. (☎436-2811).

Medical Care: Providence North Coast Clinic, 171 Larch St. (☎717-7000), in Sandpiper Sq. Non-emergency care only; nearest emergency care in **Seaside** (see p. 98). Open M-F 8:30am-noon and 1:15-4:30pm.

Internet Access: Cannon Beach Library, 131 N Hemlock (☎436-1391). $6 per hr. Open M-W, F 1-5pm, Th 1-7pm. **Copies and Fax,** 1235 S Hemlock (☎436-2000). $5 for 1st 30min., then $5 for each additional hour. Open M-F 10am-6pm.

Post Office: 163 N Hemlock St., 97110 (☎436-2822). Open M-F 9am-5pm. **Postal Code:** 97110.

▌ ACCOMMODATIONS AND CAMPING

During the winter season, inquire about specials; many motels offer two-for-one deals. In the summer, however, it's a seller's market, so most motels have 2 night minimum stays if you want a reservation. Real budget deals are a short drive away: the **Seaside International Hostel** is 7 mi. north (see p. 99), and **Oswald West State Park** (see p. 103), 10 mi. south of town, has a stunning campground. **Nehalem Bay State Park,** only a few miles farther south than Oswald West outside of Nehalem, has plentiful camping options.

McBee Cottages, 888 S Hemlock St. (☎436-2569). The office is in the **Sandtrap Inn** at 539 S Hemlock St. Bright and cheerful rooms a few blocks from the beach. Some kitchen units and cottages available. $60; winter $45. ❸

Wright's for Camping, 334 Reservoir Rd. (☎436-2347), off Hwy. 101. Tree-shaded sites make this family-owned campground a relaxing retreat from RV mini-cities. Showers, toilets. Wheelchair accessible. Reservations advised in summer. 19 sites, $17. ❶

◖ FOOD

The deals are down Hemlock St. in mid-town. **Mariner Market,** 139 N Hemlock St., holds 7000 grocery items on its expansive shelves. (☎436-2442. Open July-Sept. Su-Th 8am-10pm, F-Sa 8am-11pm; Oct.-June Su-Th 8am-9pm, F-Sa 8am-10pm.)

Lazy Susan's Cafe, 126 N Hemlock St. (☎436-2816), in Coaster Sq. This Cannon Beach favorite has an intimate, woodsy interior. Excellent homemade scones ($1.75). Omelettes $7-8. Open summer daily 7:30am-10pm; winter M, W-Th 8am-2:30pm, F-Sa 8am-8pm, Su 8am-5pm. ❷

Cafe Mango, 1235 S Hemlock St. (☎436-2393), in Haystack Sq. An up-and-coming new restaurant where Midtown Cafe used to be. Savory crepes $5-7, omelettes about $9. First-rate service. Open summer Th-M 7:30am-2:30pm. ❸

Bill's Tavern, 188 N Hemlock St. (☎436-2202.) A local spot for down-to-earth eatin'. Beer on tap is brewed upstairs. Basic pub grub $3-8.25. Pints $3. Open Th-Tu 11:30am-midnight, W 4:30pm-midnight. Kitchen closes around 9:30pm. ❶

🎵 🏞 ENTERTAINMENT AND OUTDOOR ACTIVITIES

Cannon Beach is a gauntlet of expensive, sporadically elegant galleries and gift shops. A stroll along the 7 mi. stretch of flat, bluff-framed beach suits many better. **Coaster Theater,** 108 N Hemlock St., is a small playhouse that stages theater productions, concerts, dance performances, comedy, and musical revues year-round. Schedule varies, so call or check the web site. (☎436-1242; www.coastertheater.com. Box office open W-Sa 1-8pm. Tickets $12-15.) A huge **Sand Castle Competition** will transform Cannon Beach into a fantastic menagerie on June 14, 2003. Contestants begin digging in the morning to construct their ornate sculptures.

The best place to enjoy the dramatic volcanic coastline of Cannon Beach is at **Ecola State Park,** which attracts picnickers, hikers, and surfers alike. Have a look at Ecola Point's views of hulking **Haystack Rock,** which is spotted with (and by) seagulls, puffins, barnacles, anemones, and the occasional sea lion. Follow signs from Hwy. 101. $3 entrance fee. **Indian Beach** is a gorgeous surfing destination; catch waves between volcanic rock walls, with a freshwater stream running down the beach to rinse the salt off after you're done. To surf, rent boards from **Cleanline Surf,** 171 Sunset Blvd. (☎436-9726. Surfboards and boogieboards $15 per day; wetsuits $20 per day. Open M-F 10am-6pm, Sa 9am-7pm, Su 10am-6pm; winter daily 10am-5pm.) There is also good hiking in the area:

Indian Beach Trail (2 mi., about 1hr.) leads to the Indian Beach tide pools, which teem with colorful sea life. Follow signs to "Ecola" to reach trailhead. Easy to moderate.

Tillamook Head Trail (12 mi. round-trip, several hours). Leaves from Indian Beach, and hugs the coast to the mini-cape that separates Seaside Beach from Cannon Beach. The trail passes the top of Tillamook head (2 mi. up the trail), where 5 hiker sites await those willing to make the trek for free camping. Moderate.

Saddle Mountain Trail (5 mi. round-trip, several hours), 14 mi. east of Cannon Beach on US 26, climbs the highest peak in the Coast Range. The trail leads to the mountain's 3283 ft. summit and ends with astounding views of the Pacific Ocean, Nehalem Bay, and the Cascades. Moderate to difficult.

CANNON BEACH TO TILLAMOOK   ☎ 503

The coastal mountains south of Cannon Beach culminate in a scenic section of roadway that cuts into the ocean cliffside of Neahkannie Mountain. Farther south is **Tillamook State Forest,** so named after the infamous Tillamook Burn (a series of fires in 1933) reduced 5 sq. mi. of coastal forest near Tillamook to charcoal. While nature has restored Tillamook State Forest to health, coastal towns to the west are still scarred. The coastline alongside these tiny towns is much less crowded than Seaside and Cannon Beaches. Tourist info for the area is available at the visitors center in Tillamook (see p. 103) or the Rockaway Beach Chamber of Commerce, 103 S 1st St., off US 101. (☎355-8108. Open M-F 10am-3pm.)

HUG POINT. The tidal caves, Hug Point's main claim to fame, are accessible only at low tide. The beach is framed by tall cliffs, and secluded picnic tables dot the headlands near the parking lot. The point is about 2 mi. south of Cannon Beach.

OSWALD WEST STATE PARK. Ten miles south of Cannon Beach, Oswald West State Park is a tiny headland rainforest of hefty spruce and cedars. Local surfers call the sheltered beach here **Short Sands Beach,** or Shorty's; with a first-rate break and camping so close by, the beach is a premier surf destination. The beach and woodsy campsites are only accessible by a ¼ mi. trail off US 101, but the park provides wheelbarrows for transporting gear from the parking lot to the 29 sites. (Open Mar.-Nov. Sites $15.) The campground fills quickly; call ahead. From the south side of the park, a segment of the Oregon Coast Trail leads over the headland to 1661 ft. Neahkahnie Mountain.

NEHALEM. Eight miles south of Oswald State Park, a cluster of made-in-Oregon-type shops along US 101 make up Nehalem. The **Nehalem Bay Winery,** 34965 Hwy. 53, 3 mi. south of town, has free tastings of local cranberry and blackberry vintages. The backpacker-friendly winery sponsors performances in a small theater and an annual reggae and bluegrass festival, providing a forum for general bacchanalian revelry. (☎ 368-9463. Open summer daily 9am-6pm; winter 10am-5pm.)

TILLAMOOK ☎503

Although the word Tillamook (TILL-uh-muk) translates to "land of many waters," to the Northwest it is synonymous with cheese. Tourists come by the hundreds to gaze at blocks of cheese being cut into smaller blocks on a conveyor belt at the **Tillamook Cheese Factory.** The dairy cows themselves give the town a rather bad odor; still, two good museums, hiking and biking in the nearby coastal mountains, and the Three Capes Loop redeem Tillamook for the adventurous traveler.

⬛🛈 ORIENTATION AND PRACTICAL INFORMATION. Tillamook lies 49 mi. south of Seaside and 44 mi. north of Lincoln City on **US 101.** It's also 74 mi. west of Portland on **Rte. 6** and **US 26.** Tillamook's main drag, US 101, splits into two one-way streets downtown: **Pacific Ave.** runs north and **Main Ave.** runs south. The cross streets are labeled numerically. **Ride the Wave Bus Lines** (☎ 800-815-8283) runs locally (M-Sa; $1) as well as to Portland (2½hr., 5 per week, $10). Find a list of campsites and hiking trails in Tillamook County at the **Tillamook Chamber of Commerce,** 3705 US 101 N, in the big red barn near the Tillamook Cheese Factory, 1½ mi. north of town. (☎ 842-7525. Open summer M-Sa 9am-5pm, Su 10am-4pm; winter M-F 9am-5pm, Sa 10am-3pm.) **Equipment repair** is at **Trask Mt. Cycle,** 2011 3rd St., by Pacific Ave., where they also give good advice and sell maps of mountain biking trails in the area. (Open M-Th 9am-8pm, F-Sa 9am-9pm, Su 11am-7pm.) Call ☎911 in an **emergency,** or notify the **police** at 210 Laurel St. (☎ 842-2522) in City Hall. The **Coast Guard** can be reached at ☎322-3531. **Tillamook County Library,** 210 Ivy Ave., offers 3 computers with 30min. of free **Internet access.** (☎ 842-4792. Open M-Th 9am-9pm, F-Sa 9am-5:30pm.) The **post office** is at 2200 1st St. (☎ 800-275-8777. Open M-F 9am-5pm.) **Postal Code:** 97141.

🛏 ACCOMMODATIONS AND CAMPING. Motel prices in Tillamook are steep (and aren't helped by the 7% city lodging tax), but the camping is some of the area's finest. The only reasonably priced motel in town is the **MacClair Inn ❹,** 11 Main Ave. at the center of town, which rents huge, clean rooms. Enjoy the outdoor pool, hot tub, and sauna. (☎ 842-7571 or 800-331-6857. Singles $66, doubles $73. 10% AAA discount. Credit card required.) **Kilchis River Park ❶,** 6 mi. northeast of town at the end of Kilchis River Rd., which leaves US 101 1 mi. north of the factory,

OREGON

has 35 sites between a mossy forest and the Kilchis River. The campground itself is mostly geared towards families, with a baseball field, volleyball court, horseshoes, and swimming. Mountain bikers can find excellent trails within short rides of the campground on former logging roads, hiking options abound in the mountains, and the campground offers access to one of the **best salmon-fishing** rivers in the lower 48. (☎842-6694. Water, toilets. Open May-Oct. Tent sites $10; walk-ins $3.) To sleep on the sand, try the **campgrounds** on the Three Capes Loop.

◖ FOOD. Tillamook may be a cheese-lover's paradise, but other food choices in town are lacking. Pick up some Velveeta at **Safeway,** 955 US 101, on the north side of downtown. (☎842-4831. Open daily 6am-1am.) The **Blue Heron French Cheese Company ❷,** 2001 Blue Heron Dr., north of town and 1 mi. south of the Tillamook Cheese factory, has tasty deli sandwiches. Although the sheer quantity of items for sale is almost overwhelming, sandwiches stand out at $6.25. (☎842-8281. Open summer daily 8am-8pm; winter 9am-5pm. Deli open 11:30am-4pm.)

◙ SIGHTS. Plane buffs and all who celebrate mechanical marvels will appreciate the impressive **Tillamook Naval Air Station Museum,** 2 mi. south of town. This hulking seven-acre former blimp hangar is the largest wooden clear-span structure in the world. The airy cavern is home to over 34 fully functional war planes, including WWII beauties like the P-38 Lightning and a PBY-5A Catalina. It also has some modern fighter jets on loan from the navy. (☎842-1130. Open daily 10am-5pm. $9.50, over 65 $8.50, ages 13-17 $5.50, 12 and under $2.) Downtown, the **Tillamook County Pioneer Museum,** 2106 2nd St., features exceptionally thorough collections of WWII medals, rifles, and collectibles. Also displays the head-turning work of taxidermist and big game hunter Alex Walker. (☎842-4553. Open M-Sa 8am-5pm, Su 11am-5pm. $2, seniors $1.50, ages 12-17 $0.50, under 12 free.)

◪ THE THREE CAPES LOOP ☎503/541

Between Tillamook and Lincoln City, US 101 wanders east into wooded land, losing contact with the coast. The Three Capes Loop is a 35 mi. circle that connects a trio of spectacular promontories—**Cape Meares, Cape Lookout, and Cape Kiwanda State Parks**—that will almost certainly make you linger longer than you expect; plan accordingly. The loop leaves US 101 at Tillamook and rejoins it about 10 mi. north of Lincoln City. Unless time is of the utmost importance, taking the loop is a far better choice than driving straight down US 101.

CAPE MEARES STATE PARK. Cape Meares State Park, at the tip of the promontory jutting out from Tillamook, protects one of the few remaining old-growth forests on the Oregon Coast. The mind-blowing **Octopus Tree,** a gnarled Sitka spruce with six candelabra trunks, looks like the imaginative doodlings of an eight-year-old. The **Cape Meares Lighthouse** operates as an illuminating on-site interpretive center. (Open May-Sept. daily 11am-4pm; Oct. and Mar.-Apr. F-Sa 11am-4pm. Free.) If you walk down to the lighthouse, bring binoculars or use the $0.25 viewer to look at the amazing seabird colony on the giant volcanic rock. As you drive south of Cape Meares, a break in the trees reveals a beach between two cliffs; this is a beautiful, quiet place to pull off the road and explore.

Oceanside and Netarts lie a couple miles south of the Cape, and offer overpriced gas, a market, and a few places to stay that tend to fill up fast. **The Terimore ❸,** 5103 Crab Ave., in Netarts, has the least expensive rooms in the two towns, some with ocean views. (☎842-4623 or 800-635-1821. Rooms with views $60-70, without $45-60.) Try the **Whiskey Creek Cafe ❷,** 6060 Whiskey Creek Road in Neharts. Popular for their oysters fresh from the bay; halibut and chips costs $9.25. (☎842-5117. Open Su-Th 11am-9pm, F-Sa 11am-10pm.)

CAPE LOOKOUT STATE PARK. Another 12 mi. southwest of Cape Meares, Cape Lookout State Park offers a small, rocky beach with incredible views of the surrounding sights. It also has some fine camping near the dunes and the forests behind them. (☎842-4981 or 800-551-6949. $16.) From here, the 2½ mi. **Cape Trail** heads past the 1943 crash site of a military plane to the end of the lookout, where a spectacular 360-degree view featuring **Haystack Rock** awaits. The **Cape Lookout campground ❷** offers fine camping near the dunes and the forests behind them, although sites with better privacy tend to go far in advance. 216 sites. Toilets and showers. (☎842-4981, 800-551-6949. Tent sites $16, non-camper showers $2. State park has $3 day use fee.)

CAPE KIWANDA STATE PARK. Cape Kiwanda State Park (☎800-551-6949), 1 mi. north of Pacific City, is the jewel of the Three Capes Loop's triple crown. This sheltered cape draws beachcombers, kite-flyers, volleyball players, surfers, and windsurfers, not to mention the odd snowboarder out to ride a giant sand hill. A walk up the sculptured sandstone on the north side (wear shoes with good grips) reveals a ▓**hypnotic view** of swells rising over the rocks, forming crests, and smashing into the cliffs. If the surf is up, head to **South County Surf,** 33310 Cape Kiwanda Dr., a little ways of the beach, where the walls are lined with shots of wipeouts and the Northwest's biggest surfing days. (☎503-965-7505. Surfboard rental $20 until 5pm; boogieboard $10; wetsuit $15. Open Tu-F, Su 10am-5pm, Sa 9am-5pm.)

PACIFIC CITY. The nearest town to Cape Kiwanda, Pacific City is a hidden gem that most travelers on US 101 never even see. If you plan to stay overnight, the **Anchorage Motel ❸,** 6585 Pacific Ave., offers homey rooms. (☎541-965-6773 or 800-941-6250. Rooms from $45, offseason from $37.) Camping on beaches in Oregon is illegal, but local youth have been known to camp near the beach, or on more secluded beaches north of Cape Kiwanda. The town hides away some surprisingly good restaurants; the **Grateful Bread Bakery ❷,** 34805 Brooten (BRAW-ten) Rd., creates monuments to the art of dining. Get anything from a vegetarian stuffed focaccia ($7) to one of many excellent omelettes. (☎965-7337. Summer Th-Tu 8am-8:30pm; winter Th-M 8am-8:30pm.)

LINCOLN CITY   ☎541

Lincoln City is actually five towns wrapped around a 7 mi. strip of ocean-front motels, gas stations, and souvenir shops along US 101. Most budget travelers, and this travel guide, will tell you that the Three Capes area is far superior as a destination. As one of the largest "cities" on the North Coast, Lincoln City can, however, be used as a gateway to better points north and south.

■▐ **ORIENTATION AND PRACTICAL INFORMATION.** Lincoln City lies between Devils Lake and the ocean, 42 mi. south of Tillamook, 22 mi. north of Newport, and 88 mi. southwest of Portland. The city proper is divided into quadrants: the D River ("the smallest river in the world") is the north-south divide; US 101 divides east from west. **Greyhound** buses, 3350 NW US 101 (☎800-454-2487) depart from Wendy's at the north end of town to **Newport** (50min., 2 per day, $7) and **Portland** (2½hr., 2 per day, $13). Tickets are available at the **visitors center** (801 US 101 SW #1. M-Sa 9am-4:30pm, Su 10am-3:30pm; see below.) **Robben-Rent-A-Car,** 3244 US 101 NE, rents for $28 per day and $0.15 per mi. after 50 mi. Must be 21+ with credit card. (☎994-2454 or 800-305-5530. Open daily 8am-5pm.) The **Oregon Surf Shop,** 4933 US 101 SW, rents a wetsuit and surfboard for $30 per day, or wetsuit and boogie board for $25; expert instructors offer lessons for $30 per hour. Sit-on-top kayaks are $25 per 4 hours. (☎996-3957 or 877-339-5672. Open M-F 10am-5pm, Sa 9am-5pm, Su 10am-5pm.) **Public showers** ($1.25) are yours at the **Lincoln City Pool,** 2150 NE Oar Pl. (☎994-

OREGON

FROM THE ROAD

RIDING THE DUNES

I had just crested the highest point of the "Coliseum" dune, a short walk from Umpqua Beach parking lot #3 in the Oregon Dunes, and the wind was pulling a smoky plume of sand up into my face. I grabbed my sandboard (essentially a snowboard made to ride on sand), slid my bare feet fit into the bindings, and attempted to descend. 20 or 30 ft. down the 33 degree-steep dune, I caught an edge and started cartwheeling down the hill. When I slid to a halt, I spat out the sand in my mouth, attempted (and failed) to pry sand out of my ear, jumped up, and ran to the next hill.

As my day of sandboarding wore on, the experience got better and better. I realized that waxing the board before each run was essential for a smooth ride. Furthermore, I learned that the drier the sand was, the faster the ride was; I sought out the driest terrain possible. Most of all, however, I learned that I needed a pair of goggles to guard my eyes from the relentless sand.

What does sandboarding have over snowboarding? For starters, you have to earn your rides by hiking back up the hill. The dunes are beautiful, and the powerful rays of the summer sun merely heighten the experience. Gliding down the hill and sending up billows of sand with the sun beating down on your back is one of best, and some would say only, ways to truly see the dunes. Riding the dunes is worth a shot for intermediate or better snowboarders with humility and a love for the beach... or at least for sand.

—Carleton Goold

5208. Open in summer M-F 5:30am-9pm, Sa 11am-9pm, Su noon-4:30pm; call for winter hours.) In an **emergency**, call ☎911 or contact the **police**, at 1503 East Devils Lake Rd. SE (☎994-3636). **Samaritan North Lincoln Hospital** is at 3043 NE 28th St. (☎994-3661). The **Driftwood Library**, 801 US 101 SW, provides 1hr. of free **Internet access.** (☎996-2277. Open M-W 9am-9pm, Th Sa 9am-5pm.) The **post office** is at 1501 East Devils Lake Rd. SE, 97367. (☎800-275-8777. Open M-F 9am-5pm.) **Postal Code:** 97367.

⬛⬛ ACCOMMODATIONS AND FOOD. Beautiful, small rooms await at the **Captain Cook Inn ❸**, 2626 US 101 NE. (☎994-2522 or 800-994-2522. Singles $48; doubles $52.) **Dory Cove ❸**, 5819 Logan Rd., at the far north of town, is the locals' unanimous choice for affordable seafood. Dinners start at $10 a plate. (☎994-5180. Open summer M-Sa 11:30am-8pm, Su noon-8pm; winter M-Th 11:30am-8pm, F-Sa 11:30am-9pm, Su noon-8pm.) There's a **Safeway**, 4101 NW Logan Rd., at the north end of town. (☎994-8667. Open daily 6am-midnight.)

DEPOE BAY AND THE OTTER CREST LOOP ☎541

Rest stops and beach-access parking lots litter the 30 mi. of US 101 between Lincoln City and Newport. Diminutive Depoe Bay boasts gray whale viewing along the town's low seawall, at the **Depoe Bay State Park Wayside** and the **Observatory Lookout**, 4½ mi. to the south. Go early in the morning on a cloudy day during the annual migration (Dec.-May) for your best chance of spotting the giants. **Tradewinds Charters** (☎765-2345 or 800-445-8730) has 6hr. ($70) fishing and crabbing trips, and 1hr. ($15) and 2hr. ($20) whale watching trips. **Dockside Charters** offers similar trips; turn east at the only traffic light in Depoe Bay. They're next to the Coast Guard. (☎765-2545 or 800-733-8915. 5hr. fishing $55; 1hr. whale watching $15, ages 13-17 $11, ages 4-12 $7.) Just south of Depoe Bay, detour from US 101 on the renowned **Otter Crest Loop**, a twisting 4 mi. excursion high above the shore that affords spectacular vistas at every bend and includes views of **Otter Rock** and the **Marine Gardens**. A lookout over the aptly named **Cape Foulweather** has telescopes ($0.25) for spotting sea lions lazing on the rocks. **The Devil's Punch Bowl**, formed when the roof of a seaside cave collapsed, is also accessible off the loop. It becomes a frothing cauldron during high tide when ocean water crashes through an opening in the side of the bowl. **Otter Rocks** beach is known as a great place to learn to surf; beginners can have a blast in the smaller breaks close to shore.

NEWPORT
☎ 541

After the miles of malls along US 101, Newport's renovated waterfront area of pleasantly kitschy restaurants and shops is a delight. Newport's claim to fame, however, is the world-class **Oregon Coast Aquarium**. Best known as home to Keiko the Orca of *Free Willy*, the aquarium offers several interesting exhibits. This, in addition to the Mark Hatfield Marine Science Center and loads of inexpensive seafood, make Newport a marine lover's starred attraction.

▓▓ ORIENTATION AND PRACTICAL INFORMATION

Corvallis lies 55 mi. east of Newport on **US 20**, Lincoln City is 22 mi. north of town on **US 101**, and Florence sits 50 mi. south. Newport is bordered on the west by the foggy Pacific Ocean and on the south by Yaquina Bay. US 101, known in town as the **Coast Hwy.**, divides east and west Newport. US 20, known as **Olive St.** in town, bisects the north and south sides of town. Just north of the bridge, **Bay Boulevard** (accessible via Herbert St., on the north side of the bay bridge) circles the bay and runs through the heart of the port. Historic Nye Beach, bustling with tiny shops, is on the northwest side of town in between 3rd and 6th St.

Buses: Greyhound, 956 10th St. SW (☎265-2253 or 800-454-2487), at Bailey St. Open M-F 8-10am and 1-4:15pm, Sa 8am-1pm. To Portland (4hr., 2 per day, $18); **San Francisco** (16½-21hr., 3 per day, $76); and Seattle (9hr., 2 per day, $45).

Taxis: Yaquina Cab Company (☎265-9552). $2.25 base, $2.25 per mi.

Visitor Information: Chamber of Commerce, 555 Coast Hwy. SW (☎265-8801 or 800-262-7844; www.discovernewport.com). 24hr. info board outside. Open M-F 8:30am-5pm; summer also Sa-Su 10am-4pm.

Laundry: Eileen's Coin Laundry, 1078 Coast Hwy. N (☎265-5474). Wash $1.25, dry $0.25 per 8min. Open daily 6am-11pm.

Emergency: ☎911. **Weather and Sea Conditions:** ☎265-5511.

Police: 169 SW Coast Hwy. (☎265-5331).

Coast Guard: ☎265-5381.

Hospital: Samaritan Pacific Community Hospital, 930 Abbey St. SW (☎265-2244).

Internet Access: Newport Public Library: 35 Nye St. NW (☎265-2153), at Olive St., offers 30min. of free Internet access every day on 6 computers. Open M-Th 10am-9pm, F-Sa 10am-6pm, Su 1-4pm.

Post Office: 310 2nd St. SW (☎800-275-8777). Open M-F 8:30am-5pm, Sa 10:30am-1:30pm. **Postal Code:** 97365.

▓ ACCOMMODATIONS AND CAMPING

Motel-studded US 101 provides affordable but sometimes noisy rooms. Nearby monster camping facilities often fill on summer weekends.

Beverly Beach State Park, 198 123rd St. NE (☎265-9278; reservations 800-452-5687), 7 mi. north of Newport and just south of Devil's Punch Bowl. A year-round campground of gargantuan proportions. Non-camper showers $2. 129 tent sites, $17; 76 electrical, $20; 53 full RV sites, $21; 21 yurts, $29; hiker/biker $4.25. ❶

City Center Motel, 538 Coast Hwy. SW (☎265-7381 or 800-627-9099), opposite the visitors center. Spacious but oddly empty rooms. Singles $30, doubles $45. ❷

Money Saver Motel, 861 SW Coast Hwy. (☎265-2277 or 888-461-4033). Basic rooms with friendly management. Singles $42 in summer, $32 in winter; doubles $60 summer, $45 winter. ❷

OREGON

South Beach State Park, 5580 Coast Hwy. S (☎867-4715), 2 mi. south of town. Near the quiet South Beach, the campground has sparse conifers which offer little shelter and no privacy. Offers 2 hr. kayak tours on nearby Beaver Creek, May-Sept., for $10 per person. 227 electric RV sites, $20; 22 yurts, $29; hiker/biker sites $4.28. Showers $2 for non-campers. ●

Inn at Yaquina Head, 2633 S Pacific Way. (☎888-867-3100.) Large rooms with views of the bay and marina. Continental breakfast. Jacuzzi, exercise room. Call for rates. ●

🍴 FOOD

Food in Newport is surprisingly varied, but seafood is the dining option of choice.
Oceana Natural Foods Coop, 159 2nd St. SE, has a small selection of reasonably priced health foods and produce. (☎265-8285. Open daily 8am-8pm.) **J.C. Sentry,** 107 Coast Hwy. N, sells standard supermarket stock. (☎265-6641. Open 24hr.)

Mo's Restaurant, 622 Bay Blvd. SW (☎265-2979). Just about always filled to the gills, this is the original location of what is now a regional franchise. Go for the clam chowder ($7) or fish and chips ($9). Open daily 11am-10pm. ●

April's, 749 3rd St. NW (☎265-6855), down by Nye Beach, is the pinnacle of local dining. The serene ocean view and good food are worth every penny. Tables fill early, especially on weekends. Dinners $12-19; daily specials are pricier. Towering chocolate eclairs $4. Reservations suggested. Open Tu-Su for dinner from 5pm. ●

Canyon Way Restaurant & Bookstore, 1216 SW Canyon Way (☎265-8319). Browse through the petite bookstore before or after your meal. Deli sandwiches hover around $6. Dinner entrees in the restaurant are pricier ($16-21). Restaurant open Tu-Sa: lunch 11am-3pm, dinner 5pm-9pm. Bookstore open M 10am-5pm, Tu-Sa 10am-9pm. Deli open Tu-Sa 10am-4pm. ●

Rogue Ale & Public House, 748 Bay Blvd. SW (☎265-3188). They "brew for the rogue in all of us," and bless 'em for it. Plenty of brew on tap—including "extreme ales" for the expert drinker—and garlic ale bread to boot ($2.25). Most lunch items about $10-13. Locals pack it in for F and Sa night trivia. Fish and chips with Rogue Ale batter $10. Open daily 11am-2:30am; food until 11:30pm. ●

👁 SIGHTS

■ **MARK O. HATFIELD MARINE SCIENCE CENTER.** This is the hub of Oregon State University's coastal research. The 300 scientists working here ensure rigorous intellectual standards for the exhibits, which are on fascinating topics that range from chaos—demonstrated by a paddle wheel/waterclock—to climactic change and a behavioral analysis of Wile E. Coyote's causality. While the live octopus can't be played with, a garden of sea anemones, slugs, and bottom-dwelling fish awaits your curiosity in the touch tanks. (*At the south end of the bridge on Marine Science Dr. ☎867-0100. Open daily 10am-5pm; winter Th-M 10am-4pm. Donations accepted.*)

OREGON COAST AQUARIUM. More famous, less serious, and much more expensive than the Science Center is the Oregon Coast Aquarium. This world-class aquarium housed Keiko, the much-loved *Free Willy* Orca during his rehabilitation before he returned to his childhood waters near Iceland. The **Passages of the Deep** exhibit features a 200 ft. undersea tunnel; experience being surrounded by sharks, rays, and fish. (*2820 Ferry Slip Rd. SE, at the south end of the bridge. ☎867-3474; www.aquarium.org. Open June-Sept daily 9am-6pm; Sept.-June 10am-5pm. $10.25, seniors $9.25, ages 4-13 $6.25.*)

OREGON

ROGUE ALE BREWERY. The Brewery has won more awards than you can shake a pint at. Cross the bay bridge, follow the signs to the aquarium, and you'll see it. 20 brews, including Oregon Golden, Shakespeare Stout, and Dead Guy Ale, are available at the pub in town (see **Food,** above) or upstairs at **Brewers by the Bay,** where taster trays of four beers cost $4.50. *(2320 Oregon State University Dr. SE. Brewers by the Bay ☎867-3664. Brewery ☎867-3660. Open Su-Th 11am-9pm, F-Sa 11am-10pm. Free tours of the brewery leave daily at 4pm, depending on demand.)*

NEWPORT TO REEDSPORT ☎541

From Newport to Reedsport, US 101 slides through a string of small towns, beautiful campgrounds, and spectacular stretches of beach. The **Waldport Ranger Station,** 1049 Pacific Hwy. SW, is located 16 mi. south of Newport in Waldport. The office describes hiking in **Siuslaw National Forest,** a patchwork of three wilderness areas along the Oregon Coast. Furnishes detailed maps ($4-6) and advice on the area's campgrounds. (☎563-3211. Open M-F 8am-4pm.)

CAPE PERPETUA. Cape Perpetua, 11 mi. south of Waldport and 40 mi. north of Reedsport, is the highest point on the coast (803 ft.) and arguably its high point for scenic beauty. Even if you're only passing through, drive to the top of the Cape Perpetua **viewpoint** (2 mi.) and walk the quarter-mile loop at the top. Gaze out at the ocean, as well as the headlands to the north and south. Those looking for a more challenging hike can take the difficult 1¼ mi. **St. Perpetua Trail** from the visitors center up to the same viewpoint. The **Cape Perpetua Interpretive Center,** 2400 US 101, just south of the viewpoint turn-off, has informative exhibits about the surrounding area and hilarious rangers. (☎547-3289. Open May-Nov. M-Sa 9am-5pm, Su noon-5pm, and open for whale week, Christmas-New Year's.) At high tide, witness an orgy of thundering spray in the **Devil's Churn** (¼ mi. north of the visitors center down Restless Water Trail) and **Spouting Horn** (¼ mi. south down Captain Cook Trail). The two sites, as well as the **tidal pools,** are connected; the tidal pools can also be reached from the visitors center. The **Cape Perpetua campground ❶** is an excellent place to sleep. Located at the viewpoint turn-off, it has 37 sites alongside a tiny, fern-banked creek. (☎877-444-6777 for reservations. Water, toilets. Firewood $5. Sites $15.) The **Rock Creek Campground ❶,** 8 mi. farther south, has 16 sites under mossy spruces a half-mile from the sea. (Drinking water, toilets. $14.)

ALPHA FARM. A communal alternative to the coast's bourgeois tourism. Members farm and produce giftshop-type items to support the communal purse. Drive 14 mi. east of **Florence,** a long strip of fast-food joints and expensive motels, to the tiny community of **Mapleton;** press on 30min. along Rte. 36 and then 7 mi. up Deadwood Creek Rd. Anyone willing to lend a hand with the chores is welcome to camp out or stay in the beautiful, simple bedrooms. Visitors can stay up to three days; afterward, a long-term commitment to the farm is required. The **Alpha Bit Cafe ❶,** in Mapleton on Rte. 126, is owned and staffed by the very chill and very dreadlocked members of Alpha Farm. (Farm ☎964-5102; cafe 268-4311. Cafe open Sa-Th 10am-6pm and F 10am-9pm.)

OREGON DUNES AND REEDSPORT ☎541

Nature's ever-changing sculpture, the **Oregon Dunes National Recreation Area,** presents sand in shapes and sizes unequaled in the Northwest. Formed by millennia of wind and wave action, the dunes shift constantly and the sand sweeps over footprints, tire marks, and—in years past—entire forests. Perhaps the only hotbed of "reverse conservation," the dunes are actually greening rapidly as European

OREGON

beachgrass, planted in the 1920s, spreads its tenacious roots and sparks concerns that the dunes may disappear in as few as 100 years. Get them while they're hot: the dunes have something for everyone, from the hard-partying buggy or ATV rider to the hiker seeking solitude in the endless expanses of windblown sand.

ORIENTATION AND PRACTICAL INFORMATION

The dunes stretch from Florence to Coos Bay, broken only where the Umpqua and Smith Rivers empty into Winchester Bay. On the south side of the bay is the town of **Winchester,** to the north is **Reedsport.** At the junction of **Rte. 38** and **US 101,** Reedsport is 185 mi. southwest of Portland, 89 mi. southwest of Eugene, and 71 mi. south of Newport.

Tourist Information: Oregon Dunes National Recreation Area Visitor Center, 855 US 101 (☎271-3611; www.fs.fed.us/r6/siuslaw/oregondunes.htm), at Rte. 38 in Reedsport, just south of the Umpqua River Bridge. Has displays, a 10min. video on dune ecology, and essential info on fees, regulations, hiking, and camping. Maps $4-6. Open June-Oct. daily 8am-4:30pm; Nov.-May M-F 8am-4:30pm, Sa 10am-4pm. The **Chamber of Commerce** (☎271-3495 or 800-247-2155), at the same location and open the same hours, has dune buggy rental info and motel listings.

Passes and Permits: Most parking areas in the NRA now require day-use passes, which are $5 per day or $30 per year. The **Northwest Forest Pass** can be purchased at most places where it is required. Those staying at a campground and already paying a $15 fee are exempt from day-use fees.

Laundromat: Coin Laundry, 420 N 14th St. (☎271-3587), next to McDonald's in Reedsport. Wash $1.25, dry $0.25 per 7½min. Open daily 8am-9:30pm.

Emergency: ☎911.

Police: 146 N 4th St. (☎271-2100).

Coast Guard: ☎271-2138.

Internet Access: Reedsport Public Library, 395 Winchester Ave. (☎271-3500). 1hr. of free access. Open M 2-8:30pm, Tu-W and F 10am-6pm, Th 2-6pm, Sa-11am-2pm.

Post office: 301 Fir Ave. (☎800-275-8777), off Rte. 38. Open M-F 8:30am-5pm. **Postal Code:** 97467.

ACCOMMODATIONS AND CAMPING

Although they often fill during summer, motels with singles from $40 abound on US 101. Fourteen campgrounds, many of which are very near the dunes, also dot the coast. During the summer, RVs and ATVers dominate local campsites. Permits for dispersed camping (allowed on public lands 200 ft. from any road or trail) are required year-round and available at the **Dunes Information Center.** The campgrounds that allow dune-buggy access are parking-lot style **Driftwood II ❶** (69 sites, off Siltcoos Rd. about 7 mi. south of Florence), **Spinreel ❶** (36 sites), **Horsfall ❶** (69 sites, showers), and **Horsfall Beach ❶** (34 sites, toilets, water; $15). Limited reservations at ☎800-280-2267; call five days in advance.

Harbor View Motel, 540 Beach Blvd. (☎271-3352), off US 101 in Winchester Bay, is so close to the marina that there are boats in the parking lot. A robotic frog welcomes guests to the office. Rooms are comfortable and clean, with striking color schemes. Queen $39; double occupancy $46. Kitchens $2 more. ❸

William M. Tugman State Park (☎ 759-3604; reservations 800-452-5687), 8 mi. south of Reedsport on US 101. Close to gorgeous Eel Lake. Slightly less privacy, but still well-sheltered. Wheelchair accessible. Hiker/biker camping is the most private ($4). Water and electricity. 115 sites, $15; yurts $27. Non-camper showers $2. ❶

Carter Lake Campground, 12 mi. north of Reedsport on US 101. Boat access to the lake; some sites are lakeside. The well-screened spots are as quiet as it gets out here. No ATVs. Nice bathrooms. Open May-Sept. 23 sites, $15. ❶

Eel Creek Campground, 10 mi. south of Reedsport. Sandy, spacious sites hidden from the road and each other by tall brush. Trailhead for the 2½ mi. Umpqua Dunes Trail, one of the best dune walks. Toilets, water. No RV sites or ATVs. 53 sites, $15. ❶

☐ FOOD

Cheap, tasty food prevails in Winchester Bay and Reedsport. Grab a shrink-wrapped T-bone and a box of fudgesicles at **Safeway,** right off US 101 in Reedsport. (Open daily 7am-11pm.) The **Bayfront Bar and Bistro ❸,** 208 Bayfront Loop in Winchester Bay, is a classy but casual choice on the waterfront. For lunch, a salmon burger is $6.25, and grilled oysters are $9.25. Dinner is pricey ($9-16), but tasty. (☎ 271-9463. Open Tu-Su 11am-9pm.) **Back to the Best ❷,** on US 101 at 10th St., may look dated, but the food is fresh. Sandwiches with such fineries as smoked gouda cost $6.95. (☎ 271-2619. Open M-F 6am-6pm, Sa 7am-6pm, Su 8am-5pm.)

☒ OUTDOOR ACTIVITIES

Depending on where you see them, the dunes will leave widely varying impressions. Regions that allow off-road vehicles will probably seem like mazes of madcap buggy riders, but other hiker-only areas offer timeless dreamscapes with nothing but sand, shrubs, and footprints vanishing in the wind.

OFF-ROAD RIDING. For an unmuffled and undeniably thrilling dune experience, venture out on wheels. While there are no accurately defined buggy trails through the dunes, simply following other riders can yield the best action in the sand. Plenty of shops on Hwy. 101 between Florence and Coos Bay rent and offer tours, and most either transport ATVs to the dunes or are located on them; the **National Recreation Area Visitors Center** also offers a list of places that rent. **Dune Buggy Adventures,** off Hwy. 101 in Winchester Bay, rents Suzuki Scrambler 90s for $35 per hour, and 250 Trailblazer ATVs for $40 per hour. $150 deposit required. (☎ 271-6972. Open summer 8am-last rider in, call for winter hours.)

ON-FOOT HIKING. Simply put, the dunes are beautiful and require a hiker's slow pace to be fully appreciated. Multiple ecosystems separated by the sands harbor birds, insects, and occasional larger animals such as foxes. The vast stretches of sand south of Winchester Bay and around Eel Creek represent dunes at their most primal. The experience of any dayhike is heightened by solitude: go early or late to avoid other tourists.

▨ **Umpqua Dunes Trail.** With little to guide you besides an occasional marking pole, the "trail" wanders through unparalleled beauty in the sand slopes, wind cornices and rippled surfaces of the dunes. The area is ATV-free, and you'll probably find yourself wandering along the ridgetops of the dunes while exploring an occasional patch of vegetation and being enraptured by the beauty and solitude of the area. The views are best when the sun is low in the sky and the shadows highlight the precise transitions between slopes and other wind-sculptured features. Walk as long as you like; the trail goes 2 mi. to the ocean over progressively softer sand, requiring several hours of hiking. Access the trailhead off US 101, ¼ mi. south of Eel Creek campground.

OREGON

PART OF A COMPLETE BREAKFAST Each year, over 22,000 gray whales *(Eschrichtius robustus)* migrate northward from their warm winter calving grounds in Mexico to an Arctic summer smorgasbord nurtured by increased energy from the midnight sun. During the 19th century, these whales were hunted almost to extinction. Whalers would kill a calf, wait for its mother to investigate, and then harpoon her. Today, gray whales have regained their high population levels to the point that native groups like the Makah Nation have renewed ceremonial and subsistence whale hunts with international support. The secret of the whales' success might be in their diet; unlike the slowly rebounding humpbacks, which eat major commercial fish species, the gray whales feed on creatures that would make a human's stomach turn: fish roe, mud shrimp, and crab larvae.

Oregon Dunes Overlook (Tahkenitch Creek Trail). Most tourists content themselves with stopping at the Oregon Dunes overlook. Here, they peer out at a smallish stretch of oblique dunes whose lines of shrub stretch to the ocean. 1½-3 hr. walks off the overlook are far more satisfying, though, and feature a wider variety of dunes to explore. Wildlife lovers will enjoy this hike the most—you'll experience a constant barrage of bird calls from the cover of the shrubs.

OTHER ACTIVITIES. Bird-watching is popular around Reedsport; lists of species and their seasons are available at the **visitors center.** Throughout August, the **Crab Bounty Hunt** offers a whopping $10,000 reward for catching a particular tagged crustacean. Traps can be rented in Winchester Bay; rumor has it that the crab is most often caught in Salmon Harbor.

COOS BAY, NORTH BEND, AND CHARLESTON
☎ **541**

The largest city on the Oregon Coast, Coos Bay still has the feel of a down-to-earth working town. Nearby North Bend blends in at the border, while tiny Charleston sits peacefully a few miles west on the coast. This is one of the few places on the Pacific where life slows down as you near the shore, with a string of state parks along the coastline and a pristine estuary near Charleston Bay. Coos Bay was also home to Steve Prefontaine, the US Olympian and distance running legend who died in a tragic car accident in his early 20s.

✈ 🛈 ORIENTATION AND PRACTICAL INFORMATION

US 101 jogs inland south of Coos Bay, rejoining the coast at Bandon. From Coos Bay, **Rte. 42** heads east 85 mi. to **I-5**, and US 101 continues north over the bridge into dune territory. **Coos Bay** and **North Bend** are so close together that one town merges seamlessly into the next, but street numbers start over again at the boundary; for instance, there are two Broadways, one for each city. US 101 runs along the east side of town (as Coos Bay's Broadway), and **Cape Arago Hwy.** runs along the west side, connecting Coos Bay to **Charleston** and the coast.

Buses: Greyhound, 275 N Broadway (☎267-4436), Coos Bay. Open M-Th 6:30am-5pm, F-Sa 6:30am-4pm. To **Portland** (6½hr., 3 per day, $30) and **San Francisco, CA** (14hr., 2 per day, $69-74).

Taxis: Yellow Cab (☎267-3111). $5 anywhere within town, and $1 per mi. outside.

RANDOM, USEFUL PRONUNCIATION TIP. You'll see it and mispronounce it. "Slough" is pronounced "slew."

Car Rental: Verger, 1400 Ocean Blvd. (☎888-5594), Coos Bay. Must be 23+ with credit card. Open M-F 8am-5:30pm, Sa 9am-5pm. Cars from $28, 150 mi. per day free, $0.25 per mi. thereafter.

Tourist Information: All the following cover the whole area.

Bay Area Chamber of Commerce, 50 E Central Ave. (☎269-0215 or 800-824-8486), off Commercial Ave., Coos Bay. Open M-F 9am-5pm, Sa 10am-4pm; in summer also Su noon-4pm.

North Bend Visitor Center, 1380 Sherman Ave. (☎756-4613), on US 101, south of North Bend bridge. Open in summer M-F 8am-5pm, Sa 10am-5pm, Su 12:30-5pm; winter M-F 8am-5pm.

Charleston Visitor Center (☎888-2311), at Boat Basin Dr. and Cape Arago Hwy., has brochures. Open May-Sept. daily 9am-5pm.

Outdoor Information: Oregon State Parks Information, 89814 Cape Arago Hwy. (☎888-8867), Charleston. Open M-F 8am-noon and 1-4:30pm.

Equipment Rental: High Tide Rental, 8073 Cape Arago Hwy. (☎888-3664). In Charleston, diagonally across from the Charleston Visitor Center. Rents every piece of gear necessary to fully enjoy the land and water of Coos Bay. Kayaks $20 per 2hr., bikes $15 per day, crab pots $8. Open Tu-Th 8am-4pm, F 7am-9pm, Sa 8am-9pm, Su 8am-4pm.

Rocky Point Surf and Sport (☎266-9020), Coos Bay. Rents surfboards and wetsuits, each for $15 per day. 3½hr. lesson $105. Gives directions to the local spots, Bastendorff Beach and Lighthouse Beach.

Laundromat: Wash-A-Lot, 1921 Virginia Ave. (☎756-5439), North Bend. Wash $1.50; dry $0.25 per 6min. Open 24hr.

Emergency: ☎911. **Police:** 500 Central Ave. (☎269-8911), Coos Bay.

Coast Guard: 63450 Kingfisher Dr. (☎888-3266), Charleston.

Women's Crisis Line: ☎756-7000. 24hr.

Hospital: Bay Area Hospital, 1775 Thompson Rd. (☎269-8111), Coos Bay.

Internet Access: Coos Bay Library, 525 W Anderson Ave. (☎269-1101), Coos Bay. Free 30min. of Internet access. Open M-W 10am-8pm, Th-F 11am-5:30pm, Sa 11am-5pm.

Post Office: 470 Golden Ave. (☎800-275-8777) at 4th St., Coos Bay. Open M-F 8:30am-5pm.

Postal Code: 97420.

ACCOMMODATIONS AND CAMPING

Cheap, noisy motels line Hwy. 101 for those just passing through; quieter rooms with a roof lie close to the outdoors attractions in Charleston. Campers, rejoice: the nearby state-run and private sites allow full access to the breathtaking coast.

Captain John's Motel, 63360 Kingfisher Dr. (☎888-4041), in Charleston. Escapes the highway noise and attracts anglers; this is the closest good place to the state parks and the estuary. Crab rings $2.50 per day. Queen from $46; 2 double beds from $55. ❸

Bluebill Campground (☎271-3611), off US 101, 3 mi. north of North Bend. Camping among sandy scrub; some sites with good privacy. Follow the signs to the Horsfall Beach area, then continue down the road to this US Forest Service campground. ½ mi. to the ocean and dunes. Closed in winter. 18 sites, $15. ❶

Sunset Bay State Park, 89814 Cape Arago Hwy. (☎888-4902; reservations 800-452-5687), 12 mi. south of Coos Bay and 3½ mi. west of Charleston. Akin to camping in a well-landscaped parking lot; **loop B** sites have a bit more seclusion. Sunset Beach is worth it. 138 sites, $16; full RV sites $19; yurts $27; hiker/biker sites $4. ❶

◘ FOOD

A **Safeway** is at 230 E Johnson Ave. off US 101 north, at the southern end of town. (Open daily 6am-1am.)

Blue Heron Bistro, 100 Commercial Ave. (☎267-3933), at the corner of Broadway in Coos Bay. Here, zie Germans still have a stranglehold on Europe and D-Day is only a plan in the works. Cuisine of the belligerent powers complements the war memorabilia on the walls; sandwiches $8, dinners $9-13. Open M-Sa 11am-10pm, Su 5-10pm. ❸

Cranberry Sweets, 1005 Newmark St. (☎888-9824), Coos Bay, near junction of Ocean Blvd. and Newmark St. This far-from-average candy factory serves up enough ambitious ventures (think beer squares and cheddar cheese fudge) to make lunch moot. $2-5 per lb. Cheapskates may exploit the free samples. Open M-Sa 9am-6pm, Su 11am-4pm. ❶

◙ SIGHTS AND EVENTS

Four miles south of Charleston up Seven Devils Rd., the ◪**South Slough National Estuarine Research Reserve** is one of the most fascinating and under-appreciated venues on the central coast. Spreading out from a small interpretive visitors center, almost 7 sq. mi. of salt- and freshwater estuaries nurture all kinds of wildlife, from sand shrimp to blue herons to deer. Check the interpretive center first to see if there are any guided hikes or paddles going out (free), or to start on some of the short trails leading from the center. A great way to observe wildlife close-up by canoe or kayak is to start from the Charleston marina (near the Charleston Bridge) at low tide, and paddle into the estuary with the tide and out as it subsides; much of the interior is miserable mud flats at low tide. (☎888-5558; www.southsloughestuary.com. Open June-Aug. daily 8:30am-4:30pm; Sept.-May M-F 8:30am-4:30pm. Trails open year-round dawn-dusk.)

Inland 24½ mi. from Coos Bay, at **Golden and Silver Falls State Park,** three trails lead to the awesome Golden Falls, a 210 ft. drop into the abyss, and the beautiful Silver Falls, thin sheets of water cascading down a rock face. From Coos Bay, take the Eastside-Allegany exit off US 101, and follow it along a narrow, gravel road.

For two weeks in mid-July, Coos Bay plays host to the **Oregon Coast Music Festival,** the most popular summer music event on the coast. A week of jazz, blues, and folk is followed by a week of performances by the renowned festival orchestra. (☎267-0938. Festival concerts $6-10, orchestra concerts $12-17.) Art exhibits and a free classical concert in Mingus Park spice up the festival even for the ticketless.

◤ OUTDOOR ACTIVITIES

Sunset Bay, 11½ mi. from Coos Bay on Cape Arago State Hwy., has been rated one of the top 10 American beaches. Sheltered from the waves by two parallel cliffs, the warm, shallow bay is perfect for **swimming.** The magnificent and manicured **Shore Acres State Park** rests a mile beyond Sunset Bay on the Cape Arago Hwy. (☎503-888-3732. Open summer daily 8am-9pm; winter 8am-dusk. $4 per car. Wheelchair accessible.) Once the estate of local lumber lord Louis J. Simpson, the park contains elaborate botanical gardens that outlasted the mansion and a short trail to peaceful Simpson Beach. Displays rose gardens and several rare trees: should monkeys invade, *Let's Go* suggests you find the Monkey Puzzle Tree (*Araucaria araucana*) to thwart the pestering primates. At the south end of the highway is breezy **Cape Arago,** notable for the rich life of its tide pools. Paved paths lead out toward the tip of the cape and provide an excellent view of Shell Island, a quarter-mile offshore, which is a protected elephant and harbor seal rookery.

Fishing enthusiasts can hop on board with **Bob's Sportfishing,** operating out of a small building at the west end of the Charleston Boat Basin, where they can buy one-day fishing licenses for $8. (☎ 888-4241 or 800-628-9633. 5hr. salmon fishing trip $60 mid-May to Sept.)

BANDON   ☎ 541

Despite a steady flow of summer tourists, the fishing town of Bandon-by-the-Sea has refrained from breaking out the pastels and making itself up like an amusement park. A few outdoor activities make Bandon worth a stop on a coastal tour.

⊠ PRACTICAL INFORMATION. Bandon is 24 mi. south of Coos Bay and 27 mi. north of Port Orford on US 101. The **visitors center** is at 300 SE 2nd St. in Old Town. (☎ 347-9616. Open summer daily 10am-5pm; winter 10am-4pm.) The **post office** is at 105 12th St. SE (☎ 800-275-8777. Open M-F 8:30am-4:30pm.) **Postal Code:** 97411.

⌨⌘ ACCOMMODATIONS AND FOOD. The beautiful Mediterranean exterior of the **Bandon Wayside Motel ❸,** on Rte. 42 south just off US 101, gives way to good rooms with tile floors, nice beds, and cable TV. (☎ 347-3421. Summer $45-80. Winter $20-40.) The small **Sea Star Guest House ❷,** 375 2nd St., contains the remains of a once-thriving hostel as well as several elegant guesthouse rooms overlooking the marina. (www.seastarbandon.com. 2-person dorm rooms $15; private hostel rooms $25-45; guesthouse rooms $75-105 summer, $55-75 winter.) Two miles north of town and across the bridge, **Bullard's Beach State Park** houses the **Coquille River Lighthouse ❷,** built in 1896. The 185 sites have little privacy. (☎ 347-2209. $19; yurts $27; hiker/biker sites $4 per person. Showers $2 for non-campers.)

For a tasty and healthy morsel, step into **Mother's Natural Grocery and Deli ❶,** 975 US 101, south of the junction with Rte. 42 south. Vegetarian and organic foods prevail here over pesticides and other evils. Meals cost about $3.75-4.25. (☎ 347-4086. Open M-Sa 9am-6pm.) **A&R World Cafe ❷,** adjoining the Sea Star Guest House, serves excellent gyros and other "world food" in a mellow atmosphere. (☎ 347-8204. Open Tu-Th 7am-8pm, F-Sa 7am-9pm. Breakfast $4-6, lunch $5-7, dinner $9-15.) The best seafood and a great dining room view is at **Bandon Boatworks ❸,** 275 Lincoln Ave. SW. Lunches ($6-9) are more affordable than dinners ($12-20), when the Boatworks breaks out the wine glasses. (☎ 347-2111. Open M-Sa 11:30am-9pm, Su 11am-8:30pm; winter closed M.)

◲ SIGHTS AND EVENTS. A stroll around **Old Town** is pleasant, as is exploring the beach on a horse from **Bandon Beach Riding Stables.** (☎ 347-3423. $25 for 1hr.) The well-marked beach loop road that leaves from Old Town and joins US 101 5 mi. south passes **Table Rock, Elephant Rock,** and **Face Rock,** three of the coast's most striking offshore outcroppings.

BANDON TO BROOKINGS

Whether it's because of the general lack of development in this area, or the proliferation of offshore volcanic rocks and vertiginous shorelines, this stretch of the coast is the most beautiful segment of the Oregon Coast. With exceptional beauty, though, comes a small price: economically struggling Curry County has a reputation for crime. However, in daylight hours, there is little to detract from the cliff-lined coves and grassy hills.

Cape Blanco State Park, north of Port Orford, offers a long stretch of empty beach; it is the farthest point west on the Oregon Coast and its **lighthouse** is the Coast's oldest, with miles of views north and south. Take a tour of the lighthouse and its mesmerizing lens, from the end of the road leading into the park. (Open Apr.-Oct. Th-M 10am-3:30pm.) Few stop at the **campground ❶** a few miles back from the lighthouse;

OREGON

it offers exceptional seclusion between hedges, plus access to a beautiful but iso- lated beach. Toilets. $18 electrical RV sites, $4 hiker/biker sites. Showers. **Humbug Mountain State Park ❶,** 6 mi. south of Port Orford, surrounds the heavily-forested mountain; a 3 mi., moderate trail ascends to the 1700 ft. peak with amazing views on top and lush ferns on the trail up. The trail is accessible from a campground at the foot of the mountain, which has 101 tightly packed sites with toilets. (☎ 332-6774. Tents $16; hiker/biker sites $2. Showers $2 for non-campers.)

Boardman State Park is the best example of Oregon Coast preservation, enclos- ing 15 mi. of some of the finest and most rugged coastal terrain in Oregon. The park has overlooks and trailheads at 1- to 5-mile intervals along a trail that runs through the park and beyond. With a little bit of footwork, you could easily obtain an entire pristine cove for yourself: just find an empty trailhead parking area, and see where the trail takes you. The undertouristed park begins about 8 mi. north of Brookings. At the very least, stop at the Arch Rock viewpoint, which grants a look at beautiful coves on two sides plus the unusual Arch Rock itself. A complete list of the different trail segments is available, free, at the ranger station in Brookings.

Thirty miles north of Brookings, in **Gold Beach,** you can ride a jet boat up the **Rogue River. Mail Boat Hydro-Jets,** 94294 Rogue River Rd., offers 64, 80, and 104 mi., 6-7hr. whitewater daytrips. (☎ 247-7033 or 800-458-3511. May-Oct. $30-75.) Longer trips get more whitewater; all trips offer many wildlife viewing opportunities.

BROOKINGS ☎ 541

Brookings is the southernmost stop on US 101 before California and one of the few coastal towns that remain relatively tourist-free. Here, hardware stores are easier to find than trinket shops, and the beaches are among Oregon's least spoiled. The city also sits in Oregon's "banana belt" (a.k.a. California's "arctic cir- cle"): warm weather is not rare in January, and some Brookings backyards even boast scraggly palm trees. For exhaustive coverage of all that is hot and cool down south, consult *Let's Go: California 2003.*

🛈 PRACTICAL INFORMATION. US 101 is called Chetco Ave. in town. Strictly speaking, there are two towns here, separated by the **Chetco River**—Brookings to the north and **Harbor** to the south—which share everything and are referred to as Brookings Harbor. A relatively inconspicuous strip of commercial activity is on Lower Harbor Road: to get there, take Benham Ln. towards the ocean at the south end of town. The **Greyhound** station is at 601 Railroad Ave., at Tanbark. (☎ 469- 3326. Open M-F 8:45am-noon and 4-6:30pm, Sa 8:45am-noon.) Two buses per day run to **Portland** (9hr., $46) and **San Francisco, CA** (12hr., $53). The **Brookings Wel- come Center,** 1650 US 101, welcomes from just north of town. (☎ 469-4117. Open May-Sept. M-Sa 8am-6pm, Su 9am-5pm; Apr. and Oct. M-Sa 8am-5pm, Su 9am- 5pm.) The **Chamber of Commerce,** 16330 Lower Harbor Rd., is across the bridge to the south. (☎ 469-3181 or 800-535-9469. Open summer M-F 9am-5pm, Sa-Su 10am- 2pm; winter open M-F only.) The **Chetco Ranger Station,** 555 5th St., distributes info on the **Siskiyou National Forest.** (☎ 469-2196. Open M-F 8am-4:30pm.) Clean up at **Econ-o-Wash,** next door to the Westward motel on Chetco Ave. (Wash $1.25, dry $0.25 for 7min. Open daily 7:30am-10pm, last wash 9pm.) Rent a kayak ($20) or bike ($15) at **Escape Hatch,** 642 Railroad Ave. (☎ 469-2914. Open M-F 10am-5:30pm, Sa 10am-5pm.) Get the lowdown on local surf-spots (South Jetty in town, plus Harrison Sponge beach 1 mi. north of town) at **Sessions Surf Co.,** 800 Chetco Ave. (☎ 412-0810). Guess what's responsible for that semi-circular set of dents on the board in the shop? Don't ponder too long if you're going into the water soon. Rents body board and wetsuit for $10. Get a free hour of **Internet access** at the **library,** 405 Alder St. (☎ 469-7738. Open M and F 10am-6pm; Tu and Th 10am-7pm;

W 10am-8pm, Sa 10am-5pm.) Also try **Java Java,** 612 Chetco Ave., for $5 per hr. (☎412-7444. Open M-F 7am-4pm, Sa 9am-4pm.) The **post office** is at 711 Spruce St. (☎800-275-8777. Open M-F 9am-4:30pm.) **Postal Code: 97415.**

▌▐ ACCOMMODATIONS AND FOOD. The Bonn Motel ❸, 1216 US 101, has a heated indoor pool and cable. (☎469-2161. Singles $40; doubles $45; $10 less in winter.) **Harris Beach State Park Campground ❶,** at the north edge of Brookings, has 63 good tent sites set back in the trees. (☎469-2021 or 800-452-5687. Sites $17; full RV sites $20; yurts $28; hiker/biker sites $4. Free showers.) For campsites off the beaten path, travel 15 mi. east of Brookings on North Bank Rd. to the charming **Little Redwood Campground ❶,** alongside a salamander-filled creek. (Drinking water and pit toilet. 12 sites, $10.) **Redwood Bar ❶,** across the way with drinking water, charges $5. Contact the Chetco Ranger Station for info. (☎469-2196.)

A half-sandwich and a cup of soup or chili goes for $4.50 at the **Homeport Bagel Shop ❶,** 1011 Chetco Ave. (☎469-6611. Open M-F 7am-5pm.) A number of seafood spots can be found near the harbor. The locals' favorite is **Oceanside Diner ❷,** 16403 Lower Harbor Rd. (☎469-7971. Open daily 4am-3pm.)

◪ ▨ SIGHTS AND OUTDOOR ACTIVITIES. Brookings is known statewide for its flowers. In downtown's **Azalea Park,** azaleas encircle pristine lawns and bloom from April to June, at intervals: don't visit for the blooms without calling ahead to make sure the flowers are out. The pride of Brookings is its **Azalea Festival** (☎469-3181), held in Azalea Park over Memorial Day weekend. South Beach is just north of town and offers haunting vistas of angular volcanic rocks strewn about the sea, plus sand that's soft on bare feet. It is also designated a "marine garden." Harris Beach, a bit farther north, has an equally excellent view of the rock diaspora, and has less developed views.

INLAND VALLEYS

While jagged cliffs and gleaming surf draw tourists to the coast, many Oregonians opt for the inland Willamette and Rogue River Valleys for their vacations. Vast tracts of fertile land support agriculture and a burgeoning wine industry, and for decades the immense forests maintained a healthy timber industry. Since the fortunes of logging are now uncertain, tourism has become the industry of choice in small-town Oregon. With festivals galore, Ashland, Eugene, Corvallis, and Salem all attract their fair share of visitors.

SALEM   ☎503

The home of Willamette University and the third-largest urban center in Oregon, Salem gives off the vibes of a much smaller city. Boasting fine museums, several renowned wineries, and attractions like the Oregon State Fair, Salem draws throngs of visitors, though it's hardly a hopping tourist destination.

▐ TRANSPORTATION

Salem is 51 mi. south of **Portland** and 64 mi. north of **Eugene** on **I-5. Willamette University** and the **capitol building** dominate the center of the city, and the nearby shops make up the heart of downtown. To reach downtown, take Exit 253 off I-5. Street addresses are divided into quadrants: the **Willamette River** divides east from west. **State St.** divides SE from NE.

OREGON

Trains: Amtrak, 500 13th St. SE (☎588-1551 or 800-872-7245), across from the visitors center. Open daily 6:15am-7pm. To **Portland** (1½hr., 2 per day, $8-15); **Seattle** (5-7hr., 2 per day, $27-46); and **San Francisco, CA** (17hr., 1 per day, $76-120).

Buses: Greyhound, 450 Church St. NE (☎362-2428). Open M-F 5:30am-8:30pm, Sa 5:30am-8:30pm. To: **Portland** (1½hr., 9 per day, $8-9); **Eugene** (1½-2hr., 10 per day, $10-11); **Seattle, WA** (6hr., 7per day, $25-28). Lockers $1 per day.

Local Transportation: Cherriots Customer Service Office, 220 High St. NE (☎588-2877; www.cherriots.org), provides bus maps and monthly passes. Routes leave from High St. in front of courthouse every hr. M-F 6am-9:30pm, Sa 7am-10pm. All buses have bike racks. Adults $0.75; over 60 and disabled $0.35; under 19 $0.50.

Taxis: Salem Yellow Cab Co. (☎362-2411). $2.20 base, $1.80 per mi.

AAA: 2909 Ryan Dr. NE (☎861-3118 or 800-962-5855). Open M-F 8am-5pm.

⚡ PRACTICAL INFORMATION

Tourist Information: 1313 Mill St. SE (☎581-4325 or 800-874-7012; www.scva.org), in the Mission Mill Museum complex; take I-5 Exit 253 and follow signs. Open M-F 8:30am-5pm, Sa 10am-4pm.

Equipment Rental: South Salem Cycle Works, 4071 S Liberty Rd. (☎399-9848). Rents road bikes and hybrids for $15 per day. No shop rents mountain bikes in Salem. Open M-Sa 10am-6pm.

Laundromat: Suds City Depoe, 1785 Lancaster Dr. NE (☎362-9845). Snack bar and big-screen TV. Wash $1.25, dry $0.25 per 15min. Open daily 7:30am-9pm. **Lancaster Self-Service Laundry,** 2195 Lancaster Dr. NE, next to Bi-Mart. Wash 18 lb. for $1.75, or 50 lb. for $4.25. Dry $0.25 per 10min. Open daily 8am-10pm, last load 9pm.

Emergency: ☎911.

Police: 555 Liberty St. SE (☎588-6123), in City Hall room 130.

24hr. Crisis Line: ☎581-5535.

24hr. Women's Crisis Line: ☎399-7722.

Hospital: Salem Hospital, 665 Winter St. SE (☎561-5200).

Internet Access: Salem Public Library, 585 Liberty St. SE (☎588-6315). Free ½hr. of Internet access. 15 computers. Metered parking in the garage next door. Open June-Aug. M 10-6, Tu-Th 10am-9pm, F-Sa 10am-6pm; Sept.-May also open Su 1-5pm.

Post Office: 1050 25th St. SE (☎800-275-8777). Open M-F 8am-5:30pm.

Postal Code: 97301.

🏠 ACCOMMODATIONS AND CAMPING

The visitors center has a list of B&Bs, which provide a comfortable and often classy setting (from $45). A number of cheaper hotels line Lancaster Dr. along the length of I-5, and camping options are also available.

Silver Falls State Park, 20024 Silver Falls Hwy. Rte. 214 (☎873-8681; reservations ☎800-452-5687). (See **Sights,** below, for directions.) Toilets, water, wheelchair access. 60 tent sites, $16; 44 RV sites, $20; 14 cabins, $35. Warm showers. ❶

Alden House Bed and Breakfast, 760 NE Church St. (☎363-9574 or 877-363-9573). Choose from 6 themed rooms (romantic, cowboy), all of which have private baths. Breakfast in the elegant dining room at 9am. Reservations advised. Rooms $45-65. ❸

OREGON

Cozzzy Inn, 1875 Fisher Rd. NE (☎588-5423). From I-5 Exit 256 to Lancaster Dr., take Sunnyview Rd. west to Fisher Rd. and make a left. Comfortable rooms, bargain prices (may be changing to a franchise with increased rates, though). Rooms from $37. ❸

Red Lion Hotel (☎370-7888 or 800-733-5466). Take I-5 Exit 256. This full-service chain hotel has large rooms. Jacuzzi, indoor heated pool, exercise room, restaurant downstairs. Summer queens, $70; kings, $80. Winter rooms from $50. ❹

❑ FOOD

Salem is no city for the budget gourmet, and most restaurants are somewhat bland. Groceries await at **Roth's,** 702 Lancaster Dr. NE. (☎585-5770. Open daily 6am-11pm.) Hit the **Farmer's Market,** at the corner of Marion and Summer St., for local produce and crafts. (☎585-8264. Open Sa 9am-3pm.)

Off-Center Cafe, 1741 Center St. NE (☎363-9245). Colorfully named breakfasts such as Green Chile Tortoise ($6.25) are enormously satisfying. Standard dinner fare. Open Tu-W and F 7am-2:30pm, Th 6-9pm for dinner, Sa-Su 8am-2pm for brunch. ❷

Fuji Rice Time, 159 High St. SE (☎364-5512), serves traditional Japanese food to the local lunch crowd, who enjoy watching the chef at work in the sushi bar ($4-6). Open M-F 11am-2:30pm and 5-9pm, Sa 4-9pm. ❶

Arbor Cafe, 380 High St. NE (☎588-2353), serves coffees and teas ($2-3) as well as delicious pastries ($1-2) for breakfast; panini and sandwiches for lunch and dinner ($7-8.50). Open M 7:30am-4pm, Tu-Th 7:30am-9pm, F-Sa 8am-10pm. ❷

◉ ♫ SIGHTS AND ENTERTAINMENT

STATE CAPITOL. This gigantic marble building, topped by a 23 ft. gilt-gold statue of the "Oregon Pioneer," is located in the heart of Salem. (*900 Court St. NE. Bounded by Court St. to the north, Waverly St. to the east, State St. to the south, and Cottage St. to the west. ☎986-1388. Open M-F 7:30am-5:30pm, Sa 9am-4pm, Su noon-4pm. In summer, a free tour to the top of the rotunda leaves every 30min., and tours of the various chambers leave every hour; call for off-season tours.*)

SILVER FALLS STATE PARK. A long (12 mi.) loop trail passes by 10 waterfalls. 106 ft. Middle North Falls is an easy 1 mi. hike away: were the waterfalls any closer to the trail, *Let's Go* would suggest bringing soap and shampoo. (*Take Rte. 22 east for 5 mi., then take the exit for Rte. 214 N and follow it for about 18 mi. $3 day use fee.*)

OREGON STATE FAIR. Salem celebrates the end of summer in the 12 days leading up to Labor Day with the annual Oregon State Fair. With a whirl of livestock shows and baking contests, country-folk invade the city and transform it from a picture of complacent suburbia to a barnyard celebration. (*2330 17th St. NE. At the Expo Center. ☎947-3247 or 800-833-0011; www.fair.state.or.us. Open Su-Th 10am-10pm, F-Sa 10am-11pm. $6-7, seniors $3-5, ages 6-12 $2-4.*)

SALEM ART FAIR AND FESTIVAL. During the third weekend of July, the Salem Art Association hosts the free **Salem Art Fair and Festival** in Bush's Pasture Park. While the food booths do brisk business and the local wineries pour from their most recent vintage, the artsy and crafty display their wares as bands strum away the afternoon. The visitors center has info on the fair and on local **wineries.**

SALEM CINEMA. This single-screen theater offers refreshing indie film selections. (*Pringle Plaza, 445 High St. SE ☎378-7676; www.salemcinema.com. $7, students $6, seniors 62 and over and children 12 and under $4; matinees $5.*)

CORVALLIS   ☎ 541

Unlike so many Oregon towns, this peaceful residential community in the central Willamette Valley has no historic pretensions. Covered in black and orange, the colors of Oregon State University (OSU), for nine months, Corvallis is at heart a college town. Also boasting a gigantic Hewlett-Packard facility, Corvallis keeps pace with the technological world. Life bustles downtown all year, but Corvallis mellows in the summer, hosting a few choice festivals and offering some outdoor exploration in the nearby Willamette and Deschutes National Forests. Corvallis makes for a nice stop on the way to bigger, better places.

■ ▼ ORIENTATION AND PRACTICAL INFORMATION. Corvallis is laid out in a checkerboard fashion that quickly degenerates outside the downtown area. Numbered streets run north-south; east-west streets are a test of U.S. historical knowledge, as they are named after presidents. More recent presidents are to the north, older to the south. Monroe divides the north half of town from south. **Rte. 99 W** splits in town and becomes two one-way streets: northbound **3rd St.** and southbound **4th St. 2nd St.** becomes US 20 north of town and leads to Albany and I-5.

Greyhound, 153 4th St. NW, runs to: **Portland** (2½hr., 5 per day, $14-15); **Seattle, WA** (7hr., 5 per day, $25-27); **Newport** (7½hr., 3 per day, $12); and **Eugene** (1hr., 5 per day, $8-9). Lockers $1 per day. (☎ 757-1797 or 800-231-2222. Open M-F 6am-6:15pm, Sa-Su 7am-1:30pm.) **Corvallis Transit System,** 501 SW Madison Ave., runs public transit. (☎ 766-6998; www.ci.corvallis.or.us/pw/cts. Fare $0.60. Service M-F 6:30am-6:30pm, Sa 9:30am-4:30pm.) The **Chamber of Commerce** (☎ 757-1505) and **Convention and Visitor Bureau** (☎ 757-1544 or 800-334-8118; www.visitcorvallis.com), both offer **tourist information** at 420 2nd St. NW, the first right past the bridge if you're coming from the east. The visitor bureau has maps of Corvallis and Albany, and provides an excellent map of the bike trails in the area for free. (Open M-F 8am-5pm, Sa-Su 10am-3pm.) **Oregon State University** has its main entrance and info booth at Jefferson and 14th St. (☎ 737-0123, events info 737-6445. Open M-F 8am-5pm.) **▧Peak Sports,** 129 2nd St. NW, is an incredible outdoors shop covering almost all forms of outdoors recreation in three separate, adjacent locations. Sells trail maps ($2-10) and rents mountain bikes ($25 for first day, $15 each day after) and all kinds of kayaks ($30 per day) with gear included. (☎ 754-6444; www.proaxis.com/~peak. Open M-Th and Sa 9am-6pm, F 9am-8pm, Su noon-5pm.) **Campbell's Laundry,** 1120 9th St. NW, has wash for $1.25, dry $0.25 per 10min. (☎ 752-3794. Open daily 6am-1am.) Call ☎ 911 in an **emergency,** or contact the **police,** located at 180 5th St. NW (☎ 757-6924). The **Corvallis Clinic,** 3680 Samaritan Dr. NW., has **medical services.** Take 9th St. north from downtown. (☎ 754-1150; walk-ins ☎ 754-1282. Open M-F 8am-8pm, Sa-Su 10am-5pm.) **Corvallis Public Library,** 645 Monroe St. NW, offers free Internet access on 15 computers, 1hr. max. (☎ 766-6927. Open M-F 9am-9pm, Sa 9am-6pm, Su noon-6pm.) The **post office** is at 311 2nd St. SW. (Open M-F 8am-5:30pm, Sa 9am-4pm.) **Postal Code:** 97333.

▐ ACCOMMODATIONS. The few campgrounds in and around Corvallis are not the RV mini-cities of their counterparts up and down Western Oregon. The few motels are reasonably priced, but occasionally fill during conventions or important college weekends. The **Budget Inn Motel ❸,** 1480 SW 3rd St., has decently sized rooms for undersized prices. (☎ 752-8756. Fridges, A/C, cable TV. Singles $35; doubles $45. Kitchenettes $5 extra.) **Salbasgeon Suites ❹,** 1730 NW 9th St., pampers guests with a pool and private spa. The hotel offers free Internet browsers in every room and free continental breakfast. (☎ 800-965-8808; www.salbasgeon.com. Singles from $88; doubles from $93.)

🖬🖳 FOOD AND NIGHTLIFE. Corvallis has a smattering of collegiate pizza parlors, noodle shops, and Mexican food. OSU students prowl Monroe Ave. for cheap, filling grub. **First Alternative Inc.,** 1007 3rd St. SE, is a co-op stocked with a range of well-priced, natural products. (☎ 753-3115. Open daily 9am-9pm.) The **Safeway** grocery store and pharmacy is at 450 3rd St. SW. (☎ 753-5502. Open daily 24 hr.) **Bombs Away Cafe ❶,** 2527 Monroe St. NW, goes the extra *kilometro*. A mainstay of the college crowd, the adobe facade hides great burritos ($6-7) and live music every other week. This spot's thriving bar scene explodes on Tuesday with $2 beers; don't neglect Monday $2 margaritas, either. (☎ 757-7221. Open M-F 11am-midnight, Sa 5pm-midnight, Su 5-9pm. 21+ after 10pm.) **Nearly Normal's Gonzo Cuisine ❶,** 109 15th St. NW, a purple cottage turned veggie-haven, has masses of flowers and hanging plants. The decor whets the appetite for low-price, large portion vegetarian options ($4-8). Sunburgers are $6. (☎ 753-0791. Open M-F 8am-9pm, Sa 9am-9pm.) **McMenamins ❶,** 420 3rd St. NW, has by far the best pub fare in town. Have a sandwich ($5-7) or try a taster of six hand-brewed ales. Pints cost $3.25. (☎ 758-6044. Open M-Sa 11am-1am, Su noon-midnight.) If college beer bashes are your thing, find your way to the University frat houses.

🎵 ENTERTAINMENT. Ten miles east in **Albany** (off US 20 before I-5), the **River Rhythms** concert series attracts thousands each Thursday night from mid-July through August for free music in the picturesque Monteith River Park. Musical acts vary from bluegrass to candy-coated pop. There are special shows with local performers each Monday night in July. Call the **Albany Visitor Center** for more info. (☎ 800-526-2256. Open M-F 9am-5pm, Sa 9am-3pm, Su 10am-2pm.) The musically oriented can always check the **KBBR concert line** (☎ 737-3737).

🚵 MOUNTAIN BIKING. Mountain biking is a way of life in Corvallis, and all roads seem to lead to one bike trail or another. A map of the trails around Corvallis can be found at the visitor bureau (see **Practical Information,** above). Those searching for a hard-core mountain biking experience, however, would be better served in the Willamette or Deschutes National Forests near **Sisters.** In any case, riding is no good in the winter season when rains turn the trails to soup. Maps for biking destinations are available at **Peak Sports** ($5; see **Practical Information,** above). The **Oregon State University's McDonald Forest** has marked trails that are mostly flat (with the exception of Dan's trail, a local favorite); the unmarked trails can get sick though with log drops and steep singletrack. Go west out of town on Harrison Blvd. for 4½ mi., then turn right on Oak Creek Dr. until the pavement dead-ends at OSU's lab. An easy place to get lost; a map is useful.

🛶 KAYAKING. The class IV "Concussion Run," on the **Middle Santiam,** is known as a summertime classic. The run is short but sweet, and has three rapids that get successively more difficult, culminating with Concussion itself (which must be scouted). Only runs when there's a dam release: call ☎ 541-367-5132 to get the schedule; 1300-2000 cfs is optimal. The run begins at **Green Peter Reservoir,** and ends at **Foster Reservoir,** off of Hwy. 20; ask the folks at Peak Sports for directions.

EUGENE
☎ 541

Epicenter of the organic foods movement and a haven for hippies, Eugene has a well-deserved liberal reputation. Any questions about Eugene's leftward alignment can be resolved during the hippie-rific Oregon Country Fair. Also home to the University of Oregon, and known as the track capital of the USA due to legends such as Coach Bowerman (inventor of the artificial track) and his runner Steve Prefontaine, Eugene takes due credit for its role in the running revolution of the 80s. Still,

OREGON

for all its running history, bike travel is all the rage today in Eugene, where heavy encouragement of pedal power has led to such biker friendly deals as free valet bike parking at events.

⌐ TRANSPORTATION

Eugene is 111 mi. south of **Portland** on **I-5,** just west of **Springfield. Franklin Blvd.,** also known as Rte. 129 and Rte. 99, runs from I-5 to the city center. East-west streets are numbered beginning at Willamette St. **Highway 99** splits in town—**6th Avenue** runs west and **7th Avenue** goes east. The **pedestrian mall** is downtown, on Broadway between Charnelton and Oak St. Eugene's main student drag, **13th Avenue,** leads to the **University of Oregon (U of O)** in the southeast of town. The city is a mess of one-way streets, and virtually none of the parking downtown is free; in addition, most restaurants and other sites are well spaced out, and walking the city is very time-consuming. The most convenient way to get around is by bike—every street has at least one bike lane, and the city is quite flat. The **Whittaker** area, around Blair Blvd. near 6th Ave., has a high crime rate and may be **unsafe at night.**

Trains: Amtrak, 433 Willamette St. (☎687-1383 or 800-872-7245; http://tickets.amtrak.com), at 4th Ave. To **Portland** (2½-3hr., 3 per day, $16-28) and **Seattle, WA** (6-8hr., 2 per day, $35-59). Baggage storage $1.50 per item per day. Open daily 5:15am-9pm, 11pm-midnight.

Buses: Greyhound, 987 Pearl St. (☎344-6265 or 800-231-2222), at 10th Ave. To **Seattle, WA** (6-9hr., 9 per day, $31); **Portland** (2-4hr., 9 per day, $13). Open daily 6:15am-9:35pm. Lockers $1 per day for passengers.

Public Transportation: Lane Transit District (LTD; ☎687-5555). **Maps** and timetables at the LTD Service Center at 11th Ave. and Willamette St. Runs M-F 6am-11:40pm, Sa 7:30am-11:40pm, Su 8:30am-8:30pm. Wheelchair accessible, and bike rack equipped. $1; seniors and 18 and under $0.50.

Taxis: Yellow Cab (☎343-7711). $2 base, $2 per mi. 24hr.

Car Rental: Enterprise Rent-a-Car, 810 W 6th Ave. (☎344-2020). $33 per day; unlimited mileage within OR. Out-of-state $0.25 per mi if over 200 mi. Will beat any competitor's price. 10% county tax. 21+. Credit card required for out-of-town customers. Open M-F 7:30am-6pm, Sa 9am-noon.

AAA: 983 Willagillespie Rd. (☎484-0661), near Valley River Center Mall, 2 mi. north of the U of O campus. Open M-F 8am-5:30pm.

🛈 PRACTICAL INFORMATION

Tourist Information: 115 W 8th Ave. #190 (☎484-5307 or 800-547-5445; www.visitlanecounty.org.), but the door is on Olive St. Courtesy phone. Ask for the free **map,** and get free Eugene advice from the friendly staff. Open May-Aug. M-F 8am-5pm, Sa-Su 10am-4pm; Sept.-Apr. M-Sa 8:30am-5pm. **University of Oregon Switchboard,** in the Rainier Building at 1244 Walnut St. (☎346-3111). Great info on anything, from rides to housing to directions. Open M-F 7am-6pm.

Outdoor Information: Willamette National Forest, 211 E 7th Ave. (☎465-6521), in the Federal Building. Map $6. Open M-F 8am-4:30pm.

Equipment Rental:

High Street Bicycles, 535 High St. (☎687-1775), downtown. Full-suspension mountain bikes $40 per day. Open M-Sa 9am-5:30pm. Credit card required.

Paul's Bicycle Way of Life, 152 W 5th Ave. (☎344-4105). Friendly staff. City bikes $12 per day, $60 per week. Open M-F 9am-7pm, Sa-Su 10am-5pm. Also at 2480 Alder St. (☎342-6155) and 2580 Willakenzie (☎344-4150).

OREGON

TO 5

Museum of History

Agate St.

Franklin Blvd.

E 15th Ave.

University Museum

University St.

99

126

University of Oregon

E 18th Ave.

Kincaid St.

Alder St.

Hilyard St.

E 11th Ave.

E 12th Ave.

E 13th Ave.

E 14th Ave.

E 15th Ave.

Patterson St.

Ferry St.

Mill St.

High St.

Bijou Art Cinema

Pearl St.

TO 11 (800yd.)

Oak St.

Willamette St.

Olive St.

Charnelton St.

Lincoln St.

Lawrence St.

Washington St.

Jefferson St.

Lane County Fairgrounds

Centennial Blvd.

Autzen Stadium

105

Alton Baker Park

Willamette River

Coburg Rd.

E 2nd Ave.

E 3rd Ave.

E 4th Ave.

High St. Bicycles

8th Ave.

E Broadway

Greyhound

9

City Hall

Hult Performing Arts Center

4

Saturday Market

Lane Transit

Public Library

Amtrak Station

3

5th Ave.

6th Ave.

3rd Ave.

Lawrence St.

Washington St.

2

6

7

Holliday Coin Laundromat

5

Broadway

Skinner Butte Park

Willamette River

105

Owen Memorial Rose Gardens

1st Ave.

Jefferson St.

Madison St.

Monroe St.

Adams St.

Jackson St.

Van Buren St.

W 11th Ave.

Enterprise Rent-A-Car

Blair Blvd.

126

W 7th Ave.

Adams St.

Jackson St.

11

Grand St.

N Polk St.

Railroad Blvd.

1st Ave.

2nd Ave.

Polk St.

Taylor St.

Almaden St.

Fillmore St.

Chambers St.

Grant St.

Oregon River Sports

99

99

600 yards

600 meters

0

0

Eugene

▲ ACCOMMODATIONS
Campus Inn, 9
Downtown Motel, 5
The Hummingbird (HI), 11

🍴 FOOD
Bene Gourmet Pizza, 6
Cozmic Pizza, 10
Keystone Cafe, 2
Morning Glory, 3
New Frontier Market, 7

🎵 NIGHTLIFE
Jo Federigo's Jazz Club, 4
Sam Bond's Garage, 1
The Downtown Lounge & Diablo's, 8

Oregon Riversports, 1640 W 7th St. (☎334-0696 or 888-790-7235; www.oregonriversports.com) rents whitewater gear and also arranges "social floats." Whitewater kayak rentals, all accessory gear included $25 per day, inflatable kayaks $30 per day, rafts $55-75 per day. Credit card required. Open summer M-F 9am-6pm, Sa-Su 8am-6pm; winter M-F 10am-6pm, Sa 9am-6pm.

Laundromat: Holliday Coin Laundromat, 381 W 11th St., Wash $1, dry $0.75 for 10min., detergent $0.50. Open daily 6am-11pm.

Emergency: ☎911.

Police: 777 Pearl St. #107 (☎682-5111), at City Hall.

Hospital: White Bird Clinic, 341 E 12th Ave. (☎800-422-7558). Free 24hr. crisis counseling. Low-cost medical care at the clinic's **medical center,** 1400 Mill St. Open M-F 8:30am-noon, by appt. only 1-3pm.

Internet Access: Eugene Public Library, 100 W 13th Ave. (☎682-5450), at Olive St. 1hr. free, 3 times per week. Be prepared to wait. Open M-Tu 2pm-7pm, W-Sa 2pm-5pm. **CS Internet Cafe,** 747 Willamette Ave. (☎345-0408). 1st 15min. of Internet access is $2, then $7.20 per hr. Open M-F 7am-5pm, Sa 9am-5pm.

Post Office: 520 Willamette St. (☎800-275-8777), at 5th Ave. Open M-F 8:30am-5:30pm, Sa 10am-2pm. **Postal Code:** 97401.

⚑⚑ ACCOMMODATIONS AND CAMPING

A choice hostel, inexpensive hotels, and accessible campgrounds make Eugene particularly budget-friendly. Ask at the visitors center for directions to the cheap hotel chains scattered about the town. Farther east on Rte. 58 and 126, the immense **Willamette National Forest** is packed with **campsites ❶** (sites with drinking water, $6-16; sites without water usually free). Superb campgrounds cluster around the town of McKenzie Bridge and along the river. **Paradise Campground ❶,** east of McKenzie Bridge, is surrounded by impressive greenery and great fishing. **McKenzie Bridge Campground ❶,** west of the town, has secluded sites under old-growth; loop B is best. (Reservations for both ☎877-444-6777. Sites $12.)

▨ **The Hummingbird Eugene International Hostel (HI),** 2352 Willamette St. (☎349-0589). Take Bus #24 or 25 from downtown; get off at 24th Ave. and Willamette. A wooden fence guards this once-private residence, and guests are still treated like family. A bookshelf-lined living room with a stereo complements the lovely backyard garden, and has become a gathering center for a diverse and friendly bunch of travelers. Check-in 5-10pm. Check-out at 10am. Lockout 11am-5pm. Kitchen open 7:30-9:30am and 5-10pm. Cash or traveler's check only. Members and students $13, nonmembers $16; private rooms from $30. ❶

▨ **Pine Meadows** (☎942-8657 or 877-444-6777). Take I-5 S. to Exit 172, then head 3½ mi. south, turn left on Cottage Grove Reservoir Rd., and go another 2½ mi. Alongside a reservoir with plenty of RV and jet ski traffic. Open just before Memorial Day-Labor Day. 92 sites, $12. Another 15 sites ¼ mi. down the road, $6. Free showers. ❶

Schwarz Park (☎942-1418 or 877-444-6777), off I-5 S. Exit 174, about 15min. south of Eugene. Go straight down the off-ramp and left at the first traffic light, then go past the village green for about 5½ mi. The camp lies below beautiful and swimmable Dorena Lake. Flat and quiet. Toilets and water. 82 sites, $12. ❶

Downtown Motel, 361 W 7th Ave. (☎345-8739 or 800-648-4366), located near downtown and the highway, but still quiet and peaceful. Fridges and free sweets. Strong coffee in the morning. Singles $35; doubles $40. ❸

Campus Inn, 390 E Broadway (☎343-3376), has plenty of amenities like Starbucks coffee in the spotless rooms, cable TV with HBO, and tea in the lobby. Free continental breakfast. Singles from $56; doubles from $74. AAA and AARP discounts. ❹

🔲 FOOD

Eugene offers those on a budget ample opportunity to enjoy the local cuisine. The student hang-out zone at 13th Ave. and Kincaid has cheap grab-and-go options. The **New Frontier Market**, with the **Broadway Bistro and Wine Bar**, at 200 W Broadway and Charnelton, is an organic store that also features an amazing wine bar and take-out lunch counter. (☎685-0790. Open M-Th 7am-9pm, F 7am-10pm, Sa-Su 8am-8pm.) For groceries, head to **Safeway**, 145 E 18th Ave. at Oak. (☎485-3664. Open daily 6am-2am.)

ORGANIC DINING

Perhaps most noteworthy of Eugene dining is the craze for "organically grown" products. Avoiding antibiotics, hormones, and nasty chemicals like strychnine, these restaurants only serve food that undergoes organic certification. Visit www.tilth.com for more info.

🏆 **Keystone Cafe**, 395 W 5th St. (☎342-2075). For 23 years, the creative menu has given diners a true taste of Eugene. A small kitchen and crowds of devotees make for slow service, but all will be forgiven after a mouthful of their famous pancakes ($3.25). A host of vegan and vegetarian options is available. Breakfast served all day ($3-7). Open daily 7am-5pm. ❶

Morning Glory Cafe and Bakery, 450 Willamette Ave. (☎687-0709), is decorated with provocative images of female supermodels in a mockery of mainstream sexual culture, and the waitstaff is pierced to complete the alternative feel. Though the food is a bit pricey, it gets local raves. Even a caffeine habit can be satisfied organically here, since Morning Glory shares space and a counter with **Out of the Fog Organic Coffee House**. Breakfast dishes and sandwiches $6-7.50. Open Tu-Su 7:30am-3:30pm. ❷

Cozmic Pizza, 1430 Willamette Ave. (☎338-9333), has vegetarian, organic pizzas served thin, perfectly crusted and piping hot. Offers occasional live music in the "magic garden," a central courtyard with a trickling fountain. Service can be slow. Small pizzas that serve 1 are $5, $0.25 per extra topping. Open daily 11:30am-11pm. ❶

OTHER RESTAURANTS

Bene Gourmet Pizza, 225 W Broadway Ave. (☎284-2700). This simple yet elegant cafe serves a wide range of truly gourmet pizzas, from the basic to a pie with turkey sausages, roasted peppers, and roasted hazelnuts ($12-19). The $6.50 lunch special includes a pizza slice, salad, and drink. Open M-F 11am-9pm, Sa-Su 4-9pm. ❷

The Glenwood, 1340 Alder St. (☎687-0355), near U of O, is ideally positioned to draw a large student crowd: it has huge portions at cheap prices, excellent food, and attentive service. Expect a crowd. If it's sunny, you can eat outside under shady trees. There are 2 Glenwoods in Eugene, but locals like this location best. Open daily 7am-10pm. ❶

🔳 OUTDOOR ACTIVITIES

To escape the city, Eugene residents flock to the **McKenzie River Corridor**, which harbors the clear and continuous rapids of the McKenzie River and a gentle trail along its banks. For rafting, the Upper McKenzie is a wild and scenic stretch, and is much preferred to the sometimes clear-cut lower section.

KAYAKING AND RAFTING. The McKenzie River has several stretches of class II-III whitewater. It is best enjoyed in June, when warm weather and high water conspire for a thrilling but comfortable ride. The Upper McKenzie is highly continuous, and 14 mi. can easily be paddled within 2-2½hr. One class III, 9 mi. trip begins

OREGON

at Olallie Campground and ends at Paradise Campground. Both access points are on Rte. 126; Olallie is about 12 mi. east of McKenzie Bridge. A class II+ stretch begins at the Paradise Campground and continues downstream. These are not the only options, as many campgrounds along the river offer access; put-ins upstream of Olallie Campground are feasible except during late-summer low water.

High Country Expeditions (☎ 888-461-7233; www.hcexpeditions.com), on Belknap Springs Road about 5 mi. east of McKenzie Bridge, is one of the few rafting companies that floats the Upper McKenzie. (Half-day, 14 mile trips are $50; full-day, 18-19 mile trips are $75. College student and senior discounts.)

HIKING. The 26 mi. **McKenzie River Trail** starts 1½ mi. west of the ranger station (see **Driving,** above; trail map $1) and ends north at Old Santiam Rd. near the Fish Lake Old-growth Grove. Parallel to Rte. 126, the trail winds through mossy forests, and leads to two of Oregon's most spectacular waterfalls, **Koosah Falls** and **Sahalie Falls.** Each falls also has a separate trailhead and overlook, but the two are separated by only a quarter-mile. The falls flank **Clear Lake,** a volcanic crater now filled with crystal-clear waters. The entire trail is also open to mountain bikers, and is considered fairly difficult because of the volcanic rocks. A number of Forest Service campgrounds cluster along this stretch of Rte. 126. More ambitious hikers can sign up for overnight permits at the ranger station and head for the high country, where the hiking opportunities are endless.

DRIVING. To see the country as 19th-century settlers saw it, take Rte. 126 east from Eugene. On a clear day, the mighty and snow-capped **Three Sisters** are visible. Just east of **McKenzie Bridge,** the road splits into a scenic byway loop. Rte. 242 climbs east to the vast lava fields of **McKenzie Pass,** while Rte. 126 turns north over Santiam Pass and meets back with Rte. 242 in Sisters (see p. 141). Rte. 242 is often blocked by snow until the end of June. The exquisite drive winds its narrow way between **Mt. Washington** and the **Three Sisters Wilderness** before rising to the high plateau of McKenzie Pass. Here, lava outcroppings once served as a training site for astronauts preparing for lunar landings. The Civilian Conservation Corps-built **Dee Wright Observatory** has incredible views on clear days. The **McKenzie Ranger Station,** 3 mi. east of McKenzie Bridge on Rte. 126, has more info. (☎ 822-3381. Open summer daily 8am-4:30pm; winter M-F 8am-4:30pm.) Check with rangers about hiking permits (usually free) before going to the trailheads. The **Willamette National Forest** (see **Practical Information,** p. 122) has information on the McKenzie Pass.

HOT SPRINGS. Cougar Hot Springs, also known as the Terwilliger Hot Springs on Cougar Lake, is a popular soaking spot. Three pools surrounded by old-growth soothe a colony of nude bathers. The **Blue River Reservoir,** on the way up, is being drained until 2004, so brace yourself for an ugly look into its now-dry depths. To get there, go 4 mi. east of Blue River on Rte. 126, turn right onto Aufderheide Dr. (Forest Service Rd. #19), and follow the road 7 mi. along the side of Cougar Reservoir.

◉ SIGHTS

Pay homage to the ivy-covered walls that set the scene for *National Lampoon's Animal House,* Eugene's centerpiece, the **University of Oregon.** Tours begin from the reception desk at **Oregon Hall.** (At E 13th Ave. and Agate St. ☎ 346-3014. Tours M-F 10am and 2pm, Sa 10am. Reception desk open M-F 8am-5pm.) A few blocks away, the **Museum of Natural History,** at Agate, shows a collection of relics from indigenous cultures worldwide, including the world's oldest pair of shoes. (1680 E 15th Ave. ☎ 346-3024. Open T-Su noon-5pm. Suggested donation $2.)

ENTERTAINMENT

The *Eugene Weekly* (www.eugeneweekly.com), a free mag available all over town, has a list of concerts and local events as well as features on the greater Eugene community. The *Sentient Times* (www.sentienttimes.com) is worth a read to see Eugene's liberal side in print. The **Community Center for the Performing Arts** operates the **WOW Hall,** 291 W 8th Ave., a historic dance venue on the National Register of Historic Places. All kinds of public speaking, dance, and theater events, as well as workshops and classes, are hosted here. Tickets are available at the Hall and at local ticket outlets. (☎687-2746. Open M-F 3-6pm. Tickets up to $15.) Highbrow culture finds a home at the extravagant **Hult Center for the Performing Arts,** One Eugene Center, at 7th Ave. and Willamette St. The two theater halls host a variety of music from Tool to Tchaikovsky and from blues to Bartók, as well as theater and opera. (Info ☎682-5087, ticket office 682-5000, 24hr. event info 682-5746. Free tours Th and Sa at 1pm. Tickets $8-55; some student and senior discounts. Box office open Tu-F 11am-5pm, Sa 11am-3pm, and 1hr. before curtain.) The **Bijou Art Cinema,** 492 E 13th Ave. at Ferry St., is a local favorite where indie and art films are screened in the sanctuary of an old Spanish church. (☎686-2458. Box office open 20min. before the first screening. Th-Sa $6.50, Su-W $5, seniors $4. Late night shows $3.) In the summer, a large and bustling **Saturday Market** at 8th St. and Oak Ave. has live music, street percussion groups, and produce.

■ OREGON COUNTRY FAIR. The fair takes place in **Veneta,** 13 mi. west of town on Rte. 126, and is by far the most exciting event of the summer. Started in 1969 as a fundraiser for a local Waldorf school, the fair has become a magical annual gathering of hippies, artists, musicians, misfits, and activists. From July 11-13, 2003, 50,000 people, many still living in Haight-Ashbury happiness, will flock from across the nation to experience this festival unlike any other. Hundreds of performers crowd onto seven different stages, and 300 booths fill with art, clothing, crafts, herbal remedies, exhibits on alternative energy sources, and food. Lofty tree houses, parades of painted bodies, dancing 12 ft. dolls, and thousands of revelers transport travelers into an enchanted forest of frenzy. Parking is extremely limited ($5) and the fair requires advance tickets. Most people park for free at Civic Stadium, at 19th and Willamette in Eugene. From there, free buses run every 10min. from 10am until the fairgrounds close at 7pm. (☎343-4298; www.oregoncountryfair.org. Tickets F and Su $10, Sa $15; not sold on site.) Nearby camping for the weekend is available through Fastixx. (☎800-992-8499. $30-36 per person.)

OREGON BACH FESTIVAL. The Oregon Bach Festival is entering its 32nd year. From June 27-July 13, 2003, conductor Helmuth Rilling will lead some of the country's finest orchestral musicians in a 33-year-old celebration of Bach and his contemporaries. (☎346-5666 or 800-457-1486; www.bachfest.uoregon.edu. Concert and lecture series $13; main events $20-45; ages 6-18 $10.)

NIGHTLIFE

According to some, Eugene's nightlife is the best in Oregon, outside of Portland. Not surprisingly, the string of establishments by the university along 13th St. are dominated by the college crowd. Refugees from this scene will find a diverse selection throughout town. Check out *Eugene Weekly* for club listings.

- **Sam Bond's Garage,** 407 Blair Blvd. (☎431-6603). Bus #50 or 52. A supremely laid-back gem in Whittaker neighborhood, favoring honest jam-band performances. Groove to live music almost every night with the popular "Bluegrass Tuesdays" and "Sunday Irish Jam." 8 microbrews ($3 per pint). Open daily 3pm-1am.

OREGON

The Downtown Lounge/Diablo's, 959 Pearl (☎343-2346). The **Downtown Lounge,** upstairs in the large building, offers the casually dressed, younger set four red-felt pool tables bathed in red light and a long bar and stage in back. Live music. Open daily 11am-2:30am. Downstairs, in **Diablo's,** over 500 clubbers in the hippest clothes possible party in the flame-covered space. Cover $2-3. Open W-Sa 9pm-2:30am.

Jo Federigo's Jazz Club and Restaurant, 259 E 5th Ave. (☎343-8488), across the street from 5th St. Public Market. This is an intimate jazz club and a great place to bring a date, but come with at least a few cool requests; the joint is small and you'll get to know the musicians. The club swings with live music every night (usually at 9:30pm). Upstairs, dine among upside-down umbrellas that add to the ambience. All-you-can-eat spaghetti $9. Beer $3 per glass, $3.75 per pint. W blues night. Restaurant open Tu-F 12:30pm-2pm, dinner daily 5-10pm. Jazz club open daily 8:30pm-1am.

GRANTS PASS   ☎541

Workers building a road through the Oregon mountains in 1863 were so overjoyed by the news of General Ulysses S. Grant's Civil War victory at Vicksburg that they named the town Grants Pass after the burly President-to-be. Today, the city colonizes the hot, flat valley with espresso stands and fast-food joints. A fine place to sleep, but real adventure lies in the Rogue River Valley and Illinois Valley regions.

⌐ PRACTICAL INFORMATION. The town lies within the triangle formed by **I-5** in the northeast, **Rte. 99** in the west, and the **Rogue River** to the south. In town, Rte. 99 splits into one-way **6th** and **7th St.,** which run through the heart of downtown and separate east from west. The railroad tracks (between G and F St.) divide north and south addresses. Within the confines of historic downtown, north-south streets are numbered and east-west streets are lettered. **Greyhound,** 460 NE Agness Ave. (☎476-4513; open M-Sa 6am-6:45pm), at the east end of town, runs to **Portland** (5½hr., 5 per day, $30) and **San Francisco, CA** (12hr., 4 per day, $49). **Enterprise,** 1325 NE 7th St., rents cars from $30 plus $0.25 per mi. after 150 mi.; they'll also match any price. (☎471-7800. Must be 21+ with a credit card. Open M-F 7:30am-6pm, Sa 9am-noon.)

The **Chamber of Commerce,** 1995 NW Vine St., off 6th St., provides info beneath an immense plaster caveman. (☎476-7717 or 800-547-5927. Open M-F 8am-5pm, Sa 9am-5pm, Su 10am-4pm; winter closed Sa and Su.) **MayBelle's Washtub** is at 306 SE I St. at 8th St. (☎471-1317. Wash $1.25, dry $0.25 per 8min. Open daily 7am-10pm; last wash 8:30pm.) In an **emergency,** call ☎911 or contact the **police,** 500 NW 6th St. (☎474-6370). The **hospital** is at 500 SW Ramsey Ave. (☎472-7000), just south of town. Get **Internet access** at the **Josephine County Library,** 200 NW C St., where it's free for 1hr. on one of six computers. (☎474-5480. Open M-Th 10am-7pm, F-Sa 10am-5pm.) The **post office** can be found at 132 NW 6th Ave. at F St. (☎800-275-8777. Open M-F 9am-5pm.) **Postal Code:** 97526.

⌐⌐ ACCOMMODATIONS AND CAMPING. Grants Pass supports one of every franchise motel on earth, from Motel 6 to the Holiday Inn Express. The one-of-a-kind cheapo motels are farther back from the interstate on 6th St. and cost $25-35. The owner of the huge **Fordson Home Hostel (HI) ❶,** 250 Robinson Rd., gives tours of the antique tractors and vortex on his 20 secluded acres. Perks include free bike loans and $2 off the nearby Oregon Caves entrance fee. Located 38 mi. southwest of Grants Pass; follow US 199 to Rte. 46 east, and after 6 mi., turn onto Upper Holland Loop Rd. After 1 mi., you'll hit Robinson Rd. (☎592-3203. Reservations mandatory. $12, nonmembers $15. Bicyclists, backpackers, and students with ID $2 off.) For clean and welcoming, if aging, rooms, the **Parkway Lodge ❸,** 1001 NE 6th

St. off Exit 58, fits the bill; they provide cable and fridges upon request. (☎476-4260. Singles from $32, doubles $45; cheaper in winter.) Of the camping options, **Valley of the Rogue State Park ❶** is your best choice. 12 mi. east of town off I-5 Exit 45B. The valley is just wide enough for the river, a row of tents, RVs interspersed with a few trees, and the noise of the interstate. (Tents $15; electric $17; full RV sites $18; yurts $27.)

▢ FOOD. For spatulas and spaghetti noodles, try **Safeway,** 115 NE 7th St. (☎479-4276. Open daily 6am-1am.) The **Growers' Market,** held in the parking lot between 4th and F St., is the state's largest open-air market and has arts and crafts, produce, food, and music everywhere. (☎476-5375. Sa mornings at 9am and 1pm.) **Thai BBQ ❶,** 428 SW 6th St. at J St., is decorated like an English teahouse but serves authentic Thai. Fancier than the name suggests but just as cheap: most lunch dishes are $5.25, and many dinner entrees are only a few dollars more. (☎476-4304. Open M-Sa 11am-9pm.) **Matsukaze ❷,** 1675 NE 7th St. at Hillcrest, is the best Japanese food in town. At what has become a youth hangout, traditional entrees run $4-15. (☎479-2961. Open M-Th 11am-2pm and 5-9pm, F 11am-2pm and 5-9:30pm, Sa 5-9:30pm; winter closes 30min. earlier.)

◪ RAFTING AND KAYAKING. The **Rogue River** is the greatest draw in the town of Grants Pass. A federally protected "Wild and Scenic River," the Rogue can be enjoyed by raft, jetboat, mail boat, or hiking on foot. Anglers are in good company—Zane Grey and Clark Gable used to roam the Rogue River with tackle and bait. For more information on fishing licenses and the best places to go, head to the ranger station off I-5 at Exit 58. Prime rafting and kayaking can be found on a powerfully scenic 35 mi. stretch of Class III and IV rapids starting just north of Galice. Paddling this restricted area requires a permit ($10) or guide. To get extra permits, try ☎479-3735 exactly 9 days before your trip; see www.or.blm.gov/rand for more info. Although the rest of the river near Grants Pass is very popular, it is not nearly as scenic, and can be downright residential; still, the whitewater gives plenty of thrills, especially for the uninitiated. The river can be found just outside of **Merlin,** where the necessary equipment can be procured as well. To get there, head west off I-5 Exit 61. **White Water Cowboys,** 210 Merlin Rd., rents rafts, and offers shuttle services. (☎479-0132. Discounts possible in May, early June, and late Sept., as well as for multi-day rentals. $65-95 per day.) **Orange Torpedo Trips,** in the same building, runs tours down every section of the Rogue river in orange inflatable kayaks. OTT was the first to use these interesting contraptions all the way back in 1969. (☎479-5061 or 800-635-2925; www.orangetorpedo.com. 2hr. for $30; half-day "dinner trip" for $50; full-day for $70, all on the Rogue.)

◪ SPELUNKING. To reach **Oregon Caves National Monument,** 30 mi. south of Grants Pass via US 199, drive through plush, green wilderness to Cave Junction, and then 20 mi. east along Rte. 46. Here, in the belly of the ancient Siskiyous, enormous pressure and acidic waters created some of the only caves with walls of glistening marble in North America. A typical guided cave tour ($7.50; seniors $6.50) runs 1½hr. and begins every 15min. in the summer and every hour from September to December. The temperature inside is 42°F, and the walk can be rather strenuous. Tours last 1¼hr. An "off-trail" tour for those who like their exploration a bit more extreme leaves every summer morning at 10am and lasts 4hr. (☎592-2100 or 593-3400; www.nps.gov/orca/cavetour.htm. $25; reservations recommended. Open mid-Mar. to Nov. daily 9am-6:30pm.)

OREGON

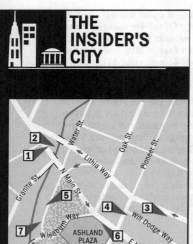

THE INSIDER'S CITY

ASHLAND PUB CRAWL

Ashland has a nightlife scene denser than the darkest of microbrewed stouts—you could easily enjoy a week of hard partying among the clubs and bars on E Main St. between 2nd St. and Water St. Most bars are dominated by students during the school year, and some bars have a reputation for frat brother patrons. Come summertime, everything is less crowded (but still hopping) and far mellower. All bars are 21+ unless otherwise noted.

1 Start your night by mellowing out with a drink on the huge outdoor deck at the **Ashland Creek Bar & Grill**, 92 N Main St. (☎482-4131). W DJ. F-Sa blues, ska and reggae. Cover $1-3. Open M-Th, Su 11am-1am, F 11am-2am, Sa 11am-8pm.

2 When you've taken in all that the Bar & Grill has to offer, head to the **Siskiyou Brew Pub**, 31 Water St. (☎482-7718), the most laid-back bar in town. Live music once or twice a week. Cover $5-10. Call or drop by for business hours.

ASHLAND
☎ **541**

Set near the California border, Ashland mixes hip youth and British literary history to create an unlikely but intriguing stage for the world-famous Oregon Shakespeare Festival. From mid-February to October, drama devotees can choose from 11 plays—several of them written by dramatists other than Shakespeare—which are performed in Ashland's three elegant theaters. But to locals and the outdoorsy, Ashland is far more than a town crazy for an old, dead bard: unexpected in every way, it's a small (pop. about 20,000, not including students) town crammed between mountains to the west and east and culturally smeared somewhere between liberal Portland and new-age Northern California; the dining and partying befit a town ten times its size. To add to the fun, Ashland and the surrounding area are packed with all the biking, boating, hiking, and beautiful people you could ever hope for. Ashland is a great place to linger a few more weeks than planned.

▛ JOURNEY'S END

Ashland is located in the foothills of the Siskiyou and Cascade Ranges, 285 mi. south of Portland and 15 mi. north of the California border, near the junction of **I-5** and **Rte. 66. Rte. 99** cuts through the middle of town on a northwest-southeast axis. It becomes **N Main St.** as it enters town from the west, and then splits briefly into **E Main St.** and **Lithia Way** as it runs through the highly walkable downtown. Farther south, Main St. changes name again to **Siskiyou Blvd.**, where Southern Oregon University (SOU) is flanked by affordable motels.

Buses: Greyhound, 2073 N Hwy. 99 (☎482-8803). Pick-up and drop-off at Mr. C's Market, at the intersection of Rte. 99 N and Valley View Rd., which extends from I-90 Exit 280. To: **Portland** (8hr., 3 per day, $43), **Sacramento, CA** (7hr., 3 per day, $45), and **San Francisco, CA** (11hr., 3 per day, $49).

Public Transportation: Rogue Valley Transportation (RVTD; ☎779-2877), in Medford. Bus schedules available at the Ashland Chamber of Commerce. The #10 bus runs between the transfer station at 200 S Front St. in **Medford** and the plaza in Ashland (35min.), then makes several stops on a loop through downtown Ashland. An in-town fare is $0.25. #10 runs through Ashland every 30min. daily 5am-7pm.

Taxis: Yellow Cab (☎482-3065, 800-527-0700), $2.50 base, $2 per mi. 24hr.

Car Rental: Budget, 3038 Biddle Rd. (☎779-0488), at the airport in Medford. $30 per day, $0.20 per mi.

after 200 mi. Must have credit card. Ages 21-24 $10 extra per day.

📷 HERE CEASE MORE QUESTIONS

Tourist Info: Chamber of Commerce, 110 E Main St. (☎482-3486; www.ashlandchamber.com). Also, there is an **info booth** in the center of the plaza. Open summer M-Sa 10am-6pm, Su 11am-5pm.

Outdoor Information: Ashland District Ranger Station, 645 Washington St. (☎482-3333), off Rte. 66 by I-5 Exit 14. Offers Pacific Crest Trail tips (and PCT maps $2 each), as well as up-to-date sno-park info. Ranger station open M-F 8am-4:30pm. For the inside scoop the outdoors, it's better to talk to the people at Ashland Mountain Supply.

Equipment Rental: 📷**Ashland Mountain Supply,** 31 N Main St. (☎488-2749; www.ashlandmountainsupply.com). Rents internal frame backpacks and many other "accessories" (ice axe, helmet, etc.) for $5 per day. Mountain bikes $13 for 2hr., $30 per day. Cash deposit or credit card required. Copious and multidisciplinary (climbing, fishing, skiing, biking) outdoors advice is free; they can refer fishing guides for almost every local river. Open daily 10am-6pm.

Laundromat: Main Street Laundromat, 370 E Main St. (☎482-8042). Wash $1.25, dry $0.25 per 8min. Open daily 7am-11pm, last wash at 10pm.

Pharmacy: Rite Aid, 2341 Ashland St. (☎482-7406). Open M-F 8am-9pm, Sa 9am-7pm, Su 10am-6pm.

Emergency: ☎911.

Police: 1155 E Main St. (☎482-5211).

Crisis Line: ☎779-4357 or 888-609-4357. 24hr.

Hospital: Ashland Community Hospital, 280 Maple St. (☎482-2441). Open 24hr.

Internet Access: The newly expanded **Ashland Library,** 410 Siskiyou Blvd. (☎482-1151), at Gresham St. Free 30min. of Internet access. Open M-Tu 10am-8pm, W-Th 10am-6pm, F-Sa 10am-5pm. **Evo's Java House,** 376 E Main St. (☎482-2261); also offers free access, and once or twice a week you can check your mail while listening to live folk, punk, metal, or maybe a duet. There might be a cover then, though.

Post Office: 120 N 1st St. (☎800-275-8777), at Lithia Way. Open M-F 9am-5pm.

Postal Code: 97520.

🏠 TO SLEEP, PERCHANCE TO DREAM

In the winter, Ashland is a budget traveler's paradise of motel vacancy and low rates; in summer, every

3 If you want to shoot pool, the place to be is **Q's,** 140 Lithia Way (☎488-4880). M Billiards tournaments in this outstanding pool hall with a mostly student patrons. No cover. Open Th-Sa 11am-2:30am, Su-W 11am-1am.

4 Once you've cleaned out your friends playing 9-ball, let the dancing begin at **Tabú,** 76 Will Dodge Way (☎482-3900). Choice acoustics and a great bar area sheltered from the dance floor give this place a trendy, classy feel. Th and Sa salsa, F house/techno. Cover $2-3. Open W-Su 11:30am-3pm, daily 5pm-10pm for dinner. Club open Th-Sa 10pm-2am, and *tapas* served until 2am.

5 After dancing, regain your saucy edge with an ale from **Black Sheep,** 51 N Main St. (☎482-6414). Follow the Union Jack into one of the only authentic English pubs in Oregon. No cover. Open daily 11:30am-1:30am.

6 If drinking ballads aren't your thing, get technological at **Kat Wok,** 62 E Main St. (☎482-0787). A mainstream club scene, with laser lights and a glow-in-the-dark pool table. Cover $3-5. Call or drop by for business hours.

7 Finally, to grab a beer, see the game, and just sample a slice of student life, check out **Louie's,** 41 N Main St. (☎482-9701), a sports bar with cheap beer that is constantly packed during the school year. No cover. Open M-Sa 11am-2:30am, Su 11am-9pm.

room in town fills in the blink of an eye and rates rise sky high. The nearest state park offering a decent-sized campground is the **Valley of the Rogue State Park** (see p. 129), about 30 mi. north on I-5.

■ **Ashland Hostel,** 150 N Main St. (☎482-9217). The Victorian parlor and sturdy bunks play host to PCT hikers, theater-goers, and other Ashland visitors in search of entertainment, outdoors or in. It's very well-positioned for living the nightlife to its fullest. Laundry, kitchen. No A/C. Check-in 5-10pm. Lockout 10am-5pm. Reservations recommended. Dorms $20, $18 winter; private rooms $50, $45 winter. ❷

■ **Mt. Ashland Campground,** about 25min. south of Ashland off I-5 Exit 6. Follow signs to Mt. Ashland Ski Area and take the high road from the far west end of the lot, at the sign for Grouse Gap Snowpeak. 7 sites in the forest overlook the valley and Mt. Shasta. Can be snowy in June. Fire pits and pit toilets, no drinking water. Suggested donation $3. ❶

Columbia Hotel, 262½ E Main St. (☎482-3726 or 800-718-2530). Oozes with charm; don't expect a full-service chain hotel. A reading alcove and morning tea round out this historic home turned Euro-style hotel. Only 1½ blocks from theaters. June-Oct. rooms $65; private baths begin at $95. Mar.-June $49-89. 10% HI discount in off-season. ❹

Relax Inn, 535 Clover Ln. (☎482-4423 or 888-672-5290), just off I-5 at Exit 14 behind a 76 gas station. The small building conceals recently remodeled rooms with cable TV and A/C. Singles $43; doubles $52. ❸

🍴 FOOD OF LOVE

The incredible selection of foods available on North and East Main St. has earned Ashland a great culinary reputation. Even the ticketless come from miles around to dine in Ashland's excellent (though expensive) restaurants. Beware the evening pre-show rush. **Ashland Community Food Store Co-op,** 237 N 1st St. at A St., has a lively spirit and great organic produce. (☎482-2237. 5% senior discount. Open M-Sa 8am-9pm, Su 9am-9pm.) Cheaper groceries are available at **Safeway,** 585 Siskiyou Blvd. (☎482-4495. Open daily 6am-midnight.)

■ **Morning Glory,** 1149 Siskiyou Blvd. (☎488-8636), deserves a medal for "most pleasant dining environment," earned either inside by the fireplace and bookcases or outside by the rose-entwined wooden porticos. Tourists, regulars, professors, and students love it; there will be a wait on weekends. Grab a book, wait, and you'll be well rewarded for your patience. Breakfast and lunch run about $8.50-11.50. Open daily 7am-2pm. ❸

Three Rivers, 1640 Ashland St. (☎482-0776). If you eat Indian food like a camel drinks water, load up here for the weeks ahead. The tandoori chicken and the rest of the buffet are quite tasty. All-you-can-eat lunch buffet $6.95, dinner buffet $7.95. Open M-Su 11:30am-2:30pm and 5pm-9pm. ❶

Pangea, 272 E Main St. (☎552-1630), offers a menu of creative, filling wraps and grilled panini sandwiches. The Wrap of Khan is a meal by itself ($7). Almost anything on the menu can be made without meat. Open daily 11:00-9pm. ❷

Natural Cafe, 358 E Main St. (☎888-5493). Vegetarian options abound. This buddhist-themed restaurant appears, ironically, to exploit its aura for financial ends. Good food, though; the outdoors deck is unbeatable for people-watching. Sandwiches (about $5) and salads ($6-7) for lunch or dinner. Open Su-Th 7am-9pm, F-Sa 7am-10pm. ❶

Bento Express, at the corner of Granite St. and N Main St., is a tiny restaurant offering large portions of rice and cheap *bento* lunches to go. *Bao* and potstickers are $1.75, *bento* meals are $4.25. Open M-Sa 11am-5pm, Su noon-4pm. ❶

Ashland

▲ ACCOMMODATIONS
Ashland Hostel, 1
Columbia Hotel, 3
Mt. Ashland
  Campground, 9
Relax Inn, 8

🍴 FOOD
Bento Express, 2
Morning Glory, 6
Natural Cafe, 5
Pangea, 4
Three Rivers, 7

OREGON

♫ 🎭 DRINK DEEP ERE YOU DEPART

Ashland remains a cultural center even after the festival ends. Local and touring artists alike play throughout the year to the town's enthused audiences. The **Oregon Cabaret Theater,** at 1st and Hagardine St., stages light musicals in a cozy former church with drinks, dinners, and Sunday brunch. Tickets $15-23, food not included; reservations required 48 hr. in advance. (☎488-2902; www.oregoncabaret.com. Box office open Th-Sa, M 11am-2pm, 3pm-6pm M, W-Sa; Th open 4pm-6pm and Su 4pm-8:00pm when there is a performance.) Small groups, such as the **Actor's Theater of Ashland** (☎535-5250), **Ashland Community Theatre** (☎482-7532), and **Southern Oregon University**'s theater department (☎552-6346) also sporadically raise the curtains year-round. Ashland also finds space for great music. When in town, the traveling **Rogue Valley Symphony** performs in the Music Recital Hall at SOU and at Lithia Park. (☎552-6398. Tickets run from $31; students $10.) In July and August, the **State Ballet of Oregon** graces the stage in a variety of venues Monday nights. The **Palo Alto Chamber Orchestra** giving hit performances at the Elizabethan Theatre, weather permitting. (☎482-4331. Tickets $10. M nights in late June.)

☾ MIDSUMMER MADNESS

The Oregon Shakespeare Festival (☎482-4331; www.osfashland.org.) was begun in 1935 by local college teacher Angus Bowmer as a nighttime complement to the daytime boxing matches in the old **Chautauqua Dome.** Today, the site of the dome is the festival's featured theater; instead of local college students, professional actors perform 11 plays in repertory, five or six of which are contemporary and classical works. Performances run on the three Ashland stages from mid-February through October and any boxing now is over scarce tickets. The 1200-seat **Elizabethan Stage,** an outdoor theater modeled after an 18th-century London design, is open from mid-June to mid-October, and hosts three Shakespeare plays per season. The **Angus Bowmer Theater** is a 600-seat indoor stage that shows one Shakespearean play and a variety of dramas. The **New Theater,** awaiting a $7 million donor for a name, seats 250-350 and serves as a modern replacement for the aging **Black Swan** theater. 2003 brings 11 plays to the Ashland stages, including *Romeo and Juliet* and *The Piano Lesson* in the Angus Bowmer, *Antony and Cleopatra* and *Lorca in a Green Dress* in the New Theater, and *Richard II* and *A Midsummer Night's Dream* in the Elizabethan.

In mid-June, the **Feast of Will** celebrates the annual opening of the Elizabethan Theater with dinner and merry madness in Lithia Park. ($12. Call box office for details.) **Festival Noons,** a mix of lectures and concerts held in the courtyard just outside the Elizabethan Theatre, occur almost every day at noon beginning in mid-June. Most are free, but some require tickets ($2-10), available at the box office.

TICKETS. Ticket purchases are recommended six months in advance. The **Oregon Shakespearean Festival Box Office,** 15 S Pioneer St., is next to the Elizabethan and Bowmer Theaters, and across the street from the New Theater. (☎482-4331; www.osfashland.org. Open Tu-Su 9:30am-8:30pm, M 9:30am-5pm. General mail-order and phone ticket sales begin in January, and many weekend shows sell out within the first week. Tickets cost $22-39 for spring previews and fall shows, summer shows $29-52, plus a $5 handling fee per order for phone, fax, or mail orders. Children under 6 are not admitted. Those under 18 receive 25% discounts in the summer and 50% in the spring and fall. For complete ticket info, write **Oregon Shakespeare Festival,** P.O. Box 158, Ashland, OR 97520, or visit the web site.)

Last-minute theater-goers should not abandon hope. At 9:30am, the box office releases unsold tickets for the day's performances. Prudence demands arriving early; local patrons have been known to leave their shoes in line to hold their places. When no tickets are available, limited priority numbers are given out. These entitle their holders to a designated place in line when the precious few returned tickets are released (1:30pm for matinees, 6pm for evening shows). For those truly desperate for their Shakespeare fix, the box office also sells twenty clear-view **standing room tickets** for sold-out shows on the Elizabethan Stage ($11, available on the day of the show). Half-price **rush tickets** are occasionally available 1hr. before performances not already sold out. Some half-price matinees are offered in the spring and in October, and all three theaters hold full-performance **previews** in the spring and summer at considerable discounts. Unofficial ticket transactions take place all the time just outside the box office, but festival employees advise those "buying on the bricks" to check the date and time on the ticket carefully and pay no more than the face value.

BACKSTAGE TOURS. Backstage tours provide a wonderful glimpse of the festival from behind the curtain. Tour guides (usually actors or technicians) divulge all kinds of anecdotes—from the story of the bird songs during an outdoor staging of *Hamlet* to the time when a door on the set used for almost every stage entrance and exit locked itself midway through the show, provoking over 30min. of hilarious improvisation before it was fixed during intermission. (Tours leave from the Black Swan Tu-Sa. Start at 10am and last 2hr. Call box office in case of changes. $12, ages 6-17 $7.50; no children under 6.)

▲ THE GILDED MONUMENTS

LITHIA PARK. Before it imported Shakespeare, Ashland was naturally blessed with **lithia water,** which contains dissolved lithium salts reputed to have miraculous healing powers. It is said that only one other spring in the world has a higher lithium concentration. To try the water, hold your nose (to avoid sulfur salts) and head for the circle of fountains in plaza center. Besides aquatic phenomena, Lithia Park features free concerts, readings, nature walks around hiking trails, a Japanese garden, and swan ponds. On summer weekends, there is an artisans' market.

EMIGRANT LAKE PARK. Scads of kids and kids-at-heart flock to the 280 ft. **waterslide** at **Emigrant Lake Park,** 6 mi. east of town on Rte. 66. Popular for boating, hiking, swimming, and fishing, the park offers fantastic views of the valley. ($3 entry fee. Ten slides for $5 or unlimited slides for 3hr. $10-12. Park open daily 8am-sunset, waterslide May-Sept. noon-6:30pm.)

MT. ASHLAND. If your muscles demand a little abuse after all this theater-seat lolly-gagging, head out to Mt. Ashland for some serious **hiking** and **biking.** One of the best options for those looking for a long day's worth of downhill is a shuttle to the Mt. Ashland Ski Lodge (elev. 6200 ft.) that allows a 15-25 mi. ride down to Ashland. (elev. 1800 ft.) **Bear Creek Bicycles,** 1988 Hwy. 99 N, offers this service and $3 Jackson County bicycle maps; unfortunately, you'll have to rent your mountain bike elsewhere. (☎488-4270. Shuttle leaves 9:30am Sa and Su, $10.) Both hiking and biking on and around Mt. Ashland require a Northwest forest pass, available at the ranger station for $5 per day. The ranger station can also provide an excellent and comprehensive guide to hiking and biking in the area for free. The folks at the **Adventure Center** (see **Equipment Rental,** p. 131) can give tips on biking trails.

Pacific Crest Trail (3½ mi. one-way, 2hr.). Forest boundary to Grouse Gap. Take Exit 6 off I-5 and follow the signs along the Mt. Ashland Access Rd. for 7¼ mi. to the sign denoting the Rogue River National Forest Boundary. This section of the Pacific Crest Trail begins to climb Mt. Ashland, passing through forests and meadows covered with wildflowers, and ends at the Grouse Gap shelter. Moderate.

Wagner Butte Trail (5¼ mi. one-way, several hours). From Ashland, take Rte. 99 north of town to Rapp Rd. in Talent. Turn left and drive 1 mi. to the junction with Wagner Creek Rd. and then 8 mi. to Forest Rd. #22. Turn left and drive 2 mi. to the trailhead across from a parking area. This trail climbs 3000 ft. through a landslide area and tufts of old-growth fir to the top of Warner Butte. Breathtaking views on sunny days. Strenuous.

Horn Gap Mountain Bike Trail (3 mi. one-way or 9 mi. loop, 1-3hr.). To reach the trailhead from Lithia Park, take Granite St. along Ashland creek 1 mi. to Glenview, and park alongside the road; the upper trailhead; the lower trailhead is 4 mi. down the road. This ride offers both incredible views of Mt. Ashland and technical fun in steep slopes and several slalom courses. It can be linked with Rd. 2060 to create the 9 mi. loop. Moderate.

SKIING

At the top of the 9 mi. road leading from I-5 Exit 6 is **Mount Ashland,** a small ski area with 23 runs, a vertical drop of 1150 ft., a new half-pipe, and over 100 mi. of free **cross-country** trails. (☎ 482-2897, snow report ☎ 482-2754; www.mtashland.com. Lift tickets $27, ages 9-17 and seniors $22, 8 and under free. Starting at the beginning of Jan., lift tickets on Tu are only $15. Ski rentals $17 per day, snowboards $25. Open from late Nov. to mid-Apr. daily 9am-4pm. Night skiing Th-Sa 4-10pm.)

RAFTING

The wild and scenic Upper Klamath offers hard-core class IV-V action all summer. Depending on water level, the run can be a technical rock-bash or a continuous wave-train ride. In general, rafters prefer the run since the especially sharp rocks have ruined many an upside-down kayaker's day (and dental work). If water color is your only criterion for a river, don't paddle here; it's brown. **The Adventure Center,** 40 N Main St. (☎ 488-2819 or 800-444-2819; www.raftingtours.com), guides rafting trips. (Half-day $69; full-day $119-139; bike tours around Mt. Ashland $69 for 3hr., $119 per day. A water release schedule is available at ☎ 800-547-1501, or http://www.pacificorp.com/applications/hydro/waterrelease.cfm.)

CENTRAL AND EASTERN OREGON

Central Oregon stretches between the peaks of the Cascades to the west, and Eastern Oregon spans gorges, desert mountain ranges, and alkali flats to the east. Except for Portlanders, most Oregonians live in Central Oregon, west of the Willamette Valley. Tourists come to eastern Oregon for the rodeos and festivals, or to toe the Oregon Trail. Backcountry hikers hit majestic Mt. Hood, Hells Canyon—the deepest gorge in the US—and the isolated volcanic features and wildlife preserves of the southeast. The severe landscape has changed little but never ceased to test the resolve of its inhabitants. The fertility of the land and the harshness of winter have nurtured and taken their toll upon game, hunters, wheat, and farmers.

THE CASCADES

The Cascade range connects California's Mt. Shasta with Washington's Mt. Rainier. Once highly volcanic, the Cascades have settled down enough for wind and water to have their way. Slicing Oregon almost completely from north to south, the Cascades create a natural barrier for moisture and lush vegetation. Central Oregon's towns are dotted throughout the mountains and receive most of the precipitation from the Pacific Ocean; more arid, less populated regions lie to the east.

BEND   ☎541

Defined by a dramatic landscape—volcanic features to the south, the Cascades to the west, and the Deschutes River running through its heart—Bend attracts its share of visitors. Settled in the early 1800s as "Farewell Bend," a pioneer trail waystation along the Deschutes, Bend is now a secret that everyone knows. SUVs with bikes, boards, or boats on top have replaced covered wagons, and the Three Sisters to the west are viewed as insurance against boredom, not a daunting obstacle.

◀ ⁊ ORIENTATION AND PRACTICAL INFORMATION

Bend is 144 mi. north of Klamath Falls on **US 97** and 100 mi. southeast of Mt. Hood via **US 26** and **Rte. 97**. The city is bisected by US 97, which becomes **3rd St.** in town. **Wall St.** and **Bond St.** are the main arteries. Downtown lies to the southwest along the **Deschutes River**. From east to west, Franklin Ave. becomes Riverside Blvd.; at the edge of Drake Park, Tumalo St. becomes Galveston Ave.; Greenwood Ave. becomes Newport Ave.; 14th St. becomes Century Dr. and is the first leg of the **Cascade Lakes Highway**. Before you explore, get a map at the **visitors center**.

Buses: Greyhound, 63076 US 97N (☎382-2151). Open M-F 8am-1:30pm and 2:30-5pm, Sa 8:30am-3pm, Su 8:30am-2pm. Call for info on other bus and van lines. To **Eugene** (2½hr.; 1 per day; $21) and **Portland** (4½hr.; 1 per day; $24).

Taxis: Owl Taxi, 1919 NE 2nd St. (☎382-3311). $2 base, $2 per mi.

Tourist Information: 63085 US 97N (☎382-3221; www.visitbend.org). Full-time ranger on duty. Offers a mother lode of brochures in addition to an "Attractions and Activities Guide" and a map of the area. Open M-Sa 9am-5pm.

Outdoor Information: The forest headquarters maintains an info desk at the visitors center. A "Recreation Opportunity Guide" covers each of the 4 ranger districts. **Deschutes National Forest Headquarters,** 1645 20E (☎383-5300) and **Bend/Fort Rock District Ranger Station,** 1230 NE 3rd St. #A262 (☎383-4000; www.fs.fed.us/r6/deschutes), have additional info on Deschutes National Forest. Both open M-F 7:45am-4:30pm. **Oregon Dept. of Fish and Wildlife,** 61374 Parrell Rd., sells fishing licenses for $8 per day; inquire about hunting permits. (☎388-6363. Open M-F 8am-5pm.)

Bike and Ski Rental:

Hutch's Bicycles, 725 NW Columbia Ave. (☎382-9253; www.hutchsbicycles.com). Front suspension bikes $20 per day, $15 per 4hr. Full $45 per day. Open M-F 9am-7pm, Sa-Su 9am-6pm.

Sunnyside Sports, 930 NW Newport Ave. (☎382-8018; www.sunnysidesports.com), has front suspension bikes for $20 per day; each additional day $10. Cross-country skis $10-20 per day; each additional day $5. Open M-Th 9am-7pm, F 9am-8pm, Sa-Su 8am-6pm.

Pine Mountain Sports, 133 SW Century Dr. (☎385-8080; www.pinemountainsports.com), has mountain bikes for $20 per day. Also rents skis and snowshoes ($25 and $10). Open M-Sa 9am-6pm, Su 10am-5pm. Full suspension models at all shops are $45 per day.

OREGON

Kayak and Canoe Rental: Alder Creek, 805 SW Industrial Way, on the river next to the Colorado Ave. bridge (☎317-9407). An excellent source of river level info and advice on boating in the area. Whitewater kayak rental $30 per day.

Laundromat: Westside Laundry and Dry Cleaners, 738 NW Columbia Ave. (☎382-7087). Wash $1.25, dry $0.25 per 10min. Open daily 6:30am-9:30pm.

Emergency: ☎911.

Police: 711 NW Bond St. (☎388-0170).

Hospital: St. Charles Medical Center, 2500 NE Neff Rd. (☎382-4321).

Internet Access: Try the ▨**Deschutes County Library,** 601 NW Wall (☎388-6679). Free, fast Internet access on the 2nd floor next to the reference desk. Open M-Th 10am-8pm, F 10am-6pm, Sa 10am-5pm, Su 1-5pm. **Cafe Internet,** 141 SW Century Dr. (☎318-8802), offers broadband Internet access and a wide variety of games. $2 for 15 minutes, $10 for an entire Saturday of network gaming. Open M-Sa 10am-6pm.

Post Office: 2300 NE 4th St. (☎800-275-8777), at Webster. Open M-F 8:30am-5:30pm, Sa 11am-1pm. **Postal Code:** 97701.

▰ ACCOMMODATIONS AND CAMPING

Bend treats budget travelers right: the hostel and B&Bs provide good deals for tuckered-out travelers. Cheap motels line 3rd St. just outside of town. **Deschutes National Forest** maintains a huge number of lakeside **campgrounds ❶** with toilets along the **Cascade Lakes Highway** west of town. Those with potable water average $8-12 per night; the rest are free. Backcountry camping in the national forest area is free. Parking permits may be required. Contact the **Bend/Ft. Rock Ranger District Office** (see above) for more info.

Bend Cascade Hostel, 19 SW Century Dr. (☎389-3813 or 800-299-3813). From 3rd St., take Greenwood west until it becomes Newport, then take a left on 14th St. Pillows, sleepsacks, and blankets are provided. Laundry $1 wash, dry $0.50. Kitchen. Lockout 9:30am-4:30pm. Curfew 11pm. $15; seniors, students, cyclists, and HI $14; under 18 with parents half-price. ❶

Tumalo State Park, 62976 OB Riley Rd. (☎382-3586 or 800-551-6949). 4 mi. north of Bend off US 20W. Riverside campsites go early, despite road noise. Though crowded with people, curious chipmunks vastly outnumber humans. Lots of tubing nearby. 65 sites, $16-18; 22 full RV sites, $20; 4 yurts, $29. Solar showers available. ❶

Rainbow Motel, 154 NE Franklin Ave. (☎382-1821 or 888-529-2877). Large, clean rooms surround a central mini-park lined with roses. TV, microwave, fridge. Free continental breakfast included. Summer queen $50. Winter single $35; double $45. ❸

◪ FOOD

Bend has a huge number of restaurants. Four mega-markets line south 3rd St. **Devore's Good Food Store and Wine Shop,** 1124 Newport NW, peddles wine, cheese, and all things organic. (☎389-6588. Open M-Sa 8am-7pm, Su 10am-6pm.)

Taqueria Los Jalapeños, 601 NE Greenwood Ave. (☎382-1402). A simple space filled by a steady stream of locals devoted to good, cheap food. Filling bean and cheese burritos for $1.75; combo plates $7. Open summer M-Sa 11am-8pm; winter 11am-7pm. ❶

Mother's Juice Cafe, 1255 NW Galveston St. (☎318-0989). Friendly staff blends exquisite smoothies ($4). Try the Mt. Everest sandwich ($5.75, $3.75 for half). Open summer M-Sa 7am-8pm; winter M-Sa 7am-7pm; Su 11am-5pm. ❶

Near Bend

Westside Bakery and Cafe, 1005 NW Galveston St. (☎382-3426). You won't be able to peel your eyes away from the tempting case of sugary desserts (under $3) on your way to the table. Burgers and sandwiches ($5.50-7). Open daily 6:30am-2:30pm. ❶

Baja Norte, 801 NW Wall St. in downtown (☎385-0611), serves delicious tacos, burritos, and other wrapped Mexican-style meals. Open daily 11am-9pm. ❶

Kuishinbo Kitchen, 114 NW Minnesota St. (☎385-9191). Grab a Japanese lunch to go. *Bento* ($5.25-6.75) is good, but most people order yakisoba noodles with tofu or meat ($4-6). Open M-F 11am-6:30pm, Sa 11am-4pm. ❶

👁 💡 SIGHTS AND FESTIVALS

▨ **HIGH DESERT MUSEUM.** The museum is one of the premier natural and cultural history museums in the Pacific Northwest. Stunning life-size dioramas recreate rickety cabins and cramped immigrant workshops. An indoor desertarium offers a peek at shy desert creatures. Hourly interpretive talks wind through river otter and porcupine habitats, and a new 7000 sq. ft. wing featuring birds of prey in their natural habitats includes the endangered spotted owl. A Native American wing with exhibits on post-reservation Indian life is insightful. *(59800 Hwy. 97 S, 3½ mi. south of Bend on US 97. ☎382-4754; www.highdesert.org. Arrive early to beat crowds. Open daily 9am-5pm. $7.75, ages 13-18 and over 65 $6.75, ages 5-12 $3.75, under 5 free.)*

DRAKE PARK AND THE CASCADE FESTIVAL OF MUSIC. Picnic by the river with Canadian geese at beautiful Drake Park. The park hosts many events and festivals, most notably the Cascade Festival of Music, a weeklong series of classical and pop concerts during the week before Labor Day. *(Between Mirror Pond and Franklin St., one block from downtown. ☎382-8381; www.cascademusic.org. Tickets $16-25, rush tickets, students, and under 12 half-price.)*

⚡ OUTDOOR ACTIVITIES

The outdoors opportunities near Bend are limitless, and without peer in Oregon. From skiing, snowboarding, and snowshoeing in the winter to hiking, biking, and whitewater in the summer, Bend can be an inexpensive outdoor adventure waiting to happen. The **Three Sisters Wilderness Area,** north and west of the Cascade Lakes Hwy., is one of Oregon's largest and most popular wilderness areas. A parking permit is required at most trailheads; pick one up at any of the ranger stations or at the visitors center ($5 per day). Within the wilderness, the South Sister can be done as a non-technical hike in late summer that threads between glaciers. The other Sisters provide more difficult technical climbs, with opportunities for multipitch ice or rock climbs.

SKIING. Those who ski the 9065 ft. **Mount Bachelor,** with its 3365 ft. vertical drop, are in good company—Mt. Bachelor has been home to the US Ski Team and the US Cross-Country Ski Team, and hosts many of the largest snowboarding competitions in the country. Many consider this the best ski resort in Oregon, with snow that's unusually dry in comparison to the soppy stuff farther west in the Cascades. The ski season runs September to June. (☎800-829-2442, snow report 382-7888. Alpine day tickets $43, ages 7-12 $22.) A shuttle bus service runs the 22 mi. between the parking lot at the corner of Simpson and Columbia in Bend and the mountain (Nov.-May; $2). Many nearby lodges offer **ski packages** (contact Central Oregon Visitor's Association at ☎800-800-8334 for info). **Chairlifts** are open for sightseers during the summer. (Open daily 10am-4pm. $10, seniors $9, ages 7-12 $6. A parking permit is necessary for all cars on the mountain; $5 per day from the ranger. See **Orientation and Practical Info,** p. 137, for equipment rental info.)

MOUNTAIN BIKING. Though biking is not allowed in the wilderness area, mountain bikers have many options for intense riding around Bend. Be forewarned: the loose "pummy dust"—ground up pumice—makes riding slow and corners sketchy. The most renowned area for biking is "Phil's Trail," which fills the space between Skyliners Rd. and the Cascade Lakes Highway west of Bend. A $9 map from one of the bike shops (see above) is necessary, as is a compass. Go west on Skyliners Road out of Bend 2½ mi., then make a left (south) on Forest Road 220. Try **Deschutes River Trail** (6 mi.) for a flat, forested trail along the biggest rapids of the Deschutes. To reach the trailhead, go 7½ mi. west of Bend on Century Dr. (Cascade Lakes Hwy.) until Forest Service Rd. 41; turn left and follow the signs to Lava Island Falls. For a technical ride, hit **Waldo Lake Loop,** a grueling 22 mi. around the lake (4-4½hr.). Take Cascade Lakes Hwy. to Forest Service Rd. 4290. A guide to mountain bike trails around Bend ($9) and *Mountain Biking in Central Oregon* (free) are available at the **Bend/Ft. Rock District Ranger Station. Cog Wild Bicycle Tours** gives half-day and full-day tours. (☎800-818-1902; www.cogwild.com.)

RAFTING AND KAYAKING. Bend has an enormous kayaking and rafting community. The powerful Deschutes River has year-round flows thanks to dam releases for irrigation, and its rapids—formed by lava flows—are unusual and range from class II to unrunnable gnar-gnar. Two good playspots satisfy boaters' everyday needs.

First Street Rapids has a mellow, class II-III wave above a recovery pool, in a non-scenic setting below a dam. To get there, cross over to the west side of the Deschutes River and work north and east via 3rd St. to 1st St, which then dead ends at First Street Rapids Park. **Big Eddy** is the other big playspot, although the recovery pools are brief at summertime high flows, necessitating either a quick roll or a facemask. The class III-IV or IV stretch, depending on flow, is accessed by taking 14th St. south 6½ mi. from Bend, and then making the next left after passing the Inn of the 7th Mountain. Take the road marked by "Big Eddy/Aspen." A common run is to put in at Aspen and take out above Lava Island Falls. Along the same road, several of the Deschutes' falls (really huge rapids, not waterfalls), including Lava Island Falls, have extreme descents.

Rafting companies take half-day trips from Aspen to above Lava Island Falls. These usually last 3hr. and cover the upper Deschutes's fairly tame waters. Full-day trips require a 1hr. drive to Maupin to run the Class III+ rapids of the lower Deschutes. **Sun Country Tours** runs half-day and full-day trips out of the Sun River Resort, 17 mi. south of Bend off US 97, and at 531 SW 13th St. in Bend. (☎ 800-770-2161. Half-day $40; full-day $95-105, ages 6-12 $80-105.) **River Drifters** offers trips on the Deschutes as well, but also has trips to other rivers close by. (☎ 800-972-0430; www.riverdrifters.net. Trips on the Deschutes are $65-75 per day for adults, $55-65 for kids. Trips to other rivers such as the Klickitat and the Sandy Gorge cost $75.)

▶ DAYTRIP FROM BEND: NEWBERRY NATL. MONUMENT

The Newberry National Volcanic Monument was established in 1990 to link and preserve the volcanic features in south Bend. Featuring such volcanic wonders as **Lava Butte, Lava River Cave, Newberry Crater,** and **the Paulina Lakes,** the Newberry National Monument offers visitors plenty of sights and a wealth of hiking. Immediately behind the **Lava Lands Visitor Center** is **Lava Butte,** a 500 ft. cinder cone from which lava once flowed. Between Memorial Day and Labor Day, you can drive 2 mi. up the narrow road (no RVs) that leads to the butte. (13 mi. south of Bend on US 97. ☎ 593-2421. Required parking fee $5, free with a Golden Eagle Passport. Open mid-May-Labor Day daily 9am-5pm; Apr. to mid-May and Labor Day to Oct. W-Su 9:30am-5pm.) The monument's centerpiece is **Newberry Crater,** the remains of what was once the Newberry Volcano, one of three volcanoes in Oregon likely to erupt again "soon." The 500 sq. mi. caldera contains Paulina Lake and East Lake. (13 mi. south of Lava Lands Visitor Center on US 97, then 13 mi. east on Rte. 21. Parking within the national monument requires a $5 permit, available from the ranger or the visitors center; parking free with a Golden Eagle Pass.)

Obsidian Flow Trail (½ mi.). This is the result one of the most recent geological events in the Cascades, the Big Obsidian Flow. Formed only 1300 years ago when the Newberry volcano erupted, 170 million cubic yards of obsidian are crossed by this trail. Easy.

Paulina Lake Trail (7 mi.). Beginning at the visitors center and circumnavigating the gorgeous Paulina Lake, this trail provides views of the wildlife surrounding the lake. Paulina Lake also offers excellent fishing. Easy to moderate.

Crater Rim Trail (21 mi.). Encircling the entire Newberry Caldera, the trail offers vistas of the entire Bend area as well as the surrounding mountains. While hikers share this trail with bikers and horseback riders, there are plenty of sights to go around. Difficult.

SISTERS
☎ 541

A gateway to the nearby **Deschutes National Forest** and **Cascade Lakes,** Sisters offers those in town and those just passing through the same warm welcome. Unfortunately, it sometimes seems like *everyone* is just passing through. Authentic or not,

Sisters features a refined old West look, which is bolstered by the annual Sisters Rodeo. Sisters also provides access to climbing facilities in nearby Smith Rock State Park and the sights of the Warm Springs Indian Reservation.

■■ ■ **ORIENTATION AND PRACTICAL INFORMATION.** From Sisters, **Rte. 126** heads east to **Redmond** (20 mi.) and **Prineville** (39 mi.), and joins **US 20** to cross the Cascades to the west. **Rte. 242** heads southwest over McKenzie Pass (see p. 142) to rejoin Rte. 126 and blend into **Cascade St.** The **visitors center,** 164 N Elm St., is one block from Cascade St. (☎549-0251; www.sisters-chamber.com. Open M-F 9am-5pm; Sa-Su hours vary, call ahead.) Sisters' **Deschutes National Forest Ranger District Station,** on the corner of Cascade and Pine St., has info on nearby campgrounds, local dayhikes, and biking trails, and sells the required $5 parking permit for the park. (☎549-7700. Open summer M-F 7:45am-4:30pm, Sa 8am-4pm; winter M-F 7:45am-4:30pm.) **Eurosports,** 182 E Hood St., **rents** mountain bikes, snowshoes, snowboards, and cross-country and alpine skis. (☎549-2471. Bikes: front suspension $20 per day, $100 per week; full suspension $25 per day, $125 per week. Snowshoes, shaped skis, and snowboards $12-25 per day. Open summer daily 9am-5:30pm; winter M-F 9am-5:30pm, Sa-Su 8am-5:30pm.)

■■ ■ **CAMPING AND FOOD.** Budget travelers generally pass up expensive Sisters for Bend's cheap lodging (see **Bend Accommodations,** p. 138). Camping, however, is as good as it gets in the Deschutes National Forest. The Ranger District maintains many spectacular **campgrounds** near Sisters; most of them cluster around **Camp Sherman,** a small community on the Metolius River 16 mi. northwest of Sisters. Two noteworthy sites are **Riverside ❶,** 10 mi. west on Rte. 20 and 4 mi. northeast on Rd. 14 (pumped water; 16 sites, $10), and **Allingham ❶,** 1 mi. north of the Camp Sherman store on Rd. 14 (piped water; 10 sites, $12). Both are maintained by **Hoodoo Recreation Services** through the ranger. Contact Hoodoo at ☎822-3799 or www.hoodoo.com for more info. Riverside's walk-in sites provide refuge from motor vehicles, and Allingham's drive-in sites perch right on the river, with ample fishing opportunities (with an $8 license).

Plan on exploring Sisters during the daylight hours; things are slow at 6pm and dead by dark. Overpriced food is available anytime at the faux-western tourist joints, but delis that close by 5, or even 3pm, are better for purse and palette. **Sisters Bakery ❶,** 251 E Cascade St., has all kinds of baked goods, including $2.25 marionberry cobbler, $3 loaves of top-notch bread, and $2.50 tasty chocolate eclairs. (☎549-0361. Open M-Sa 5am-6pm; in summer also open Su 6am-4pm.) **The Harvest Basket ❷,** 110 S Spruce St., features organic groceries and fresh fruit smoothies. (☎549-0598. Open M-F 9am-7pm, Sa 9am-6pm, Su 10am-5pm.)

■ **SIGHTS AND EVENTS. The Museum at Warm Springs** is located off Hwy. 26 north of Sisters and Bend (look for the signs), on the **Warm Springs Indian Reservation.** A stunning piece of architecture, it documents the tribal history of the Wasco, Paiute, and Warm Springs Indians with interactive and informative exhibits. (☎553-3331. Open daily 10am-5pm. $6, seniors $5, ages 5-12 $3.) The annual **Sisters Rodeo,** over the second weekend in June, draws big-time wranglers to this tiny town for 3 days and nights of bronco-riding, calf-roping, and steer-wrestling, all in pursuit of the $100,000 purse. Have a rip-roaring time at the Rodeo Parade and the Buckaroo Breakfast. (☎549-0121 or 800-827-7522. $8-12. Shows often sell out.)

■ **HIKING.** A 45 mi. segment of the Pacific Crest Trail runs from Lava Lakes through the Three Sisters Wilderness, with numerous opportunities for side-hikes. A $5 per day permit, available at the trailheads or from the ranger in Sisters, is required for most activities. The ranger station in Sisters also offers free guides to popular hiking and biking trails in the region.

Metolius River Trail (10 mi.). Go west on Rte. 20 from Sisters, then make a right at the sign for Camp Sherman (Rd. 14). Proceed 7 mi. on Rd. 14 past the "Head of the Metolius" and park at the Wizard Falls Fish Hatchery, right on the Metolius River. This trail is also open to mountain biking, and is considered superlative though difficult for that purpose. (☎595-6611. Open daily 8am-5pm.) An easy hike, but a tricky bike.

Black Butte Trail (2 mi. one way, 2hr. up; can be pushed in 45min.). The view on top is the attraction: alongside an active fire lookout, survey 180 degrees of Cascades from Mt. Adams to Broken Top. Bring binoculars if you want to see glaciers. Moderate.

Black Crater (8 mi.). About 11 mi. west of sisters off the left side of Rte. 242. Deeper in the mountains, the strenuous round-trip hike up Black Crater offers unsurpassed views of snow-capped peaks and lava flows on McKenzie Pass, and intimate encounters with volcanic debris. Access is often limited due to snow.

McKenzie Pass (15 mi.). West of Sisters on Rte. 242. The site of a relatively recent lava flow that created barren fields of rough, black **A'A** (AH-ah) lava. The ½ mi. trail from the Dee Wright Observatory winds among basalt boulders, cracks, and crevices.

⚑ OTHER OUTDOOR ACTIVITIES. Opportunities for both novice and hard-core **mountain biking** abound near Sisters. No bikes or motor vehicles are allowed in official wilderness areas, but most other trails and little-used dirt roads are open to bikes. The ranger station distributes a packet detailing local trails; the friendly people at Eurosports also have info on the best trails (see **Practical Information,** p. 142). Half an hour from Sisters, the majestic rock spires of **Smith Rock State Park** are a popular **rock climbing** destination. Pick up a trail guide from the ranger, or at the park. For learning climbers, **First Ascent** has lessons. To get there, take Rte. 126 to Redmond, then go north for 9 mi. on US 97, and follow the signs from the town of Terrebonne.(☎800-325-5462. $175 per day; $95 per person per day for 2 people; $80 per person per day for 3 or more people.)

CRATER LAKE AND KLAMATH FALLS ☎541

The deepest lake in the US, the 7th deepest in the world, and one of the most beautiful anywhere, Crater Lake is one of Oregon's signature attractions. Formed about 7700 years ago in an eruption of the huge Mt. Mazama, it began as a deep caldera and gradually filled itself with centuries worth of melted snow. The circular lake plunges from its shores to a depth of 1936 ft.; though it remains iceless in the winter, its banks, which loom as high as 2000 ft. above the 6176 ft. lake surface, are snow-covered until July. Visitors from all over the world circle the 33 mi. Rim Drive, carefully gripping the wheel as the impossibly blue water enchants them. Klamath Falls, one of the nearest cities, makes a convenient stop on the way to the park and contains most of the services, motels, and restaurants listed below.

⬛ TRANSPORTATION

Rte. 62 skirts the park's southwestern edge as it arcs 130 mi. between Medford in the southwest and Klamath Falls, 56 mi. southeast of the park. West of the park, Rte. 62 follows the Upper Rogue River. To reach Crater Lake from Portland, take **I-5** to Eugene, and then **Rte. 58** east to **US 97** south. From US 97, **Rte. 138** leads west to the park's north entrance, but Crater Lake averages over 44 ft. of snow per year, and snowbound roads usually keep the northern entrance closed as late as July; the roads to **Rim Village** stay open year-round. Before July, enter the park from the south. **Rte. 62** runs west from US 97 about 40 mi. south of the park, through the small town of **Fort Klamath,** and on to the south access road that leads to the caldera's rim. Another 20 mi. of southward travel from the intersection of Rte. 62 and US 97 brings you to Klamath Falls.

OREGON

Trains: Amtrak (☎884-2822 or 800-872-7245; www.amtrak.com). Follow Klamath Ave. until you see signs for the station. Open daily 7:30am-11am and 8:30pm-10pm. Once a day to **Portland** ($36-60); trains continue north.

Buses: Greyhound, 3817 US 97 N, in Mollie's Truck Stop (☎882-4616. Open M-F 8am-1:00am, Sa 6-9am and midnight-12:45am.). Once a day to **Bend** (3hr., $20), **Eugene** (10hr., $40), and **Redding, CA** (4hr., $30).

Public Transportation: Basin Transit Service (☎883-2877) runs 6 routes. Runs M-F 6am-7:30pm, Sa 10am-5pm. $0.90, seniors and disabled $0.45.

Taxis: Classic Taxi (☎850-8303). $2 base, $2 per mi. 24hr.

Car Rental: Budget (☎885-5421), at Klamath Falls airport. From S 6th St., go south on Washburn Dr. and follow the signs. $30 per day M-F, $0.25 per mi. after 100 mi. $26 per day Sa-Su, 100 free mi. per day. Open M-F 7am-10pm, Sa-Su 8:30am-6pm.

🛈 PRACTICAL INFORMATION

Tourist Information: Chamber of Commerce, 507 Main St. (☎884-0666 or 800-445-6728; www.klamath.org). Open M-F 8am-5pm.

Outdoor Information: William G. Steel Center (☎594-2211, ext. 402), 1 mi. from the south entrance. Open daily 9am-5pm. **Crater Lake National Park Visitors Center** (☎594-3100), on the lake shore at Rim Village. Open daily June-Sept. 8:30am-6pm. Park main phone ☎594-3000; www.nps.gov/crla.

Park Entrance Fee: Cars $10, hikers and bikers $5. Free with Golden Eagle Passport.

Laundromat: Main Street Laundromat, 1711 Main St. (☎883-1784). Wash $1.25, dry $0.25 per 12min. Open M-Sa 8am-8pm; last wash 7pm.

Emergency: ☎911.

Police: 425 Walnut St. (☎883-5336).

Crisis and Rape Crisis Line: ☎800-452-3669. 24hr.

Hospital: Merle West Medical Center, 2865 Daggett Ave. (☎882-6311). From US 97 N, turn right on Campus Dr., then right onto Daggett. 24hr. emergency room.

Internet Access: Klamath County Library, 126 S 3rd St. (☎882-8894). Has 6 slow computers with 1hr. free Internet access. Open M, Tu, and Th 10am-5pm, W 1pm-8pm, F-Sa 10am-5pm, Su 1pm-5pm.

Post Office: Klamath Falls, 317 S 7th St. (☎800-275-8777) at Walnut St. Open M-F 7:30am-5:30pm, Sa 9am-noon. **Crater Lake,** in the Steel Center. Open M-Sa 9am-noon and 1-3pm. **Postal Code:** 97604.

🏠🏕 ACCOMMODATIONS AND CAMPING

Klamath Falls has plenty of affordable hotels that make easy bases for Crater Lake. If you'd rather live in the trees, **Forest Service campgrounds** ❶ (usually about $5) line **Rte. 62** through Rogue River National Forest to the west of the park. The park itself contains two campgrounds, both of which are closed until roads are passable. **Backcountry camping** is allowed in the park; a backcountry permit, free from the Steel Center, is required.

Mazama Campground (☎594-2255), near the park's south entrance off Hwy. 62. Tenters and RVs swarm this monster facility when it opens in mid-June, and some don't leave until it closes in Oct. Mostly tent sites. Few electrical RV sites. **Loop G** is more secluded and spacious, but opens later in the year. Toilets, laundry, telephone. A general store, and gas, open 7am-10pm daily. Wheelchair accessible. No reservations. 213 sites, tents $15, RVs $17, electric RV sites $19. Showers $0.75 for 4min. ❶

Townhouse Motel, 5323 S 6th St. (☎882-0924). 3 mi. south of Main, on the edge of Klamath Falls' strip-mall land, offers clean, comfy rooms at good prices. Cable, A/C, no phones. Double bed $30; 2-bed rooms $35. ❷

Lost Creek Campground (☎594-2255), in the southeast corner of the park, 3 mi. on a paved road off Rim Dr. 16 mid-sized sites set amid pines. Water, toilets. No reservations. Usually open mid-July to mid-Sept.; check with Steel Center. Tent sites $10. ❶

Cimarron Motor Inn, 3060 S 6th St. in Klamath Falls (☎882-4601), has clean and comfortable rooms, plus continental breakfast. 1 or 2 people $65; 3 or 4 $75. ❹

Collier Memorial State Park and Campground (☎783-2471), 30 mi. north of Klamath Falls on US 97, offers small tent and RV sites with little privacy just off the Williamson River. The brilliant green lichen hanging off the timber is a highlight, ironically, as a logging museum is just south of the campground. Toilets and laundry. Sites $15; Full RV sites $18. Showers. Down the same road, the **Williamson River Campground** offers tent sites with pit toilets and no water for $6 per night. ❶

🄵 FOOD

Eating cheap ain't easy in Crater Lake, with dining limited to a cafeteria, restaurant, and cafe in Rim Village. **Klamath Falls** has some affordable dining and a **Safeway** at Pine and 8th St., one block north of Main St. (☎882-2660. Open daily 6am-11pm.) A lot of eats in Klamath Falls go hand in hand with billiards; if you're a pool shark, Main St. between 5th and 7th St. is the place to go. The **Fort Klamath General Store,** 52608 Hwy. 62, offers canned goods, sells gas, and houses a cafe. (☎381-2263. Open summer daily 7am-10pm; winter 7am-8pm.)

Waldo's Mongolian Grill and Tavern, 610 Main St. (☎884-6863). This large restaurant and lounge might play techno or reggae even if most patrons are wearing stetson hats. The food is standard Mongolian BBQ (you choose the ingredients, they cook them); the lounge has just about every equipment-intensive bar game (pool, shuffleboard, etc.) known to man. Youthful bar scene weekends. Medium bowl is $8.50, all-you-can-eat $10. Grill open M-Sa 11am-9pm; tavern M-Th 11am-11:30pm, F-Sa 11am-1am. ❷

Plentiful Bakery, 2918 Altima Dr. off S 6th St. (☎273-6622). Basic, homemade goodness hits the spot in this small cafe. Be like the locals and have soup and a sandwich for $5.50 or stick with salad ($3-6). Open daily 6am-9pm. ❶

Cattle Crossing Cafe (☎381-2344) on Hwy. 62 in Fort Klamath. Waffle breakfasts ($3-7), burgers ($5-7), and dinners ($7-14) are capped off by mouth-watering homemade pie ($2.75 a slice). Open Apr.-Oct. daily 9am-6pm. ❷

Beckie's Cafe, in the tiny town of Union Creek just south of the Rogue River Gorge (☎560-3563), is a decent place to fuel up en route to or from the lake on Rte. 62, west of the lake. Specialty burgers $6.25. Open summer 8am-9pm. ❷

🄽 OUTDOOR ACTIVITIES

The area around Crater Lake is filled with all sorts of outdoor adventures. With ample options for hiking and biking, as well as easy access to the backcountry regions outside the park, you may feel overwhelmed with options. A good jumping off point is the Steel Center (see **Outdoor Information,** p. 144), or the Rim Village, where the information center and the Crater Lake Lodge are located. **Crater Lake Lodge** (☎594-2255; 830-8700 for reservations) is a few hundred yards east of Sinnott Memorial Overlook in the Rim Village. Rooms are very expensive, but fun in the lodge can be had for free: make a quick visit to the rustic "great hall," rebuilt from its original materials, and warm yourself by the fire or relax in a rocking chair on the observation deck. The friendly staff will be happy to help you find any info on the Lake that you need.

DRIVING. Rim Dr., usually not open until mid-July, loops 33 mi. around the rim of the caldera, high above the lake. Pull-outs are strategically placed along the road wherever a view of the lake might cause an awe-struck tourist to drive off the cliff. Don't despair when the caldera walls block sight of the lake: the views of Cascade volcanoes as distant as Mt. Shasta, 100 mi. south, will console your eyes.

HIKING. Most visitors never stray far from their vehicles as they tour the lake, so hiking provides a great way to get away from the crowds. Trailheads are scattered along the rim, so just park and hike away from the road. The Steel Center has a trail map and info about which trails are closed due to weather.

   Watchman Peak (¾ mi. one-way, 1hr.). Begins on the lake's west side. Short, but yields a great view of Wizard Island. One of the lake's two active cinder cones. Moderate.

   Mt. Scott (5 mi. round-trip, 2-3hr.). The trailhead is 17 mi. clockwise from Rim Village. Although steep, the ascent to the top of 9000 ft. Mt. Scott and the historic fire tower on top affords a beautiful panoramic view of the lake. Moderate to strenuous.

   Cleetwood Cove Trail (2¼ mi. round-trip, 2hr.), leaves from the north edge of the lake and is the only route down to the water and the park's most traveled trail. It drops 700 ft. in 1 mi. to get to the shore. Moderate to strenuous.

ON THE LAKE. In the summer, park rangers lead hour-long boat tours from the Cleetwood Cove trailhead. Aside from giving a comprehensive history of the lake and its formation, the tours provide breathtaking views of both **Wizard Island,** a cinder cone rising 760 ft. above the lake, and **Phantom Ship Rock,** a spooky rock formation. (Tours run 7 times daily 10am-4:30pm between late June and mid-Sept. $19.25, under 11 $11.50.) The boat tours provide foot access to the island, which can be hiked for a view into its crater. Land-lubbers may prefer picnics and fishing (artificial lures only) at the bottom of the trail. Though the lake (supposedly without outlet, though many contend the Rogue River drains out the bottom) was virtually sterile when modern man found it; it has since been stocked with rainbow trout and kokanee. Those who walk down to the lake at Cleetwood Cove can take a dip, but the water reaches a maximum temperature of only 50°F (10°C).

BACKCOUNTRY EXPLORATION. A hiking trip into the park's vast **backcountry** leaves all the exhaust and tourists behind. Hiking or climbing inside the caldera is prohibited. Other than near water sources, dispersed camping is allowed anywhere in the area but is complicated by the absence of water and the presence of bears. Get info and required backcountry permits for free at either visitors center. The **Pacific Crest Trail** begins from the trailhead ¾ mi. west of the south entrance. The ultimate backcountry trail passes through the park and three backcountry campsites, giving great views of mountain meadows, old-growth timber, and, of course, the lake. Another excellent loop begins at the **Red Cone trailhead** on the north access road, passing the less-traveled **Crater Springs, Oasis Butte,** and **Boundary Springs trails.** However, it is impaired by the snow until July and opens only at the discretion of the ranger. Contact the Steel Center for more information.

UPPER ROGUE RIVER. If you prefer your water more vertical than anything the lake can offer, try the Upper Rogue, easily accessible from Rte. 62 southwest of Crater Lake. Emerging from a spring on the northern slope of Mt. Mazama, the river contends with the area's many lava flows by raging through scenic gorges, passing through huge waterfalls and cataracts, and even going underground for a stretch. Despite all this, the fish are doing alright, especially in places like **Casey State Park,** 46 mi. SW of the park; here, the angling is good but crowded.

Mill Creek Falls drops 173 ft. into a deep canyon downstream of the **Avenue of Giant Boulders,** where a huge jumble of rocks offers navigational puzzles for the feet and sublime **sunning** for your back. The pools formed between cascades also make for equally great **splashing around.** From Rte. 62, easy, short trails to both sites are accessed from a trailhead; follow signs to "Mill Creek Falls/Prospect Access Road," about 32 mi. SW of Crater Lake on Rte. 62.

Things get steamier for the Rogue as it approaches Mt. Mazama: lava flows are clearly at work in both the **Natural Bridge** and the **Rogue River Gorge.** The river performs a natural, but still frightening, disappearing act under the bridge, where it descends into a lava tube and reappears 200 ft. downstream. In the Gorge, the river is forced through a lava flow and gets angry about it, smashing through in a series of short but raging waterfalls. The gorge has been kayaked, amazingly, and advanced/ expert kayakers may put in *below* the Natural Bridge for unusual, lava-formed class IV rapids. Class VI Therapy Falls, after a right jog about 0.5-1.5 mi. into the run, with an absolute must portage before the jog on river left, could very well be lethal for any party that goes without knowing the run, especially at high water in spring. The Gorge and Natural Bridge are about 20 and 23 mi. SW of Crater Lake on Rte. 62, respectively.

HELLS CANYON AND WALLOWA MTNS. ☎541

The northeast corner of Oregon is the state's most rugged, remote, and arresting country, with jagged granite peaks, glacier-gouged valleys, and azure lakes. East of La Grande, the Wallowa Mountains (wa-LAH-wah) rise abruptly, looming over the plains from elevations of more than 9000 ft. Thirty miles east, North America's deepest gorge plunges to the Snake River. It may take a four-wheel-drive vehicle to get off the beaten path, but those with the initiative and the horsepower will find stunning vistas and heavenly solitude in the backcountry.

▐ TRANSPORTATION

There are three ways to get to the **Wallowa Valley,** which lies between the **Hells Canyon National Recreation Area** and the **Eagle Cap Wilderness.** From **Baker City,** Rte. 86 heads east through **Halfway** (also known as **Half.com,** the world's first dot-com city) to connect with Forest Rd. 39, which winds north over the southern end of the Wallowas, meeting Rte. 350 (also known as Little Sheep Creek Hwy.) 8 mi. east of **Joseph**. From **La Grande,** Rte. 82 arcs around the north end of the Wallowas, through the small towns of Elgin, Minam, Wallowa, and Lostine, continuing through **Enterprise** and **Joseph,** and terminating at **Wallowa Lake.** From **Lewiston, Idaho,** Rte. 129 heads south into Washington, then over Rattlesnake Pass, becoming Rte. 3 in Oregon and joining Rte. 82 in Enterprise.

◀▶ ❷ ORIENTATION AND PRACTICAL INFORMATION

Three main towns offer services within the area: Enterprise, Joseph, and Halfway. Joseph lies 6 mi. east of Enterprise on Rte. 82. In **Enterprise,** Rte. 82 is called North St., and in Joseph it goes by Main St. **Halfway** is about 65 mi. south of Joseph. To get there, take E Wallowa Rd., off Main St. in Joseph, and follow the signs to Halfway (the drive takes 2hr., the majority of which is on **Forest Rd. 39,** a paved but brutally curvy route). Other major roads in the area are **Rte. 350,** a paved route from Joseph 30 mi. northeast to the tiny town of **Imnaha,** and the **Imnaha River Rd.** (a.k.a. Country Rd. 727 and Forest Rd. 3955), a good gravel road that runs south from Imnaha to reconnect with Forest Rd. 39 about 50 mi. southeast of Joseph. The invaluable and free Wallowa County Visitor Map is available in visitors centers and ranger stations, as are current road conditions information.

Hells Canyon Region

▲ CAMPING
Copperfield, **3**
McCormick, **4**
Saddle Creek, **1**
Wallowa Lake, **2**
Woodhead, **5**

Buses: Moffit Brothers Transportation (☎ 569-2284) runs the **Wallowa Valley Stage Line,** which makes one round-trip M-Sa between **Joseph** and **La Grande.** Pickup at the **Chevron** on Rte. 82 in Joseph, the **Amoco** on Rte. 82 in Enterprise, and the **Greyhound terminal** in La Grande. Will stop and pickup at Wallowa Lake with advance notice. One-way from **La Grande** to: **Enterprise** ($10); **Joseph** ($11); and **Wallowa Lake** ($15).

Visitor Information: Wallowa County Chamber of Commerce, 936 W North St. (☎ 426-4622 or 800-585-4121), in Enterprise. General tourist info as well as the comprehensive and free *Wallowa County Visitor Guide.* Open M-F 8am-5pm. **Hells Canyon Chamber of Commerce** (☎ 742-4222), in the office of Halfway Motels (see **Accommodations,** below), provides info on accommodations, outfitters, and guides.

Outdoor Information: Wallowa Mountains Visitor Center, 88401 Rte. 82 (☎426-5546; www.fs.fed.us/r6/w-w), on the west side of Enterprise. $6 map a necessity for navigating area roads. Open Memorial Day to Labor Day M-Sa 8am-5pm, Su noon-5pm; Labor Day to Memorial Day M-F 8am-5pm. **Hells Canyon National Recreation Area Office,** 2 mi. south of Clarkston, WA on Rte. 129 (☎509-758-0616), carries all sorts of information on Hells Canyon. Open M-F 7:45-11:30am and 12:30-4:30pm.

Laundromat: Joseph Laundromat and Car Wash, on Rte. 82 in Joseph, across from the Indian Lodge Motel. Wash $1, dry $0.25 per 8min. Open daily 6am-10pm.

Emergency: ☎911. **Police:** State police ☎426-3036. In Enterprise, 108 NE 1st St. (☎426-3136), at the corner of North St.

Fire: ☎426-4196.

Hospital: Wallowa Memorial, 401 NE 1st St. (☎426-3111), in Enterprise.

Internet Access: The **Enterprise Public Library,** 101 NE 1st St. (☎426-3906), at Main St., charges $4 for 30min. and $6 per hr. Open M, F noon-6pm, T-Th 10am-6pm.

Post Office: 201 W North St. (☎426-5980), on Rte. 82 in Enterprise. Open M-F 9am-4:30pm. **Postal Code:** 97828.

■ ACCOMMODATIONS AND CAMPING

Most of the towns along Rte. 82 have motels with plenty of vacancy during the week. On weekends rooms are more scarce. Campgrounds here are plentiful, inexpensive, and sublime. Pick up the free *Campground Information* pamphlet at the Wallowa Mountains Visitor Center (see p. 148) for a complete listing of sites in the area. Many **free campgrounds** are not fully serviced, and recent improvements to some (water and pit toilets) have resulted in fees ($5-8) for formerly free sites. Insect repellent is a must during summer, when most campgrounds are open.

Indian Lodge Motel, 201 S Main St. (☎432-2651 or 888-286-5484), on Rte. 82 in Joseph. Elegant rooms with dark wood furniture and plush blue carpet. A/C, cable, coffeemakers, fridges. Singles $37; doubles $49. Winter singles $32; doubles $40. ❷

Country Inn Motel, 402 W North St. (☎426-4986 or 877-426-4986), in Enterprise. Reminiscent of a country farmhouse. Rooms stay remarkably cool without A/C. Cable, coffeemakers, fridges. Singles $50, doubles $54. Rates lower in winter. ❸

Wallowa Lake State Park Campground (☎432-4185; reservations 800-452-5687), at the eastern end of Rte. 82. Books 11 months in advance. Full-service camping. Flushing toilets, potable water. Tent sites $17, full RV sites $21. Showers. ❶

Snake River Campgrounds (☎785-3323). Only three are open year-round: **Copperfield,** at the northern end of Hwy. 86; **McCormick,** 12 mi. south of Copperfield off Hwy. 71; and **Woodhead,** 4 mi. south of McCormick on Hwy. 71. Restrooms. No reservations. Tent sites $6, RV sites $10. Hot showers at Woodhead. ❶

Saddle Creek Campground. From Rte. 82, turn on E Wallowa Rd. (a.k.a. Rte. 350) in Joseph. Drive 19 mi. on the unpaved and steep Hat Point Rd. 7 sites perched on the lip of Hells Canyon feature unbelievable views. No water. Wheelchair accessible. Free. ❶

▐ FOOD

If you're heading out onto the roads of Hells Canyon, bring some provisions—a flat or breakdown could require a roadside meal or two. Find groceries at **Safeway,** 601 W North St., on Rte. 82 in Enterprise. (☎426-3722. Open daily 6am-10pm.)

OREGON

■ **Wildflour Bakery,** 600 N Main St. (☎ 432-7225), in Joseph, offers an amazing selection of scrumptious baked goods, as well as giant sourdough and cornmeal pancakes ($2 per cake). Sit on the patio and enjoy the day with a chicken sausage sandwich or giant burrito ($5). Open M and W-Sa 7am-3pm, Su 7am-noon. Breakfast til 11am. ❶

Embers Brew House, 207 N Main St. (☎ 432-2739), in Joseph. In the summer, the patio is packed outside this popular dinner spot. Sample 5 of 17 microbrews ($5). Fries $4. Open June-Sept. daily 11am-11pm; winter Su-Th 11am-8pm, F-Sa 11am-11pm. ❶

Old Town Cafe, 8 S Main St. (☎ 432-9898), in Joseph. Sit in the outdoor grotto and dig into a bottomless bowl of homemade soup ($3) or a giant fresh baked cinnamon roll ($1.75). Breakfast all day. Open F-W 7am-2pm. ❶

Vali's Alpine Delicatessen Restaurant, 59811 Wallowa Lake Hwy. (☎ 432-5691), in Wallowa Lake. For 28 years in this small, alpine-esque cottage, Mr. Vali has cooked one authentic European dish each night and Mrs. Vali has served it. Hungarian Kettle Goulash $8.50; schnitzel $12. Reservations required for dinner. Breakfast W-Su 9-11am, dinner seatings W-Su at 5 and 8pm. After Labor Day, open Sa and Su only. ❷

▲ OUTDOOR ACTIVITIES: HELLS CANYON

The canyon's endearing name comes from its legendary inaccessibility and hostility to human habitation. The walls of Hells Canyon drop over 8000 ft. to the **Snake River,** which makes it the deepest canyon in North America.

LOOKOUTS. Hells Canyon Overlook, the most accessible of the lookout points, is up Forest Rd. 3965. The road departs Rd. 39 about 5 mi. south of the Imnaha River crossing. The broadest and most eye-popping views are from the **Hat Point Lookout Overlook,** where visitors can climb a 90 ft. wooden fire lookout. To get there, go 24 mi. up a steep but well-maintained gravel road (not recommended for trailers) from Imnaha (Forest Rd. 4240, a.k.a. Hat Point Rd.), and follow the signs. There are pit toilets at the overlook and several picnic sites for day use. The **Buckhorn Lookout** lies far off the beaten path, 42 mi. northeast of Joseph, and offers lofty views of the Imnaha River Valley. Take Rte. 82 north 3 mi. out of Joseph or 3 mi. south out of Enterprise, and look for the green sign for Buckhorn. Turn off and follow Zumwalt Rd. (a.k.a. Country Rd. 697, which turns into Forest Rd. 46) for approximately 40 bumpy miles to Buckhorn—about a half-day round-trip. Also at that end of the canyon, the immense **Hells Canyon Dam** lies 23 mi. north of Oxbow on Rte. 86 (turns into Forest Rd. 454). This drive is one of only three ways to get near the bottom of the canyon by car, and the dam is the only place to cross.

HIKING. There are over 1000 mi. of trails in the canyon, only a fraction of which are maintained. Most are only open in April. The dramatic 56 mi. **Snake River Trail** runs by the river for the length of the canyon. At times, the trail is cut into the side of the rock with just enough clearance for a horse's head. This trail can be followed from **Dug Bar** in the north down to the Hells Canyon Dam or accessed by steep trails along the way. From north to south, **Hat Point, Freezeout,** and **P.O. Saddle** are access points. To reach Dug Bar, get a high-clearance 4WD vehicle and hit the steep, slippery Forest Rd. 4260 for 27 mi. northeast from **Imnaha.** Bring snakebite kits, boots, and water. Rangers patrol the river by boat at least once a day.

WATER. The easiest way to see a large portion of the canyon is on the Snake River by jet boat or raft; both pursuits are guaranteed to drench. Numerous outfitters operate out of Oxbow and the dam area; the Wallowa Mountains Visitors Center (see p. 148) and all local chambers of commerce have a list of the permittees. **Hells Canyon Adventures,** 4200 Hells Canyon Dam Rd., 1½ mi. from the Hells Canyon Dam in Oxbow, runs a wide range of jet boat and raft trips. (☎ 785-3352 or 800-422-3568. Jet boats 2hr. $30, 3hr. $40, full day $105. Whitewater rafting $140 for a day trip.)

⚠ OUTDOOR ACTIVITIES: WALLOWA MOUNTAINS

Without a catchy, federally approved name like "Hells Canyon National Recreation Area," the Wallowas often take second place to the canyon. They are equally magnificent, however, as their canyons echo with the rush of rapids and their jagged peaks cover with wildflowers in spring.

HIKING. Over 600 mi. of **hiking trails** cross the **Eagle Cap Wilderness** and are usually free of snow from mid-July to October. Deep glacial valleys and high granite passes make hiking this wilderness difficult. It often takes more than a day to get into the most beautiful areas, so carry adequate supplies and prepare for sudden weather changes. The 5 mi. hike to **Chimney Lake** from the **Bowman** trailhead on the Lostine River Rd. (Forest Rd. 8210) traverses fields of granite boulders sprinkled with a few small meadows. A little farther on lie the serene **Laverty, Hobo,** and **Wood Lakes,** where the road is less traveled. The **Two Pan** trailhead at the end of the Lostine River Rd. is the start of a forested 6 mi. hike to popular **Minam Lake,** which makes a good starting point for those heading to other backcountry spots.

By far the most popular area in the Eagle Cap Wilderness is the **Lakes Basin** (a 7-9 mi. hike from the Two Pan trailhead), where explorers can find unsurpassed scenery, good fishing, and hikes to Eagle Cap Peak. While it is possible to escape the crowds in the basin during the week, the lake is packed on weekends. **Steamboat, Long,** and **Swamp Lakes** (also accessible from the Two Pan trailhead) are as magnificent as the Lakes Basin but receive only half as many visitors. Rangers at the visitors center can also recommend more secluded routes. Many excellent dayhikes to **Lookingglass, Culver, Bear, Eagle, Cached, Arrow,** and **Heart Lakes** start from the Boulder Park trailhead, on Forest Rd. 7755, on the southern side of the Eagle Cap Wilderness (accessible from Baker City and Halfway).

FISHING. Fishing in the alpine lakes of Eagle Cap is incredible, but it's illegal even to catch and release without a permit. Some fish, such as bull trout, are entirely protected. Get permits ($8 per day, $49 per year) and the *Oregon Sport Fishing Regulations* booklet at any local sporting store.

BURNS ☎ 541

Tiny Burns and its even tinier neighbor Hines serve as traveler waystations and supply centers. Packed with cheap motels and fast food joints, Burns offers sustenance, shelter, and a wealth of information on the surrounding country. And what great outdoor country it is: ideally situated between the Ochoco and Malheur National Forests, Steens Mountain, the Alvord Desert, and the Malheur National Wildlife Refuge, Burns is the center for outdoor activities in the otherwise uninhabited wilderness of southeastern Oregon.

🖪🛈 ORIENTATION AND PRACTICAL INFORMATION. US 20 from Ontario
and **US 395** from John Day converge 2 mi. north of Burns, continue through Burns and Hines as one, and diverge about 30 mi. west of town. US 20 continues west to Bend and the Cascade Range; US 395 runs south to Lakeview, OR and California; Rte. 205 runs south to Frenchglen and Fields (see below). Although buses and vans run to and from some of the nearby towns, you're better off making like Moses and heading for the desert than waiting for public transportation there. **Harney County Chamber of Commerce,** 76 E Washington St., has excellent maps and info on both towns. (☎573-2636. Open M-F 9am-5pm.) Even more useful are the **Burns Ranger District (Malheur National Forest)** and **Snow Mountain Ranger District (Ochoco National Forest),** in Hines. These outdoor

OREGON

resources share an office on the main drag about 4½ mi. south of Burns, and provide information on camping, hiking, and every other wilderness activity imaginable in the surrounding countryside. (☎ 573-4300. Open M-F 8am-4:30pm.) **Burns Bureau of Land Management (BLM),** on US 20 West, is a few miles west of Hines. The BLM office and the BLM web site provide essential information on the federally controlled areas of southeastern Oregon, including Steens Mountain and the Malheur Wildlife Refuge. The office also has a nifty relief map, and sells recreation maps for $4. (☎ 573-4400; www.or.blm.gov/burns. Open M-F 7:45am-4:30pm.) Call ☎ 911 in an **emergency,** or contact the **police,** 242 S Broadway (☎ 573-6028). The **hospital,** at 557 W Washington St. (☎ 573-7281), has 24hr. emergency care. The **post office** can be found at 100 S Broadway. (☎ 800-275-8777. Open M-F 8:30am-5pm.) **Postal Code:** 97720.

⌐⌐ ACCOMMODATIONS AND FOOD. The **Bontemps Motel** ❷, 74 W Monroe St., provides comfortable rooms with firm beds and some cool jungle-style lampshades. Cable TV and A/C; kitchenettes are about $5 more. (☎ 573-2037 or 800-229-1394. Singles $30; doubles $35; pets $5.) There's a **Days Inn** ❸ at 577 W Monroe St. (☎ 573-2047. Singles $52, doubles $57.) **Joaquin Miller** ❶ campground, just off of US 395 19 mi. north of town, has free camping surrounded by Ponderosa pines. Pit toilets; no water. **Safeway** is at 246 W Monroe St. (☎ 573-6767. Open daily 6am-11pm.) **Broadway Deli** ❶, 528 N Broadway Ave., sells cheap but good and filling sandwiches ($4.75) and homemade soups ($2 per bowl). It's a great alternative to fast food fare. (Open M-F 8am-4pm. Sa 11am-3pm.) **Elk Horn Cafe/Linda's Thai Room** ❷, 457 N Broadway, juxtaposes Thai cuisine and greasy spoon fare, ornate chandeliers and Thai spiritual figures against elk wallpaper. Decent Thai or Chinese dinners $8-12. (☎ 573-3201. Open daily 8am-2pm, 5-9pm.)

NEAR BURNS ☎ 541

MALHEUR NAT'L WILDLIFE REFUGE & DIAMOND CRATERS

About 40 mi. south of Burns, miles of sagebrush give way to the grasslands and marshes of **Harney** and **Malheur Lakes,** where thousands of birds end their migratory flight paths each year at **Malheur National Wildlife Refuge.** Stretching 35 mi. south along Rte. 205, the refuge covers 185,000 acres and is home to 58 mammal species and over 320 species of birds, including grebes, ibis, plovers, shrikes, owls, wigeons, and waxwings. The best time to see the birds is in April; bald eagles are best seen in the coldest months. The refuge takes 2hr. to traverse, and some areas require a 4WD vehicle.

The refuge headquarters, 6 mi. east of Rte. 205 on a well-marked turn-off between Burns and Frenchglen, houses a useful **visitors center** that provides trail directions and area info. (☎ 493-2612. Open M-Th 7am-4:30am, F 7am-3:30pm, Sa-Su 8am-4pm.) No camping is allowed within the refuge, but **accommodations** are available at the **Malheur Field Station** ❷, an old government training camp 5 mi. west of headquarters. Make reservations well in advance, especially for spring, fall, and holiday weekends. Toilets and potable water. Meals are available in high season (April and May) when large groups are eating. Basic housekeeping is expected of the guests. (☎ 493-2629. Spartan bunks $20; available for large groups. Kitchenette singles $23, $18 if shared. Singles in a trailer $40; doubles $60; RV sites $16.) The Field Station occasionally teaches classes on wildlife in the refuge; these are open for large groups only, but extra space is sometimes available. Call to inquire.

OREGON

HIKING. Hiking is generally allowed only along roads. Two short trails depart from the visitors center. Also, the largely unmarked and primitive **Loop Trail** (11 mi. loop, several hr.) departs from "P-Ranch" just before Frenchglen. This moderately difficult trail offers great opportunities to see migratory birds.

DIAMOND CRATERS. A well-marked turn-off 30 mi. south of Burns on Hwy. 205 leads to the **Diamond Craters,** located just east of the Malheur Refuge. This outstanding national area has more than meets the eye, and is a geologist's playground of craters, lava flows, and cinder bomb piles. For laypeople, the BLM's self-guided tour (available at any visitors center, ranger station, or at the hotel or mercantile in Frenchglen) and a fair bit of patience are essential to make any sense of the volcanic history here. The **Lava Pit Crater** is most worth a stop. Bring water and watch out for rattlesnakes; the nearest medical facilities are in Burns, 55 mi. to the northwest.

The 100-year-old **Hotel Diamond** ❹, 12 mi. east of Rte. 205 on Diamond Lane, seems young in relation to the craters but proves a sophisticated rest stop for the dedicated explorer. (☎ 493-1898; www.central-oregon.com/hoteldiamond. Breakfast $1.50-4.75; dinner $10-15, for guests or by reservation only. No children allowed. A small double with shared bath starts at $55; with private bath $90.)

FRENCHGLEN   ☎ 541

An hour south of Burns along Rte. 205, Frenchglen provides access to wildlife refuges and the western side of the Steens Mountain via the Steens Mtn. Loop. **Fields,** 55min. farther south of Frenchglen on Rte. 205, at the southern tip of the mountain, provides access to the eastern face and the Alvord Desert. Both towns are little more than a few buildings along the highway, but they can provide food, shelter, and sound advice. **Frenchglen Mercantile** ❶, on Rte. 205, has gas, some groceries, and, from June through August, big deli sandwiches for $4.50 (☎ 493-2835). (Open daily 7am-8pm.) The owners also run a bar and a **guesthouse** ❹ connected to the main store, with two very comfortable rooms. (☎ 493-2738. $65.) The **Steens Mountain Resort,** North Steens Mtn. Loop Rd. just 3 mi. outside of town, also has a small general store with canned goods, ice cream, and laundry facilities. (☎ 493-2415. Wash $0.75, dry $0.50 for 20min. Showers $5. Open daily 8:30am-6pm.)

FIELDS   ☎ 541

About 5 mi. northwest of Fields, Rte. 205 squeezes through a small pass and the scenery rapidly evolves from rugged to lunar, with hulking fault-block mountains all around. Consisting of only a few houses, the rambling **Fields Station** is home to four businesses owned by the same family: they've lived here 30 years. The general store and gas station are the last of each for miles. The **cafe** ❶ serves remarkably large burgers ($4.25), scrumptious onion rings ($2), and 6000 milkshakes a year ($3). The **hotel and campground** ❸ next door to the cafe rent very nice rooms and sites. (☎ 495-2275. Singles $40; doubles $55; RV sites $10; tenting areas $2.)

STEENS MOUNTAIN   ☎ 541

Oregon's most unearthly landscape lies in the southeast, where the **Steens Mountain** rises to an elevation of nearly 10,000 ft. and reaches a vertical mile above an uninhabited, bone-dry alkali flat to the east. Although its fault block geology might seem a let-down from the western view—the sloped road ascends very gradually—on the substantially more remote east side, the incredible 30 mi. north-south stretch of mountain presents huge cliffs and deep canyons. Contact the Burns District BLM for road info and get **maps** of the area at the **Frenchglen Hotel** and the **Steens Mountain Resort** (see above). There are four campgrounds on the west side,

OREGON

all with pit toilets and drinking water; they charge $6-8 per night. Each is just off the Steens Mtn. Rd., which leaves from Frenchglen. **Page Springs ❶**, only 5 mi. from Frenchglen, is accessible year-round and has 36 grassy sites surrounded by cliffs; **Fish Lake ❶**, 19 mi. in and 1½ mi. up toward the mountain, has 23 sites and a boat ramp to access the best fishing in the area; **Jackman Park ❶**, 3 mi. farther in, has 6 mountainside sites; and **South Steens ❶**, a few miles farther, features 21 sites and 15 equestrian sites. The campgrounds on the east side are free and offer plenty of solitude; as a major plus, the stargazing doesn't get any better. **Pike Creek ❶** has a pit toilet and a creek nearby. It's 1½ mi. north of the Alvord Hot Springs (see below). Make a left after the second creek north of the desert (marked by a line of trees), and drive up the *very* rough road. Keep your eyes peeled; it's easy to miss.

DRIVING. Don't think that driving is a cop-out—the 66 mi. dirty track **Steens Mountain Loop Rd.** (open July-Oct.) is rutted, washboardy, and bound to be a full-on adventure for any 2WD vehicle. It climbs the west slope of the mountain from Rte. 205 near Frenchglen, and rejoins the highway only 8 mi. farther south.

OTHER EXPLORATION. Though hot, dusty, and chock full of rattlesnakes, the canyons of the mountain, gouged deep into the rock by glacial activity, are beautiful and difficult hikes. **Pike Creek** trail (see above for directions; the trail and road are unmarked) begins as an old mining road, goes past an abandoned mining shack and under towering rock spires, and then gradually fades about 1½ mi. in as it switchbacks and continues to the mouth of Pike Creek's canyon. To find the trail, just walk up the creek. Follow the cairns in the canyon. The trail ends at the mouth, but the summit arête can be attained by a very difficult scree scramble—there's no trail—to the top. (Hiking to the mouth is moderate to strenuous. To the summit is very strenuous and takes 1-1½ days.)

Another trip, lasting four days, ascends the **Big Indian Creek Gorge** on the west side to the summit, and then descends via the **Little Blitzen River Gorge,** also on the west side. Filterable water is usually available. The canyons are also good for shorter dayhikdayhikes, returning via the ascent route. A popular and moderately difficult hike is along the **Blitzen River trail** (4 mi. one-way, several hours) which follows along the river, crossing in certain places to avoid steep cliffs, to some great places to fish. The river passes through the Steens Mtn. Resort.

ALVORD DESERT

The utterly flat and barren Alvord Desert supports no terrestrial life. On the other hand, if a giant metal craft lands while bearing beings from outer space, don't worry: the Alvord Desert is reportedly the US space shuttle's 4th-choice landing spot. It's also a favored place for sand yachting, where the wheeled sailcraft can achieve speeds up to 100 mph. Regattas are held occasionally. For those piloting more mundane craft, roads lead out onto the desert plain, allowing car access to the desert. Regardless of your recreational intentions, a gaze over this *bona fide* wasteland is worth the long trip—although enjoying the desert requires a sense of humor. Drive 25 mi. north on the East Steens Rd., a dirt road just west of Fields. Continue north past the Alvord Desert about 1½hr. to Rte. 78, which can be taken west back to Burns. Make sure to bring lots of water and plenty of gas.

The borate-rich **Alvord Hot Springs** emerges next to the desert; a couple of enterprising, and probably reclusive, miners once extracted the cleaning agent borax up a dirt road opposite the springs. A tin shack houses a small pool for bathing, kept much cooler than the 174°F of the spring. It's on the right side of the road, about 200 ft. north of a cattleguard. About 20 mi. farther north, **Mann Lake** is open to excellent fishing and **free camping ❶** with pit toilets but no piped water. For those in search of a burly, multi-day desert adventure well beyond anything a car could give, the Desert Trail runs through the area. **Trail guides** and info are available from the Desert Trail Association (☎475-2960) in Burns.

JOHN DAY FOSSIL BEDS

☎541

The John Day Fossil Beds National Monument is one of Eastern Oregon's most precious gems. A place where paleontological reputations are made, the beds hold the bones of ancient monsters from saber-tooths to ever-elusive gomphotheres. Though no original fossils are on display outdoors in the Monument, the beds lack nothing in topographical exuberance. The **Sheep Rock, Painted Hills,** and **Clarno** units each depict one facet of a 40-million-year geological history. The nearby town John Day is at best a stopover.

█ ACCOMMODATIONS. Magone Lake ❶ (mah-GOON) is a popular campground with fishing, hiking, and swimming. To get there from John Day, take US 26 east 9 mi. to Keeney Forks Rd. N and follow the signs for 15 mi. to the campground. (Potable water. 23 sites, $5.) **Clyde Holiday State Park ❶**, 7 mi. west of town on US 26, has grassy sites and a less-than-primitive aura. It offers electricity, carpeting, and foam mattresses. (☎932-4453, reservations 800-452-5687. Hiker and bicyclist sites $4; 30 sites with RV sites, $16; 2 tepees, $28. Showers for non-campers $2.)

For those preferring a bed and a roof, **Dreamer's Lodge ❸**, 144 N Canyon Blvd., has large rooms with A/C, fridges, microwaves, and cable TV. (☎575-0526. Singles $52; doubles $56; $7-9 more for a kitchenette. AAA and AARP discounts.) **Little Pine Inn ❸**, 250 E Main St., is less expensive and has free breakfast deals at a local restaurant. (☎575-2100. Singles $41; doubles $46.)

▐ FOOD. Pick up groceries at **Chester's Thriftway**, 631 W Main St., in John Day Plaza. (☎575-1899. Open daily 7am-9pm.) Sit down and have a burger or a steak at the **Grubsteak Mining Co. ❶**, 149 E Main St. Pool and beer ($2 bottles) are available at the saloon in the back. (☎575-1970. Open daily 7am-10pm.) Enjoy a sit-down meal at **Dayville Cafe ❷**, 212 W Franklin St. (Rte. 26) in Dayville. Big breakfasts, grilled sandwiches ($5-6) and country dinners ($10-15) are served in a calico country atmosphere. Everything is fresh and homemade by mom and pop. (☎987-2132. Open Tu-Sa 7am-8pm, Su 8am-5pm. No credit cards.)

▨ OUTDOOR ACTIVITIES. The **Sheep Rock Unit** has some of the best hiking in the area, with trails that show off prehistoric fossils. It also contains the **visitors center** on Rte. 19, 2 mi. north of US 26. The center has displays, exhibits, and an award-winning video produced by high school students that explains the history of the fossil beds. (☎987-2333. Open daily 9am-5pm.) The **Blue Basin** area (3 mi. up the road from the visitors center) provides two distinct hiking opportunities: the **Island in Time Trail,** an easy 1 mi., 1 hr. round-trip into the canyon that passes by a blue-green rock formation, and the **Blue Basin Overlook Trail,** a more challenging 3 mi., 2½hr. loop up to the basin's rim and a view of the John Day River Valley. The former's fossil replicas of sea turtles and saber-toothed carnivores are intriguing, but are surpassed by the latter's views of brightly colored badland spires.

Five miles north of US 26 from the turn-off, 3 mi. west of Mitchell, the **Painted Hills Unit** offers several short hikes that present a better way to examine the beautifully colored mounds, once tropical rainforests. It focuses on an epoch 30 million years ago, when the land was in geologic transition. Smooth mounds of brilliant red, yellow, and black sediment are most vivid at sunset and dawn, or after rain when the whole gorge glistens with brilliantly colored layers of claystone.

The **Clarno Unit,** the monument's oldest section, on Rte. 218, is accessible by US 97 to the west or Rte. 19 to the east. Its trails wind through ancient ash-laden mudflows from volcanic eruptions. While all of the hikes are short, and many of them more scenic than strenuous, all offer up ample opportunities to witness the stark beauty of this national monument.

STRAWBERRY MOUNTAIN WILDERNESS

Tall, rocky peaks make the Strawberry Mountains a great cure for any case of desert blues. Needle-sharp summit ridges, snow-lined cliffs, and forested lakes make it a justly popular destination for Oregon city-folk. Though it can get slightly crowded (by wilderness standards) with vacationers and their angry dogs, a weekday trip will offer refreshing views and clean (but thin) air. To squeeze in the best views in the least time, try dayhikes and overnight camping in the **lakes basin,** around **Strawberry Lake.** Backpackers enjoy more solitude in the west side of the wilderness, accessible from forest roads south of John Day. Ask at the ranger station for details; in any case, wilderness maps are essential as trail signs are perplexing. Get one at the Prairie City **ranger station** (☎ 820-3311), located on the right as you come into from John Day, for $3. In case of emergency, **Blue Mtn. Hospital** is in John Day, 170 Ford Rd. (☎ 575-1311).

To get to **Strawberry Campground** and the trailhead for the lakes basin, make a right on Main St. in Prairie City, 13 mi. east of John Day. Take the next left, and then drive straight at the mountains on Road 60, which becomes Road 6001; follow it until the end. The **campground ❶** itself is a decent campsite with potable water (sites $8). A better, cheaper option is to hike up into the high country. **Free camping ❶** is allowed anywhere in the wilderness; many people camp around Strawberry Lake, fewer at the more rugged **Little Strawberry Lake** and its surrounding streams.

Strawberry Lake, a moderate 1½ mi. hike from Strawberry Campground, is the base of most of the popular trails. A strenuous 6 mi. (4hr. up) trail through the lake to the top of Strawberry Mountain passes through ghostly-white burns and subalpine meadows peppered with wildflowers. The windy and razor-sharp 9000 ft. summit ridge has a view across the rest of the Strawberry wilderness and the Monument Rock wilderness. To get there, head up the trail to Little Strawberry Lake from the south side of Strawberry Lake.

WASHINGTON

Washington State Capital: Olympia. **Population:** 5,685,300. **Area:** 66,582 sq. mi. **Motto:** *"Alki,"* "by and by" in Salish. **Nickname:** Evergreen State. **Flower:** Coast rhododendron. **Gem:** Petrified wood. **Tree:** Western hemlock. **Folk Song:** "Roll On, Columbia, Roll On." **Fishing Hotline:** 360-902-2500. **Shellfish Hotline:** 360-796-4601.

What is now Washington was home to only some 400 settlers when Oregonians rallied for territorial recognition in the 1840s. The indigenous nations of the coast and plains still outnumbered the newcomers when Washington was made a territory in 1853 (encompassing much of present-day Idaho and Montana). By 1863, 4000 settlers had journeyed along the Oregon Trail and the state had attained roughly its present shape. Over the 20th century, the development of the state's towns depended on the course of railroads linking the west with the east. During World War II, Seattle's resource-driven economy was transformed by the nation's need for ships and aircrafts.

On Washington's western shore, concert halls and art galleries offer cosmopolitan entertainment within easy reach of Puget Sound, its gorgeous islands, and the temperate rainforests of the Olympic Peninsula. Seattle is the home of coffee, grunge, Microsoft, scattered hilly neighborhoods, fantastic parks, and miles of waterfront. The lush San Juan Islands boast puffins, sea otters, and sea lions. Pods of orcas circle the islands, followed by pods of tourists in yachts and kayaks. East of Puget Sound, the North Cascades rise up with fury and the Columbia River flows from the Canadian border to the Pacific Ocean, interrupted by numerous dams providing the state with water and electricity.

Buses cover most of Washington, although navigating the Olympic Peninsula requires some dexterity with a patchwork of county schedules. The train from Los Angeles to Vancouver makes many stops in western Washington; another line extends from Seattle to Spokane and on to Chicago.

⬛ WASHINGTON'S HIGHLIGHTS

ROCK out at the Experience Music Project in Seattle (p. 171).

EXPLORE The micro-environments of ONP, on the Olympic Peninsula (p. 203).

BURN with envy at the North Cascades Smokejumpers Base (p. 233).

CONQUER spectacular Mt. Rainier (p. 234).

ADMIRE the work of Tacoman glass artists at the Tacoma Museum of Glass (p. 181).

SCALE the dramatic peaks of North Cascades National Park (p. 203).

SEATTLE ☎ 206

Seattle's serendipitous mix of mountain views, clean streets, espresso stands, and rainy weather proved to be the magic formula of the 1990s. Although a slowdown in the tech sector has turned some computer magnates' smiles into frowns, the setting and culture continue on in Seattle without missing a beat. The city is one of the youngest and most vibrant in the nation, and Seattle has the country's highest percentage of residents with a college degree. A nearly epidemic fixation on coffee

Washington

WASHINGTON

CANADA
USA

IDAHO

OREGON

Vancouver Island

Victoria

Sidney

Strait of Georgia

San Juan Islands

Strait of Juan de Fuca

Neah Bay

Olympic Nat'l Forest

Forks

Quinault

Olympic National Forest

Olympic Nat'l Park

Port Angeles

Port Townsend

Oak Harbor

Whidbey Island

Anacortes

Bellingham

Sedro Woolley

Mt. Vernon

Everett

Bremerton

Shelton

Montesano

Aberdeen

South Bend

Long Beach

Astoria

Cathlamet

Longview

Kelso

Vancouver

Portland

Mount Baker Nat'l Forest

North Cascades Nat'l Park

Mount Baker-Snoqualmie Nat'l Forest

Stehekin

Pasayten Wilderness

Okanogan Nat'l Forest

Okanogan Nat'l Forest

Colville Nat'l Forest

Colville National Forest

Newport

Chewelah

Colville

Tonasket

Winthrop

Twisp

Brewster

Lake Chelan

Wenatchee Nat'l Forest

Leavenworth

Wenatchee

Ellensburg

Yakima

Toppenish

Goldendale

Trout Lake

Gifford Pinchot Nat'l Forest

Mount St. Helens Nat'l Volcanic Monument

Mount Rainier Nat'l Park

Randle

Morton

Elbe

Chehalis

Centralia

Olympia

Tacoma

Bellevue

Seattle

Puget Sound

CASCADE MOUNTAINS

Columbia River

Grand Coulee

Republic

Wilbur

Davenport

Spokane

Coeur d'Alene

Moscow

Pullman

Colfax

Pomeroy

Dayton

Walla Walla

Umatilla Nat'l Forest

Lewiston

Pasco

Kennewick

Richland

Prosser

Pendleton

Columbia River

Snake River

Washtucna

Ritzville

Sprague

Moses Lake

Ephrata

Othello

Columbia River

Sidney

Stevenson

Kelso

0   60 miles

0   60 kilometers

31

20

25

395

21

155

97

20

20

5

20

101

112

101

101

109

8

9

4

101

5

12

3

405

90

2

2

97

97

12

90

504

503

14

14

141

84

84

12

395

240

26

243

28

17

174

21

2

155

97

28

17

26

14

82

82

90

26

195

270

129

3

12

90

95

has also made it one of the most caffeinated. The droves of newcomers provide an interesting contrast to the older residents who remember Seattle as a city-town, not a thriving metropolis bubbling over with young millionaires. Computer and coffee money have helped drive rents sky high in some areas, but the grungy, punk-loving street culture still prevails in others. In the end, there is a nook or cranny for almost anyone in Seattle.

The Emerald City sits on an isthmus, with mountain ranges to the east and west. Every hilltop in Seattle offers an impressive view of Mt. Olympus, Mt. Baker, and Mt. Rainier. To the west, the waters of Puget Sound glint against downtown skyscrapers and nearly spotless streets. The city's artistic landscape is as varied and exciting as its physical terrain. Opera always sells out, and the *New York Times*

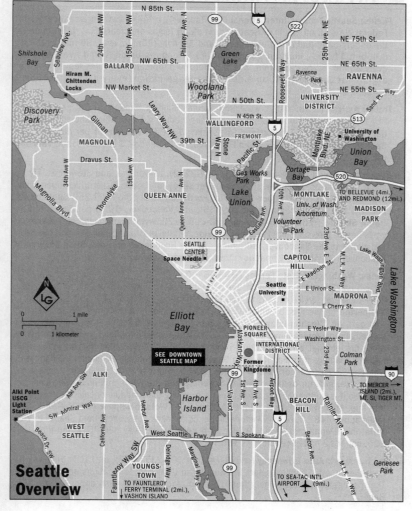

WASHINGTON

Seattle
Overview

has complained that there is more good theater in Seattle than on Broadway. When Nirvana introduced the world to their discordant sensibility, the term "grunge" and Seattle became temporarily inseparable, and the city that produced Jimi Hendrix again revitalized rock 'n' roll. Good bands thrive in grunge's wake, keeping the Seattle scene a mecca for edgy entertainment. Bill Gates of Microsoft and Howard Shultz of Starbucks have built vast and perhaps only marginally evil empires on the backs of software and coffee beans, but Seattle's residents go about their lives in a state of caffeinated bliss.

■ INTERCITY TRANSPORTATION

Flights: Seattle-Tacoma International (Sea-Tac; ☎ 431-4444; www.portseattle.org), on Federal Way, 15 mi. south of Seattle, right off **I-5** (signs are clear). Bus #194 departs the underground tunnel at University St. and 3rd Ave. (30min., every 30 min. 5:25am-8:45pm, $1.25-2, children $0.50) and #174 departs Union & 2nd Ave. (45min., every 30min. 5:25am-3:30am, $1.25-2) for the airport. These routes leave from the airport for Seattle from outside the baggage claim (every 15min. 4:45am-2:45am, $1.25-2).

Trains: Amtrak (☎ 382-4125; www.amtrak.com), King St. Station, at 3rd and Jackson St., 1 block east of Pioneer Square next to the stadiums. Ticket office and station open daily 6am-10:30pm. To: **Portland** (4 per day, $33-36); **Tacoma** (4 per day, $9-14); **Spokane** (4 per day, $41-85); **San Francisco, CA** (1 per day, $100-167); and **Vancouver, BC** (1 per day, $23-35).

Buses: Greyhound (☎ 628-5526 or 800-231-2222), at 8th Ave. and Stewart St. Try to avoid night buses, since the station can get seedy after dark. Ticket office open daily 6:30am-2:30am, station open 24 hr. To: **Portland** (11 per day, $22.25); **Spokane** (5 per day, $31.25); **Tacoma** (8 per day, $5); and **Vancouver, BC** (8 per day, $24.25. **Quick Shuttle** (☎ 604-940-4428 or 800-665-2122; www.quickcoach.com) makes 8 cross-border trips daily from Seattle (Travelodge hotel at 8th and Bell St.) and the Sea-Tac airport to the **Vancouver, BC** airport and the Holiday Inn on Howe St. in downtown Vancouver (4-4½hr.; $31 from downtown, $39 from Sea-Tac).

Ferries: Washington State Ferries (☎ 464-6400 or 888-808-7977; www.wsdot.wa.gov/ferries) has 2 terminals in Seattle. The main terminal is downtown, at Colman Dock, Pier 52. From here, service departs to **Bainbridge Island** (35min.; $5.10, $10-12 with car), **Bremerton** on the Kitsap Peninsula (1hr.; passenger-only boat 40min; $5.10, $10-12 with car), and **Vashon Island** (25min., passengers only, $7.10). From the waterfront, passenger-only ferries leave from Pier 50. The other Seattle terminal is in **Fauntleroy;** to reach the terminal, drive south on I-5 and take Exit 163A (West Seattle) down Fauntleroy Way. Sailings from Fauntleroy to **Southworth** on the Kitsap Peninsula (35min.; $4, with car $8.75); **Vashon Island** (15min; $3.30, with car $13-15.) If ferry travel is in your plans, pick up both the *Sailing Schedule* and the *Fares* pamphlet. Services are tricky, so it is worth spending a few minutes perusing the schedule or calling the toll-free info line. Most ferries leave, frequently 6am-2am. **Victoria Clipper** (☎ 800-888-2535, reservations 448-5000; www.victoriaclipper.com) takes passengers from Seattle to **Victoria** only. Departs from Pier 69 (3hr.; 2-4 per day; one-way $60-75, round-trip $99-125, under 12 half-price; bicycles $10.)

Car Transport: Auto Driveaway (☎ 878-7400 or 800-235-5052), on Pacific Highway S, near the airport. Recruits "select individuals" to drive cars to locations across the US. The management loves to hear from *Let's Go* readers. $300 cash deposit. Open M-F 8am-5pm.

■ ORIENTATION

Seattle stretches from north to south on an isthmus between **Puget Sound** to the west and **Lake Washington** to the east. The city is easily accessible by car via **I-5,** which runs north-south through the city, and by **I-90** from the east, which ends at I-5 southeast of downtown. Get to **downtown** (including **Pioneer Square, Pike Place Market,** and the **waterfront**) from I-5 by taking any of the exits from James St. to Stewart St. Take the Mercer St./Fairview Ave. exit to the **Seattle Center;** follow signs from there. The Denny Way exit leads to **Capitol Hill,** and, farther north, the 45th St. exit heads toward the **University District.** The less crowded **Rte. 99,** also called **Aurora Ave.** or the Aurora Hwy., runs parallel to I-5 and skirts the western side of downtown, with great views from the Alaskan Way Viaduct. Rte. 99 is often the better choice when driving downtown or to **Queen Anne, Fremont, Green Lake,** and the northwestern part of the city. For more detailed directions to these and other districts, see the individualized neighborhood listings under **Food** (p. 165), **Nightlife** (p. 176), and **Sights** (p. 170).

▐ LOCAL TRANSPORTATION

Even the most road-weary drivers can learn their way around the Emerald City. Street parking creates many blind pull-outs in Seattle, so be extra careful when turning onto cross roads. Downtown, **avenues** run northwest to southeast and **streets** run southwest to northeast. Outside downtown, everything is simplified: with few exceptions, avenues run north-south and streets east-west. The city is in **quadrants:** 1000 1st Ave. NW is a far walk from 1000 1st Ave. SE.

When driving in Seattle, **yield to pedestrians.** They will not look, so make sure you do. Locals drive slowly, calmly, and politely; police ticket frequently. Downtown driving can be nightmarish: parking is expensive, hills are steep, and one-way streets are ubiquitous. Read the street signs carefully, as many areas have time and hour restrictions; ticketers know them by heart. **Parking** is reasonable, plentiful, and well lit at **Pacific Place Parking** between 6th and 7th Ave. and Olive and Pine St., with hourly rates comparable to the meters and at **Seattle Center,** near the Space Needle. (☎652-0416. 24hr. $2 per hr.; $19 per day.) Park at the Needle and take the monorail to the convenient **Westlake Center** downtown. If you are driving in Seattle, prepare yourself for heavy traffic, especially on I-5, at almost any hour of the day. Public transportation on the whole in Seattle is not stellar. Inhabitants and visitors alike must settle for above-ground transportation. Although buses are large and schedules are flexible, the transit is slow and infrequent.

The **Metro ride free zone** includes most of downtown Seattle (see **Public Transportation,** below). The **Metro** buses cover King County east to North Bend and Carnation, south to Enumclaw, and north to Snohomish County, where bus #6 hooks up with **Community Transit.** This line runs to Everett, Stanwood, and into the Cascades. Bus #174 connects to Tacoma's Pierce County System at Federal Way.

Seattle is a **bicycle-friendly** city. All buses have free, easy-to-use bike racks (bike shops have sample racks on which to practice). Between 6am and 7pm, bikes may only be loaded or unloaded at stops outside the ride free zone. Check out Metro's *Bike & Ride*, available at the visitors center. For a bike map of Seattle, call **City of Seattle Bicycle Program** (☎684-7583).

Public Transportation: Metro Transit, Pass Sales and Information Office, 201 S Jackson St. (☎553-3000 or 24hr. 800-542-7876). Open M-F 9am-5pm. The bus tunnel under Pine St. and 3rd Ave. is the heart of the downtown bus system. Fares are based on a 2-zone system. **Zone 1** includes everything within the city limits (peak hours $1.50, off-peak $1.25). **Zone 2** includes everything else (peak $2, off-peak $1.25).

Ages 5-18 always $0.50. **Peak hours** in both zones are M-F 6-9am and 3-6pm. Exact fare required. Weekend day passes $2.50. Ride free daily 6am-7pm in the downtown **ride free area**, bordered by S Jackson on the south, 6th and I-5 on the east, Blanchard on the north, and the waterfront on the west. Free **transfers** can be used on any bus, including a return trip on the same bus within 2hr. Most buses are **wheelchair accessible** (info ☎ 684-2046). The **Monorail** runs from the Space Needle to Westlake Center every 15min. 9am-11pm. ($1.50, seniors $0.75, ages 5-12 $0.50.)

Taxi: Farwest Taxi (☎ 622-1717), $1.80 base, $1.80 per mi.; **Orange Cab Co.** (☎ 522-8800), $1.80 base, $1.80 per mi.

Car Rental: U Save Auto Rental, 16223 Pacific Hwy. S (☎ 242-9778). $34 per day for compacts, plus $0.22 per mi. over 100 mi. Unlimited mileage in BC and WA. Must be 21 with a major credit card. **Enterprise,** 11342 Lake City Way NE (☎ 364-3127). $36 per day for compacts, plus $0.20 per mi. over 150 mi. Their **airport location,** 15667 Pacific Hwy. S (☎ 246-1953), charges an additional 10%.

⑦ PRACTICAL INFORMATION

TOURIST AND FINANCIAL SERVICES

Tourist Information: Seattle-King County Visitors Bureau (☎ 461-5840), at 7th and Pike St., on the 1st floor of the convention center. Helpful staff doles out maps, brochures, newspapers, and Metro and ferry schedules. Open June-Oct. M-F 8:30am-5pm, Sa 10am-4pm; Nov.-May M-F 8:30am-5pm.

Outdoor Information: Seattle Parks and Recreation Department, 100 Dexter Ave. N (☎ 684-4075). Open M-F 8am-5pm for info and pamphlets on city parks. **Outdoor Recreation Information Center,** 222 Yale Ave. (☎ 470-4060), in REI (see **Equipment Rental,** below). A joint operation between the Park and Forest services, this station is able to answer any questions that might arise as you browse REI's huge collection of maps and guides. Unfortunately, the desk is not set up to sell permits. Free brochures on hiking trails. Open M-F 10:30am-7pm, Sa-Su 10am-7pm.

Equipment Rental:

REI, 222 Yale Ave. (☎ 223-1944 or 888-873-1938), near Capitol Hill. The mothership of camping supply stores rents everything from camping gear to technical mountaineering equipment (see **Outdoor Activities,** p. 178). Open M-F 10am-9pm, Sa-Su 10am-7pm.

The Bicycle Center, 4529 Sand Point Way (☎ 523-8300), near the Children's Hospital, rents mountain and hybrid bikes ($3 per hr., $15 per day; 2hr. min.). Credit card deposit required. Open M-Th 10am-8pm, F 10am-7pm, Sa 10am-6pm, Su 10am-5pm.

Gregg's Greenlake Cycle, 7007 Woodlawn Ave. NE (☎ 523-1822). Wide range of bikes conveniently close to Green Lake and Burke-Gilman bike trails ($7 per hr., $25-30 per day, $30-35 per 24hr., $120 per week). Photo ID and cash or credit card deposit required. Also rents in-line skates ($7 per hr., $20 per day, $25 per 24hr.). Overnight rentals require deposit. Open M-F 10am-9pm, Sa-Su 10am-6pm.

Currency Exchange: Thomas Cook Foreign Exchange, 400 Pine St. (☎ 682-4525), on the 3rd floor of the Westlake Shopping Center. Open M-Sa 9:30am-6pm, Su 11am-5pm. Also behind the Delta Airlines ticket counter and at other airport locations.

Travel Agencies: Council Travel, 4311 University Way (☎ 632-2448). Open M-F 10am-6pm, Sa 10am-5pm. Also at 424 Broadway Ave. E (☎ 329-4567), in Capitol Hill. Open M-F 10am-6pm, Sa 10am-5pm. **STA Travel,** 4341 University Way (☎ 633-5000; www.statravel.com), at NE 45th. Open M-F 10am-6pm, Sa 10am-5pm.

Short-term Work Opportunities: City of Seattle Personnel Department, 710 2nd Ave., 12th fl. (job hotline ☎ 684-7999, www.cityofseattle.net/jobs/).

LOCAL SERVICES

Bookstores: Elliott Bay Books, 101 S Main St. (☎624-6600), in Pioneer Sq. Vast collection with 150,000 titles. Sponsors a reading and lecture series almost every day, all year long. Most readings are weekdays at 7:30pm or weekend afternoons. Coffeehouse in the basement. Open M-F 9:30am-10pm, Sa-Su 10am-10pm.

Ticket Agencies: Ticketmaster (☎628-0888) in Westlake Center and every Tower Records store. **Ticket/ Ticket,** 401 Broadway E (☎324-2744), on the 2nd floor of the Broadway Market, sells half-price day-of-show tickets for theatres, music, clubs, cruises, tours, and more. Cash only. Sales only done in person. Open Tu-Sa noon-7pm, Su noon-6pm. Also in **Pike Place Market information booth** at 1st Ave. and Pike St. 30min. free parking in garage under Harrison St. with ticket purchase. Open Tu-Su noon-6pm.

Laundromat: Sit and Spin, 2219 4th St. (☎441-9484). A laundromat local hot spot (see **Nightlife,** p. 176). Wash $1.25, dry $0.25 per 10min. Open Su-Th 11am-midnight, F-Sa 11am-2am.

EMERGENCY AND COMMUNICATIONS

Emergency: ☎911.

Police: 810 Virginia St. (☎625-5011).

Crisis Line: ☎461-3222.

Rape Crisis: King County Sexual Assault Center (☎800-825-7273). Crisis counseling and advocacy. **Harborview Medical** (☎731-3000), **Harborview Center for Sexual and Traumatic Stress** (☎521-1800). All 24hr.

Medical Services: International District Emergency Center, 720 8th Ave. S, Ste. 100 (☎461-3235). Medics with multilingual assistance available. Clinic 9am-6pm, phone 24hr. **U.S. Health Works,** 1151 Denny Way (☎682-7418). Walk-in. 7am-6pm. **Swedish Medical Center, Providence Campus,** 500 17th Ave. (☎320-2111), for urgent care and cardiac. 24hr.

Internet Access: The Seattle Public Library, 800 Pike St. (☎386-4636; TDD 386-4697), is stashed away in a temporary building near the convention center until fall 2003, when a brand-new Rem Koolhaas building will open. A visitor's library card (must have local address) lasts 3 months ($10). One-time visitors can use Internet for free with photo ID. Open M-Th 9am-9pm, F 10:30am-6pm, Sa 9am-6pm, Su 1-5pm. **Capitol Hill Net,** 216 Broadway Ave E (☎860-6858), charges $6 per hr. 15min. free with food purchase of $1.50. *Let's Go* readers and all hostelers get 15min. free. Open M-Su 8am-midnight.

THE LOCAL STORY

WHEN BEARS THROW FISH BACK

*Part of the quintessential Seattle experience is a trip to the historic Pike Place Market. Let's Go Researcher-Writer Posy Busby spoke to **the Bear,** one of the famous Pike Place fish-throwers, in July of 2002.*

Q: Do you throw fish?
A: Yes, all day long.
Q: How long have you been working here?
A: 16 years.
Q: How many fish do you throw per day?
A: Lots.
Q: Have you ever hit someone with a fish?
A: Yes. There was the Amish woman one day. I hit her right in the forehead.
Q: What did she do?
A: Nothin', what could she do? She was Amish.
Q: Has anyone had a serious injury from a hit?
A: Nobody has died yet.
Q: What do you throw the most of here?
A: Fish.
Q: What kind?
A: Dead ones for the most part.
Q: What's a popular fish?
A: The monk fish, with its mouth open. Everybody gotta look at that one when they come in... all you gotta do is hang out and you'll have a fun experience.

Post Office: 301 Union St. (☎ 748-5417 or 800-275-8777) at 3rd Ave. downtown. Open M-F 8am-5:30pm, Sa 8am-noon. General delivery window open M-F 9am-11:20am and noon-3pm. **Postal Code:** 98101.

PUBLICATIONS

The city's major daily, the *Seattle Times* (☎ 464-2111; www.seattletimes.com), lists upcoming events in its Thursday "Datebook" section. Its major "competitor" (actually its partner), the *Seattle Post-Intelligencer*, has an award-winning sports section and great news coverage, but does not publish on Sunday. The Thursday listings of the *Seattle Weekly* (www.seattleweekly.com) are free and left-of-center. Even farther over is *The Stranger* (free), which covers music and culture, materializing Thursdays at music, coffee, and thrift shops. *The Rocket*, a bimonthly publication, relays music and entertainment info from all over the Northwest. *Arts Focus*, free at most bookstores, covers performing arts. *Seattle Arts*, published by the Seattle Arts Commission, is especially good on visual arts. Both are monthlies. The weekly *Seattle Gay News* sells on Fridays at newsstands.

▌ ACCOMMODATIONS

Seattle's hostel scene is not amazing, but there are plenty of choices and establishments to fit all types of personalities. The **Vashon Island Hostel** is probably the best bedding in the area and most certainly the most relaxing (see **Accommodations**, p. 188). **Pacific Bed and Breakfast Association** arranges B&B singles in the $50-65 range. (Info ☎ 439-7677, booking ☎ 800-684-2932; www.seattlebedandbreakfast.com. Open M-F 8am-5pm.)

DOWNTOWN

Seattle International Hostel (HI), 84 Union St. (☎ 622-5443 or 888-622-5443), at Western Ave., right by the waterfront. Take Union St. from downtown; follow signs down the stairs under the "Pike Pub & Brewery." Great location overlooking the water, but the space itself can feel like a cramped dorm on full nights. Coin laundry. Internet access $0.15 per min. 7-night max. stay in summer. Reception 24hr. Check-out 11am. No curfew. Reservations recommended. 199 beds; $22, nonmembers $25. $2 extra for bathroom in dorm room. Private rooms sleep 2-3; $54, nonmembers $60. ❶

Green Tortoise Backpacker's Hostel, 1525 2nd Ave. (☎ 340-1222; fax 623-3207), between Pike and Pine St. on the #174 or 194 bus route. A young party hostel downtown; lots of people, lots of activities. Free beer on F, free dinner on M, free breakfast daily (7am-9:30am), and free Internet access. Kitchen, library, patio, and laundry. Bring your own bedding; blanket $1 with $9 deposit. $20 cash key deposit required. Reception 24hr. Dorm beds $22 with credit card, $21 with cash; private rooms $50. ❶

Moore Hotel, 1926 2nd Ave. (☎ 448-4851 or 800-421-5508; www.moorehotel.com), at Virginia, 1 block east from Pike Place Market, next to historic Moore Theater. Built in 1905, the Moore Hotel beckons visitors with an open lobby, cavernous halls, and attentive service. Singles $49, with bath $59; doubles (1 bed) $59, with bath $68. Big room with 2 beds and bath $86. Large suites, some with kitchen, $150. ❸

Commodore Hotel, 2013 2nd Ave. (☎ 448-8868), at Virginia. Pleasant decor and only a few blocks from the waterfront. Front desk open 24hr., but no visitors past 8pm. Singles $59, with bath $69; 2 beds and bath $79. ❸

West Coast Vance Hotel, 620 Steward St. (☎ 441-8612). Built in 1926, the West Coast Vance offers charming rooms starting at $119. The hotel is located within walking distance from Pike Place Market as well as the 5th Ave. shopping district. ❺

OUTSIDE DOWNTOWN

For inexpensive motels farther from downtown, drive north on Hwy. 99 (Aurora Ave.) or take bus #26 to the neighborhood of Fremont. Budget chain motels like the **Nites Inn ❸**, 11746 Aurora Ave. N, line the highway north of the Aurora bridge. (☎365-3216. Singles from $42; doubles $46.) Look for AAA approval ratings.

Corona Apartments, 715 2nd Ave. N (☎856-8630), on the south slope of Queen Anne Hill, 3 blocks east from the Space Needle and the Seattle Center. Long-term accommodations for travelers. Backyard, kitchen, garden, and laundry. Applications available at the Green Tortoise Hostel (allow a few days for processing). Single studios from $495 per month (3-month min. stay).

The College Inn, 4000 University Way NE (☎633-4441; www.collegeinnseattle.com), at 40th St. NE. Quiet place near UW campus and its youthful environs. This European-style inn offers charming rooms with classy brass fixtures. All rooms share bathrooms. Free continental breakfast. Singles from $45; doubles $55-75. Credit card required. ❸

🍴 FOOD

Although Seattleites appear to subsist solely on espresso and steamed milk, they do occasionally eat. The finest fish, produce, and baked goods are at **Pike Place Market.** The **University District** supports inexpensive and international cuisine. The **Chinatown/International District** offers tons of rice, pounds of fresh fish, and enough veggies to keep your mother happy, all at ridiculously low prices. **Puget Sound Consumer Coops (PCCs)** are local health food markets at 7504 Aurora Ave. N (☎525-3586), in Green Lake, and at 6514 40th NE (☎526-7661), in the Ravenna District north of the university. Capitol Hill, the U District, and Fremont close main thoroughfares on summer Saturdays for **farmers markets.**

PIKE PLACE MARKET AND DOWNTOWN

In 1907, angry citizens demanded the elimination of the middle-man and local farmers began selling produce by the waterfront, creating the Pike Place Market. Business thrived until an enormous fire burned the building in 1941. The early 1980s heralded a Pike Place renaissance, and today thousands of tourists mob the market daily. (Open M-Sa 9am-6pm, Su 11am-5pm. Produce and fish open earlier; restaurants and lounges close later.) In the **Main Arcade,** on the west side of Pike St., fishmongers compete for audiences as they hurl fish from shelves to scales. The market's restaurants boast stellar views of the sound.

An **information booth** faces the bike rack by the Main Arcade, at 1st Ave. and Pike St. (☎461-5800. Open Tu-Su 10am-noon.) Restaurants south of Pike Place cater mostly to suits on lunch breaks and tourists, but there are many sandwich and pastry shops covering downtown.

Piroshki, Piroshki, 1908 Pike St. (☎441-6068), across the street from the front entrance of the market building. The *Russian Piroshki* is a croissant-like dough baked around sausages, mushrooms, cheeses, salmon, or apples doused in cinnamon. Watch the *piroshki* process in progress while awaiting your order. Open daily 8am-7pm. ❶

Soundview Cafe (☎623-5700), on the mezzanine in the Pike Place Main Arcade. The sandwich-and-salad bar is a good place to enjoy a view of Puget Sound. Breakfast and lunch $3-6. Open M-F 8am-5pm, Sa 8am-5:30pm, Su 9am-3pm. ❶

Garlic Tree, 94 Stewart St. (☎441-5681), 1 block up from Pike Place Market. The smell will drag you in. Loads of fabulous veggie, chicken, and seafood stir-fry ($7-9). Try the tofu chapche ($6.95). Open M 11am-8pm, Tu-Th 11am-9pm, F-Sa 11am-10pm. ❷

Emmett Watson's Oyster Bar, 1916 Pike Place (☎448-7721). Oyster Bar Special—2 oysters, 3 shrimp, bread, and chowder—is $6.25. Shelves of bottles show off the selection of brews. Open M-Th 11:30am-8pm. F-Sa 11:30am-9pm. Su 11:30am-6pm. ❷

THE WATERFRONT

Budget eaters, steer clear of Pioneer Square: instead, take a picnic to **Waterfall Garden,** on the corner of S Main St. and 2nd Ave. S. The garden sports tables and chairs and a man-made waterfall that masks traffic outside. (Open daily 8am-6pm.)

Mae Phim Thai Restaurant, 94 Columbia St. (☎624-2979), a few blocks north of Pioneer Sq. between 1st Ave. and Alaskan Way. Slews of pad thai junkies crowd in for cheap, delicious Thai cuisine. All dishes $5.50. Open M-F 11am-7pm, Sa noon-7pm. ❷

Ivar's Fish Bar, Pier 54 (☎467-8063), north of the square. A fast-food window that serves the definitive Seattle clam chowder ($2). Clam and chips ($4.99). Open M-Th and Su 11am-12pm, F-Sa 11am-2am. ❶ For a slightly more upscale seafood meal, check out **Ivar's Restaurant** next door (same hours). ❸

INTERNATIONAL DISTRICT

Along King and Jackson St., between 5th and 8th Ave. east of the Kingdome, Seattle's International District is packed with great eateries. Competition keeps prices low and quality high, and unassuming facades front fabulous food. Lunch specials are particularly appealing, and the long lines move quickly.

🔳 **Uwajimaya,** 600 5th Ave. S (☎624-6248). The Uwajimaya Center is a full city block of groceries, gifts, videos, and CDs; it's the largest Japanese department store in the Northwest! There is even a food court, plying Korean BBQ and Taiwanese-style baked goods. Open M-Sa 9am-11pm. ❷

Tai Tung, 655 S King St. (☎622-7372). Select authentic Chinese and Mandarin cuisine from one of the largest menus around. Grab a bite at the bar, where menus are plastered on the wall. Entrees $5-12. Open Su-Th 10am-11:30pm, F-Sa 10am-2am. ❷

Ho Ho Seafood Restaurant, 653 S Weller St. (☎382-9671). Generous portions of tank-fresh seafood. Stuffed fish hang from the ceilings. Lunch $5-7 (until 4pm), dinner $7-12. Open Su-Th 11am-1am, F-Sa 11am-3am. ❷

CAPITOL HILL

With bronze dance-steps on the sidewalks and neon storefronts, **Broadway** is a land of espresso houses, imaginative shops, elegant clubs, and plenty of eats. Although not the cheapest place to eat, it has a great variety of cuisine options catering to most budgets and taste buds. Bus #7 runs along Broadway; bus #10 runs through Capitol Hill along more sedate **15th St.** Free parking is behind the reservoir at Broadway Field, on 11th Ave.

🔳 **Bimbo's Bitchin' Burrito Kitchen,** 506 E Pine (☎329-9978). The name explains it, and the decorations (fake palm trees and lots of plastic) prove it. Walk right on through the door to the **Cha Cha,** a similarly-decorated bar (tequila shots $3.50). Spicy Bimbo's burrito $4.25. Open M-Th noon-11pm, F-Sa noon-2am, Su 2-10pm. ❶

Ristorante Machiavelli, 1215 Pine St. (☎621-7941), right across the street from Bauhaus (see **Cafes,** below). A small Italian place that locals fiercely love. Pasta $8-10. Open M-Sa 5-11pm. ❷

HaNa, 219 Broadway Ave. E (☎328-1187). Packed quarters testify to the popularity of the sushi here. Lunch sushi combo platter with rice and soup $7.25. Dinner $9-10. Open M-Sa 11am-10pm, Su 4-10pm. ❷

Honey Hole Sandwiches, 703 E Pike (☎ 709-1399). The primary colors and veggie-filled sandwiches make you feel healthy and happy. The hummus-loaded "Daytripper" is a treat ($5.50). Open M-Sa 10am-11pm, Su 10am-5pm. ❶

UNIVERSITY DISTRICT

The neighborhood around the immense University of Washington ("U-Dub"), north of downtown between Union Bay and Portage Bay, supports funky shops, international restaurants, and yes, coffeehouses. The best of each lies within a few blocks of University Way, known as "Th' Ave." Restaurants run rampant here. The Ave. supports everything from Denny's to bubble tea. Think student budget: this is probably the cheapest place to eat in the city. On Saturdays (June-Oct.) a **farmers market** at 50th and University Way NE sells fresh fruit and veggies to eager students. To get there, take Exit 169 off I-5 N, or take one of buses #70-74 from downtown, or #7 or 9 from Capitol Hill. (Open 9am-2pm).

Flowers, 4247 University Way NE (☎ 633-1903). This 20s landmark was a flower shop; now, the mirrored ceiling tastefully reflects an all-you-can-eat vegetarian buffet ($7.50). Great daily drink specials: $2 tequila shots W, $3 well sours Th, $3 margaritas Sa. Open M-Sa 11am-2am, Su 11am-midnight. ❶

Neelam's, 4735 University Way NE (☎ 523-5275), serves up the best authentic Indian cuisine in the University District, and the price is right. Open for lunch (buffet $5.95) daily 11:30am-3pm, dinner Su-Th 5pm-10pm, F-Sa 5pm-10:30pm. ❷

Araya's Vegan Thai Cuisine, 4732 University Way NE (524-4332). Consistently rated among the top vegan restaurants in Seattle, Araya's will satisfy any vegetarian or vegan desire. Lunch buffet ($5.99) 11:30am-3:30pm. Open M-Th 11:30am-9pm, F-Sa 11:30am-9:30pm, Su 5pm-9pm. ❷

🄲 CAFES

The coffee bean is Seattle's first love. One cannot walk a single block without passing a Starbuck's or Tully's. But if you're looking for a more unique experience, check out the funky cafes on Capitol Hill or in the University District.

CAPITOL HILL

Bauhaus, 301 E Pine St. (☎ 625-1600). The Reading Goddess looks from above the towering bookshelves, protects patrons, and oversees service of drip coffee ($1) or Kool-Aid ($1). Open M-F 7am-1am, Sa-Su 8am-1am.

The Globe Cafe, 1531 14th Ave. (☎ 324-8815). Seattle's next literary renaissance is brewing here. Quotes overheard at the Globe are plastered on the tables. Fabulous all-vegan menu. Stir-fry tofu $4-6. Open Tu-Su 7am-4pm.

UNIVERSITY DISTRICT

Espresso Roma, 4201 University Way NE (☎ 632-6001). A pleasant patio, and quasi-former-warehouse interior result in spacious tables with an open air feel. The Ave.'s cheapest coffee. Mocha $1.95. Internet access $0.15 per min. After 7pm, get a grande for the price of a tall. Open M-F 7am-10pm, Sa-Su 8am-10pm.

Ugly Mug, 1309 43rd St. (☎ 547-3219), off University Way. Off-beat in a 10,000 Maniacs-thrift store sort of way. Eclectic chair collection is quite comfortable. Wide sandwich selection (turkey foccaccia $4). Open M-F 7:30am-6pm, Sa and Su 9am-6pm.

Gingko Tea, 4343 University Way NE (☎ 632-7298). If you dig tea over coffee, you'll find a niche at Gingko's. Classical music supplies the background; wood furniture and floral cushions provide the foreground. 5 types of chai ($2.55). Bubble tea $2.45. Open M-Th 10:30am-11pm, F-Sa 10:30am-12pm, Su 11am-10pm.

WASHINGTON

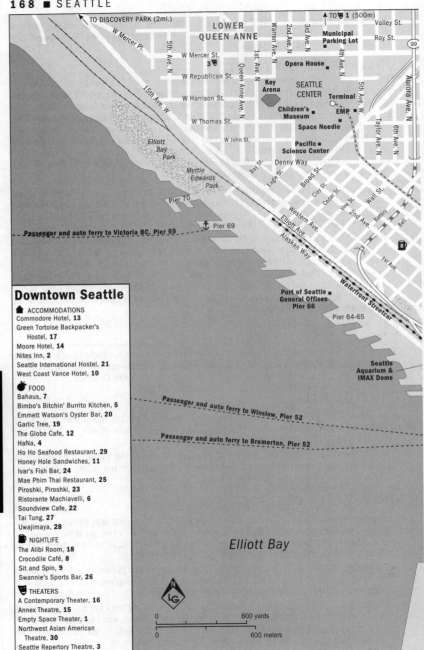

TO DISCOVERY PARK (2mi.)

W Mercer Pl.

LOWER QUEEN ANNE

TO 1 (500m)

Valley St.
Roy St.

W Mercer St.
3
W Republican St.
W Harrison St.
W Thomas St.
W John St.

5th Ave. N
1st Ave. N
Warren Ave. N
2nd Ave. N
3rd Ave. N
4th Ave. N
Queen Anne Ave. N

Municipal Parking Lot

99

Opera House

Key Arena

SEATTLE CENTER

Terminal

Children's Museum
Space Needle
EMP

5th Ave. W
Taylor Ave. N
6th Ave. N
Aurora Ave. N

Pacific Science Center

Denny Way

15th Ave. W

Elliott Bay Park

Myrtle Edwards Park

Bay St.
Eagle St.
Broad St.
Clay St.
Cedar St.
Vine St.
2nd Ave.
Wall St.
Battery
Bell

Pier 70

Western Ave.

Pier 69

Passenger and auto ferry to Victoria BC, Pier 69

Elliott Ave.

Alaskan Way

1st Ave.

Waterfront Streetcar

8

Downtown Seattle

ACCOMMODATIONS
Commodore Hotel, **13**
Green Tortoise Backpacker's Hostel, **17**
Moore Hotel, **14**
Nites Inn, **2**
Seattle International Hostel, **21**
West Coast Vance Hotel, **10**

FOOD
Bahaus, **7**
Bimbo's Bitchin' Burrito Kitchen, **5**
Emmett Watson's Oyster Bar, **20**
Garlic Tree, **19**
The Globe Cafe, **12**
HaNa, **4**
Ho Ho Seafood Restaurant, **29**
Honey Hole Sandwiches, **11**
Ivar's Fish Bar, **24**
Mae Phim Thai Restaurant, **25**
Piroshki, Piroshki, **23**
Ristorante Machiavelli, **6**
Soundview Cafe, **22**
Tai Tung, **27**
Uwajimaya, **28**

NIGHTLIFE
The Alibi Room, **18**
Crocodile Café, **8**
Sit and Spin, **9**
Swannie's Sports Bar, **26**

THEATERS
A Contemporary Theater, **16**
Annex Theatre, **15**
Empty Space Theater, **1**
Northwest Asian American Theatre, **30**
Seattle Repertory Theatre, **3**

Port of Seattle General Offices
Pier 66

Pier 64-65

Seattle Aquarium & IMAX Dome

Passenger and auto ferry to Winslow, Pier 52

Passenger and auto ferry to Bremerton, Pier 52

Elliott Bay

N

0   600 yards
0   600 meters

WASHINGTON

↑ TO **2**
(5mi.)

TO LAKE UNION & UNIVERSITY DISTRICT ↑
(3mi.), VOLUNTEER PARK (.5mi.)

E Roy St.

Mercer St.

Republican St.

Harrison St.

CAPITOL HILL

E Harrison St.

E Thomas St.

John St.

*Denny
Park*

Denny Way

E John St.

**REI/National
Park Information**

E Denny Way

E Howell St.

E Howell St.

Monorail

E Olive St.

E Olive St.

BELLTOWN

Greyhound

*Broadway
Playfield*

E Pine St.

E Pine St.

Olive Way

Pine St.

E Pike St.

E Union St.

Seattle Public Library

**State Convention
and Trade Center**

E Union St.

E Spring St.

**FIRST
HILL**

**Seattle
University**

E Marion St.

**PIKE PLACE
MARKET**

**Virginia Mason
Medical Center**

**Swedish Medical
Center**

E Columbia St.

E Cherry St.

*Water-
front
Park*

**Seattle
Art Museum**

E Jefferson St.

Pier 56

Pier 54

Columbia Tower

E. Terrace St.

Alder St.

**Harborview
Medical
Center**

E Spruce St.

E Fir St.

**Washington
State Ferry
Terminal**

**Underground
Tours**

**PIONEER
SQUARE**

**Smith
Tower**

Yesler Way

E Yesler Way

Pier 48

**Klondike Gold Rush
National History Museum**

S Washington St.

S Main St.

**Eliott Bay
Books**

**King Street
Station**

**Union
Station**

S Jackson St.

Pier 46

**Wing Luke
Asian American Museum**

S King St.

S King St.

S Weller St.

S Weller St.

**INTERNATIONAL
DISTRICT**

S Dearborn St.

S Lane St.

TO **90**
MERCER
ISLAND

Charles St.

S Dearborn St.

S Royal Brougham Way

WASHINGTON

◉ SIGHTS AND FESTIVALS

It takes only three frenetic days to get a decent look at most of the city's major sights, since most are within walking distance of one another or the Metro's ride free zone (see p. 161). Seattle taxpayers spend more per capita on the arts than any other Americans, and the investment pays off in unparalleled public art installations throughout the city (self-guided tours begin at the visitors center), and plentiful galleries. The investments of Seattle-based millionaires have brought startlingly new and bold architecture in the Experience Music Project and International Fountain. Outside cosmopolitan downtown, Seattle boasts over 300 areas of well-watered greenery (see **Waterways and Parks,** p. 178).

DOWNTOWN

SEATTLE ART MUSEUM. Housed in a grandiose building designed by Philadelphia architect and father of Postmodernism Robert Venturi, the SAM balances special exhibits with the region's largest collection of African, Native American, and Asian art and an eclectic bunch of contemporary western painting and sculpture. Call for info on special musical shows, films, and lectures. Admission is also good for the **Seattle Asian Art Museum** (a branch housed in the museum's former building; see p. 172) for a week. *(100 University Way, near 1st Ave. Recording ☎ 654-3100, person 654-3255, or TDD 654-3137. Open Tu-Su 10am-5pm. Free tours 1 and 2pm, as well as several later in the day. $10, students and seniors $7, under 12 free; first Th of the month free.)*

SEATTLE ART MUSEUM GALLERY. Inside the Museum Plaza Building at 1st Ave., the free **Seattle Art Museum Gallery** displays and sells work by local artists. *(☎ 654-3176. Open M-Sa 11am-5pm.)*

THE WATERFRONT

The **Pike Place Hillclimb** descends from the south end of Pike Place Market past chic shops and ethnic restaurants to the Alaskan Way and waterfront. (An elevator is available.) The waterfront is lined with vendors and people; needless to say, you will not be lonely in the harbor.

▓THE SEATTLE AQUARIUM. The aquarium's star attraction is a huge underwater dome, but harbor seals, fur seals, otters, and plenty of fish don't disappoint, either. Touch tanks and costumes delight kids. A million-dollar salmon exhibit and ladder teaches about the state's favorite fish. Feedings occur throughout the day and shouldn't be missed. Next door, the **IMAX Dome** cranks out Imax films, many of them focusing on natural events or habitats. *(Pier 59, near Union St. ☎ 386-4320, TDD 386-4322. Open daily 9:30am-8pm; last admission 1hr. before closing. $9.75, seniors $8.75, ages 6-18 $7, ages 3-5 $5. IMAX Dome ☎ 622-1868. Films daily 10am-10pm. $7, seniors $6.50, ages 6-18 $6. Aquarium and IMAX Dome combo ticket $15.25, seniors and ages 13-18 $14.25, ages 6-13 $11.75, ages 3-5 $5.)*

THE SEATTLE CENTER

The 1962 World's Fair demanded a Seattle Center to herald the city of the future. Now the Center houses everything from carnival rides to ballet, although Seattle residents generally leave the Center to tourists and suburbanites. The Center is bordered by Denny Way, W Mercer St., 1st Ave., and 5th Ave., and has eight gates, each with a model of the Center and a map of its facilities. It is accessible via a short **monorail** which departs from the 3rd floor of the Westlake Center. The center's anchor point is the Center House, which holds a food court, stage, and **Information Desk.** A brand-new International Fountain squirts water 20 ft. in the air from all angles off its silver, semispherical base. The grass around it is a wonderful place to sit and relax.

WASHINGTON

(Monorail: every 15min. M-F 7:30am-11pm, Sa-Su 9am-11pm. $1.50, seniors $0.75, ages 5-12 $0.50. Info Desk: open daily 11am-6pm. For info about special events and permanent attractions, call ☎ 684-8582 (recorded info) or 684-7200 for a real live person.)

■ **EXPERIENCE MUSIC PROJECT (EMP).** Undoubtedly the biggest and best attraction at the Seattle Center is the new, futuristic, abstract, and technologically brilliant Experience Music Project. The museum is the brainchild of Seattle billionaire Paul Allen, who originally wanted to create a shrine to worship his music idol Jimi Hendrix. But nothing this man does is small. Splash together the technological sophistication and foresight of Microsoft, dozens of ethnomusicologists and multimedia specialists, a collection of musical artifacts topping 80,000, the world-renowned architect Frank Gehry, and enough money to make the national debt appear small (fine, it was only $350 million), and you guessed it, you have the rock 'n' roll museum of the future. The building alone—consisting of sheet metal molded into abstract curves and then acid-dyed gold, silver, purple, light-blue, and red—is enough to make the average person gasp for breath. Walk in and strap on your personal computer guide (MEG) that allows you to interact with the exhibits. Hear clips from Hendrix's famous "Star Spangled Banner" as you look at the remnants of the guitar he smashed on a London stage. Move into the Sound Lab and test your own skills on guitars, drums, and keyboards linked to computer teaching devices and cushioned in state-of-the art sound rooms. When you are ready, step over to On Stage, a first-class karaoke-gone-haywire, and blast your tunes in front of a virtual audience. Expect to spend several hours testing your creativity, jamming to punk/hip-hop/blues/folk, and much, much more—in fact, locals tend to make a day out of it, using readmission to go in and out several times. Unfortunately this much to do does come with a hefty price tag. *(325 Fifth St. at Seattle Center. From I-5, take Exit 167 and follow signs to Seattle Center. Bus #3, 4, or 15. ☎ 367-5483 or 877-367-5483; TDD 770-2771; www.emplive.com. Open in summer daily 9am-11pm; winter Su-Th 9am-6pm, F-Sa 9am-9pm. $20, seniors and ages 13-17 $16, children $15. Free live music Tu-Sa in the lounge; national acts perform for a price almost every F and Sa in the Sky Church.)*

SPACE NEEDLE. The Space Needle was built in 1962 for the Seattle World's Fair. When this 607 ft. rotating building was constructed it was hailed as futuristic and daring. Today, the EMP has stolen part of the Needle's glory, but the Space Needle is still recognized internationally as a symbol of Seattle. The Needle provides a great view (on a clear day) and an invaluable landmark for the disoriented. The elevator ride itself is a show—operators are hired for their unique talents. The needle houses an observation tower and a high-end 360° rotating restaurant. *(☎ 905-2100. $12, seniors $10, ages 5-12 $5.)*

PACIFIC SCIENCE CENTER. The get-down-and-dirty approach of this museum ropes kids into loving to learn. Ride a high-rail bike, tread water in a giant hamster wheel, or play virtual basketball. The tropical butterfly garden is fantastic and the Center also houses a **laserium** that quakes to rock as well as two **IMAX theaters.** *(200 2nd Ave. N. Monorail or bus #1, 2, 3, 4, 6, 8, 19, 24. ☎ 443-2001; www.pacsci.org. Exhibits open in summer daily 10am-6pm; winter Tu-F 10am-5pm, Sa-Su 10am-6pm. $9, seniors and ages 3-13 $6.50, under 3 free. Laserium ☎ 443-2850. Laser shows nights Th $5, F-Su $7.50, matinee $2.50. IMAX ☎ 443-4629. Shows daily from 10am-7pm. $7.50, seniors or ages 3-13 $6.50. Various combo tickets are sold, ranging from $12.50-24.50 for adults.)*

PIONEER SQUARE AND ENVIRONS

From the waterfront or downtown, it's just a few blocks south to historic **Pioneer Square,** centered around Yesler Way and 2nd Ave., home of the first Seattleites. The 19th-century buildings, restored in the 1970s and now home to chic shops and

WASHINGTON

trendy pubs, retain their historical intrigue. Pioneer Square is extra busy on game day as baseball moms and dads walk their children to Safeco Field Baseball Park to see the Mariners in action.

UNDERGROUND TOUR. Originally, downtown stood 12 ft. lower than it does today. The tour guides visitors through the subterranean city of old. Be prepared for lots of company, comedy, and toilet jokes. Tours depart from Doc Maynard's Pub, 610 1st Ave. "Doc" Maynard, a charismatic and colorful early resident, gave a plot of land here to one Henry Yesler to build a steam-powered lumber mill. The logs dragged to the mill's front door earned the street its nickname, **Skid Row,** and the smell of the oil used to lubricate the slide was so overwhelming that the self-respecting Seattleites of the day left the neighborhood to gamblers and prostitutes. (☎ 682-4646 or 888-608-6337; www.undergroundtour.com. 1½hr. tours daily, roughly hourly 10am-6pm. $9, seniors and students ages 13-17 $7, children $5. Cash only, AAA and HI 10% discount. No reservations—arrive early on weekends.)

THE INTERNATIONAL DISTRICT/CHINATOWN

Seattle's **International District/Chinatown** is three blocks east of Pioneer Square, up Jackson on King St.

▨ **WING LUKE MEMORIAL MUSEUM.** This hole-in-the-wall gives a thorough description of life in an Asian-American community, investigates different Asian nationalities in Seattle, and shows work by local Asian artists. Special exhibits add even more to the tight space. The museum also hands out the helpful *Walking Tour of the International District.* (407 7th Ave. S ☎ 623-5124. Open Tu-F 11am-4:30pm, Sa-Su noon-4pm. $4, seniors and students $3, ages 5-12 $2. Free 1st Th of the month.)

▨ **SEATTLE ASIAN ART MUSEUM.** What do you do when you have too much good art to exhibit all at once? Open a second museum; which is just what SAM did, creating a wonderful stand-on-its-own attraction. The collection is particularly strong in Chinese art, but most of East Asia is admirably represented. (In Volunteer Park, just beyond the water tower. ☎ 654-3100. Open Tu-Su 10am-5pm, Th 10am-9pm. $3, under 12 free; free with SAM ticket from the previous 7 days; SAAM ticket good for $3 discount at SAM.)

▨ **UNIVERSITY OF WASHINGTON ARBORETUM.** The Arboretum nurtures over 4000 species of trees, shrubs, and flowers, and maintains superb trails. Tours depart the **Graham Visitor Center,** at the southern end of the arboretum on Lake Washington Blvd. (10 blocks east of Volunteer Park. Bus #11 from downtown. ☎ 543-8800. Open daily sunrise to sunset, visitors center 10am-4pm. Free tours Sa and Su at 1pm.)

PUBLIC ART. Landmarks of the International District include the abstract Tsutakawa sculpture (corner of Maynard and Jackson), and the gigantic dragon mural and red-and-green pagoda in Hing Hay Park (S King and Maynard St.). Although you will not find many trees in the park, the pagoda provides a nice respite from the sun (or rain).

VOLUNTEER PARK. Although it is unsafe (and closed) at night, the park is a popular afternoon destination. The **outdoor stage** often hosts free performances on summer Sundays. Scale the **water tower** at the 14th Ave. entrance for a stunning 360° panorama of the city and the Olympic Range. The **glass conservatory** houses dazzling orchids. (Between 11th and 15th Ave. at E Ward St., north of Broadway. Open daily in summer 10am-7pm; winter 10am-4pm; Free.)

UNIVERSITY DISTRICT, FREMONT, AND BALLARD

The northern districts of Seattle include neighborhoods that seem to be entirely at odds with each other, and yet somehow eek out a peaceful co-existence. The

University district is a young and multi-cultural scene revolving around the main drag "The Ave." Fremont is a small community, busy with plans of secession from the nation. Scandinavians have concentrated in Ballard.

HENRY ART GALLERY. Specializing in modern and contemporary, the Henry reflects its curators' enthusiasm with unconventional installations and rarely-seen artists. In 2003, check out contemporary art from Mexico's past decade, including Frida Kahlo and Diego Rivera (Oct.-Jan.), and "Out of Site: Fictional Architectural Spaces" (Nov.-Feb.). *(Located at the intersection of 41st NE and 15th NE Ave.* ☎ *616-9894; www.henryart.org. Open Tu-Su 11am-5pm, Th 11am-8pm. $6, seniors $4.50, all students free. Free Th after 5pm.)*

THOMAS BURKE MUSEUM OF NATURAL HISTORY AND CULTURE. Savor the chance to see the only dinosaur bones on display in Washington and a superb collection on Pacific Rim cultures. You will enjoy kid-friendly explanations of the natural history of Washington's formation. Across the street, the astronomy department's old stone **observatory** is open to the public. *(45th St. NE and 17th Ave. NE. In the northwest corner of the U Washington campus.* ☎ *543-5590; observatory* ☎ *543-0126. www.washington.edu/burkemuseum. Open daily 10am-5pm and until 8pm on Th. $6.50, seniors and students $3, under 5 free. Special exhibits occasionally more.)*

FREMONT. This area is home to residents who pride themselves on their love of art and antiques, and the liberal atmosphere of their self-declared "center of the world" under Rte. 99. Twice in the past 10 years Fremont has applied to secede from the United States. A statue entitled **"Waiting for the Inner-City Urban"** laments the loss of the neighborhood's public transportation to downtown. The **immense troll** beneath the Aurora Bridge on 35th St. grasps a Volkswagen Bug with a confounded expression. Some say kicking the bug's tire brings good luck; others say it hurts the foot. A flamin' **Vladimir Lenin** resides at the corner of N 36th and N Fremont Pl.; this work from the former Soviet Union will be around until it's bought by a permanent collection, presumably of Soviet artwork.

NORDIC HERITAGE MUSEUM. Just east of the U District, the primarily Scandinavian neighborhood of **Ballard** offers a wide variety of Scandinavian eateries and shops along Market St. The museum presents realistic exhibits on the history of Nordic immigration and influence in the US. Stumble over cobblestones in old Copenhagen, or visit the slums of New York City that turned photographer and Danish immigrant Jacob Riis into an important social reformer. The museum hosts a **Viking festival** (☎ 789-5708) the weekend after the 4th of July and a series of **Nordic concerts** by national and international musicians throughout the year. *(3014 NW 67th St. Bus #17 from downtown or bus #44 from the U District, transferring to #17 at 24th and Market.* ☎ *789-5707. Open Tu-Sa 10am-4pm, Su noon-4pm. $4, seniors and students $3, ages 6-18 $2.)*

ANNUAL EVENTS

Pick up a copy of the visitors center's *Calendar of Events*, published every season, for event coupons and an exact listing of innumerable area happenings. The first Thursday evening of each month, the art community sponsors **First Thursday,** a free and well-attended gallery walk. Watch for **street fairs** in the University District during mid- to late May, at Pike Place Market over Memorial Day weekend, and in Fremont in mid-June. The International District holds its annual two-day bash in mid-July, featuring arts and crafts booths, East Asian and Pacific food booths, and presentations by a range of groups from the Radical Women/Freedom Socialist Party to the Girl Scouts. For more info, call **Chinatown Discovery** (☎ 382-1197), or write P.O. Box 3406, Seattle 98114.

Puget Sound's yachting season begins in May. **Maritime Week,** during the third week of May, and the **Shilshole Boats Afloat Show** (☎ 634-0911), in August, give area boaters a chance to show off their crafts. Over the 4th of July weekend, the Center for Wooden Boats sponsors the free **Wooden Boat Show** (☎ 382-2628) on Lake Union. Blue blazers and deck shoes are *de rigeur.* Size up the entrants (over 100 wooden boats), then watch a demonstration of boat-building skills. The year-end blow-out is the **Quick and Daring Boatbuilding Contest,** when hopefuls try to build and sail wooden boats of their own design, using a limited kit of tools and materials. Plenty of music, food, and alcohol make the sailing smooth.

Opening Day (☎ 325-1000), 1st Sa in May. A celebration of spring, water, and boats. Highlight is the Montlake Cut parade of yachts and the Windermere Cup crew races. Free.

Northwest Folklife Festival (☎ 684-7300), on Memorial Day weekend. One of Seattle's most notable events, held at the Seattle Center. Dozens of booths, artists, musicians, and dancers celebrate the area's heritage. $5 suggested donation.

Bite of Seattle (☎ 232-2982), in mid-July. Bite size to full meals from free to $8. Decide for yourself what is the best of Seattle. Free.

Seattle Seafair (☎ 728-0123; www.seafair.com), spread over 4 weeks beginning in early July. The biggest, baddest festival of them all. Each neighborhood contributes with street fairs, parades large and small, balloon races, musical entertainment, and a seafood orgy. Major city wide torch run culminates the event.

Bumbershoot (☎ 281-7788; www.bumbershoot.org), over Labor Day weekend. A massive 4-day arts festival that caps off the summer, held in the Seattle Center. Attracts big-name rock bands, street musicians, and a young, exuberant crowd. 4 days $48-52; 2 days $28-34; 1 day $15-20. Tickets are cheaper if you buy them in advance. Additional tickets needed for certain big-name concerts or events. Prices subject to change.

🎵 ENTERTAINMENT

Seattle has one of the world's most famous underground music scenes and the third-largest theater community in the US (second to New York and Chicago), and supports performance in all sorts of venues, from bars to bakeries. The big performance houses regularly sell half-price tickets and alternative theaters offer high-quality drama at downright low prices. The free **Out to Lunch** series (☎ 623-0340) brings everything from reggae to folk dancing to downtown parks, squares, and office buildings during summer (June-Sept., M-F). The **Seattle Public Library** screens free films as part of the program and hosts daily poetry readings.

MUSIC AND DANCE

The **Seattle Opera** performs favorites from August to May. In October 2003, the Opera House will re-open after renovations (until then all Opera House performances will be in the **Mercer Arts Arena**). Buffs should reserve well in advance, although rush tickets are sometimes available. (☎ 389-7676; www.seattleopera.org. Students and seniors can get half-price tickets 1½hr. before the performance. Open M-F 9am-5pm; tickets from $35.) The **Pacific Northwest Ballet** performs at the Opera House (Sept.-June). In 2003, look for the *Merry Widow* (Sept.-Oct.), *Russian Nights* (Jan.-Feb.), and *Sleeping Beauty* (May). (☎ 441-2424. Half-price rush tickets available to students and seniors 30min. before showtime. Tickets from $15.) The **Seattle Symphony** performs in the new Benaroya Hall, 200 University St. at 3rd Ave., from September to June. (☎ 212-4700, tickets 215-4747; www.seattlesymphony.org. Ticket office open M-F 10am-6pm, Sa 1-6pm. Tickets from $15, most from $25-39; seniors half-price; students (day of show) $10.) Even if you won't be hearing the symphony, drop by the new concert hall to take in Chihuly glass chandeliers and a Rauchenberg mural. (☎215-4895. Tours M-F noon and 1pm.) Free organ concerts bring out large crowds on the 1st Monday of the month at 12:30pm as well. The **University of Washington** offers its own program of student recitals and concerts by visiting artists. The **World Series** showcases dance, theater and chamber music (tickets $25-40). Some lectures and dances are much cheaper ($5-10). Contact the Meany Hall box office, 4001 University Way. Half-price student rush tickets are available half an hour before show at the box office. (☎543-4880. Open Oct.-May M-F 10am-6pm; summer M-F 10:30am-4:30pm.)

THEATER

The city hosts an exciting array of first-run plays and alternative works, particularly by talented amateur groups. Rush tickets are often available at nearly half price on the day of the show (cash only) from **Ticket/Ticket** (see p. 163).

■ **The Empty Space Theatre,** 3509 Fremont Ave. N (☎547-7500; www.emptyspace.org), 1½ blocks north of the Fremont Bridge. Comedies in the small space attract droves. Season runs Oct. to early July. Tickets $20-30. Under 25 $10 and previews (first 4 shows of a run) $22. Half-price tickets 30min. before curtain. Box office open on show days Tu-Su noon-5pm, Tu-F 12am-5pm non-show days.

Seattle Repertory Theater, 155 Mercer St. (☎443-2222; www.seattlerep.org), at the wonderful Bagley Wright Theater in the Seattle Center. Contemporary and classic winter productions (and Shakespeare). Tickets $15-45 (cheaper on weekdays), seniors $32, under 25 $10. Rush tickets 30min. before curtain $20. Box office open daily noon-8pm during season (Sept.-June).

A Contemporary Theater (ACT), 700 Union St. (☎292-7676). Summer season (April-Nov.) of off-beat premieres. $28-45. Under 25 $10. Office open Tu-Su noon-7pm.

Annex Theatre (☎728-0933). A rogue theater group without a regular space—call their number to find out where they are performing. Refreshing emphasis on company-generated material and unconventional theater. Pay-what-you-can previews. Tickets $10-12. Shows usually Th-Sa at 8pm and Su at 7pm.

Northwest Asian American Theater, 409 7th Ave. S (☎340-1445), in the International District next to the Wing Luke Asian Museum. Excellent new theater with pieces by Asian Americans. Year-long season. Tickets $15, students $12. Open M-F 10am-6pm.

CINEMA

Seattle is a cinematic paradise. Most of the theaters that screen non-Hollywood films are on Capitol Hill and in the University District. Large, first-run theaters are everywhere, including the 16-screen **Loews Cineplex Meridian** (☎223-9600) at 7th Ave. and Pike. **Seven Gables,** a local company, has recently bought up the Egyptian, the Metro, the Neptune, and 25 other theaters. $28 buys admission to any five films at any of their theaters. Call ☎443-4567 (movie phone) for local movie times and locations. On summer Saturdays, **outdoor cinema** in Fremont begins at dusk at 670 N 34th St., in the U-Park lot by the bridge, behind the Red Door Alehouse. Enter as early as 7pm to catch live music that starts at 8pm. **TCI Outdoor Cinema** shows everything from classics to cartoons for free at the Gasworks Park. (☎694-7000. Live music 7pm-dusk.) Aspiring independent filmmakers or actors/actresses should check out the Alibi Room for readings (see **Nightlife,** below).

The Egyptian, 801 E Pine St. (☎323-4978), at Harvard Ave. on Capitol Hill. This Art Deco art-house is best known for hosting the **Seattle International Film Festival** in the last week of May and 1st week of June. The festival's director retrospective features a personal appearance by said director. Festival series tickets available at a discount. $8.25, seniors $5.25.

The Harvard Exit, 807 E Roy St. (☎323-8986), on Capitol Hill, near the north end of the Broadway business district. Quality classic and foreign films. Converted women's club that has its own ghost and an enormous antique projector. $8.25, students and seniors $5.25. Cash only.

Seven Gables Theater, 911 NE 50th St. (☎632-8820), in the U District just off Roosevelt, a short walk west from University Way. Another art-house cinema in an old house showing art, independent, and international films. Entrance is shaded by trees. $8.25, 1st show of the day $5.25, seniors $5.25. Cash only.

Grand Illusion Cinema, 1403 NE 50th St. (☎523-3935), in the U District at University Way. Plays world cinema flicks and exciting international films. Frequently revives old classics and hard-to-find films. One of the last independent theaters in Seattle. $7, seniors and children $5, matinees $4.50.

Little Theatre, 608 19th Ave. (☎675-2055), at Mercer St. on Capitol Hill. A non-profit theater showing documentaries and independent films. $7, seniors and children $5, matinees $4.50.

SPORTS

Seattleites cheered recently when the home team, the **Mariners,** moved out of the Kingdome, where in 1995 sections of the roof fell into the stands. The "M's" are now playing baseball in the half-billion dollar, hangar-like **Safeco Field,** at 1st Ave. S and Royal Brougham Way S, under an enormous retractable roof. Saving the game from frequent rain-outs is simply a matter of pushing a single button labelled "Go" and costs a mere $1.50 in electricity. (Tickets ☎622-4487; www.ticketmaster.com. From $10.) Seattle's football team, the **Seahawks,** are stuck playing in UW's Husky Stadium until construction on their stadium is finished. (Tickets ☎628-0888. From $10.)

On the other side of town and at the other end of the aesthetic spectrum, the sleek **Key Arena** in the Seattle Center hosts Seattle's NBA basketball team, the **Supersonics** (☎628-0888). The men now share their turf with their female counterparts: the WNBA expansion team, the **Seattle Storm** (☎628-0888; www.storm.wnba.com). The **University of Washington Huskies** football team has dominated the PAC-10 for years and doesn't plan to let up. Call the Athletic Ticket Office (☎543-2200) for Huskies schedules and prices.

◪ NIGHTLIFE

Seattle has moved beyond beer to a new nightlife frontier: the cafe-bar. The popularity of espresso bars in Seattle might lead one to conclude that caffeine is more intoxicating than alcohol, but often an establishment that poses as a diner by day brings on a band, breaks out the disco ball, and pumps out the microbrews by night. Many locals tell tourists that the best spot to go for guaranteed good beer, live music, and big crowds is Pioneer Square, where UW students from frat row dominate the bar stools. You may prefer to go to Capitol Hill, or up Rte. 99 to Fremont, where the atmosphere is usually more laid-back than in the Square. Wherever you go, but especially downtown, do stay alert—Seattle is big city, and has the homelessness, crime, and dark alleys that come with size.

DOWNTOWN

▨ **The Alibi Room,** 85 Pike St. (☎623-3180), across from the Market Cinema, in the Post Alley in Pike Place. A remarkably friendly local indie filmmaker hangout. Bar with music open 7 nights. A downstairs dance floor open F and Sa. Brunch Sa and Su. No cover. Open daily 11am-4pm and 5pm-2am.

Sit and Spin, 2219 4th Ave. (cafe and laundromat ☎441-9484), between Bell St. and Blanchard St. Board games keep patrons busy while they wait for their clothes to dry or for bands to stop playing in the back room. F-Sa nights cover $6-10. Artists cut albums in the **Bad Animal** studio down the street, where R.E.M. once recorded. Open Su-Th 9am-midnight, F-Sa 9am-2am. Kitchen opens daily at 11am.

Crocodile Cafe, 2200 2nd Ave. (☎448-2114; www.thecrocodile.com), at Blanchard in Belltown. Cooks from scratch by day, and features live music by night (Tu-Sa). Shows usually start 9:30; some require advance ticket purchase. 21+ after 9pm. Cover $6-22. Open Tu-Sa 8am-2am, Su 9am-11pm.

PIONEER SQUARE

Pioneer Square provides a happening scene, dominated by twentysomethings, frat kids, and cover bands. Most of the area bars participate in a joint cover (F-Sa $10, Su-Th $5) that will let you wander from bar to bar to sample the bands. The larger venues are listed below. Two smaller venues, **Larry's Blues Cafe,** 209 1st Ave. S (☎624-7665) and **New Orleans,** 114 1st Ave. S (☎622-2563) feature great blues and jazz nightly (no cover weekdays). Not part of the Pioneer Square joint cover because it's often free, **J and M Cafe and Cardroom,** 201 1st Ave. (☎292-0663) is in the center of Pioneer Square, often blasting rock and blues (Th, no cover) or disco and top 40 (W, $6).

Bohemian Cafe, 111 Yesler Way (☎447-1514), pumps reggae every night. 3 sections— a cafe, a bar, and a stage—are all adorned with art from Jamaica. Live shows 6 nights per week, often national acts on weekends. Happy hour 4-7pm. Part of the joint cover, but no cover Tu-Th. Open M-F 4pm-2am, Sa 6pm-7am.

Central Tavern, 207 1st Ave. S. (☎622-0209), One of the early venues for grunge has now become a favorite for bikers. Live rock 6 nights a week at 9:30pm. Tu open mic. Part of the joint cover. Open daily 11:30am-2am, kitchen closes 8ish.

Last Supper Club, 124 S. Washington St. (☎748-9975), at Occidental. 2 dance floors, DJed with everything from 70s disco (F) to funky house, drum & bass, and trance (Sa). Su nights salsa at 8:30pm. Cover F-Sa $10; W, Th and Su $5. Open W-Su 4pm-2am.

Swannie's Sports Bar, 222 S Main St. (☎622-9353). Share drink specials with pro ball-players who stop by post-game. Any Seattle sports junkie will swear this is the place to be. Drink specials change daily. Open M-Su 11:30am-2am.

CAPITOL HILL

East off of Broadway, Pine St. is cool lounge after cool lounge. Find your atmosphere and acclimatize. West off of Broadway, Pike St. has the clubs that push the limits (gay, punk, industrial, fetish, dance) and break the sound barrier.

Linda's, 707 Pine St. E (☎325-1220). A very chill post-gig scene for Seattle rockers. On Tu night a live DJ plays jazz and old rock. W is movie night. Expanded menu, liquor, and breakfast on weekend. No cover. Open M-F 2pm-2am, Sa-Su 10am-2am.

Neighbors, 1509 Broadway (☎324-5358; www.neighboursonline.com). Enter from the alley on Pike. A gay dance club for 20 years, Neighbors prides itself on techno slickness. Midnight drag shows (W, Th, and Su). House (M, W, and F-Sa), 80s (Tu, Th), Latin (Su). Cover Su-Th $1; F-Sa $5. Open Su-W 9pm-2am, Th 9pm-3am, F-Sa 9pm-4am.

Garage, 1130 Broadway (☎322-2296), between Union and Madison. An automotive warehouse turned upscale pool hall, this place gets suave at night. Happy hour 3-7pm, $3 microbrew. 18 pool tables $6-14 per hr.; $4 per hr. during happy hour, $5 per hr. M; free for female sharps on Ladies' Night (Su). Open daily 3pm-2am, kitchen M-F 4pm-midnight, Sa-Su 4pm-1am.

Elysian Brewing Co., 1211 E Pike St. (860-1920), serves microbrews to a young crowd. "The Immortal" Indian Pale Ale and Dragon's Tooth Oatmeal Stout are two favorites. Try the gourmet bar food (Ahi taco $8.95). Open M-Sa 11am-2am, Su noon-midnight.

◪ WATERWAYS AND PARKS

Thanks to the foresight of Seattle's early community and the architectural genius of the Olmsted family, Seattle enjoys a string of parks and waterways.

LAKE UNION. Sailboats fill Lake Union, situated between Capitol Hill and the University District, and the **Center for Wooden Boats** can supply boats, with a moored flotilla of new and restored craft for rent. (*1010 Valley St. ☎382-2628; www.cwb.org. Open daily 11am-7pm. Rowboats from $23, sailboats from $16.*) **Gasworks Park,** at the north end of Lake Union, fills the grounds of a retired oil-refining facility, necessitating frequent EPA checks. Fittingly, the park hosts a ◪**4th of July Fireworks show,** and is a celebrated kite-flying spot. (*Take bus #26 from downtown to N 35th St. and Wallingford Ave. N.*) **Gasworks Kite Shop** provides the high-flying vehicles. (*3420 Stone Way ☎633-4780. Open M-F 10am-6pm, Sa 10am-5pm, Su 11am-5pm.*) **Urban Surf** rents surfboards, in-line skates, snowboards and kiteboards. (*2100 N Northlake Way, opposite park entrance. ☎545-9463. Boards $15 per day. Skates $5 per hr., $16 per day. Open M-F 10am-7pm, Sa 10am-5pm, Su 11am-5pm.*)

WOODLAND PARK AND WOODLAND ZOO. Woodland Park is mediocre, but the zoo has won a bevy of AZA awards (the zoo Oscars, if you will) for best new exhibits. The African Savanna and the Northern Trail exhibits are both full of zoo favorites: grizzlies, wolves, lions, sasquatch, giraffes, and zebras. (*5500 Phinney Ave. N I-5 50th St. exit or N 50th St. Bus #5 from downtown. ☎684-4800. Park open daily 4:30am-11:30pm. Zoo open May to mid-Sept. daily 9:30am-6pm; mid-March to April and mid-Sept. to mid-Oct. 9:30am-5pm; winter 9:30am-4pm. $9.50, seniors $8.75, ages 6-17 $6.50.*)

DISCOVERY PARK. Across the canals and west of the locks lie the 534 bucolic acres of Discovery Park, at 36th Ave. W and W Government Way, on a lonely point west of the Magnolia District and south of Golden Gardens Park. Grassy fields and steep, eroding bluffs, while dangerous for hikers, provide a haven for birds forced over Puget Sound by bad weather around the Olympic Mountains. A **visitors center** is right by the entrance. A popular beach and lighthouse are also open for exploration, but only via free **shuttle.** The **Daybreak Star Indian Cultural Center** at the park's north end is operated by the United Indians of All Tribes Foundation as a social, cultural, and educational center. (*Discovery Park: ☎386-4236. Open daily 6am-11pm. Visitor Center: 3801 W Government Way. Bus #24 or 33. Open Tu-Su 8:30am-5pm. Beach: open June-Sept. Sa-Su 11:45-4:30pm. Donation requested. Cultural Center: ☎285-4425. Open M-F 9am-5pm, Sa 10am-noon, Su noon-5pm. Free.*)

◪ OUTDOOR ACTIVITIES

BIKING. Seattle has more bike-commuters than any other American city. The city prides itself on 30 mi. of bike-pedestrian trails, 90 mi. of signed bike routes, and 16 mi. of bike lanes on city streets. Over 1000 **cyclists** compete in the 190 mi. **Seattle to Portland Race** in mid-July. Call the **bike hotline** (☎522-2453) for info. On five **Bicycle Sundays** from May to September, Lake Washington Blvd. is open exclusively to cyclists from 10am to 6pm. Call the **Citywide Sports Office** (☎684-7092) for info. The **Burke-Gilman Trail** makes for a longer ride. It runs from the University District along Montlake Blvd., then along Lake Union and all the way west to Chittenden Locks and Discovery Park. Runners also enjoy the Burke-Gilman.

DROP THE PACK. After a few months backpacking it's no surprise that your shoulders start bruising like unrefrigerated steaks. Fortunately, there is a cure: sea kayaks. Kayaking is the perfect way to explore the nooks of Washington's labyrinthine Puget Sound, and rental boats are readily available. A truly unique resource is the Cascadia Marine Trail, a network of seaside campsites and launching spots maintained specifically for paddlers and sailors. The trail stretches from the San Juans south to Olympia, has over 40 places to pitch a tent along the way, and has been recognized as one of 16 Millennium Trails in the country. Routes in the south of the Sound tend to be shorter and more protected, perfect for beginner and intermediate boaters. Paddling in the north sound can be dangerous due to ship traffic and fast tides, so be sure you know your stuff before biting this off. Companies that rent often offer moderately-priced guided trips for anywhere from half-day to multi-day excursions. Fees for camping vary site to site (free-$10). For information and help planning a trip contact the Washington Water Trails Association, 4649 Sunnyside Ave. N, Room 305 Seattle, WA 98103 (☎ 545-9161; www.wwta.org).

HIKING. 4167 ft. **Mt. Si** is the most climbed mountain in the state of Washington, and with good reason. Just an hour from downtown Seattle, hikers can reach a **lookout** that showcases Mt. Rainier, the Olympic Mountains, and Seattle in just a few hours (1 mi. one-way). A 4hr. hike (4 mi. one-way) brings you to **Haystack Basin,** the false summit. Don't try climbing higher unless you have rock-climbing gear, though. To get to Mt. Si, take I-90 East to SE Mt. Si Rd. (2 mi. from Middle Fork). Cross the Snoqualmie River Bridge to the trailhead parking lot. **Tiger Mountain** is another great day-hike near Seattle. A 4hr. hike (5½ mi. round-trip) leads to the summit of West Tiger Mountain (2522 ft.). Take I-90 to Tiger Mountain State Forest. From the Tradition Plateau trailhead, walk to Bus Road-Trail and then to West Tiger Trail. If you parked outside the gated lot, stay for sunset! For additional information, check out *55 Hikes around Snoqualmie Pass*, by Harvey Manning.

WHITEWATER RAFTING. Although the rapids are hours away by car, over 50 **whitewater rafting** outfitters are based in Seattle and are often willing to undercut one another with merciless abandon. **Washington State Outfitters and Guides Association** (☎ 877-275-4964) provides advice; although their office is closed in summer, they do return phone calls and send out info. The **Northwest Outdoor Center,** 2100 Westlake Ave., on Lake Union, gives $50-70 instructional programs in whitewater and sea kayaking. (☎ 281-9694. Kayak rentals $10-15 per hr. Weekdays 3rd and 4th hours are free. Make reservations. Open M-F 10am-8pm, Sa-Su 9am-6pm.)

⚡ DAYTRIPS

EAST SOUND. Seattleites leave the city en masse to play in this bikers', picnickers', and suburbanites' paradise rolled into one. Entirely unnecessary Range Rovers and outdoor shopping plazas litter the landscape. Companies buy up expanses of East Sound land, smother them in sod and office complexes, and call them "campuses"—witness **Microsoft,** which has nearly subsumed the suburb of Redmond. Rapid growth has had its benefits, though. The wealthy and beautiful suburb of **Bellevue** is home to Bill Gates, among others. The small but interesting **Bellevue Art Museum** stands strong in a new building surrounded by malls and parking lots. The museum focuses mainly on contemporary art, and makes a good destination for a rainy day. (*510 Bellevue Way NE. In central Bellevue just south of NE 8th St., west of I-405.* ☎ *425-519-0770. Open Tu, W, F, Sa 10am-5pm, Th 10am-8pm, Su noon-5pm. $6, students and seniors $4; free first Th and last Sa of every month.*) The July **Bellevue Jazz Festival** attracts both local cats and national acts. *(Cross Lake Washington on one of 2 floating bridges to arrive in East Sound.)*

JIMI HENDRIX'S GRAVE. Rock pilgrims trek out to the grave of Seattle's first rock legend, **Jimi Hendrix,** to pay homage to the greatest guitarist who ever lived. Jimi's grave is in Greenwood Cemetery, in the town of Renton. Plan on spending some time driving down labyrinthine streets. Once you find the cemetery, look for the grave toward the back, just in front of the sun dial. *(Bus #101 from downtown to the Renton Park 'n' Ride, then switch to #105 to Greenwood Cemetery. Drivers take the Sunset Blvd. exit from Rte. 405—follow Sunset Blvd., not Park—turn right onto Branson, and right again on NE 4th. The Cemetery is on a hill, just next to a McDonalds.)*

LAKE SAMMAMISH STATE PARK AND FURTHER EAST. The exits along I-90 east of the city contain several hidden treats. Swim, water-ski, and play volleyball to your heart's content within **Lake Sammamish State Park,** a weekend hot spot on the eastern shores of the lake. *(Take I-90 east to Exit 15, and follow the very large brown signs.)*

Just outside of **Snoqualmie,** 29 mi. east of Seattle, is the astounding **Snoqualmie Falls.** Formerly a sacred place for the Salish, the 270 ft. wall of water has generated electricity for Puget Power since 1898. Five generators buried under the falls work hard to provide energy for 1600 homes. It is particularly spectacular in spring, when the falls are swollen with melt-off. *(Take the Snoqualmie Parkway exit from I-90.)*

As I-90 leaves the sound, the road rises into mountains that offer some fantastic **dayhikes.** You can really take your pick—for information, contact the **Issaquah Chamber of Commerce** (☎425-392-7024), at 155 NW Gilman in downtown Issaquah, just past the State Park. They sell maps ($5-6) and can help set you up with a route.

BOEING. The Seattle area is surrounded by the vast factories of **Boeing,** the city's most prominent employer and site of the largest covered structure in North America. Boeing offers **public tours** of the facilities in Everett, about 15min. north of the city, where 747s, 767s, and 777s are made. Just seeing how such large pieces are moved and assembled makes the tour worth it. Arrive early because the limited tickets often run out in the summer. The tour includes a theater show and a short walk through the facilities. *(Take I-5 north to exit 189 and then go west on 526. Signs are clear. ☎800-464-1476; www.boeing.com. Tours 9, 10, 11am, 1, 2, and 3pm. $5, seniors or under 16 $3. Tours M-F 9am-3pm. Ticket reservations $10, cash only.)*

MUSEUM OF FLIGHT. South of Seattle at Boeing Field is the **Museum of Flight.** The huge structure enshrines flying machines, from canvas biplanes to chic fighter jets, under a 3-story roof. Tour Eisenhower's old Air Force One, or fly in a nauseatingly realistic flight simulator and explore the red barn where William E. Boeing founded the company in 1916. Photographs and artifacts trace the history of flight from its beginnings through the 30s. *(9404 E Marginal Way S. Take I-5 south to Exit 158 and turn north onto E Marginal Way S and follow for ½ mi. Bus #174. ☎206-764-5700. Open M-Su 10am-5pm, 1st Th of month, 10am-9pm. Free tours of the museum every 30min., 10am-3:30pm. $9.50, seniors $8.50, ages 5-17 $5, under 5 free. Free after 5pm on 1st Th of the month.)*

BREMERTON. Nosing into Puget Sound between the Olympic Peninsula and Seattle, the Kitsap Peninsula's deep inlets seemed a natural spot in which to park a fleet of nuclear-powered submarines. The instant you set foot in **Bremerton,** the hub of the peninsula, you see that is exactly what happened. *(Washington State Ferries ☎206-464-6400 or 800-843-3779; www.wsdot.wa.gov/ferries. 2 boats run between downtown Seattle and Bremerton. A regular ferry runs daily (1hr.; $5.10, car and driver $11.25). Passenger only ferry runs M-F (40min.; $6.10; departs Pier 50). Bremerton Area Chamber of Commerce, 301 Pacific Ave. ☎360-479-3579; www.bremertonchamber.org. Open M-F 9am-4pm; booth at ferry dock open on weekends.)*

BREMERTON NAVAL MUSEUM AND USS TURNER JOY. The museum, replete with WWII photos, 10 ft. models of ships, and a 14th-century wicker basket from Korea believed to be the world's oldest existing cannon, is sure to please any Navy buff. (☎360-479-7447. Open M-Sa 10am-5pm, Su 1-5pm. Donations appreciated.)

Behind the museum, explore the destroyer **USS Turner Joy,** the ship that fired the first American shots of the Vietnam War. It is managed by the Bremerton Historic Ships Association. For a closer view of the retired ships that fill Bremerton harbor, join the **Navy Ship Tour** at the *Turner Joy* and scoot along mothballed submarines and aircraft carriers. Tours leave from the Ship's Store in Port Orchard, across the harbor, but stop in Bremerton before heading to the boats. (USS Turner Joy: ☎360-792-2457. Self-guided tours $7, seniors $6, children $5, military in uniform free; buy tickets at Turner Joy gift shop. Navy Ship Tour: ☎360-792-2457. Open June-Aug. daily; May and Sept. Sa and Su only. Tours last 45min. $9, seniors $8, children $6.)

▶ DAYTRIP TO TACOMA

Tacoma, founded as a sawmill town in the 1860s, was called "The City of Destiny" when it was designated the western terminus of the first railroad to reach the Northwest. In the 20th century, however, Seattle became the industrial and cultural hub of the region. Recently, however, Tacoma has emerged from Seattle's shadow. In July 2002, Tacoma opened the Museum of Glass to showcase the city's native and internationally renowned glassblower, Dale Chihuly. The Museum of Glass is linked to the Washington State History Museum and the Tacoma Art Museum by the awesome Chihuly Bridge of Glass across I-705.

Tacoma is Washington's third largest city and lies on **I-5,** 32 mi. (30min.) south of Seattle and 28 mi. (30min.) northeast of Olympia. Take Exit 132 from I-5 and follow the signs to the city center. There are several public transportation options for getting to Tacoma; **SoundTransit** runs two of these. The **Sounder** is a commuter train that runs from Tacoma in the morning, and from Seattle in the evening (1hr.; $4). Pick up a schedule booklet from Union Station in Seattle. Both SoundTransit options arrive at the Puyallup Ave. Station in Tacoma, which is shared with **Greyhound.** (510 Puyallup Ave. ☎383-4621. Open daily 8am-9pm.) They also run buses to **Portland** (8 per day, $21.25) and **Seattle** (8 per day, $5). Point Defiance is Tacoma's ferry terminal. Get the skinny on Tacoma at the **Visitor Information Center,** 1119 Pacific Ave., 5th floor (☎253-627-2846 or 800-272-2662; open M-F 9am-5pm), or from the desk in the back of the Washington State Museum gift shop (see **Sights,** below; open M-Sa 10am-4pm, Su noon-5pm). The superb *Pierce County Bicycle Guide Map* shows bike routes and lists trails near Mt. Rainier. Tacomans are bicycle enthusiasts.

MUSEUM OF GLASS. In 2002, the much anticipated, $63-million Museum of Glass and International Center for Contemporary Art opened its doors to visitors. The highlight inside is the "hot shop," an amphitheater and glassblowing studio where visitors can watch art-in-action. The outdoor draw is the 500 ft. long Chihuly Bridge of Glass. The bridge displays 1700 works by renowned glass artist Dale Chihuly. (1801 E. Dock St. ☎866-468-7386, www.museumofglass.org. Open Tu-W and F-Sa 10am-5pm, Th 10am-8pm, and Su noon-5pm. $8, seniors and students $6, children $3. Free every 3rd Th 5pm-8pm.)

WASHINGTON STATE HISTORY MUSEUM. The shiny $40-million museum houses interactive, stereophonic exhibits on Washington's history through the 1800s. A sprawling model train on the 5th floor is a highlight for children, railroad buffs, and child railroad buffs. (1911 Pacific Ave. ☎888-238-4373; www.wshs.org. Open Tu, W, F 10am-4pm, Th 10am-8pm (free 4-8pm), Sa 10am-5pm, Su noon-5pm. $7, seniors $6.50, students $5, children under 5 free.)

WASHINGTON

POINT DEFIANCE PARK. The 698-acre park is a wonderful place to pass time on a warm day, but it's a secret everyone knows about. Besides being a spot to relax, the park is excellent for other more active and visual pursuits. A 5 mi. driving and walking loop passes all the park's attractions, offering postcard views of Puget Sound and access to miles of woodland trails. In spring, the park is bejeweled with flowers; a rhododendron garden lies nestled in the woods along the loop. **Owen Beach** looks across at Vashon Island and is a good starting place for a ramble down the shore. The park's prize possession is the **Point Defiance Zoo and Aquarium.** The zoo boasts more than 5000 animals, including penguins, puffins, polar bears, beluga whales, and sharks. The meticulously restored **Fort Nisqually** was built by the British Hudson Bay Company in 1832 as they expanded their trade in beaver pelts. The series of 19th-century cabins contains museum-like exhibits of the lives of children, laborers, and natives. *(Park: take Rte. 16 to 6th Ave., go east on 6th Ave., then head north on Pearl St. ☎ 305-1000. Open daily from dawn until 30min. after dusk. Zoo: 5400 N Pearl St. ☎ 404-3678 or 591-5337; www.pdza.org. Open Jan.-Mar. 9:30am-4pm, Apr. 9:30am-5pm, May-Sept. 9:30am-7pm, Oct.-Dec. 9:30am-4pm. $7.75, seniors $7, youth $6, students $4. Fort: ☎ 591-5339. Open daily June-Aug. 11am-6pm; Sept.-Apr. W-Su 11am-4pm. $3, seniors $2, ages 5-12 $1.)*

PUGET SOUND

Stretching from Admiralty Inlet to Whidbey Island, this unusually deep body of water runs a full 100 mi. up to the Straits of Juan de Fuca and Georgia. The Sound was originally discovered by George Vancouver, who generously decided that an island was good enough for him and granted the naming rights to his second lieutenant Peter Puget. Sharing the seas with the shipping trade and frequenting the harbors of Seattle, Tacoma, Everett, and Port Townsend, modern US Navy submarines and battleships are now based in Bremerton. The Alaska Marine Highway also ends its voyage here in the Sound.

OLYMPIA   ☎ 360

Inside Olympia's seemingly interminable network of suburbs, there lies a festive downtown area known for its art, antiques, liberalism, and of course, irresistible microbrews. Evergreen State College lies a few miles from the city center, and its highly-pierced, tree-hugging student body spills into the mix in a kind of chemistry experiment that gets progressively weirder when politicians join in. Named Olympia because of its superb view of the Olympic mountains, the city is also a logical launching pad into Olympic National Park.

█ TRANSPORTATION

Settled at the junction of **I-5** and **US 101** between **Tumwater** (to the south, I-5 Exit 102) and **Lacey** (to the east, I-5 Exit 108), Olympia makes a convenient stop on any north-south journey. I-5 Exit 105 leads to the **Capitol Campus** and **downtown** Olympia. **Capitol Way** divides the city's East and West downtown streets. The west side of downtown borders freshwater **Capitol Lake** and salty **West Bay,** also known as **Budd Bay.** The **4th Ave.** bridge divides the two bodies of water and leads to the city's fast-food-chain-infested section. Navigating Olympia's one-way streets on **bike** or **foot** is easy, and all public buses have bike racks.

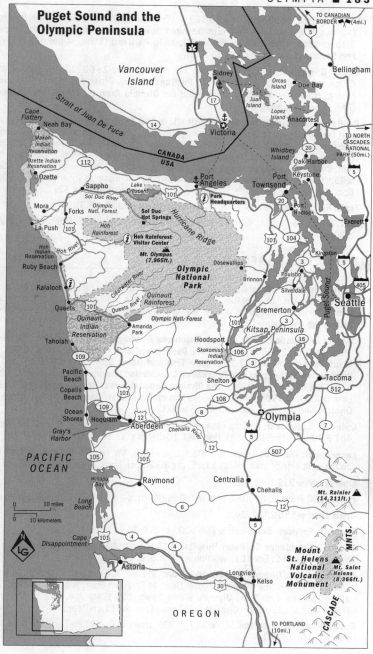

Puget Sound and the Olympic Peninsula

WASHINGTON

Trains: Amtrak, 6600 Yelm Hwy. (☎923-4602 or 800-872-7245). In neighboring Lacey (I-5 Exit 108), but bus #64 runs between downtown and the station. Open daily 8:15am-noon, 1:45-3:30pm, 5:30-8:30pm. To **Portland** (2½hr., 4 per day, $15-25) and **Seattle** (1¾hr., 4 per day, $11-20).

Buses: Greyhound, 107 E 7th Ave. (☎357-5541 or 800-231-2222), at Capitol Way. Office open daily 8:30am-10pm. To **Portland** (2¾hr., 7 per day, $21.25); **Seattle** (1¾hr., 6 per day, $9.25; but check out the **Olympia Express,** below); and **Spokane** (9hr., 3 per day, $31.25).

Public Transportation: Intercity Transit (IT; ☎786-1881 or 800-287-6348). Reliable and flexible service to almost anywhere in Thurston County, even with a bicycle. Schedules at the visitors center or at Transit Center, 222 State Ave. Open M-F 7:30am-5:30pm. $0.75 per ride. Day passes $1.50. The most useful route is #42, which runs from the Capitol Campus to downtown, eastside, and westside (every 15min., 6:45am-5:45pm). **Olympia Express** runs between Olympia and **Tacoma** (55min., M-F 5:50am-6pm, $2; Tacoma to Seattle $1.50; Olympia and Lacey to Sea-Tac $2).

Taxis: Red Top Taxi (☎357-3700). **Capitol City Taxi** (☎357-4949).

AAA: 2415 Capitol Mall Dr. (☎357-5561 or 800-562-2582). Open M-F 8:30am-5:30pm.

▐ PRACTICAL INFORMATION

Tourist Information: Washington State Capitol Visitor Center (☎586-3460), on Capitol Way at 14th Ave., south of the State Capitol; follow the signs on I-5, or from Capitol Way turn west at the pedestrian bridge. The center has tourist information for Olympia as well as the entire state. Open M-F 8am-5pm.

Outdoor Information: State Natural Resources Building, 1111 Washington St. (☎902-1000 or 800-527-3305), houses the **Department of Natural Resources (DNR).** The **Maps Department** (☎902-1234), the **Fish and Game Office** (☎902-2200), and the **Washington State Parks and Recreation Commission Information Center** (☎800-233-0321) are on the ground floor. **The Olympic National Forest Headquarters,** 1835 Black Lake Blvd. SW (☎956-2400), provides info on forest land. Open M-F 8am-4:30pm. For Olympic National Park info, call ☎565-3000.

Outdoors Equipment: Pick up essentials or go on a buying spree at Olympic Outfitters, 407 E 4th Ave. (☎943-1114). Open M-F 10am-8pm, Sa 10am-6pm, Su noon-5pm.

Laundromat: Westside Laundry, 2103 Harrison Ave. NW (☎943-3857), in a strip mall on the west side of town. Wash $1.75, dry $0.25 per 7min. Open daily 9am-10pm.

Emergency: ☎911.

Police: 900 Plum St. SE (8am-5pm ☎753-8300; 5pm-8am ☎704-2740), at 8th Ave.

Crisis Line: ☎586-2800. 24hr.

Women's Services: Safeplace ☎754-6300 or 800-364-1776.

Hospital: Providence St. Peter Hospital, 413 Lilly Rd. NE (☎491-9480). Follow signs northbound on I-5, Exit 107; southbound Exit 109. Emergency 24hr.

Internet Access: Olympia Timberland Library, 313 8th Ave. SE (☎352-0595), at Franklin St. Up to 1hr. free Internet access. Open M-Tu 10am-9pm, W-Th 11am-9pm, F-Sa 10am-5pm, Su 1pm-5pm. **Olympia World News,** 116 E 4th Ave. (☎570-9536), off Washington St. $3 per hr. Open M-Sa 11am-11pm, Su 11am-9pm.

Post Office: 900 Jefferson SE (☎357-2289). Open M-F 7:30am-6pm, Sa 9am-4pm. **Postal Code:** 98501

Olympia

▲▲ ACCOMMODATIONS
Capital Forest Area, **10**
Golden Gavel Motor Hotel, **7**
Grays Harbor Hostel, **8**
Millersylvania Park, **9**

🍴 FOOD
Saigon Rendez-Vous, **5**
Santosh, **2**
The Spar Cafe & Bar, **1**

🍸 NIGHTLIFE
4th Ave. Alehouse, **3**
Eastside Club&Tavern, **4**
Fishbowl Brewpub, **6**

ACCOMMODATIONS AND CAMPING

Olympia motels cater to policy-makers ($60-80), but options in Tumwater are more affordable. Try **Motel 6** ❸, 400 W Lee St. (☎754-7320. Singles $40; doubles $45.) For free camping, head to the **Capital Forest Multiple Use Area**.

🖼 **Grays Harbor Hostel,** 6 Ginny Ln. (☎482-3119), just off Rte. 8 in Elma, 25 mi. west of Olympia. Bus #40 (Grays Harbor) from Olympia, or take the Grays County Fairground Rd. exit off Rte. 8 (reached via 101), and make the 1st right. Kitchen (complete with produce from the garden), 2 common rooms, a disc golf course, and shed for bike repairs. Check-in 5-9pm. Lockout 9:30am-5pm. The Klemps are working on moving the hostel to Olympia, so call ahead (call hours 6:30-8:45pm and 5-9pm). 14 beds. Dorms $14; private rooms available. (Motor)cyclists can camp on the lawn for $10. ❶

The Golden Gavel Motor Hotel, 909 Capitol Way (☎352-8533). A few blocks north of the Capitol building. Clean, spacious, 70s-style rooms are a siren call for travelers not on the corporate account. Singles $46; doubles $54. AAA/senior discount $2. ❸

Millersylvania State Park, 12245 Tilly Rd. S (☎753-1519; reservations 888-226-7688), 10 mi. south of Olympia. Take Exit 95 off I-5 N or S, turn onto Rte. 121 N, then take a left at the stop sign. A few secluded sites, most in the back of the park. Some kitchens available. 20-day max. stay. Wheelchair accessible. 148 sites. $14; RV sites $22; sites for bicyclists $6. Showers $0.25 per 3min. ❶

Capital Forest Multiple Use Area, 15 mi. southwest of Olympia. Take Exit 95 off I-5. Grab a forest map at the state DNR office (see **Practical Information,** above). 90 camp-sites spread among 7 campgrounds, administered by the DNR. All sites have bathrooms and water. Free. No showers. ❶

FOOD

Diners, veggie eateries, and Asian quick-stops line bohemian 4th Ave. east of Columbia. Get slightly upscale groceries at the 24hr. **Safeway,** 520 Cleveland Ave. (☎943-1830), off Capital Blvd. in Tumwater, a quarter-mile south of the Capitol

WASHINGTON

building. The **Olympia Farmer's Market,** 700 N Capitol Way, is a great place to stroll, people-watch, and grab cheap eats from small vendors. (☎352-9096. Open Apr.-Oct. Th-Su 10am-3pm; Nov.-Dec. Sa-Su 10am-3pm.)

The Spar Cafe & Bar, 114 E 4th Ave. (☎357-6444), has been a hot spot for beer, burgers ($7), and cigars for decades. A national historic monument and still operating to the tunes of live jazz every Sa night (8pm-midnight). Cafe open M-Th 6am-10pm, F-Sa 6am-11pm, Su 6am-8pm. Bar open M-Th 11am-midnight, F-Sa 11am-2am. ❷

Saigon Rendez-Vous, 117 W 5th Ave. (☎352-1989). The queen of Olympia's many Vietnamese restaurants with a huge vegetarian menu (but meat eaters will be able to find a tasty meal here, too). Entrees $5-8. Open M-Sa 10:30am-10:30pm, Su noon-9pm. ❶

Santosh, 116 W 4th Ave. (☎943-3442), west of Capitol Way. All-you-can-eat Indian lunch buffet $6.95. Regular dishes $8-12. Open Su-F 11.30am-2:30pm, 5-9:30pm, Sa 11am-2:30pm and 5-10pm. ❷

▣ NIGHTLIFE

Olympia's nightlife seems to have outgrown its daylife. Labels like K Records and Kill Rock Stars, with their flagship band Bikini Kill, have made Olympia a crucial pitstop on the indie rock circuit. *The Rocket* and the city's daily *Olympian* list shows.

▣ **Fishbowl Brewpub & Cafe,** 515 Jefferson St. SE (☎943-3650), 2 blocks south off 4th. With fish painted on outside walls and an indoor aquarium, this brewpub captures Olympia's love for the sea, art, and beer. The British ales ($3.25) are named after fish. Kitchen, open daily until 11pm, offers sandwiches and pasta ($3.50-7). Occasional live music. Open M-Sa 11am-midnight, Su noon-10pm.

▣ **Eastside Club and Tavern,** 410 E 4th Ave. (☎357-9985). Old and young come to play pool and sip pints of microbrews. Pints $2.50. Frequent drink specials. M pints $1.75, Th $2. Happy hour daily 4-7pm, pints $1.75. Open M-F noon-2am, Sa-Su 3pm-2am.

4th Ave. Alehouse & Eatery, 210 E 4th Ave. (☎786-1444). Townfolk gather for "slabs" of pizza ($2.75), seafood baskets ($5-6), and one of the 30 regional draft microbrews. Pints $3, $2 during happy hour (5pm-7pm). Live tunes, from blues to rock to reggae (Th-Sa 9pm). Cover $3-10. Open M-F 11:30am-2am, F-Sa noon-2am.

⊙ SIGHTS AND EVENTS

Olympia's main draw is definitely its political scene, so don't miss the chance to see WA state tax dollars in action.

STATE CAPITOL. Olympia's crowning glory is the State Capitol, a complex of state government buildings, carefully sculpted gardens, veterans' monuments, and fabulous fountains, including a remarkable replica of Copenhagen's Tivoli fountain. Get a free tour of the **Legislative Building,** constructed in 1927 and styled after Rome's St. Peter's Basilica. The newly renovated interior enshrines a six-ton Tiffany chandelier and six bronze doors depicting the state's history. *(I-5 to Exit 103. Visitors Center ☎586-3460. Call 586-8687 for more info and options for the disabled. Free tours depart from front entrance daily on the hr. 10am-3pm; 11am tour is most in-depth. Open for tourists to explore M-F 8am-5:30pm, Sa-Su 10am-4pm.)*

WOLF HAVEN INTERNATIONAL. This sanctuary provides a permanent home for captive-born gray wolves (reclaimed from zoos or illegal owners). During the summer weekly **Howl-ins** are a sort of vaudeville-inspired wolf-and-human romp. *(3111 Offut Lake Rd. 10 mi. south of the capitol, near Millersvania Park. Take Exit 99 off I-5, turn east, and follow the brown signs. ☎264-4695 or 800-448-9653; www.wolfhaven.org. Open May-Sept. W-M 10am-5pm; Oct. and Apr. 10am-4pm. Nov.-Jan. and Mar. Sa-Su 10am-4pm. 45min. tours on the hr.; last tour leaves 1hr. before closing. $6, seniors $5, ages 5-12 $4. Howl-ins summer Sa evenings, reservations required; $10, children $8.)*

ZOUNDS! MOUNDS! Baffling scientists since the mid-1800s, Mima (my-mah) Mounds have spawned wild speculation about their origins. An evenly spaced network of small, perfectly rounded hills covers the prairies just outside the Capital Forest, 12 mi. southwest of Olympia. Anthropology fanciers attribute the mounds' existence to the arcane labors of a nation of yesteryear, biology buffs cite giant gophers, and delusional paranoids cry government conspiracy. The scientific community is torn among hypotheses ranging from glacial action to seismic shock waves; by 1999, no fewer than 159 Mima-related papers had been published. Today, the Mounds inhabit some of the last remaining prairie in the Pacific Northwest, providing visitors with an opportunity to learn about the region's natural history and mystery. To reach the Mounds, take Exit 95 off I-5 and follow the signs to Littlerock. From Littlerock, follow more signs to the Capital Forest and watch for the marked dirt road to the parking lot and trailhead. (Open daily 8am-dusk. For info, call the DNR ☎ 748-2383.)

NISQUALLY NATIONAL WILDLIFE REFUGE. Nisqually National Wildlife Refuge shelters 500 species of plants and animals and miles of open trails. People come to walk and above all, bird-watch. Bald eagles, shorebirds, and northern spotted owls nest here. The trails are open daily from dawn to dusk and are closed to cyclists, joggers, and pets. The visitors center offers free binocular loans and info packets—just leave behind an ID. *(Off I-5 between Olympia and Tacoma at Exit 114. ☎ 753-9467. Visitors centers office open W-Su 9am-4pm. Park office open 7:30am-4pm. Park open dawn to dusk. $3 per person or family.)*

VASHON ISLAND
☎ 206

Although it's only a 25min. ferry ride from Seattle and an even shorter hop from Tacoma, Vashon (VASH-in) Island remains inexplicably invisible to most Seattle tourists. This artists' colony feels like the San Juan Islands without the tourists or an economy to cater to them. Vashon is the perfect place for a one-day trip, a multi-day exploration, or a base from which to explore Seattle.

⬛ **TRANSPORTATION.** Vashon Island stretches between **Seattle** and **Tacoma** on its east side and between **Southworth** and **Gig Harbor** on its west side. The town of **Vashon** lies at the island's northern tip; ferries stop at both the south and north ends of the island. **Washington State Ferries** (☎ 464-6400 or 888-808-7977; www.wsdot.wa.gov/ferries) runs ferries to Vashon Island from 4 different locations. A passenger ferry departs downtown **Seattle** (25min., 8 per day M-F, $5.50), while ferries from **Fauntleroy** in West Seattle and **Southworth** in the Kitsap Peninsula take cars and walk-on passengers. (Fauntleroy ferries 15min., Southworth ferries 10min.; both $3, car and driver $10-13.) A fourth ferry departs from **Point Defiance** in Tacoma and arrives in Tahlequah (15min.; $3, car and driver $10-13). To get to the Fauntleroy terminal on the mainland from Seattle, drive south on I-5 and take Exit 163A (West Seattle/Spokane St.) down Fauntleroy Way. To get to Point Defiance in Tacoma, take Exit 132 off I-5 (Bremerton/Gig Harbor) to Rte. 16. Get on 6th Ave. and turn right onto Pearl St.; follow signs to Point Defiance Park and the ferry. Seattle's **King County Metro** services the downtown ferry terminal, Fauntleroy ferry terminal, and Vashon Island. Buses #54, 116, 118, and 119 run between Seattle and Fauntleroy. Bus #54 picks up at 2nd and Pike St. Save your transfer for the connection on Vashon. Buses #118 and 119 service the island's east side from the north ferry landing through Vashon to the south landing. Bus #117 services the west side of the island. The island is in a different fare zone than Seattle. (☎ 553-3000 or 800-542-7876. 30min., buses every 30min. 5:15am-1:40am. One zone $1.25. Between zones $1.75.)

⑦ PRACTICAL INFORMATION. The **Thriftway** (see **Food,** below) provides maps, as does the Vashon-Maury **Chamber of Commerce,** 17637 SW Vashon Hwy. (☎463-6217). **Joy's,** 17318 Vashon Hwy., has laundry facilities. (☎463-9933. Wash $1.50, dry $0.25 per 10min. Open M-F 7am-8:30pm, Sa-Su 8am-8pm.) Other services include: **Vashon Pharmacy,** 17617 Vashon Hwy. (☎463-9118. Open M-F 9am-7pm, Sa 9am-6pm, Su 11am-1pm.); **emergency,** ☎911; **police,** ☎463-3783. The **library,** 17210 Vashon Hwy., has free **Internet access.** (☎463-2069. Open M-Th 11am-8:30pm, F 11am-6pm, Sa 10am-5pm, Su 1-5pm.) The **Post office** is at 1005 SW 178th St. (☎800-275-8777. Open M-F 8:30am-5pm, Sa 10am-1pm.) **Postal Code:** 98070.

⌂⌂ ACCOMMODATIONS AND FOOD. The ▧**Vashon Island AYH Ranch Hostel (HI) ❶,** 12119 SW Cove Rd., 1½ mi. west of Vashon Hwy., is an oasis just 30min. away from Seattle. Though this frontierland packed with teepees and log-cabin bunkhouses is a destination in its own right, the hostel is also a perfect place to dump a car so you can ferry downtown Seattle. 100 acres call for hiking and biking. (☎463-2592. Free pancake breakfast. Free 1-gear bikes, mountain bikes $6 per day. Sleeping bag $2. 24hr. check-in. Open May-Oct. Bicyclists $11, members $13, nonmembers $16. Teepee and covered wagons also $13/$16. Private double $45; nonmembers $55; $10 per extra person.) A shuttle to the morning ferry is $1.25. The hostel's new B&B, **The Lavender Duck ❸,** 16503 Vashon Hwy., just north on Vashon Hwy., has pleasant, themed rooms and a beautiful living room and kitchen. (☎567-5646. Check in at the hostel. $60.) The meadows are the island's only legal place to **camp ❶,** and campers can use the hostel's kitchens, showers, and common space. ($9 per person, children half-price.) Get creative in the hostel's kitchens with supplies from the large and offbeat **Thriftway,** downtown at 9740 SW Bank Rd. The bulk food section is a camper's dream come true. All buses from the ferry terminal stop there, and a free phone connects to the hostel. (☎463-2100. Open daily 8am-9pm.) The **Stray Dog Cafe ❷,** 17530 Vashon Hwy., has tasty vegetarian and vegan options. (☎463-7833. Open M-Tu 7am-3pm, W-F 7am-3pm and 6-9pm, Sa 8am-3pm, Su 8am-4pm.) **Bishop's Cafe and Lounge ❷,** 17618 Vashon Hwy., has plenty of meals for meat-lovers (burger mania on Monday is $4.25) and many options for the night owl in all of us, as well: video games, pool, big screen TVs, and pints of beer. (☎463-5959. Restaurant open daily 10am-10pm. Bar 11am-2am.) **Fred's Homegrown Restaurant,** 17614 Vashon Hwy SW., serves Vashon locals fresh and healthy meals daily. Breakfast $3-5, lunch $6-7, dinner $7-10. (☎463-6302. Open M-F 8am-3pm, Tu-Sa 5pm-9pm, Sa-Su 8am-2pm.)

◐⌖ SIGHTS AND OUTDOOR ACTIVITIES. Vashon Island provides wonderful but strenuous biking, a sometimes-unbalanced relationship celebrated at the **Bicycle Tree,** off the Vashon Hwy. past Sound Food, where a misbehaving little two-wheeler is lodged in the woods. To get to **Point Robinson Park,** a gorgeous spot for a picnic, take Ellisburg Rd. off the Vashon Hwy. to Dockton Rd. to Pt. Robinson Rd. **Free tours** of the 1885 **Coast Guard lighthouse** are available (☎217-6123. Summer weekends noon-3:30pm.) **Vashon Island Kayak Co.,** at Burton Acres Park, Jensen Point Boat Launch, runs guided tours ($65) and rents sea kayaks. (☎463-9257. Open F-Su 10am-5pm. Call and leave a message for weekday rentals. Singles $14 per hr., $50 per day; doubles $20, $65.) More than 500 acres of woods in the middle of the island are interlaced with mildly difficult **hiking trails.** The **Vashon Park District,** 17130 Vashon Hwy., can tell you more. (☎463-9602. Open daily 8am-4pm.) Count on some culture no matter when you visit—one in 10 residents of Vashon is an artist.

WASHINGTON

WHIDBEY ISLAND   ☎ 360

Clouds wrung dry by the mountains west of Seattle release a scant 20 in. of rain
each year over Whidbey Island, a beach-ringed strip of land that offers peaceful
relaxation in the San Juan islands. The town of **Coupeville**, in Whidbey's middle, is
a great place to start exploring the four state parks and historic reserve, where
rocky beaches meet bluffs crowded with wild roses and blackberries. **Oak Harbor**,
northeast of Coupeville, is a much larger town offering chain stores and a Thursday farmers' market. MacGregor's free *Whidbey Island* is full of maps and info on
coastal towns.

⬛ TRANSPORTATION. Washington State Ferries (☎206-464-6400 or 800-843-3779;
www.wsdot.wa.gov/ferries) provides frequent service from the mainland to the
island. One ferry connects mainland **Mukilteo**, 10 mi. south of Everett and 19 mi.
north of Seattle, with **Clinton**, on the south end of the island (20min.; every 30min.;
$2.70, car and driver $5-6.25, bike $0.90). The other connects **Port Townsend** on the
Olympic Peninsula with the **Keystone terminal** near Ft. Casey State Park (see **Accommodations**, below), at the "waist" of the island (30min.; every 45min.; $2, car and
driver $7-8.75, bike $0.35). You can drive onto the island along Rte. 20, which
heads west from **I-5**, 12 mi. south of Bellingham, at Exit 230. **Rte. 20** and **Rte. 525**
meet near Keystone and form the transportation backbone of the island, linking
significant towns and points of interest. **Island Transit** (☎678-7771 or 321-6688) provides free, hourly public transportation all over the island and has info on connections to and from **Seattle**, but no service Sundays. All buses have bike racks that
hold up to two bikes. Flag a bus down anywhere that is safe for it to stop. The **Visitor Info Center**, 207 Main St., is a self-serve station filled with maps and brochures.
Just look for the tiny building with a giant American flag. For **Traveler Info**, tune to
1610AM. The **Coupeville Public Library**, 788 NW Alexander, provides free **Internet
access**. (☎678-4911. M, W 10am-8pm; Tu, Th-Sa 10am-5pm.)

⬛ ACCOMMODATIONS. Ebey's Landing National Historic Reserve, a Department of the Interior protected beach, covers much of the peninsula and has great
views of the islands, the surrounding Olympic Mountains, and Port Townsend.
Two State Parks lie near Ebey's Landing. **Fort Ebey State Park ❶** lies just north and
east off Rte. 20 (☎678-4636. Open daily 6:30am-dusk, booth hours Su-Th 6am-7pm,
F-Sa 9am-10am, 2pm-3pm, 6pm-8pm. 50 sites. $16, RV $22, hiker/biker $6.) **Fort
Casey State Park ❶**, just south of Fort Ebey, is home to old bunkers and military
paraphernalia on a peninsula with unsheltered, slightly crowded sites with views
of the straits. (☎800-452-5687. $16; no RV sites. Showers $0.25 per 3min.) An interpretive center lies at the **Admiralty Point lighthouse**. (Open Apr.-Oct. Th-Su 11am-
5pm.) To avoid the busier state parks, try **Rhododendron campground ❶**, 1½ mi.
before Coupeville; look for the small tent sign on eastbound Rte. 20/525; if you see
the recycling plant you've just passed it. (☎679-7373; ballfields, picnic sites,
restrooms. 6 primitive sites. $8.) The beautiful **South Whidbey State Park ❶**, amid
old-growth forest by the beach, was once a favorite camp of the Skagit and Snohomish tribes. Numerous trails cut through the woods and beach. (☎206-321-4559,
reservations 888-226-7688. 46 sites; $16, RV sites $22, hiker/biker $8.) If you prefer
a B&B to a tent, the **Anchorage Inn ❹**, 807 North Main Street in Coupeville, offers
comfortable Victorian rooms. (☎678-5581. $80.)

⬛ FOOD. La Paz ❷, 8898 Hwy. 525 right off of the ferry dock, is a Baja-style Mexican restaurant in Clinton, replete with loud colors and beans. A tasty seafood taco
with rice is $7. (☎341-4787. Open daily noon-3pm for lunch and 5-8pm for dinner;
open F-Sa until 9pm for dinner.) Seaside **Coupeville**, Washington's 2nd-oldest town,

WASHINGTON

makes for a nice stroll. At the bakery, **Knead and Feed ❷**, 4 Front St., you can eat a fabulous lunch ($3-8). (☎678-5431. Open M-F 10am-3pm, Sa-Su 9am-4pm.) For coffee, a pizza ($4), and a great patio view, walk down the stairs to **Great Times Espresso ❶**, 12 Front St. (☎678-5358. Open M-F 7am-7pm, Sa-Su 8am-7pm.)

◧ 🏔 SIGHTS AND OUTDOOR ACTIVITIES. At the north tip of the island, on Rte. 20, the crowded **Deception Pass Bridge,** the nation's first suspension bridge, connects Whidbey Island to Fidalgo Island. A secret cave at one end held 17th-century prisoners who were forced to make wicker furniture. Deception Pass itself is a thin sliver of water that can be brought to the boil by tides; white-water kayakers come here to test their mettle against the salt-water rapids. **Deception Pass State Park,** 41229 SR (☎675-2417), surrounds the pass itself, and is the most heavily used of Whidbey's four state parks (especially on weekends). There are camping facilities, a saltwater boat launch, and a freshwater lake good for swimming, fishing, and boating. The **campground ❶** is subjected to jet noise from EA6B Navy attack aircraft from nearby Whidbey Island Naval Air Station, in Oak Harbor. (☎888-226-7688. Reservations suggested. 250 sites; $16, RV sites $22, hiker/biker $5.)

BELLINGHAM   ☎360

Situated between Seattle and Vancouver, Bellingham (pop. 67,000) is a dream city for the outdoor adventurer—Mt. Baker and the North Cascades are just a stone's throw to the east, and Bellingham Bay offers an array of ocean adventures, from kayaking to whale watching. Historic Bellingham was an industrial port city reliant upon rich mineral and timber resources. Today, Bellingham's port still thrives, but is home to a large fishing fleet and ferry boats, while the town also accommodates **Western Washington University** (14,000 students).

▟▛ ORIENTATION AND TRANSPORTATION. Bellingham lies along **I-5,** 90 mi. north of **Seattle** and 57 mi. south of **Vancouver, BC.** Downtown centers on **Holly St.** and **Cornwall Ave.,** next to the Georgia Pacific pulp mill (Exits 252 and 253 off I-5). **Western Washington University (WWU)** sits atop a hill to the south. The hip town of **Fairhaven,** where ferries, buses, and trains stop, is south of Bellingham and serviced by public transit. Catch a train at **Amtrak,** 401 Harris Ave., in the bus and train station next to the ferry terminal. (☎734-8851 or 800-872-7245. Counter open daily 8:45am-12:30pm and 1-4:30pm.) Two per day to **Seattle** (2½hr., $20) and **Vancouver, BC** (1½hr., $14.) **Greyhound** is in the same station next to the ferry terminal. (☎733-5251 or 800-231-2222. Open M-F 8am-6pm, Sa-Su 8am-5pm.) Buses run to **Seattle** (2hr.; 5 per day, 7 on F, $14-15); **Mt. Vernon** (30min.; 5 per day, $6-8); and **Vancouver, BC** (2hr.; 4 per day, $12.) Private shuttles run ferries to the nearby San Juan Islands (see p. 194). **Public Transportation** routes all start at the Railroad Avenue Mall terminal, between Holly and Magnolia St. (☎676-7433. M-F 5:50am-6:30pm. $0.50, under 6 or over 84 free. No transfers. Buses run every 30 or 60min.) **City Cab** (☎773-8294 or 800-281-5430) and **Yellow Cab** (☎734-8294) service the town.

🛈 PRACTICAL INFORMATION. Services include a friendly, well-organized **Visitors Info Center,** 904 Potter St. Take exit 253 (Lakeway) from I-5. (☎671-3990. Open daily 8:30am-5:30pm.) **Equipment Rental: Fairhaven Bikes,** 1103 11th St., rents bikes ($20-30 per day) and in-line skates. (☎733-4433. Open M-Th 9:30am-7pm, F 9:30am-8pm, Sa 10am-6pm, Su 11am-5pm.) **Bellingham Cleaning Center,** 1010 Lakeway Dr., offers washing for $1.50 and drying for $0.25 per 8min. (☎734-3755. Open daily 6am-10pm). Other services include: **emergency,** ☎911; **police,** 505 Grand Ave. (☎676-6913. Open M-F 8am-5:30pm.); **crisis Line,** ☎800-584-3578; **St. Joseph's General Hospital,** 2901 Squalicum Pkwy. (☎734-5400. Open 24hr.)

Access the **Internet** at the **library**, 210 Central Ave., at Commercial St. opposite City Hall. (☎676-6860. Open M-Th 10am-9pm, F-Sa 10am-6pm; also Sept.-May Su 1-5pm.) The **Post Office** is at 315 Prospect St. (☎800-275-8777. Open M-F 8am-5:30pm, Sa 9:30am-3pm.) **Postal Code:** 98225.

☗ ACCOMMODATIONS. Bellingham does not have a hostel, but Blaine, 17 miles north, offers the **Hostelling International-Birch Bay ❶**, 7467 Gemini Street, which is within walking distance of Birch Bay. (☎371-2180. Office open 7:30am-9:30am and 5pm-10pm. 49 beds. $14 HI members, $17 nonmembers.) In Bellingham proper you can pick from a strip of budget motels on N. Samish Way (2min. off exit 252). The **Bay City Motor Inn ❸** is at 116 N. Samish Way. (Singles from $40; doubles $50.) If you prefer to stay in the heart of the downtown area, the **Bellingham Inn ❸**, 202 E Holly St. off I-5 Exit 253, has queen beds, clean rooms, and cable TV. (☎734-1900. Singles $42; doubles $50.) If you want to camp close to the city, head to **Larrabee State Park ❶**, on Chuckanut Dr., 7 mi. south of town. Larrabee offers 14 mi. of trails with views of the San Juan Islands, bouldering, a boat launch, restrooms and showers, and even clamming. (☎902-8844; reservations 1-888-226-7688. 85 sites, $14; RV sites $20. Reservations suggested. Park open daily 6:30am-dusk.)

Bellingham

🏠🏕 ACCOMMODATIONS
Bay City Motor Inn, **6**
Bellingham Inn, **5**
Hostelling International-
   Birch Bay, **1**
Larrabee State Park, **8**
🍎 FOOD
Boundary Bay Brewery
   Bistro, **4**
Casa Que Pasa, **3**
Old Town Cafe, **2**
Tony's, **7**

◘ FOOD. The **Community Food Co-op,** 1220 N Forest St., at Maple St., has all the essentials for the healthy eater, plus a tasty cafe in the back. (☎734-8158. Open daily 8am-9pm, cafe closes at 8pm.) The Saturday **Bellingham Farmer's Market,** at Chestnut St. and Railroad Ave., has 115 vendors selling fruit, vegetables, seafood, and homemade doughnuts. (☎647-2060. Apr.-Oct. Sa 10am-3pm.) Locals feast on huge burritos starting at $3 at **Casa Que Pasa ❶,** 1415 Railroad Ave. Gallery space for local artists. (☎738-8226. Open daily 11am-11pm, tequila bar open until 1am.) For a taste of local brew, check out the **Boundary Bay Brewery & Bistro ❷,** 1107 Railroad Ave. (☎647-5593.) Pints are $3.25, while burgers and nachos cost $7. Bang out a few songs on the piano at **The Old Town Cafe ❶,** 316 West Holly St., which makes delectable breakfasts. Buttermilk pancakes are $3.75; breakfast specials start at $5 and are served all day. (☎671-4431. Open M-Sa 6:30am-3pm, Su 8am-2pm.) **Tony's ❷,** 1101 Harris Ave., is in Fairhaven Village, just blocks from the ferry. This garden and cafe serves ice cream, bagels, and the infamous $4.50 Toxic Milkshake, made with espresso grounds. (☎738-4710. Open M-F 7am-9pm, Sa-Su 7:30am-9pm.)

◙ ♫ SIGHTS AND ENTERTAINMENT. The **Whatcom Museum of History and Art,** 121 Prospect St., occupies four buildings along Prospect St., most notably the bright red former city hall. Photographs of turn-of-the-century Pacific Northwest logging scenes by Darius Kinsey are a highlight. (☎676-6981. Open Tu-Su noon-5pm. Wheelchair accessible. Free.) The ARCO Exhibits Building and Whatcom Children's Museum are also worth a visit. **Big Rock Garden Park,** 2900 Sylvan St., is a 3-acre Japanese-style sculpture garden, featuring mostly contemporary work. Take Alabama St. east and then go left on Sylvan for several blocks. Call ahead for a schedule. (☎676-6985. Park open in summer 7am-9pm, winter 8am-6pm.)

In the second week of June, lumberjacks from across the land gather for axe-throwing and log-rolling at the **Deming Logging Show.** To reach the show grounds, take Rte. 542 (Mt. Baker Hwy.) 12 mi. east to Cedarville Rd. and then turn left and follow signs. (☎592-3051. $5, ages 3-12 $3.) The **Bellingham Festival of Music** brings symphony, chamber, folk, and jazz musicians from around the world during the first two weeks of August. All concerts are in Western Washington University Auditorium at 8pm. (☎676-5997. Tickets $18-23; students half-price.) Also in August is the **Mount Baker Blues Festival** (☎671-6817) at Rivers Edge Tree Farm in Deming. Memorial Day weekend sees the mother of all relays, the **Ski to Sea Race** (☎734-1330.) Participants sand-ski, run, canoe, bike, and sea kayak 85 miles from Mt. Baker to the finish line at Bellingham Bay. Families, friends, and spectators join the participants in a grand parade and festival at the race's conclusion.

▨ OUTDOOR ACTIVITIES. The 2½ mi. hike up **Chuckanut Mountain** leads through a quiet forest to a view of the islands that fill the bay. On clear days, Mt. Rainier is visible from the top. The trail leaves from the North Chuckanut Mountain Trailhead off Old Samish Hwy., about 3 mi. south of city limits. Alternatively, from Clayton Beach, you can hike a mile to an excellent vista of the San Juan Islands. From the viewpoint, hike the **Fragrance Lake Trail** if you're interested in an afternoon swim (1 mi. from viewpoint to lake). The beach at **Lake Padden Park,** 4882 Samish Way, has the warmest water in the Puget Sound; take bus #44 1 mi. south of downtown. The park also has tennis courts, playing fields, hiking trails, a boat launch (no motors allowed), and fishing off the pier. (☎676-6985. Open daily 6am-10pm.) The popular **Rotary Interurban Trail** (great for biking and running) travels 7 mi. from **Fairhaven Park** to **Larrabee State Park** along the relatively flat route of the old Interurban Electric Railway. Breaks in the trees permit a glimpse of the San Juan Islands. Several trails branch off the main line and lead into the Chuckanut Mountains or down to the coast; get a map from the visitors center at Larrabee.

NEAR BELLINGHAM: BLAINE AND BIRCH BAY

A small border town 20 mi. north of Bellingham, Blaine is home to the west's busiest border station between Canada and the US. Directly on the US border, Blaine's main attraction is the **Peace Arch State Park**. To reach the park, take I-5 Exit 276, then turn north onto 2nd St. The Peace Arch contains relics of early US and Canadian ships of discovery and commemorates the Treaty of Ghent, which ended the War of 1812 and inaugurated the long era of peace between Canada and the US. (☎ 332-8221. Open daily 8am-dusk.) The **Harbor Cafe ❸**, 295 Marine Dr., halfway down Blaine's main pier, serves the best seafood in town. (☎ 332-5176. Open M-F 7am-9pm, Sa-Su 7am-10pm.)

MOUNT BAKER ☎ 360

Rising 10,778 ft. above sea level, Mt. Baker is the crown of the 1.7 million-acre Mt. Baker-Snowqualmie National Forest. Mt. Baker hasn't erupted for 10,000 years, but occasional steam rises from this active volcano. A yearly average of 615 in. (51¼ ft.) of snowfall makes for excellent snowboarding and skiing. No high speed lifts here; just great bowls, chutes, glades, and cheap lift tickets. During the summer, hikers and mountaineers challenge themselves on its trails.

⛭ TRANSPORTATION AND PRACTICAL INFORMATION. To get to this hotbed of outdoor activity, take I-5 Exit 255, just north of Bellingham, to Rte. 542, known as the Mt. Baker Hwy.; 58 mi. of roads through the foothills afford views of Baker and other peaks in the range. The highway ends at Artist Point (5140 ft.), with spectacular wilderness vistas. The road closes at Mt. Baker Ski Area in winter. For trail maps, backcountry permits, or further info about both the National Forest and National Park, stop by the Glacier Ranger Station, located on 542 just before the National Forest. (☎ 599-2714. Open daily May-Oct. 8am-4:30pm.)

⛺ CAMPING. Silver Lake Park ❶, 9006 Silver Lake Rd., is 3 mi. north of the highway at Maple Falls. The park has 73 sites, 4 mi. of hiking trails, swimming, and fishing. Buy a 2-day license in Maple Falls for $7, and catch a few of the 17,000 trout stocked yearly in Silver Lake. (☎ 599-2776. Sites $17; RV sites $19.) More primitive and closer to the mountain is **Douglas Fir Campground ❶**, past Glacier at Mile 36 off Rte. 542 (30 sites, $12), and **Silver Fir Campground ❶**, at Mile 46 off Rte. 542. (Water. 21 sites, $12.) **Glacier Creek Lodge ❸**, 10036 Mt. Baker Hwy. is a fine option for the night. Free breakfast and a steamy hot-tub are pluses. 2 night min. stay on weekends during ski season. (☎ 599-2991. Reservations essential during peak winter and summer seasons. Singles or doubles $44, cabins $115-165.)

⛷ WINTER SPORTS. Baker is arguably the birthplace of the snowboard, and boards are wildly popular here. The volcano packs soft powder for longer than any other nearby ski area, staying open from early November through May. The ski area has seven diesel-powered lifts and the lowest lift ticket rates in the Northwest. There is no snow-making or shaping on the mountain's 1500 vertical feet of runs. Contact the **Mt. Baker Ski Area Office** in Bellingham for more info. (☎ 734-6771; www.mtbakerskiarea.com. Lift tickets Sa-Su and holidays $35, Th-F $27, M-W $25; under 16 and seniors $27, $22, $21.) In the winter many trails become impromptu cross-country ski trails and snowshoe tracks.

⛰ HIKING. Many roads and trails are covered in snow well into the summer so call ahead to check which trails are accessible. In June, you can access the Glacier Overlook along **Heliotrope Ridge** (Road 39 off Hwy. 542). This 3 mi. trail is the starting point for mountaineers heading up Baker, and offers hikers an excellent view of the mountain. The **Lake Ann Trail** (5 mi., multi-day) is one of the favorites in the area. This steep trail leads 5 mi. to the lake of the same name, then continues to the Lower Curtis Glacier. **Skyline Divide,** on Road 37 off Hwy. 542, is also a great day-hike that provides stunning views of the North Cascade range (3½ mi. one way.) Hikers can make the inevitable Robert Frost references along the **Fire and Ice Trail,** a picturesque half-mile loop beginning on Rte. 542. The first part of the trail is wheelchair accessible. For a hike up to a beautiful, remote lake, head up to **Tomyhoi Lake Trail** (4 mi. one-way, full day). Take forest service road 3065 north from the highway as far as it will go.

♥ MOUNTAINEERING. If you're looking to summit a peak in the North Cascades, considerable experience in mountaineering and glacier travel is necessary. Check out Fred Beckey's *Cascade Alpine Guide: Climbing and High Routes* or contact the **American Alpine Institute,** 1515 12th St. (☎ 671-1505; www.aai.cc.) Both provide information on routes, and the American Alpine Institute provides guides.

SAN JUAN ISLANDS

With hundreds of tiny islands and endless parks and coastline, the San Juan Islands are an explorer's dream. The islands enjoy nothing less than perfect weather: between May and September the average daily high temperature is in the upper 60s to low 70s, the sun shines almost every day, and only 1 in. of rain falls each summer month in this "rain-shadow" of the Olympic Mountains. The scattered small towns showcase each islands' uniqueness. Tourists storm the islands in July and August, so plan a visit in late spring or early fall. The *San Juanderer* has tide charts and ferry schedules, and is free on ferries or at visitors centers. A trip to the San Juan Islands requires thinking ahead as the info you need may be available only in Seattle; be sure to book early if you are planning a summertime visit to the San Juan Islands.

◄ INTER-ISLAND TRANSPORTATION

Washington State Ferries (☎ 206-464-6400 or 888-808-7977; www.wsdot.wa.gov/ferries) has frequent daily service to **Lopez** (40min.), **Orcas** (50min.), **San Juan Island** (1hr.), and **Shaw** (30min.) from **Anacortes;** check the schedule available at visitors centers in Puget Sound. Travel time to the islands depends on the number of stops. To save on fares, travel directly to the westernmost island on your itinerary, then return: eastbound traffic travels for free. The ferries are packed in summer, so call ahead to ask when to arrive. Generally, you should get there at least 1hr. (2hr. on weekends) prior to departure. (Passengers $8-10 from Anacortes to Friday Harbor, vehicles $30-36 from Anacortes to Friday Harbor. Eastbound inter-island: passengers free, vehicles $13. Cash and credit cards accepted in Anacortes, inter-island ferries cash only.) To reach the terminal from Seattle, take **I-5** north to Mt. Vernon, then **Rte. 20** west to Anacortes, and then follow signs. The **Bellingham Airporter** (☎ 800-235-5247) runs shuttles between **Sea-Tac** (see p. 160) and **Anacortes** (8 per day; $31, round-trip $56).
   Victoria Clipper (☎ 1-800-888-2535; www.victoriaclipper.com), departs **Seattle's** Pier 69 daily for San Juan Island, arriving at Spring St. Landing, one block north of the state ferry dock in **Friday Harbor** (2½hr.; $38, round-trip $59), or at **Rosario Resort,** on Orcas Island (3¼hr.; mid-May to mid-Sept.; $58, round-trip $89; 1 week advance discount; children half-price). **Island Commuter** (☎ 734-8180 or 888-734-8180) departs **Bellingham**

San Juan Islands

▲ ACCOMMODATIONS

Discovery Inn, **7**
Doe Bay Resort, **3**
Hotel de Haro, **5**
Lakedale Campgrounds, **6**
Lopez Farm Cottages and Tent
  Camping, **11**
Lopez Islander Marina Resort, **13**
Moran State Park Campgrounds, **2**
Obstruction Pass Campgrounds, **4**
Odlin Park Campgrounds, **8**
Outlook Inn, **1**
San Juan County Park, **9**
Spencer Spit State Park
  Campgrounds, **12**
Wayfarer's Rest, **10**

WASHINGTON

for **Rosario Resort** (1¼hr.), **Friday Harbor** (2¼hr.), and islands on the way ($25, round-trip $35, ages 6-12 half-price, under 6 free; bicycles $5). **Kenmore Air** (☎ 800-543-9595) flies to San Juan from Seattle (4-5 times per day; one-way $96-105, round-trip $159-169).

SAN JUAN ISLAND   ☎ 360

San Juan Island is the longest trek from Anacortes, yet it is the most popular tourist destination. Ferries drop off passengers in Friday Harbor, the largest town in the archipelago. San Juan Island is the easiest island to explore on a budget since the ferry docks right in town, the roads are good for cyclists, and a shuttle bus services the island. San Juan is home to a National Historic Park and **Lime Kiln State Park,** the only designated whale watching park in the world.

⊏ LOCAL TRANSPORTATION

With bicycle, car, and boat rentals within blocks of the ferry terminal, **Friday Harbor** is a convenient base for exploring San Juan. Miles of poorly marked roads access all corners of the island. It's wise to carefully plot a course on the free **map** available at the visitors centers, real estate offices, and gas stations.

Buses: San Juan Transit (☎378-8887 or 800-887-8387; www.san-juan.net/transit.com). Travels from Friday Harbor to Roche Harbor on the hr. and will stop upon request ($4, return trip $7; from Friday Harbor to Westside $4, return trip $7; day pass $10, 2 day pass $17. Tours $17, depart Friday Harbor at 11am and 1pm. Call ahead for reservations.)

Ferries: Washington State Ferries; see **Transportation,** above.

Taxis: San Juan Taxi (☎378-3550). $4 base, $1 per person, $1 per mi. after the 1st mi.

⊓ PRACTICAL INFORMATION

Visitor Information: Chamber of Commerce, 1 Front St. 2a (☎378-5240; www.sanjuanisland.org or www.guidetosanjuans.com), is upstairs on the corner of Front St. and Spring St. Stop in for a map and information on tours.

Outdoor Information: San Juan National Historic Park Information Center (☎378-2240; www.nps.gov/sajh), on the corner of First St. and Spring St. Open daily in summer 8:30am-4:30pm; winter 8:30am-4pm.

Tours: A host of companies offer tours; shopping around (especially looking at fliers at the tourist office) pays dividends. **San Juan Boat Tours** (☎800-232-6722), at Spring St., docks a block right from ferry, has a 66-passenger boat with speakers to pick up the Orcas' chat. (3hr., departs daily at 12pm; $39, children $29). **Sea Quest Expeditions** (☎378-5767), a non-profit education, research, and conservation group, runs kayaking tours daily all year. Call to arrange trips. Day-trip $59; multi-day trips available.

Equipment Rental: Island Scooter and Bike Rental, 85 Front St. (☎378-8811) next to Friday's Crabhouse, rents scooters for $17 per hr., $51 per day. Bikes $6 per hour, $30 per day. Open daily 9am-6pm.

Laundromat: Sail-In Laundromat, on East St. behind the waterfront strip. Wash $2.50, dry $2.50. Open daily 7am-8pm.

Emergency: ☎911.

Police: 135 Rhone St. (non-emergency ☎378-4151), at Reed St.

Domestic Violence/Sexual Assault Services: ☎378-8680.

Pharmacy: Friday Harbor Drug, 210 Spring St. (☎378-4421). Open M-Sa 9am-7pm, Su 10am-4pm.

Red Tide Hotline: ☎800-562-5632.

Medical Services: Inter-Island Medical Center, 550 Spring St. (☎378-2141), at Mullis Rd. Open M-F 8:30am-4:30pm, Sa 10am-1pm. **Crisis:** ☎378-2345. 24hr.

Internet Access: San Juan Island Library, 1010 Guard St. (☎378-2798), provides visitors 30min. of free emailing, or 1hr. general **Internet** use.

Post Office: 220 Blair Ave. (☎378-4511), at Reed St. Open M-F 8:30am-4:30pm. **Postal Code:** 98250.

ACCOMMODATIONS AND CAMPING

The popularity of San Juan and its few budget accommodations makes finding a cheap bed challenging. The campgrounds are wildly popular; reservations are imperative. While beautiful, the B&Bs are also prohibitively expensive; contact **San Juan Central Reservation** (☎888-999-8773; www.fridayharbor.com) for help. If you miss out on hosteling and camping options, your best bet may be to take the ferry back to Anacortes where a plethora of cheap motels line Commercial Ave., the main street leading up to the ferry. Prices are less than half of those on the island. The **Gateway Motel ❸**, 2019 Commercial Ave., is a reasonable deal. (☎293-2655. Singles $49; doubles $55; with kitchen $10 more.)

Wayfarer's Rest, 35 Malcolm St. (☎378-6428), a 10min. walk from the ferry up Spring onto Argyle St. and turn left at the church. This house-turned-hostel has beautiful home-made driftwood bunks, a comfortable living area with TV, a patio and garden, and a full kitchen. Coin showers, washers, and dryers ($2 wash, $2 dry). Bike rental $15 per day. Check-in 2-9pm. Bunk room $22; private room and cabins $55. ❷

San Juan County Park, 380 Westside Rd. (☎378-1842), 10 mi. west of Friday Harbor, along the bay. 20 sites are perched on a bluff with a fantastic sunset view. Water, toilets. Open daily 7am-10pm. Office open daily 9am-7pm. Make reservations 7-90 days ahead. Vehicle sites $22; walk-ins $6. ❶

Lakedale Campgrounds, 4313 Roche Harbor Rd. (☎378-2350 or 800-617-2267), 4 mi. from Friday Harbor, just west of Egg Lake Rd. Some sites near lakes. Office hours 8am-10pm. Reservations suggested, but campers can almost always find spots. Fishing permits $4 per day, non-campers $8 per day. Boat rental. Open Mar. 15-Oct. 15; cabins year-round. Vehicle sites $24, plus $5.75 per person after 2; hiker/biker sites $8 per person; 4-person tent-cabins from $45. Cheaper rates in off-season. ❶

Hotel de Haro, Roche Harbor, 248 Reuben Memorial Drive (☎378-2155 or 800-451-8910). This hotel was built in 1886 and overlooks a busy harbor and beautiful formal garden. Classic hotel rooms with shared bath $69 (Oct.-May), $79 (May-Sept.). ❹

Discovery Inn, 1016 Guard St. (☎378-2000 or 1-800-822-4753), located about a mile from the buzz of Friday Harbor. Offers an outdoor jacuzzi, sauna, sun decks, and gardens. Singles and doubles in off season $79, summertime $105. ❺

FOOD

Both the quality and quantity of food at **King's Market,** 160 Spring St., will trick you into thinking you're on the mainland; once you see the bill, however, reality will strike. (☎378-4505. Open in summer M-Sa 7:30am-10pm, Su 7:30am-9pm.) Plan ahead to avoid missing a meal; many cafes and restaurants close early.

Thai Kitchen, 42 1st St. (☎378-1917), next to the Whale Museum. A popular dinner spot with a beautiful patio for flower-sniffing or star-gazing. Try the fresh lime juice with the popular Pad Thai. Lunch dishes around $7, dinners $8-12. Open for lunch Tu-Sa 11:30am-2:30pm, dinner M-F 5pm-9pm. ❸

San Juan Donut Shop, 209 Spring St. (☎378-2271). Stop in for bottomless coffee ($1.25) and fresh donuts ($0.75) while you wait for the ferry. Open daily 6am-3pm. ❶

Hungry Clam Fish and Chips, 130 1st St. (☎378-3474), serves up excellent fresh beer-battered Alaskan Cod (fish and chips $5.50-8.50). Open daily 11am-7pm. ❷

Blue Dolphin Cafe, 185 1st St. (☎378-6116), is a local favorite for a hearty breakfast or lunch. Tall stack of pancakes $3.50, hot sandwiches from $6. Daily specials are a good bet if you've got a few extra bucks. Open daily 5am-2pm. ❷

Vic's Drive Inn, 25 2nd St. (☎378-8427), serves up the cheapest burger in Friday Harbor ($2). You'll also find a quarter pizza pie or apple pie for $2.50. Open M-F 7am-7pm, Sa 7am-2pm. ❶

Front Street Ale House, 1 Front St. (☎378-2337), serves cold brews from the San Juan Brewing Co. located just next door. San Juan local micro-brews taste fantastic after a long day of biking or paddling. Pints $4, Open daily 11am-11pm. ❷

👁 SIGHTS

Driving around the 35 mi. perimeter of the island takes about 2hr.; on bike, it makes for the perfect day-long tour. The **West Side Rd.** traverses gorgeous scenery and provides the best chance for sighting **orcas** from three resident pods. To begin a tour of the island, head south and west out of Friday Harbor on Mullis Rd. (Bikers may want to do this route in the opposite direction, as climbs heading counterclockwise around the island are much more gradual.)

WHALE MUSEUM. The museum has a collection of artifacts and whale skeletons as well as modern tools used for whale research. Step into a phone booth and listen to the sound of orcas, dolphins or walruses. Local whale art adds a colorful backdrop to the experience. Call their whale hotline at ☎800-562-8832 to report sightings and strandings. *(62 First St. N. ☎378-4710 or 800-946-7227. Open June-Sept. daily 10am-5pm; call for winter hours. $5, seniors $4, students and ages 5-18 $2, under 5 free.)*

SAN JUAN ISLAND NATIONAL HISTORICAL PARK. Two national historic parks preserve a living memory of tensions between the British and American camps co-occupying San Juan Island in the mid-19th century. The American army built its barracks on Cattle Point, located on southeastern San Juan Island. Today, **American Camp** is the more elaborate of the park's two halves. The **visitors center** explains the history of the curious conflict, while a self-guided trail leads from the shelter to an excellent view of Mt. Baker at the Redoubt. For a slightly longer hike, head to the top of Mt. Finlayson. You'll see Mt. Rainier to the southeast, the Olympic Mountains to the south, and BC to the west (Mt. Finlayson trail). **English Camp,** on the island's north end, exhibits a greater number of historic buildings, and contains one of Washington's largest Big Leaf Maple trees. The Bell Point trail is a pleasant 2 mi. loop. During the summer on Saturday afternoons, the two camps alternate re-enacting Pig War-era life. *(To get to American Camp, follow Cattle Point Rd. south from Friday Harbor. British Camp can be reached by Roche Harbor Rd. ☎378-2902. Camp open daily June-Aug. dawn-11pm; Sept.-May Th-Su. Visitors center open daily 8:30am-5pm. Guided walks June-Sept. Sa 11:30am. Re-enactments June-July 12:30-3:30pm. Free.)*

🏔 OUTDOOR ACTIVITIES

Tourism on San Juan Island are centered around Orca whales. The San Juan Islands are home to three pods of Orcas, creatively dubbed pods J, K, and L. San Juan Island receives the majority of whale watching attention due to the whales' travel patterns north and south through the Haro Strait. In the summer, whales are seen daily from **Lime Kiln Point State Park,** along West Side Rd. This location is renowned as the best **whale watching** spot on the island. Take the short hike to the whale watching balconies, where cliffside crowds watch as killer whales prowl for salmon between occasional acrobatics. More determined whale watchers might prefer a cruise; see **San Juan Boat Tours,** p. 196. Keep in mind, San Juan has almost as many whale watching boats as it does whales, and whale watching can sometimes feel like whale boat-watching. When choosing a company, ask about boat size; smaller boats can usually get closer to the whales. Kayak tours will also seek out Orcas; see **SeaQuest Expeditions** and **Crystal Seas Kayaking,** p. 196.

The island provides several laid-back hiking trails as well as picturesque beaches, both relaxing options for the afternoon. If the sky is clear, make the half-mile jaunt down the road to **Cattle Point** for views of the distant Olympic Mountains, or stop by **South Beach,** a stretch of dazzling shoreline. Also in the south, **Eagle Beach** and **Grandma's Cove** are considered two of the finest beaches on the island. Heading east from West Side Rd., Mitchell Bay Rd. leads to a steep half-mile trail to **"Mount" Young,** a good tall hill within viewing range of Victoria and the Olympic Range. The gravel False Bay Rd., heading west from Cattle Point Rd., runs to **False Bay,** where **bald eagles** nest. During spring and summer, nesting eagles are visible at low tide along the northwestern shore.

ORCAS ISLAND ☎ 360

Mount Constitution overlooks much of Puget Sound from its 2407 ft. summit atop Orcas Island—this high point is touted as the best 360 degree marine viewpoint in North America. A small population of retirees, artists, and farmers dwell here in understated homes surrounded by green shrubs and the bronze bark of madrona trees. With a commune-like campground and resort, and the largest state park in Washington, Orcas Island has the best budget tourist facilities in the San Juans. Unfortunately, much of the beach is occupied by private resorts and closed to the public. Moran State Park offers a relaxing wilderness experience while Eastsound provides a movie theater, several restaurants, a museum, and shopping.

ORIENTATION AND PRACTICAL INFORMATION

Orcas is shaped like a horseshoe, lending a commonsensical name to the main thoroughfare, **Horseshoe Hwy.** The ferry lands on the southwest tip at **Orcas Village. Eastsound,** the main town, is at the top of the horseshoe, 9 mi. northeast. **Olga** and **Doe Bay** are another 8 and 11 mi. down the eastern side of the horseshoe, respectively. Pick up a map in one of the four shops at the ferry landing.

Ferries: Washington State Ferries, see p. 194.

Taxis: Orcas Island Taxi (☎376-8294). $3.50 flat rate, $1.50 per mi.

Visitor Information: San Juan Island houses the more official tourist facilities. **Pyewacket Books** (☎376-2043), in Templin Center, in Eastsound at N Beach Rd., has good island books.

Equipment Rental: Wildlife Cycles 350 North Beach Rd., (☎376-4708), at A St. in Eastsound. Bikes $7.50 per hr., $30 per day. Open M-Sa 9am-6pm, Su noon-3pm. **Dolphin Bay Bicycles** (☎376-4157), near the ferry. $25 per day, $55 for 3 days.

Sporting Goods: Eastsound Sporting Goods, 1 Main Street (☎376-5588), Templin Center #4. Caters to all your outdoor equipment needs and rents fishing rods for $10 per day. Open in summer daily 9:30am-9pm.

Emergency: ☎911.

Domestic Violence/Sexual Assault Services: ☎376-1234.

Pharmacy: Ray's (☎376-2230, after-hours emergencies 376-3693), Templin Center #3, in Eastsound at N Beach Rd. Open M-Sa 9am-6pm.

Internet Access: Library (☎376-4985), at Rose and Pine in Eastsound. Walk up the path from Prune Alley. Open M-Th 10am-7pm, F-Sa 10am-5pm. **Orcas Online,** 254 N Beach Rd. (☎376-4124), in Eastsound. $5 per 30min. Open M-Sa 9am-5:30pm.

Post Office: 221 A St. (☎376-4121), in Eastsound. Open M-F 9am-4:30pm. **Postal Code:** 98245.

ACCOMMODATIONS AND CAMPING

B&Bs on Orcas charge upwards of $85 per night; call ☎376-8888 for advice. Camping is the cheapest option on Orcas. Reservations are important during summer.

Doe Bay Resort (☎376-2291), off Horseshoe Hwy. on Pt. Lawrence Rd., 5 mi. east of Moran State Park. A former commune and then Human Potential Center, this retreat keeps the old feel in its guise as vacation spot. Cafe (open daily 8:30am-12pm, 6pm-9pm), treehouse, and a co-ed clothing-optional hot tub and steam sauna. Sauna $4 per day. Office open 11am-9pm. Kayak rentals through Shearwater Adventures (see **Outdoors Information,** below). Private rooms start at $55; yurts $75; camping $25. ❸

Moran State Park, State Rte. 22 (ranger ☎376-2326, reservations 1-888-226-7688 or www.parks.wa.gov). Follow Horseshoe Hwy. straight into the park, 14 mi. from the ferry on the east side of the island. The most popular camping in the islands, but sites are often reserved months in advance (you can reserve as early as 9 months prior to your stay). At Cascade Lake, you can rent rowboats and paddleboats ($12-13 per hr., $35-45 full day). 4 campgrounds throughout the park contain 151 sites. About 12 sites are open year-round. Car sites $16, hiker/biker sites $6. ❶

Obstruction Pass. Accessible by boat or foot. Turn off the Hwy. just past Olga, and head south (right) on Obstruction Pass Rd. Follow the gravel road marked Obstruction Pass Trailhead to the trailhead and parking lot. Some of the only free camping in the San Juan Islands. Pit toilets, no water. Access to nice pebble beaches on Puget Sound. 11 sites. ❶

Outlook Inn (☎376-2200), on Horseshoe Hwy. in Eastsound, just West of N. Beach Rd. (☎376-2200), offers rooms with shared baths from $64-84. A good budget option if you want a room in town. ❹

FOOD

Essentials can be found in Eastsound at **Island Market,** 469 Market St. (☎376-6000. Open M-Sa 8am-9pm, Su 10am-7pm.) For a large selection of groceries, medicines, and vegan cheeses, make a bee-line for **Orcas Homegrown Market,** on N Beach Rd. Try their deli and seafood specials for lunch; most specials are $5-6 and there are always vegetarian options. (☎376-2009. Open daily 8am-9pm.) For loads of fresh local produce, visit the **Farmer's Market** in front of the museum. (Sa 10am-3pm.)

Cafe Jama (☎376-4949), in Eastsound Sq. on N Beach Rd. Perhaps the only place you'll find a Sunday *New York Times* on Orcas Island, Cafe Jama serves up a Northwest breakfast (specialty coffees and homemade muffins) as well as a variety of tasty lunch options: soups, salads and sandwiches $6-8. ❷

Chimayo (☎376-6394), in Our House Building on N Beach Rd. Portions are large, the salsa is fresh, and prices are lower than across the street. Design your own burritos and tacos ($5-9), or get 2 tacos for $3.75. Vegetarian options abound. Open M-F 11am-7pm, Sa 11am-3pm. ❷

Lower Tavern (☎378-4848), at the corner of Horseshoe Hwy. and Prune Alley. One of the few cheap spots open after 5pm. Dig into burgers and fries from $7. Seven beers on tap, pints $2.50-$3.75. Happy hour M-F 4:30-6:30pm. Bar open M-Th 11am-midnight, F-Sa 11am-1am, Su 12pm-7pm. Kitchen open M-Sa 11am-9pm, Su noon-5pm.

Roses Bread and Specialties (☎376-5805) in Eastsound Sq. Those who visit this gem will be rewarded with a huge selection of cheeses, fresh bread, and sweet baked goods. If you aim to make a gourmet picnic lunch for Moran State Park, Roses will provide all you need. Open M-Sa 10am-5pm.

🌀 SIGHTS

The **Orcas Island Historical Museum,** 181 N. Beach Rd., is composed of six clustered homesteads constructed between the 1870s and the 1890s. View Lummi and Samish Native American artifacts and explore early colonial life on the islands. Check out the fruit picking exhibit. (☎376-4849. Open Tu-Su 1pm-4pm, F 1pm-7pm. $2, students $1.) The **Rosario Resort,** 1400 Rosario Rd., is home to the mansion of Robert Moran, an industrialist and politician who donated the land that is now Moran State Park. The mansion totals 35,000 sq. feet and cost $2.5 million when it was built in 1905. The fine Honduran Mahogany woodwork is worth a look, as is the largest pipe organ built in a private home in 1905. (☎376-2222. Free.)

🏔 OUTDOOR ACTIVITIES

Travelers on Orcas Island don't need to roam with a destination in mind; half the fun lies in rambling around, although those who stray too far from designated trails will often find themselves on private property. The trail to **Obstruction Pass Beach** is the best way to clamber down to the rocky shores. Taking up the majority of Orcas' eastern half, **Moran State Park** is the last large undeveloped area on the San Juans, making it a star outdoor attraction. This is a must-see during even a brief sojourn on the island. Ample trails, steep mountains, and several lakes create a landscape with diverse options for outdoor activity.

HIKING & BIKING

With 5252 acres, Moran offers over 30 mi. of hiking and biking trails. Find a good map and detailed trail descriptions in the free *Treasure in the San Juans: Your Guide to Moran State Park,* available at the registration station. (☎376-2326. Open daily 10am-9:30pm.) Biking in Moran State Park is restricted in the summer months, so be sure to check with the ranger or contact Wildlife Cycles for information (☎376-4708). Roads on Orcas are also a pleasant way to explore the island.

Cold Springs Trail (4¼ mi. one-way, 1 day), goes from the North End Campground up to the summit of Mt. Constitution. Since a road also runs to the summit, those with a little less spunk can catch a ride back down to the camping areas. 2000 ft. gain. Difficult.

Mountain Lake Trail (4 mi. loop, 2-3hr.) starts from the cabin near Mountain Lake campground and loops around Mountain Lake, the larger and more secluded of the parks 2 big lakes. A more mellow trail, great for an easy hike or trail run.

WATER SPORTS

Within the park, two freshwater lakes are accessible from the road, and rowboats and paddleboats can be rented at **Cascade Lake.** ($12-14 per hr.) Anglers also hit Moran's water with glee; Mouton and Cascade Lakes are both stocked with silver cutthroat, rainbow trout, and eastern brook trout. Outside of the park and on salt water, Orcas is probably the best place to kayak in the San Juans, with a wide variety of conditions and far fewer crowds than San Juan Island. **Shearwater Adventures** runs fascinating **sea kayak tours** and classes, and their store in Eastsound is a great information source for more experienced paddlers. (☎376-4699. 3hr. tour with 30min. of dry land training $45. Full-day and multi-day trips available.) **Crescent Beach Kayak,** on the highway 1 mi. east of Eastsound, rents kayaks for paddling the mellow waters of the East Sound. (☎376-2464. $10 per hr., $25 per half-day. Open daily 9am-5pm. Owner will not rent when there are white caps in the water.)

WASHINGTON

LOPEZ ISLAND   ☎ 360

Smaller than either Orcas or San Juan, "Slow-pez" lacks some of the tourist facilities of the larger islands; still, what it lacks in size it more than makes up for in lethargy. This island is a blessing for those looking for solitary beaches, bicycling without car traffic, rolling farmland, and a small-town atmosphere.

■ ⁊ **ORIENTATION AND PRACTICAL INFORMATION. Lopez Village,** the largest town, is 4½ mi. from the ferry dock off Fisherman Bay Rd. To get there, follow Ferry Rd. and then take a right onto the first street after Lopez Center (before the Chevron station). It's best to bring a bicycle, unless you're up for the hike. To rent a bike or kayak, head to **Lopez Bicycle Works** and **Lopez Kayak,** both south of the village next to the island's Marine Center. Get an excellent map here or at the **visitors center.** (☎ 468-2847, 2845 Fisherman Bay Rd. Bikes open July-Aug. daily 9am-9pm Apr.-June and Sept.-Oct. 10am-5pm. Kayaks open daily 10am-5pm. Bikes $5 per hr., $25 per day. Single kayaks $12-25 per hr., $40-60 per day; doubles $20-35 per hr., $60-80 per day. 2hr., 3hr., and day-long trips available.) **Lopez Island Pharmacy** is at 157 Village Rd. (☎ 468-2616. open M-F 9am-6pm, Sa 10am-5pm.) The **Lopez Island Library,** 2225 Fisherman Bay Rd., has free **Internet** access. (☎ 468-2265. Open M and Sa 10am-5pm, W 10am-9pm, and Tu, Th-F 10am-6pm.) For a taxi, call **Angie's Cab** (☎ 468-2227). Keep it so at **Keep It Clean,** south of the winery. (Wash $2, dry $0.25 per 5min. Open M-F 8:30am-7pm, Sa-Su until 5pm.) Other services include: **domestic violence/sexual assault services,** ☎ 468-4567; **emergency,** ☎ 911; **clinic,** ☎ 468-2245; **post office,** on Weeks Rd. (☎ 468-2282. Open M-F 8:30am-4:30pm.) **Postal Code:** 98261.

⁊⁊ **ACCOMMODATIONS AND FOOD.** When spending the night on Lopez, camping is the only bargain. Luckily, there are many great sites to pitch a tent. **Spencer Spit State Park ❶,** on the northeast corner of the island about 3½ mi. from the ferry terminal, has seven sites on the beach, 30 nicely secluded wooded sites up the hill, two group sites, and a bunkhouse. Spencer Spit offers good **clamming** in the late spring, unless there is red tide (☎ 800-562-5632; permit required). The park is closed Nov. 1-Feb. 2. (☎ 468-2251; reservations 888-226-7688. Toilets, no showers or RV sites. Reservations necessary for summer weekends. Open until 10pm. Sites $15, biker/hiker sites $6, bunkhouse $22.) Voted one of the 10 best places to woo by MSNBC, **Lopez Farm Cottages and Tent Camping ❶,** just north of town on Fisherman Bay Rd., is an agrarian dreamland. Each campsite has a hammock and chairs. Min. age 14. Free morning coffee. Showers that open to the sky. (☎ 800-440-3556. Sites $28 for double occupancy, "Northwest Scandinavian" cottages $99-150 depending on time of year). **Odlin Park ❶** is close to the ferry terminal, 1 mi. south along Ferry Rd., and offers running water, a boat launch, volleyball net, and baseball diamond as well as nice beaches and pleasant walks. (☎ 468-2496; reservations 378-1842. 30 sites: beach sites $19, forest sites $16, hiker/biker sites $11.) If you're looking for a roof, **Lopez Islander Marina Resort ❹,** on Fisherman Bay Road, offers rooms with mini-refrigerators and color TV. (☎ 468-2233. Rooms from $89.50.)

Although Lopez doesn't boast the selection of restaurants that the other two islands do, a good meal is easy to find. Play *boules* while brown-bagging in the grassy park adjacent to the **Village Market,** which has a complete meat and produce department. (☎ 468-2266. Open daily 8am-8pm.) Across the street, sample fresh pastries, bread, and pizza at **Holly B's ❷.** Try the french bread baked with caramelized onions and brie cheese. Bargain breads go for $2, pastries for $0.80. (☎ 468-2133. Open W-M 7am-5pm.) For a delicious vegetarian meal, head straight to **Vortex Juice Bar & Good Food ❶,** located in the Old Homestead with Blossom Natural Foods in Lopez Village. You'll smell the wraps, burritos, and homemade soups and salads ($4-8) from across the street. (☎468-4740. Open M-Sa 10am-7pm.) The **Farmer's Market** showcases Lopez island arts and crafts, as well as jams, baked goods, and potted plants. (Open Sa 10am-2pm.)

⚠ ⬛ SIGHTS AND OUTDOOR ACTIVITIES. Lopez is attractive to many for the total lack of things to do—the opportunity to spend the day exploring at a snail's pace is a large part of the island's appeal. The small **Shark Reef** and **Agate Beach County Parks**, on the southwest end of the island, have tranquil and well-maintained hiking trails. Watch in wonder at the waves crashing against the rocky beaches at Shark Reef Park, or stroll down Agate's calm and deserted shores. The 2 mi. round-trip hike to **Iceberg Point** promises dramatic ocean scenery. For an agrarian adventure, get a copy of the *Guide to Farm Products on Lopez Island* and visit sheep, cattle, and fruit and vegetable farms. **Lopez Island Vineyards,** 724 Fisherman Bay Rd., San Juan's oldest vineyards, permits visitors to sample all of their wines for $2 per person. (☎468-3644. Open in summer W-Sa noon-5pm, year-round by appointment.)

Lopez Island is ideal for **biking.** The car traffic is minimal and the scenery is top notch. Pick up a copy of the *Bicyclists' Touring Companion for the San Juan Islands* to plan out your route. Circling the island in a day is definitely an attainable goal. Pick up a 2-day **clamming/crabbing** permit at the **Lopez Island Marine Center** on Fisherman Bay Rd. for $8. Then head to Odlin Park or Spencer Spit State Park for some of the best clamming and crabbing in all of Washington.

OLYMPIC PENINSULA

Due west of Seattle and its busy Puget Sound neighbors, the Olympic Peninsula is a remote backpacking paradise. Olympic National Park dominates much of the peninsula, and it prevents the area's ferocious timber industry from threatening the glacier-capped mountains and temperate rainforests. With the pick of three ecosystems—rainforest, beach, or mountain—outdoors enthusiasts have a full plate. Outside of the park, a smattering of Indian reservations and logging and fishing communities lace the peninsula's coastline along US 101. To the west, the Pacific Ocean stretches to a distant horizon; to the north, the Strait of Juan de Fuca separates the Olympic Peninsula from Vancouver Island; and to the east, Hood Canal and the Kitsap Peninsula isolate this sparsely inhabited wilderness from the sprawl of Seattle.

WASHINGTON

OLYMPIC NATIONAL PARK

AT A GLANCE	
AREA: 1400 sq. mi.	**GATEWAYS:** Forks, Port Angeles, Port Townsend.
CLIMATE: Fair summers (65-75°F), mild winters (30-40°F). Heavy precipitation.	**CAMPING:** 14-day camping limit.
FEATURES: Olympic National Forest, Hoh Rainforest, Olympic Mountain Range.	**FEES AND RESERVATIONS:** Permit Registration Fee $5, Individual Nightly Fee $2.

Olympic National Park (ONP) is certainly the centerpiece of the Olympic Peninsula, sheltering one of the most diverse landscapes of any region in the world. With glacier-encrusted peaks, river valley rainforests, and jagged shores along the Pacific Coast,

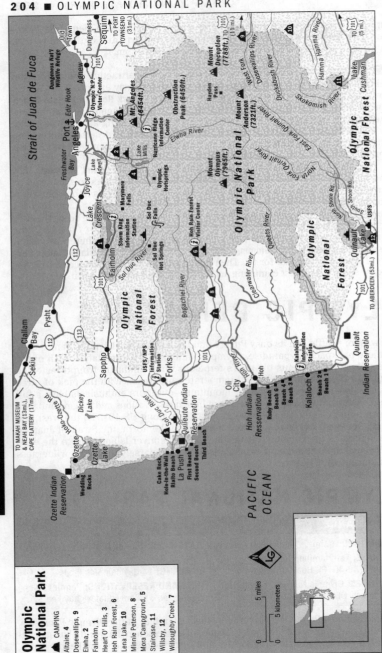

WASHINGTON

Olympic National Park

▲ CAMPING

Altaire, **4**
Dosewallips, **9**
Elwha, **2**
Fairholm, **1**
Heart O' Hills, **3**
Hoh Rain Forest, **6**
Lena Lake, **10**
Minnie Peterson, **8**
Mora Campground, **5**
Staircase, **11**
Willaby, **12**
Willoughby Creek, **7**

the park has something to offer to everyone. Roads lead to many corners of Olympic National Park, but they only hint at the depths of its wilderness. A dive into the backcountry leaves summer tourists behind and reveals the richness and diversity of the park's many faces. Many try to make this trip in a day or two, but beware: the breadth and distances in the park make it difficult to enjoy in under three or four days.

✴ ORIENTATION

The entire **Olympic Mountain Range** is packed into the peninsula's center, where conical peaks ring huge quantities of moisture from heavy Pacific air. Average precipitation in the park varies, but an annual 12 ft. of rain and snow is common. At altitudes above 3500 ft. it is not rare to encounter snow in late June. The mountains steal so much water that some areas are among the driest in Washington.

Temperate rainforests lie on the west side of ONP, along the coast, and in the **Hoh, Queets,** and **Quinault River valleys.** Moderate temperatures, loads of rain, and summer fog support an emerald tangle dominated by Sitka spruce and Western Red cedar. The rest of the park is populated by lowland forests of Douglas fir and hemlock, with silver fir at higher elevations. Ancient Native American **petroglyphs** and boxy offshore bluffs called **sea stacks** lend a sacred quality to the beaches along the coastline. Swaths of **Olympic National Forest** and private land separate these seaside expanses from the rest of the park. The park's perimeters are well-defined but are surrounded by **Forest Service** land, **Washington Department of Natural Resources (DNR)** land, and other public areas. It's important to remember that the ONP and ONF are maintained by separate organizations. Their usage, purposes, facilities, rules, and regulations differ accordingly.

Each side of the park has one major settlement—**Port Townsend** in the east, **Port Angeles** to the north, and **Forks** in the west. The size of the towns and the services they offer decline as you go west, as does the traffic. The park's vista-filled eastern rim runs up to Port Townsend, from where the much-visited northern rim extends westward. Along a winding detour on Rte. 112, off US 101 westward, the tiny town of **Neah Bay** and stunning **Cape Flattery** perch at the northwest tip of the peninsula; farther south on US 101, the slightly larger town of Forks is a gateway to the park's rainforested western rim. Separate from the rest of the park, much of the peninsula's Pacific coastline is gorgeous.

July, August, and September are the best months for visiting Olympic National Park. Much of the backcountry remains snowed-in until late June, and only summers are relatively rain-free. The Park Service runs free interpretive programs such as guided forest hikes, tidepool walks, and campfire programs out of its ranger stations. For a schedule of events, pick up a copy of the *Bugler* from ranger stations or the visitors center (see below). Erik Molvar's *Hiking Olympic National Park* ($15) is a great resource for hikers, with maps and step-by-step trail logs for over 585 mi. of trails. Although it lacks coverage of coastal areas and can be slightly outdated, Robert Wood's comprehensive *Olympic Mountains Trail Guide* ($15) is the classic book for those planning to tackle the backcountry. *Custom Correct* maps provide detailed topographic information on various popular hiking areas. However, because of the density of helpful ranger stations and adequate signs, most visitors who are sticking to park campgrounds will have little need to purchase additional literature.

▟ TRANSPORTATION

The peninsula provides quite a few transportation options for a place so remote. Highway 101 forms an upside-down "U", passing through almost every place listed. A combination of roads also heads straight west from Olympia, allowing one to bypass the park and then head north on 101, skipping the crowds and going straight to the rainforest. Local buses link Port Townsend, Port Angeles, Forks, and Neah Bay, cost $0.50-$1, and accommodate bicycles. From there rides can be cobbled together to get farther into the park. Vans lines, ride-sharing, and taxis are all options. When combined with bus travel, bicycling can move a traveler around quickly. Be aware, though: the stretch of 101 that runs along Lake Crescent is poor for bikers. Roads into the park are accessible from US 101 and serve as trailheads for over 600 mi. of hiking.

Actually getting to the peninsula to begin the trip requires a bit of planning, but can be rewarding: the trip from Seattle to the farthest end of Olympic National Park can cost as little as $7 (7hr. via Pierce, Grays Harbor, and West Jefferson Transits). A ferry is probably the fastest bet and can work well for those driving too. For more info, contact **Washington State Ferries** (☎888-808-7977 or 206-464-6400); **Greyhound** (☎800-231-2222); **King** in Seattle (☎800-542-7876); **Pierce** in Tacoma (☎206-581-8000); **Intercity** in Olympia (☎800-287-6348); or **Kitsap** in Kitsap and Bainbridge (☎360-373-2877). For service on the peninsula, contact **Jefferson** in Port Townsend (☎360-385-4777); **Clallam** in Port Angeles (☎800-858-3747); **Grays Harbor** in Aberdeen (☎800-562-9730); **West Jefferson** in the southwest (☎800-436-3950); or **Mason** in the southeast (☎800-374-3747). The hostels around the peninsula know the terrain and will help anyone navigate transit routes around the park.

⛏ PRACTICAL INFORMATION

Emergency: ☎911. **Park Headquarters** (☎565-3000). Staffed daily 7am-midnight; winter 7am-5:30pm. Or call the nearest ranger station and report your exact location.

Tourist Information: Olympic National Park Visitor Center, 3002 Mt. Angeles Rd. (☎565-3130; www.nps.gov/olym/home.htm), off Race St. in Port Angeles (see p. 212). ONP's main info center. Contains a children's natural history room, extensive exhibits, and plays a 12min. movie that gives an overview of the park. The info center also distributes an invaluable **park map.** Open in summer daily 9am-5:30pm; winter 9am-4pm. **Park Headquarters,** 600 E Park Ave. (☎565-3000), in Port Angeles, is an administrative office but can answer questions by phone. Open M-F 8am-4:30pm. For the many local **ranger stations,** see specific regions below.

Backcountry Information: Olympic National Park Wilderness Information Center (☎565-3100; www.nps.gov/olym/wic), behind the visitors center, provides trip-planning help and info on food storage and leave-no-trace techniques. Call here for backcountry reservations. Pay the ONP wilderness user fee here or at any ranger station. Quota area permits must be purchased at Ranger Stations. Open Apr.-June 8am-4:30pm; June-Sept. Th-Sa 7:30am-8pm, Su-W 7:30am-6pm; Oct.-Mar. hours vary.

Fees and Reservations: $10 per car; $5 per hiker or biker. Charged at Hoh, Heart o' the Hills, Sol Duc, Staircase, and Elwha entrances. Covers 7 days access to the park; keep that receipt! Backcountry users must pay a $5 permit fee as well as $2 extra per person per night to ranger offices. The National Forest requires a Northwest Forest Pass at most parking areas ($5 daily, $30 annually). **Fishing:** Fishing within park boundaries requires a license except when along the Pacific Ocean. A booklet with all of the park's regulations is available at stations upon request.

Park Weather: ☎565-3131. 24hr.

Park Radio: 530 AM for road closures and general weather conditions. 610 AM for general park rules and information, 1610 AM in Lake Crescent and Quinault areas.

🏕 CAMPING

Competition for sites on the peninsula can get fierce, but there would be sufficient space for the entire population of Washington to camp there at once if it so chose. It just takes a little driving to uncover all the treasures of hidden sites. In addition to numerous national park sites, there is a network of state and county sites and several hostels well spaced across the peninsula.

STANDARD CAMPING. Ask at the Olympic National Forest Headquarters in Olympia (see p. 184) about **ONP** campgrounds within its boundaries (sites $8-12). **ONF** maintains six free campgrounds in the Hood Canal Ranger District and other campgrounds within its boundaries; sites at **Seal Rock, Falls View,** and **Klahowga** can be reserved. (☎800-280-2267; www.reserveusa.com. Open daily 8am-midnight. Sites $8-12.) In addition to **Ft. Worden** and **Ft. Flagler,** there are four **state parks** on the peninsula. (Reservations ☎800-452-5687. Sites $14; RV sites $20; hiker or biker $6.) **Dosewallips** (☎796-4415) and **Lake Cushman** (see **Eastern Rim,** below) are to the east. **Sequim Bay** is northeast of Sequim. (☎683-4235. Table and stove at each site. Restrooms.) Most **drive-up camping** is first come, first served.

BACKCOUNTRY CAMPING. Whether in rainforest, high country, or along the coast, backcountry camping in the park requires a **backcountry permit.** Park offices maintain **quota limits** on backcountry permits for popular spots, including **Lake Constance** and **Flapjack Lakes** in the eastern rim (see below); **Grand Valley, Badger Valley,** and **Sol Duc** in the northern rim (see p. 212); **Hoh** in the western rim (see p. 216); and the coastal **Ozette Loop.** Make **reservations** in advance, especially for the Ozette area, where reservations are required. Contact the Wilderness Info Center to secure a spot. Backpackers should prepare for varied weather conditions. Even in the summer, parts of the park get very wet. Pack appropriately for the weather. **Giardia,** a nasty diarrhea-inducing bacterium, lives in the water here. Water purification tablets are available at the visitors center and most outfitters. **Black bears** and **raccoons** pose another backcountry hazard; when issuing backcountry permits, ranger stations instruct hikers on hanging food out of animals' reach. Cougars have also become a concern, and ranger officials will give you extensive advice on how to maximize your safety. For more on wilderness safety, see p. 38. Above 3500 ft., **open fires** are prohibited; below 3500 ft., maps and signposts indicate if they are allowed. Before any trip, inquire about **trail closures;** winter weather often destroys popular trails.

EASTERN OLYMPIC PENINSULA

The area of the peninsula most accessible from Puget Sound City, the Olympic's eastern edge suffers from a heavy traffic of weekend cabin-renters and daytrippers. Still, the eastern edge of the park, generously padded with a thick strip of National Forest, houses some fun (and generally dry) trails. The big draw, though, is the town that serves as the peninsula's social capitol, Port Townsend. PT is the one settlement west of Olympia that doesn't qualify as "sleepy," making it a welcome change of pace for travelers who have been taking advantage of the park's solitude for a little too long.

PORT TOWNSEND   ☎ 360

Set apart from the rest of the Olympic Peninsula on a small peninsula of its own, Port Townsend is the local cultural hot spot. During the late 1800s, the city's predominance in the entire state of Washington seemed secure. Every ship en route to Puget Sound stopped here for customs inspection, and speculation held that the bustling port would become the capital of the new state. When rumors circulated that rail would connect the town to the east, wealthy families flocked to the bluffs overlooking the port, constructing elaborate Victorian homes and stately public buildings. When rail passed the town by, "the inevitable New York" was left a ghost town, perched on the isolated northeast tip of the Olympic Peninsula and made to subsist by paper-milling and logging. In the 1970s, Port Townsend's neglected Victorian homes were discovered by artists and idealists who turned the town into a vibrant, creative community. Now the business district stands restored, recently declared a national landmark, and the town takes advantage of its 19th-century feel to entice those heading to the park onto Rte. 20 and into town. It is a turn that few who make it regret.

■■ 🖈 ORIENTATION AND PRACTICAL INFORMATION

Port Townsend sits at the terminus of **Rte. 20** on the northeastern corner of the Olympic Peninsula. It can be reached by **US 101** on the peninsula, or from the Kitsap Peninsula across the Hood Canal Bridge. **Kitsap County Transit** meets every ferry and runs to Poulsbo. From Poulsbo, **Jefferson County Transit** runs to PT. The ferry also crosses frequently to and from Keystone on Whidbey Island (see p. 189). Ferries dock at **Water St.**, west of touristy downtown, along **Water** and **Washington St.**, where restaurants, hotels, and motels are located. Laid-back uptown, with a small business district of its own, is four steep blocks up, on **Lawrence St.**

Local Transportation: Jefferson County Transit (JCT; ☎385-4777; www.jeffersontransit.com). Peninsula towns are serviced by JCT and neighboring transit systems. Buses run between Ft. Worden and downtown, and also connect to Port Angeles and Seattle. $0.50; seniors, disabled travelers, and ages 6-18 $0.25; extra-zone fare $0.25. Day passes $1.50. A **shuttle** runs between downtown and the Park 'n' Ride lot, right next to the Safeway. There is usually ample parking in town, although usually limited to 2hr.

Taxis: Peninsula Taxi, ☎385-1872. $2 base plus $1.75 per mi.

Visitor Information: Chamber of Commerce, 2437 E Sims Way (☎385-2722 or 888-365-6978; www.ptguide.com), lies 10 blocks southwest of town on Rte. 20. Open M-F 9am-5pm, Sa 10am-4pm, Su 11am-4pm.

Equipment Rental: P.T. Cyclery, 100 Tyler St. (☎385-6470), rents mountain bikes for $7 per hr., $25 per day. Maps $1.75. Ages 100+ free. Open M-Sa 9am-6pm. **Kayak Port Townsend,** 435 Water St. (☎385-6240 or 531-1670; www.kayakpt.com), is part of PT's burgeoning sea-kayaking scene. Rents singles $25 per 4hr.; doubles $40 per 4hr. Windrider sailing craft $25 per hr., $60 per day; ages 84+ free. Open M-F 10am-6pm, Sa 9am-7pm, Su 9am-5pm.

Emergency: ☎911.

Police: 607 Water St. (☎385-2322), at Madison. 24hr.

Crisis Line: ☎385-0321 or 800-659-0321. 24hr. **Sexual Assault Line:** ☎385-5291.

Pharmacy: Safeway Pharmacy, 442 Sims Way (☎385-2860). Open M-F 8:30am-7:30pm, Sa 8:30am-6pm, Su 10am-6pm.

Hospital: 834 Sheridan (☎385-2200 or 800-244-8917), off Rte. 20 at 7th St.

Internet Access: Library, 1220 Lawrence (☎385-3181). Free Internet access, 15min. drop in, up to 1¼hr. by appointment. Open M-W 11am-8pm, Th-Sa 11am-6pm. **Cyber Bean,** 2021 E Sims Way (☎385-9773). 2min. free with latte, $6 per 15min. Open M-F 8:30am-6pm, Sa-Su 8:30am-2:30pm.

Post Office: 1322 Washington St. (☎385-1600). Open M-F 9am-5pm, Sa 10am-2pm. **Postal Code:** 98368.

WASHINGTON

Port Townsend

■▲ ACCOMMODATIONS
Ann Starrett Mansion, **2**
Fort Flagler Hostel, **4**
Fort Flagler State Park, **5**
Olympic Hostel, **1**
Water Street Hotel, **11**

The Elevated Ice Cream, **13**
Food Coop, **3**
Waterfront Pizza, **10**

🍴 FOOD
Bread and Roses, **8**
Burrito Depot, **9**

🍷 NIGHTLIFE
Rose Theatre, **7**
Sirens, **12**
Upstage, **6**

🏠🏨 ACCOMMODATIONS AND CAMPING

Port Townsend is a B&B mecca; many of the historic Victorian homes now offer rest to weary travelers. If you're looking to splurge, the striking **Ann Starrett Mansion ❺**, built in 1889, offers rooms starting at $105 (see **Sights**, below).

Olympic Hostel (HI; ☎385-0655; www.hiayh.org), in Fort Worden State Park, 1½ mi. from town. Follow the signs to the park at "W" and Cherry St. A converted WWII barracks, the Olympic offers nice clean beds, but the biggest attractions are the surrounding park (over 400 acres!) and beaches. Laundry, tennis courts, frequent concerts, trails, and free pancake breakfast. Private rooms available. Check-in 5-10pm, check-out 9:30am. Book ahead, especially in summer. Beds $14; nonmembers $17. ❶

Fort Flagler Hostel (HI; ☎385-1288), in Fort Flagler State Park, on gorgeous **Marrowstone Island,** 20 mi. from Port Townsend. Take State Rte. 20 to State Rte. 19 South, go 3 mi., and turn left on State Rte. 116 for 9 mi. into Fort Flagler State Park. The hostel is an old military building just a short hop from the beach. Check-in 5-10pm, lockout 10am-5pm. Call if arriving late. Book ahead for weekends. Open Mar.-Sept. Beds $14, nonmembers $17, hikers/bikers $2 off. ❶

Fort Flagler State Park (☎385-1259). Camping in same place as the hostel. Some sites on the beach. 115 sites. Tents $16; RVs $22; hikers/bikers $6. Book ahead. ❶

Water St. Hotel, 635 Water St. (☎385-5467 or 800-735-9810), is a newly renovated Victorian building with fabulous views of the water and Port Townsend streets. $45-100 in winter, $50-135 in summer. ❸

🄫 FOOD

The **Food Coop,** 414 Kearney St., is in a converted bowling alley. Every Wednesday from 3:30-6pm there is a market in their parking lot. (☎385-2883. Open M-Sa 8am-9pm, Su 9am-7pm.) **Safeway,** 442 Sims Way (☎385-2860), is open 24hr.

■ **The Elevated Ice Cream Co.,** 627 Water St. (☎385-1156), ironically on the ground floor. Serves homemade ice cream that receives rave reviews. Single scoop $2. If you don't want frozen treats, try the sweet shop next door. Open daily 10am-10pm. ❶

Waterfront Pizza, 953 Water St. (☎385-6629), offers little historic ambiance but churns out a damn good pizza on a sourdough crust (12 in. pie $8-14). 12 in. Focaccia $4. Open Su-Th 11am-10pm, F-Sa 11am-11pm. ❷

Bread and Roses, 230 Quincy St. (☎385-1044). Serves baked goods, sandwiches ($3-7), and muffins in cozy environs; the garden is gorgeous. Open M-Sa 6:30am-5pm, Su 6:30am-4pm. ❶

Burrito Depot, 609 Washington St. (☎385-5856). Quick, tasty Mexican food, and Thai thrown in, too. Big burritos $4-6. Open M-Sa 10:30am-8pm, Su 11am-7:30pm. ❶

👁 SIGHTS

Port Townsend is full of huge Queen Anne and Victorian mansions, many of which now serve as B&Bs. The **Ann Starret Mansion,** 744 Clay St., is renowned for its frescoed ceilings and three-tiered spiral staircase. (☎385-3205 or 800-321-0644. Tours daily noon-3pm. $2.)

Point Hudson, where Admiralty Inlet and Port Townsend Bay meet, is the hub of a small shipbuilding area and forms the corner of Port Townsend. Check out boatbuilders crafting sea kayaks and sailboats. North of Point Hudson are several miles of **beach** and the beautiful **Chetzemoka Park,** a (guess what) Victorian park at Garfield and Jackson St.

Fort Worden State Park is a sprawling complex most easily accessed through the gates at "W" and Cherry St. (Open daily 6:30am-dusk.) In the 1900s, Fort Worden was part of the "Triangle of Fire," a defense for Puget Sound formed by **Worden** (☎344-4400), **Fort Flagler** across the bay, and **Fort Casey** on Whidbey Island. Fort Worden re-entered service in 1981 as the set for *An Officer and a Gentleman.* Three museums are on the grounds. The **Commanding Officer's Quarters** is stuffed with Victorian furniture. (Open daily June-Aug. 10am-5pm; Mar.-May and Sept.-Oct. Sa-Su 1-4pm. $1.) The **Coast Artillery Museum** is clean-cut. (☎385-0373. Open M-Su 10am-4pm; closed Oct.-Mar. $2.) Sea life lives above the Fort Worden pier at the **Marine Science Center.** (☎385-5582. Open W-M 11am-5pm. $3, children $2.)

🎵 ENTERTAINMENT

Port Townsend's music scene is surprisingly lively. *This Week* has the scoop on the nightlife. Steep-side **Sirens,** 823 Water St., hosts live folk and blues (F-Sa) on the deck, which has a great view. (☎379-1100. Happy hour 4-6pm. Occasional cover. Open M-Th 4pm-2am, F-Sa noon-2am.) **Upstage,** 923 Washington St., supports music from classical to country from Thursday to Saturday. (☎385-2216. Cover $3-14. Open daily 4pm-midnight.) The **Rose Theatre,** 235 Taylor St., is one fine art house theater that claims to make the best popcorn in the Northwest. (☎385-1089. $6, seniors $5, children $4; matinees $5.)

THE GIFT THAT JUST WON'T STOP GIVING

In the early part of this century, elk were shipped from Washington to Alaska in an effort to provide more game for hunting, and mountain goats were sent from Alaska to Washington in return. The goats proliferated in Olympic National Park long after hunting was prohibited, damaging endangered native plants by grazing, trampling, wallowing, and loitering. Park Service authorities tried many ways of removing the goats, including live capture and sterilization darts, but nothing really worked. In 1995, they resolved to eliminate the goats once and for all by shooting them from helicopters. Washington Congressman Norm Dicks got this measure postponed, and has since proposed reintroducing the native gray wolf to the park. Wolves were banished in the early part of this century in an effort to provide more game for hunting. To add to the mess, a 2000 study concluded that the goats neither belong in, nor do they substantially damage, the environment. For now, the goats are left hiding deep in the interior of the park.

Every summer, **Centrum Foundation** (☎385-5320 or 800-733-3608; www.centrum.org) sponsors festivals in Fort Worden Park, including the **Port Townsend Blues Festival** (tickets $20) at the beginning of August, the **Festival of American Fiddle Tunes** (tickets $14) in early July, and **Jazz Port Townsend** (tickets $19-24) the third week of July. The **Port Townsend Writer's Conference** in mid-July is one of the finest in the Northwest. Well-attended guest-readings and lectures cost $5-6. Port Townsend's biggest gathering is the **Wooden Boat Festival** (☎385-3629), held the first weekend after Labor Day. It is organized by **The Wooden Boat Foundation**, 380 Jefferson St. (☎385-3628), an institute that supports lessons and races.

THE REST OF THE EASTERN PENINSULA

NEAR HOODSPORT. The first info area one passes on US 101 coming in from Olympia is the Hood Canal Ranger Station, just off of the highway in Hoodsport. (☎877-5254. Open in summer daily 8am-4:30pm; winter M-F 8am-4:30pm.) This station is run jointly between the Forest and Park services, so it can answer questions about almost any destination on the peninsula. The station's turnoff also leads to two of the whole peninsula's most popular destinations. The first is a camping and hiking area on Lake Cushman known as Staircase. **Staircase Campground ❶** is a major hub 16 mi. northwest of Hoodsport; take a left after 9 mi. on Rte. 119 and follow the signs. (☎877-5491. RV accessible. 56 sites. $10.) The other much sought-out place is the summit of **Mt. Ellinor,** also past the station. Follow Rte. 119 for 9 mi. to Forest Rd. 24, turn right, and continue to Forest Rd. 2419, following signs to Upper/Lower Trailhead. Look for signs to the Upper Trailhead along Forest Rd. 2419-144. Once on the mountain, hikers can choose either the three-mile path or an equally steep but shorter journey to the summit. Those hiking on the mountain before late July should bring snow clothes.

HAMMA HAMMA RECREATION AREA. Fourteen mi. north of Hoodsport, 8 mi. west off FS Road #25, lies the Hamma Hamma Recreation Area. A 3 mi. hike leads to **Lena Lake,** one of the most popular backcountry lakes on the Olympic Peninsula. From Lena Lake, trails lead to Upper Lena Lake and The Brothers Wilderness. The **Hamma Hamma Campground ❶,** at the Lena Lake Trail-head, has 15 sites. ($10.) For backcountry camping, try **Lena Lake Campground ❶,** located on the west shore of Lena Lake, which offers 29 free sites with compost toilets but no water.

North of the Hamma Hamma, hike 6 mi. to **Royal Lake** for a breathtaking waterfall, summertime wildflowers, and views of the second-highest peak in the Olympics, Mt. Deception. Permits are required for backcountry camping.

WASHINGTON

QUILCENE. Thirty miles north of Hoodsport, the **Quilcene Ranger Station** (☎765-2200) is available to answer any questions about the National Forest. (Open daily 8am-4:30pm. Closed on weekends in winter.) Nearby, the **Mt. Walker Viewpoint,** 5 mi. south of Quilcene on US 101, is a very popular destination. A one-lane gravel road leads 4 mi. to the lookout, the highest viewpoint in the forest accessible by car. The road is steep, has sheer drop-offs, and should not be attempted in foul weather or with a temperamental car. Picnic tables perch on the east side; feast there while gazing at the north face of 7743 ft. **Mt. Constance.**

NORTHERN OLYMPIC PENINSULA

On the north side of the peninsula, the mountains creep towards the shore, leaving only a thin strip of land that people have settled. Along this stretch of US 101, spur roads regularly reach south into the park, delivering travelers to hot springs, trailheads, and mountain passes. The north strikes a good balance between the isolation of the west and the traffic of the east—solitude can be found, yet transportation is still easy to figure out, especially when using Port Angeles as a base. It is the right balance for someone with only a day or two to see the park, or who is looking to recover from a stint in the isolation of the western park.

PORT ANGELES   ☎360

Port Angeles is the "gateway" to the Olympic National Park. The administrative headquarters and main info center are both located here. As US 101 turns west on the peninsula, the traffic thins as only those headed to ONP remain. Port Angeles (PA) is the final stop, the point where the weekend traffic drops off and those here to explore remain. With the park headquarters, transportation connections, and a small, walkable downtown, it has always been a logical stop, but with the addition of a new hostel and several good places to eat, PA is now at least as much a place to recharge batteries and rest aching muscles as it is a place to pass through.

▛ TRANSPORTATION

Buses: Olympic Bus Lines, 221 N Lincoln (☎417-0700), in the Doubletree Hotel parking lot. To **Seattle** (2½hr., 4 per day, $49 round-trip) and **Sea-Tac Airport** (3hr., 3-5 per day, $58 round-trip). **Olympic Van Tours (OVT;** ☎452-3858) runs from the Olympics to **Hoh Rainforest** ($32) and **Hurricane Ridge** ($20). OVT also shuttles to trailheads.

Ferries: 2 different vessels (1 passengers-only) shuttle across the straits to **Victoria, BC. M.V. Coho,** 101 E Railroad Ave. (☎457-4491; www.northolympic.com/coho), runs Mar.-Jan. The Coho does NOT take reservations, so call ahead to find out how early to arrive. (1¾hr.; 4 per day; $8, with bicycle $11.50, with car $31; children $4). **Victoria Express,** 115 E Railroad Ave. (☎800-633-1589; www.victoriaexpress.com), has passenger-only service and does take reservations. (1hr., $12.50, ages 5-11 $7.50, under 5 free). US and Canadian citizens crossing into Canada, children included, need valid proof of citizenship. Other internationals should check their own visa requirements. Day parking lots line Railroad Ave. near the docks ($7-10 per day).

Public Transportation: Clallam Transit System, 830 W Lauridsen Blvd. (☎800-858-3747 or 452-4511; www.clallamtransit.com), serves **Port Angeles** and **Clallam County,** as far as **Neah Bay** and **Forks,** from the transport center on Railroad Ave. at Oak St., a block west of the ferry. Operates M-F 4:20am-9pm, Sa 10am-7pm. Downtown $0.75, ages 6-19 $0.50, seniors $0.25; day pass $2; $0.25 per zone passed.

Taxis: Peninsula Taxi, ☎385-1872. $2 base plus $1.75 per mi.

WASHINGTON

Car Rental: Evergreen Auto Rental, 808 E Front St. (☎452-8001). From $33 per day plus $0.20 per mi. after 100 mi. Must be 21+ with proof of insurance.

🎐 PRACTICAL INFORMATION

Tourist Information: Chamber of Commerce, 121 E Railroad Ave. (☎452-2363 or 877-465-8372; www.portangeles.org), near the ferry. Ask for a guide to the town's art for a fun walking route. Open daily 10am-4pm, longer depending on staff size; winter M-F.

Outdoor Information: The **Olympic National Park (ONP) Visitor Center,** 3002 Mt. Angeles Rd. (☎565-3130), is just outside of town. Open 8:30am-5:30pm; see p. 203 for details. **Port Brook and News,** 104 E 1st St. (☎452-6367), has maps and advice on the region. Open M-Sa 9am-9pm, Su 10am-5pm.

Equipment Rental: Olympic Mountaineering, 140 W Front St. (☎452-0240; www.olymtn.com), rents sturdy gear (external frame pack $15 per day) with lower weekly rates. Offers guided hiking and climbing trips in the ONP (from $150 for 2 people). The shop also features an indoor climbing wall. Open M-Sa 9am-6pm, Su 10am-5pm. **Brown's Outdoor Store,** 112 W Front St. (☎457-4150), rents at low daily rates. Packs $10 per day, tents $10 per day. Call ahead. Open M-Sa 9:30am-6pm, Su noon-4pm. **Sound Bikes and Kayaks,** 120 E Front St. (☎457-1240), rents bikes for $9 per hr.; $30 per day. Leads half-day kayak trips for $40, kayak rentals alone $12 per hr. Open M-Sa 9am-5:30pm.

Laundromat: Peabody St. Coin Laundry, 212 Peabody St. at 2nd St. Wash $1.75, dry $0.25 per 10min. 24hr.

Emergency: ☎911.

Police: ☎452-4545. 24 hr.

Sexual Assault: Safehome, 1914 W 18th St. (☎452-4357).

Pharmacy: Safeway (☎457-0599; see **Food,** below).

Medical: Olympic Memorial Hospital, 939 Caroline St. (☎417-7000) at Washington St. on the waterfront. Open 24hr.

Post Office: 424 E 1st St. (☎452-9275). Open M-F 8:30am-5pm, Sa 9am-noon. **Postal Code:** 98362.

🏠🏕 ACCOMMODATIONS AND CAMPING

Countless motels are found in PA, and, keeping in mind that cleanliness is proportional to price, you can pay what you will. The least expensive motels line US 101 west of town, so cruise First St. to price-shop. Winter rates drop $5-15. West on US 101, halfway between Port Angeles and Lake Crescent, a 6 mi. spur road leads south to two **campgrounds** along the waterfall-rich Elwha River: **Elwha Valley** (40 sites) ❶ and the nearby **Altaire** (30 sites) ❶. Both have drinking water, toilets, and fishing. (☎452-9191. Sites $10.)

🏠 **Thor Town Hostel,** 316 N Race St. (☎452-0931), a friendly refuge 7 blocks east of the city center and 1 mi. north of ranger station. This "work-in-progress" hostel is located in a renovated 100-year old house. Linens and towels provided, laundry $1. Features bike rentals ($8 per day), trailhead shuttles, and bus info. $12, private room $28. ❶

Ruffles Motel, 812 E 1st St. (☎457-7788), is slightly ahead in terms of the price-grime curve. Nice rooms and cable, but no A/C. Singles $47; doubles $55. ❸

Heart o' the Hills Campground, just after the park entrance, overflows with vacationers poised to take Hurricane Ridge by storm. The campground has no RV sites or showers but offers plenty of giant trees, fairly private sites, drinking water, and wheelchair access. (105 sites. $10.) ❶

🌀 FOOD

Cheap buffets are ubiquitous in Port Angeles. For a breakfast buffet, try the **Best Western Olympic Lodge ❶**, 140 Del Guzzia (☎452-4995), a $6 all-you-can-eat joint. There is plenty of seafood in town—finding a cheap place to eat is the trick. Picnickers can shop at **Safeway**, 110 E 3rd St., at Lincoln St. (☎457-0788. Open 24hr.)

Thai Peppers, 222 N Lincoln. A new restaurant in town, this place keeps PA natives happy; the seafood is excellent. Lunch specials $6, dinners $8-10. Open M-Sa 11am-2:30pm and 4:30-9pm. ❶

India Oven, 222 N Lincoln (☎452-5170). Before (or after) catching the ferry to Victoria, fill up at the $7 lunch buffet. Regular dishes $8-11. Open daily 11am-10pm. ❷

La Casita, 203 E Front St. (☎452-2289). Regular burritos $5, or spice it up with crab, shrimp, and fish ($9.95). Free, all-you-can-eat tortilla chips to snarf between margaritas ($2). Open M-Th 11am-10pm, F-Sa 11am-11pm, Su noon-10pm. ❶

Bella Italia, 118 E 1st St. (☎457-5442). Hungry vegetarians can sit down to lasagna ($10) or a plate of spaghetti ($7). Open M-Sa 11am-10pm, Su 10:30am-10pm. ❷

👁 🏔 SIGHTS AND OUTDOOR ACTIVITIES

The main draw of Port Angeles is the National Park, which looms behind the town in the form of Mt. Angeles. Nevertheless, there are several places to enjoy outside of the park if a change of pace is what you are looking for.

The **Fine Arts Center and Sculpture Park**, 1203 E Lauridsen Blvd., near the national park visitors center, has exhibits by Northwest artists in a small space. The surrounding five acres show sculpture in a very entertaining art park. (☎457-3532; www.olympus.net/community/pafac. Gallery open Tu-Su 11am-5pm, art outside open daylight hours year-round. Both free.) Take US 101 east about 4 mi. and turn left. A 5 mi. (2hr.) trail out on the 7 mi. **Dungeness Spit** is the world's longest natural sand spit, extending 6 mi. into the Strait of Juan de Fuca. Over 200 species of birds inhabit this area, as well as loads of indigenous crabs and clams. (Open from 9am until 2hr. before sunset.) The Dungeness Spit also houses a small **campground ❶**. Nearby, the **Olympic Game Farm**, 1423 Ward Rd. off Woodcock St., is a retirement home for animal movie stars. Drive by zebras, llamas, rhinos, and bears, or take a guided walking tour. (☎683-4295 or 800-778-4295; www.olygamefarm.com. Open daily 9am-5pm for driving (until 6pm on Sa); 10am-3pm for walking. Driving tour 4 mi.; $9, children $7. Walking tour 1hr.; $10, $8. Both driving and walking $15, $12.)

While most come to the ridge just to gawk, getting out on your feet is the best way to take in the views without the chatter of families and rangers. Before July, walking on the ridge usually involves snow-stepping. On weekends from late December to late March the Park Service organizes free guided **snowshoe walks** atop the ridge. **High Ridge** (½ mi. loop, 30min.) is a paved trail just off of the Hurricane Ridge parking lot, with access to a view north from **Sunset Point. Klahhane Ridge** (¾ mi., 5hr.) is a more strenuous hike, leading 2¾ mi. on flat ground, and then turning for 1 mi. of tough switchbacking to actually get to Klahhane.

Accessible by road directly from Port Angeles, **Hurricane Ridge** boasts the best drive-up views of the park's mountainous interior. Clear days promise splendid views of Mt. Olympus and Vancouver Island against a foreground of snow and indigo lupine. RVs and tourists crowd the ridge by day, but seclusion can be found at dawn. To get into the park, take Race Rd. south from US 101 and turn right shortly after the **ONP Visitors Center** (☎565-3132).

LAKE CRESCENT. A massive body of water located in the north-central region of the peninsula, just off US 101, Lake Crescent is often ignored by travelers. The lake offers brisk swimming, blissful picnicking, and frequent sunshine. Storm King Ranger Station is on a small peninsula in the center of the lake and offers all of the regular services. (☎ 928-3380. Open in summer daily 10am-5pm.)

At the west end of the lake, just past the Fairholm General Store, there is a small road that heads to **Fairholm Campground ❶,** which has wheelchair access, beautiful moss-covered trees, picnic areas, and some sites right on the lakeshore. (☎ 928-3380. 87 sites, $10.) Several strenuous hikes head out from the lake up the steep slopes. The **Lake Crescent Lodge,** next to the Storm King Station, rents rowboats to help in summertime seduction. (☎ 928-3211. Rentals 7am-8pm. $8.50 per hr., $20 half-day, $30 full day.) Swimming and trout **fishing** are both popular on the water—but only catch-and-release is allowed (no permit required).

SOL DUC HOT SPRINGS. Just west of the tip of Lake Crescent, a road turns south and follows the Sol Duc river south for 12½ mi. into a large green valley. At the end lies a beacon for tired travelers—hot baths in the **Sol Duc Hotsprings Resort.** The hot springs are in the National Park (so be prepared to fork up a $10 park entrance fee), but operated by the Resort. Hiking is also good in the area; to get information and permits, stop at the **Eagle Ranger Station,** just before the springs. (☎ 327-3534. Open in summer daily 8am-4:30pm.) With its location, it is no surprise that the **Sol Duc Hot Springs Campground ❶** often fills by 3pm. (☎ 327-3534. Picnic sites. 78 sites, $12.)

With trails leaving the resort, ranger station, and **Sol Duc Trailhead** (at the end of the road, 1 mi. from the campground), Sol Duc is a good leaping-off point, or better yet given the hot baths, return point. **Lover's Lane Trail** (6 mi. loop, 2½hr.) departs the resort and leads to Sol Duc falls before looping back. The lazy or busy just go from the Sol Duc trailhead and make it there in 1½ mi. (1hr.). **Mink Lake** (2½ mi., 5hr.) climbs through a dense forest to a small mountain lake. After this there will be no guilt about pampering oneself in a hot spring. (1500 ft. gain. Strenuous.)

The **Resort ❺** is not inexpensive, but still affordable, with special-end-of-day rates and all-day admission. (Cabins $123; RV sites $22.) Natural spring water is filtered into three man-made mineral pools. To avoid the hot water and sulfur smell, you can also jump in the large chlorinated swimming pool. (☎ 327-3583; www.northolympic.com/solduc. Open late May-Sept. daily 9am-9pm; spring and fall Th noon-6pm, F-Su 9am-6pm. $10; ages 4-12 $7.50; last 2 hr. twilight rate $6.50. Suit, locker, and towel rental $3 each.)

NEAH BAY AND CAPE FLATTERY

At the westernmost point on the Juan de Fuca Strait and well away from the National Park is **Neah Bay,** the only town on the **Makah Reservation.** The community has recently become famous for its revival of its gray-whale hunt and is renowned for the "Pompeii of the Pacific," a remarkably-preserved 500-year-old Makah village buried in a landslide. Gorgeous **Cape Flattery** is the most northwesterly point in the contiguous US. James Cook gave the Cape its name in 1778, because it "flattered us with the hopes of finding a harbor." Flattery got them nowhere; the nearest port is Port Angeles, 50 mi. away.

You can reach Neah Bay and Cape Flattery by an hour-long detour from **US 101.** From Port Angeles, **Rte. 112,** a National Scenic Byway, leads west 72 mi. to Neah Bay. From the south, **Rte. 113** runs north from Sappho to **Rte. 112. Clallam Transit System** runs from Port Angeles; take bus #14 from Oak St. to Sappho (1¼hr.), then #16 to Neah Bay. (☎ 452-4511 or 800-858-3747. 4-5 times per day. $1; seniors $0.50; ages 6-19 $0.50.)

⌐⌐ ACCOMMODATIONS AND FOOD. If you're eager to spend a night on a Native American reservation, try the few motels and campgrounds here. The **Cape Motel ❸**, on Rte. 112, offers small but clean rooms, or sack out in a rustic shanty or tentsite. (☎645-2250. Office open 7:30am-10pm. Rooms $50-75; shanty singles $18, $25 as doubles; sites $12.) **Hobuck Beach Campground ❶** is 3 mi. northwest of Neah Bay—follow signs to Ocean Beaches. (20 sites, $10.)

Neah Bay doesn't offer many dining options. A few mediocre cafes line Front St. Pick up picnic materials at **Washburn's General Store,** also on Front St. (☎645-2211. Open M-Sa 8am-9pm, Su 8am-7pm.)

◪ SIGHTS. The **Makah Cultural and Research Center,** in Neah Bay on Rte. 112, is just inside the reservation, opposite the Coast Guard station. The center presents beautiful artifacts from the archaeological site at Cape Alava. The Makah Nation, whose recorded history is 2000 years old, lives, fishes, and produces artwork on this land. (☎645-2711. Open June-Aug. daily 10am-5pm; Sept.-May M-F 10am-5pm. $5, seniors and students $4, under 5 free. Free tours W-Su at 11am.) During Makah Days, in the last weekend in August, Native Americans from around the region come for canoe races, dances, and bone games (a form of gambling). Visitors are welcome and the salmon is delightful. Call the center for details.

Cape Flattery can be reached through Neah Bay, 8 mi. further northwest. Pick up directions at the Makah Center, or just take the road through town until it turns to dirt. Follow the "Marine Viewing Area" sign once you hit gravel, and continue for another 4 mi. to a small circular parking area, where a trailhead leads half a mile to Cape Flattery. At 3pm, a free, short guided hike leaves from the trailhead. You'll know you're close to the amazing views of **Tatoosh** and **Vancouver Island** when you hear the sound of Tatoosh's bullhorn. The road is excruciatingly bumpy, but the hike reveals some of the more beautiful stretches of ocean around. To the south, the Makah Reservation's **beaches** are solitary and peaceful; respectful visitors are welcome to wander.

Outside the reservation, to the south, dayhikers and backpackers adore the 9 mi. boardwalk loop that begins at Ozette Lake, an ONP area 21 miles off Hwy. 112. The boardwalks alone are a marvel; cedar shakes cut from old-growth red cedar form the attractive walk-ways. One heads toward sea stacks at **Cape Alava,** the other to a sublime beach at **Sand Point.** A 3 mi. hike down the coast links the two legs, passing ancient native petroglyphs. The entire area is mostly prairie and coastal forest, but presents plenty of sand to slog through. Overnighters must make permit reservations in advance; spaces fill quickly in summer. The **Ozette Ranger Station** has further info. (☎963-2725. Open intermittently.) Call the visitors center outside of PA at ☎565-3100 for permit reservations.

WESTERN OLYMPIC PENINSULA

Swinging wildly between rainforest, clear cuts, and dramatic coastline, US 101 traces a manic path through what is a truly stunning landscape. Travelers who drive the extra distance to this side of the peninsula will be rewarded with seclusion and almost unimaginable natural beauty.

FORKS ☎360

Between ONP's northern and western rims lies the logging town of Forks. Once the king timber town in the region, Forks both embraces and mourns its historic legacy. If you're passing through town or grabbing a bite to eat, take time to visit the **Forks Logging Museum.** (☎374-2531. Open M-Su 10am-4pm, logging and mill tours M, W, and F at 9am.) Check out forestry research in action at the **Olympic Natural Resources Center,** just south of the Logging Museum. Students and faculty from the University of Washington (and beyond) use this research facility to experiment with forest management techniques. Forks lies two hours west of Port Angeles and offers the widest selection of services in the western peninsula. Visit during the dry season (summer) if possible; Forks gets more rain than any other city or town in Washington.

◪ ⏻ ORIENTATION AND PRACTICAL INFORMATION. Clallam Transit (☎452-4511 or 800-858-374) Rte. #14 serves Forks from **Port Angeles** (M-F; 7 per day; $1.25, disabled, seniors, and ages 6-19 $1). The **Forks Chamber of Commerce,** south of town, offers advice and maps, as well as tours through a real saw mill. (☎374-2531 or 800-443-6757. Open M-F 9am-5pm, Sa 10am-2pm.) The **Department of Natural Resources Main Office,** just off US 101 on the north side of Forks, right next to Tillicum Park, hands out maps of state land on the peninsula. Since tourists who actually stop here are a rarity, the DNR is happy to help. (☎374-6131. Open M-F 8am-4:30pm.) Check your email at the **Library** on 224 S Forks Ave. (☎374-6402. Free. Open M, Tu, W noon-8pm, Th-Sa 10am-5pm.) The **police** are in the City Hall on E Division. (☎374-2223. Open daily 6am-6pm.) The **hospital** (☎374-6271) is just west of 101 on Bogachiel Way. The **post office** is at Spartan Ave. and A St., east of US 101. Open M-F 9am-5pm, Sa 10am-noon. **Postal Code: 98331.**

⬛ ⬚ ACCOMMODATIONS AND FOOD. In Forks you'll find a row of motels offering budget prices. The **Town Motel ❸,** 1080 S Forks Ave., has a beautiful garden and comfortable rooms. (☎374-6231. Singles $37-45; doubles $47-55.) Twenty mi. south of Forks on US 101, between Hoh Rain Forest and Kalaloch, you'll find the **Rainforest Hostel ❶,** 169312 US 101. To get there, follow hostel signs off US 101, 6 mi. south of the Hoh turnoff or 4 mi. north of Ruby Beach; buses go to the hostel from North Shore Brannon's Grocery in Quinault daily at 9am, 1pm, and 4:35pm. Family rooms and dorms are available, as are outside trailers for couples or people allergic to the resident dog and cat. The Hostel is a true resource for travelers, with laundry ($2), snacks, ride-sharing, info on buses, and parking. (☎374-2270. Morning **chore** required. Beds $12; family rooms $1 plus $12 per adult, $6 per child. Camping available for bikers, hikers, and busers for $6 per person.)

Off the highway, grab groceries and coffee at **Forks Thriftway,** 950 S Forks Ave. (☎374-6161. Open M-Su 8am-10pm.) The **Raindrop Cafe ❷,** 111 E A St. at S Forks Ave., serves breakfast until 11am, names its burgers after clouds ($3.75-7.50), and serves seriously delicious $7 salads. (☎374-6612. Open in summer M-Sa 6am-9pm, Su 6am-8pm; winter daily 6am-8pm.)

MORA

A quiet beach and campsite that doubles as a trailhead for long beach-following hikes is just 10 mi. west of Forks. In the morning, a haze hangs over the beach, making this area a perfect place to camp. This area is reached by taking US 110 west from just north of Forks.

Mora Campground ❶ is a sprawling 95-site campground that sees quite a bit of traffic from beach-goers. It offers evening programs on weekend nights, as well as toilets and water. (☎374-5460. Sites $10.) **Beach camping** is permitted both north and south of the **Mora Ranger Station.** To camp south of Mora a permit is required, in addition to a short drive to just before **La Push** (permit $5, plus $2 per person). From there, a trail leads down the beach—camping is permitted south of Third Beach and north of Oil City. Before hiking or camping on the coast, pick up a required overnight permit, a park map, a tide table, and the useful *Olympic Coastal Strip Info* brochure at a ranger station. Set up camp well above the highest line of tidal debris. North from Mora's **Rialto Beach,** 17 mi. of secluded beach snakes up to **Shi-Shi Beach.** Camping is allowed anywhere north of Ellen Creek

WASHINGTON

THE CITY OF (NO) LIGHT. You may notice dim lights in state buildings and supermarkets across the Northwest. An altruistic move by an environmentally-conscious state? Alas, young idealist, we fear the world is not so selfless; the motivation is less about altruism and more about blackmail. Because the western United States is connected by an electrical network, the northwest quickly felt the spring 2001 power shortage in California. Utilities demanded 10% reductions in usage or threatened to raise prices up to 300%. Folks responded with a lot of grumbling, especially about their (least) favorite state down south, but they have made changes, stalling drastic price raises.

with an overnight backcountry permit. Overnight options are numerous, and dayhikers often choose to take an abbreviated version of the same route, stopping at **Hole-in-the-Wall** (1½ mi. round-trip, 2hr.). Rialto beach is a sight in itself. To get there, head 1½ mi. west from Mora Campground.

HOH RAIN FOREST

The place to go to see the western rain forests, Hoh Rainforest sees plenty of guests. The average yearly rainfall in the Hoh Valley is 142 in. (Seattle gets 34 in. annually). The sights are spectacular, the growth is amazing, and the 18 mi. drive into the park from US 101 is an enjoyable patchwork of old-growth, wildflowers, and riverbeds. Turn off from 101 onto the Hoh Valley Rd., and drive about 12 mi. to the park entrance booth. Check out the **Hoh Rainforest Visitors Center** for backcountry permits and assistance in designing a backcountry route. (☎374-6925; www.nps.gov/olym. Open daily mid-June to Labor Day 9am-6pm.) The park maintains 88 campsites ❶ near the visitors center ($10) with drinking water and toilets, but has limited facilities for the handicapped. 70 backcountry **campsites** ❶ lie along the 17 mi. Hoh River Trail, which stretches between the Visitors Center and the Blue Glacier at Mt. Olympus (permit required, $5 plus $2 per person). Two free DNR campsites closer to 101, **Minnie Peterson** (7 sites) and **Willoughby Creek** (3 sites), are primitive and without treated water. No reservations are taken, so they are worth checking out to see what is open.

Hikers regularly file into the Hoh parking lot, returning from several popular routes that thread into the park's interior from the rainforest. The Hoh River Trail parallels the Hoh River for 17 mi., a three-day trip that traces through old-growth forests and lowlands to **Blue Glacier** on the shoulder of **Mount Olympus.** Shy Roosevelt elk, the ever-contested northern spotted owl, and the gods of ancient Greece inhabit this area. Closer by, the three-quarter-mile wheelchair-accessible **Hall of Mosses Trail** offers a whirlwind tour of rainforest vegetation. The slightly longer **Spruce Nature Trail** leads 1¼ mi. through old-growth forest, passing more varied vegetation along the banks of the Hoh River.

LAKE QUINAULT

Less visited than the Hoh Rain Forest, Lake Quinault offers its own rain forest and a large, beautiful lake. This lake, at the southwestern corner of ONP, sustains a small enclave of weekend getawayers, anglers, and hikers, many of them bypassing the rest of the peninsula and coming straight north to the lake via Aberdeen. On the southern, more populated side of the lake, the Forest Service operates an info center at the **Quinault Ranger Station,** 353 S Shore Rd. (☎288-2525. Open in summer M-F 8am-4:30pm, Sa-Su 9am-4pm; winter M-F 9am-4:30pm.) On the northern side of the lake, the **Quinault River Ranger Station** performs similar services, but from within the national park, 6 mi. from the highway. (☎288-2444. Open in summer daily 8:30am-5pm.) Campers can drop their gear lakeside in **Willaby Campgrounds ❶**, a quarter-mile before the Forest Service Ranger Station along the south shore of the lake. (☎288-2213. Sites $14.) Be aware—like those in the rest of the area, this campsite fills quickly. The **Lake Quinault Lodge** (☎288-2900 or 800-562-6672), next to the southern ranger station, rents canoes ($13 per hr.), seacycles ($18), rowboats ($11), and kayaks ($16) from their posh establishment.

Lake Quinault is surrounded by a great trail network. Stop at either ranger station for a detailed photocopy of trails in the area. **The North Fork trailhead** is 20 mi. up North Shore Rd. and starts one of the park's most popular multi-day hikes. It stretches 44 mi. north across the park, finishing at **Whiskey Bend** on the north rim near Elwha campgrounds. The week-long trip is one of the easier ones into the heart of the Olympics and has 17 campsites along the way (back-country permit required). The **Skyline Ridge Trail** (6½ mi. one-way), just south of the North Fork trailhead, leads to the Park's largest yellow cedar. **Three Lakes Point** is an exquisite summit that often remains covered with snow into July. The 7 mi. hike (one-way) from North Fork runs through yellow cedar and prime amphibian habitat. Give the trip several days. **Dayhikes** depart the Quinault Ranger Station, including the 4 mi. **Quinault Lake Loop** and the half-mile **Maple Glade Trail.** Many more are found on the north of the lake, including the new 1 mi. **Kestner Homestead Trail.**

PACIFIC COAST

Approaching its northern terminus, US 101 travels along beautiful coastal shores. Small towns, phenomenal shellfish, and sparkling beaches beckon. Unfortunately, red tide plagues the shellfish population with a bacteria that can be fatal to humans. Check with the visitors centers or www.doh.wa.gov/ehp/sf/biotoxin.htm to see which beaches are open.

WILLAPA BAY   ☎360

Willapa Bay stretches between the Long Beach Peninsula and the Washington mainland just north of the Washington-Oregon border and the mouth of the Columbia River. Home to the last unpolluted estuary in the nation, this is an excellent place to watch birdlife, especially in late spring and early fall. **US 101** passes the bay as it winds along the Pacific Coast toward Oregon. From Olympic National Park to the north, the highway passes Grays Harbor and the industrial cities of Aberdeen and Hoquiam at the mouth of the Chehalis River. As US 101 passes through Willapa Bay's sparkling sloughs, the quiet forests of Long Island lure seekers of solitude and lovers of wildlife. From the north, stop at the headquarters of the **Willapa National Wildlife Refuge,** just off US 101 on the left, 12 mi. north of the junction between US 101 and Rte. 103 by Chinook. The headquarters offers info on Canada geese, loons, grebes, cormorants, and trumpeter swans. (☎484-3482. Open M-F 7:30am-4pm.) Rangers can give directions and maps to several accessible hiking trails in the region, including Leadbetter Point at the tip of the Long Beach Peninsula. Long Island is home to five limited-use campgrounds, all inaccessible by car. Reaching the island, although it is only a stone's throw away from the mainland, requires finding a boat or bumming a ride on one (boats launch from the headquarters). Because of the difficulty of access, the bulk of tourist traffic is left stranded on the mainland.

WASHINGTON

RAINIER AREA KAYAKING: HOW TO GET HURT

Creeks and rivers in the Rainier area suck in all lovers of "adventure" and "fun," which can be translated out of the Northwest kayaker's vernacular as "self-punishment" and "pain." When I descended two rivers in the shadow of Rainier and Adams, I had all the "fun" I could handle, and more.

First came McCoy Creek. Everything went more or less okay (not counting when I slipped off a rock and nearly got swept into an undercut slot) until we got to an unportageable (read: no way out but down the river), virtually unscoutable, two-tiered 25 ft. beast of a waterfall. I plopped off okay, but the paddler behind me, Chad, blew a crucial move to cross the current and got recirculated in a vicious monster of a hole. Forced out of his boat but still trapped in the hole, he was underwater so long I started to remind myself how many pumps per minute to do in CPR. After an hour or so of recovery, Chad revealed the Northwest boater's attitude towards thrashings: "Whatever, I'll be back here next year."

I could only convince one of the four guys who had paddled with me on McCoy to come back out to Rainier the next day. Perhaps a bit reluctant, my friend Dan showed up an hour and a half late, and we put on Johnson Creek at 4:30 in the afternoon. The scenery was beautiful, mossy, and wooded. After the first portage (an hour-long mission to traverse 150 ft. of logs and thorns), though, we knew we might get more than we bargained for. Actually, we

After reaching the island, hike 2½ mi. along the island's fern-lined main road to pay your respects to the **Ancient Cedars.**

LONG BEACH PENINSULA   ☎ 360

The 28 mi. of unbroken sand that is Long Beach Peninsula is a frenzy of kitsch and souvenir shops sporadically broken up by calm forests and beautiful ocean views. Just don't let the looks deceive you into taking a dip—the water is very cold and carries lethal riptide currents. Accessible by US 101 and Rte. 103, every town has a clearly marked beach access road (unmarked roads end in private property). Fishing, boating, and kite-flying are how residents recuperate from pounding winter storms. Clamming season lasts from October to mid-March (but beware red tide). **Short Stop,** in the Shell Station across from the visitors center, sells non-resident licenses (annual license $23, two-day license $8) along with tips and tide tables.

Like most other towns along the bay, **Ilwaco** was nearly devastated when depleted salmon stocks required a shutdown of the fishery for several years. Salmon steaks are plentiful along the waterfront, where the industry is beginning to recover (barring a ban on fishing). **Pacific Salmon Charters** leads 8hr. fishing tours. (☎ 642-3466 or 800-831-2695. From $70. Open daily at 5:30am.) The **Long Beach Peninsula Visitors Bureau** is 5min. south of Long Beach on US 101. (☎ 642-2400 or 800-451-2542; www.funbeach.com. Open M-Sa 9am-5pm, Su 9am-4pm. Call for winter hours.) **Pacific Transit** sends buses from Long Beach as far north as Aberdeen. (☎ 642-9418. 85¢; exact change required.) Local buses run up and down the peninsula all day. Schedules are available in post offices and visitors centers on the peninsula (local service Sa-Su only). During the last week in August, flyers from Thailand, China, Japan, and Australia compete in the spectacular **International Kite Festival.**

Among the cheap places to hit the hay on the Peninsula is the **Sand-Lo-Motel ❸,** 1910 N Pacific Hwy. (☎ 642-2600. Rooms from $50; rates drop in winter.) **My Mom's Pie Kitchen ❷,** 1113 S Pacific Hwy., is a delicious respite from steak houses and greasy spoons. (☎ 642-2342; open W-Sa 11am-6pm.) **Mary's Traditional Dinners ❷** has tasty entrees for $10-14. (Open M-W 4:30-8pm, W-Su 8am-2pm.) For the best meal around, head down Hwy. 103 in Ocean Park to historic **Oysterville.** The star draw of this tiny, whitewashed town is **Oysterville Sea Farms ❸,** at 1st and Clark, which raises and dishes out its namesake mollusk. (☎665-6585. Open daily 10am-5pm.) For some entertainment, head to **Marsh's Free Museum,** 409 S Pacific Way, home to a mechanical fortune teller, Jake the petrified alligator-man, and honky-tonk souvenirs. (☎642-2188; open, ironically, whenever tourists bring money.)

THE COLUMBIA RIVER ESTUARY ☎360

Several miles south of Long Beach on Washington's southern border, **Cape Disappointment** guards the **Columbia River Estuary.** Over the last 300 years, almost 2000 vessels have been wrecked, stranded, or sunk at Cape Disappointment, and even today the Coast Guard is kept busy during the frequent squalls in the area. **Fort Columbia State Park** lies on US 101 northwest of the Astoria Megler Bridge, 1 mi. east of Chinook on the west side of the highway. The park interpretive center recreates life at the fort and showcases numerous artifacts on the indigenous Chinook people as well as on the white soldiers. (☎777-8221. Open Memorial Day to Oct. 1 daily 10am-5pm; call for winter hours.)

Three miles southwest of Ilwaco, at the southern tip of the Peninsula, **Fort Canby State Park ❶** offers camping and a megadose of Lewis and Clark. The park was the dynamic duo's final destination, and now boasts two lighthouses and a well-pruned campground packed with RVs. The sites fill up quickly in summer. (☎642-3078 or 800-452-5687. Open daily dawn-dusk. 240 sites, $12; RV sites $17; hiker/biker sites $6; cabins and yurts sleep 4 for $35. Reservation fee $6.) At the end of the main road, the spaceship-shaped **Lewis and Clark Interpretive Center** hovers above the ruins of the fort. Inside, a winding display documents their expedition from Missouri to their arrival at the mouth of the Columbia. (Open daily 10am-5pm.) **The North Head Lighthouse,** built in 1898, is accessible by a gravel path in the northwest corner of the park, off Hwy. 103; the path has great views down the breakers. The **Cape Disappointment Lighthouse,** built in 1856, is the oldest lighthouse in the Pacific Northwest. In the southeast corner of the park, its distinctive red light can be reached by walking up a steep hill from the Coast Guard station parking lot, or by following a narrow, fairly steep trail from the interpretive center. For a magnificent beach-level view of both lighthouses, drive through the campground area past Waikiki Beach on the North Jetty. Waikiki is the only beach safe for swimming and is a solitary spot for winter beachcombing and ship watching.

anything, since all we knew to expect was a runnable 20 ft. waterfall in the middle of a deep canyon. Our certainty turned to shock, though, when we realized the falls was blocked by logs and was clearly unrunnable—hitting any of them would mean certain death. One glance at the imposing rock walls around us led to a quick, inescapable conclusion. "Dude, we're screwed," I explained to Dan.

With no other choice, we began tackling the walls inch by inch, hauling our boats by rope over mud, rocks, and brush. Two and a half hours later and well past dark, I wedged my 40 lb. boat into a tree, curled up in the fetal position, and mumbled something incoherent. In addition to the steepness of the canyon walls (if I had pushed hard enough against the wall, I would have tumbled backwards off the face), the arrangement of fallen logs was so devilish that it slowed our pace to a few feet per minute and produced a combination of rage, frustration, and resignation. As it turned out, when I had lost all hope we were only 100 ft. below a forest road on the canyon rim—my friend, in a burst of superhuman endurance, had pressed on and discovered it. So, after a mild 1½ hr. stumble down the road, we reached Dan's car and some oh-so-tasty PB&J sandwiches.

—Carleton Goold

***WILLKOMMEN IN* LEAVENWORTH!** A true experiment in tourism. After the town's logging industry collapsed and the railroad switching station moved to nearby Wenatchee, Leavenworth needed a new *Weltanschauung*. Desperate officials launched "Project Alpine," a gimmick to transform the town into a German village: zoning and building codes necessitated Bavarian-style buildings, waiters learned about bratwurst, polka blasted over the loudspeakers, and German beer flowed. It worked: more than 1.5 million Americans came in 2000, with influxes peaking during the city's three annual festivals. Tasty pretzels and *Schnitzel*, oddly enough, complement the nearby world-class rock climbing and camping. On the eastern slope of the Cascades, Leavenworth is near Washington's geographic center. To get there from Seattle, follow I-5 North to Everett (Exit 194), then US 2 East (126 mi., 2½hr.). From Spokane, follow US 2 West (184 mi., 4hr.). The Chamber of Commerce/Visitor Information Center, 220 9th St. at Commercial St., provides a plethora of pamphlets and brochures. (☎548-5807. Open M-Th 8am-5pm, F-Sa 8am-6pm, Su 10am-4pm; winter M-Sa 8am-5pm.) Indulge in the fabulous location of Bindlestiff's Riverside Cabins, 1600 Hwy. 2. Eight private cabins rest just feet from the beautiful Wenatchee River where you can watch the rafters drift by, borrow the BBQ, and grill on your own private porch. (☎548-5015. Fridge. TV. No phones. 1- and 2-room cabins $63-83.) Camping is also available 8 mi. out of town on Icicle Creek Rd. at a National Forest Campground ($10). Predictably, Leavenworth's food mimics German cuisine; surprisingly, it often succeeds. German *Wurst* booths are tucked between buildings everywhere. When you've had your fill of tourist-watching and sausage-scarfing, embark on an adventure into Leavenworth's extensive hiking, biking, and climbing opportunities in the Wenatchee National Forest.

THE CASCADE REGION

WASHINGTON

Sprawling in the rain shadow of the Cascades, the hills and valleys of the Columbia River Basin foster little more than sagebrush, tumbleweed, and tiny wildflowers among unirrigated dunes. Where the watershed has been tapped, however, a patchwork of farmland yields bumper crops of fruit and wine. Seeking the best of the region, travelers take high alpine routes through the Cascades, where dry hills give way to uncommonly green beauty in the mountains. The Cascades are most accessible in July, August, and September. Many high mountain passes are snowed in during the rest of the year, making access difficult and anything beside skiing and snowshoeing just about impossible. Mounts Baker, Vernon, Glacier, Rainier, Adams, and St. Helens are accessible by four major roads. The North Cascades Hwy. (Rte. 20) is the most breathtaking and provides access to North Cascades National Park. Scenic US 2 leaves Everett for Stevens Pass and descends along the Wenatchee River. Rte. 20 and US 2 are often traveled in sequence as the Cascade Loop. US 12 approaches Mt. Rainier National Park through White Pass and provides access to Mt. St. Helens from the north. I-90 sends four lanes from Seattle to the ski resorts of Snoqualmie Pass and eastward. From the west the state is accessible by bus on I-90 and US 2, and the train parallels I-90. Rainstorms and evening traffic can slow hitching; locals warn against thumbing Rte.20

MOUNT ST. HELENS ☎ 360

After two months of mounting volcanic activity, Mount St. Helens erupted with a cataclysmic blast on May 18, 1980, transforming what had been a perfect mountain cone into a crater one mile wide and two miles long. The force of the ash-filled blast crumbled 1300 ft. of rock and razed forests, strewing trees like charred matchsticks. Ash from the crater rocketed 17 mi. upward, circling the globe and blackening the region's sky for days. Debris from the volcano flooded Spirit Lake and choked the region's watersheds. Today, Mt. St. Helens is made up of the middle third of the Gifford Pinchot National Forest, as well as the Mount St. Helens National Volcanic Monument. The monument is part national park, part laboratory, and encompasses most of the area around the volcano affected by the explosion. Parts of the monument are off-limits to the public due to experiments, and hikers are obliged to keep to the handful of trails through such areas. Due to federal budget cuts many of the services currently offered on the mountain are slated to be cut back or cancelled. Call ahead to be sure, especially regarding early morning and winter hours.

✈ ORIENTATION

To make the **western approach** (the most popular and worthwhile of the approaches, see p. 225), take Exit 49 off **I-5** and use **Rte. 504,** otherwise known as the **Spirit Lake Memorial Hwy.** The brand-new 52 mi. road has wide shoulders and astounding views of the crater. For most, this is the quickest and easiest daytrip to the mountain, and includes the Mount St. Helens Visitor Center, the Coldwater Ridge Visitor Center, and the Johnston Ridge Observatory. A **southern approach** (see p. 226) on **Rte. 503** skirts the side of the volcano until it connects with **Forest Service Rd. 90.** From there, **Forest Service Rd. 83** leads to lava caves and the Climber's Bivouac, a launch pad for forays up the mountain. Views from the south side don't show the recent destruction, but the green glens and remnants of age-old lava and mud flows make up for it with great hiking and camping. To make a **northern approach** (see p. 227), take **US 12** east from I-5 (Exit 68). The towns of Mossyrock, Morton, and Randle along US 12 offer the **closest major services** to the monument. From US 12, **Forest Service Rd. 25** heads south to Forest Service Rd. 99, which leads 16 mi. into the most devastated parts of the monument. Travelers can stop by the famous and majestic Spirit Lake, and marvel at the huge expanses of blown down forest. Although the monument itself contains no established **campgrounds,** a number are scattered throughout the surrounding national forest. See individual approaches for listings of campgrounds. Talking to a ranger is always your best option.

⁊ PRACTICAL INFORMATION

Entrance Fee: There are 2 main types of fees associated with Mt. St. Helens. The first is the **Monument Pass**—this one-day, multi-site pass allows access to almost every center on the western approach, as well as Ape Cave. It can be purchased as a multi-site pass everywhere it is needed ($6, ages 5-15 $2, 4 and under free), or it can be purchased as a single site pass, which allows access to only one area ($3, ages 5-15 $1, 4 and under free). Areas of the monument that do not require a Monument Pass most likely require the second fee, a **Northwest Forest Pass,** which will take care of the entire northern approach, as well as most of the southern area ($5 per day, $30 annually). Climbing the mountain requires a whole separate set of permits (see **Climbing** p. 227).

Mt. St. Helens, Mt. Rainier, and Vicinity

ACCOMMODATIONS
Cowlitz River Lodge, **7**
Hotel Packwood, **8**
Serenity's, **22**
Shade Tree Inn, **17**
Whittaker's Bunkhouse, **4**

CAMPING
Beaver, **19**
Cougar, **18**
Cougar Rock, **3**
Guler-Mt. Adams County Park, **21**
Ike Kinswa, **10**
Iron Creek, **12**
Lewis & Clark State Pk., **11**
Ohanapecosh, **6**
Peterson Prarie, **20**
Seaquest State Park, **14**
Sunshine Pt., **5**
Swift, **15**
Takhlakh Lake, **13**
Trout Lake Creek, **16**
White River, **1**

FOOD
Club Cafe, **9**
Highlander, **2**
KJ's Bear Creek Cafe, **23**
Time Out, **24**

Visitors Information: There are 9 visitors centers and info stations, listed below by approach. Those on the western approach are the most popular.

Publications: *The Volcano Review,* free at all visitors centers and ranger stations, contains a map, copious information, and schedules of activities. The *Road Guide to Mount St. Helens* ($6), available at visitors centers, is more thorough.

Forest Service Information: Gifford Pinchot National Forest Headquarters, 10600 NE 51st Circle, Vancouver, WA 98682 (☎891-5000, recording 891-5009; www.fs.fed.us/gpnf). Info on camping and hiking within the forest. Additional **ranger stations** and **visitor information** at **Randle,** 10024 US 12 (☎497-1100) and **Packwood,** 13068 US 12 (☎497-1172), both north of the mountain on US 12.

Monument Headquarters, 42218 NE Yale Bridge Rd., Amboy, 98601 (☎247-3900), 4 mi. north of Amboy on Rte. 503. This is *the* place to call or write for any questions prior to the trip: road conditions, permit availability, access, etc. Open daily 7:30am-5pm.

Radio: 530 AM. Road closures and ranger hours. Only in winter.

Emergency: ☎911.

WESTERN APPROACH: RTE. 504

▣ VISITORS CENTERS

Mount St. Helens Visitor Center (☎274-2100), opposite Seaquest State Park. A great introduction to the explosive events of 1980. See the film, a manmade lava cave, and other interactive geological displays. Learn how a volcano works before you see its aftermath. A mile-long hike through 2500-year-old wetlands is also offered. Open daily 9am-5pm. 16min. film shown twice per hour.

Forest Learning Center (☎414-3439). The Weyerhaeuser Lumber Company sponsors this center, which houses interesting exhibits on logging and the reforestation of the surrounding timber downed by the explosion. Take the time and watch the video that explains how logging is done. Open May-Oct. 10am-6pm. Free.

Coldwater Ridge Visitor Center (☎274-2131). Superb view of the crater, along with trails leading to **Coldwater Lake.** Emphasis on the area's recolonization by living things through exhibits, a short film, and a ¼ mi. trail. Picnic areas, interpretive talks, and a gift shop and snack bar. Open daily 10am-6pm. Call for winter hours.

Johnston Ridge Observatory (☎274-2140), at the end of Rte. 504. Geological exhibits and the best view from the road of the steaming lava dome and crater. The center is named for David Johnston, a geologist who predicted the May 18, 1980 eruption, stayed to study it, and was killed. Fantastic 22min. wide screen film and exhibits emphasizing survivors of the blast. Open daily May-Oct. 10am-6pm.

▮▯ ACCOMMODATIONS AND FOOD

The only non-camping options close to the park are a few expensive motels that cluster around I-5, Exit 49, near the intersection of Rte. 504. Despite high prices, they book solid in the summer. Try the **Mt. St. Helens Motel ❸,** 1340 Mt. St. Helens Way NE in Castle Rock, 5 mi. from the Mt. St. Helens Visitor Center on Rte. 504. Enjoy free local calls, fridge, TVs, morning coffee, and laundry facilities. (☎274-7721. Singles $55; doubles $75.) **Seaquest State Park ❶,** opposite the Mt. St. Helens Visitor Center, is easy to reach off I-5, and the closest campground with facilities to the park. (☎274-8633, reservations 888-226-7688. Reservations essential. Wheelchair accessible. 92 sites, $14; 16 full RV sites, $20; 4 primitive walk-in sites, $5. Pay showers.) If your coolers and stomachs are empty, Castle Rock is the best place to refuel.

Supermarkets and convenience stores lie on the west side of Hwy. 5, while fast food joints and a few restaurants sit on the east. Papa Pete throws a mean and inexpensive pizza at **Papa Pete's Pizza ❷**, 1163 Mt. St. Helens Way NE. A large cheese is $17. (☎274-4271. Open daily 10am-11pm.)

🄢 HIKING

The 1hr. drive from the Mt. St. Helens Visitor Center to Johnston Ridge offers spectacular views of the crater and rebounding ecosystem, with plenty of opportunities to park the car and walk along short, well-marked trails. The **Boundary Trail** (3 mi. to the Lake) leads from the Johnston Ridge Observatory to Spirit Lake, and continues 52 mi. to Mt. Adams through sensitive terrain. Moderate to difficult.

SOUTHERN APPROACH: RTE. 503

🄻 VISITORS CENTERS

Pine Creek Information Station, 17 mi. east of Cougar on Rd. 90, shows a short interpretive film of the eruption. Also the only place in the south of the park with free water to fill up bottles. Open June-Sept. daily 9:30am-5:30pm.

Apes' Headquarters, at Ape Cave on Rd. 8303, 3 mi. north of the Rd. 83-Rd. 90 junction (15min. from Cougar). Rangers dish out rental lanterns and guide 45min. lantern walks into the 1900-year-old lava tube daily from 10:30am-4:30pm, every hour on the half hour. On the weekends arrive early to snag a spot. Dress warmly—cave is 42°F. Open late-May to Sept. daily 10am-5:30pm.

🄰 CAMPING

Swift Campground ❶ (☎503-813-6666), 30min. east of Cougar on Rd. 90 and just west of the Pine Creek Information Station, has spacious sites on Swift Reservoir. It is one of the most popular campgrounds in the area. 93 sites, $12.

Cougar Campground and **Beaver Bay,** 2 and 4 mi. east of Cougar respectively, along Yale Lake; Cougar Lake has 60 sites ($15) that are more spread out and private than Beaver Bay's 78 sites ($15).

🄾 OUTDOOR ACTIVITIES

SPELUNKING

The **Ape Cave** lies 5 mi. east of Cougar, just off of Road 83. The cave is a broken 2½ mi. lava tube formed by an eruption over 1900 years ago. When exploring the cave, wear a jacket and sturdy shoes, and take at least two flashlights or lanterns. The Lower Cave's easy travel attracts most visitors, but the Upper Cave offers a more challenging scramble over rock rubble and lava breakdown. Budget 1¼hr. for the Lower Cave, 3hr. for the Upper Cave. A Monument Pass is required. Rangers lead guided cave explorations every day (see **Apes' Headquarters,** above), as well as rent lanterns. (Rentals $2 each, and stop at 4pm.) No free water is available at Apes.

HIKING

A quarter-mile before Ape Cave on Rd. 83 is the **Trail of Two Forests,** a lava-strewn and wheelchair-accessible boardwalk path above the forest floor. A beautiful forest has emerged, engulfed in lava from thousands of years ago. (Easy.) Rd. 83 continues 9 mi. farther north, ending at **Lahar Viewpoint,** the site of terrible mudflows that followed the eruption. On Rd. 83, 11 mi. northeast of its junction with Rd. 90, the **Lava Canyon Trail #184** hosts a range of challenges: an easy, wheelchair-accessible 40min. stroll yields spectacular views of the **Muddy River Gorge** and **Waterfall;** a more difficult route leads 3 mi. to the site of a now-defunct footbridge over Lava Canyon. Only the brave should venture farther; the trail then continues along a cliff and down a 25 ft. ladder to reach the canyon floor.

CLIMBING

The recently reshaped Mt. St. Helens draws hordes of people eager to gaze into the crater to see the source of so much power. It is now the most climbed mountain in the Northwest. The biggest challenge to climbing an otherwise very easy route is getting a permit. Between May 15 and Oct. 31, the Forest Service allows 100 people per day to hike to the crater rim. $15 permits are required to climb anywhere above 4800 ft. ($30 for an annual pass; reservations still required). Reserve in person or write to the Monument Headquarters (see **Practical Information**). Fifty permits per day may be reserved in advance after Feb. 1. Write early; weekends are usually booked by March, and weekdays often fill up as well. The reservation-less can enter a 6pm lottery for the next day's remaining permits at **Jack's Restaurant and Country Store**, 13411 Louis River Rd., on Rte. 503, 5 mi. west of Cougar. (☎231-4276. I-5 Exit 21. Open daily 5:30am-9pm.)

Although not a technical climb, the route up the mountain is a steep pathway of ash strewn with boulders. Often, the scree on the steep grade is so thick that each step forward involves a half-step back (5hr. up; 3hr. down). The view from the lip of the crater, encompassing Mt. Rainier, Mt. Adams, Mt. Hood, Spirit Lake, and the lava dome directly below, is magnificent. Bring sunglasses, sunscreen, sturdy climbing boots, foul-weather clothing, plenty of water, and gaiters to keep boots from filling with ash. Snow covers parts of the trail as late as early summer, making an ice axe a welcome companion. Free camping (no water) is available at the **Climber's Bivouac ❶**, the trailhead area for the **Ptarmigan Trail #216A,** which starts the route up the mountain. The trail is located about 4 mi. up Rd. 83. Note: entry into the crater is strictly prohibited.

WINTER ACTIVITIES

The southern area of Mt. St. Helens has several **SnoParks** along Rte. 90 and Rte. 83, connected by semi-groomed trails. They are popular with cross-country skiers, snowshoers, and snowmobilers. Pick up a pass before going out; they are available in Cougar and Randle during the winter. Another SnoPark is found along Rd. 25, accessible only from Randle.

NORTHERN APPROACH: US 12

🚩 VISITORS CENTERS

Woods Creek Information Station, 6 mi. south of Randle on Rd. 25, from US 12. A small station that is designed mainly for drive-through-style quick questions. It is, however, the north's best option past the Randle station (see p. 228). Open June-Aug. daily 9am-4pm.

Windy Ridge Interpretive Site, at the end of Rd. 99 off Rd. 25, 1¼hr. from Randle. Rangers give 30min. talks about the eruption in the outdoor amphitheater before the stunning backdrop of the volcano. Talks every hour on the half-hour between 11:30am-4:30pm. The route to Windy Ridge is lined with several viewpoints, all of them looking onto the area most damaged by the eruption. Stopping is well worth the extra time.

THE LOCAL STORY

UT OF THE FLYING PLANE, INTO THE FIRE

*Smoke jumpers, or firefighters who parachute from planes to combat blazes, have some of the coolest jobs on earth. Let's Go Researcher-Writer James Pinto spoke with **Scott Wicklund**, a smoke jumper based out of Winthrop, WA, in August of 2002.*

Q: A lot of people would say this is an insane job. How would you respond?
A: People would say this is an insane job because they don't realize all the safety precautions that go into it. It seems crazy because you're jumping out of a perfectly good airplane... into a forest fire! But the reality is that you've got a perfectly good parachute and you know fire behavior. So you land in a place where you're safe from any sort of fire activity, and take the proper measures to control the fire.
Q: What made you decide that you wanted to do this?
A: I guess growing up my mom said, "Don't get dirty; don't play with fire." I found a job that paid me to do both.
Q: Do you have a particularly scary, crazy, or weird story from your job?
A: The weirdest thing that ever happened to me? One time I landed in an 80 ft. tree, but the parachute didn't catch on the branches. I slid down the side of the tree, picking up speed until I basically knew I was going to break my leg in half a second. All of a sudden, the parachute catches on a branch and I was just hanging there a foot away from the ground. Hanging there perfectly fine. Which was a great feeling.

CAMPING

Iron Creek Campground ❶, just south of the Woods Creek Information Station, is the closest campsite to Mt. St. Helens, and has good hiking and beautiful forest along with a good location. All 98 sites can fill up on busy weekends. (Reservations ☎ 877-444-6777, strongly recommended in summer. Water. $12.50 per site, $14.50 for premium sites, $6 per extra vehicle.) The first stop for visitors traveling south on Rd. 25 from Randle and US 12 should be the **Woods Creek Information Station.**

HIKING

Independence Pass Trail #227, a 3½ mi. hike with overlooks of Spirit Lake and superb views of the crater and dome. (Moderate.) A serious hike continues past the intersection with **Norway Pass Trail,** running through the blast zone to the newly reopened **Mt. Margaret peak.** Considered the best hike in the park, the trail is 8 mi. (7hr.) to the peak and back. (Difficult.) Farther west, **Harmony Trail #224** provides a steep hike (2 mi. round-trip) to Spirit Lake. (Moderate to difficult.) Spectacular **Windy Ridge** is the exclamation point of Rd. 99. From here, a steep ash hill grants a magnificent view of the crater 3½ mi. away. The **Truman Trail** (7 mi.) meanders through the Pumice Plain, where hot flows sterilized the land. The area is under constant scrutiny by biologists, so stay on the trail at all times. (Easy to moderate.)

COWLITZ VALLEY/US 12   ☎ 360

The Cowlitz Valley is a broad, flat area that stretches from the south of Rainier west to Interstate 5. The Valley's location between Rainier, St. Helens, and Adams guarantees that anyone touring the southern Cascades will end up there at some point. Several lakes, services, plenty of inexpensive accommodations, and roads leading to all of the major peaks make the Valley a good stop on almost any itinerary. Exploring tiny back roads is not recommended, as a large population of marijuana farmers in Lewis County might not take kindly to being discovered.

The main road running through the valley is US 12. To figure out the next stop on your tour of the area, drop in at the **Cowlitz Valley Ranger Station,** 10024 US 12, located in Randle, near the center of the valley. The ranger station has lots of information on trails and other outdoor activities. (☎ 497-1100. Open June-Aug. daily 8am-4:30pm; Sept.-May, closed Sa-Su.) Info is also available 16 mi. to the east, at the Packwood Visitor Information Center, 13068 US 12.

(☎497-1172. Open summer daily 7:45-11:30am and
12:30-4:30pm; winter closed Sa-Su.) **Packwood** has
groceries and other essentials. **Mossyrock** and **Morton**
are settlements with services nearer I-5; Morton has
a laundromat and grocery near the intersection of
Rtes. 7 and 12.

There are several options for camping, including
Northwest Forest Pass sites— ask at a station for
info. **Ike Kinswa State Park ❶**, on Mayfield Lake's Rte.
122, a 30min. drive west of Randle, about 18 mi. off
US 12 from the west, offers camping, swimming (to
non-campers, too), and trout fishing year-round. It
boasts 101 private sites with full access to a lake that
attracts bald eagles and ospreys. (☎983-3402. Reservations are strongly recommended in summer; call
888-226-7688. Sites $16, full RV sites $22, extra vehicle $6. Showers $0.50 per 3min.) Thirteen miles to the
west of Ike Kinswa along Rte. 12 on Jackson Hwy.,
the **Lewis and Clark State Campground ❶** has sites amid
old-growth forests, plus BBQs and kitchens. (☎864-
2643, reservations 800-452-5687. Group sites available. 25 sites, $13.)

There is excellent **fishing** in the Cowlitz area. Spots
downstream of the **Barrier Dam** are crowded for good
reason. To get there, travel to Salkum off Rte. 12, go
south down Fuller Rd., and follow signs to the Barrier Dam boat launch. There is a tackle shop on the
road down. Locals claim that **Mineral Lake** is the best
place around to catch fish and that **Riffe Lake** is also
worth a cast.

MOUNT ADAMS ☎509

At 12,276 ft., Mt. Adams is the second highest peak in
Washington but still one of the least visited. Overlooked throughout its history, it was named after the
2nd U.S. President by Lewis and Clark only because
other volcanic heavy-hitters Hood, Rainier, and
Baker had already been claimed for British admirals.
Still, Mt. Adams's lack of fame works to the advantage of those seeking solitude on its rugged volcanic
terrain. Unfortunately, part of the reason Adams
lacks recognition is that it's hard to access: it is connected by pavement only to the south, and the gravel
roads traveling to the north are closed much of the
year due to snow.

**■+🖈 ORIENTATION AND PRACTICAL INFORMA-
TION.** The Mt. Adams District is formed by the
southern third of the Gifford Pinchot National Forest, as well as the Mt. Adams Wilderness. The entire
area is most accessible from the south, by following
Hwy. 141 north from Hood River via White Salmon.
One can also approach from the north, along Forest

Q: Can you describe the feeling of
crashing into a tree from the sky at 12
miles per hour?

A: You jump out of the airplane, you
see the meadow below that you're
supposed to be going for, and you're
aiming for that; then the wind picks
up, and you know you're not going to
make it. At that point you start looking for some shorter trees to land in,
so you're not hung up too high off the
ground. Then you try and cap that tree
with your canopy so you're hung up
well; they train you to do that. But
there's still a bit of chaos. At that
point you don't know exactly what's
going to happen. A lot of times it's a
soft landing, because you go in there
and the canopy catches the tree perfectly. Other times, your feet get
kicked out from underneath you,
you're upside-down and falling, you're
not sure that your canopy hung up,
your heart's racing a million miles per
hour, and then *jerk,* you're hanging.

Q: What's the injury rate like?

A: I have never been injured jumping.
We might get two or three sprained
ankles, maybe a blown ACL, maybe a
broken femur, maybe a broken wrist
every year.

Q: Would you say working here is a
team effort?

A: It is every day. The first thing you
do after you land is check with your
partner and make sure he's okay. We
always jump two at a time.

Q: Would you recommend this job to
a lot of people?

A: Yeah, I'd recommend it to anyone
who likes having adventures but
doesn't want to make a whole lot of
money.

Rd. 23 (this road is largely unpaved, and usually blocked with snow until June or July). **Amtrak** (☎ 800-872-7245) is also an option, stopping 20 mi. away in Bingen at the foot of Walnut St., with routes from **Portland** (2hr., $10-17) and **Spokane** (5½hr., $34-60).

If you're coming from the south, your last stop before heading into the great unknown should be Trout Lake, found on Highway 141. Trout Lake's main draw is the **Mt. Adams District Ranger Station,** 2455 Hwy. 141, whose rangers dispense advice, the proper permits, detailed topographic maps of the area for $4, and guides to hiking trails for $6. (☎ 395-3400; station open M-F 8am-4:30pm, additional weekend hours during summer.) Trout Lake also has a gas station and **General Store,** 2383 Hwy. 141, which sells a small supply of food and essentials at a price that will make you regret not getting them elsewhere. (☎ 395-2777. Open summer daily 8am-8pm, winter 8am-7pm.) Another option is to pick up provisions on your way up Hwy. 141, at a grocery store in **BZ Corner** or any of the other towns.

Information about the area is available in White Salmon, at the **Mt. Adams Chamber of Commerce Information Center,** just west of the toll bridge from Hood River on Rte. 14. (☎ 493-3630; Open summer daily 9am-5pm, Oct.-May M-F 9am-5pm.) Equipment rental is best taken care of in Hood River (see **Columbia River Gorge,** p. 89). For road conditions, call ☎ 360-905-2958. **Emergency:** ☎ 911. **Police:** 180 W Lincoln, White Salmon (non-emergency ☎ 493-2660). **Post office:** 2393 Hwy. 141, in Trout Lake. (☎ 395-2108; open M-F 8:30am-12:30pm, 1-5pm.) **Postal Code:** 98650.

🏕 🍴 ACCOMMODATIONS AND FOOD. The Mt. Adams area is crawling with places to pitch a tent, many of them requiring only a Northwest Forest Pass. The best plan is to stop at the ranger station and tell them what you want to do; they will tell you the best site to use as a base. The closest to Trout Lake is the **Guler-Mt. Adams County Park ❶,** one of the few areas with showers. To get there, take a left at the post office and follow the signs. (Sites with water $10, water and electricity $14.) The biggest pay area near Trout Lake is **Peterson Prairie ❶;** head about 5 mi. past Trout Lake on 141 and another 3 mi. into the National Forest, and look for signs to your right. (30 sites, $11.) On the way, check to see if there is room at **Trout Lake Creek,** a forest-pass-only site just off 141; take a right on Forest Rd. 88 and follow the signs. Both sites put you near the Natural Bridges and Ice Caves, which are off Hwy. 141 on the left and worth a quick stop. Perhaps the best camping is 1hr. north of Trout Lake, in the Takhlakh Lake area. There are several different spots, but the best is 🌄**Takhlakh Lake Campsite ❶,** which offers amazing views of Mt. Adams presiding over the lake. ($11 per site, $13 for prime sites.) To get there, take the Mt. Adams Rec. Hwy. out of Trout Lake, and then take Forest Road 23 for 1hr. until you see signs—call the ranger station to ask about road openings.

The one budget option that will put a hard roof overhead is found in Glenwood, a 16 mi. drive from Trout Lake. To get there, take the Mt. Adams Rec. Hwy. out of Trout Lake, and then take the first right—a small sign will say Glenwood. Look for the small but friendly **Shade Tree Inn ❷,** 105 E Main St. A motel with attached restaurant, convenience store, and laundromat, it also has excellent views of the mountain from a back balcony. Satellite TV, A/C. (☎ 364-3471. Reception and store open daily 7am-9:30pm, restaurant 7am-7pm. Singles $45; doubles $55.)

A broader range of luxuries can be found at **Serenity's ❸,** 2291 Hwy. 141, just south of town and across from Trout Lake School. The four spacious cabins with full bath (jacuzzis in 3 cabins), kitchenettes, gas log fireplaces, TV and VCR are geared toward romantic couples, though as many as 6-8 can fit comfortably in the large, lofted bedroom. (Minimum 2 night stay on weekends. Chalets $90-150.)

Get basic foods at **BZ Corner Grocery,** on the left when going north on Hwy. 141 in BZ Corner, about 10 mi. south of Trout Lake. (☎ 493-2441; open M-Sa 6am-9pm, Su 7am-8pm.) In Trout Lake, **KJ's Bear Creek Cafe ❶,** 2376 Hwy. 141 at the fork of Hwy.

141 and the Mt. Adams Recreational Hwy., has greasy but reasonably priced food. Breakfast meals $4-5, burger $3.60. (☎395-2525; open summer 6am-8pm daily.) Just south of the Trout Lake school is **Time Out ❶**, 2295 Hwy. 141, which serves pizza (small $7) and burgers. (☎395-2767; open M-F 11am-7pm, Sa-Su noon-8pm.)

HIKING AND MOUNTAIN BIKING.
The best resources in the Mt. Adams area for hiking are available at the ranger station: supplement the rangers' advice with the **Forest Services Trail Guide** ($6). Hiking is generally very rewarding—most trails meander in and out of broken-up lava flows and occasionally open up onto good views. If you're driving, many trailheads require a **Northwest Forest Pass** ($5 per day, $30 annually; available at the ranger station). The area can get very dry in the summer, so be sure to bring adequate water; also note that **compasses don't work in lava beds** due to the abundance of underground mineral deposits. A long thaw leaves many trails closed through spring, and bugs can make early summer very uncomfortable.

The half-mile trail to **Sleeping Beauty Peak** starts off at a small trailhead on the left side of Rd. 8810-040, about a quarter-mile from the Rd. 8810 junction (see directions to Trout Lake campground, above). The **Indian Heaven Wilderness Trail** is a mild 10 mi. loop through forest and meadow. Other dayhiking options abound in the Adams area. For multi-day hikes, the most popular is the **Round-the-Mountain Trail**. It does not go around the mountain at all, but rather stretches 8 mi. to the south of Mt. Adams, eventually ending at the border of the Yakama Indian Reservation. This area is closed to hikers lacking tribal permission, so most parties turn around at this point, yielding a 2-3 day 16 mi. journey (although permits to use Yakama land are available from rangers at Bird Lake, off the trail). Mountain biking is permitted on many of the trails in the National Forest. Bikeable trails are clearly marked and are listed in the trail guide available at the ranger station.

CLIMBING.
Mt. Adams is laced with at least a dozen mountaineering routes, including the very popular (and relatively easy) **South Spur** and **Mt. Adams Summit Route**. All routes require crampons and an ice axe year-round, and usually do not even open up until June. In addition, climbers should stop at the ranger station to register and purchase a **Cascade Volcano Pass** ($10 for trips on M-Th, $15 for a trip that touches either F, Sa, or Su), required for all parties going higher than 7000 ft. up the mountain. Get climbing info at ☎891-5015.

RAFTING AND KAYAKING.
Three rivers pour off the flanks of Mt. Adams, through volcanic rock and down to the Columbia River. The **White Salmon River** has several classic runs. The class III-IV section, from BZ Corner to Husum, dives into a craggy gorge with lichen-draped old-growth trees and crumbling lava cliffs. The **Farmlands Run** courses through a beautiful, dark, and vertical-walled canyon, whose flat rim belies the raging class IVs (two V+) below. First-timers should go with a veteran. Immediately downstream of the Farmland's last rapid lurks the class V-VI **Green Truss** section, where the Gorge Games' races are held on its sometimes-lethal waterfalls. A class II+ section from Husum down to Northwestern lake is a popular after-work run.

Other nearby boating options include the **Klickitat River,** famed for its columnar basalt formations and isolated, roadless sections, as well as the **Wind River.** For extreme kayakers, the **Little White Salmon River** has the best paddling in the Northwest. But it's no cakewalk: veterans estimate that only 10% of runs finish without mishap. For rafters, guiding companies line Hwy. 141 around BZ Corner, taking patrons to most rivers in the area. **River Drifters** (☎800-972-0430; www.riverdrifters.net) has lots of options. Two companies operate out of White Salmon—**Zoller's Outdoor Odysseys** (☎800-366-2004) and **All Adventures** (☎877-641-7238). **River Riders,** in Hood River, also has competitive prices (☎800-448-7238). A day of rafting can cost anywhere between $45 and $70.

Weaving its way through the craggy peaks and lush valleys of Washington's North Cascades Range, Rte. 20 is nothing short of a blissful driving experience—the road seems to have been designed to afford drivers unadulterated pleasure. Spectacular vistas await at every turn, and a string of small towns scattered along the road provide services. Rte. 20 runs east-west through Northern Washington, traveling through the spectacular scenery of Mt. Baker Snoqualmie National Forest, North Cascades National Park, and Okanogan National Forest.

TIME: 2hr. driving time
DISTANCE: 70 mi.
SEASON: Apr.-Nov.

WEST OF NORTH CASCADES NATIONAL PARK

The westernmost town of note on Rte. 20 is **Sedro Woolley,** a logging town nestled in the rich farmland of the lower Skagit Valley. Sedro Woolley is home to the **North Cascades National Park and Mt. Baker-Snoqualmie National Forest Headquarters,** at 810 State Rte. 20, near the intersection with Rte. 9. The helpful rangers and info on activities in the park can help you move out of Sedro, which should be done as quickly as possible, considering the spectacular landscape farther west. (☎856-5700. Open daily 8am-4:30pm; closed in winter Sa-Su.)

Forty miles west of Sedro Woolley is the town of **Marblemount,** whose major attraction is the **Marblemount Wilderness Information Center,** 1 mi. north of West Marblemount on a well-marked road. This is the best resource for backcountry trip-planning in the North Cascades. It is best to explore the park on a multi-day hiking trip. The Information Center is the only place to pick up backcountry **permits,** and they have updates on trails and weather. Permits must be picked up in person no earlier than the day before trip date. (☎873-4500, ext. 39. Open July-Aug. Su-Th 7am-6pm, F-Sa 7am-8pm; in winter call ahead.) Once you leave Marblemount, there are **no major service stations** for more than 69 mi. west—you are entering the wild land of the National Park.

NORTH CASCADES NATIONAL PARK

East from Marblemount and across the Skagit River, Rte. 20 enters the wildest, most rugged park in Washington. The North Cascades National Park is unlike any other—as amazing as the views seem from the car, you can't experience this park's flavor from a vehicle, so make sure to hop out and explore; the area is rife with hiking trails.

The dramatic rocky pinnacles rising abruptly from the park's deep glacial valleys make for the most complex and challenging moutaineering in the continental United States—the region is commonly referred to as "the Alps of North America." Those determined to penetrate the park should allot a stout pair of boots and several days toward that goal. As with every national park in Washington, North Cascades is surrounded by ample national forest. Know which forest you are headed into, as different agencies, permits, and rules apply. The **Marblemount Wilderness Information Center,** 4 mi. west of the park, provides backcountry permits (required for any overnight travel in the park) and info on hikes. Another source for hiking info is the **North Cascades Visitors Center and Ranger Station.** (☎386-4495. Open in summer daily 8:30am-6pm; winter Sa-Su 9am-4:30pm.) The National Park is divided into four sections. The **North Unit** reaches up to the Canadian border, and is the most remote area of the park. The few trails that do cross it begin mainly near **Mt. Baker** or **Hozemon,** a small camp accessible from British Columbia. The **Ross Lake National Recreation Area** runs along Rte. 20 and north along Ross Lake. This is the most highly used area of the park, and the one to which most confine their stay. **South Unit** is pocked by glaciers and is accessible from trails leaving Rte. 20 along its north and east sides, making it an inviting wilderness to explore. Finally, at the park's southernmost tip, the **Lake Chelan National Recreation Area** protects the beautiful wilderness around Stehekin and the northern tip of Lake Chelan.

The park's **Goodell Creek Campground ❶,** at Mile 119 just west of Newhalem, is a beautiful, small area, with leafy sites suitable for tents and small trailers, and a launch site for white-water rafting on the Skagit River. (Pit toilets. 21 sites, $10. Water shut off after Oct., when sites are free.) **Newhalem Creek Campground ❶,** at Mile 120, shares a turn-off with the visitors center. It is a larger facility geared toward RV folk (111 sites, $12).

Route 20 Scenic Drive

The amazing **Cascade Pass Trail** begins 22 mi. from the bridge, and continues to Stehekin Valley Rd. The 3hr. hike gains 1700 ft. of elevation in 3½ mi. (Moderate to difficult.) **Thunder Creek Trail** is among the most popular hikes in the area. The 1½ mi. meander through old-growth cedar and fir begins at Colonial Creek Campground at Mile 130 of Rte. 20. (Easy.) A more challenging variation is the 3¼ mi. **Fourth of July Pass Trail.** It begins 2 mi. into the Thunder Creek trail and climbs 3500 ft. toward stupendous views of glacier-draped Colonial and Snowfield peaks. (Moderate to difficult.)

EAST OF NORTH CASCADES NATIONAL PARK

The stretch of road from **Ross Lake,** near the Eastern border of North Cascades National Park, to **Winthrop,** in the Okanogan National Forest, is the most beautiful section of Rte. 20. The frozen creases of a mountain face stand before you. Snow and granite rise on one side of the road, sheer cliffs plummet on the other. Leaving the basin of Ross Lake, the road begins to climb, revealing the craggy peaks of the North Cascades.

The **Pacific Crest Trail** crosses Rte. 20 at **Rainy Pass** (Mile 157) on one of the most scenic and difficult legs of its 2500 mi. course from Mexico to Canada. Near Rainy Pass, scenic trails of 1-3 mi. can be hiked in sneakers, provided the snow has melted (about mid-July). Just off Rte. 20, an overlook at **Washington Pass** (Mile 162) rewards visitors with one of the state's most dramatic panoramas, an astonishing view of the red rocks exposed by **Early Winters Creek** in **Copper Basin.** The area has many well-marked trailheads off Rte. 20 that lead into the desolate wilderness. The popular 2½ mi. walk to **Blue Lake** begins half a mile east of Washington Pass—it's usually snow-free by July and provides a gentle ascent through meadows. An easier 2 mi. hike to Cutthroat Lake departs from an access road 4½ mi. east of Washington Pass. From the lake, the trail continues 4 mi. farther and almost 2000 ft. higher to **Cutthroat Pass** (6820 ft.), treating determined hikers to a breathtaking view of towering, rugged peaks.

About 5 mi. east of Winthrop, the ◪ **North Cascades Smoke Jumper Base** is staffed by courageously insane smoke jumpers who give thorough and personal tours of the base, explaining the procedures and equipment they use to help them parachute into forest fires and put them out. To get there, drive east through Winthrop. At the bridge, instead of turning right to follow Hwy. 20, go straight and follow all the curves of the main road. After about 5 mi., the base will be on your right. (☎997-2031. Open in summer and early fall; daily tours 10am-5pm.)

RUMBLE IN THE MOUNTAINS A long time ago, when wishing still mattered and mountains fought for love, three rumples in the Earth's crust were caught in a love triangle. Legend holds that Pah-toe (Mt. Adams) fought and defeated his brother Wy'East (Mt. Hood) for the love of Squaw Mountain. Dismayed, the broken-hearted Squaw Mountain laid at the feet of Pah-toe and fell asleep, becoming Sleeping Beauty Mountain. Pah-toe, once proud and tall, bowed his head in shame—thus taking his current shape.

BIRD-WATCHING, HUNTING, AND FISHING. Though the prolific elk population in the area around Glenwood is conducive to hunting, marksmen beware: the beasts are protected in the nearby Conboy Lake Wildlife Refuge. The elk are familiar with its boundaries and are known to gloat from inside at frustrated hunters. Duck and other fowl can be hunted from within the refuge, however, and many of the streams in the area are fishable for trout and bullheads. Pick up the "Sport Fishing Rules" and "Big Game Hunting Seasons and Rules" guides at local stores for info on all the complex details and seasons. For those who prefer to merely observe wildlife, the refuge is home to nesting sites of rare Sandhill cranes, and guided bird-watching trips leave the ranger station every Friday morning. Bird-watching is reputed to be best right around the first spring break-up.

MOUNT RAINIER NATIONAL PARK ☎360

AT A GLANCE	
AREA: 235,625 acres	**GATEWAYS:** Ashford, Packwood.
CLIMATE: Characterized by random stormy weather.	**CAMPING:** Extensive backcountry options, see p. 236.
FEATURES: Mount Rainier, large backcountry.	**FEES:** $10 per car, $5 per hiker. Permits good for 7 days. Backcountry permits free.
HIGHLIGHTS: Climbing Rainier, Silver Falls during snowmelt.	

At 14,411 ft., Mt. Rainier (ray-NEER) presides over the Cascade Range. The Klickitat native people called it Tahoma, "Mountain of God," but Rainier is simply "the Mountain" to most Washington residents. Perpetually snow-capped, this dormant volcano draws thousands of visitors from all around the globe. Clouds mask the mountain for at least 200 days per year, frustrating those who come solely to see its distinctive summit. Rainier is so big it creates its own weather by jutting into the warm, wet air and pulling down vast amounts of rain and snow. Its sharp ridges, steep gullies, and 76 glaciers combine to make Rainier an inhospitable host for the thousands of determined climbers who attempt its summit each year. The non-alpinists among us can explore the old-growth forests and alpine meadows of **Mt. Rainier National Park.** With over 305 mi. of trails through wildflowers, rivers, and hot springs, Mt. Rainier has options for nature lovers.

▐ TRANSPORTATION

To reach Mt. Rainier from the northwest, take I-5 to Tacoma, then go east on Rte. 512, south on Rte. 7, and east on Rte. 706. This road meanders through the town of **Ashford** and into the park by the Nisqually entrance, which leads to the visitors centers of **Longmire** and **Paradise.** Rte. 706 is the only access road open year-round;

snow usually closes all other park roads from November through May. Mt. Rainier is 65 mi. from Tacoma and 90 mi. from Seattle.

Gray Line Bus Service, 4500 S Marginal Way, Seattle (☎206-624-5208 or 800-426-7532; www.graylineofseattle.com), has buses that run from **Seattle** to Mt. Rainier daily May to mid-Sept. (1-day round-trip $54, under 12 $27). Buses leave from the Convention Center at 8th and Pike in Seattle at 8am and return at 6pm. The trip up takes 3½-4hr. (with a few stops at picturesque viewpoints) and allows 2½hr. at Paradise. Rainier Shuttle (☎569-2331) runs daily between **Sea-Tac Airport** and **Ashford** (2hr., 2 per day, $40), or **Paradise** (3hr., 1 per day, $45).

All major roads offer scenic views of the mountain, with numerous roadside lookouts. The roads to Paradise and Sunrise are especially picturesque. Stevens Canyon Rd. connects the southeast corner of the national park with Paradise, Longmire, and the Nisqually entrance, revealing superb vistas of Rainier and the Tatoosh Range. The summer draws hordes of visitors, making parking very difficult at many of the visitors centers and trailheads throughout the afternoon hours.

Rainier weather changes quickly, so pack warm clothes and cold-rated equipment. Before setting out, ask rangers for mountain-climbing, hiking, and equipment recommendations. Group size is limited in many areas, and campers must carry all waste out of the backcountry. Potable water is not available at most backcountry campsites. **All stream and lake water should be treated** for giardia with tablets, filters, or by boiling it before drinking. For more information on preparing for the outdoors, see **Camping and Hiking Equipment,** p. 38.

🛈 PRACTICAL INFORMATION

The section of the Mt. Baker-Snoqualmie National Forest that surrounds Mt. Rainier on all but its southern side is administered by **Wenatchee National Forest,** 301 Yakima St., Wenatchee, WA 98807 (☎509-662-4314). The **Gifford Pinchot National Forest** (☎425-750-5000), to the south, has headquarters at 6926 E Fourth Plain Blvd., P.O. Box 8944, Vancouver, WA, 98668. The Packwood ranger station is nearest, at 13068 US 12. (☎494-0600. Open 10am-5pm.) The main web site for the park is www.nps.gov/mora.

Visitor Information:

Longmire Wilderness Center (☎569-4453, backcountry reservations only), 6 mi. east of the Nisqually entrance in the southwest corner of the park, is the best place to plan a backcountry trip. Open Su-Th 7:30am-6:30pm, F-Sa 7am-7pm.

The Jackson Memorial Visitors Center, at Paradise, has 360 degrees of windows, an information desk, exhibits on the mountain's mischievous ways, and a predictably expensive and not-so-good cafeteria. Open 10am-6pm daily, permits available.

White River Ranger Station (☎663-2273), off Rte. 410 on the park's east side, on the way to Sunrise, is also very good for information. Open Su-Th 8am-4:30pm, F-Sa 7am-7pm.

The Wilkeson "Red Caboose" Ranger Station (☎829-5127) is at Carbon River. Open M-Th 8am-4:30pm, F 8am-7pm, Sa 7am-7pm, Su 8am-6pm. These stations all distribute backcountry permits.

The Park Headquarters, Tahoma Woods, Star Rte., Ashford, OR 98304 (☎569-2211; www.nps.gov/mora) is the best place to call with phone inquiries. Open M-F 8am-4:30pm. Free map. *Tahoma News,* distributed at park entrances and ranger stations, is a useful source of maps, hiking recommendations, and safety precautions.

Equipment Rental: Rainier Mountaineering, Inc. (☎569-2227, www.rmiguides.com), in Paradise across from the Paradise Inn and in Ashford next to Whittaker's Bunkhouse. Expert RMI guides lead summit climbs, seminars, and special programs (for dear prices). Open May-Oct. daily 9am-5pm. Rents ice axes ($13), crampons ($13), boots ($24), packs ($24), and helmets ($10) by the day.

Climbing: Glacier climbers and mountain climbers intending to scale above 10,000 ft. must register in person at Paradise, White River, or Wilkeson Ranger Stations to be granted permits. Cost-recovery fee $15 per person. Annual pass $25.

Emergency: ☎911.

Hospital: The nearest medical facilities are in **Morton** (40 mi. from Longmire) and **Enumclaw** (5 mi. from Sunrise). **Tacoma General Hospital,** 315 Martin Luther King Way (☎253-552-1000), has 24hr. emergency facilities.

Internet access: See **Whittaker's Bunkhouse,** below. $3 per 30min.; $5 per hr.

Post Office: In the **National Park Inn,** Longmire. Open M-F 8:30am-noon and 1-5pm. Located in the **Paradise Inn** (see below). Open M-F 9am-noon and 12:30-5pm, Sa 8:30am-noon.

Postal Code: Longmire 98397, Paradise 98398.

ACCOMMODATIONS

Longmire, Paradise, and Sunrise offer expensive accommodations. For a bed, stay in Ashford or Packwood. Alternatively, camp and convince yourself that your tent has a roof and heating, and is a hostel.

Hotel Packwood, 102 Main St. (☎494-5431), in Packwood 20min. south of Ohanapecosh or 1hr. south of Nisqually. Charming since 1912. A sprawled-out grizzly graces the parlor. Grr. Singles $32; doubles $54. Private bath extra. ❸

Whittaker's Bunkhouse (☎569-2439), 6 mi. west of the Nisqually entrance. Owned by Lou Whittaker, a long-time RMI guide. View his accomplishments (he was in the first party to climb the North Face of Everest) in the photos hanging from nearly every wall. Espresso bar, but no kitchen or bedding. Book ahead. Spacious co-ed dorms with 2 baths. Dorms $25; private rooms $65-90. ❸

Paradise Inn (☎569-2413; reservations ☎569-2275), in Paradise. Built in 1917 from Alaskan cedar at 5400 ft. Large dining facility with exquisite-looking, and expensive, food. Open late May-Oct. Book ahead. Very popular during the summer. Small singles and doubles from $75, each extra person $12. ❹

The Cowlitz River Lodge, 13069 US 12 (☎494-7378), on the east end of Packwood right across from the Packwood Information Center. The Lodge offers very nice rooms for a decent price. Singles $50; doubles $67. ❸

CAMPING

Backcountry camping requires a **permit,** free from ranger stations and visitors centers. Get them in person 24hr. beforehand, or by reservation up to two months in advance. (☎569-4453. $20 per group, ask about group size limits.) Inquire about trail closures before setting off. Hikers with a valid permit can camp at well-established trailside, alpine, and snowfield sites (most with toilets and water source). Fires are prohibited except in front-country campgrounds.

Camping in national forests outside the park is free. Avoid eroded lakesides and riverbanks; flash floods and debris flows are frequent. Campfires are prohibited, except during the rainy season. Check with ranger stations for details. There are six campgrounds within the park. For reservations, apply in person at the visitors centers; after February, call ☎800-365-2267 (international ☎301-722-1257) or visit http://reservations.nps.gov. National Park campgrounds are handicapped-accessible, but have no RV sites or showers. Coin-op showers are available at **Jackson Memorial Visitors Center,** in Paradise. Alternatively, the **Packwood RV Park** has pay showers for $3 at the corner of Main St. and US 12 in Packwood. **Sunshine Point ❶,** a quarter-mile beyond the Nisqually entrance, is a quiet site to the south. (Open year-round. Quiet hours 10pm-6am. 18 sites, $10.) **Cougar Rock ❶**, 2¼ mi. north of Longmire in the southwest, is near a glacial river. (Quiet hours 10pm-6am. Open June-Sept. Reservations required June 28 to Labor Day. 173 individual sites, $15. Winter season $12. 5 group sites, $3 per person.) **Ohanapecosh ❶**, 11 mi. north of Packwood on Rte. 123, in the southeast, provides secluded sites with great scenery. (Open May-Sept. Reservations required, often booked solid. 205 sites, $15; winter $12.) About 150 ft. outside of the Ohanapecosh entrance, a dirt road descends from the highway and turns into a T. Either fork takes you to free camping spots under tall trees. **White River ❶** is 5 mi. west of White River on the way to Sunrise in the northeast. (Open late June-Sept. 112 sites, $10.)

🍴 FOOD

The general stores in the park sell only last-minute trifles like bug repellent (well worth it). An extra state-park tax is charged, so stock up before you arrive. **Blanton's Market**, 13040 US 12 in Packwood, is the closest decent supermarket to the park and has an ATM in front. (☎494-6101. Open summer daily 6am-9pm, winter 7am-8pm.) **Highlander ❷**, in Ashford, serves standard pub fare in a single dimly-lit room with a pool table. Burgers $6-7. (☎569-2953; open daily 7am to anytime between 10pm and 2am. Restaurant closes at 9pm.) **Club Cafe ❷**, 13016 Hwy. 12, is in Packwood. A small, down-home diner. Their omelettes always elicit oohs and ahhs. (☎494-5977; open daily 7am-7pm.)

🏔 OUTDOOR ACTIVITIES

Rainier's moody weather makes it a tricky destination. Clouds and freezing rain can sweep in at any time, making the fireplace at **Paradise Inn** the mountain's most attractive destination. In the winter, huge volumes of snow close most of the park (almost 70 ft. fell at Paradise in 2002), and trails often remain snow-covered well into summer. But hit Rainier on a good day, and the rewards are huge. Hiking is probably the best bet, as ample views and fascinating terrain are ubiquitous.

HIKING. The hiking trails are far too numerous to list—Rainier is easily Washington's most versatile area. One option is a **ranger-led interpretive hike,** which can delve into anything from area history to local wildflowers. Each visitors center conducts hikes and most of the campgrounds have evening talks and campfire programs. **Camp Muir** (9 mi. round-trip), the most popular staging ground for a summit attempt, is also a challenging dayhike. It begins on Skyline trail (which is itself a popular dayhiking option), and then heads north on Pebble Creek Trail. The latter half of the hike is covered in snow for most of the year.

A beautiful, and easier, half-day hike wanders along the Ohanapecosh River by **Silver Falls** (a sight to behold during spring snowmelt), then up to the **Grove of the Patriarchs,** whose stately cedars have patiently awaited your arrival since the days of feudalism and the Magna Carta. A trail leads to the falls from Ohanapecosh campground, and a shorter route begins at a pulloff on the west side of Rte. 123, just south of the intersection with 706. The Grove can be accessed just inside the Ohanapecosh entrance.

CLIMBING. A trip to the summit of Rainier requires substantial preparation and expense. The ascent involves a vertical rise of more than 9000 ft. over 9 mi., and usually takes two days with an overnight stay at **Camp Muir** on the south side (10,000 ft.) or **Camp Schurman** on the east side (9500 ft.). Each camp has a ranger station, rescue cache, and toilet. Permits cost $15 per person. Only experienced climbers should attempt the summit, and no one should try going solo;

novices can be guided to the summit with the help of **Rainier Mountaineering, Inc.** after a day-long basic climbing course. For details, contact Park Headquarters or RMI (see **Practical Information,** p. 235).

CHELAN ☎509

The serpentine body of Lake Chelan (sha-LAN) undulates some 55 mi. southeast through the Wenatchee National Forest and the Lake Chelan National Recreation Area toward the Columbia River and US 97. Here, the green mountains of North Cascades National Park transform into the bone-dry brown hills and apple orchards that surround the town of Chelan. Unfortunately, the town itself is disappointingly touristy—the economy is structured around family tourism that usually involves renting a house for an extended stay. There is little the in town to draw the budget traveler. The real attraction of Chelan is at the docks, where several ferries leave for the beautiful wilderness farther up the lake.

■✚🗹 **ORIENTATION AND PRACTICAL INFORMATION.** The town of Chelan rests on the southeast end of Lake Chelan, along Hwy. 97, 190 mi. (4hr.) east of Seattle and west of Spokane. **US 97** cuts through the town along the lake and becomes its main street, **Woodin Ave.** Look out for speed traps near the lake.

Link, the local bus service, runs Rte. 21 and 31 hourly between the Chamber of Commerce and Wenatchee. (☎662-1155; www.linktransit.com. 1¼hr., M-F 6am-6pm, $0.50-1.) **Northwest Trailways** (☎800-366-3830, or through Greyhound 800-231-2222) departs Wenatchee for **Seattle** (3½hr., 2 per day, $23) and **Spokane** (3½hr., 1 per day, $23). For **ferry** service, see **Stehekin,** p. 240. The **Chamber of Commerce,** 102 E Johnson, off Manson Hwy., has info on the town. (☎682-3503 or 800-424-3526; www.lakechelan.com. Open summer M-F 9am-5pm, Sa-Su 10am-3pm; winter M-F 9am-5pm.) The **Chelan Ranger Station,** 428 W Woodin Ave. on the lake, is the place to buy maps ($4) or Northwest Forest Passes ($5) for parking. (☎682-2549. Open June-Sept. daily 7:45am-4:30pm; Oct.-May M-F 7:45am-4:30pm.) **Chelan Boat Rentals,** 1210 W Woodin, is one of the shops on the lake that rents small fishing boats ($15 per hr.), jet skis (from $30 per hr., $100 per day), and bikes ($15 per hr.). (☎682-4444. Open daily 9am-8pm.) **Town Tub Laundry** is by the Pennzoil station on the east end of Woodin Ave. (Wash $1.75, dry $0.25 per 10min. Open daily 8am-9pm.) **Electrik Dreams,** 246 W Manson Rd., Suite 1, provides **Internet access** for $9 per hour. (☎682-8889. Open M-Th 11am-10pm, F-Sa 11am-9pm.) Call ☎911 in an **emergency,** or contact the **police,** located at 207 N Emerson St. (☎682-2588). A 24hr. **crisis line** can be reached at ☎662-7105, and there's a 24hr. **pharmacy** at Safeway (☎682-4087. Open M-F 9am-7pm, Sa 8am-6pm, Su 10am-6pm.) A **hospital** is at 503 E Highland St. (☎682-3300. Open 24hr.) The **post office** is at 144 E Johnson St. (☎682-2625. Open M-F 8:30am-5pm.) **Postal Code:** 98816.

🗝 **ACCOMMODATIONS AND CAMPING.** Most Chelan motels and resorts are rather pricey. The **Apple Inn ❸,** 1002 E Woodin, boasts a hot tub, pool, and shuttle service. (☎682-4044. Singles $49; doubles $59. Winter $35, $39.) **Mom's Montlake Motel ❸,** 823 Wapato, south off Woodin Ave. on Clifford, is a summertime mom-and-pop operation with clean, microwave- or kitchen-equipped rooms. (☎682-5715. Singles $49; doubles $59.) Most campers head for **Lake Chelan State Park ❶,** a pleasantly grassy, but crowded, campground 9 mi. up the south shore of the lake with a beach, swimming area, small store, picnic sites, a boat launch, playing fields, and jet ski rentals. (☎687-3710 or reservations 800-452-5687. Bus #21. Sites $14; full RV sites $20.) **Twenty-Five Mile Creek State Park ❶** is a smaller, but no less crowded, site; it boasts a beach, a boat launch, and small store.

(☎ 687-3610 or 800-452-5687. Reservations recommended Apr.-Sept. 63 sites, $14; 23 RV sites, $20.) Campers are also free to pitch tents anywhere in the national forest, but may only light fires in established fire rings.

◘ FOOD. The cheapest food in Chelan is at local fruit stands, although a few good places can be found slightly outside of town on E Woodin. **Safeway,** 106 W Manson Rd., has groceries. (☎ 682-2615. Open daily 6am-11pm.) **Bear Foods** (a.k.a. Golden Florin's General Store), 125 E Woodin Ave., provides health food. (☎ 682-5535. Open M-Sa 9am-7pm, Su noon-5pm.) Behind the unassuming facade of ▓**Local Myth ❶,** 122 Emerson St., Art and the gang create mind-blowing pizzas from whole-wheat dough and fresh ingredients. The pizzas ($7 and up), calzones ($6-9), and conversations are unbeatable. (☎ 682-2914. Open Tu-Sa 11:30am-9pm.) Pick up baked goods and throw down shots of wheatgrass ($2.50) or espresso ($1) over at **The Rising Sun Bakery ❶,** 514 E. Woodin Ave. (☎ 682-8938. Open M-F 9am-5pm.) **Flying Saucers ❶,** 116 S Emerson, has mocha, chai tea, cinnamon rolls (all $2), and aura galore in a converted 50s diner with flying saucers hanging from the ceiling. (☎ 682-5129. Open summer M-Sa 7am-8pm; winter M-F 7am-4pm.)

▓ DAYTRIP FROM CHELAN: GRAND COULEE DAM

As the climate warmed 18,000 years ago, a small glacier blocking a lake in Montana gave way, releasing floodwaters that swept across eastern Washington, gouging out layers of soil and exposing the layers of granite and basalt below. The washout carved massive canyons, called coulees, into a region now known as the Channeled Scab Lands, which composes most of the striking, mesa-filled country south of the dam across its largest canyon, the Grand Coulee.

From 1934 to 1942, 7000 workers toiled on the construction of the **Grand Coulee Dam,** a local remedy for the agricultural woes of the drought and the Great Depression, but a travesty for conservationists and Native Americans. Nearly a mile long, this behemoth is the world's largest solid concrete structure and irrigates the previously parched Columbia River Basin, all while generating more power than any other hydroelectric plant in the United States. The amount of concrete used to construct Grand Coulee would be enough to construct a standard 6 ft. wide sidewalk around the globe at the equator. The Columbia River, raised 350 ft. by the dam, forms both **Franklin D. Roosevelt Lake** and **Banks Lake,** where "wet-siders" from western Washington flock for swimming, boating, and fishing.

The dam hulks at the junction of Rte. 174 and Rte. 155, about 75 mi. east of Chelan and 90 mi. west of Spokane. The rotund **Visitor Arrival Center,** on Rte. 155 just north of Grand Coulee, is filled with disconnected exhibits on the construction, operation, and legacy of the dam. A guided tour of the third and newest powerplant begins every 30min. between 10am and 5pm (contact the visitors center for more info). On summer nights, a spectacularly cheesy yet technically amazing 36min. laser show chronicles the structure's history on the spillway of the dam. Watch from the visitors center for guaranteed sound (and arrive at least an hour early to beat the crowds), or park at Crown Point Vista off Rte. 174 and tune in to 89.9 FM. (☎ 509-633-9265. Open June-July daily 8:30am-11pm; Aug. 8:30am-10:30pm; Sept. 8:30am-9:30pm; Oct.-May 9am-5pm. Show late May-July daily 10pm; Aug. 9:30pm; Sept. 8:30pm. Free.) If you plan to spend the night after the light show, head to the only federal campground in the area, **Spring Canyon Campground ❶,** 5 mi. east of the damn. Tent sites $10.

STEHEKIN

☎**509**

Stehekin (steh-HEE-kin) counts among the most magical places in Washington. An isolated village at the wetter, quieter, more welcoming northern end of Lake Chelan, its main connection to the rest of the world is a 50 mi. ferry route; the only other option is hiking in on the extensive Pacific Crest Trail or float-planing in. This isolation has preserved a wild, beautiful place. With McGregor Mountain looming and total silence just a 5min. walk out of the small settlement, Stehekin is a destination that entertains the outdoorsy for days on end.

■ **INTERCITY TRANSPORTATION.** Three **ferries** ply the lake in summer. The ferries proceed along a shoreline where mountain goats and brown bears roam: this alone makes the ride worthwhile. All are operated by the **Lake Chelan Boat Company**, 1418 W Woodin, about 1 mi. west of downtown Chelan. (☎682-2224 or reservations 682-4584; www.ladyofthelake.com. Open May-Oct.) The *Lady of the Lake II*, a 350-person ferry, makes one round-trip to Stehekin per day. (4hr. with a 1½hr. layover, 8:30am, $25.) This ferry also picks up from Fields Point, 16 mi. up South Shore Rd. near **Twenty-Five Mile Creek State Park** (9:45am; parking $3 per day, $17 per week). You can request that the ferry stop at Prince Creek or Moore Point campgrounds along the Lakeshore Trail (see **Outdoor Activities,** below). Arrange in advance to be picked up, then flag them down with a bright article of clothing. The smaller *Lady Express* makes an express trip to Stehekin (2¼hr. with a 1hr. layover, $44). A combination ticket for the *Lady Express* or *Lady of the Lake II* to Stehekin and back also runs $41, and allows just over 3hr. in Stehekin. A new high-speed catamaran, the *Lady Cat*, makes two round-trips per day (1¼hr. with a 1½hr. layover, 7:45am and 1:30pm, $89). Book ferry tickets in advance on summer weekends; they will not accept credit cards on the day of travel.

■ **LOCAL TRANSPORTATION.** Stehekin itself is small enough that two legs and two minutes are all one needs to cross it—transport isn't a problem. Getting further up the road to trailheads and campsites can be an issue, though. **Discovery Bikes** rents two-wheelers. (☎884-4844. $3.50 per hr., $10 per half-day, $15 per day.) From mid-May to mid-October, a shuttle leaves from the ferry and runs up Stehekin Valley Rd. to High Bridge campground (45min., 4 per day). The $6 NPS shuttles continue on to Bridge Creek campground (30min.) and Glory Mountain (1hr.) from July to mid-October. From mid-May to mid-June, the NPS shuttle runs to High Bridge upon request. (☎856-5700, ext. 340. Reservations recommended.)

■ **CAMPING AND FOOD.** The Park Service maintains 12 **campgrounds** along the Stehekin River off Stehekin Valley Rd. All except the area closest to Stehekin are geared toward the hiker. **Purple Point** ❶, right next to the ferry landing, is unique in its amenities: it has water, bathrooms, and free showers. All need reservations, so stop at the ranger station and have them help you figure out how to get there. **Permits** are free, and required for backcountry camping and hiking. (Permits available at the **visitors center;** call ☎856-5700, ext. 340.) The **Stehekin Valley Ranch** ❸ offers more expensive lodging than the camping alternative. (☎800-536-0745. Cabins $60 for stays of 5 days or more; price includes meals and transportation.) A delicious **dinner** ❸ at the Ranch costs about $14. (☎682-4677. Reserve ahead. Open M-F 9am-5pm.) The **Lodge Restaurant** ❸, at the landing, serves dinner that runs $6-17. (☎682-4494. Open 7:30am-8pm.) Two miles up the road, the **Stehekin Pastry Company** ❶ lures hikers out of the hills for sticky buns. (Open June 1-Sept. 23 daily 8am-5pm; May 26-June 15 and Sept. 24-Oct. 8 Sa-Su 8am-5pm.)

△ OUTDOOR ACTIVITIES. Some short, scenic dayhikes surround the landing. The simple ¾ mi. **Imus Creek Trail** is an interpretive hike that offers great views of the lake, starting behind the Golden West Visitor Center. (Easy.) The moderately steep **Rainbow Loop Trail** offers stellar valley views. The 4½ mi. trail begins 2½ mi. from Stehekin; shuttles run to the trailhead five times a day, but it's close enough to walk. (Moderate.) From Purple Creek, take a right turn to reach the switch-backs of the steep 15 mi. (round-trip) **Purple Creek Trail.** The 5700 ft. climb is tough, but the rewards include glimpses of nearby glaciers. (Difficult.) The 17½ mi., 2- to 3-day **Lakeshore Trail** begins by the Visitor Center and follows the north shore of Lake Chelan to Prince Creek, never rising more than 500 ft. above the lake but offering splendid views of the surrounding peaks. (Easy.)

An unpaved road and many trails probe north from Stehekin into **North Cascades National Park.** Two hikes begin at High Bridge. The mellow **Agnes Gorge Trail** is the second trailhead on the left, 200 yards beyond the bridge, and travels a level 2½ mi. through forests and meadows with views of 8115 ft. Agnes Mountain. (Easy.) Behind the ranger cabin, the **McGregor Mountain Trail** is a strenuous straight shot up the side of the mountain, climbing 6525 vertical feet over 8 mi. and ending with unsurpassed views of the high North Cascades peaks. (Difficult.) The last half-mile is a scramble up ledges. This extremely challenging trail is often blocked by snow well into July; check at the visitors center before starting out. The shuttle to Bridge Creek provides access to the **Pacific Crest Trail,** which runs from Mexico to Canada. The North Cascades portion of this trail has been called its most scenic by many who have completed the colossal journey. (Moderate to difficult.)

The **Rainbow Falls Tour,** in Stehekin, is a guided bus tour that coincides with ferry arrival times. It zooms through the valley and its major sights: the Stehekin School, the last one-room schoolhouse in Washington; the Stehekin Pastry Company; and Rainbow Falls, a misty 312 ft. cataract. ($7, ages 6-11 $4, under 6 free. Tickets available on ferries.)

EASTERN WASHINGTON

WASHINGTON

Lying in the Cascade's rain shadow, the hills and valleys of the Columbia River Basin foster little more than browning grass, sagebrush, and tumbleweed. Where the construction of dams and canals has made irrigation possible, the desert has bloomed into a land of bountiful fruit crops and their dazzling by-product: tasty, high-quality wines. Sunshine fills the days and attracts the moody and depressed "wetsiders" from rainy Western Washington. The calm beauty and dry, hot air of the region invite a pleasant and lazy vacation of wine-tasting and apple-munching.

SPOKANE   ☎ 509

Ah, 1974: Gerald Ford in the White House, Elvis in the white suit, and Spokane (spoe-KAN) in the world's spotlight. Built on silver mining and made prosperous as an agricultural rail link, Spokane found fame when the World's Fair came to town in 1974. Parks, department stores, and skyways sprang up in preparation for the city's promising future. Today, cafes catering to a college crowd and 50s-style burger joints make for a suburban atmosphere, and the melancholy remains of Spokane '74 slumber in Riverfront Park. A small-town America feel, pleasant outdoor parks, and the culture of a larger city make Spokane '03 worthy of a stopover.

Spokane

▲▲ ACCOMMODATIONS
Boulevard Motel, **10**
Downtowner Motel, **7**
Riverside State Park, **1**

🍴 FOOD
Brooklyn Deli, **6**
Dick's, **9**

Frank's Diner, **8**
The Onion, **2**

■ & ★ NIGHTLIFE &
ENTERTAINMENT
Dempsey's Brass Rail, **4**
Satellite Diner & Bar, **5**
Avista Stadium, **3**

WASHINGTON

▐ TRANSPORTATION

Spokane is 280 mi. east of Seattle on I-90, between Exits 279 and 282. Avenues run east-west parallel to the **Spokane River,** streets run north-south, and both alternate directions one-way. The city is divided north-south by **Sprague Ave.** and east-west by **Division St.** Downtown is the quadrant north of Sprague Ave. and west of Division St., wedged between I-90 and the river.

Airplanes: Spokane International Airport (☎ 624-3218), off I-90 8 mi. southwest of town. Most major carriers service **Seattle, Portland,** and beyond.

Trains: Amtrak, 221 W 1st Ave. (☎ 624-5144; 800-USA-RAIL), at Bernard St. Counter open daily 10pm-6am. All trains depart 1-3am. 1 train per day to **Portland, OR** ($35-75, depending on season and availability) and **Seattle.**

Buses: Greyhound, 221 W 1st Ave. (☎ 624-5251), at Bernard St., in the same building as Amtrak. Ticket office open daily 7:30am-6:20pm and 12:15-2:20am. One-way to: **Portland, OR** (8-10hr., 3 per day, $40) and **Seattle** (6hr., 5 per day, $30.25). **Northwestern Trailways** (☎ 838-5262 or 800-366-3830) shares the same terminal, serving other parts of WA and large cities. Ticket office open daily 8am-6:45pm. Senior discounts.

Taxis: Checker Cab (☎ 624-4171). **Yellow Cab** (☎ 624-4321). Both run 24hr.

Car Rental: U-Save Auto Rental, 918 W 3rd St. (☎455-8018), at Monroe St. Cars from $39 per day, $195 per week. Unlimited mileage within WA for more than 3 days; otherwise $0.20 per mi. after 200 mi. Must be 21+ with major credit card; $5 per day if under 25. Open M-Su 7am-7pm.

PRACTICAL INFORMATION

Tourist Office: Spokane Area Convention and Visitors Bureau, 201 W Main St. (☎800-248-3230). Exit 281 off I-90. Offers free Internet access and local phone calls. Open May-Sept. M-F 8:30am-5pm, Sa 9am-5pm, Su 10am-3pm; Oct.-Apr. M-F 8:30am-5pm.

Equipment Rental: Mountain Gear, 2002 N Division St. (☎325-9000 or 800-829-2009; www.mgear.com) rents canoes ($45 per day), kayaks ($25-45 per day), and snowboards ($24). Open M-F 9:30am-8pm, Sa 9:30am-6pm, Su 11am-5pm.

Laundromat: Otis Hotel Coin-Op, 110 S Madison St. (☎624-3111), at 1st Ave. $1 wash, dry $0.25 per 20min. Open daily 7am-7pm.

Washington Road Conditions: ☎800-695-7623.

Emergency: ☎911.

Police: ☎456-2233. 24hr. crime-report line.

Crisis Line: ☎838-4428. 24hr.

Medical Services: Rockwood Clinic, 400 E 5th Ave. (☎838-2531 or 459-1577), at Sherman St. Open daily for walk-ins 8am-8pm.

Internet Access: Spokane **Library,** 906 W Main St. (☎444-5333). 15min. free. Open M and Tu noon-8pm, W-F 10am-6pm. Also see the **Visitors Bureau,** above.

Post Office: 904 W Riverside. Ave. (☎800-275-8777). Open M-F 6am-5pm. **Postal Code:** 99210.

ACCOMMODATIONS AND CAMPING

Cheaper motels are sprinkled among the chains along Rte. 2 toward the airport, and others can be found on the north end of town along Division Ave.

Boulevard Motel, 2905 W Sunset Blvd. (☎747-1060). Take 4th Ave. southwest from downtown to the I-90 Business Loop, which becomes Sunset Blvd. The recently-renovated rooms are so clean you could eat off the floor. Singles $35; doubles $46. ❷

Downtowner Motel, 165 S Washington St. (☎838-4411), at 2nd Ave. Aging exterior and a mint-green ivy motif. This motel's prices and convenient downtown location can't be beat. Continental breakfast and cable included. Singles $33; doubles $37. ❷

Riverside State Park (☎800-233-0321; reservations ☎800-452-5687), 6 mi. northwest of downtown. Take the Maple St. Bridge north and turn left at the brown park sign; follow signs to Rte. 291 (Nine Mile Rd.), turn left onto Rifle Club Rd. and follow to the park. 101 newly rebuilt sites in a sparse ponderosa forest near the river. Sites $14; RV sites $20; hiker/biker sites $6. Showers $0.25 per 3min. ❶

FOOD

The **Spokane Marketplace,** 1100 N Ruby St., at DeSmet St., sells fresh fruit, baked goods, and crafts. (☎456-0100. Open Apr. Sa 9am-4pm; May-Dec. W and Sa 9am-4pm.) Groceries are at **Safeway,** 1617 W 3rd St. (☎624-8852. Open 24hr.)

▨ **The Onion,** 302 W Riverside Ave. (☎624-9965), at Bernard St., serves amazing burgers ($6-8) and huckleberry shakes ($3) amid throngs of locals and visitors who've been coming here since 1978. Open daily 11am-about 11pm. ❷

Frank's Diner, 1516 W 2nd Ave. (☎747-8798), at Walnut St., operates out of a 1906 observation railroad car. Breakfast all day long. More elegant than most pricier restaurants. Breakfast $4-8. Open Th-Sa 6am-9pm, Su-W 6am-7pm. ❶

Dick's, 10 E 3rd Ave. (☎747-2481), at Division St. Look for the huge panda sign near I-90 and find burgers by the bagful. A time warp—customers eat in their parked cars and pay 1950s prices (burgers $0.63; fries $0.63; shakes $0.93). Open M-Th 8am-midnight, F-Sa 8am-1am, Su 9am-midnight; mid-June to Aug. open 1hr. later. ❶

Brooklyn Deli, 122 S. Monroe (☎835-4177). This small, friendly joint serves turkey avocado and tasty vegetarian sandwiches (don't forget to ask for a pickle!). Half-sandwich $4.25, whole $6.50. Open M-F 10am-7pm, Sa 10am-5pm. ❶

🎭🎵 NIGHTLIFE AND ENTERTAINMENT

For local happenings, pick up the *Spokesman-Review* Friday "Weekend" section, or look for the *Inlander* or the *Wrap*, both available at the library.

Dempsey's Brass Rail, 909 W 1st Ave., has a hot dance floor, flashy decor, and free Internet access by the bar. Drag Diva shows (F-Sa) and rainbow-striped beer taps make Dempsey's "the place to be gay." Happy hour 3-7pm daily. (☎747-5362. Kitchen serves dinner daily 3-8pm. Open Su-Th 3pm-2am, F-Sa 3pm-4am.) **Satellite Diner and Bar,** 425 W Sprague Ave., is a great place to people-watch until 4am over biscuits and gravy ($3.25). Microbrews $3. Happy hour daily 4pm-7pm. (☎624-3952. Open M-F 7am-4am, Sa-Su 6pm-4am; bar closes at 2am.)

The **Spokane Indians** play single-A baseball in the Northwest League of Professional Baseball from June to August in **Avista Stadium,** at the Spokane Fairgrounds, 602 N Havana St. (☎535-2922; www.ticketswest.com. Great seats only $4, seniors $3.) The minor league **Spokane Chiefs** play hockey in the Canadian Hockey League September through March in **Spokane Memorial Arena,** 720 W Mallon Ave. To get there, follow signs from the Maple St. exit off I-5. (☎535-7825. Box office open M-F 10am-6pm. Seats $7-15.)

👁 SIGHTS

■ **MANITO PARK.** One of the most beautiful spots in Spokane, this park boasts five sections of lovingly-maintained flowerbeds. Commune with the carp in the **Nishinomiya Japanese Garden,** sniff the blooming roses on **Rosehill** in late June, relax in the elegant **Duncan Garden,** or sniff around in the **David Graiser Conservatory** and the **Joel Farris Perennial Garden.** *(4 W 21st Ave. From downtown, go south on Bernard St. and turn left on 21st Ave. ☎625-6622. Open 24hr.; buildings locked from dusk-8am. Free.)*

RIVERFRONT PARK. The centerpiece of downtown, the park is Spokane's civic center and the place for a pleasant stroll. Developed for the 1974 World's Fair, the park's 100 acres are divided down the middle by the rapids that culminate in Spokane Falls. In the park, the **IMAX Theater** houses your basic five-story movie screen and a projector the size of a Volkswagen Bug. **Serendipity Cycles,** in the park, rents surrey cycles. The park hosts **ice-skating** in the winter. *(Park: 507 N Howard St., just north of downtown. ☎456-4386; www.SpokaneRiverfrontPark.com. Theater: ☎625-6686. Shows June-Sept. on the hour; call for winter schedule. Open daily 11am-9pm. $7, under 12 $5, over 62 $6. Carousel: Open Su-Th 11am-8pm, F-Sa 11am-10pm. $1.75 per whirl, under 12 or over 62 $1. A 1-day pass, $15, covers both, plus a ferris wheel, park train, sky ride, and more. Cycling: Open daily June-Aug. 10am-9pm. $12 per hr., $20 per hr. with trailer. Ice skating: $4.50, under 12 and over 62 $3.50; skate rental $2.)*

MUSIC. Spokane Symphony Orchestra calls the **Opera House** home. The opera house also hosts traveling **Broadway shows** and special performances. Check out *Rent* and *South Pacific* in 2003. *(Opera House: 334 W Spokane Falls Blvd. Ticket Office: 601 Riverside in the Mezzanine of the Bank of America building. ☎326-3136. Open M-F 9:30am-5:30pm. Box office at the Opera House: open M-F 10am-5pm. Orchestra: www.spokanesymphony.com. Symphony tickets $11-13.)* Known for locally produced shows, the **Civic Theater** has a downstairs space for experimental productions. *(1020 N Howard St., opposite the Spokane Veteran's Memorial Arena. ☎325-2507 or 800-446-9576. Musicals $18, plays $15.)* The **Spokane Interplayers Ensemble** is a resident professional theater troupe. *(174 S Howard St. ☎455-7529. Season runs Sept.-June Tu-Sa. $20, students $10, seniors 20% off.)*

BRITISH COLUMBIA

Before Europeans plunked themselves down for frontier lives in the huge territory now known as British Columbia, tribal nations (including the Kwakwaka'wakw, Nuu-cha-nulth, and Coast Salish, had already developed complex societies all across the land. Eventually, gold was discovered north and east of Vancouver in 1858, bringing in a flood of prospectors. Vancouver blossomed into the metropolis it is today on account of the Canadian Pacific Railroad, which made the town its western terminus in 1886.

Today, residents swear backwards and forwards that BC is the most beautiful place on earth, and most visitors share the opinion upon their departure. It's easy to see why. Small, developed communities surround the metropolitan areas, and breathtaking wilderness is never more than a short drive away. Vancouver's relaxed populace enjoys the most diverse nightlife in western Canada, and gets two full months of summer to enjoy Burrard Inlet's sweeping beaches and snow-capped horizons. Vancouver's location on the mainland side of the Strait of Georgia affords immediate access to the Gulf Islands and Vancouver Island. Sechelt Peninsula, north along the mainland, is less developed than its surroundings and boasts amazing diving, kayaking, and hiking amid the largest trees in Canada.

BRITISH COLUMBIA'S HIGHLIGHTS

EDUCATE yourself in Vancouver's famous **Museum of Anthropology** (see p. 260).

SKI to your heart's content at **Whistler/Blackcomb** (see p. 265).

PICNIC by the beach at **Lighthouse Park** (see p. 262).

SOAK away your sorrows in **Radium Hot Springs** (see p. 322).

LEAP off a bridge in **Nanaimo** (see p. 284).

CHILL with the Haida on **Moresby Island** (see p. 347).

SCUBA DIVE off the **Sechelt Peninsula** (p. 263).

VANCOUVER ☎ 604/778

Like any self-respecting city on the west coast of North America, Vancouver boasts a thriving multicultural populace; the Cantonese influence is so strong that it is often referred to by its nickname, "Hongcouver." With Vancouver supporting North America's third largest Chinatown and plenty of the world's other major cultures and ethnicities, visitors are never hard-pressed to find delicious representations of foreign culinary traditions. As a bonus for adventurous visitors, Vancouver's diversity and urban excitement are so closely hemmed by mountains, forest, and ocean that the city almost feels like a wilderness town; for better or worse, it is hard to avoid the outdoors.

When the city incorporated in 1886, logging was its economic mainstay. Since then, Vancouver has been routinely reshaped by waves of immigration. Thousands of Chinese immigrants (whose work at the turn of the century made the completion of the trans-Canada railroad possible) settled at the line's western terminus, founding the city's Chinatown.

More recent developments on the cultural landscape include a trend among young Canadians from all points east to migrate to this western city. This ongoing influx of immigrants has ensured that the city's landscape remains peppered with

BRITISH COLUMBIA

**Vancouver
Overview**

▲ ACCOMMODATIONS
Vancouver Hostel Jericho Beach, **2**
Pacific Spirit Hostel, **14**
◉ UBC Lodgings, **13**

◉ FOOD
Belgian Fries, **8**
Benny's Bagels, **11**
The Excellent Eatery, **10**
Hon's Wun-Tun House, **1**
The Naam, **5**
Nuff-Nice-Ness, **7**
Soupspoons, **6**
Mongolian Teriyaki, **9**
WaaZuBee Cafe, **4**
■ NIGHTLIFE
The King's Head, **3**
Koerner's Pub, **12**

1 mile
1 kilometer

Skytrain

new folks and their cultural contributions. And while there is some degree of self-segregation among the city's neighborhoods, Vancouverites largely appreciate the diversity. Perhaps the best evidence of (and maybe even the reason for) this is the abundance of fine ethnic restaurants of every imaginable cuisine and budget level.

> **PHONE CODES** In 2001, Vancouver switched to 10-digit dialing. All the old numbers will remain 604, but new numbers will have the area code 778. Should you encounter problems, confirm the area code of the number you are trying to reach at www.addthecode.com.

■ INTERCITY TRANSPORTATION

Flights: Vancouver International Airport (☎604-207-7077; www.vancouverairport.com), on Sea Island, 23km south of the city center. A **Visitors Center** (☎604-303-3601) is on level 2. Open daily 8am-11:30pm. To reach downtown, take bus #100 "New Westminster Station" to the intersection of Granville and 70th Ave. Transfer there to bus #20 "Fraser." An **Airporter** (☎604-946-8866 or 800-668-3141) bus leaves from airport level 2 for downtown hotels and the bus station. (4 per hr.; 6:30am-midnight; $12, seniors $8, ages 5-12 $5.

Ferries: BC Ferries (☎888-BC-FERRY; www.bcferries.com) connects Vancouver to the **Gulf Islands,** the **Sechelt Peninsula,** and **Vancouver Island.** Fares are lowest in the winter off-season. Ferries to the **Gulf Islands, Nanaimo** (2hr.; 4-8 per day; $9.50, $8 in winter; car $24-33.50), and **Victoria** (1½hr.; 8-16 per day; $9.50, $8 in winter; bikes $2.50, car $24-33.50) leave from the **Tsawwassen Terminal,** 25km south of the city center (take Hwy. 99 to Hwy. 17). To reach downtown from Tsawwassen by bus (1hr.), take #640 "Scott Rd. Station," or take #404 "Airport" to the Ladner Exchange, then transfer to bus #601. More ferries to **Nanaimo** (1½hr.; 8 times per day; $9.50, $8 in winter; car $24-33.50) and the **Sechelt Peninsula** (fare charged only from Horseshoe Bay to Langdale; 40min.; 8-10 per day; $8-9.50, ages 5-11 less, car $24-33.50; off-season slightly cheaper) depart the **Horseshoe Bay Terminal** at the end of the Trans-Canada Hwy. in West Vancouver. Take "Blue Bus" #250 or 257 on Georgia St. to get there from downtown. (40min.)

Trains: VIA Rail, 1150 Station St. (☎800-561-8630; US ☎800-561-3949; www.viarail.com) runs eastbound trains. Open M, W, Th, and Sa 9:30am-6pm; Tu, F, and Su 9am-7pm. 3 trains per week to eastern Canada via **Edmonton, AB** (23hr., $258) and **Jasper, AB** (17hr., $193). **BC Rail,** 1311 W 1st St. (☎800-663-8238; www.bcrail.com), in North Vancouver just over the Lions Gate Bridge at the foot of Pemberton St., runs to **Whistler** and northern BC. Take the **BC Rail Special Bus** on Georgia St. (June-Sept.) or the **SeaBus** to North Vancouver, then bus #239 west. Open daily 8am-8pm. Trains to **Prince George** (14½hr.; Su, W, F at 7am; $247); **Whistler** (2¾hr., daily, $49); and **Williams Lake** (10hr.; W, F, Sa at 7am; $165).

Buses: Greyhound Canada, 1150 Station St. (☎604-482-8747 or 800-661-8747; www.greyhound.ca), in the VIA Rail station. Open daily 5am-12:30am. To **Banff, AB** (14hr., 5 per day, $112); **Calgary, AB** (15hr., 5 per day, $125); and **Jasper, AB** (2 per day, 106). **Pacific Coach Lines,** 1150 Station St. (☎604-662-8074; www.pacificcoach.com), runs to **Victoria** every time a ferry sails (3½hr., $29 includes ferry). **Quick Shuttle** (☎940-4428 or 800-665-2122; www.quickcoach.com) makes 8 trips per day from the Holiday Inn on Howe St. via the airport to **Bellingham, WA** (1½hr.; $22, $16 with student ID), **Seattle, WA** (3½hr.; $34, $25 with student ID), and the **Sea-Tac airport** (4hr.; $44, $34 with student ID). **Greyhound USA** (☎800-229-9425 or 402-330-8552; www.greyhound.com) goes to **Seattle** (3-4½hr.; one way $20, round-trip $38).

Downtown Vancouver

⚡ ORIENTATION

Vancouver lies in the southwestern corner of mainland British Columbia. It is divided into distinct regions, mostly by waterways. South of the city flows the **Fraser River** and to the west lies the **Georgia Strait,** which separates the mainland from Vancouver Island. **Downtown** juts north into the Burrard Inlet from the main mass of the city and **Stanley Park** goes even further north. The **Lions Gate** suspension bridge over Burrard Inlet links Stanley Park with North and West Vancouver **(West Van)**, known collectively as the **North Shore;** the bridges over False Creek south of downtown link downtown with **Kitsilano ("Kits")** and the rest of the city. West of Burrard St. is the **West End**. Gastown and **Chinatown** are just east of downtown. The **University of British Columbia (UBC)** lies to the west of Kitsilano on Point Grey, while the **airport** is on Sea Island in the Fraser River delta tucked between S. Vancouver and **Richmond** to the south. **Hwy. 99** runs north-south from the US-Canada border through the city along **Oak St.,** through downtown, then over the Lions Gate bridge. It joins temporarily with the **Trans-Canada Hwy. (Hwy. 1)** before splitting off again and continuing north to Whistler (see p. 265). The Trans-Canada enters from the east, cuts north across the **Second Narrows Bridge** to the North Shore, and ends at the Horseshoe Bay ferry terminal. Most of the city's attractions are grouped on the peninsula and farther west.

Downtown Vancouver

🏠 ACCOMMODATIONS
Cambie Int'l Hostel, 5
C&N Backpackers Hostel, 14
Seymour Cambie Hostel, 4
Global Village Backpackers, 11
Vancouver Hostel Downtown, 10

🍴 FOOD
La Luna Cafe, 1
Subeez Cafe, 12
Kam's Garden Restaurant, 8

🍸 NIGHTLIFE
The Irish Heather, 6
Odyssey, 13
The Purple Onion, 2
Sonar, 3
Sugar Refinery, 15
Wett Bar, 16

⭕ OTHER
Dr. Sun Yat-Sen Classical
  Chinese Garden, 9
Granville Island Brewing Co., 17
World's Skinniest Building, 7

Vancouver is a major point of entry for heroin, with an active street trade in this drug and marijuana; there is a high addict population. While incidences of armed assaults, armed robbery, and murder are low by US standards, the rates for crimes are higher than in most other Canadian cities. Walking around by day is safe most anywhere and downtown is relatively safe at night on main streets. The area east of Gastown, especially around **Hastings** and **Main St.,** is home to many of Vancouver's down, out, and addicted, and should be avoided late at night if possible.

▣ LOCAL TRANSPORTATION

If you're on the outskirts of Vancouver with a car, consider using the **Park 'n' Rides.** These are cheap or free parking lots at major transit hubs where you can leave your car for the day and take public transit into town. From the southeast, exit Hwy. 1 at New Westminster and follow signs for the Pattullo Bridge. The lot is over the bridge and to the right, on the corner of Scott Rd. and King George Hwy. Park for $1 per day and take the **SkyTrain** downtown.

Public Transit: Transit timetables are available at public libraries, city hall, community centers, and **Vancouver Travel Infocentre** (see **Practical Information,** p. 251). The pamphlet *Discover Vancouver on Transit* lists bus numbers for every major site in the city. **Coast Mountain Buslink** (☎ 604-953-3333; www.translink.bc.ca) is the bus system that covers most of the city and suburbs, with direct transport or easy connections to airport and the ferry terminals (see **Intercity Transportation,** above). The city is divided into 3 concentric zones for fare purposes. Riding in the **central zone,** which encompasses most of Vancouver, costs $2. During peak hours (M-F before 6:30pm), it costs $3 to travel between 2 zones and $4 for 3 zones. During off-peak hours, all zones are $2. Ask for a **free transfer** (good for 90min.) when you board buses. **Day passes** $8; sold at all 7-11 and Safeway stores, SkyTrain stations, and HI hostels. Seniors and ages 5-13 for 1 zone or off-peak $1.50; 2 zones $2; 3 zones $3; day pass $6. Bikes can travel on the rack-equipped #404/#601 combination to the Tsawwassen ferry terminal. **SeaBus** and **SkyTrain:** Same contact information as the buses, above. Included in the normal bus fare. The SeaBus shuttles passengers across the busy waters of Burrard Inlet from the foot of Granville St. downtown (Waterfront SkyTrain station) to **Lonsdale Quay** at the foot of Lonsdale Ave. in North Vancouver. The SkyTrain is a light rapid transit system, with a 28km track from Vancouver to **Burnaby, New Westminster,** and **Surrey** in 40min. 20 stations with service every 5min. **Bikes** may be brought on board the SeaBus, but not on the SkyTrain.

Car Rental: Most car rental services, located at the airport, require that you be 21+ to rent a vehicle. **EZ Car Rentals** (☎ 604-240-5383) has no such requirement.

Taxis: Yellow Cab, ☎ 604-681-1111 or 800-898-8294. **Vancouver Taxi,** ☎ 604-871-1111. **Black Top and Checker Cab,** ☎ 604-731-1111.

▣ PRACTICAL INFORMATION

LOCAL SERVICES

Tourist Information: 200 Burrard St., plaza level (☎ 604-683-2000), near Canada Place. BC-wide info on accommodations, tours, and activities. Courtesy reservation phones. Open daily 8am-7pm.

Travel Outfitter: The Travel Bug, 2667 W Broadway (☎604-737-1122). Everything you need to get around, from maps to bags to guides. 10% HI discount on accessories. Open M-Tu 10am-6pm, W-F 10am-7:30pm, Sa noon-5pm, Su 10am-6pm.

Tours: The Gray Line, 255 E 1st Ave. (☎879-3363 or 800-667-0882). Narrated bus tours. The Double Decker Bus stops at over 20 sights. Unlimited use for 2 days $26; seniors $25, ages 5-12 $14. Buses run 8:30am-4:30pm. Hostels run sporadic tours.

Consulates: Canadian Consulate General, 412 Plaza 600 (☎604-443-1777). **British Consulate General,** 900 4th Ave., Ste. 3001 (☎604-622-9255). **U.S. Consulate General,** 1095 W. Pender (☎604-685-4311).

Equipment Rental: Stanley Park Cycle, 766 Denman (☎604-688-0087), near Stanley Park. Mountain bikes or 21-speed from $3.50 per hr., $10.50 per 5hr. Open daily 8am-8pm. The immensely popular and knowledgably staffed **Mountain Equipment Co-op (MEC),** 130 W Broadway (☎604-872-7858; www.mec.ca), rents tents, sleeping bags, and kayaks. Open M-W 10am-7pm, Th-F 10am-9pm, Sa 9am-6pm, Su 11am-5pm.

Laundry: Davie Laundromat, 1061 Davie St. (☎604-682-2717), $2.50 per load. Open daily 8am-8pm.

Gay and Lesbian Information: The Centre, 1170 Bute St., offers counseling and info. *Xtra West* is the city's gay and lesbian biweekly, available here and around Davie St. in the West End. Open M-F 9:30am-7pm. Try www.gayvancouver.bc.ca for events.

Weather: ☎604-664-9010; www.weatheroffice.com.

Road Conditions: Talking Yellow Pages ☎604-299-9000. Select #7623.

EMERGENCY AND COMMUNICATIONS

Emergency: ☎911.

Police: 312 Main St. (☎604-665-3321), at Powell.

Crisis Center: ☎604-872-3311. 24hr. **Rape Crisis Center:** ☎604-872-8212. 24hr.

24hr. Pharmacy: Shoppers Drug Mart, 2979 W Broadway (☎604-733-9128), and 1125 Davie St. (☎604-669-2424). Open 24hr.

Hospital: Vancouver General Hospital, 899 W 12th Ave. (☎604-875-4111). **UBC Hospital,** 221 Westbrook Mall (☎604-822-7121), on the UBC campus.

Internet Access: Library: 350 W Georgia St. (☎604-331-3600). Free Internet. Open M-Th 10am-8pm, F-Sa 10am-5pm. Free email at 20 other branches; check White Pages.

Post Office: 349 W Georgia St. (☎604-662-5725). Open M-F 8am-5:30pm. **Postal Code:** V6B 3P7.

▓ ACCOMMODATIONS

Greater Vancouver B&Bs are a viable option for couples or small groups (singles from $45, doubles from $55). Agencies like **Town and Country Bed and Breakfast** (☎604-731-5942) or **Best Canadian** (☎604-738-7207) list options. **HI hostels** are a good bet for clean and quiet rooms; some non-HI options can be seedy or rowdy.

DOWNTOWN AND WEST END

▓ **Vancouver Hostel Downtown (HI),** 1114 Burnaby St. (☎604-684-4565 or 888-203-4302), in the West End. Sleek and clean 225-bed facility between downtown, the beach, and Stanley Park. Library, kitchen, rooftop patio. Pub crawls W, F; frequent tours of Granville Island. Travel agency in the lobby. Reception open 24hr. Reservations crucial in summer. $20, nonmembers $24; private doubles $55, nonmembers $64. ❷

■ **Global Village Backpackers,** 1018 Granville St. (☎604-682-8226 or 888-844-7875; www.globalbackpackers.com), on the corner of Nelson, next to Ramada Inn. Shuttle from bus/train station; call for details. Airporter Bus stops at Granville St. Funky technicolor hangout in an area with great nightlife. Internet, pool, laundry. HI, ISIC, other hosteling members $21; doubles $57, with bath $62. Nonmembers $3 more. ❷

Seymour Cambie Hostel, 515 Seymour St. (☎604-684-7757). The quieter of 2 downtown Cambie hostels. Pub crawls, movie nights (Su-M), soccer games during summer season (Sa), free tours of Granville Island Brewery (Tu at noon, 2pm, and 4pm). Laundry, kitchen, and Internet access. No lockers, storage available for $2 per day. July-Sept. dorm $22.50. Oct.-June dorms $20; singles $40; weekly rates $130. ❷

C&N Backpackers Hostel, 927 Main St. (☎ 604-682-2441 or 888-434-6060), 300m north on Main St. from the train station. Cheap meal deals with the **Ivanhoe Pub** ($2.50 breakfast all day) make this recently renovated hostel a bargain. Kitchen, laundry ($1 per wash or dry), bikes ($10 per day). May-Sept. dorms $14; single, double, or family room $35. Weekly rates available, monthly rates available in winter. ❶

GASTOWN

Cambie International Hostel, 300 Cambie St. (☎604-684-6466 or 877-395-5335). Free airport pickup 9am-8pm. The Cambie offers easy access to the busy sights and sounds of Gastown. Common room, laundry. No kitchen, but free hot breakfast. Pool tables in the pub. 24hr. reception. June-Sept. dorms $20, singles $45. Oct.-May dorms $17.50, singles $40. ❷

KITSILANO AND OTHER NEIGHBORHOODS

Vancouver Hostel Jericho Beach (HI), 1515 Discovery St. (☎604-224-3208 or 888-203-4303), in Jericho Beach Park. Follow 4th Ave. west past Alma, bear right at the fork, or take bus #4 from Granville St. downtown. Peaceful location with a great view across English Bay. 280 beds in 14-person dorm rooms. 10 family rooms. Free linen, kitchens, TV room, laundry, cafe (breakfasts around $6, dinner $7-8), parking $3 per day. Bike storage free for guests. Stay-and-ski package with Grouse Mountain (see below) for $37. Reservations imperative in summer. $17.50, nonmembers $21.50; family rooms $50-60. ❷

Pacific Spirit Hostel/UBC Lodgings, 1935 Lower Mall (☎604-822-1000), at Place Vanier on the University of British Columbia campus. Bus #4 or #10 from city center. Continue down University Blvd. from bus loop until you turn right on Lower Mall. Standard dorm singles for a hostel price. Free linen, laundry, TV lounges, shared microwave and fridge; pubs and food on campus. Free Internet. Open May-Aug. Singles $24-84. 10% HI or ISIC discount at hostel. ❸

▟ CAMPING

Capilano RV Park, 295 Tomahawk Ave. (☎604-987-4722), at foot of Lions Gate Bridge in North Van. Pool, laundry. Reception open daily 8am-11pm. 2-person sites $28-38, extra person $3.50; full RV sites $38 and up with auto club membership, $46 and up without. Showers. ❸

Richmond RV Park, 6200 River Rd. (☎604-270-7878 or 800-755-4905), near Holly Bridge in Richmond, a 30min. drive from Vancouver. Follow the Westminster Hwy. west into Richmond from Hwy. 99, turn right on No. 2 Rd., then right on River Rd. Limited privacy. Open Apr.-Oct. 2-person sites $17.50; RV sites $24 and up. Showers. 10% AAA/ CAA discount. ❷

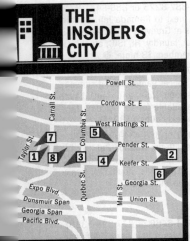

THE INSIDER'S CITY

CHINATOWN HIGHLIGHTS

Savvy tourists should take a break from downtown's slick hot spots and experience Chinatown, Vancouver at its most raw and energized.

1 Gawk at the impossibly narrow **Sam Kee Building,** said to be the narrowest in the world.

2 Barter, bicker, and haggle at the **Chinatown Night Market.** Open June-Sept. F-Su 6:30-11:30pm.

3 Let the tranquil **Dr. Sun Yat-Sen Classical Chinese Garden** (☎604-689-7133) ease your stress.

4 Enjoy great Chinese food on the cheap at **Kam's Garden Restaurant** (☎604-689-7133).

5 Recognize the trials and successes of Chinese Canadians at the **Winds of Change Mural.**

6 Choose your meal from hundreds at **Hon's Wun-Tun House** (☎604-688-0871).

7 Visit the huge **Western Han Dynasty Bell.**

8 Explore the permanent and changing exhibitions at the **Chinese Cultural Center** (☎604-658-8865).

Hazelmere RV Park and Campground, 18843 8th Ave. (☎604-538-1167, fax 604-538-1080), in Surrey, a 45min. drive from downtown. Close to the US/Canada border. Off Hwy. 99A, head east on 8th Ave. Quiet sites on the Campbell River, 10min. from the beach. Full RV sites $26; 2-person sites $23; additional person $3; under 7 free. Showers $0.25 per 5min. ❷

ParkCanada, 4799 Hwy. 17 (☎604-943-5811), in Delta 30km south of downtown, near Tsawwassen ferry terminal. Take Hwy. 99 south to Hwy. 17, then go east for 2.5km. The campground, located next to a waterslide park, has a pool. 2-person sites $18.50; RV sites $21 and up; additional person $2. Free showers. ❷

◘ FOOD

The diversity and excellence of Vancouver's international cuisine makes the rest of BC seem positively provincial. Vancouver's **Chinatown** and the **Punjabi Village** along Main and Fraser, around 49th St., both serve cheap, authentic food. Every type of world cuisine, from Vietnamese noodle shops to Italian cafes to succulent yet-cheap-sushi, seems represented along **Commercial Drive,** east of Chinatown.

Restaurants in **downtown** compete for the highest prices in the city. The **West End** caters to diners seeking a variety of ethnic cuisines (check out the globe-spanning lineup on Denman Street), while **Gastown** lures tourists fresh off the cruise ships. Many cheap and grubby establishments along Davie and Denman St. stay open around the clock. Dollar-a-slice, all-night **pizza places** pepper downtown. In Kits, **Buy-Low Foods,** at 4th and Alma St., keeps it real. (☎604-222-8353. Open daily 9am-9pm.) Downtown, **SuperValu** is at 1255 Davie St. (☎604-688-0911. Open 24hr.)

WEST END, DOWNTOWN, AND GASTOWN

▣ **Subeez Cafe,** 891 Homer (☎604-687-6107), at Smithe, downtown. Serves hipster kids in a cavernous, casual setting. Eclectic menu, from vegetarian gyoza ($7) to organic beef burgers ($9), complements a lengthy wine list and home-spun beats (DJs W, F, and Sa from 9pm to midnight). Weekly specials. Entrees $7-15. Open M-F 11:30am-1am, Sa 11am-1am, Su 11am-midnight. ❸

Ukrainian Village, 815 Denman St. (☎604-687-7440). Three kinds of fresh borscht ($4.75 each) complement traditional dishes like schnitzel or Kiev cutlet (each $10.50). $5.95 combo lunch specials bring you back

CANNABUSINESS British Columbia's buds fare well at Amsterdam's Cannabis Cup (the World Cup of pot smoking), and at an estimated $1.1 billion, generate half as much annual revenue as the province's logging industry. Most ganja dollars come from exports, and most exports go straight to the US. In 1998, Canada legalized hemp plants containing very low levels of the psychoactive compound THC, giving visitors and locals full legal freedom to enjoy fibrous rope. At some Vancouver cafes, however, public marijuana smoking is commonplace. What's the source of such seeming herbal impunity? Vancouver police don't seem to treat small-time pot smoking behind closed doors as a criminal offense, despite federal law. The police do tend to have moments of forgetfulness, though, at which point they raid the shops. For a connoisseur's perspective and news on further legalization efforts, tune in to the mind-altering www.cannabisculture.com or www.pot-tv.net. Educate yourself on the issues by visiting the BC Marijuana Party Bookshop and HQ at 307 W. Hastings St., which has literature, clothing, and other party paraphernalia. (☎604-682-1172. Open M-Th 10:30am-6pm, F-Sa 10:30am-7pm, Su 11am-6pm.)

to the Dnieper in savory style. Open daily for lunch 11:30am-5pm, dinner 5pm-10pm. F and Sa dinner runs until 11pm. ❷

La Luna Cafe, 117 Water St. (☎604-687-5862), in Gastown. Loyal patrons swear by the coffee, which is roasted on-site. Cheap, satisfying sandwiches ($3.95-4.95), home-made soups ($3). Internet $1 per 12min. Open M-F 7:30am-5pm, Sa 10am-5pm. ❶

COMMERCIAL DRIVE AND EAST VANCOUVER

Mongolian Teriyaki, 1918 Commercial Dr. (☎604-253-5607). Diners fill a bowl with meats, veggies, sauces, and noodles, and the chefs fry everything up and serve it with miso soup, rice, and salad for only $5 (large bowl $5.95). Take-out menu available. Open daily 11am-10:30pm. ❶

WaaZuBee Cafe, 1622 Commercial Dr. (☎604-253-5299), at E 1st St. Sleek, metallic decoration, ambient music, and artwork accompany the inventive food. New brunch menu boasts Belgian waffles and other classics ($5-8). Veggie spinach and ricotta agnoilotti pasta $13, Thai prawns $8, veggie burger $7. Open M-F 11:30am-1am, Sa 11am-1am, Su 11am-midnight. ❸

Nuff-Nice-Ness, 1861 Commercial Dr. (☎604-255-4211), at 3rd. Nice price and no fuss in this small Jamaican deli. Large jerk chicken with salad and rice $7.50; beef, chicken, or veggie patty $2; oxtail $7.72. Open M-Sa noon-9pm, Su noon-8pm. ❷

Belgian Fries, 1885 Commercial Dr. (☎604-253-4220). If you've never had it, try what CBC Montreal calls the "Best Poutine in BC," a concoction of fries, curds, and gravy. Huge portions serve two ($5). Open M-F 11:30am-10pm, Su 11:30am-9pm. ❶

KITSILANO

▨ **The Naam,** 2724 W 4th Ave. (☎604-738-7151), at MacDonald St. Bus #4 or 7 from Granville Mall. One of the most diverse vegetarian menus around, with great prices to boot. Crying Tiger Thai stir fry $9; several kinds of veggie burgers under $7; tofulati ice cream $3.50. Live music nightly 7-10pm. Birthday discounts equal your new age (e.g., 25 years old means 25% off!). Open 24hr. ❷

▨ **Benny's Bagels,** 2505 W Broadway (☎604-731-9730). Every college student's dream. Serves the requisite beer ($3 per glass), bagels ($0.75, $2.25 with cream cheese), and sandwiches and melts ($5.50-7.50). Open Su-Th 7am-1am, F-Sa 24hr. ❶

The Excellent Eatery, 3431 W Broadway (☎604-738-5298). Candlelight, sushi, and pop art. Reserve 1 of 2 canopied booths. Sushi $3.50-6. Mango-tuna-avocado sushi $4.25. Open M-Th 5pm-12:30am, F-Sa 5pm-1am, Su 5-11:30pm. ❶

Soupspoons, 2278 W. 4th Ave. (☎604-328-7687). This Parisian bistro offers panini and sandwiches ($6), salads ($3), and 10 ever-changing soups. The Beachpack gets you a chilled soup, baguette sandwich, and drink for $6.50. Open daily 10am-9pm. ❶

CHINATOWN

The prettiest are usually the priciest in Chinatown and adjacent **Japantown**. For guaranteed good food, stop in restaurants that are crowded with locals. Lively afternoons make this a better place for lunch than dinner.

▓ **Hon's Wun-Tun House,** 268 Keefer St. (☎604-688-0871). This award-winning Cantonese noodle-house is the place to go (bowls $3.50-6). Over 300 options make reading the menu take almost as long as eating from it. Attentive service. Open daily 8:30am-10pm; in summer F-Su until 11pm. Cash only. ❷

Kam's Garden Restaurant, 509 Main St. (☎604-669-5488). Authentic, no-frills Chinese food and plenty of it. Huge noodle platters $5-9. Open daily 10:30am-8pm. ❶

🎵 ENTERTAINMENT

MUSIC, THEATER, AND FILM

The renowned **Vancouver Symphony Orchestra** (☎604-684-9100) plays September to May in the refurbished **Orpheum Theatre** (☎604-665-3050), at the corner of Smithe and Seymour. In summer, tours of the theater are given ($5). The VSO often joins forces with other groups such as the **Vancouver Bach Choir** (☎604-921-8012).

Vancouver has a lively theater scene. The **Vancouver Playhouse Theatre Co.** (☎604-873-3311), on Dunsmuir and Georgia St., and the **Arts Club Theatre** (☎604-687-1644), on Granville Island, stage low-key shows, often including local work. **Theatre Under the Stars** (☎604-687-0174), in Stanley Park's Malkin Bowl, puts on outdoor musicals in the summer. Have some laughs at the **Theatresports League** at the Arts Club New Revue Stage on Granville Island. The world-famous improvisational theater company performs competitive improv, comedies, and improv jam sessions W-Sa at 8pm and F-Sa at 10pm. (Box office ☎687-1644. Open M-Sa 9am-showtime. Tickets $15, students $12.)

The **Ridge Theatre,** 3131 Arbutus, shows arthouse, European, and vintage film double features. (☎604-738-6311. $7, seniors and children $4; Tu $5, seniors and children $3; seniors free on M.) The **Hollywood Theatre,** 3123 W Broadway, shows a mix of arthouse and second-run mainstream double features for cheaper than the other theaters around downtown. (☎515-5864. $5, on M $3.50, seniors and children $3.50.) The **Blinding Light!! Cinema,** 36 Powell St., shows indie films and hosts special events such as the monthly Multiplex experimental music and film series. (☎604-878-3366; www.blindinglight.com. $5.) The **Paradise,** 919 Granville (☎604-681-1732), at Smithe, shows triple features of second-run movies for $4.

SPORTS

One block south of Chinatown on Main St. is **BC Place Stadium,** at 777 S Pacific Blvd., home to the Canadian Football League's BC Lions and the world's largest air supported dome (tickets from $15). The NHL's **Vancouver Canucks** call the nearby **GM Place** home. Tickets for both are often available as late as game day (from $40). The **Vancouver Canadians** play AAA baseball in Nat Bailey Stadium, at 33rd. Ave. and Ontario, opposite Queen Elizabeth Park, offering some of the cheapest sports tickets going (tickets from $8). For tickets and info call **Ticketmaster** at ☎ 604-280-4400 or visit www.ticketmaster.ca.

ANNUAL EVENTS

As with almost everything else, buying tickets in advance for these festivals often results in drastically reduced prices.

Chinese New Year will fall on Feb. 23, 2003. Fireworks, music, and dragons in the streets of Chinatown and beyond.

Alcan Dragon Boat Festival. End of June each year. (☎ 604-696-1888; www.canadadragonboat.com). Traditional food and dance from around the world, and dragon boat racing on False Creek. $9, seniors and youth $5, family $20.

Du Maurier International Jazz Festival Vancouver, June 21-July 1, 2003 (☎ 604-872-5200 or 888-438-5200; www.jazzvancouver.com). Draws over 500 performers and bands for 10 days of jazz, from acid to swing. Free concerts in Gastown, at the Roundhouse on Davie St., and around Granville Island. Other events range from $10-60.

Vancouver Folk Music Festival, July 18-20, 2003 (☎ 604-602-9798 or 800-985-8363; www.thefestival.bc.ca). Performers from around the world give concerts and workshops in July. Very kid-friendly. $35-50 per day, $110 for the weekend. Ages 13-18 $22-25, $55; ages 3-12 $12 for the weekend or $7 per day. Under 2 and over 65 free.

HSBC-Power Smart Celebration of Light, late July-early Aug. (☎ 604-738-4304; www.celebration-of-light.com). Pyrotechnicians light up the sky over English Bay on Sa and W nights. Hundreds of thousands gather to watch, closing off downtown streets.

Holy Pride! Late July to early Aug. (www.van-pride.bc.ca). This is Vancouver's gay and lesbian festival. Events include dances, parties, games, music, and a parade. Tickets and info from Ticketmaster or Little Sisters (see above).

Vancouver International Film Festival, late Sept.-early Oct. (☎ 604-685-0260; www.viff.org). This event showcases 275 movies from over 50 countries, with particular emphasis on Canadian films, East Asian films, and documentaries. $6-8.

Vancouver International Comedy Festival Late July-early Aug. (☎ 604-683-0883; www.comedyfest.com). Comics from all over the world converge on Granville Island in late July for 11 days of chortles and antics. Expect to pay big for the big acts, and much less for the unknowns. $10 and up.

IN RECENT NEWS

CRIME AND NO PUNISHMENT

Any nighttime walk through the streets east of Gastown reveals Vancouver's entanglement in illicit drugs. Aside from the trade in BC marijuana, parts of Vancouver are awash in harder substances, especially heroin.

Since 1990, Vancouver-area police have logged over 50 homicides related to gangland battles and turf wars beween Indian-led gangs, including the brazen 1998 nightclub assassination of reputed gangster kingpin Bindy Johal. Despite Johal being shot dead in the middle of a crowd of more than 300, no suspects have been named in his murder—and a good deal of the killings go unsolved.

This is due in large part to a not unjustifiable fear of violent reprisals against those who choose to cooperate with law enforcement authorities. The dismal conviction rate against those suspects who are actually tried in court also dampens potential witness cooperation—four years before his assassination, Johal and several associates were acquitted for the murder of another suspected drug cartel leader.

The continued violence has distressed community activists and has led the Vancouver Police Department to create a special task force. But with four more murders in the opening months of 2002, and with the fierce demand for drugs in Vancouver, these efforts must overcome substantial obstacles.

◨ NIGHTLIFE

Vancouver's nightlife centers around dance clubs playing beats and DJs spinning every night. Local pubs inundate communities with relaxed options for a post-work drink. The free weekly **Georgia Straight** publishes comprehensive club and event listings, restaurant reviews, and coupons. **Discorder** is the unpredictable monthly publication of the UBC radio station CITR. Both are available in local cafes, and *Georgia Straight* can be found around town in newspaper bins.

GASTOWN

▨ **Sonar,** 66 Water St. (☎604-683-6695). A popular beat factory. Sa House, W hip-hop and reggae, and F turntablist. Pints $3.75-5. Open M-Sa 8pm-2am, Su 9pm-midnight.

▨ **The Irish Heather,** 217 Carrall St. (☎604-688-9779). The 2nd-highest seller of Guinness in BC, this true Irish pub and bistro serves up memories of the Emerald Isle. Full 20oz. draughts ($5.20 before tax), mixed beer drinks ($5.60 before tax), and a helping of bangers and mash ($14) will keep those eyes smiling. Lots of veggie dishes, too. Live music in the evening, Tu-Th. Open M-Th 3-11:30pm, F-Su 11:30am-12:30pm.

The Blarney Stone, 216 Carrall St. (☎604-687-4322). For a more raucous Irish experience, join the mostly university crowd for live music by a band called Killarney, a fixture for 18 years. Cover $5-7, Th $5 cover goes to charity. Open W-Sa 7pm-2am.

Purple Onion, 15 Water St. (☎604-602-9442). Sucks in the crowd with an eclectic music selection and inviting lounge chairs. DJs spin acid jazz, disco, soul, and funk in the back room. The lounge features live blues, R&B, jazz, and funk acts W-Sa. Don't miss the frenetic "Platinum Saturdays," followed by the more relaxed "Sanctuary Sundays." M and W-Sa $3-8 cover; Tu no cover, Su $1. Open M-Th 9pm-2am, F-Sa 8pm-2am, Su 9pm-midnight.

DOWNTOWN

▨ **Sugar Refinery,** 1115 Granville St. (☎604-683-2004). Where those involved in film, art, and music go to relax. An ever-changing program of events, music, and spoken word entertains while the tasty vegetarian meals please the stomach. Entrees $7.50-9, big sandwiches $5-7.50, tap beers served in mason jars $4.25-5.75. Open M-F 5pm-12pm, Sa-Su 5pm-2am, kitchen open throughout.

Wett Bar, 1320 Richards St. (☎604-662-7707). Candlelit dining booths and a weekend dress code. Wields one of the most advanced stereo and light systems in Vancouver. F Hip-hop, Sa top 40, W house. Open M and W-Sa 8pm-2am, Tu 9pm-1am.

Odyssey, 1251 Howe St. (☎604-689-5256). Embark on a high-energy journey. F-Sa cranks out beats to a mainly gay crowd. Male go-go dancers spice it up F. Su and W Drag Night. $3-6. Open daily 9pm-2am.

The Drink, 398 Richards St. (☎604-687-1307). Nightclub with a diverse repertoire including alternative Tu, "Noche Havana" latin W, House Party Th with $2.50 drinks, and hip-hop and reggae Sa. Open W 8pm-2am, Th-Sa 9pm-2am, Su noon-2am.

KITSILANO

The King's Head, 1618 Yew St. (☎604-738-6966), at 1st St., in Kitsilano. Cheap drinks, cheap food, relaxing atmosphere, and a great location near the beach. Bands play acoustic sets on a tiny stage. Daily drink specials. $3 pints. Open M-F 7am-1am, Sa 7:30am-2am, Su 7:30am-midnight.

Koerner's Pub, 6371 Crescent Rd. (☎604-822-0983), on UBC campus. Owned and operated by the Graduate Student Society, this is the place to meet a smart special someone. Mellow M's with live music and open jam, W techno night. Open late Aug. to mid-Apr. M-F noon-1am, Sa 4pm-1am; summer M-Sa 4pm-midnight.

◎ SIGHTS

DOWNTOWN

▨VANCOUVER ART GALLERY. This gallery is host to fantastic temporary exhibitions and home to a good collection of contemporary art. (*750 Hornby St. in Robson Square.* ☎604-662-4700. *Open M-Su 10am-5:30pm, Th 10am-9pm; call for winter hours. $12.50, seniors $9, students $7, under 12 free; Th 5-9pm pay-what-you-can; 2-for-1 HI discount.*)

CHINATOWN

The neighborhood bustles with restaurants, shops, bakeries, and **the world's narrowest building** at 8 W Pender St. In 1912, the city expropriated all but a 1.8m (6 ft.) strip of Chang Toy's property in order to expand the street; he built on the land anyhow. The serene **Dr. Sun Yat-Sen Classical Chinese Garden** maintains imported Chinese plantings, carvings, and rock formations in the first full-size authentic garden of its kind outside China. (*578 Carrall St.* ☎604-689-7133. *Open May to mid-June daily 9:30am-5:30pm; mid-June to Aug. 9:30am-6:30pm; Sept. 9:30am-5:30pm; Oct.-Apr. 9:30am-4pm. Admission to part of the garden is free, while another section is $7.50, students $5, seniors $6, children free, families $18. Tours every hr. 10am-6pm.*) Don't miss the sights, sounds, smells, and tastes of the weekend **night market** along Pender and Keefer St., the first in North America. (*Open F-Su 6:30-11am.*) Chinatown itself is relatively safe, but its surroundings make up some of Vancouver's more unsavory sections. (*Chinatown is southeast of Gastown. Bus #22 north on Burrard St. leads to Pender and Carrall St., in the heart of Chinatown.*)

GARDENS

The city's temperate climate, which also includes ample rain most months of the year, allows floral growth to flourish. Locals take great pride in their private gardens, and public parks and green spaces also showcase displays of plant life.

▨VANDUSEN BOTANICAL GARDEN. 55 acres (22 hectares) of former golf course have been converted into an immense garden showcasing 7500 taxa from six continents. An international **sculpture** collection is interspersed with the plants, while more than 60 species of **birds** can be seen in areas such as the Fragrance Garden, Children's Garden, Bonsai House, Chinese Medicinal Garden, or the Elizabethan Maze, which is planted with 3000 pyramidal cedars. Daily tours given at 2pm; alternatively, follow a self-guided tour tailored to show the best of the season. The Flower & Garden Show is the first weekend of June. (*5251 Oak St. at W 37th. From downtown take #17 Oak bus and get off at West 37th and Oak.* ☎604-878-9274; *www.vandusengarden.org. Free parking. Mostly wheelchair accessible. Apr.-Sept. $7, ages 65+ or 13-18 $5, 6-12 $3.50, family $16; Oct.-Mar. up to 50% off. Open June to mid-Aug. 10am-8pm; mid-Aug.-Labor Day 10am-8pm; Labor Day-Sept. 30 10am-6pm; Oct.-Mar. 10am-4pm; Apr. 10am-4pm, May 10am-8pm.*)

BLOEDEL FLORAL AND BIRD CONSERVATORY. Journey from tropics to desert in 100 paces inside this 43m diameter triodetic geodesic dome, constructed of plexiglass bubbles and aluminum tubing. The conservatory, maintained at a constant 18°C (65°F), is home to 500 varieties of exotic plants and 150 birds. Its elevation also affords great views of downtown Vancouver. (*In the center of Queen Elizabeth Park on Cambie and 37th Ave., a few blocks east of VanDusen.* ☎604-257-8570. *$3.75, ages 65+ $2.25, ages 13-18 $2.85, ages 6-12 $1.85, under 5 free. Open Apr.-Sept. M-F 9am-8pm; Sa-Su 10am-9pm; Oct.-Mar. daily 10am-5pm.*)

UNIVERSITY OF BRITISH COLUMBIA (UBC)

The high point of a visit to UBC is the breathtaking ■**Museum of Anthropology.** The high-ceilinged glass and concrete building houses totems and other massive carvings, highlighted by Bill Reid's depiction of Raven discovering the first human beings in a giant clam shell. The actual site of the discovery is in the Queen Charlotte Islands (see p. 338). *(6393 NW Marine Dr., bus #4 or 10 from Granville St. Museum.* ☎ *604-822-3825 or 604-822-5087; www.moa.ubc.ca. Open July-Aug. M and W-Su 10am-5pm, Tu 10am-9pm; Sept.-May W-Su 11am-5pm, Tu 11am-9pm, closed M. $7, students $4, seniors $5, under 6 free; Tu after 5pm free.)* Across the street caretakers tend to **Nitobe Memorial Garden,** the finest classical Shinto garden outside of Japan. *(☎ 604-822-6038. Open mid-Mar. to Oct. daily 10am-6pm; Nov. to mid-Mar. M-F 10am-2:30pm. $2.75, ages 65+ and students $1.75, under 6 free.)* The **Botanical Gardens** are a collegiate Eden encompassing eight gardens in the central campus, including the largest collection of rhododendrons in North America. *(6804 SW Marine Dr.* ☎ *604-822-9666. Same hours as Nitobe Garden. $4.75, ages 65+ and students $2.50, under 6 free.)*

STANLEY PARK

Established in 1889 at the tip of the downtown peninsula, the 1000-acre **Stanley Park** is a testament to the foresight of Vancouver's urban planners. The thickly wooded park is laced with cycling and hiking trails and surrounded by an 10km **seawall** promenade popular with cyclists, runners, and rollerbladers. *(☎ 257-8400. To get to the park, take #23, #123, #35, or #135 bus. A free shuttle runs between major destinations throughout the park June-Sept. 10am-6pm.)*

■**VANCOUVER AQUARIUM.** The aquarium, on the park's eastern side not far from the entrance, features exotic aquatic animals. BC, Amazonian, and other ecosystems are skillfully replicated. Dolphin and beluga whales demonstrate their advanced training and intelligence by drenching gleeful visitors in educational wetness. The new Wild Coast exhibit allows visitors to get a close-up view of marine life. Outside the aquarium, an **orca fountain** by sculptor Bill Reid glistens black. *(☎ 604-659-3474; www.vanaqua.org. Open July-Aug. daily 9:30am-7pm; Sept.-June 10am-5:30pm. Shows throughout the day from 10am-5:30pm. $14.75, students, ages 13-18 and seniors $11.95; ages 4-12 $8.95; 3 and under free.)*

WATER. The **Lost Lagoon,** brimming with fishies, birds, and the odd trumpeter swan, provides a utopian escape from the skyscrapers. **Nature walks** start from the **Nature House,** underneath the Lost Lagoon bus loop. *(Walks ☎ 604-257-8544. 2hr. Su at 1pm. $5, under 12 free. Nature House open June-Aug. F-Su 11am-7pm.)* The park's edges boast a few restaurants, tennis courts, a cinder running track with hot showers and a changing room, swimming beaches staffed by lifeguards, and an outdoor theater, the **Malkin Bowl** *(☎ 604-687-0174).* For warm, chlorinated water, take a dip in the **Second Beach Pool.** *(Next to Georgia St. park entrance. Pool ☎ 604-257-8370. $4, ages 13-18 $3, ages 65+ $2.40, ages 6-12 $2. Towels $2, lockers $0.25. Open May 19-June 10 M-F noon-8:45pm; June 11-Sept. 3 M-F 10am-8:45pm; May 19-Sept. 3 Sa-Su 10am-8:45pm.)*

FALSE CREEK AND GRANVILLE ISLAND

GRANVILLE ISLAND BREWING COMPANY. Canada's first micro-brewery offers daily tours of the facility, including free samples. *(Under the bridge at the southern tip of the island.* ☎ *604-687-2739. Tours at noon, 2pm and 4pm, hourly noon-5pm on weekends. $7. Includes samples of 4 brews and a souvenir glass. Call for store hours.)*

H.R. MACMILLAN SPACE CENTRE. Housed in the same circular building as the **Vancouver Museum,** the space center runs a motion-simulator ride, planetarium, and exhibit gallery, as well as frequent laser-light rock shows. *(1100 Chestnut St. Bus #22 south on Burrard St. from downtown.* ☎ *604-738-7827. Open July-Aug. daily 10am-5pm,*

Sept.-June closed M. $12.75, students and seniors $9.75; laser-light show $9.25. Vancouver Museum ☎604-736-4431. Open daily 10am-5pm; winter closed M. $8, under 19 $5.50, seniors $7. Combined admission to both museums $17, youth $11.)

◪ BEACHES

Vancouver has kept its many beaches relatively clean (for an urban area). Follow the western side of the Stanley Park seawall south to **Sunset Beach Park,** a strip of grass and beach extending all the way along **English Bay** to the Burrard Bridge. The **Aquatic Centre,** 1050 Beach Ave., at the southeast end of the beach, is a public facility with a sauna, gym, and 50m indoor pool. (☎604-665-3424. Call for public swim hours, generally M-Th 9am-4:20pm and 8pm-9:55pm, F 9am-4:20pm and 8:20-8:55pm, Sa 10am-9pm, Su 1-9pm. $4, ages 13-18 $3, ages 6-12 $2, ages 65+ $2.40.)

 Kitsilano Beach ("Kits"), across Arbutus St. from Vanier Park, is another local favorite for tanning and beach volleyball. For fewer crowds, more young 'uns, and free showers, visit **Jericho Beach** (head west along 4th Ave. and follow signs). A cycling path at the side of the road leads to the westernmost end of the UBC campus. West of Jericho Beach is the quieter **Spanish Banks;** at low tide the ocean retreats almost a kilometer, allowing for long walks on the flats. Most of Vancouver's 31km of beaches are patrolled daily by lifeguards from late May to Labour Day between 11:30am and 9pm.

◪ LOCAL MOUNTAINS

Three local mountains loom above the city on the North Shore, bringing the locals out year-round. In winter, all three offer night skiing and heavier snow than mountains farther from the ocean. Their size and impact on your wallet are much smaller than Whistler, which is a 2hr. drive north on Hwy. 99 (see p. 265). In summer, all offer challenging hiking and beautiful views of the city from the top.

GROUSE MOUNTAIN. The ski hill closest to downtown Vancouver has the crowds to prove it. Take bus #236 from the North Vancouver SeaBus terminal, which drops passengers off at the Super Skyride, an aerial tramway open daily from 9am-10pm. The slopes are lit for skiing until 10:30pm from mid-November to mid-April. (☎604-984-0661; snow report 986-6262; www.grousemountain.com; . Lift tickets $35, youths $25, seniors $19, children $15; night passes at a reduced rate. Tramway $21.95, seniors $19.95, ages 13-18 $12.95.) The steep 2.9km **Grouse Grind Trail** is popular among Vancouverites in the summer; it climbs 853m to the top of the mountain and takes a good 2hr. The Skyride back down costs $5.

CYPRESS BOWL. Cypress Bowl in West Vancouver provides a less crowded ski alternative. It boasts the most advanced terrain of the local mountains on its 23 runs. Head west on Hwy. 1, and take Exit 8 (Cypress Bowl Rd.). A few minutes before the downhill area, the 16km of groomed trails at Hollyburn **cross-country ski area** are open to the public. In summer, the cross-country trails are excellent for **hiking** and **berry-picking.** (☎604-922-0825; snow report 604-419-7669; www.cypressbowl.com. Discount tickets available at Costco supermarkets.)

MOUNT SEYMOUR. Take bus #211 from the Phibbs Exchange at the north end of the Second Narrows Bridge to **Mt. Seymour Provincial Park.** Trails leave from Mt. Seymour Rd., and a paved road winds 11km to the top. The Mt. Seymour ski area is the cheapest skiing around. Its marked terrain is also the least challenging, although the spectacular backcountry is the preferred terrain of many top pro snowboarders. (www.mountseymour.com. Midweek lift tickets $19, seniors $15, ages 6-12 $9; weekends and holidays $29, ages 6-12 $12, seniors $19.)

⚒ WILDLIFE ADVENTURES

The Lower Mainland of British Columbia hosts a huge variety of wild critters, including mule deer, black bear, wolves, cougars, and more than a few bird species. The **Guide-Outiftters Association of British Columbia,** 7580 River Rd., Suite 250, Richmond, BC (☎604-278-2688) is a BC-wide information and contact clearinghouse for those interested in hunting game. Those interested in importing firearms into Canada should consult the Canadian government's **Firearms Centre** (☎800-731-4000). If you'd rather seek a communion with the water, contact the **Deep Cove Canoe and Kayak Center,** 2156 Banbury Rd., North Vancouver, which offers 2hr. canoe and kayak rentals for $28 or 2hr. twin rentals for $40. 3hr. introductory lessons for novices are $60, and overnight kayak trips up to campsites on Indian Arm are also available. (☎604-929-2268; www.deepcovekayak.com. Reservations suggested in summer. Apr.-Oct. 9am-9pm)

⚒ DAYTRIPS FROM VANCOUVER

EAST OF NORTH VAN. East of the city center, the town of **Deep Cove** in North Vancouver luxuriates in saltiness, and sea otters and seals ply pleasant **Indian Arm. Cates Park,** at the end of Dollarton Hwy. on the way to Deep Cove, has popular swimming and scuba waters and makes a good bike trip out of Vancouver. Trails leave from Mt. Seymour Rd., and a paved road winds 11km to the top for access to hiking and biking. See also **Local Mountains,** p. 261. *(Bus #210 from Pender St. to the Phibbs Exchange on the north side of Second Narrows Bridge. From there, take bus #211 or 212 to Deep Cove. Bus #211 also leads to Mount Seymour Provincial Park.)*

▨ LIGHTHOUSE PARK. If you only get out of Vancouver once, go to gorgeous **Lighthouse Park.** Numerous trails, including an easy 3km loop that covers most of the park (plan to spend a couple hours walking it), criss-cross the 185-acre park. To reach one of the best picnic spots in the world, walk down the path toward the lighthouse, hang a left at the buildings, keep right at the fork in the trail, and walk to a large flat rock. Some **rock climbing,** consisting of sea cliff top-roping and bouldering, can be found at Juniper Point on the west side of the park. *(Head across Lions Gate Bridge from Stanley Park and west along Marine Dr. for about 10km through West Van. 50km round-trip from downtown; blue bus #250 goes right to the park's entrance. For a park map stop by the West Van. Parks & Community Services Office at 750 17th St., 2nd floor. ☎604-925-7200. Open M-F 8:30am-4:30pm.)*

REIFEL BIRD SANCTUARY. Reifel Bird Sanctuary is on 850-acre Westham Island. The marshland supports 265 bird species, and spotting towers are set up for extended bird-watching. April, May, October, and November are the best months to visit. *(Westham Island lies northwest of the Tsawwassen ferry terminal and 16km south of the city. ☎604-946-6980. Open daily 9am-4pm. $4, seniors and children $2.)*

LYNN CANYON. An idyllic setting that provides easy hiking for city escapists. Unlike the more famous Capilano (below), the suspension bridge here is free, uncrowded, and hangs 50m above the canyon. The park offers more trails than Capilano; several are 10-20min., but longer hiking trails are also plentiful. Swimming is not recommended; many have died over the years from the treacherous currents and falls. *(SeaBus to Lynn Canyon Park, in North Vancouver. Take bus #229 from the North Vancouver SeaBus terminal to the last stop (Peters Rd.) and walk 500m to the bridge. ☎604-981-3103. Open summer 7am-9pm; spring and fall 7am-8pm; winter 7am-6pm.)*

CAPILANO SUSPENSION BRIDGE. You and every other Vancouver tourist will enjoy crossing the precarious Capilano Bridge. Although the bridge was built in 1889, it remains awe-inspiring, spanning 137m and swaying 70m above the river. A few short trails meander through the surrounding old-growth forest. Guided tours every 15min. in summer. *(3735 Capilano Rd. North Van. 10min. from town. Drive through Stanley Park, over the Lions Gate Bridge, north 1km. on Capilano Rd. From Hwy. #1 take Exit 14 and go north.5km. Or take bus #246 from downtown to Ridgewood stop and walk 1 block north to park. ☎ 985-7474; www.capbridge.com. Open in summer daily 8:30-dusk; winter 9am-5pm. $13.95, seniors $10.75, students $7.95, child 6-12 $3.75, under 6 free. CAA, AAA 20% discount; HI members get student rate.)*

SECHELT PENINSULA   ☎ 604

Tucked between the Strait of Georgia and Porpoise Bay, Sechelt (SEE-shelt) is one of BC's greatest secrets. Only 1½hr. by road and ferry from downtown Vancouver, this quiet seaside paradise remains miles away in attitude, lifestyle, and even climate. The region offers a rich array of outdoor activities: world-class kayaking, hiking, scuba diving, biking, and even skiing are close-by.

█▌ ORIENTATION AND PRACTICAL INFORMATION. Sechelt is the largest community on the Sunshine Coast, 27km west of the **BC Ferries**, Langdale Ferry Terminal (☎ 886-2242 or 888-223-3779). The fare on the ferry between Langdale and Horseshoe Bay is only charged on the way from the mainland to Sechelt (40min.; 8-10 per day; $8, under 12 $4, car $30; off-season slightly cheaper). **Malaspina Coach Lines** (☎ 885-3666) runs to **Vancouver** (2 per day, $10.75 plus ferry fare). **Sunshine Coast Transit System** (☎ 885-3234) buses run from Sechelt to the ferry terminal (adult $1.50, students and seniors $1). **National Tilden**, 5623 Wharf St., rents cars. (☎ 885-9120. From $50 per day; $0.25 per km over 100km; winter rates start at $44.) Hail a **Sunshine Coast Taxi** at ☎ 885-3666. The **visitors center** is located in the Trail Bay Centre at Trail Ave. and Teredo St. next to Home Hardware. (☎ 885-0662 or 877-633-2963. Open year-round M-Sa 9:30am-5:30pm, Su 10am-4pm; off season closed on Su.) **Trail Bay Sports**, at Cowrie St. and Trail Ave., rents mountain bikes and sells fishing gear and permits as well as other useful outdoor gear. (☎ 885-2512. Bikes $10 per hr., $45 per 8hr. Open in summer M-Th and Sa 9am-6pm, F 9am-9pm, Su 10am-4pm; winter M-Sa 9:30am-5:30pm.) **Sechelt Coin Laundry** is on Dolphin St. at Inlet Ave. (☎ 885-3393. Open daily 9am-9pm. Wash $1.75, dry $0.25 per 5min.) **Call** ☎ 911 in an **emergency**, or get to **St. Mary's Hospital** (☎ 885-2224), on the highway at the east end of town. The **Sechelt Public Library**, 5797 Cowrie St., has **Internet access** for $1 per 30min. (☎ 885-3260. Open Tu 10am-5pm, W-Th 11am-8pm, F and Su 1pm-5pm, and Sa 10am-4pm.) The **post office** is on Inlet Ave. at Dolphin St. (☎ 885-2411. Open M-F 8:30am-5pm, Sa 8:30am-12:30pm.) **Postal Code:** V0N 3A0.

╔ ACCOMMODATIONS AND CAMPING. Most of Sechelt's accommodations are pricey, but deals can be found. The comfortable **Moon Cradle Backpacker's Retreat ❶**, 3125 Hwy. 101 across from the golf course, 10km east of Sechelt, is situated on 10 acres of woodland property with a firepit, sauna, laundry, Internet, and bike rentals ($6 per hr.). It can turn into a hangout for the locals, so idyllic silence isn't always the norm. (☎ 885-2070. $25, students and seniors $22; singles $40, $37; doubles $55, $49.) **Eagle View B&B ❸**, 4839 Eagle View Rd., 5min. east of Sechelt, has rooms with private bath, sitting room with TV/VCR and video collection, an ocean view, complimentary tea and biscuits, and delightful hosts. (☎ 885-7225. Singles $45-50, doubles $70.)

The provincial parks in the area are dreamy. The family-oriented **Porpoise Bay Provincial Park ❶**, 4km north of Sechelt along Sechelt Inlet Rd./E Porpoise Bay Rd., offers a forested campground with toilets, showers, firewood, playground, and a lovely beach and swimming area. (Reservations ☎ 800-689-9025. Wheelchair accessible. 84

regular sites, $18; cyclist campsites by the water $9. Gate closed 11pm-7am.) For more seclusion, **Roberts Creek Provincial Park ❶**, 11km east of Sechelt, has private sites amid old-growth Douglas Firs. (Pit toilets, firewood, water. 24 sites, $12.) **Smuggler Cove Provincial Park ❶** has five primitive, free walk-in sites (pit toilets, no water). The sites are accessible by boat, and the cove is an excellent base for kayaking. Head west out of town towards Halfmoon Bay and turn left on Brooks Rd., which leads 3.5km to a parking area. The campsite is 1km along a trail.

☐ FOOD. Claytons, in the Trail Bay Centre, is the place to go for groceries. (☎ 885-2025. Open M-Th 9am-7pm, F 9am-9pm, Sa-Su 10am-6pm.) **The Gumboot Garden Cafe ❶**, 1059 Roberts Creek Rd., 10km east of Sechelt in Roberts Creek, serves delicious meals with organic ingredients. Lunch and breakfast favorites include fries and miso gravy ($3.50) and Thai salad with chicken, salmon, or tofu ($6-7). A variable dinner menu is uniformly excellent and always includes vegan options. (☎ 885-4216. Open M-W 8am-8pm, Th-Sa 7:30am-10pm, Su 7:30am-6pm.) In Sechelt, the **Old Boot Eatery ❸**, 5520 Wharf St., serves up generous portions of Italian food and local hospitality; pasta entrees are $9-15. (☎ 885-2727. Open in summer M-Sa 11am-9:30pm; winter 11am-9pm.) **Wakefield Inn ❷**, on the highway (number 6529) 5min. west of Sechelt, dishes out pub fare and live music with a great view of the ocean. Pints are $4-5. (☎ 885-7666. Music F-Sa 9pm-1am.)

☐ ◪ SIGHTS AND OUTDOOR ACTIVITIES. The eight wilderness marine parks in the protected waters of **Sechelt Inlet** make for fantastic sea kayaking and canoeing and offer free camping along the shore. **Pedals & Paddles**, at Tillicum Bay Marina, 7km north of town, rents vessels. (☎ 885-6440. Single kayaks $23 per 4hr., doubles $46; canoes $27. Full-day single kayaks $40, doubles $75; canoes $45.) The intersection of Sechelt and Salmon Inlets is home to the **S.S. Chaudiere artificial reef**, one of the largest wreck dives in North America. **Suncoast Dive Center** rents equipment, teaches lessons, and charters boats (☎ 740-8006; www.suncoastdiving.com. Regular rental $45 per day; full rental $75 per day; 1 day charter $85). On the other side of the peninsula, **Pender Harbor** offers equally impressive diving; Jacques Cousteau considered this site second only to the Red Sea. **Skookumchuck Narrows** is a popular destination by water or by land to view tidal rapids that bring waves standing 1.5m at peak tides. Tidal schedules are available at the Info Centre or at the trailhead. To get there, drive 54km west to **Earl's Cove** and then 4km towards **Egmont** (about 1hr.). From the parking area, it's a 4km walk to four viewing sites (allow 1hr.). The route to the first site is wheelchair-accessible.

Dakota Bowl and Wilson Creek 4km east of Sechelt have hiking and free cross-country skiing trails. From Sechelt, turn left on Field Rd. and drive 8km to the trailhead. Sechelt's lumber legacy has left it with an extensive system of former logging roads suitable for hiking and mountain biking. The intermediate **Chapman Creek Trail** passes huge Douglas firs en route to **Chapman Falls**. The trailhead is at the top of Havies Rd., 1km north of the Davis Bay Store on Hwy. 101, or access at Brookman Park on the highway. The **Suncoaster Trail** extends over 40km from **Homesite Creek**, near Halfmoon Bay northwest of Sechelt, through the foothills of the **Caren Range**, home of Canada's oldest trees (some as old as 1835 years).

Indoors, the **Sunshine Coast Arts Centre**, on Trail Ave. at Medusa St., showcases local talent in a log building. (☎ 885-5412. Open July-Aug. Tu-Sa 10am-4pm, Su 1-4pm; Sept.-June W-Sa 11am-4pm, Su 1-4pm. Admission by donation.) They also organize the Hackett Park Crafts Fair, held during the Sechelt's big event, the **Sunshine Coast Festival of the Written Arts**, which attracts talented Canadian and international authors to give **readings** (August 8-11, 2002). Panels are held in the **botanical gardens** of the historic Rockwood Centre, and tickets go early. (☎ 885-9631 or 800-565-9631. Grounds open daily 8am-10pm.) The **Roberts Creek Community Hall** (☎ 886-3868 or

740-9616), on the corner of the highway and Roberts Creek Rd., attracts excellent musicians on weekends, from reggae to Latin funk. Tickets ($10-20) can be purchased at the **Roberts Creek General Store** (☎ 885-3400).

ALONG HWY. 99: SEA TO SKY HWY.

Winding around the steep cliffs on the shore of Howe Sound from Horseshoe Bay to Squamish and then continuing inland to Whistler, the Sea to Sky Hwy. (Hwy. 99) is one of the loveliest, most dangerous, and best loved drives in British Columbia. Sinuous curves combine with brilliant vistas of the Sound and Tantalus Range.

VANCOUVER TO WHISTLER

Numerous provincial parks line the rocky drive to Whistler, providing excellent hiking and climbing opportunities. One worth stopping for is **Shannon Falls,** just off the highway, 3km past the museum. The park affords a 2min. walk (350m) to a spectacular view of a 335m waterfall, the third highest in BC. Steep but well-maintained trails from the falls make for difficult **dayhiking** up to the three peaks of the **Stawamus Chief** (11km round-trip), the second largest granite monolith in the world, which bares a 671m wall of solid granite. The face of the Chief is a popular climb for expert hikers. **Squamish Hostel** ❶, 38490 Buckley Rd., in downtown Squamish, is a common stopover for those tackling the local geography. In summer, the hostel is packed with wandering climbers, as the region between Squamish and Whistler boasts over 1300 excellent routes. (☎ 892-9240 or 800-449-8614 in BC. Shower, kitchen, linen. $15; private rooms $25.) At **Eagle Run**, a viewing site 4km north of the hostel along the Squamish River, thousands of bald eagles make their winter home along the rivers and estuaries of Squamish Valley. BC Parks runs a spotless **campground** ❶ 13km north of Squamish at **Alice Lake**. (Reservations ☎ 800-689-9025; www.discovercamping.ca. Hot water, firewood. $18.50. Showers.) Nearby **Garibaldi Park** contains a vast number of stunning hikes, including an 18km (round-trip) trail up to **Garibaldi Lake.** The backcountry campgrounds at the lake provide further access to Black Tusk and Cheakamus Lake (trailhead at Rubble Creek parking lot, 25km north of Squamish). The **BC Parks District Office** in Alice Lake Park has trail maps. (☎ 898-3678. Open M-F 8:30am-4:30pm.) The **BC Forest Service office**, 42000 Loggers Ln., has maps of local logging roads and primitive campgrounds and sells the $10 permits needed to camp at them. (☎ 898-2100; www.for.gov.bc.ca/Vancouver/district/squamish. Open M-F 8:30am-4:30pm.)

WHISTLER   ☎ 604

This skiers' and snowboarders' utopia is among the top ski destinations in the world, and for good reason: over 7000 acres of ski-able terrain make it the largest ski area on the continent. The mountains are part of Garibaldi Provincial Park, and it takes little effort to get off the beaten path. When the snow melts, bikes (the primary recreation on the summer slopes), boots, horses, and rafts usually fill in for skis, and bundled up ski junkies are replaced by people in baggy shorts who look like they want to be skiing. The town itself is pretty enough, but its shops and restaurants earn it a deserved reputation as an overpriced, outdoor mall.

⚒ 🛈 ORIENTATION AND PRACTICAL INFORMATION

Whistler is located 125km north of Vancouver on the beautiful, if dangerously twisty, Hwy. 99. Services are located in **Whistler Village**, most of which is **pedestrian-only. Whistler Creek**, 5km south on Hwy. 99, offers a smaller collection of accommodations and restaurants. The first thing to do upon arriving in town is obtain a map. Otherwise, all is lost.

Greyhound Bus Lines: (☎932-5031 or 800-661-8747; www.whistlerbus.com.) To **Vancouver** from the **Village Bus Loop** (2½hr.; 7 per day; $21.50, round-trip $43). The Activity Centre sells tickets.

BC Rail: (☎984-5246). **Cariboo Prospector** departs North Vancouver at 7am for Whistler Creek and returns at 6:40pm daily. ($39 one-way. The train station is on Lake Placid Rd. in Creekside; free connecting bus service to the Village.)

Taxi: Whistler Taxi (☎932-3333).

Tourist Office: Activity Centre (☎932-3928), in the Conference Centre, provides maps and booking services. Open daily 8:30am-5pm. The **Chamber of Commerce** and **Info Centre** (☎932-5528. Open daily summer 9am-6pm; winter 9am-5pm) are in a log cabin at the corner of Hwy. 99 and Lake Placid Rd. in Creekside. Alternatively, call **Whistler/Blackcomb** (☎932-3434 or 800-766-0449; www.whistlerblackcomb.com).

Laundry: Laundry at Nester's, 7009 Nester's Rd. (☎932-2960). $2.25 wash, $0.25 per 4min. of drying. Open 8:30am-8:30pm.

Weather Conditions: ☎664-9033.

Emergency: ☎911.

Police: 4315 Blackcomb Way (☎932-3044), in the Village.

Telecare Crisis Line: ☎932-2673.

Medical Services: Whistler Health Care Center, 4380 Lorimer Rd. (☎932-4911).

Internet Access: Whistler Public Library (932-5564), located between Main St. and Northlands Blvd. Free, but long waits. Open M-Tu and Th 10am-8pm, F-Su 10am-5pm.

Post Office: (☎932-5012), in the Village Marketplace. Open M-F 8:30am-5:30pm, Sa 8:30am-12:30pm. **Postal Code:** V0N 1B4.

ACCOMMODATIONS AND CAMPING

Whistler offers great hostels and campgrounds. The Forest Service office in Squamish (see p. 265) has maps for other camping options.

■ **Whistler Hostel (HI),** 5678 Alta Lake Rd. (☎932-5492). BC Rail from Vancouver stops right in front on request. 5km south of Whistler Village off Hwy. 99. The Rainbow Park bus runs to the Village ($1.50). The lakeside timber building has a kitchen, fireplace, ski lockers, pool table, Internet, and sauna. Bikes $18 per day. Canoes free on Alta Lake. Check in 8am-11am and 4pm-10pm. Reserve ahead. Bunks $20; nonmembers $24; under 13 half-price; under 6 free. Private rooms $10 surcharge. ❷

The Fireside Lodge, 2117 Nordic Dr. (☎932-4545), 3km south of the Village. Caters to a quiet, easygoing crowd. The spacious and spotless cabin, filled with funky, angular bedrooms, comes with mammoth kitchen, lounge, sauna, coin laundry, extensive and lively game room, storage (bring your own lock), and parking. Check-in 3:30-8:30pm. 24 bunks: Apr. to mid-Dec. $20; mid-Dec. to Mar. $30. Singles $40. ❸

Shoestring Lodge, 7124 Nancy Greene Dr. (☎932-3338), 1km north of the Village. Cable, private bath, laundry, and Internet. Small fee for kitchen use. In-house pub can lead to late-night ruckus outside. Free shuttle to slopes Dec.-Apr. Check-in 4pm, check-out 11am. 4-person dorm $17-30; doubles $90-140; more expensive in winter. ❸

FOOD

Cheap food is hard-won in the Village with the exception of the popular **IGA** supermarket in the Village North. (Open daily 9am-9pm.) Pub food is the most affordable way to find sustenance (meals usually around $10, with a pint $15). Pubs are in almost every other building throughout the Village.

■ **South Side Deli**, 2102 Lake Placid Rd. (☎932-3368), on Hwy. 99 by the Husky station 4km south of the Village. Heaping breakfasts, mammoth lunches, and deliciously greasy dinners. Be sure to try the B.E.L.T.C.H. (bacon, egg, lettuce, tomato, cheese, and ham). Open Th-Su 6am-10pm, M-W 6am-3pm. ❷

Uli's Flipside Restaurant, 4433 Sundial Plaza (935-1107). Right next to the main Village Square. Getting closer to the upscale side of things, Uli's offers hearty and worthy Mediterranean-Canadian fare, with almost all dishes falling between $10-15. Worth the splurge after a long day's workout. M-Sa 5pm-1am. ❸

Moguls Coffee Beans, 4208 Village Square (☎932-4845). Right on the Village Square, a tasty and thrifty option. Delectable home-baked goods ($2.25 or less) and sandwiches ($4.50). Open daily 6:30am-9pm. ❶

🏔 OUTDOOR ACTIVITIES

WINTER SPORTS. Thirty-three lifts (15 of them high-speed), three glaciers, over 200 marked trails, a mile (1609m) of vertical drop, and unreal scenery makes **Whistler/Blackcomb** a top destination for snow enthusiasts. Parking and lift access for this behemoth are available at six points, but Whistler Creekside offers the shortest lines and the closest access for those coming from Vancouver. A **lift ticket** is good for both mountains and depending on the timing, costs between $112-141 for three days, with better deals for longer trips. (☎932-3434 or 800-766-0449.) A **Fresh Tracks** upgrade ($15), available every morning at 7am, provides a basic breakfast in the mountaintop lodge on Blackcomb along with the chance to begin skiing as soon as the ski patrol has finished avalanche control. **Cheap tickets** are often available at convenience stores in Vancouver, and rates are sometimes cheaper midweek and early or late in the season. While Whistler offers amazing alpine terrain and gorgeous bowls, most **snowboarders** prefer the younger Blackcomb for its windlips, natural quarter-pipes, and 16-acre terrain park. Endless **backcountry skiing** is accessible from resort lifts and in Garibaldi Park's **Diamond Head** area. Equipment rentals are available through Whistler-Blackcom and through Affinity Sports, located next to Moguls Coffee on the Village Square (☎932-6611).

 The BC Parks office in Alice Lake Park (see p. 265) has avalanche info. Avalanches kill people every year, and there are no patrols outside resort boundaries. Always file trip plans and stay within the limits of your experience.

SUMMER ACTIVITIES. While skiing is God in Whistler and lasts until August on the glaciers, life goes on in the summer as the **Whistler Gondola** continues to whisk sightseers to the top of the mountain, providing access to the resort's extensive **hiking trails** and **mountain bike park.** ($22 for hiking only, $32 for mountain bike park.) Hiking trails tend to be short dayhikes, with lengths ranging from 20min. to 5-6hr. and most trails taking less than an hour to complete. For more info on trails and the multitude of other options—such as rafting, fishing, kayaking, off-road tours, mountain climbing, and horseback riding—that make Whistler/Blackcomb famous in the summer, check their web site at www.whistlerblackcomb.com or call the tourist info line (see **Tourist Office**, p. 266).

NORTH OF WHISTLER

JOFFRE LAKES. For a fantastic **dayhike** 65km north of Whistler, climb to the **Joffre Lakes** along a popular 11km path round-trip that passes three glacially-fed lakes and affords spectacular views of **Joffre Peak** and **Slalok Mountain** (accessible in the summer months only, look for the entrance 32km north of Pemberton).

LILLOOET. Little traffic continues north along Hwy. 99 and the drive is eerily remote. **Lillooet** ("B.C's Little Nugget"), 135km north of Whistler, was originally Mile 0 of the historic **Cariboo Gold Rush Wagon Trail,** which led 100,000 gold-crazed miners north to Barkerville between 1862 and 1870. The town itself is small, but oozes with history. The **Chamber of Commerce** (☎256-4364; fax 256-4315) will help you find a place to crash. In the second weekend in June, the town celebrates its heritage during **Lillooet Days** with a host of events including a staged train robbery, mock trial, and execution.

FARTHER NORTH. From Lillooet, Hwy. 99 meanders north another 50km, snaking with the Fraser River until it meets Hwy. 97 11km north of **Cache Creek.** The weary can break half-way for trout fishing and swimming in **Crown Lake** beneath the red limestone cliffs of **Marble Canyon Provincial Park ❶** (camping $12).

VANCOUVER ISLAND

Vancouver Island stretches almost 500km along continental Canada's southwest coast and is one of only two points in Canada extending south of the 49th parallel. The Kwagiulth, Nootka, and Coastal Salish shared the island for thousands of years until Captain Cook's discovery of Nootka Sound in 1778 triggered European exploration and infiltration. The current culture of Vancouver Island bespeaks its hybrid heritage, presenting a curious blend of totems and afternoon teas. The cultural and administrative center is Victoria, BC's capital, on its southernmost tip.

The Trans-Canada (Hwy. 1) leads north from Victoria to Nanaimo, the transportation hub of the island's central region. Once you get out of Victoria and Nanaimo, wilderness takes over and towns shrink in size, creating a haven for hikers, kayakers, and mountaineers. Pacific Rim National Park, on the island's west coast, offers some of the most rugged and outstanding hiking in North America. On the northern third of the island, crumpets give way to clamburgers, and 4x4 pickups and logging caravans prowl dirt roads.

VICTORIA ☎250

Although many tourist operations would have you believe that Victoria fell off Great Britain in a neat little chunk, its high tea tradition actually began in the 1950s to draw American tourists. Before the invasion of tea, Fort Victoria, founded in 1843, was a fur trading post and supply center for the Hudson Bay Company. But the discovery of gold in the Fraser River Canyon pushed it into the fast lane in 1858, bringing international trade and the requisite frontier bars and brothels. The government soon followed. Victoria became the capital in 1868.

Clean, polite, and tourist-friendly, Victoria is a homier alternative to cosmopolitan Vancouver. Its namesake British monarch and her era of morals and furniture aside, Victoria is a city of diverse origins and interests. Galleries selling native arts operate alongside new-age bookstores, tourist traps, and pawn shops. Double-decker bus tours motor by English pubs while bike-taxis pedal past the markets, museums, and stores that make up the rest of downtown. Victoria also lies within easy striking distance of the rest of Vancouver Island's "outdoor paradise."

▐ TRANSPORTATION

The **Trans-Canada Hwy. (Hwy. 1)** runs north to Nanaimo, where it becomes **Hwy. 19,** stretching north to the rest of Vancouver Island. **The West Coast Hwy. (Hwy. 14)**

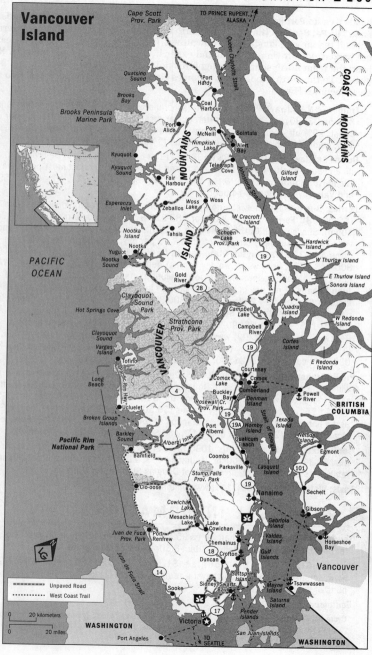

Vancouver Island

PACIFIC OCEAN

BRITISH COLUMBIA

Unpaved Road
West Coast Trail

0   20 kilometers
0   20 miles

WASHINGTON

Cape Scott Prov. Park
TO PRINCE RUPERT, ALASKA
Queen Charlotte Strait

Quatsino Sound
Port Hardy
Brooks Bay
Coal Harbour
Brooks Peninsula Marine Park
Port Alice
Port McNeill
Sointula
Alert Bay
COAST MOUNTAINS

Nimpkish Lake
Kyuquot
Telegraph Cove
Kyuquot Sound
Gilford Island
Fair Harbour
MOUNTAINS
Esperanza Inlet
Woss Lake
Zeballos
Woss
Johnstone Strait
W Cracroft Island

Nootka Island
Tahsis
Schoen Lake Prov. Park
Sayward
Hardwick Island
Nootka
Yuquot
Nootka Sound
ISLAND
Gold River
W Thurlow Island
19
E Thurlow Island
Sonora Island

28
Island Hwy.

Clayoquot Sound Park
Campbell Lake
Quadra Island
W Redonda Island

Hot Springs Cove
Strathcona Prov. Park
Campbell River
19
Cortes Island
E Redonda Island

Clayoquot Sound
VANCOUVER
Vargas Island
Tofino
Courtenay
Comox
W Redonda Island

Long Beach
Pacific Rim Hwy.
Comox Lake
Cumberland
Denman Island
Powell River
BRITISH COLUMBIA

Ucluelet
4
Buckley Bay
Rosewall Cr. Prov. Park
19
Hornby Island
Texada Island

Broken Group Islands
Port Alberni
19A
Qualicum Beach
Nelson Island

Pacific Rim National Park
Barkley Sound
Alberni Inlet
Coombs
Lasqueti Island
Egmont

Bamfield
Parksville
Strait of Georgia
101

Clo-oose
Stump Falls Prov. Park
19
Nanaimo
Sechelt

Cowichan Lake
Gabriola Island
Gibsons

Mesachie Lake
Lake Cowichan
Valdes Island

Juan de Fuca Prov. Park
Port Renfrew
Chemainus
18
Crofton
Gulf Islands
Horseshoe Bay

14
Duncan
Saltspring Island
Vancouver

Sooke
Sidney
Swartz Bay
Mayne Island
Tsawwassen

17
Pender Islands
Saturna Island

Victoria
San Juan Islands

Juan de Fuca Strait
Port Angeles
TO SEATTLE
WASHINGTON

BRITISH COLUMBIA

heads west to **Port Renfrew** and the West Coast Trail unit of the **Pacific Rim National Park. The Pat Bay Hwy. (Hwy. 17)** runs north from Victoria to Swartz Bay ferry terminal and the airport, 30min. from downtown. Driving in Victoria is relatively easy, but **parking** downtown is difficult and expensive. Victoria surrounds the **Inner Harbour;** the main north-south thoroughfares downtown are **Government St.** and **Douglas St.** To the north, Douglas St. becomes Hwy. 1. **Blanshard St.,** one block to the east, becomes Hwy. 17.

Trains: E&N Railway, 450 Pandora St. (schedule ☎383-4324, general info and tickets 800-561-8630), near the Inner Harbour at the Johnson St. Bridge. 10% senior discount. 25% off when booked 7 days in advance. Daily service to **Courtenay** (4½hr.; $44, students with ISIC $29) and **Nanaimo** (2½hr.; $23, students with ISIC $15).

Buses: Laidlaw, 700 Douglas St. (☎385-4411 or 800-318-0818), at Belleville St., and its affiliates, **Pacific Coach Lines** and **Island Coach Lines,** connect most points on the island. To: **Nanaimo** (2½hr., 6 per day, $17.50), **Port Hardy** (9hr., 1-2 per day, $93), and **Vancouver** (3½hr., 8-14 per day, $29).

Ferries: Bus #70 runs between downtown and the Swartz Bay and Sidney ferry terminals ($2.50). **BC Ferries** (☎386-3431 or 888-223-3779; www.bcferries.com. Call 7am-10pm). Service to all **Gulf Islands** (see p. 276). Ferries depart **Swartz Bay** to Vancouver's **Tsawwassen** ferry terminal (1½hr.; 8-16 per day; $8-9.50, bikes $2.50, car and driver $24-34). **Washington State Ferries** (☎656-1831; in the US 206-464-6400 or 800-843-3779; www.wsdot.wa.gov/ferries) depart from **Sidney** to **Anacortes, WA.** A ticket to Anacortes allows free stopovers along the eastward route, including the **San Juan Islands** (2 per day in summer, 1 per day in winter; US$9, car with driver US$41). **Victoria Clipper,** 254 Belleville St. (☎800-888-2535; www.victoriaclipper.com), runs passenger ferries direct to **Seattle** (2-3hr.; 4 per day May-Sept., 1 per day Oct.-Apr.; US$79-125, seniors US$90-103, ages 1-11 $50-56). **Black Ball Transport,** 430 Belleville St. (☎386-2202; www.northolympic.com/coho), runs to **Port Angeles, WA** (1½hr.; 4 per day mid-May to mid-Oct., 2 per day Oct.-Dec. and mid-Mar. to mid-May; US$7.75, car and driver US$30, ages 5-11 US$4, bicycle US$3.50).

Public Transportation: BC Transit (☎382-6161; www.bctransit.com). City bus service with connections at the corner of Douglas and Yates St. Single-zone travel $1.75; multizone (north to Swartz Bay, Sidney, and the Butchart Gardens) $2.50; seniors $1.10 and $1.75; under 5 free. Get day passes ($5.50, seniors $4) and a free *Rider's Guide* at the library, from any driver, or with maps at **Tourism Victoria. Disability Services** for local transit (☎727-7811) is open M-Th and Su 7am-10pm, F-Sa 7am-midnight.

Car Rental: Island Auto Rentals, 1030 Yates St. (☎384-4881). Starting at $20 per day, plus $0.12 per km after 100km. Insurance $13. 21+. The big companies with comparable rates are located at the bottom of Douglas St. near the Museum.

Taxis: Victoria Taxi (☎383-7111; www.victoria-taxi.com).

🔢 PRACTICAL INFORMATION

Tourist Information: 812 Wharf St. (☎953-2033), at Government St. Also a Ticketmaster outlet. Open July-Aug. daily 8:30am-6:30pm; winter 9am-5pm.

Tours: Grayline, 700 Douglas St. (☎388-5248 or 800-663-8390; www.victoriatours.com). Runs several tours in double-decker buses through different parts of the city ($18-87).

Equipment Rental:

Cycle BC Rentals, 747 Douglas St. (☎885-2453; www.cyclebc.ca), guarantees the best prices in town. Bikes from $6 per hr., $19 per day; scooters $12, $45. Motorcycles available. Look for coupons at hostels and hotels. Open summer daily 9am-6:30pm, winter 9am-5pm.

Victory

♦▲ ACCOMMODATIONS
Cat's Meow, **6**
Ocean Island Backpackers Inn, **5**
Victoria Backpackers Hostel, **3**
Victoria Youth Hostel (HI), **7**

▲ CAMPING
Goldstream Provincial Park, **1**

TO 🌸
SOOKE (35km),
PORT RENFEW (80km),
NANAIMO (111km)

TO HWY. 17,
BUTCHART GARDENS
& ⓘ (20km), FERRY
TERMINAL (30km)

Burnside E. St.
Cecelia St.
Manchester St.
Lutland St.
Dunedin St.
Topaz St.
Quadra St.
Garbally St.
Queens St.
Nanaimo St.
Wark St.
Bridge St.
Gorge Rd. E
Market St.
Ellice St.
Hillside Ave.
Ross Hill St.
Dowler St.
Wark St.
David St.
Hillside Ave.
Douglas St.
King St.
Rock Bay Ave.
John St.
Bay St.
West-bourne St.
Pleasant St.
Turner St.
Bridge St.
Ludgate St.
Field St.
Blanshard

ESQUIMALT

Skinner St.
Galloping Goose Trail

Selkirk Water

Selkirk Trestle (footbridge)

Edward St.
Alston St.
Bay St.
Tyee Rd.
Pt. Ellice Bridge
Queens Ave.
Princess St.
Henry St.
Wilson St.
Pembroke St.
Pembroke St.

Upper Harbour

Store St.
Government St.
Discovery St.
Caledonia St.
Chatham St.
Herald St.

TO 2 (200m)

Sitkum St.
Esquimalt St.
Harbour Rd.
Saghalie
Cooperage Pl.

VICTORIA WEST

Kimta Rd.
Songhees Rd.

Johnson St. Bridge

E&N Railway Station
Pandora St.

CHINATOWN

Swift St.
Fisgard St.
North Park St.
Julia St.
Balmoral St.

MARKET SQ.
Johnson St.
Cormorant St.
Amelia St.
Mason St.

7 8
9

BASTION SQ.
Broad St.
Douglas St.
Yates St.
TO 6 (1km)

Inner Harbour

Trounce St.
View St.
Blanshard St.
Quadra St.

Langley St.
Fort St.

DOWNTOWN

Victoria Harbour

Wharf St.
Broughton St.

Courtney St.
Courtney St.
Library
10

Gordon St.
Humboldt St.

TO ART GALLERY
OF GREATER
VICTORIA (900m),
CRAGDARROCH
CASTLE (1km),
OAK BAY (8km)

ⓘ
Erie St.
Kingston St.
Montreal St.
Belleville St.
Cross St.
Pendray St.

Victoria Clipper
Ferry to
Seattle ⚓

Victoria Star
Ferry to
Bellingham
(seasonal) ⚓

Ferry to
Port Angeles
(seasonal) ⚓

Empress
Hotel

Pemberton St.
Pennell St.
Terr St.
Fairfield Rd.

Ontario St.
Oswego St.
Quebec St.
Parliament
Buildings

Kingston St.
Superior St.

Royal
British Columbia
Museum

Elliot

11

Montreal St.
Simcoe St.
Aimo Pl.
Michigan St.
Menzies St.
Government St.
Academy St.
Southgate St.
Humboldt St.
Convent Pl.

11
Superior St.

Michigan St.
Reindall St.
Croft St.
Simcoe St.
Powell St.
Heather St.
Young St.
Toronto St.
Douglas St.
Haywood St.

*Beacon
Hill
Park*

🍎 FOOD
Blue Fox Cafe, **10**
James Bay Tea Room, **11**
John's Place, **4**

🍺 NIGHTLIFE
Steamer's Public House, **8**
Spinnakers, **2**
Suze, **9**

0   200 meters
0   200 yards

Vancouver St.

BRITISH COLUMBIA

Harbour Rental, 811 Wharf St. (☎995-1211), opposite the visitors center. Rowboats and single kayaks $15 per hr., $49 per day; doubles $25, $69; canoes $19, $49. Open summer daily 10am-8pm; winter 9am-5pm.

Sports Rent, 1950 Government St. (☎385-7368), rents camping equipment. Sleeping bags from $9, tents from $15, packs from $12. Open Tu-Sa 9am-6pm, Su 10am-5pm, M 9:30am-5pm.

Laundromat and Showers: Oceanside Gifts, 102-812 Wharf St. (☎380-1777). Wash $1.25, dry $1. Showers $1 per 5min. Open daily 7am-10pm.

Emergency: ☎911.

Police: 850 Caledonia (☎995-7654), at Quadra St.

Crisis Line: ☎386-6323. 24hr.

Rape Crisis: ☎383-3232. 24hr.

Pharmacy: Shoppers Drug Mart, 1222 Douglas St. (☎381-4321). Open M-F 7am-8pm, Sa 9am-7pm, Su 9am-6pm.

Hospital: Royal Jubilee, 1900 Fort St. (☎370-8000).

Internet Access: $3 per hr. at the **library,** 735 Broughton St. (☎382-7241) at Courtney St. Open M, W, and F-Sa 9am-6pm, Tu and Th 9am-9pm.

Post Office: 621 Discovery St. (☎963-1350). Open M-F 8am-6pm. **Postal Code:** V8W 2L9.

🖪🖪 ACCOMMODATIONS AND CAMPING

Victoria has a plethora of budget accommodations. A number of flavorful hostels and B&B-hostel hybrids make a night in Victoria an altogether pleasant experience. More than a dozen campgrounds and RV parks lie in the greater Victoria area. It's wise to make reservations ahead of time in the summer.

🎐 Ocean Island Backpackers Inn, 791 Pandora St. (☎385-1788 or 888-888-4180), downtown. This colorful hostel boasts a better lounge than many clubs, tastier food than many restaurants, a fantastic staff, and accommodations comparable to many hotels. Undoubtedly one of the finest urban hostels in Canada. Laundry and e-mail. Limited parking, $5. 140 dorms, $17.25. Singles $23; doubles $40-50. ❶

The Cat's Meow, 1316 Grant St. (☎595-8878). Take bus #22 to Victoria High School at Fernwood and Grant St. 3 blocks from downtown. This mini-hostel earns its name with 12 quiet beds, friendly conversation, and 2 welcoming cats. Breakfast included. Coin-op laundry, free street parking, discounts on kayaking and whale watching. Dorms $18.50; private rooms $40-45. ❶

Victoria Backpackers Hostel, 1608 Quadra St. (☎386-4471), close to downtown. A funky old house with a small yard, lounge, and kitchen. Newly renovated dorms, lounge, and kitchen. Free linens, towels, and soap. Laundry $2. Dorms $15 or $40 for 3 nights; private rooms $45. ❶

Victoria Youth Hostel (HI), 516 Yates St. (☎385-4511), at Wharf St. downtown. Big and spotless barracks-style dorms. Foosball, pool, video games, TV room, and info desk. Kitchen, free linen. Storage $3 per week. Laundry $2, towel $0.50. Reception 24hr. Dorms July-Sept. $17.25, nonmembers $21.25; private rooms $39-45. ❶

Goldstream Provincial Park, 2930 Trans-Canada Hwy. (☎391-2300; reservations ☎800-689-9025), 20km northwest of Victoria. Riverside area with dayhikes and swimming. Toilets, firewood. Follow the trail on the other side of the highway to a railway trestle in the woods. Gates closed 11pm-7am. 167 gorgeous, gravelly sites, $19. ❶

Seattle

Vancouver

Skytrain

Burrard Inlet

First Narrows

Prospect Point

TO BC RAIL STATION (1km.)

Lions Gate Bridge

Lions Gate Bridge Rd.

Stanley Park

Stanley Park Dr.

Seawall Promenade

Brockton Point

Deadman's Island

Seawall Promenade

Brockton Oval

Vancouver Aquarium

Zoo

Malkin Bowl

Stanley Park Dr.

Pipeline Rd.

Beaver Lake

Coal Harbour

Lost Lagoon

Lost Lagoon Dr.

Lost Lagoon Rd.

1A 99

Georgia St.

Powell St.
Hastings St.
Pender St.
Jackson Ave.
Prior St. East

CHINA TOWN

Main St.
Columbia St.
Carrall St.
Abbott St.

GAS-TOWN

Waterfront Rd.

SeaBus Terminal
SeaBus

Canada Place

Waterfront

Canada Place

Coal Harbour Rd.

Pender St.

Cordova St.

Burrard

Granville

ROBSON

Public Library

Vancouver Art Gallery

YMCA

Stadium
Dunsmuir St.

Hastings St.
Pender St.
Georgia St.
DOWNTOWN
Smithe St.

Beatty St.
Cambie St.
Homer St.
Richards St.
Seymour St.
Granville Mall
Granville St.
Howe St.
Hornby St.
Burrard St.
Thurlow St.

Bute st.
Jervis St.
Robson St.
Haro St.
Barclay St.
Nelson St.
Pendrell St.
Comox St.
Denman St.
Gilford St.

WEST END

Broughton St.
Nicola St.
Cardero St.

Beach Ave.

Davie St.
Burnaby St.
Harwood St.
Pacific St.

Nelson Park

Bute st.

Aquatic Centre

Sunset Beach Park

Stadium

BC Place Stadium

Plaza of Nations

Science World

VIA Rail Station

Terminal Ave.
Mainland Ave.

Main

1A
99A

Main St.
Quebec St.
2nd Ave. W
4th Ave. W
6th Ave. W
Broadway W
10th Ave. W
12th Ave. W
14th Ave. W
16th Ave. W

Columbia St.
Yukona St.
Cambie St.
Ash St.
Heather St.
Willow St.
Laurel St.
Oak St.

6th Ave. W
9th Ave. W

Charleson St.

Charleson Park

False Creek

David Lam Park

YALETOWN

Pacific Blvd.

Cambie Bridge

False Creek Ferries

99

99

Hornby St.

Granville Bridge

Old Bridge St.

99

Granville Island

Public Market

Burrard Bridge

Granville Bridge

Laurel's Mill Rd.

False Creek Ferries

Vanier Park

Vancouver Museum and H. R. MacMillan Planetarium

Maritime Museum

English Bay

0   500 yards
0   500 meters

◘ FOOD

A diverse array of food awaits in Victoria, if you know where to go. Many **Government St.** and **Wharf St.** restaurants raise their prices for summer tourists. **Chinatown** extends from Fisgard and Government St. to the northwest. Coffee shops can be found on every corner. Cook St. Village, between McKenzie and Park Sts., offers an eclectic mix of creative restaurants. **Fisherman's Wharf**, at the end of Erie St., has the day's catch. For groceries, try **Thrifty Foods**, 475 Simcoe St., six blocks south of the Parliament Buildings. (☎544-1234. Open daily 8am-10pm.)

■ **John's Place,** 723 Pandora St. (☎389-0711), between Douglas and Blanshard St. Dishing up Canadian fare with a little Mediterranean flair and a Thai twist. Try your hand at an appallingly large breakfast in the presence of greatness (the walls of John's are adorned with the images and autographs of some of North America's finest athletes). Extra selections on Thai night (M) and perogie night (W). Open M-F 7am-10pm, Sa 8am-4pm and 5-10pm, Su 8am-4pm and 5-9pm. ❷

Blue Fox Cafe, 101-919 Fort St. (☎380-1683). Walk 3 blocks up Fort. St. from Douglas St. A local favorite. Breakfast all day, every day; specials until 11am for under $6. Try the "Bubble & Squeak," sautéed veggies and panfries drowned in cheese and baked ($7). Open M-F 7:30am-4pm, Sa 9am-4pm, Su 9am-3pm. ❶

James Bay Tea Room & Restaurant, 332 Menzies St. (☎382-8282) behind the Parliament Buildings. At James Bay, the sun never sets on the British Empire; a trip to Victoria is improper without a spot of tea. The sandwiches and pastries that accompany tea service ($7.25) or high tea on Sunday ($10.25) are a lower-key version of the archaic High Tea served at the Empress Hotel. Open M-Sa 7am-8pm, Su 8am-8pm. ❷

◉ SIGHTS

If you don't mind becoming one with the flocks of tourists heading to the shores of Victoria, wander along the **Inner Harbour.** You'll see boats come in and admire street performers on the Causeway as the sun sets behind neighboring islands.

■ **ROYAL BRITISH COLUMBIA MUSEUM.** This museum houses thorough exhibits on the biological, geological, and cultural history of the province. The First Nation exhibit features a totem room and an immense collection of traditional native art. The museum's **National Geographic IMAX Theater** runs the latest action documentaries on a six-story screen. **Thunderbird Park** and its many totems loom behind the museum and can be perused for free. (*675 Belleville St.* ☎*356-7226. Open daily 9am-5pm; IMAX 9am-9pm. $10; students, youths, and seniors $7; under 6 free. IMAX $10, seniors $8.50, youth $6.50, child $3.50. Combo prices available.*)

■ **BUTCHART GARDENS.** The elaborate and world-famous Butchart Gardens, founded by Robert P.'s cement-pouring fortune, sprawl across 50 acres 21km north of Victoria off Hwy. 17. Immaculate landscaping includes the magnificent **Sunken Garden** (a former limestone quarry), the Rose Garden, Japanese and Italian gardens, and fountains. The gardens sparkle with live entertainment and lights at night. Outstanding fireworks on Saturday evenings in July and August draw out the locals. (*Bus #75 Central Saanich runs from downtown at Douglas and Pandora. ($2.50, 1hr.) The Gray Line,* ☎*388-6539, runs a round-trip, direct package including admission ($42, youth $32, child $13.25; 35min. each way).* ☎*652-4422. Open daily July-Aug. 9am-10:30pm. $19.25, ages 13-17 $9.50, ages 5-12 $2, under 5 free.*)

BUTTERFLY GARDENS. Close to the Butchart Gardens, this enclosure devoted to winged insects is maintained at 20-28°C (80-85°F) and 80% relative humidity. Hundreds of specimens of over 35 species float around visitors' heads alongside (non-butterfly-eating) canaries, finches, and cockatiels, while caterpillars munch on the profusion of tropical plants thriving in the moist environment. The gardens successfully breed giant Atlas Moths, which, with a wingspan of up to 30cm (1 ft.), are the largest species of moth in the world. Perhaps most appealing to the eye, however, are the iridescent hues of the famous morpho butterflies that live the good life in the gardens. *(1461 Benvenuto Ave. Open Mar.-Oct. daily 9am-5pm. $8, seniors and students $7, ages 5-12 $4.50. 10% AAA or family discount.)*

VANCOUVER ISLAND BREWERY. After a few days of hiking, biking, and museum-visiting, unwind with a tour of the **Vancouver Island Brewery.** The 1hr. tour has 20min. of touring and 40min. of drinking. *(2330 Government St. ☎361-0007. 19+. Tours F-Sa 3pm. $6 covers five 4 oz. samples.)*

🎭 ENTERTAINMENT

The **Victoria Symphony Society,** 846 Broughton St. (☎385-6515), performs regularly under conductor Kaees Bakels. The highlight of the season is the **Symphony Splash,** which is played on a barge in Inner Harbour. The performance concludes with fireworks and usually draws 50,000 listeners (first Su in Aug.; free). For the last 10 days of June, Victoria bops to **JazzFest.** (☎388-4423. $35 per day, or 5-day pass $90.) **Folkfest** hosts multicultural entertainment with food and dancing at Market Square and Ship's Point. (☎388-4728. Late June to early July. $2-12.)

   Cineplex Odeon, 780 Yates St. (☎383-0513), rolls out the reels of blockbuster hits every night with all tickets under $8. Around the corner is the **Famous Players** theater, which complements its list of current hits (☎381-9300). To experience the cheapest movies available, visit **The Roxy,** 2657 Quadra St., an old airplane hangar turned movie theatre. (☎382-3370. $5, seniors $2.50; Tu $2.50.) For off-beat and foreign films, head to the **University of Victoria's Cinecenta** in the Student Union. (☎721-8365. Bus #4, 26, 11, or 14. $6.75, seniors and students $4.75, Sa-Su matinees $3.75.) July and August bring **free outdoor screenings** of classic movies to the **Boardwalk Restaurant** at the Ocean Pointe Resort on Wednesday and Thursday at dusk. Those who wish can reserve at the restaurant and get a table at the front, a good meal (expensive), and free blankets (☎360-5889). The Ocean Pointe Resort is the first right after crossing the blue Johnson St. bridge. Parking and screen are around the back to the right. In June, **Phoenix Theaters** (☎721-8000) at UVIC, puts on term-time live theater performances. Victoria goes Elizabethan when the **Annual Shakespeare Festival** lands in the Inner Harbour. (☎360-0234. Mid-July to mid-Aug.)

🌙 NIGHTLIFE

English pubs and watering holes abound throughout town. The free weekly *Monday Magazine*, out on Wednesdays, lists who's playing where and is available at hostels, hotels, and most restaurants.

   Steamers Public House, 570 Yates St. (☎381-4340). Locals and visitors alike dance nightly to live music, from world-beat Celtic to funk. The best Su entertainment in town. Open stage M, jazz night Tu. Cover $3-5 at night, free M-Tu. Open Tu-Sa 11:30am-2am, Su 11:30am-midnight, M 11:30am-1am.

   Suze, 515 Yates St. (☎383-2829). Trendy lounge and restaurant serves creative pizzas ($11.50-13.50) and Asian-inspired items such as the popular pad thai ($9). Nightly martini specials. Open Su-W 5pm-midnight, Th-Sa 5pm-1am.

   Spinnakers Brew Pub, 308 Catherine St. (☎384-6613, office 384-0332). Take the Johnson St. bridge from downtown and walk 10min. down Esquimalt Rd., or stick to the waterfront and you'll walk right by it. The oldest brew pub in Canada is a great place to shoot pool and boasts the best view of the Inner Harbor. Open daily 11am-11pm.

⚑ OUTDOOR ACTIVITIES

The flowering oasis of **Beacon Hill Park,** off Douglas St. south of the Inner Harbour, pleases walkers, bikers, and the picnic-inclined; it borders the gorgeous Dallas Rd. scenic drive. The **Galloping Goose,** a 100km trail beginning in downtown Victoria and continuing to the west coast of Vancouver Island, is open to cyclists, pedestrians, and horses. Ask for a map, which includes Transit access info, at the Info Centre. The trail is a part of the **Trans-Canada Trail** (still in progress), which will be the longest recreational trail in the world. When it is finished, it will cover 16,000km and stretch from Coast to Coast.

The **beach** stretches along the southern edge of the city by Dallas St. **Willows Beach** at Oak Bay has particularly white sand—take Fort St. east, turn right on Oak Bay St., and follow to the end. Victoria is a hub for sailing, kayaking, and whale watching tours. The folks at **Westcoast Activities Unlimited,** 1140 Government St., will help you find somewhere or someone to help you do anything, free of charge. (☎412-0993. Open daily 8am-7:30pm.) **Ocean River Sports,** 1437 Store St., offers kayak rentals, tours, and lessons. (☎381-4233 or 800-909-4233. Open M-Th and Sa 9:30am-5:30pm, F 9:30am-8pm, Su 11am-5pm. Singles $42 per day, doubles $50. Multi-day discounts available.) Most whale watching companies give discounts for hostel guests. **Ocean Explorations,** 532 Broughton St., runs tours in very fast, very fun, very wet Zodiac raft-boats that visit resident pods of orcas in the area. (☎383-6722. Runs Apr.-Oct. 3hr. tours $69, hostelers and students $55, children $49, less in early season. Reservations recommended. Free pickup at hostels.)

▶ DAYTRIP FROM VICTORIA: SOOKE

About 35km west of Victoria on Hwy. 14. To find Hwy. 14, take Hwy. 1 north to the junction. To get to Phillips Rd. from the city, take bus #50 to the Western Exchange and transfer to #61. The potholes are located 5km north of Hwy. 14 on Sooke River Rd.

The **Sooke Region Museum,** 2070 Phillips Rd., just off the highway, houses a **visitors center** and delivers an excellent history of the area. (☎642-6351. Open daily July-Aug. 9am-6pm; Sept.-June Tu-Su 9am-5pm. Admission by donation.) The **Sooke Potholes** are a chain of deep swimming holes naturally carved out of the rock in the narrow Sooke River gorge. These popular and sun-warmed waters reputedly host some of the best cliff jumping in the area and draw people from all over. Access is through private property owned by **Deertrail Campground and Adventure Gateway ❶** and costs $10 per vehicle; bikes and hikers free. (☎382-3337. 63 sites, $15-20. Includes entrance fee.) North of Sooke, Hwy. 14 continues along the coast, stringing together two provincial parks and their rugged, beautiful beaches. **Juan de Fuca Provincial Park** is home to China Beach and Loss Creek. **China Beach campground ❶** has 78 drive-in sites. (☎800-689-9025. $12.) **French Beach Provincial Park ❶** has tent sites. (☎391-2300. $12.) The **Juan de Fuca Marine Trail** starts at China Beach and heads 47km north to Botanical Beach at Port Renfrew. Trails connect beaches with the road, which is still far enough away to keep the seaside wild. Camping in wide open sites is free at the popular **Jordan River Recreation Area ❶,** 10min. past French Beach. The **Galloping Goose** bike and horse trail (see **Outdoor Activities,** above) passes a day-use area and trails heading east and west across the island's southern tip. The **Sooke River Flats Campsite ❶,** on Phillips Rd. past the museum, has open sites with a large picnic area, showers, toilets, and running water. On **All Sooke Day,** the third Saturday in July, the campsite hosts competitions centered around logging and family fun. (☎642-6076. Gates locked 11pm-7am. Sites $15; sani-dump $5 for non-guests.) Those in

BRITISH COLUMBIA

search of a roof over their heads will find their needs met within easy striking distance of the village at the **Pacific Trails Hostel ❶**, 8959 W Coast Rd., local name of Highway 14 (642-7007; www.pacifictrailshostel.com. $19.). Blend in with the locals at **Mom's Cafe ❷**, 2036 Shields Rd., in town. Driving from Victoria, turn right after the stoplight. (☎ 642-3314. Open summer daily 8am-9pm; winter Su-Th 8am-8pm, F-Sa 8am-9pm.)

NEAR VICTORIA: GULF ISLANDS

Midway between Vancouver and Victoria, the Gulf Islands are a peaceful retreat from urban hustle, and much less overrun by summer tourists than the nearby San Juan Islands. While the beaches are uniformly rocky with little sand, the islands are known for a contagiously relaxing lifestyle, as well as excellent kayaking and sailing opportunities. The chain's five main islands, **Galiano, Mayne, Pender, Salt Spring,** and **Saturna,** are visited by BC Ferries at least twice a day.

SALT SPRING ISLAND   ☎ 250

Named for a dozen brine springs discovered on its northern end, **Salt Spring** is the largest (185 sq. km) and most populous of the islands, with the widest range of activities and accommodations. Today, the island is a haven for artists whose medium of choice varies from clay to paint to metal to wood. Visitors will enjoy the vibrant downtown of Ganges, as well as peaceful natural areas in the southern regions of the island.

◼◼ ORIENTATION AND PRACTICAL INFORMATION. Life on Salt Spring Island is centered around the small village of **Ganges;** all of the listings below are in Ganges unless otherwise specified. **BC Ferries** (☎ 386-3431 or in BC 888-223-3779; www.bcferries.bc.ca), based on **Vancouver Island,** runs two ferries to Salt Spring. One departs **Crofton** and arrives in **Vesuvius** (12-15 times per day; $6 per person, cars $20 round-trip.) The other ferry leaves from **Swartz Bay** and arrives in **Fulford Harbour,** 14.5km south of Ganges (8 per day; $6 per person, cars $20 round-trip). Ferries from **Vancouver** and the other Gulf Islands dock at the **Long Harbor** wharf, 6km northeast of town. In summer, the **Gulf Island Water Taxi** connects Salt Spring Island to both Mayne and Galiano Islands. W and Sa. (☎ 537-2510. Runs June-Aug. Departs W and Sa 9am, returns 4:40pm. $15 round-trip, bikes free.) The **Info Centre,** 121 Lower Ganges Rd., will help travelers find a place to stay. (☎ 537-5252. Open July-Aug. daily 9am-6pm; call for winter hours.) **Silver Shadow Taxi** (☎ 537-3030) tends to the carless. **Marine Drive Car Rentals,** 124 Upper Ganges (☎ 537-6409), next to **Moby's** (see **Food,** below), rents vehicles starting at $50 per day. The **Bicycle Shop,** 131 McPhillips Ave., rents bikes. (☎ 537-1544. $5 per hr., $20 per 24hr. Open Tu-F 9am-5pm, Sa 10am-4pm.) **New Wave Laundry,** 124 Upper Ganges Rd., is next to Moby's Marine Pub. (☎ 537-2500. Wash $2.50, dry $0.25 per 8min. Open M and Th 8am-8pm, Tu-W 8am-6pm, F 10am-6pm, Sa and Su 9am-6pm. Other services include: **public showers,** beneath Moby's ($1 per 5min.); **Pharmasave,** 104 Lower Ganges Rd. (☎ 537-5534; open M-Sa 9am-6pm, Su 11am-5pm); **emergency,** ☎ 911; **Internet access** at **Corlnternet Cafe,** 134 McPhillips Ave. (☎ 537-9932; $1 per 15min., youths and seniors $0.50 per 15min.; open Tu-Th 1-8pm, F-Su noon-5pm) or **Salt Spring Books,** 104 McPhillips Ave. (☎ 537-2812; $0.10 per min.; open M-Sa 8:30am-6pm, Su 9:30am-6pm in summer, and M-Sa 8:30am-5:30pm, Su 9:30am-5pm in winter); **police** (☎ 537-5555), on Lower Granges Rd., on the outskirts of town; and the **post office,** 109 Purvis Ln., in the plaza downtown (☎ 537-2321. Open M-F 8:30am-5:30pm, Sa 8am-noon.) **Postal Code:** V8K 2P1.

ⒽⒾ ACCOMMODATIONS AND FOOD. Salt Spring offers a wealth of both food and B&Bs (from $70) despite its small size. The least expensive beds on the island are 8km south of Ganges in the **Salt Spring Island Hostel (HI) ❶**, 640 Cusheon Lake Rd.—look for the tree-shaped sign that says "Forest Retreat." In addition to three standard dorms in the lodge, the hostel's 10 acres also hide 3 tepees that sleep 3 and 2 hand-crafted **treehouses** that sleep 2-4. Treehouses are wildly popular and reservations are essential. The sparkling clean outdoor composting toilet is brand new. (☎537-4149. Rent bikes from $15 per day, scooters from $20 per 2hr. Linens $2. Open Mar. 15-Oct 15. Tepees $17; dorms $17, nonmembers $20; doubles $40-60; treehouse double $60, nonmembers $70. MC only.) Island bikers will love the overwhelming breakfast at the **Wisteria Guest House ❸**, 268 Park Dr., a short walk from the village. (☎537-5899. Singles $60, doubles $75.)

◪Ruckle Provincial Park ❶, 23.5km southeast of Ganges, offers some of the best oceanside campsites in British Columbia. Its 78 walk-in sites on the unsheltered Beaver Point overlook the ocean. 8 RV sites are also available. Gate closed 11pm-7am. (☎391-2300 or 877-559-2115. Dry toilets, free firewood. Sites $12.)

If you want to cook up your own fresh halibut, red snapper, rock cod, or king salmon, check out **The Fishery,** 151 Lower Ganges Rd. (☎537-2457). For all other food needs, head to **Thrifty Foods,** 114 Purvis Ln. (☎537-1522. Open June-Sept. daily 8am-9pm; Oct.-May daily 8am-8pm.) **Barb's Buns ❶**, 1-121 McPhillips, sells all kinds of baked goods, including spelt bread and delicious chocolate-hazelnut sticky buns ($2.75). Vegetarians will dig the $5 sandwiches. (☎537-4491. Open in summer M-Sa 6:30am-6pm; winter M-Sa 7am-5:30pm.) The **Tree House Cafe ❶**, 106 Purvis Ln., delivers interesting and tasty sandwiches ($5-7) in the shade of an old plum tree and has open-mic Thursdays (7pm) in addition to live music every night in summer. (☎537-5379. Kitchen open daily 8am-9:30pm. 10% HI discount.)

◪ SIGHTS. Salt Spring Island is perhaps best known for its resident artists. A self-guided **studio tour** introduces visitors to the residences of 36 artisans around the island; pick up a brochure at the visitors center (see **Tourist Information,** p. 276). The century-old **Fall Fair** (☎537-8840), held the 2nd weekend of September, draws farmers from all over the islands to display their produce, animals, and crafts with pride. The **Saturday Market** is a smaller version of the fall fair held in downtown's **Centennial Park** from Easter to Thanksgiving, and is a big deal on the island.

◪ OUTDOOR ACTIVITIES. Wallace Island and **Prevost Island** are two excellent kayaking daytrips from Salt Spring. **Sea Otter Kayaking,** on Ganges Harbor at the end of Rainbow Rd., rents boats to experienced paddlers only. They also run 2hr. introductory certification courses ($40), tours including 3hr. sunset ($35) and full-moon trips ($40), and multi-day excursions. (☎537-5678 or 877-537-5678. Singles $25 per 2hr., $55 per day; doubles $40, $80. 15% discount for hostel guests. Open in summer daily 9am-6pm; reservations preferred in winter.) Five of Salt Spring's 10 freshwater lakes are open for swimming. **Blackburn Lake,** 5km south of Ganges on Fulford-Ganges Rd., is one of the less crowded spots, and is clothing-optional. **Hiking** and **biking** options are limited on Salt Spring due to the small and residential nature of the islands. **Ruckle Provincial Park** offers 200 acres of partially settled land and an 11km waterfront trail. **Mt. Maxwell,** 11km southwest of Ganges on Cranberry Rd., offers a stunning vista, and you can drive to the top!

PACIFIC RIM NAT'L. PARK ☎ 250

The Pacific Rim National Park stretches along a 150km sliver of Vancouver Island's remote Pacific coast. The region's frequent downpours create a lush landscape rich in both marine and terrestrial life. Hard-core hikers trek through enormous old-growth red cedar trees and along rugged beach trails. Long beaches on

AT A GLANCE	
AREA: 193 sq. mi.	**HIGHLIGHTS:** Kayaking in the Broken Group, hiking the West Coast Trail.
CLIMATE: Cool foggy summers, mild wet winters; heavy precipitation.	**FEES AND RESERVATIONS:** $10-$20 camping fee; $95 West Coast Trail fee.
FEATURES: The West Coast Trail, Long Beach, the Broken Group Islands, Juan de Fuca Provincial Park.	**GATEWAYS:** Port Renfrew (p. 278), Bamfield (p. 280), and Tofino (p. 281).

the open ocean draw beachcombers, bathers, kayakers, and surfers year-round. Each spring, around 22,000 gray whales stream past the park. Orcas, sea lions, bald eagles, and black bears also frequent the area. From October to April, the Pacific Rim area receives 22 rain days per month. In the summer, however, only 10 in. fall each month (the average annual rainfall in the park is 122 in.). The park is comprised of three distinct geographic regions. The southern portion is home to the **West Coast Trail,** which connects the towns of Bamfield and Port Renfrew. The park's middle section—known as the **Broken Group Islands**—is comprised of roughly 100 islands in Barkley Sound. Finally, the northern region of the Park, known as **Long Beach,** is northwest of Barkley Sound. The villages of Ucluelet and Tofino are on the boundaries of this region. The park's administrative office is in Ucluelet, 2185 Ocean Terrace Rd. (☎726-7721).

WEST COAST TRAIL

A winding, 1½hr. drive up Hwy. 14 from Hwy. 1 near Victoria lands you in Port Renfrew. Spread out in the trees along a peaceful ocean inlet, this isolated coastal community of 400 people is the southern gateway to the world-famous ▨**West Coast Trail.** The other end of the trail lies 75km north, in Bamfield. Most hikers take 7 days to travel the entire length of the trail, but it can be done in less. The route weaves through primeval forests of giant red cedars and spruce, waterfalls, rocky slopes, and rugged beach. The uniqueness of the trail lies not

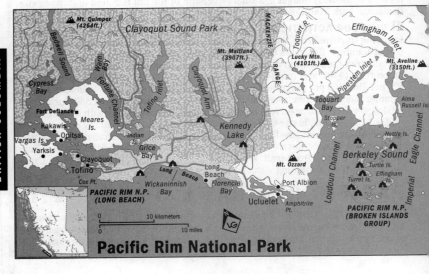

Pacific Rim National Park

only in its spectacular terrain, but also in the man-made scenery. Exciting challenges lie at every bend, but the combination of wet weather and slippery terrain over a long distance means that challenges can also be dangerous. Each year dozens of hikers are evacuated or rescued by park rangers. Most injuries are ankle or knee related, caused by rough and muddy forest trails; on the beach, hikers must be wary of surge channels. Only experienced backpackers should attempt the trail, and never alone. The trail is regulated by a strict and unforgiving quota system; reservations are necessary to hike it and can be made as early as two months prior to departure date. Campsites at the southern end tend to be crowded since they are fewer than in the northern section of the trail. Each day between May 1 and September 30, 52 hikers are allowed to begin the journey from the two trailheads, Pachena Bay in the north and Gordon River in the south (26 from each trailhead; 20 reserved and 6 wait-listed). The maximum group size is 10 people. For more info on the illustrious trek, call **Tourism** (☎800-435-5622) or **Parks Canada** (☎726-7721), or write to Box 280, Ucluelet, BC, V0R 3A0. Hikers pay about $120 per person for access to the trail (reservation fee $25, trail-use fee $70, ferry-crossing-fee $25). Seek out maps, information on the area, and registration info at one of the two **Trail Information Centres:** in **Port Renfrew** (☎647-5434), at the first right off Parkinson Rd. (Hwy. 14) once in "town"; or in **Pachena Bay** (☎728-3234), 5km south of Bamfield. (Both open daily May-Sept. 9am-5pm.) David Foster Wayne's *Blisters and Bliss* is an excellent guide to the trail ($11).

⊡ TRANSPORTATION. West Coast Trail Express runs daily from **Victoria** to **Port Renfrew** via the **Juan de Fuca** trailhead. (☎888-999-2288 or 477-8700; www.trailbus.com. Runs May-Sept.; 2¼hr., $35.) Buses also run from **Nanaimo** to **Bamfield** (3½hr., $55), **Bamfield** to **Port Renfrew** (3hr., $50), and **Port Renfrew** or **Banfield** to **Nitinat** (2hr., $35). Reservations are recommended, and they can be made for beaches and trailheads along the route from Victoria to Port Renfrew. The **Juan de Fuca Express** operates a water taxi between Port Renfrew and Bamfield. (☎888-755-6578 or 755-6578. 4-7 hr., $85.)

BRITISH COLUMBIA

FROM THE ROAD

CAMPING AND FOOD. Accommodations are limited outside the park campgrounds, but you can drive to Sooke, near Victoria on Hwy. 14, for numerous B&Bs. Near Port Renfrew and adjacent to the West Coast Trail registration office lies the **Pacheedaht Campground ❶**. (☎647-5521. Tent sites $10; RV sites $16; beach campers $8.) Laundry ($2) can be done at the **Port Renfrew Hotel ❷**. (☎647-0116. Singles from $39. Showers for non-guests $2 for 10min.) A new motel in town, the **West Coast Trail Motel ❸** on Parkinson Rd., provides hikers with a hot tub to soothe aching muscles. (☎647-5565. Singles $65; doubles $74.) On the other end of the West Coast Trail, in Bamfield, camp at the **Pachena Bay Campground ❶**, adjacent to the registration office. (☎728-1287. Sites $18; RV sites $20-25.) The **General Store** on the main road into town has basic groceries. (☎647-5587. Open daily 10am-8pm, winter 11am-5pm.) Almost all of the restaurants in Port Renfrew are inexpensive and offer the usual fare. The **Lighthouse Pub & Restaurant ❸** (☎647-5505), on Parkinson Rd., serves up tasty fish and chips.

OUTDOOR ACTIVITIES. If you only want to spend an afternoon roughing it, visit the gorgeous **Botanical Beach Provincial Park.** Visit at low tide or don't expect to see much (info centers will have tide charts). **Botanical Beach** forms one end of the 47km **Juan De Fuca Marine Trail,** connecting Port Renfrew with **Juan de Fuca Provincial Park** to the east. The trail can be traveled in 4-6 days. Compared to the West Coast Trail, the Juan de Fuca has more forest hiking and fewer opportunities for beach walks. The Juan de Fuca Trail is also cheaper than the West Coast Trail, with no user fee or registration fee. There are a number of **campsites ❶** along the way; overnight permits are required ($5 for a party of 4; self-register at trailheads). For more info on the trail and day-use information, look at the **map** in the Botanical Beach or China Beach parking lots for directions, or call ☎391-2300.

THE BROKEN GROUP

The **Broken Group**'s 100 islands stretch across Barkley Sound and make for some great sea kayaking, as well as expensive **scuba diving.** This is the wettest spot on the island; expect lots of liquid sunshine.

PRACTICAL INFORMATION. Driving hours of logging roads or traveling by water are the only two ways into **Bamfield.** Gravel roads wind toward Bamfield from **Hwy. 18** (west from Duncan) and from **Hwy. 4** (south from Port Alberni). Be sure to watch for logging trucks. **West Coast Trail Express** (see above) runs daily from **Victoria** to **Bamfield** (4½hr., $55) and from **Nanaimo** to **Bamfield** (3½hr., $55); reservations are recommended. Because Bamfield lies on two sides of an inlet, water transit is necessary to cross town. **Alberni Marine Transportation** (☎ 723-8313 or 800-663-7192; Apr.-Sept.) operates a passenger ferry from **Port Alberni** to **Bamfield** (4½hr., $23) and **Ucluelet** (4½hr., $25). Other services include: **emergency,** ☎ 911; **hospital,** ☎ 728-3312; and the **post office,** near the Bamfield Inn, by the General Store (open M-F 8:30am-5pm). **Postal Code:** V0R 1B0.

⌖▯ ACCOMMODATIONS AND FOOD. Accommodations are limited; motels and B&Bs are expensive (singles $50-180; doubles $70-180; the majority are at the higher end). **Marie's B&B ❸** is at 468 Pachena Rd. (☎ 728-3091. Singles $50; doubles $80. On the mainland, camping is the cheapest option; head to **Pachena Bay Campground ❶** (see above) for tree-rich sites just a short walk from the beach. (☎ 728-1287. Sites $24; sani-dump only $26; full RV sites $31.) Eight islands in the archipelago contain primitive campsites ($5 per person.) The **Tides and Trail Market,** 242 Frigate Rd. in Bamfield near the public dock, offers groceries, supplies, and an amazing selection of candy. (☎ 728-2000. Open daily 8am-8pm.)

▨ OUTDOOR ACTIVITIES. While the Nuu-cha-nulth have navigated these waters for centuries, the Sound can be dangerous to those with less experience. A maze of reefs and rocky islands, combined with large swells, tidal currents, and frigid waters, makes ocean travel in small craft hazardous (but adventuresome). **Alberni Marine Transport** (see **Practical Information,** above) and other operators transport from Ucluelet and Port Alberni to the Broken Group. (3 hr.; one per day M, W, F; $20.) For guided trips, contact **Broken Island Adventures** (☎ 888-728-6200). For kayak rentals, check with the **Bamfield Kayak Centre** (☎ 877-728-3535). Several short hiking trails pass through shore and forest at **Pachena Bay, Keeha Beach,** and the **Pachena Lighthouse.**

LONG BEACH

The northern third of Pacific Rim National Park begins where Hwy. 4 hits the west coast after a 1½hr. drive from Port Alberni. Ucluelet (yew-KLOO-let) remains a quiet fishing village until it floods with travelers every July and August. Tofino, with its predominantly surfer-dude populace, is an increasingly popular resort destination, attracting backpackers and wealthy weekend-warriors alike.

✴ ▮ ORIENTATION AND PRACTICAL INFORMATION

The two towns of Ucluelet and Tofino lie 40km apart at opposite ends of the **Pacific Rim Hwy.,** separated by the lovely and trail-laden Long Beach. **Chinook Charters** (☎ 725-3431) connects **Victoria** and **Nanaimo** with Tofino and Ucluelet through Port Alberni. Two buses leave daily in summer from **Victoria** to **Tofino** (7hr., $55) via **Ucluelet** (6½hr., $53). The **Long Beach Link** (☎ 726-7790) connects Tofino with **Long Beach** and Ucluelet in the summer (6 per day; $10 round-trip from either town to Long Beach, $12 round-trip between the two towns). **Lady Rose Marine Services** operates a passenger freighter in summer from Port Alberni to Ucluelet (☎ 723-8313 or 800-663-7192; 1 per day M, W, and F; leaves at 8am from Port Alberni and 2pm from Ucluelet; 5hr., $25). **Ucluelet Taxi** (☎ 726-4415) services both towns and everything in between. A trio of **Info Centres** guides visitors. The first is located where Hwy. 4 splits into a road to each town. (☎ 726-7289. Open Victoria Day to Labor Day daily 11am-7pm.) The Tofino **Info Centre** is at 351 Campbell St. (☎ 725-3414. Open July-Aug. daily 9am-5pm; winter hours sporadic.) Ucluelet's **Info Centre** is at 227 Main St. (☎726-4641. Generally open daily 10am-5pm; call for hours. Off-season weekends closed.) **Parks Canada Visitor Info** has two branches, one off the Pacific Rim Hwy. inside the park (☎726-4212; open mid-June to mid-Sept. daily 9:30am-5pm), and the other farther in at Wickaninnish Beach. (☎726-7721. Open year-round daily 10:30am-6pm.) The **CIBC Bank** is on 301 Campbell St. (**24hr. ATM**; no currency exchange. Open M-Th 10am-3pm, F 10am-4:30pm.) **Storm Light Marine Station**, 316 Main St., rents sleeping bags for $12 per day and tents for $15 per day. (☎725-3342. Open June-Oct. daily 9am-9pm, Nov.-May 10am-6pm). **Fiber Options**, at the corner of 4th and Campbell, rents bikes for $6 per hr. or $25 per day, credit card required. (☎725-2192. Open June-Sept. daily 9:30am-10pm, Oct.-May 10am-6pm.) For the **weather**, call ☎726-3415. Other services include: **police**, 400 Campbell St. (☎725-3242); **People's Drug Mart**, 460 Campbell St. (☎725-3101; open M-Sa 9.30am-5pm, Su 11am-5pm); and a **hospital**, 261 Neill St. (☎725-3212). Get **Internet access** at the **Blue Raven Coffee House and Cyber Cafe**, 1627 A Peninsula Rd., in Ucluelet. (☎726-7110. $2.50 per 20min. or $7 per hr. Open daily 7am-10pm.) In Tofino, head to **Caffe Vincente**, 441 Campbell St. (☎725-2599. $3.72 for 20 min. Open in summer 7am-6pm.) The **post office** is at 161 1st St., at Campbell. (☎725-3734. Open M-F 8:30am-5:30pm, Sa 9am-1pm.) **Postal Code:** V0R 2Z0.

🅿️🅘 ACCOMMODATIONS AND FOOD

Tofino is the place to be, but there are options in Ucluelet and outside the park. In general, there is no free camping, and in the summer both campsites and cheap motels fill up quickly. Reservations are a must after mid-March.

IN UCLUELET. Prices are steep, especially in the summer. Travelers without reservations might get shut out of reasonably priced accommodations and forced into a motel room (singles from $75). The Info Centre gives out a pamphlet listing the many **B&Bs** in town. **Radfords ❷**, 1983 Athlone St. (☎726-2662), off Norah St., is close to town. The owners rent two quaint singles ($40) and a double ($80, $15 per additional guest), and offer fresh muffins, fruit, and a view of the harbor. **Matterson House Restaurant ❹**, 1682 Peninsula Rd., has homemade Canadian fare. Locals love the $14 Matterson Chicken with raspberry cream sauce. (☎726-2200. Open daily 7:30am-9pm.) Taste the northwest in the $9 salmon burgers at **Blueberries Restaurant ❸**, 1627D Peninsula Rd. (☎726-7707. Open daily 7:30am-9:30pm.) For cheaper eats, head to **Roman's Restaurant ❶**, 6-1636 Peninsula Rd., in Davison Plaza. Deli-style subs ($6) and yummy pizza (from $12) are the main draws. (☎726-2888. Open M-F 11am-noon, Sa-Su 4pm-midnight.)

IN AND AROUND THE PARK. While there are a number of private **campgrounds** between the park and the towns, they average at least $22 to camp and $30 for RV sites. The ones on the Ucluelet side tend to be cheaper. The **Park Superintendent** (☎726-7721) can be contacted year-round for advance information. **Greenpoint Campground ❶**, 10 km north of the park info center, is the only campground in the park itself and is often full. Greenpoint has 94 regular sites and 20 walk-ins and is equipped with toilets and fire rings. Despite swarms of campers in the summer, it offers hedge-buffered privacy and great beach access. (Reservations essential; call ☎800-689-9025. Walk-in sites are un-reserveable, so arrive at 11am to nab a spot. Walk-in sites $14; drive-in sites $20.) **Ucluelet Campground ❶**, off Pacific Rim Hwy. in Ucluelet, offers sites in the open (better for sun than for privacy) with showers and toilets. (☎726-4355. Open Mar.-Oct. $23; full RV sites $29. Showers $2.) The **golf course** in the park often has private, showerless gravel sites ($15).

IN TOFINO. ▨**Whalers on the Point Guesthouse (HI) ❶**, 81 West St., voted the best hostel in Canada by HI, has room for 64. To get there, turn right on 1st St. from Campbell St. and then left on Main St. (follow to West St.). They offer free sauna, billiards, linen, and harborside views. Check inside for HI discounts around town. Internet $1 for 10min. (☎725-3443. Check-in 7am-2pm and 4-11pm. $22, nonmembers $24; private rooms $66, $70.) **Wind Rider Guesthouse ❶**, 231 Main St., is all female (except for kids under 12) and drug and alcohol free. A gleaming kitchen, jacuzzi, and TV room make this a welcoming haven. (☎725-3240. Check-in 3-6pm. Free linen. Dorms $25; private rooms from $60.) Shop for groceries at the **Co-op**, 140 1st St. (☎725-3226. Open M-Sa 9am-8pm, Su 10am-6pm.) **Salals Co-op ❶**, near 4th St. on Campbell, sells organic groceries and has an all-vegetarian menu that includes all-day breakfast ($4.50-10) and lunches for $6-8. (☎725-2728. Open M-Sa 10am-6pm, Su 1pm-6pm.) The **Common Loaf Bake Shop ❶**, 180 1st St., is the best place in Tofino to get a cup of coffee. Thai and Indian dinners are $7-9. (☎725-3915. Open in summer daily 8am-8:30pm; winter 8am-6pm.) The adjacent **Alleyway Cafe ❷**, 305 Campbell, has outdoor seating on driftwood benches. Breakfast is dished up all day until the place reopens as the festive **Costa Azul** with Mexican dinners for under $10. (☎725-3105. Open daily 9am-3pm and 5:30pm-9:30pm.)

OFF ISLAND. On Vargas Island, 20min. off Tofino, the **Vargas Island Inn ❷** rents guest rooms in a classy lodge and two beach cabins. (☎725-3309. Tent sites $15; hostel beds $30; private rooms from $40; cabins from $30.) The boat shuttle is free for guests, but hikers can pay $25 and hike to **free camping** at Ahous Bay (no facilities). For some out of the way R&R, try **Nielson Island Inn ❷**, the only establishment on 20-acre Nielson Island, a 5min. boat ride from Crab Dock. Enjoy the benefits of a small kitchen (the owner will cook dinner with your ingredients), a lush yard, and a trail around the island. (☎726-7968. Free pickup. Singles $35; doubles $50.)

◪ OUTDOOR ACTIVITIES

HIKING. Hiking is a highlight of the trip to the west side of the Island. The trails grow even more beautiful in the frequent rain and fog. The **Rainforest Centre**, 451 Main St. (☎725-2560), in Tofino, has assembled an excellent trail guide for Clayoquot Sound, Tofino, Ucluelet, the Pacific Rim, and Kennedy Lake (available by donation). Park passes cost $3 per 2hr. or $8 per day (available in all parking lots); seasonal passes are also available ($45). Long Beach is, fittingly, the longest beach on the island's west coast, and is the starting point for numerous hikes. The Parks **Canada Visitor Centre** and **Info Centres** (see **Orientation and Practical Information**, p. 281) provide free maps of nine hikes ranging from 100m to 5km in length. On the **Rainforest Trail** (two 1km loops), boardwalks off the Pacific Rim Hwy. lead through gigantic trees and fallen logs of old-growth rainforest. **Bog Trail** (1km) illuminates little-known details of one of the wettest, most intricate ecosystems in the park. You can even view tiny carnivorous plants. (Wheelchair accessible.)

SURFING AND KAYAKING. Exceptional **surf** breaks invitingly off **Long Beach** and **Cox Bay** (5km south of Tofino). These two coves funnel large and occasionally dangerous waves toward hordes of young diehards; just don't forget your wetsuit. **Storm Surf Shop** has locations in both Tofino and Ucluelet and rents everything you'll need. (In Tofino: 171 4th St., ☎725-3344. Full wetsuits $13 half-day, $20 full day; surfboard $15, $25.) It is possible to kayak to Meares Island and throughout the sound, although the trailhead is difficult to find. **Pacific Kayak**, at Jamie's Whale Station (see above), provides a map, has the best rates in town, and rents to experienced paddlers. (☎725-3232. Singles $40 per day, doubles $65; 4hr. guided tour $52; multi-day discounts.)

WHALE WATCHING. Every March and April, gray whales migrate past Clayoquot Sound north of Tofino. Six or seven stay at these feeding grounds during the summer. There are more tour companies than resident whales. **Jamie's Whale Station,** 606 Campbell St., just east of 4th St. in Tofino, runs smooth rides in large boats, but rough-riders choose Zodiacs to ride the swells at 30 knots. (☎725-3919 or 800-667-9913. Whale watching $80 per 3hr., students and seniors $70, youths $50; Zodiacs $59 per 2hr., students $53; bear watching $59, students and seniors $53, youths $45.) They also have an outlet in Ucluelet at the bottom of Main St.

HOT SPRINGS. Hot Springs Cove, 1hr. north of Tofino by boat, is one of the least crowded hot springs in all of British Columbia. The Matlahaw Water Taxi, operated by the Hesquiaht First Nation, makes a run or two each day to the cove. (☎670-1106. $35 per person one-way.) The springs are near an exceptionally quiet and lush **campground ❶**, and a footpath to more secluded beaches in the Maquinna Marine Park. (15 private sites, $20.) Seaside Adventures, at 300 Main St. in Tofino, makes two 6hr. trips leaving in the morning and whale watches on the way. All the whale watching companies have trips as well. (☎725-2292 or 888-332-4252. $90, students and seniors $80, children $60.)

UP ISLAND

To a Victorian, anything north of town constitutes being "up Island." 'Nuff said.

NANAIMO   ☎250

Primarily a ferry terminal stopover for travelers en route to the rainforests of northern and western Vancouver Island, Nanaimo (na-NYE-moe) appears along the highway as a strip of motels, gas stations, and chain stores. While the city contains several beaches and parks, the semi-urban setting lacks the natural splendor of Vancouver Island's more secluded locations. The silver lining of city life is Nanaimo's ridiculous annual bathtub boat race and legalized bungee jumping.

✴ 🛈 ORIENTATION AND PRACTICAL INFORMATION

Nanaimo lies on the east coast of Vancouver Island, 111km north of Victoria on the **Trans-Canada Hwy. (Hwy. 1),** and 391km south of **Port Hardy** via the **Island Hwy. (Hwy. 19).** Hwy. 1 turns into **Nicol St.** and **Terminal Ave.** in Nanaimo before becoming Hwy. 19A. **Nanaimo Parkway** (Hwy. 19) circumvents the town.

Trains: VIA Rail, 321 Selby St. (☎800-561-8630). To **Victoria** (1 per day, $20).

Buses: Laidlaw (☎753-4371), at Comox Rd. and Terminal Ave., behind Howard Johnson Inn. To: **Port Hardy** (7½hr., 1-2 per day, $82.50); **Tofino** and **Ucluelet** (4hr., 2 per day, $33); and **Victoria** (2¼hr., 6 per day, $20).

Ferries: BC Ferries (☎753-1261 or 888-223-3779), at the northern end of Stewart Ave., 2km north of downtown. To Vancouver's **Horseshoe Bay** (1½hr.; 8 times per day; $8-9.50, car $24-34) and **Tsawwassen** terminals (2hr.; 4-8 per day; $9, car $30-32). The **Scenic Ferry** (☎753-5141) runs from the Maffeo-Sutton Park in downtown to Newcastle Island just offshore (on the hr. 10am-6pm; $5). No vehicles are permitted on the island and the passenger ferry runs only in summer months.

Car Rental: Rent-A-Wreck, 227 Terminal Ave. S (☎753-6461). From $33 per day plus $0.16 per km after 150km. Must be 21+ with major credit card. Free pickup. Open M-F 8am-6pm, Sa 9am-4pm, Su 10am-4pm.

Visitor Info: 2290 Bowen Rd. (☎ 756-0106), west of downtown. Head south from Terminal Ave. on Comox Rd., which becomes Bowen Rd., or go north from Hwy. 19 on Northfield Rd. Open in summer daily 8am-7pm, winter 9am-5pm.

Laundromat: 702 Nicol St. (☎ 753-9922), at Robins Rd. in Payless Gas Station. $2.50 per load. Open 24hr.

Equipment Rental: Chain Reaction, in The Realm at 2 Commercial St. (☎ 754-3309), rents bikes and in-line skates. Bikes $20 per day, $10 for Nicol St. Hostel Guests; $35 per week. In-line skates $15 per day. Open M-Sa 9:30am-6pm.)

Emergency: ☎ 911.

Police: 303 Prideaux St. (☎ 754-2345), at Fitzwilliam St.

Crisis Line: ☎ 754-4447. 24hr.

Pharmacy: London Drugs, 650 Terminal Ave. S (☎ 753-5566), in Harbour Park Mall. Open M-Sa 9am-10pm, Su 10am-8pm.

Hospital: Nanaimo Regional General Hospital, 1200 Dufferin Crescent (☎ 754-2141). Open 24hr.

Internet: Free at **Literacy Nanaimo**, 19 Commercial St. (754-8988). Open M-F 9am-4pm, Sa 10am-4pm. A visitor's Internet pass is $5 at the **library,** 90 Commercial St. (☎ 753-1154.) Open M-F 10am-8pm, Sa 10am-5pm, Su noon-4pm.

Post Office: 650 Terminal Ave. S (☎ 741-1829), in Harbour Park Mall. Open M-F 8:30am-5pm. **Postal Code:** V9R 5J9

▌ ACCOMMODATIONS AND CAMPING

Travelers should never be at a loss for a room in Nanaimo. Cheap motels are packed in like sardines along the main drag.

Nicol St. Hostel, 65 Nicol St. (☎ 753-1188). A quick walk from the ferry, bus station, or downtown. Lots of freebies: parking, linens, and Internet are just a few. Living room, small tidy kitchen, and laundry facilities. 25 beds; tent sites and ocean views in backyard. Reservations recommended. Dorms $17; doubles $34; sites $10 per person. ❶

Cosmic Cow Guesthouse, 1922 Wilkinson Rd. (754-7150), is a hop, skip, and a jump from the Nanaimo River, 10km south of Nanaimo. From downtown Nanaimo, head south on Hwy. 1 & Nanaimo Pkwy. (#19). Take a left (east) on Cedar Rd. and make a right turn onto Wilkinson Rd. before the bridge. This quiet farmhouse retreat offers solitude, nature trails, bonfires, and free breakfast. Dorms $18, cabins $20. ❶

Living Forest Oceanside Campground, 6 Maki Rd. (☎ 755-1755), 3km southwest of downtown. 193 large, spacious sites; several amid cedars overlooking the ocean. Clean bathrooms. Sites $17-19; full RV sites $20-23. Showers $1 per 5min. ❶

▌ FOOD

The highway attracts dives and fast-food joints, many open late or 24hr. Get groceries from **Thrifty Foods** in the Harbour Park Mall. (☎ 754-6273. Open daily 8am-10pm.) The **Farmer's Market** runs on F (10am-2pm) and W (3pm-7pm) at the Pioneer Waterfront Plaza on Front St. in downtown Nanaimo.

The Dar, 347 Wesley St. (☎ 755-6524). Up Franklyn from City Hall, take a right on Wesley. A quiet respite from downtown, with tasty Greek and Indian cuisine. Open M-Sa 10am-midnight, Su 4pm-midnight. 15% discount for Nicol St. Hostel guests. ❷

Gina's Mexican Cafe, 47 Skinner St. (☎ 753-5411). A bright pink landmark on Nanaimo's skyline, Gina's offers unique Mexican fare at a great price with stellar service. Experiment with creative items like the Don Juan, a veggie and cheese omelet in a grilled tortilla ($8). Vegetarian options are plentiful, and the margaritas are stellar. Open M-Th 11am-9pm, F 11am-10pm, Sa noon-10pm, Su noon-8pm. ❷

BRITISH COLUMBIA

NANAIMO BARS were once sent in care packages from the United Kingdom to hard-working sons in Nanaimo coal mines. **Layer 1:** ½ cup butter, ¼ cup white sugar, 1 egg, 1 tsp. vanilla, 1 tbsp. cocoa, 2 cups graham cracker crumbs, 1 cup unsweetend coconut, ½ cup walnut pieces. Combine butter, sugar, egg, vanilla, and cocoa in the top of a double boiler, over medium heat, and stir until slightly thickened. Combine crumbs and coconut in a bowl, then pour the hot mixture over top. Stir, and then press into the bottom of a shallow 6x9 in. rectangular pan. Refrigerate. **Layer 2:** 2 tbsp. custard powder, 2 cups icing sugar, ¼ cup soft butter, 3 tbsp. milk. Blend the butter, sugar, milk, and powder until smooth. Spread over first layer. **Layer 3:** 5oz. semi sweet chocolate, 1 tbsp. butter. Melt chocolate and butter in double boiler. Spread the chocolate over layer 2. Chill.

Yum. Heart attack in a dish—a worthy claim to fame for a small town.

👁 SIGHTS AND EVENTS

SIGHTS. The **Nanaimo District Museum,** 100 Cameron Rd., pays tribute to Nanaimo's First Nation communities with an interactive exhibit on the Snuneymuxw (SNOO-ne-moo) and a section on the coal mining origins of the town. (☎753-1821. Open in summer daily 9am-5pm, in winter Tu-Sa 9am-5pm. $2, students and seniors $1.75, under 12 $0.75.) The **Bastion** up the street was a Hudson's Bay Company fur-trading fort, and it fires a cannon every weekday at noon. (Open July-Sept. W-M 10am-4:30pm. Free.)

EVENTS. The multi-day **Marine Festival** is held the last weekend in July, with many events leading up to the actual festival. Highlights include the **Bathtub Race,** in which contestants race tiny boats built around porcelain tubs with monster outboards from Nanaimo harbor, around Entrance and Winchelsea Islands, and finish at Departure Bay. Officials hand out prizes to everyone who makes it, and they present the "Silver Plunger" to the first tub to sink. The organizer of this bizarre and beloved event is the **Royal Nanaimo Bathtub Society** (☎753-7223).

⚡ OUTDOOR ACTIVITIES

BUNGEE JUMPING. Adrenaline-junkies from all over the continent make a pilgrimage to the **Bungy Zone,** 35 Nanaimo River Rd., the only legal bungee bridge in North America. To reach the Zone, take Hwy. 1 south to Nanaimo River Rd. and follow the signs, or take the free shuttle to and from Nanaimo. Plummet 42m (140 ft.) into a narrow gorge (water touches available); variations include a zipline, high-speed rappel, and the Swing. (☎716-7874 or 888-668-7874; nanaimo.ark.com/~bungy. $95, same-day jumps $35. 20% HI discount. **Campsites ❶** $10 per person.)

HIKING. The serene 🏝**Newcastle Island Provincial Park,** accessible only by boat, has 756 automobile-free acres filled with hiking trails, picnic spots, and campsites. (☎754-7893. **Scenic Ferries** run only in summmer, on the hr. 10am-6pm; $5.) The **Shoreline Trail** that traces the island's perimeter offers great vantage points of Departure Bay. **Petroglyph Provincial Park,** 3km south of town on Hwy. 1, protects carvings inscribed by Salish shamans. A menagerie of animals and mythical creatures decorates the soft sandstone.

WATER. The waters of **Departure Bay** wash onto a pleasant, pebbly beach in the north end of town on Departure Bay Rd., off Island Hwy. Jacques Cousteau called the waters around Nanaimo "The Emerald Sea," and they offer top diving opportunities. The **Nanaimo Dive Association** (☎ 729-2675) helps visitors find charters, lessons, or equipment. **The Kayak Shack,** 1840 Stewart Ave., near the ferry terminal, rents kayaks, canoes, and camping equipment. (☎ 753-3234. Singles and canoes $10 per hr., $40 overnight; doubles $15, $60.)

HORNBY ISLAND
☎ 250

In the 1960s, large numbers of draft-dodgers fled the US to settle peacefully on Hornby Island, halfway between Nanaimo and Campbell River. Today, hippie holdovers of all manners and origins and a similarly long-haired and laid-back younger generation mingle on the island with descendants of 19th-century pioneers. Low tide on Hornby uncovers over 300m of the finest sand in the strait of Georgia. **Tribune Bay,** at the end of Shields Rd., is the more crowded of the two beaches **(Li'l Tribune Bay,** next door, is clothing-optional). The alternative, **Whaling Station Bay,** has the same gentle sands and is about 5km farther north, off St. John's Point Rd. On the way there from Tribune Bay, Helliwell Rd. passes stunning **Helliwell Provincial Park,** where well-groomed trails lead through old-growth forest to bluffs overlooking the ocean.

■ ☷ ORIENTATION AND PRACTICAL INFORMATION. There are two main roads on Hornby: the coastal **Shingle Spit Rd.** (try saying *that* 10 times fast) and **Central Rd.,** which crosses the island from the end of Shingle Spit. The island has no public transit and is hard to cover without a bike or car. On-foot travelers have been known to ask friendly faces for a lift at Denman or on the ferry (*Let's Go* does not recommend hitchhiking). The **Laidlaw** (☎ 753-4371) bus has a flag stop at **Buckley Bay** on Hwy. 19, where the ferry docks. **BC Ferries** has sailings all day from **Buckley Bay** to **Denman** and from Denman to **Hornby.** To reach the Hornby ferry, follow Denman Rd. all the way to end, on the other side of the island. (☎ 335-0323; www.bcferries.com. $4.50-4.75 per adult; $15-17 with car.) The **visitors center** (☎ 335-0313; open daily 10am-3pm) and the **Hornby Island Off-Road Bike Shop** (☎ 335-0444; $8 per hr., $30 per day; children $5, $20; open daily 10am-5pm) are located in the island's **Ringside Market. Hornby Ocean Kayaks** transports kayaks to the calmest of seven beaches and provides guided tours, lessons, and rentals. (☎ 335-2726. Tours starting at $30; full-day $65. Rentals $24 for 4hr.; $40 per day.) The island's only **24hr. ATM** is at the **Hornby Island Resort** (See **Accommodations and Food,** below). The **post office** is also at the Ringside Market in the Co-op. (Open M-Sa 9:30am-4:30pm; closed 1-1:30pm.) **Postal Code:** V0R 1Z0.

▐▌◖◗ ACCOMMODATIONS AND FOOD. At the earthy heart of Hornby sits the grocery-bearing **Co-op** in the Ringside Market. (☎ 335-1121. Open daily 9am-6pm.) The colorful market, at the end of Central Rd. by Tribune Bay, is also home to artisan **gift shops,** a beach-gear store, and two budget- and vegetarian-friendly restaurants. Most **B&Bs ➍** cluster around the **Whaling Station, Galleon Beach, and Sandpiper Beach** areas and cost $65-175 per night, with the majority in the $80-90 range. The **Hornby Island Resort ➊,** right at the ferry docks, is a pub/restaurant/laundromat/hotel/campground. The fare at the resort's **Thatch Pub** is standard, but the view from the outdoor deck is not. The **Wheelhouse Restaurant ➋,** with ocean views from a shared deck, has breakfasts from $9 and burgers for $7-8.50. (☎ 335-0136. Pub open daily 11:30am-midnight; live jazz every F night at 7pm. Restaurant open daily 9:30am-9pm. Sites $20; RV sites $19. Jan.-Mar. sites $14. Private rooms from $75.) **Tribune Bay Campsite ➋,** on Shields Rd., offers 118 sites a quick walk from the island's popular beach. Showers, toilets, and playground. Reservations are necessary July-Aug. (☎ 335-2359. Sites $24, power $27, cyclists with tent $19.)

■ **FESTIVALS.** For one day in the first week of July, the **Hornby Festival** celebrates classical music with a small touch of the popular variety. In addition, island
residents offer a $15 walking tour of many local studios, homes, and galleries to
raise money for the festival. Call the festival office for info. (☎335-2734;
www.mars.ark.com/~festival. Performances $5-15, full pass $165.)

DENMAN ISLAND   ☎250

The Denman village center, perched above the Buckley Bay ferry terminal, offers
crucial amenities. **Denman Island General Merchants** houses the **visitors center** and
the **post office** (postal code V0R 1T0; open 8:30am-4:30pm M-Sa), and sells basic
groceries. (☎335-2293. Open summer M-Th 7am-9pm, F-Sa 7am-11pm, Su 9am-
9pm; winter hours shorter.) Next door, the **Cafe on the Rock** ❶ serves delicious
food at delicious prices. Full vegetarian breakfast $6, homemade pie $4, sandwiches $4. (☎335-2999. Open same hours as general store.) The ⬛**Denman Island
Guest House/Hostel** ❶, 3806 Denman Rd., has a super-relaxed family feel. Check
out the gargantuan and amazingly sweet-smelling composting toilet. Features a
kitchen, home-baked treats, and a hot tub. (☎335-2688; www.earthclubfac-
tory.com. $17. Bikes $10 per day.) You can pitch a tent at beach-side **Fillongley Provincial Park** ❶, just off Denman Rd., halfway to the Hornby Ferry. (☎335-2325.
Reservations recommended; call 800-689-9025. Pit toilets, water. $15.) You can
camp for free at **Sandy** ❶ or **Tree Island** ❶ at the north end of the island. To get
there, take a short hike along NW Rd. from the village center, make a left onto
Gladstone Way, and head north toward the island with all the trees. (No campfires;
access at low tide only.) The island's two lakes, **Graham Lake** and **Chickadee Lake,**
offer fine freshwater swimming.

COMOX VALLEY   ☎250

With fine hiking, fishing, and skiing, and the southern regions of Strathcona Provincial Park just a hike away, the tourist season never ends in this self-proclaimed
"Recreation Capital of Canada." The area's beaches, trails, extensive cave network, and forested swimming holes would take weeks to explore. Sheltering the
towns of Courtenay, Comox, and Cumberland, the Comox Valley boasts the highest concentration of artists in Canada and offers many free museums and galleries.
In addition, the 1989 discovery of the 80 million-year-old "Courtenay Elasmosaur,"
which swam in the valley back when the valley was a lake, has transformed the
region into a minor mecca of paleontology.

■ ■ **ORIENTATION AND PRACTICAL INFORMATION. Courtenay,** the largest
town in the Valley, lies 108km (1hr.) north of Nanaimo on the **Island Hwy.** (Hwy.
19). In Courtenay, the Island Hwy. heading north joins **Cliffe Ave.** before crossing
the river at 5th St., intersecting with **Comox Rd.,** and then once again heading north.
Laidlaw (☎334-2475) buses run from Courtenay at 2663 Kilpatrick and 27th St. by
the Driftwood Mall to **Nanaimo** (2hr., $20), **Port Hardy** (5hr., $64), and **Victoria** (5hr.,
$40). The **Comox Valley Transit System** connects the valley's three towns. (☎339-
5453. Buses run 6:40am-10:20pm. $1.25; seniors $1.) **BC Ferries** links Comox with
Powell River. (☎888-223-3779; www.bcferries.com. 1¼hr.; 4 per day; $8, car $22-25.)
The **visitors center,** 2040 Cliffe Ave., is in Courtenay. (☎334-3234. Open summer M-
F 9am-6pm, Sa-Su 9am-5pm; shorter hours in winter.) **Comox Valley Kayaks,** 2020
Cliffe Ave. beside the visitors center, rents, transports, and leads workshops and
full-moon paddles. (☎334-2628 or 888-545-5595; www.comoxvalley.com. Singles
$35 per day, doubles $50-63. Open summer daily 10am-6pm; by appointment in
winter.) Do **laundry** at **The Pink Elephant,** 339 6th St. (☎897-0167. Wash $1.75; dry

$0.25 for 5min. Open M-F 8:30am-7pm, Sa-Su 9am-7pm.) In an **emergency, call** ☎911 or the **police** at ☎338-1321. The **hospital** can be reached at ☎339-2242. For **weather**, call ☎339-5044. Get free **Internet access** at the **library**, on 6th St. next to Thrifty's. (☎338-1700. Open M-F 10am-8pm, Sa 10am-5pm.) The **post office** is at 333 Hunt Place. (☎334-4341. Open M-F 8:30am-5pm.) **Postal Code:** V9N 1G0.

⌂⌂ ACCOMMODATIONS AND FOOD. The **Comox Lake Hostel ❶**, 4787 Lake Trail Rd., about 8km from town, is within hiking distance of Strathcona Provincial Park. To get there, take 5th St. toward the mountains to Lake Trail Rd., turn west, and just keep going. Free linen, plus kitchen and laundry. Great local swimming. (☎338-1914. Beds $16; tent sites $10 per person.) The new **Courtenay Riverside Hostel ❶**, 1380 Cliffe Ave., provides beds right in town by the river. Private rooms are available. (☎334-1938. Linen, towels, laundry. Dorms $16. Winter ski-and-stay package $50.) The **Mt. Washington Guest House and Hostel ❷** offers rooming right by the ski resort. (898-8141. Hot tub, laundry, free linen. $17-20. Doubles $45-55.) Campers hit **Kin Beach ❶** campground, on Astra Rd. past the Air Force base in Comox. To get there, turn left at the four-way stop in front of the base, take your first right and follow it for 5min. (☎339-6365. Tennis, pit toilets, water. 18 wooded sites, $8.) Despite the trek 25km north from Courtenay, family-oriented **Miracle Beach ❶** on Miracle Beach Dr. is often full. (☎337-5720, reservations 800-689-9025. Sites $19. Showers.) **Comox Valley Farmers' Market** occurs three times per week at different locations: W at 4th St. and Duncan St., F at the Comox Marina, and Sa at the fairground on Headquarters Rd. (May-Sept. 9am-noon). Thaw a TV dinner from **Safeway** on 8th St. in Courtenay. (Open M-Sa 8am-9pm, Su 9am-9pm.) The surprisingly hip **▨Atlas Cafe ❶**, 250 6th St., serves delicious quesadillas ($5.75-7) and light entrees. (☎338-9838. Open Tu-Th and Sa-Su 8:45am-10pm, F 8:45am-11pm.) **Bar None Cafe**, 244 4th St. off Cliffe Ave. in Courtenay, stocks exceptional vegetarian fare. Open mic on Tu-F, 6-9pm. (☎334-3112. Open M-Sa 8am-7pm.)

◨ SIGHTS. The area's largest draw is the **Mt. Washington** ski area, on the edge of Strathcona Provincial Park (see p. 291). It's only a 30min. drive to the base of the lifts from Courtenay, so staying in a cheap motel is a viable way to avoid the mountain's stratospheric prices. The **Queneesh Gallery**, 3310 Comox Rd., displays the work of some of the finest traditional Salish and Kwakwaka'wakw carvers on northern Vancouver Island. (☎339-7702. Open daily 10am-5pm; Jan.-Feb. closed Su-M.) Inquire at the visitors center about other galleries. The **Cumberland Museum**, 2680 Dunsmuir Ave., displays exhibits on the coal-mining town that in 1920 was home to large Chinese and Japanese communities. (☎336-2445. Open daily 9am-5pm; Oct. to mid-May closed Su. Admission by donation.)

◪ OUTDOOR ACTIVITIES. The snowmelt-fed **Puntledge River** at **Stotan Falls**, a long stretch of shallow waters racing over flat rocks, is a great place for **swimming**; test the current and depths before wading or jumping. Coming from Courtenay on Lake Trail Rd., turn right at the stop sign onto the unmarked road at the first "hostel" sign. Take the next left at the logging road Duncan Bay Main, cross the pipeline, and then park on either side of the one-lane bridge. Comox Lake Hostel (see **Accommodations,** above) can provide a map. For longer trails through the woods, try breath-taking **Nymph Falls**, upriver. From Duncan Bay Main, go left on Forbidden Plateau Rd. to the "Nymph" sign. **▨Horne Lake Caves Provincial Park**, 55km south of Courtenay off the Island Hwy. on Horne Lake Rd., offers superb caving tours—a genuinely other-worldly experience—for beginners (1½hr., $15; 3hr., $39), and 5 and 7hr. tours involving crawlways, rappelling and the ethics of spelunking. (☎757-8687; reservations www.hornelake.com. $79-109. 15+, bring heavy, non-cotton clothing.) Hikers can explore two short, highly damaged caves for free. **Tiderunner Charters** (☎337-2253 or 334-7116) rents boat and rods.

BRITISH COLUMBIA

CAMPBELL RIVER
☎ **250**

A big rock covered with graffiti welcomes visitors to Campbell River, another of BC's many "Salmon Capitals of the World." Jacques Cousteau called Campbell River's incredible fishing and scuba diving "second only to the Red Sea." The number of gas stations and motels along the old Island Hwy. (Hwy. 19A) confirms Campbell River's role as the transportation hub of the island's north. It provides easy access to Strathcona Provincial Park, Port Hardy, and the Discovery Islands.

■ ⓘ **ORIENTATION AND PRACTICAL INFORMATION.** Campbell River lies 45km north of Courtenay on the **Island Hwy.** (Hwy. 19). **Laidlaw** (☎ 287-7151), at 13th and Cedar, sends buses to **Nanaimo** (4 per day, $24.75) and **Port Hardy** (1-2 per day, $58), as well as **Victoria** (4 per day, $44). **BC Ferries** (☎ 888-223-3779) runs to Quadra Island (all day; $4.50-4.75, cars $10.50-12, ages 5-11 $2.25-2.50). The **visitors center** is off the Island Hwy. near the Tyee Mall, adjacent to the Marina. (☎ 287-4636. Open summer daily 8am-6pm; winter M-F 9am-5pm.) Call ☎ 287-4463 for **weather,** and ☎ 911 in an **emergency.** The **police** can be reached at ☎ 286-6221, and a **crisis line** at ☎ 287-7743. The **hospital** is at 375 2nd Ave. (☎ 287-7111).

▐ ⓒ **ACCOMMODATIONS AND FOOD.** B&Bs ❹ in Campbell River tend to be a bit expensive (singles $45-70; doubles $60-90), but the Info Centre can help you find a bed to sleep in. The best camping near town is at **Quinsam Campground ❶,** in Elk Falls Provincial Park on Hwy. 28, with space among firs. (Pit toilets. 122 sites, $12.) The **Beehive Cafe ❷,** 921 Island Hwy., has a deck overlooking the water. Breakfast and lunch run $6 and up. For an amazing local treat, try the smoked salmon bagel sandwich. (☎ 286-6812. Open summer daily 6:30am-10pm; winter 7am-8pm.) Shop for honey at **Super Valu** in the Tyee Mall. (☎ 287-4410. Open daily 8:30am-9:30pm.) **Spice Island ❷,** 2269 Island Hwy., offers customized meat, seafood, or tofu dishes at 5 levels of spiciness. (☎ 923-0011. Open Tu-Sa 4:30pm-closing.) Sockeye, coho, pink, chum, and chinook **salmon** are hauled in by the boatload from the waters of the Campbell River. The savvy can reap the fruits of the sea from **Discovery Pier** in Campbell Harbour, and the unskilled can at least buy rich ice cream and frozen yogurt on the pier, which has an artificial reef built to attract fish. (Fishing $2; rod rentals $2.50 per hr., $6 per half-day.) Get a **fishing license** ($6-8 per day, salmon $6.50 extra) at the visitors center or any sports outfitter in town.

▣ ⓚ **SIGHTS AND OUTDOOR ACTIVITIES.** Tour the **Quinsam River Salmon Hatchery,** 4217 Argonaut Rd., and see a wealth of "natural" resources. The hatchery nurtures little fish to adolescence. (☎ 287-9564. Open daily 8am-4pm.) **Scuba** gear rentals can be pricey and require proper certification, but **Beaver Aquatics,** 760 Island Hwy., offers a nifty $25 **snorkeling** package that includes suit, mask, snorkel, and fins; they also have a $50 full dive package. (☎ 287-7652. Open M-Sa 9am-5pm, Su 10am-12pm.) Beaver only supplies equipment, so if you have charter needs, give a call during business hours to **Abyssal Charters** (☎ 285-2420) for some guided, bubble-blowing, spear-gunning good times.

QUADRA ISLAND

Quadra boasts pleasing landscapes that rival her southern Gulf Island cousins, a European history that is older than that of most settlements on Vancouver Island, and a thriving First Nation community around Cape Mudge. It is one of the world's more relaxing places. The ▨**Kwagiulth Museum and Cultural Centre,** at 37 Weeway Rd., in the village of Cape Mudge just south of Quathiaski Cove, houses a spectacular collection of potlatch regalia confiscated by the government early this century and not returned until as late as 1988. (☎ 285-3733; www.island.net/~kmccchin.

Open M-Sa 10am-4:30pm; in summer also Su noon-4:30pm. $3, seniors $2, children $1. Tours $1 extra.) Quadra is a 10min. ferry ride from Campbell River (see p. 290). **BC Ferries** sail to Quadra every hour on the half hour from Campbell River (see **Orientation,** above). **Quadra Credit Union** (☎285-3327; **24hr. ATM**) and a **visitors center** with maps of island trails and rental info await at the first corner of Harper Rd, across from **Quadra Foods,** which will satisfy your grocery needs and sell you a **fishing license.** (☎285-3391. Open daily 9am-8pm. Licenses $6-8 per day, $6.50 extra for salmon.) Call ☎911 or the **police** (☎285-3631) in an **emergency.** Travel- and world-weary sojourners will find a welcome place to relax at the ◼**Travellers' Rural Retreat ❶,** where remarkable hosts welcome you into their home for as long as you need. Ask for a tour of Jim's driftwood sculptures. (☎285-2477. Call for directions; pick-up available. $16.) Several minutes down Heriot Bay Rd. from the beauty of **Rebecca Spit Provincial Park** and **Heriot Bay,** the **We Wai Kai Campsite ❶** lies on the water. (☎285-3111. Toilets, water, laundry. Sites $15-17. Coin showers.) **Spirit of the West** rents kayaks and runs guided trips that explore Quadra Island's wildlife-rich shores and beyond. (☎800-307-3982; www.kayakingtours.com. Singles $40 per 8hr. day; doubles $55. Full-day tour $89, including a huge lunch; sunset tour $59 with snack; 4-day kayaking with killer whales $857.)

STRATHCONA PROVINCIAL PARK ☎250

Elk, deer, marmots, and wolves all inhabit Strathcona's over 2000 sq. km; it's one of the best-preserved wilderness areas on Vancouver Island and the oldest provincial park in BC. The park spans the land just west of the Comox Valley, reaching north to connect with Campbell River via Hwy. 28. It stretches from sea-level to the highest point on Vancouver Island, 2200m **Golden Hinde.**

◼◼ **ORIENTATION AND PRACTICAL INFORMATION.** The park is accessible from Courtenay or Campbell River. The two **BC Parks** offices are on **Buttle Lake** (open summer only F-Su 9am-4pm), on Hwy. 28 between Gold River and Campbell River, and **Mt. Washington/Forbidden Plateau,** outside Courtenay off Hwy. 19. For park info, contact the BC Parks District Manager (☎954-4600).

◼◼ **ACCOMMODATIONS AND CAMPING.** The two frontcountry **campgrounds,** with 161 sites between them, are Buttle Lake and Ralph River. Both are on the shores of Buttle Lake and accessible by **Hwy. 28** and secondary roads (follow the highway signs). **Buttle Lake ❶,** 50km from Campbell River (about 45min. of scenic, but winding driving), has comfortable sites, a playground, and sandy beaches on the lake (pit toilets, water; $15). Less crowded **Ralph River ❶,** 75km (1½hr. drive) west of Campbell River, provides convenient access to the park's best hiking trails ($12). Five smaller marine campsites are accessible only by trails (pick up a map at the park entrance). The **Ark Resort ❶,** 11000 Great Central Lake Rd., just west of Port Alberni off Hwy. 4, rents canoes for the 35km water journey to the Della Falls trailhead (see **Hiking,** below) or provides a water taxi for $85 per person round-trip. (☎723-2657. Sites $19; rooms $45.) For outfitting and outdoor guidance on the doorstep of the park, **Strathcona Park Lodge ❷,** 30km from Campbell River on Hwy. 28, offers equipment rental and experienced guides. The lodge has roomy lakefront houses and a dining hall that serves three meals a day. (☎286-3122. Single kayaks $9 per hr., $37 per day; doubles $14, $53; 17 ft. sailboats $20, $70. Dining hall 7am-9am, noon-2pm $10; 5:30-7pm $17; summer 6-9pm a la carte.)

◼ **HIKING.** The park offers a great variety of trails of all lengths and difficulties. Visitors who wish to explore Strathcona's **backcountry areas** must camp 1km from main roads and at least 30m away from water sources; campfires are discouraged.

Those entering the undeveloped areas of the park should notify park officials of their intended departure and return times and should be well equipped (maps and rain gear are essential). Be sure to check back in with wardens upon your return.

Karst Creek Trail (2km, 45min.). Leaves from the Karst Creek day-use area and passes limestone sinkholes and waterfalls. Easy.

Myra Falls Trail (1km, 20-40min.) starts 1km past Thelwood bridge at the south end of Buttle Lake at a signed parking area. The trail features a walk through old-growth forest and a steep hill with loose rock on the way to the immense, pounding falls. Moderate.

Phillips Ridge (12km round-trip, 7-8hr.). Trailhead at the parking lot just south of the campsite along the highway. The trail leads to Arnica Lake and wildflower-strewn alpine meadows, passing 2 waterfalls and ascending 700m along the way. Difficult.

Elk River Trail (11km one-way, 4-6hr.). This popular trail starts just before Drum Lakes along Hwy. 28; follow signs to trailhead on the left. A campsite at 9km has bear food caches. The trail gains 600m in elevation as it follows an old elk trail to Landslide Lake, where part of Mt. Colonel Foster fell into the water. Moderate.

Della Falls (16km one-way, 7hr.). Splendid in its scenery and remoteness, this trail is accessible only by boat from the west end of Great Central Lake and follows Drinkwater Creek to the base of big, beautiful Della Falls. Moderate.

🏂 **OUTDOOR ACTIVITIES.** Skiers and snowboarders hit the slopes just outside the park boundaries at **Mt. Washington** to take advantage of 10m of annual snowfall. The mountain is accessible from Courtenay; follow Cliffe St. to the end, take a right on 1st St., a left at the end of 1st, and follow signs. A few years ago, one of the nearby lodges actually caved in from too much snow, and lifts have been known to close on occasion because of excess precipitation. (☎338-1386, reservations 888-231-1499; www.mtwashington.ca. $44, over 65 and ages 13-18 $36, ages 7-12 $23, 6 and under free. Night skiing F-Sa 4:30-9pm. $6, 6 and under free.) A lift is open in the summer to satiate the appetites of vista-hungry bikers. ($10, youth and senior $8, under 6 free; with bike $15.) The mountain also offers 40km of cross-country and snowshoe trails; the lodge has rentals. (Alpine ski package $22; cross country $16; over 65 and ages 13-18 $12. Snowboards $36; snowshoes $9.)

THE PORT McNEILL AREA   ☎250

The protected waters and plentiful fish of Johnstone Strait provide a fine summer home for orca pods. Mainland and island settlements near Port McNeill provide fine quiet waterside trips. Sighting charters run $60 for 3-4hr., but lucky visitors can glimpse orcas from the ferry between Port McNeill, Sointula, and Alert Bay, or even from the shoreline. For good whale watching, head 25km south of Port McNeill to the boardwalk town of **Telegraph Cove.** Turn left south of town on the Island Hwy.; over the last 5km, it becomes an unpaved road. **North Island Kayaks,** in Port Hardy (see below), will drop off and pick up kayaks in the cove. (☎949-7707 or 877-949-7707. Kayaks $50 per day; doubles $70; daytrips $125.)

Tiny Cormorant Island and the town of **Alert Bay** is home to a fabulously rich repository of native culture. The cultural legacy of several groups of the **Kwakwaka'wakw** peoples (ka-kwak-QUEW-wak; formerly known as the Kwakiutl or Kwagiulth) sets the fishing village apart from its aquatourist siblings. By the Big House stands a 173 ft. totem pole, the largest in the world. Two kilometers north of the ferry terminal, the pole towers over the **U'mista Cultural Centre,** which houses an astonishing array of Kwakwaka'wakw artifacts repatriated decades after Canadian police pillaged a potlatch. *U'mista* means "the return of a loved one taken captive by raiding parties." (☎974-5403. Open daily 9am-5pm; winter M-F 9am-5pm.) **Sointula,** on the coast of Malcolm Island, is a modern artist and fishing community with Finnish roots known for its December Christmas bazaar.

⚑ PRACTICAL INFORMATION. Laidlaw (☎956-3556) runs one bus per day to **Port McNeill** from **Victoria** (8hr., $84.75). **BC Ferries** (☎956-4533 or 888-223-3779; www.bcferries.com) runs from Port McNeill to **Sointula** on Malcolm Island (25min.) and **Alert Bay** (45min.; 6 per day; round-trip $5.50-6, car $15). **Visitors centers** are stationed at 351 Shelley Crescent in Port McNeill (☎956-3131; open in summer daily 9am-5pm) and 118 Fir St. in Alert Bay (☎974-5024; open June-Sept. daily 9am-6pm). In an **emergency,** call ☎911. The **hospital** is at 2750 Kingcome Pl. (☎956-4461) in Port McNeill.

⚑☖ ACCOMMODATIONS AND FOOD. The **Sun Spirit Hostel and Guesthouse ❶**, 549 Fir St. in Alert Bay, is a welcome spot to play piano and whale watch from the living room. (☎974-2026. $17, cash or traveler's checks only.) Beautiful camping, with a view of the mainland coastal range, is available across the island at **Bere Point Regional Park ❶** near Sointula. (Pit toilets, no water. 12 sites, by donation.) The budget-mindful eschew island restaurants for the hardtack at **ShopRite Grocery,** 99 Fir St. (☎974-2777. Open M-Sa 9am-6pm, Su 10am-5pm.) The **Killer Whale Cafe ❸** in Telegraph Cove is all yellow cedar and stained glass. High prices and erratic service. (☎928-3155. Dinner from $11. Open daily 8am-2:30pm and 4-10pm.)

PORT HARDY   ☎250

Port Hardy, an idyllic logging and fishing community, is the southern terminus for the BC Ferries route up the Inside Passage. The northernmost major town on the island, it has a vested interest in tourism. You will be welcomed by a chainsaw-carved sign, erected for the 1500 passengers who sleepily disembark the ferry every other night. These transients join a surge of fishermen preparing for unpredictable fall fisheries on the west coast of BC and a growing indigenous population drawn from more remote towns for schooling and employment.

▤ TRANSPORTATION. Port Hardy, on Vancouver Island, is perched 36km north of Port McNeill and 238km (2½hr.) north of Campbell River on **Hwy. 19. Market St.** is the main drag, running through the shopping district and along a scenic seaside path. **Laidlaw** (☎949-7532), opposite the visitors center on Market St., runs to **Victoria** (8¾hr., $94.15) via **Nanaimo** (6hr., $83) each day at 9am and when the ferry arrives. **BC Ferries** (☎949-6722 or 888-223-3779; www.bcferries.com) depart 3km south of town at **Bear Cove,** for **Prince Rupert** (every other day June-Sept.; winter every Sa and 2nd W $53-106, car $124-218). The Discovery Coast Passage route between Port Hardy and **Bella Coola** runs from mid-June to mid-Sept. ($70-110, car $140-220). Book months ahead for cars. **North Island Taxi** (☎949-8800) services the ferry from all over town for $5.25 per person, $6.50 to the airport.

▣⚑ ORIENTATION AND PRACTICAL INFORMATION. To reach the **visitors center,** 7250 Market St., follow Hwy. 19 until the end and take a right on Market St. (☎949-7622. Open M-F 8:30am-6pm, Sa-Su 10am-5pm; winter M-F 8:30am-5pm.) The **Port Hardy Museum** (see **Sights and Outdoor Activities,** below) also has in-depth info on the region. The **CIBC bank,** 7085 Market St., has a **24hr. ATM.** (☎949-6333. Open M-Th 10am-4pm, F 10am-6pm.) **North Star Cycle and Sports,** at Market and Granville St., rents road bikes. (☎949-7221. $20 per day. Open daily 9:30am-6pm.) For all else, there's **Jim's Hardy Sports,** in the Thunderbird Mall on Granville St. (☎949-8382. Open M-Sa 9am-6pm.) Diving rentals can be found at **North Island Diving and Water Sports,**

at Market and Hastings St. (☎ 949-2664. Open Tu-Sa 10am-6pm; full setup $89.) Wash up at the **Shell Gas Station,** on Granville St. (☎ 949-2366. Wash $1.75; dry $0.25 per 7min. Open 24hr.) **Internet access** is $5 at the **library,** 7110 Market St. (☎ 949-6661. Open M, W, F noon-5pm and 7-9pm; Tu and Th noon-5pm). Other services include: **Police,** 7355 Columbia St. (☎ 949-6335); **crisis line,** ☎ 949-6033; and **hospital,** 9120 Granville St. (☎ 949-6161). The **postal code** is V0N 2P0.

▐ **FOOD.** Stock up on groceries before the long ferry ride or trip down the island at **Glenway Foods,** 8645 Granville St. (☎ 949-5758; open M-Sa 9am-9pm). The burger is this town's budget meal. One of the best is $6 at **I.V.'s Quarterdeck Pub ❶,** 6555 Hardy Bay Rd., on the fishing dock. Their great vegetarian fare is balanced by F prime rib night ($15 with all the trimmings) and $0.25 wings on W and Su. (☎ 949-6922. Open daily 11am-12:30pm.) The **Oceanside Restaurant & Pub ❶,** 6435 Hardy Bay Rd., just down from I.V.'s at the Glen Lyon Inn, has a terrific view and serves $0.25 wings on W and F. (☎ 949-7115. Open daily 6:30am-9pm.) Your best breakfast bet is at **Snuggles Restaurant ❶,** 4965 Byng Rd., by the Quatze River Campground. (☎ 949-7494. Full breakfast starting at $5. Open daily 7:30am-9:30pm.)

▐▟ **ACCOMMODATIONS AND CAMPING.** The visitors center will reserve B&B rooms for free. (☎ 949-7622. Call ahead on ferry nights.) The ▟**Dolphin House B&B ❸,** 297 Harbor Rd. in Coal Harbor, is a short excursion (20min.) from Port Hardy. This hidden gem offers incredible ocean views, an array of outdoor activities, and proximity to native villages. Take Island Hwy. 19 to Coal Harbor Rd., turn right at the coffee shop in town, and head past the whale bones. (☎ 949-7576. Free pickup from ferry, bus station, airport. Singles $50; doubles $60.) **This Old House ❶,** 8735 Hastings, is downtown by the bus station. They rent cozy rooms with balconies upstairs. Free linen, laundry. Backyard BBQ, shared bath. (☎ 949-8372. 5 hostel beds $20; singles $40; doubles $70.) The proprietors of **The Hudson's Home B&B ❸,** 9605 Scott St., provide all the TLC and custom breakfasts you can handle. Hot tub, Internet, and pickup and drop-off from the bus station. (☎ 949-5110. Singles $60; doubles $75; mention *Let's Go* and get 10% off.) **Bonita B&B ❸,** relatively new on the scene, offers guests privacy and their own sparkling kitchen to use. (☎ 949-6787. Singles $50; double $65-70.) Quiet, wooded sites at **Quatse River Campground ❶,** 8400 Byng Rd. (☎ 949-2395. toilets, laundry; $14, full RV sites $18. Free showers) are a 25min. walk from town but just minutes from **Snuggles Restaurant** (see **Food,** below). Internet access $1.50 per 15min. The camp shares space with a fish hatchery. (☎ 949-9022. Tours are best Sept.-Nov.) Sites amid an overgrown garden at **Wildwoods Campsite ❶** lie off the road to the ferry, a walk to the terminal, but a hike from town. (☎ 949-6753. Tent sites $7, RV sites $18.)

▐▟ **SIGHTS AND OUTDOOR ACTIVITIES.** The **Port Hardy Museum and Archives** is at 7110 Market St., beneath the library. The museum's sea-creature remnants, 19th-century Cape Scott pioneers' personal effects, 8000-year-old tools from Hardy Bay, and erudite curator merit a visit. (☎ 949-8143. Open M-Sa 10:30am-4:30pm; shortened hours in winter. Donation requested.) A 15min. drive from town brings picnickers to the hard sand of **Storey's Beach,** a good place to put in a kayak or stroll along the rocky shore. Turn left off the Island Hwy. when driving out of town onto Byng Rd. and then take a left on Beaver Harbour Rd. to the water. Nearby, the **Copper Maker,** 114 Copper Way, commissions some of the finest Kwakiutl carvers in the region. From Byng Rd., turn left onto Beaver Harbour Rd., right on Tsak'is Way, and right again. (☎ 949-8491. Call for hours.) Farther down Tsak'is Way, a ceremonial and community **bighouse** overlooks the sea from the heart of Fort Rupert village, a site inhabited by the Kwakiutl for thousands of years. **Petroglyphs** adorn rocks near **Fort Rupert;** ask at the museum for advice in locating them at low tide. At the north end of the village stands the decaying stone chimney of Fort Rupert, an outpost built in 1849 by the Hudson's Bay Company.

A map of logging roads from the visitors center will allow you to explore the **geological curiosities** of the region's limestone bedrock or just get out into the woods: Devil's Bath sinkhole, the Vanishing and Reappearing Rivers, and several spelunkable caves are all located toward **Port Alice** (40min. from town). **Odyssey Kayaking** can equip and transport you. (☎902-0565. Singles $35 per day; doubles $55. Must have one experienced paddler in your group.) They also offer guided day trips for $95, including a delicious lunch. The Port Hardy area is known for some of the world's best **cold-water diving. Sun Fun Divers** (☎956-2243; www.sunfundivers.com) rents gear ($60 first day, $25 second day), and runs half-day ($45) and full-day ($90) trips out of Port Hardy and Port McNeill.

INTERIOR BRITISH COLUMBIA

From the jagged snow-capped Rocky Mountains, the Fraser River courses and hurdles its way through 1300km of canyons and plateaus on its journey toward a land more arid than the Pacific. The sweeping agricultural basin in the middle of BC between the Rockies and the Coast Range mountains sees much more sun than the coast and is a vacation hot spot for city-slickers and backcountry adventurers alike. The Rockies form the boundary that was finally breached by rail lines to unite Canada, and the mountains still constitute a large part of western Canada's identity. Today they are home to hugely popular national parks and thousands of square kilometers of hiking, climbing, and camping. Bus and train routes cross the interior and pass by various means through the mountains.

FRASER RIVER CANYON

In 1808, Simon Fraser enlisted the help of native guides to make the perilous expedition down the river from Mt. Robson to Vancouver. Today's route from Cache Creek to Hope on the Trans-Canada Hwy. (Hwy. 1) makes his trailblazing seem like a distant dream. Up close, the canyon is a good place to feel small, with 200km of pounding rapids below and pine sprouting out of near-vertical rock walls above.

In quiet **Hope,** travelers will find a tranquil town despite its fame as the Chainsaw Carving Capital. Hope's location at the intersection of several highways ensures easy arrival and departure. The **Trans-Canada Hwy. (Hwy. 1)** originates in Vancouver, passes through Hope, and then bends north to Yale and eventually Cache Creek, where it meets the **Cariboo Hwy. (Hwy. 97;** see p. 325). **Hwy. 7** runs west along the north bank of the Fraser River to Vancouver's suburbs. **The Crowsnest Hwy. (Hwy. 3)** winds east through breathtaking country including Manning Provincial Park, through Kootenay Country to Nelson, and over Crowsnest Pass into Alberta. The **Coquihalla Hwy. (Hwy. 5)** is a new toll road ($10) running north to Kamloops, and preferred by most heading to the Rockies in a hurry—it's faster as long as the miles of grueling 8% grade don't get the best of the cars.

Southern
British Columbia

HOPE

☎ 604

Buses arrive in Hope at the **Greyhound** station, 677 Old Hope-Princeton Way, a hub for bus travel throughout the region. (☎ 869-5522. Open 7:30am-1pm, 2:10pm-2:40pm, and 4pm-9pm.) Buses run north on the Coquihalla to **Kamloops** (2½hr., 3 per day, $32), then east to **Banff** (10½hr., 3 per day, $94), **Calgary** (12hr., 3 per day, $112), and **Jasper** (8½hr., 2 per day, $87); north on Hwy. 1 along the Fraser Canyon to **Cache Creek** (2¾hr., 2 per day, $30); east on Hwy. 3 to **Penticton** (3½hr.; 2 per day, 1 on Sa; $37) and points east; and west to **Vancouver** (2½hr., 8 per day, $21). Many try and hitch north on Hwy. 1, where rides are reputedly easy to find (*Let's Go*, however, does not recommend hitchhiking). **Gardner Chev-Olds**, 945 Water Ave., rents cars. (☎ 869-9511. $40 per day, 7th day free. $0.13 per km after 100km. Must be 25+ with credit card. Open M-Sa 8am-6pm.) For biking, hiking, fishing, and hunting needs, stop by **Cheyenne Sporting Goods**, 267 Wallace St. (☎ 869-5062). The **Visitors Centre**, 919 Water Ave., provides the riveting, self-guided **Rambo Walking Tour** (*First Blood* was filmed here) in addition to sharing info on Fraser River Canyon and Manning Park. (☎ 869-2021 or 800-435-5622. Open M-F 9am-5pm.) Ask about the **Carving Walking Tour** through downtown, and make sure to take a break from the tour in Memorial Park, the city's pleasant green spot. The **police** are located at 690 Old Hope-Princeton Way (☎ 869-7750), and the **post office** at 777 Fraser St. **Postal Code:** V0X 1L0.

There's a motel on every corner downtown in Hope (singles $45-55). On the outskirts of town, **Holiday Motel ❸**, 63950 Old Yale Rd., offers an outdoor swimming pool, playground, volleyball court and fire-pit. (☎ 869-5352. Rooms with cable TV start at $40. Tent sites $15; RV sites $22; both include showers.) Campers can head for the big trees at the spacious **Coquihalla Campsite ❶**, 800 Kawkawa Lake Rd., off 6th Ave., on the east side of town along the banks of the Coquihalla River. (☎ 869-7119 or 888-869-7118. Open Apr.-Oct. 122 sites, $17; river sites $20; RV sites $23.) Shop for groceries at **Buy and Save Foods,** 489 Wallace St. (☎ 869-5318. Open July-Aug. daily 8am-10pm; Sept.-June 8am-9pm.) Locals love the generous portions and homemade cherry pie ($3.50 per slice) at the **Home Too Restaurant ❷**, 665 Hope Princeton Hwy. (☎ 869-5558.)

AROUND HOPE

☎ 604

A number of excellent hikes begin in or near Hope. Find the lush **Rotary Trail** (20min.) on Wardle St. at the confluence of the Fraser and Coquihalla Rivers. **Mt. Hope Loop** (45min.) offers an impressive view of the town and surrounding area (hike begins at intersection of Hwy. #1 and Old Hope Princeton Way, across from Rainbow Junction). To reach **Lookout Trail** (3½-4hr. round-trip), turn right under the Hwy. 1 overpass at Old Hope-Princeton Way. (Challenging.) Pause for a pleasant diversion at **Kawkawa (a.k.a. Suckers) Creek,** off Union Bar Rd., enhanced in 1984 to aid the late summer and mid-fall salmon spawning. The boardwalk along the creek leads to a swimming hole and popular picnicking spot. **Manning Provincial Park** (☎ 840-8836), 15min. east of Hope on Hwy. 3, has more extensive hiking options with over 70,000 hectares of cedar rainforest and flowering alpine meadows. Set up your tent at one of four **campgrounds ❶** throughout the park (Lightning Lake Campground, Coldspring, Mule Deer and Hampton; 350 sites total, $12-18.50). **Paintbrush Nature Trail,** at Blackwall Peak, provides a rare opportunity to enjoy subalpine meadows (bloom late July to early August). The path is wheelchair-accessible. (1km, 20 min.) For a more difficult hike, the **Pacific Crest Trail** passes through Manning beginning at Windy Joe. Parking lot on the Gibson Pass Road. (13km one way.)

BRITISH COLUMBIA

OTHELLO-QUINTETTE TUNNELS. The **Coquihalla Canyon Recreation Area** is a 5-10min. drive out of Hope along Kawkawa Lake Rd. Here the **Othello Quintette Tunnels,** blasted through solid granite, provide mute evidence of the daring engineering that led to the opening of the **Kettle Valley Railway** in 1916. The dark tunnels lead to narrow bridges over whitewater that shoots through the gorge. These tunnels set the backdrop to many Hollywood adventure-classics: *First Blood (Rambo)*, *Shoot to Kill*, and *Far from Home: Adventures of Yellowdog*. To get there, turn right on Othello Rd. off Kawkawa Lake Rd. and right again on Tunnel Rd.; allow 30min. to walk through the tunnels.

LADY FRANKLIN ROCK AND RAFTING. For an even closer view of the Fraser River, head 36km north on Hwy. 1 to the town of **Yale.** Take the first right after the stop light, then follow the gravel road for about 1km to a view of the majestic **Lady Franklin Rock,** which splits the river into two sets of heavy rapids. **Fraser River Raft Expeditions,** south of town, runs full-day whitewater trips almost daily on the Fraser and its tributaries. Travelers can stay the night in their oversized teepee or in the B&B. (☎ 863-2336 or 800-363-7238 for reservations. Class III-IV rapids; $110 includes lunch. **Camping** $5 per person; teepee $10 per night; B&B double $70.)

HELL'S GATE AIRTRAM. When Simon Fraser made his pioneering trek down the river, he likened one tumultuous stretch of rapids, 25km north of Yale on Hwy. 1, to the Gates of Hell—where "no human beings should venture." The Hell's Gate Airtram, 43111 Hwy. 1, carries the vertigo-immune 500 ft. down into the canyon in four minutes, although acrophobes and budgeteers may prefer the nearby 1km trail down to the river. (☎ 867-9277. $11, seniors $9.50, ages 6-18 $7, families $29.)

KAMLOOPS   ☎ 250

T'Kumlups, a Shuswap word meaning "where the waters meet," fits the town well, as it surrounds the convergence of the North and South Thompson rivers, and the heavily traveled Hwys. 5 and 1. The landscape looks something like California (complete with wineries!); in addition, over 200 lakes lie within an hour's drive of town. That, combined with a fine hostel, outdoor live music in the summer, and numerous outdoor adventure opportunities, makes the town a great base for day-tripping in the area, or a good waystation on long highway voyages.

◼◼◼ ORIENTATION AND PRACTICAL INFORMATION. Kamloops lies 356km east of Vancouver and 492km west of Banff, anchoring the junction of the heavily traveled Yellowhead (Hwy. 5) and Trans-Canada (Hwy. 1). **VIA Rail** (☎ 800-561-8630) trains stop at North Station, 11km north of the city center off Hwy. 5, making three runs per week to **Edmonton, AB** (15hr., $20) and **Vancouver** (8½hr., $92). **Greyhound,** 725 Notre Dame Ave. (☎ 374-1212), departs Kamloops for **Vancouver** (4½hr., 5 per day, $49); **Jasper, AB** (6hr., 3 per day, $60); and **Calgary, AB** (9hr., 4 per day, $82). **Kamloops Transit System** (☎ 376-1216) buses cost $1.50. **Cycle Logical,** 194 Victoria St. (☎ 828-2810), rents bikes for $25 per day. Kamloops claims to be the largest (think: area) city in North America; a free transit map from the visitors center is handy. The **Visitors Centre** is just off the Trans-Canada Hwy at Exit #368. (☎ 374-3377 or 800-662-1994. Open mid-May to Aug. daily 9am-6pm; Sept.-May M-F 9am-5pm.) **McCleaners,** 437 Seymour St. (☎ 372-9655), is a McLaundry. The **police** are at 560 Battle St. (☎ 828-3000 or ☎ 911) in the city center. Free **Internet access** is at the **public library,** 466 Victoria St. (☎ 372-5145. Open Tu-Th 10am-9pm, M and F-Sa 10am-5pm, Su noon-4pm.) The **post office** is at 217 Seymour St. (☎ 374-2444. Open M-F 8:30am-5pm.) **Postal Code:** V2C 5K2.

▐▌ ACCOMMODATIONS AND FOOD. The excellent ▨**Kamloops Old Court-house Hostel (HI) ❶**, 7 W Seymour St., is in fact a turn-of-the-century courthouse. The giant common room still sports a jury box, judge's bench, and witness stand, compensating for the tightly-packed dorm rooms. (☎828-7991. Check-in 8am-noon and 5-10pm. 75 beds. $16, nonmembers $20; private rooms $5 surcharge.) Campers can stay the night 8km east of the city center at **Kamloops View Tent & Trailer Park ❶**, 1-4395 Trans-Canada Hwy. E. Features forty sites, flush toilets, and laundry. (☎573-3255. Sites $16; full RV sites $25. Free showers.) A huge variety of foods lines Victoria St., the main strip downtown. For the best breakfast in Kamloops, try **Amsterdam Pancake House ❶**, 369 Victoria St., which serves Dutch-style *pannenkoeken* ($5-9) and $5-6 grilled sandwiches. (☎377-8885. Open daily 8am-3pm.)

◧ SIGHTS. Every night in July and August at 7:30pm there is "Music in the Park," as bands perform in **Riverside Park** on the banks of the Thompson River. The **Wanda Sue Paddle Boat,** 2472 Thompson Dr., gets you up close and personal with the river on a 2hr. cruise. (☎374-7447. 1-3 cruises per day. $12, seniors $11, ages 6-12 $7.) **Secwepemc Museum and Heritage Park,** 355 Yellowhead Hwy., is devoted to preserving the culture and heritage of the Shuswap people. It contains the reconstructed remains of a 2000-year-old Shuswap village. Located near the site of a school from which the Canadian government removed native children as late as the 1970s, the museum is a testament to the historical endurance of the First Nations. (☎828-9801, www.secwepemc.org. Open Memorial Day to Labor Day M-F 8:30am-8pm, Sa-Su 10am-6pm; Labor Day to Memorial Day M-F 8:30am-4:30pm. Summer $5, youths and seniors $4; off-season $1 less.) The annual **Cattle Drive** (☎800-288-5850) gives you the opportunity to live an expensive Western dream from Nicola Ranch to Kamloops. Would-be ranchers lacking mounts have to pay a hefty ransom ($745-1315, "posse" rates available) for rentals. The cattle drive runs once a year in mid-July. Booking early is essential.

▟ OUTDOOR ACTIVITIES. Sun Peaks, 1280 Alpine Rd., a 45min. drive north of Kamloops, is a powdery magnet for snowboarders and skiers. The mountain's large vertical drop (881m) and annual snowfall (559cm), as well as the six glades, justify the somewhat pricey tickets. In summer, the lift carries hikers and bikers up to trails and wildflower meadows. (☎800-807-3257; www.sunpeaksresort.com. Hiking $12, seniors and ages 13-18 $11, ages 6-12 $9; mountain biking $26, $22, $12; winter $48, $34, $28.) To get to Sun Peaks, take Hwy. 5 north from Kamloops, turn right at Heffley Creek and continue 31km. The resort also hosts the annual **Ice Wine Festival** (☎861-6654; www.owfs.com) in late January. The **Stake Lake Trails** form a network of cross-country skiing terrain, with a good selection of beginner and intermediate options. Take Exit 366 from Hwy. 1 south of Kamloops, and follow Lac Le Jeune Rd. for 20min. Ask for a map at the visitors center or get one at the hut in winter. (Snow report ☎372-5514. $7 per day, $30 per 5 days. Summer usage for biking or hiking is free.)

For an up-close look at the creatures inhabiting the area surrounding the rails, check the **Wildlife Park,** 15min. east of Kamloops along Hwy. 1, a non-profit organization devoted to rehabilitating local wildlife. (☎573-3242. $8, ages 65+ and 13-16 $6, ages 3-12 $5.) Local climbers head out to **rock climb** at a crag about 25km west of Kamloops on Hwy. 1. Always in the shade, these 35 easy to moderate sport climbs offer a scenic view of Kamloops Lake. **Ropes End** climbing gym, 975 B Laval Cres. (☎372-0645), has more details. Cheap fly-fishing trips start at $20 through **Ark Park Trout Fishing.** Call for transportation info (☎573-3878; www.arkpark.com). In winter, call **Alaskan Husky Adventures** in nearby Clearwater to get your mushing on with frighteningly efficient blue-eyed dogs. Multiple tours available. (☎866-587-0037; www.dogsleddingadventures.com.)

SHUSWAP LAKE REGION ☎ 250

From the dugout canoes of the Shuswap to the RVs of today's vacationers, the warm waters and productive fisheries of the sublime Shuswap Lake have attracted people for centuries. The area is a peaceful place to stay for the night or to stop and enjoy the scenery. Salmon Arm, a metropolis compared to the nearby villages, is still unexceptional but for its lakefront situation and its poster-perfect backdrop of rolling, forested mountains. Beware: if you are going to try and find your way through Salmon Arm off the highway, have a good map—the streets are confusing. The area is rich in camping and fishing opportunities, making it a popular destination for British Colombians looking for a relaxing weekend getaway.

■ 🚺 **ORIENTATION AND PRACTICAL INFORMATION.** Shuswap Lake is shaped like a sideways 'H.' Hwy. 1 hugs the northern arm of the lake before dipping south and following the southern arm east from Salmon Arm. The **Salmon Arm Transit System** (☎832-0191) has scheduled ($1.25, M-Sa) and door-to-door service ($1.50, M-F). The **visitors center** is at 751 Marine Park Dr. (☎832-6247 or 877-725-6667; fax 832-8382. Open May-Sept. M-Su 9am-7pm; Oct.-Apr. M-F 9am-5pm.) **Greyhound** is located at 50 10th St. SW (☎832-3962). Wash clothes at **Shuswap Laundry**, 330 Ross St. (☎832-7300. Open daily 7am-10pm.) In an **emergency,** call ☎911. Free **Internet** is at the **library,** in Picadilly Pl. Mall on 10th Ave. SW. (☎832-6161. Open M, W-Th, and Sa 10am-5pm; Tu and F 10am-8pm.) The **post office** is at 370 Hudson St. NE. (☎832-3093. Open M-F 8:30am-5pm.) **Postal Code:** V1E 4M6.

🚺🚾 **ACCOMMODATIONS AND CAMPING.** ▩**Squilax General Store and Caboose Hostel (HI) ❶,** 10km east of Chase, 8km west of Sorrento on Hwy. 1, sleeps travelers on board three Canadian National Railway cabooses. All three were specially outfitted for hosteling with kitchenettes and restrooms. Ample lounge space, a "sweat lodge," and laundry facilities are also part of the package. (☎675-2977. 24 beds, $14; nonmembers $18. Tent sites by the river $8. Showers.) **B&Bs ❹** are the way of Salmon Arm; for help finding a cheap one (prices range $45-100), visit or call the visitors center or Chamber of Commerce (see above). Campgrounds in Salmon Arm, especially those on Shuswap Lake, are often crowded and cramped. There are a handful of them on the lake side of Hwy. 1, about 10km west of Salmon Arm. For a much more peaceful stay, take the extra 30min. to drive to **Herald Provincial Park ❶,** 27km northwest of Salmon Arm by following signs off Hwy. 1. The park maintains 119 campsites with a large swimming area and access to dayhiking along Margaret Falls. (Reservations ☎800-689-9025. $18.50 includes firewood, hot showers, and toilets. See **Entertainment and Outdoor Activities,** below.)

🚹 **FOOD.** The best food deal for miles around awaits at the **Real Canadian Wholesale Club,** 360 Hwy. 1. Even the non-bulk items cost less than at a supermarket. (☎804-0258. Open M-F 9am-9pm, Sa 9am-6pm, Su 10am-5pm.) Farther west on Hwy. 1, **De Mille Fruits and Vegetables,** 3710 10th Ave. SW, markets local produce and, in August and September, incredible sweet corn. (☎832-7550. Open June-Sept. daily 8am-8pm; Oct.-May 8am-6:30pm.) To try bannock, a type of bread eaten by natives, stop at the **B&B Bannock Booth ❶.** It is located across the bridge on Squilax-Anglemont Rd., north of the hostel. The Smoked Salmon Bannock ($3) is sure to convert you. Satisfy your sweet tooth at **Wee Willie's Deli ❶,** 160 Lakeshore Dr. They also have freshly baked bread. (☎832-3888. Open M-Sa 7:30am-5:30pm.)

🚹🎭 **ENTERTAINMENT AND OUTDOOR ACTIVITIES. Caravan Farm Theatre,** 8km northwest of Armstrong and 45min. from Salmon Arm, presents top-notch performances during summer. Tickets are available from the Squilax General

Store and Hostel. (☎546-8533. Call for show times. $6-12.) The Farm overflows with remnant hippie charm, and organic produce, and musical instruments dangle from the trees. For an outstanding Native Dance Competition, see the Powwow in July; the visitors center has show times. The mystery of curds is solved in a tour at ▩**Gort's Gouda Cheese Factory**, 1470 50th St. SW. The tour is short and filled with tasty samples. Skip the tour, stock up on bargain cheeses, and watch the cheese-making process through viewing windows, from cow to wax package. (☎832-4274. Tours mid-June to Aug. M-W and F 10am, store M-Sa 9am-5pm.)

The area's outdoors attractions revolve around the waterways that surround town, and range from fishing for kokanee and rainbow trout in Lake Shuswap to taking a 10min. walk through **Herald Park** (see **Accommodations**, above) and viewing the lovely **Margaret Falls**. When doing the latter, be careful to stay on the path; the habitat is recovering from excessive trampling. Closer to town, many trails mean-der along the nature preserve on the banks of Lake Shuswap, where you can catch a glimpse of the rare Western grebe. Call Shuswap Lakes Tourism Assoc. (☎800-661-4800) for the date of this year's spring **Grebe Festival. Interior Whitewater Expedi-tions,** in Scotch Creek, leads 2hr. trips on the reasonably gentle (Class II-IV) **Adams River.** (☎800-661-7238. $44, under 16 $34; 15% HI discount.) The paths along the river can be hiked or mountain-biked on an 18km round-trip trail. Take Squilax-Anglemont Rd. north across the bridge, just west of the Squilax General Store, and the trail heads upriver across the first narrow bridge on the road.

THE OKANAGAN VALLEY

Known throughout Canada for its bountiful fruit harvests, the Okanagan (oh-kuh-NAH-gan) Valley lures visitors with summer blossoms, ample sun, plentiful winer-ies, and tranquil lakes. The **Okanagan Connector** (Hwy. 97C) links Vancouver to the valley in a 4hr. drive, making the valley a popular vacation destination among sun-starved coastal British Columbians. In the winter, **Big White Ski Resort** and **Apex Mountain** resort attract skiers looking to avoid long lines and pricey lift tickets at Whistler. Travelers looking to earn cash can sign on to pick fruit at one of the many orchards stretching south from Penticton to the US border along Hwy. 97.

KELOWNA ☎250

In the heart of the Okanagan Valley, Kelowna (kuh-LOW-nuh) is one of Canada's richest agricultural regions and a popular tourist destination. Kelowna (pop. 105,000) lies on the east shore of 170km long Okanagan Lake, halfway between Penticton in the south and Vernon in the north. The town's fruit stands, acclaimed wineries, unique blend of chains and independent shops, and sunshine draw thou-sands of vacationing Vancouverites every summer. And in the winter, those not skiing in Whistler find the slopes of Big White Ski Resort equally rewarding.

▐ TRANSPORTATION

Kelowna lies 400km east of Vancouver, 602km west of Calgary, and 86km north of Penticton on **Hwy. 97** at the eastern shore of Okanagan Lake. Hwy. 97, **Harvey Ave.** in town, runs east-west across the lake and bisects the town. The floating bridge across the lake is one-of-a-kind in Canada.

Buses: Greyhound, 2366 Leckie Rd. (☎860-3835 or 860-2364), off Harvey Ave. next to the Best Western, runs buses to: **Calgary, AB** (10hr., 3 per day, $85); **Hope, BC** (3 hr., 5 per day, $37); **Penticton, OR** (1½hr., 6 per day, $13); and **Vancouver, BC** (6½hr., 6 per day, $58). Ticket office open 7am-7pm M-Su, depot open 7am-1am M-Su.

Public Transportation: Kelowna Regional Transit System (☎860-8121) services town. Runs M-F 6am-10pm, Sa 8am-10pm, Su 9am-5pm. Adults $1.25, students $1; day pass: $3.25, students $3.

Taxis: Kelowna Cabs, 1180 Graham St. (☎762-2222 or 762-4444). $1.60 base, $2.60 1st km., $1.45 per additional km. 24hr.

Car Rental: Rent-A-Wreck, 2787 N Hwy. 97 (☎763-6632) at McCurdy Rd., will supply your means about town. Must have a major credit card. 19+. From $30 per day, $0.12 per km over 100km. Open M-Sa 8am-5pm, Su 9am-4pm.

🛂 PRACTICAL INFORMATION

Tourist Office: Visitor Center, 544 Harvey Ave. (☎861-1515). Brochures, bathrooms, and a doggie watering trough. Open in the summer M-F 8am-7pm, Sa-Su 9am-7pm, and in the winter M-F 8am-5pm, Sa-Su 10am-3pm.

Equipment: Sports Rent, 3000 Pandosy St. (☎861-5699). City bikes $18 per day, mountain bikes $22 ($26 with shocks), in-line skates $11, kayaks $30, canoes $35, water skis $20 per day. Open May-Sept. daily 9am-6pm, Oct.-Apr. 9am-8pm.

Laundromat: Cullen's Cleaning Carousel, 2660 Pandosy St. Wash $2, dry $0.25 per 6min. Open M-Th 8:30am-8pm, F 8:30am-7pm, Sa 8:30am-6pm, Su 9am-5pm.

Emergency: ☎911.

Police: 350 Doyle Ave. (☎762-3300).

Hospital: 2268 Pandosy St. (☎862-4000), 7 blocks south of Harvey Ave.

Internet Access: Kelowna Public Library, 1380 Ellis St. (☎762-2800), offers 1hr. of free Internet access. Open M and F-Sa 10am-5:30pm, Tu-Th 10am-9pm; Oct.-May also Su 1-5pm. The **SameSun Hostel** charges $1 for 10min., and **Kelowna International Hostel** offers 30 min. for $2 (both see below.)

Post Office: Town Centre Postal Outlet, 101-591 Bernard St. (☎868-8480). Open M-F 8am-5:30pm, Sa 9am-5:30pm. **Postal Code:** V1Y 7G0.

🏠🏠 ACCOMMODATIONS AND CAMPING

Warm, dry summer days attract thousands of soggy Vancouverites, so be sure to make reservations (at campgrounds too) or you'll be stuck in a chain hotel 5km out of town.

Kelowna International Hostel (HI), 2343 Pandosy St. (☎763-6024). Only 1 block from the beach in a colorfully painted, restored home, this laid-back hostel is a budget paradise. Kitchen, free pancake and coffee breakfast, laundry ($1.25 wash, $1.25 dry), Internet access ($2 for 30min.), and pick-up from bus station. Reception 7am-11pm, checkout 11am. 30 dorm beds total. $17 with hosteling membership, passport, or student card; nonmembers $20. Private rooms $38, $40. ❶

SameSun International Hostel, 245 Harvey Ave. (☎763-9814 or toll-free 1-877-562-2783). Just across the floating bridge, you'll find this brand-new youth hostel featuring keg parties and BBQs ($10 unlimited beer, $5 hamburgers) almost every summer night. For daytime fun, join a bike trip to Kettle Valley ($25, includes bike rental) or spend the day on the SameSun houseboat ($25 afternoon, $40 overnight). Huge kitchen, fresh linens and laundry facilities. Key deposit $10. Reception 8am-11pm. Call ahead if you'll arrive after-hours. Pickup from bus terminal $5, from airport $10. Dorm beds $20; private rooms $49. ❶

Kelowna
▲■ ACCOMMODATIONS
Bear Creek Provincial Park, 7
By the Bridge B&B, 5
Kelowna International Hostel, 8
SameSun International Hostel, 4
🍴 FOOD
The Bohemian Cafe, 2
Doc Willoughby's Downtown, 1
The Pier, 6
Tripke Bakery, 3

By the Bridge B&B, 1942 McDougall St. (☎ 860-7518), at the east end of Okanagan Lake Bridge, minutes from the beach and downtown. Cozy rooms, private baths, and a continental breakfast including freshly baked bread, jam, and fruit. Checkout 11am. Singles $49-69; doubles $59-79; triples $79-89; quads $89-99. ❸

Bear Creek Provincial Park (☎ 1-800-689-9025 or ranger 494-6500), 9km north of Hwy. 97 on Westside Rd. Day use/picnic area and camping. Unique features include shaded lakeside sites, 400m of Okanagan lake shore, boat launch, and an Apple Triathlon in Aug. Lakeside sites go quickly in summer season. Toilets, water, and firewood. 122 sites, $18.50. Campground gate closed 10pm-7am. Free showers. ❶

🗲 FOOD

Kelowna overflows with fresh produce. Find juicy delights at the stands outside town along **Benvoulin Rd.** and **KLO Rd.**, or head south on **Lakeshore Dr.** to the u-pick cherry orchards. In town, the shelves groan beneath big carrots and cucumbers at **Safeway,** 697 Bernard Ave. (☎ 860-0332. Open daily 8am-midnight.) **Bernard Ave.** is lined with restaurants and cafes.

The Bohemian Cafe, 363 Bernard Ave. (☎ 862-3517). This cafe features delectable food in a comfortable atmosphere right on the main drag. Try the mango-chutney turkey salad ($5.95), homemade bread and soup ($4.75), or huge sandwiches (starting at $5). Open M-F 7:30am-3:30pm, Sa 9am-3pm. ❷

The Pier, Marine Pub, 2035 Campbell Rd. (☎ 769-4777), just across the floating bridge outside Kelowna. This unassuming joint serves up unbelievable daily specials: Tu 12oz. Sirloin steak ($7.50); Tu, W, Th $0.10 wings; Sa and Su seafood specials (Alaska King Crab $12.99). Nine beers on tap all the time ($3.75 pint). Take your meal outside to the patio for an incredible lake view. Open Su-W 11am-midnight, Th-Sa 11am-1am. ❸

Doc Willoughby's Downtown, 353 Bernard Ave. (☎ 868-8288). A new pub-style restaurant with live music ranging from Celtic to blues on F-Sa nights. Food starts around $8, W $0.25 wings, F double highballs ($4.95). Hostelers get 20% off. Open M-Su 11:30am-1am. ❷

Tripke Bakery Donditorei & Cafe, 567 Bernard Ave. (☎ 763-7666). You'll smell this European style bakery from across Lake Okanagan. Grab a loaf of health bread ($2.79) before taking off for an outdoor adventure. Or try one of their myriad pastries (cinnamon buns $0.85). Open M-Sa 8am-5:30pm. ❷

👁 ⚠ SIGHTS AND OUTDOOR ACTIVITIES

The sun is Kelowna's main attraction, warming Okanagan parks and beaches for an average of 2000hr. per year. **City Park,** on the west end of downtown, is a popular hangout for locals and tourists alike. **Boyce Gyro Park,** on Lakeshore Rd. south of the Okanagan Bridge, features beach volleyball. **Sports Rent,** a short walk from the lake, rents camping, boating, and sporting equipment (see **Practical Information,** p. 302). **Kelowna Parasail Adventures,** 1310 Water St. (☎868-4838), at the docks of Grand Okanagan Resort north of City Park, transforms patrons into kites, floating them high above the lake.

HIKING, BIKING, AND SKIING. While Kelowna's main attraction is Okanagan Lake, surrounding areas offer excellent opportunities for terrestrial fun. Ponderosa pines dominate this hot and dry landscape. You'll also find bluebunch wheatgrass, bitterroot (a pink flower) and balsamroot (a bright yellow flower). **Knox Mountain,** just north of the city, features many hiking trails as well as a paved road to the summit. Hike, bike, or drive to the top for a spectacular view of Kelowna and Okanagan. Hikers will also find trail opportunities throughout **Bear Creek Park** and **Okanagan Mountain Park.** Bikers head to **Wildhorse Canyon** in the southern end of Okanagan Mountain Park for technically challenging rides. Another popular biking trail is the **Kettle Valley Railbed** (12-41km, 2-8hr.), which passes through scenic Myra Canyon and then through the only desert in Western Canada. To access Myra Canyon from downtown, go east on the K.L.O. Rd. (off Pandosy) to McCulloch Rd., follow McCulloch to June Springs Rd., take June Springs to Little White Forest Service Rd., and follow Little White 4.5km to the parking lot. The railbed through Myra Canyon stretches 12km, but the bike trail continues all the way to Penticton. (Easy to moderate).

In the winter, downhill skiing is the most popular outdoor activity in the Okanagan Valley. **Big White Ski Resort,** on a clearly marked access road off Hwy. 33, east of town, offers over 100 trails throughout 7000 acres of terrain. With two hostels and plenty of cheap eats surrounding the slopes, Big White is a great place for skiers on a budget. (☎765-3101, snow report 765-7669; www.bigwhite.com. Open mid-Nov. to late Apr. Adult day pass $55, youth 13-18 $47. Night-skiing 5-8pm, $16. Multi-day discounts. Ski rental $26; snowboard $35.)

WINE AND FRUIT. Over the past few years, the Okanagan valley has become the center of the British Columbian, and therefore Canadian, **wine** industry. Kelowna and the surrounding area is home to 12 of the valley's more than 25 wineries, all of which offer tastings, and many of which have tours. Contact the visitors centers or call ☎868-9463 for a complete list of tours. Wine and cheese parties are common at the **Okanagan Wine Festival** (☎861-6654; www.owfs.com) for 10 days in early October, for four days at its lesser counterpart in late April, and for three days at the new **Ice Wine Festival** in late January. **Mission Hill,** 1730 Mission Hill Rd., on the west bank of Okanagan Lake, is one of Kelowna's most respected local wineries. To get there, cross the bridge west of town, turn left on Boucherie Rd., and follow the signs. The winery overlooks Lake Okanagan. Free tours of a unique underground wine cavern, bell tower, and outdoor amphitheater. (☎768-7611. Open daily 10am-5pm, July-Sept 10am-7pm. $5 tasting for those over 19.) The posh **Summerhill Estate Winery** lets you taste five sparklers and join a tour to get a peek into an aging replica of the Cheops pyramid. Take Lakeshore Dr. to Chute Lake Rd. (☎800-667-3538. Open daily 9am-6pm; tours every hr. on the hr. 1-4pm. Free.)

Kelowna Land and Orchard, 2930 Dunster Rd., off KLO Rd. on E Kelowna, is the town's oldest family-owned farm, and offers a 45min. hayride and a tour that explains farming techniques and technologies. Indulge in delicious produce at the end of the tour. (☎763-1091. Open May-Oct. daily 8am-5pm; call for winter hours. Tours run 11am, 1 and 3pm; $5.25, students $2, under 12 free.)

PENTICTON

☎250

Indigenous peoples named the region between Okanagan and Skaha Lakes Pen-tak-tin, "a place to stay forever." Today, Penticton (pop. 33,000) is known more commonly as the "Peach City." However, Penticton is more than an agricultural mecca. The city bustles with tourists during the summer months. With endless outdoor adventures and an inviting downtown, one is still tempted to stay forever, although the rise in prices due to the ever-encroaching tourist industry may strain the budget traveler's wallet.

▐ TRANSPORTATION

Penticton lies 395km east of Vancouver at the junction of **Hwy. 3** and **Hwy. 97,** at the southern extreme of the Okanagan Valley. **Okanagan Lake** borders the north end of town, while smaller **Skaha Lake** lies to the south. **Main St.** bisects the city from north to south, turning into **Skaha Lake Rd.** as it approaches Skaha Lake.

Buses: Greyhound, 307 Ellis St. (☎493-4101), runs buses to **Kelowna** (1½hr., 7 per day, $12) and **Vancouver** (6-7hr., 6 per day, $52). Open M-Sa 6am-5pm, Su 7am-5pm.

Public Transportation: Penticton Transit System, 301 E Warren Ave. (☎492-5602), services town. $1.50, students and seniors $1.20; day pass $3.25, $2.75. Runs M-Sa 6:15am-10pm, Su 9am-6pm.

Taxis: Courtesy Taxi (☎492-7778). $2 base, $1.40 per km. 24hr.

Car Rental: Rent-a-Wreck, 130 W Industrial Ave. (☎492-4447), rents cars from $35 per day, then $0.12 per km over 100km. Major credit card required. Open M-Sa 8am-5pm.

▐ PRACTICAL INFORMATION

Tourist Office: Penticton Wine and Information Center, 888 W Westminster Ave. (☎493-4055 or 800-663-5052; www.penticton.org), at Power St. The info center does not, unfortunately, serve wine. Open M-F 8am-8pm, Sa-Su 10am-6pm.

Equipment: Freedom: the Bike Shop, 533 Main St. (☎493-0686). Bikes $30 per day, $20 half day, $5 HI discount. Open M-Sa 9am-5:30pm.

Laundromat: The Laundry Basket, 976 W Eckhardt Ave. (☎493-7899), next to the golf course. Wash $1.50, dry $0.25 per 7min. Open daily 8am-8pm.

Hospital: Penticton Regional, 550 Carmi Ave. (☎492-4000).

Emergency: ☎911.

Police: 1101 Main St. (☎492-4300).

Crisis Line: ☎493-6622. Women's Shelter: (☎493-7233). 24hr.

Internet Access: Penticton Public Library, 785 Main St. (☎492-0024), offers free access for 30min. Open in summer M, W, F, and Sa 10am-5:30pm; Tu-Th 10am-9pm; in winter Su 1pm-5pm. **Mousepad Coffee Bar,** 320 Martin St. (☎493-2050), charges $3.50 per ½hr., $6 per hr. Open M-F 6am-10pm, Sa 8am-10pm, Su 8am-8pm.

Post Office: 56 W Industrial Ave. (☎492-5769). Open M-F 8:30am-5pm. **Postal Code:** V2A 6J8.

▐ ACCOMMODATIONS AND CAMPING

Penticton is a resort city year-round; cheap beds are few and far between, and it's essential to make reservations in summer. If possible, avoid the expensive yet decrepit hotels that lurk along Skaha Lake Rd., and benefit from the beautiful hostel. Campground sites along Skaha Lake are expensive and often tightly packed. If you're camping, head north to Okanagan Lake Provincial Park for a lakeside site.

BRITISH COLUMBIA

Penticton Hostel (HI), 464 Ellis St. (☎ 492-3992). A large, well-maintained youth hostel with roof-top solar panels for hot water. Join a hostel bike tour ($44, includes bike), wine tour ($32), lake cruise ($10), or simply walk 10min. to the beach. Comfortable lounge, kitchen, TV room with cable, patio, free linen, and laundry facilities ($1 wash, $1 dry). Reception 8am-noon and 5-10pm. $16, nonmembers $20; private singles (without private bath) $36, $40. Ask about multi-day discounts. ❶

Riordan House, 689 Winnipeg St. (☎ 493-5997), rents lavishly decorated rooms with shared bathrooms in a Penticton heritage home. Scrumptious "Okanagan breakfast" of fresh muffins and fruit cobbler made from local peaches. Free pickup from Greyhound depot. Singles $50; doubles with TV/VCR and fireplace $60-85. ❶

Okanagan Lake Provincial Park, (☎ 494-6500 or 800-689-9025), 24km north of town on Hwy. 97. 168 sites total on 2 campgrounds (north and south). The north park is more spacious, and the beach is good for swimming. Reservations recommended. Free firewood, and toilets. $19. Free showers. ❶

Executive Inn, 333 Martin St. (☎ 492-3600). This newly renovated hotel is centrally located downtown just 2 blocks from Lake Okanagan. Indoor pool, fitness center and restaurant. Singles $109; doubles $119. ❺

🍴 FOOD

Find your staples at **Safeway,** 801-1301 Main St. (☎ 487-2103). The **Penticton Farmer's Market** sells local produce and baked goods. (In Gyro Park at the corner of Westminster and Main St. Open June-Oct. Sa 8:30am-noon.) You can also find **fruits and vegetables** at family stands (look for signs on the side of the road) both north and south of town of Hwys. 97 and 3A.

Il Vecchio Delicatessen, 317 Robinson St. (☎ 492-7610), just across the street from the Greyhound station. Locals, including the mayor, line up daily for delicious sandwiches that are an incredible value. Ask for the "mortadella capicollo," a 2-meat, 2-cheese sandwich for $2.95. Or try the vegetarian sandwich with sun-dried tomatoes and fresh pickles. Homemade soup $1.89. Open M-Sa 8:30am-6pm. ❶

The Dream Cafe, 74 Front St. (☎ 490-9012), is an organic oasis. Try the gypsy spring salad rolls ($4.95), the mango roasted chicken sandwich ($6.50), or szechuan prawns with rice and roasted veggies ($9.75). Live every week. Open M-Su 9am-10pm (closed M during winter). ❷

🏔 SIGHTS AND OUTDOOR ACTIVITIES

To check out the history of Penticton's gold trails and the Kettle Valley Railway, head to the **Penticton Museum,** 785 Main St. (☎ 490-2451. Open M-Sa 10am-5pm.)

In the summer, the Penticton tourist trade revolves around both **Lake Okanagan** and **Lake Skaha.** Youths tend to gravitate toward Skaha Lake Park to the south. Floating down the Okanagan River canal from Lake Okanagan to Lake Skaha is an excellent way to cool down on a hot summer afternoon. **Coyote Cruises,** 215 Riverside, rents tubes for $10 and provides a free shuttle for the return. (☎ 492-2115. Open in summer daily 10am-6pm.) **Pier Water Sports,** 45 N Martin St., rents more advanced water vessels for those with an active spirit and a few extra bucks. (☎ 493-8864. Jet skis $70 per hr., canoes $15 per hr., and kayaks $20 per hr.)

Although the lakes are the star attractions, those looking for land based adventures will not be disappointed. Visit **Munson Mountain,** an extinct volcano, for a bird's eye view of the valley. The mountain also has "PENTICTON" spelled out in letters 50 ft. high and 30 ft. wide. (Take Vancouver Ave. north of town, turn right on Tupper Ave. then left on Middle Bench Rd., to Munson Mt. Rd. The road takes you within minutes of the summit.

Bikers, walkers, and runners will enjoy the **Kettle Valley Railway,** which runs through Penticton. Traveling north, you'll pass through orchards, vineyards, and wineries, all with a fantastic view of Lake Okanagan. To access the KVR from downtown take Vancouver Ave. north to the intersection with Vancouver Pl. Those looking for a day trip from Penticton can travel 21 km at a gradual 2% ascent to Glenfir, or 41 km to Chute Lake. For shuttle service, contact **Vista Treks Tours and Shuttle** (☎ 496-5220; www.kettlevalleytrail.com).

The **Skaha Bluffs,** southeast of town on Valley View Rd., feature some of Canada's best sport and traditional rock-climbing. For hikers and spectators there are trails throughout the park. Check out *Skaha Rock Climbs,* by Howie Richardson (1997, Elaho Publishing), for detailed information on climbs. **Skaha Rock Adventures** (☎ 493-1765), 113-437 Martin St., offers guiding and instructional services. A resource for gear and advice is **Ray's Sports Den,** 101-399 Main St. They rent rock climbing shoes for $10, but not harnesses or other climbing equipment. In the winter, you can rent cross-country skis and snow-shoes for $13 per day. (☎ 493-1216. Open M-F 9:30am-6pm, Sa 9:30am-5pm, Su 10am-4pm.)

If you're visiting Penticton in the winter, **Apex Mountain Resort,** off an access road west of Penticton on Hwy. 3, offers the best downhill **skiing** in the area. Apex has downhill, cross-country, and night skiing (W and F-Sa 4:30-9:30pm) on over 60 runs with a 2000 ft. drop, and a new half pipe and terrain park for boarders. For a $12 round-trip bus ride from Penticton to Apex, contact Tim Horton's Magic Ski Bus (www.apexresort.com/skibus.htm). In the summer, ski slopes transform into a dream-come-true for mountain bikers. (☎ 292-8222 or 877-777-2739. Adult day pass $46, youth 13-18 $38, child 1-12 $29; night skiing $12. Adult rental equipment $29, youth $16, child $13.)

NELSON   ☎ 250

The history of Nelson is sobering, as it depicts the all too familiar disappearance of a native population in the wake of speculation, disease, and the mining industry. But today Nelson is not just another mining development, and tellingly, mining itself has become a very minor industry here. The town of just over 9,000 is a fascinating combination of Canadian culture, Bohemia, and the surrounding beauty of Kootenay Lake and its neighboring mountains. The sport of curling is all the rage for locals, granola devotees eat scrambled tofu for breakfast, and during summer and winter the town is awash with eager hikers and skiers in search of nature at its most extreme. But for all this, Nelson remains a mellow and alternative locale, one with a charm independent of its surrounding natural splendors.

▐ TRANSPORTATION

Nelson lies at the junction of **Hwy. 6** and **3A**, 624km southwest of Calgary, 454km southeast of Kamloops, and 657km east of Vancouver. From Nelson, Hwy. 3A heads 41km west to Castlegar. Hwy. 6 leads 65km south to the US border, where it becomes Washington's Rte. 31 and continues 110 mi. south to Spokane.

Buses: Greyhound, 1112 Lakeside Dr. (☎ 352-3939), in the Chako-Mika Mall. Terminal open M-F 6am-8:30pm, Sa 6-11am and 4-8:30pm, Su 7:30-8:30am and 4:30-8:30pm. Runs buses to: **Banff, AB** (13½hr. with a 1-5am layover in Cranbrook, 1 per day, $73); **Calgary, AB** (12hr., 2 per day, $83); **Vancouver** (12hr., 2 per day, $94).

Public Transportation: Nelson Transit Systems (☎ 352-8201) has 5 bus lines that cover the city and lake. Runs M-F 7am-11:30pm, Sa-Su 8:30am-7:30pm. $1-3.

Taxis: Glacier Cabs (☎ 354-1111). 24hr. $2 base, $2 per km in Nelson.

Car Rental: Rent-a-Wreck, 524 Nelson Ave. (☎352-5122), in the Esso station. 18+. $40 per day, $0.12 per km after 200km.

⚡ PRACTICAL INFORMATION

Outdoor information is generally available at the **West Kootenay Visitor Centre** (☎825-4723), in Kokanee Creek Provincial Park, 20km east of Nelson on Hwy. 3A. Recent funding cuts, however, have made the Visitor Centre's hours (and existence) unpredictable. If the West Kootenay Centre is closed, some park information can be obtained from **BC Parks, Kootenay District** at ☎422-4200.

Tourist Office: Visitor Information, 225 Hall St. (☎352-3433; www.discovernelson.com), provides an unusually good map of the city and surrounding area. Open June-Aug. daily 8:30am-8pm; Sept.-Oct. daily 8:30am-5pm; Nov.-May, M-F 8:30am-5pm.

Equipment: The Sacred Ride, 213 Baker St. (☎354-3831), rents front suspension bikes for $35 per day and full-suspension bikes for $55-75. Maps sell for $5, and helpful trail advice is free. Open M-Sa 9am-5:30pm. **Gerick Cycle and Sports,** 702 Baker St. (☎354-4622; www.gericks.com), rents front-suspension bikes for $29 per day, $133 per week, and features cross-country ski packages for $15 per day. Hours vary from season to season and even month to month; call ahead for details.

Laundromat: Found at the **Esso Station,** 524 Nelson St. (☎352-3534). Open Su-F 7am-9:30pm. Wash $2-4, dryers free.

Showers: Nelson City Tourist Park (see below). $2 for non-campers.

Emergency: Dial ☎911.

Police: 606 Stanley St. (☎352-2266). Right next to the library.

Hospital: 3 View St. (☎352-3111). 24hr.

Internet Access: Nelson Library: 602 Stanley St. (☎352-6333). M, W, and F 1-8pm, Tu and Th 10am-6pm, Sa 11am-6pm. $2 per 30min. The **Dancing Bear Inn** (see below) charges $1 per 10min., as does the **Flying Squirrel Hostel** (see below).

Post office: 514 Vernon St. (☎352-3538). Open M-F 8:30am-5pm.

Postal Code: V1L4EO.

📛 ACCOMMODATIONS AND CAMPING

▨ **Flying Squirrel Hostel,** 198 Baker St. (☎352-7285 or 866-755-7433; www.flyingsquirrelhostel.com). Superlatives abound here: younger, hipper, cooler. Catering, and catering well, to the more youthful outdoorsy crowd, this recent addition provides Nelson with a social scene unto itself. With foosball, a full kitchen, laundry, and free pickup from the bus station, they do it all. Internet access $1 per 10 min. Reception 8am-noon and 4-9pm. Checkout by 11am. $17-20, private rooms from $42. ❶

Dancing Bear Inn (HI), 171 Baker St. (☎352-7573 or 877-352-7573). This place just might remind you of grandma's house (don't forget to take off your shoes!) with its cozy, fire-warmed common room, art-decked and book-covered walls, full supply of board games and movies, and bountiful hospitality services. Super-helpful staff. Laundry, kitchen, free parking, and Internet access $1 per 10min. Reception 7-11am and 4-10pm. Reservations recommended June-Aug. Dorm rooms $17, nonmembers $20, under 10 half-price. Private rooms $34-45, nonmembers $40-54. ❶

Kokanee Creek Provincial Park, (☎825-4212; reservations ☎800-689-9025; www.discovercamping.ca). 20km north of town on Hwy. 3A. Shaded, spacious sites with decent privacy are near the lake. Flush toilets, running water. Wheelchair accessible. 166 sites; half for reservations, $25; half first come, first served, $19. ❷

Nelson City Tourist Park, (☎352-9031) on High St., is convenient for camping, backyard-style. Take Vernon St. to its eastern end and follow signs. Flush toilets. Wash $1, dry 50¢ for 30min. 40 sites. $15, power $18, with water $20; showers free. ❶

🏠 🎭 FOOD AND NIGHTLIFE

Basic groceries can be found at **Extra Foods,** 708 Vernon St. (Open M-Sa 9am-9pm, Su 9am-6pm.) Fresh bread, vegan brownies, and organic goodies abound at the **Kootenay Bakery** on 295 Baker St. (☎352-2274. Open M-Sa 7:30am-6pm.)

■ **Baci's Bistro,** 445 Baker St. (☎354-0303). Founded and operated by a couple of native Nelson boys, Baci's is sure to appease even the most famished traveler with fresh dishes made entirely from scratch ($8-12). Regardless of why you came to Nelson, you can't leave without trying the Tiramisu ($4.50). Open daily 11am-10pm. ❷

Redfish Grill, 479 Baker St. (☎352-3456), offers an eclectic menu alongside eclectic local artwork. Both are in very good taste. Thai-influenced wraps start at $5.50; the unadventurous can try burgers that run $6-8. Open daily 7am-1am. ❷

The Outer Clove, 536 Stanley St. (☎354-1667). Vegetarians, rejoice! Those who sleep next to them, cringe! This "Garlic Cafe" puts garlic in everything from tapas ($4-8) to ice cream ($2). For those with problems other than garlic breath (maybe a desire to suck blood), the vampire-killer chili is only $7. Open M-Sa 11:30am-9pm. ❶

Max and Irma's Kitchen, 515 Kootenay St. (☎352-2332). More chic than its mom and pop name implies, Max and Irma's serves up gourmet 10 in. pizzas from a wood-fired oven ($10-13), and serves enticing sandwiches like *croque monsieur* for $8. Open Su-Th 11am-9pm, F-Sa 11am-10pm. ❷

Mazatlan, 198 Baker St. (☎352-1388). Run by the super-friendly Medina family, this place offers excellent (the salsa's green!) platters ($10-16) of authentic Mexican food. Tortilla está buena, eh? Open M-F 5-10pm, Sa 3-11pm, Su 3-10pm. ❷

Nelson

🏠 ▲ ACCOMMODATIONS
Dancing Bear Inn, **7**
Flying Squirrel Hostel, **10**
Kokanee Cr. Prov. Park, **1**
Nelson City Tourist Park, **2**
🍎 FOOD
Baci's Bistro, **5**
Extra Foods, **3**
Kootenay Bakery, **6**
Max and Irma's Kitchen, **8**
The Outer Clove, **9**
Redfish Grill, **4**
Mazatlan, **11**

West Arm of Kootenay Lake

TO LAUNDRY (1km)
(20km)
Chatham St.
Willow St.
High St.
Front St.
Simpson Rd.
Morgan St.
Gyro Park
Kootenay Lake District Hospital
Vernon St.
Lakeside Dr.
McDonald Dr.
Lake St.
Baker St.
Herridge Ln.
Victoria St.
Silica St.
Carbonate St.
Falls St.
Kootenay St.
Cottonwood Creek
■ Library
Mill St.
Latimer St.
Josephine St.
Ward St.
Stanley St.
Hall Mines Rd.
Vancouver St.
TO 3A CASTLEGAR (41km)
TO US BORDER (65km)
Hendryx St.
Cedar St.
Park St.
S. Pine St.
View St.
Pine St.
Hoover St.
Observatory St.
Robson St.
Gore St.
Innes St.
Houston St.
0   250 meters
0   250 yards

⚡ OUTDOOR ACTIVITIES

Bordering Nelson on the north, the watery **West Arm** seems huge, but it's just a tiny segment of enormous **Kootenay Lake**. Dolly varden, rainbow trout (up to 14kg according to local legend), and kokanee cruise the lake, while sturgeon up to 1.5m long inhabit the nearby **Kootenay River**. The best time to find the big ones is from October to February. Licenses and bait are available at the **Balfour Dock,** 30min. north of town on Hwy. 3A.

HIKING

Hiking is plentiful in the hills around Nelson. Maps of brief hikes from the city center can be obtained at the **Dancing Bear Inn** (see above). Some of the area's best hiking can be found in **Kokanee Glacier Provincial Park,** which is generally uncrowded because it's so hard to reach. Various entrances off Hwy. 31 (which heads north off Hwy. 3A east of town) are not regularly maintained; these roads are not for the weak-willed driver or the low-riding vehicle and can be closed well into June. For a complete list of trails, check out *Don't Waste Your Time in the West Kootenays*, a worthwhile trail guide published by Voice in the Wilderness Press and available at most bookstores.

Old-growth Trail (2km, 1-2hr.) begins 12km up the Kokanee Creek Rd 20km out of town on Hwy. 31. Pass the Kokanee Creek campground turnoff on your right; the road is an unmarked, easily missable left turn about 500m further on. Trailhead on the left. Following the **Cedar Grove Loop,** this trail wanders through a cedar forest and offers views of the surrounding mountains and an old mining tramway. Easy.

Gibson Lake to Slocan Chief Cabin Trail (10km round-trip, 3-4hr.) lies another 4m up Kokanee Creek Rd. at the Gibson Lake Trailhead. If you're parking, wrap it with chicken wire to prevent porcupine damage (more info at the West Kootenay Visitor Center). From the trailhead, a 4km trail leads up and across the mountainside to **Kokanee Lake** and continues 3km to the **Kaslo Lake** campground, which consists of 10 sites that have pit toilets and good fishing. Another few kilometers and the path reaches the 12-person **Slocan Chief cabin** below **Kokanee Glacier.** (Campgrounds $5. Cabin $15 per person or $30 for group.) **Do not walk on any glacier without a guide.** Moderate.

Silver Spray Trail (8km, several hours). On Hwy 31, take the Woodbury Creek turnoff 10km north of Ainsworth Hot Springs (a few kilometers beyond Woodbury Creek itself) and drive 13km to the trailhead. This difficult trail passes through several avalanche areas and prime grizzly bear feeding zones en route to the Silver Spray Cabin (wood fireplace, sleeps 4-8) and the circa 1920s Violet mine and blacksmith shop. The views of the glacier are simply unbelievable. Strenuous.

HOT SPRINGS

Several kilometers northeast of Nelson, at 3609 Hwy. 31, the **Ainsworth Hot Springs** are a source of healing for the rheumatic and source of relaxation for everyone else. The water in the main swimming area hovers around body temperature and contains low levels of 10 healthful minerals. A second pool contains water 10 minutes melted from the glacier above (40° F). Jumping from pools of radically different temperatures is rumored to be good for the skin. Watching other swimmers jump from pool to pool is rumored to be wildly funny. The real highlights here are the humid limestone caves, naturally filled with water that reaches 112° F. It's like the batcave, only filled with steam and really hot water. (☎ 229-4212 or 800-668-1171. Open daily 10am-9:30pm. All day passes $11.)

SKIING

In winter, the soft powder of **Whitewater Ski Resort**, 12km southeast of town off of Hwy. 6, draws skiers and boarders to 32 well-maintained runs, some of Canada's best bowls, and 400m of vertical drop. With an average snowfall of 15m, Whitewater has over 12km of groomed cross-country trails. (☎354-4944 or 800-666-9420, snow report ☎352-7669; www.skiwhitewater.com. Lift tickets $37, ages 13-18 $28, ages 7-12 $21, under 7 free. Full package ski or snowboard rentals $25 per day.)

VALHALLA PROVINCIAL PARK ☎250

Valhalla stretches up from the enchantingly turquoise and trout-filled waters of Slocan Lake, then continues through a lush and temperate rain forest before arriving at a curtain of craggy alpine peaks. Once a homeland to the Sa-al-tkw't Indians, who left pictographs on the bluffs above the lake, the park has now been largely given over to feral pikas, mountain goats, and bears. Residents of nearby New Denver fought for countless years to have this treasure declared a park protected from logging interests before finally achieving success in 1983. Much of the park is accessible only by boat; the only roads to the park leave from the miniscule town of Slocan. Twenty-two separate camping areas, many with bear caches and pit toilets, are spread throughout the park. Motorists and cyclists beware—no mechanized vehicles of any kind, including mountain bikes, are allowed. Dogs must be leashed and are only allowed in certain areas of the park; fires also are allowed only in designated areas and must be made with driftwood from the beaches. Many trails require expert-level route-finding skills; others allow for a less strenuous journey through the amazing scenery. With cars, jet skis, and snowmobiles prohibited for miles, this is truly a place where the valiantly slain Norseman (or the odd traveler) can rest in peace.

✴ 🛈 ORIENTATION AND PRACTICAL INFORMATION

Valhalla lies on the west shore of Slocan Lake, 150km south of Revelstoke and 286km east of Kelowna. In the south, a bridge from **Slocan** provides access to southern trailheads, most at the end of long and bumpy forest roads. In the north, the town of **New Denver** provides food and shelter to weary wanderers as well as water access to the northern trailheads. The towns are linked by Hwy. 6, which runs north from Nelson. Back in the 1940s, New Denver was one of many Japanese internment camps set up by the Canadian government during WWII. The **Nikkei Internment Memorial Center**, at 306 Josephine St. just off 3rd Ave., has exhibits on the living conditions and culture of the nearly 20,000 interned Japanese-Canadians. (☎358-7288. Open May-Sept. daily 9:30am-5pm. $4, students and seniors $3.)

Without a designated visitor's center, the best information about New Denver comes from the townspeople themselves. Many shops carry brochures on the area, but nothing seems to trump good old local know-how. For **outdoor info**, visit the folks who led the crusade to preserve Valhalla as a national park, the **Valhalla Nature Center/Valhalla Wilderness Society**, 307 6th Ave., in the building that says Valhalla Trading Post (☎358-2333. Open M-F 10am-5pm, Sa 11am-3pm.) If the office appears closed, knock anyway; someone working late may answer and provide you with their invaluable park trail guide ($4). To get to the park from New Denver, rent a kayak at **Sweet Dreams Guesthouse** ($40 per day, $25 for half day, or $180 per week; see **Accommodations**, below) or ask around about the local water taxi service. There is no 911 service for this area (which includes Valhalla park and New Denver). For emergencies call the **police:** 407 Slocan Ave. (☎358-2222), south of 6th St. **Post office:** 219 6th Ave. (☎358-2611. Open M-F 9am-5pm, Sa noon-4pm.) **Postal Code:** V0G 1S0.

▮▯ ACCOMMODATIONS AND FOOD

Those who don't wish to camp in the park can stay in luxury at the **Sweet Dreams Guesthouse ❸**, 702 Eldorado Ave. Take 6th Ave. toward the lake and turn left on Eldorado Ave. This B&B is located in a cozy country home with a beautiful view of the lake (Room 4 is famous for its view). Three-course dinners are available by reservation and run about $20. (☎358-2415. Singles $45-55, doubles $70-85, triples $85. Multiple-day rates are often available.) Another lodging option is the **Valhalla Inn ❷**, on Hwy. 6 in town, which offers spare but spacious and spotless motel rooms, as well as a restaurant (entrees run $6-15) and a pub with $4 pints. (☎358-2228. Singles $55, doubles $60, can accommodate up to seven in one room with an initial price of $70 for 2 people, $10 for each additional person.) Convenient but unaesthetic (aside from the view) camping is available at the **municipal campground ❷** at Centennial Park, on the south side of town by the lakeshore between 3rd and 1st Ave. Forty small sites, most filled with RV toting boaters, cluster around showers and a boat launch. (Tents $13, on the water $14, electricity and water $16.) **Valhalla Park ❶** itself is filled with free backcountry sites.

Basic supermarket goods can be found at **Eldorado Market**, 402 6th Ave. (☎358-2443. Open M-Sa 9am-6pm, Su 10am-5pm.) **Ann's Natural Foods**, 805 Kildare St., has a small selection of natural food products. (☎358-2552. Open M-Sa 9am-5:30pm.) Meals abound on 6th Ave., where you can find the renowned **Appletree Cafe ❶**, 210 6th Ave. The tiny cafe is home to a colorful local crowd promising, and honoring its promise of, "up to the minute gossip" and other essential small-town services including homemade soups ($3.50), and build-your-own $6-8 sandwiches. (☎358-2691. Open M-F 7am-4pm, Sa 11am-4pm.)

▧ HIKING

Explorers of Valhalla's outdoor paradise must take a few important precautions. First off, Slocan Lake, while usually placid and eerily mirror-like, occasionally bears the brunt of winds funneled down the valley. Talk to locals about weather conditions and be sure to learn about "the black line" (talk about eerie). The temperate rain forest of Valhalla is often very wet, and hypothermia is a real concern, even in the summer. Extra layers of warm clothing are a good idea. Additional safety gear is always recommended when camping, and a whistle is particularly handy in Valhalla because it can be heard across the lake. Be aware of the possibility of bear encounters. Most camping areas provide bear-proof food caches, but if none are available, bear-bagging supplies are necessary. Finally, remember that forest roads may be impassable as late as June due to winter-like weather conditions. One popular activity, which arose in response to this problem, is kayaking along the lake's shore and camping near the beach.

Bannock Burn to Gimli Ridge (4km, 2-3hr.). Turn off Hwy. 6 at Slocan City, cross the river, and follow the gravel road 13km south. Turn right onto Bannock Burn Creek logging road and follow it to the parking lot. It is an unsurpassed hike with opportunities for world-class **rock climbing.** Camping is available along the trail. Moderate to strenuous.

Sharp Creek to New Denver Glacier (8.8km, day-long). The trail begins along the west shore of Slocan Lake, directly across from New Denver, and is accessible only by boat. A very steep climb through several hanging valleys of lush moss, monumental cascades, and old-growth forest. There's a campground about half way up and stunning views of the glacier and surrounding area from the top. Strenuous.

Evan's Creek Trail (8km, 2-3hr.). Park on the Slocan City side of the Slocan River bridge, walk across, then turn right to walk 200m to the trailhead. The trail passes along the lakeshore and past moss-carpeted waterfalls. A cabin and tent pads are available at the creek, and ample fishing awaits at Cahill and Beatrice Lakes. Easy to moderate.

⚠ OTHER ACTIVITIES

Newly constructed trails have made biking an increasingly common and popular activity. Pathways have been carved from old rail beds 50km in the direction of Nakusp to the north, and 50km to Kaslo to the east. Fairly flat, these trails offer a relaxing, leisurely, and quiet way to see the West Kootenays. Bike rental is a fairly informal affair usually run from someone's back porch. Ask locally for a map of the trails and rental information; **Sweet Dreams Guest House** (see above) is a good place to start. Kayaking, though often seen as a means of transportation by locals, is a perfect Slocan Lake recreation unto itself. Countless inlets are well worth exploration, filled with loons, wrecked ships, and pictographs. Winter sports are also available in the area. Cross-country skiing is the primary activity, but snow-mobiling has also become popular.

FERNIE ☎ 250

Those willing to go the extra kilometer will be rewarded with the best snow around. A magnet for mountain bikers and snowboarders, Fernie combines the familiarity of small-town life with the commercialism of franchised strip malls, plus the breadth of outdoor activities found in Jasper and Banff. While not as familiar as Banff or Whistler, Fernie has begun to attract the attention of travel guides and snow-lovers alike. During the summer, Fernie offers everything you would expect from a city set in the Rockies: gorgeous hiking, superior mountain biking, and world-class trout fishing. Add to these a range of excellent, cheap hostels, and you have a locale that's destined for discovery.

◼▮ ORIENTATION AND PRACTICAL INFORMATION. Fernie is located on Hwy. 3, 1hr. east of Cranbrook and 3½hr. southwest of Calgary. Local services cluster along Hwy. 3 and in downtown Fernie, 5km north of the ski resort. The **Visitors Center,** with free pamphlets and a few free books, is set beneath a wooden oil rig 1km east of town on Hwy. 3. (☎423-6868. Open winter M-F 9am-5pm, summer daily 9am-7pm.) **Greyhound,** 742 Hwy. 3 (☎423-6871) in the Park Place Lodge, runs two buses per day to **Calgary** (6½hr.; $47, students $42) and **Vancouver** (18hr.; $100, students $90). **Kootenay Taxi** (☎423-4408) runs 24hr. and ferries powder-heads to the slopes in winter ($10 one-way). In an **emergency,** call ☎911 or contact the **police,** at 496 13th St. (☎423-4404). The **Fernie District Hospital** is at 1501 5th Ave. (☎423-4453). **Fernie Library,** 492 3rd Ave., offers **Internet access** for $5 per hr. (☎423-4458. Open T-Th 11am-8pm, Sa noon-5pm.) **Raging Elk Hostel** has access for $2 per 20 min. **Ski and See Adventure Lodge** offers free Internet access to guests. The **post office** is at 491 3rd Ave. (☎423-7555. Open M-F 8:30am-5pm.) **Postal Code:** V0B 1M0.

▮▯ ACCOMMODATIONS AND FOOD. Ski and See Adventure Lodge ❶, 301 2nd Ave. above the Grand Central Hotel, is the latest addition to the Fernie travel scene. This new European-style hotel offers shared and private rooms, comfortable common areas, and a huge outdoor patio with a hot tub. (☎423-7367. In winter shared rooms $30, private rooms $60; in summer $19/30.) The **Raging Elk Hostel (HI) ❶,** 892 6th Ave., is a converted motel offering both dorm-style lodging and private rooms with a healthy dose of ski culture on the side. In addition to the cozy living quarters, it boasts private baths, a large common area, a kitchen, laundry, Internet access, and a free pancake breakfast. Reservations are crucial during the December to April ski season. (☎423-6811. Reception daily 8-11am and 5-11pm. In winter $18, private bath $22; in summer $15, nonmembers $18.) **Mount Fernie Provincial Park ❶** (☎422-4200), 3km south of town on Hwy. 3, offers 38 private and shaded sites as well as flush toilets and water for $12.

COAL-HEARTED ROMANCE Local Fernie legend holds that town founding father William Fernie had the hots for a local native princess. Being something of a shallow man, his interest was focused below her head—specifically, on the black stone in her necklace. When he finally discovered the valuable local coal deposits (the source of the necklace), he abandoned the woman. In retribution, a local medicine man placed a curse upon the entire valley. Two massive fires, a devastating flood, and a mining disaster later (all in the course of thirteen years), the curse seemed real enough. To exorcise the demons, local tribes were finally gathered in 1964. They lifted the hex, sharing a symbolic peace pipe with the mayor of the town. However, as tour guides are very ready to point out, on Mt. Hosmer, a peak to the west of town, afternoon shadows create the remarkably distinct image of a horse with two riders—the princess and her father still remind the residents of Fernie of the pain their ancestor caused.

Find groceries at **Overwaitea Foods** on 2nd Ave. (☎423-4607. Open Sa-Th 8am-8pm, F 8am-9pm.) **The Curry Bowl** ❷, 931 7th Ave., offers "enlightened Asian cuisine" like curry ($8-12) and large bowls of noodles for $5. (☎423-2695. Open Tu-F 5-11pm, Sa-Su 4-11pm.) **The Arts Station** ❷, 1st Ave. and 6th St., is a former train depot that now acts as a staging point for local artists; it also serves homemade soups ($3) and $7.50 sandwiches. (☎423-4842. Open daily 7am-2pm except W.) **Mug Shots Bistro** ❷, 592 3rd Ave., is a small cafe offering Internet access alongside its blueberry pancakes ($4.50), homemade (but homely) sandwiches ($5.50-8), and $8 bag lunches. (☎423-8018. Open daily 7am-4pm.) Unwind after snowboarding at **The Grand Central Hotel** ❶, 301 2nd Ave., with $4 pints, and on Monday nights, $0.15 wings. (☎423-3343. Open M-Sa noon-2am, Su noon-midnight.)

🎿 **SKIING.** The engine driving Fernie's expansion is the **Fernie Alpine Resort** and its 2500+ acres of feathery powder. With a 875cm/29 ft. annual snowfall, the Fernie Alpine Resort embarrasses the competition. Over 100 trails spread out across the Lizard Range, creating a winter wonderland of gullies, ravines, five alpine bowls, a terrain park, a vertical-drop, and tree-skiing. (☎423-4655, snow report 423-3555; www.skifernie.com. $56; students 18-24, ages 13-17 or 65+ $45; ages 6-12 $15.) **Fernie Sports**, 1191 7th Ave., on Hwy. 3, offers **ski and snowboard rental** packages for $22 and $25. (☎423-3611; www.ferniesports.com. Open in winter daily 8:30am-7pm; summer M-F 10am-6pm.)

🥾 **OUTDOOR ACTIVITIES.** The April thaw, while heralding the end of ski season, also uncovers Fernie's abundant hiking trails. Many trails leave from the Alpine Resort, where free maps are provided. The **Fernie Ridge Walk** (11 mi., at least 8hr.) begins in the parking lot of the ski resort and offers spectacular views of alpine meadows and jagged limestone peaks before returning to the valley floor. Cheaters can take the lift part way up the mountain in the summer ($8, bikes $3), but won't avoid the steep **Snake Ridge** or a 15m/50 ft. fixed-rope climb. (1000m/3300ft. gain. Strenuous.) Fernie and the mountain resort offer various trails. **The Guides Hut,** 671 2nd Ave., is happy to recommend equipment and trails, and rent front-suspension bikes. (☎423-3650 or 888-843-4885. Open in summer M-Sa 9:30am-6pm, Su noon-5pm; call for winter hours. $25 per day, $130 per week.) The **Bike Base**, 432 2nd Ave., and neighboring **Ski Base** rent trade-ins at great prices. (☎423-6464. Full-suspension $40 per day. Open Sa-Th 9:30am-5:30pm, F 9:30am-8pm.) The Elk river and its tributaries provide 180km of world-class **fly-fishing** for bulltrout and cut-throat. Follow the crowd and fish along

Hwy. 3, or head off the beaten path and farther along the river. A good start, the **Kootenay Fly Shop and Guiding Company,** 821 7th Ave., rents rods for $20 per day and sells maps and books for $10-17. (☎423-4483. Open M-Sa 9am-5:30pm; July-Aug. also open Su.)

REVELSTOKE   ☎250

In the 19th century, Revelstoke was a town straight out of an old west movie, complete with dust-encrusted misers maiming one another amid the gold-laden Selkirk and Kootenay Mountains. Located on both the Columbia River and the Canadian Pacific Railway, the town was born as a transfer station for boats and trains. Although still a stopover for travelers to the Rockies, Revelstoke is finally coming into its own. The first sign of excellent outdoor opportunities is that the town is empty during the day. Revelstoke's uniquely laid-back social life complements the physical rigors of the area. Excellent hostels, free and suprisingly lively outdoor entertainment in the town center, and extensive outdoor pursuits make Revelstoke a particularly welcoming destination.

▟ ❼ ORIENTATION AND PRACTICAL INFORMATION

Revelstoke is on the **Trans-Canada Hwy.** (Hwy. 1), 285km west of Banff, 210km east of Kamloops, and 565km east of Vancouver. The town is easily navigated on foot or by bike, as evidenced by the lack of traffic and abundance of parking spaces downtown. **Mount Revelstoke National Park** lies just out of town on Hwy. 1.

Buses: Greyhounds depart from 1899 Fraser Dr. (☎837-5874). To get there, turn away from the city center at the traffic lights on Hwy. 1 and take your 1st left. Open M-Sa 8am-7pm, Su 11am-1pm and 3-5pm. To **Calgary, AB** (6hr., 4 per day, $57); **Salmon Arm, BC** (1½hr., 5 per day, $17); and **Vancouver** (8-10hr., 5 per day, $69).

Taxi: ☎837-4000.

Visitors Info: Visitors Centre (☎837-3522; www.revelstokecc.bc.ca), located at junction of Hwy. 1 and Hwy. 23 N. Open daily July-Aug. 9am-6pm; May-June 9am-5pm. An additional, smaller information center is located at 204 Campbell Ave. in central Revelstoke (☎837-5345; open M-Sa 9am-5pm). **Parks Canada** (☎837-7500), at Boyle Ave. and 3rd St. Open M-F 8:30am-noon and 1-4:30pm.

Bike Rental: High Country Cycle and Sports, 118 Mackenzie Ave. (☎814-0090; fax 814-0091). $7-8 per hr., $35-40 per day. Open 9:30am-5:30pm.

Laundry: Family Laundry, 409 1st St. W (☎837-3938), just behind the Samesun Hostel. $1.50 for single load wash, $4 for massive loads, dry $0.25 per 5min. Open M-Sa 8am-7pm, Su 9am-5pm.

Emergency: ☎911.

Police: 320 Wilson St. (☎837-5255).

Ambulance: ☎837-5885.

Hospital: Queen Victoria Hospital, 6622 Newlands Rd. (☎837-2131).

Internet Access: Free at the **library,** 600 Campbell Ave. (☎837-5095; open Tu and F 1-8pm, W and Sa 10am-4pm, Th 1-5pm). Also at **Woolsey Creek Cafe** (p. 316) and **Bertz Outdoor Equipment and Cafe** (p. 316).

Post Office: 307 W 3rd St. (☎837-3228). Open M-F 8:30am-5pm.

Postal Code: VOE 2S0.

▶ ACCOMMODATIONS AND CAMPING

Samesun Hostels Revelstoke, 400 2nd St. W (☎877-562-2783). The friendly staff successfully walks the fine line between providing a youthful hostel scene and offering decent private rooms to an older crowd. Several kitchens, full bathrooms, living room with TV, and a constant mellow soundtrack. Internet $1 for 10 min. Deals with some local restaurants and the Powder Springs Resort. 24hr. check-in. Dorms $20; singles $43, winter $39; groups of 6+ $18 per person. ❶

Daniel's Guest House, 313 1st St. E (☎837-5530), a 2min. walk from downtown. A home-turned-hostel, the comfortable beds, couch-filled common room, and porch make the place feel, well, homey. Kitchen, laundry ($1.50), satellite TV, 2 bathrooms, and pick-up from the bus station. 24hr. check-in. 20 beds in single-sex 6-person dorms and private rooms. Dorms $17; doubles $34; private rooms $30. HI discount; kids free. ❶

Williamson's Lake Campground, 1818 Williamson Lake Rd. (☎837-5512 or 888-676-2267), 5km southeast of town on Airport Way. Farther from the highway than competitors, it is next to a peaceful and popular swimming hole. Laundry and general store. Closed Nov. to mid-Apr. 41 sites, $14.50; 20 full RV sites, $18. Free showers. ❶

▶ FOOD

The town's local market is **Cooper's Supermarket,** 555 Victoria St. (☎837-4372. Open daily 8am-9pm. On the east side of town lies **Southside Grocery,** 900 4th St. (☎837-3517. Open daily 9am-9pm.)

Luna Taverna, 102 2nd St. E (837-2499). Titanic helpings of Greek and Mediterranean fare. Meals like souvlaki dish up far more deliciously tender meat than the average mortal can handle. Appetizers run $4-8, full meals $11-16. Staying at Samesun Hostel earns free cheesecake. Open Tu-Sa 11am-2pm and 5pm-10pm; Su-M 5pm-10pm. ❷

Woolsey Creek Cafe, 212 Mackenzie Ave. (837-5500), offers three solid meals a day in a relaxed, toy-strewn atmosphere. Internet access $1 for 10min. Breakfast runs $1.50-9, lunch $3.50-8.50, dinner $6-15. Open Tu-Su 8am-10pm, but schedule varies. ❷

Chalet Deli and Bakery, 555 Victoria St. (☎837-5552), across the parking lot from Cooper's. The complete package for lunch and baked goods. Offers a hot deli, pizza by the slice ($2.50), and sandwiches on fresh bread ($4.50). Open M-Sa 6am-6pm. ❶

The Ol' Frontier Family Restaurant, 122 N Hwy. 23 (☎873-5119), at Hwy. 1 and 23 N, next to the visitors center. Serves ¼ lb. burger with the works and the "Ain't No Bull" mushroom-and-peppers veggie burger, each for $6. Open daily 5am-10pm. ❶

Bertz Outdoor Equipment and Cafe, 217 Mackenzie Ave. (☎837-6575), will supply you with food, outdoor equipment, and advice on local climbing and mountaineering. Large bagel sandwiches ($4.50). Internet access $4 for 30min., $7 per hr. Open in summer M-F 8am-5pm, Sa 9am-4pm, Su 10am-4pm; winter M-F 8am-5pm. ❶

▶ ▶ SIGHTS AND ENTERTAINMENT

Revelstoke Railway Museum, 719 W Track St. off Victoria Rd., tells of the construction of the Trans-Canada line, which was completed in 1885. Other exhibits include a real steam engine and a full passenger car. (☎877-837-6060; www.railwaymuseum.com. Open July-Aug. daily 9am-8pm; May-June and Sept. daily 9am-5pm; April and Oct. M-Sa 9am-5pm; Nov. M-F 9am-5pm; Dec.-Mar. M-F 1pm-5pm. $6, 60+ $5, ages 7-16 $3, under 7 free, family $13.) The quite interesting mechanical marvels of the **Revelstoke Dam,** 5km north of Hwy. 1 on Hwy. 23, along with the latest in utility company propaganda, are illustrated in a free talking-wand tour. Wheelchair accessible.

(☎837-6515. Open May to mid-June and mid-Sept. to mid-Oct. daily 9am-5pm; mid-June to mid-Sept. 8am-8pm.) The town also boasts a **blues festival** in late June, a lumberjack competition in early July, and a railroad festival in August. Call the visitors center for dates. Also, from late June through August, the town's main square rings with quality bands from a cappella to ska. Weeknight shows tend to be more family oriented, while weekends rock a little harder.

◤ OUTDOOR ACTIVITIES

SUMMER ACTIVITIES. Canyon Hot Springs, between Mt. Revelstoke National Park and Glacier National Park on Hwy. 1, sports two spring-fed pools that simmer at 26°C and 40°C. (☎837-2420. May-June and Sept. 9am-9pm; July and Aug. 9am-10pm. $6.50, seniors and under 14 $5.50, under 4 free.) The neighboring **Apex River** runs 2hr. and 4hr. whitewater rafting tours on the Illecillewaet's Class II-III rapids. (☎837-6376 or 888-232-6666. $69, under 17 $59.) A more relaxing aquatic experience can be found with **Revelstoke Kayaking Adventures.** (☎866-405-2925; www.revelstokekayaking.com. Open daily June-Sept. 9am-6pm. Double and single kayak rentals are available, as are half-day and weekend tours.) **Grizzly Country Tours** (☎837-3020 or 837-3010; reservations taken dawn to dusk) can take fisherfolk out on the Columbia to raft for various rates depending on numbers. The 140 bolted routes on Begbie Bluffs offer exceptional **sport climbing** (from the small parking area almost 9km down 23 South from Hwy. 1, the bluffs are a 10min. walk; take the left fork). Rogers Pass and the surrounding peaks offer a lifetime of year-round opportunity to hone one's **mountaineering** skills.

WINTER SPORTS. Winter in Revelstoke brings excellent **downhill skiing. Powder Springs Resort** (☎800-991-4455; www.catpowder.com) is only 5km outside town and maintains one chairlift and 21 trails (2000 ft. vertical drop) on the bottom third of Mt. MacKenzie. Tickets cost $28-32, but inquire about money-saving accommodation packages (see **Samesun Hostels Revelstoke,** p. 316). Local companies offer heli-skiing and cat-skiing on the upper two-thirds of this and other local mountains. Ask at the visitors center (see **Practical Information,** p. 315) for more information on where the cheapest equipment rentals can be found. Parks Canada offers excellent advice and brochures on area nordic trails and world-class backcountry skiing. They also provide information and brochures on area snowmobiling.

MT. REVELSTOKE NATIONAL PARK. Adjacent to town, Mt. Revelstoke National Park furnishes a quick and satisfying nature fix with its astounding scenery. It is a favorite of mountain bikers and hikers. **Summit Cycle Tours** drives customers to the summit of Mt. Revelstoke and provides bicycles and a guided tour on the 2hr., 27km descent. (☎888-700-3444; www.summitcycle.com. $54, under 16 $49; group discounts.) The park is too tiny to offer extensive backcountry opportunities, but does boast two **backcountry campgrounds** (permit $6); get details from the **Revelstoke Parks Canada** office or the **Rogers Pass** visitors center (see p. 318). For hiking, two boardwalks off Hwy. 1 on the east side of the park access the trails. **Skunk Cabbage Trail** (1.2km, 30min.) leads through acres of stinking perfection: skunk cabbage plants tower at heights of over 1.5m. **Giant Cedars Trail** (500m, 15min.) has majestic trees over 600 years old growing around babbling brooks. **Meadows in the Sky Parkway** (Summit Rd.) branches off Hwy. 1 about 1.5km east of town, leading to a 1km hike up Mt. Revelstoke to subalpine meadows. A wheelchair-accessible shuttle is available (summer only, 10am-4:20pm). The **Summit Trail** (10km one-way, full day) leaves from the trailer drop-off parking lot at the base of Summit Rd. and climbs steadily to the summit of Mt. Revelstoke, where the weary traveler will be joined by everyone who drove up. **Jade Lake Trail** (9km one-way, full day) cuts up from the Heather Lake parking lot on Summit Rd. to the parks most photographed, most jade-colored lakes.

GLACIER NATIONAL PARK   ☎250

This aptly named national park is home to over 400 monolithic ice floes that cover one-tenth of its 1350 sq. km. area. The jagged peaks and steep, narrow valleys of the Columbia Range not only make for breathtaking scenery but also prevent development in the park. An inland rain (although it feels more like snow) forest, Glacier receives significant precipitation every other day in the summer, but the clouds of mist that encircle the peaks and blanket the valleys only add to the park's astonishing beauty. In late summer, brilliant explosions of mountain wild-flowers offset the deep green of the forests. In the winter, brilliant explosions of Howitzer shells shake the calm of the valleys. Glacier is Canada's prime avalanche research and prevention area; scientists fire 105mm shells into mountain sides to create and observe controlled avalanches. This makes winter travel dangerous for multiple reasons, and consultation with park rangers is necessary. Roger's Pass, the park's main tourist attraction, has quite a history itself, as it was the last great obstacle of nature overcome by the Canadian Pacific Railroad in 1882.

■ ▮ **ORIENTATION AND PRACTICAL INFORMATION.** Glacier lies 350km west of Calgary and 723km east of Vancouver. **Greyhound buses** make one trip from Revelstoke. (☎837-5874. 1hr., $14.70.) For details on the park, including great trail suggestions, talk to the Parks Canada staff or buy a copy of *Footloose in the Columbias* ($2) at the **Roger's Pass Information Center,** on the highway in Glacier. (☎814-5232. Daily **park passes** cost $4, ages 65+ $3, 6-16 $2, group of 2-7 $10 (see p. 36). Open daily Dec.-Mar. 7am-5pm, Apr. to mid-June, Sept.-Oct. 9am-5pm; mid-June to Aug. 8am-7pm; during Nov. Th-M 9am-5pm.) For more info about Glacier, write to the Superintendent, P.O. Box 350, Revelstoke, BC V0E 2S0, or call ☎837-7500. In an **emergency,** call the **Park Warden Office.** (☎837-7500. Open daily 7am-5pm; winter hours vary; 24hr. during avalanche control periods.)

▰ **CAMPING.** Glacier has 2 frontcountry campgrounds: **Illecillewaet ❶** (ill-uh-SILL-uh-way-et), 3½km west of Roger's Pass (wheelchair accessible, 60 sites open mid-June to early Oct.), and **Loop Brook ❶,** another 3km west on Hwy. 1 (20 sites, open July-Sept.). Both offer toilets, kitchen shelters with cook stoves, and fire-wood. (Sites at both $14.) Backcountry campers must purchase a **backcountry pass** ($6 per day) from the Parks Canada office in Revelstoke (☎837-7500) or from the Rogers Pass Information Center. Food is limited; stock up in **Golden** or **Revelstoke.**

▨ **OUTDOOR ACTIVITIES. Biking** and **fishing** in Glacier are prohibited. **Backcountry skiing** at Roger's Pass and Balu Pass is legendary. Contact the Roger's Pass Information Center for registration and info on areas and avalanche conditions. Glacier also boasts the **Nakimu Caves,** located off the Balu Pass Trail near the info center, an extensive limestone wonderland open only to experienced cavers. Access to the caves is granted a couple times per summer, depending on condi-tions, to groups led by a park officer; interested parties need to apply to the park superintendent (see **Orientation and Practical Info,** above) by early summer or hope for an empty spot at the last minute (not recommended).

HIKING. More than 140km of rough, often steep trails lead from the highway, inviting mountaineers to conquer the unconquerable. While the highway works its way through the park's lush valleys, a majority of the area in the parkland lies above the treeline, providing for incredible high altitude, highly aesthetic hikes.

Meeting of the Waters Trail (2km one-way). A gentle hike that leads to the impressive confluence of the Illecillewaet and Asulkan Rivers. Easy.

Avalanche Crest Trail (8½ km round-trip, 6hr.) offers spectacular views of Roger's Pass, Hermit Range, and Illecillewaet River Valley. The treeless slopes below the crest attest to the destructive power of winter snowslides and endanger the highway. Moderate.

Balu Pass Trail (10km round-trip, 4hr.). Trailhead is at the west edge of Rogers Centre parking lot, near Roger's Pass info station. The Ursus Major and Ursus Minor peaks provide the best chance of seeing wildlife. (*Balu* is Inuit for bear, while *Ursus* is Latin for it.) This trail is prime bear habitat; check with park wardens before embarking. Difficult.

Copperstain Trail (16km, 6hr.). Beaver River Trailhead, 10km east of the Glacier Park Lodge uphill through alpine meadows. From early July to late August, the park staff run sporadic interpretive hikes at 8:30am. Contact the visitors center for details. Moderate.

Illecillewaet Trails (varies, 1km-6.5km one-way). A plethora of trails leave from the campground (see **Camping**, above) and climb to the retreating Illecillewaet and Asulkan Glaciers. Dramatic views of the valley behind and opportunities to extend the hikes to the toes of the glaciers make these trails well worth the rigorous climbs. Difficult.

YOHO NATIONAL PARK ☎ 250

A Cree expression for awe and wonder, Yoho is the perfect name for this small, superlative-laden park. It sports some of the most engaging names in the Rockies, such as Kicking Horse Pass, named after Captain John Hector who, struggling to find a mountain pass for the Canadian Pacific Railroad, was kicked in the chest by his horse. Driving down Yoho's narrow pass on Hwy. 1, visitors can see evidence of geological forces: massive bent and tilted sedimentary rock layers exposed in sharply eroded cliff faces, and natural rock bridges formed by water that has carved away the stone. Beneath these rock walls, Yoho overflows with natural attractions, including the largest waterfall in the Rockies—Takakkaw Falls—and paleontolologically illuminating 500 million-year-old fossils.

⌂⚑ TRANSPORTATION AND PRACTICAL INFORMATION. The park lies on the Trans-Canada Hwy. (Hwy. 1), next to Banff National Park. Within Yoho, the town of **Field** is 27km west of Lake Louise on Hwy. 1. **Greyhound** (☎800-661-8747) stops for travelers waving their arms on the highway at the Field junction as long as they call first. **Hostelling International** runs a shuttle connecting hostels in Yoho, Banff, and Jasper National Parks and Calgary ($8-65). The **Visitors Centre** in Field is on Hwy. 1. (☎343-6783. Open in summer daily 8am-7pm; spring and fall 9am-5pm; winter 9am-4pm.) Other services include **bike rentals** (see **Equipment Rental** for Banff) and **park pass** sales ($6, senior $4.50, child $3, groups $12. Valid for Glacier and Revelstoke.) In case of **emergency**, call ☎911 in the Field area; the **Park Warden Office** (☎343-6142, 24hr.; ☎762-1473 for non-emergencies); or the **RCMP** (☎344-2221) in nearby Golden. The **post office** is at 312 Stephen Ave. (☎343-6365. Open M-F 8:30am-4:30pm.) **Postal Code:** V0A 1G0.

⌂⚑ ACCOMMODATIONS AND CAMPING. With one of the best locations of all the Rocky Mountain hostels, the ▓**Whiskey Jack Hostel (HI) ❶**, 13km off the Trans-Canada on the Yoho Valley Rd., perfectly blurs the line between civilization and nature. Located in one of Canada's most scenic spots, the hostel offers a kitchen, campfires, plumbing, propane light, easy access to Yoho's best high-country trails, and the splendor of the Takakkaw Falls right from the front porch. Reserve through the Banff Hostel. (☎403-762-4122. Open mid-June to mid-Oct., depending on snow. Su-Th $18, nonmembers $22; F-Sa $21, nonmembers $25.)

The four official **frontcountry campgrounds** offer a total of 200 sites, all easily accessible from the highway. All sites are first come, first served, but only Monarch and Kicking Horse fill up regularly in summer. ◨**Takakkaw Falls Campground ❶** is situated beneath mountains, glaciers, and the magnificent falls 14km up curvy Yoho Valley Rd. It offers only pump water and pit toilets, and campers must park in the Falls lot and haul their gear 650m to the peaceful sites. (Open late June until the snow flies. 35 sites, $13.) **Hoodoo Creek ❶**, on the west end of the park, has kitchen shelters, running hot water, flush toilets, a nearby river, and a playground. (Open June-early Sept. 30 sites, $13.) **Monarch Campground ❶** sits at the junction of Yoho Valley Rd. and Hwy. 1. (Open late June-early Sept. 46 sites and 10 walk-ins, $13.) **Kicking Horse ❶**, another kilometer up Yoho Valley Rd., has toilets and is wheelchair accessible. (Open mid-May to mid-Oct. 86 sites, $18. Hot showers.) Reserve one of two backcountry **alpine huts ❶** through the Alpine Club of Canada. (☎403-678-3200. $16.) The group campground at splendid **Lake O'Hara ❶**, in the east end of the park, can only be reached by a 13km trail or on a park-operated bus. (Bus reservations ☎343-6433, up to 3 months in advance. Round-trip $12. Permit required for camping.)

◪ FOOD. The most convenient food stop in Yoho, and potentially a sit-all-day-stop, is the ◨**Truffle Pigs Cafe and General Store ❶**, on Stephen Ave. in Field. Sells basic foodstuffs, microbrews, wine, and camping supplies. Local crafts line the walls, and the owners peddle home-made sandwiches ($4.25), breakfast ($4.50-7), and eclectically delicious $8-15 dinners. (☎343-6462. Has the only **ATM** in the area. Open daily 8am-10pm; winter M-Sa 10am-7pm.)

◪ OUTDOOR ACTIVITIES. The Great Divide is both the boundary between Alberta and BC as well as the Atlantic and Pacific watersheds. Here a stream forks with one arm flowing 1500km to the Pacific Ocean, and the other flowing 2500km to the Atlantic via Hudson's Bay. It is also the site of the **Burgess Shale,** a layer of sedimentary rock containing the world's most important animal fossils, imprints of the insect-like, soft-bodied organisms that inhabited the world's oceans prior to an intense burst of evolution known as the **Cambrian Explosion.** Discovered in 1909, the unexpected complexity of these 505 million-year-old specimens changed the way paleontologists thought about evolution. Larger, clumsier animals known as humans have since successfully lobbied to protect the shale from excessive tourism. Educational hikes led by the **Yoho-Burgess Shale Foundation** (☎800-343-3006) are the only way to see it. A full-day, 20km hike costs $45, under 12 $25. A steep 6km loop to the equally old and trilobite-packed **Mt. Stephen Fossil Beds** runs $25. (July to mid-Sept. only. Reservations required.) For easier sightseeing, follow the 14km of the Yoho Valley Rd. to views of the **Takakkaw Falls,** Yoho's most splendid waterfall, and the highest-altitude major falls in the Canadian Rockies.

HIKING. The park's six **backcountry campgrounds** and 400km of trail make for an intense wilderness experience, with countless quickly accessed trails exhibiting scenery equal to and beyond that of the larger parks. Before setting out, pick up **camping permits** ($6 per person per day), maps, and the free *Backcountry Guide to Yoho National Park* at the visitors center. Whiskey Jack Hostel (see above) is also well stocked with trail information. The park's finest terrain is in the Yoho Valley and is accessible only after the snow melts in mid- to late summer.

> **Iceline Trail** (via Little Yoho 19.8km, via Celeste Lake 17km). Starts at the hostel. Takes hikers briefly through forests of alder, spruce, and fir before leading them on an extended trip above the tree line, over glacial moraines, and past the striated rock and icy pools of Emerald Glacier. Moderate.

Emerald Triangle (21.5km round-trip). The route travels through the Yoho Pass (see *Backcountry Guide*) to the Wapta Highline trail, Burgess Pass, and back to the start. Most of the journey is above treeline with breathtaking views over much of Yoho's diverse landscape. Moderate.

Mt. Hunter Lookout to Upper Lookout (12.8km). Cuts through Yoho's lush lower altitudes, but manages a nice view of Kicking Horse and Beaverfoot valleys. Moderate.

Wapta Falls (4.8km round-trip). The trailhead is not marked on Hwy. 1 for westbound traffic as there is no left-turn lane. Continue 3km to the west entrance of the park, turn around, and come back east. Highlights include seeing the Kicking Horse River drop 30m. The least ambitious and least spectacular of the Yoho hikes. Easy.

KOOTENAY NATIONAL PARK ☎ 250/453

Kootenay National Park hangs off the Continental Divide on the southeast edge of British Columbia, bordering Alberta. Many visitors travel through Kootenay to get to or from Banff National Park on the majestic Banff-Windermere Hwy. (Hwy. 93), the first road to cross the Canadian Rockies. The federal government built the road in 1920 in exchange for the 8km of land on either side that now constitutes the park. Kootenay's biggest attraction is its lack of visitors: unlike Banff and Jasper, Kootenay has not been developed at all. The only civilization is found at the **Radium Hot Springs,** on the park's western border. The park's stately conifers, alpine meadows, and pristine peaks hide in Banff's shadow, allowing travelers to experience the true solitude of the Canadian Rockies while still in a national park.

✈ ？ ORIENTATION AND PRACTICAL INFORMATION

Kootenay lies southwest of Banff and Yoho National Parks. **Hwy. 93** runs through the park from the **Trans-Canada Hwy.** in Banff to **Radium Hot Springs** (see **Hot Springs,** p. 322) at the southwest edge of the park, where it joins **Hwy. 95.** One **Greyhound bus** per day stops at the **Esso station,** 7507 W Main St. (☎347-9726; open daily 7am-11pm.), at the junction of Hwy. 93 and Hwy. 95 in Radium Hot Springs, on the way to **Banff** (2hr., $22) and **Calgary** (3½hr., $39). The **park information center** and **Tourism BC Info Centre** are both located at 7556 Main St. W in Radium. They supply free maps and a backcountry hiking guide. (Parks Canada: ☎347-9505; Tourism BC: ☎347-9331. Open July-Aug. daily 9am-7pm; Sept.-June approximately 9am-4pm.) The **Kootenay Park Lodge** operates another visitors center 63km north of Radium. (☎403-762-9196. Open July-Aug. daily 9am-8pm; reduced hours in June and early Sept.) The **Park Administration Office,** on the access road to Redstreak Campground, dispenses the backcountry hiking guide and is open in the winter. (☎347-9615. Open M-F 8am-noon and 1-4pm.) An **ambulance** can be reached at ☎342-2055. In an **emergency,** call the Banff Park Warden (☎403-762-4506) or the **police** in either Invermere (☎342-9292) or Radium Hot Springs (☎347-9393). **Windermere District Hospital** is in Invermere, 850 10th Ave. (☎342-9201), 15km south of Radium on Hwy. 95. The **post office** is on Radium Blvd in Radium Hot Springs. (☎347-9460. Open M-F 9am-5pm.) **Postal Code:** V0A 1M0.

♠ ♥ ACCOMMODATIONS AND FOOD

The **Misty River Lodge (HI) ❶,** 5036 Hwy. 93, is the first left after you exit the park's West Gate. Offers bike rentals for $10 per day. (☎347-9912. Dorms $17, nonmembers $22; private room with bath $42, nonmembers $65.) There's also a **B&B ❹** upstairs. ($69-79, 10% HI discount.) Downtown, Radium features over 30 other motels, with high-season doubles starting at $40. The park's only serviced campground is **Redstreak ❶,** on the access road that departs Hwy. 95 near the south end of Radium Hot Springs, which boasts 242 sites, including 50 fully-serviced sites and 38 with electricity only. Features toilets, firewood, and playgrounds. Arrive early to secure a spot. (Open mid-May through mid-Oct. $17; full RV sites $22. Free showers.) **McLeod Meadows ❶,** 27km north of the West Gate entrance on Hwy. 93, offers more solitude and wooded sites on the banks of the very blue Kootenay River, as well as access to hiking trails. (Open mid-May to mid-Sept. 98 sites, $13.) From September to May, snag one of the seven free winter sites at the **Dolly Varden ❶** picnic area, 36km north of the West Gate entrance, which boasts free firewood, water, toilets, and a shelter. Ask at the visitors centers for details on **Crooks Meadow ❶,** which is available for groups (75 people max.), and cheap ($8), unserviced camping in the nearby Invermere Forest District.

There is little affordable food in Kootenay, with the exception of a few basic staples at the **Kootenay Park Lodge.** Radium supports a few inexpensive eateries on Main St. The bst selection of groceries is at **Mountainside Market,** 7546 Main St. E. right next to the Visitor Centre. (☎ 347-9600. Open M-Sa 9am-9pm, Su 9am-8pm.)

🔏 OUTDOOR ACTIVITIES

The 95km **Banff-Windermere Highway (Hwy. 93)** forms the sinuous backbone of Kootenay. Stretching from Radium Hot Springs to Banff, the highway follows the Kootenay and Vermilion Rivers, passing views of glacier-enclosed peaks, dense stands of virgin forest, and green, glacier-fed rivers. The wild landscape of the Kootenay River Valley remains unblemished but for the ribbon of road.

HOT SPRINGS
The park's main attraction is **Radium Hot Springs,** named after the radioactive element detected there in trace quantities. The crowded complex is responsible for the traffic and towel-toting tourists just inside the West Gate. Natural mineral waters fill two swimming pools—a hot one for soaking at 40°C (open 9am-11pm) and a cooler one for swimming at 27°C (open noon-9pm). The hot pool is wheelchair accessible. (☎ 347-9485. Single entry $6.25, children and seniors $5.25; winter $5.25/$4.75; group and family rates available. Lockers $0.25, towel rental $1.25, swimsuit rental $1.50.) The **Lussier Hot Springs** in Whiteswan Lake Provincial Park offer a more natural alternative to Radium's lifeguards and ice-cream vendors. The springs flow directly from the riverbank into the Lussier River, and engineered rock walls form shallow pools that trap the water at varying temperatures. To find this diamond in the rough, turn onto the rough dirt logging road 66km south of Radium and follow it for 17km.

HIKING
The **Rockwall Trail** in the north of the park is the most popular backcountry area in Kootenay. All **backcountry** campers must stop at a visitors center (see **Orientation and Practical Info,** p. 321) for the hiking guide, which has maps, trail descriptions, and topographical profiles, and sells a mandatory **wilderness pass.** ($6 per person per night, $38 per year.) A number of shorter trails lead right off Hwy. 93 about 15km from the Banff border. Two fire roads, plus all of Hwy. 93, are open for **mountain biking,** but Kootenay lacks the extensive trail systems of its larger siblings. Icy water and rock flour from glaciers make for lousy fishing.

Marble Canyon Trail (750m, 15min.). Many tourists enjoy this path, which traverses a deep limestone gorge cut by Tokumm Creek before ending at a roaring waterfall. Easy.

Paint Pots Trail (1.6km, 30min.). 3.2km south of Marble Canyon on Hwy. 93. This partially wheelchair-accessible trail leads to springs rich in iron oxide. Tourist-heavy. Easy.

Stanley Glacier Trail (5.5km, 4hr.). Starts 3.5km from the Banff entrance and leads into a glacier-gouged valley, ending 1.6km from the foot of Stanley Glacier. One of the hot springs' most astounding and therapeutic powers is their ability to suck travelers out of the woods, leaving Kootenay's many longer hiking trails uncrowded. Considered the "best dayhike in the park." Moderately difficult.

Kindersley Pass (16.5km). The 2 trailheads at either end of the route, Sinclair Creek and Kindersley Pass, are less than 1km apart on Hwy. 93, about 10km inside the West Gate entrance. Trail climbs more than 1000m to views of the Columbia River Valley in the west and the crest of the Rockies in the east. Strenuous.

NORTHERN BRITISH COLUMBIA

Northern BC remains among the most remote and sparsely inhabited regions of North America. Averaging one person per 15 sq. km, the land's loneliness and sheer physical beauty are overwhelming. Native peoples have lived here for thousands of years, adapting their lifestyles and culture to patterns of animal migration and the uncompromising climate. White settlers began migrating West in the early 19th century, attracted by the wealth of natural resources. While furs were lucrative, it wasn't until several gold rushes hit, that stampedes rushed in to settle permanently. Since then, the lumber and mining industries have brought a steady flow eager to extract the wealth of the land. Despite some tell-tale signs of logging and mining, the land remains mainly unspoiled. Unfortunately the area is often blown through by travelers hell bent on Alaska. Their loss; the stark mountains, yawning canyons, roaring rivers, and clear lakes are left all that more pristine for those who will stop to appreciate them.

ALONG HWY. 20: CHILCOTIN HWY.

WILLIAMS LAKE TO BELLA COOLA ☎250

The allure of the Chilcotin Hwy. lies not in its lackluster endpoint, Bella Coola, but in the rugged and scenic lands along the 457km highway (a 5-7hr. drive). Most of the drive is smooth sailing, but the unforgettable "Hill" is an unforgettably guard-rail-less 21km of gravel (see below). Leaving Williams Lake, the Chilcotin Hwy. heads west across the **Fraser River** and climbs briefly before flattening out through forests and pastures dotted with cattle ranches. Warning to unsuspecting travelers: cattle at large. Watch for them on roads to avoid unplanned barbecues.

Alexis Creek (Km 110), **Nimpo Lake** (Km 300), and **Anahim** (Km 305) are stops with gas, cafe, lodging, and a general store. **Bull Canyon Provincial Park ❶**, 8km past Alexis Creek, features fishing on the Chilcotin River as well as two dozen tent sites with pit toilets ($12). Lakeside resort turn-offs are sprinkled along the highway with a concentration worth visiting at **Puntzi Lake.** The best meal can be consumed around Nimpo Lake at the **Chilcotin's Gate ❷.** Burgers $7-8, sandwich and fries $7, steak dinner $13. (☎742-3720. Open daily June-Sept. 6am-9pm; winter 7am-7pm.)

Low-priced, convenient camping is across the highway at **Vagabond RVs ❶**, but bring earplugs to sleep through the early morning take-offs of floatplanes. (Tent $10, RV $15, free shower, coin laundry.) **Nimpo Towing** aids the Chilcotin-traveler in need

(☎ 742-3484, M-Sa 8am-6pm) or feeds the hungered traveler at the bakery and cafe (open M-Sa 6am-6pm). **Chilko River Expeditions** runs **rafting** expeditions along the Chilcotin and Chilko Rivers from Williams Lake lodging. (☎ 354-2056 or 877-271-7626. $100 for daytrip.) Whatever you do and wherever you stay, bring enough insect repellant to permanently damage your skin.

PUNTZI LAKE. A 5km turn-off along a gravel road at Chilanko Forks (Km 175) leads to the 9km long **Puntzi Lake,** surrounded by several affordable resort options. Summer activities include fishing for kokanee and rainbow trout while watching white pelicans. Smiling owners dole out campsites, cabins, and canoe rentals at **Puntzi Lake Resort ❶** (☎ 481-1176 or 800-578-6804; sites $15; cabins $50-90; full RV sites $17-21) and **Barney's Lakeside Resort ❶** (☎ 481-1100; sites $15; cabins $45 for 2, $5 each additional person).

PARKS. South of the Chilcotin Hwy., **Tsylos Provincial Park** (sigh-LOSS) boasts Canada's first grizzly bear refuge, the glacier-fed, trout- and salmon-rich Lake Chilko. To reach the **Gwa da Ts'ih campground** on the north side of the park, turn off at Tatla Lake (Km 220) and drive 63km on washboard gravel roads (4-6hr. from Williams Lake). The highway enters the southern portion of **Tweedsmuir Provincial Park** (☎ 398-4414) at Heckman's Pass, 360km west of Williams Lake. The park protects the Atnarko River, Hunlen Falls, Monarch Glacier, and the colorfully streaked shield volcanoes of the Rainbow Mountains. Unfortunately, road trippers' introduction to the park is the final 21km of gravel road, commonly referred to as "The Hill": a one-lane, brake-burning, head-turning, windshield-cracking, free-falling, no-barrier, roller-coaster ride with steep (18%) grades and switchbacks exceptionally notable for their sharpness and susceptibility to avalanches, in addition to undeniably spectacular views (*Let's Go* always recommends that drivers keep both eyes on the road, but especially recommends it here) of the Coast Range and the valley below (road conditions ☎ 900-565-4997).

For decades, Hwy. 20 ended at **Anahim Lake,** 315km west of Williams Lake. In 1955, frustrated by inaction from a government that said the road to the sea could not, financially and physically, be completed, locals got two bulldozers, borrowed money, and finished the job themselves. The route's alternate name is the "Freedom Highway." After the hill, the highway is paved again for its most scenic 75km, following the **Bella Coola River** into town along the Hwy. 20 corridor through the rest of Tweedsmuir Park and into Bella Coola. Perhaps the biggest thing in Tweedsmuir is the terminus of the 25- to 30-day **Alexander Mackenzie Heritage Trail,** reserved for those hikers beyond hard-core and off the deep end. Its 420km stretch from **Blackwater River,** just west of Quesnel, across western British Columbia to **Burnt Creek Bridge** on Hwy. 20, traces the final leg of Mackenzie's 1793 journey across Canada to the West Coast. Mackenzie reached the Pacific more than a decade before Lewis and Clark, although the Americans continue to hog all the glory. The southern end of the park overflows with more hiking opportunities. One multi-day trip goes to **Hunlen Falls;** a difficult, grizzly inhabited 16.4km one-way (9hr.) hike. Trailhead access by 4WD next to the gate at the bottom of "The Hill." Depending on whom you ask, the cataract holds numerous records (is it second highest in BC? fourth highest in the Canada? the world? Locals disagree; but they are really, really big, loud, and supremely majestic in their misty descent).

After hiking into the falls, visitors can spend the night at **Turner Lake ❶** (all lake campsites $5) before renting canoes on the snow-capped-peak-studded **Turner Lakes Chain.** ($30 per day, 3-5 days. Canoe reservations, cabin rentals ($50), and flights for three people out to the lake ($210) are all available through **Tweedsmuir Air Services,** ☎ 800-668-4335, out of Nimpo Lake.) One can also walk the gorgeous alpine tundra wonderland up to and beyond **Ptarmigan Lake** (12km one-way, 5hr., two backcountry campsites). Summertime daytrippers can explore **Rainbow Ridge Trail** (trailhead before "the Hill," 8km one-way, 2-3hr.) or for a shorter trip follow the **Valley Loop/Burnt Bridge Trail** (5km round-trip, 1-2hr.) from the Mackenzie Heritage Trailhead (50km east of Bella Coola). The viewpoint overlooks the Bella Coola Valley. The park has two campgrounds along Hwy. 20; **Atnarko ❶**, right at the bottom of the hill (28 sites), and **Fisheries Pool ❶**, at the western end of the park (14 sites), both costing $10. Call the park for details (see above) and look for brochures in the Williams Lake Visitor Centre and at the campgrounds.

BELLA COOLA. The pot of pewter at the end of the Chilcotin rainbow is the coastal village of Bella Coola, homeland of the Nuxalk Nation. Salmon fishery restrictions and the pull-out of the logging industry over the last three years have severely depressed the local economy. This has made the town increasingly dependent on the tourism from the **BC Ferries'** *Discovery Passage* route, which links Bella Coola with Port Hardy, on the northern tip of Vancouver Island, from mid-June to mid-September. (☎888-223-3779. Adults $103, ages 5-11 $51, under 5 free. Car $205.) The **Shell Station,** across from the Valley Inn on McKenzie Rd., does repairs and has the only gas in town. (☎799-5314. Open daily 8am-8pm.) The **visitors center** is located in the *Tweedsmuir Travel* office (the place to make BC Ferries reservations) downtown. (☎799-5638, 800-515-8998. Open M, W, and F 9:30am-4:30pm, Tu and Th 9:30am-6pm, Sa 2-6pm.) Getting a room in town is expensive, but the **Bella Coola Motel ❹**, downtown, has **camping ❶** on its large back lawn. (☎799-5323; www.bcadventure.com/bellacoolamotel. Double rooms for $65. Tents $10; RV $12, no RV sites. Toilets, free showers.) For shaded and forested sites, head to **Gnome's Home Campground and RV Park ❶**, in Hagensborg 16km east of Bella Coola along the highway. (☎982-2504. Sites $12; full RV sites $15. Showers included.)

For a bite to eat, try the **Bay Motor Hotel ❶** coffee shop, on Hwy. 20 in Hagensborg, or the small grocery store across the street. (☎982-2212. Open daily 6am-9pm; F and Sa to 6am-10pm.) In Bella Coola, sit on the deck and enjoy pricier dinner options at the **Bella Coola Valley Inn ❸**. (☎799-5316. Open daily 7am-9pm.)

WILLIAMS LAKE TO QUESNEL   ☎250

Williams Lake, 90km north of 100 Mile House, is the Cariboo's largest town, but certainly not its most appealing. Fortunately, it's easy to leave, with Hwy. 20 meandering 457km west to **Bella Coola** (see p. 323) and Hwy. 97 continuing north to the rough-hewn lumber towns of **Quesnel** and **Prince George.** The biggest thing happening in town is the celebration of its cowboy heritage over Canada Day weekend (July 1) with the **Williams Lake Stampede.** Festivities include a rodeo, mountain race, wild cow milking, barn dance, and live music. (☎800-717-6336. $11-15, cheaper if bought before June 14.) **Tourist information** in town is available on Hwy. 97. (☎392-5025. Open June-Aug. daily 9am-5pm; Sept.-May M-F 9am-4pm.) The town **library** at the corner of 3rd Ave. N and Proctor St. has free **Internet access** for 30min. (☎392-3630. Open Tu-Th 10am-8pm, F-Sa 10am-5pm.)

The **Slumber Lodge,** 27 7th Ave., is cheap with a small indoor pool, phones, and cable. (☎392-7116 or 800-577-2244. Singles $45; doubles $50.) For a cheap thrill, pitch tent on the **Stampede grounds** in the center of town. To get there, cross the bridge on Hwy. 20 from the junction with Hwy. 97 and take first right on Mackenzie Rd.; the grounds are on your right. (☎392-6585. $8, full RV sites $15.)

To escape the bustle, bask on the beach at **Blue Lake Holiday Campgrounds** (☎297-6505), turn off at Blue Lake Rd. 32km north of town and 3km up a gravel road. Campsites ($12) and canoes ($5 per hr.) on the bright blue-green lake are at your disposal. Corral your buckin' bronco and hightail it to the all-you-can-eat chock-full salad and hot entree buffet at **Fraser Inn,** Hwy. 97 north of intersection. (☎398-7055. Salad bar only $6, whole shebang $8. M-F 11am-1:30pm, Sa and Su 11am-4pm.) If looking to fill your saddlebag with an overflowing sub or wrap, the deli **Zesto's,** 86 3rd Ave. N, has every option under the western sun. (☎398-9801. Open M-Sa 8:30am-10pm, Su 10am-10pm.)

The 122km drive north to Quesnel can be a little dull, but those willing to subject their car to a little gravel can make it more interesting. About 35km north of Williams Lake, the **Soda Creek Townsite Rd.** splits from Hwy. 97 for 20km of rustic splendor alongside the **Fraser River.** The road returns to the highway several kilometers south of the free **Marguerite Ferry,** which shuttles drivers across the river to a gravel road paralleling Hwy. 97 for the remainder of the trip to Quesnel. (Open May-Oct. 5min., on demand 7-11:45am, 1-4:45pm, and 6-6:45pm.)

QUESNEL ☎ 250

The town of Quesnel, 123km north of Williams Lake and 116km south of Prince George, takes great pride in its gold-driven past and forestry-propelled present. The town itself has little to offer but provides relatively close access to other options. After being welcomed into town by the world's largest (and purplest) goldpan on the north end of town on Hwy. 97, it's only a 10min. drive to **Pinnacles Provincial Park:** cross the river on Marsh Rd., then turn right on Baker Dr., and follow it for 5km. Park at the gate walk 1km to the hoodoos—volcanic rock formations that look like giant sand dribble castles—and impressive views. Every third weekend of July, crowds flock to Quesnel for the wholesome family fun of **Billy Barker Days,** featuring a rodeo, live entertainment, and a "Crash-to-Pass" demolition derby. The logging industry maintains a very strong presence (and odor) in this industrial oasis.

■ ◪ **ORIENTATION AND PRACTICAL INFORMATION.** Hwy. 97 becomes Front St. in Quesnel and wraps along the river. One block over the main road, Reid St., is the parallel Front St. in the "city centre." The **Greyhound** depot is on Kinshant between St. Laurent and Barlow. (☎992-2231 or 800-661-8747. Open M-F 6am-8pm, Sa 6am-noon and 6-7:30pm, Su 6-10:30am and 6-7:30pm.) Buses run to **Prince George** (1½hr.; 3 per day; $19, students and seniors $17) and **Vancouver** (10hr.; 3 per day; $87, students and seniors $78). The **visitors center,** 705 Carson Ave., is just off Hwy. 97 at the south end of town. (☎992-8716 or 800-992-4922. Open July-Aug. daily 8am-6pm; mid-May to June and Sept.-Oct. daily 9am-4pm; Nov. to mid-May W-Su 9am-4pm.) **Market and pharmacy: Safeway,** 445 Reid St. (☎992-6477. Open daily 8am-10pm.) **Free Internet access** is at the **library,** 593 Barlow Ave. on two computers. Reserve in advance. (☎992-7912. Open Tu-Th 10am-8pm, F-Sa 10am-5pm.) Call ☎911 in an **emergency,** or contact the **police** at ☎992-9211. The **post office** is at 346 Reid St. (☎992-2200. Open M-F 8:45am-5:15pm.) **Postal Code:** V2J 2M0.

◪ ◪ **ACCOMMODATIONS AND FOOD.** With a nod to Quesnel's history, the **Gold Pan Hotel ❸,** 855 Front St., at the north edge of downtown, offers cheap rooms with dingy bedspreads but clean bathrooms, cable, coffee, and phones. (☎992-2107. Singles $40; doubles $44.) Treat yourself to the **Caribou Hotel ❸,** 254 Front St., downtown. Ten more bucks will land you a river view, continental breakfast, TV, phone, and whirlpool bath. Request rooms 1-3 when a live band plays downstairs in the pub. (☎992-2333 or 800-665-3200. Live music W-Sa. Open M-Sa 11am-1am, Su 11am-midnight. Check monthly calendar for nightly drink and food bargains. A **drive-in liquor store** keeps the place hoppin'.) For more ambience than the cheap RV parks on either end of town, try **Robert's Roost Campground ❷,** 3121 Gook Rd., 8km south of town and 2km off Hwy. 97, which offers elegantly landscaped lakeside sites. Features include coin showers, laundry, playground, and fishing; row boat and canoe rentals are $5. (☎ 747-2015. Sites $17; full RV sites $22.) Pub food can be found throughout Quesnel and south on Hwy. 97. A burlap-bag-ceilinged alternative for any meal, **Granville's Coffee ❶**, Reid St., bakes gigantic ham and cheese muffins ($1.50) and sells heaping sandwiches (under $6—try the Hungry Hobo) and $5 mac and cheese. (Open daily 7am-10pm.)

◙ 🖉 SIGHTS AND OUTDOOR ACTIVITIES. The long-defunct mining town of **Barkerville,** 90km east of Quesnel along Hwy. 26, was established in 1862 after Billy Barker found gold on Williams Creek and sparked BC's largest gold rush. For the rest of the 19th century, Barkerville was the benchmark against which the rest of western Canada was measured. Since 1958 the town has been operated as an educational **"living museum,"** housing only residents who run the local B&Bs. (☎ 994-3332. Open daily 8am-8pm in summer. 2-day pass $8, students and seniors $6.25, youth $4.75, children $2.25, under 5 free. 30% off from late May to mid-June. Additional fee for shows and stagecoach rides.) Although brochures ask that you "plan to spend enough time to re-live a century of time," most modern folks find that one day is enough to see it all. However, those staying a while might find services 8km towards Quesnel in the mining town of **Wells.** The visitors center has the scoop on mill tours at **West Fraser Lumber** (times arranged on demand).

Bowron Lakes Provincial Park is a paddling paradise located 25km north of Barkerville. This necklace of lakes forms a 116km loop in the heart of the **Cariboo Mountains,** which takes most canoers 10 days to complete. The park service charges $50 per person to canoe the circuit and $25 per person to canoe the westside to Unna Lake (three to four days) to help maintain the 54 lakeside camping areas. Reservations are required through **Super, Natural BC** (☎ 800-435-5622); two walk-ons per day. **Becker Lodge** rents canoes and kayaks (☎ 992-8864 or 800-808-4761; $130-230 for the circuit), as does the **Bowron Lake Lodge** (☎ 992-2733; $100-225). Both also offer camping and cabins within a stone's throw of the loop's starting point. **Tent sites ❶** overlooking the lake are more private at Becker (tents $15, RVs $20) while lodging in the **Bowron Lake Motel ❹** is the cheapest option with a hard roof ($60).

Anyone traveling between Prince George and Quesnel on Hwy. 97 will live a better life for having stopped at **◪Cinema Second Hand General Store,** 32km north of Quesnel on Hwy. 97. Cash-strapped road warriors will find everything they need (except an actual cinema), plus a wide variety of things they could never possibly need, like old-fashioned snowshoes and disco LPs. The store also offers **free camping** with a pit toilet. (☎ 998-4774. Open daily 9am-9pm.)

PRINCE GEORGE ☎ 250

Prince George stands at the confluence of the Nechako and Fraser Rivers, the banks of which play host to the pulp and lumber mills that crowd the valley floor in an impressive display of industrial *forte*. Prince George is a crucial point of transport for goods and services heading in all directions, a true nerve center for the Northwest. But even with recent additions to the town—a civic center, a national university, and a Western League hockey team—Prince George is most definitely a stopover, not a destination.

✦ ◱ ORIENTATION AND TRANSPORTATION

Hwy. 97 cuts straight through Prince George just to the west of the city center. **Hwy. 16** runs through the city center, becomes **Victoria St.** in town, and crosses Hwy. 97 to the south of town. Running the width of the city, **15th St.** is home to most of the shopping centers and terminates on the east end downtown.

HOW MUCH WOOD DOES A CANUCK
CHUCK?
About 76 million cubic meters a year. That's enough to bring BC 15.3 billion loonies from exports, employ a group of people three times the population of the Yukon (nearly 100,000), and dole out $4 billion in wages and salaries. The majority of BC's chopped riches make their way to Canada's North American next-door neighbor—the USA—in the form of softwood lumber. Before you get your tree-hugging self heading to BC to tie yourself to a sapling in protest, note this: it's been done before and with some success. As a result of such a protest, stringent forest management laws were passed leading to careful planning and reforestation efforts. Over 200 million baby trees are plopped in the soil each year, and tree planters earn their wages by the tree. Eat your heart out, Johnny Appleseed.

Greyhound, 1566 12th Ave. (☎564-5454 or 800-661-8747; www.greyhound.ca), opposite the Victoria St. Visitors Center, is open M-Sa 6:30am-5:30pm and 8pm-midnight; Su 6:30-9:30am, 3:30-5:30pm, and 8:30pm-midnight. Buses to **Edmonton** (10hr., 2 per day, $101); **Dawson Creek** (6hr., 2 per day, $56); **Prince Rupert** (10hr., 2 per day, $96); and **Vancouver** (12hr., 3 per day, $104). **BC Rail,** 1108 Industrial Way (☎561-4033; www.bcrail.ca. Open M-F 3-11:30pm, Su 6-10pm and M, Th, Sa 6-10am), 2km south off Hwy. 97 at the end of Terminal Blvd., runs the scenic Cariboo Prospector to **Vancouver** (14hr.; M, Th, Sa at 7am; $247, over 59 $222 children $148; 3 meals included.

ⓩ PRACTICAL INFORMATION

Tourist Information: Visitors Center, 1198 Victoria St. (☎562-3700 or 800-668-7646; www.tourismpg.bc.ca), at 15th Ave. Open M-F 8:30am-6pm, Sa 9am-6pm. Another center (☎563-5493) is at the junction of Hwy. 16 and Hwy. 97 beneath a huge "Mr. P.G." logger. Open daily May-Sept. 9am-8pm.

Equipment Rental: Centre City Surplus, 1222 4th Ave. (☎564-2400), rents and sells outdoor gear at competitive prices. Open M-Sa 9am-6pm, Su 11am-4pm.

Market: The Real Canadian Superstore, 2155 Ferry Ave. (☎960-1335), at Hwy. 16, has loads of fresh produce, aisles of bulk bins, ethnic foods, a pharmacy, clothes, and gas. (Open M-F 9am-10pm, Sa 8am-10pm, Su 10am-8pm.)

Laundromat: Whitewash Laundromat, 231 George St. (☎563-2300). Wash $1.50, dry $0.25 per 8min. Open M-Sa 7:30am-6pm.

Emergency: ☎911.

Police: 999 Brunswick St. (☎561-3300).

Fire: ☎561-7664

Crisis Line: ☎563-1214. 24hr.

Hospital: 2000 15th Ave. (☎565-2000; emergency 565-2444).

Internet Access: Free 1hr. daily at the **library,** 887 Dominion St. (☎563-9251). 12 computers. Open in summer M-Th 10am-9pm, F-Sa 10am-5:30pm; winter Su 1-5pm. **Internet Cafe** (☎561-0011), inside London Drugs in the Parkwood Mall, at Victoria and 15th St. $3.20 per 30min. Open M-Sa 9am-10pm, Su 10am-8pm.

Post Office: 1323 5th Ave. (☎561-2568). Open M-F 8:30am-5pm. **Postal Code:** V2L 3L0.

⌂ ACCOMMODATIONS AND CAMPING

During the summer, the **College of New Caledonia Student Residence ❶**, 3330 22nd Ave. (turn off Hwy. 97 west of downtown and take the second right), offers the best deal in town, boasting clean rooms and a young crowd. Rooms include a fridge and microwave. With kitchen, lounge, BBQ, sundeck, and cheap laundry, the price is unbeatable. (☎561-5849 or 800-371-8111. Linen $5. Wash $1.50, dry $0.50. Singles $20; doubles $25.) To upgrade to a queen bed and cable TV, a good bet is the **Queensway Court Motel ❸**, 1616 Queensway, one motel over from 17th Ave., close to downtown. Well-kept rooms come with fridges and cable. (☎562-5068. Singles $36; doubles $40.) The **Log House Restaurant and Kampground,** located on the shores of Tabor Lake, pleases adults with its impeccable grounds, proximity to fishing, and a costly German-owned steakhouse. To reach this slice of Europe, head out of town on Hwy. 16 E; after 3km, turn right on "Old Cariboo Hwy.," left on Giscome Rd. and follow the signs (15min. from downtown). Rowboats, canoes, and pedal boats can be rented. (☎963-9515. Boats all $8 per hr. Sites $15; full RV sites $22; cabins with kitchenettes $45; teepees $10 per person.) To secure a bed and breakfast room, call the helpful **B&B Hotline** (☎888-266-5555).

◉ FOOD AND NIGHTLIFE

While it is hard to escape chains and interchangeable pasta joints on George St., a few alternatives stand out. Freshness exudes from the **1085 Cafe ❷**, 1085 Vancouver St., tucked away at 11th Ave. near the mall. Enjoy vegetable pita pizzas ($6.75), wraps ($4-6), salads, or chai ($3.50) on the flowered patio. (☎960-2272. Open M 7am-4pm, Sa 9am-4pm, Tu-F 7am-7pm.) Hit up hip **Javva Mugga Mocha Cafe ❶**, 304 George St., for the best coffee in town. (☎562-3338. Open M-F 7am-5:30pm, Sa 8am-5:30pm.) An oasis for the big appetite, **Esther's Inn ❸**, 1151 Commercial Crescent, off Hwy. 97 near 15th Ave., has an all-you-can-eat spread laid out next to a waterfall in the tropical dining area. Main dish theme varies. Lunch $9, dinner M-Th $12, F-Sa $14. (Open for lunch 11am-2pm, dinner 4-10pm.)

There's no shortage of taps in Prince George. **JJ's Pub,** 1970 S Ospika off 15th Ave. heading from Hwy. 97 to UNBC, reminds its loyal Canadian crowd and visitors that "Canadians kick ass." (☎562-2234. Open daily 11am-midnight.) Cowboys congregate for live country rock at **Cadillac Ranch,** 1390 2nd Ave., and two-step under disco lights. (☎563-7720. Open M-Th 9pm-2am, F-Sa 8pm-2am.) Clubs and bars teem with college students during the academic year; in summer, twentysomethings line up outside **Sgt. O'Flaherty's,** 770 Brunswick at 7th Ave., under the Crest Hotel. Thursday nights, pints fill up for $3. Live music nightly, except for when the live acts are pre-empted by special events—then you'll see the crowds swell up even more than usual. (☎563-0121. Open M-Sa 4pm-1am.)

⚑ ♫ OUTDOOR ACTIVITIES AND EVENTS

PARKS. Fort George Park, on the banks of the Fraser River off 20th Ave., offers an expansive lawn, beach volleyball courts, picnic tables, and barbecue pits. It also makes a perfect starting point for the 11km **Heritage River Trail,** which wanders through the city and along the Fraser and Nechako Rivers. After meandering through **Cottonwood Island Nature Park,** off River Rd., you'll get a sense of Prince George at its rawest and most industrial. For a bird's eye view of Prince George— the cement jungle—scramble up to **Connaught Hill Park,** with picnic tables and ample frisbee-throwing space. To reach the park, scale the yellow metal staircase across 15th Ave. from the visitors center or take Connaught Dr. off Queensway. **McMillan Regional Park** is right across the Nechako River, off Hwy. 97 N and features a deep ravine with a view of the city from the river's cutbanks. Two parks farther out of town have wide trails that are wheelchair accessible and double as cross-country skiing paths in the winter. The lush **Forests for the World,** only 15 min. away (take Hwy. 97 N, turn left on 15th Ave., right on Foothills Blvd., left onto Cranbrook Hill Rd., and finally left on Kueng Rd.), will pump the fresh woodsy air right back into your lungs. To take advantage of the web of trails, pick up a map at the Visitors Center first. The trails at **Esker's Provincial Park** (☎ 565-6340), off Hwy. 97 (12km north) and 28km down Ness Lake Rd., circle three lakes.

FISHING. With more than 1600 lakes within a 150km radius, fishing is excellent near Prince George. The closest spot is **Tabor Lake,** where the rainbow trout all but jump into boats in spring and early summer. Tabor is east on Hwy. 16; follow the directions to the Log House Restaurant and Kampground described above. For a complete listing of lakes and licensing information, contact the Visitors Center.

EVENTS. Imagine finding organic produce, baked goods, jams, salsas, and tofu concoctions in this town of chain food. Each Saturday these unexpected treats are available on tables at the **Farmers Market,** Courthouse Plaza on George Ave. (☎ 563-3383. Open May-Sept. 8:30am-1pm.) **Mardi Gras** (☎ 564-3737) lasts for 10 days in late February and features such events as snow golf, dog-pull contests, and bed races. You'll swear you're in New Orleans. **Sandblast** (☎ 564-9791) sends daredevils down the steep, snowless Nechako Cutbanks on the third Sunday in August. Anyone can participate, using almost any contraption—see how well your couch fares against the bikers, if you've got the guts.

JOHN HART (HWY. 97): PRINCE GEORGE TO DAWSON CREEK

For most travelers, the highlight of a stay in Prince George is departing for points elsewhere. To get to Mt. Robson, Jasper, or points farther east, take the Yellowhead Hwy. (Hwy 16) eastbound out of town. To connect to the Cassiar Hwy. (Hwy 37) and go to places like Prince Rupert or the Queen Charlotte Islands, take Hwy. 16 westbound out of Prince George. If Dawson Creek or the Alaska Highway is your thing, then roll north on Hwy. 97 (the 'Hart' or 'John Hart' Hwy.). Neon lights and strip malls become a distant memory a few kilometers into the 402km stretch from Prince George to Dawson Creek (Mile 0 of the Alaska Hwy.). The road cuts a lonely swath along a winding path through the forests of northern British Columbia. The first outpost of civilization is the micropolis of **Bear Lake,** 74km along Hwy. 97, which offers a motel, RV park, restaurant, and gas.

CROOKED RIVER AND WHISKERS POINT PROVINCIAL PARKS

Situated on **Bear Lake,** 2km south of town, **Crooked River Provincial Park** ❶ offers a great beach for swimming and picnicking, as well as 90 secluded, wooded campsites. The trails around the lake make this park well-suited for winter activities such as tobogganing, snowshoeing, and cross-country skiing. For park conditions or ski and weather info, call ☎ 562-8288 during business hours. (Campground ☎ 972-4492. Toilets. Gates locked 11pm-7am. $15.) **Whiskers Point Park** ❶, 51km past Bear Lake, has the same lakefront charm and the same amenities as Crooked River on a slightly smaller scale. The park provides a boat launch for the large **McLeod Lake.** (Toilets. Gates locked 11pm-7am. $15.)

MACKENZIE

Blink and you'll miss **MacKenzie Junction,** 26km past Whiskers Point. From the junction, it's 149km to the next town of note, Chetwynd, and almost 80km to the next gas station, **Silver Sands Gas.** (☎788-0800. Open daily 9am-10:30pm.) The junction also provides a turn-off to the town of **MacKenzie,** 29km north on Hwy. 39, the largest town in the area and home to the closest hospital. Barring medical emergency, MacKenzie is probably not worth the detour unless it has been your life's dream to see the world's largest tree crusher.

CHETWYND

Pause to eat your picnic directly in front of the stubby but voluminous Bijoux Falls, 115km before Chetwynd at **Bijoux Falls Provincial Park.** 300km from Prince George, **Chetwynd** is the Chainsaw Sculpture Capital of the World. It's worth cruising downtown to see what's not visible from the highway. Ask at the **visitors center** for a town guide to see what chopped wood dreams are made of. (☎401-4100. Open daily 9am-5pm.) **Wildmare Campground ❶,** 5km before town along the highway, provides toilets, laundry facilities, and budget rates for basic sites. (☎788-2747. Tents $8; RV $18. Showers $2.) If clean and affordable is what you desire, head for the **Chetwynd Court Motel ❸,** 5104 North Access Rd. right off Hwy. 94, which offers TV and kitchenettes. (☎788-2271. Rooms $45.) After Chetwynd, Dawson Creek is 102km away.

MONKMAN PROVINCIAL PARK

The overlooked **Monkman Provincial Park** (☎787-3407) covers a gorgeous slab of the Rockies foothills and a few peaks as well. The park is home to the **Kinuseo Falls,** which are taller than Niagara Falls and totally surrounded by wilderness. Several dayhikes provide views and some easy paddling below the falls. The 4.5km Stone Corral Trail leads along a high cliff, past various fossils, to two caves. A 50km trail to Monkman Lake and ten spectacular waterfalls beyond takes 3 days and begins at the campground below. BC Parks volunteers maintain 42 sites at **Kinuseo Falls Campground ❶** on Murray River. Pit toilets, water, and firewood. ($12). To reach Monkman, take Hwy. 29 south to the coal town of **Tumbler Ridge,** 94km from Chetwynd. Monkman is another 60km due south on a gravel road, past a huge anthracite coal mining operation.

ALONG HWY. 16: YELLOWHEAD HWY.

PRINCE GEORGE TO MT. ROBSON   ☎250

East of Prince George, the pristine terrain that lines the 319km of road to Mt. Robson gives little indication of the logging that drives the regional economy, thanks to scenic, sightline-wide strips of forest left untouched alongside the route. Lakeside campsites can be found at **Purden Lake Provincial Park ❶,** 59km east of Prince George. (☎565-6340. Toilets and free firewood. Gate closed 11pm-7am. $15. One wheelchair-accessible site.) **Purden Lake Resort ❶** (☎565-7777), 3km east, offers tent sites ($12), RV sites ($22-24), a cafe (open 7am-8pm), and the last gas before **McBride,** 140km east. Tenters find refuge, toilets, showers, and laundry at the **Beaverview Campsite ❶,** 1km east of McBride. (☎569-2513. $13; partial RV sites $17.)

From McBride, the Yellowhead weaves up the **Robson Valley,** part of the Rocky Mountain trench stretching north-south the length of the province. **Tête Jaune Cache** lies 63km east of McBride, where Hwy. 5 leads 339km south to Kamloops and the Okanagan beyond. **Tête Jaune Motel and RV Park ❶** offers no-frills lodging right off the highway. (☎566-9815. Camping $12; RV sites $14. Showers $1.) Just 2km east of the intersection, the diminutive **Rearguard Falls** (a 20min. walk) marks the terminus of the chinook salmon's migration from the Pacific.

As Hwy. 16 continues east, the scenery reaches a crescendo at towering **Mt. Robson,** 84km west of Jasper and 319km east of Prince George. Standing 3954m tall, Robson is the highest peak in the Canadian Rockies; mountaineers reached its summit in 1913 only after five unsuccessful attempts. Less ambitious folk can appreciate the mountain's beauty from the parking lot and picnic site beside the **Mt. Robson Provincial Park Headquarters.** (☎566-4325, reservations 800-689-9025. Open June-Aug. daily 8am-8pm; May and Sept. 8am-5pm.) Sedentary types are accommodated at **Robson River Campground ❶** and the larger **Robson Meadows Campground ❶,** both opposite the headquarters. (Toilets. $18. Free showers.). Five nearby **hiking trails,** ranging from 2km walks to 66km treks, are the park's main draws (backcountry camping permit $5 per person per night; under 13 free). The 22km trail to **Berg Lake** (two days; trailhead at the parking lot by Robson River, 2km from the visitors center) is a luscious, well-maintained path along the milky-blue Robson River past Lake Kinney and **Valley of a Thousand Falls.** Berg Lake is the highest of five campsites along the route, and can be used as a base to explore options from alpine ridge-running to wilderness camping.

PRINCE GEORGE TO TERRACE   ☎250

As Hwy. 16 winds its way westward 575km (8hr.) toward Terrace from Prince George, towering timbers gradually give way to the gently rolling pastures and the tiny towns of British Columbia's interior **Lakes District.** To escape city camping, stop 1½hr. outside Prince George at **Beaumont Provincial Park ❶,** on Fraser Lake. There are 49 roomy sites, clean facilities, a playground, a swimming area, and firewood. (☎565-6340. $15.)

NEW HAZELTON. The town of New Hazelton is 68km past Smithers. The **'Ksan Village & Museum,** 7km along Churchill Ave. towards Old Hazelton, displays a rich collection of totem poles, longhouses, and artwork of the Gitskan. Gitskan dancers perform every Friday at 8pm from July to August. (☎842-5544. Tours every 30min. Open July to mid-Aug. daily 9am-6pm; reduced hours in winter. Wheelchair accessible. $10, seniors and children 6-18 $6.50.) Another 44km west of New Hazelton is the junction with the Cassiar Hwy. (Hwy. 37; see p. 349), which leads 733km north to the Yukon Territory and the Alaska Hwy. (see p. 356). The **Petrocan** sells the last gas before Terrace. (☎849-5793. Open daily 7am-9pm.)

TERRACE   ☎250

The site of a World War II army mutiny, Terrace is now known for its wildlife. The area is the habitat of the world's largest Chinook salmon (weighing in at 92½ lb.), and the infamous Kermodei bear, a member of the black bear family recognizable by a coat that ranges from light chestnut blond to steel blue gray in color. Terrace itself is a straightforward working-class town, but its backyard is the big wilderness. The locals will tell you all about the great fishing, but rodless hikers can still find their peace in the hills and on the curvy banks of the Skeena River.

🛈 PRACTICAL INFORMATION. Terrace is 144km east of Prince Rupert on the Yellowhead Hwy. (Hwy. 16) and 91km southwest of the junction of the Yellowhead and the Cassiar Hwy. (Hwy. 37). **VIA Rail** (☎800-561-8630), sends three trains per week to **Prince George** (10hr., $81) and **Prince Rupert** (2½hr., $19). **Greyhound,** 4620 Keith St. (☎635-3680), also runs twice daily to **Prince George** (8hr., $80) and **Prince Rupert** (2hr., $24). **Canadian Tire,** at 5100 Hwy. 16, will get your wheels back in action. (☎635-7178. Open M-F 7am-9pm, Sa 7am-6pm, Su 10am-5pm.)

The **visitors center,** 4511 Keith St., is off Hwy. 16 just east of town. (☎635-0832 or 800-499-1637. Open in summer daily 9am-5pm; winter M-F 8am-4:30pm.) The **24hr. ATM** is in the city center at **Bank of Montreal,** 4666 Lakelse Ave. (☎615-6150). The **Women's Resource Centre,** 4542 Park Ave., by the Aquatic Centre, has referral services, advocacy, lay counseling, and a library. (☎638-0228. Drop-in M-Th 10am-4pm.) **Richard's Cleaners,** 3223 Emerson St., has washers ($2) and dryers ($0.25 per 5min.). (☎635-5119. Open M-Sa 7:30am-9pm, Su 8am-9pm.) **Terrace Aquatic Center,** on Paul Clark Dr., has a pool, hot tub, saunas, and gym facilities. (☎615-3030. $4.50, students and seniors $2.50, ages 2-14 $1.75.) The **market** and **pharmacy** are at **Safeway,** 4655 Lakelse Ave. (☎635-7206. Open daily 8am-10pm.) For super cheap produce, and one-hour photo hit **The Real Canadian Wholesale Club,** located behind the visitors center off Hwy. 16. (☎635-0995. Open M-F 9am-9pm, Sa 9am-6pm, Su 10am-5pm.) **Mills Memorial Hospital:** 4720 Haugland Ave. (☎635-2211). **Emergency:** ☎911. **Police:** 3205 Eby St. (☎635-4911). **Sexual Assault Crisis Line:** ☎635-1911. (Staffed daily 8:30am-4:30pm.) **Internet access** is free at the **library,** 4610 Park Ave. for 1hr.; call ahead. (☎638-8177. Open M 1-9pm, Tu-F 10am-9pm, Sa 10am-5pm, Su 1-5pm; closed Su in July and Aug.) The **Post Office** is at 3232 Emerson St. (☎635-2241. Open M-F 8:30am-5pm.) **Postal Code:** V8G 4A1.

▐▐ ACCOMMODATIONS AND FOOD. Motels in the $45-75 range abound along the highway outside of the city centre. **Kalum Motel ❷,** 5min. west on Hwy. 16 is a bargain. (☎635-2362. Big TV, local phone calls, and coffee maker included. Singles or doubles $40. Kitchenettes $5 extra.) The **Alpine House Motel ❷,** 4326 Lakelse Ave., is also removed from noisy downtown. Take the Alternate Route across the one lane bridge as you enter on Hwy. 16 from the east. (☎635-7216 or 800-663-3123. Singles $45, doubles $55; Oct.-Apr. $10 less. Kitchenettes available for no extra charge.) **Ferry Island Municipal Campground ❶,** lies just east of Terrace on Hwy. 16 with big sites under big trees and lush walking trails. The island's prime fishing spot is a short walk away and is lined with eager anglers. The community pool is half-price for Ferry Island campers. (☎615-3000. Pit toilets, water, firewood. Sites $12; RV sites $14.) **Kleanza Creek Provincial Park ❶** is the site of an abandoned gold mine, 19km east of the town on Hwy. 16, with sites nestled in towering evergreens along the rushing creek. (Pit toilets, water, firewood. $12.)

Terrace offers a handful of welcome breaks from the dreariness of highway diner cuisine. **◪Don Diego's ❷,** 3212 Kalum St., is a fun, laid-back joint that serves Mexican, Greek, and whatever's in season. Fresh, new menu with each meal. (☎635-2307. Lunch $7-9. Dinner $10-15. Open M-Sa 11:30am-3pm and 5-9pm, Su 4:30-9pm.) For authentic and affordable Indian cuisine, drive 5min. west of town along Hwy. 16 to **Haryana's Restaurant ❷,** in the Kalum Motel. Vegetarian entrees cost $10-12 and succulent chicken tikka masala is $13. (☎635-2362. Open M-Th 5-9pm, F 5-11pm, Sa 11am-11pm, Su 11am-9pm.) Food, beer, and big TVs await at the **Back Eddy Pub,** 4332 Lakelse Ave., next to the Alpine House Motel. Chess boards and pool tables add class. (☎635-5336. Open daily 11am-midnight.)

◙ SIGHTS. The **Falls Gallery,** 2666 Hwy. 37, just east of town, has an impressive collection of native masks and art. Take the Hwy. 37 turn-off south towards Kitimat, and turn in the driveway before the Volkswagen dealer. (☎638-0438. Open daily 10am-5pm.)

Gruchy's Beach, 13km south of Terrace on Hwy. 37, is a 1.5km hike from the parking lot and is big, sandy, and begging to be picnicked upon. Check out the locals cliff-jumping at **Humphrey Falls.** Take Hwy. 37 south towards Kitimat and after about 35km, turn left on a gravel road and then drive or walk to the water. The **Nisga'a Memorial Lava Bed,** Canada's youngest lava flow, lies 100km north of Terrace. To reach this 54 sq. km swath of moonscape, follow Kalum Lake Dr. (also called the Nisga'a Hwy.), which intersects Hwy. 16 just west of downtown, through the scenic valleys of the **Tseax** (T'SEE-ax) and **Nass Rivers.** At the end of the long trek, you can sleep amid the lava for $12 in a BC Parks **campground ❶** near the Lava Bed visitors center. **Hayatsgum Gibuu Tours** leads 4hr. hikes and guided tours of the lava bed. (☎ 633-2150. Hikes May-Aug. W-Su 10am and 3pm; reservation required. $12, students $10, children $5.)

⚠ OUTDOOR ACTIVITIES. The **Terrace Mountain Nature Trail** is a popular climb of moderate difficulty, beginning at Johnstone Ave. in the east end of town. The route (10km, 1½-2½hr.) offers spectacular views of plateaus and the surrounding valley. For an easy stroll, visit the **Redsand Lake Demonstration Forest,** 26km north on West Kalum Forestry Rd., a well-maintained gravel route found 200m past the Kalum River Bridge, west of town off Hwy 16. The three trails meander around beautiful Redsand Lake, and through a variety of forested areas. A steep, old skidder trail awaits mountain bikers who make it up to **Copper Mountain**—directions to the logging roads that lead up the mountain are complex. Get maps at visitors center.

Anglers can strap on their waders and try their luck on the east shore of **Ferry Island** (see above). Ask for tips at the **Misty River Tackle Shop,** 5008 Agar Ave. (☎ 638-1369. Open in summer M-Sa 7am-10pm, Su 8am-10pm; winter daily 7am-10pm.) A convenient eight-day angling license for non-Canadians costs $30 and can be purchased from any tackle shop or hardware store in town. To find the hottest fishing spots, watch for where the locals clump. The latest regulations are always posted at www.bcfisheries.gov.bc.ca. Click on the link for Skeena Region 6.

In winter, groomed **cross-country** trails stretch halfway to Kitimat (about 30km down Hwy. 37) around the enigmatic (depth-testing has yet to detect its bottom) **Onion Lake** (☎ 798-2227 or 615-3000). World-class **downhill skiing** is but 35km west on Hwy. 16 at **Shames Mountain.** Locals go nuts every winter on Shames' double chair and handle tow, the 18 trails on over 130 acres, and the 500m vertical drop.

PRINCE RUPERT   ☎ 250

In 1910, railway magnate Charles Hays made a covert deal with the provincial government to purchase 10,000 acres of choice land at the western terminus of the Grand Trunk Pacific Railway. When the shady operation was exposed two years later, Hays was already under water—not drowned in his dire financial straits, but in the wreckage of the *Titanic.* The sole fruit of Hays' illegal labors was the town of Prince Rupert, victim of a nationwide naming contest lacking in creativity. Nowadays, the famous Cow Bay waterfront gets chicer by the month, while RV caravans blend much of the rest of town into strip-malled suburban mush. But that's a minor point. With exceptional hiking and sea kayaking available in the area, Prince Rupert offers a smooth blend of tasteful urbanism and access to the outdoors.

⌐ TRANSPORTATION

Prince Rupert is a gateway to Southeast Alaska. Both BC Ferries from Vancouver Island and the Alaska Marine Hwy. from Bellingham (see p. 190) have made this town a stop on their coastal routes, providing access to nearby villages like Metlakatla (see p. 431), and farther ports in the Inside Passage. The only major road

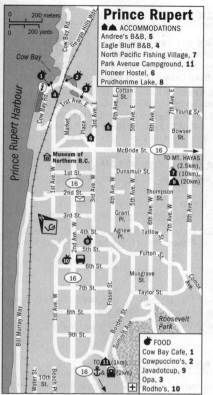

Prince Rupert

🏠▲ ACCOMMODATIONS
Andree's B&B, 5
Eagle Bluff B&B, 4
North Pacific Fishing Village, 7
Park Avenue Campground, 11
Pioneer Hostel, 6
Prudhomme Lake, 8

🍴 FOOD
Cow Bay Cafe, 1
Cowpuccino's, 2
Javadotcup, 9
Opa, 3
Rodho's, 10

into town is the Yellowhead Hwy. (Hwy. 16), known as **McBride St.** within the city. At the north end of downtown, Hwy. 16 makes a sharp left and becomes **2nd Ave.** At the south end, Hwy. 16 becomes **Park Ave.**, continuing to the **ferry docks.** Avenues run parallel to the waterfront with McBride splitting the east from west. Building numbers ascend from this central point as well. Streets run perpendicular and ascend numerically from the waterfront. Many of the city's businesses are located on 2nd and 3rd Ave. **Cow Bay** is off to the right as you enter town.

Flights: Prince Rupert Airport is on Digby Island. The ferry and bus to downtown costs $11 (seniors $7, children $4) and takes about 45min. **Air Canada** (☎888-247-22620) runs to **Vancouver** (2-3 per day; $401, under 25 $230). Book 14 days in advance.

Trains: VIA Rail (☎627-7304 or 800-561-8630) at the BC Ferries Terminal. To **Prince George** (12hr., 3 per week, $78). A **BC Rail** (in BC ☎800-339-8752; elsewhere 800-663-8238 or 604-984-5500) train continues the next morning from Prince George to **Vancouver** (14hr., $247).

Buses: Greyhound, 6th St. at 2nd Ave. (☎624-5090). To **Prince George** (11 hr., 2 per day, $100) and **Vancouver** (24hr., 2 per day, $201). Station open M-F 8:30am-12:30pm and 4-8:45pm, Sa-Su 9-11am and 7-8:45pm.

Ferries: The docks are at the end of Hwy. 16, a 30min. walk from downtown. Ferrygoers may not park on Prince Rupert streets; check with the ferry company or visitors center for paid parking options. **Seashore Charter Services** (☎624-5645) runs shuttle buses between the terminal and the hotels and train station for $3. **Alaska Marine Hwy.** (☎627-1744 or 800-642-0066; www.akmhs.com) runs to **Ketchikan** (6hr., US$43) and **Juneau** (26hr., US$119). **BC Ferries** (☎624-9627 or 888-223-3779; www.bcferries.bc.ca). To **Port Hardy** (15hr.; every other day; $99, car $233) and **Queen Charlotte Islands** (6-7hr.; 6 per week; $23.50, car $86.50). Reserve for BC ferries well in advance. If the ferry is full, you can get on the standby list over the phone.

Public Transportation: Prince Rupert Bus Service (☎624-3343) runs downtown Su-Th 7am-6:45pm, F until 10:45pm. $1, students $0.75, seniors $0.60; day pass $2.50, seniors and students $2. Buses from downtown leave from 2nd Ave. West and 3rd. About every 30min., the #52 bus runs to near the **ferry terminal.** Twice per day, a bus runs to **Port Edward** and the **North Pacific Cannery.** $2.50, students $2.

⚡ PRACTICAL INFORMATION

Tourist Information: (☎624-5637 or 800-667-1994) at 1st Ave. and McBride St., in a cedar building modeled after a traditional Tsimshian (SIM-shian) longhouse. Ask for maps and useful packets on accommodations, attractions, and trails. Open May 15 to Labour Day M-Sa 9am-8pm, Su 9am-5pm; Labour Day to May 14 M-Sa 10am-5pm.

Equipment Rental: Far West Sporting Goods (☎624-2568), on 3rd Ave. near 1st St., rents bikes, including lock and helmet. $8 per hr., $25 per day. Open M-Sa 9:30am-5:30pm. **Eco-Treks** (☎624-8311), on the dock in Cow Bay, rents **kayaks** and gear. Singles $35 per hr., double $45 per hr.; $40/$70 per day. No rentals to novices or soloists. 3hr. guided tours for any ability level leave at 1 and 6pm with safety lessons for novices ($45).

24hr. ATM: Banks line 2nd Ave. W and 3rd Ave. W; all have **24hr. ATM**s.

Market: Safeway, at 2nd St. and 2nd Ave. (☎624-2412), offers everything from a florist to a deli. Open daily 8am-10pm.

Laundromat: Mommy's Laundromat, 6th St. between 2nd and 3rd Ave. Offering the cheapest wash in the land: $1, dry $0.75 per 15min. Open daily 9am-9pm.

Showers and pool: Earl Mah Pool, 1000 McBride St. (☎624-9000). Pool, showers, and gym $4, students $3. Call for schedule. **Pioneer Hostel,** see below. Showers $3.

Emergency: ☎911.

Police: 100 6th Ave. (☎624-2136).

Hospital: 1305 Summit Ave. (☎624-2171).

Internet Access: Library, 101 6th Ave. W at McBride St. (☎624-8618). First 30min. free, then $2 per hr. Open M-Th 10am-9pm and F-Sa 10am-5pm.

Post Office: (☎624-2353), in the mall at 2nd Ave. and 5th St. Open M-F 9:30am-5pm. **Postal Code:** V8J 3P3.

🏠 ACCOMMODATIONS AND CAMPING

Most of Prince Rupert's hotels nestle within the six-block area bordered by 1st Ave., 3rd Ave., 6th St., and 9th St. Everything fills to the gills when the ferries dock, so call a day or two in advance. Most motels are pricey—a single costs at least $60.

▨ **Andree's Bed and Breakfast,** 315 Fourth Ave. E (☎624-3666). Set in a spacious 1922 Victorian-style residence overlooking the harbor and city—check out the sunsets from the deck. Singles $50; doubles $65; twins $70. $15 per extra person. ❸

▨ **Eagle Bluff Bed and Breakfast,** 201 Cow Bay Rd. (☎627-4955 or 800-833-1550), on the waterfront in the loveliest part of town. Attractively furnished with bright rooms and private deck on the bay. Rooms come with TVs and a common kitchen area. Singles $45, doubles $55; $10 extra for private bath in single, $20 for double. ❸

Pioneer Hostel, 167 3rd Ave. E (☎624-2334 or 888-794-9998), 1 block east of McBride St. Rupert's only hostel keeps things simple and clean. Microwave, TV, gazebo, and BBQ. Laundry $3. Dorms $17; singles $25; doubles $35. ❶

North Pacific Historic Fishing Village (☎628-3538), at the Cannery Museum in Port Edward. Live for cheap in the renovated cannery workers' quarters, although it is inconvenient without wheels. Bunkhouse rooms $10; modest inn rooms with shared bath $45; small 1-bedroom units with kitchens $65. ❶

Prudhomme Lake, 20km east of town on Hwy. 16, run by BC Parks. Camp along the shore, under shady trees. Worth the drive to escape the RVs. Fishing, water, wood, and pit toilets. Sites $12. ❶

Park Avenue Campground, 1750 Park Ave. (☎624-5861 or 800-667-1994), 1km east of the ferry on Hwy. 16. An RV metropolis! Laundry. Sites $10.50; RVs $13.50, with RV sites $18.50. Showers free for guests. ❶

FOOD

▨ **Cow Bay Cafe,** 201 Cow Bay Rd. (☎627-1212), shares the waterfront corner of Cow Bay with Eagle Bluff B&B. This popular hot spot switches the menu around on a whim but always keeps the lunches ($8-10) and dinners ($12-17) fresh. Lots of wine. Reservations necessary. Open Tu noon-2:30pm, W-Sa noon-2:30pm and 6-8:30pm. ❸

▨ **Opa,** 34 Cow Bay Rd. (☎627-4560), upstairs. Pottery studio and sushi bar in old fishing net loft. Drink free tea out of handspun mugs. Spin a bowl at the in-house pottery studio, and while it's firing, hang out on the deck enjoying fresh sushi. Tuna rolls $3, miso soup $1.50. Open Tu-F 11:30am-2pm and 5-9pm, Sa noon-3pm and 5-9pm. ❸

Cowpuccino's, 25 Cow Bay Rd. (☎627-1395). Caffeinate while taking in the cow pics from around the world. Try colossal muffins ($1), bagel sandwiches ($4.50), or Sex in a Pan ($4.75). Open M-Sa 7am-10pm, Sa 8am-8pm. ❶

Rodho's (☎624-9797), on 2nd Ave. near 6th St. Huge menu of pleasing Greek entrees ($13-17), pastas ($9-10), and pizzas ($14 for a loaded medium). Open daily 4pm-1am. Free delivery in town. ❸

Javadotcup, 516 3rd Ave. W (☎622-2822). Internet cafe with speedy computers, coffee, and quick lunches ($3). Smoothies $3. Internet $1.75 per ½hr. Open M-Th 7:30am-10:30pm, F 7:30am-11pm, Sa 8am-11pm, Su 7:30am-10pm. ❶

SIGHTS AND OUTDOOR ACTIVITIES

Prince Rupert's harbor has the highest concentration of archaeological sites in North America. Archaeologists have unearthed materials from Tsimshian settlements dating back 10,000 years. **Archaeological boat tours** leave from the visitors center. (2½hr. tours depart daily mid-June to early Sept. $28, children $15.) A local expert interprets several sites from the boat, with a stop at the village of **Metlakatla** across the harbor. The **Museum of Northern British Columbia,** in the same building as the visitors center, displays haunting Tsimshian artworks. (☎624-3207. Open late May-early Sept. M-Sa 9am-8pm and Su 9am-5pm; mid-Sept. to late May M-Sa 9am-5pm. $5, students $2, children 6-12 $1; includes guided tour of collection and totem pole and heritage walking tours.)

The best time to visit Prince Rupert may be during **Seafest** (☎624-9118), an annual four-day event planned for June 6-9, 2003. Surrounding towns celebrate the sea with parades, bathtub races, and beer contests. The **Islandman Triathlon** (☎624-6770), a 1000m swim, 35km bike, and 8km run, is also held around the time of Seafestivities and was won in 1997 by an intrepid *Let's Go* researcher. Later in June, Prince Rupert hops during the **National Aboriginal Day.**

A number of attractive small parks line the hills above Prince Rupert. Tiny **Service Park,** off Fulton St., offers views of downtown and the harbor beyond. An even wider vista awaits atop **Mt. Oldfield,** east of town, for serious hikers (8.4km, 5-6hr.). The trailhead is at Oliver Lake Park, about 6km from downtown on Hwy. 16. The **Butze Rapids trail** (5km, 2½-3½hr.) teaches walkers about plants and then plants them in front of rushing tidal rapids. The trailhead is across the highway.

Freshwater anglers can enjoy the great **fishing** in the Skeena and pull up big steelhead or salmon. Get permit and hotspot info at the visitor's center.

Prince Rupert is hemmed in by dozens of sandy little islands, and sea kayaking is a great way to explore them. **Eco-Treks** (see **Equipment Rental**, above) specializes in kayak introductions and rents to experienced paddlers, who can put in at Cow Bay, paddle north around Kaien Island—home to Prince Rupert—and brave the challenging **Butze Reversing Tidal Rapids**. One of the most incredible wilderness experiences in all of BC is the **Khutzeymateen/K'tzim-a-Deen Grizzly Bear Sanctuary**. Hiking is not permitted within the sanctuary, leaving the surrounding wilderness incredibly untouched. Access is through the Khutzeymateen River, and takes 6-10hr. from Rupert. For more information, contact BC Parks at ☎798-2277.

◪ NIGHTLIFE

Drinking establishments in Prince Rupert compete for ferry tourists and fishing boat crews. Come sundown, the town is a-crawl with sea life come to shore. The **Surf Club**, 200 5th St., attracts a younger set later in the evening with space to dance and alternating nights of live music and karaoke. (☎624-3050. Open M, Th-Sa 10pm-2am.) The **Empress Hotel**, 716 3rd Ave. W (☎624-9917), has the best house band, but is not recommended for the pub-naive. **Shooters Bar and Grill** at The Commercial Inn, 901 1st Ave., and **Breaker's Pub**, 117 George Hills Way in Cow Bay overlooking the small boat harbor, are full of local color. (Shooters ☎624-6142. Open Su-M noon-midnight, Tu-Th noon-1:30am, F-Sa noon-2am. Breaker's ☎624-5990. Open M-Th 11:30am-midnight, F-Sa 11:30am-1am, Su noon-midnight.)

QUEEN CHARLOTTE ISLANDS/HAIDA GWAII

Nothing in Haida Gwaii is ever far from rainforest or foggy coast. A full 130km west of Prince Rupert, two principal islands and 136 surrounding inlets form the archipelago known as "the Canadian Galápagos." Graham, the northern island, is home to all but one of the islands' towns, a potent strain of hallucinogenic mushroom, and an eclectic population of tree-huggers, tree-cutters, First Nations people, and fishermen. Few tourist-huggers inhabit Haida Gwaii; in fact, locally drawn postcards poke fun at visitors. But the beaches and rainforests can't help but mellow folks out just a touch. To the south, hot springs steam from mountainous Gwaii Haanas (Gwaii-HAH-nus; Moresby Island on many maps), where the wooden totem poles of the islands' first inhabitants decay. Remote wilderness envelopes the kayakers and boaters who approach Haida Gwaii's lonely sandbars, outcroppings, coves, and shoals. The Islands' chief employer is the timber industry, edging out the Canadian government. In the 1980s, the Islands attracted global attention when environmentalists from around the globe joined the Haida Nation in demonstrations to stop logging on parts of Gwaii Haanas. In 1988, the Canadian government established the Gwaii Haanas National Park Reserve now managed co-operatively by the government of Canada and the Haida Nation.

▐ TRANSPORTATION

The **BC Ferry** from Prince Rupert docks at Skidegate Landing on Graham Island, which is between **Queen Charlotte City** (4km west of the landing) and the village of **Skidegate** (SKID-uh-git), 2km to the northeast. All of the towns of Graham Island lie along Hwy. 16, which continues north from Skidegate through **Tlell, Port Clements**, and **Massett**. Be wary of deer while driving—they're everywhere, and they bolt at all the wrong times. Each town does its own thing. Hit Queen Charlotte City for eating and hostels, or trek north toward hikes and beaches near Tlell and Masset. To the south, Gwaii Haanas is home to **Sandspit** and the Islands' only commercial airport. From Skidegate Landing, 12 ferries per day make the 20min. crossing between the big islands. The lack of public transportation and the exorbitant cost of car rentals bankrupt backpackers, but residents are supposedly generous in picking up hitchhikers. *Let's Go* does not recommend hitchhiking.

QUEEN CHARLOTTE CITY   ☎ 250

Queen Charlotte City's central location and size make it the base for exploring both main islands. "Size" is relative, however; this community of just over 1000 people is not the city its name claims it to be. Most locals either work the sawmills, the trawlers, or for the government.

▐ TRANSPORTATION

Towns on the island line one waterfront road; in Charlotte that road is **3rd Ave.**

Ferries: BC Ferries (☎559-4485 or in BC 888-223-3779; www.bcferries.bc.ca), in Skidegate Landing, 3km east of Queen Charlotte City. To **Prince Rupert** (6hr.; July-Aug. 6 per week, Oct.-June 4 per week; $23.50, bike $6, car $86.50). Reserve at least 3 weeks in advance for cars; car fares do not include driver. Ferries also run between **Skidegate Landing** on Graham Island and **Alliford Bay** on Gwaii Haanas (20min.; 12 per day; round-trip $4.75, car $12.60, off-season car $9.50). No reservations.

Taxis: Eagle Cabs (☎559-4461). $8-11 between Charlotte and the ferry terminal. Open Su-W 7am-9pm, Th-Sa 7am-close.

Car Rental: Rustic Rentals (☎559-4641), west of downtown at Charlotte Island Tire. Must be 21+ with credit card. Will pick up at the ferry terminal in Skidegate. $41 per day, $0.15 per km. Office open daily 8am-7pm, but cars available 24hr.

Auto Repair: Charlotte Tire (☎559-4641), along Hwy. 33, provides 24hr. towing. Open daily 8am-7pm.

▐ PRACTICAL INFORMATION

Tourist Information: (☎559-8316; www.qcinfo.com), on Wharf St. at the east end of town. Ornate 3D map of the islands and a creative natural history presentation. The free *Guide to the Queen Charlotte Islands* has detailed maps. Holds **mandatory orientations** for visitors to Gwaii Haanas Park every day at 8am and 7:30pm (see **Gwaii Haanas,** below). Open mid-May to mid-Sept. daily 10am-7pm; early May and late Sept. daily 10am-2pm.

Outdoor Information: Gwaii Haanas Park Information (☎559-8818; www.fas.sfu.ca/parkscan/gwaii), on 2nd Ave. off 2nd St. above city center. A trip-planning resource. Open M-F 8am-noon and 1-4:30pm. For registration info, see **Gwaii Haanas National Park Reserve,** p. 347. **Ministry of Forests** (☎559-6200), on 3rd Ave. at the far west end of town, has info on Forest Service campsites and logging roads on both islands. Open M-F 8:30am-4:30pm. Get a saltwater **fishing license** at **Meegan's Store,** 3126 Wharf St. (☎559-4428). Open M-Sa 9am-6pm. Freshwater licenses are available only from the **Government Agent** (☎559-4452 or 800-663-7867), 1½ blocks west of the city center.

Equipment Rental: Premier Creek Lodge has bikes. $15 per half-day, $30 per full day.

Bank: Northern Savings Credit Union (☎559-4407), on Wharf St., has a **24hr. ATM**. Many businesses don't take credit cards. Bank open Tu-Th 10am-5pm, F 10am-5:30pm, Sa 10am-3pm. The only other bank is in Massett.

Market: Food is more expensive on the islands. Stock up off-island. The only fully-stocked grocery in town is **City Centre Stores** (☎559-4444), in the City Centre Mall (open M-Sa 9:30am-6pm). **Isabel Creek Store**, 3219 Wharf St. (☎559-8623) opposite the visitors center, offers organic foods. Open M-Sa 10am-5:30pm.

Laundromat: 121 3rd Ave. (☎559-4444), in the City Centre Mall. Wash $1.50, dry $0.25 per 5min. Open daily 9am-9pm. At **Premier Creek Lodging**, $4 including soap.

Emergency: ☎559-8484. **No 911. Ambulance:** ☎800-461-9911.

Police: 3211 Wharf (☎559-4421).

Pharmacy: (☎559-4310), downstairs in the hospital building. Open M-Tu and Th-F 10:30am-12:30pm and 1:30-5:15pm, W 1:30-5:15pm.

Hospital: (☎559-4300), on 3rd Ave. at the east end of town.

Internet Access: Free at the **Library**, 138 Bay St. (☎559-4518), under the community hall. Open M and W 10:30am-12:30pm, 1:30-5:30pm, and 6:30-8:30pm., Sa 10:30am-12:30pm and 1:30-5:30pm. **Premier Creek Lodging**, $2 for 10min.

Post Office: (☎559-8349), in the City Centre Mall on 3rd Ave. Open M-F 9am-5pm, Sa noon-4pm. **Postal Code:** VOT 1SO.

▗ ACCOMMODATIONS AND CAMPING

Indoor accommodations in town cater to tourists who want to relax. During the summer, make reservations or arrive early in the day to secure a room.

▨ **The Premier Creek Lodging,** 3101 3rd Ave. (☎559-8415 or 888-322-3388). Bunk beds in a creekside cottage behind the main hotel with shared kitchen, bath, common room, and campfire pit. Fresh breakfast $6-8. Laundry $4. Bed in hostel $20. Clean rooms in hotel $30, with kitchenette $45. Large rooms with kitchen and couches, overlooking the ocean $65 single, $75 double. Campsites $15. Credit cards accepted. ❶

Dorothy and Mike's Guest House, 3125 2nd Ave. (☎559-8439), centrally located up the hill behind the downtown Rainbow Gallery. A standing hammock chair, library, breakfast, and kitchen use. Call ahead. Singles $45; doubles $65. ❸

Joy's Campground (☎559-8890), halfway between the ferry terminal and Charlotte. Camp in Joy's waterfront backyard (which runs alongside 3rd Ave.), and drink from the spring. No toilets. To secure space, go to Joy's Island Jewelers, 3rd Ave., next to Sea Raven Restaurant. Tent sites $5; RV sites $9; electrical $15. ❶

Haydn-Turner Community Campground, 5min. drive west of town. Turn left down a short dirt road labeled "campground" as the main drag turns to gravel. Pleasant and forested. Water, firewood, pit toilets. 6 sites $10; walk-in beach front site $5. ❶

Sea Raven Motel, 3301 3rd Ave. (☎559-4423). Tidy rooms with TV, private bath, phones, and a central location overlook Bearskin Bay. Fishing licenses sold on premises. Singles $45; doubles $65. With kitchen $10 extra. ❸

◖ FOOD

▨ **Hanging by a Fibre** (☎559-4463), on Wharf St., beside the Howler's building. Hang out in this artsy, popular coffee shop. Take in the local art shows that change each month and a Starving Artist lunch ($4.50) of fresh bread and soup. Wraps or quiche with salad ($8). Lunch served 11:30am-4pm. Open M-Sa 9am-5:30pm and Su noon-4pm. ❶

Howler's Bistro (☎559-8602), on 3rd Ave. Dine on a deck overlooking the water. Fully loaded Howler burger or veggie burger $9. Sandwiches $7. Mexican dishes $8-10. Open in summer daily 11am-11pm; in winter 11am-10pm. **Howler's Pub,** downstairs, will get you good and liquored up. Open daily 1pm-2am. ❷

Oceana, 3119 3rd Ave. (☎559-8683), offers a huge menu of Asian cuisine ($10-14). Lunch specials $7-10. Open daily 11:30am-2pm and 5-10pm. ❷

Sea Raven, 3301 3rd Ave. (☎559-8583), offers an airy, sun-washed dining area and glimpses of the ocean through alder trees. Large seafood selection and the best salmon clam chowder on the island at $4.50 a bowl. Expensive at dinner ($15-22) but reasonable lunches ($8-10). Open daily 7am-2pm and 5-9pm. ❸

Summerland Pizza and Steakhouse (☎559-4588), west on 3rd Ave. about 1km from the center of town. A local pizza joint with Mediterranean and Greek mixed in. Pizza lunch special $6. Sandwiches with fries $6-9. Steak, seafood, or Greek dinners $14-20. Open daily 11am-3pm and 4:30-9pm. ❷

🄸 SIGHTS

Few Haidas survived the smallpox plague that hit the once-thriving villages in the southern islands in late 1800s. Still, today the Haida history of 10,000 years on the Queen Charlotte Islands, or "Haida Gwaii," which means "Islands of the People," remains alive. Six impressive cedar **totem poles** were raised in June 2001 on Second Beach, 1km east of the ferry landing on Hwy. 16, as a symbolic demonstration of the continuation of Haida culture. Traditionally, totem poles were built in Haida villages for a variety of reasons, spiritual and secular. The local poles represent each of the six southern Haida villages, now in ruins, which can be visited by boat in Gwaii Haanas Haida Heritage Site (see p. 347). Behind the poles, a shed protects a 50 ft. cedar canoe, the **Lootaas,** carved for Vancouver's Expo '86 by renowned Haida artist Bill Reid (open M-F 9am-4:30pm). Next door, the **Haida Gwaii Museum at Qay'llnagaay** houses totem poles alongside haunting Haida paintings. (☎559-4643. Open June-Aug. M-F 10am-5pm, Sa-Su 1-5pm; May and Sept. closed Su; Oct.-Apr. closed Tu as well. $4, students and seniors $3, children under 12 free.)

The Haida town of **Skidegate,** known as "the village," lies 1km beyond the museum. This community of 695 people is the nexus of Haida art and culture. Residents are sensitive to tourists and expect that visitors will exhibit discretion and respect concerning local culture and practices. Bald eagles often perch atop the totem pole out front of the **Skidegate Community Hall** near the water, a Haida longhouse built in 1979 according to ancient design specifications. Visitors must get permission from the **Skidegate Band Council Office** (☎559-4496), between the Gwaii Coop on the main highway, to photograph the cemetery or to camp and hike in certain areas; ask for details from the receptionist at the **Haida Gwaii Watchmen,** next to the museum. (☎559-8225. Open M-F 9am-noon and 1-5pm.)

🄽 OUTDOOR ACTIVITIES

Queen Charlotte offers the easiest road access to the west coast of the island. Following 3rd Ave., it turns to gravel; multiple west coast destinations are listed on a sign less than a kilometer down the road. Multiple **forestry recreation sites** on Rennell Sound, 27km down feisty lumber roads, provide a true escape ($8 permit for overnight use). Watch out for the 22% grade as the road dips down toward the sound—if your brakes have given you any problems in the past, shy away.

Hiking the tangle of local logging roads is easier with a few good maps from the **Tlell Watershed Society** (see **Tlell,** below). Even on a two- or three-day hike, it's important to leave a **trip plan** with the visitors center before setting out.

BRITISH COLUMBIA

The visitors center issues crucial information on **tides** and **scheduled logging road activity.** It's very dangerous for hikers or 4x4s to vie for trail space with an unstoppable logging truck. For the most part, logging road use is restricted to industrial traffic from M-Sa 6am-6pm. Ignoring this restriction isn't just illegal, it's idiotic.

The **Spirit Lake Trail** network (several loops and 3km of trail, 1-2hr.) departs from a parking lot beside the George Brown Recreation Centre off Hwy. 16, in Skidegate. The network leads up a hill side and to the lake (1000m), where it breaks off into various loops that are all well maintained and clearly marked. A guide pamphlet is available at the visitors center. **Balance Rock** teeters on a roadside beach 1km north of Skidegate. A group of brawny loggers once failed in an attempt to dislodge the boulder, so it's unlikely to topple from its precarious perch.

Numerous outfitters rent boats and kayaks, with rates varying according to the length of your journey and your level of experience. **Queen Charlotte Adventures,** 34 Wharf St., offers a $125 guided day paddle of Skidegate Inlet perfect for island newcomers. It'll be tough to keep your mind on the paddling as otters, seals, salmon, and birds all sidle up alongside to investigate you. (☎ 559-8990 or 800-668-4288. Kayaks $40 per day, $200 per week.)

TLELL ☎ 250

Tlell (tuh-LEL), 40km north of Queen Charlotte City, is a line of houses and farms spread thinly along a 7km stretch of Hwy. 16. The quasi-town enjoys some of Graham Island's best beach vistas, plus a population of artisans who earn Tlell a reputation as the Charlottes' hippie zone. Tlell hosts its own Woodstock, **Edge of the World Music Festival,** in early July. Here, the rocky beaches of the south give way to sand, and the Tlell River offers fishing and water warm enough for swimming.

⚑ PRACTICAL INFORMATION. Visitors center, outdoors information, and flora and fauna displays are put together by the Tlell Watershed Society at **Naikoon Park Headquarters,** right before the campground. (Open Su-Th and Th-Sa 11am-5pm.) Tlell's **bookstore** is in the Sitka Studio (at the end of Richardson Rd.), which shows local art and sells art supplies. (☎ 557-4241. Open daily 10am-6pm.) **Wrench Tech,** on the Port Clements turnoff, offers some of the only auto service between Queen Charlotte and Masset. (☎ 557-4324. Open M-Sa 8am-6pm.) Other services include: **emergency/ambulance,** ☎ 800-461-9911, **no 911; police,** (☎ 559-4421) in Queen Charlotte City; and the **post office,** on Hwy. 16, 2km south of Wiggins Rd. (Open M-F 2:30-5:30pm.) **Postal Code:** V0T 1Y0.

⛺⌂ ACCOMMODATIONS AND FOOD. Sea breezes and birds singing in the spruces await at ▨**Cacilia's B&B/Hitunwa Kaitza ❸,** snuggled against the dunes just north of Richardson Ranch on the ocean side of the road. Friendly cats, driftwood furniture, and hanging chairs give character to the common living space. Rooms are skylit and comfortable. (☎ 557-4664. Singles $40; doubles $60; grassy tent site and campfire pit near dunes $15.) Pitch a tent or park an RV at the beautiful **Misty Meadows Campground ❶,** in Naikoon Provincial Park, 2km beyond Cacilia's, just south of the Tlell River bridge. (Pit toilets, water, picnic tables, beach access. 14-night max. stay. Sites $12.)

Lunch ($5-8) can be found at **Dress for Less ❶,** 1km south of Richardson Ranch in a pink building. Sidle up to the pink coffee bar nestled among racks of vintage clothing. Enjoy your pick of local artists' wares or sip coffee on the deck. (☎ 557-2023. Open daily 9am-5pm.) Turn off for Port Clements, 22km north of Tlell, for a good-sized dinner ($12-18) at a good old diner, the **Hummingbird Cafe ❹.** (Open Tu-Su 11am-3pm, 5-8pm.)

FALL AND RISE OF THE GOLDEN SPRUCE

For years, oddity-seekers of the world drove, biked, hiked, and ran to Port Clements, where the planet's only Golden Spruce basked in singular glory. Due to a rare genetic mutation, the 300-year-old tree contained only a fraction of the chlorophyll present in an ordinary Sitka spruce, causing its needles to be bleached by sunlight. The striking 50m giant glowed fiery yellow in the sun, beaming its way into Haida creation myths and horticulturists' dreams. In January 1997, however, a disgruntled ex-forestry worker arrived at the site with an axe and a mission. To protest the logging industry's destruction of British Columbia's forests, he chopped down the tree. These actions won him no prize for logic, but certainly drew province-wide attention.

While islanders reacted with astonishment at their beloved tree's untimely demise, the University of British Columbia revealed another shocker: there had been not one but *three* Golden Spruces—two, created in 1977 from clippings of the original, were growing peacefully in the botanical gardens of the UBC Victoria campus. University authorities donated these golden saplings to the Haida nation, and their future looks good. Concurrent with the fall of the Golden Spruce, an albino raven was born on the island, an event that locals took as a sign foretelling a continuation of the Spruce's three-century history.

OUTDOOR ACTIVITIES. One of the most popular trails around Tlell leads to the **Pesuta Shipwreck,** the hulking remains of a 246 ft. lumber barge that ran aground during a gale in 1928. The 2hr. hike to the site leaves from the Tlell River picnic area off Hwy. 16, just north of the river. When the trail branches, follow the "East Beach" sign up the ridge, or walk the whole way at low tide along the river. Hwy. 16 cuts inland just north of Tlell, leaving over 90km of pristine beach exclusively to backpackers. Allow four to six days to reach the road access at the north end of the route, 25km east of Massett. Before setting out on the East Beach hike, register at **Naikoon Provincial Park Headquarters,** in a brown building on the right side of the highway, just before the Tlell River bridge. (☎557-4390; call ahead.) **Tlell Watershed Society** leads hikes throughout the island to local secret spots, such as Pretty John's Hike. Hikes are on island time so return time may be later than estimated. (Call Berry Wijdeven for information ☎557-4709; www.tlellwatershed.org.)

Visitors to Port Clements often mistakenly assume that the body of water surrounding town is a lake. It's actually the oceanic **Masset Inlet,** and has some of the most uncrowded fishing on the islands. Cast right off the docks or head down the rocky shore for total seclusion. Local shops along the Bayview Dr. waterfront can set you up with permits and whatever gear you need.

MASSETT   ☎250

At Mile Zero of the Yellowhead Hwy. (Hwy. 16), Masset isn't a showy city. The mixture of loggers, Haidas, and hippies leads to the occasional culture clash and a sometimes volatile political and social scene. Spectacular scenery surrounds the town; the rainforest of Tow Hill and the expansive beachfront of the Blow Hole, east of town in Naikoon Provincial Park, more than justify the northward trek.

ORIENTATION AND PRACTICAL INFORMATION

Massett is about 108km (1¼hr. on a good, although narrow and deer-filled, road) north of Skidegate on Hwy. 16. To get downtown, take a left off the highway onto the main bridge, just after the small boat harbor. After the bridge, **Delkatla Rd.** is on the left. **Collision Ave.,** the main drag, is the first right off Delkatla. To reach the campgrounds (see below), continue on Hwy. 16 without crossing the bridge.

Taxis: Vern's Taxi (☎ 626-3535). Open daily 8am-6pm.

Car Rental: Tilden Rentals, 1504 Old Beach Rd. (☎ 626-3318), at the Singing Surf Inn. From $40 per day; $0.25 per km. Must be 25+. Open M-Sa 7am-9pm, Su 8am-9pm.

Car Repair: TLC (☎ 626-3756), on Collision Ave. Open daily 8am-6pm. 24hr. towing.

Tourist Information: Tourist Information Centre, Old Beach Rd. (☎ 626-3982 or 888-352-9242), at Hwy. 16. History, maps for bird-watching, extensive Massett packet. Open daily July-Aug. 10am-8pm; Sept.-June F-M 9am-2pm. The **Village Office** (☎ 626-3955) has advice year-round. Open M-Th 9am-4pm, F noon-4pm.

Bank: Northern Savings (☎ 626-5231), Main St. north of Collision Ave. Only bank and **24hr. ATM** outside Queen Charlotte City. Open Tu-Th and Sa 10am-3pm, F noon-5pm.

Laundromat: (☎ 626-5007), just north of Collision on Orr St. Wash $1.75, dry $1.75. Open Tu-Sa 9am-9pm.

Pool: Massett Rec Centre (☎ 626-5507). Pay to use pool, fitness room, weights, and squash courts. Open M-F 8:30am-9pm, Sa noon-9pm, Su 3-9pm. $5, seniors and children under 18 $2.50.

Ambulance: ☎ 800-461-9911, **no 911.**

Police: (☎ 626-3991), on Collision Ave., at Orr St.

Hospital: (☎ 626-4700; emergency 626-4711). The clinic (☎ 626-4702 or 626-4703) is on Hodges Ave., on the right just over the main bridge into Massett. Call ahead.

Internet Access: Free at the **Library** (☎ 626-3663), at Collision Ave. and McLeod St. 30min. limit. Call ahead. Open Tu 2-6pm, Th 2-5pm and 6-8pm, Sa noon-5pm. Available daily but costly ($4 per 20min.) at **Tourist Information Centre** (see above).

Post Office: (☎ 626-5155), on Main St. north of Collision. Open M-F 9am-5:30pm, Sa 1-4pm. **Postal Code:** V0T 1M0.

■ ■ ACCOMMODATIONS AND CAMPING

Massett campsites are scenic, cheap, and everywhere. There is **free beach camping** on North Beach, 1km past Tow Hill, 30km east of Massett, in Naikoon Provincial Park. Look for signs marking the end of Indian Reserve property. Call ahead for favored indoor lodging.

■ **Rapid Richie's Rustic Rentals** (☎ 626-5472; www.beachcabins.com), 18km east of Massett on Tow Hill Rd. Self-sufficient accommodation on a wild northern beach. 6 airy cabins with water collected from roof, propane lights, wood or propane heating, kitchen, cookstove, and pit toilets. Sleeps 2-4. Reservations recommended. $40-70 per day for 2; $15 per extra person. ❸

Singing Surf Inn, 1504 Old Beach Road (☎ 626-3318 or 888-592-8886), next to visitors center before crossing bridge into Massett. Revamped rooms are clean and modern. Attached bar and restaurant keep you fed and tipsy. TV, kitchenette, and queen bed in most singles. Singles from $59; doubles $65. ❹

Copper Beech House, 1590 Delkatla Rd. (☎ 626-5441), at Collision Ave. by small boat dock. Dine off Beijing china, share a bath with carved wooden frogs from Mexico, and snuggle under comforters from Finland. Singles $75; doubles $100; loft in the garden shed for $25 or make use of that shovel next to your pillow and stay for free. ❹

Village of Massett RV Site & Campground (☎ 888-352-9292), 2km east of town on Tow Hill Rd. The name belies nothing about this straightforward campground. The 22 sites crowd between forest and ocean. Sites $10-20. Electricity included. ❶

◘ FOOD

Snag yourself a big crab for free on the North Beach. Razor clams are free too, but gathering them is a little more strenuous and the clams are potentially toxic. Call the **Department of Fisheries and Oceans** (☎ 626-3316) before harvesting mollusks and then stop by Christie St. behind the visitors center to pick up a free permit and harvesting tips. Lemons and seafood garnishes are sold at **Delmos Co-op,** on Main St., south of Collision Ave. (☎ 626-3933. Open M-Sa 10am-6pm.)

Moon Over Naikoon, 18km on the left on the Tow Hill Rd. Whale bones and other beachcomb finds decorate this small cafe. Edibles include whole wheat flaxseed bread ($5), melt-in-your-mouth butter tarts ($1), and marine-inspired lunch dishes. Open F-M 11am-7 or 8pm. ❷

Marj's (626-9344), on Main St. next to the post office. This little diner is the heart of Massett town and a local hangout where most of the village's problems are solved (or at least discussed) over all-day breakfast ($6-8), burgers ($6-8), NY steaks ($12), and gargantuan slices of fresh pie ($3). Open daily 7am-3:30pm. ❷

Sandpiper Gallery, 2062 Collision Ave. (☎ 626-3672). The owners happily *plaudern* with homesick Germans and serve *lecker* chicken burgers ($8). Open M-Sa 8:30am-9pm. ❷

Haidabucks (☎ 626-5548), on Main St. across from the Rec. Center. Haida art decorates this big, airy coffeehouse. Sandwiches run $5-7, but the big dessert pans behind the counter clinch repeat business. Open M-F 9am-5pm, Sa and Su 10am-4:30pm. ❶

◪ SIGHTS AND OUTDOOR ACTIVITIES

Tow Hill, an incredible outcrop of volcanic basalt columns about 26km east of town, rises out of nowhere at the far end of Agate Beach, and presides over Massett as the area's reigning attraction. Continue 1km past Agate Back Campsite to **Tow Hill Viewpoint trailhead.** Hustle up the tar paper-covered boards to a fabulous overlook (unless it's foggy) 100m above the rocky shoreline (30min. to ascend). On a clear day, miles of virgin beach and even the most southerly reaches of Alaska spread out below; slow summer sunsets hang in the horizon for hours. On the way back down (10min.), take a detour to loop past the **Blow Hole** (25min.), a small cave that erupts with 15ft. high plumes of water at mid-tide.

Two less-traveled trails depart from the Tow Hill Viewpoint parking lot: an 11km beach walk to **Rose Spit** (2½-3hr. one-way) at the island's northeast corner, and a 10km hike on the **Cape Fife trail** (3½-4hr. one-way), which passes through some of the island's most varied vegetation and accesses to the East Coast Beach and the long hiking route out of Tlell (see p. 342). A lean-to at the end of the Cape Fife trail allows tireless backpackers to link the two routes, exploring the entire island in a 4- to 6-day trek. Inform **Naikoon Park Headquarters** (☎ 557-4390 in Tlell; see p. 342) before multi-day trips, and contact them for advice. Across the Hiellen River, **North Beach** is where Raven discovered a giant clam containing the first men in the Haida creation myth and where clam and crab catchers congregate today.

Closer to town, red-breasted sapsuckers, orange-crowned warblers, glaucous-winged gulls, and binocular-toting bird-watchers converge on the **Delkatla Wildlife Sanctuary,** off Tow Hill Rd. The best paths for observing 113 local species begin at the junction of Trumpeter Dr. and Cemetery Rd. Continue on Cemetery Rd. past the sanctuary to reach **Oceanview Cemetery,** in a lush green forest on the beach.

Once the crabbing's done, grab your rod and permit (available at virtually any store in town) and **fish** off the docks. Locals regularly pull up bucketfuls of fresh catch in only a few hours. But be courteous—outsiders are too often rude when they visit town, and Massett folk won't take kindly to dock-hogs.

SANDSPIT   ☎250

Sandspit is the only permanent community on Gwaii Haanas. The town sprawls alongside the beach, misting everything (people and bald eagles alike) with salty seaspray. Mother Nature buffets the community with a perpetual west wind and provides sprawling sunsets over a porpoise-filled bay each evening. This well-groomed hub houses the only commercial airport on the islands, and serves as a major launching point for kayak and boat trips to Gwaii Haanas National Park Reserve (see p. 347).

■ ☒ ORIENTATION AND PRACTICAL INFORMATION. Having a car or bike is handy in Sandspit, since the town is spread over the long **Beach Rd.** parallel to the seashore. There isn't much traffic on the 13km road between Sandspit and **Alliford Bay,** where the ferry docks; those hitching to catch a late ferry report that it is often hard to find a ride. Bringing a bike over on the ferry is free, and the trip to town is an idyllic, easy 1hr. ride along the ocean.

Sandspit Airport is near the end of the spit on Beach Rd. **Air Canada** (☎888-247-2262) flies to **Vancouver** ($495, youth standby $180). **BC Ferries** (☎223-3779 or 888-559-4485; www.bcferries.bc.ca) runs between **Skidegate Landing** on Graham Island and **Alliford Bay** on Gwaii Haanas (20min.; 12 per day; round-trip $4.75, car $12.60, kayak or canoe $2). **Eagle Cabs** runs a shuttle from the airport across to Queen Charlotte City twice per day. (☎559-4461 or 877-547-4461. 1 shuttle Sa. $14 includes ferry. Reservations recommended.)

Tourist and outdoor information is available at the airport. Register and gather trail information or buy topographical maps here before heading into the park. **Park orientations** are held daily at 11am during the summer. (☎637-5362. Open mid-May to mid-Sept. daily 9am-6:30pm; May 1-16 and mid-Sept. to Sept. 30 daily 9am-1pm.) **Budget,** 383 Beach Rd., by the post office, rents autos. (☎637-5688 or 800-577-3228. $50 per day plus $0.35 per km. Must be 21+ with a credit card. **Bayview Sales and Services,** at the west end of town, pumps gas and sells camping fuel. (☎637-5359. Open M-F 9am-noon and 3-7pm, Sa 9am-noon and 1-6pm, Su 9am-1pm and 6-8pm.) **The Trading Post,** on Beach Front Rd., before the gas station when heading out of Sandspit, sells fishing licenses and outdoor gear. (Open M-Sa 9am-noon and 1-6pm.) The **Supervalu Supermarket,** 383 Alliford Bay, in the mini-mall near the spit, carries some produce and sells alcohol. (☎637-2249. Open M-Sa 9:30am-6pm, Tu 9:30am-7:30pm, Su 10am-4pm.) Call an **ambulance** at ☎800-461-9911. The **police** (☎559-4421) are in Queen Charlotte City. The **health clinic** is on Copper Bay Rd., in the school building. (☎637-5403. Open M-F 10am-noon.) After hours, call the **Queen Charlotte General Hospital** (☎559-4506). The **post office** is at Beach and Blaine Shaw Rd. (☎637-2244. Open M-F 9am-5pm, Sa 11am-2pm.) **Postal Code:** V0T 1T0.

☒ ☒ ACCOMMODATIONS AND CAMPING. Sandspit rooms are more affordable and less crowded than most on the islands. The ☒**Seaport Bed and Breakfast ❷,** just up the road toward Spit Point, offers island hospitality with guest pickup at the airport. Rooms in two cottages with kitchens and cable TV common rooms. (☎637-5698. Reservations are essential in summer. Singles $35; doubles $40.) Identical accommodations are provided by Bonnie's daughter two blocks away on Beach Rd. at ☒**Bayside Bed and Breakfast ❷** (☎637-2433). Not quite as homey but nearly as economical, **Moresby Island Guest House ❷,** on Beach Rd. next to the post office, has 10 rooms with shared washrooms, a kitchen, and coin-operated laundry facilities. Make-your-own-breakfast is provided, but further kitchen use costs $10. (☎637-5300. Singles $30; doubles from $60; cots $15.) **501 RV and Tent Park ❶,** 501 Beach Rd., has the only public showers on the island. (☎637-5473. Open daily 8am-9pm. 5 tent sites $8; 10 RV sites $10. Showers $1 per 2min.)

BRITISH COLUMBIA

Along the west coast of the island, BC Parks and the Forestry Service maintain two campgrounds. The first at **Mosquito Lake ❶**, about 35km (1hr.) from Sandspit, is every tenter's dream with mossy sites in wooded seclusion. About another 7km down the road, **Moresby camp ❶** has mowed sites with fewer bugs but lots of loud boat traffic into Gwaii Haanas. Both require an $8 permit. Follow Alliford Bay Main past the ferry docks to South Bay Main to Moresby Rd. to get there. **Grey Bay,** 20km south of town (30min.), offers a virtually uninterrupted expanse of sand. Twenty primitive forestry **campsites ❶** line the long expanse of the beach and afford tons of privacy. Obtain directions and logging road activity updates at the visitors center. Arrive early on weekends. ($8 permit only.)

◖◗ FOOD. For a nice, long round of golf ($20) and loaded burgers or veggie burgers ($7-9), head to **Willows Golf Course Clubhouse ❷**, near the end of Copper Bay Rd. (☎ 637-2388. Open W-Su 11:30am-8pm.) More pleasant inside than out, **Dick's Wok Restaurant and Grocery ❸**, 388 Copper Bay Rd., serves a heaping plate of fried rice ($9.50) next to a tank filled with monster goldfish. Dick also offers a limited selection of groceries. (☎ 637-2275. Open daily 5-10pm.) The **Sandspit Inn,** opposite the airport near the spit's end, houses the town's only **pub.** (☎ 637-5334. Open daily 11:30am-11pm, F-Sa 11:30am-1am.)

◪◩ OUTDOOR ACTIVITIES AND EVENTS. Spectacular sunrises and sunsets reward those who wander to the end of the **Spit,** where anglers surf-cast for silver salmon. Beachcombers should stay below the tide line if possible, since the spit is legally airport property. Several trails depart from the road between the ferry docks and the spit. In May take the easy stroll on **Onward Point trail** (30min.) to a grey whale watching outlook and a fossil bed. The **Dover Trail** (2hr.) begins 40m west of the Haans Creek Bridge across from the small boat harbor and passes giant cedars with ancient Haida markings. The **Skyline Loop** runs an hour to the shore over more difficult terrain. Although the trail system is marked, it goes through dense brush and crosses other trails, making the return trip more difficult.

Dirt logging roads lead south and west of town into some bogglingly scenic areas. If you plan on using **logging roads** between 6am and 6pm during the week, you must check in at the visitors center for active logging status; in winter call Teal Jones (☎ 637-5323). Ten kilometers past where Copper Bay Rd. turns into gravel are the rocky shores of **Copper Bay,** a haven for bald eagles.

The roads are perfect for **mountain biking.** The closest rentals are in Charlotte, and bikes are allowed free on ferries. The 24km Moresby Loop is a popular route that runs from Sandspit down to an old train trellis over Skidegate Lake and on to an abandoned Cumshewa Inlet logging camp. Logging in the area has slowed but locals still celebrate **Logger Sports Day** in July. The festival features pole-climbing, caber-tossing, axe-throwing, and other vigorous lumber-related activities.

GWAII HAANAS NATIONAL PARK RESERVE/HAIDA HERITAGE SITE

Roadless Gwaii Haanas corrals visitors with its haunting calm. Paddlers who reach the park's lonesome Haida villages, abandoned and rotting in the rainforest, clear nothing but mile and mile of quickening water and the steady thrum of ocean pounding the empty shore. Provincially owned Crown Land for most of the 20th century, the territory has been disturbed only by sporadic logging and occasional tourist visits to deserted Haida villages. In the mid-80s, the timber industry, the Haida nation, environmentalists, and the provincial government came to heads over land use on the island. In 1988, the federal government interceded, purchasing the southern third of the Queen Charlotte Islands to create a National Park Reserve. A 1993 agreement united the Haida Nation and the Government of Canada in the management of Gwaii Haanas. The Canadian Parks Ministry now patrols the islands, while the Haida Gwaii Watchmen guide visitors with the goal of protecting their cultural heritage.

✈ ORIENTATION

By air or by sea, each summer a few thousand visitors make the long ocean journey south from Moresby Camp (about 25km). **No trails** penetrate Gwaii Haanas and most exploration remains close to the 1600km of shoreline. The seas on the rocky west coast pound, making travel treacherous. On the east coast, the serene, remote waters teem with marine life and birds, peaking in Burnaby Narrows with the highest density of animal and vegetable protein per square meter in the world. Gaze up to see bald eagle nests in dead trees and paddle silently along shore at dawn to spot the strong-jawed sub-species of **black bears** unique to Haida Gwaii.

The islands hold treasures as inspiring as the seascape. Old-growth forest stands tall in **Hik'yah (Windy Bay)**, where Haida stood up to loggers. Chains of lakes and waterfalls span Gwaii Haanas. At **Gandll K'in (Hotsprings Island)**, three pristine seaside pools steam, soothing ocean-weary muscles.

Haida Gwaii Watchmen share the history of their culture at settlements being permitted to "return to the land," in keeping with Haida tradition. Totem poles slowly decay at **K'uuna (Skedans)** on Louise Island, north of Gwaii Hanaas, and the UNESCO World Heritage site of **Nan Sdins (Ninstints)**. Both Haida villages were deserted after late-19th-century epidemics of smallpox and tuberculosis. At **T'aanuu (Tanu)**, a moss grown longhouse village can be envisioned from the depressions and fallen poles. The grave of the recently deceased, famous Haida carver Bill Reid can be visited on the point next to the grave of the anonymous "Charlie."

🛈 PRACTICAL INFORMATION

Three hundred people can enter the park without licensed tour operators each year; they face unique planning and preparation concerns. These experienced kayakers and small craft owners may reserve dates to enter and exit the park by calling **Super, Natural British Columbia.** (In Canada and the US ☎ 800-663-6000; elsewhere 250-387-1642. Reservations $15 per person.) The park also provides six standby entries daily, although if you secure one of these spots, you still may not be able to enter the park for another couple of days. All visitors must attend the 1½hr. **orientation session** before they depart: these are held daily from May to Sept. at 8am and 7:30pm at the **Queen Charlotte City visitor center** (see p. 339) and at 11am at the **Sandspit visitor center** (see p. 346). Call at least a day ahead to arrange sessions. Park user fees are $10 per day (under 17 free; $80 max.). For a **trip-planning** package with a list of charter companies, contact **Parks Canada** (☎ 250-559-8818). Ask the park management about camping locations to avoid traditional Haida sites. Kayakers venturing into the park alone should file a **sail plan** with the **Prince Rupert Coast Guard** (☎ 250-627-3081), but should be aware that rescue may not be possible for many hours after a distress incident due to the park's remoteness. Contact **Fisheries and Oceans** (☎ 559-4413) before sampling shellfish. Freshwater fishing is not allowed; saltwater licenses are available in Charlotte (see p. 339).

> ## SIREN'S CALL
> Pause from paddling or cut off your Zodiak engine. Break the silence with a bull kelp horn! Snatch a piece of the kelp and cut the kelp to a length of 1-2 meters. You should see daylight through the ends. Now hold your horn in a "U" shape, buzz as you would to play a brass instrument, and hear it echo! The kelp is freshest and most prevalent in the spring and early summer.

Weather reports are broadcast on VHF channel 21. Two **warden stations** are staffed from May to September, at Huxley Island (about halfway down the park) and at Rose Harbour (near the south tip of Gwaii Haanas). They can be reached on VHF channel 16. Five **watchmen sites** (VHF 6) are staffed during the same period, and will offer assistance upon request, although their role is not to act as tour guides. To visit a cultural site, contact the watchmen a day in advance. No more than 12 people are permitted ashore at any one time.

🅰 OUTDOOR ACTIVITIES

To avoid the exposed north portion of Gwaii Haanas and to begin your trip in shelter of coastal islands, **Moresby Camp,** on the west side of the island, is a logical place to enter the park. Check with the info center in Sandspit (see p. 346) before traveling the potentially hazardous logging roads to this access point. **Bruce's Taxi** will run you down the gravel roads to Moresby Camp. (☎ 637-5655. 1hr. one-way; $150; fits 7 people and 2 kayaks; pre-arranged pickup.) **Moresby Explorers** (☎ 800-806-7633) will transport kayakers, kayaks, and gear from Sandspit into Gwaii Hanaas ($125 per person to Juan Perez Sound) or to their float camp at the north edge of Gwaii Haanas to pickup rental kayaks ($320 per week to rent and be transported). **Queen Charlotte Adventures** (see p. 342), in Queen Charlotte City, offers sea kayak rentals (singles $40 per day, $200 per week) and marine transport ($135 from Queen Charlotte to Juan Perez Sound). A round-trip kayak voyage down the length of the Gwaii Haanas takes two weeks; a guided voyage all the way down and back will run you at least $3000.

To experience Gwaii Haanas quickly and easily, **tour operators** guide visitors and take care of all logistics for entering Gwaii Haanas. Guided visitors do not have to make independent reservations or attend an info session. Run by energetic Doug Gould, 🅰**Moresby Explorers,** on Beach Rd. in Sandspit, just west of Copper Bay Rd., offers chartered trips. (☎ 637-2215 or 800-806-7633; www.moresbyexplorers.com. Trips $125, 2 days with overnight at float camp $350.) **South Moresby Air Charters** (☎ 559-4222) flies over many of the heritage sites.

APPROACHING THE YUKON

If you want to drive up through the deep north of BC, you have two main options: the Alaska Hwy. and the Cassiar Hwy. The Alaska Hwy. will lead you and a few trillion RVs through eastern BC before curving west as it crosses into the Yukon. The less-developed Cassiar Hwy. runs straight up north into the Yukon through BC's western half. The Cassiar is accessed from the south from Hwy. 16. You'll still have to tussle with the motorhomes, though—the Cassiar's northern terminus is the Alaska Hwy. A smattering of small towns line each road.

ALONG HWY. 37: CASSIAR HWY.

A growing number of travelers prefer the Cassiar Hwy. to the Alaska Hwy., which has become an RV institution. Built in 1972, the Cassiar slices through charred forests and snow-capped ebony peaks, passing scores of alpine lakes on its way from the Yellowhead Hwy. (Hwy. 16) in British Columbia to the Alaska Hwy. in the Yukon.

Three evenly spaced provincial **campgrounds** ❶ right off the highway offer beautiful camping, and lodges in the provincial parks section in the middle provide resort-like accommodation at prices lower than highway motels on the Alaska Hwy. Any waiter or lodging owner along the Cassiar's 718km will readily list its advantages: less distance, consistently intriguing scenery, and fewer crowds. Be prepared, however, to sacrifice the frequent gas stations and hardtop pavement that come with tourists. Large sections of the road past Meziadin Junction are dirt and gravel and become slippery when wet, causing plenty of tire blowouts. Trucks often barrel up and down the highway; drive at dawn, dusk, and on Sundays to keep in sight of wildlife and out of the way of these gravel-spitting behemoths.

HWY. 16 TO MEZIADIN JUNCTION

Just north of the junction of Hwy. 37 and Hwy. 16 stand the totem poles of **Gitwengak,** which relate the history of the First Nation fort that stood on nearby **Battle Hill** until 1800. The 2.5km **Kitwanga Loop Rd.,** 4km north of the junction, leads through Kitwanga to the **National Historic Park,** where the Hill is located. Once a stronghold for the mighty warrior **Nekt,** Battle Hill has become demure. Its intricate tunnel system has given way to stairs and guided walkways. The totem poles in the small native village of **Gitanyom** lie another 19km to the north and 3km off the highway.

The first gas stop is 139km north at **Meziadin Lake General Store** (meh-zee-AD-in), where produce, deli sandwiches, mail, and fishing stuff can be found. (☎636-2657. Open in summer daily 7am-11pm; winter 7am-9pm.) **Postal Code:** V0J 3S0. **Meziadin Lake Provincial Park** ❶ lies another 16km north, with plenty of fishing but tightly packed sites. (Water, free firewood, and pit toilets. 66 sites, $12.) The gravel sites are better geared to RVs, but tenters endure for the fishing; Meziadin Lake is one of three lakes in BC where salmon spawn. You might want to pick up a BC fishing regulations summary (available at nearly every BC visitors center) before you head out - unless you hire an outfitter, you'll have trouble finding one out in the wilderness. Violation fines are not trivial.

Make minor **tire repairs,** grab gas, and shoot the bull with truckers at **Meziadin Junction.** (☎636-2390. Open in summer daily 6am-10pm; winter 8am-7pm.) The nearby **cafe** ❶ serves up inexpensive burgers and whatnot. (☎636-9240. Open daily in summer 7am-7pm.) Don't get confused by the "T" in the road. Turn right to **Whitehorse, YT,** which lies 953km (12-15hr. of solid driving) to the north. Or, turn left to **Stewart, BC,** and **Hyder, AK,** which are 62km (45min. on paved roads) west, along Hwy. 37A. The road to Stewart and Hyder is known as the "Glacier Highway"; sprawling, calving plates of pale blue ice spill off the mountains and nearly jam into the roadway, chilling the whole valley.

STEWART, BC AND HYDER, AK ☎250

"It's the prettiest place on earth," profess most Hyderites. So as long as you keep your view trained above the dumpy townsite and toward the glacier-welted mountains on every side, you'll see why. **Stewart, BC** is positioned in the jaws of one of the world's longest fjords, among tidal flats. Its cross-border partner, the former ghost town of **Hyder, AK** looks like an old-west village plopped down in the mountains. Horses and townsfolk alike roam the unpaved streets. Although Hyder is technically in Alaska, its currency is Canadian (except at the US Post Office), its clocks tick to Pacific Standard Time, and its area code is 250. During International Days, from Canada Day to Independence Day (July 1-4), the two tiny communities erupt in an extravaganza of fellowship that is North America's longest birthday party, and visitors are heartily welcomed to bond in local bars. Stewart provides most modern amenities in contrast with Hyder, which sports frontier-style nightlife and dirt roads. Although the past economy has been based on the mining and timber industries, with attractions like the world's largest road-accessible glacier, Hyder and Stewart are becoming tourist centers. Visit before the tourist rush gets any more frenzied—the towns still don't depend tourists for most of their revenue, and the prevailing flavor is still local.

◼ ◪ ORIENTATION AND PRACTICAL INFORMATION

Hwy. 37A becomes **Conway St.** in Stewart. It intersects **5th Ave.**, which is the main drag on the waterfront, and leads along the bay into Hyder. On your return from Hyder, beware: Canadian customs patrols the border to curb smuggling. Be prepared to show ID and be asked how long you were in "America." Humorless officers don't flinch at the typical response of "about 5 minutes."

Airplanes: Taguan Air (☎636-2800) flies a mail plane that carries passengers to **Ketchikan** (45min., M and Th, $100). Call well ahead.

Local Transportation: Seaport Limousines (☎636-2622), in Stewart, drives to Terrace (4hr., daily 10am, $30) and takes sightseers to Salmon Glacier for $34 per person.

Auto Repair: PetroCan (☎636-2307, after hours ☎636-2456), at 5th Ave. and Conway, has the only gas in either town. Open daily 7:30am-8pm, repairs 8am-4:30pm. 24hr. road service.

Tourist Information: In **Stewart** (☎636-9224; www.stewartcassiar.com), on 5th Ave. heading to Hyder. Open June-Aug. daily 9am-7pm; in winter M-F 1-5pm. In **Hyder** (☎636-9148), at the **Hyder Community Association Building;** bear right at the Sealaska Inn downtown. Open June-Aug. M 10am-2pm, Th noon-4pm.

Outdoor Information: Forest Service (☎636-2367), down the hall from Hyder visitors center. Open May 1-Sept. 15, usually 10am-2pm. Call ahead.

Bank: Canadian Imperial Bank of Commerce (☎636-2235), on 5th Ave. in Stewart, has a **24hr. ATM.** Open M and W noon-3pm.

Laundromat and Public Showers: Shoreline Laundromat (☎636-2322), on Brightwell and 6th, behind the post office, in Stewart. Wash $1.75, dry $0.25 per 4min. Showers $1 per 1½min. Open daily 7am-11pm. In **Hyder**, beside the Sealaska Inn. Wash $2, dry $1.75. Showers $3 per 8min. Open 24hr.

Emergency: ☎911.

Police: (☎636-2233) at 8th Ave. and Conway St.

Ambulance: ☎800-461-9911.

Fire: ☎636-2345.

Health Centre: (☎636-2221), at Brightwell and 9th. Open M-F 9am-5pm.

Internet Access: A cheap $2 per hr. at **Stewart Public Library.** Turn left on 9th Ave. as you drive into Stewart from highway. Open in summer M-Th 1-4:30pm and 6-8pm, Su 1:30-4:30pm. **Toast Works,** see **Food,** below. $6 per hr.

Post Office: (☎636-2553) In Stewart, at Brightwell St. and 5th Ave. Open M-F 8:30am-5pm, Sa 9am-noon. In Hyder, 1 Hyder Ave. (☎636-2662), past the Community Building towards Fish Creek. US currency only. Open M-F 9am-1pm and 2-5pm, Sa 10:30am-12:30pm. **Postal Codes:** Hyder: 99923. Stewart: V0T 1W0.

⌂ ◖ ACCOMMODATIONS AND FOOD

Reasonably priced B&Bs are popping up all over Stewart and Hyder. **Kathi's B&B** ❸, at the corner of 8th and Brightwell, provides placid accommodations and a full breakfast. (☎636-2795. Singles $60; doubles $70.)

INTERNATIONAL DAYS Celebrated in Stewart, BC, and Hyder, AK, International Days run from Canada Day, July 1st, to Independence Day, July 4th. The four days of wild festivities are kicked off with the wet t-shirt contest at the Sealaska. International Days features such events as the ax throw and the broom kick and culminates with the annual Bush Woman Classic. The strong-armed women of Hyder and Stewart come together to flex their muscles, trying to post the fastest time and highest accuracy over a course that includes hanging laundry, shooting a bear, chopping wood, diapering a baby, and finally sprinting while applying lipstick. Beware, these women take no prisoners, and spectators are often rallied into competing.

Stewart's **Rainey Creek Campground ❶,** located at the end of Brightwell St., is orderly, quiet, and woodsy, with putting-green quality grassy tent sites, forested sites with electricity, and impeccably clean showers. (☎636-2537. Tents $11 for 2 people, $3 per extra person. Dry RV sites $15, sites with electricity $18. Showers $1 per 4min.) Less appealing **Camp Runamuck ❶,** in Hyder, has tent-sites ($12) separated from a gravelly RV park (RV sites $18) with coin showers and laundry in the **Sealaska Inn ❷.** The Inn has **camping ❶** as well as cubicle-like "sleeping rooms" and regular rooms. (☎636-2486 or 888-393-1199. Tents $10; RV sites $18. Sleeping rooms with shared bath $36; singles $52; doubles $58.) It's upstairs from a night lounge famous for its wet t-shirt contests during **International Days.**

The **Bitter Creek Cafe ❶,** in Stewart on 5th Ave., keeps an array of thick, fresh sandwiches and sweets in a great building adorned with historical photos and frontier appliances. (☎636-2166. Open May-Oct. daily 11:30am-2pm and 5-8pm; July-Aug. 8am-9pm.) Across the street, **Toast Works ❶** has an interactive appliance bar and serves fruit smoothies. Two dollars will get you into toaster-lover's heaven, dedicated to the history of the toaster. (Open daily mid-May to mid-Sept. noon-5:30pm.) **Rainey Mountain Bakery and Deli ❶,** also on 5th Ave. will tempt you with low-priced, fresh-baked treats and breads. (☎636-2777. Open daily 8am-8pm.) **Cut-Rate Foods,** on 5th Ave. in Stewart, lives up to its name. (☎636-2377. Open daily 9am-9pm. No credit cards.) **Wildflour Cafe ❷,** on Hyder's main drag, will feed you the vast Hungry Lumberjack breakfast for $12 or the merely enormous Country Road Special for $8. (☎636-2875. Open daily 6:30am-noon.)

👁 🔺 SIGHTS, NIGHTLIFE, AND OUTDOOR ACTIVITIES

SIGHTS. The Stewart Historical Society runs a **museum,** on Columbia St. The classic horror flick *The Thing* was filmed in Stewart, and the museum's got the gory photos to prove it. (☎636-2568. In winter, call ☎636-9029 for appointment. Open mid-May to mid-Sept. daily 11am-7pm. $4, ages 6-12 $2, under 6 free.)

NIGHTLIFE. The principal activity in Hyder is sidling up to the bar in the historic **Glacier Inn** and asking to be "Hyderized." Over $45,000 in signed bills line the tavern walls, where early miners would tack up cash to insure themselves against returning to town too broke to buy a drink. A sign over the door reminds youth that the drinking age in the US is 21. (☎636-9092. Open in summer 10am-close; winter 2pm-close.) If you want to catch a ballgame on TV or master the Grand Lizard pinball machine, head over to the **Sealaska.** (Take a left at the "intersection." ☎636-2486. Open 11am-close.)

OUTDOOR ACTIVITIES. The chilling **Salmon Glacier,** 20 mi./32km from Hyder on the Salmon River Rd., is the fifth-largest glacier in Canada and the largest accessible by road. Beginning at Mile 19, the road creeps along a ridge almost directly above the glacier for several miles, providing eagle-eye views. The rocks above the road make for good hiking as the glacier lays beneath the setting sun. The road to the glacier is rocky and winding, but navigable for most vehicles. There are many scenic pull-outs. Check road conditions with the Forest Service and get a self-guided tour brochure. **Bear Glacier,** 35km east of Stewart, sits in plain and glorious view of Hwy. 37A. Most anglers let the bear population work the creeks and streams, but for a hefty sum, deluxe fishing boats can be chartered for the hour, day, or week. If you already possess boating prowess, you can rent your own craft.

Each year during the salmon spawning season (late July-Aug.), bears congregate at **Fish Creek,** 5 mi./8km down the road in Hyder, to feed on bloated, dying Alaskan chum salmon. Come early in the morning to avoid tourist crowds. The only maintained trail on the Hyder side is the **Titan Trail,** a challenging 16km (round-trip) hike up from the valley with creek crossings. It gains 1200m of elevation, becoming rocky and difficult toward the end (check with the Forest Service for trail conditions). Heading away from Hyder, the trailhead is on the right about half a mile past Fish Creek. Check with the forestry gang for trail conditions and bear density. 8 mi./13km north of Stewart along Hwy. 37A, the **Ore Mountain Trail** is a shorter, but still challenging 4 mi./7km (round-trip) climb to a viewpoint overlooking the Bear River Valley. Hunters near Hyder should note that the Canadian borderline is always very, very close—pay attention to topo maps to avoid huge fines.

MEZIADIN JUNCTION TO ISKUT ☎ 250

This stretch of the Cassiar Hwy. has hands-down the best lodging and roadside bear-viewing around and also closest access to the two provincial parks. The area around the small village of **Iskut,** 256km north of Meziadin Junction, presents a range of resorts, earning it the unremarkable title "Resort Capital of NW BC."

The first stop after the junction is 90km north at **Bell II Lodge ❷,** the posh heliskiing jump-off point that caters to summer road-trippers searching for gas and food at reasonable prices. Big breakfasts are $8 and burgers are $6-8. (☎ 604-881-8530 or 800-655-5566. Sites $10; RV sites $22. Showers and dump station. Gas and coffee shop open daily 7am-10pm. Dining room open daily 7am-8pm.) Another 117km north is **Kinaskan Lake Provincial Park ❶,** where an immaculately kept campground includes water, pit toilets, firewood, and a boat launch onto the rainbow trout-stocked lake. (Wheelchair accessible. 50 lakeside sites, $12.) Pick up fishing permits before you arrive. At the far end of the lake is the head of a 24km hiking trail to **Mowdade Lake** in **Mount Edziza Provincial Park** (see below). There is gas, car repairs, lodging, boat rentals, and the last food for a long while among the moose antlers of the "wilderness oasis" of **Tatogga Lake Resort ❷,** another 25km north. (☎ 234-3526. Canoes $20 for 2hr., $40 per day. Boat and motor $65 per day. Meat lover's sandwich $4.75. Laundry $2.50 wash or dry. (Open May-Sept. daily 7am-10pm, winter 7am-7pm). Cabins with woodstoves $32, cabins with amenities $45 for 1 bed, $65 for 2 beds. Tent sites $10-12. RV sites $19. Showers $3.) A bit farther is the **Ealue Lake** (EE-lu-eh) turn-off on Spatsizi Rd., which leads to trailheads pointing deep into the virgin backcountry of the **Spatsizi Plateau Wilderness.**

Everyone heartily approves of ▧**The Red Goat Lodge,** 3km south of Iskut on **Eddontenajon Lake.** The **hostel ❶** in the basement boasts a full kitchen, spacious common room, wood stove, coin showers, and laundry. The hosts' kids and llamas keep the place lively even when it's not packed. The **B&B ❸** upstairs is equally impressive. (☎ 234-3261. Wash $2, dry $1. Hostel $17; B&B singles $65, doubles $85. Cabins $90-105. Showers $1 per 3½min.) **Tent sites ❶** are on the loon-inhabited lake. (Canoes $10 per half-day. Rentals for trips on the **Stikine** and **Spatsizi Rivers** start at $35 per day. Sites $14; RV sites $20.)

BRITISH COLUMBIA

At Iskut, travelers can get gas and groceries at **Kluachon Centre.** (☎234-3241. Open June-Aug. daily 8am-10pm; winter M-Sa 9am-6pm, Su noon-5pm.) It doubles as the **post office** (open M, W, and F 9am-4pm, Tu 1-4pm). **Postal Code:** V0J 1K0.

Just north of Iskut, **Mountain Shadow RV Park and Campground ❶** has lovely campsites nestled in the mountain forest near trails to the lake and hikes into the woods. (☎234-3333. Boat rental $15. Sleeping cabin with electricity $45, cabin with stocked kitchen and bathroom $65. Tent sites $15; RV electric RV sites $18; Full RV sites $20.)

DEASE LAKE   ☎250

Dease Lake, 84km north of Iskut, became a Hudson Bay Company outpost in the late 1800s, although it had been long known by the local indigenous Tahltan as "Tatl'ah" ("Head of the Lake"). When the early gold rush glory petered out, so did the town's allure. There's little to draw road-trippers to Dease Lake besides gas and food. The traveler in search of accommodations should stay outside of Dease Lake in resort-like, lake-front accommodations in the **Iskut** area that cost less and have more character.

🛈 PRACTICAL INFORMATION. The **Dease Lake Tourist Information Office** is in the Northern Lights College, a small series of buildings on Cassiar in the middle of town (☎771-3900). The **Forest Service** (☎771-8100) occupies the building next door and offers info on local trails or campsites; call ahead. Fishing and camping supplies can be found at **McLeod Mountain Supply Ltd.,** on Boulder St. past **Tanzilla Bar.** (☎771-4699. Open M-Sa 9am-5pm, Su 10am-4pm.) The **TD Bank** is in the Government building across the highway from the college. (Open M, W, and F 10am-noon and 1-3pm.) **Dease Gas Station** has **showers** ($4; includes towel, soap, and shampoo) and a **laundromat** (☎771-5600; wash $3, dry $0.25 per 5min.; open daily 7am-8pm). The **Stikine Health Center** is just off the Cassiar at the north end of town. (☎771-4444. Walk-in M-F 8:30am-4:30pm.) Other service include: **police,** ☎771-4111; and **ambulance,** ☎771-3333. Free **Internet access** is available at the Northern Lights College. (Open M-F 8:30am-noon and 1-4:30pm.) The **Post office** is in the Dease Gas Station. (☎771-5013. Open M-F 8:30am-1pm and 2-5pm.) **Postal Code:** V0C 1L0.

🖃🍴 ACCOMMODATIONS AND FOOD. The spacious, pine-furnished **Arctic Divide Inn ❹,** right on the Cassiar, features clean rooms with private bath, phones, TV, and access to a shared kitchen. (☎771-3119. Generous continental breakfast is included. Singles and doubles $68.) You can camp in town at **Allen Lake ❶.** From Boulder St., go left on 1st Ave. and follow it to the end ($8 camping permit only; no real sites, no water, pit toilets). Be warned—the road down to the lake is steep. For camping outside of town, head south to the **Tanzilla River Lion's Club Campground ❶** ($7 for a site with fire pit and pit toilets, $3 per bundle of wood) or drive an hour south for true camping paradise.

Northway Country Kitchen ❷, or "the restaurant," offers big portions in a spacious setting. Feel your arteries clog for only $9.50 with "pierogies & smokies," cheese-filled dumplings with four sizeable sausages. (☎771-4114. Open May-Oct. daily 7am-9pm.) Stock up on the best-priced and fullest selection of **groceries** for quite a distance at the **Supervalu.** (☎771-4381. Open mid-June to Sept. daily 8am-8pm; winter M-Sa 9am-7pm, Su 9am-6pm.)

NEAR DEASE LAKE: TELEGRAPH CREEK. Lying 119km from Dease Lake on Telegraph Creek Rd., Telegraph Creek is the only remaining settlement along the **Stikine River** (stuh-KEEN). The highest navigable point on the Stikine, the site was

BRITISH COLUMBIA

an important rendezvous for the coastal Tlingit and interior Tahltan people. Telegraph Creek's 400 residents are still mostly Tahltan.

The biggest attraction for thrill-seeking travelers is the 112km **Telegraph Creek Rd.** The gravel road is well maintained and offers magnificent views of the **Stikine Grand Canyon.** It is no place, however, to lug a clumsy RV or give a failed brake system a second chance. The second half of the road features 20% grades and hairpin turns along the steep obsidian outbanks of the Tuya and Stikine River canyons. Travelers should allow 2½hr. to drive each way, with time to de-frazzle in between. A rest stop, 88km from Telegraph Creek, offers a view of the canyon and a chance to stop and check on your car. If you don't know much about checking your car, learn the basics before tackling this road.

The modern village of Telegraph Creek revolves around the historic **Stikine River-Song.** Today, the RiverSong acts as Telegraph Creek's **hotel ❸, cafe ❸,** gas station, and general store. Rooms are clean, with cedar finishing and a common kitchen. (☎235-3196. Showers $4. Open May-Sept. M-Sa 11am-7pm, Su noon-7pm. Singles $55, doubles $65; $10.50 per additional person.) Free **camping ❶** is available 15 mi. toward **Glenora** past Winter Creek. Outdoors adventurers need to be respectful of tribal lands, which have different access, fishing, and hunting regulations than the rest of BC. Tribal land holdings speckle the surrounding wilderness. Topo maps help identify their boundaries, but you'll need mapsheets anyway if you plan to do much hiking—there are few developed trails in the region.

The community welcomes its infrequent visitors, but those keen to explore should seek permission from the **Tahltan Band** (☎235-3151) before crossing onto tribal lands. For **tire repair,** contact **Henry Vance** (☎235-3300). Locals have been known to stop and help motorists stalled by the road. Call the **police** at ☎235-3111. Follow signs for Glenora to find the **health clinic** (☎235-3212 or 235-3171). On your way into town from the south, the **post office** is on the right. (Open M and W 9:30-11:30am, Tu and Th 1-4pm, F 9:30-11:30am and 1-4pm.) **Postal Code:** V0J 2W0.

DEASE LAKE TO THE ALASKA HWY.

This stretch of highway follows the old Cassiar Gold Route, where some dredges are still in use. **Moose Meadow Resort ❶,** 85km north of Dease Lake, is a roomy lakeside campground with access to canoe routes. (Firewood, water. Sites $8; cabins from $25. Showers $2.50.) **Jade City ❶,** 113km past Dease Lake, offers free RV and tent sites in addition to an impressive jade stash. (Open daily 8am-9pm.)

Kididza Services, at Good Hope Lake, 23km past Jade City, is the last gas for 98km, when you hit the Alaska Hwy. (☎239-3500. Open M-Sa 8am-9pm, Su 10am-4pm.) **Boya Lake Provincial Park ❶** is 152km north of Dease Lake and the final campground before the Alaska Hwy. (85km later), situated on a magnificent turquoise lake with a boat launch and swimming dock. Grab some reading material at the book exchange box at the entrance. (Pit toilets, firewood, water. 45 sites, $12.) Having crossed into Yukon 3.5km back and reached the end of this 718km odyssey at the junction of the Cassiar Hwy. and the Alaska Hwy., travelers can find showers, munchies, gas, and minor repairs at the **PetroCan Station,** which doubles as the office for the **RV park ❶** and **motel ❷** next door. (☎536-2794. Sites $13-16, full RV sites $20. In motel, baths are shared. Singles and doubles $40. Showers free, $3 for non-guests.) If the office is closed, check in at the **saloon.** (☎536-2796. Open daily 11am-midnight.) The station also operates a **24hr. laundromat** (wash $1.50, dry $0.50 per 14min.). Travelers can chomp on a Junction Melt ($8) at the **Junction 37 Cafe ❷,** next to PetroCan. (☎536-2795. Open May-Oct. M-Sa 6am-midnight, Su 7am-10pm; winter daily 7am-10pm.) **Whitehorse** lies another 435km (5hr.) west on the Alaska Hwy. (see below).

HWY. 97: THE ALASKA HWY.

Built during World War II in reaction to the Japanese bombing of Pearl Harbor and the capture of two Aleutian Islands, the Alaska Hwy. served to calm Alaskan fears of an Axis invasion. Due to the speed with which it was built, the highway stands as one of the most incredible engineering feats of the 20th century. Army troops and civilians pushed from both ends—Dawson Creek and Fairbanks—and bridged the 2451km at Mile 1202 (near Beaver Creek) in 8 months and 12 days.

While the original one lane dirt track has evolved into a "highway," the potholes that develop after the winter thaw and the patches of loose gravel give drivers a taste of the good old days. In recent years, the US Army has been replaced by an annual army of over 250,000 tourists and RV-borne senior citizens from the US and Europe. For those with the time to stop, there are countless opportunities to hike, fish, and view wildlife off the highway. However, if your priority is to beat the quickest path to the Yukon border, the **Cassiar Hwy.** (Hwy. 37; see p. 349) may be a better route for you. Another scenic option is on the far side of the Yukon border, on the **Campbell Hwy.** (Hwy. 4; see p. 364).

For daily Alaska Hwy. **road conditions** call ☎ 867-667-8215. Mileposts put up along the highway in the 1940s are still used as mailing addresses and reference points, although the road has been rebuilt and rerouted so many times that they are no longer accurate. Washouts sometimes occur in the spring, and other hazards include forest fires, falling rock, and construction delays. Motorists should always be aware of wildlife on the road, keep headlights on, carry spare tires and spare parts, and be prepared to slow down for graders, potholes, and general road breakup and gravel patches.

DAWSON CREEK ☎ 250

Mile 0 of the Alaska Hwy. is Dawson Creek, BC. First settled in 1890, it was just another pip-squeak frontier village of a few hundred people among the flaming canola fields of Peace River. Then the Alaska Highway came through, and so did nearly every senior citizen in North America with a motor home. The 13,000-odd residents are serious about their home's role as the womb of the Alaska Hwy., and visitors who pause to enjoy the town's history and hospitality can easily get caught up in the enthusiasm. Dawson draws a hardy Alaska-bound crew and caters more to the pure tourist than the outdoorsman.

✈ ⬅ ORIENTATION AND TRANSPORTATION

There are two ways to reach Dawson Creek from the south. From Alberta, drive northwest from Edmonton along **Hwy. 43,** through Whitecourt to Valleyview; turn left on **Hwy. 34** to Grande Prairie, and continue northwest on **Hwy. 2** to Dawson Creek for a total journey of 590km. From Prince George, drive 402km north on the John Hart section of **Hwy. 97** (see p. 330). Both drives take the better part of a day.

Greyhound, 1201 Alaska Ave. (☎ 782-3131 or 800-661-8747), is open M-F 6am-5:30pm and 8-8:30pm; Sa 6-11am, 2:30-4:30pm, and 8-8:30pm; Su 6-10:30am, 3-4:30pm, and 8-8:30pm. Buses run to **Whitehorse, YT** (20hr.; June-Aug. M-Sa; $186); **Prince George** (6½hr., 2 per day, $58); and **Edmonton** (8hr., 2 per day, $78).

🛈 PRACTICAL INFORMATION

Tourist Information: Stop at the **visitors center,** 900 Alaska Ave. (☎ 782-9595), next to the big red grain elevator, for daily road reports, maps to just about everything in the city, and a small museum (donation requested). Open May 15-Labour Day daily 8am-7pm; winter Tu-Sa 9am-5pm.

Bank: CIBC (☎ 782-4816), 10200 10th St. **24hr. ATM.**

Markets: Groceries at **IGA,** 1100 Alaska Ave. (☎ 782-5766). Open daily 8am-11pm. **Safeway,** 1200 8th St. (☎ 800-723-3929). Open daily 8am-11pm.

Laundromat: King Koin Laundromat, 1220 103rd Ave. (☎ 782-2395). Wash $2.50, double load $3, dry $0.25 per 5min. Showers $2.75. Open daily 8am-9pm. At the **Mile 0 Campground,** loads are a buck apiece (see **Accommodations,** below).

Auto Repair: J&L Mechanical Services (☎ 782-7832) does **24hr. road service.**

Hospital: 1100 13th St. (☎ 782-8501). **Ambulance:** ☎ 782-2211.

Police: (☎ 782-5211), at Alaska Ave. and 102nd Ave.

Crisis Line: ☎ 877-442-2828

Internet access: Free 1hr. at the **library,** 10 St. and McKellar Ave. (☎ 782-4661). Open Tu-Th 10am-9pm, F 10am-5:15pm, Sa and Su 1:30-5:15pm; closed Su summer.

Post Office: (☎ 782-9429), at 104th Ave. and 10th St. Open M-F 8:30am-5pm. **Postal Code:** V1G 4E6.

▐ ACCOMMODATIONS AND CAMPING

Those willing to trade a few amenities for bargain prices, great location, and an offbeat aura should head straight for the historic **Alaska Hotel ❸.** It is located above the Alaska Cafe & Pub (see **Food,** below) on 10th St., 1½ blocks from the visitors center. The comfortable rooms are carefully decorated, some with pictures of Marilyn Monroe and Elvis. Shared bath; no TV or phone. (☎ 782-7998. Singles $32; doubles $37; winter $5 less.) The newer **Voyageur Motor Inn ❸,** 801 111th Ave., facing 8th Ave., offers motoring voyagers phones, cable TV, and fridges at no extra charge in sterile boxy rooms. (☎ 782-1020. Singles $45; doubles $50.) Folks willing to spend more can get all sorts of services at the **Inn On The Creek ❹,** 10600 8th St.: cable TV, fridge and microwave, and a location close to downtown. (☎ 782-8136. Singles $55-65; doubles $60-70.) The popular but RV-laden **Mile 0 Campground ❶** is 1km west of Alaska Hwy., adjacent to the Pioneer Village. (☎ 782-2590. Coin laundry $1.25. Sites $12; full RV sites $17. Free showers.) Campers can also head for the convenient **Alahart RV Park ❶,** 1725 Alaska Ave., at the intersection with the John Hart Hwy., for a dump station and laundry. The friendly owners rival the visitors center for maps and suggestions on entertainment and food. (☎ 782-4702. Sites $10; full RV sites $20. Free showers.)

▐ FOOD

The **Alaska Cafe & Pub ❷,** "55 paces south of the Mile 0 Post" on 10th St., serves excellent burgers and fries from $7. The pub offers live music nightly at 9pm (mostly country), and travelers can sing at Monday night karaoke amidst stuffed cougars, elk, and marmots. (☎ 782-7040. Open Su-Th 10am-10pm, F-Sa 11am-11pm; pub open daily noon-3am.) Eating too many sandwiches ($5.50) at **PotBelly Deli ❶,** 1128 102nd. Ave., will give your tummy some chub too, but you won't regret it. Each night a new international cuisine inspires the chef. (☎ 782-5425. Open M-F 10am-7pm, Sa 10am-5pm.) Dine old-school style in **Mile One Cafe ❷.** Select your entree from the chalkboard as you relive 1940s Dawson Creek in the Pioneer Village. (See **Sights.** Open Tu-Su 8am-7pm.) Pick up a loaf for the road at the **Organic Farms Bakery,** 1425 97th Ave. From the visitors center, drive west along Alaska Ave. and take a right at 15th St. You can't miss it; the building is huge. Breads are baked fresh from local grain and start at $2; cakes and cookies are also available. (☎ 782-6533. Open F 9:30am-5:30pm, Sa 9am-4pm.)

👁 ⚠ SIGHTS AND OUTDOOR ACTIVITIES

This town boomed during construction. Literally. On February 13, 1943, 60 cases of exploding dynamite leveled the entire business district save the **COOP** building, now Bing's Furniture, opposite the Mile 0 post. Travelers cruising through Dawson Creek can't miss the photo ops at **Mile 0 Cairn** and **Mile 0 Post** near the visitors center. Both commemorate the birth of the Alaska Hwy., and are within a stone's throw of the visitors center. The **Art Gallery** in the old grain elevator next door displays a photo essay on the Alaska Hwy. creation saga. (☎ 782-2601. Open daily June-Aug. 9am-5pm; winter Tu-Sa 10am-noon and 1-5pm.)

The **Pioneer Village**, 1km west of Mile 0, is an excellent re-creation of Dawson Creek life from the 1920s to the 40s, with antique (read: rusted) farm equipment, an antler carver hard at work, nine gardens tended by the Horticultural Society, and a play area for children. (☎ 782-7144. Open May-Aug. daily 8am-8pm. Donation requested.) In early August, the town plays host to the **Fall Fair & Stampede** (☎ 782-8911), with a carnival, fireworks, chuckwagon races, and a professional rodeo.

Travel 10km out of town to the highland marshes of ▓**McQueen's Slough** and follow the trail to the left across a boardwalk and around the water. Take Hwy. 49 east from the visitors center, turn left onto Rd. 3. (Rolla Rd., not to be confused with Parkhill Dr., which is also marked "Rolla Rd.," and which is still in town), and take the second left at the driveway across from the binocular signpost. The slough is filled with a broad spectrum of birds.

DAWSON CREEK TO FORT NELSON ☎ 250

The Alaska Hwy. between Dawson Creek and **Fort St. John** (76km and about 45min. up the Alaska Hwy.) offers little more than cows and rolling hills. It runs through a region more concerned with industry (natural gas and timber) than tourism. Ride a 10km loop of the Old Alaska Hwy. over the curved Kiskatinaw Bridge (the only original timber bridge still in existence), 28km from Dawson Creek, and you'll appreciate the condition of the new highway.

TAYLOR AND FORT ST. JOHN

In early August, gold-grubbers converge 20km south of Fort St. John in **Taylor** to pan for prizes and fame at the **World Invitational Gold Panning Championships** (☎ 789-3392) in Peace Island Park. The **visitors center,** 9923 96th Ave. at 100th St., is adjacent to the park and museum. (☎ 785-3033. Open June-Aug. M-F 8am-8pm, Sa and Su 9am-6pm; Sept.-May M-F 8am-5pm.) The people of Fort St. John take deep pride in their gargantuan **North Peace Leisure Pool,** containing every imaginable aquatic delight. (☎ 787-8178. Wave pool, sauna, hot tub, water slide, and steam room. $4.95, ages 13-18 $3.85, under 13 $2.75.)

SIKANNI

Sikanni River RV Park ❶, at Alaska Hwy. Mile 160, has full amenities in a mountain setting. Grassy tent sites along the river have picnic tables and fire pits. (☎ 774-1028. Toilets, laundry. Sites $12; full RV sites $19. Free showers.) The best sites for camping along the way are at **Buckinghorse Provincial Park ❶,** 27km from Sikanni, along the river, although they are not particularly private. (Pit toilets. $12.) Two kilometers past Buckinghorse, **River Lodge** allows **free tenting** on its grassy lawn. (☎ 773-6468. Showers $3.)

FORT NELSON

☎ 250

Four hundred and fifty-six kilometers north of Dawson Creek and 210km east of Toad River is Fort Nelson, a bastion of natural resource extraction. The **visitors center**, in the Recreation Centre/Curling Rink on the west edge of town, provides **daily Alaska Hwy. road reports.** (☎774-6400. Open daily May-Sept. 8am-8pm.) The **Library,** right behind the Phoenix Theater off S 50 Ave., has free Internet. (☎774-6777. M-W noon-5pm, 7pm-9pm; Th, F 10am-5pm; Sa, Su noon-5pm.) The **Fort Nelson Heritage Museum,** across the highway from the visitors center, features an impressive collection of stuffed game, as well as remnants from the era of highway construction. (☎774-3536. Open daily 9am-6pm. $3, ages 6-16 and seniors $2.) The **First Nations Craft Center** is on 49th Ave. From 50th St., off 50th Ave. S, take a right on 49th Ave.; it's on the right. (☎774-3669. Open M-F 8:30am-4:30pm.)

Rest at the **Mini-Price Inn ❸,** 5036 51st Ave. W, one block off the highway near the visitors center. No phones. Cable TV. (☎774-2136. Singles $45; doubles $50; kitchenettes $5 extra.) The **Almada Inn ❹** is by the CIBC Bank off the Alaska Hwy. (☎774-2844. Free breakfast. Singles $69; doubles $79.) The **Westend Campground ❶,** across from the visitors center, has dusty sites in a pretty, wooded area, but the place is more RV-oriented than tent friendly. (☎774-2340. Laundry: wash $2, dry $1 per 30min. Sites $17; full RV sites $22. Showers $1 per 9min.)

There aren't many choices for dining in Fort Nelson. **Dan's Pub ❷,** at the southern end of town, offers nightly drink specials, pool, and an extensive menu in a dark pub. (☎774-3929. Open M-Th 11am-12:30am, F-Sa 11am-1:30am, Su 11am-midnight. After 8pm, 19+.) **Blue Bell Restaurant ❶,** opposite Dan's in the Blue Bell Inn, serves a $5 breakfast. (☎774-3550. Open M-Sa 6am-9pm, Su 8am-4pm.)

FORT NELSON TO THE BC/YUKON BORDER

Small towns, usually composed of one gas pump, one $50-60 motel, and one cafe, pock the remainder of the highway to Whitehorse. Fortunately for the glassy-eyed driver, highway scenery improves dramatically a few miles out of Fort Nelson.

STONE MOUNTAIN. About 150km north of Fort Nelson, the stark naked **Stone Mountain** appears. Next, **Summit Lake** lies below the highest summit on the highway (1295m). The neighboring **Stone Mountain Campground ❶** makes a superb starting point for hiking in the area. (New-fangled composting outhouse, firewood, water. Sites $12.) The steep **Summit Peaks Trail** begins across the highway from the campground, ascending 5km along a ridgeline to the breathtaking crest. A more moderate trail climbs 6km to the alpine Flower Springs Lake. Each hike takes about 5hr. round-trip. If you're ready for the challenge, a 70km loop leads from km 632 of the Alaska Hwy. through the craggy MacDonald Creek Valley and back out the hoodoo-lined Wokkpash Valley Gorge. Expect to spend 5-7 days on this lavish route. Gas and accommodations are available roadside 7km past the lake.

TOAD RIVER. Toad River, a town of 75, lies 45km north of Summit. The **Toad River Cafe ❷,** on the highway has some 5900 hats dangling from the ceiling. Tasty burgers from $7. Headwear donations accepted. (☎232-5401. Open in summer daily 6:30am-10pm; winter 7am-9pm.) An Alaska Hwy. odyssey—a grassy, RV- and tent-friendly campground with private, new sites—**Poplars Campground and Cafe ❶** springs up 5km after Toad River. (☎232-5465. Tents $14; full RV sites $20.)

MUNCHO LAKE. Fifty kilometers north of Toad River, Muncho Lake Provincial Park delights even the weariest drivers. Muncho ("big lake" in Tagish) is a 7 mi. long azure mirror. **Strawberry Flats Provincial Campground ❶** and **MacDonald Provincial**

Campground ❶, 8km farther on, have the best camping in the area with sweet lake-front sites. (Pit toilets, fire wood, water. Sites $12.) If you don't want to camp, stay at the **Muncho Lake Lodge ❸**, 10km north of Strawberry Flats. Rooms are well-kept, and the service is good. (☎ 776-3456. Singles $45; tents $14; RV sites $16.)

LIARD RIVER HOT SPRINGS. Near the 775km mark are the Liard River Hot Springs. These two naturally steamy and sulfurous pools are a phenomenal place to sooth a driver's derriere. For a bit more privacy and deeper water, skip the Alpha pool and head up to Beta. The park service manages campsites and free day-use of the springs. Arrive early, as non-reservation campsites are in extremely high demand. (Reservations ☎ 800-689-9025. Water, toilets, firewood. Gates closed 11pm-6am. Sites $15.) About 10km after Liard Hot Springs, a rough, 3km gravel road thwarts RVs and leads to the hidden and largely untouristed **Smith River Falls.** Watch carefully for the turn-off sign. A steep trail with rickety staircases leads right to the base of the huge cascade, and grayling can be fished from the Smith River with a permit. For permit info, contact BC Parks at ☎ 250-787-3407.

ALBERTA

ALBERTA'S... **Drinking age:** 18. **Sales Tax:** 7% national sales tax (GST). **Traffic Laws:** Seatbelt required. Bicycle helmets required. **Capital:** Edmonton. **Tartan:** Forest green, wheat gold, sky blue, rose pink, coal black.

With its gaping prairie, oil-fired economy, and conservative politics, Alberta is the Texas of Canada. Petrodollars have given birth to gleaming, modern cities on the plains. In 1988, the Winter Olympics temporarily transformed Calgary into an international mecca, and the city hasn't yet stopped collecting tourist interest off the legacy. Calgary is also the stomping grounds for the Stampede, the world's largest rodeo and meeting place for the most skilled cowboys in the West. Alberta's capital, Edmonton, is slightly larger than Calgary, its hockey rival to the south, and serves as the trusty transportation hub for the stunning national and provincial parks that line the Alberta-British Columbia border.

For adventurous outdoor enthusiasts, Alberta is a year-round playground. Hikers, mountaineers, and ice climbers will find a recreational paradise in the Canadian Rockies in Banff and Jasper National Parks and Kananaskis Country. The parks represent Alberta's most consistent draw, and with good reason: they pack enough scenic punch, exhilarating thrills, and luxurious hostels to knock travelers of all ages flat. The province boasts thousands of prime fishing holes, internationally renowned fossil fields, and centers of indigenous Canadian culture.

☒ ALBERTA'S HIGHLIGHTS

MEANDER through breathtaking **scenery** between Banff and Jasper on the Icefields Parkway; this area is best seen from a bike (see p. 385).

SWAGGER into town for the **Calgary Stampede** (see p. 372).

DIG for dinosaur bones in the **Badlands** (see p. 373).

LEARN time-tested methods for killing tens of thousands of buffalo using only ingenuity and gravity at **Head-Smashed-In Buffalo Jump** (see p. 373).

HIT the slopes at **Lake Louise** (p. 385).

EDMONTON ☎ 780

The provincial capital of Alberta may not have claim to the amazing scenery of Banff and Jasper, or the spectacle that is the Calgary Stampede, but Edmonton has a variety of other things to offer a wide spectrum of tastes. This popular travel destination hosts the Canadian Finals Rodeo in November, and is home to the world's largest shopping mall. A plethora of museums attracts children and art lovers alike, while the Saskatchewan River valley draws hikers and bikers. A perpetual stream of music, art, and performance festivals brings summer crowds to the self-proclaimed "City of Festivals." A happening strip on Whyte Avenue transforms Edmonton into a pleasant urban oasis near the almost overpowering splendor of the neighboring Rockies.

ALBERTA

Alberta

BRITISH COLUMBIA

SASKATCHEWAN

Lake Athabasca

Wood Buffalo Nat'l Park

Athabasca R.

Peace R.

Fort MacKay
63

TO YUKON TERRITORY, ALASKA

97 Dawson Creek
97

35

88

Peace R.

Peace River
2
2

49 Spirit River
43
49

Grande Prairie
43

Valleyview
43

49 High Prairie
2A
Triangle

Utikuma Lake

Lesser Slave Lake

Slave Lake
63

33

Swan Hills

44 Atmore
55

Athabasca
2

Primrose Lake

Cold Lake
55

Cold Lake
41

Fox Creek
32

Willmore Wilderness Prov. Park

Hinton
16

Whitecourt
43
33

Westlock
36

Elk Island Nat'l Park

Pocahontas

Mt. Robson (3954m)
Jasper
Milette Hot Springs

Drayton Valley
22

Edmonton
39
2

Vegreville
16

TO PRINCE GEORGE

Jasper Nat'l Park

Icefields Pkwy

20
13

Wetaskiwin

Mt. Robson Prov. Park

22

Rocky Mtn. House
12
11

21

56 Stettler
36
13

Provost

5
Mt. Revelstoke Nat'l Park

93
11
Saskatchewan River Crossing

Banff Nat'l Park

Red Deer

12
Castor

Hanna
9

Glacier Nat'l Park

Yoho Nat'l Park
93
Lake Louise

2

21
56

TO VANCOUVER (350km)

Revelstoke

Golden
Castle Junction
1A
Bow Valley Prov. Park

9
Drumheller

Kamloops

95
Banff
Canmore

Ghost Lake

Calgary
24

Bragg Creek Prov. Park
23

Brooks
36

Kootenay Nat'l Park

Radium Hot Springs

Rocky Mtn. Forest Reserve

23

Medicine Hat

BRITISH COLUMBIA

95
93

N
LG

0   50 kilometers
0   50 miles

Chain Lakes Prov. Park

Kimberley
95A

Fernie

Head-Smashed-In-Buffalo-Jump
Crowsnest Pass

Lethbridge
3
Taber
36

Bow Island

41

CANADA
USA

Cranbrook
3

Waterton Lakes Nat'l Park

6
Fort Macleod
5
4

Cardston

WASHINGTON

MONTANA

Glacier Nat'l Park

IDAHO

ALBERTA

TRANSPORTATION

The city lies 294km north of Calgary, an easy but tedious 3hr. drive on the **Calgary Trail (Hwy. 2).** Jasper is 362km to the west, a 4hr. drive on Hwy. 16. Edmonton's streets run north-south, and avenues run east-west. Street numbers increase to the west, and avenues increase to the north. The first three digits of an address indicate the nearest cross street: 10141 88 Ave. is on 88 Ave. near 101 St. The **city center** is quite off-center at 105 St. and 101 Ave.

Flights: The **airport** (☎890-8382) sits 29km south of town, a $35 cab fare away. The **Sky Shuttle Airport Service** (☎465-8545 or 888-438-2342) runs a shuttle downtown, to the university, or to the West Edmonton Mall for $11 ($18 round-trip). Cheapskates have been known to hop on free airport shuttle buses to downtown hotels.

Trains: VIA Rail, 12360 121 St. (☎422-6032, reservations 800-561-8630) is a 10min. drive NW of downtown in the CN tower. 3 per week to **Jasper** (6hr.; $138, students $90) and **Vancouver, BC** (23hr.; $258, students $168). No train service to Calgary.

Buses: Greyhound, 10324 103 St. (☎420-2412). Open daily 5:30am-midnight. To **Calgary** (nearly every hr., $43); **Jasper** (5hr., 4 per day, $54); **Vancouver, BC** (14-16hr., 2 per day, $140); and **Yellowknife, NWT** (22½hr.; 2 per day M-F, winter 3 per week; $194). Locker storage $2 per day. **Red Arrow,** 10010 104 St. (☎468-6771), at the Holiday Inn. Open M-F 7:30am-8pm, Sa 8am-8pm. 10% discount with hosteling card. To **Calgary** (6 per day, $46) and **Fort McMurray** (2 per day, $54).

Public Transportation: Edmonton Transit (schedules ☎496-1611, info 496-1600; www.gov.edmonton.ab.ca). Buses and **Light Rail Transit (LRT)** run frequently. LRT is **free downtown** between Grandin Station at 110 St. and 98 Ave. and Churchill Station at 99 St. and 102 Ave. Runs M-F 9am-3pm and Sa 9am-6pm. $1.65, over 65 or under 15 $1.05. No bikes on LRT during peak hours traveling in peak direction (M-F 7:30-8:30am and 4-5pm); no bikes on buses. Info booth open M-F 8:30am-4:30pm.

Taxis: Yellow Cab (☎462-3456). **Alberta Co-op Taxi** (☎425-8310). Both 24hr.

Edmonton Overview

ACCOMMODATIONS
Edmonton Int'l Hostel, 5

FOOD
Chianti, 1
Dadeo's, 2
Pita Pit, 6

NIGHTLIFE
The Billiard Club, 1
Blues on Whyte, 5
Club Malibu, 3
Cook County Saloon, 8
Iron Horse, 7
Squire's, 1

ALBERTA

Car Rental: Budget, 10016 106 St. (☎448-2000 or 800-661-7027); call for other locations. From $46 per day, with unlimited km; cheaper city rates with limited km. 21+. Ages 21-24 $12 per day surcharge. Must have major credit card. Open M-F 7:30am-6pm, Sa 8am-5pm, Su 9am-5pm.

⑦ PRACTICAL INFORMATION

Tourist Information: Edmonton Tourism, Shaw Conference Centre, 9797 Jasper Ave. (☎496-8400 or 800-463-4667), on Pedway Level. Info, maps, and directions. Open M-F 8:30am-4:30pm. Also at **Gateway Park** (☎496-8400 or 800-463-4667), on Hwy. 2 south of town. Both open summer daily 8am-8pm; winter M-F 8:30am-4:30pm, Sa-Su 9am-5pm. **Travel Alberta** (☎427-4321 or 800-661-8888) has province-wide info. Open M-F 7am-7pm, Sa-Su 8:30am-5:30pm.

Equipment Rental: The **Edmonton International Youth Hostel** (see below) rents bikes. $7 per half-day, $12 per day. **Campus Outdoor Centre** (☎492-2767), NW corner of the Butterdome at U of A, rents a variety of equipment including cross-country skis ($7 overnight), camping gear, and bikes ($15 per day). Open Apr.-Aug. M-Tu 9am-7pm, W 10am-5pm, Th-F 9am-8pm, Sa-Su noon-4pm; call for hours in winter.

Gay and Lesbian Services: Gay/Lesbian Community Centre, 10612 124 St. #103 (☎482-2855). Community listings, youth services, on-site peer counseling. Open M-F 7-10pm; events hotline plays during non-business hours. **Womenspace** (☎482-1794) is Edmonton's lesbian group. Call for a recording of local events.

Emergency: ☎911.

Police: ☎423-4567.

Crisis Line: ☎482-HELP. **Sexual Assault Centre** ☎423-4121. Both 24hr.

Pharmacy: Shoppers Drug Mart, 11408 Jasper Ave. (☎482-1011), or 8210 109 St. (☎433-2424) by Whyte Ave. Open 24hr.

Hospital: Royal Alexandra Hospital, 10240 Kingsway Ave. (☎477-4111).

Internet Access: Dow Computer Lab, 11211 142 St. (☎451-3344), at the Odyssium (see **Sights,** below); free with admission. Free at the **library,** 7 Sir Winston Churchill Sq. (☎496-7000); 1hr. per day for a week. Open M-F 9am-9pm, Sa 9am-6pm, Su 1-5pm.

Post Office: 9808 103A Ave. (☎944-3265), adjacent to the CN Tower. Open M-F 8am-5:45pm. **Postal Code:** T5J 2G8.

⌂ ACCOMMODATIONS

The hostel is the liveliest place to stay in Edmonton; St. Joseph's College and the University of Alberta provide a bit more privacy. For B&B listings, contact **Alberta B&B Association,** 3230 104A St. (☎438-6048).

▨ **Edmonton International Youth Hostel (HI),** 10647 81 Ave. (☎988-6836). Bus #7 or 9 from the 101 St. station to 82 Ave. You'd never know that this hostel is in a renovated convent, but for the abundance of private 2-person bedrooms with the dimensions of a nun's cell. Facilities include a kitchen, game room, lounge, new bathrooms, laundry, and a small backyard. Just around the corner from the clubs, shops, and cafes of Whyte Ave. $18, nonmembers $23; semi-private rooms $20, $25. Family rooms available. ❶

St. Joseph's College, 89 Ave. at 114 St. (☎492-7681). The rooms here are smaller than those at the university. Library, huge lounges, rec room, and laundry, and close to U sports facilities. Reception open M-F 8:30am-4pm. Call ahead; the 60 dorms often fill up quickly. Rooms available early May to late Aug. Singles $30, with full board $50. ❷

ALBERTA

Downtown Edmonton

ACCOMMODATIONS
St. Joseph's College, **2**
University of Alberta, **3**

FOOD
The Silk Hat, **1**

University of Alberta, 87 Ave. between 116 and 117 St. (☎492-4281). Generic dorm rooms. Dry cleaning, kitchen, free Internet access, convenience store, and buffet-style cafeteria downstairs. Check-in after 3pm. Reservations strongly recommended. Rooms available late Apr.-Aug. Singles $30. Weekly and monthly rates available. ❷

FOOD

Edmonton locals tend to swarm into the coffee shops and cafes of the Old Strathcona area along Whyte (82) Ave., between 102 and 106 St.

Dadeo's, 10548 Whyte Ave. (☎433-0930). Cajun and Louisiana-style food away from the bayou at this funky 50s diner. Gumbo $4.50. M-Tu Po' Boys $7. Su $4 for a pint or a plate of wings. Spicy dishes make you sweat just right. Open M-W 11:30am-11pm, Th-Sa 11:30am-midnight, Su 3-10pm. ❷

The Silk Hat, 10251 Jasper Ave. (☎425-1920). The oldest restaurant in Edmonton maintains enough character and sass to out-survive the competition. This diner in the heart of downtown serves a huge array of food, from seafood to veggie-burgers ($6.25) to breakfast all day. Happy Hour M-F 4-6pm. Open M-F 8am-5:45pm, Sa 10am-8pm. ❶

Chianti, 10501 Whyte Ave. (☎439-9829). Daily specials, desserts, and coffees accompany an expanse of pasta, veal, and seafood. Pastas $6.60-10; veal $10-13. M-Tu all pasta dishes $6. Open Su-Th 11am-11pm, F-Sa 11am-midnight. ❷

The Pita Pit, 8109 104 St. (☎435-3200), near Whyte Ave. Surprisingly delicious pitas, fast-food style. Souvlaki $5.25. Students don't pay sales tax. Open Th-Sa 11am-4am, Su noon-3am, M-W 11am-3am. ❶

Kids in the Hall Bistro, 1 Sir Winston Churchill Sq. (☎413-8060), in City Hall. This lunchroom is truly one-of-a-kind. Every employee, from waiter to chef, is a young person hired as part of a cooperative community service project. Various entrees ($5-10) and sandwiches ($5-7). Takeout available. Open M-F 8am-4pm. ❷

ALBERTA

☺ SIGHTS

WEST EDMONTON MALL. Yet another blow against Mother Nature in the battle for tourists, the $1.3 billion **West Edmonton Mall** engulfs the general area between 170 St. and 87 Ave. No ordinary collection of stores, the **world's biggest mall** contains water slides and the world's largest indoor wave pool, an amusement park with a 14-story roller coaster, miniature golf, dozens of exotic caged animals, over 800 stores, an ice-skating rink, 110 eating establishments, a full-scale replica of Columbus's *Santa Maria*, an indoor bungee jumping facility, a casino, a luxury hotel, a dolphin show, swarms of teenage mall rats, multiple movie theaters, and twice as many submarines as the Canadian Navy. One note of caution: remember where you park. *(Bus# 1, 2, 100, or 111. ☎ 444-5300; www.westedmontonmall.com. Open M-F 10am-9pm, Sa 10am-6pm, Su noon-6pm. Amusement park stays open later.)*

FORT EDMONTON PARK. At the park's far end sits the fort proper: a 19th-century office building for Alberta's first capitalists, the fur traders of the Hudson Bay Company. Between the fort and the park entrance are three streets—1885, 1905, and 1920 St.—bedecked with period buildings from apothecaries to blacksmith shops, all decorated to match the streets' respective eras. *(Park: On Whitemud Dr. at Fox Dr. Buses #2, 4, 30, 31, 35, 106, and 315 stop near the park. ☎ 496-8787; www.gov.edmonton.ab.ca/fort. Open mid-May to late June M-F 10am-4pm, Sa-Su 10am-6pm; late June to early Sept. daily 10am-6pm; rest of Sept. wagon tours only from M-Sa 11am-3pm, Su 10am-6pm. $8, seniors and ages 13-17 $6, ages 2-12 $4.25, family $24.50.)*

ODYSSIUM. The reincarnated Space and Science Centre still appeals to the curiosities of all ages with exhibits on the human body and the environment, including a **Gallery of the Gross** and a hands-on **Crime Lab.** Housed in a building shaped like an alien spacecraft, the largest **planetarium dome** in Canada uses a booming 23,000 watts of audio during its laser light shows. The **IMAX theater** makes the planetarium seem like a child's toy. *(11211 142 St. ☎ 451-3344; www.odyssium.com. Open summer daily 10am-9pm, winter Su-Th 10am-5pm, F-Sa 10am-9pm. Day pass includes planetarium shows and exhibits: $10, students and seniors $8, ages 3-12 $7, family $39. General admission and IMAX show $16, students and seniors $13, ages 3-12 $11, family $60.)*

RIVER VALLEY. The best part of Edmonton would have to be the longest stretch of urban parkland in Canada. Edmonton's **River Valley** boasts over 50km of easy to moderate paved multi-use trails and 69km of granular and chip trails for hiking and cycling. Any route down the river leads to the linked trail system; pick up a map at the Ranger Station. *(12130 River Valley Rd. ☎ 496-2950. Open daily 7am-1am.)*

◑ ♫ FESTIVALS AND ENTERTAINMENT

Edmonton proclaims itself "Canada's Festival City" (www.festivalcity.com); celebrations of some kind go on year-round. The **Jazz City International Music Festival** packs 10 days with club dates and free performances by top international and Canadian jazz musicians (☎ 432-7166; June 20-29, 2003). Around the same time is a visual arts celebration called **The Works.** (☎ 426-2122; June 20-July 2, 2003.) In August, the **Folk Music Festival,** considered one of the best in North America, takes over Gallagher Park (☎ 429-1899; Aug. 7-10, 2003). All the world's a stage in Old Strathcona for the **Fringe Theater Festival,** when top alternative music and theater pours from parks, stages, and streets. This is the high point of Edmonton's festival schedule, and 500,000 travelers come to the city just to find the Fringe. (☎ 448-9000; www.fringe.alberta.com; Aug. 14-24, 2003.)

ALBERTA

The Edmonton Oilers, the local NHL franchise, remain in an extended rebuilding period following their glorious Wayne Gretzky-led Stanley Cup runs of the 1980s. But this is Canada, and it is hockey. The Oilers play at 11230 110th St. (☎451-8000; www.edmontonoilers.com. Season runs Oct.-April.)

IN RECENT NEWS

 NIGHTLIFE

Edmonton, like many big cities, has a variety of clubs; like other Alberta cities, many of them are cowboy-themed. The happening clubs are lined up along Whyte (82) Ave. in Old Strathcona. For club listings, see *Magazine*, published every Thursday and available in free stacks at cafes.

Squire's, 10505 82 Ave. (☎439-8594), lower level by Chianti. Popular with the college crowd. Specials include M $2.50 bottles of Canadian, Tu $2 highballs, and Th half-price from 7-11pm. Enjoy $0.09 wings on W. Open M-Sa 4pm-3am.

Club Malibu, 10310 85 Ave. (☎432-7300). This well-known dance club shows Edmonton's younger crowd how to party. Th $0.50 Coronas until 10pm, $2 everything all night; F $1-3 drinks. Sa offers $0.25 bottles of Canadian beer until 10pm. M is ladies' night, with male entertainers. Open M and Th-Sa 8pm-3am.

The Billiard Club, 10505 82 Ave. (☎432-0335), 2nd fl., above Chianti. A busy bar packed with a diverse crowd of young up-and-comers and some older already-theres. Pool tables and outdoor patio. Open daily 11:30am-2:30am.

Blues on Whyte, 10329 82 Ave. (☎439-5058). If blues is what you want, blues is what you'll get. Live blues and R&B from top-notch performers every night; Sa afternoon jam 3pm-8:30pm. This joint may deserve its reputation as a biker bar; these blues are anything but sedate. 8 oz. glasses of beer for just $1. Open daily 10am-3am.

Cook County Saloon, 8010 103 St. (☎432-2665). Bring your hat and your best boots to Edmonton's rootinest, tootinest country bar. W night dance lessons. Happy Hour F-Sa 8-9pm. M oil wrestling. Hosts hot live concerts on many nights. Open W-Su 8pm-2am.

Iron Horse, 8101 103 St. (☎438-1907). A full restaurant turned Top 40 dance club at night. Live music Su, "Extreme Karaoke" Th, and "Love Train" (singles night) W. Popular with a younger crowd. Happy Hour M-F 4-8pm. Open daily 11:30am-2am.

THE BUSK STOPS HERE

Being a good citizen in Calgary doesn't mean giving the corner guitarist a dollar—it means turning him in to the police. Busking (giving street performances) is illegal, and has been since the government tightened its policy on performers in 2002. The move was innocently designed to ease major congestion problems on the city's byways, but it has infuriated supporters of Calgary's open music scene. Designated "Busk Stops," or spots performers can sign up for in advance, have eased the tension somewhat; still, police maintain a zero-tolerance policy toward buskers who are caught anywhere that is not the south side of Olympic Plaza or the Eau Claire Market Amphitheater. People on both sides of the issue claim that the system is imperfect and will require additional modifications. The city makes references to opening more Busk Stops, but where and when they'll do it is not entirely clear. So, the future of public music in Calgary hangs in the balance. For now, most of the streets of downtown Calgary lack music and life beyond the drone of passing cars.

CALGARY

☎ 403

Mounties founded Calgary in the 1870s to control Canada's flow of illegal whisky, but oil made the city what it is today. Petroleum fuels Calgary's economy and explains why the city hosts the most corporate headquarters in Canada outside of Toronto. As the host of the 1988 Winter Olympics, Calgary's dot on the map grew larger; already Alberta's largest city, this thriving young metropolis is the second fastest-growing in all of Canada. No matter how big its britches, however, the city still pays annual tribute to its original tourist attraction, the "Greatest Outdoor Show on Earth," the Calgary Stampede. For 10 days in July, the city dons cowboy duds for world-class bareback riding, country music, and Western art.

▐ TRANSPORTATION

Calgary is 126km east of Banff along the Trans-Canada Hwy. (Hwy. 1). It is divided into quadrants (NE, NW, SE, SW): **Centre St.** is the east-west divider; the **Bow River** splits the north and south. Avenues run east-west, streets north-south. Cross streets can be derived by disregarding the last two digits of the street address: 206 7th Ave. SW would be on 7th Ave. at 2nd St.

Flights: The **airport** (☎735-1372) is 17km northeast of the city center. Take Bus #57.

Buses: Greyhound, 877 Greyhound Way SW (☎265-9111 or 800-661-8747). To: **Banff** (1¾hr., 4 per day, $22); **Drumheller** (1¾hr., 2 per day, $24); **Edmonton** (3½hr., 8 per day, $43), with lower student rates. Free shuttle from Calgary Transit C-Train at 7th Ave. and 10th St. to bus depot (every hr. near the ½hr. 6:30am-7:30pm). **Red Arrow,** 205 9th Ave. SE (☎531-0350), goes to **Edmonton** (7 per day, $46) and points north. 10% HI discount; student and senior rates. **Brewster Tours** (☎221-8242), from the airport or the downtown Marriot at 808 Centre St. S, to **Banff** (2hr., 4 per day, $40) and **Jasper** (8hr., 1 per day, $75). 10% HI discount.

Public Transportation: Calgary Transit, 240 7th Ave. SW (☎262-1000). Open M-F 8:30am-5pm. C-Trains free in downtown zone on 7th Ave. S from 3rd St. E to 10th St W. Buses and C-Trains outside downtown $1.75, ages 6-14 $1.10, under 6 free. Day pass $5, ages 6-14 $3. Book of 10 tickets $14.50, ages 6-14 $9. Runs M-F 6am-midnight, Sa-Su 6am-9:30pm. Tickets at stops, the transit office, or Safeway stores.

Taxis: Checker Cab (☎299-9999). **Yellow Cab** (☎974-1111).

Car Rental: Rent-A-Wreck, 113 42nd Ave. SW (☎287-1444). $35 per day. $0.12 per km over 250km. 21+ need credit card. Open M-F 8am-6pm, Sa-Su 9am-5pm.

▐ PRACTICAL INFORMATION

Tourist Information: 220 8th Ave. SW (☎750-2397; www.tourismcalgary.com). Open in summer daily 9am-5pm; winter 9:30am-5:30pm.

American Express: Canada Trust Tower, 421 7th Ave. SW (☎261-5085) on main floor.

Equipment Rental: Outdoor Program Centre, 2500 University Dr. (☎220-5038), at U of Calgary, rents tents (from $10), canoes ($18), and downhill skis ($19). Open daily 8am-8pm. **Mountain Equipment Co-op** (☎269-2420) rents watercraft ($25-30 per day, including all safety equipment and paddles), camping gear ($4-21), rock- and ice-climbing gear ($4-18), and snow sports equipment ($8-35). Both companies have weekend specials. Be prepared to shell out a large deposit.

Laundromat: Inglewood Laundromat, 1018 9th Ave. SE (☎269-1515). Wash $2, dry $0.35 for 7min. Open daily 8am-5:30pm.

Gay and Lesbian Services: Events and clubs ☎234-9752. Counseling ☎234-8973.

ALBERTA

Calgary Overview

Weather: ☎ 299-7878.

Emergency: ☎ 911.

Police: 133 6th Ave. SE (☎ 266-1234).

Pharmacy: Shopper's Drug Mart, 6455 S Macleod Trail (☎ 253-2424). Open 24hr.

Hospital: Peter Lougheed Centre, 3500 26th Ave. NE (☎ 291-8555).

Internet Access: At the **Library,** 616 Macleod Trail SE (☎ 260-2600). $2 per hr. Open M-Th 10am-9pm, F-Sa 10am-5pm; mid-Sept. to mid-May also Su 1:30-5pm.

Post Office: 207 9th Ave. SW (☎ 974-2078). Open M-F 8am-6pm. **Postal Code:** T2P 2G8.

🏠 ACCOMMODATIONS

Lodging prices skyrocket when tourists pack into the city's hotels for the July Stampede; call far in advance. Calgary's downtown lacks cheap places to sleep; finding a hotel bed for under $100 is virtually impossible. As a result, hostels and alternative accommodations are undoubtedly the way to go. For a more homey feel, contact the **B&B Association of Calgary** for info and availability. (☎ 543-3900. Singles from $30; doubles from $50.)

ALBERTA

Downtown Calgary

♣ FOOD
Pongo's, **9**
Take 10 Cafe, **2**
Thi-Thi Submarine, **3**
Wicked Wedge, **8**

♠ NIGHTLIFE
Nightgallery Caberet, **7**
Vicious Circle, **6**

♠ ACCOMMODATIONS
Calgary Int. Hostel, **5**
University of Calgary, **1**
YWCA, **4**

City
Quadrant Deliniation
LRT

TO ZOO (1km)

Olympic Way SE
3rd St. SE
Stampede Park
5 St. SE
4 St. SE
Macleod Trail
1 St. SE
SE

Library
Olympic Plaza
Glenbow Museum
Red Arrow
Calgary Tower
Devonian Gardens
Eau Claire Market
Riverfront Ave.
Centre St.
1 St.
2 St.
3 St. SW (Barclay Mall)
4 St.
5 St.
6 St.
7 St.
8 St. SW
9 St. SW

5 Ave. SW
Eau Claire Ave.
1 Ave. SW
2 Ave. SW
4 St.
6 Ave. SW
7 Ave. SW
8 Ave. SW
9 Ave. SW
10 Ave. SW
11 Ave. SW
12 Ave. SW
17th Ave. SW
1 St. SW
2 St. SW
4 St. SW
5 St. SW
6th St. SW
7 St. SW
16 Ave. SW
8 St. SW
13 Ave. SW
14 Ave. SW
15 Ave. SW
10 St. SW
11 St. SW
12 St. SW
11th Ave. SW
10th Ave. SW

Downtown Safeway

SW

Prince's Island Park
Bow River

NE
Edmonton Trail
7 Ave. NE
5 Ave. NE
4 Ave. NE
3 Ave. NE
2 Ave. NE
1 Ave. NE
6 Ave. NE
7 Ave. NE
7 St. NE
6A St. NE
6 St. NE
4 St. NE
3 St. NE
2 St. NE
1 St. NE
2 Ave. NE
1 Ave. NE
5 Ave. NE
4 Ave. NE
McDougall Rd. NE
Marsh Rd. NE
Meredith Rd. NE
Memorial Dr. NE

NW
Memorial Dr. NW
1 St. NW
3 St. NW
4A St. NW
5 St. NW
5A St. NW
1 Ave. SW
2 Ave. SW
1 Ave. NW
2 Ave. NW
3 Ave. NW
5 Ave. NW
8 St. NW
9 St. NW
9A St. NW
10th St. NW
10A St. NW
11 St. NW
11A St. NW
12 St. NW
13 St. NW
14 St. NW
15 St. NW
16 St. NW
16A St. NW
18 St. NW
18A St. NW
19 St. NW
Kensington Rd. NW
Westmount Rd.
Bowness Rd.
Broadview Rd. N
Westmount Blvd.
Gladstone Rd. NW
Riley Park
7 Ave. NW
6 Ave. NW
2 Ave. NW
1 Ave. NW
7 Ave. NW

Greyhound

1A

TO (5km)

0   400 meters
0   400 yards

Bow River

Calgary International Hostel (HI), 520 7th Ave. SE (☎269-8239), near downtown. Walk east along 7th Ave. from the 3rd St. SE C-Train station; the hostel is on the left just past 4th St. SE. Busy and sometimes impersonal, this urban hostel has some nice accessories; the clean kitchen, lounge areas, laundry, and backyard with BBQ are pluses. Helpful information desk, occasional guest activities. Wheelchair-accessible. 120 beds. $16, nonmembers $20; Oct. 16-May 1: $15, $19. Private rooms $4 extra. ❶

University of Calgary, the ex-Olympic Village in the NW quadrant, far from downtown if you're walking. Accessible by bus #9 or a 12min. walk from the University C-Train stop. Popular with conventioneers and often booked solid. Coordinated through **Cascade Hall,** 3456 24th Ave. NW (☎220-3203). Rooms available May-Aug. only. Shared rooms $21, students (with ID, May and June only) $17; singles $34-100, students $28; generous suites with private bath about $45 per person. ❶

YWCA, 320 5th Ave. SE (☎263-1550). Walk 2 blocks north of the 3rd St. SE C-Train station. 2 newly renovated residential floors. Women only. 150 beds available. Singles from $40; doubles from $50; triples $130; quads $140; seniors 10% discount. ❸

▶ FOOD

It seems fitting that most of the affordable restaurants with good food in Calgary are not found downtown. The most gloriously satisfying and cheap eats are located in ▨**Chinatown,** concentrated in a four block area at the north end of Centre St. S and 1st St. SE. Six dollars gets you a feast in any Vietnamese noodle-house or Hong Kong-style cafe, many of which don't even close until the wee hours. Some budget chow-houses also hide out among the trendy, costlier spots in the popular **Kensington District,** along Kensington Rd. and 10th and 11th St. NW; still others can be found on **17th Ave.** between 2nd St. SW and 14th St. SW. **Downtown Safeway** (☎800-723-3929), 813 11th Ave. SW, sells groceries. (Open daily 8am-11pm.) Restaurants, produce, international snack bars, and flowers grace the plaza-style, upscale **Eau Claire Market** mall, at the north end of 3rd St. SW.

▨ **Thi-Thi Submarine,** 209 1st St. SE (☎265-5452). Some people have closets larger than Thi-Thi, but this place manages to pack in 2 plastic seats, a bank of toaster ovens, and the finest Vietnamese submarines in Calgary. Most meaty subs are sub-$5; the veggie sub is an unreal $2.25. Open daily 10am-7pm. ❶

▨ **Peter's Drive In,** 219 16th Ave. NE (☎277-2747). Peachy keen! A generational anomaly and worthy destination, Peter's is one of the city's last remaining drive-ins. Hordes of chummy patrons attest to the swell quality. Drive-in or walk to the service window. Famous milkshakes under $3 and burgers under $4. Open daily 10am-midnight. ❶

Pongo's, 524 17th Ave. SW (☎209-1073). Pongo's sterile, futuristic decor seems at odds with the large portions of quality Asian food they serve. Huge helpings of pad thai are $8. Takeout available. Open Su-Th 11:30am-midnight, F-Sa 11:30am-4am. ❷

Take 10 Cafe, 304 10th St. NW (☎270-7010). Take 10 became a local favorite by offering dirt-cheap, high-quality food. All burgers are under $5.75, and the menu also sports some sizzling Chinese food (under $8). Open Tu-Sa 9am-6pm, Su 9am-3pm. ❷

Wicked Wedge, 618 17th Ave. SW (☎228-1024). Serves large, topping-heavy slices of pizza ($3.75) to Calgary's post-party scene. 3 varieties of pie dished out nightly. Open M-Tu 11am-1am, W-Sa 11am-3am, Su noon-midnight. ❷

▶ SIGHTS

OLYMPIC LEFTOVERS. For two glorious weeks in 1988, the world's eyes were on Calgary for the Winter Olympics. Almost fifteen years later, the world has moved on, but the city still has some very exciting facilities, and relentlessly clings to its two weeks of Olympic stardom. Visit the **Canada Olympic Park** and its looming ski jumps and twisted bobsled and luge tracks. The **Olympic Hall of Fame,** also at Olympic Park, honors Olympic achievements with displays, films, and a ▩bobsled simulator. In summer, the park opens its hills and a lift to **mountain bikers.** *(A 10min. drive northwest of downtown on Hwy. 1. ☎ 247-5452. Open daily 9am-8pm. $10 ticket includes chairlift and entrance to ski-jump buildings, Hall of Fame, and icehouse. Self-guided tour $15, $45 per family. Mountain biking open May-Oct. daily 9am-9pm. Hill pass $7 for cyclists. Front-suspension bike rental $12 per hr., $31 per day.)* Keep an eye out for ski-jumpers, who practice at the facility year-round. The miniature mountain (113m vertical) also opens up for recreational **downhill skiing** in winter. *(Snow report ☎ 289-3700. $21.)* The **Olympic Oval,** an enormous indoor speed-skating track on the University of Calgary campus, remains a major international training facility. Speedskaters work out in the early morning and late afternoon; sit in the bleachers and observe the action for free. *(☎ 220-7890; www.oval.ucalgary.ca. Public skating hours vary, so call ahead. $4.50, children and seniors $2.50, family $10, under 5 free. Skate rental under $5.)*

PARKS AND MUSEUMS. Footbridges stretch from either side of the Bow River to **Prince's Island Park,** a natural refuge only blocks from the city center. In July and August, Mount Royal College performs **Shakespeare in the Park.** *(☎ 240-6374 or 240-6908. Various matinees and evening shows; call for shows and times.)* Calgary's other island park, **St. George's Island,** is accessible by the river walkway to the east or by driving. It houses the **Calgary Zoo,** including a botanical garden and children's zoo. For those who missed the wildlife in Banff and Jasper, the **Canadian Wilds** exhibit has recreated animal habitats. For those who missed the Cretaceous Period, life-sized plastic dinosaurs are also on exhibit. *(Parking is off Memorial Dr. on the north side of the river. ☎ 232-9300. Open daily 9am-5pm. $12, seniors and under 17 $10.)*

STAMPEDE. The more cosmopolitan Calgary becomes, the more tenaciously it clings to its frontier roots. The Stampede draws one million cowboys and tourists each summer, in the first couple weeks of July, when the grounds are packed for world-class steer wrestling, bareback and bull-riding, pig and chuck wagon races. Check out the livestock shows, cruise the midway and casino, ride the roller coaster, or hear live country music and marching bands. The festival spills into the streets from first thing in the morning (free pancake breakfasts all around) through the night. Depending on your attitude, the Stampede will either be an impressive spectacle rekindling the Western spirit or an overpriced, slick carnival where humans assert their hegemony over lesser animals. *(Stampede Park is just southeast of downtown, bordering the east side of Macleod Trail between 14th Ave. SE and the Elbow River. The C-Train features a Stampede stop. Tickets and info ☎ 269-9822 or 800-661-1767; www.calgarystampede.com. $10, ages 65+ and 7-12 $5, under 7 free. Rodeo and evening shows $21-62, rush tickets $10, on sale at the grandstand 1½hr. before showtime.)*

◤ NIGHTLIFE

Nightclubs in Alberta only became legal in 1990, and Calgary is making up for lost time. The city is crawling with bars and nightclubs that cater to waves of visitors and young locals. Live music in Calgary ranges from national acts and world-famous DJs to some guy with a guitar. The best areas in town for finding pubs, clubs, and live music are the **Stephen Ave. Walk** (8th Ave. SW), **17th Ave. SW,** and **1st and 4th St. SW.** Wherever you head, finding cheap liquor is not a problem; many bars in town offer unbelievable drink deals. Last call in Alberta is at 2am, and is strictly observed. For listings of bands and theme nights, check *The Calgary Straight* or *Calgary's Ffwd.* Both come out on Thursday and are free. *Outlooks,* the city's gay and lesbian events publication, offers information on different bars. All are available at local clubs and cafes.

HEAD-SMASHED-IN BUFFALO JUMP Some 5700

years ago, plains-dwelling Blackfoot began using gravity to kill bison. Disguised as calves, a few men would lure a herd of the short-sighted animals into lanes between stone cairns. Hunters at the rear, dressed as wolves, then pressed forward, whipping the bison into a frenzy. When the front-running bison reached the cliff and tried to stop, the momentum of the stampede pushed their one-ton bodies over the edge. Each year, the communities obtained food, tools, and clothing from the bodies of the bison. The particular cliffs of Head-Smashed-In Buffalo Jump were an active hunting site for nearly 8,000 years, but only earned their modern name at one of the site's final jumps 150 years ago when a thrill-seeking warrior watching the massacre from under the cliff ledge was crushed. As European settlement spread over the plains, the bison that once numbered 60 million continent-wide were nearly extinct in 1881. A century later, the United Nations named Head-Smashed-In a UNESCO World Heritage Site; ten-meter-deep beds of bone and tools make this one of the best-preserved buffalo jumps in North America. The magnificent **interpretive center** explores the hunting, history, and rituals of the Plains people. (☎553-2731. Open daily May 15 to Labour Day 9am-6pm; off-season 10am-5pm. $6.50, seniors $5.50, ages 7-17 $3, family $15, under 7 free.) Head-Smashed-In Buffalo Jump lies 175km south of Calgary and 18km north-west of Fort Macleod, on Secondary Rd. 785 off Hwy. 2.

Nightgallery Cabaret, 1209B 1st St. SW (☎269-5924, www.nightgallerycabaret.com). A large dance floor, a bar, and a diverse program attract clubbers. Has the best House in town on Th and at "Sunday Skool." Reggae-Dub on M draws a slightly older crowd. Live music F and Sa. $1.50 highballs before 11pm. Cover $5. Open daily 8pm-3am.

Vicious Circle, 1011 1st St. SW (☎269-3951). A very relaxing bar, "The Vish" offers a solid menu, colored mood lights, and a disco ball, plus pool tables, couches, eclectic local art, and TV. All kinds of coffee, a full bar, and 140 different martinis. Summer patio seating. Happy Hour all night Su, movie nights M, live music Tu. Open daily 11am-2am.

Eau Claire Market IMAX (☎974-4629). Pit your imagination against a large-screen feature that claims to be bigger. Box office open M-F 11:30am-10pm, Sa and Su 10:30am-10pm. IMAX films $9, ages 65 and up $7.50, under 13 $6.50, night double feature $13. Also at Eau Claire, Cineplex Odeon shows regular films; call for times (☎263-3166).

⚡ DAYTRIP FROM CALGARY: ALBERTA BADLANDS

Once the fertile shallows of a huge ocean, the Badlands are now one of the richest dinosaur fossil sites in the world. After the sea dried up, wind, water, and ice molded twisting canyons into sandstone and shale bedrock, creating the desolate splendor of the Alberta Badlands. The **Royal Tyrrell Museum of Paleontology** (TEER-ull), with its remarkable array of dinosaur exhibits and hands-on paleontological opportunities, is the region's main attraction. **Greyhound** runs from Calgary to **Drumheller** (1¾hr., 2 per day, $24), which is 6km southeast of the museum.

ROYAL TYRRELL MUSEUM OF PALEONTOLOGY. The world's largest display of dinosaur specimens is a forceful reminder that *Homo sapiens* missed out on the first 2½ billion years of life on earth. From the Big Bang to the present, the museum celebrates evolution's grand parade with quality displays, videos, computer activities, and towering skeletons, including one of only 12 reconstructed *Tyrannosaurus rex* skeletons in existence. You cannot miss the Predator Room, which features cunning dinosaurs and creepy background lighting. It does not, at any point in earth's evolution, ever get cooler than this. (*6km northwest of Drumheller,*

ALBERTA

THE HIDDEN DEAL

KANANASKIS COUNTRY: DIAMOND IN THE CROWD

Between Calgary and Banff lie 4200 sq. km of provincial parks and multi-use recreational areas collectively known as **Kananaskis Country** (KAN-uh-NASS-kiss). The landscape rolls down from the Canadian Rockies through undulating foothills less than an hour from Banff. Kananaskis has a majesty comparable to the national parks, but thankfully with few of their crowds and none of their entrance fees. This is truly a gem of the Rockies—don't mention it to anyone.

Though harmed by recent budget cuts, the best source of local info is still **Barrier Lake Visitor Centre**, 6km south of Hwy. 1 on Hwy. 40. (☎673-3985. Call for hours.) **Ribbon Creek Hostel (HI)** ❶ is 24km south of the Trans-Canada Hwy. (Hwy. 1) on Hwy. 40. The common room has a fireplace and comfy couches. Firepit, BBQ, volleyball court, and huge kitchen. (Reservations ☎866-762-4122. $15, nonmembers $19. Private rooms $42, nonmembers $50. Free showers.) The hostel has winter-time lift ticket and lodging deals with nearby Nakiska. Over 38 **campgrounds** ❶ are accessible via K-Country roads more than a dozen group campgrounds also exist).

The area is divided into nine provincial parks. The three most popular are the meadows and forests of **Bow Valley Provincial Park** (☎673-3663), the grasslands of **Elbow River Valley** (☎949-3754) on Hwy. 66 near Bragg Creek, and the towering peaks of **Peter Lougheed Provincial Park** (☎591-6322), 1hr. south on Hwy.

which itself lies 138km northeast of Calgary. Get there by driving east on Hwy. 1 from Calgary, then northeast on Hwy. 9. ☎403-823-7707 or 888-440-4240; www.tyrrellmuseum.com. Open daily Victoria Day to Labour Day 9am-9pm; Labour Day to Thanksgiving 10am-5pm; Thanksgiving to Victoria Day Tu-Su 10am-5pm. $10, seniors $8, ages 7-17 $6, under 7 free, families $30.)

DIGS. The museum's hugely popular 12-person **Day Digs** include instruction in paleontology and excavation techniques, and a chance to dig in a fossil quarry. The fee includes lunch and transportation; participants must also agree that all finds go to the museum. (Daily, July-Aug. Weekends only in June. Digs depart at 8:30am, returning at 4pm. $90, ages 10-15 $60. Reservations required; call the museum.)

DINOSAUR PROVINCIAL PARK AND BADLANDS BUS TOUR. The Badlands, a UNESCO World Heritage Site, are the source of many finds on display at the Tyrrell Museum; more fossil species—over 300, including 35 species of dinosaurs—were discovered here than anywhere else in the world. The museum's **Field Station**, 48km east of the town of **Brooks** in **Dinosaur Provincial Park,** contains a small museum, but the main attraction is the **Badlands Bus Tour.** The bus chauffeurs visitors into a restricted hotspot of dinosaur finds. Many fossils still lie within the eroding rock. The park's **campground** ❶ is shaded from summer heat, and grassy plots cushion most sites. Although it stays open year-round, the campground only has power and running water in summer. (To reach the **Field Station** from Drumheller, follow Hwy. 56 south for 65km, then take Hwy. 1 about 70km to Brooks. Once in Brooks, go north along Hwy. 873 and east along Hwy. 544. Field Station ☎378-4342. Open daily Victoria Day to Labour Day 8:15am-9pm; Labour Day to Victoria Day M-F 9am-4pm. **Museum** admission $2.50, ages 7-17 or 65+ $1.50, under 7 free. Tours Victoria Day to Thanksgiving. 2-8 per day. $4.50, ages 7-17 $2.25, under 7 free. Reservations ☎378-4344. Sites $13, with power $15.)

DINOSAUR-FREE ACTIVITIES. The Badlands also offer a variety of other recreational activities. The staff of **Midland Provincial Park** (☎823-1749), located halfway between the Tyrrell Museum and Drumheller, leads free 75min. natural history walking tours, departing from the museum one or two times per day. To see **hoodoos** in the making, go 15km east on Hwy. 10 from Drumheller. These limestone columns are relatively young: the stone caps on their tops have not yet eroded away. In **Horseshoe Canyon**, about 20km west of Drumheller on Hwy. 9, **hiking and biking trails** wind below the prairie through red rock layers carved into bizarre, rounded formations.

Several trails located in Dinosaur Provincial Park take hikers over and through the eroded landscape, including the **Coulee Viewpoint Trail** (1km, 45min., moderate) and the **Cottonwoods Flats Trail** (1.4km, 2hr., easy), which weaves around Deer River. Carry plenty of water during hot weather, and be sure not to hop fences onto private property. Stock up on groceries at **IGA Market**, at N Railroad Ave. and Centre St. (☎823-3995. Open daily 24hr.)

THE ROCKIES

The five national parks of the Canadian Rockies comprise one of Canada's top tourist draws, and with excellent reason. Every year, some five million visitors make it within sight of the parks' majestic peaks, stunning glacial lakes, and myriad varieties of wildlife. Thankfully, much of this traffic is confined to highway-side gawkers, leaving infinite backcountry trails and mountains where one can escape the flocks of tourists. Of the big two parks—Banff and Jasper—the latter feels a little farther removed from the droves of tourists. The hostels that line both parks are among the country's best, and are usually booked up as a result. It's also well worth diving into the quieter Yoho (see p. 319), Glacier (see p. 318), and Kootenay National Parks (see p. 321), as well as Kananaskis Country (see p. 375), the locals' free playground that separates Calgary from the Rockies.

▐▄ TRANSPORTATION

BY CAR, BUS, AND TRAIN. Alberta's extensive highway system makes travel between major destinations easy, and provides the traveler with beautiful roadside scenery. The north-south **Icefields Parkway (Hwy. 93)** runs between **Banff** and **Jasper**. The east-west **Yellowhead Hwy. (Hwy. 16)** connects **Edmonton** with **Jasper**, and continues across British Columbia. The **Trans-Canada Hwy. (Hwy. 1)** completes the loop, linking **Calgary** with **Banff**. The easiest way to get here is to drive yourself or explore the bus options. **Buses** (Greyhound, Brewster, and Red Arrow) travel all of these routes; VIA Rail **trains** run from **Edmonton** to **Jasper**.

BY BIKE. Icefields Parkway is a popular trail, although the trip is best suited to experienced cyclists. Inquire at the rental shops (see **Equipment Rental**, below) about their service to return bikes after one-way trips. The 291km separating Jasper and Banff is swelling with hundreds of glaciers, dramatic mountain peaks, and fantastic hostels located on and off the highway.

Descriptions of Kananaskis Country's abundant activities give outdoor enthusiasts goose bumps. With over 1000km of trails, hiking in K-Country can provide anything from a 1hr. quick fix to a full-blown Rocky Mountain High. Pick up the $1 trail guide at one of the visitor centers. Gillean Dafferns's *Kananaskis Country Trail Guide* ($17), published by Rocky Mountain Books and available at any area information center, is a definitive, detailed source of information on longer trails. **1982 Canadian Mt. Everest Expedition Trail** (2km) starts at the White Spruce parking lot in Peter Lougheed Park 10km south of the visitors center. Climb through forest to a lookout point that provides a majestic view of both Upper and Lower Kananaskis Lakes. **Upper Lake Trail** (15km loop, 4.5km to campsite) circumnavigates the Upper Lake and provides incredible views of the surrounding mountains, reflected in the Lake's still waters. **Ribbon Creek Trail** (8km to falls, 10km to lake; 350m gain) starts half a kilometer south of the hostel parking lot and passes through the waterfall-rich canyon land between **Mt. Kidd** and **Mt. Bogart**, arriving at the Ribbon Falls campground.

Cliffs throughout the park offer excellent climbing opportunities. **Barrier Bluffs** has dozens of bolted routes up the wall. The foothills of the **Sibbald Area** in the northeast of K-country (30min. off Hwy. 1) offer wide expanses of terrain to horseback riders, hikers, and cyclists.

The Rockies (Banff, Yoho & Kootenay National Parks)

■ ACCOMMODATIONS

Castle Mountain, **13**
Lake Louise, **9**
Mosquito Creek, **3**
Rampart Creek Hostel, **1**
Whiskey Jack Hostel, **5**

Lake Louise, **8**
Lake O'Hara, **10**
McLeod Meadows, **18**
Monarch, **7**
Mosquito Creek, **2**
Protection Mountain, **11**
Redstreak, **19**
Takakkaw Falls, **4**
Tunnel Mountain, **16**
Two Jack, **15**

▲ CAMPING

Dolly Varden, **17**
Hoodoo Creek, **12**
Johnston Canyon, **14**
Kicking Horse, **6**

BY TOUR. Without a car, guided bus rides may be the easiest way to see some of the park's main attractions, such as the **Great Divide,** the **Athabasca Glacier,** and the spiral railroad tunnel. **Brewster Tours** offer 9½hr. guided trips on the Icefields Parkway. (☎ 762-6767. Mid-May to Oct. at 8:10am. $95, child $47.50. Spring and fall $72/$36. 10% HI discount. A visit to the Columbia Icefields is $27 extra, $13.50 children.) **Bigfoot Tours** runs fun, two-day, 11-passenger van trips between Banff and Jasper with an overnight stop at the **Mt. Edith Cavell Hostel.** (☎ 888-244-6673; www.bigfoottours.com. $95, not including food or lodging.) Trips have three departures a week; trips east stop at the **Squilax General Store Hostel** and trips west stop at the **Old Courthouse Hostel** in Kamloops.

ALBERTA

BANFF NATIONAL PARK   ☎ 403

Banff is Canada's best-loved and best-known natural park, with 6641 sq. km of peaks, forests, glaciers, and alpine valleys. It also holds the title of Canada's first National Park, declared so only days after the Canadian Pacific Railway's completion in 1885. The park's name comes from Banffshire, Scotland, the birthplace of a certain two Canadian Pacific Railway financiers. These men convinced Canada's first Prime Minister that a "large pecuniary advantage" might be gained from the

AT A GLANCE

AREA: 6641 sq. km.

CLIMATE: Alpine and subalpine.

FEATURES: Cave and Basin Mineral Springs, Tunnel and Sulphur Mountain.

HIGHLIGHTS: Backcountry hiking (p. 383), watersports (p. 383).

GATEWAYS: Calgary (p. 368).

CAMPING: Plenty of options. Most sites are between $10 and $17 per night. (p. 380).

FEES: Park fee: Adult $5, senior $4, 6-16 $2.50, family $10.

region, telling him that "since we can't export the scenery, we shall have to import the tourists." Their plan worked to a fault, but even streets littered with gift shops and chocolatiers cannot mar the beauty of the wilderness outside of the Banff townsite. Outdoors lovers arrive with mountain bikes, climbing gear, and skis, but a trusty pair of hiking boots remains the park's most widely-used outdoor equipment. Banff's natural beauty, along with the opportunities for excitement and laid-back attitude it affords, have turned Banff into one of Canada's youngest towns.

▛ TRANSPORTATION

Banff National Park hugs the Alberta side of the Alberta/British Columbia border 128km west of Calgary. The **Trans-Canada Hwy. (Hwy. 1)** runs east-west through the park, connecting it to Yoho National Park in the west. The **Icefields Parkway (Hwy. 93)** connects Banff with Jasper National Park to the north and Kootenay National Park to the southwest. Civilization in the park centers around the towns of **Banff** and **Lake Louise**, 58km apart on Hwy. 1. The more serene **Bow Valley Parkway (Hwy. 1A)** parallels Hwy. 1 from Lake Louise to 8km west of Banff, offering excellent camping, hosteling, sights, and wildlife. The southern portion of Hwy. 1A is restricted at night in the late spring and early summer to accommodate the wildlife on the road. All listings apply to Banff Townsite, unless otherwise specified.

Buses: Brewster Transportation, 100 Gopher St. (☎762-6767). Depot open daily 7:45am-9pm. To: **Calgary** (2hr., $40); **Jasper** (5hr., $54); **Lake Louise** (1hr., $12). Ages 6-15 half-price. See **The Rockies,** p. 375, for info on tours to, from, and within parks. **Greyhound** (☎800-661-8747) uses Brewster's station. 4 per day to **Lake Louise** (1hr., $12) and **Vancouver, BC** (14hr., $105); 5 per day to **Calgary** (1½hr., $22).

Public Transportation: Banff Transit runs between the Banff Springs Hotel, the RV parking area, and Banff Hostel on Tunnel Mountain Rd., as well as between the Tunnel Mountain Campground, downtown, and the Banff Park Museum. $1, children $0.50. Mid-May to Sept. 7am-midnight; late Apr. to early May and Oct.-Dec. noon-midnight.

FLOUR POWER Passing by the many lakes and streams in the Rockies, you may notice that they have an unusual color. When looking at the swimming-pool turquoise or glowing blue color of these bodies of water, you might wonder if this is some kind of gimmick perpetuated by the park wardens to bring in the tourists. Many years ago, one visitor to Lake Louise claimed that he had solved the mystery of the beautiful water: it had obviously been distilled from peacock tails. Turns out he was a bit off the mark. The actual cause of the color is "rock flour." This fine dust is created by the pressure exerted by the glacier upon rocks trapped within the ice; the resulting ground rock is washed into streams and lakes in the glacial meltwater. Suspended particles trap all colors of the spectrum except for the blues and greens that are reflected back for your visual pleasure.

ALBERTA

Taxis: Banff Taxi (☎726-4444). 24hr. **Lake Louise Taxi** (☎522-2020). Runs 6am-2:30pm.

Car Rental: Available from several establishments with rates ranging from $50-60 per day, with 100-150 free km. Ask at the visitors center for a comparison chart.

Tours: Bigfoot Adventure Tours (☎888-244-6673; www.bigfoottours.com) runs fun 10-day trips from Vancouver to Jasper and Banff. Passengers can get on and off any of their 3 tour vans. (Daily from July-Sept.) A $410 ($400 with ISIC card) fee covers transportation and park fees, but not the HI accommodations, food, or entertainment.

▣ PRACTICAL INFORMATION

Tourist Information: Banff Visitor Centre, 224 Banff Ave. Includes **Banff/Lake Louise Tourism Bureau** (☎762-8421; www.banfflakelouise.com) and **Parks Canada** (☎762-1550). Open June-Sept. daily 8am-8pm; Oct.-May 9am-5pm. **Lake Louise Visitor Centre** (☎522-3833), at Samson Mall on Village Rd. Open mid-June to Sept. daily 8am-6pm; Oct. to mid-June 9am-5pm.

Equipment Rental:

Mountain Magic Equipment, 224 Bear St. (☎762-2591) is one of the few places in Banff to rent packages for Telemark ($25 per day) and mountaineering ($50 per day). They also offer the usual bike, ski, and snowboard rentals. Open Dec.-Mar. daily 8am-9pm; Apr.-Nov. 9am-9pm.

Bactrax Rentals, 225 Bear St. (☎762-8177), rents mountain bikes for $6-10 per hr., $22-36 per day. Bike tours $15 per hr. including all equipment. Ski packages from $16 per day, snowboard packages $28. 20% HI discount. Open Apr.-Oct. daily 8am-8pm; Nov.-Mar. 7am-10pm.

Performance Sports, 208 Bear St. (☎762-8222), rents tents ($20-26 per day), fishing gear ($16-30 per day), cross-country ski or snowshoe packages ($12 per day, $31 for 3 days), avalanche packages ($23 per day), and snow or rainwear ($8-17 per day). 10% HI or Real Big Adventures discount. Open daily July-Aug. 9:30am-8pm; Sept.-June 10am-6pm.

Wilson Mountain Sports (☎522-3636) in the Lake Louise Samson Mall, rents bikes ($15 per hr., $35 per day) and camping and fishing gear. They also offer mountaineering packages ($35 per day), rock climbing packages ($15 per day) and sell fishing permits. Open daily mid-June to Sept. 9am-9pm; Oct. to Apr. 8am-8pm; May to mid-June 9am-8pm.

Laundry: Johnny O's, 223 Bear St. (☎762-5111). $2.75 for regular wash, $6 for huge load (more than 2 regular loads). $2.50 for dry. Open in summer daily 9am-10pm, until 9pm in winter.

Weather: ☎762-2088.

Road Conditions: ☎762-1450.

Emergency: ☎911.

Police: Banff Police (☎762-2226. Non-emergency 762-2228). On Lynx St. by the train depot. **Lake Louise Police** (☎522-3811. Non-emergency 522-3812). **Banff Park Warden** (☎762-4506. Non-emergency 762-1470). 24hr. **Lake Louise Park Warden** (☎522-1200).

Hospital: Mineral Springs, 301 Lynx St. (☎762-2222), near Wolf St. in Banff.

Internet Access: Library, 101 Bear St. (☎762-2611). Sign up in advance. Open daily 10am-8pm. Closed Su from late May-early Sept. **Cyber Web** (☎762-9226), 215 Banff Ave. $3 per 15min., $8 per hr., $5 per hr. from 9:30pm-close. Open daily 10am-midnight. For laptops, open M-Th 10am-8pm, F 10am-6pm, Sa 11am-6pm, Su 1-5pm. $1 per 15min.

Banff Townsite

▲ ACCOMMODATIONS
Banff International Hostel, **3**
Tunnel Mts. Campgrounds, **2**
Two Jack Campground, **1**

🍴&🍺 FOOD & NIGHTLIFE
Aardvark's, **6**
Sunfood Cafe, **5**
Aurora, **8**
Rose and Crown, **7**
St. James's Gate, **4**

- - - - - Trails/Bikes
────── Trails/No Bikes

Post Office: 204 Buffalo St. (☎ 762-2586). Open M-F 9am-5:30pm. **Postal Code:** TOL
0C0.

🏔 ACCOMMODATIONS

Finding a cheap place to stay in Banff has become increasingly difficult; the number of visitors soars into the millions every year. Townsite residents offer rooms in their homes, occasionally at reasonable rates ($75-140, winter $60-100). Check the list at the back of the *Banff and Lake Louise Official Visitor Guide*, available free at the visitors centers.

Mammoth **modern hostels** at Banff and Lake Louise anchor a chain of cozier hostels from Calgary to Jasper. **Rustic hostels** provide more of a wilderness experience (read: no electricity or flush toilets), and often have some of the park's best hiking and cross-country skiing right in their backyards. HI runs a **shuttle service** connecting all the Rocky Mountain hostels and Calgary ($8-90). Wait-list beds become available at 6pm, and the larger hostels try to save a few stand-by beds for shuttle arrivals. Beds go quickly, especially during the summer, so make your reservations as early as possible. The hostels below are listed from south to north, and all reservations are made through the southern Alberta HI administration at ☎ 866-762-4122 or online at www.hostellingintl.ca. Free reservations are held until 6pm,

ALBERTA

but can be guaranteed until later with a credit card. Because of a recent move towards centralizing the administration of these hostels, information regarding prices, closures, and facilities will be in flux for some time.

▨ **Lake Louise International Hostel (HI)** (☎ 522-2200), 500m west of the Info Centre in Lake Louise Townsite, on Village Rd. toward the Park Warden's office. Ranked 4th in the world by HI, and rightly so. More like a resort than a hostel, it boasts a reference library, a stone fireplace, 2 full kitchens, a sauna, and a quality cafe. Internet access $2 per 20min. Hub for mountaineering tours. Check-in 3pm, check-out 11am. $26, nonmembers $30; private rooms available. ❶

▨ **Rampart Creek Wilderness Hostel (HI),** 34km south of the Icefield Centre. Close to several world-famous ice climbs (including Weeping Wall, 17km north), this hostel is a favorite for winter mountaineers and anyone who likes a rustic sauna after a hard day's hike. Wood-burning sauna, full-service kitchen. A steep climb behind the hostel leads to a hammock with free access to the visual orgy of the entire valley. 2 co-ed cabins with 12 beds each. $18, nonmembers $22; F-Sa $21, nonmembers $25. ❶

▨ **Castle Mountain Wilderness Hostel (HI),** in Castle Junction, 1.5km east of the junction of Hwy. 1 and Hwy. 93 south, between Banff and Lake Louise. One of the hardest hostels to find, Castle Mountain offers a smaller, quieter alternative to the hubbub of its big brothers. Comfortable common area with huge bay windows. A library, collection of games, and fireplace. Friendly staff, hot showers, kitchen, laundry, electricity, and volleyball. Check-in 5-10pm; check-out 10am. Sleeps 28. Su-Th $18, nonmembers $22; Fr-Sa $21, nonmembers $25. ❶

▨ **Mosquito Creek Wilderness Hostel (HI),** 103km south of the Icefield Centre and 26km north of Lake Louise. Across the creek from the Mosquito Creek campground. Close to the Wapta Icefield. Enormous living room with wood stove, wood-burning sauna, kitchen, and pump water. 2 co-ed cabins of 16 beds each. $18, nonmembers $22; F-Sa $21, nonmembers $25. ❶

Banff International Hostel (HI) (☎ 762-4122), 3km uphill from Banff Townsite on Tunnel Mountain Rd. Walk or take Banff Transit from downtown ($1). This monster hostel has 3 lounges and kitchens. Check-in 3pm. Check-out 11am. Laundry and hot showers. Sleeps 215. $26 nonmembers $30; for better rooms in new building add $1.50. ❷

🏕 CAMPING

A chain of campgrounds stretches between Banff and Jasper. Extra-large, fully hooked-up grounds lie closer to the townsites; for more trees and fewer vehicles, try the more remote sites farther from Banff and Lake Louise. At all park campgrounds, a campfire permit (includes firewood) is $4. Sites are first come, first served; go early. The sites below are listed from south to north and have wheelchair access but no toilets or showers unless otherwise noted.

Tunnel Mountain Village, 4km from Banff Townsite on Tunnel Mountain Rd. With nearly 1200 sites, this facility is a camping metropolis. Trailer/RV area has 321 full RV sites, Village 2 has 188 sites, and Village 1 houses a whopping 618 sites. Fires allowed in Village 1 only; all villages have showers. Village 2 is open year-round; 1 and 3 closed Oct.-early May. $17; power only $21; full RV sites $24. ❶

Two Jack, 13km northeast of Banff, across Hwy.1. Open mid-May to Aug. The 381 sites in the main area ($13) have no showers or disabled access, while the 80 lakeside sites ($17) do. ❶

Johnston Canyon, 26km northwest of Banff on Bow Valley Pkwy. Access to Johnston Canyon Trail (see below). Open mid-June to mid-Sept. 140 sites, $17. Showers. ❶

Protection Mountain, 15km east of Lake Louise and 11km west of Castle Junction on the Bow Valley Pkwy. (Hwy. 1A). 89 spacious and wooded sites (14 trailer) in a basic campground. Open late June-early Sept. Sites $13. ●

Lake Louise, 1½km southeast of the visitors center on Fairview Rd. On Bow River, not the lake. Plenty of hiking and fishing awaits near this tent city. 189 trailer sites with electricity, open year-round; $21. 220 tent sites, open mid-May to Sept.; $17. Showers. ●

Mosquito Creek, 103km south of the Icefield Centre and 26km north of Lake Louise. 32 sites with hiking access. Pit toilets. Sites $10. ●

Rampart Creek, 147km north of Banff, 34km south of the Icefield Centre, across the highway from Rampart Creek hostel and amazing ice climbing. Pit toilets. Open late June-Aug. 50 sites, $10. ●

🎭 🎬 FOOD AND NIGHTLIFE

Like everything else in the park, Banff restaurants tend toward the expensive. The Banff and Lake Louise hostels serve affordable meals in their cafes ($3-10). Groceries await at **Safeway,** at Marten and Elk St. just off Banff Ave. (☎ 762-5378. Open daily 8am-11pm.) Bartenders maintain that Banff's true wildlife is in its bars. Check the paper or ask at the visitors center to find out which nightspots are having "locals' night," featuring cheap drinks. Banff Ave. hosts more bars, restaurants, kitschy gift shops, ATMs and banks than there are mountains. The fun doesn't stop after Saturday night, either: Banff Sundays boast great nightlife.

🍴 **Rose and Crown,** 202 Banff Ave. (☎ 762-2121), upstairs on the corner of Banff and Caribou. Ample room for dancing, and pool-playing ($1.25), even on busy nights. Couch-adorned living room for watching sports and live music every night at 10pm. Happy hour M-F 3:30-6:30pm. $2 cover Sa, Jam Night Su with happy hour 9pm-close. Open daily 11am-2am. ❷

Laggan's Deli (☎ 522-2017; fax 522-3299), in Samson Mall in Lake Louise. Always crowded. Thick sandwiches ($4-5) or fresh-baked loaves ($3). Open June-Sept. daily 6am-8pm; Oct.-May 6am-7pm. Cash or traveler's checks only. ●

Sunfood Cafe, 215 Banff Ave. (☎ 760-3933), 2nd floor of the Sundance Mall. A very relaxed vegetarian cafe hidden upstairs in a touristy mall. Veggie burger with the works $6.25. Daily specials, takeout available. Beer and wine. Open M-Sa 11am-9pm. ●

Aardvark's, 304A Caribou St. (☎ 762-5500 or 762-5509). Does big business after the bars close. Skinny on seating. Small-ish slices of pizza $3. Small pie $6-9; large $13-21; buffalo wings $5 for 10. Open daily 11am-4am. ❸

Aurora, 110 Banff Ave. (☎ 760-5300). This neon-lit, ultra-modern club caters to the 25+ crowd with a martini and cigar bar in back. House, hip-hop, and trance dance floor; sports area with big-screen; 5 bars. Highballs and beer Sa. Open daily 9pm-2am.

Lux Cinema Centre, 229 Bear St. (24hr. cinema info ☎ 762-8595). Fun for the whole family. Call for movies and times.

St. James's Gate, 205 Wolf St. (☎ 762-9355). A laid-back Irish Pub with friendly staff. Ask the bartenders which of the 32 beers on tap to try. Live jigs and reels F-Sa completes the Irish ambience. Open daily 11am-2am.

👁 SIGHTS

MUSEUMS. Visitors can purchase a pass to gain admission to all of the following sites for $9, seniors and students $6.50, family $20. The **Whyte Museum of the Canadian Rockies** explores the history and culture of the Canadian Rockies over the last two centuries in the Heritage Gallery, while temporary exhibits focus on the natural history of the region. Displays include works done by Canadian painters. *(111 Bear St. ☎762-2291. Open daily 10am-5pm. $6, students and seniors $4, 5 and under free.)* The **Banff Park Museum National Historic Site** is western Canada's oldest natural history museum, with rooms of stuffed specimens dating to the 1860s. *(☎762-1558. Open mid-May to Sept. daily 10am-6pm; Oct. to mid-May 1-5pm. Tours in summer daily 3pm, weekends in winter. $2.50, seniors 65 $2, children $1.50.)* Banff National Park would not exist if not for the **Cave and Basin Mineral Springs,** once rumored to have miraculous healing properties. The **Cave and Basin National Historic Site,** a refurbished bath house built circa 1914, is now a small museum detailing the history and science of the site. Access to the low-ceilinged cave containing the original spring is inside the building. Five of the pools are the only home of the park's most endangered species: the small Banff Springs snail—*Physella johnsoni*. *(☎762-1566. Open in summer daily 9am-6pm; winter M-F 11am-4pm, Sa-Su 9:30am-5pm. Tours at 11am. $2.50, seniors $2, children $1.50.)* The **springs** are southwest of the city on Cave Ave. For an actual dip in the hot water, follow the egg smell to the Upper Hot Springs pool, a 40°C (104°F) sulfurous cauldron on Mountain Ave. *(☎762-1515. Open mid-May to mid-Oct. daily 9am-11pm; mid-Oct. to mid-May Su-Th 10am-10pm, F-Sa 10am-11pm. Summer rates $7.50, seniors and children 3-17 $6.50, families $21.50. Winter $5.50, $4.50, $15. Swimsuits $1.50, towels $1.25, lockers $0.50.)*

EVENTS. In summer, the **Banff Festival of the Arts** keeps tourists occupied. A wide spectrum of events, from First Nations dance to opera, are performed from May to mid-August. Some shows are free; stop by the visitors center for a schedule. The **Banff Mountain Film Festival,** in the first week of November, screens films and videos that celebrate mountains and mountaineers. *(For times and info, call ☎762-6301.)*

◪ OUTDOOR ACTIVITIES

A visitor sticking to paved byways will see only a tiny fraction of the park and the majority of the park's visitors. Those interested in the seemingly endless outdoor options can hike or bike on more than 1600km of trails. Grab a free copy of the "Mountain Biking and Cycling Guide" or "Dayhikes in Banff" and peruse park maps and trail descriptions at information centers. For still more solitude, pick up "The Banff Backcountry Experience" and an **overnight camping permit** at a visitors center and head out to the backcountry ($6 per person per day, up to $30; $38 per year). Be sure to check with the park rangers at the information center for current weather, trail, and wildlife updates.

BANFF TOWNSITE AREA

HIKING

Two easy trails are within walking distance of Banff Townsite, but longer, more rigorous and escapist trails abound farther away. The best escapes and incomparable experiences are found in the backcountry.

Fenland (2km, 1hr.). Follow Mt. Norquay Rd. to town outskirts, look for signs across the tracks on road's left side. The trail winds through a flat area shared by beaver, muskrat, and waterfowl, but is closed for elk calving in late spring and early summer. Easy.

Tunnel Mountain (2.5km, 2hr.). Follow Wolf St. east from Banff Ave., and turn right on St. Julien Rd. to reach the head of the steep trail. Provides a dramatic view of the **Bow Valley** and **Mt. Rundle.** Tunnel Mountain has the unfortunate distinction of being the Rockies' smallest mountain. Not that it matters. Easy to moderate.

Aylmer Pass (26.5km round-trip, 8hr.) The trail leaves from the shore of Lake Minnewanka on Lake Minnewanka Rd. (the extension of Banff Ave. across the Trans-Canada from town). Parking just above tour boat area. A steep climb to the summit yields a panoramic view of the lake and surrounding scenery. The trail can be abridged by hiking only 11.6km to the lookout, cutting the final 250m ascent. Strenuous.

Johnston Canyon (5.5km). West of the Norquay Interchange on Hwy. 1, then 18km along the Bow Valley Pkwy. (Hwy. 1A). A very popular half-day hike. A catwalk along the edge of the deep limestone canyon runs 1.1km over the thundering river to the canyon's lower falls, then another 1.6km to the upper falls. The trail continues for a more rugged 3.2km to seven blue-green cold-water springs, known as the **Inkpots,** in an open valley above the canyon. More than 42km of trails beyond the Inkpots are blissfully untraveled and punctuated with campgrounds roughly every 10km. Moderate to strenuous.

Sulphur Mountain (5.5km, 2hr.). Winds along a well-trodden trail to the peak, where a spectacular view awaits; the **Sulphur Mountain Gondola** doesn't charge for the 8min. downhill trip. (☎ 762-2523. Uphill $19, ages 6-15 $9.50, under 6 free.) The **Panorama Restaurant** (☎ 762-7486), perched atop the mountain, serves breakfast ($10) and lunch buffets ($13) from mid-May to mid-August. Moderate.

BACKCOUNTRY

Backcountry trekking is the way to see Banff as the masses of travelers cannot. Banff's backcountry, replete with picture-postcard, mind-boggling scenery, belies the kitschy tourist trap that the townsite has become. Amateurs and experts alike should beware of dangerous and changing conditions on strenuous trails that do not receive as much maintenance as more accessible routes; consult park rangers for information. Trails to ask about include **Egypt Lake** (12.5km one-way, 2 days), **Twin Lakes** (9km one-way, 2 days), **Mystic Pass** (37km, 3 days), **Skoki Loop** (34km, 3 days), **Assiniboine Loop** (55km, 4 days), **Sunshine-Assiniboine-Bryant Creek Trail** (56km, 4 days, two cars recommended), **Sawback Trail** (74km, 5 days), and **Mystic Pass-Flint's Park-Badger Pass Trail** (76km, 5 days).

BIKING

Biking is permitted on public roads, highways, and certain trails in the park. Spectacular scenery and a number of hostels and campgrounds make the **Bow Valley Parkway (Hwy. 1A)** and the **Icefields Parkway (Hwy. 93)** perfect for extended cycling trips. Every other store downtown seems to rent bikes; head to **Bactrax** or **Performance Sport** (see **Equipment Rental,** p. 378) for HI discounts. Parks Canada publishes a "Mountain Biking and Cycling Guide" that describes trails and roadways where bikes are permitted (free at bike rental shops and visitors centers).

WATERSPORTS

Fishing is legal in most of the park's bodies of water during specific seasons, but live bait and lead weights are not. Get a **permit** and check out regulations at the info center. (7-day permit $6, annual permit valid in all Canadian National Parks $13.) **Bourgeau Lake,** a 7km hike in, is home to a particularly feisty breed of brook trout. Closer to the road, try **Herbert Lake,** off the Icefields Pkwy., or **Lake Minnewanka,** on Lake Minnewanka Rd. northeast of Banff. Lake Minnewanka Rd. passes **Johnson Lake,** where shallow warm water makes a perfect **swimming hole.**

    Hydra River Guides runs **whitewater rafting** trips along the **Kicking Horse River.** (☎ 762-4554 or 800-644-8888; www.raftbanff.com. 22km, 2½hr; 6hr. including transportation. Up to Class IV+ rapids. $90, includes lunch, transportation, and gear; HI members $76.) **Blast Adventures** leads half-day, 1- to 2-person **inflatable kayak** trips on the rowdy Kananaskis River. (☎ 609-2009 or 888-802-5278; www.blastadventures.com. $64 per person including transportation, gear, and snacks.)

ALBERTA

THINGS THAT GO BANFF IN THE NIGHT Bear
sightings are common in the Canadian Rockies, but one black bear took it upon himself to give Banff residents an uncommon reminder of whose park it really is. Imaginatively known as Bear 16 (numbers are used to discourage personification), this ursine vagabond moved into town, disrupting everyday activity by foraging in front lawns and lazing in the road, blocking traffic. Bear 16 crossed the line when the scent from a bakery lured him too close to human territory. The park staff ultimately removed Bear 16 from the park, had him castrated, and relocated him to the Calgary Zoo.

While most travelers to the park are eager to see its wildlife, few want as intimate an encounter as Bear 16 offered. The safest bet is to talk, sing, or yodel loudly while hiking, especially on windy days or near running water. The number of bear attacks actually ranks low among the total number of attacks by park animals; dozens of visitors are bitten each year by rodents pursuing human food. By far the most dangerous of Banff animals, however, are people—road accidents are the most common cause of death for large wildlife in the park.

LAKE LOUISE TOWNSITE AREA

The highest community in Canada (1530m), Lake Louise and the surrounding glaciers have often passed for Swiss scenery in movies and are the emerald in the Rockies' tiara of tourism. Once at the lake, the hardest task is escaping fellow gawkers at the posh, though aesthetically misplaced, **Chateau Lake Louise.** The chateau's canoe rentals are an unheard of $30 per hr.

HIKING

If you don't want to succumb to the town's prices, you can view the water and its surrounding splendor from several hiking trails that begin in the neighborhood and climb along the surrounding ridgelines. As any celebrity can attest, with beauty comes crowds; expect masses of tourists (and bears).

Lake Agnes Trail (3.5km, 2½hr. round-trip), and the **Plain of Six Glaciers Trail** (5.5km, 4hr. round-trip) both end at teahouses and make for a lovely, if sometimes crowded, dayhike with views down to the Lake. Open summer daily 9am-6pm.

Moraine Lake, 15km from the village, at the end of Moraine Lake Rd. and off Lake Louise Dr. (no trailers or long RVs). Moraine lies in the awesome **Valley of the Ten Peaks,** opposite glacier-encrusted **Mt. Temple.** Join the multitudes on the **Rockpile Trail** for an eye-popping view of the lake and valley and a lesson in ancient ocean bottoms (10min. walk to the top). To escape the camera-wielding hordes, try one of the Lake's more challenging trails, either **Sentinel Pass** via Larch Valley (6km one-way, 5-6hr.), with stunning views from flower studded meadows, or **Wenkchemna Pass** via Eiffel Lake (10km one-way, full day), which carries hikers the length of the Valley of the Ten Peaks with incredible views in both directions. Moraine packs more scenic punch than its sister Louise; be sure to arrive before 10am or after 4pm to see the view instead of the crowds. If you don't visit Moraine, just get your hands on an old $20 bill; the Valley of Ten Peaks is pictured on the reverse.

Paradise Valley, depending on which way you hike it, can be an intense dayhike or a relaxing overnight trip. From the **Paradise Creek Trailhead,** 2.5km up Moraine Lake Rd., the loop through the valley runs 18.1km through subalpine and alpine forests and along rivers (7½hr., elevation gain 880m). One classic backpacking route runs from Moraine Lake up and over **Sentinel Pass,** joining the top of the Paradise Valley loop after 8km. A **backcountry campground** marks the mid-point from either trailhead. Campers aren't the only admirers of the scenery: grizzly activity often forces the park wardens to close the area in summer. Check with the wardens before hiking in this area.

WINTER SPORTS

Winter activities in the park range from world-class ice climbing to ice fishing. Those 1600km of hiking trails make for exceptional **cross-country skiing** (**Moraine Lake Rd.** is closed to vehicle traffic in the winter, and is used for cross-country skiing, as are the backcountry trails), and three allied resorts offer a range of **skiing and snowboarding** opportunities from early Nov. to mid-May. All have terrain parks for snowboarders. Shuttles to all the following three resorts leave from most big hotels in the townsites, and Banff and Lake Louise hostels typically have ticket and transportation **discounts** available for guests. Multi-day passes good for all three resorts are available at the **Ski Banff/Lake Louise** office, 225 Banff Ave., lower level, and at all resorts. Passes include free shuttle service and an extra night of skiing at Mount Norquay. (☎762-4561; www.skibanfflakelouise.)

Sunshine Mountain (☎762-6500, snow report 760-7669, in Calgary 277-7669; www.skibanff.com). Spreading across 3 mountains, with the most snowfall (9.9m) in the area, this mountain attracts loyal followers to its 3168 acres. $56; students under 24, ages 13-17, and over 65 $46; ages 6-12 $20.

Lake Louise (☎522-3555, snow report in Banff 762-4766, in Calgary 244-6665; www.skilouise.com). The 2nd-largest ski area in Canada (4200 ski-able acres), with amazing views, over 1000m of vertical drop, and the best selection of expert (double-black) terrain. Some simpler slopes cover plenty of the mountain. $59; students under 25 and adults over 65 $47; ages 6-12 $15.

Mt. Norquay (☎762-4421). A local's mountain: smaller, closer to town, and less manic. Draws like F night-skiing and 2-5hr. tickets. ($47; students, ages 13-17 and 55+ $37; ages 6-12 $16. Night-skiing $23; students, youth, and seniors $21; ages 6-12 $12.)

SIGHTSEEING

The **Lake Louise Sightseeing Lift,** up Whitehorn Rd. and across the Trans-Canada Hwy. from Lake Louise, cruises up **Mt. Whitehorn.** (☎522-3555; www.skilouise.com. Open daily May 9am-4pm; June and Sept. 8:30am-9pm; July and Aug. 8am-6pm. $19, students and seniors $17, ages 6-12 $9, under 6 free. To enjoy breakfast at the top, add $2; for lunch, add $6, under 6 $2.)

BANFF TO JASPER: ICEFIELDS PARKWAY (HWY. 93)

The Icefields Parkway began in the Great Depression as a work relief project. The 230km Parkway is one of the most beautiful rides in North America, heading north from Lake Louise in Banff National Park to Jasper Townsite in Jasper National Park. Drivers may struggle to keep their eyes on the road as they skirt stunning peaks, aquamarine glacial lakes, and highwayside glaciers, not to mention all the wonders of Rocky Mountain fauna, visible from the safety of a car window.

🚩 **PRACTICAL INFORMATION** Parks Canada manages the parkway as a scenic route, so all users must obtain a **Park Pass,** available at entrance gates and information centers. ($10 per day, seniors $8; $38 per year, $70 for 2-7 persons. Valid at all Canadian national parks.) Free maps of the Icefields Parkway are available at park visitors centers in Jasper, Lake Louise, and Banff. They are also available at the **Icefield Centre,** at the boundary between the two parks, 132km north of Lake Louise and 103km south of Jasper Townsite. (☎780-852-6288. Open May to mid-Oct. daily 9am-5pm; July and Aug. 9am-6pm.) Although the center is closed in winter, the Parkway is only closed for plowing after heavy snowfalls. Thanks to the extensive campground and hostel networks that line the Parkway, longer trips between Banff and Jasper National Parks are convenient and affordable. Cyclists should be prepared to face rapidly changing weather conditions and some very steep hills.

⚡ OUTDOOR ACTIVITIES. The Icefields Parkway has 18 trails into the wilderness and 22 scenic points with spectacular views. **Bow Summit,** 40km north of Lake Louise, is the Parkway's highest point (2135m); there, a 10min. walk leads to a view of fluorescent, aqua **Peyto Lake.** The Icefield Centre (see above) lies in the shadow of the tongue of the **Athabasca Glacier.** This gargantuan ice floe is one of six major glaciers that flow from the 200 sq. km **Columbia Icefield,** the largest accumulation of ice and snow in the Canadian Rockies. The icefield's runoff eventually flows to three oceans: the Pacific, Atlantic, and Arctic.

Columbia Icefield Snocoach Tours carry visitors over the Athabasca Glacier in monster-truck-like buses for an 80min. trip. (☎877-423-7433; www.columbiaicefield.com. Open mid-Apr. to mid-Oct. daily 9am-5pm; $28, ages 6-15 $14.) Visitors can also drive close and take a 10min. walk up piles of glacial debris onto the glacier's mighty toe. Dated signposts mark the glacier's speedy retreat up the valley over the last century. The trail onto the glacier is limited to a very small "safe zone," and all hikers are warned that glacial crevices are a very real concern; two people have died on Athabasca in the last decade. For more geological tidbits, sign up for an **Athabasca Glacier Icewalk.** The daily "Ice Cubed" hike provides 3hr. of fun and education on the ice. ($45, ages 7-17 $23.) Sunday and Thursday at 11am, the "Icewalk Deluxe" hike takes the eager out for a 5-6hr. tour higher up on the glacier, though snow may limit these trips to July and August. ($50, ages 7-17 $25.) Contact the Icefield Centre. (☎780-852-3803. Tours run mid-June to mid-Sept.)

The **Wilcox Pass Trail** begins 3km south of the Icefield Centre at **Wilcox Creek Campground** (see p. 388). After 2.5km, the path reaches a ridge with astounding views of Athabasca Glacier and Mt. Athabasca. Considered one of the best hikes in Jasper, it's 8km to the pass and back, and 11km one-way from the trailhead to a later junction with the Icefields Parkway, requiring either two vehicles or good hitchhiking skills. *Let's Go* does not recommend hitchhiking. The **Parker Ridge Trail** leads 2.5km away from the road and up above treeline, where an impressive view of the **Saskatchewan Glacier** awaits. The trailhead is 1km south of the **Hilda Creek Hostel's** burned down remains, and 8.5km south of the Icefield Centre.

JASPER NATIONAL PARK   ☎780

AT A GLANCE	
AREA: 10,878 sq. km	**GATEWAYS:** Banff (p. 376), Edmonton (p. 361)
CLIMATE: Alpine, subalpine	
FEATURES: Columbia Icefields, Maligne Lake	**CAMPING:** First come, first served (p. 389)
HIGHLIGHTS: Hiking the 2 Mt. Edith Cavell trails, visiting the Athabasca Glacier	**FEES:** Day pass $6, $4.50 senior, $3 ages 6-16

Northward expansion of the Canadian railway system led to further exploration of the Canadian Rocky Mountains and the 1907 creation of Jasper, the largest of the National Parks in the region. The area went virtually untouristed until 1940, when the Icefields Parkway paved the way for the masses to appreciate Jasper's astounding beauty. The Parkway is popular with cyclists, making for a remarkable, albeit long, bike journey. In summer, caravans of RVs and charter buses line the highway jostling for the chance to take photos of surprisingly fearless wildlife. Because 40% of the park is above the treeline, most visitors stay in the sheltered vicinity of Jasper Townsite, smaller than its nearby counterpart, Banff. Every summer, the tourists quadruple the town's population to over 20,000. In the face of this annual bloat, Jasper's permanent residents struggle to keep their home looking and feeling like a small town. In the winter, crowds melt away, snow descends, and a modest ski resort welcomes visitors to a slower, more relaxed town.

TRANSPORTATION

All of the addresses below are in **Jasper Townsite,** near the center of the park at the intersection of **Hwy. 16,** which runs east-west through the northern reaches of the park, and the **Icefields Parkway (Hwy. 93),** which connects Jasper with Banff National Park in the south. Many bike shops rent one-way between the two parks. Hitching is popular and reportedly easy along the Parkway, but *Let's Go* does not recommend hitchhiking. The two front streets in Jasper hold all the shops and stores, while the hostels and campgrounds are several kilometers out from town.

Trains: VIA Rail, 607 Connaught Dr. (☎800-561-8630). 3 per week to **Edmonton** (5hr., $142), **Vancouver, BC** (17hr., $198), and **Winnipeg, MB** (1 day, $288).

Buses: Greyhound (☎852-3926), in the train station. To **Edmonton** (4½hr., 3 per day, $54) and **Vancouver, BC** (10½hr., 2 per day, $106), via **Kamloops, BC** (5hr., 2 per day, $60). **Brewster Transportation** (☎852-3332), in the movie theater, across the street from the train station. To **Calgary** (8hr., $75) via **Banff** (6hr., $54).

Taxis: Heritage Cabs (☎852-5558). Metered for short local trips. 24hr.

Car Rental: Hertz (☎852-3888), in the train station. $50 per day, $0.23 per km after 150km. Must be 24+ with credit card. Open M, W, F 9am-7pm, and Tu, Th, Sa-Su 9am-5pm. **Budget,** 638 Connaught Dr. (☎852-3222), in the Shell Station. $53 per day, $0.23 per km after 150km; $33 per 6hr. with 50km free and $0.23 per km thereafter. Open daily 8am-7pm.

Car Repair: Petro Canada, 300 Connaught Dr. (☎852-3366).

Tours: Bigfoot Adventure Tours (see p. 378) run between Vancouver, Jasper, and Banff.

PRACTICAL INFORMATION

Tourist Information: Park Information Centre, 500 Connaught Dr. (☎852-6176), has trail maps, trail reports, and backcountry permits. Lists local accommodations, homestay and activity options. Offers free local calls. Open mid-June to early Sept. daily 8am-7pm; early Sept. to late Oct. and late Dec. to mid-June 9am-5pm.

Bank: CIBC, 416 Connaught Ave. (☎852-3391), by the visitors center. Open M-Th 10am-3pm, F 10am-5pm. **24hr. ATM.**

Equipment Rental: Freewheel Cycle, 618 Patricia Ave. (☎852-3898; www.freewheeljasper.ca). Hi-end mountain bikes $8 per hr., $24 per day, $32 overnight. Snowboards $28 per day. Watch for twin-tip ski demo deals. Open summer daily 9am-9pm; spring and fall 9am-6pm; call for winter hours. **Jasper International Hostel** rents mountain bikes. $8 per half-day, $15 per day. Snowshoes $8 per day.

Laundromat and Public Showers: Coin Clean, 607 Patricia St. (☎852-3852). Wash $2, dry $1.50. Showers $2 per 10min. Open daily 8am-9:30pm.

Local Work Opportunities: Jasper Employment Centre, 622 Connaught Dr. (☎852-5982). Open M-F 10am-4pm.

Weather: ☎852-3185. **Road Conditions:** ☎852-3311.

Emergency: ☎911.

Police: 600 Pyramid Lake Rd. (☎852-4421).

Women's Crisis Line: ☎800-661-0937. 24hr.

ALBERTA

Jasper Townsite

🍴 FOOD
CoCo's Cafe, **6**
Jasper Pizza Place, **1**
Mountain Foods and Cafe, **4**
Scoops and Loops, **3**
Soft Rock Cafe, **5**
Super A Foods, **2**

Pharmacy: Cavell Value Drug Mart, 602 Patricia St. (☎852-4441). Open May to Sept. daily 9am-11pm; Sept. to May M-Sa 9am-9pm, Su 10am-6pm.

Hospital: Corner of Miette Ave. and Turret St. (☎852-3344).

Internet Access: Soft Rock Cafe (see **Food,** below). $2 for 15 min, $8 per hr. The **library,** 500 Robson St. (☎852-3652), charges $5 per hr. Open M-Th 11am-9pm, F-Sa 11am-5pm. Also available at **Coin Clean,** see **Laundromat,** above, $2 for 15min.

Post Office: 502 Patricia St. (☎852-3041), across from the townsite green and the visitors center. Open M-F 9am-5pm. **Postal Code:** T0E 1E0.

🏠 ACCOMMODATIONS

The modern Jasper International Hostel, just outside Jasper Townsite, anchors a chain of **Hostelling International (HI)** locations throughout Jasper National Park. The rustic hostels farther into the park offer fewer amenities, but lie amid some of Jasper's finest scenery and outdoor activities. HI runs a shuttle service connecting the Rocky Mountain hostels with Calgary. Reservations are necessary for most hostels in summer, but wait-list beds become available at 6pm. In winter, Jasper International, Athabasca Falls, and Maligne Canyon run normally; guests at other hostels must pick up the key at Jasper International and give a deposit. For couples or groups, a B&B may prove more economical (doubles summer $40-130; winter $30-95). Many are in town near the train station; ask for a list at the park information center or the bus depot.

Jasper International Hostel (HI) (☎852-3215 or 877-852-0781), known as Whistlers Hostel, is 3km up Whistlers Rd. from its intersection with Hwy. 93, 4km south of the townsite. Closest hostel to the townsite. Attracts a gregarious breed of backpackers and cyclists. 88 often-full beds (get ready for some sharing—it's possible to have as many as 43 roommates). 2 private rooms available with at least 2 people. 2am curfew. Sun Dog Shuttle (☎852-4056) runs from train station to hostel en route to Jasper Tramway ($3). $18, nonmembers $23. ●

Maligne Canyon Hostel (HI), on Maligne Lake Rd. north of the Maligne Canyon parking lot, 11km east of town off Hwy. 16. Small, recently renovated cabins sit on bank of Maligne River, with access to the Skyline Trail and the Maligne Canyon. Manager is on a first-name basis with several local bears. Electricity, fridge, pay phone, potable water. Check-in 5-11pm. Closed W Oct.-Apr. 24 beds. $13, nonmembers $18. ●

Mt. Edith Cavell Hostel (HI), 12km up Edith Cavell Rd., off Hwy. 93A. Cozy quarters heated by wood-burning stoves. A postcard view of Mt. Edith Cavell and her glaciers, with easy access to the mountain and trails. Propane light, spring water (filter in the newly-painted kitchen), private wash area, firepit, and the best smelling outhouses in the park. Road closed in winter, often until late June, but the hostel is open to anyone willing to pick up the keys at Jasper International Hostel and ski uphill from the highway. Check-in 5-11pm. 32 beds $13, nonmembers $18. ❶

Athabasca Falls Hostel (HI), on Hwy. 93 just south of the 93-93A junction, 32km south of the townsite. A hostel in a quiet setting that still has the comforts of town—electricity, e-mail, and ping pong. However, the only running water around is the beautiful Athabasca Falls, which are a 500m stroll away. Propane heat. 40 beds in 3 cabins. $13, nonmembers $18. ❶

Beauty Creek Hostel (HI), on Hwy. 93, 87km south of the townsite. On the banks of the glacier-fed Sunwapta River and close to the Columbia Icefields. ½km south of the 3.2km Stanley Falls trailhead. Poetry on the outhouse walls and views of the whole valley from the solar shower. Check-in 5pm-11pm. 22 beds, $12; nonmembers $17. ❶

⛰ CAMPING

These government-run campgrounds are listed from north to south. Most are primitive sites with few facilities. All are first come, first served, and popular. Call the park info center (☎852-6176) for details. Fire permits are $4. All campgrounds except for Pocahontas also offer kitchen shelters.

Pocahontas, on Hwy. 16 at the northern edge of the park, 44km northeast of the townsite. Closest campground to Miette Hot Springs. Flush toilets. Open mid-May to mid-Oct. 130 sites and 10 walk-in tent sites. $13. ❶

Snaring River, on Hwy. 16, 16km north of Jasper Townsite. Right on the river. Come early for choice spots. 56 sites and 10 walk-in tent sites, dry toilets. Open mid-May to late Sept. $10. ❶

Whistlers, on Whistlers Rd., 3km south of the townsite off Hwy. 93. This 781-site behemoth is the closest campground to Jasper Townsite and has all the amenities. Public phones, dump station. Wheelchair accessible. Open early May to mid-Oct. Sites $15; full RV sites $24. Free showers. ❶

Wapiti, on Hwy. 93, 3.8km south of Whistlers, along the Athabasca River. Plentiful brush separates tenters from RVers. Pay phone, sani-dump, and electric RV site. Wheelchair accessible. Mid-June to early Sept.: 362 sites, $15-18. Oct.-early May: 91 sites, $13-15. Coin showers. ❶

Columbia Icefield, 109km south of the townsite. Lies close enough to the Athabasca Glacier to intercept an icy breeze and even a rare summer night's snowfall. Difficult and steep access road makes sites tents-only. Dry toilets and pay phones. Open mid-May to mid-Oct. 22 sites and 11 walk-ins. $10. ❶

🍴 FOOD

Food prices in Jasper range from the affordable to the outrageous. However, cheap options can be found and lots of places offer good lunch deals. **Super A Foods,** 601 Patricia St., satisfies basic grocery needs. (☎852-3200. Open daily 8am-10pm.) A larger selection and the bakery at **Robinson's IGA Foodliner,** 218 Connaught Dr., is worth the 5min. walk. (☎852-3195. Open summer daily 9am-9pm.) **Nutter's Bulk Foods,** 622 Patricia St., offers bulk snacks, vitamins, and fresh $5 sandwiches. (☎852-5844. Open daily 8am-11pm.)

ALBERTA

Mountain Foods and Cafe, 606 Connaught Dr. (☎852-4050). Offers a wide selection of sandwiches, salads, home-cooked goodies, and take-out lunches for the trail. Turkey focaccia sandwich and assorted wraps $7.50. Fantastic breakfast special for $5.50. Open daily 8am-6pm. ❷

Jasper Pizza Place, 402 Connaught Dr. (☎852-3225). Has both draft and bottle beer. Free delivery in Jasper area (min. order $5). Large wood-oven pizzas $9-13, sandwiches $3-8. Open daily 11am-midnight. ❷

Coco's Cafe, 608 Patricia St. (☎852-4550). A small, vegetarian-friendly cafe downtown. Homemade items include tasty soups, baked goods, and smoothies ($3.50). Breakfast wraps are served all day ($5.25). A variety of tasty sandwiches from $4.75. Open in summer daily 7am-8pm; winter 7am-6pm. ❶

Scoops and Loops, 504 Patricia St. (☎852-4333). Not just an ice-cream parlor. Sandwiches ($3-4), sushi ($3-7), *udon* ($8). Open M-Sa 10am-11pm, Su 11am-11pm. ❶

Soft Rock Cafe, 622 Connaught Dr. (☎852-5850). Internet access, but no trademark t-shirts. Baguette sandwiches $4.25-8. Breakfast all day: sizable omelette, homefries, and thick toast $8. Open summer daily 7am-11pm; winter 7am-7pm. ❷

⚠ OUTDOOR ACTIVITIES

HIKING

Jasper National Park offers excellent dayhiking. This means nature writ large and exotic wildlife that includes bears and bighorn sheep. Remember, it's illegal to feed wildlife. Short, aesthetically mind-boggling walks make the postcard-perfect scenery of the Canadian Rockies easily accessible. For more info, stop by the Information Centre for a copy of their "Summer Hiking" pamphlet and trail condition updates. As a supplement to hiking, check out **The Jasper Tramway** (☎852-3093), just past the hostel on Whistlers Rd., 4km south of the townsite on Hwy. 93. Climbing 973m up Whistlers Mountain, the tramway leads to a panoramic view of the park and, on clear days, far beyond it. From the upper station, you can join hikers on the Whistlers Trail for the last 200m elevation gain to the summit. ($19, ages 5-14 $9.50, under 5 free. Open daily Apr. 13-May 17 and Oct. 9:30am-4:30pm; May 18-June 25 and Sept. 9:30am-9pm; June 26-July 8:30am-10pm.) **Sun Dog Tours** (☎852-4056; fax 852-9663) offers a shuttle from town and tram ride to the top ($24).

Path of the Glacier Loop (1.6km, 45min.). The trailhead is 30km south of the townsite; take Hwy. 93 to 93A to the end of the bumpy, twisty, and quite often closed (see Mt. Edith Cavell Hostel) 15km Mt. Edith Cavell Rd. One of the 2 paths features **Mt. Edith Cavell,** the glacier-laden peak named after an English nurse executed by the Germans for providing aid to the Allies during World War I. An easy path leads to a rewarding view of a glacier receding into a lake littered with icebergs. Open June-Oct.; no trailers or vehicles over 6m long.

Cavell Meadows Loop (8km, 3-6hr.). Trailhead is same as Path of the Glacier Loop. A more strenuous ascent past the treeline and through a carpet of wildflowers (from mid-July to Aug.), with striking views of the towering north face and the Angel Glacier. Be careful to stay on the trail as steep cliffs make for dangerous slide conditions. 400m gain. Open June-Oct.; no trailers or vehicles over 6m long.

Sulphur Skyline Trail (9.6km round-trip, 4-6hr.). This challenging hike enables the hardy to summit a peak in a day and attain views of the limestone Miette Range and Ashlar Ridge. The trail leaves from the parking lot of the Miette Hot Springs. If you have lunch at the peak, guard it from the courageous golden-mantled ground squirrels. Beware afternoon thunderstorms and serious wind gusts at the peak. 700m gain.

Maligne Canyon (2.1km one-way, 1-2hr.). The spectacular, over-touristed Maligne Canyon (mah-LEEN) is 8km east of the townsite on the Maligne Lake Rd. The best way to view the Canyon is by parking at the 5th Bridge parking area, crossing the bridge, and bearing right at every possible opportunity. From the trailhead, the path follows the Maligne River as it plunges through a narrow and intricately sculpted limestone gorge. Be sure to make it all the way to the first Bridge for views of the ground-shaking, breathtaking upper waterfall—truly a must-see. Along the walk, look for springs pouring into the Canyon. The water flows underground from Medicine Lake, 15km away, making this the longest underground river in North America.

Whistlers Trail (7.9km one-way; 3-5hr. up, 2-3hr. down) is a strenuous hike beginning next to the Jasper International Hostel basketball court. Bring extra layers, as weather conditions change rapidly at the 2470m summit. Worth the effort; the summit features an incredible 360-degree view of mountain range after mountain range. 1200m gain.

MALIGNE LAKE

Maligne Lake, at the end of the road, is the longest (22km) and deepest (97m) lake in the park. A flotilla of water vessels allows escape from fellow tourists (except those who also rent a boat) and the plastic geraniums of Maligne Lake Chalet. **Maligne Tours,** 627 Patricia St. (☎852-3370), rents kayaks ($70 per day) and leads canoe trips ($15 per hr.) and narrated scenic cruises (90min.; $35, seniors $29.75, children $17.50). Free maps to hiking trails are available at the Maligne Tours office or by the lake; bookings for whitewater and sightseeing trips are available at the office. Perhaps the best way to see the Lake's scenery is to escape into the surrounding hills on foot. The **Opal Hills Trail** (8.2km round-trip, 4-6hr.), which starts at the northeast corner of the first parking area, winds through subalpine meadows and ascends 460m in only 3km to views of the lake. The truly strong of stamina and mammoth of calf muscle can follow one of the drainages away from the lake at the halfway point of the hike in the high, tundra valley. At the ridge overlooking the valley, follow the rough footpath (avoid trampling the delicate alpine tundra) that leads up to **Opal Peak,** the highest in the vicinity. Note that this is not a maintained trail, and the loose shale makes for dangerous hiking, but the champion of the mountain will be rewarded with a view hard to surpass in this or any region. **Shuttle service** from Jasper to the area is available from Maligne Tours. (To the canyon $8; to the lake $12; round-trip with cruise $56; 3-6 per day, 8:30am-5:30pm.)

BACKPACKING

An extensive network of trails weaves through the park's backwoods, providing respite from tourist-land. The trails cover three different ecological regions. The **montane zone,** which includes Jasper Townsite, blankets valley floors with lodgepole pine, Douglas fir, white spruce, and aspen; it hosts elk, bighorn sheep, and coyotes. Subalpine fir and Engelmann spruce share the **subalpine zone** with porcupines and marmots, while fragile plants and wildflowers struggle against mountain goats and pikas in the uppermost **alpine zone.** To avoid trampling endangered plant species, hikers should not stray from trails in the alpine area.

Kick off any foray into the wilderness with a visit to the visitors center in the townsite, where rangers distribute the free *Backcountry Visitors' Guide* and plentiful advice. Overnight hikers need to register and pay the $6 per night fee, either at the Visitor Centre or by calling ☎852-6177; many buy *The Canadian Rockies Trail Guide* ($15). Before hitting the trail, ask about road and trail closures, water levels (some rivers cannot be crossed at certain times of the year), and snow levels at high passes. The Icefield Centre (see p. 385), on Hwy. 93 at the southern entrance to the park, provides similar services.

Trails particularly worthy of recommendation include the **Skyline Trail** (45km, 3 days), **Maligne Pass** (48km, 3 days), **Tonquin Valley** (42km, 3 days), **Jonas Pass** (53km, 4 days), **Athabasca Pass** (51km one way, 7 days), **North Boundary Trail** (192 km, 10 days), and **South Boundary Trail** (176km, 10 days). Backpackers should know their skill level and recognize the dangers that accompany trips of these durations in such mountainous conditions.

HOT SPRINGS

The **Miette Hot Springs,** 42km north of the townsite on Hwy. 16 and 15km along Miette Hot Springs Rd., blends heat therapy with a panoramic view of the surrounding limestone mountains. Once a rudimentary log bath-house in 1913, the waters—the hottest in the Canadian Rockies—are now chlorinated, filtered, and cooled before they arrive in three outdoor swimming pools at temperatures ranging from 39-41°C or 6-22°C. The road to Miette is, sadly, closed in winter. (☎ 866-3939. Open early May to mid-Oct. daily 8:30am-10:30pm. $6, children and seniors $5. Mid-Oct to Apr. open 10:30am-9pm, $1 cheaper. Swimsuit $1.50, towel $1.25.)

SKIING

Winter brings 4m of snowfall and plenty of skiing opportunities to the slopes of **Marmot Basin,** 19km south of Jasper via Hwy. 93, 93A, and the Marmot Basin Rd. The upper half of the slope's 897m vertical drop is above the treeline, creating room for bowls and a modest snowboard park. (☎ 852-3816; www.skimarmot.com. Full-day lift ticket $49, 65 and over $35, ages 13-17 and students up to age 25 $41, ages 6-12 $20, under 6 free.) Bargain **ski rental** is available at **Totem's Ski Shop,** 408 Connaught Dr. (☎ 852-3078. Open winter daily 8am-6pm; summer 9:30am-10pm. Ski package $9-20; snowboard package and boots $25; cross country skis from $9 per day.) **The Sports Shop,** 406 Patricia St., offers the same hours and ski rental prices and rents ice skates as well as camping and fishing equipment. (☎ 852-3654. Skates $4 per hr., $10 per day.) Maligne Lake offers **cross-country ski trails** from late November through May. **Everest Outdoor Stores,** 414 Connaught Dr., also has ski rentals. (☎ 852-5902. Open daily 9:30am-10pm, winter 8am-6pm. Cross-country skis from $12 per day, downhill skis and boots $25-35 per day, snowshoes $10 per day.)

FISHING

The key to finding a secluded **fishing hole** in Jasper is to hike somewhere inaccessible to cars. **The Sports Shop** (see above) rents rod, reel, and line for $10, or a fly fishing rig for $20. **Currie's,** in the Sports Shop, offers one-day boat or canoe rental ($30; after 2pm $20, after 6pm $15. Pick-up and drop-off service or guided trips available; half-day $149, full-day $189.) **Permits** are available at fishing shops and the Park Information Center ($6 per week, $13 per year). Pick up a copy of the *Parks Canada Fishing Regulations Summary* to establish where, when, and how one may fish in the park.

OTHER OUTDOOR ACTIVITIES

Paul Valiulis teaches half-day ($59) and full-day ($89) **rock climbing** courses (☎ 852-4161; www.icpeaks.com). **Peter Amann** teaches 2-day introductory climbing classes for $150 as well as 2-3 day ice climbing classes for $220-300. (☎ 852-3237. May-June and Sept.) Both companies lead ice climbing and mountaineering trips. **Gravity Gear,** 618 Patricia St. (☎ 888-852-3155), has rentals for mountain adventures and offers multi-day discounts. **Rocky Mountain Unlimited,** 414 Connaught Dr., serves as a central reservation service for most local outdoor businesses. They provide prices and recommendations for rafting, fishing, horseback riding, wildlife safaris, and all your outdoor pursuits. (☎ 852-4056.

Open summer daily 8:30am-9pm; winter 9am-6pm.) **Whitewater** leads two trips on the Athabasca River and one on the faster Sunwapta River. (☎852-7238. 2-3½hr. From $43. Register by phone.) **Rocky Mountain River Guides,** 626 Patricia St., offers similar rides. (☎852-3777. 2-3hr. $40.) **Boat rentals** are available at **Pyramid Lake Resort,** 7km from town off Pyramid Ave. from Connaught Dr. (☎852-4900. Open daily 8am, last boat out at 8:30pm. Canoes $15, pedal boats $24 for 1hr., both $15 per additional hr.)

THE YUKON

> **YUKON TERRITORY'S... Drinking Age:** 19. **Capital:** Whitehorse. **Population:** 32,635. **Caribou Population:** 100,000. **Attempted Coups by the Under-represented Caribou Population:** 5. **Area:** 478,970 sq. km. **Bird:** Raven. **Flower:** Fireweed. **Holiday:** Discovery Day, on the third Monday in Aug. For **emergencies** outside the Whitehorse area, 911 may not work; call the local police detachment or ☎867-667-5555.

If you want to be alone with the land, the Yukon is where you ought to be. Yukon vistas cross glaciated, sawtooth mountain ranges and ease down into lakes, tundra, gigantic forests, and arid plateaus. And best of all for many travelers, the area is all but unpopulated. Glaciation left much of the Yukon untouched, creating an ice-free corridor for vegetation, wildlife, and early hunters. Although summer here is spectacular, Yukoners have been suffering payback for the ancient fair weather ever since, enduring what's often described as "nine months of winter and three months of bad snowmobiling." Fur traders in the 1800s came looking for faster routes and new partners. The gold seekers of 1898 came charging to Carcross from Skagway, then down the Yukon River to Whitehorse, Dawson City, and the goldfields beyond. A second territorial rush occurred during the construction of the Alaska Highway. These days, logging, mining, and the federal government support the region's economy. Yukon First Nations are presently negotiating with the federal government for land, self-government, and funding for innovative projects to rebuild their communities. But the human footprint on the land evaporates meters away from any Yukon road, and the highway system is but a tiny skeleton laid over a huge area. It's an intimidating area, but one that demands exploration.

▣THE YUKON TERRITORY'S HIGHLIGHTS

JAM with musicians at the **Dawson City Music Festival** (see p. 414).

DIP your toes in the Arctic Ocean after driving up the **Dempster Hwy.** (see p. 416).

FLY over **Kluane National Park** (see p. 404) to enjoy all its splendor.

RETRACE prospectors' foot steps on the **Chilkoot Trail** (see p. 404).

BASK under the **aurora borealis** in the winter (see p. 401), and the **midnight sun** in the summer.

WHITEHORSE ☎867

Whitehorse was born during the Klondike Gold Rush, when the gold-hungry used it as a layover on their journey north. Miners en route to Dawson coined the name, claiming that whitecaps on the rapids downstream resembled galloping white stallions. With a population of 24,000, Whitehorse is home to 70% of the territory's population. The capital of the Yukon shifted from Dawson to here in 1953, and now the majority of government employees call Whitehorse home. The town itself is clogged with acres of RVs during the summer, and an adventure traveler's best bet is to head on out into the surrounding wilds—the drone of city life disappears just a kilometer or two outside city limits.

Yukon Territory

TRANSPORTATION

Whitehorse lies 1500km northwest of Dawson Creek, BC, along the **Alaska Hwy.** (see p. 356), and 535km south of Dawson City. The city is an oblong grid of numbered avenues running north-south and streets running east-west.

Flights: The **airport** is off the Alaska Hwy., southwest of downtown. **Air Canada** (☎888-247-2262 or 668-4466) flies to **Calgary** and **Edmonton, AB** via **Vancouver, BC** (3 per day; prices fluctuate between $400 and $1100, so call ahead). Expect to pay through the roof for short-notice flights, especially in the summer.

Buses: The bus station is on the northeast edge of town. **Greyhound,** 2191 2nd Ave. (☎667-2223; www.greyhound.ca), runs to: **Dawson Creek, BC** (18hr., $187) and **Vancouver, BC** (41hr., $340). A **Dawson City** route (5hr.) is run by **Dawson City Courier** (☎393-3334; open M-F 8am-5pm, Sa 4-8am). No service to AK. Buses run daily from late June to early Sept.; rest of year M, W, and F departures. **Alaska Direct,** 509 Main St. (☎668-4833 or 800-770-6652), runs to: **Anchorage, AK** (15hr., 3 per week, $165); **Fairbanks, AK** (13hr., 3 per week, $140); and **Skagway, AK** (3hr.; reservation only; M, Th, and F; $50). In winter, 1 bus per week to above destinations.

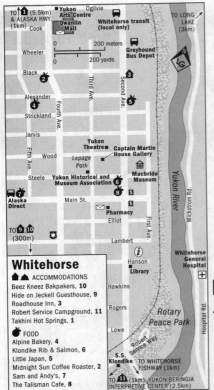

Whitehorse

▲■ ▲▲ ACCOMMODATIONS
Beez Kneez Bakpakers, 10
Hide on Jeckell Guesthouse, 9
Roadhouse Inn, 3
Robert Service Campground, 11
Takhini Hot Springs, 1

🍎 FOOD
Alpine Bakery, 4
Klondike Rib & Salmon, 6
Little Japan, 5
Midnight Sun Coffee Roaster, 2
Sam and Andy's, 7
The Talisman Cafe, 8

Public Transportation: Whitehorse Transit (☎668-7433). Limited service to downtown, the airport, Robert Service campground, and Yukon College. Buses arrive and depart next to the Canadian Tire on Ogilvie St. $1.50. Runs M-Th 6:15am-7:30pm, F 6:15am-10:30pm, Sa 8am-7pm.

Taxis: Yellow Cab (☎668-4811) or **Global Taxi** (☎633-5300). Both 24hr.

Car Rental: Norcan Leasing, Ltd., 213 Range Rd. (☎668-2137; from western Canada 800-661-0445; from AK 800-764-1234; www.norcan.yk.ca). Cars from $50 per day, winter prices lower, $0.25 per km after 100km per day. Must be 21+ with credit card.

Auto Repair: Petro Canada, 4211 4th Ave. (☎667-4003 or 667-4366). Full service. Oil and lube approx. $45. Open daily 7am-10pm; gas pumps open 24hr.

🛈 PRACTICAL INFORMATION

TOURIST, LOCAL, AND FINANCIAL SERVICES

Tourist Information: 100 Hanson St. (☎667-3084) off 1st Ave., in the Tourism and Business Centre at 2nd Ave. Free 15min. film every ½hr. daily. English, German, French, and Dutch spoken. Open mid-May to mid-Sept. daily 8am-8pm; winter M-F 9am-5pm.

Outdoor Information: Yukon Conservation Society, 302 Hawkins St. (☎668-5678; www.yukonconservation.org), offers maps and great ideas for area hikes along with titles such as *The Yukon Hiking Guide* ($20). Open M-F 10am-2pm.

Equipment Rental: Several upscale equipment shops line Main St. between 2nd and 3rd Ave. **Kanoe People** (☎668-4899), at Strickland and 1st Ave., rents mountain bikes ($15 per half-day), canoes ($25 per day, $150 per week), and kayaks (plastic $35 per day, fiberglass $45). Pick-up 20km downstream $30. Open daily 9am-6pm.

Bank: Bank of Montreal (☎668-4200) or **CIBC** (☎667-2534), at the corner of Main St. and 2nd Ave. **24hr. ATM.**

Bookstore: Mac's Fireweed Bookstore, 203 Main St. (☎668-2434). Open daily 8am-midnight. Used books, CDs, and videos across from library at **Zack's New & Used Books,** 2nd Ave. and Hawkins (☎393-2614). Open M-Sa 11am-6pm.

Market: Extra Foods, 4th Ave. and Ogilvie St. (☎667-6251), in the Qwanlin Mall. Open M-W and Sa 8:30am-7pm, Th-F 8:30am-9pm, Su 10am-6pm.

Laundromat: Public Laundromat at Family Motel, 314 Ray St. (☎668-5558), at 4th Ave. next to Qwanlin Mall. Wash $2, dry $0.25 per 5min.

Public Pool: Whitehorse Lions Pool, 4051 4th Ave. (☎668-7665), next to the High Country Inn. $4.50, seniors and children $2, students $3.50. Call for swim times.

EMERGENCY AND COMMUNICATION

Emergency: ☎911.

Police: 4100 4th Ave. (☎667-5555). 24hr.

24hr. Refuge: Tim Horton's, 2210 2nd Ave. (☎668-7788), at the far northern end of downtown, 1 block from river.

Pharmacy: Shoppers Drug Mart, 211 Main St. (☎667-2485). Open M-F 9am-9pm, Sa 9am-6pm, Su 10am-6pm.

Hospital: Whitehorse General (☎393-8700) is the big green building across the river from downtown on Hospital Rd., just off Wickstrom Rd.

Internet Access: Library, 2071 2nd Ave. (☎667-5239), at Hanson. Free 30min. Internet access twice daily; reserve in advance or stop in for first-come, first-served 15min. of access. Open M-F 10am-9pm, Sa 10am-6pm, Su 1-9pm. **Wired Cabin,** 402 Hawkins (☎250-309-1225), at 4th Ave. $2 per 10min. or $5 per hr. Also scanning, CD burning, and color copies. Open daily 8am-midnight.

Post Office: General services, 211 Main St. (☎667-2485), in the basement of **Shopper's Drug Mart.** Open M-F 9am-6pm, Sa 11am-4pm. Also in **Qwanlin Mall** (☎667-2858) at 4th Ave. and Ogilvie St., in **Coffee, Tea and Spice.** Open M-Th and Sa 9:30am-6pm, F 9:30am-8pm. **General delivery** at 300 Range Rd. (☎667-2412). **Postal Code** for last names beginning with the letters A-L is Y1A 3S7; for M-Z it's Y1A 3S8. Open 10am-1:40pm and 2:15-4:45pm.

▐▐▝ ACCOMMODATIONS AND CAMPING

Interchangeable motels around town charge upwards of $70, but fear not; the hostel and campground options are superb.

▨ **Hide on Jeckell Guesthouse,** 410 Jeckell (☎633-4933), between 4th Ave. and 5th Ave., 1 block from Robert Service Way. Stay in the continent-themed room of your choice and pick your endangered species-labeled bed. Amenities include coffee, kitchen, bikes, Internet, local calls, linens, lockers, and BBQ night. No curfew. 22 beds, 6 rooms. $20. 10% discount for cyclists, 20% for tandem. ❷

Beez Kneez Bakpakers Hostel, 408 Hoge St. (☎456-2333), off 4th Ave., 2 blocks from Robert Service Way. Weary backpackers find refuge in this hostel equipped with Internet, BBQ deck, washer ($2) and dryer ($2). 8 bunks, $20 each. Private rooms $50. ❷

Robert Service Campground (☎668-3721), 1km from town on Robert Service Way along the Yukon River. A home for university students who tan on the lawn and gear up for the outdoors. Food trailer, firewood ($2), drinking water. Gates open 7am-midnight. Open late May to early Sept. 68 sites. $14 per tent. Showers $1 per 5min. ❶

Takhini Hot Springs (☎633-2706). Follow the Alaska Hwy. northwest from downtown about 10km, turn right on North Klondike Hwy., and left after 6.5km onto Takhini Hot Springs Rd. Drive 10km to the end for tent camping and thermal relief. Separate $4-5.50 admission charge for daily pool use in winter or summer. Restaurant, horseback riding ($20 per hr.). Pools open May-Sept. daily 10am-10pm. 88 sites. $12.50, with electricity $15. Showers. ❶

Roadhouse Inn, 2163 2nd. Ave. (☎667-2594), at Black St. An affordable downtown alternative to pricier tourist havens. Rooms are straightforward and simple; the saloon next door keeps the taps flowing until 2am. Phones and private bathrooms. Motel units start at $45 for singles; from $50 for doubles. Hotel units with cable TV $10 more. ❹

🏠 🎵 FOOD AND ENTERTAINMENT

While Whitehorse gives the impression of catering only to the fast food-craving Alaska Hwy. driver, hip musicians and tourists hungering for the frontier will find good grub, too. An excellent selection of top-quality fruits and veggies can be found at **The Fruit Stand**, at 2nd Ave. and Black St. (☎ 393-3994. Open in summer M-Sa 10:30am-7pm.) **Alpine Bakery**, 411 Alexander St., between 4th and 5th Ave., turns out exquisite bread. (☎ 668-6871. Open M-Sa 8am-6pm; winter closed M.) Those looking for bars can choose from a wide variety on Main Street. Most have nightly live music, and the scene varies from 20-year-old pop fans at **Lizard Lounge** to classic rock at the **Roadhouse Saloon** to Canadian rock at **Capitol Hotel**.

■ **The Talisman Cafe**, 2112 2nd Ave. (☎ 667-2736). Decorated with local First Nations and local art. Vegetarians, ethnic food lovers, and carnivores will all leave happy and full. Serves heaps of fresh food ranging from Mexican to Middle Eastern for $10-14. Open daily 9am-8pm. ❸

■ **Klondike Rib and Salmon Barbecue**, 2116 2nd Ave. (☎ 667-7554). In an old wall-tent structure, these down-home folks will call you "sweetie" and serve you friendly-like. Worth its weight in (Yukon) gold, the rich salmon-dip lunch ($13) comes with a big ole hunk of homemade bread. The dinner menu is pricey. Open May to Sept. M-F 11:30am-9pm, Sa-Su 5-9pm. ❸

Sam and Andy's, 506 Main St. (☎ 668-6994), between 5th and 6th. Tex-Mex on a jumpin' patio. Generous build-your-own fajitas are mid-range entrees ($13). You can save money by ordering the veggie version. Thrifty Thursdays mean $1 drafts, $2 pints. Open M-Sa 11am-11pm, Su 11am-10pm. ❷

Midnight Sun Coffee Roaster, 4168 4th Ave. (☎ 633-4563). Offers every coffee drink under the sun ($3-8) to sip among stained-glass art in comfy chairs or in funky outdoor booths. Internet $3 for 30min., $5 per hr. Open M-F 7am-10pm, later on weekends. ❷

Little Japan, 2157 2nd Ave. (☎ 668-6620). Offers affordable sushi (five salmon rolls $6.50) and western fare for the squeamish (small $15 "Meatzza" pizzas are not that small). Open M-F 6:30am-9pm, Sa-Su 11am-9pm. ❷

🅢 SIGHTS

YUKON BERINGIA INTERPRETIVE CENTRE. Huge woolly mammoths, saber-toothed tigers, and other reconstructed Ice Age critters make you realize how rough the north's first settlers had it. Even the bears were bigger back then—see for yourself. (*On the Alaska Hwy., 2km northwest of the Robert Service Way junction.* ☎ 667-8855; www.beringia.com. *Open mid-May to June, and Sept. daily 9am-6pm; July-Aug. daily 8:30am-7pm; winter Su 1-5pm and by appointment. $6, seniors $5, students $4.*)

WHITEHORSE FISHWAY. If you think you're a weary traveler, meet the chinook salmon who swim 27,740km upstream before reaching the fish ladder—designed to save them from death by dam. You're most likely to see them climbing the 370m ladder from late July through August. (*2.4km from town, over the bridge by the S.S. Klondike.* ☎ 633-5965. *Open June W-Su 10am-6pm. Open early July to early Sept. daily 8:30am-9pm. Wheelchair accessible. Admission by donation.*)

VISUAL ARTS. Government patronage and an inspired population make Whitehorse a northern epicenter of the arts. The Yukon Government's **permanent collection** is housed throughout the administrative and public spaces of the capital. (☎ 667-5264.) Pick up a free **ArtWalk** brochure at the **visitors center**, or at the nonprofit, Yukon-artwork-adorned **Captain Martin House Gallery**. (*305 Wood St.* ☎ 667-4080. *Open* *summer M-F 10am-8pm, Sa 10am-5pm, Su noon-5pm; winter M-Sa 11am-5pm; closed Jan.)* The Yukon's only public art museum, the **Yukon Arts Centre Art Gallery,** typically shows Canadian contemporary art every 6-10 weeks. *(300 College Drive, Yukon College. ☎ 667-8578. Open June-Aug. M-F 11am-5pm, Sa-Su noon-5pm; Sept.-May Tu-F 11am-5pm, Sa-Su 1-4pm. Adult $3, students and seniors $2, children under 12 free. Su free.)*

EVENTS. Two Whitehorse festivals draw crowds from all over the world: the **Yukon International Storytelling Festival** *(☎ 633-7550),* to be held May 30-June 2 2003, and the **Frostbite Music Festival** *(☎ 668-4921),* in February. The **Commissioner's Potlatch** gathers indigenous groups and visitors in June for traditional dancing, games, artistry, and a feast. Locals, transients, and native artists perform for free at noon with **Arts in Lepage Park** on weekdays. *(At Wood St. and 3rd Ave. ☎ 668-3136. From June to mid-Aug.)* Call the **Yukon Arts Centre Theatre** for stage updates. *(☎ 667-8574; www.yukonartscentre.org.)* The **Yukon River** hosts the popular **Rubber Duckie Race** on Canada Day, July 1. *(☎ 668-7979. $5 per duck. Proceeds go to charity.)*

OUTDOOR ACTIVITIES

HIKING. There seem to be more trails than people around Whitehorse. Seasoned hikers can simply wander (respecting the bear population, of course). **Kluane National Park** (see p. 404) beckons from the west, but there is plenty of accessible dayhiking near town. *Whitehorse Area Hikes and Bikes* ($19), published by the **Yukon Conservation Society,** and the *Whitehorse Area Hikes* map ($10) are both available at Mac's Fireweed Books (see **Practical Information,** p. 396). Discover where to spot a golden eagle or the boreal birds with the aid of the **Yukon Bird Club** *(☎ 667-4630)* or take an easy-paced, free birding trip into the wetlands during the summer.

Grey Mountain. Take Lewes Blvd. across the bridge by the S.S. Klondike, then take a left on Alsek Ave. Turn left again at the Grey Mt. Cemetery sign and follow the gravel road to its end. Partially accessible by gravel road, Grey Mountain is a fairly vigorous dayhike. Moderate to difficult.

Miles Canyon Trail Network. Take Lewes Blvd. to Nisutlin Dr. and turn right; just before the fish ladder, turn left onto the gravel Chadbum Lake Rd. and continue 4km up to the parking area. The Network parallels the Yukon River and is frequented by joggers, bikers, and cross-country skiers alike. The Conservation Society leads free hikes daily July-Aug. Schedule available at office. (Open M-F 10am-2pm). Easy to moderate.

Lookout Hill. Go down to the Whitehorse Fishway on Nisultin Dr.; the trailhead is across from the fishway's information building. This short 1.5km trail takes you to an outstanding lookout over Schwatka Lake and surrounding mountains. Easy.

WATER. The **M.V. Schwatka,** on Miles Canyon Rd. off Robert Service Way, floats folks on a relaxing, historical ride through Miles Canyon. *(☎ 668-4716. 2hr. cruises. 2pm daily from June to early Sept. 7pm tour added in July. $21, ages 2-10 $10.50, under 2 free. Wheelchair accessible.)* **Up North Boat and Canoe Rentals,** 103 Strickland St., lets you paddle 25km to Takhini River or take a longer trip. *(☎ 667-7035; www.upnorth.yk.ca. 4hr. $30 each for 2 or $60 solo, including transportation.)* An 8-day trip on the Teslin River costs $200, but you can rent sea kayaks and canoes by the day ($30-35). The waterways around **Sanfu Lake** (1½hr. south of Whitehorse on Atlin Rd.) are ideal for kayaking among tiny islands. **Tatshenshini Expediting,** 1602 Alder St., leads intense whitewater rides. (Take the Alaska Hwy. north 2km, turn left on Birch, and left again on 15th St., which becomes Alder. ☎ 633-2742. Full day $115.)

JUSTICE TO GO, TRIBAL STYLE As in many remote regions, law in the Yukon is administered with a long arm. While Whitehorse is the seat of the territorial government, the work of frontier justice is carried out on the frontier: once a week a judge, a clerk, and a recorder climb into a single-engine plane and depart for outlying towns, where a prosecuting and defending attorney will meet them, themselves arriving by car in long, cross-country odysseys between clients. Court is then set up in community centers and recreation halls. This system has evolved in recent years from a transplanted version of a courthouse's formal proceedings to a truer reflection of the traditions of the mostly indigenous communities it serves. Increasingly, elements of traditional justice are changing how community members are punished: friends and family are in more and more cases invited to sit down in a "sentencing circle," in which everyone has a say in how the criminal can be cared for and reintegrated into society. The circle has done amazing work, greatly reducing recidivism, and creating a team-building attitude in the makeshift halls of justice.

WINTER. In winter, the Whitehorse area is criss-crossed by 300km of groomed and ungroomed **snowmobile trails. Up North Boat and Canoe Rentals** (see above) rents snowmobiles and skis. Whitehorse is also a **cross-country skiing** paradise. The **Whitehorse Cross Country Ski Club,** beside Mt. McIntyre, off Hamilton Blvd. near the intersection of Two Mile Hill and the Alaska Hwy., grooms 50km of world-class trails; 5km of trails are lit at night. Club facilities include saunas and showers. (☎668-4477. Day passes $9, under 19 $4; 3 days $22; 5 days $35.) In February, "the toughest race in the world," the **Yukon Quest 1000 Mile International Sled Dog Race** (☎668-4711), follows gold rush routes between Whitehorse and Fairbanks.

THE ALASKA HWY.: BC BORDER TO WHITEHORSE

WATSON LAKE ☎867

Switchbacking between the Yukon and British Columbia, the Alaska Hwy. (see p. 356) winds through tracts of young forest that stretch in all directions. Just after it crosses into the Yukon for the second time, at km 1021, the highway runs through **Watson Lake,** site of the zany **Sign Post Forest.** In the 1940s, a homesick WWII Army G.I. posted the mileage from Watson to his hometown of Danville, Illinois. The 50,000 signs that subsequent travelers put up make this site a gigantic, mind-boggling oddity than should not be missed. Find the distance to your hometown buried somewhere in the wacky forest. The **visitors center** is hidden inside this forest of signs, along the Robert Campbell Hwy. (☎536-7469. Open May-Sept. daily 8am-8pm.) If finding the distance to your hometown fails to smother your homesickness, email your pals for free on one of the computers at the new **library,** in the town office on Adela Trail. (☎536-7517. Open Tu-F 10am-8pm, Sa noon-6pm.)

Scan for mountain bluebirds on **Wye Lake** from the 3km boardwalk trail running from the Town Center to **Wye Lake Park.** Watson Lake also lures passers-by with the **Northern Lights Centre** opposite the visitors center, which dispenses scientific and cultural explanations for the aurora borealis. (☎867-536-7827; www.watsonlake.net. Call ahead for hours. 50min. shows 6 times daily. $10; seniors and students $9; children $6. Exhibits free.)

The **Liard Canyon Recreation Site** on **Lucky Lake,** 8km before town, makes for great picnicking and swimming. A 2km trail down the canyon is a relaxing and scenic stroll. Accommodations in Watson Lake are plentiful but pricey. A budget

THE YUKON

BRIGHT LIGHTS, NO CITY Many travelers come to Alaska to get away from all the bright lights and noise of the big city, only to find themselves falling under the spell of the most awesome of natural light shows: the aurora borealis (northern lights). Some bands of Native Americans believed these Christmas-colored clouds and arcs were the torches of spirits, lighting the way to heaven for those who had died a voluntary or violent death. Scientists, however, point the finger at violent solar flares which hit the earth, sweeping streams of electrically charged particles into the atmosphere. As the earth's magnetic field deflects these particles away from the Equator and up toward the poles, the particles enter the atmosphere and begin to glow. Oxygen atoms create either the brilliant yellow-green, or if higher in the atmosphere, a burning red. Ionized nitrogen particles cast a blue hue, while neutral nitrogen creates a cloud of purplish-red. But such scientific mumbo-jumbo can't detract from the supernatural mystery of the northern lights. A few onlookers claim to be able to even *hear* the lights overhead, although no scientist has yet to record these sounds or come up with an explanation. Some Inuit tribes interpreted these noises as the whisperings of the spirits. So prick up your ears as you next stare skyward, and you may discover that no matter how far away you think you've gotten from civilization, there might still be someone to spoil your quiet.

traveler's best bet is the **Watson Lake Campground ❶,** 3km west of town along the highway and then 4km down a well-marked gravel road, with primitive private sites ideal for tenting. ($8 camping permit only.) Campers can swim on the lake and hike several trails of varying difficulty. If you continue out of Watson Lake 21km northwest, you'll find accommodations at the **Cassiar Hwy.** junction. Dining options in town are restricted to highway fare. The **Pizza Place ❸,** at the **Gateway Motor Inn,** is a somewhat pricey gem. Medium specialty pies start at $15, but ambitious eaters go right for the $22 "Yukoner," loaded with all manner of meats and vegetables. For the tighter budget, meals from the grill range from $6.50 to $9. (☎536-7722. Open daily 6:30am-10pm.) **Groceries** and an **ATM** can be had at **Tags Foods,** by the visitors center. (☎536-7422. Open daily 6am-midnight.) Gas pumps and convenience store open 24hr. CIBC Banking Center (☎536-7495) in the shopping center on the east side of the visitors center has a **24hr. ATM.** Next door is the **post office.** (Open M-F 8:30am-5:30pm, Sa 8:30am-12:30pm.) **Postal Code:** Y0A 1C0.

Hardcore travelers **fish** for dinner. In mid-summer, grayling swim in the back eddies of tiny streams west along the Alaska Hwy., and both **Lucky Lake** (5½km east of town) and **Hour Lake** (at the east end of town behind the RCMP) are full of rainbow trout. Check in at the visitors center to purchase the appropriate permits.

Here at Watson Lake, the **Campbell Hwy.** (Hwy. 4) begins an alternate route into the Yukon Territory toward Whitehorse via Ross River and Johnson's Crossing, or to Dawson City via Ross River, Little Salmon, and Carmacks. For coverage of this wonderful side track, see p. 414. Km 1043 (or Mile 649) marks the Alaska Hwy.'s junction with the **Cassiar Hwy** (Hwy. 37; see p. 349), which leads south to the **Yellowhead Hwy.** (Hwy. 16; see p. 331). For coverage of this junction, see p. 356.

TESLIN LAKE   ☎867

About 260km west of Watson Lake, the **Dawson Peaks Resort** on **Teslin Lake** dishes up delectable burgers in its restaurant ($7) and offers a number of accommodation choices. (☎390-2244. Open daily 7:30am-10pm. Showers $2. Toilets, firewood, water. Sites $10; full RV sites $18; canvas tent platforms $35; private cabins $82.) The friendly hosts lead **river runs,** (4-5 days, $400) organize guided **fishing charters,** ($50 per hr.) and rent canoes ($8 per hr.) and powerboats ($25 per hr.).

The Alaska Highway

Teslin, 11km west of the resort, tells its story at the duly acclaimed **George Johnston Museum,** on the Alaska Hwy. at the west end of town. Born in Alaska in 1889, George Johnston was a Tlingit man who ran a trap line and a general store while experimenting with photography on the side. Johnston left a series of stunning photographs documenting Tlingit life in Teslin from 1910 to 1940. The museum also displays a moose skin boat, Teslin's first automobile (bought by Johnston when the town was roadless), and an excellent video about the Alaska Hwy.'s effect on native culture. (☎390-2550. Open daily mid-May to early Sept. 9:30am-5:30pm. $4, students and seniors $3.50, children 6-15 $2, families $10. Wheelchair accessible.) RV travelers bond over food and the free house boat rides at **Muklak Annie's ❹,** 7km east of Teslin. There's nothing miniature about a mini-salmon plate ($15) or kids' portion ($9), but the big-eaters can pay $19 for loads of salmon, all-you-can-eat salad, fresh rolls, coffee, and dessert. Ribs, pork chops, and burgers are also served on the checked cloths in the gift shop decor dining hall. (☎667-1200. Open daily 7am-9pm. Free campsite, house boat ride, RV wash, dump station, and water fill-up with meal. Showers $4, cabins with shared bath $40, motel $50.) From Teslin, the 183km (2hr.) drive to Whitehorse is interspersed with a few **gas stops** and **provincial campgrounds**.

CARCROSS
☎867

Carcross, shortened from "Caribou Crossing," perches on the narrows between Bennett and Nares Lakes, surrounded by snow-capped peaks and pristine waterways. At the turn of the century, Carcross served as a link in the gold seekers' treacherous route between Skagway and the Yukon River, and during the 1940s Carcross was a supply depot for the construction of the Alaska Hwy. But the heyday passed decades ago, and recent years have roughed the town up quite a bit. The few shops in town now cater to tour buses from the Skagway cruise ships, and the best attractions are outside the town, in the nearby wildlands.

🖂🖻 TRANSPORTATION AND PRACTICAL INFORMATION. Carcross lies 74km south of Whitehorse, YT, and 106km north of Skagway, AK, on the **Klondike Hwy.** (Hwy. 2). Turn right off the highway into town. **Atlin Express Buses** (☎250-651-7575) run to **Atlin, BC** (2hr.; $23, seniors $20, ages 5-11 $11.50, under 5 free) and **Whitehorse** (1¼hr.; $17, seniors $15, ages 5-11 $8.50, under 5 free). **Tourist information** and daily highway or weather reports are available inside the depot. (☎821-4431. Open daily mid-May to mid-Sept. 8am-8pm.) **Montana Services,** in the Shell Station on Hwy. 2, has **laundry, public showers,** and the only **ATM** in town. (☎821-3708. Open daily 7am-11pm, winter 8am-8pm. Wash $2.25, dry $0.25 per 4min. Shower $3.) A **health station** (☎821-4444) is inside the two-story red building behind the Caribou Hotel. For an **ambulance,** call ☎821-3333; for the **police,** call ☎821-5555 or 667-5555. The **library** on Tagish St. has free **Internet access.** (☎821-3801. Open summer M-Th noon-4:30pm.) The **post office,** with a free paperback exchange, is in the red-trimmed white building on Bennett Ave. (☎821-4503. Open M, W, and F 8am-noon and 2:30-4pm, Tu and Th 10-11:45am.) **Postal Code:** Y0B 1B0.

🏠🛏 ACCOMMODATIONS AND FOOD. The Yukon Government maintains 14 **campsites ❶** by the airstrip across Hwy. 2 from the Shell station with potable water, firewood, and pit toilets. (Requires an $8 Yukon government camping permit.) **Spirit Lake Wilderness Resort ❶,** 10km north of town on Hwy. 2, has lakeside accommodations and rents canoes for $8 per hour. (☎821-4337. Toilets, coin laundry. Tent sites $14, with power $20; cabins on the jade-colored lake $72 for 1-2 people, $81 for 3-4 people. Free showers.) If you don't mind parking lots, stay at **Montana Services ❶,** which offers RV hook-ups ($12) and car tent sites ($7).

THE CHILKOOT TRAIL A valuable coastal trade route protected by the Tagish and Tlingit for thousands of years, the Chilkoot Trail bore the great torrent of gold-seekers hungering for the Yukon interior in the late 1890s. First led by native packers and later accompanied by hordes of their fellow stampeders, north-country novices slogged back and forth 33 mi. between Skagway, Dyea, and Lake Bennett, transporting 1000 pounds of provisions each to satisfy Canadian officials that they were prepared for the country ahead. Hikers take to the trail today for a rigorous 3-5 dayhike past the horse skeletons and gold-rush relics that still litter the precipitous pass. The trail departs from the coast and travels through a dramatic variety of climate, terrain, and vegetation, both above and below the timberline, before descending into the forests of northern British Columbia within reach of Lake Bennett and Carcross. For more hike info, see p. 466.

Just up the road from the Spirit Lake Resort (9km north of town), the **Cinnamon Cache ❶** is a gem among Dall sheep and bluebirds. Homemade cinnamon buns, survival cookies for the trail (both $2.50), hot pies, and soup and sandwiches make tummies happy. (☎821-4331. Open Feb.-Sept. daily 7am-7pm.) Another choice is the small **Koolsen Place ❷**. Watch the river wash by and munch on one of the few items on the menu. (Open daily 10am-7pm.)

⚠ OUTDOOR ACTIVITIES. Legendary big-game guide Johnny Johns led countless trips out of the Carcross area in the direction of the Yukon Mountains, the Upper Rockies, and the Coastal Range, which are all visible from town. While outfitting companies such as his no longer operate, hiking in the Carcross area garners justifiable acclaim. Pick up a copy of *Whitehorse Area Hikes and Bikes* at the visitors center or in Whitehorse before setting out. The most popular hike in the area is the **Chilkoot Trail** (see p. 466), a moderately difficult 3-5 day adventure beginning at Skagway and ending at the far end of Lake Bennett. The lake's two sandy beaches are understandably popular with locals in July and August. Overlooking the town, **rough mining roads** snake around Montana Mountain. To access them, follow Hwy. 2 south and take the first right after crossing the bridge. Take the first left and drive until you reach the washout. From there, it's all on foot to astounding views. (Round-trip 21km, 8hr. including drive; 1000 ft. gain.) The adventurous can play in the sand of an exposed glacial lake bottom in the world's smallest desert, **Carcross Desert,** 3km north of town on the highway.

KLUANE NATIONAL PARK   ☎867

AT A GLANCE	
AREA: 22000 sq. km	**GATEWAYS:** Haines Junction, Klukshu.
CLIMATE: Cool and dry; often extreme cold in winter.	**CAMPING:** No limit on length of stay.
FEATURES: Mt. Logan (Canada's highest peak), Kathleen Lake.	**FEES AND RESERVATIONS:** Wilderness permit $5 per day. Fishing permit $5 per day.

Dizzyingly massive glaciers spill off of huge mountains and keep going for dozens of kilometers, wedging into the surrounding forests like waves of cold crystal. Lakes thick with fish ("Kluane" means "place of many fish" in the Southern Tutchone language) speckle unbroken tracts of raw forest wilderness, and bears mingle with Dall Sheep beneath soaring eagles. Kluane doesn't shy from natural spectacle.

Kluane National Park

---- Seasonal Road
--- Maintained Trail
·-·- Unmaintained Trail

Together with Glacier National Park, the adjacent Wrangell-St. Elias National Park in Alaska (see p. 484), and Tatshenshini/Alsek Provincial Park in BC, Kluane is part of one of the world's largest protected wilderness areas. Canada's massive mountain range, the St. Elias Mountains, divides into two separate ranges within the park. The smaller Kluane Range runs right along the Alaska Hwy. (p. 356). The soaring giants of the Icefield Range, including Canada's highest peak, Mt. Logan (5959m), and the most massive non-polar ice fields in the world are separated from the Kluane range by the Duke Depression. The ice-blanketed mountains of Kluane's interior are a haven for experienced expeditioners, but their remoteness renders two-thirds of the park inaccessible (except by plane) to humbler hikers. Fortunately, the northeastern section of the park (bordering the Alaska Hwy.) offers splendid, easily accessible backpacking, rafting, biking, fishing, and dayhiking. Many routes follow original Southern Tutchone and Tlingit trails and old mining roads left over from Kluane's brief and disappointing fling with the gold rush in 1904-05. Most ventures into Kluane begin from **Haines Junction.**

ORIENTATION AND PRACTICAL INFORMATION

Kluane's 22,015 sq. km are bounded by the **Kluane Game Sanctuary** and the **Alaska Hwy.** (Hwy. 1; see p. 356) to the north, and the **Haines Hwy.** (Hwy. 3) to the east. **Haines Junction** (pop. 800), 158km west of Whitehorse at the park's eastern boundary, is the gateway to the park. There is also access to trails in the north of the park from **Sheep Mountain,** 72km northeast of Haines Junction on the Alaska Hwy.

Buses: Alaska Direct (☎800-770-6652, in Whitehorse ☎668-4833) runs a summer schedule from **Haines Junction** on Su, W, and F to **Anchorage, AK** (13hr., US$145); **Fairbanks, AK** (11hr., US$125); **Skagway, AK** (16hr., 12hr. overnight in Whitehorse, US$90, reservations required); and **Whitehorse, YT** (2hr., US$40).

Auto Repair: Source Motors Ltd. (☎634-2268), 1km north of Haines Junction on the Alaska Hwy. Does just about everything and offers 24hr. emergency road service. Open M-F 7am-9pm, Sa-Su 9am-9pm.

Tourist Information:

Kluane National Park Visitor Reception Centre (☎634-7207; www.parkscanada.gc.ca/kluane), on Logan St. in Haines Junction (Km 1635 on the Alaska Hwy.). Provides **wilderness permits** ($5 per night, $50 per season); **fishing permits** ($5 per day for non-Yukoners, $25 per season for Canadians, $35 for non-Canadians); **topographical maps** ($12); **trail and weather info,** and registers overnight visitors to the park. Open May-Sept. daily 9am-7pm; Oct.-Apr. M-F 10am-noon and 1-5pm.

Yukon Tourism (☎634-2345) gives information on activities inside and outside the park. Open mid-May to mid-Sept. daily 8am-8pm. Inquire about guided tours in late June and Aug.

Sheep Mountain Information Centre lies 72km north of town at Alaska Hwy. Km 1707. Registers hikers headed for the northern area of the park, sells hiking guides for $1, and rents bear canisters. Open daily May-Labour Day 9am-5pm. Overnight registrations until 4:30pm only.

Bank: Toronto Dominion (☎634-2820), in Madley's Store. Exchanges foreign currency and cashes traveler's checks. Open M-F 12:30-4:30pm. **ATM** available 8am-9pm daily.

Laundromat and Showers: Gateway Motel (☎634-2371), at the junction. Wash $2, dry $0.25 per 6 min. Shower $4. Open daily 8:30am-10pm. Comparable prices at **Kluane RV Kampground** (☎634-2709), north from the junction on the Alaska Hwy. 24hr. access to laundry and showers on the meter.

Emergency and Police: ☎634-5555; **no 911.**

Fire: ☎634-2222.

Ambulance/Health Clinic: ☎634-4444. Across from Madley's. Open M-F 9am-noon and 1-5pm.

Internet Access: Free at the **library** (☎634-2215), located next door to Madley's. Book ahead if possible. Open Tu-F 1-5pm and Sa 2-5pm. Better hours but a fee at **Village Bakery.** (☎634-2928). $3 per 30 min. Open in summer daily 7am-9pm.

Post Office: (☎634-3802), in Madley's. Open M-F 8:15am-noon and 1-5pm. **Postal Code:** Y0B 1L0.

ACCOMMODATIONS AND CAMPING

Camping by a gorgeous lakeside beats staying at a clean-but-forgettable highway motel or RV park any day (see also **Kluane Lake** below).

Stardust Motel, (☎634-2591), 1km north of town on the Alaska Hwy. The Stardust offers spacious rooms with satellite TV and private bath. No phones. Kitchenettes extra. Reservations recommended. Open mid-May to mid-Sept. Singles $55; doubles $65. ❸

Bear Creek Lodge (☎634-2301), 11km north of Haines Junction towards Sheep Mountain on the Alaska Hwy. Forgoing the location in town rewards visitors with cheaper rooms. Singles from $50 (without private bathrooms); doubles from $60. ❸ The Lodge also offers **camping** at bargain rates on simple sites. Sites $5 for 1 person, $10 for 2. RV sites $15. ❶

Pine Lake, 7km east of town on the Alaska Hwy. The closest government-run campground to Haines Junction and very popular. Features a sandy beach with a swim float, a pit for late-night bonfires, and a snazzy interpretive trail along the river. Water, firewood, pit toilets. $8 with Yukon camping permit only. ❶

Kathleen Lake Campground, National Park land off Haines Rd. 27km south of Haines Junction. The base for many of the area's hikes. Water (boil before drinking), toilets, fire pits, and firewood. Wheelchair accessible. Open mid-May to mid-Sept. 39 sites, $10. ❶

🍴 FOOD

Most Haines Junction restaurants offer standard highway cuisine. But the ■**Village Bakery** ❷ breaks the trend, offering fresh veggie dishes, beefy sandwiches, and tray upon tray of novel fudge and sweets. Substantial soups with bread ($3.50), sourdough cheese dogs ($2.25), sushi (on F only; $4.50 for 5 pieces), and espresso fudge ($1.75). Make reservations to enjoy live music and salmon-BBQs ($13.50) on Monday nights. (☎634-2867. Open daily May-Sept. 7am-9pm.) "We got it all"—the motto of **Madley's General Store**—is an understatement. Find star fruit, tackle, hardware, and a butcher block. (☎634-2200. Open May-Sept. daily 8am-9pm; Oct.-Apr. daily 8am-6:30pm.)

🎵 SIGHTS AND ENTERTAINMENT

Visit the **Kwaday Dan Kenji** traditional camp of the Champagne people, recently constructed with the help of local elders, and enjoy a mug of fresh brewed tea ($1.25). Kwaday Dan Kenji is a few minutes east of the village of Champagne, situated 70km west of Whitehorse and 88km east of Haines Junction on the Alaska Hwy. **Camping** ❶ facilities have pit toilets and fresh water, and there is a guided tour of the traditionally-made shelters and animal traps. (Shop with artifacts and local crafts open daily May-Oct. 9am-7:30pm. $10, children $6. Sites $10.)

Reserved little Haines Junction lets it all hang out in late June for back-to-back festivals. During the second weekend in June, music-loving rowdies from all over the area gather for "the function at the junction" to hear northern artists perform at the **Alsek Music Festival.** (☎634-2520; ask about the Kidzone for children.)

🥾 HIKING

Kluane's trails are varied and very accessible. The visitors centers are great sources for trail maps, information, and conditions. A $1 pamphlet lists about 25 trails and routes ranging from 500m to 96km. Routes, as opposed to trails, are not maintained, do not have marked paths, are more physically demanding, and require backcountry navigation skills. Overnight visitors must register and pay at one of the visitors centers ($5 per night for adults), and use bear-resistant food canisters, which the park rents for $5 per night (with $150 cash or credit refundable deposit).

Dezadeash River Loop (DEZ-dee-ash, 5km). The trailhead is downtown at the day-use area across from Madley's on Haines Rd. This flat, forested trail will disappoint anyone craving steepness, but it makes for a nice stroll. As always when in bear country, use a noise-maker or belt out tunes to warn bears that you're coming. Easy.

Auriol Loop (15km, 4-6hr., 400m gain). The trail begins 7km south of Haines Junction on Haines Rd. and cuts through boreal forest, leading to a subalpine bench just in front of the Auriol Range. Divided by a primitive campground halfway along, this is a popular overnight trip, although it can easily be hiked in a day without heavy packs. Moderate.

THE YUKON

King's Throne Route (10km round-trip, 1220m gain). This rewarding dayhike with a panoramic view begins at the Kathleen Lake day-use area (see p. 407). Difficult.

Sheep Creek Trail (10km round-trip, 430m gain). Down a short gravel access road just north of the visitors center for **Sheep Mountain.** This satisfying dayhike gives you a good chance to see Dall sheep during the summer months. Sheep Mountain boasts more excellent hiking near the park's northern section. An easy 500m jaunt up to **Soldier's Summit** starts 1km north of the Sheep Mountain Info Centre and leads to the site where the Alaska Hwy. was officially opened on Nov. 20, 1942. Moderate.

The Deep Backcountry. Backcountry hiking can quickly become a dangerous and challenging enterprise in the undeveloped, glaciated Kluane interior. Be sure to carry twice as much food as you expect to need, buy the proper topographic maps, and always consult rangers before you head out. Don't underestimate the bears, either. **Donjek** and **Kaskawulsh** glaciers are the most accessible to backcountry travelers–consult the visitor's center for more detailed advice on specific approaches. Extreme.

◤ OTHER OUTDOOR ACTIVITIES

WATER. Anglers can readily put the park's many-fished reputation to the test at **Kathleen Lake** (see p. 407), home to lake and rainbow trout (catch and release only), grayling, and rare freshwater Kokanee salmon (usually in season mid-May to early June). Less-crowded **St. Elias Lake** is an easy 3.5km hike from the trailhead, 60km south of Haines Junction on Haines Rd. **Pine Lake,** the popular territorial campground, is a good spot to put in a canoe for a paddle, as it is less windy than Kathleen Lake. Fishing here requires a Yukon permit from Madley's, while Kluane waters require a National Parks **fishing permit,** available at the visitors center in Haines Junction (see p. 406). Be sure to pick up the essential **Yukon Fishing Regulations Summary Booklet** for free from the visitor's center to avoid any uncomfortable incidents with the law and fines.

TOURS. If you've got the cash, guides are invaluable for area information, bear security, and navigation skills. In addition to guiding services, **PaddleWheel Adventures,** directly down the road from the Village Bakery, arranges flightseeing over the glaciers, hike-out helicopter rides to the **Kluane Plateau,** and full-day rafting trips on the Class III and IV rapids of the **Blanchard** and **Tatshenshini Rivers.** They also rent the gear you'd need to explore the park on your own, including tents, packs, and bear spray. (☎634-2683. Flightseeing $95 per person for 30min. flight over the Kaskawulsh. Rafting $100 per person including lunch. Helicopter rides vary depending on what you want to see. Bikes $25 per day, canoes $25. Guides $150 per day for up to 6 people and $25 per additional person; fishing guides $150 per day for one person.) Call **Kluane Ecotours** for custom-fitted hiking, canoeing, or kayaking guides. (☎634-2626. $85 per person; minimum $150 per day.)

MOUNTAIN BIKING. The **Alsek River Valley Trail,** which follows a bumpy old mining road for 14km from Alaska Hwy. Km 1645 to Sugden Creek, is popular with mountain bikers who crave rugged terrain. The rocky road crosses several streams before gently climbing to a ridge with a stellar view of the Auriol Mountains. More insider tips on the park's bike-friendly trails are available from PaddleWheel Adventures (see above).

WINTER ACTIVITIES. For winter use of the southern portion of the park, call ahead for snow conditions (☎634-7207) and stop by the visitors center for free, detailed maps of **cross-country ski routes.** The **Auriol, Dezadeash,** and **St. Elias trails** (see above) are all local favorites. Bound through the trails with snowshoes, or pick up dogmushing regulations at the information center and round up a team. Camping is available at day-use area in town in the winter.

SHEEP MOUNTAIN TO ALASKA

THE YUKON

KLUANE LAKE. The drive northwest from Haines Junction to the Alaska border is broken up by a smattering of tiny pit stops, the most scenic of which lie along Kluane Lake. The lake's spectacular aquamarine color is due to suspended "glacier flour" particles in the water that reflect blue light waves. Spanning 478 sq. km, Kluane Lake is the largest in the Yukon. **Congdon Creek Campground ❶,** at Km 1723 on the Alaska Hwy., is the nicest campground before the US border, with a long stone beach for evening strolls and romantic mountain views. Prime lakeside sites fill up early. Be warned—sometimes the camp shuts down from mid-July to September due to the ripening soapberries and the bears which eat them. (Water, pit toilets, firewood. 80 sites, $8 with Yukon camping permits.) If lake spots at the territorial campground are all taken or you prefer showers and laundry, stop 6km short of Congdon at the beautiful **Cottonwood RV Park and Campground ❶.** Melt away your woes in the hottub ($4 for 30min.) or tool around on the mini-golf course. (No phone. Full RV site $24; dry site $18.)

BURWASH LANDING. Sixteen kilometers north of Destruction Bay is Burwash Landing, home to the world's largest gold pan at the **Kluane Museum of Natural History.** This noisy museum plays animal sound effects to accompany the Yukon's largest wildlife display and a collection of Southern Tutchone garb. The mammoth teeth are enormous. (☎841-5561. Open daily late May and early Sept. 10am-6pm; June-Aug. 9am-9pm. $3.75, seniors $3.25, children 6-12 $2.) Stop at Kluane First Nation's **Dalan Campground ❶** for secluded campsites on the lake. (☎841-4274. Wood, water, pit toilets. 25 sites, $10.) The **Burwash Landing Resort ❹** offers rooms with TV and private bath. **Tenting ❶** or dry RV is free on the lawn or parking lot. The lakeside resort houses a **diner ❷** in the lodge that serves up hefty $7 sandwiches. (☎841-4441. Open in summer daily 7am-11pm. Singles $70; doubles $80. RV sites $18. Showers $4.)

Between Burwash and Beaver Creek, break up the monotonous mountain-viewing miles at **Pine Valley Bakery and RV ❸** (Km 1845) and grab some grub, shower, gas, tire repair, or relatively cheap ($50 and up) lodging at this busy jack-of-all-trades stop. (☎862-7407. Open mid-May to mid-Sept. 24hr.)

BEAVER CREEK. The westernmost community (Km 1935) in Canada is by far the liveliest of all these roadside wonders. Get a sales pitch about Beaver Creek offerings, such as the oddly shaped historic church, at the **visitors center.** (☎862-7321. Open daily in summer 8am-8pm.) Most of what you need can be found at the log **1202 Motor Inn,** from **camping ❶** (dry sites $10; RV sites $15) and **motel rooms ❷** ($35 for "plain jane" with shared bath, $65 for the works) to a grocery store, **restaurant ❷** with giant sandwiches ($6.50-8), and an **ATM.** (☎800-661-0540. Open daily 6:30am-1am.) A heated indoor public **pool** is open June-Aug. (☎862-7702.) Lodging is a steal at the **Beaver Creek Hostel** in the **Westmark Inn ❶,** which has a bar and rec room for fun. (☎862-7501. Open May-Sept. Rooms $22.)

ENTERING THE US. Past Beaver Creek, 20 mi. of highway and prime moose-viewing wilderness separate US and Canadian customs and immigration, although several signs and landmarks can be found at the official border on the 141st meridian. Alaska time is 1hr. behind Pacific time, and gas a few miles into US territory is considerably cheaper than anything in Canada. From the border it's 80 mi. (1½hr.) to Tetlin Junction, where the Alaska Hwy. meets the Taylor Hwy. (see p. 559), and 92 mi. (2hr.) to Tok (see below).

ALONG HWY. 9: TOP OF THE WORLD HWY.

The majestic 127km (1½hr.) highway earns its name--visit and see. Starting across the Yukon River from Dawson City, it climbs for several kilometers and then follows the spine of a series of mountains. The trip affords staggering views of the Southern Ogilvies and the North Dawson Range before connecting with the Taylor Hwy. at **Jack Wade Junction** in Alaska. Unmarked trails head into the bush from rest stops, and the bare hills make for simple climbs up to expansive views. The road is open May-September, although the mountainous Yukon-Alaska border crossing at Km 108 is only open 9am-9pm Pacific (i.e., Yukon) time. The only services on the Canadian side are the links at the **Top of the World Golf Course** (☎867-667-1472), about 10km past the ferry. The 5min. ferry runs 24hr. from June to July (peak traffic 7-11am from Dawson and 2-8pm to Dawson). The US side of the road is full of pocks in the gravel, while the Canadians lay down some asphalt in between their pocks. Just over the border in the US, the **Boundary Cafe** sells snacks and will trade a gallon of gasoline for US$2.

DAWSON CITY   ☎867

Born in a frenzied lust for dust, Dawson City booms today by telling its own history. On August 17, 1896, three men stumbled upon thick ribbons of gold in a stream outside of today's Dawson City. Within weeks, gold-diggers flooded town. Shops, saloons, and hotels quickly sprung up all over the boomtown. For 12 boggling months from 1898-1899, this was the largest Canadian city west of Toronto, known as "the Paris of the North." After that year of frenzied claim-staking and legend-making, most of the gold seekers realized that the early birds had scooped up all the prime claims before their arrival; they packed up and headed to Nome. Dredges took over and corporate mining trudged on from its center in Bear Creek, 13km south of Dawson, until sputtering out in 1966. In the early 1960s the Klondike Visitors Association and the Canadian government set out to return Dawson City to its gold-rush glory, restoring dirt roads, long boardwalks, and wooden store fronts, and in the process transforming the town into the lively summer RV and college student destination that it is today.

▐▀ TRANSPORTATION

To reach Dawson City, take the **Klondike Loop (Hwy. 2)** 533km (6hr.) north from **Whitehorse,** or follow the majestic **Top of the World Hwy. (Hwy. 9)** 108km east from the Alaska border (see **Taylor Hwy.,** p. 559).

Buses: Dawson City Taxi and Courier Service (☎993-6688, www.dawsonbus.ca), at the corner of 2nd and York. To **Whitehorse** (7½hr., June-Aug. M-F, $82.50). **Parks Hwy. Express** (☎888-600-6001, www.alaskashuttle.com) will take you across the "top of the world" and to **Fairbanks** (11hr., 3 daily, $145).

Cruise: Yukon Queen II River Cruises (☎993-5599), on Front St. next to the Keno. Office open daily 8am-8pm. Departs daily at 9am for **Eagle, AK** along the Yukon River. Includes hot meals. (10-11hr. round-trip. One-way standby US$91, CDN$130; round-trip US$149, CDN$215. Returns canoes from Eagle for US$50 (see p. 560).

Car Rental: Budget, 451 Craig St. (☎993-5644), in the Dawson City B&B. $60 per day, $0.20 per km after 100km. Free pick-up and delivery. Must be 21+ with a credit card.

Auto Repair: Esso (☎993-5142) on the Klondike Hwy. (Hwy. 2) immediately before town. Open in summer daily 7am-11pm.

Dawson City

▲▲ ACCOMMODATIONS
The Bunkhouse, **11**
Bombay Peggy's, **12**
Dawson City River Hostel, **1**
Gold Rush Campground, **3**
Yukon River Campground, **2**

🍴 FOOD
General Store, **6**
Klondike Kate's, **4**
Midnight Sun Hotel
 Restaurant, **7**
Riverwest Bistro, **9**
Rio, **5**

■ NIGHTLIFE
Bombay Peggy's, **12**
Pit Tavern & Lounge, **10**
Sun Tavern & Lounge, **8**

🛈 PRACTICAL INFORMATION

Tourist Information: (☎993-5566), at Front and King St. Movies, inexpensive tickets and pick-a-pack tour tickets (see **Sights**, below). Open mid-May to mid-Sept. daily 8am-8pm. The **Northwest Territories Visitors Centre** (☎993-6167) opposite, knows the Dempster Hwy. Open May-Sept. daily 9am-8pm.

Bank: Canadian Imperial Bank of Commerce, at 2nd Ave. and Queen. St. has a **24hr. ATM.** Open M-Th 10am-3pm, F 10am-5pm.

Equipment Rental: Dawson City River Hostel (see **Accommodations**, p. 412). Bikes $20 per day, canoes $20. Non-hostelers must use passport as deposit.

Bookstore: Maximilian's Goldrush Emporium (☎993-5486), on Front near Queen St., stocks every word ever written by local stars Jack London and Robert Service. Open in summer M-Sa 9am-8pm, Su 10am-8pm; winter M-Sa 9am-6pm, Su noon-6pm.

Laundromat and Public Showers: The Wash House Laundromat (☎993-6555), on 2nd Ave. between Princess and Queen. Wash $2.50, dry $0.25 per 4min. Showers $1 per 4min., towels $0.50. Open in summer daily 9am-9pm; winter 10am-6pm.

Pool: (☎993-7412), on 5th next to Museum. Adults $4, college students $3.50, youth and seniors $3, child $2, family $9. Reduced after 8pm. Call for exact hours.

Weather: ☎993-8367.

Women's Shelter: (☎993-5086). 24hr.

Police: (☎993-5555 or 667-5555), at Front St. and Turner St., in the south of town.

Ambulance: ☎993-4444.

Medical Services: Nursing Station (☎993-4444), at 6th Ave. and Church. Open M-F 8:30am-5pm.

Internet Access: Free 30min. at the **Library** (☎993-5571), in the school at 5th Ave. and Princess St. Call ahead. Open in summer Tu-Th 10am-9pm, F-Sa 10am-5pm; winter Tu-Th 1-9pm, F-Sa noon-5pm. Also at **Grubstake** (☎993-6706), 2nd Ave. between King St. and Queen St. $5 per hr. Open Su-Th 10am-10pm, F-Sa 10am-11pm.

Post Office: (☎993-5342), 5th Ave. near Princess St. and Queen St. Open M-F 8:30am-5:30pm, Sa 9am-noon. The **Historical Post Office,** at 3rd and King St., gives historical service nearer downtown. Open daily noon-3pm and 3:30-6pm. **Postal Code:** Y0B 1G0.

ACCOMMODATIONS AND CAMPING

The hostel and campground on the west side of town, across the Yukon River, are by far the most attractive options in town. A hotel room in town will rarely go for much less than $90. The ferry to float you and your wheels across the river is free and runs 24hr. Hop on at Front and Albert St., in the north end of town. The **tent city,** in the woods next to the hostel, remains popular with the town's summer college crowd, despite the $100 per person per summer price tag. Contact the Northern Network of B&Bs (☎993-5644) for the town's listings.

Dawson City River Hostel (HI; ☎993-6823), across the Yukon River from downtown; take the first left off the ferry. Sun on lounge chairs overlooking the Yukon, bathe in wood-stove-heated creek water, stir-fry in the outdoor kitchen, or snuggle in the cozy lounge. Open mid-May to Sept. Beds $15, nonmembers $18; tent sites $10, additional tent occupants $7 per person; private rooms $38. No credit cards. ❶

The Bunkhouse (☎993-6164), on Princess at Front St. Basic, clean wood-planked rooms with comfy firm beds. Best option actually *in* town. Open mid-May to mid-Sept. Singles $50, with bath $80; doubles $60, $90; quads with bath $120. ❸

Bombay Peggy's (☎993-6969), on Princess at 2nd St. Each of the rooms in this historic restored brothel has its own distinct decoration and ambience. Though the madame and her ladies are long gone, the pub below will mellow you out long past the midnight sun. Reservations recommended. Rooms $89-$109; most are doubles. ❺

Yukon River Campground, first right off the ferry. Roomy, secluded sites are a haven for nature-lovers, who can peer at the peregrine falcons nesting across the river. An escape from the RV-mania across the river. Water, pit toilets. Requires $12 Yukon Camping Permit available from local vendors or the visitors center. ❶

Gold Rush Campground (☎993-5247), at 5th and York St. Right downtown. Pure RV, baby. Laundry $3, dry $1.50. Dump station. Gravel tent sites $14; RV sites $23-26; pull-through sites $22. Shower $2 per 6min. ❶

FOOD

On Thanksgiving Day in 1898, a turkey in Dawson City cost over $100. Snag one today (or any other grocery product) for much less at the **Dawson City General Store,** on Front St. (☎993-5475. Open M-Sa 8am-8pm, Su 10am-7pm.)

Riverwest Bistro (☎993-6339), Front St. between Princess and Queen. Dawson's artists, tourists, and hipsters converge here for fresh sandwiches ($4.95) and specialty sweets like pecan streusel ($1.50). Open M-Sa 7am-7pm, Su 8am-6pm. ❶

Klondike Kate's (☎993-6527), at 3rd and King St. A favorite of Dawson Sourdoughs. Daily specials add to the full menu of pita wraps ($6), salads ($6-8), burgers ($8), and a hummus plate ($6). Vegetarians and martini connoisseurs ($5.75) rejoice. Open mid-May to mid-Sept. daily 6:30am-11pm. ❶

Rio (☎993-4683), on Front St. between King and Queen. A burger shack that attracts the summer college crowd with its patty creations and tasty fries ($8-9) and pool table on the deck. The best milkshakes in the north run $4.50. Open daily 11am-10pm. ❷

Midnight Sun Hotel Restaurant (☎993-5495), at 3rd and Queen St. Chinese entrees from $11. Burgers and more $6-8. Lunch smorgasbord on F $10. Close enough to the lounge to hear locals belting out their favorite tunes at the hottest karaoke joint in town (see **Debauchery,** p. 413). Open Su-Th 6am-1am, F-Sa 6am-3am. ❷

◎ SIGHTS

Parks Canada looms large, overseeing the sights in town. Scope information and buy ticket packages at the visitors center (see **Practical Information,** p. 411).

GOLD. Nearly 16km of maintained gravel road follow Bonanza Creek to the former site of **Grand Forks,** which was chewed up when the dredges came through, leaving monster-size gopher tunnels. Along the way are **Gold Dredge #4,** a gigantic machine used to exhaust Bonanza Creek when corporate mining replaced hand-mining, and **Discovery Claim,** the site of the first discovery of gold in Dawson. *(Gold Dredge #4: gold-info rich tours on the hour daily 9am-4pm, except 11am; $5. Discover Claim: interactive gold-staking program daily 11am. $5.)* **Goldbottom Mining Tours and Gold Panning,** 30km south of town, offers a tour of an operating mine and an hour of panning. (☎ 993-5023. Open June to freeze-up daily 11am-7pm. $12.) Pan for free at the confluence of the Bonanza and Eldorado Creeks beyond the Discovery Claim site; panning anywhere else could lead to an unpleasant encounter with the owner of the claim you're jumping. Pans sold at local hardware stores for about $10.

ROBERT SERVICE. Before stopping by Robert Service's cabin for an animated account of his life and poetry, catch the Robert Service Show given by the magnificent Tom Byrne, who recounts the life of Robert Service as he weaves in Service's famous poems, "The Cremation of Sam McGee" and "The Shooting of Dan McGrew." The poems' wit and Byrne's story-telling make the show a feature attraction in Dawson. *(Cabin on 8th near Hanson. Free viewing daily 9am-noon and 1-5pm. Shows at 10am and 1:30pm. $5 includes Jack London talk. Robert Service Show at corner of Front St. and Prince. Shows June-Aug. daily at 3pm and 8pm. $8, 10-16 $4, under 10 free.)*

JACK LONDON. Examine the traces of frontier literary genius Jack London at his **cabin,** where the great California author's life and brief stint in the Yukon are described in letters, photographs, and a talk by London fanatic and Canadian author Dick North. *(On 8th Ave. and Firth St. Open daily 10am-1pm and 2-6pm. 30min. tours daily 11:15am and 2:45pm. Exhibit and talk $2 or free with Robert Service cabin talk.)*

DEBAUCHERY. Diamond Tooth Gertie's was Canada's first legal casino and the stuff movies are made of. Gamblers fritter the night away with roulette, blackjack, and Texas Hold 'em against local legends such as Johnny Caribou and No Sleep Filippe. Madame Gertie belts out tunes and can-can dancing at 8:30pm, 10:30pm, and midnight. *(☎ 993-5575. At 4th and Queen St: 19+. Open nightly 7pm-2am. $6 cover or $20 season pass. No cover after 11pm. Happy hour midnight-2am. On-site ATM for those who need to really clean out their nest eggs.)* The **Gaslight Follies,** a high-kicking vaudeville revue, is held in **Palace Grand Theatre.** *(King St., between 2nd and 3rd. ☎ 993-6217. Up to 2 shows nightly. Reservations available. Box office open daily 11am-9pm. $15-17, under 12 $7.50.)* As the night winds down, karaoke winds up at the **Sun Tavern and Lounge.** Young and old alike pack in to check out the local talent. Though no longer Dawson's roughest bar, the Sun is still no place to sip fruity drinks. Pints are $4. *(3rd St. and Queen. ☎ 993-5495. Open daily noon-2am.)* See grown men cry to home-spun country tunes at **The Pit Tavern and Lounge.** Barnacle Bob plays the tavern from 4pm, and the much-acclaimed country and blues house band plays the lounge Wednesday-Saturday at 10pm. *(At the old Westminster Hotel on 3rd. ☎ 993-5339. Tavern open 9am-11pm; lounge open noon-2am. Happy hour 4:45-5:45pm.)* For a less rowdy glass of sangria, head to **Bombay Peggy's.** Sangria pitchers are $12 from 7-9pm. *(2nd St. and Princess. ☎ 993-6969. Happy hour 5-6pm, sangria pitchers $12 7-9pm. Open in summer 2pm-1:30am; winter 4pm-1am.)*

TR'ONDEK HWECH'IN CULTURAL CENTRE. The **Tr'ondek Hwech'in Cultural Centre,** celebrated for its architecture since its completion in 1998, is a striking and innovative home for exhibits on First Nations culture. The center is open for visitors to browse displays, watch videos, or participate in various cultural activities and demonstrations. *(On Front St. ☎ 993-6564. Open daily 10:30am-6pm. Donations welcome. Tours of gallery and slide show Offered 3 times a day. $5, under 5 free.)*

OUTDOOR ACTIVITIES. Dawson is a jungle-gym for outdoors-lovers. Find trail maps for **Moosehead Slide** and **Midnight Dome** at the visitors center. The Dawson region is surrounded by a network of loop roads and trails perfect for hiking and biking (but watch out for jeeps and ATVs on the wider ones). The trailhead for the **Ridge Road Trail** (32km), which runs up some wilderness hills before connecting with Bonanza Creek Rd., is located by the Callison Industrial Area—the visitors center has essential maps. **Hunker, Dominion,** and **Sulphur Creek Rds.** also provide hiking challenges—but pack well, because the full loop is 164km. Fishers will find angling on the Yukon or its tributaries difficult without the *Regulations Summary.* Pick it up for free at the visitors center. The Dawson City River Hostel (see p. 412) sells topographic maps of the region ($12) and arranges four-day **canoe rentals** to Eagle, AK (US$110), or ten-day trips to Circle, AK .

🎵 EVENTS

A trip up the **Midnight Dome,** 7km along Dome Rd., just past the Esso gas station on the way into town, is a Yukon-wide tradition on the **summer solstice,** on which the sun dips below the horizon for just 20min. around 12:30am. The Midnight Dome makes for a panoramic picnic spot or sunset photo op. Drive up or take the steep 7km trail that ascends over 600m leaving from the end of King St. (2hr. one-way, map at visitors center). Race it on the Saturday of Music Fest and then head riverside for a salmon barbecue.

During the third weekend of July, Gold Fever becomes Dance Fever as Canadians bust their move at the 🎵**Dawson City Music Festival** for three days of fantastic music and energy. Kid Fest events thrill the younger crowd. Tickets to see 20-plus pop, rock, and folk bands, go on sale in April, and usually sell out by mid-June. The ticketless eavesdrop outside venues and in the beer garden. (☎ 993-5584; www.dcmf.com. July 18-20, 2002. $70 for 3 days of workshops, performances, and dancing.) Mid-August sees Dawson explode in Sourdough charm during **Discovery Days,** with a parade, pancake breakfasts, and an entire town in gold-rush period costume. Be prepared to face down the columns of tourist RVs. Labour Day visitors will not want to pass up watching the **Great International Outhouse Race.** Teams of contenders tow occupied outhouses on wheels through the streets of Dawson. (Visitors Association ☎ 993-5575. Sept. 1, 2003.)

ALONG HWY. 4: CAMPBELL HWY. ☎ 867

Unlike drivers on the Alaska Hwy., those who travel the Campbell Hwy. (Hwy. 4) feel like they are truly penetrating the wild and powerful north alone. They are following the footsteps of the highway's namesake, Robert Campbell, the first white man to brave the Yukon. From the south, the Campbell Hwy. runs 602km from **Watson Lake** to **Carmacks** (8hr.). Faltering mining ventures have turned the towns along the highway into ghost-towns. Only anglers, solitude-seekers, and wildlife buffs lured by Faro's eco-tourism venture on the road, and the land is devoid of RVs. From the tiny, largely native community of Ross River (originally a 19th-century fur-trading post), a finger of road cuts off towards the Northwest Territories (NWT) wilderness. Other roads off the Campbell service smaller mining and prospecting operations. Indeed, much of the activity and sparse settlement found along the Campbell seems to be dedicated to its maintenance; the 383km (5-5½hr.; no services on this stretch) of graded dirt road from Watson

Lake in the south (on the Alaska Hwy.) to Ross River runs through wilderness broken only by year-round highway servicing camps. **This stretch is not to be taken lightly:** tires are sliced and windshields are cracked at high speeds. Unless you want to be stranded roadside for hours, carry extra auto-fixing gear with you. As you get closer to Ross River, you start to catch views of the velvet-puckered green Pelly Range to the south and strange, rounded, high dirt cliffs. On the way to Carmacks from Faro, the greatly improved road continues on high bluffs and eventually follows the Yukon River with some forceful views approaching town. Five government campsites lie on the route (Kms 80, 177, 376 at the turnoff for Ross River, 428 up toward Faro, and 517 on Little Salmon Lake; $8 permit camping only), and three more on the short Frenchman Rd. This road branches off the Campbell at Km 551, near Carmacks, and leads 60km to the **Klondike Hwy.**

ROSS RIVER. Ross River is 370km of gravel road and two campsites away from Watson Lake and the Alaska Hwy. Camping awaits just beyond the Ross River at **Lapi Canyon Territorial Campground ❶,** above the river that flows between the sandy cliffs of the canyon. (Pit toilets, firewood, water. $8.) The sole **gas station** doubles as a **general store** with groceries. (☎969-2212. Open daily 8am-6pm.) **Medical emergencies:** ☎969-4444. **Police:** ☎867-667-5555.

FARO. One hour northeast of Ross River and a jaunt down 10km of road will land you in the almost-ghost-town of **Faro.** When active, the town's mine held the world's largest open-pit lead and zinc production complex. If you do make the trip to Faro, there is spectacular wilderness fit for **fishing** and **hiking.** The underdeveloped nature of the land means that most hiking ventures will become backcountry treks—bring appropriate gear and maps.

You may catch a view of rare black-and-white **Fannin sheep** from one of the town's specially constructed **viewing platforms.** The closest platform to town is at the corner of Blind Creek Rd. and Lorna Blvd.; ask at the visitors center for directions to others. Take the short hike from the visitors center over to **Van Gorder Falls,** a beautiful spot not requiring backcountry hiking. To reach the **nursing station,** take a left on Bell Ave. of Campbell St. For the **police,** (☎994-5555), turn right immediately upon entering town. The **post office** is on the left past Hoang's. (open M-F 8:30am-5:30pm, Sa 8:30am-noon). If you need car repair, try **Shell.** (☎994-2538. **24hr. road service** ☎994-3019 or 994-2538).

The **Johnson Lake Territorial Campground ❶** lies 6.5km back toward the highway. (Pit toilets, pump water, and firewood. $8.) Down the road from the visitors center, **Redmond's Hotel ❹** has the only rooms in town. **Hoang's ❷** is the only restaurant in town, attached to the hotel on your left past the visitors center. Meals $6-13. (Open M-Sa 11am-8pm).

CARMACKS. Little Salmon Lake ❶ lies 85km before Carmacks and offers awesome lakeside campsites. (Permit required. Pit toilets, firewood, water. $8.) Signs from here will guide you down the Campbell's paved 180km (2hr.) to **Faro.** Stop at **Eagle's Nest Bluff,** about 30km from Carmacks, to hear the aspens rustle and get a wide-ranging view of the wide Yukon River and its surroundings. The end of the Campbell meets the North Klondike Hwy. (Hwy. 2); turn left for Carmacks. The final approach to Carmacks delivers in-town **camping** along the Nordenskiold River at the popular **Tantalus Public Campground ❶,** and a meandering stretch of riverside boardwalk. (Pit toilets, water. $12.) Eat with local characters at the **Gold Panner Cafe ❷,** part of the Hotel Carmacks complex below the highway. (☎863-5221. Open daily 6am-10pm; winter reduced hours.) North of town, the new **Tage Cho Hudan Cultural Centre** preserves the Tutchone culture and displays the world's only mammoth snare model. (☎863-5830. Open daily 9am-5pm.

Donation requested.) The **visitors center** is beside the campground (☎ 863-6330. Open M-F 8:30am-5pm.) Other services include: **police,** ☎ 863-5555 and **ambulance/health clinic,** ☎ 863-4444. From **Carmacks,** the smooth **North Klondike Hwy.** (Hwy. 2) runs 175km south to Whitehorse and 360km north to Dawson City.

MT. HALDANE. 179km north of Carmacks on Hwy. 2, Hwy. 11 branches off to the mining towns of **Mayo, Elsa,** and **Keno.** A 76km detour down the rough, gravel-surfaced Hwy. 11 leads hikers toward the Mt. Haldane trailhead—the trail winds steeply toward the mountain's nearly 2000m summit and some of the best lookouts in all of the central Yukon, since Haldane juts starkly alone out of the vast McQuesten Valley. The trail's remoteness keeps it largely off the tourist track, and weeks often pass without any hiker traffic. Plan to spend 3hr. each way on the 6km trail. To get to the trailhead, look for the Mt. Haldane Trail sign after heading north from Mayo toward Elsa—it is about 26km from Mayo.

APPROACHING THE NORTHWEST TERRITORIES: THE DEMPSTER HWY. ☎ 867

If you have ever dreamed of a day in which the sun never sets, or a sunset that lasted for hours before slowly flowing into a gorgeous sunrise, then the Dempster Hwy. will fulfill your Arctic Circle fantasies. The residents of the towns above the Arctic Circle shed their watches during the summer; while it may be perfectly fine to knock on your neighbors door at 2am, 10am may be late in the day. The experience is entirely worthwhile, but be prepared to pay for it—prices on everything rise along with the latitude.

THE ROAD. The Dempster Hwy. begins in the Yukon as Hwy. 5. It winds a spectacular 734km toward Inuvik, becoming Hwy. 8 when it crosses into the Northwest Territories (Km 465). Construction of the highway began in the 1950s when oil and gas were discovered near the Arctic Circle at Eagle Plains. It was not until 1979, however, that Canada's isolated Mackenzie River Delta towns of **Fort McPherson, Tsiigehtchic,** and **Inuvik** (ih-NOO-vik) finally had road access. These communities are largely indigenous Inuvialuit and Gwich'in.

THE REALITY. The Dempster presents its drivers with naked wilderness, huge tracts of wholly undeveloped forest, plains, and tundra. Though recent improvements have made it easier to drive close to the 90km speed limit most of the way, you won't want to—amazing vistas await at every curve and pass. The road is not to be taken lightly. Part of the Dempster is built on a bed of sharp, graded shale, which pops right up through the toughest 18-ply truck tires. The drive should be approached with careful planning. Services are limited to Klondike River Lodge (Km 0), Eagle Plains (Km 369), Fort McPherson (Km 550), and Inuvik (Km 734), Although a trip to Tombstone makes a pleasant overnight, the full drive takes around 12hr. (two days each way to be fully and safely appreciated). The weather is erratic. Quick rainstorms or high winds can make portions of the route impassable (watch for flashing red lights that denote closed roads) and can disrupt ferry service to Inuvik for as long as two weeks, leaving travelers stranded.

■ **SCENERY ORIENTATION.** The spectacular first 150km of the Dempster pass through the crags of the **Ogilvie Mountains,** whose curvy, barren slopes are shaped like glaciers. The dramatic peaks of the southern ranges gradually round out to the gentler, gravel-covered, unglaciated **Northern Ogilvies** near Engineer Creek (Km 194). The road then descends into forests and velvet tundra as it approaches the **Arctic Circle** (Km 405). The northernmost stretch of the Rockies, the Richardson Mountains,

DESTRUCKTION: (deh-STRUK-shun) n. the act of semis racing along the Dempster Highway at high speeds, spitting gravel at the windshields of oncoming vehicular traffic. Vehicles can best avoid cracks from destrucktion by playing Dempster Chicken. Hug the center of the road and begin braking as the truck approaches, thus encouraging the steamroller to slow down. Before the truck passes, pull to the side of the road and stop so flying gravel will be less likely to crack the windshield.

parallel the road in the distance. The trees become more stunted the farther north you go, due to the permafrost that covers much of the Yukon. The trees are forced to dig their roots in the "active layer" above the ice. There are only a handful of settlements to distract drivers from the wonder of gazing.

🖪 PRACTICAL INFORMATION. Road and Ferry Report (☎ 800-661-0752; in Inuvik 777-2678) provides up-to-date road info. The **NWT Visitor Centre** (see p. 410) in Dawson City has free regional brochures, a map of the highway, a short video, and reports from recent drivers. A full tank of gas, dependable tires (6-ply or better), a good spare or three, extra oil and coolant, and emergency supplies (food, water, clothes, a first aid kit, and a can of gas) are necessary Dempster companions. The **Klondike River Lodge** (☎ 993-6892; open daily 7am-10:30pm, garage services limited to tire repair on Su) has full services and will rent you a gas can for $5 with a $15 deposit. Bring powerful bug repellant—even 100% DEET won't thwart every skeeter bite—and some form of netting if camping. If you lack wheels or doubt yours will survive the trip, **Dawson City Courier** (☎ 993-6688) drives up Mondays and Fridays and returns Wednesdays and Sundays for $230 each way.

TOMBSTONE. Some drivers from Dawson stay in Tombstone, a beautiful range of igneous rock, overnight. The **Interpretive Centre** at **Tombstone Campground** (Km 72) has wise staff, trails, and expansive displays including real specimens of local flora and fauna. The migrating **Porcupine caribou herd** north of Tombstone is, at 150,000 head, the largest in North America.

CAMPING. Several Yukon **government campgrounds ❶** ($8) line the route north to Inuvik (Km 72, 194). At the foot of Sapper Hill and Rock River, **Engineer Creek ❶** (Km 194) provides the most scenic camping. In **Nitainlii** (just before Ft. McPherson at Km 541), there is an excellent Gwich'in **interpretive center** and **campground ❶.** (Center open June-Sept. daily 9am-9pm. Sites $15.)

BACKCOUNTRY. The mesmerizing landscape tempts **backcountry** trippers but does not play kindly with the under-prepared. The Ogilvie and Blackstone Rivers are favored by backcountry paddlers. *Paddling the Yukon* ($24, available at **Maximillian's**, see p. 411) is a comprehensive guide. Only a handful of paths access this wilderness. The road guide *Along the Dempster* describes routes accessible from the highway. Updated descriptions of routes that have become trails due to use, *Yukon's Tombstone Range and Blackstone Uplands: A Traveler's Guide* is well-worth the $20. Backcountry hikers should carry maps of where they intend to travel, however—much of the terrain lining the highway is Vuntut Gwich'in settlement land, and hiking, hunting, fishing, or camping on it requires tribal authorization. If the visitors centers can't answer your questions, you can contact the **Gwich'in Land Administration** directly. (☎ 867-777-4869, fax 867-777-4538.)

DAYHIKES. At Km 58, a small road behind the gravel pit becomes the **Grizzly Valley** trail (3hr. one-way), leading through spruce forest to an alpine ridge with a fine view. The hike to **Tombstone Mountain** (known in Gwich'in as **Ddhah Ch'aa Tat,**

"among the sharp, ragged, rocky mountains") begins just north of the interpretive centre or at Grizzly Creek, takes three to four days, and requires self-reliance, a compass, and topo maps. For a day-long adventure in the Northern Ogilvies, try the **Mt. Distincta trail** ("Windy Pass") at Km 154, which heads over craggy boulders to one of the area's highest peaks (1800m). From the highway, walk southeast across a narrow ribbon of tundra to the ridge base. Follow the ridge south 6km, past a radio tower, and up a slope to the west to the true summit. From there, hike north 6km and then descend back to the highway where you'll emerge 5km west of the trailhead. This trail rises about 1000m/3274 ft. **Sapper Hill**, with its yellow-gray ridge, is one of the best half-day hikes along the highway. It begins just after Engineer Creek (Km 194) and takes 4hr. Avoid walking along the fishbone crest of the ridge; the chunky limestone near the summit can be tricky to navigate. Once the road descends into the river delta lowlands of the Northwest Territories, hiking becomes nearly impossible due to the swampy top layer of permafrost—even worse, the mosquitoes will sap pint after pint out of any hiker unbowed by soggy feet.

EAGLE PLAINS HOTEL. Gas, food, a coin laundry and showers, and accommodations are available at the well-kept **Eagle Plains Hotel ❺**, halfway to Inuvik at Km 369—rooms have monopoly pricing and a comfy 70s decor. Parking lot-style camping is available. Gas in the summer of 2002 topped out at over a buck a liter, but driving through the middle of nowhere is no time to be picky. The next pump is 197km away and the price is not much better. (☎993-2453. Singles $112; each extra person $14. Sites $10. Electricity $15.) **Food ❷** at the hotel is of disarmingly good value. A Bushfire burger (onions, hot peppers, and horseradish) with thick fries costs $8. (Restaurant open daily 7am-9pm. Lounge open daily 4:30pm-2am.)

ARCTIC CIRCLE. Just past Eagle Plains at Km 405, the Dempster crosses the Arctic Circle. Here lies an imaginary dotted line in the tundra. A sign provides photographic proof that you've reached the **Land of the Midnight Sun.**

NORTHWEST TERRITORIES. Set your watch to **Mountain Time** upon entering the Northwest Territories at Km 465. From mid-June to mid-October, **free ferries** cross **Peel River** (Km 539; runs daily on demand) and **Arctic Red River/MacKenzie River** (Km 608; departs daily from south shore 25min. past the hour 9am-12:25am). In winter, cars can drive across the thick ice. No crossing is possible during fall freeze or spring thaw. Call ☎800-661-0752 for ice status. Travelers who wish to visit the community of Tsiigehtchic should note that the MacKenzie River ferry does not dock there by default (the Dempster skirts Tsiigetchic by a few hundred meters), and that ferry operators must be notified to make a landing at Tsiigetchic.

FORT MCPHERSON. The small community of Ft. McPherson doesn't have a lot to offer travelers, but it does have the only **ATM** and auto repair between Eagle Plains and Inuvik. Pick up some groceries or an axe at the **Tetlit Co-op,** located in

THE LOST CITY OF INUVIK Around Inuvik, all the houses rest on pilings, though not, as one may suspect, to protect the abodes in case of flood. These high rises protect the ground and the precious permafrost beneath it from the heat houses radiate. Houses sitting on the ground risk melting the permafrost, thus sinking into their own foundations and gradually shrinking in height. The protective, temperamental permafrost, which varies in depth from a few centimeters to many meters, requires not only that houses be suspended awkwardly in the air, but also that water be kept in tanks above ground, so that the town does not disappear.

THE YUKON

the big white building on the right a ways down the Ft. McPherson turnoff. (☎952-2417. Open M-Sa 10am-6pm; **public phone** available.) Thank God for **Wolf Creek Services** and their $25 tire repair, along with garage, wash, and tow services. To get there, drive a few dozen meters down the Ft. McPherson turnoff to the intersection with C Wilson St.—it's the garage building on the right. If you get to the Co-op, you've driven too far. (☎867-952-2139. Open daily 9am-9pm.) In emergencies, call the **police** ☎952-2551, **fire** ☎952-5555, or **Health Center** ☎952-2586.

INUVIK, NT   ☎867

Inuvik ("living place") has 3600 residents, mostly from two Arctic tribes: Inuvialuit of the Beaufort Sea coast and the Gwich'in of the Mackenzie River Delta. During the long winter, Inuvik's houses are painted bright colors, and during the summer, the community hosts a renowned 10-day Great Northern Arts Festival. A recent upsurge in petroleum exploration has caused traffic jams and sent housing prices even farther north. While most shops try to operate on a night and day schedule, the town is usually out and about for the sun's lowest point in the sky (2:30am).

⊠ PRACTICAL INFORMATION. Just about everything in town is on Mackenzie St., starting with the welcoming **Western Arctic Visitor Centre.** (☎777-4727. Open daily 9am-8pm.) Stop here on arrival and receive your **free Arctic Adventurer certificate** for driving the Dempster and visit its extensive display for a crash course on the area. **Arctic Tire,** 80 Navy Rd., offers 24hr. road service and 24hr. gas pumps. (☎777-4149. Open M-Sa 8am-6pm.) Both the **CIBC bank** and the **post office** have **24hr. ATMs.** A great book selection and amazing topo maps are available at **Boreal Books,** 181 Mackenzie Rd. They also carry the coveted "We drove the Dempster Highway" bumper stickers. (☎777-3748. Open daily 10am-6pm.) Other services include: **police** (☎777-2935); **ambulance** (☎777-4444); and **Inuvik Regional Hospital** (☎777-8000). Free **Internet** access is available at the **library,** 100 Mackenzie Rd., for 1hr. (☎777-2749. Open M-Th 10am-6pm and 7-9pm, F 10am-6pm, Sa-Su 2-5pm.)

⌂⊡ ACCOMMODATIONS AND FOOD. The four hotels in town charge prices north of outrageous. For an unparalleled Arctic experience, stay with twenty sled dogs at the **⊠Arctic Chalet ❷.** Walk your favorite dog in the summer or pay for a thrilling sled ride in the winter. (Single cabin $45; large cabins with kitchen, private toilet, and shared bathhouse from $85.) **Robertson's Bed and Breakfast ❹,** 41 Mackenzie Rd., offers the cheapest rooms in town. (☎777-3111. Singles $70; doubles $80.) Pretty camping awaits at **Chuk Campground ❶,** right outside town. (☎777-3613. Toilets. Sites $15, day use $5, electric RV sites $20. Free showers.)

While in town, eat up like the natives do. The cheapest caribou and musk-ox burgers ($6-8) and greasy food are at **To Go's,** 71 Mackenzie St. (☎777-3030. Open M-Th 7am-midnight, F and Sa 9am-3am, Su 11am-11pm.) Get Inuvik's best falafel ($6.95) and *shwarma* ($9.95) at the diverse **Fast Food Cafe ❷,** across from the Igloo Church (☎777-2020. Open daily 11:30am-2:30am.) The **Cafe Gallery ❷** serves baked goods (big muffins $2.50) and light lunches (sandwich and soup $10) in a studio with comfy chairs. (☎777-2888. Open M-Sa 8am-6pm, Su noon-6pm.) On a late night hit **The Zoo,** the Arctic's rowdy hot spot in the Mackenzie Hotel. (Open daily 11am-2am. Dance party F and Sa.) Recently-opened **Frosty's Arctic Pub,** also across from the Igloo Church, draws crowds with its live music and freewheeling party atmosphere. (☎777-5194. Open daily 11:30am-2am.)

⊡⚐ EVENTS AND OUTDOOR ACTIVITIES. Begun in 1989, the **Great Northern Arts Festival** brings over 100 artists and entertainers to Inuvik for performances, workshops, and a world-class art sale. (☎777-3536. Mid-July, 2003.) The **Midnight Sun**

Tundra Nature Hike (2hr. one-way) begins at the Marine Bypass Rd. on the north side of Inuvik and follows mountain ridges for 6km to **Three Mile Lake**. The ridges are a perfect spot to watch the sun in its lowest arc and to survey the **Richardson Range**. To explore the Mackenzie Delta, contact **Western Arctic Adventures and Equipment,** 38 Sprucehill Dr. (☎777-2594), for canoes, kayaks, air charters, and trip-planning help. Canoes and kayaks can be put in behind the house for $35 a day with paddles, jackets, and friendly advice. **Arctic Nature Tours** (☎777-3300; www.arcticnaturetours.com), beside the Igloo church, mobilizes outfitters and community contacts to lead nature and culture tours. Explore Inuvik (1½hr., $25); cruise the Mackenzie River and visit an Inuvialuit camp (4hr., 1hr. tour in camp, $75); have tea and bannock with an elder (3½ hr., $65); or fly to Herschel Island Territorial Park to see abandoned whaling towns (5hr., $228). **Aurora Research College Research Centre** offers a naturalist's canoe tour of the Delta. At the research station, at Duck Lake St. and Mackenzie Rd., you can peruse the arctic library, browse the **Internet** for free, or catch a free slideshow on the region. (☎777-3838. Open M-F 8:30am-noon and 1-5pm. Tour 4hr.; summer M 6pm, Th 1pm; $32.)

THE PANHANDLE

THE PANHANDLE'S HIGHLIGHTS

WRANGELL The ice-choked **Stikine River** and **Chief Shakes Hot Springs** are cold and hot, respectively, in a valley called a "Yosemite that keeps going..." (see p. 434).

JAM with folk fests, fiddles, and blues at **Juneau's Alaskan Hotel** (see p. 450).

EXPLORE hidden **Tlingit totem poles** in the forest around Sitka (p. 441).

SURF off the black sands of Yakutat (see p. 467).

Southeast Alaska, known as "the Panhandle," spans 500 miles from the wet peaks of Misty Fjords National Monument (see p. 431), past the state capital of Juneau (see p. 447), to Skagway (see p. 462) and the foot of the Chilkoot Trail. Snow-capped coastal ranges separate it from the Interior and countless straits divide thousands of islands, inlets, and fjords, collectively known as the Inside Passage. Panhandle towns typically cling to narrow pockets of coast that provide little room for growth.

Boasting a mild, wet climate year-round, fantastic salmon runs, enormous halibut, the Tongass National Forest, and the largest old-growth temperate rainforest in the world, fishing and logging are the economic mainstays of the region. However, come summer, tourism is king. Cruise ships, charter boats, and ferries might clog the waterways, but it's still possible to slip away from the mayhem with a short hike to a quiet beach, cloud-swathed mountain, or lush rain forest. To avoid the cruise ship hordes (and the prices that go along with them) winter is the best time to travel. Unfortunately, many businesses close shop in winter due to little traffic. Wilderness camping is always free within the Tongass, and remote, well-maintained Forest Service cabins are a steal (from $25 per night), although many of these, along with some of the region's most vaunted sights—Misty Fjords, the Stikine River, LeConte Glacier, Glacier Bay—require fly-in or boat-in service. Such service can be expensive, but charter groups will often offer last-minute discounted fares for empty seats; good news for single travelers.

The Panhandle is accessible by boat and plane, but it is most often reached by the Alaska Marine Highway ferry system (see p. 425). The Marine Highway's late-night departures, delays, and occasional long layovers require patience and flexibility. By night, the deck is littered with mummy-bagged travelers camping under the stars to avoid pricey accommodations. By day, however, the views are spectacular—the Southeast is home to more bald eagles than anywhere else in the world, and most of the humpback whales in the Pacific summer here.

KETCHIKAN
☎ 907

Ketchikan is Alaska's fourth-largest city (population 14,000), but you wouldn't know it. One reason, immediately observed by most travelers to this area, is that Ketchikanians *want* to live here. Ketchikan is surrounded by the Tongass National Forest and Misty Fjords National Monument, and provides an excellent home base for some of the most outstanding hiking, kayaking, fishing, and flightseeing opportunities in Southeastern Alaska.

Alaska

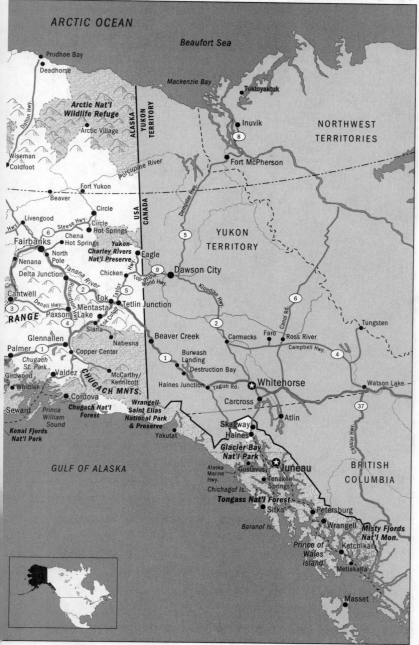

ARCTIC OCEAN

Beaufort Sea

Prudhoe Bay
Deadhorse

Mackenzie Bay

Tuktoyaktuk

Arctic Nat'l
Wildlife Refuge

Inuvik

NORTHWEST
TERRITORIES

8

Arctic Village

Dalton Hwy.

ALASKA

YUKON TERRITORY

Porcupine River

Wiseman
Coldfoot

Fort McPherson

Fort Yukon

USA
CANADA

Beaver

Circle

5

YUKON
TERRITORY

Livengood

Steese Hwy.

Circle
Hot Springs

Hwy. 1

6

Chena
Hot Springs

Fairbanks

Dempster Hwy.

North
Pole

Yukon-
Charley Rivers
Nat'l Preserve

Eagle

9

Dawson City

6

Nenana

Tanana River

Chicken

Top-of-the
World Hwy.

Tungsten

Delta Junction

2

Richardson Hwy.

Tok

5

Taylor Hwy.

Tetlin Junction

Klondike Hwy.

Cantwell

Denali Hwy.

Mentasta
Lake

Tok Cutoff

2

Carmacks

Faro

Campbell Hwy.

RANGE

Paxson

4

Slana

Beaver Creek

Ross River

6

Glennallen

4

Palmer

1

Copper Center

Nabesna

1

Burwash
Landing

Destruction Bay

Watson Lake

Chugach
St. Park

Valdez

CHUGACH MNTS.

McCarthy/
Kennicott

Haines Junction

Tagish Rd.

Whitehorse

37

Girdwood

Cordova

Chugach Nat'l
Forest

Wrangell-
Saint Elias
National Park
& Preserve

Carcross

Whittier

Seward

Prince
William
Sound

Skagway

Atlin

Kenai Fjords
Nat'l Park

Yakutat

Haines

Cassiar Hwy.

GULF OF ALASKA

Glacier Bay
Nat'l Park

Alaska
Marine
Hwy.

Gustavus

Juneau

BRITISH
COLUMBIA

Tenakee
Springs

Chichagof Is.

Tongass Nat'l Forest

Sitka

Baranof Is.

Petersburg

Wrangell

Misty Fjords
Nat'l Mon.

Prince of
Wales
Island

Ketchikan

Metlakatla

Masset

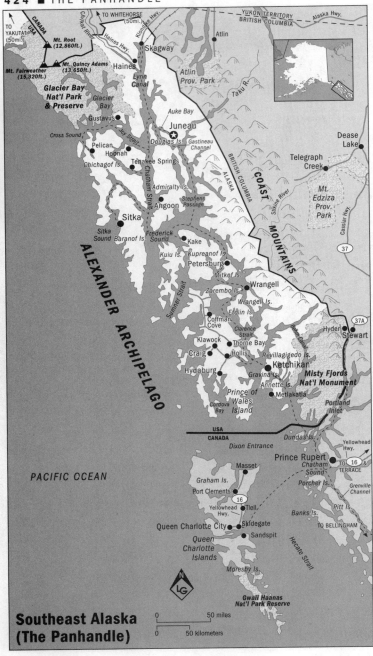

**Southeast Alaska
(The Panhandle)**

0   50 miles

0   50 kilometers

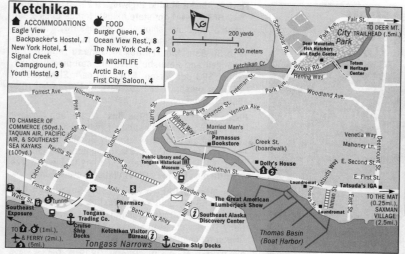

Ketchikan

♠ ACCOMMODATIONS
Eagle View
Backpacker's Hostel, 7
New York Hotel, 1
Signal Creek
Campground, 9
Youth Hostel, 3

🍴 FOOD
Burger Queen, 5
Ocean View Rest., 8
The New York Cafe, 2

🍸 NIGHTLIFE
Arctic Bar, 6
First City Saloon, 4

Every summer day, the town is dwarfed by cruise ships making their first stop in Alaska. Try to arrive in the evening (after 6pm), after the cruise ships have gone, to experience Ketchikan as the Ketchikanians live it, not as four thousand tourists chew it up and spit it out. A revamped "historical district" is dressed for the tourists who support the newest growth industry, but parts of Ketchikan remain economically depressed. The adjustment to a tourism-based service economy has not been easy for many of the town's residents, who would prefer to turn back the clock to the days when fishing and logging were the only shows in town.

▌ TRANSPORTATION

Ketchikan rests on the west side of Revillagigedo Island (ruh-VIL-ya-GIG-a-doe), 235 mi. southeast of Juneau and 90 mi. northwest of Prince Rupert, BC. Reset your watch to **Alaska Time,** which is an hour behind Pacific Standard Time. Public transportation is inconvenient, but many sights are within walking distance. Renting a bike is a good idea if you want to reach the sights outside of town.

Flights: Ketchikan's **airport** is located on nearby Gravina Island. A small ferry runs from the airport to town, arriving just north of the state ferry dock (every 30min., $6 one-way and round-trip if you return the same day). **Alaska Airlines** (☎800-225-2752) makes daily flights around Alaska and to **Juneau** (from $100). **ProMech Air** (☎225-3845 or 800-860-3845) makes regular flights to **Metlakatla** ($66 round-trip, seniors and children $59) and **Prince of Wales Island** ($198 round-trip). **Taquan Air,** 1007 Water St. (☎225-8800 or 800-770-8800; www.taquan.com), specializes in flights to **Misty Fjords** (see below; $179 for a 1½ hour flightseeing adventure). Much of the surrounding wilderness can be reached only by boat or float plane, for hire through the visitors center. **Pacific Air, Taquan Air,** and **Island Wings** (☎225-2444 or 888-854-2444) will fly charter-flight routes for groups of 2 or more (approx. $400 per hr. with $250 per hr. standby rate). To get the benefit of a flightseeing tour for less money, consider hopping on the mail plane for a bush pilot flight. See **Outdoor Activities,** p. 429.

FROM THE ROAD

UNEXPECTED NEW FRIENDS

In the last five minutes of the flight from Seattle to Ketchikan, I met my neighbor. She was a Sitka resident who, upon hearing that I would be in her town three weeks later, gave me her number, and offered the free use of her car and her home. Being a New Yorker, I was flabbergasted and almost melted in thanks as she preceeded me down the aisle. On the three minute ferry ride from the Ketchikan airport to Ketchikan proper I met John, who gave me a ride to the hostel, protested that I needn't pay for a bed, and insisted that I share his family's freshly-caught halibut dinner. Later that night, I met two pilots who offered to take me flying. And did. Four times. Two nights later I met a woman who offered to have me crash with her when I got back from a few days on Prince of Wales. I called when I got back to Ketchickan, but hung up when I got her business machine. A few hours later, I tried again, this time listening to the full message. After the typical message ended, there was a brief pause and then, "and if this is Catherine, we're at [insert address]. The house is open—please make yourself at home and we'll see you tonight." Now, I don't mean to suggest that you cancel your hostel reservations, but people are awfully friendly here. I have never encountered such casual and natural generosity. Southeastern Alaskans thrive on sharing the wealth.

—Catherine Gowl

Ferries: Alaska Marine Highway (☎225-6181 or 800-642-0066; www.dot.state.ak.us), ferries dock 2 mi. north of the cruise ships on N Tongass Hwy. "The Bus" stops here (see below). Call hours M-F 8am-5pm, Sa and Su 8am-4pm. Ferries to: **Juneau** (stopping in Wrangell and Petersburg, 18 hr.; stopping in Sitka, 36hr., $83 per person, $181 per car); **Sitka** (23hr., $61 per person, $131 per car); and **Wrangell** (5½-6hr., $26 per person, $55 per car).

Public Transportation: "The Bus" runs a loop between the airport parking lot near the ferry terminal, the dock, and Saxman Village. M-Sa every 30min. 6am-11pm, Su every hr. 9am-3pm. $1.50; seniors and children ages 5-12yrs, under 4 free. Exact fare required. A **free shuttle** runs from SEADC to **Walmart** every 30min.

Taxis: Alaska Cab (☎225-2133), **Sourdough Cab** (☎225-5544), and **Yellow Taxi** (☎225-6800) offer charter rates ($25 per 30min.). From downtown to the ferry $8, downtown to Saxman $10. Check the visitors center for charter tours ($25 per 2hr.).

Car Rental: Alaska Car Rental, 2828 N. Tongass Ave (☎225-5000 or 800-662-0007). Free local pick-up and delivery; unlimited mileage. Must be 21+ or have full insurance.

🛈 PRACTICAL INFORMATION

Tourist Information: 131 Front St. (☎225-6166 or 800-770-3300; www.visit-ketchikan.com), on the cruise ship docks. Each charter or touring company has its own kiosk and offers maps, info and reservations. **ATM, public restrooms,** and pay phones. Open daily 8am-5pm and when cruise ships are in. **Southeast Alaska Discovery Center (SEADC),** 50 Main St. (☎228-6220; www.fs.fed.us/r10/tongass), caters to the independent traveler and is an essential stop for outdoor adventurers traveling anywhere in Southeast Alaska. The trip-planning room is run by the **US Forest Service** and features a bookstore, maps, and brochures. A knowledgeable staff gives advice for free. Open May-Sept. daily 8am-5pm; Oct.-Apr. Tu-Sa 10am-4:30pm. **Southeast Reservations** (☎800-287-1607) is the ultimate resource for finding high value in adventure trips.

Equipment Rental: In general, it is best to call ahead for equipment rental, since the guides are often out exploring: a walk-in may yield nothing but the sound of your knock. **Southeast Sea Kayaks** (☎225-1258 or 800-287-1607) has a kiosk in the visitors center and an office on Water St. by Taquan and Pacific Air. Singles $35 per day for plastic, $40 for fiberglass, doubles $55 per day; discounted rates for longer trips. $200 damage deposit. They also sell a trip-planning guide to Misty Fjords that includes map, hiking, kayaking, and sheltering information ($16).

Work Opportunities: The **Chamber of Commerce,** 744 Water St., upstairs (☎225-1388 and 225-3184, www.ketchikanchamber.com), provides information on job listings. The **Alaskan Jobs website** (www.jobs.state.ak.us) is a resource for finding seasonal, part-time, and full-time work. Open M-F 8am-5pm (sometimes closed M 9-10am for staff meetings and W 11:30-1:30 for chamber luncheon). The **Ketchikan Daily News** (www.ketchikandailynews.com) is a good source for job listings. The help wanted board to in **Potlatch,** 126 Thomas St. (☎225-4855), advertises employment on the boats.

Bookstores: Village Source, 807 Water St. (☎225-7600). Open M-Sa 11:30am-5:30pm.

Market: Tongass Trading Company, on the main cruise ship dock. Everything from kerosene to quick dry towels. Open M-Sa 8am-6pm, Su 8am-5pm.

Laundromat/Public Showers: The Mat, 989 Stedman St. (☎225-0628). The TV and arcade should keep you glued to your spot. 10 lb. of laundry, $2.25. Showers $2.50 per 15min. Towels $0.75; soap $0.29. Open daily 6:30am-10pm.

Weather: ☎800-472-0391.

Emergency: ☎911.

Police: ☎225-6631, at Main and Grant St. across from the hostel.

Pharmacy: Downtown Drugstore, 300 Front St. (☎225-3144). Open daily 9:30am-6:30pm.

Hospital: Ketchikan General Hospital, 3100 Tongass Ave. (☎275-5171). 2 mi. north of town, just short of the ferry terminal.

Internet Access: Soapy's Station, 425 Water St. (☎247-9191), by the tunnel. They sell access cards for $4 per 15min., $6 per 50min., $10 for 100min. The cards are reusable and transferable to other stores in Juneau and at Salmon Landing by the SEADC. Open May-Sept. M-Sa 8am-6pm, Su 8am-2pm or whenever a cruise ship is in.

Post Office: (☎225-9601). Next to the ferry terminal. Open M-F 8:30am-5pm. There is a **substation** (☎225-7678) in the Great Alaskan Clothing building, on Mission St. near the library. Open M-Sa 9am-5:30pm. **Postal Code:** 99901.

▚ ACCOMMODATIONS AND CAMPING

Budget lodging is sparse in Ketchikan. The **Ketchikan Reservation Service** provides info on B&Bs. (☎800-987-5337; fax 247-5337. Singles from $69.) The bus doesn't service most B&Bs, so you'll have to hike or catch a cab. For more info on Forest Service campgrounds and cabins, call the reservations hotline (☎877-444-6777) or check www.reserveusa.com. Forest Service Cabins in the area are generally accessible only by boat or floatplane and cost $25-45 per night.

Ketchikan Youth Hostel (☎225-3319), at Main and Grant St. in the First Methodist Church. The impeccably clean men's and women's dorm rooms are spare but functional. Linens $1.25. 4-night max. stay. Strict lockout 9am-6pm. Curfew 11pm. No alcohol. Open June-Aug. $12, nonmembers $15. ❶

New York Hotel, 207 Stedman St. (☎225-0246, toll-free 866-225-0246), offers quiet and spotlessly clean dark-wood rooms with cable TV, data ports, and full bath. (Singles $89 per night, $79 for 2 or more nights; doubles $99, $89). ❹ The hotel management recently acquired several 2 story units on Creek St. These offer kitchenettes, DVD and VHS players, and jacuzzis, not to mention seals swimming by the window. $139 for the 1st 2 people, and $10 for each additional person up to 6. ❸

Eagle View Backpacker's Hostel, 2303 5th Ave. (☎225-5461). From Tongass, take Jefferson Ave. uphill and turn right on 5th Ave. Less than 1 mi. from ferry docks. Kitchen, shared bath, deck, TV, and sauna. Great harbor views. 3 rooms with space for 5 males, 3 females, and 1 couple. Laundry $3 per load. $25 plus tax per person. ❷

Signal Creek Campground (USFS), 5¼ mi. north of ferry dock, Mile 1 on Ward Lake Rd. 24 units with water, toilets, and fire pits. Bring your fishing gear. Self-registration. Strict 14-day max. stay. Open early May-late Sept. Sites $10. ❶

🍴 FOOD

Grocery stores are your best bet for affordable food in this tourist town. **JR's,** closest to downtown at 407 Dock St., is essentially a convenience store. (Open daily 7am-11pm.) **Tatsuda's IGA,** at the corner of Stedman and Deermount, stocks groceries, liquor, and deli products. (Open daily 7am-11pm.) **Carr's,** at the Plaza Shopping Center on Tongass near the ferry docks, is huge, has a pharmacy, and is open 24hr.

■ **New York Cafe,** 207 Stedman St. (☎225-1800). At the south end of Creek St. Incredible soup, healthy lunch specials (around $8), and frequent poetry readings in the evening make this an excellent and comfortable place to bide your time when locked out of the hostel. There is always a veggie option. Open M-F 6am-8pm, Sa-Su 6am-11pm. ❷

■ **Ocean View Restaurante,** 1831 Tongass Ave. (☎225-7566). In a new location, this local favorite continues its tradition of good food and large portions, but now offers more seating and a gorgeous view. Italian and Mexican specialties start at $7. Free chips and salsa. If your view is better at home, they'll deliver. Reservations recommended. Open daily 11am-11pm. ❷

Burger Queen, 518 Water St. (☎225-6060). North side of the tunnel. The best burgers in town ($5.50-8.50) were served out of a truck for 15 years. Now they are served in a building with less character; Ketchikanians, however, still swear by the quality of the food. Get your halibut and chips ($10) delivered across the street to the Arctic Bar for a harbor view. Open M-Sa 11am-7pm. ❷

🎭🎵 NIGHTLIFE AND ENTERTAINMENT

The annual **Timber Carnival** enlivens a boisterous 4th of July with speed-chopping, axe-throwing, and other fantastic lumberjack feats. On the second Saturday in August, the **Blueberry Arts Festival** brings art, food, music, and wackiness to the streets, when locals race slugs and have chewing gum competitions.

First City Saloon, 830 Water St. (☎225-1494), ¼ mi. north of the tunnel. With 3 bars, pool tables, video games, and a dance floor, this is the youngest hangout in town. Guinness ($5) and a variety of microbrews ($2-4) flow liberally, and the halibut tacos ($6) are famous. Leave your mark on the ceiling with one of the markers kept behind the bar. Live local music Tu-Su with a $3 cover. Open M-Sa noon-2am, Su 4pm-2am.

Ketchikan Brew Pub, 602 Dock St. (☎247-5221), serves the only beer brewed in town. Try the Spruce Tip Beer, steeped with hand-picked Sitka Spruce tips. If you bring any bottle that seals, they'll fill it with beer to go. Open M-Sa 10am-2am, Su 12:30pm-2am.

Arctic Bar, 509 Water St. (☎225-4709). This popular bar is distinguished by a logo that features copulating bears and a deck that features a harbor view. Open daily until 2am.

👁 SIGHTS

Every summer day, thousands of cruise travelers tumble down gangplanks into Ketchikan, attracting horse-drawn carriages and charter boats that cart them all over the island. The official walking tour (available at the information center and most establishments) does little to improve the lot of disoriented tourists, although the town has much to offer.

SAXMAN TOTEM PARK. A Tlingit village founded in 1894, Saxman was accessible only by boat until a few decades ago and houses the state's largest collection of totems. The community's longhouse is surrounded with brightly colored recent and historic carvings (up to 150 years old); you can't get in, however, unless you are on a tour. Each pole's story is described in a $1 guide, available at the **Saxman Arts Co-op** down the hill. Come during the day to view master carvers working at the **Edwin C. Dewitt Carving Center,** next door to the park. Several companies in town offer 2hr. tours that include dancing and descriptions of the totems. **Cape Fox,** a Native company, has the best tour, even if it is a bit more expensive ($35). Call Rebecca at Saxman City Hall (☎225-4846) for more information; tours are organized around the cruise ships. *(2½ mi. SW of town on Tongass Hwy.; a short ride on the highway bike path, a ride on The Bus, or a $10 cab. Wheelchair accessible. The park is always open. Free.)*

TOTEM POLES. The **Totem Heritage Center** presents 33 original 19th-century totem poles and many fragments in their raw, unrestored state gathered from around Ketchikan. The surrounding museum serves as an excellent introduction to totem carving traditions. *(601 Deermount St. Up Park St. on the hill above downtown. Open May-Sept. daily 8am-5pm; Oct.-Apr. Tu-F 1-5pm. Wheelchair accessible. $4, under 12 free. $9.95 with admission to the Hatchery (see below.).)* For more totem madness, check out the **Totem Bight State Historical Park,** where the poles look out to the sea from a natural forest setting. Consider biking and packing a picnic, since taxis operate on exorbitant charter rates of $55 round-trip. Go early to beat the tour buses. *(10 mi. north of the ferry docks on the N Tongass Hwy. Wheelchair accessible. Free.)*

DEER MOUNTAIN TRIBAL HATCHERY AND EAGLE CENTER. The hatchery is run by the Ketchikan Indian Corporation and offers a glimpse into modern fishing raise and release practices. While a pair of injured eagles are permanent residents, young salmon and trout are shipped off as soon as they come of age. Come in July to see the adult salmon return. *(1158 Salmon Rd. Located across the creek from the Totem Heritage Center. ☎225-6026. In summer open daily 8:30am-4:30pm. Wheelchair accessible. $6.95, $9.95 includes admission to Totem Heritage Center.)*

🏔 OUTDOOR ACTIVITIES

The wilderness around Ketchikan offers boundless opportunities for the fisher, hiker, or kayaker, but you'll need transportation and a little dough. Kim at Southeast Reservations and Sea Kayaks and the SEADC Trip Planning room (see **Tourist Information,** p. 426) are great first stops. The US Forest Service (☎877-444-6777) maintains **cabins** ($25-45 per night) and **shelters** in the Tongass National Forest, generally accessible only by boat or floatplane, that can be reserved in advance.

HIKING. Many great fishing, swimming, and outdoor activities are found along the hiking trails. The trail difficulties range from an easy walk to a strenuous climb. Many of the maintained trails in Southeast Alaska are boardwalks that protect the muskeg (and protect you from the muskeg: you can sink in up to your thighs).

Deer Mountain Trail (2½ mi. or 10 mi.). From downtown: Park St. becomes Fair St. which becomes the hairpin turns of Ketchikan Lakes Rd. At the crossroads follow signs and veer left to the trailhead. Most hikers stop at the peak after 2½ mi., but the trail continues for 7½ more mi. past Blue Lake, John Mountain, Little Silvis Lake, and Beaver Falls Fish Hatchery to emerge 12 mi. south of Ketchikan at the Beaver Falls Powerhouse parking lot.

During the latter 7½ mi., snow and ice remain even in the summer and the trail is less maintained. A steep climb yielding sparkling rewards, the trail gains 3350 ft. An A-frame **cabin** between Deer Mountain and John Mountain can be reserved through the Forest Service (☎877-444-6777). Open June-Sept. Moderate to difficult.

Perseverance Lake Trail (2½ mi.). 100 ft. past the entrance to the 3C's Campground. A less strenuous, family-oriented hike that climbs the 450 ft. to Perseverance Lake. The boardwalk trail passes through muskeg, Sitka spruce, hemlock, and cedar. The lake is great for trout fishing. Open Mar.-Nov. Easy.

Ward Lake (1 mi.). Head to the Signal Creek Campground for this easy walk around the grassy pond. Once there, outdoors activities abound for bikers, swimmers, and even tanners. Open year-round. Easy.

Connell Lake Trail (2½ mi. one-way). Turn right of Revilla Rd. onto Connell Lake Rd. (past the entrance to the Last Chance Campground) and follow for ½ mi. This hike starts at the parking area opposite the dam. The trail traverses old-growth forest where berries and bird-watching opportunities abound. Open year-round. Easy to moderate.

Naha River Trail (5½ mi. one-way). This trail is accessible only by boat or floatplane from Naha Bay. The trail winds along the Naha River through a series of lakes and provides access to some of the best stream fishing in the Ketchikan area. There are 2 forest service cabins along the trail, 1 at the final destination, Heckman Lake, which can be reserved in advance. Open Mar.-Oct. Difficult.

KAYAKING. Although kayaks are easy to rent, anyone who is not a seasoned paddler should never venture into the water on their own. All kayak rentals are dependent upon an assessment of a kayaker's experience. That said, the area around Ketchikan offers several launch points and truly outstanding paddling.

Naha Bay is located 25 mi. north of Ketchikan, has the largest remaining stretch of old-growth temperate rainforest in the world, and is closed to all commercial activity. Southeast Sea Kayaks (see **Practical Information,** p. 426) will transport to the launch and pick up for $20 per person. Consult the kayaking outfitters for the best means of navigating this area.

Moser Bay is 4 mi. north of Settler's Cove launch point (18 mi. north of Ketchikan at the end of the road). Moser is a deep, well-protected inlet that also houses the **Wolf Lake Trail,** which leads to a shelter on Upper Wolf Lake. A good day or overnight trip.

George Inlet, a long arm of the sea that stretches into Revillagigedo Island south of Ketchikan, offers numerous coves and islands to explore. The water is calm even on windy days, largely untrafficked by other boats, and easily accessibly by road.

The Tatoosh Islands lie just west of **Bretton Island** and boast many beaches for camping and exploration. Bretton Island has 10 mi. of shoreline and provides excellent opportunities for viewing bald eagles, cormorants, seals, porpoises, and orca whales. You can camp on a Tatoosh beach if you want to stay over. **Southeast Exposure** offers a 4hr. day-trip to the Tatoosh Islands for $85 per person, a 4-day tour of the Misty Fjords for $708 per person, and a 6-day tour for $950 per person. Southeast Sea Kayaks (see **Practical Information,** p. 426) drops off and picks up kayakers anywhere on the Ketchikan roads for $20 per person each way. They also offer a 4-day trip to Misty Fjords for $799.

FLIGHTSEEING. The landscape visible from the air around Ketchikan is extraordinary. One of the best ways to see the area is to hop on the mail plane. **Taquan Air** will let you fly with the mail for cheaper rates than most companies. For the best viewing of the Misty Fjords, ask for the **Bush Pilot** flight to the tiny town of **Hyder** (population 200). The mail goes on Tu and Th mornings around 6:30am; going along with it will cost around $159. Call the night before to reserve; availability is dependent upon the weight of the mail.

SPORTFISHING. Fishing is a way of life in Ketchikan and there are plenty of salmon, dolly varden, steelhead, halibut, red snapper, and trout. The fishing off nearby Prince of Wales Island is the best around (see below). **Ketchikan Charter Boats, Inc.** (☎ 800-272-7291 or 225-7291) by the tunnel has guided boats, offers information on unguided boats, and sells fishing licenses. A 4hr. guided trip averages $135 per person; call for overnight quotes.

METLAKATLA   ☎ 907

Fifteen minutes by float plane from Ketchikan's cruise ship docks, Metlakatla, or "calm channel where the fog drifts in and out" in Tsimshian (SIM-she-an), is perched on the western flatlands of the **Annette Islands Reserve.** Sights such as the Fish Packing Company, the Duncan Cottage Museum and the Longhouse are open to tourists only during tours. **Traditional tribal dancing** is the finale worth waiting for. Tours are generally scheduled under contracts for cruise ships, and run at varying times that often clash with the ferry and flight schedules. The independent traveler can join a tour by calling the Tourist Director's Office in advance. (☎ 886-8687. Open M-F 8am-4:30pm. $40.) West of Metlakatla proper rises what appears to be a transplant from the American Southwest. **Yellow Hill** (named for the unique color of its rusting iron ore deposits), offers vistas of Annette Island. **Leask Market,** at 1st and Milton, is a fully stocked grocery store. (☎ 886-4881. Open M-F 10am-6pm, Sa 10am-5:30pm, Su noon-5pm.) **The Metlakatla Hotel and Restaurant ❹,** 1807 3rd and Lower Milton, has large, attractive rooms with microwave, coffeemaker, cable TV, full bath and minifridge for $88. The **restaurant ❷** is the only one in town. It serves $6 sandwiches and burgers and a sunday brunch buffet. (Restaurant open May-Sept. Tu-Sa and Oct.-Apr. Su-F 11:30am-6pm.) The hotel also organizes fishing trips for $100-$150 a day, some of the best prices around. **Pro-Mech Air** flies several 15min. trips a day from Ketchikan to "Met"; frequency and number vary, so call ahead. (In Metlakatla ☎ 886-3845, in Ketchikan ☎ 225-3845 or 800-860-3845. $68 round-trip, offers specials.) The **Alaska Marine Highway** (☎ 800-624-0066; www.dot.state.ak.us) visits the island six times a week and twice on Saturdays (1¼hr., $15). The ferry terminal is a short walk from town.

MISTY FJORDS NATIONAL MONUMENT   ☎ 907

The jagged peaks, plunging valleys, and dripping vegetation of **Misty Fjords National Monument,** 20 mi. east of Ketchikan, make biologists dream and outdoor enthusiasts drool. Accessible only by kayak, power boat, or float plane, the 2.3 million-acre monument offers superlative camping, kayaking, hiking, and wildlife viewing. More than 12 ft. of annual rainfall and a flood of runoff from large icefields near the Canadian border feed the streams and waterfalls that empty into two long fjords, **Behm Canal** (117 mi.) and **Portland Canal** (72 mi.), on either side of the monument.

KAYAKING. Misty Fjords has superlative kayaking. **Walker Cove, Punchbowl Lake,** and **Rudyard Bay,** off Behm Canal, are choice destinations for paddlers. Bear in mind, however, that the waters are frigid and wide stretches of the coast lack good shelter or dry firewood. Seasoned **kayakers** navigate the harsh currents between Ketchikan and Behm Canal and paddle straight into the monument. For the less expert, transportation into and orientation in the Fjords is provided by **Southeast Sea Kayaks** (see **Equipment Rental,** p. 426). They charge $150-300 for drop-off and pickup at the entrance to the Fjords, and also sell a trip planning package, including maps, suggested routes and area information ($16). The folks at **SEADC** are a great resource for planning the trip yourself, and can also give you details on the minimal but outstanding hiking in the monument (see **Tourist Information,** p. 426).

CAMPING. Wilderness camping is permitted throughout the monument, and is best on the sandy beaches. The Forest Service maintains four remote, free, first-come, first-served shelters and 14 **cabins ❶** ($25). Call far in advance to the **Misty Fjords Ranger Station** (☎ 225-2148) to choose a cabin, or talk to the folks at SEADC (see **Tourist Information,** p. 426). To reserve cabins, call the **Forest Service Hotline** (☎ 877-444-6777) or go to www.reserveUSA.com

PRINCE OF WALES ISLAND   ☎ 907

Prince of Wales Island sits less than 30 mi. west of Ketchikan, beneath a thick temperate rainforest canopy broken by mountain peaks, patches of muskeg, and swaths of clear-cut land. Tongass National Forest rangers and Native American tribal groups manage most of the island's real estate, which is criss-crossed with logging roads. On an island this large—smaller only than Hawaii and Kodiak in the US—exploration requires a set of wheels. The 1800 mi. of logging roads are perfect for mountain biking (but there is no rental on the island, so rent bikes in Ketchikan or bring your own) or tooling around in an all-terrain vehicle. Acquire permits for and know where tribal lands end and the National Forest begins.

There are three main towns on Prince of Wales: **Craig, Klawock,** and **Thorne Bay.** Craig, on the west side of the island, has most of the tourist resources. The tribal community of Klawock lies 7 mi. north, while the more remote town of Thorne Bay is 43 mi. east of Klawock on the other side of the island. There are a few B&Bs here, but all cost $90 or more per night. **Hollis,** where the ferry docks, is 31 mi. east of Craig and has only a mini-mart and a library. Although Craig caters mainly to big-time fishermen and hunters, others use the town as a starting point for their exploration of Prince of Wales Island.

◧ TRANSPORTATION. Float planes fly directly into Craig from Ketchikan, although schedules vary; call for more detailed information. **Promech Air** (☎ 826-3845 or 800-860-3845) flies the route for $99 each way. The snazzy new **Interisland Ferry** makes the 2½hr. trip twice daily from Ketchikan. (☎ 866-308-4848. Leaves Ketchikan at 10:35am and 5:45pm; leaves Hollis at 7am and 2:10pm. May-Sept. $29, seniors $14, 15 ft. car $57, 19 ft. car $68. Oct.-Apr. $25, senior $12, 15 ft. car $51, 19 ft. car $60.) **Jackson Cab** (☎ 755-2557) runs between Hollis and Craig for about $25. **Holiday Rentals,** 333 Cold Storage Rd. at the TLC Laundromat, rents cars for $49.95 per day plus $0.30 per mi., or for $75 per day with unlimited mileage. (☎ 826-2966. Open 24hr.) **Log Cabin Sporting Goods,** 1 Easy St., is an all around outfitter that rents canoes and kayaks. You can also get your **hunting and fishing licenses** here. (☎ 826-2205. Open Apr.-Sept. M-Sa 6am-6pm, Su 10am-4pm; Oct.-May daily 9am-5:30pm. Canoes $25 per day; single kayaks $40, doubles $50.)

◪ PRACTICAL INFORMATION. Tourist information is available from the **Forest Service Office** at 9th Ave. and Main St. Craig. They give the skinny on caves, camping, 20 wilderness cabins, and recreation sites on the island (☎ 826-3271. Open M-F 7am-5pm.) **Brown Bear,** in Klawock off the highway, sells fishing gear. (Open daily 4am-midnight.) The **Wells Fargo Bank** (☎ 826-3040), by the post office on Craig-Klawock Hwy. in Craig, and **Klawock IGA** both have **ATMs. JT Brown's,** on Front St. is a general store. Open daily 7:30am-6pm, but hours vary in the winter. **Voyageur Bookstore,** on Cold Storage Rd. in the Southwind Plaza, sells books and has **Internet** access. (☎ 826-2333. $4 for the 1st 15 min. $10 for an hr. credit that can be used any time. Open M-F 7:30am-7pm, Sa 9am-7pm, Su 12-4pm.) The **library** (☎ 826-3281), on 3rd St., has free **Internet access** if you sign up in advance. In an **emergency,** call ☎ 911. The **police** (☎ 826-3330) are opposite the library; **state police** ☎ 755-2918. The **Alicia Roberts Medical Clinic** (☎ 755-4800), is in Klawock, off the highway. The **post office** is on Craig-Klawock St. beside the Thompson Supermarket. (☎826-3298. Open M-F 8:30am-5pm, Sa noon-2pm.) **Postal Code:** 99921.

ACCOMMODATIONS AND CAMPING. Although most of the island falls within the free camping zone of Tongass National Forest, Craig is surrounded by private tribal lands where camping is **prohibited.** The **TLC Laundromat and Rooms ❸,** on Cold Storage Rd. past the supermarket, offers affordable slumber space with cable TV, shared bath, public showers, and communal refrigerator and microwave. (☎826-2966. Wash $2.25, dry $0.25 per 5min. Detergent $0.75. Showers $2.25 per 5min. Open M-Sa 7am-9pm. Singles $41.95; doubles $49.95.)

Visits to **Tongass National Forest** may last up to one month, as long as campers spend no longer than two weeks at any one site. Contact the **Forest Service Station** in Craig (see **Practical Information,** above) or **Thorne Bay** (☎828-3304) for more information on the 20 **wilderness cabins** they maintain. (☎877-6777; www.reserveusa.com. Advance reservations required. $25-45 per night). Most cabins can only be reached by boat or floatplane. Two cabins, **Control Lake** and **Sweetwater Lake,** can be reached by road, trail, and then row-boat. The Forest Service maintains two campgrounds on Prince of Wales Island: the newly built **Harris River Campground ❶,** halfway between Hollis and Craig, and the **Eagle's Nest Campground ❶,** halfway between Craig and Thorne Bay. Both campgrounds have gravel sites, toilets, water, cooking grates, picnic tables, and RV parking. (Sites $8 in summer).

FOOD. The **Klawock IGA,** on Craig-Klawock St. in Klawock, is cheap. **Dockside ❷,** at the corner of Third and Front St., serves homecooked yumminess to a loyal local clientele, and opens every morning for coffee at 5:30am. Massive omelettes and burgers are $6-8, but people come from near and far for the famous homemade pie ($3.50). Open Su-W 6am-3pm, Th-Sa 6am-8pm. **Ruth Ann's ❸,** on Front St., has affordable breakfast and lunch "stuff" (as their menu says; $6-9), but dinner prices skyrocket upwards of $18. (☎826-3377. Open daily 7am-9pm. Lunch menu closes at 3:30pm.)

OUTDOOR ACTIVITIES.

HIKING. Hiking is not the primary activity on Prince of Wales Island. A more extensive trail network has been years in the making. There is one trail right outside of town, the **Mt. Sunnahae Trail** (2hr.), but it is not maintained by the Forest Service. The trail is part mud, part log-balance-beam through the remaining forested section of a clear-cut area. To get there, take the Craig-Klawock Hwy. about a quarter-mile toward Klawock, and look for it on the right side of the road at the end of one of the guardrails past the last entrance to the trailer park. The **Harris River Trail** (1½ mi.) starts two miles east of the intersection of the Craig-Klawock Hwy. and Hydaburg, right next to the Harris River Campground. The trail ends at the river and has excellent wildlife-viewing and fishing possibilities. The road to Hydaburg offers several more trailheads. Two miles south of the intersection with Craig-Klawock Hwy. on Hydaburg Rd. lies **One Duck Trail** (1½ mi.), a steady, manageable, and boardwalked hike that climbs up a steep 1200 ft. to outstanding views of the Klawock Mountains. A 3-sided shelter with room for four is located at the edge of the alpine vegetation zone, which itself begs exploration. Contact **Craig Parks and Recreation** for more hiking ideas and trail info (☎826-3405), or go to www.fs.fed.us/r10/tongass/recreation for more information on recreation ideas in the Tongass National Forest.

KAYAKING AND DIVING. Prince of Wales Island is a kayaker's paradise. It is surrounded by smaller islands and has plenty of internal coves and lake chains to navigate. The tides are often ferocious, however, and whirlpools are not uncommon. Consult with your outfitter before taking off. Craig offers several kayak launching locations near Graveyard Island, Fish Egg Island, and Ballenas Islands: the boat ramp at North Cove, the beach by the helipad on the south side of "old town," and the City Park on and near Graveyard Island. Ask outfitters about the route to **Canoe Point** (approx 7 mi. one-way), north of Craig, where a giant waterfall—which you can walk behind—crashes into the water. From Thorne Bay, there is a launch for the **Honker Divide Route** (30 mi. one-way, 3-5 days), a challenging route that travels up the Thorne Bay River through Thorne, Twin, Galea, Honker, Butterfly, and Hatchery Lakes. It is best to begin the trip during a period of high water or after a heavy rain. There is a Forest Service **cabin** on Honker Lake (approx 23 mi. along the route). Call ahead (☎877-444-6777) to reserve. The **Sarkar Route** is a 15 mi. loop route which accesses five major lakes within a roadless area. There is a Forest Service **cabin** about one mile in on Sarkar Lake. Call ahead (☎877-444-6777) to reserve. The Sarkar parking area is located off Forest Service Road 20 on road 2050 about two thirds of the way between Craig and El Capitan Cave. For canoe and kayak rentals in Craig, go to **Log Cabin Sporting Goods** (see **Transportation,** p. 432). **Craig Dive Center,** at 1st and Main St. offers a two-tank dive for groups of four. (☎826-3481 or 800-380-3483. $125 per person.) Contact Craig Ranger District for more ideas and tide conditions.

SPELUNKING. The northern part of Prince of Wales Island is riddled with over 300 uncharted caves. One of the deepest known caves in North America, **El Capitan Cave** is one of the most striking sights on the island. Speleologists recently found grizzly bear bones there that they dated at nearly 12,295 years old. Free 2hr. tours start behind the gate 150 ft. inside the cave, and require a hard-hat and flashlight (hard-hat provided, you bring the flashlight). It's cold and damp inside, so dress accordingly. The cave is a 3hr. drive from Craig or Thorne Bay, largely on unpaved roads. Follow Forest Rd. 20 to Forest Rd. 15, take a left, and drive about a mile to the cave. (☎828-3304. Tours late May-early Sept. Th-Sa 9-11am, noon-2pm, 2-4pm; Children under 7 not permitted. Call at least a week in advance for a schedule of tours and to make reservations with the Thorne Bay Ranger's Office.)

MOUNTAIN BIKING. Prince of Wales Island's 1800 mi. of logging roads offer bountiful terrain for mountain bike exploration. There is no bike rental on the island, so you'll have to bring one over on the ferry. A Forest Service Road Guide is essential to navigate the web of roads. They are $4 at the SEADC in Ketchikan, or at the Forest Service office in Craig at 9th Ave. and Main St.

FISHING. There are numerous charter fishing companies on the island. The **Fireweed Lodge** across from St. Johns Catholic Church in Klawock offers fishing, room and meal packages. (☎755-2930; www.fireweedlodge.com. May 15-Sept. 30 a 4-night, 3-day fishing package with 4 people per boat costs $1613 per person. 2 people per boat is $2142 per person. Does not include cost of fishing license.) Consult the chamber of commerce (see p. 432) for more options.

WRANGELL   ☎907

Wrangell was the staging area for three gold rushes during the late 1800s and is the only town in Alaska to have been ruled by four nations—the Tlingit nation, Russia, Britain and the United States. Enamored with the town's surroundings, John Muir spent over sixty pages writing on the Stikine River, calling it "a Yosemite that just kept going and going." Wrangell is now trying to diversify its economy by attracting ecotourism; the newly founded **Convention and Visitors Bureau (CVB)** emphasizes Wrangell's natural wonders, which are too many to count.

◪ TRANSPORTATION

Wrangell rests on the northern tip of 30 mi. long Wrangell Island, 85 mi. north of Ketchikan and 150 mi. south of Juneau. The town is small and easily walkable. The **ferry** docks are at the north end of town; the **airport** is 1½ mi. east.

Flights: Alaska Airlines (☎874-3308 or 800-426-0333) is the only carrier with regular air service to and from Wrangell. Daily flights to: **Juneau** ($137.50); **Ketchikan** ($116.50); and **Petersburg** ($92.50). **Sunrise Aviation** (☎874-2319) offers flightseeing over the **Stikine River, LeConte Glacier, Tracy Arm and Endicott Arm,** and **Anan Bear Observatory** (prices depend upon number in party; call for rates).

Ferries: Alaska Marine Highway (☎874-2021 or 800-642-0066, www.alaska.gov/ferry), at Stikine Ave. and McCormack St. Service to: **Juneau** (13-26hr., $63); **Ketchikan** (6hr., $26); and **Sitka** (13hr., $43). Open 1hr. before arrivals. Lockers $0.25.

Taxis: Star Cab (☎874-3622) and **Northern Lights Taxi** (☎874-4646). $5 to the airport, $8-10 to the Rainbow Falls Trail.

Car Rental: Practical Rent-A-Car (☎874-3975; fax 874-3911), on Airport Rd. near the airport. Compacts $44.95 per day, vans $54.95 per day; unlimited mileage. 21+.

◪ PRACTICAL INFORMATION

Tourist Information: Chamber of Commerce (☎874-3901; www.wrangellchamber.org), on Front St. by the cruise ship docks. A huge calendar across the street lists events. Open M-F 10am-4pm or whenever a cruise ship is in.

Outdoor Information: District Forest Service Station, 525 Bennett St. (☎874-2323), ½ mi. east of town, off Church St. past the hospital. Free walks guided by a naturalist run every Sa. in July and Aug. Open M-F 8am-5pm. **Ottesen's True Value** (☎874-3377), on Front St., sells licenses. The service desk is to the right of the entrance. Open M-Sa 8am-6pm, Su 10am-3pm.

Equipment Rental: There are several operators in town that have formed a cooperative and matched their prices. They all rent bikes, kayaks, canoes, and skiffs, and all operate from the **Wrangell Tours** booth across from the Chamber of Commerce. They are **Alaska Waters** (☎800-347-4462, www.alaskawaters.com, no bikes), **Rainwalker Expeditions** (☎874-2549 or 874-0400, www.rainwalkerexpeditions.com), and **Solo Cat Sports** (☎877-874-2923). Bike rental: $27 half-day, $45 full day. Kayak rental: singles $24 half-day, $40 full day; doubles $40, $60. Aluminum skiffs: $150 per day. Longer rentals are discounted. Alaska Waters also rents camping kits for $15 per day.

Laundromat and Public Showers: Churchill Laundromat, on Front St., near Shakes Island. Wash $2, dry $0.25. Showers $2.50 per 10min. Open daily 8am-8pm.

Emergency: ☎911.

Police: ☎874-3304. In the Public Safety Building on Zimovia Hwy.

Pharmacy: Stikine Drug, 202 Front St. (☎874-3422). Open M-F 10am-5pm, Sa 10am-2pm.

Hospital: ☎874-3356. At Bennett St. and 2nd Ave.

Internet Access: Library (☎874-3535), on 2nd St. Free, but must sign up ahead. Open M and F 10am-noon and 1-5pm, Tu-Th 1-5pm and 7-9pm, Sa 9am-5pm.

Post Office: (☎874-3714), at the north end of Front St. Open M-F 8:30am-5pm, Sa 11am-1pm. **Postal Code:** 99929.

ACCOMMODATIONS AND CAMPING

If you've got a car or other means of transportation, well-maintained, well-located, and free Forest Service campgrounds are the best places to sleep. **Shoemaker Bay ❶**, 4½ mi. south of town across from the Rainbow Creek trailhead, has a tennis court, a beach, a harbor for pleasure craft, and accommodates tenters and RVs. **Nemo ❶**, 14 mi. south on Zimovia Hwy., sits on a ridge with breathtaking views of Zimovia Strait and the surrounding area. Wheelchair accessible. **Free forest service shelters ❶** are first-come, first-served and are located only a few miles up the trail from the **Rainbow Falls trailhead** (see **Outdoor Activities**, below).

Wrangell Hostel, 220 Church St. (☎874-3534), 5 blocks from the ferry terminal in the Presbyterian Church. Showers, large kitchen with free common food, and a common room with TV/VCR. No daytime lockout. 11pm curfew extended for late ferry arrivals. Closed Sept.-early Jun. $15. ❶

Rooney's Roost (☎874-2026), at the corner of McKinnon and Church St., 4 blocks from the ferry terminal. Rooney's offers beautiful, richly-colored rooms. Large common rooms, big-screen TV. Full breakfast included. Free rides to airport and ferry. Call ahead for reservations. Doubles $75; with private bath $95. ❹

Zimovia B&B, 319 Webber St. (874-2626), 4 blocks from downtown, has a private entrance, a sauna, cable TV, and kitchenette. Rooms $65. Weekly rates available. ❸

FOOD

Wrangell is not known for its restaurants, and most people eat at home. The **IGA Supermarket ❶**, 223 Brueger St. off Outer Dr., has groceries, the cheapest sandwiches in town ($3-5), and free coffee for patrons. (☎874-2341. Open M-Sa 8am-8pm.) **Zak's Cafe ❷**, 314 Front St. has a surprisingly eclectic menu and portions big enough for two. Dinners are expensive, but the cheap lunch menu ($6-10) is available all day and there are plenty of vegetarian options. (Open M-Sa 11am-9pm, Su noon-9pm.) In June, locals head to Front St. for **"Queen food"**--the daily specials prepared by contestants for Wrangell's homequeen. Proceeds go toward Wrangell's famous 4th of July celebrations.

SIGHTS AND EVENTS

There are a few worthwhile cultural attractions in town that could easily be seen in a day. See them, and then get yourself in a boat or on a trail.

SHAKES ISLAND. Here you'll find a replica of turn-of-the-century Tlingit Chief Shakes's **clanhouse,** built during the Depression by the Civilian Conservation Corps without the aid of a sawmill or a single nail. Surrounding the longhouse are replicated **totem poles.** (Walk south on Front St. toward the edge of town, past the Marine Bar, and walk across the bridge. Longhouse usually opens 30min. after a cruise ship docks. $2, by appointment $20. Totems can be visited anytime at no charge.)

PETROGLYPH BEACH. Walking the beach, which is littered with ancient rock carvings made anywhere from 2000-8000 years ago, is like a treasure-hunt. The more than 50 petroglyphs have faded, but splashing them with water makes them stand out. Even at high tide, the **Killer Whale petroglyph** to the right of the boardwalk and the **owl petroglyphs** under the tree are fairly easy to find. (¾ mi. north of town on Evergreen Ave. Best viewing 1hr. before and 1hr. after high tide. Wheelchair accessible. Free.)

EVENTS. To break the monotony of dreary winter, the first weekend in February brings the **Tent City Festival** to Wrangell. The event is one big party, replete with beard-growing and long-john contests. The **Garnet Festival** that heralds the arrival of spring is actually a birding festival with informational speakers on wildlife, a golf tournament, and live bands. The end of May and beginning of June brings the **Annual King Salmon Derby.** For the **Fourth of July,** Wrangell pulls out all the stops, boasting the largest, best celebration in Southeastern Alaska. Locals compete in the Soap Box Derby, log rolling, and other events, beginning on July 3.

⚡ HIKING

Wrangell's **Forest Service Station** offers free guided flora and fauna excursions every Saturday during the summer, and is an invaluable trip-planning resource. In addition to information on hiking, biking, and kayaking, rangers have descriptions and access options for Forest Service cabins ($25-35) and shelters (free). Marie at **Rainwalker Expeditions** will conduct guided tours and hikes through some of the island's beautiful sites for $10 per hr. or $60 per day, including transportation and a bag lunch (see **Equipment Rental,** above).

Mt. Dewey Trail (½ mi. round-trip, ½hr.). Head uphill on Church St., turn left on McKinnon, and follow the hiker signs. A short, quiet trail which winds its way to the top of Mt. Dewey, overlooking the town and Zimovia Strait. To get to all the other trails around Wrangell you will need some sort of transportation. Easy.

Rainbow Falls Trailhead, 3 mi. beyond City Park on Zimovia Hwy., is the opening spur for some of the best hiking in the area. **Rainbow Falls Trail** itself (¾ mi., 500 ft. gain, 20 min. one-way) starts on the spongy floor of an old-growth rain forest and climbs to a scenic view of the 100 ft. Rainbow Falls. On the right is the turnoff for the **Institute Trail** (2.7mi one-way, 1000ft gain, 1¾hr.), which climbs through old-growth forest to the Shoemaker Bay. (Moderate to difficult.) At the 1.5 mark, the Institute Trail intersects with the **North Wrangell High Country Trail** (2½ mi. loop, 1100ft. gain, 3hr.), which climbs to rewarding views of Southeast Alaska. (Moderate to difficult.)

The Anan Creek Trail, 31 mi. south of Wrangell, access by boat or float plane. This ½ mi. trail leads to excellent wildlife viewing at the **Anan Bear Observatory** during July and Aug. Forest service interpreters are on duty at the trailhead to brief you on safety. **Alaska Waters, Rainwalker Expeditions** and **Breakaway Adventures** all offer 6 hr. tours of the observatory for $165 per person.

⚓ WATERSPORTS

Most sightseers who spend a full day or more in Wrangell try to tackle the Stikine River. Many kayak, but only very experienced paddlers should attempt to run the river. The Forest Service has maps and info. There are six Forest Service cabins in the Stikine Delta and two bathing huts at **Chief Shakes Hot Springs,** a few miles upriver. The 160 mi. route on the Stikine River to **Telegraph Creek,** British Columbia, is a phenomenal trip of natural beauty. Unfortunately, because the rapid current makes upstream travel impossible, the only way to get to these and other attractions on the Stikine, such as **Shakes Glacier,** is by charter boat or plane. **Breakaway Adventures** (☎ 874-2488) charges $135-150 per person (depending on trip length), but often runs specials as low as $65 in July and Aug. They also offer full day fishing trips for the same price. **Alaska Waters** (☎ 800-347-4462 or 874-2378) runs the same route for $145. Call ahead to either charter for special prices to Telegraph Creek. For the less-experienced kayakers who don't run the Stikine, there are still plenty of paddling options in the Wrangell area. Starting at Earl West Cove is a 7mi. trip to **Berg Bay.** Four miles into the bay there is a Forest Service cabin (call ahead to reserve). From the cabin, you can paddle 13 mi. down the narrows to the **Anan Creek Trail** and the **Bear Observatory** (see above).

PETERSBURG
☎ 907

There is something achingly beautiful about Petersburg. Surrounded by fierce, breathtaking mountains, Petersburg's vivacious and simple friendliness seems out of joint with its environment. Petersburg supports one of the world's largest halibut fleets, and the tiny Wrangell Narrows leading to Petersburg spare the town from cruise ship crowds. For any travelers who squeeze through the Narrows, though, plentiful summer work, gorgeous hiking, breathtaking mountains, and generous, fiercely independent people await.

▐ TRANSPORTATION

Petersburg is on **Mitkof Island**. The **airport** is a mile east of the waterfront on Haugen Dr.; ferries dock a mile south of downtown at Nordic Dr. The town is circumnavigated by the main roads: **Nordic Dr.** becomes **Sandy Beach Rd.** becomes **Haugen Dr.** The **Mitkof Hwy.** leads south out of town to the free camping and trailheads.

Flights: Alaska Airlines, 1506 Haugen Dr. (☎772-4255 or 800-426-0333), flies direct once a day to **Juneau** ($147) and **Seattle, WA** ($401.69). Next door, **LAB** (☎772-4300) flies 3 daily flights to **Juneau** ($144) and services **Kake** ($64). **Pacific Wing** (☎772-4258) runs 45min. flightseeing tours of **LeConte Glacier** ($90 per person for 3 people, $75 per person for 6 people).

Petersburg

🍎 FOOD

🏠▲ ACCOMMODATIONS
Petersburg B&B Hostel, **3**
Tent City, **7**

Coastal Cold Storage, **1**
Hammer and Wikan, **6**
Helse, **5**
Alaskafe, **2**

🍷 NIGHTLIFE
Kito's Cave, **4**

Ferries: Alaska Marine Highway (☎772-3855 or 800-642-0066), Mile 0.9 Mitkof Hwy., 1 mi. from the town center. Open 1hr. before ferry arrivals. To: **Juneau** (8hr., $48); **Sitka** (10hr., $30); **Ketchikan** (10hr., $43); and **Wrangell** (3hr., $21).

Taxis: City Cab (☎772-3003), and **Maine Cab** (☎772-6969). Rates start at $4 around town, $5 anywhere to Tent City.

Car and Boat Rental: Scandia House 110 Nordic Dr. (☎772-4281 or 800-722-5006). Rents cars ($52 per day) and skiffs ($160).

▐ PRACTICAL INFORMATION

Tourist Information: (☎772-4636; www.petersburg.org) at 1st and Fram St. Open in summer M-Sa 9am-5pm, Su noon-4pm; winter M-F 10am-2pm.

Outdoor Information: Forest Service (☎772-3871), on 1st St., above the old post office, offers an extensive and essential free booklet on hiking trails in the area and info on the local forest service cabins. Open M-F 8am-5pm.

Dept. of Fish and Game (☎772-3801), Sing Lee Alley. Licenses available at **Sing Lee Alley Bookstore** (☎772-4440), on Sing Lee Alley. Open M-F 9:30am-5:30pm, Sa 9:30am-5pm, Su noon-4pm.

Work Opportunities: Petersburg Employment Service (☎772-3791), at Haugen Dr. and 1st St. Petersburg is a great place to find temporary work in the canneries. Most jobs for the duration of summer; **day labor** occasionally needed. Open M-F 10am-2pm.

Laundromat: Glacier Laundry (☎772-4144), at Nordic and Dolphin. Wash $2, dry $0.25 per 5min. Open 24hr., but bathrooms locked after 10pm.

Public Showers: The harbormaster at North Harbor (☎772-4688) has hot showers ($1 per 7½min.). Also at **Glacier Laundry** ($2 per 7min.; towels $1), and **Tent City**.

Emergency: ☎911.

Police: 16 S Nordic Dr. ☎772-3838.

State Police: ☎772-3100.

Hospital: Petersburg Medical Center (☎772-4291), at Fram and N 1st St.

Internet Access: Free at the **Library,** at Haugen and Nordic Dr. above the Fire Hall; sign up the day before. Open M-Th noon-9pm, F-Sa 1-5pm.

Post Office: 1300 Howkan (☎772-3121) off Haugen Dr. Open M-F 9am-5:30pm, Sa 11am-2pm. **Postal Code:** 99833.

◤ ACCOMMODATIONS AND CAMPING

Outside of Tent City and **LeConte RV Park ❶** (off of Haugen Dr.; $10 to pitch tent under the neighboring trees), the nearest campground, **Ohmer Creek ❶**, is 22 mi. south of the ferries. (Water and pit toilets. $6, season pass $30.) The **Raven's Roost Cabin ❶**, 4 mi. up the Raven's Roost trail (see below), the only forest service cabin on Mitkof Island, offers stellar views.

Petersburg Bunk & Breakfast Hostel, 805 Gjoa St. (☎772-3632), east of 8th St., between the airport and downtown. The cheapest beds in town. Free Internet and breakfast with homemade bread. Laundry $3. Lockout 9am-5pm. Open May 15-Sept. 15. Groups of 4 or more accommodated in winter. $25 per person. ❷

Yurtsville, 415 Mitkoff Highway (☎772-2921). 4 mi. south of town you can stay in yes, a yurt. Traditional circular Nordic houses with all the modern amenities: queen bed, sofa, fridge and stove. In a quiet, secluded wooded area. Yurts $65. ❸

Tent City (☎772-9864), on Haugen Dr. ½mi past the airport, 2 mi. from the ferry. Hordes of cannery workers bunk here in summer. Amenities include pay phone, water, toilets, lockers, and fire pits. Quiet hours 10pm-noon. No alcohol or guests midnight-6am. Open May-Sept. $5 per night, $125 per month. Showers $0.75. ❶

◖◗ FOOD AND NIGHTLIFE

Most of the fish that comes in off the boats goes straight to the cannery or is frozen and shipped, leaving restaurant seafood pricey. Grocery shopping at **Hammer & Wikan,** 1300 Haugen Dr., two blocks past the hostel, earns a free shuttle ride and cup of coffee. (☎772-4246. Open M-Sa 7am-8pm, Su 7am-7pm.) The downtown option is the **IGA** on Nordic Dr. Open M-Sa 7am-7pm, Su 9am-5pm.

▨ **Alaskafe** (☎772-5282), on Excel St. off of Nordic Dr., has the best food in town. Home-made bakery goodies, fresh salads, sandwiches, and soups ($5-8) are made before your eyes. Dinner entrees are expensive but worth the splurge ($11-18). Open M 8-11am, Tu 7am-3pm, W-F 7am-8:30pm, Sa 8am-3pm. ❷

■ **Coastal Cold Storage,** 306 N Nordic Dr. (☎772-4177). Serves fresh seafood at reasonable prices ($5-8). Open M-Sa 7am-5:30pm, Su 7am-3pm. ❷

Helse, 17 Sing Lee Alley (☎772-3444). Homemade soups and bread and a variety of eclectic, veggie-heavy sandwiches ($3.75-$8.25, half portions available). Open M-F 7:30am-5pm, Sa 10am-3pm. ❷

Kito's Kave (☎772-3207), on Sing Lee Alley, is the liveliest place in town, catering to young cannery workers. *Rolling Stone* once recognized Kito's for having the best Sa night music in Alaska. Open M-F 10am-2am, Sa 10am-3am, Su noon-2am.

🜛 🎵 SIGHTS AND ENTERTAINMENT

This is one of the best places on the Panhandle to see a fishing town at work. The heart of the year-round operations is down at **North Harbor,** near the middle of town on Excel Ave., where you can wander the docks, talk to local fishermen, read the bulletin boards, and savor the smells. Many of the fish processing companies will give tours to cruise ship passengers and other groups. Of the approximately 1000 whales that summer in Southeast Alaska, about 500 feed in Frederick Sound, just north of Petersburg. **Kaleidoscope Cruises** (☎800-868-4373 or 772-3736) will take you to see the whales with a retired marine biologist. (8hr. $180, min. group of 2). For saucy, cheap tours of **LeConte Glacier** and whale watching trips, ride with Brooklyn-born Sean Reilly of **Hook and Eye Charters.** (☎772-3400. $95 per person.)

For a hands-on experience of Petersburg's history, **Sandy Beach** at low tide reveals 8000-year-old petroglyphs to the left of the cove and perfectly preserved ancient heart-shaped fish traps reach out from the mud. Watch out for flying fish on the **4th of July:** celebrations feature a competitive herring toss.

🜚 OUTDOOR ACTIVITIES

Petersburg's best outdoors options are kayaking and hiking. **Tongass Kayak Adventures** (see **Equipment Rental,** p. 439), rents sea kayaks and offers guided tours up Petersburg Creek (4hr. tours daily June-Aug.; $55 per person), and to LeConte Glacier. **Pacific Wing** makes a 45min. flightseeing tour of the LeConte. (☎772-4258. $80.) Scandia House rents skiffs for $160.

Only a handful of Petersburg's many trails are readily accessible by foot. The Forest Service has a free book of trail descriptions, maps of logging roads suitable for mountain biking, and makes reservations for cabins. A great way to get a sense of Petersburg's diversity and natural beauty is to walk **"the loop,"** the 4.5 mi. road that makes a circle of downtown. After the Canneries, Nordic Dr. rounds a corner and continues to Hungry Point, where it becomes Sandy Beach Rd. At Sandy Beach Park, take a right onto Haugen, which traverses the muskeg and returns to downtown. Many locals **walk the beach** beyond Eagle's Roost Park and out around Hungry Point. The two Petersburg trails, among others, begin at the state dock in the neighboring Kupreanof Island and are accessible only by boat. Many charter operators in town ferry folks across the narrows and rent skiffs, but this can cost more than $100. Try asking at the harbormaster's office for suggestions: many fishermen and Kurpeanof-ites make the back and forth trip several times a day, and are willing to take passengers. Make sure you have a ride back to Miktof, though: residents on Kupreanof have grown impatient with unprepared visitors who knock on their doors to beg for a skiff ride back to town.

Raven's Roost Trail (4 mi. one-way, 5hr.). Take Haugen Rd. out past the airport and make a right at the orange and white water towers before Tent City. This beautiful trail with pitch varying from level to near-vertical leads to a popular **cabin** ❶ ($35). Moderate to difficult.

Three Lakes Trail (4½ mi., 2-3hr.). Drive south from Petersburg on the Mitkof Hwy. The Three Lakes Loop Rd. meets the Hwy. 10 mi. and 20 mi. from Petersburg. The three trailheads are 15 mi. from the north end of the Loop Rd. and 6 mi. from the south end. A boardwalk hike that makes a figure eight passing 4 lakes, all but one of which has a small rowboat available for public use. Easy.

Petersburg Lake Trail (10½ mi. one-way). Boat from Petersburg across the Narrows to the state dock on Kupreanof Island. You need a tide of 14 ft. or higher to reach the upper trailhead. The trail begins to the west of the dock and leads west up to Petersburg Lake, through a wilderness area to a Forest Service cabin. 4 mi. past the cabin is an entrance to the Petersburg Creek-Duncan Salt Chuck Wilderness. The trail continues through the wilderness for another 6½ mi. Moderate.

Petersburg Mountain Trail (3½ mi. one-way, 4-5hr.). From the lowtide dock, take a right at the top of the stairs and walk 3 mi. to the base of the mountain. A challenging trek ending with a steep climb to spectacular views of nearby glaciers. Difficult.

SITKA
☎ 907

Sitka was established as a Tlingit settlement thousands of years before Russian traders decreed it the outpost of "New Archangel" in 1799, making it the capital of Russian America. The Tlingit refused to accept the unwelcome foreign invasion, however, and fought for their land until 1804, when the Russians drove the Tlingits further inland. In 1867, Russia sold Russian America to the United States, signing the treaty that created Alaska in Sitka. A strong community of college students, anglers, artists, environmentalists, and Tlingits share the town, its unusually rich and diverse cultural offerings, and its mountain peaks.

▐ TRANSPORTATION

Sitka is one of the westernmost cities in the Southeast. The **ferry terminal** is 7 mi. out of town. The **airport** is just a mile away across the O'Connell Bridge, on Japonski Island. The main drag is **Lincoln St.,** which starts at Sitka National Historical Park, turns at St. Michael's Cathedral, and continues down to the waterfront.

Flights: Alaska Airlines (☎966-2422 or 800-426-0333; www.alaskaair.com). To **Juneau** ($113.50; 6am, 1:47pm and 7:30pm) and **Ketchikan** ($155.50; 11:34am, 1:47pm, and 7:30pm; the last 2 go through Juneau).

Ferries: Alaska Marine Highway, 7 Halibut Rd. (☎747-8737 or 800-642-0066; www.dot.state.ak.us), 7 mi. from town. To **Juneau** (9hr., $30); **Ketchikan** (20hr., $61); and **Petersburg** (10-14hr., $30). Open 1hr. before arrival.

Local Transportation: Sitka Tours (☎747-8443 or 747-7510 to arrange return-trip pickup), meets most ferries ($5, round-trip $7) and planes ($3, round-trip $5) and will drop you off just about anywhere; call ahead for a ride from town.

Taxis: Sitka Taxi (☎747-5001), and **Arrowhead Taxi** (☎747-8888). About $15 per person from Sitka to the ferry. $6.50 to the airport; $0.50 per additional person.

Car Rental: A&A Car Rental/Baranof Motors (☎747-8228), on Sawmill Creek Hwy., has the lowest rates. $44 per day, unlimited miles. 21+. Open M-F 8am-6pm, Sa 10am-2pm.

▐ PRACTICAL INFORMATION

Tourist Information: A small, busy **visitors center** in the Harrigan Centennial Building, 330 Harbor Dr. (☎747-3225), has printed information on sights and performance schedules.

Open in summer daily from 8am until the cruise ships leave. **Sitka Convention and Visitors Bureau,** 303 Lincoln St., Ste. 4 (☎747-5940; www.sitka.org) has oodles of information on accommodations. Open M-F 8am-5pm.

Outdoor Information: Sitka Ranger District, 204 Siginaka Way (☎747-6671), off Katlian Ave., by Thompsen Harbor. Pick up detailed information on trails, geological history, and Forest Service cabins ($35-45 per night). Open M-F 8am-4:30pm.

Fish and Game Dept., 304 Lake St. #103 (fishing ☎747-5355, hunting ☎747-5449). Open M-F 8:30am-5pm. **Mac's,** 213 Harbor Dr. (☎747-6970), sells licenses for both fishers and gamers. Open M-F 8am-7pm, Sa 8am-6pm, Su 9am-5pm. In exchange for filling out a trip plan, the **fire station,** 209 Lake St. (☎747-3233), will loan you a VHF radio for use on extended backpacking and kayaking trips.

Banks: Nations Bank of Alaska (☎747-3226), on Lincoln St. behind the church. Open M-Th 9:30am-5:30pm, F 9:30am-6pm. **24hr. ATM,** plus others on Lincoln St.

Work Opportunities: The **Sitka Sentinel** (☎747-3219) Friday edition has classified ads. The **Alaska Job Center Network,** 304 Lake St. (☎747-3423), has job postings and a **job hotline** (☎747-7989).

Equipment Rental: Southeast Diving and Sports, 105 Monastery St. (☎747-8279), rents 5-speeds and mountain bikes. $5 per hr., $20 per day. Open M-Sa 10am-5pm. **Sitka Sound Ocean Adventures** (☎747-6375), in the bus by the Centennial Building. Single kayaks $28 per half-day, $45 per day; doubles $35, $65. Guided 2hr. tours $60 per person, $50 per person for 3 or more people; skiffs for $140. Open daily 8am-5pm.

Luggage Storage: Duds and Suds Laundromat, 906 Halibut Pt. Rd., stores packs during the day for free. The **fire station,** 209 Lake St., also stores packs for free.

Bookstore: Old Harbor Books, 201 Lincoln St. (☎747-8808). Marine charts, topo maps, and info on local events. Open M-F 9am-6pm, Sa 9am-5pm, Su 10am-3pm.

Laundromats and Public Showers: Duds 'n' Suds Laundromat, 906 Halibut Point Rd. (☎747-5050), convenient to the hostel. Wash $1.75, dry $0.50 per 10min. Shower $2 per 10min. Open M-F 7am-8pm, Sa-Su 8am-8pm.

Pharmacy: Harry Race Pharmacy, 106 Lincoln St. (☎747-8006). Open M-F 10am-5pm.

Hospital: Sitka Community Hospital, 209 Moller Dr. (☎747-3241). Take Halibut Pt. Rd. out to Moller Dr. and take a right; the hospital is across from the ballfields.

Internet Access: Kettleson Memorial Library, 320 Harbor Dr. (☎747-8708). Free access, but show up early. Open M-Th 10am-9pm, F 10am-6pm, Sa-Su 1-5pm.

Post Office: 338 Lincoln St. (☎747-8491). Open M-Sa 8:30am-5:30pm. **Postal Code:** 99835.

ACCOMMODATIONS AND CAMPING

The two park service campgrounds are both far away. The Convention and Visitors Bureau has a list of Sitka's many **B&Bs** (from $60). **Sitka Sound Ocean Adventures** rents a **floating cabin** ❷ that sleeps 10, equipped with a skiff and kayaks (☎747-6375. $160 for one night, $150 per night for several nights.)

Sitka Youth Hostel (HI), 303 Kimshan St. (☎747-8661), in the United Methodist Church. A laid-back community atmosphere with plenty of communal food in the kitchen and free local calls. Basement dorms with comfy cots. Sign up for a chore. Lockout M-Sa 9:30am-6pm and Su 9am-6pm. Curfew 11pm. 3-night max. stay or until the next ferry leaves. Open June-Aug. $11, nonmembers $14. ❶

THE PANHANDLE

Sitka

▲ ACCOMMODATIONS
Sawmill Creek, 1
Sitka Hotel, 9
Sitka Youth Hostel, 2

FOOD
Alaska Native Brotherhood, 3
Backdoor, 5
Pizza Express, 4

NIGHTLIFE
Ernie's Old Time Saloon, 6
Pioneer Bar, 7

TO VERSTOVIA
TRAILHEAD & (1.25mi.)

Raptor Center

Sitka National Historical Park

Indian River

National Historic Park Visitor Center

Metlakatla

Kelly

Library

College

Sheldon-Jackson College and Museum

TO INDIAN RIVER TRAILHEAD (.3mi.)

Indian River Rd.

Crescent Harbor

Sitka Sound

Bartow

Tim Way

Lincoln St.

Jeff Davis

Etolin St.

Oja St.

Park

Bjorka St.

Baranof St.

Market Center

Russian Bishop's House

Geodetic Way

Sawmill Creek Rd.

Monastery St.

Hollywood St.

Lake St.

Merrill

Detroit

Gavan Hill & Harbor Mt. Trailhead

Hirst

Kincaid

Cemetery

Arrowhead

Shennent

1st

Pherson

Charles

Austin

Banit

Verstovia

2nd

A St.

Sirstad

Lake St.

Swan Lake

Hemlock St.

Erler

Spruce St.

Marine St.

De Armond

Andrews

New Archangel

Tlingit Way

Kogwanton St.

ANB Hall

Russian Cemetery

Etolin St.

SEE INSET

O'Connell Bridge

ANB Harbor

Crabappl

Osprey

Halibut Point Rd.

Katlian Ave.

Lakeview

Ocean St.

Lakeside Grocery

Forest Service Office

Signaka Way

Moller Field

Gavan Hill

Molter

TO 2 (330yds.), FERRY TERMINAL (6mi.)

Thomsen Harbor

Sitka Channel

University of Alaska Southeast

Japonski Island

Airport Rd.

TO (.5mi.)

Seward Ave.

Alice Island

O'Connell Bridge

Aleutski Island

INSET

Hartigan Centennial Building & Visitor Center

Kettleson Memorial Library

Harbor Dr.

Maksoutof St.

Castle Hill

O'Connell Bridge

Lincoln St.

St. Michael's Cathedral

Seward

Lake St.

American St.

Barracks St.

Harbor Books

Evergreen Natural Foods

Observatory

Russian Cemetery

Marine St.

Kogwanton St.

Katlian St.

ANB Harbor

300 yards

300 meters

0

0

Sitka Hotel, 118 Lincoln St. (☎747-3288). Convenient downtown location. Established in 1939, this Victorian-style hotel offers comfortable and simple rooms with small shared bathrooms. Free cable and local calls. Laundry facilities. Reserve 2 months ahead. Singles in winter $75, doubles $80; winter $70, $75. ❹

Sawmill Creek Campground (☎747-4216), 8½ mi. south of town. Take Halibut Point Rd. to Sawmill Creek Rd., and follow Sawmill Creek to the pulp mill; take left spur for 1½ mi. Trees, stream, solitude, picnic tables, fire rings, pit toilets, and fishing in nearby Blue Lake. Treat water from the creek. 14-night max. stay. 11 sites, free. ❶

🍴📺 FOOD AND NIGHTLIFE

Market Center, 210 Baranof St., is a source of groceries close to downtown. (☎747-6686. Open daily 5am-midnight.)

▨ **Alaska Native Brotherhood (ANB) Hall,** 205 Katlian Ave. (☎747-3359). The ANB has always been about interracial understanding and native community development. Tasty traditionally prepared local fish and game ($5). Proceeds go to scholarships for local Native youth. Mouth-watering fry bread $1. Open in summer M-F noon-5pm. ❶

The Backdoor, 104 Barracks St. (☎747-8856), behind Old Harbor Books. Diverse lunch specials await at this popular local vegetarian-friendly hangout. Mouth-watering lunch specials $3. Open M-Sa 6:30am-5pm, Su 9am-3pm. ❶

Pizza Express, 236 Lincoln St. (☎966-2428), serves up (despite its name) huge portions of affordable, authentic Mexican food. Dinner $7.25-14.95. Open M-Sa 11am-10pm, Su noon-10pm. ❸

Pioneer Bar, 214 Katlian St. (☎747-3456). The bartender is an ex commercial fisherwoman who can help you find the best fishing spots. Don't ring the bell at the bar—it means a free round on you. $4 pints. Open M-Sa 8am-2am, Su noon-2am.

Ernie's Old Time Saloon, on Lincoln St. (☎747-3334) across from the Pioneer Home, is known for strange trophies such as the half salmon, half deer over the bar. Pints $4. Live music Th-Su. Pool, darts. Open M-Sa 8am-2am, Su noon-2am.

👁🎵 SIGHTS AND EVENTS

Sitka's multi-faceted history manifests itself in a plethora of sights of cultural interest. **Tribal Tours** has a **Visitors Transit System** (☎747-7290) which services major attractions, although most sights are within easy walking distance of one another. $7 per day. Every 30min., M-F 12:30-4:30pm, mornings and weekends if cruise ships are in port.

RUSSIAN BISHOP'S HOUSE. One of the four remaining Russian colonial buildings in Alaska, this was the home of the Russian Bishop from the 1840's until 1969 when the Russian Orthodox Church sold the site to the Park Service. Bishop (and later Saint) Innocent was the first inhabitant and the founder of St. Michael's Cathedral. A man of the people, he traversed his 2000 mi. parish by kayak. The upstairs is only accessible through the tours run by the Park Service every half hour. *(2 blocks past the cathedral on Lincoln St. Open mid-May to early Oct. daily 9am-5pm; call for off-season access. Tours every 30min. $3, $10 family rate; free for children under 12 and seniors. Entrance fee includes tour.)*

SHELDON-JACKSON MUSEUM. The museum boasts a world-class collection and world-class interpretation of Athabascan, Aleutian, Inuit, and Northwest Coast Native American artifacts. Daily summer demonstrations by visiting Native artists. *(Located at 104 College Dr., east of town on Lincoln St. ☎747-8981. Open in summer daily 9am-5pm. $4, under 18 free. Winter Tu-Sa 10am-4pm. $3.)*

SITKA NATIONAL HISTORIC PARK. The site of the battle for Sitka between the Tlingit and the Russians in 1804. A leisurely path through woods and along the shore's tidal pools leads to 11 totem poles and the site of the **Tlingit Fort.** The raven helmet Chief Katlean wore is now on display at the Sheldon-Jackson Museum. At the **Southeast Alaskan Native American Cultural Center,** carvers and weavers demonstrate their crafts, and a visitors center offers orientation, a film, and a small bookstore. (Located ½ mi. east of St. Michael's on Lincoln St. ☎ 747-6281. Trails open daily 6am-10pm. Visitors and cultural centers open daily 8am-5pm.)

ALASKA RAPTOR REHABILITATION CENTER. Half of the bald eagles in the world live in Southeast Alaska. They can frequently be spotted in Thomsen Harbor when the fishing boats come in. For intimate encounters with these magnificent birds, head to the Raptor Center, which treats injured birds of prey with the hope of re-releasing them into the wild. Those birds that cannot be re-released are used for educational purposes. There are 21 permanent raptor residents, some with 8 ft. wingspans. (Raptor Way off Sawmill Creek Rd., ¾ mi. from downtown. Also accessible over the bridge from the Historical Park. ☎ 747-8662. Open daily 8am-5pm. $10, children under 12 $5.)

FESTIVALS. During the first three weeks of June, the **Sitka Summer Music Festival,** one of Alaska's most popular musical events, will draw 15 of the world's best classical musicians for a chamber music series. (☎ 747-6774. All shows $15, under 18 $8.) Other annual events include the **Gathering of the People** in April (a cultural exchange with native dance groups from across Alaska), and the **Whalefest,** the first week in November. The visitors center has more info.

🏔 OUTDOOR ACTIVITIES

HIKING. Many hikes just outside of town gain significant elevation and provide spectacular views. The Sitka Ranger Office has detailed information about each trail and its conditions. They can also direct you to a number of **remote trails** in the region, most accessible only by boat or floatplane, and many leading to **wilderness cabins** ($25-45 per night).

Mt. Verstovia Trail (2½ mi. one-way, 3-4hr., 2550 ft. gain). The trailhead is about 2 mi. east of town at 1617 Sawmill Creek Rd., next to Rookie's Sports Bar and Grill. This steep, often slippery hike boasts the best panoramic views of the area. Vegetation changes dramatically from hemlock forest to a rocky alpine area. If you continue to Arrowhead (confusingly named Verstovia on the USGS map, which calls what the locals call Verstovia "peak 2550"), the elevation gain jumps to 3300 ft. Difficult.

Indian River Trail (4½ mi. one-way, 4-5hr., 700 ft. gain). Take Sawmill Creek Rd. out of town and turn on Indian River Rd. before the bridge. After traveling a short distance to the parking lot, walk around the gate and follow the road about ½ mi. to its end at the pumphouse. The views are less dramatic than from steeper trails, but finding the base of Indian River Falls pleases most hikers. Easy.

Harbor Mountain/Gavan Hill Trail (6 mi. one-way, 4-6hr., 2500 ft. gain). The Gavan Hill Trail begins at the end of Baranof St., near downtown. Those who persevere up the stairs on this trail are rewarded by a sensational view of the sound. In the saddle between Gavan Hill and Harbor Mountain is a Forest Service shelter, which operates on a first-come, first-served basis. Moderate to difficult.

Beaver Lake Trail (1 mi. one-way, 1hr., 250 ft. gain). Take Sawmill Creek Rd. 5½ mi. east. Turn left across from the pulp mill onto the uphill gravel road. Go 1½ mi. to the Sawmill Creek Campground. The trailhead is across the bridge over the creek on the south side of the open area. This boardwalk trail is the easiest of the popular trails, flattening out after a moderately steep beginning. Platforms overlooking the serene lake offer great fishing. A boat is available for public use. Moderate.

Mt. Edgecombe Trail (7 mi. one-way, 8-12hr., 3189 ft. gain). Accessible only by boat, about a ½hr. skiff ride from Sitka. The trailhead is behind Fred's Creek cabin on the southeastern shore of Kruzof Island. A full-day clamber to the crater of Sitka's very own volcano. A shelter sits 4 mi. up the trail. The last 3 mi. of the hike are steep and end at the timber line. To reach the crater rim, continue straight up. Stunning views and a close look at eons-old red volcanic ash reward you at the summit. Difficult. The best way to get there is by watertaxi; **Esther G Sea Taxi** (☎ 747-6481) has the best rates.

KAYAKING. The clear waters around Sitka allow kayakers to spy purple, orange, and yellow starfish, as well as other wildlife along the coast. Due to its proximity to the open ocean, kayaking here requires more caution and forethought than on the inside passage. For good advice on routes and to rent any equipment, contact **Sitka Sound Ocean Adventures** (☎ 747-6375).

TENAKEE SPRINGS   ☎ 907

The third-largest town on the largely uninhabited Chichagof Island, Tenakee Springs' one street is a dirt path populated by children pushing grocery-laden wheelbarrows, older fisherman lolling outside the Mercantile, and ATVs traveling under 10 mph—the town's 100 citizens have banned cars. Residents thrive on the slow pace of this close-knit community, and are quick to welcome visitors, even those heavy of pack and light of wallet.

🛈 PRACTICAL INFORMATION. Alaska Seaplanes (☎ 789-3331) flies from **Juneau** (every M, W and F at 1pm; $85). **Wings of Alaska** (☎ 736-2247) flies twice daily from Juneau (M-Sa at 7:30am and 1:45pm, Su at 1:45pm; $84). The state ferry *LeConte* makes a short stop in Tenakee twice a week on its route between **Juneau** and **Sitka** (7-8hr.; $24 each way). There are **no banks** in Tenakee and limited groceries. The **post office** is right off the dock. (☎ 736-2236. Open M-F 7:30am-noon and 1-4pm, Sa 7:30-11:30am.) **Postal Code:** 99841.

🛏🍴 ACCOMMODATIONS AND FOOD. The only affordable option is to rent one of **Snyder Mercantile's ❸** six cabins. Each cabin is within steps of the hot spring and overlooks the water. Basic cabins sleep one to two comfortably ($50); a larger cabin sleeps four to five ($55). A $70 cabin sleeps seven, with carpeting, fireplaces, and—my stars—a flush toilet. Reservations at least a month in advance are essential in summer. (☎ 736-2205. Outside toilet, cooking facilities, no bedding, credit cards accepted.) **Camping** around Tenakee is bear-intensive; Chichagof Island has about one bear per sq. mi.; only Admiralty Island has a denser population. Walking from the ferry dock, make a right turn on the dirt street. After about three-quarters of a mile, a boardwalk to the left leads to **Indian River ❶**. Camping is technically not permitted along this trail, but there are tent sites, a shelter, and a picnic table. If there have been bear sightings, though, it isn't wise to camp near the river. Big brown beasts have been known to torment tenters during the night.

Food options apart from the salmonberries along the path include **Snyder Mercantile,** next to the ferry dock, which stocks a limited supply of groceries. (Open M-Sa 9am-noon and 1-5pm, Su 9am-2pm.)

🛁 THE HOT SPRING. What better way is there to meet the locals than naked in a tub? Tenakee's namesake and epicenter is a natural sulfuric hot spring that feeds the public bathhouse at the end of the ferry dock. You won't find this unglamorous blue concrete building on any postcards, but natives, miners, and fishers have been soaking out aches and worries in these therapeutic 106°F (41°C) waters for more than a century. Visitors can get in on the town gossip by bathing when the spring is busiest, which is at the start of each new shift. Bathers are required to be naked and reasonably clean. (Women-only 9am-2pm and 6-10pm; men-only 2-6pm and 10pm-9am. Free; donations accepted at Snyder Mercantile.)

◙ ♫ SIGHTS AND OUTDOOR ACTIVITIES. The rocks 15min. out from shore by kayak are home to dozens of **seals, land otters, and sea lions.** More seasoned paddlers ply **Tenakee Inlet,** at the end of which a 100-yard portage leads to **Port Frederick Inlet** and the town of **Hoonah.** This 40 mi. trip offers unbroken shorelines, hidden coves, and local wildlife. Only the experienced should attempt it, since the waterways are often subject to high winds and bears are likely at beachside campsites. Kayaks are not available for rent and must be brought over on the ferry ($9). For **chartered expeditions** to fish, view wildlife, and learn about the area from someone who has been on the water around Tenakee all his life, contact **Jason Carter** (☎736-2311). Jason runs traveling trips ($300 per person per day) and occasional daytrips (call for prices), and will transport kayaks upon request. Fishing and hunting licenses are available at **Snyder Mercantile.**

JUNEAU   ☎907

In 1880, Tlingit Chief Kaawa'ee led Joe Juneau and Richard Harris to the mouth of what is now Gold Creek, so named for the gold-spangled rocks they found at its source. Word spread, the Gold Rush began, and Juneau became one of the world's greatest hard-rock mining capitals and the first town founded after the U.S. purchase of the territory. Alaska's capital city is still quite literally built upon the products of its mines (tailings were poured into Gastineau Channel to serve as a foundation for the downtown area), but it has the most diverse economy, cultural sights and population of any city in Southeast Alaska. Juneau is an eclectic mix of adventurers, fishermen, artists, musicians, politicians, business leaders, and a governor who runs his dog on one of the local trails almost daily. There are 40 trailheads within a half mile of downtown, a small indication of the extensive trail network that stretches along Juneau's 50 or so miles of main road. Although downtown businesses cater to the cruise ship crowds, there are some largely undiscovered establishments farther up the hills and great escapes to easily accessible trails, nearby Mendenhall Glacier, and Glacier Bay.

IN RECENT NEWS

DON'T PUT YOUR ROAD IN MY BACKYARD

As a completley landlocked capital city with no more than 150 mi. of road, Juneau's transportation options are limited. Especially when considering that only 50 of those miles are highways, its easy to see why many of the politicians from across the state have been pushing to build a road from Juneau to Skagway to open Juneau to more tourism, broaden the economy, and offer more transportation options.

Local Juneau-ites are not thrilled by the idea of a steady caravan of RVs streaming south from Skagway. Such tourist traffic would demand more large, RV-ready campgrounds that Juneau currently does not boast (at least not in sufficiently large amounts). Creating more RV campgrounds would mean clearing land, which most Juneau residents don't want to do.

Traffic patterns and travelers aside, the road itself seems manifestly impractical. It would cost a small fortune to build, and it would have to traverse mountain passes that are impassable eight months out of the year. Although petitions are circulating both in favor of and against construction, it seems that the road is going nowhere fast.

—Catherine Gowl

▐ TRANSPORTATION

Juneau sits on the Gastineau Channel opposite Douglas Island, 650 mi. southeast of Anchorage and 900 mi. northwest of Seattle. **Franklin St.** is the main drag downtown. **Glacier Hwy.** connects downtown to "the valley": the residential, primary commercial area of the Mendenhall Valley.

Flights: Juneau International Airport, 9 mi. north of town on Glacier Hwy. **Alaska Airlines** (☎789-9539 or 800-426-0333; www.alaska-air.com) has daily flights until Labor Day to **Anchorage** ($270), **Gustavus** ($49), and **Ketchikan** ($163). **LAB Air** (☎789-9160 or 800-426-0543) flies smaller planes daily to **Haines** ($65), **Petersburg** ($144), and **Skagway** ($75). **Wings of Alaska** (☎789-0790) also services **Haines** ($84) and **Skagway** ($96).

Ferries: Alaska Marine Highway, 1591 Glacier Ave. (☎465-3941 or 800-642-0066 M-F 8am-5pm). Ferries dock at the Auke Bay terminal, 14 mi. northwest of the city on Glacier Hwy. To: **Haines** (4½hr., $26); **Ketchikan** (18-36hr., $83); and **Sitka** (9hr., $30). **Lockers** $0.25 per 48hr. Open 2hr. before all departures. Walk-ons should arrive 1hr. prior to departure.

Buses: Capital Transit (☎789-6901) runs hourly from downtown to Douglas Island, and every ½hr. to Mendenhall Valley and Auke Bay. From the airport, take the hourly express service from the terminal's north end. Evenings and weekends, catch the non-express from Nugget Mall, a 10min. walk; ask at the airport for directions. The stop closest to the ferry dock is 2 mi. away, at "DeHart's/Auke Bay," across from DeHart's General Store. The Nugget Mall is the place to switch from the local to the express bus on weekdays. Schedules at municipal building, airport, the visitors center, library, and on buses. $1.25, under 5 free; exact change only. Runs M-Sa 7am-10:30pm, Su 9am-6:30pm, express bus M-F 8:10am-5pm.

Taxis: Taku (☎586-2121) and **Alaska** (☎780-6400). **Capital Cab,** (☎586-2772), has 24hr. service. All average about $30 to the airport from downtown.

Car Rental: Rent-A-Wreck, 2450 Industrial Blvd. (☎789-4111 or 789-1302), next to the airport. $35 per day, $0.30 per mi. after 100 mi. 21+. Free pickup. If paying cash, there is a $200 damage deposit, and you must buy their $15 per day insurance policy. Extra driver $5. If taking an early/late ferry, you can lock the car at the ferry terminal and they will retrieve it for $10. Open M-F 8am-6pm, Sa-Su 9am-5pm.

▐ PRACTICAL INFORMATION

Tourist Information: Visitors Center, 101 Egan Dr. in Centennial Hall (☎586-2201 or 888-581-2201; www.traveljuneau.com), has info on local happenings and walks. The **Forest Service** has a desk here with more extensive hiking maps, information on Forest Service cabins, and wildlife viewing in the area. Open June-Sept. M-F 8:30am-5pm, Sa-Su 9am-5pm; Oct.-May M-F 9am-4pm. The Forest Service Desk closes at 3pm.

Capital City Weekly (www.capweek.com), available at most establishments, has the lowdown on free local events, concerts, and screenings.

Outdoor Information: Trail maps are available at the Visitors Center (see above). Trail Mix publishes a book called *90 Short Walks Around Juneau,* available at Hearthside Books (see below) for $6.95. **Foggy Mountain Shop** (see below) also gives outdoors advice. For trail conditions, call the **trail hotline** (☎856-5330). **Alaska Dept. of Fish and Game,** 1255 W 8th St. (☎465-4112; licensing 465-2376), close to the bridge. Open M-F 8am-5pm. **Sport fishing hotline** (☎465-4116).

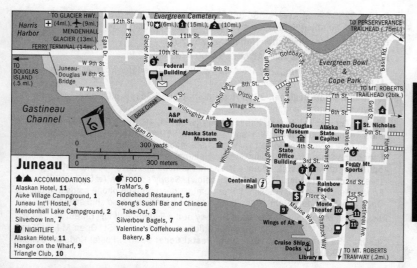

Juneau

♠♠▲ ACCOMMODATIONS
Alaskan Hotel, **11**
Auke Village Campground, **1**
Juneau Int'l Hostel, **4**
Mendenhall Lake Campground, **2**
Silverbow Inn, **7**

■ NIGHTLIFE
Alaskan Hotel, **11**
Hangar on the Wharf, **9**
Triangle Club, **10**

♥ FOOD
TraMar's, **6**
Fiddlehead Restaurant, **5**
Seong's Sushi Bar and Chinese Take-Out, **3**
Silverbow Bagels, **7**
Valentine's Coffeehouse and Bakery, **8**

Outdoor Equipment: Cycle Alaska (☎ 321-2453 or 780-2253) rents bikes for $30 per day, $20 per half day. 10-20% off longer rentals. Guided day tours for $50 per person per day. **Alaska Boat and Kayak** (☎ 586-8220), on Douglas Island, delivers kayaks anywhere in the area. Singles $40 per day, $15 per hr.; doubles $55, $20. Open daily Apr.-Sept. 8am-6pm.

Banks: On Sa, only banks by the airport are open. **AlaskaUSA**, 8201 Glacier Hwy. (☎ 789-1361), is the closest. **24hr. ATM** at Seward and Front St. and Seward and 2nd.

American Express: 8745 Glacier Hwy. (☎ 800-770-2750). Open M-F 10am-7pm, Sa 10am-6pm.

Luggage Storage: The **Alaskan Hotel** stores bags (see p. 450). Lockers at ferry terminal are less convenient (see above).

Work Opportunities: Find job listings in the classified section of the **Juneau Empire** and **Capital Weekly**. A folder on the desk of the **Juneau Public Library** (see below) also lists job announcements and contact information.

Bookstore: Hearthside Books, 254 Front St. (☎ 789-1726), caters to all tastes. Variable summer hours due to cruise ships; usually M-F 9am-9pm, Sa 9am-8:30pm, Su 9am-7pm. Winter hours: M-Sa 10am-6pm, Su noon-4pm. A more comprehensive store is in the Nugget Mall. Open year-round M-F 10am-9pm, Sa 10am-6pm, Su noon-5pm.

Gay/Lesbian Information: Southeast Alaska Gay and Lesbian Alliance (☎ 586-4297). Juneau has about the only "out" gay and lesbian community in southeast Alaska, and SEAGLA is trying to raise awareness in the community by starting a Gay Pride Carnival. SEAGLA publishes *Perspective*, available at **Rainbow Foods** and **Silverbow Bagel.**

Laundromat and Public Showers: Dungeon Laundrette (☎ 586-2805), at 4th and Franklin. Wash $1.50, dry $1.50; free detergent, bring quarters. Open daily 8am-8pm. **Alaska Laundry,** 1114 Glacier Ave. (☎ 586-1133), offers showers ($2 per 10min.) and laundry. Wash $2, dry $0.25 per 5-8min.

Weather: ☎ 586-3185.

Emergency: ☎ 911.

Police: 6255 Alaway Ave. (☎586-0600). Drive northwest from town on Glacier Hwy. (not Egan Rd.) for about 6 mi., then make a left on Alaway (before the K-Mart).

Crisis and Suicide Prevention Hotline: ☎586-4357.

Rape and Abuse Crisis Line (AWARE): ☎800-478-1090. 24hr.

Pharmacy: Juneau Drug, 202 Front St. (☎586-1233), across from McDonald's. Open M-F 9am-9pm, Sa-Su 9am-6pm.

Hospital: Bartlett Regional, 3260 Hospital Dr. (☎586-2611), off Glacier Hwy., halfway between downtown and the airport.

Internet Access: The **Juneau Public Library** (☎586-5249) sits over a parking garage at the confluence of Marine Way and S Franklin St. Free 30min. Internet access. Call ahead to reserve. Open M-Th 11am-9pm, F-Su noon-5pm. The **State Library,** on the 8th floor of the State Office Building, has free Internet access with less wait. Open M-F 9am-5pm. The **Juneau Hostel, Triangle Bar,** and **Pelmeni** also have free Internet for patrons (see **Accommodations** and **Nightlife,** below). **Soapy's Station** (☎586-8960), in the Senate Building at 175 Franklin. $5 for 50min. Cheap prepaid phone cards and copies. Open May-Sept. daily 9am-10pm, but fluctuates based on cruise ship schedule.

Post Office: Main office and General Delivery at the Federal Building on 9th St. and Willoughby. Open M-F 9am-5pm. Branch office at 127 Franklin St. Open M-F 8:30am-4:30pm, Sa 9am-2pm, Su 10am-2pm. **Postal Code:** 99801. Postal Code for General Delivery: 99802.

🔼🔽 ACCOMMODATIONS AND CAMPING

The Juneau Hostel is about as good as they come, but other affordable accommodations are limited; book ahead if possible. The **Alaska B&B Association** (www.accommodations-alaska.com) can help you find a room (from $65). The two beautiful Forest Service campgrounds are easily accessible by car, and fairly close to the bus.

🏅 **Juneau International Hostel (HI),** 614 Harris St. (☎586-9559), at 6th St. Follow signs up the steep hill on Franklin St. Spacious house with comfy common room, dining room, kitchen, and laundry facilities (wash $1.25, dry $0.25). Free Internet. Minimal chore required. Strict lockout 9am-5pm. Midnight curfew. 4-night max. stay if full, which it often is. $10 advance deposit by mail for phone reservations. 48 beds, $10. ❶

Silverbow Inn, 120 Second St. (☎586-4146 or ☎800-586-4242). Free baked goods from the restaurant (see below) are always available, and a full breakfast appears every morning. 5-6pm is daily wine and cheese hour to meet other guests. Summer $120-135, Winter as low as $60-88. ❺

Alaskan Hotel, 167 Franklin St. (☎586-1000 or 800-327-9347), in the heart of downtown. This restored 1913 hotel is furnished with antiques, kitchenettes and cable TVs. Laundry machines for guests. Rooms with shared bath (toilet, shower, and tub all in separate rooms) $67.50; private bath $85. Weekly rates for $225. ❹

Mendenhall Lake Campground, Montana Creek Rd. From town, take Egan Dr. north 10 mi. and turn right onto Mendenhall Loop Rd. the 2nd time it connects with Glacier Hwy. Turn left on Montana Creek after 3½ mi; the campground is a mile down on the right. Bus drivers stop at the intersection of Montana Creek Rd. and Mendenhall Loop Rd. upon request (7am-10:30pm only). 6 mi. from ferry. Stunning views of the oh-so-close glacier. Firepits, water, toilets, and free firewood. No reservations. 14-night max. stay. Open June to mid-Sept. 60 sites. Tents $10; RVs $20. Showers. ❶

Auke Village Campground (☎586-8800), 15 mi. from town on Egan Dr. (1½ mi. west of the ferry docks). 12 secluded sites near a scenic beach. Firepits, water, toilets, tables. No reservations. 14-night max. stay. Open early May-late Sept. $8, seniors $4. ❶

Echo Cove, at the "end of the road," Mile 40, on Egan Drive. Free, unlimited-stay camping. However, it is also amenity-free. Bring your own wood and water. ❶

🔴 FOOD

Juneau has the most diverse culinary options in Southeastern Alaska. **Juneau A&P Market,** 631 Willoughby Ave. near the Federal Building, is the place to go groceries and an **ATM.** (☎586-3101. Open daily 6am-10pm.) For organic produce and lunch options (soup $3-4, salad bar $5.49/lb.), check out **Rainbow Foods** at 2nd and Seward St. (☎586-6476. Open M-F 9am-7pm, Sa 10am-6pm, Su noon-6pm.)

◪ **Silverbow Bagels** (☎586-9866) and **The Back Room** (☎586-4146), 120 2nd St., at Main. These 2 establishments are housed in the same purple building. The oldest operating bakery in Alaska. Sandwiches ($5-7) are quality noontime chow. Open M-F 7am-5:30pm, Sa 8am-4:30pm, Su 9am-3:30pm. ❶ The Back Room has backside barstools, a trendier feel, and an eclectic menu (Indonesian peanut pasta $12). (Brunch Sa 8am-2pm, Su 9am-2pm; lunch Tu-F 11:30am-2pm; and dinner Tu-Sa 5:30pm-9pm.) ❸

Fiddlehead Restaurant, 429 Willoughby Ave. (☎586-3150), has the best gourmet vegetarian options in town at the best prices. Dinner can get pricey, but the humbler offerings ($7.95-11.95) are also delicious. Lunch ($6-11). The entryway houses a bakery section with enormous scones ($1.75) and espresso. Open 7am-10pm daily.

Seong's Sushi Bar and Chinese Take-Out, at the corner of 9th and Willoughby. Great sushi, which doesn't happen much in Southeast Alaska. Always packed. $3.50-$30, lunch specials $7-9. Open M-F 10am-8pm, Sa 4-9pm. ❷

Valentine's Coffee House and Bakery, 111 Seward St. (☎463-5144). Provincial flavor in the heart of the capital. Fresh-baked calzones ($6) are huge; happily, half portions are available for $3.95. Salads $5. Sandwiches $6.25 or half for $4.25. All sorts of breads and veggie options. Open M-F 7am-5:30pm, Sa 8am-4pm. ❷

TraMar's (☎463-5091), at the corner of Franklin and 4th. A hidden secret among locals. Breakfast is affordable ($4-11) and portions are bafflingly generous. Open daily 6am-9pm. Breakfast served all day. ❷

🔵 SIGHTS AND EVENTS

ALASKA STATE MUSEUM. An excellent museum that sets the standard for presenting and interpreting Native Alaskan artifacts. Provides in-depth exhibits on natural and state history. The first floor introduces visitors to the history and culture of Alaska's major native groups through time. Upstairs explores the discovery of Alaska, Russian Alaska, the Gold Rush years, and contemporary art. (395 Whittier St. ☎465-2901. Open mid-May to mid-Sept. daily 8:30am-5:30pm; mid-Sept. to mid-May Tu-Sa 10am-4pm. $5 in summer, $3 in winter, under 18 free.)

GASTINEAU SALMON HATCHERY. Between mid-July and September the Hatchery is packed with tourists and fish. Impressive views of the spawning ladder and a brief talk are both available outside for free. (2697 Channel Dr. ☎463-5113. Open M-F 10am-6pm, Sa-Su noon-5pm. Indoor aquarium $3, children $1.)

ALASKA BREWING CO. The ale here is based on a Gold Rush recipe found in an antique. It has won more gold medals than any other brewery, and because the beer is cold-fermented, it contains more alcohol than most. The tour begins and ends at the bar, with five 6oz. glasses of free goodness. (5429 Shaune Dr. Request the city bus to stop at Costco; turn onto Anka Rd. from the Glacier Hwy., then make a right onto Shaune Dr. ☎780-5866. Bring ID. Tours every 30min. 6-packs $6.99. Open May-Sept. M-Sa 11am-5pm; Oct.-Apr. Th-Sa 11am-4:30pm.)

PERFORMING ARTS. The **Perseverance Theater** has high-quality productions. Shows workshopped here have gone straight to Broadway. Call for shows and performance times. *(914 3rd St. On Douglas Island. ☎364-2421.)* Talented local and visiting musicians, from guitar-strumming folkies to salsa bands that get the whole crowd dancing, put on **free concerts** at Marine Park on the waterfront by the cruise ship docks. *(Summer F 7-8:30pm.)* The yearly, eagerly anticipated **Alaska Folk Festival** brings crowds to Juneau and free, all-night jam sessions to Centennial Hall. *(☎364-2658. April.)*

⬛ HIKING

Juneau's trail system is extensive, and offers access to the numerous hike-accessible glaciers in the area (**Mendenhall Glacier** is the largest and most obvious, but not necessarily the most stunning when it comes to close encounters with ancient ice). The visitors center in town as well as the Mendenhall Glacier Visitors Center offer free printed information on trails. Local bookstores and outfitters have lots of insight and thorough descriptions, and sell the somewhat less thorough and occasionally unclear **90 Short Walks Around Juneau** ($6.95). As always, beware of bears and dress in layers to prepare for elevation changes.

◼ **Mt. Roberts Trail** (5 mi., 3200 ft. elevation gain, 3-5hr.). Begins at the end of 6th St., up a stairway. This outstanding, well-maintained, and often steep trail starts downtown, winds through old-growth forest, and ascends past tree line to alpine meadows and rocky outcroppings. Clearings in the trees offer stellar views of the city, Gastineau Channel, and Mt. Juneau. A tram offers access to the vista at an overlook halfway up, but requires $20 round-trip. Hikers can ride down for $5 or a $5 purchase at the gift shop. 2 mi. to the tram stop, 2½ mi. to Father Brown's Cross (2500 ft.), 4 mi. to Gastineau Peak (3700 ft.), 5 mi. to Mt. Roberts summit (3800 ft.). Moderate to difficult.

◼ **West Glacier Trail** (6¾ mi. round-trip, 1300 ft. gain, 5-6hr.). Request that the bus take you as close as possible to the West Glacier Trail. From the Mendenhall Loop Rd., take Montana Creek Road and veer right, following signs for Skater's Cabin. Entrance to the trail is past the Mendenhall Campground, at the end of the road, through the parking lot, and to the left. This much-vaunted trail yields stunning views of **Mendenhall Glacier** and the endless ice-fields above from the first step to the final outlook. The hike parallels the glacier, crosses a creek, and appears to end at an overlook. The trail actually continues up the rocks and ends above the timberline. A primitive route continues to Mt. McGinnis, but is only recommended for experienced hikers with ice axes. The **East Glacier Trail** is a 3 mi. loop that leaves from the Mendenhall Visitors Center. It also offers stunning views of the Glacier and is a more moderate hike. Moderate to difficult.

◼ **Herbert Glacier Trail** (4½ mi. one-way, 100 ft. gain, 3-5hr.). The trailhead is to the right just after the Herbert River bridge at Mile 26.6 on Glacier Highway. No public transportation available. This relatively flat trail cuts through beautiful moss-covered cottonwood, hemlock, and spruce forest, bounces off the milky-green runoff of the Herbert River, and then yields an up-close and personal look at the Herbert Glacier. Easy.

Dan Moller Trail (3 mi. one-way, 1600 ft. gain, 3hr.). Ask the bus to Douglas to drop you on Cordova St. Go to the end of the street, turn left on Pioneer Avenue to the parking lot opposite house #3184. Most of this peaceful, flower-laden trail is a boardwalk through muskeg. The trail ends at the bottom of a glacier-carved bowl with the **Dan Moller Cabin** (reserve through the Forest Service, www.reserveusa.com). A brief hike from the cabin takes you to the ridges of the bowl for excellent views in both directions. At Mile 1 the trail intersects with the **Treadwell Ditch Trail,** which runs the length of the island at a consistent altitude with frequent outlet trails leading back to town. Easy to moderate.

Treadwell Ditch Historic Loop Trail (2 mi., 40 ft. gain, 1hr.). Take the Douglas bus to the end and get off at Sandy Beach. The trailhead is at the end of the beach. This historic trail threads through the remains of a ghost town complete with mining equipment. Stay on the trails: the area was honeycombed with tunnels. Easy.

Perseverance Trail (3 mi. one way, 700ft. gain, 3-4hr.). Take Gold St. by the hostel to Basin Rd. and follow the road past the Last Chance Mining Museum. The trail starts at the cul-de-sac. This trail leads to the ruins of the **Silverbowl Basin Mine** and booming waterfalls. Avalanche danger in winter and early spring; call the Forest Service (see p. 448) for trail conditions. Easy. The **Granite Creek Trail** (1½ mi., 900 ft. gain, 1-2hr.) is a spur trail to the left at the 2 mi. mark on Perseverance Trail. It follows a clear stream to a glacier-carved basin. Easy to moderate.

⚡ OTHER OUTDOOR ACTIVITIES

Known as "the poor man's Glacier Bay," **Tracy Arm** offers much of the spectacular beauty and wildlife at nearly half the cost. A day cruise leads through Stephen's Passage to Tracy Arm Fjord. The ships pass blue icebergs that offer safety to nursing harbor seal pups. The tour's climax is the stop at the Sawyer Glacier, where passengers gawk at the 10 mi. long sheet of ice and listen for the "white thunder" of pieces calving into icebergs. **Auk Nu Tours**, 76 Egan Dr., is the biggest tour company and has a naturalist on board. (☎ 800-820-2628. 8hr. tour $110.25, under 18 $71.81; includes lunch, snacks, and binoculars. Departs 9am from the Seam Drome Building, returns 5-5:30pm.) **Adventure Bound**, 245 Marine Way, runs a mid-sized boat, carrying 37 passengers and knowledgeable staff. (☎ 463-2509 or 800-228-3875. 8hr. tour. $100, under 18 $60.)

Fifteen miles southeast of Juneau is **Admiralty Island**, which boasts a spectacularly high density of Alaskan Brown Bears—about one bear per square mile. The **Pack Creek Bear Viewing Area** is accessible by boat and floatplane from Juneau. Viewing is possible from the tower (3hr. max.), a 1 mi. walk from the landing area; and from a viewing spit, accessed along the beach. The bears fish, graze, clam, and, in June, display mating behavior. A permit is required for access to the island, and a ranger is always around to check them. (July 5-Aug. 25 $50 per day, seniors and children under 16 $25; June 1-July 4 and Aug. 26-Sept. 10 $20 per day, seniors and children under 16 $10). Transportation is provided by charters and guides. Floatplane charters are offered by **Alaska Coastal Airlines** (☎ 789-7818), **Alaska Seaplane Services** (☎ 789-3331), and **Wings of Alaska** (☎ 789-0790). Fares fluctuate, so call around and ask for seat fares if available. 50% of visitors to Admiralty choose to go with a hired guide. Floatplane guides are offered by **Alaska Fly N' Fish Charters** (☎ 790-2120) and **Thayer Lake Lodge** (☎ 789-5646). **Alaska Discovery** (☎ 586-1911) is a **kayak guide** offering day and multi-day camping and paddle trips. These trips include float plane transportation from Juneau. Prices vary enormously so call ahead. The **Cross Island Canoe Route** connects Mole Harbor to the Tlingit village of **Angoon**, and passes through eight lakes connected by portage trails. Some of the lakes have Forest Service cabins (call ahead to reserve); the others have three-sided shelters. If camping, set up your tent well away from the cooking area and do not take food near it. Burn all food scraps and trash, and pack whatever remains. Hang food at least 12 ft. above the ground when not in use. Note: "intentionally" leaving food unattended and accessible to bears is considered feeding and is a violation of Alaskan law. Firearms and bear spray are permissible; however, after 70 years of bear-viewing here, no visitor has ever been harmed. The Forest Service desk at the Juneau Visitors Center (see **Practical Information,** above) is extremely helpful for information and trip planning.

There are many excellent trails for **mountain biking,** but off-road is sometimes prohibited. Check with **Cycle Alaska** for difficulty ratings and suggestions. Very few companies run **kayak** tours of the area, and it'll cost you. Most kayakers make the trip to Glacier Bay and spend their time in the East Arm. For those who remain in Juneau, **Alaska Boat and Kayak** rents kayaks and gives lessons and information. Good secluded kayak routes are available: **Endicott Arm,** next to Tracy Arm, has much less traffic and gets you right up to the glacier.

Juneau Sportfishing and Sightseeing, above the wharf on Egan Dr., offers half-day and full-day fishing trips (lunch provided) and **whale watching** trips of varying lengths. (☎586-1887; www.JuneauSportfishing.com. Fishing: full-day $225.75 per person, half-day $131.35 per person. Whale watching: 2½hr. $95 per person, 4hr. $131.25 per person.)

Wings of Alaska runs 45min. **flightseeing** tours over the Mendenhall Glacier and the Juneau and Suicide Icefields. (☎586-6275. $135 per adult, $100 per child.) **Coastal Helicopters** ($168 per person) and **Temsco Helicopters** ($189 per person) run 1hr. **helicopter tours** over the same territory, spending 20min. over the glacier.

Southeast Alaska's only **ski area,** community-owned **Eaglecrest,** on Douglas Island, offers chutes, bowls, and marked runs. (☎586-5284. $25 per day, high-schoolers $17, under 12 $12. Ski rental $20, children $14.) The Eaglecrest ski bus departs from the Baranov Hotel at 8:30am and returns at 5pm on winter weekends and holidays (round-trip $6). In summer, the Eaglecrest **Alpine Summer Trail** is a good way to soak in the mountain scenery of virtually untouched Douglas Island.

◪ NIGHTLIFE

Unsurprisingly, the biggest city in the Southeast has the best nightlife. Local musical talent is surprisingly good.

- **Alaskan Hotel,** 167 Franklin St. (☎586-1000). This former bordello is hugely popular with local twenty-somethings. Open mic night on Th is always packed. Live cajun and blues tunes every weekend. $4.50 pints. Su-Th noon-1am, F-Sa noon-3am.

- **Triangle Club,** 251 Front St. (☎586-3140). Senators come here in the afternoon for wheeling and dealing. Free Internet access.

- **Hangar on the Wharf** (☎586-5018), in the Wharf on Marine Way. View of the water and floatplane comings and goings amid a slightly older crowd. Local bands play F-Sa. 110 beers served. Open Su-Th until midnight, F-Sa until 2 or 3am, depending on the crowd.

GUSTAVUS
☎907

The gateway to the gateway to Glacier Bay National Park, Gustavus is generally ignored by tourists on the way to Bartlett Cove, where trips into the Bay originate. Friendly locals are quick to reveal the secrets of the land, however, and their enthusiasm for the outdoors is infectious. Come prepared. There are no banks, ATMs, or liquor stores in Gustavus. Bear Track Mercantile sells last-minute food stuffs, but its best to bring provisions with you.

◪◪ ORIENTATION AND PRACTICAL INFORMATION. Gustavus is situated on a crossroads called "Four Corners," the intersection of Gustavus Rd. and State Ferry Rd., known by locals as "the road" and "the other road." **Glacier Bay Lodge** and **Bartlett Cove,** the entrance to the park, lie 10 mi. west of Four Corners; the **airport** lies 1 mi. east and the ferry arrives 1 mi. south. Gustavus is accessible only by boat or plane. The cheapest way to get there is on one of the four daily **Alaska Airlines** flights (☎697-2203 or 800-426-0333; $49 one-way from Juneau). **Wings of Alaska**

(☎697-2201) offers two daily flights to Juneau ($60). **Skagway Air** (☎983-2218) flies from Gustavus to Haines ($85) or Skagway ($95). **Auk Nu Tours** runs a 3½hr. ferry from Juneau (☎800-820-2628. Su, M, W, and F departs Juneau for Gustavus at 9am, returns at 5pm. $69. Kayaks $40, bikes $10.) Once in Gustavus, a **bus** from the Glacier Bay Lodge (see p. 455) meets most flights and rolls on to Bartlett Cove ($12). **TLC Taxi** (☎697-2239) charges $12 for one, $20 for two, and $8 per person if there are three or more of you, plus $5 per bike and $10 per kayak. **Bud** (☎697-2403) rents midsize cars for $60 a day. There is no visitors center in Gustavus, but you can ask questions by calling the **Gustavus Visitors Association** (☎697-2475, no set hours). Otherwise, try the Glacier Bay Lodge in Bartlett Cove where there is always someone by the phone. Other services include: **Gustavus Community Clinic,** ☎697-3008; **emergency,** ☎911; and the **post office,** next to the library. (☎697-2202. Open M-F 8am-noon and 1:30-4pm, Sa noon-2pm.) **Postal Code:** 99826.

⌐⌐ ACCOMMODATIONS AND FOOD. Gustavus offers little in the way of budget accommodations. There are **no campgrounds** in town, although tenters sometimes crash on the beach near the ferry dock. The free campgrounds at Bartlett Cove aren't too far away, are easy to get to, and are the destination for most people anyway. **Good River Bed and Breakfast ❹** lends bikes, fishing gear, and rain gear. Also has cozy bedrooms with handmade quilts. (☎697-2241. $95 for doubles). The only provider of (expensive) groceries in town is **Bear Track Mercantile,** a quarter-mile south of Four Corners. (☎697-2358. Open M-Sa 9am-7pm, Su 10am-4pm.) The **Strawberry Point Cafe ❶** next door makes filling sandwiches for $6-8. (☎697-2227. Lunch Tu-Sa 11:30am-3pm. Dinner F-Sa 5:30-8pm.) The **Bear's Nest Cafe ❹,** a quarter-mile north of Four Corners, serves lasagna, enchiladas (both $12), and espresso ($1.50). Expect $20 dinners. (☎697-2440. Open daily 11am-8pm.)

⚡ OUTDOOR ACTIVITIES. Wolf Track Expeditions (☎697-2326), on State Ferry Rd., offers **bike rentals** for $35 per day, whale watching charters for $100, and a combined bike rental and shuttle service to Couverden Point on Chichagof Island, across the Icy Straits, for $160. **Hikers** can walk the 10 mi. rocky beach from Gustavus to Bartlett Cove in a long day. The trip is easiest at low tide and bears may join you for portions (see p. 38). Kayakers can also depart Gustavus instead of Bartlett's Cove; contact **Sea Otter Kayaks.** (☎697-3007. Singles $40 per day; doubles $50, less for longer trips. Includes tide tables, dry bags, and boots.) Hard-core **golfers** tee off at the nine-hole **Mt. Fairweather Golf Course.** (☎697-2214. $15; $6 new club rental, $3 older club rental. Open year-round.)

GLACIER BAY NATIONAL PARK ☎907

The landscape of Glacier Bay changes daily as about a dozen of its glaciers advance and retreat at geologically rapid speeds. Only 200 years ago, the Park Headquarters was completely covered in ice. Now, the daily cruise takes visitors just a few hours to reach spectacular views of icebergs and glaciers and experience close encounters with wildlife. Besides glacier gawkers, the park attracts outdoor purists to the wild backcountry and isolated inlets, accessible only by boat or float plane. The bay is divided into two major arms: the **West Arm** reaches north to the termini of the **Grand Pacific Glacier,** with its 2 mi. face, and **Margerie Glacier,** which advances 6 ft. every year, calving frequently. The **East Arm** is closed to most motorized boat traffic and is a haven for kayakers who cut among the icebergs, sharing the icy waters with harbor seals, humpback whales, orcas, puffins, sea lions and otters, and 45 species of birds. **The Fairweather Range,** to the west, is the highest coastal range in the world and humbles the soul.

TRANSPORTATION. Getting to **Bartlett Cove**, the principle access point to the bay, is relatively easy. A plane or ferry takes visitors to **Gustavus** (see p. 454), and from there a taxi or shuttle (about $10) goes to **Glacier Bay Lodge** and the **Visitor Information Center** at the **National Park Service office**, both close to the campground in the immediate Bartlett Cove area. Once at the Bay, transportation is either self-powered and the purpose of your visit (kayaking), or a sight in itself (cruising). Backcountry hiking and kayaking are also possible in the Dry Bay area, as is **rafting** down the Alsek River. For info, contact the **Yakutat District Office** of the National Park Service, P.O. Box 137, Yakutat, AK 99689 (☎784-3295).

ORIENTATION AND PRACTICAL INFORMATION. The park offers great opportunities for independent explorers. The **Spirit of Adventure** transports kayakers and hikers to two drop-off points while cruising the Bay. Reserve through the **Glacier Bay Lodge.** (☎697-2225 or 800-451-5952. One-way $84, round-trip $159.50, bay pass $189.50.) Because there are boat quotas in the summer, people with their own boats must call ahead to the **National Park Service Office** (☎697-2230) to book a visit. Other cruise ships and charter flightseeing tours operate from outside the park boundaries—get a full list of these by writing to the **Superintendent**, P.O. Box 140, Gustavus, AK 99826-0140 (☎907-697-2230).

Any visit to the park begins at the **Visitor Information Station,** 10 mi. north of Gustavus, a quarter-mile past Glacier Bay Lodge, next to the dock in **Bartlett Cove.** Rangers give a mandatory orientation, announce areas restricted by conservation or bear activity, and distribute permits, maps, and bear-proof food caches. A building next to the station has a gas and food exchange, plus overnight bag storage. (☎697-2230. Open daily 7am-9pm.) Another **Visitors Center,** in the lodge itself, is geared towards less adventurous visitors. (☎697-2661. Open daily 12:30-8:45pm.)

ACCOMMODATIONS AND CAMPING. The **Glacier Bay Lodge** is the center of tourist activity, boasting a restaurant, comfy couches by the fire, visitor information, and nightly Ranger talks and films. All of these features are available to the camper and dormer. Showers ($1 per 8min.) and laundry ($2 wash, $1.25 dry) are adjacent to the Lodge. Bag storage available for $5 per day.

Rooms at the lodge ❺ are almost as much as transportation upbay (singles $149, doubles $179, quads $199). The Lodge also boasts comfy dorm **beds** ❷ ($30). Backpackers and kayakers can stay in the free **campground** ❶ ¼ mi. from the dock, in the lush forest that meets the shore of the bay. The 25 sites are rarely full. (Outhouses, water, food cache for bear-proofing, campfire rings, wood, warming hut. Register at the Visitors Station, where the only water tap is.) **Backcountry camping** is permitted throughout the park—once you have an actual permit. To make sure Look for clearings behind the cottonwoods to avoid being soaked by the tides.

The best bet for food is to bring your own groceries from Juneau and have dinner on the beach. Dinner entrees at the Lodge ❸ are on the pricey side ($15-20), but the deck menu ($6-9) serves nachos built in the shape of the Fairweather Mountains and large sandwiches until 9:30pm.

OUTDOOR ACTIVITIES. The options are endless in this enormous and underused park. The *Spirit of Adventure* is owned by the Lodge (see above) and offers a daily boat tour all around the Bay with a naturalist crew. Most visitors choose this 8hr. trip; few are disappointed. Wildlife sightings and views of 200 ft. glaciers calving are the daily routine. ($157. Includes lunch, snack, and warm beverages. Sightseeing and lodging packages are also available.) **Fjord Flying** (☎697-2377) and **Air Excursions** (☎697-2375) offer aerial views of the glaciers deeper into the park and offer phenomenal views on clear days. They both have 5-person planes for around $350. Air Exursions also has a 3-person plane for $300. The tours last 1½hr.

Kayaking in Glacier Bay is, in short, phenomenal. It is the least expensive and most spectacular way to explore the backcountry over several days. The waters here, although nothing to take lightly, are less challenging than many areas in the inside passage. Most wilderness travelers prefer the East Arm of the bay, because it is off-limits to motorized traffic, and, most importantly, to cruise ships that create large wakes. Many also enjoy the closer, less expensive trip to the **Beardslee Islands,** closed to all non-kayak traffic, which boasts outstanding wildlife. Head to the **Visitor Information Station** for registration, tidal charts, and bear containers. **Kayak rental** is available at **Sea Otter Kayaks.** (☎967-3007. Singles $40 per day; doubles $50. Includes rain gear, rubber boots, drybags, and charts. Reservations recommended.) **Alaska Discovery** (☎800-586-1911) offers guided trips from Bartlett Cove to the Beardslee Islands (full day trip $125, 3hr. evening trip $50).

There are three short and fairly easy hiking trails near the lodge: **The Forest Trail** (1 mi.), **Bartlett River Trail** (24 mi. one-way), and **Bartlett Lake Trail** (4 mi. one-way). All are designed with the meandering nature-viewer in mind, rather than the thrill-seeking climber. The Visitors Center, Station, and the Lodge itself all have maps. The Lodge keeps a schedule of ranger-led walks. There are no other trails throughout the park. Backcountry hiking is accessible only by boat or plane, and is difficult and disorienting because of the thick forest. Other backcountry hikes require ice-climbing gear or skis and should only be approached by experienced climbers. Inquire at the Visitor Information Station for suggestions.

HAINES ☎907

Just south of the terminus of the Inside Passage, Haines offers a natural alternative to the touristy theme town of Skagway. Snow-capped mountains and the crystal blue waters of the Lynn Canal surround Haines with beauty, and an eclectic collection of lifers, fishermen, and newly transplanted post-university students make up the population. Called "the sunny spot of the Southeast," Haines gets *only* about 60 inches of precipitation per year, making the mountains all the more appealing. Haines' cruise ship traffic has recently been controversially reduced, and the town is complimented by travelers for its lack of crowds and for its genuineness. A site of cultural importance to Tlingits throughout Southeast Alaska, the tribal village of Klukwan remains in a strategic riverside location, isolated from Haines.

▐ TRANSPORTATION

Haines lies on a thin peninsula between the **Chilkat** and **Chilkoot Inlets,** just southwest of Skagway on the Chilkoot Inlet. **Main St.** and the **Haines Hwy.** and their perpendiculars, **2nd** and **3rd Avenues,** define downtown. Ft. Seward lies to the south. Below this peninsula, two inlets merge into **Lynn Canal.** There are US and Canadian **customs offices** at Mile 42 of the Haines Hwy. (US: ☎767-5511. Open 24 hr. Canadian: ☎767-5540. Open daily 7am-11pm.) Travelers must have valid proof of citizenship to enter Canada. Rental cars are not always allowed across the border.

Flights: Wings of Alaska (☎766-2030) has the best rates to **Juneau** (5 flights per day, $84). **LAB Air** (☎766-2222) and **Skagway Air** (☎983-2218) fly to **Skagway** ($48). Also service **Gustavus** ($85). Airlines provide free shuttle service to and from town.

Buses: R.C. Shuttles (☎877-479-0079) is based out of Mountain View Motel and will drive anywhere, as long as there are 2 passengers. **Delta Junction** ($120), **Fairbanks** ($140), and **Tok** ($150). Call for fares to other destinations. Book in advance.

Ferries: Alaska Marine Highway (☎766-2111 or 800-642-0066; www.akmhs.com). Terminal on Lutak Rd., 4 mi. from downtown. 1 per day to **Juneau** (4½hr., $28) and **Skagway** (1hr., $20). Parking for ferry passengers $5 per day, $25 per week.

Taxis: Ride with the entertaining Patrick from **24/7 Taxi Service** (☎766-2676). $7 between downtown and the ferry.) **Haines Taxi** (☎766-3138).

Car Rental: Eagle's Nest Car Rental (☎766-2891 or 800-354-6009), at Eagle's Nest Motel, west of town on the Haines Hwy. $45 per day, plus $0.35 per mi. over 100 mi. Must be 25+ with a credit card.

ⓩ PRACTICAL INFORMATION

Tourist Information: On 2nd Ave. near Willard St. (☎766-2234 or 800-458-3579; www.haines.ak.us). Open M-Tu and F 8am-8pm, W-Th 9am-10pm, Sa-Su 9am-6pm.

Outdoor Information: State Park Information Office, 259 Main St. (☎766-2292), above Helen's Shop, between 2nd and 3rd Ave. Open Tu-Sa 8am-4:30pm, but call ahead. The **Fish and Game** folks are in the same building. Open M-F 9am-5pm.

Equipment Rental: Sockeye Cycle (☎766-2869), on Portage St., above the cruise ship docks in Ft. Seward. Bikes $12 per hr., $20 for 4hr., $30 for 8hr. Open in summer M-Sa 9am-6pm, Su 1-5pm. **Deishu Expeditions and Alaska Kayaks** (☎766-2427, www.seakayaks.com) is the town's kayak rental joint. Call for prices.

Alaska Sport Shop (☎766-2441), sells fishing licenses. Open in summer M-Sa 8:30am-6pm, Su 10am-4pm; winter M-Sa 9am-5:30pm.

Bank: First National Bank of Anchorage, on Main St., is the only bank in town. Open M-F 10am-5pm. **24hr. ATM.**

Bookstore: The Babbling Book (☎766-3356), on Main St., near Howser's Supermarket. Open in summer M-Sa 10am-5:30pm, Su noon-5pm; in winter M-Sa 11am-5pm.

Laundromat and Public Showers: Port Chilkoot Camper Park, see **Accommodations and Camping,** below. **Haines Quick Laundry,** behind the Outfitter on the Haines Hwy. Wash $2.50, dry $1.50 for 45min. or $1 for 30min., detergent $0.75. Showers $0.25 per min. up to 15min. Open 7am-9pm.

Weather: ☎766-2727.

Emergency: ☎911.

Police: (☎766-2121), on the Haines Hwy., between 2nd and 3rd Ave.

Medical Services: Health Clinic (☎766-2521), on 1st Ave., next to the visitors center.

Internet Access: The **Library** (☎766-2545), on 3rd Ave. offers 20min. free. Sign up early. Open M, Tu, and Th 10am-9pm, W noon-9pm, F 10am-4:30pm, Sa noon-4:30pm, Su 1-4pm.

Post Office: 55 Haines Hwy., between 2nd Ave. and Front St. Open M-F 8:30am-5pm, Sa 1-3pm. **Postal Code:** 99827.

🏠🏕 ACCOMMODATIONS AND CAMPING

The weather is better in Haines than almost anywhere else in Southeast Alaska, making camping a pleasure. **Chilkat State Park ❶,** 7 mi. south on Mud Bay Rd., has guided walks and good king salmon and halibut fishing (32 sites, 3 beachfront sites, $6.) **Chilkoot Lake ❶,** 12 mi. north of town on Lutak Rd., provides views, sockeye salmon, toilets, and water. (32 sites, $10). **Mosquito Lake ❶,** 27 mi. north on the Haines Hwy., earns its name in late summer. (7 sites, $6.) To reserve, call the State Park Information Office (☎877-444-6777).

Bear Creek Camp and International Hostel (☎766-2259), on Small Tracts Rd., 1½ mi. out of town. From downtown, follow 3rd Ave. out Mud Bay Rd. to Small Tracts. A ring of cabins in a remote location. Call ahead for ferry terminal pickup. Laundry available. Tent sites behind cabins. Bikes $10 per day. Sites $10; dorms $15; cabins $40. ❶

Hotel Hälsingland (☎ 766-2000 or 800-542-6363). Located in Ft. Seward, down the hill from where 3rd Ave. meets Mud Bay Rd. This old officers' quarters' simple white rooms have been newly renovated and come with cable TV. Open May-Sept. and during Nov. for the Bald Eagle Festival. Singles $69. ❸

Portage Cove, almost a mile south of town on Beach Rd., offers the only legitimate free camping in town. Backpackers and cyclists only. Tenters share a grassy space overlooking the water. Rarely crowded. Water, pit toilets. 7-night max. stay. ❶

Port Chilkoot Camper Park (☎ 766-2000 or 800-542-6363), opposite Hotel Hälsingland. Centrally located with gravelly and crowded sites. Water, dump station, laundry ($2, dry $0.25 for 5min., detergent $0.75; open 7am-9pm), and coin showers ($0.50 for 3min). Open Apr.-Sept. 60 sites, $9.75 ($50 per week) for backpackers with no vehicle; full RV sites $23 ($138 per week). ❶

🍴 FOOD

Howser's IGA Supermarket, on Main St., is the town's grocer. (☎ 766-2040. Open daily 8am-9pm.) You may find dungeness crab on the dock, but salmon ($7 per lb.), halibut ($6.95-9.95) and prawns ($7.95-14) are always at **Bell's Seafood,** on 2nd Ave. (☎ 766-2950. Open year-round, hours vary.)

🏛 **Mountain Market,** 151 3rd Ave. (☎ 766-3340), at the Haines Hwy. This health food grocery store and cafe brews their own coffee and serves sandwiches overflowing with fresh ingredients ($4-6.50, with soup $6.95). Internet access $2 for fifteen minutes. Open in summer M-F 7am-7pm, Sa-Su 7am-5:30pm; winter daily 7:30am-6pm. ❶

🏛 **Chilkoot Coffee Company,** in a little booth with a porch on Portage St. This local coffee company serves the cheapest coffee and lunch special in town. The once-a-week Thai Curry lunch special ($1.75) will blow your mind. Open daily 7am-3 or 4pm. ❶

Fireweed Bakery and Cafe (☎ 766-3838), on Blacksmith Rd., up the hill behind Lutak Lumber, near Ft. Seward. The eclectic menu ranges from gourmet pizzas to halibut burgers to Vietnamese spring rolls ($6-12). Eat inside or on the deck overlooking the harbor. Open M-Sa 7am-9pm. ❶

Bamboo Room (☎ 776-2800), on 2nd Ave. near Main St. No bamboo in sight—the name comes from the screen that used to separate the bar from the bordello. Fishermen stop in for a hearty breakfast (omelettes $8) and locals come to splurge on the pricey fish and chips ($17). Open daily 6am-midnight. ❸

👁 SIGHTS

FORT WILLIAM SEWARD. Fort Seward's rectangle of colonial-style buildings dominates the southern hillside above Haines. The fort was built in 1902 and became the first permanent Army post in Alaska. The post quickly became known as a gentle assignment, as hunting and fishing became part of the usual soldierly duties. Today, the buildings are mostly B&Bs and private living quarters with the exceptions of the replicated **Totem Village** (☎ 766-2160; in summer 766-2004), in the middle of the parade ground. The Village is home to Sea Wolf Studio-Gallery (☎ 766-2540. Open daily 10am-5:30pm), where Tlingit artist Tresham Gregg carves the masks that appear in his **New Chilkat Dancers' Storytelling Theater Show.** The play itself is less than thrilling, but the costume and movements are worth the price of admission. (Open M, W, and F at 5pm, W and Th at 7:30pm. $10, children $5. Call the gallery for more information.) The Hotel Halsingland hosts salmon bakes after the late shows ($20). In the neighboring, welcoming **Alaska Indian Arts Center,** artists work in open workshops, and an annual apprenticeship trains future master carvers. Head to the back studio to see the totem pole carvers at work. (☎ 766-2160; www.alaskaindianarts.com. M-F 9am-5pm and evenings during ship dockings.)

CHILKAT BALD EAGLE PRESERVE. The world's largest group of bald eagles congregates here each fall—two dozen or more eagles in a single tree is not uncommon. Generally, eagle activity reaches its height in Nov., tapering off in Feb. The Bald Eagle Preserve is 48,000 acres of land set aside for the protection of eagles; unfortunately, you will need wheels to get there. Chilkat Cruises (see **Transportation,** above), runs a 2½hr. native history and interpretive tour of the reserve for $44 per person. *(Mile 9 to Mile 32 on Haines Highway.)*

AMERICAN BALD EAGLE FOUNDATION. The Foundation is dedicated to providing educational facilities and materials about bald eagles. They run a **Natural History Museum** in town with 180 stuffed specimens of Alaskan wildlife. The map of active eagle nests in the Chilkoot Valley makes this a worthwhile stop on the way to the preserve. *(At the intersection of Haines Hwy. and 2nd Ave. ☎ 766-3094. Open May-Sept. Sa-Su 1-4pm, M-W 9am-5pm, Th 9am-10pm. $3, ages 8-12 $1, under 8 free.)*

🅰🅾 NIGHTLIFE AND FESTIVALS

The three main watering holes in town are **The Fogcutter** on Main St., opposite the bank; **Harbor Bar,** by the small boat harbor; and the **Hälsingland Hotel Bar.** In a unique system, all of them close depending on where the action is: once the party-spot has established itself sometime after midnight, the favored barkeep calls the other two bars and they close up early. A good bet is to start at the Fogcutter for a wide selection on tap and $0.50 pool. (Opening times vary even within each bar; however, the chosen bar is open until 5am or when the activity dies down.)

The biggest annual event in Haines is the **Alaska Bald Eagle Festival** (Nov. 7-10, 2003), when thousands of eagles gather on the Chilkat River. A winter salmon run provides food for hungry eagles; who in turn provide food for hungry photographers. Wildlife experts give lectures. Contact the **American Bald Eagle Foundation Center** (☎766-3094) for more information. The **Bald Eagle Music Festival and State Fair** is a major attraction throughout the region (Aug. 14-18, 2003).

🏔 OUTDOOR ACTIVITIES

The **Haines Hwy.** winds 40 mi. from Haines into the **Chilkat Range,** running north through the Yukon, with views guaranteed bound to blow your mind. The road stretches for 160 mi. until Haines Junction, Canada, where it connects with the Alaska Highway. (Bear in mind that the you need proof of citizenship to cross the border into Canada, and rental cars are sometimes denied crossing.)

The **White Pass and Yukon Route Railroad** follows the same route as the Haines Hwy. on the other side of the ravine. Visitors can ride the wooden train over wooden rails either as an actual means of transportation into Canada or as a day-trip from Haines or Skagway. There are some trails only accessible via the railway (see **Hiking,** below). **Chilkat Cruises** offers a round-trip ferry to Skagway and a round-trip on the train to White Pass Summit and back for $95. The return ticket is open, so you can hang around heavily cruise-shipped Skagway as long or as short as your heart desires (see **Transportation,** above).

BIKING. The Haines vicinity is great for serious cyclists or those who just want a daytrip. The brawny can ride the Haines Hwy., and daytrippers can head to Chilkoot Lake (10 mi. one way) or Chilkat State Park. **Sockeye Cycle** has suggestions and pricey bikes for the renting. If you have your own, it is best to bring it with you.

MOUNTAINS. Alaska Mountain Guides and Climbing School, Inc. (☎800-766-3396; www.alaskamountainguides.com) is staffed by hard-core climbers. They will help you prepare for Everest or take you sea kayaking for a half-day ($85). Give them a call for tips on where to climb. **Out of Bounds Adventure** (☎800-HELL-YEA (seriously); alaskaheliskiing.com) runs heliskiing trips in the Haines area.

WATER. A favorite swimming hole is **Chilkoot Lake,** 10 mi. north on Lutak Rd. The Chilkat River is a late August salmon run, and is choice for canoeing and kayaking. **Deishu Expeditions** (☎800-552-9257) runs guided tours in the area, some up around the Davidson glacier. **Chilkat Guides** runs a rafting trip down the Tsirku river for eagle viewing in isolated surroundings. (☎766-2491. $75.) **Alaska Mountain Guides,** on Blacksmith Rd., runs trips ranging from 1-12 days in the Inside Passage, Glacier Bay, and the Yukon River. (☎800-766-3396. Double kayak rentals $50 per day; call for guide prices.) Sean Dog and Fishbone from Out of Bounds Adventure (see **Mountains,** above) rent a 54 ft. boat **surfing** charter out of Haines and will put it anywhere you want along the Southeast Alaskan coast. **Yeshua Guided Tours** (☎766-2334; yeshuaguidedtours.com), on 2nd Ave. by the visitors center, offers a 3hr. fishing trip for $90, $70 per person if there is more than one person.

FLIGHTSEEING. Haines is actually closer to the glaciers of Glacier Bay than the town of Gustavus (see p. 454). The views of all-white mountain peaks and miles of glaciers may trick you into believing you have traveled back in time to an ice age. Although most of the small airlines also cater to their clients' flightseeing needs, **Mountain Flying Service** (☎766-3007 or 800-954-8747), on 2nd St., has the most hospitable crew and specializes in this business. Each tour is well worth the money. (1hr. $115; 80min. $159; 2hr. $259.) Glacier landings ($75 extra) are available, but at the discretion of the pilot. There is a 2-person minimum for all flights.

🖾 HIKING

Haines' surrounding mountains are stunning and views from their summits are superb. Ask for the free *Haines is for Hikers* at the visitors center.

Mt. Ripinsky Trail (4½ mi. one-way, 3650 ft. gain, 6-8hr.) Follow 2nd Ave. north, then take Young St. uphill, veer left along the hillside at the fork in the road. After Young Rd. becomes a dirt road, the trailhead is on the left in front of a gate. This 3650 ft. summit offers panoramic views of snow-capped peaks, glacial fields, and alpine meadows. Mt. Ripinsky has 2 peaks: the South and North. After the North and higher peak (which has a register), the trail joins the **Skyline Trail** (10 mi. from Main St. in town to Mile 7 on Haines Hwy., 8-10hr.; 300 ft. gain from Ripinsky Peak), which traverses the ridgeline, ascends to Peak 3920, and then cuts down into a saddle, ending at Mile 7 on Haines Hwy. Camping is good in the saddle, and there are springs for water. Weather can make the top especially slippery, requiring good boots. Difficult.

Mt. Riley Trail (2.8mi. one-way, 1760 ft. gain, 4½hr.) also leaves right from town, and offers similarly spectacular family-accessible views. The trail can be accessed at mile 3 on Small Tracts Rd. (1½ mi. past the hostel) for the steepest and most direct route, or by turning left on FAA Rd. off of Mud Bay Rd. and following it about a mile to the end. Turn right shortly before the city dump. Moderate.

Mud Bay Road (2¾ mi. one-way, 1760 ft. gain, 3½hr.). Follow 3rd Ave. south, then follow Mud Bay Rd. for about 3 mi. The trailhead is at the top of a bank across from the parking area. Follow the steep trail and turn right at the intersection with the Lily Lake trail. The trail follows old-growth forest to open muskeg and excellent views. Difficult.

Seduction Point Trail (7 mi. one-way, 9-10hr.). Take Mud Bay Rd. out of Haines 7 mi. to Chilkat State Park. Time the last part of the hike along David's Cove to coincide with low tide. Offers birds, beaches, ocean bluffs, berry picking, wildflowers, and alluring views of Rainbow and Davidson Glaciers. Camping along the trail is permitted. No water. Connect with the Ripinsky/Skyline trails for several days of back-country hiking. Moderate.

THE PANHANDLE

Battery Point Trail (2 mi. one-way, 2hr.). Trailhead is 1½ mi. from the City Dock. Follow Beach Rd. east around Portage Cove. Turn right at the end of the road. Follow the Battery Point trail for about a mile and continue straight to open meadow and beaches. This is the easiest and briefest hike, but still accesses serene shoreline. Easy.

SKAGWAY ☎907

Only the foolhardy skip over Skagway and the beautiful mountains surrounding it on every side. Skagway's rich history began thanks to gold mines and persists due to cruise lines. Five hundred miles from Skagway, in August 1896, a Tlingit man named Skookum Jim was washing a pan in a tributary of the Klondike River when he discovered strips of gold so thick they looked "like cheese in a sandwich." By October, 20,000 stampeders from Skagway had set off for the site of Jim's discovery. The prospectors are gone now, but the railroad carries tourists to see historic Broadway St. or hike the Chilkoot Trail. The winter population of 850 swells to 1600 residents in the summer, and the tourist-centric Broadway boardwalk is trampled by nearly 800,000 visitors each year.

⌐ TRANSPORTATION

At the northernmost tip of the Inside Passage, Skagway is a terminus of the **Alaska Marine Hwy.** Skagway is also at the end of the **Klondike Hwy.** (Rte. 98 in AK and Hwy. 2 in YT), 113 mi. (2½hr.) south of Whitehorse and 66 mi. (1½hr.) south of Carcross. Canadian and US **customs** are passable 24 hours a day, although the US office is not staffed from midnight to 6am. There are no services between Skagway and Carcross. **Haines** is 15 mi. away by water, 360 mi. by land. The **ferry dock** is at the southern end of downtown. Skagway's main drag, **Broadway St.**, runs inland from the docks with **Spring St.** on the right and **State** and **Main St.** on the left. Numbered **avenues** intersect the streets. The road into town runs straight to State St.

Flights: Skagway Air Service (☎983-2218), on Broadway between 4th and 5th Ave. Open daily summer 7am-9pm; winter 7am-5pm. 8 flights per day to **Gustavus** (1hr., $95); **Haines** (10min., $45); and **Juneau** (45min., $85). Tours **Glacier Bay** (1½hr., 2-person min., $130).

Trains: White Pass and Yukon Route (☎983-2217 or 800-343-7373; www.whitepassrailroad.com), on 2nd Ave. One of North America's steepest and most scenic railroads. Round-trip daily excursions to **Summit** ($82), **Lake Bennett** ($128 on Su, M, and F; $156 on Sa), or **White Pass.** Also accesses remote trailheads (see **Outdoor Activities**, p. 466). Train and bus service daily to **Whitehorse, YT** (5hr.; 8am; $95, ages 3-12 half-price for all fares). Buses may not be wheelchair accessible. Reservations recommended.

Buses: Alaska Direct (☎800-770-6652) runs vans by appointment from the ferry terminal, visitors center, and hostel to **Whitehorse, YT** (3½hr.; $50, round-trip $90). Connections on W, F, and Su to **Anchorage** ($215) and **Fairbanks** ($190); requires an overnight stay in Whitehorse (accommodation not provided). **Alaskan Express** (☎983-2241 or 800-544-2206), in the Westmark Inn on 3rd Ave. between Broadway and Spring St., runs in summer once daily to **Whitehorse, YT** (3hr., 8:45am, $46) and from mid-May to mid-Sept. Su and W to **Anchorage** ($219) and **Fairbanks** ($216). Both trips require overnighting in Beaver Creek, YT (23hr.; accommodation not provided).

Ferries: Alaska Marine Highway (☎983-2941 or 800-642-0066). The dockside ticket booth is open when the ferry is in, 1:30-3:30pm. Ferry schedule often varies, so check online: www.state.ak.us/ferry. Typically, in July and Aug., 6 per week leave for **Haines** (1hr.; $20 for walk-on, $39-62 for vehicle and driver) and **Juneau** (6½hr.; $35, add $45-109 for vehicle depending on size). **Water Taxi** (☎983-2083 or 888-766-3395).

A SINKING INDUSTRY?
Commercial Salmon Fishing in Alaska

Salmon has long been an important staple in the Pacific Northwest. The fish provides a source of food for an entire region, and its popularity and prevalence has created jobs in the fishing industry for thousands of fishermen and women, changing quiet little villages into booming fishing towns. The years of prosperity that salmon have brought to the Pacific Northwest, however, could be ending, as the fish face an increasingly sophisticated level of attack and the market for wild salmon becomes smaller and smaller.

Modern fishermen use everything from depth finders to fish finders to spotting planes to find fish. Harvesting their catch either by encircling entire schools of fish with a net, or by strategic placement of nets, fishermen have perfected maximizing their catch in the shortest time. The populations of the small communities near the fishing grounds, mere hamlets during the winter, swell to ten times their normal size when the fish are running. For years the richness of the fishery attracted hundreds of migrant workers, both to the boats themselves and to the canneries they served. After the advent of the limited entry system in 1973, the cost of just a permit (the right to put a boat in the water), could reach $300,000. In recent years, however, all that has come to an end.

The deadly efficiency of modern fishing techniques has taken its toll on salmon populations. Salmon runs in most of the Pacific Northwest dwindled decades ago. In 2001, fishermen received a mere 40 cents per pound, the lowest price in eighteen years, and this despite a weak run. According to the ADF&G web site, the projected harvest for 2002 is a mere 9.7 million fish; 63% smaller than the previous 10-year mean harvest of 26.3 million. The permits that once cost so much now sit on the market with asking prices of $20,000, unsold.

The reasons for this collapse are varied: over-fishing is clearly one, despite regulatory efforts and an extensive network of hatcheries supplementing wild runs. What really makes the lowered runs sting, though, is the lowered price of salmon. The weakened market is due in part to the downturn of the Japanese economy in the late nineties (Japan had been a strong consumer of Alaskan salmon for years), but can be traced even more directly to the anathema of all fishermen: farmed fish.

The process of farming salmon was first perfected in Norway in the 1960s, but since then it has been spreading rapidly. Today's farmed fish are predominantly Atlantic salmon (distinct from Pacific salmon) and constitute the vast majority of salmon on the market. Raised mostly in Chile (which controls about 50% of the US import market) and Canada (which controls another 35% of the market), these farmed fish are replacing what in many cases was the main industry of small Alaskan villages. With prices low and processing plants closing, Alaskan fishermen find themselves in a grim situation.

The story isn't one of passive defeat, however. In 1990 the Alaska State Legislature passed the Fish and Game Act, which stated: "a person may not grow or cultivate finfish in captivity or under positive control for commercial purposes." Since then, the Alaskan Seafood Marketing Institute (ASMI) has been emphasizing the benefits of wild salmon, both as a healthy food and as a renewable resource. In light of the worsening state of the industry, ASMI has gone even further and, in press releases like "Not All Salmon Are Created Equal" started to point out the problems of salmon farming: the increased spread of disease due to confinement (frequently treated with heavy doses of antibiotics), the disruption of ecosystems by release of concentrated salmon waste, the weakening of genetic diversity and the possibility of escaped farm fish contaminating wild strains, and (perhaps most importantly for the consumer) the inferior quality and flavor of farm fish.

Will the Alaskan salmon industry be able to reinvent itself and survive? Does wild salmon really taste better? There's only one way to find out...

Nathaniel Brooks, a native of Homer, Alaska, is the Map Editor for this book. He was a Researcher-Writer for Let's Go Peru, Ecuador, and Bolivia 2002, and has traveled extensively throughout Alaska and the Pacific Northwest and Europe.

Open May-Sept. daily 7:30am-4:30pm. Runs twice per day to **Haines** (1hr.; $24; round-trip with 4hr. stopover $45; under 12 half-price). Buy tickets at **Dijon Delights**, on Broadway at 5th Ave.

Local Transportation: SMART (☎983-2743) runs shuttles 7:30am-9pm year-round, making stops on Broadway for a maximum fare of $3. Other local pick-ups and drop-offs accommodated. Call for reservations.

Car Rental: Sourdough Van & Car Rentals (☎983-2523, in AK 800-478-2529), 6th Ave. at Broadway. From $60 with unlimited mileage. Drop-offs at Haines and Whitehorse by arrangement. Must be 21+ with credit card.

■ PRACTICAL INFORMATION

Tourist Information: Skagway Convention and Visitors Bureau (☎983-2854; www.skagway.org), on Broadway off 2nd Ave. in historic **Arctic Brotherhood Hall**, constructed of a reputed 10,000 pieces of driftwood. Open May-Sept. daily 8am-6pm; Oct.-Apr. M-F 8am-5pm. **Klondike Gold Rush National Historical Park** (☎983-2921), at 2nd Ave. and Broadway. Open June-Aug. daily 8am-8pm; May and Sept. 8am-6pm.

Skagway

▲▲ ACCOMMODATIONS
Dyea Camping Area, **4**
Golden North Hotel, **3**
Skagway Home Hostel, **5**

🍴 FOOD
Haven Cafe, **1**
La Sabrosa, **2**
Red Onion Saloon, **6**

Outdoor Information: The **Parks Trail Center** (☎983-3655), on Broadway, sells **overnight permits** for the Canadian side of the Chilkoot trail. (CDN$35, under 16 CDN$17.50.) Knowledgeable staff prepare hikers. Open late-May to mid-Sept. daily 8am-4:15pm. The staff at **The Mountain Shop** (see **Equipment Rental**) can also provide advice on local outdoors opportunities.

Equipment Rental: The Mountain Shop (☎983-2544), on 4th Ave. between Broadway and State St., rents reasonably-priced gear for water and snow sports, camping, and hiking the Chilkoot. Kayaks $40 per day, snowshoes $5, tents $20, camp stoves $6. Rates substantially reduced for multi-day usage. **Sockeye Cycle** (☎983-2851), on 5th Ave. off Broadway St. Bikes from $6 per hr. or $30 per day. Open daily May-Sept. 9am-6pm. **Skagway Hardware** (☎983-2233), on Broadway St. at 4th Ave., sells fishing permits ($10 per day), guns and ammo, and outdoor gear. Open mid-Apr. to Sept. M-F 8am-6pm, Sa-Su 8am-5pm; winter M-Sa 8am-5pm.

Bank: National Bank of Alaska (☎983-2265), at Broadway and 6th Ave. Open M-F 9:30am-5pm. **24hr. ATM.**

Market: You Say Tomato (☎983-2784), on State St. at 9th Ave. Open Apr.-Oct. M-Sa 10:30am-7:30pm, Su noon-5pm; call for winter hours. **Fairway Supermarket** (☎983-2000), at 4th Ave. and State St. Open summer M-Sa 8am-9pm, Su 8am-6pm; winter M-Sa 9am-6pm, Su 10am-4pm.

Bookstore: Skagway News Depot (☎983-3354), Broadway between 2nd Ave. and 3rd Ave. Open daily 8:30am-7pm.

Laundromat: Services Unlimited Laundromat (☎983-2595), at 2nd Ave. and State St. attached to the gas station. Wash $2, dry $0.25 per 5min. Open summer daily 7am-9pm, last load 7pm; winter 8am-6pm.

Public Showers: Garden City RV Park (☎983-2743), on State and 15th Ave. $0.75 per 5min.

Emergency: ☎911.

Police: (☎983-2232), on State St. toward the water past 1st Ave.

Hospital: Skagway Medical Service (☎983-2255; emergency 983-2418), on 11th Ave. between State and Broadway. Clinic open M-W 9am-noon, 1-4pm, Th 9am-noon.

Internet Access: Free at the **library** (☎983-2665) at 8th Ave. and State St. (one terminal for research, one for email). Book ahead. Open M-F 1-9pm and Sa 1-5pm.

Post Office: (☎983-2330), at Broadway and 6th, next to bank. Open M-F 8:30am-5pm. **Postal Code:** 99840.

■ ACCOMMODATIONS

Several reasonably priced and unique accommodations are reason enough for the non-cruise ship passenger to visit Skagway. Make reservations unless you're camping. **Dyea,** 9 mi. away, has the only free tenting.

Skagway Home Hostel (☎983-2131), on 3rd Ave. near Main St. Does, indeed, feels just like home. Shared kitchen. Sign up for dinner before 4:30pm ($5; free if you cook). Showers, kitchen, bike use, and plenty of Chilkoot Trail stories and advice. Sheets and towels $1. Laundry $3. Chore required. Check-in 5:30-10:30pm. Curfew 11pm (late ferries accommodated). Beds $15; private double $40. No credit cards. ❶

Golden North Hotel (☎983-2491), at 3rd Ave. and Broadway St. The oldest hotel in the state of Alaska (est. 1898). Each room is decorated in a period style, with canopy beds and antique furniture. Singles $65, with bath $95; doubles $75, $105. ❹

Dyea Camping Area, 9 mi. northwest of Skagway on winding Dyea Rd., near start of Chilkoot Trail. Well-maintained. Pit toilets, fire pits, and bear poles. The tough drive is hard on RVs. 14-night max. stay. 22 spacious, woodsy sites. Free. No showers.❶

◗ FOOD

Skagway's status as a cruise ship magnet can make eating and shopping pricey.

▩ **La Sabrosa** (☎983-2469), on Broadway and 6th Ave. The fat, meaty burrito ($9) is a challenge to finish, while the salad ($6) and sandwich ($7) are also great options. Open M-F 6am-4pm, Sa-Su 7am-2pm. ❷

▩ **Red Onion Saloon** (☎983-2222), on Broadway between 2nd and 3rd Ave. At Skagway's classiest former bordello, built in 1898, the bawdy waitresses entertain the daytime tourist crowd. Tasty sandwiches ($6-8) and pizzas ($7.50). The dinner scene is much more mellow, with frequent live music. Many Alaskan beers on tap (pint $4.25). Open daily 10am-close. ❷

Haven Cafe (☎983-3553), State St. and 9th Ave. The only espresso shop in town far enough from crowds that you can settle on the couch and enjoy a book. Baked goodies (scones $2), panini sandwiches ($8), and delectable desserts (cake $5). Sunday night is open mic night, 8pm-close. Open M-Sa 6am-10pm, Su 6am-midnight. ❷

👁 🎵 SIGHTS AND ENTERTAINMENT

KLONDIKE. Many of the pristine buildings on Broadway St. from the 1900s are leased to local businesses by the Park Service as part of the **Klondike Gold Rush National Historical Park.** Guided walking tours or a self-guided tour map available (see **Tourist Information,** above). Polish up on gold rush trivia and Alaskan culture at the **Skagway Museum and Archive,** housed in both the oldest and newest granite buildings in Alaska, on 7th Ave. and Spring Street. (☎ 983-2420. Open summer M-F 9am-5pm, Sa and Su 1-5pm. $2, students $1, under 12 free.)

BARS. The **Red Onion Saloon,** Skagway's first bordello features live afternoon jazz (courtesy of cruise ship musicians), a tour upstairs with Madame Chilkoot, or a game of pool. (☎ 983-2222. Open May-Sept. daily 10am-close.) For less ambience but great Skagway brews, visit the **Skagway Brewing Company** in the Golden North Hotel, which serves up six drafts from its in-house microbrewery. (Open May-Sept. daily 11am-close.)

🏔 OUTDOOR ACTIVITIES

■ CHILKOOT TRAIL. Skagway offers phenomenal dayhikes and multi-day trips. The highly acclaimed **Chilkoot Trail** starts at the nearby Dyea Camping Area. Backpackers on the Chilkoot benefit from the Alaska National History Association's complete *Hiker's Guide to the Chilkoot Trail* ($2), available at the **Trail Center.** Hikers must register at the Trail Center to use any portion of the Chilkoot. Reservations for the Chilkoot are accepted for the coming year starting in January and are recommended if hiking between July and August. 50 people per day are allowed to cross into Canada; there is space for only eight walk-ons. Hikers are advised to allow 3-6 days to hike the Chilkoot (the record is a mere 16 hours). Rangers are stationed at the Dyea Trailhead, Sheep Camp, and Lindeman City. Upon completion, hikers must go to Canadian customs in **Fraser, BC** (☎ 867-821-4111), or **Whitehorse, YT.** (☎ 867-667-3943. CDN$35 for the whole trail, CDN$18 for children. Reservations CDN$10.)

In Whitehorse, call ☎ 800-661-0486 or 867-667-3910 to make Chilkoot reservations. Information is available in Skagway, too. (☎ 907-983-3655; open daily 8am-4:15pm.) There are a number of ways to get between Skagway or Carcross and the Chilkoot trailheads at Dyea and Bennett Lake. **Frontier Excursions** (☎ 983-2512) and **Dyea Dave** (☎ 983-2731) run taxis between Skagway and Dyea ($10) and between Skagway and the road access end at Log Cabin ($25 for both drop-off and pick-up). **The White Pass & Yukon Route** runs trains between Skagway and Lake Bennett, the traditional end. (☎ 983-2217. $65. Reservations required.)

■ GLACIERS. Outdoor accessibility knows no limit in Skagway—glaciers can be reached easily, and cozy cabins await visitors. The White Pass and Yukon Railroad (see **Trains,** p. 462) drops the glacier-bound at **Laughton Glacier** (easy 2½ mi. hike from Milepost 14; $54 round-trip) and **Denver Glacier** (5½ mi. hike from Milepost 6; $27 round-trip). Getting up next to the glaciers, huge slabs of ice jammed up against the mountainsides, is bound to be the highlight of any trip to Skagway. Reservations for the **Laughton Cabin ❷** (1½ mi. from train stop) or the noisier **Caboose Cabin ❷** (at Denver train stop) can be made through the U.S. Forest Service. (☎ 586-8751 or 877-444-6777. Pit toilets, no water. $35.)

DEWEY LAKE. Although the Chilkoot Trail is the marquee name in Skagway hiking, shorter local trails have inspiring views and less traffic. The **Dewey Lake Trail System** provides some of the best nearby hiking, from a leisurely 2hr. stroll to a strenuous climb reaching alpine lakes at 3700 ft./1130m. Pick up a free guide to the local hikes at the Trail Center, The Mountain Shop, or the visitors center (see **Outdoor Information,** p. 464). To reach the trails, walk east along 2nd Ave. and follow the dirt path just before the railroad tracks to the left. Look for trailhead signs on the right. After passing the outhouse, hikers find refuge from the railroad, helicopter, and cruise ship noise. One trail branches to the lake (2 mi./3km), and another heads to **Icy Lake** and **Upper Reid Falls** (1½ mi./2.5km). Both walks are gentle, with little change in elevation. A third trail to **Upper Dewey Lake** branches off the Icy Lake trail near the northern end of Lower Dewey Lake. The first section of the trail (2¼ mi./3.5km) is brutal until the climb mellows out into switchbacks to the site of the lake, in a stunning amphitheater of peaks. The total ascent from town takes 2-3hr. A cramped **cabin** with bunk space for 4 is available on a first-come, first-served basis. The best tenting sites are along the far shore. **Fishing** is available at both Upper and Lower Dewey Lakes. The **Skyline Trail** leads up **AB Mountain,** named for the pattern created on its face by spring meltwater. Both the directions to the trailhead and the trail itself are confusing; pick up a **Skagway Trail Map** at the Trail Center or at the Klondike Gold Rush National Historical Park Visitor Center (see **Tourist Information,** p. 464). From town, it's about 5 mi. to the panoramic 3500 ft. summit; allow 4-5hr. for the steep ascent. A free **camping permit** is necessary in the Skagway area and is available at the police station.

YAKUTAT   ☎907

There is no actual town of Yakutat, but there are numerous lodges that cater to the testosterone-heavy sportfishermen and hunters that come every summer to take home their body weight in halibut, salmon, and trout. While Yakutat's ocean-front weather can be treacherous (frequent storms bring up to 200 in. of rain and 200 in. of snow yearly), hardy surfers come here for some of the best waves in Alaska. Backpackers beware: budget travel has yet to establish itself in Yakutat. Food here is the most expensive in the Panhandle, and the weather usually makes camping a cold, wet proposition. On a sunny day, though, the 180° views of jagged peaks will make you forget your light purse.

TRANSPORTATION. Since Yakutat has nothing akin to a downtown, a car is required. The **airport** is 5 mi. south of the ferry dock on Monti Bay. The smallest community in the world with daily jet service, Yakutat receives **Alaskan Airlines** (☎784-3366 or 800-426-0333) Flights #61 and 66 on their way between **Seattle** and **Anchorage.** Short hops to **Juneau** ($168) and **Cordova** ($168) are also available. Twice a month in summer, the **Alaska Marine Hwy.** stops in on its way from Juneau to Valdez, if and only if there are vehicle reservations in Yakutat. **Situk Leasing,** affiliated with the Yakutat Lodge (see **Accommodations,** below) meets flights and rents beat-up old trucks that suit Yakutat's dirt roads. ($65-85 per day.) They also provide transportation to the Situk River ($35 per person, and $35 for any extra vehicles needed to transport your massive amounts of gear.) (☎784-3316. Unlimited mileage; must have insurance and major credit card.)

⚡ PRACTICAL INFORMATION. The **Yakutat Chamber of Commerce** (☎784-3933; www.yakutatalaska.com) has an office in the **National Park Service Ranger Station/ Visitors Center**, on Mallott Ave., which serves Wrangell-St. Elias and Glacier Bay National Parks. (☎784-3295. Open M-F 8am-5pm, but call ahead.) Get info on wilderness cabins at the **Yakutat Ranger District Forest Service**, on Ocean Cape Rd. (☎784-3359. Open M-F 8am-5pm.) The **Alaska Dept. of Fish and Game** office is near the airport. (☎784-3255. Open M-F 8am-5pm.) **Yakutat Hardware**, on Mallott Ave. downtown, sells licenses, hunting tags, gear, and supplies. (☎784-3203. Open M-Sa 10am-5:30pm.) **Alaska Pacific**, on Mallott Ave., is the only bank in town. (☎784-3991. Open M-Th 10am-3pm, F 10am-5pm.) **Monti Bay Foods** has the **ATM**. Other services include: **weather**, ☎800-662-6622; **emergency**, ☎911; **police**, (☎784-3206) in the hangar-shaped Public Safety Office on Max Italio Dr.; **pharmacy: 24hr. Health Center**, under Forest Service office. (☎784-3275. Pharmacy open M-F 9am-noon and 1-4:30pm.); and **post office**, on Mallott Ave. (☎784-3201. Open M-F 9am-5pm, Sa 9am-1pm.) **Postal Code:** 99689.

⚡⚡ ACCOMMODATIONS AND FOOD. Yakutat doesn't do hotels. They do lodges that cater to sport fishermen and offer expensive packages including food, vehicles, boats, and guides. **Yakutat Lodge ❸**, next to the airport, rents cabins that sleep four or more. Without a reservation, this is the cheapest in town. With a reservation, prices skyrocket to $250 per night. (☎784-3232. $25 per person; $50 min.)

There are no established campgrounds around Yakutat; however, good camping is available to those with wheels. About 3 mi. from the airport, **Cannon Beach** stretches 10 mi. In the summer, surfers create a bit of Hawaii in Alaska and camp on the beach, especially around Ocean Cape. The old-growth forest behind the beach provides shelter, both to you and the bears—be careful. Take a left a quarter-mile from the airport onto the gravel road, follow it 2 mi. over the bridge, and drive through the forest and onto the beach.

Yakutat is not known for its restaurants—most visitors eat what they catch. **Mallott's General Store**, on Max Italio Dr., a quarter-mile from the turn-off after Monti Bay, is where locals get groceries. (☎784-3355. Store open in summer daily 8am-8pm; winter M-Sa 8am-7pm, Su 10am-3pm.) **The Yakutat Lodge ❶** has an affordable restaurant with lunch running $4.95-10.

⚡ OUTDOOR ACTIVITIES. Dangerous River Rd. ends after 18 mi. at the trailhead for **Harlequin Lake** (¾ mi. one way, 15min.), where **Yakutat Glacier** crowds the 10 mi. lake with icebergs. To extend the day, walk the rock beach to the right, or bushwhack down to the water to hike the beach all the way around the point to the left. The Harlequin Lake Forest Service **cabin** sits by the lake. Beware, very big bears are known to roam these parts (see p. 38). The Forest Service and the National Park Service have more extensive info on local hikes and cabins.

Yakutat is *the* place to **surf** in Alaska, with rolling turquoise waves breaking off **Ocean Cape**, nicknamed "the graveyard," or **Point Munoz**, on Khantaak Island along **Cannon Beach**'s 10 mi. stretch. **Icy Waves Surf Shop** (☎784-3226) offers advice and sells wetsuits and boards; you'll need a 3-5mm suit for the 40-50°F water.

The least expensive way to go **fishing** is to camp on the Situk river and fish from shore. Only unbaited artificial lures are allowed in the 9 Mile Bridge area. Most charter operations in the area offer non-motorized drift boats for $65, and will drop you off at 9 Mile Bridge to float on down the river. The trip lasts between 8 and 14hr. depending on the current, and how often you tie up to fish a particular spot. You also have to pay a spotter ($35-65) to pick you up at the delta. Contact the Chamber of Commerce for a full list of charter operations.

Although no **kayak or canoe** rentals are available in town, extensive waterways in the region are great for kayaking and canoeing. The Forest Service can suggest some spectacular trips for experienced paddlers. Camping is permitted on some of the islands of Monti Bay.

CENTRAL ALASKA

ALASKA'S...Capital: Juneau. **Population:** 626,932. **Area:** 586,412 sq. mi. **Motto:** Cut Alaska in two and Texas will be the THIRD largest state! **Real Motto:** North to the Future. **Flower:** Forget-me-not. **State Fish:** King salmon. **Tree:** Sitka spruce. **Mineral:** Gold. **Gem:** Jade. **Sport:** Dog mushing. **Holiday:** Alaska Day, Oct. 18. **Drinking Age:** 21.

Southcentral Alaska stands alone as the region by which many outsiders gauge the entire state. Anchorage, the transportation hub, can be a daunting place to visit; strip malls and skyscrapers unsuccessfully vie for their place in a skyline dominated by mountain ranges. Major highways shuttle hordes of tour buses and campers from site to site come summer, while long winters enshroud locals in a blanket of white and provide yet another playground for the adventurous. Outdoor opportunities

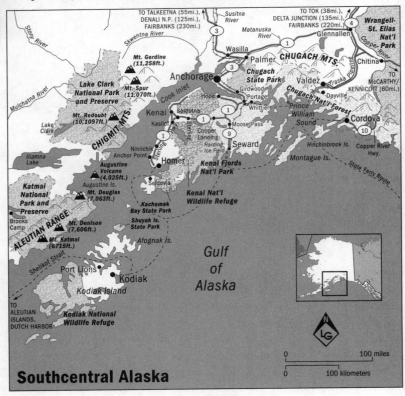

Southcentral Alaska

abound and whet the hungry nature-lover's appetite, with rock climbing, hiking, backpacking, mountaineering, ice climbing, mountain biking, fishing, hunting, kayaking, sailing, skydiving, canoeing, paragliding, sightseeing, bungee jumping, snow-machining, skiing, snowshoeing, glacier trekking, rafting, horseback riding, birding, whale watching, windsurfing, flying, and more among the many offerings. From the Kenaі Peninsula's salmon-choked streams to the solitary beauty found in the numerous National Parks, visitors get to experience a slice of the Alaskan way of life. This multi-faceted environment cultivates an attitude of independence and adventure, combined with a love for the land and self-sufficiency. Here, oil and fishing cowboys, off-beat flower-children, and Alaskan Natives all bring their traditions and distinctive ways of life together.

▨ CENTRAL ALASKA'S HIGHLIGHTS

GLACIERS calve into the waters in Cordova (see p. 497).

DENALI'S breathtaking peak must be enjoyed, whether from up close or from afar, whether by car, by foot, or by plane (see p. 534).

ALASKAN MICROBREW FESTIVAL combines hot water and hops in early August at **Chena Hot Springs Resort** (see p. 554).

GODLINESS is next to the Shoup glacier in Valdez, where Sunday services are held afloat at the foot of the ice (see p. 496).

ANCHORAGE ☎ 907

Anchorage, Alaska's foremost urban center and only metropolis, is home to 260,000 citizens, two-fifths of the state's population. Anchorage doesn't have the most scenic city design, but it reigns as the hub of travel and commerce for a state that has moved swiftly and decidedly into the 21st century, breaking barriers and stereotypes along the way. Long winters are softened by a mild coastal climate that significantly harshens only 40 mi. inland, and long summer days stretch out over Cook Inlet and the Chugach Mountains that encircle the "Anchorage Bowl."

It's impossible to pigeon-hole such a diverse city, one with strong Alaskan native and Pacific island populations that shrug off the wild Alaskan image, only to be juxtaposed with coffee shops and high rises. Anchorage may only be a momentary jumping-off point for many travelers, but locals know they're within shouting distance of any outdoor adventure, yet still undeniably urbane.

▣ TRANSPORTATION

Anchorage is the transportation hub of southcentral Alaska, 127 mi. (2½hr.) north of Seward on the **Seward Hwy.** (Rte. 9), 358 mi. south of Fairbanks on the **George Parks Hwy.** (Rte. 3), and 304 mi. west of Valdez along the **Glenn Hwy.** (Rte. 1) and **Richardson Hwy.** (Rte. 4). The city sprawls across some 50,000 acres of the Anchorage Bowl, framed by military bases **Fort Richardson** and **Elmendorf Air Force Base** to the north, the **Chugach Mountains** to the east, and the **Knik** and **Turnagain Arms** of the **Cook Inlet** to the west and south. Downtown Anchorage is laid out in a grid: numbered avenues run east-west, with addresses designated east or west from **C St.** North-south streets are lettered alphabetically to the west and named alphabetically to the east of **A St.** The **University of Alaska Anchorage** lies on 36th Ave., off Northern Lights Blvd. Buses run infrequently and the city is too spread out to walk everywhere. Renting a bike is a wise move; trails connect most of the city.

CENTRAL ALASKA

Anchorage

0 ½ mile
0 ½ kilometer

Knik Arm

Ocean Dock Rd.

Loop Rd.

Ship Creek

E Whitney Rd.

N

Viking Dr.

Post Rd.

Alaska Railroad Depot

W 1st Ave. | E 1st Ave.

Resolution Park — W 2nd Ave.

Alaska Public Lands Information Center ℹ

Saturday Market

❸

E 3rd Ave.

Gambell St.

Hyder St.

TO 1⃣ (2mi.)

Anchorage Visitors Center

E 4th Ave.

W 4th Ave.

❷

❺ ℹ

Imaginarium 🏛

E 5th Ave.

Free Fare Zone

TO NATIVE HERITAGE MUSEUM, GLENN HWY., FAIRBANKS (360mi.)

Tony Knowles Coastal Trail

Elderberry Park

❼ 🚌 Performing Arts Center

E 6th Ave.

Memorial Cemetery

Fairbanks St.

E 7th Ave.

City Bus Station 🚌

❽

Anchorage Museum of History and Art 🏛

Barrow St.

E 8th Ave.

N St.

L St.

K St.

F St.

E St.

D St.

E 9th Ave.

W 8th Ave.

Cordova St.

Denali St.

Eagle St.

Juneau St.

Karluk St.

W 9th Ave.

W 10th Ave.

Delaney Park

I St.

H St.

G St.

E 10th Ave.

E 11th Ave.

Latouche St.

Medfra St.

W 11th Ave.

Barrow St.

M St.

W 12th Ave.

E 12th Ave.

Gambell St.

TO ALASKA REGIONAL HOSPITAL ✚ (1.5mi.)

❾

W 13th Ave.

F St.

C St.

B St.

A St.

E 13th Ave.

E 14th Ave.

Ingra St.

L St.

K St.

W 14th Ave.

W 15th Ave.

E 15th Ave.

W 16th Ave.

E 16th Ave.

Mulcahy Stadium ■

E 17th Ave.

Westchester Lagoon

W 17th Ave.

Chester Creek Greenbelt

Sullivan Arena ■

E 19th Ave.

Juneau Dr.

W 19th Ave.

W 20th Ave.

W 21st Ave.

Arctic Blvd.

W 22nd Ave.

Chester Creek

W 20th Ave.

W 22nd Ave.

C St.

A St.

E 21st Ave.

E 21st Ave.

Eagle St.

Bannister Dr.

Aspen Way

Spenard Rd.

Hillcrest Dr.

TO 🔟 (3mi.)

W Fireweed Ln.

W 24th Ave.

Barrow St.

Cordova St.

Fairbanks St.

Gambell St.

Ingra St.

Juneau Dr.

TO UNIVERSITY OF ALASKA & PROVIDENCE HOSPITAL ✚ (2mi.)

Redwood St.

La Touche St.

Minnesota Dr.

1⃣1⃣

W 25th Ave.

1⃣2⃣

W 26th Ave.

W 27th Ave.

Elde St.

Bluebird Rd.

Northern Lights Blvd. E

TO EARTHQUAKE PARK (1.5mi.), WORZENOF POINT (3.5mi.)

Sears Mall ■

Benson Blvd.

W 30th Ave.

W 31st Ave.

Benson Blvd.

E 32nd Ave.

Denali St.

1⃣3⃣

W 32nd Ave.

Arctic Blvd.

Bering St.

Dawson St.

Cheechako St.

Eureka St.

31st Ave.

32nd Ave.

E 33rd Ave.

E 34th Ave.

1⃣4⃣

Cape St.

W 34th Ave.

C St.

W 36th Ave.

E 36th Ave.

Chugach Way

TO 1⃣5⃣ (1mi.)

Indiana St.

N. Star St.

Wilson St.

Cope St.

W 40th Ave.

W 41st Ave.

W 42nd Ave.

Eureka St.

Loussac Public Library ■

University Center ■

E 40th Ave.

42nd Ave.

Seward Hwy.

Old Seward Hwy.

1

Spenard Rd.

Credit Union Dr.

Tudor Rd.

A St.

W 45th Ave.

TO LAKE HOOD & LAKE SPENARD (2mi.), TED STEVENS INTERNATIONAL AIRPORT ✈ (3mi.)

TO ANCHORAGE ZOO (6mi.), FLAT TOP MOUNTAIN (11mi.)

Anchorage

🔺 ACCOMMODATIONS	🍸 NIGHTLIFE
Anchorage Guesthouse, 10	Bears Tooth, 12
International	Bernie's Bungalow Lounge, 8
Backpacker's Hostel, 1	Chilkoot Charlie's, 11
Spenard Hostel, 15	Pioneer Bar, 2
🍴 FOOD	🎭 THEATERS
Great Harvest Bread Co., 13	Alaska Experience Theater, 7
Moose's Tooth, 14	Cyrano's Off Center
New Sagaya's City Market, 9	Playhouse, 6
Snow City Cafe, 4	4th Avenue Theatre, 5
Sweet Basil Cafe, 3	

Flights: Ted Stevens Anchorage International Airport (☎266-2525). Serviced by 8 international and 15 domestic carriers. Small airlines like **ERA Aviation** (☎800-866-8394 or 248-4422 in town) have cheap deals. Nearly every airport in Alaska can be reached from Anchorage, directly or via Fairbanks.

Trains: Alaska Railroad, 411 W 1st Ave., downtown (☎265-2494; outside AK 800-544-0552; www.alaskarailroad.com). 1 per day to **Fairbanks** (12hr., $175) via **Talkeetna** (3hr., $75) and **Denali** (8hr., $125); also 1 per day to **Seward** (4hr., $90). No service to Seward in winter. Bikes up to $20. Tickets can be bought on board, but it's wise to book ahead. Station open daily 6am-5pm.

Buses: Grayline Alaska (☎800-544-2206). Daily to **Valdez** (10hr., $71). To **Skagway** (2 per week; $219; overnight in **Beaver Creek**). **Homer Stage Lines** (☎563-0800). To **Homer** via Soldotna and Cooper Landing (M-Sa; $48 one-way, $85 round-trip; service less frequent Sept.-May). **Parks Highway Express** (☎479-3065 or 888-600-6001), runs daily to **Denali** ($54) and **Fairbanks** ($74) May-Sept. Call for winter service. For buses along the **George Parks Hwy.,** see p. 542.

Ferries: Alaska Marine Highway, 605 W 4th Ave. (☎800-642-0066; www.akhms.com), in the Old Federal Building. No terminal, but ferry tickets sold and reservations granted. Open in summer daily 7:30am-4:30pm; winter M-F 7:30am-4:30pm.

Public Transportation: People Mover Bus (☎343-6543), in Transit Center on 6th Ave. between G and H St. **Free fare zone** bordered by 5th Ave., Eagle St., 7th Ave., and L St. Runs hourly M-F 6am-10pm; less often Sa-Su. $1, ages 5-18 $0.50, over 60 $0.25. Transit Center sells tokens ($0.90), day passes ($2.50), schedules ($1), and maps ($0.50). Open M-F 8am-5pm.

Taxis: Yellow Cab (☎272-2422). **Checker Cab** (☎276-1234). **Alaska Cab** (☎563-5353). About $15 from the airport to downtown, $8 to Spenard Hostel.

Car Rentals: Affordable Car Rental, 4707 Spenard Rd. (☎243-3370), opposite the Regal Alaskan Hotel. Must be 22+ with major credit card. Free drop-off and pick-up. $39 per day, $330 per week; unlimited mileage.

Ride Board: At the Anchorage Youth Hostel (see **Accommodations,** p. 474).

🔼 PRACTICAL INFORMATION

TOURIST AND LOCAL SERVICES

Tourist Information: (☎274-3531; events 276-3200) on W 4th Ave. at F St. The **bike trails guide** ($4) is helpful. Open June-Aug. daily 7:30am-7pm; May and Sept. 8am-6pm; Oct.-Apr. 9am-4pm. Also at the airport (☎266-2437 or 266-2657).

Outdoor Information: Alaska Public Lands Information Center, 605 W 4th Ave. (☎271-2737; www.nps.gov/aplic/center), in the Old Courthouse Bldg. between F and G St. Here the **Park Service, Forest Service, Division of State Parks,** the **Fish and Wildlife Service,** and the **Alaska Marine Highway** reservation desks reside under one glorious roof. Popular topo maps ($4-7), regional Alaskan exhibits, movies, and live presentations on Alaska's outdoor attractions. Open daily 9am-5:30pm.

Maps: All you could ever want at the **United Stated Geological Survey Office (USGS),** 4230 University Dr. (☎ 786-7011), in Alaska Pacific University's Grace Hall. Take bus #11, 36, or 45; get off by Providence Hospital. Open M-F 8:30am-4:30pm.

Equipment Rental:

Downtown Bicycle Rental, 333 W 4th St. (☎ 279-5293), between C and D St., 5 blocks from the Coastal Trail (see p. 476). Bikes $15 for 3hr., $19 for 5hr., $29 per day. Credit card required. Open daily 8am-7pm.

Recreational Equipment, Inc. (REI), 1200 Northern Lights Blvd. (☎ 272-4565), near Spenard. Has a wealth of backcountry maps ($4-10) and a myriad of outdoor gear rentals (canoes $40 1st day, $22 after; kayaks $50, $30). Open M-Sa 10am-9pm, Su 10am-7pm.

Alaska Mountaineering and Hiking (AMH), 2633 Spenard St. (☎ 272-1811), between Northern Lights and Fireweed. Find hiking or climbing partners, tons of rentals, and great outdoor advice. Open M-F 9am-7pm, Sa 9am-6pm, Su noon-5pm.

Bookstore: Metro Music and Book Store, 530 E Benson Blvd. (☎ 279-8622), across from **Carrs** and **Sears.** A good place to be on a rainy afternoon. Bus #3•or #4, get off at Benson and C St., walk east on Benson; it's in the strip mall. Open 9am-9pm.

Services for the Disabled: Challenge Alaska (☎ 344-7399).

Laundromat: K-Speed Wash, 600 E 6th St. (☎ 279-0731), at Fairbanks. Wash $1.75, dry $0.25 per 5min. Open M-Sa 7am-8pm.

Public Showers: Fairview Community Recreational Center, 1121 E 10th St. (☎ 343-4130), between Karluk and Latouche. Untimed showers $3 (includes sauna and weight room access). Open M-F 9am-10pm, Sa 10am-10pm, Su 11am-4pm.

Weather: ☎ 936-2525. **Marine Weather:** ☎ 936-2727. **Road Conditions:** ☎ 273-6037.

EMERGENCY AND COMMUNICATION

Emergency: ☎ 911.

Police: 4501 S Bragaw St. (☎ 786-8500). 24hr.

Gay and Lesbian Helpline: (☎ 258-4777). Open daily 6-11pm.

Rape Crisis Line: (☎ 276-7273 or 800-478-8999). 24hr. Office at 1057 W Fireweed #230, at Spenard St. Bus #6, 7, or 60. Open M-F 8am-5pm.

Hospital: Columbia Alaska Regional Hospital, 2801 DeBarr Rd. (☎ 276-1131). 24hr. emergency (☎ 264-1222). **Providence Hospital,** 3200 Providence Dr. (☎ 562-2211). 24hr. emergency (☎ 261-3111).

Internet Access: Loussac Library (☎ 343-2975), at 36th Ave. and Denali St., is a great local library and architectural oddity. Free 1hr. **Internet access.** Open M-Th 10am-8pm, F-Sa 10am-6pm; winter also Su noon-6pm.

Post Office: (☎ 800-275-8777), at W 4th Ave. and C St. on lower level of the banana-yellow mall. Open M-F 10am-5:30pm. **Stamp machine** 24hr. **Postal Code:** 99510.

▐ ACCOMMODATIONS AND CAMPING

Anchorage has large hostels, some with more drawbacks than others. Hotels, B&Bs, and even "cheap" motels are expensive, especially downtown. Try **Alaska Private Lodgings** (☎ 888-235-2148; open M-Sa 9am-6pm) or the **Anchorage reservation service** (☎ 272-5909) for out-of-town B&Bs (from $80). Tent options are available at some of the hostels and outside of town; make sure you're not on private or military land. Pick up *Camping in the Anchorage Bowl* (free) at the visitors center for crowded in-town options, or head to nearby **Chugach State Park** (☎ 354-5014).

■ **Anchorage Guesthouse,** 2001 Hillcrest Dr. (☎ 274-0408). Bus #3, 4, 6, 36, or 60 from downtown; get off at West High School and go west on Hillcrest. Guests take pride in the elegant kitchen and common area, and gladly earn their keep with a chore. Bikes $2.50 per hr., $20 per day. Breakfast included. Wash, dry $1.50 each. $5 key deposit. No alcohol. 1-week max. stay. Bunks $25; private rooms $75. ❷

■ **Spenard Hostel,** 2845 W 42nd Pl. (☎248-5036). Bus #7 from downtown to 1st stop past Gwennie's. Originally a commune, this friendly house still retains its original character without sacrificing cleanliness. Guests love the 3 lounges, kitchens, big yard, and Internet access. 6-day max. stay. Reception 9am-1pm and 7-11pm. Chore requested; free stay for 3hr. work. Bunks $16; private rooms $64. ❶

International Backpackers Hostel, 3601 Peterkin Ave. (☎274-3870). Parks Highway Express and Denali Shuttle buses stop here every day. Bus #45 or #76 from downtown to Mountain View Carwash on Commercial Ave. Towels $1, laundry $3. Bike rental $10 per day (15min. bike ride from downtown). $10 key deposit. Shuttle travels to and from airport (15min.; $14 for 1, $17 for 2). Dorms $15; sites $10, $2 per extra person. ❶

◖ FOOD

Anchorage presents the most affordable and varied culinary fare in the state. **Great Harvest Bread Company,** 570 E Benson Blvd. in Benson Mall, stocks excellent fresh bread; loaves run $4-7, but hefty slices with butter and honey are free. (☎274-3331. Open M-Sa 7am-6pm.) **Carr's** sells groceries 24hr. in the Aurora Village Shopping Center, 1650 W Northern Lights Blvd., and at 1340 Gambell St.

■ **Moose's Tooth,** 3300 Old Seward (☎258-2537). Bus #2 or 36 to the corner of Old Seward and 36th. Named for one of Denali's mountain neighbors, this relaxed joint serves an array of pizzas (personal $9) and brews ($3.75) as hearty as the climbers who come here. Hot bands usher in new brews the 1st Th of every month. Be prepared to wait; it's popular. Open M-Th 11am-midnight, F-Sa noon-1am, Su noon-midnight. ❸

■ **Sweet Basil Cafe,** 335 E St. (☎274-0070). The owner-chefs who must wake up bright and early to make the fresh pastries, breads, and pastas. Killer vegetable and fruit juices ($3.50), smoothies, and lunches ($6). Open M-F 8am-3pm, Sa 9am-3pm. ❶

Snow City Cafe, 1034 W 4th St. (☎272-2489), at L St. Art-bedecked and acoustically blessed by live music F-Sa. One of the best breakfasts in town, served until 4pm. Pizza from $8, sandwiches from $5. Open M-Tu 7am-4pm, W-Su 7am-4pm and 5-9pm. ❷

New Sagaya's City Market 900 W. 13th St. (☎274-6173). Offers gourmet variety—pizza, wraps, sandwiches, and Asian cuisine as well as espresso, freshly baked treats, and groceries. Open M-F 6am-9pm, Sa 7am-9pm, Su 8am-7pm. ❷

◉ SIGHTS

■ **ANCHORAGE MUSEUM OF HISTORY AND ART.** Probably the finest museum in the state. Exhibits of Native Alaskan artifacts and art mingle with national and international works. *(121 W 7th Ave. at A St. ☎343-4326 or 343-6173; www.anchoragemuseum.org. Open May-Sept. F-W 9am-6pm, Th 9am-9pm. Tours daily at 10, 11am, 1, and 2pm. 1hr. films daily at 11am and 3pm. $6.50, seniors and military $6, under 18 free.)*

■ **THE ALASKA NATIVE HERITAGE CENTER.** Great informational displays of the five Alaskan native traditions complement daily cultural shows and dances. Learn how each tradition has sustained itself, from the past to contemporary times. *(8800 Heritage Ctr. Dr. ☎330-8000 or 800-315-6608; www.alaskanative.net. From the Glenn Hwy., 1st right off the North Muldoon exit. Open daily 9am-6pm. Dance and music performances throughout the day. Adults $20, ages 7-16 $15, 6 and under free.)*

FROM THE ROAD

FISHING THE KENAI RIVER FOR RED SALMON

What's the most exciting fish to catch on a fly rod? In my opinion, it's the sockeye (red) salmon, named for its bright red meat. I've had 10+ lb. reds hooked to the end of the rod, jumping and splashing, making a run and swimming downstream with the line zinging out of the reel. I reel in fast as the fish turns around so that the hook doesn't slip out of its mouth, only to feel tension on the line once more. The salmon rockets out of the water, showing its brilliant silver skin, and then dives back down to start the whole process over again. The rod tip jiggles with the fish's every movement. Trying to control the rod in one hand and hold extra line in the other, with a silver bullet on the other end of the action, makes the whole experience into a sort of river rodeo.

I've seen the reds in the Kenai River so thick that they swim no more than a few feet in front of you, and I've even had them swim into my hip boots as I cast. But having fished this river for 15 years, I'm noticing frequent changes. The once serene water is often crowded with guides zooming up and down stream, and getting the right fishing spot is now a competitive venture. I prefer to avoid all the fuss and compete with just the fish—they don't cause stream erosion like reckless guides, and poaching freshly caught reds with wild chives is the perfect way to end a successful day.

—*Sarah Murphy*

ALASKA ZOO. If you don't see Alaska's animals in the wild, you can spot them at the Alaska Zoo. Binky the Polar Bear mauled a tourist here in 1994 and remains somewhat of a local hero years after his death. *(4731 O'Malley Rd. Turn toward mountains off Seward Hwy., or take Minnesota which becomes O'Malley. ☎346-2133 or 346-3242. Open daily 9am-6pm. Summers bring Tu night education programs, 6pm-9pm. $8, seniors $7, ages 12-17 $5, 3-11 $4.)*

⚑ OUTDOOR ACTIVITIES

Watching over Anchorage from Cook Inlet is **Mt. Susitna,** known to locals as the "Sleeping Lady." Legend has it that this marks the resting spot of an Athabascan maid who dozed while awaiting her lover's return from war. When peace reigns in the world, she will awake. From mountain peaks to coastal waterways, you are never more than a quick ride from great outdoor activities. Just 30min. south along the **Sterling Hwy.** (Rte. 9), skiing awaits at **Girdwood** (see p. 481); the drive past the tidal bores of **Turnagain Inlet** shouldn't be missed (see p. 480); 2hr. south on the Seward Hwy. and across the Sterling Hwy., the Kenai River supports unstoppable fishing near **Cooper Landing** (see p. 526). Hikes near Exit Glacier, flightseeing tours, and a tour of the **Kenai Fjords National Park** are still more reasons to venture south (see p. 506). North of town, Talkeetna offers access to Denali, and routes to Glennallen promise views of the **Wrangell Mountains** (see p. 486).

IN TOWN

Walk, skate, or bike to the **Tony Knowles Coastal Trail,** a 13 mi. wheelchair-accessible track that skirts Cook Inlet on one side and the backyards of Anchorage's upper crust on the other. This is one of the best urban bike paths in the country, groomed in winter for **cross-country skiing.** Pick up the trail on 2nd Ave. or Elderberry Park on the west edge of downtown. The coastal trail's southern terminus is at **Kincaid Park** (see **Biking,** below), a haven for cross-country runners and mountain bikers in the summer. Nordic skiers take over after snowfall.

WATER ACTIVITIES

Nancy Lake State Recreation Area, just west of the Parks Hwy. (Rte. 3) at Mile 67.3 and just south of **Willow,** is well known for its **canoeing.** The **Lynx Lake Loop** takes one to two days, weaving through 8 mi. of lakes and portages with designated campsites along the way. The loop begins at Mile 4.5 of the Nancy Lake Pkwy., at the Tanaina Lake Canoe Trailhead. For **canoe rental** or **shuttle service** in the Nancy Lake area,

LET'S MUSH The celebrated Iditarod dog sled race begins in Anchorage on the first weekend in March. Dogs and their drivers ("mushers") traverse a trail over two mountain ranges, along the mighty Yukon River, and over the frozen Norton Sound to Nome. State pride holds that the route is 1049 mi., in honor of Alaska's status as the 49th state, but the real distance is closer to 1150 mi.

The Iditarod ("a far-off place") Trail began as a dog sled supply route from Seward on the southern coast to interior mining towns. The race commemorates the 1925 rescue of Nome, when drivers delivered 300,000 units of life-saving diphtheria serum from Nenana. The first race, in 1967, was a 27 mi. jaunt; today, up to 70 contestants speed each year from Anchorage to Nome, competing for a $450,000 purse.

The race has come under fire from animal rights activists because of the hardships borne by the dogs, some of whom have died en route to Nome. Nevertheless, the race goes on, and Anchorage turns out in force for the ceremonial start. For more info, contact the Iditarod Trail Committee (☎376-5155; www.iditarod.com), Dept. M, P.O. Box 870800, Wasilla, AK 99687, or visit the Iditarod Headquarters (with museum, video presentations, gift shop, and free admission) at Mile 2.2 Knik Rd. in Wasilla.

call **Tippecanoe.** (☎495-6688. Open M-F 10am-7pm, Sa-Su 8am-8pm. Canoes $33 per day, $53 for 2 days, $78 for 7 days; shuttle free for backpackers.) **Lifetime Adventures,** at the Eklutna Campground, rents **bikes** and **kayaks.** (☎746-4644. Bikes $8 for 2hr.; $15 for 4hr.; $25 per day. Double kayaks from $25 per half-day, $45 per day.) **NOVA Riverrunners** runs whitewater rafting down the **Matanuska Valley.** (☎800-746-5753. 4hr. Class III and IV trips $75.)

SKIING AND SNOWBOARDING

Skiing and **snowboarding trails** weave around Anchorage. **Alyeska Ski Resort** is a short drive away along the Seward Hwy. (Rte. 9; see **Girdwood,** p. 481), offering world-class terrain. **Hatcher Pass** to the north and **Turnagain Pass** to the south both contain some of the best backcountry skiing in the region (for Turnagain Pass, see **Seward Hwy.,** p. 480.) North of Wasilla and Palmer, the best alpine skiing in the Hatcher Pass area is off of **Archangel Rd.** Check at **AMH** and **REI** (see **Anchorage, Equipment Rental,** p. 474) for conditions. At the end of Raspberry Rd. and the Tony Knowles Coastal Trail lies **Kincaid Park,** the largest cross-country skiing area in the US and a popular stop for hundreds of skiers from the Anchorage bowl. Another popular destination for Nordic skiers is the set of hillside trails that include the Lighted Loop. To reach them, take Seward Hwy. east to the Dimond exit (towards mountains), which turns into Abbott Rd., and follow it for about 3 mi.

HIKING

In 1969, a grassroots organization headed by a 19-year-old asked for and received almost every square inch it proposed for the 495,000-acre **Chugach State Park.** The park surrounds the city on three sides and has enough land and trails to keep an avid hiker busy for years. Check out the **Park Headquarters** (☎345-5014) at Mile 115 of the Seward Hwy. to learn about fees and usage information. Call to reserve any of the park's public use cabins. (☎800-280-2267. $25 per night plus $8.25 reservation fee.) Chugach has 25 established **dayhiking** trails, which leave from different points in Anchorage and along the Glenn Hwy.

Flattop Mountain (3½ mi. one-way, 4hr.). Take O'Malley, the continuation of Minnesota, toward the mountains off the Seward, turn right on Hillside, turn left on Upper Huffman for 4 mi. to the Glen Alps Trailhead mile, and then turn right onto Toilsome and drive 2 mi. to the flight of steps on the right side of the parking lot. Provides an excellent view of the inlet, the mountains of the Aleutian Chain, and during (rare) clear episodes, Denali. Flattop is the most frequently climbed mountain in Alaska, with a steep and occasionally slippery 3½ mi. hike to its crowded summit. Parking $5; bus #92 drops you off at the foot of a 2000 ft. battle up to the trail. 4500 ft. elevation gain. Strenuous.

O'Malley Peak (8 mi. round-trip, 5-8hr.). From the Flattop parking lot, follow signs to the Powerline Trail and turn east. After ¼ mi., turn left at the Middle Fork Loop Trail. After following the trail down to the footbridge at Campbell Creek, take the unmarked right fork to go to O'Malley Peak. A less crowded trail that towers over 5000 ft. above town, offers views that could rival any in the park. Moderately difficult.

Bird Ridge (5 mi. round-trip to Point 3505, 3-5hr.). Drive south on the Seward Hwy. to the trailhead at Mile 102, just south of Indian. A sign marks the trailhead parking lot on the highway. A commanding position offers jaw-dropping views across Turnagain Arm in this fairly difficult (3400 ft. elevation gain) but short climb.

BIKING

A multitude of trails for bikers of all skill levels surround Anchorage, both in the city and along the more well-maintained trails of **Chugach State Park.** The trails of **Kincaid Park** are an excellent collection of rolling hills and hard cornering that all riders find enjoyable. Follow the Raspberry Rd. entrance into the **chalet** lot and check out the trail maps that rate trails by difficulty and length. The **Bird Creek** trails offer bikers a fun romp through a dense forested valley along old logging roads. Head south of Anchorage at Mile 100.4 of the Seward Hwy., turn left at the Bird House Bar, and travel down a gravel road for 1 mi. to the trailhead.

■ ENTERTAINMENT

The visitors center (☎ 276-3200) has a calendar of events. ◼**Cyrano's Off Center Playhouse,** at 413 D St. between 4th and 5th, contains a cafe, a bookshop, the stage of the **Eccentric Theatre Company,** and a cinema that screens foreign and art films. Storytellers spin Alaskan tales here on summer afternoons, amid poetry readings and film discussion groups. Check the cafe for the events schedule. (☎ 274-2599. Theater at 7pm, summer F-Tu, winter Th-Su. Tickets $15; students $10.) The **Alaska Experience Theater,** 705 W 6th Ave., shows "Alaska the Greatland," a 40min. presentation of scenery, wildlife, and Alaskan culture projected on a 180° omniscreen (think IMAX). The theater's **earthquake exhibit** rumbles for a full 15 fun-filled minutes. (☎ 276-3730 or 272-9076. Movie on the hour 9am-9pm. $7, ages 5-12 $4. Earthquake exhibit every 20min. 8:50am-9:30pm. $5, ages 5-12 $4. Both $10, ages 4-12 $7.) The **4th Avenue Theatre,** 630 4th Ave., 1 block west of the Log Cabin Visitors Center, features a restored 1940s decor. This, the first million-dollar building in Anchorage, hosts trolley tours and concerts. The nightly musical (8pm) is free with a trolley tour. (☎ 257-5609. Tours of town start at $10.)

The **Anchorage Bucs** (☎ 561-2827) and the **Anchorage Glacier Pilots** (☎ 274-3627) play baseball against teams like the Hawaii Island Movers and the Mat-Su Miners in **Muicahy Stadium,** at 16th and Cordova. Featuring some of the best college talent in the nation, Mulcahy boasts a history of sports heroes, including Mark McGwire, John Olerud, and Tom Seaver, all of whom played here before making it big.

◼ NIGHTLIFE

Microbrews gush from Anchorage's taps like oil through the Pipeline, fueling a nightlife that can be either laid-back or rowdy, depending on your preference. All bars are 21+ unless otherwise noted.

CENTRAL ALASKA

Bears Tooth Theater and Pub, 1230 W 27th St. (☎276-4200), at Spenard St. Bus #7, get off at Chilkoot Charlie's and walk to 27th. Recently renovated, this brew-pub theater offers an alternative to the standard bar scene. Catch recent and classic flicks while enjoying your favorite pint ($3.75). Pizza $2.50 per slice. A balcony for those under 21. $3 cover for movie. Open daily 11am until the movies end.

Pioneer Bar, 739 W 4th. Ave. (☎276-7996), near the corner of 4th and A St., downtown. 2 pool tables, dart boards, and shuffleboard start to go unnoticed as the weekend nights wear on and the drinks keep coming. Bottles $3. Open daily 10am-2am.

Bernie's Bungalow Lounge, 626 D St. (☎276-8808), at 7th St. Relax in a swingback chair as you sip your lemon-drop martini ($5) or puff on a cigar ($3-10). Frequented by the young and retro. Outdoor patio and lawn (summer only, of course). Live music or DJ Th-Sa. Open in the summer daily noon-2am, winter 3pm-2am.

Chilkoot Charlie's, 2435 Spenard St. (☎272-1010), at Fireweed. Bus #7. "Koots" is the place to begin or end a wild night out; don't come for a classy evening. $1 drink specials until 10pm. Cover $3-6. Open Su-Th 10:30am-2:45am, F-Sa 11am-2:45am.

ALONG RTE. 1: GLENN HWY.   ☎907

The **Glenn Highway** is the only major thoroughfare that goes north from Anchorage. At the Palmer/Wasilla cutoff (around mile 37), it meets the George Parks Highway. (Rte. 3), turns northwest to Denali, and eventually reaches Fairbanks. The Glenn Highway continues another 152 mi. east to Glenallen (see p. 486), and from there runs into Tok and the Richardson Highway (Rte. 4). **Tip:** When asking directions, highways should be referred to by name, not by number. While the lower 48 may get their kicks on Route 66, Alaskans cruise the Glenn.

ANCHORAGE TO PALMER

Leaving Anchorage from the east on 6th Ave., the highway traces the western edge of **Chugach State Park. Eklutna (ee-KLOOT-na) Historical Park** is at Mile 26 about half a mile off the Eklutna Exit, and houses the remains of a Dena'ina (or Tanaina) village that dates back to 1650. The park is an example of the confluence of Russian Orthodox and Athabascan traditions in Alaska.

From Eklutna, the Glenn Hwy. heads into the **Matanuska-Susitna Valley (Mat-Su Valley).** The Roosevelt administration relocated 200 families here during the Great Depression, hoping to promote agricultural growth in the state by having Alaskans work the land and feed themselves. The program didn't produce enough food for the state but the long summer daylight produced extremely large vegetables (100+ lb. cabbages were not unusual). The valley is still famous for its produce, legal and illegal: those in the know claim that **Matanuska Valley Thunderfuck** is some of the world's best marijuana. *Let's Go* does not recommend getting thunderfucked.

PALMER

After passing the George Parks Highway (Rte. 3, see p. 542), the Glenn Highway rolls eastward into the agricultural hamlet of Palmer. This town hosts the **Alaska State Fair** (☎745-4827) every August, a festival that has awarded ribbons to vegetables larger than many adults. Past winners have included a 303 lb. squash and a 347 lb. pumpkin. Palmer's **Visitors Center,** 723 S Valley Way, provides info on the valley's plethora of outdoor opportunities. **Hatcher Pass** (Mile 49) is an area that offers excellent hiking, mountain biking, camping, rock climbing, and Nordic and alpine skiing (inquire at Palmer Visitors Center). In autumn, after the fair, the center displays specimens of the region's defensive lineman-sized legumes. (☎745-2880. Open May to mid-Sept. daily 9am-6pm.) For fishing, canoeing, and overnight camping, check out the **Kepler Family Park ❶,** Glen Hwy., Mile 37.

(☎ 745-0429. $10 tent sites; $6 per hr. canoe.) For info on **B&Bs** in the area (starting at $50-60), contact the visitors center. After hours, they leave a list of available rooms out front next to the courtesy phone. For cheaper beds, most backpackers find their way to the hostel in nearby Wasilla. If you can't make it that far, try the **Alaska Choice Inn Motel** ❸, at Mile 40 off the Glenn Hwy and across from the fairground. (☎ 745-1505. Singles $65; doubles $75.) ▨**Vagabond Blues** ❷, 642 S Alaska St., four blocks from the visitors center, is Palmer's artsy alternative to agriculture. This bar and restaurant has an entirely homemade vegetarian menu, live music, and an open wall for local upstart artists. (☎ 745-2233. Live music F-Sa 8-10pm, tickets free-$15, depending on the band. Open M-Th 7am-9pm, F and Sa 8am-11pm, Su 9am-5pm.)

PALMER TO GLENNALLEN

The **Matanuska Glacier** is visible near Mile 100 as the highway narrows and begins to wind, and drivers divide their time between scanning the colored ridge lines for Dall sheep, marveling at the glacier, and watching the road. After turning off at Mile 102 and paying an entrance fee at the **Matanuska Glacier Park Resort,** you can walk on the ice of the "Mat"—the most accessible glacier in the US. (☎ 745-2534. $8; seniors $6, children 6-14 $4.) For those with a desire for adventure, **MICA Guides** (☎ 800-956-6422) offers an introductory 1½hr. glacier trek complete with equipment and a glaciology lesson ($30 per person, 4 person min.), as well as more involved trips for those wishing to pursue the snowy experience.

Mile 113 is home to the **Sheep Mountain Lodge** ❶, where road-weary travelers can rejuvenate themselves by relaxing in the hot tub or wood sauna, or by hiking one of the nearby trails. The restaurant serves three meals a day for $6-8. (☎ 745-5721 or 877-645-5121. Bunks $15.) Those seeking the comfort of a trail can hike along the **Belanger Creek-Nelchina River.** The trailhead at Mile 126.4 heads 1½ mi. to Eureka Creek, eight miles to Goober Lake, and 9 mi. to the Nelchina River. Simply look for the little hiker sign. The highway climbs to the **Eureka Summit** (3322 ft.), Mile 129, where the river unfolds in the valleys below. The **Little Nelchina State Recreation Site,** at Mile 137.5, has free creek-side campsites, toilets, and firepits, but no water. The **Kamping Resort of Alaska** (☎ 822-3346), at Mile 153, is an all-purpose rest stop. At Mile 160, the turn-off for **Lake Louise Recreation Area,** 19 mi. off the highway, provides access to services and fishing licenses. This area is known for trout, cross-country skiing, and plump berries. **Ryan Lake,** at Mile 149, is known for grayling and rainbow trout. Big grayling await in the **Tolsona Creek** at Mile 173.

ALONG RTE. 9: SEWARD HWY.

Considered one of America's most scenic roads, the Seward Hwy. out of Anchorage provides spectacular views of mountain and water as it twists and turns its way along the **Turnagain Arm** of **Cook Inlet,** an area known for dramatic tidal fluctuations second only to Canada's Bay of Fundy. Miles of the arm are uncovered at low tide, only to be inundated by 10 ft. **bores,** walls of water created as the 15 mph tide races in. The Seward Hwy. is narrow and has many blind turns; drivers stopping to view animals near the highway cause accidents. Use the turnouts and keep your headlights on—it's required by law.

> The area exposed at low tide turns into **extremely dangerous quicksand.** Regardless of its cement-like composition when the water is out, be warned that deaths have occurred due to the sand's suction capabilities when wet, trapping the unlucky adventurer in the Arm's tidal waters. **Do not walk on the sand!**

Potter Marsh, just miles outside of Anchorage (Seward Mile 117.4), is a tranquil bird sanctuary and a magnet for wildlife photographers. The info station, located in a train car next to **The Chugach State Park Headquarters,** at Mile 115.2, will help you navigate the innumerable trails along the Seward. (☎345-5014. Open M-F 8am-noon and 1-4:30pm.) Dall sheep sightings are virtually guaranteed, so keep your eyes peeled for white dots on the cliffs around Mile 110. **Beluga Point,** at Mile 110.4, is so named because of the white whales that frequent the area in search of smelt.

Immediately to the left off the Girdwood turn-off at Mile 90 is the **Chugach National Forest Glacier Ranger District Office,** which is an office, not a visitors center. Rangers can still provide info on hikes in the national forest, which stretches from just south of Anchorage to Prince William Sound. (☎783-3242. Open M-F 7:30am-5pm.) The turn-off for the next visitors center is another 10 mi. down the Seward Hwy. in **Portage** (see p. 482). There are well-marked trails at nearly every turn-off and a paved bike path that runs parallel to the highway.

Kayakers are in luck in this creek-rich region. **Bird Creek,** at Mile 101.2, is a narrow Class V run. (Hike up the trail to put in, and take out at the highway). **Ingram Creek,** at Mile 75.2, is another Class V chute with challenging waterfalls. **Class V Whitewater** (see **Girdwood,** p. 481) offers rafting and kayaking trips and information on every bit of moving water around. With snow depths that can exceed 12 ft. in the winter, **Turnagain Pass,** at Mile 68.5, is a backcountry skier and snowmachiner's mecca. There are bathrooms and an emergency phone at the turn-off at the pass. The Alyeska Resort (see **Girdwood,** p. 481) runs just off the highway.

GIRDWOOD ☎907

Tucked in at the base of Mt. Alyeska and encircled by the Chugach Mountains, Girdwood's charm comes from its sense of humor. With possibly the highest rate of preferred unemployment in the U.S., this bohemian ski town has successfully avoided the development of Anchorage only 35 mi. north and retained its comfortable character. You won't find souvenir shops in this town—only fine restaurants, hiking, skiing, mountain vistas, and wonderful, slightly toasted people.

🔁 **PRACTICAL INFORMATION.** Girdwood Ski and Cyclery, (☎783-2453) on the Alyeska Hwy., rents **bikes** ($25 per day), snow shoes ($15 per day), and telemark and cross-country skis ($25-30 per day); the staff provides a wealth of local knowledge for all-season sports. For supplies, visit **Crow Creek Mercantile.** (☎783-3900. Open M-F 7am-midnight, Sa-Su 8am-midnight.) Past the mercantile is a **health clinic** (☎783-1355). There is free **Internet access** at the **municipal library,** in the school at the end of Hightower Rd. (☎783-2565. Open Tu 1-6pm, W 1-8pm, Th 10am-3pm, F-Sa 10am-6pm.) Farther on lies the **post office.** (☎783-2922. Open M-F 9am-5pm, Sa 9am-noon.) **Postal Code:** 99587.

🏠 **ACCOMMODATIONS AND FOOD.** The **Girdwood-Alyeska Home Hostel ❶** is a rustic wooden cabin in a wide valley hemmed in by mountains. From the Seward Hwy., drive 2½ mi. down the Alyeska Hwy., turn right on Timberline Dr., and then right again on Alta. The hostel, on the left, has 11 beds. (☎783-2099. 4-night max stay. Reservations encouraged. $12.50.) Showers, swimming, and a hot tub are available for $5 at the **Alyeska Prince Hotel.** Below the resort, turn left at the end of the Alyeska Access Rd. and then up the hill on Olympic to visit the 🔲**Bake Shop ❶.** Folks statewide sing the praises of its $3 sourdough, $4.50 bottomless bowls of soup, and $3 mountain-sized sweet rolls. (☎783-2831. Open Su-F 7am-7pm, Sa 7am-8pm.) **Chair 5 Restaurant and Bar ❷,** right by the post office, serves the cheapest dinner in town, including small pizzas (from $7.50), burgers ($6.75), and steak or seafood entrees ($14). This local hangout boasts a perfect jukebox, $0.50 pool table, and many microbrews. (☎783-2500. Open daily 11am-10pm; bar open until 2am.) About a quarter-mile up Crow Creek Rd., you'll find the **Double Musky Inn ❺**, which has been called one of Alaska's best restaurants. A steep Cajun-style dinner ($18-30) shouldn't distract you from the Double Musky pie ($4) and the garden outside. (☎783-2822. Open Tu-Th 5-10pm, F-Su 4:30-10pm.)

⚠ OUTDOOR ACTIVITIES **Class V Whitewater** (☎783-2004 or 800-783-2004; www.alaskanrafting.com) leads moderate to truly intense rafting, kayaking, and fishing trips. Float trips from $50, rafting from $75. If you ever wondered where all the hippies went, they're at the **Girdwood Forest Fair**, (☎566-3039) a free, three-day outdoor fair every July 4th weekend. Wander through the woods and check out non-stop musical acts on two stages, crafts and artwork from local artists, tasty—if pricey—cuisine, and beautiful people of all ages as they gather in the woods. Also see **Outdoor Activities** in Portage, below.

PORTAGE ☎907

Flattened by the 1964 Good Friday earthquake, Portage has done little to rebuild itself and is now primarily an access road for the Chugach State forest and the town of Whittier. The well-paved **Portage Glacier Hwy.**, beginning at Seward Mile 78.9, runs for five of its miles through the magnificent **Portage Valley.** Four roadside glaciers carve the steep walls of the valley, extending into the nearby ocean. The **Begich and Boggs Visitor Center,** at Mile 5, provides ranger-led **iceworm safaris** to Byron Glacier in search of the tiny, mysterious, algae-eating beasts, and offers exhibits on glaciers and the Whittier tunnel. (☎783-2326. Safaris May-Sept. Tu and Sa at 2:45pm and 3:45pm. Open in summer daily 9am-6pm; winter Sa-Su 10am-4pm. Free.) **Portage Glacier** has receded almost half a mile since the building's construction, so you have to drive through the first tunnel en route to Whittier to see it. In winter, a mile hike over the frozen lake brings you to the glacier's base; check with the ranger station to make sure the ice is frozen.

⚲ CAMPING In the national forest, camping is free anywhere that isn't an official campground or otherwise marked. About four miles off the highway, two state-run campgrounds—**Black Bear ❶** (tents $10) and **Williwaw ❶** ($12)—have water, toilets, bear-proof food lockers, and views of the glacier. With 12 wooded sites, **Black Bear** is the more tent-friendly of the 2, compared with **Williwaw's** 50+ paved pull-ins. (☎877-444-6777; www.reserveusa.com.)

⛷ SKIING. Great cross-country skiing can be found at **Moose Meadows** between the airstrip and the ski resort, and at **Winter Creek** just north of Moose Meadows. **Alyeska Ski Resort** has 7 chairlifts and a 3934 ft. vertical drop's worth of world-class skiing. (☎754-7669. Open Nov.-Apr. as snow conditions permit. Half-day $31, full-day $44; ages 14-17 $22-26, ages 8-13 or 60-69 $19, under 8 and over 69 $7.) A tram goes up in the summer for lunch. ($19; without lunch $16. Children $7, seniors $15.) Intrepid hikers can ride the tram down for free, but no bikes are allowed.

🥾 HIKING. Several easy, enjoyable hikes depart the Portage Hwy. **Moose Flats** has fishing ponds and interpretive displays along a wooden boardwalk, and **Middle Glacier** and salmon-spawning areas are accessible from **The Williwaw Nature Trail** that begins at **Williwaw Campground.** For more trail info, contact Chugach National Forest Offices; either the Girdwood Office, right off the Alyeska Hwy., or the Anchorage office, 3301 C St., Anchorage 99503. (☎271-2500. Open M-F 8am-5pm.)

CENTRAL ALASKA

Crow Pass (8 mi. round-trip to the pass, 26 mi. to Eagle River Nature Center). Drive 2 mi. east on the Alyeska Hwy., turning left (north) on Crow Creek. Follow 6mi. to trailhead. The most spectacular short hike in Girdwood climbs from the end of Crow Creek Rd. to a spectacular view of **Raven Glacier.** The trail continues 21 mi. past **Crow Creek in Chugach State Park** to the **Eagle River Visitor Center.** Strenuous.

Winner Creek Gorge Trail (5mi. round-trip), at the terminus of the Alaska Hwy. Turn left onto Arlberg Rd., following signs to the Alaska Prince Hotel. Follow signs for trailhead from the hotel parking lot, to the right of the tram ticket office. This hike leads through lush spruce-hemlock forest at an easy pace, passing over the spectacular **Winner Creek Gorge** before ending at an historic mining cabin. Easy.

Moraine Nature Trail (½ mi. round-trip; 30min.). This wheelchair accessible loop has fine views of the glacier and the lush, green valley. Trail begins past the Portage Glacier Visitor Center near the restrooms. Moderate.

Byron Glacier Trail (2 mi. round-trip; 1hr.). Park in the Glacier Cruise lot and walk out the south end of the parking lot. The trail is spectacular, beginning in an alder forest and continuing past the rushing Byron Creek to a snowfield near the foot of the glacier. Beware of avalanches in winter and early spring; climbing on the glacier can be dangerous due to hidden crevasses. Moderate to strenuous, depending on conditions.

WHITTIER ☎ 907

Named for the poet John Greenleaf Whittier, this tiny seaport town was the military's main Alaskan port for troops and cargo during World War II. Until June 7, 2000, the only way to reach Whittier was by plane, railroad from Portage or Anchorage, or via boat through Prince William Sound. That year, the 2½ mi. railroad tunnel was made into a one-lane vehicle tunnel, the longest in North America. Despite the increased access to the town, Whittier's charm continues to lie in its solitude and off-the-beaten-path feel. The tunnel is only open to one direction of traffic at a time, so check out the schedule at the Portage **visitors center** or at www.dot.state.ak.us/whittier.tunnel to avoid long waits. Hourly service begins at 6am (one-way passenger vehicles to Whittier $12; from Whittier free).

There are no banks in town, but an **ATM** is located at the **Outpost Liquor Store,** in the triangle business park. **Laundry** can be done at the **Anchor Inn,** off Whittier St. (☎472-2354. Wash $1.50, dry $0.25 for 10min.) Get **tunnel conditions** by calling ☎822-5511. You can reach the local **police** at ☎472-2340 or the **state police** at ☎783-0927, in Girdwood. The **Whittier Health Clinic** can be reached at ☎472-2303 or 472-2303. The **Alaska Marine Highway** ferry dock (☎800-642-0066) is located straight off the tunnel road, just past the triangle business park. **Fishing** charters, **tours,** and guided **kayaking** trips are available out of Whittier for the adventurous. **Bread n' Butter Charters** offers halibut or salmon charters ($180-200 per person) and sight-seeing trips into the Sound. (☎472-2396; $145.) Sea kayaking trips in Prince William Sound vary in price from $70 to $250. Call **Alaska Sea Kayakers** (☎472-2534; www.alskaseakayakers.com), **Prince William Sound Kayak Center** (☎472-2452; www.pwskayakcenter.com), or **Lazy Otter Charters** (☎472-887 or 800-587-6887; www.lazyotter.com). Lazy Otter also offers escorted **scuba diving;** call or check the web site for detailed information. After a day on the water, hit **Varly's Swiftwater Seafood Cafe ❶** for a $4.50 bowl of hearty seafood chowder. (☎472-2550. Open Su-Th 11:30am-9pm, F-Sa 11:30am-10pm.)

HOPE

Settled at the turn of the century as a Gold Rush offshoot, the town of Hope sits at the end of the Hope Hwy., just past Turnagain Pass off the Seward Hwy. 18 mi. in, the Chugach Mountains push Hope into Turnagain Arm, making the town's lights visible to motorists between Anchorage and Girdwood after dark. Few amenities exist in this town of 200, which is primarily used for its access to the immensely popular **Resurrection Pass Trail,** and other hiking and biking trails. (Near Hope Hwy. At Mile 16 take a left onto Palmer Cr. Rd., and make a right ½ mi. later to reach the northern trailhead; 4 mi.) **Gull Rock** is a popular long dayhike or overnight with both coastal and forest scenery along its flat, 10 mi. round-trip trail. (Accessible from Porcupine Campground at the terminus of the Hope Hwy. A bike trail as well. See **Girdwood, Practical Info,** p. 481 for bike rentals. Camping $10.)

WRANGELL-ST. ELIAS NATIONAL PARK
☎907

AT A GLANCE

AREA: 13.2 million acres.	Blackburn, bungee jumping over the Kuskulana River, backcountry hiking.
CLIMATE: Continental, marine.	**GATEWAYS:** Glennallen (p. 486), McCarthy and Kennicott (p. 489).
FEATURES: Mt. Sanford, Mt. Drum, Mt. Blackburn, Mt. St. Elias; Kuskulana and Kennicula Rivers.	**CAMPING:** Along McCarthy Rd. (p. 489).
HIGHLIGHTS: Flightseeing over Mt.	**FEES:** None.

In a state where the enormous is commonplace, Wrangell-St. Elias remains unique. The largest national park in the US, it is so big that six Yellowstone National Parks could fit within its boundaries. The Wrangell, St. Elias, Chugach, and Alaska mountain ranges all converge within its 13.2 million acres. Nine of the 16 tallest peaks in the United States can be found here, led by Mt. St. Elias, which at 18,008 ft. kowtows only to Denali. The **Malaspina Glacier,** by itself, is larger than the state of Rhode Island. Also of interest is Mt. Wrangell, a huge, active shield volcano that last erupted in 1900 and today emits steam visible to motorists on the Glenn Hwy. Beyond towering peaks and extensive glaciers, Wrangell-St. Elias teems with wildlife. Bears, Dall sheep, caribou, moose, sea lions, and a host of birds all make the park their home. With only two rough roads that penetrate its interior and almost no established trails, Wrangell keeps most tourists at bay. Only a fraction of Denali's visitors even make it within Wrangell-St. Elias boundaries, much less into the mind-bogglingly beautiful backcountry. The land that surrounds the two roads into the park was prospected for copper and gold at the turn of the 20th century; mining ruins, reeling railroad trestle bridges, and homesteaders' cabins still remain. McCarthy Rd. and Nabesna Rd. hikers should inquire about tracts of private property to avoid trespassing, but those who venture farther into the backcountry may find themselves where literally no one has ever walked before.

◀◘ ▮▬ ORIENTATION AND TRANSPORTATION

Wrangell-St. Elias is in the southeast corner of Alaska's mainland, bordered by the **Copper River** to the west, the Yukon's **Kluane National Park** to the east (see p. 404), and **Yakutat Bay** to the southeast. Two challenging routes to the park's interior are the **Nabesna Rd.** (see p. 487), which extends 46 mi. from Slana into the park's northern portion, and **McCarthy Rd.** (see p. 488), which rattles 61 mi. from Chitina (CHIT-nuh) to McCarthy. If you don't have a set of wheels, or don't want to jeopardize the ones you have, take **Backcountry Connection,** which shuttles people up to McCarthy

Wrangell-St. Elias National Park & Preserve

for around $80 from Chitina (see p. 489). There are numerous airfields that flight companies service for backcountry drop-offs. Dayhikers generally set out from points along or at the termini of the Slana-Nabesna or Chitina-McCarthy roads.

🛈 PRACTICAL INFORMATION

Camping is allowed anywhere in the park except on private property (check with ranger stations). For overnight trips, rangers request a written itinerary. There are ranger stations in and around the park (all open May-Sept. daily; limited hours in winter) and the **park headquarters** is in **Copper Center,** south of Glennallen. (☎822-7261. Open mid-May to mid-Sept. daily 8am-6pm; mid-Sept. to mid-May M-F 8am-4:30pm.) Additional info booths are at the park-run campground near **McCarthy** (open 11am-5:30pm) and at **Kennicott** (open 9am-5:30pm) in the Jurick Building. Both sell topographic maps ($10, quadrants $4).

⚑ OUTDOOR ACTIVITIES

Mountaineers and climbers will revel in the park's many glaciers, icefields, and mountains. Most popular and vaunted among the peaks are **Sanford, Drum, Blackburn,** and **St. Elias.** The Copper and Chitina rivers offer the best **rafting** opportunities in the park.

WALK THE WALK. Backcountry hikers in Wrangell-St. Elias will meet untouched wilderness, but they must have extensive survival skills and experience in route-finding and stream-fording. Be aware of the park's large **brown and black bear** populations and take appropriate precautions. All backcountry trekkers should come prepared with wilderness first-aid knowledge; the closest **medical care** is to the west in Glennallen and to the east in Yakutat. Evacuations (even by air) are difficult.

Kayakers can navigate some of the inland rivers and streams, but the bays, inlets, and coasts in the Yakutat (see p. 467) and Icy Bay areas are perhaps the park's most beautiful and underused waterways. **Cross-country skiing** and **snowshoeing** are best in March, April, and May—after the winter's most severe cold weather, but before the snow has melted off the lowlands. **Mountain bikers** should rush to the networks of wagon roads around McCarthy and Kennicott.

GLENNALLEN ☎ 907

Glennallen serves mostly as a means of entering **Wrangell-St. Elias National Park** and accessing the fishing 20 mi. north or 14 mi. south of town. The local land is better for hunting mosquitoes than for hiking, and much of it is privately owned.

■ 🗹 ORIENTATION AND PRACTICAL INFORMATION. Glennallen stands 115 mi. (2½hr.) north of Valdez on the Richardson Hwy. (see p. 557) and 189 mi. (3½hr.) east of Anchorage on the Glenn Hwy., making it a stop for countless RVs. The two roads that lead into Wrangell-St. Elias are conveniently close. The **Nabesna Rd.** lies 75 mi. to the north (see p. 487), and the turn-off for the **Edgerton Hwy.** (leading to the **McCarthy Rd.;** see p. 488) is 32 mi. south on the Richardson.

The **Wrangell-St. Elias Park Headquarters** is 9 mi. south of Glennallen in Copper Center, off the Richardson Hwy. (☎822-5235; www.nps.gov/wrst. Open summer daily 8am-6pm; winter 8am-4:30pm.) Information on Wrangell-St. Elias and the surrounding area can be found at the **Glenallen Visitors Center.** Found at the intersection of the Glenn and Richardson Hwys. on the east side of town. (☎822-5558. Open daily May 15-Sept. 15 8am-7pm.) **Winter** visitor information is available at the Chamber of Commerce on the Richardson Hwy. in the Ahtna building. (☎822-5558. Open daily 10am-4pm.)

The **Wells Fargo Bank** is located off the Glenn Hwy. at Birch Rd. **24hr. ATMs** are located in the bank and at the **Hub Maxi Mart,** at the highway intersection. The **laundromat** is next to Park's Place. Wash $2, dry $0.25 for 10min. Open daily 8am-11pm. Get **road conditions** by calling ☎822-5511 or contact the **state police** at ☎822-3263. The **Crossroads Medical Clinic** is 1 mi. west of the crossroads on the Glenn. (☎822-3203. Open M 9am-5:30pm, T-F 10am-4:30pm, closed daily 11:30am-1pm.) The **library,** 1½ mi. west of the crossroads on the Glenn Hwy., on Ballpark Rd., has **free Internet access.** (☎822-5226. Open Tu-Th 1-6pm, F 1-8pm, Sa 11am-6pm.) The **post office** is on Glennallen Schools Rd., two blocks east of the Caribou Hotel, north of the Hwy. (☎822-3273. Open M-F 9am-5pm, Sa 9am-11:55am.) **Postal Code:** 99588.

🏕 🍴 ACCOMMODATIONS AND FOOD. Northern Nights Campground and RV Park ❶, a half-mile west of the crossroads on the Glenn Hwy., has 18 wooded sites for RVs and five tent sites. Water and pit toilets. (☎822-3199. Tents $10, RV sites $19.) **The Sports Page ❷** offers "Cabins on the Glenn," at Mile 187 of the Glenn Hwy., and lets tenters use their unfilled RV sites. Cabins sleep up to four. (☎822-5833. Tents $10, cabins $65. Showers $5, free with stay.) **Carol's B&B ❸,** on the right side of Birch St. off the Glenn Hwy. about 1½ mi. west from the visitors center, serves a

> **PRIVATE PROPERTY.** Local Athabascan tribes own a large amount of land returned to them through the Alaska Native Claim Settlement Act of 1971. Since then, trespassing has been a significant problem. Much land that lines the Richardson Hwy. to the north and south of Glennallen, including some river access on the Gulkana, Klutina, and Copper Rivers, is Ahtna land, and some of it is not marked. Before camping or fishing, check in with the **Ahtna Inc. Headquarters,** across from the visitors center, which sells maps and has info on camping and river access. (☎ 822-3476; www.ahtna-inc.com. Open M-F 8am-5pm.)

"true Alaskan breakfast" with sourdough pancakes and moose sausage. (☎822-3594 or 822-3600. Singles $60, winter $40-50; doubles from $80.) For info on other affordable B&Bs, contact the **Chamber of Commerce** (☎822-5558).

The only supermarket around for park-bound trippers is **Park's Place Groceries ❶,** just west of the crossroads on the Glenn Hwy. Try their loaded deli sandwiches for $5. (☎822-3334. Open M-Sa 7am-11pm, Su 9am-11pm.) There are several restaurants in town, but the **Rendezvous Cafe ❷,** located ½ mi. north of the crossroads on the Richardson Hwy., really does the trick. Munch on a huge $9 sandwich or try the $6 all-you-can-eat salad bar. (☎822-5353. Open daily 6am-10pm.)

INTO THE PARK: SLANA AND THE NABESNA RD.

TRANSPORTATION. The Nabesna Rd. into Wrangell-St. Elias National Park is shorter (1½hr.) and more scenic than the McCarthy Rd., and offers access to nearly a dozen established trails of varying lengths and difficulties. The turn-off for the Nabesna Rd. is located at **Slana** (rhymes with "bandana"), 65 mi. southwest of **Tok** (see p. 558) on the Tok Cutoff. Slana is the place to make last-minute preparations for a journey into the park, since **Nabesna,** at the end of the 46 mi. road, is little more than a mining ghost town populated by one family. The gravel Nabesna Rd. is passable for most cars up to mile 29; past that, there are several stream crossings. Four-wheel drive cars are recommended. In the summer, ask at the ranger station about the water levels of the streams that cross the road, and stop to assess the streams before attempting to cross. It's best to charge through low water at between 10 and 20 mph to avoid getting mired in wet gravel, but use your best judgment; roadside assistance is not readily accessible.

🛂 PRACTICAL INFORMATION. The **Slana Ranger Station,** right off the Tok Cutoff, sells topo maps ($10, quadrants $4) and provides info on weather, road conditions, and bear behavior. (☎822-5238. Open daily 8am-5pm; winter hours by appointment.) For **emergencies,** call ☎911 or a ranger station. Slana's **post office** is 1 mi. down Nabesna Rd. (Open M, W, and F 10am-1pm.) **Postal Code:** 99586.

🛏🍴 ACCOMMODATIONS AND FOOD. Stop in to see Jay and Debbie at **Midway Services ❶,** about 1 mi. northeast of the Nabesna Cutoff (on the Tok Cutoff) where the "tent camping, coffee and bullshit are free." They also have groceries, showers, coin laundry, **Internet access,** and **fishing permits,** and make minor car repairs. (☎822-5877. Internet $3 per 30min. Open M-Sa 10am-6pm. RV sites $10. Showers $3.) If you're not sleeping for free in the mountains and need to snooze in Slana, **Hart D Ranch ❸,** down the Nabesna Rd. next to the post office, has camping and showers. (☎822-3973. Tents and RV sites $20; spacious rooms $137. Showers $5 or free with stay.) Nestled in the forest, family-run **Huck Hobbit's Homestead Retreat and Campground ❷** rents cabin bunks and tent sites. (☎822-5312. Bunks $15, with linen $20. Tents $2.50.) To get there, head south on the Nabesna Rd., turn left at Four Mile Rd., and then take the first right; follow the signs to the trailhead and hike in three-quarters of a mile (or call ahead for an ATV lift). The secluded two- and six-person cabins sport trapping decor, are heated with wood-burning stoves, and are filled with relics from the last federal homestead. A fresh spring provides cold water. The friendly owners cook meals for guests with advance notice and rent **canoes** for use on the Slana River. (☎ 822-3196. Breakfast $7, dinner $10. Canoes $30 per day, including drop-off and pickup.)

To quench your need for **gas** or good food, stop by the oasis that is **Duffy's Cafe and Bar ❶**, about 3 mi. northeast of the Nabesna Cutoff, and chat with locals over a meal and a brew. Try the $4.50 grilled cheese or a $6 burger. (Cafe open summer 7am-9pm, winter noon-9pm. Bar open until midnight or "whenever.")

📷 **HIKING.** The **Slana Ranger Station** has a list of hikes beginning at Nabesna or along the road. Most are ATV trails and are flat, wet, and muddy; they serve well as access points into the mountains along the road. Be wary of bears and mosquitoes in the brushy areas, and savor the rare opportunity to sing as loudly and poorly as you want while dousing yourself from head to toe with bug spray. The area's most pristine hiking is in the backcountry, where you will see few, if any, other people. Popular fly-in destinations in the Nabesna area are **Grizzly Lake, Jeager Mesa,** and **Cooper Pass;** climbers prefer **Mt. Gordon, Nabesna Glacier,** and **Copper Glacier.**

Skookum Volcanic Trail (5 mi. round-trip, 6-8hr.). Trailhead leaves from Mile 36.2. Highly popular and recently cleared by the Sierra Club, the trail rises about 2000 ft. up a forested alluvial fan. It follows rock cairns along a stream and into the tundra-covered tussocks in the crater of extinct Skookum Volcano. At the windy pass you can camp or continue alongside another creek down to the road again. Moderately strenuous.

Caribou Creek Trail (4 mi., 2-3hr.). Park in the gravel quarry at Mile 18.9 and walk to the trailhead at Mile 19.2. The walk weaves across the creek 3 times before coming upon an old tin cabin with first-come, first-served bunks. From this cabin, you can forge your own trails into the surrounding Mentasta Mountains, some of which offer good views of Mt. Blackburn, Mt. Wrangell, and Mt. Sanford on clear days. Easy.

Lost Creek Trail (21 mi., 2-4 days). Starts at Lost Creek Trail at Mile 31 and loops back to Trail Creek Trail at Mile 29. Trackless ridge-walking with gorgeous glimpses of alpine meadows, canyons, Dall sheep, and a 6000 ft. pass. The 2 creeks are not directly connected; chat with the rangers before setting out. Map skills are essential. Strenuous.

INTO THE PARK: THE MCCARTHY RD.

CHITINA. Chitina (CHIT-nuh) lies at the western gates of Wrangell-St. Elias. Once the largest town in Alaska and heralded as its future capital, Chitina bucked the yoke of greatness. When the copper mines dried up in the 1930s, the town virtually followed suit. Now, it's a flower-child community of only 110 year-round residents.

The town has a **ranger station** (☎ 823-2205; open daily 10am-6pm) and a **post office** (☎ 823-2225; open M-F 8am-4pm, Sa 10am-2pm). The last fuel stop on the McCarthy Rd. is at the **general store.** (☎ 823-2211. Open daily 8pm-10pm.) Nightlife is comprised of several nondescript bars. The **Chitina Burger Bar ❶** serves salads ($7), sandwiches ($5) and ice cream ($1.50) from a trailer. (Open mid-May to mid-Sept. 8am-10pm daily.) Penniless campers will delight in the spacious, free **campground ❶** across the **Copper River** (pit toilets, no water).

NUGGET CREEK. At Mile 13.5, across from the air strip, a small wagon-wheel sign on the left marks the Nugget Creek/Kotsina Rd. The **Nugget Creek Trail** begins 2½ mi. up this road, immediately across Strelna Creek. This unremarkable 14 mi. ATV route leads to a first-come, first-served **public-use cabin** at the foot of beautiful

Mt. Blackburn and the Kuskulana Glacier. Stream crossings may prove difficult; be prepared to turn back. Dayhikes from here pursue the canyons of Nugget Creek and the mining ruins in the hills behind the cabin. The Nugget Creek/Kotsina Rd. will also lead you to the **Dixie Pass Trail,** which follows Strelna Creek through scenic canyons and a narrow, breathtaking pass over the mountains. This route joins the **Kotsina Trail,** which leads back to the road in a 45 mi. loop.

KUSKULANA RIVER. At Mile 17, the Kuskulana Bridge passes 238 ft. above the raging **Kuskulana River.** Summer thrill-seekers can **bungee jump** from the bridge thanks to **Club Way North.** (☎783-1335. Call ahead. 1 jump $50, 2 jumps $80; jumps are free if you jump naked.) After jolting and rattling for 44 mi. more, the road terminates on the western edge of the Kennicott River; travelers going to McCarthy must cross a footbridge and walk a half-mile farther. A **Park Service Information Desk** is located ¾ mi. before the river on the north side; all the rangers are residents and give frank advice. (Open daily mid-May to mid-Sept. 11am-5:30pm.) The **parking lot** at the Copper Point Tram Station beside the river charges $6 per day.

MCCARTHY AND KENNICOTT ☎907

Deep in the heart of Wrangell-St. Elias National Park, abandoned, log-hewn buildings and roads straying off to points unknown bear witness to the ghost towns of McCarthy and Kennicott. In the early 1900s, thousands of miners swarmed to the site of the purest copper ore ever discovered, a vein running between the Kennicott Glacier and McCarthy Creek. In its heyday, the Copper River and Northwest Railway (CR&NW) transported nearly $200 million worth of ore to points south. McCarthy sprouted as a free-wheeling, sin-celebrating alternative to stick-in-the-mud Kennicott, a company town where strict rules of conduct were enforced. In 1938, operations came to a halt, and the last train out marked the end of an era. Since the establishment of the national park in 1980, McCarthy has been revived as the hub of the summer tourist industry, and Kennicott provides visitors with a look into the area's mining history, as well as access to popular hikes.

🛈 PRACTICAL INFORMATION. Backcountry Connection (☎822-5292 or 800-478-5292) runs 15-passenger **vans** daily from **Glennallen** (4hr.; $70, round-trip same day $99, different day $105) and **Chitina** (3hr.; $55, round-trip same day $80, different day $90) to McCarthy. **Wrangell Mountain Air** flies to McCarthy twice daily from **Chitina** and farther afield by arrangement. (☎554-4411 or 800-478-1160; www.wrangellmountainair.com. Round-trip $140.) A flight straight from Anchorage is offered by **Ellis Air Taxi,** which leaves Anchorage at 8am on Wednesday and Friday only. (☎822-3368. Round-trip $400.) Relatively regular traffic makes hitchhiking possible for some travelers, although getting stranded is also entirely possible. *Let's Go* does not recommend hitchhiking. For **Internet,** head to **The Lodge** for their wireless connection. ($1.50 for the first 30min., $0.15 for each additional min.) Many McCarthy locals still get their water from **Clear Creek,** so please don't pollute the water (use the outhouses). Fill your water bottles at your own risk.

🛈🛏 ACCOMMODATIONS AND FOOD. The cheapest and most convenient accommodations in the area are at or near the end of the McCarthy Rd. Several campgrounds line the side of the road, among them the **Glacier View Campground ❶,** a half-mile before the river. It has campsites and showers and serves nondescript barbecue food (burgers $6) all day long. (☎554-4490. Open daily Memorial Day to Labor Day 7am-10pm. Sites $10. Showers $5.) The **bike rentals** here are the area's cheapest. ($10 per half-day, $20 per day.) Right next to the bridge and closest to town, **Copper Point Campground ❶** has sites back in the woods with pit toilets and water or out by the river and away from the bugs ($10). Since most of the land around McCarthy and Kennicott is privately owned, camping is prohibited in most areas east of the river. If in doubt, check with a Park Service employee. Six miles north of McCarthy and 2 mi. north of Kennicott, a Park Service **campground** with no amenities overlooks the Root Glacier. The few, small tent sites on the hillside are hard to find, but some have stunning views. Regardless of where you camp, be sure to keep a tight camp, set up 50 ft. off trail, and store food in bins and cars. Bear sightings have been on the increase in recent years. McCarthy's cheapest beds, six-person cabins, and a cozy common room await a quarter-mile before the river on the left at the **Kennicott River Lodge and Hostel ❷**. (☎554-4441, winter 479-6822. Rooms $25; cabins $85. Showers $5 with room, $7 without.)

The food in town is expensive due to the high cost of delivery; bring groceries with you. **The Potato ❷**, a street away from the main drag, serves up spicy breakfast food, a strong cup-a-joe, and good tunes. Try the $5 spudniks and gravy. (Open 7:30am-4pm.) After a day of hiking and sight-seeing, wind down with pizza and beer at **Tailor Made Pizza ❷**, at the far end of town. (Open daily 7am-9pm.)

◙ **SIGHTS.** The first building you'll see houses the **McCarthy-Kennicott Historical Museum**, filled with mining pictures and artifacts. A walking tour map is available here. (Open in summer daily 9am-6pm. Suggested donation $1.) Kennicott is 4 mi. north of McCarthy along the road, or a bit farther on the **Old Wagon Trail** (a moderately strenuous, uphill bike to Kennicott. 45-60min.; see McCarthy campgrounds for rentals). It's recommended that bikers save the **Wagon Trail** for the trip back, as its uphill climbs can make it difficult to outride the mosquitoes. Kennicott is the gateway to the **Root Glacier** and home to the spooky ruins of the **old mill**. A shuttle runs the 5 mi. road between the towns. (9am-7:30pm. Round-trip $10.)

🔼 OUTDOOR ACTIVITIES

FLIGHTSEEING. If you go flightseeing anywhere in Alaska, do it here. Even a short flight to 16,390 ft. Mt. Blackburn and the surrounding glaciers offers magnificent views. In addition to its scheduled flights, **Wrangell Mountain Air** (see **Practical Information**, above) makes a 35min. tour of the amazing icefalls of the Kennicott and Root Glaciers ($60). The best bargain is a 70min. trip up the narrow Chitistone Gorge to view the thundering Chitistone Falls, and then on to a slew of glaciers and peaks ($105 per person; min. 2 people). **McCarthy Air** specializes in fly-in charters and flightseeing, and offers equally enthralling tours for comparable prices. (☎554-4440 or 888-989-9891. $60 for 35min., $100 for 1hr.; min. 2 people.)

ADVENTURE TRIPS. Copper Oar and **St. Elias Alpine Guides** run comparable day-long **whitewater rafting** trips down the Class III Kennicott River with a flightseeing jaunt back from Chitina. (**Copper Oar** ☎554-4453 or 800-523-4453. $235. **St. Elias** ☎554-4445 or 888-933-5427; www.steliasguides.com. $245) **Kennicott-McCarthy Wilderness Guides** (☎800-664-4537) lead 3hr. tours of Kennicott that give visitors their only chance to see inside a 14-story mill ($25). A full-service backcountry trip will cost participants about $150-200 per day. Popular choices from both St. Elias Alpine Guides and the Kennicott-McCarthy Wilderness Guides are a day of **ice climbing** (about $100) or **glacier hiking** ($50-100 depending on length).

MOUNTAIN BIKING. Wagon trails between McCarthy and Kennicott and into the bush are great for riding. One good route is the semi-strenuous 9 mi. ride along the wooded **Nizina Rd.**, beginning across McCarthy Creek and continuing to the Nizina River. There the fractured Old Nizina River Bridge rests, a victim of glacial flooding.

The **Nugget Creek Trail** is a well-defined path that gains significant elevation in its 34 mi. round-trip, making it a fairly taxing ride. **Nugget Creek** begins 13½ mi. east of Chitina on the McCarthy Rd. The creek road leads to the north; park out of the way and expect a 5-7hr. ride. See above for bike rentals.

DAYHIKES. The **Root Glacier Trail** (2-3hr.) begins in Kennicott, 2 mi. from the glacier itself, and runs alongside the glacier for 2 mi. past a Park Service campground (see above). **Exercise extreme caution** if you choose to climb onto the glacier where the gravel covers it; these areas are very slick, and deep crevasses await hikers with careless footwork. The steep **Bonanza Peak Trail** is a gem, climbing 4000 ft. over 4 mi. to a commanding view of the Kennicott and Root Glaciers and the Donoho Peak between them. To access this strenuous trail, continue a quarter-mile east of Kennicott and take a right at the junction.

BACKCOUNTRY. As is true of most parts of Wrangell-St. Elias, the best hikes in the McCarthy area are backcountry hikes along routes established by miners and wildlife. Accessible hiking trails depart town and the McCarthy Rd. At Mile 13.5 of the McCarthy Rd., outside Chitina, a small wagon-wheel sign on the left marks the Nugget Creek/Kotsina Rd. For descriptions of the **Nugget Creek Trails** and 45 mi. **Dixie Pass Trail-Kotsina Trail** loop, which can be accessed from the same point, stop at the Chitina Ranger station for the National Park Service **trip reports.** The darling of backcountry McCarthy is the **Goat Trail,** an early miners' route from McCarthy to the Chisana gold fields. The trail starts at **Skolai Pass,** home to the Golden Horn and Hole in the Wall glaciers, and traverses the ridge high above Chitistone Gorge and Falls, one of the park's most spectacular features. The route continues 25 mi. to Glacier Creek, with fantastic views of the Wrangell and St. Elias mountain ranges. The Goat Trail requires crossing the sometimes-impassable Chitisone River. Check with rangers for river conditions, which change daily, and be prepared to turn back if necessary. Many backcountry excursion require fly-in drop-offs and cover unmarked trails, so plan ahead.

PRINCE WILLIAM SOUND

In Prince William Sound, George Vancouver left his mark once again, this time honoring the grandson of King George III. The Sound lies within the Chugach National Forest, which provides ample natural resources. With its abundant fish and wildlife, fjords, glaciers, and outdoor activities, Prince William Sound is a destination for people of all ages and interests.

VALDEZ   ☎ 907

The northernmost ice-free port in Alaska, Valdez (val-DEEZ) is the terminus of the Alaska pipeline, and oil runs the show. Natural and human disasters have fixed Valdez in the popular imagination; the 1964 Good Friday earthquake, an 8.6 on the Richter scale, created 100 ft. tall waves that hammered the docks and flooded the town. Exactly 25 years later, disaster struck the relocated settlement again when the infamous Exxon *Valdez* tore open on the Bligh Reef. Although no oil actually made it into the port, 11 million gallons spread across 1640 sq. mi. of Prince William Sound and over 1500 mi. of shoreline, wreaking havoc on the ecosystem. The $2 billion clean-up lasted over three years and tripled the town's population. Efforts continue in the sound to recuperate from the spill.

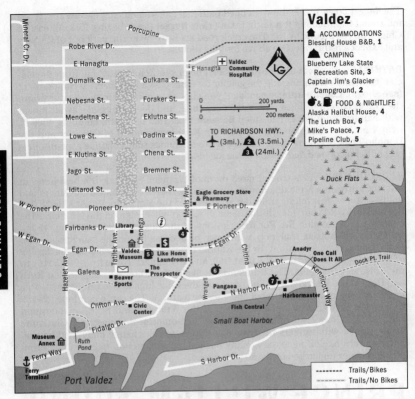

Disaster, however, has failed to spoil Valdez's charm. College-aged adventurers annually seek very small fortunes in fish canneries, or "slime houses," while sport fishermen seek a fresher catch. A handful of backpackers pass through, camping in the hills outside the city while exploring its misty forests and streams. An absurd amount of snow—330 in. on average—makes Valdez "The Snow Capital of Alaska," and draws winter purists seeking powdered ski runs.

TRANSPORTATION AND ORIENTATION

Valdez lies in the northeast of Prince William Sound, 304 mi. east of Anchorage. From Valdez, the spectacular **Richardson Hwy.** (Rte. 4, see p. 557) runs 119 mi. north through Thompson Pass to Glennallen (2½hr. from Valdez). There, it intersects the **Glenn Hwy.** (Rte. 1, see p. 478) and runs southeast to Anchorage. Most of downtown Valdez lies on **Egan St., Fairbanks St., Pioneer Dr.** and **North Harbor Dr.**, all of which run east-west between the north-south **Hazelet Ave.** and **Meals Ave.**

Flights: The **airport** is 4 mi. from town on Airport Rd., off the Richardson Hwy. **ERA Aviation** (☎835-4282) flies to **Anchorage** (40min.; M-F 3 per day, S-Su 2 per day; $130).

Buses: Parks Highway Express (☎888-600-6001; www.alaskashutle.com) runs 3 times a week to **Fairbanks** ($89).

Ferries: Alaska Marine Highway (☎835-4436 or 800-526-6731; www.akferry.com), at the city dock at the end of Hazelet Ave. Service for people and autos to **Bellingham, WA** (twice a week, $356) via **Juneau** (1½ days; $103, ages 6-11 $52.) Also runs to **Whittier, AK** (M, Tu, Th, Sa, and Su. $65, cars from $53).

Taxi: Valdez Yellow Cab (☎835-2500).

Car Rental: Valdez-U-Drive (☎835-4402 or 800-478-4402), at the airport. 25+ or 21+ if insured. Cars, trucks, and vans $49-89 per day. $0.25 per mi. after the first 100 mi.

🛈 PRACTICAL INFORMATION

Tourist Information: (☎835-2984 or 800-770-5954) at Fairbanks St. and Chenega. Open in summer daily 8am-8pm; winter M-F 9am-5pm. Free tour and lodging calls.

Outdoor Information: Most fishing stores sell **fishing licenses** and offer free advice. Check with **Fish Central** (see below) or any local bartender or bouncer for hot spots. **Harbormaster,** 307 N. Harbor Dr. (☎835-4981), has information on fishing, license requirements, weather, moorage, and storage of boats as well as showers. Open 7:30am-10:30pm. Showers $4, open 24hr. Buy tokens during office hours.

Work Opportunities: Alaska Employment Service (☎835-4910), on Meals Ave. in the Courthouse, Room 22. M-F 8am-noon and 1-4:30pm.

Equipment Rental and Sales:

The Prospector, 141 Galena Dr. (☎835-3838), beside the post office, has an immense supply of outdoor and sportsman gear. Open M-F 8am-9pm, Sa 8am-8pm, Su 9am-6pm; opens and closes an hr. earlier in winter.

Beaver Sports, 316 Galena Dr. (☎835-4727). Carries high-quality backpacking and climbing gear. Cross-country ski, snowshoe, and bike rentals. Bikes $6 per hr.; $16 per 6 hr.; $20 per day, 1-4 days. All rentals require $250 deposit. Open M-Sa 10am-7pm; winter 10am-6pm.

Fish Central, 217 N. Harbor Dr. (☎835-5090), rents boats and rods.

Anadyr Adventures, 217 N. Harbor Dr. (☎835-2814), next to Fish Central, rents kayaks. Singles $45 per day for 2 days, $35 each day after; doubles $65 1st day, $55 each day after. Cash deposit or credit card required.

Banks: First National Bank of Anchorage, 101 Egan Dr. (☎834-4800). Open M-Th 10am-5pm, F 10am-6pm. **24hr. ATM.**

Laundromat and Public Showers: Like Home Laundromat, 121 Egan St. (☎835-2913). Wash $1.50, dry $0.25 per 7min. $4 for 10min. shower. Open daily 8am-11pm. The **Harbormaster** has $4 showers (see **Outdoor Information,** above).

Weather: ☎835-4505.

Emergency: ☎911.

Police: ☎835-4560.

Pharmacy: Village Pharmacy (☎835-3737), in the same building as Eagle Quality Center, at Pioneer Dr. and Meals Ave. Open M-Th 9am-6pm, F 9am-7pm, Sa 10am-1pm.

Hospital: Valdez Community Hospital, 911 Meals Ave. (☎835-2249).

Internet Access: The **library** at 260 Fairbanks Dr. (☎835-4632), beside the museum. Outstanding 3 fl. building, with well-stocked Alaska Room and book selection. **Free 1hr. access;** call ahead. Open M and F 10am-6pm, Tu-Th 10am-8pm, Sa noon-5pm.

Post Office: (☎835-4449), at Galena Dr. and Tatitlek St. Open M-F 9am-5pm, Sa 10am-noon. **Postal Code: 99686.**

CENTRAL ALASKA

ACCOMMODATIONS

Finding a roof in Valdez can be expensive and time-consuming. The visitors center provides non-prioritized options, brochures, and a phone. With the hostel closed, the cheapest indoor options are B&Bs (from $60), which become even cheaper if travelers band together and share rooms. The free reservation center, **One Call Does It All** (☎835-4988 or 888-304-4988; www.alaska.net/~onecall), arranges B&B visits (as well as glacier tours, rafting trips, fishing charters, rental cars, and helicopter rides) and gives friendly advice on any of the local happenings. Valdez forbids camping in non-designated areas, but insolvent sojourners sometimes camp illegally along Mineral Creek, a 15min. walk from downtown. Most turn-offs at least 5 mi. out of town on the **Richardson** should be fair game for **free camping** (see p. 557).

Blessing House B&B (☎835-5333 or 888-853-5333), at the corner of Meals Ave. and Dadina St. Near downtown. The friendly hosts have 5 cheery rooms ($65-85) and continental breakfast, as well as complete use of a kitchen and piano. ❸

Blueberry Lake State Recreation Site, 24 mi. up the Richardson Hwy. from town. Camp, hike, and fish in the mountains near the top of Thompson Pass. May have snow late into the season. Pit toilets, water. 15 well-spaced sites, $12. ❶

Captain Jim's Glacier Campground (☎835-2282). With a natural waterfall and full picnic area, Capt. Jim's rests against the mountains 1 mi. past the airport. Turn north at the blinking light 3 mi. outside of town. Store all food in cars or away from tents because of bear activity. Pit toilets, water. 101 RV and tent sites, $10. ❶

FOOD AND NIGHTLIFE

Low-key eating and drinking abounds in Valdez. The **Eagle Quality Center** (☎835-2100), at 313 Meals Ave. and Pioneer Dr., supplies grocery-store items 24hr.

Mike's Palace (a.k.a. Pizza Palace), 201 N Harbor Dr. (☎835-2365). Good seafood and great pizza keep locals happy at the harborside. Sit down for Greek, American, Mexican, or Italian fare. Great soup ($3), burgers ($5), halibut ($14), and 12 in. pizza ($9). Open daily 11am-11pm. Closes at 10pm in winter. ❷

The Lunch Box (☎835-9500). Though there is no such thing as a free lunch, these made-to-order sandwiches and boxed lunches are a great deal for those planning all-day excursions. Sandwiches $5.25. Open M-F 10am-5pm, Sa 11am-4pm. ❶

Alaska Halibut House, 208 Meals Ave. (☎835-2788). The closest thing to fast food in Valdez, the Halibut House offers up some of the cheapest fresh seafood in the state. It ain't glamorous, but it's quick and filling. Catch of the day $5, halibut basket (huge!) $9. Open daily for breakfast 6am-11am, lunch and dinner 11am-10pm. ❶

Pipeline Club, 112 Egan St. (☎835-4332). With a local flavor that isn't too over-the-top, the Pipeline serves up cold Alaskan brews in a comfortable setting. Shoot some pool with a local cannery worker, or ask the bouncer where the fishing hot spots are while kicking back to live music. Su-W 1pm-midnight, Th-Sa 1pm-1am. ❷

SIGHTS

VALDEZ MUSEUM. This small museum packs an impressive informational punch for its size, with excerpts from prospectors' diaries, exhibits on the Good Friday disasters, and an entire bar from Old Town. *(217 Egan St. ☎835-2764. Open May-Sept. M-Sa 9am-6pm, Su 8am-5pm; Oct.-Apr. M-F 10am-5pm, Sa noon-4pm. $3, seniors $2.50, ages 14-18 $2, under 14 free.)*

ALASKA CULTURAL CENTER. A huge collection of Native Alaskan artifacts is housed here, alongside a 15min. earthquake video that plays every hour. *(At airport.* ☎*834-1690. Open daily 9am-8pm. Call for winter hours. $3, under 12 $1.)*

THEATER. The Prince William Sound Community College Last Frontier Theatre Conference, at the Civic Center in June, sponsors workshops with guest playwrights, holds performances, and features the noted playwright Edward Albee. *(*☎*834-1612; www.uaa.alaska.edu/pwscc.)*

🎪 FESTIVALS AND EVENTS

Gold Rush Days (☎835-5821) are a feast for budget travelers. The visitors center hosts a free salmon and halibut fry, plus fashion shows, dances, bed races, and an **ugly vehicle contest.** (1st W-Su in Aug.) Valdez makes the most of winter and its immense amounts of snow with the annual **Snowman Festival** (☎835-2330) during the first weekend in March. While the sculptures are assembled, a drive-in movie is projected onto a giant snowbank. Make sure to wear your "frosty fever" buttons during festival days for good deals at local establishments. Competitors at the **Valdez Ice Climbing Festival** (☎835-5182) race up the frozen waterfalls of Keystone Canyon, while competitors at the **World Freeskiing Championships** (☎650-888-9311) race down the powdered slopes of the Chugach Mountains. The **Mountain Man Snowmobile Hill Climb** (☎835-2372; www.valdezsnow.com) tests the courage and skill of drivers as they head straight up the snowy walls of Thompson Pass.

🏔 OUTDOOR ACTIVITIES

FISHING. Though expensive, charter companies offer the best access to the halibut, salmon and rock fish in Prince William Sound. Halibut charters are full-day ($165-200 per person) and salmon charters are half-day ($80-100 per person). Try **One Call Does It All** (☎835-4988 or 888-304-4988) to compare prices. To prepare your catch for travel, **Easy Freeze** (☎835-4208) will seal and flash-freeze for $1.50 per lb. and also offers shipping; call for prices. Derbies boast big prizes all summer (call the Chamber of Commerce at ☎835-2330 for info). If the charter option is too pricey, pink and silver salmon have been known to bite as close as the town docks through August. Ask at the **Harbormaster's Office** (see **Outdoor Information,** p. 493) or **Fish Central** (see **Equipment Rental,** p. 493) for nearby hot spots.

KAYAKING. Kayaking in Prince William Sound is the best way to travel. Moving along at a good clip with enough time to savor the sights, an extended trip among towering mountains and calving glaciers is enough to draw the queasiest landlubber out to the seas. Both **Anadyr Adventures** (see **Equipment Rental,** p. 493) and **Pangaea Adventures,** 101 N. Harbor Dr., offer similar half- and full-day sea kayaking trips. (☎835-8442 or 800-660-9637. Half-day: 3hr. Duck Flats $55; 6hr. Gold Creek Coast $75. Full-day: 8-10hr. trips start around $150. Multi-day and mothership supported packages navigate inner channels to remote glaciers. River kayakers will be thrilled by the Class IV middle portion or the Class IV upper stretch of the Tsaina River. **Keystone Adventures** (☎835-2606 or 800-328-8460) leads kayaking and **rafting** trips, including a 4½ mi. (45min.; $35) route on the Lowe River through Class II and III rapids and past the vast Bridal Veil Falls. Get dressed up in a dry suit and helmet for the Class IV Tsaina run ($75), and be prepared to swim.

TOURS. By boat, helicopter, or plane, and for a hefty price, visitors can view Prince William Sound's most prized possession: **Columbia Glacier.** The best budget option is the ferry (see **Ferries,** p. 493), which pauses in front of the face of the 3 mi.

wide ice monstrosity for 10min. on its way to and from Whittier ($64). For private tours, try **One Call Does It All**, 241 N. Harbor Dr. (☎ 835-4988 or 888-304-4988), a free reservation and info service that will match you with trips with rates in your range.

CHURCH. The Chapel of the Sea allows the pious and penniless aboard the *Lu-Lu Belle* for a 1hr., non-denominational church service in the Sound. Show up Sunday by 7:45am at the dock adjacent to the Westmark Hotel. (☎ 800-411-0090. First-come, first-served. 65 seats. Free, but offering is collected.)

HIKING. Local hiking is first-rate. Inquire at the visitors center or **Beaver Sports** for more info on Valdez hiking opportunities.

■ **Solomon Gulch Trail** (3¾ mi. round-trip). Begins 150 yards northeast of the hatchery on Dayville Rd. toward the Alyeska Terminal. Covers 2 steep inclines, ending at Solomon Lake with excellent views of Valdez Bay and the pipeline. The more rigorous **Goat Trail,** farther from the city, follows a Native Alaskan footpath that was once the only route from Valdez to the Interior. As it weaves through Keystone Canyon, the trail follows the Lowe River and features glimpses of waterfalls.

Mineral Creek Trail (8 mi.). Pull off the highway at Bridalveil Falls and follow the posted directions. 1st 6 mi. accessible by car along a gravel road and also easily accessible by car at Mile 18.2, just north of downtown. A gentle 2 mi. round-trip footpath leads farther through the mountains past waterfalls and wildlife to the **Old Gold Mine.**

Shoup Bay Trail (12 mi.). Starts from the parking area located on the left at the west end of Egan St. Leads along the mountainside with views of the bay and distant mountains, but is muddy and mosquito-infested in places. About 6 mi. in, this level trail crosses Gold Creek. A mile-long turn-off to the right leads to spectacular waterfalls. Another 6 mi. along the trail leads to a remarkable view of the distant **Shoup Glacier.**

SKIING AND SNOWBOARDING. Valdez's plentiful snowfall and prime coastal location, which warms up to a balmy 25°F in January, together make the town and the surrounding Chugach Mountains a **powder paradise.** Experienced skiers and snowboarders charter helicopters to **Mt. Odyssey** and any of the other 450 designated heli-skiing runs, or drive and "snow machine" (Alaskan for "snow-mobile") to **Thompson Pass** to ski back. Most outfits in Valdez and Thompson Pass offer daily heli-skiing packages ($500-600, average 6 runs), including **Valdez H2O Heli Adventures** (☎ 835-8418; www.h2oguides.com), **Valdez Heli-Camps, Inc.** (☎ 835-5898; www.valdezhelicamps.com), and **Valdez Heli-Ski Guides** (☎ 835-4528; www.valdezheliskiguides.com). For those looking specifically to telemark or Nordic ski, try **Thompson Pass Treks** (☎ 835-4817; www.alaska.net/~chalet). They also offer guided backcountry touring trips for skiers and snow-boarders willing to snowshoe their skis/boards up the runs. **Phatz Ski Rental** (☎ 835-4727; www.alaska.net/~pcprice) offers daily rates on alpine skis ($25), snowboards ($25), and safety packages which include an avalanche beacon ($35). The avid Nordic skier will enjoy **cross-country ski trails,** which lead to the left and right off Mineral Creek Rd. and along the road itself. Advanced runs are in the Tsaina Valley at the north base of Thompson Pass. Moderate trails begin at the Coast Guard Housing on Anchor Crest St. at the western end of town. **Beaver Sports** (see **Practical Information,** p. 493) has cross-country skis as well as snow shoes for rent ($18 skis, $14 snowshoes; $10 each additional day). Check out www.valdezalaska.org/winter, the most informative web site on guided ski-ing opportunities in Valdez. For more details on all winter activities, pick up the free *Valdez Winter Guide* at the visitors center.

CORDOVA ☎907

Surrounded by rugged mountains and waters teeming with salmon, Cordova lures nature lovers and anglers alike. Modern Cordova sprang to life at the turn of the century when a huge copper deposit was discovered in the Wrangell Mountains, and is now a commercial fishing town. Cordovans still use the old copper railroad bed to access the enormous Childs Glacier through the Copper River Delta, the largest wetland on the Pacific Coast. Accessible only by sea and air, the town of 2800 has preserved blissfully uncrowded hiking, biking, skiing, bird-watching, and fishing opportunities. Cordova's only drawback is the weather: many cloudy days and 150 in. of annual precipitation make this a damp paradise.

▐▀ TRANSPORTATION

Cordova, on the east side of Prince William Sound at **Orca Inlet,** starts at the shore and climbs up the steep hillside. **Railroad Ave.** begins at water level, and numbered streets parallel the ocean. **First St.** is the downtown shopping district and leads out of town toward the ferry terminal. Railroad Ave. becomes the **Copper River Hwy.** out of town toward the airport and the Childs Glacier.

Flights: The **airport** is 13 mi. east of town on the Copper River Hwy. **Alaska Airlines** (☎424-3278 or 800-426-0333) flies once per day to **Anchorage** ($142.50) and **Juneau** ($259.50). They also contract **Era Aviation** (☎800-866-8394) to fly to Anchorage 2 more times a day (except on Su) from June-Sept. ($162.50). The **Airport Shuttle** (☎424-3272) meets scheduled flights and runs to town for $11.

Ferries: Alaska Marine Highway (☎424-7333 or 800-642-0066; www.akmhs.com), 1 mi. north of town on Ocean Dock Rd., off 1st St. Regular service to **Valdez** (5½hr., M and F night, $34) and **Whittier** (7hr., W morning, $65).

Taxis: Wild Hare Taxi Service (☎424-3939). $16 to airport.

Car Rental: Cordova Auto Rentals (☎424-5982), at the airport. $70 per day; unlimited free mileage. Big cars $80 per day. Hefty taxes added. Must be 21+ with a credit card. **Northern Lights Inn** also rents cars to its guests (see **Accommodations,** below).

▐▉ PRACTICAL INFORMATION

Visitor Information: Cordova Historical Museum, 622 1st St. (☎424-6665). Open in summer M-Sa 10am-6pm, Su 2-4pm; winter Tu-F 1-5pm, Sa 2-4pm. **Cordova Chamber of Commerce** (☎424-7260), on 1st St. Open M-F 10am-5:30pm.

Outdoor Information: Forest Service Cordova District Ranger Station (☎424-7661), on 2nd St. between Browning and Adams, 2nd fl. Research Forest Service cabins here. Open M-F 8am-5pm. Fishing licenses are available at A.C. Value (see **Food,** below).

Equipment Rental: Cordova Coastal Outfitters (☎424-7424), on the dock in the small boat harbor. Mountain bikes $15 per day; single kayaks $15, doubles $50; skiffs (fishing gear and gas included) $135. **Cordova Auto Rentals** rents canoes for $35 per day.

Bookstore: Orca Book Store (☎424-5305), on 1st St. Houses a collection of 1st edition Alaskan books. Open M-F 7am-5pm, Sa 8am-5pm. No credit cards.

Laundromat and Showers: Club Speedwash, in the alley behind the Club Bar on 1st. St. Wash $2, dry $0.25 per 15min. Open daily 8am-8pm. **Harbormaster,** 602 Nicholoff Way (☎424-6400). Dry $3 per 10min. Tokens available M-F 8am-5pm and other irregular hours. Call ahead. Showers open 24hr.

Emergency: ☎911.

Police: (☎424-6100). Beside the post office on Railroad Ave.

Pharmacy: Cordova Drug Co. (☎424-3246), on 1st St. Open M-Sa 9:30am-6pm.

Hospital: 602 Chase Ave. (☎424-8000), off the Copper River Hwy.

Internet Access: At the **library** (☎424-6667), on 1st St., next to the museum. Open Tu-F 1-8pm, Sa 1-5pm. Free, but slow.

Post Office: (☎424-3564), at Council St. and Railroad Ave. Open M-F 10am-5:30pm, Sa 10am-1pm. **Postal Code:** 99574.

ACCOMMODATIONS AND CAMPING

Although Cordova itself has several cheap options for rooms, the city and surrounding area is largely devoid of places to pitch a tent or park an RV. The **City RV Park ❶**, 1 mi. from downtown on Whitshed Rd., offers minimal space and maximal noise. These sites are mainly used by summer cannery workers. (Reserve through the harbormaster at ☎424-6400. Sites $3; RV sites $12.) The next-closest option is **Childs Glacier ❶**, 50 mi. from town on the Copper River Hwy. The sites allow you to listen to the glacier calve throughout the night. (Pit toilets, no water. Sites $5.) Contact the Forest Service (☎424-7661) to find out whether **day-use sites ❶** on the highway may be open for overnight use.

Alaskan Hotel and Bar (☎424-3299), on 1st St. Look for the upside down sign. Above the not-so-muffled sounds of the bar's jukebox, these rooms are simple, spacious, and centrally located. Ask for a room on the 2nd floor; they're quieter. Singles and doubles $35; with private bath $55; add $10 for 3 or more people. ❷

The Salvation Army ("The Lighthouse"), 514 1st St. (☎424-3581 or 424-3134), behind the thrift store. Clean, new, and private rooms are off the street and include a large kitchenette, private bath, 2 double beds, TV, and phone. May to mid-Sept. $67.50; mid-Sept. to Apr. $50. No credit cards. ❹

Northern Nights Inn (☎424-5356), at 3rd St. and Council Ave. Look for the flowers. 4 homey rooms, all with kitchenette and full bath. Bikes $12 per day. Ask about the room and car deal. A 4-person apartment downstairs is a steal at $80 a night. Other rooms $60, $50 in winter. ❸

FOOD

Cordova offers a variety of delectable lunch options, but at night, the few places still open charge nearly $20 for a mediocre meal. If possible, buy and cook your own dinner. The best selection of groceries is the colossal **A.C. Value,** on Nicholoff St., in the small boat harbor. (☎424-7141. Open M-Sa 7:30am-10pm, Su 8am-9pm.)

▨ **Baja Taco** (☎424-5599). In a red bus by the small boat harbor, surrounded by a collection of outdoor furniture reminiscent of driftwood, sits a woman who can add some spice to your life. Fish tacos with fresh halibut ($2.75) are outstanding. Filling meals range $3-8. Open May-Sept. (weather permitting) M-Th 8am-8pm, Su 10am-8pm. ❶

Killer Whale Cafe (☎424-7733), on 1st St. in the back of the groovy Orca Bookstore. The Killer Whale stands out over other towns earthy, espresso-steeped cafes. The sandwiches are on croissants and the views are of books, not mountains. Homemade soup and croissant $2.75; killer sandwiches $6-9. Open M-F 7am-4pm, Sa 8am-3:30pm. ❶

Cordova Lighthouse Cafe, 212 Nicholoff Way (☎424-7080), bakes arguably the best bread in South Central Alaska. Open Tu-Sa 7am-2pm. ❷

🜚 🎵 SIGHTS AND ENTERTAINMENT

Cordova's **docks** are always bustling and occasionally feature fresh fish for sale. In the heart of winter, Cordovans escape cabin fever by honoring the little squirmers who love the dark days and cold temperatures. **The Iceworm Festival** (the first week-end in February) has become a huge deal over the years. Events include art shows, a food festival, and the coronation of the ever-coveted title Miss Iceworm Queen. (☎424-3982.) During the second week of May, bird-watchers flock to Cordova for the annual **Shorebird Festival,** when the largest accumulation of shorebirds in the world (about 14 million) rests in the Copper River Delta for its journey to the Arctic. (Call the visitors center at ☎424-6665 for details.)

Cordova's nightlife is concentrated at the **Alaskan Hotel and Bar,** where the original oak bar has been hospitable to local fishermen since 1906. Beer costs $2.25-4.50. (☎424-3288. Open M-Th 8am-2am, F-Sa 8am-4am, Su 10am-2am.)

🜨 HIKING

Hiking in the Copper River Delta is often wet and tough, but the neighboring **Chugach Mountains** provide well-maintained dry trails and excellent climbing opportunities. Get a copy of *Take a Hike!*, a great pamplet on hiking in the area, from the Forest Service. A series of trails stretches 12 mi. out of town. These trails can be accessed by several trailheads along Power Creek Rd. or from the base of Eyak Ski Mountain at the end of 6th St. Becky at **Copper River and Northwest Tours** will drop hikers anywhere. (☎424-5356. $1 per mi.)

The Mount Eyak Trail (3 mi. one-way, 1½ hr.) starts at the end of Sixth St. and climbs around the back and more scenic side of the mountain. It continues past the top of the chairlift to a fork. The left side goes up to the peak of Mt. Eyak proper. (Moderate to difficult.) The right fork connects to the **Crater Lake Trail** (2½ mi. one-way, 1500 ft. gain, 2hr.) after 1 mi. Crater Lake is a popular hike that leads to views of the Copper River Delta, Prince WIlliam Sound, and the Chugach Mountains, as well as to the Crater Lake alpine bowl. (Difficult.) At the lake itself, the trail becomes **Ridge Route Intertie** (6 mi., 500 ft. gain from Crater Lake, 3-4hr.), which connects Crater Lake and Power Creek. Views from the ridge are outstanding. A shelter is available midway. (Difficult.) The **Power Creek Trail** (5 mi. one-way, 1500 ft. gain, 3-5 hr.) can be accessed via a trailhead 7 mi. from Cordova on Power Creek Rd. The trail passes through diverse scenery, with lots of waterfalls, a hanging glacier, and berry-picking. Allow plenty of time, wear rubber boots, and consider reserving the **Forest Service Cabin.** (Difficult.) **McKinley Lake** (2½ mi. one-way, 2hr.) can be accessed by a trailhead at Mile 21.6 of Copper River Hwy. The Lucky Strike Mining Co. began the construction of this trail in 1927. It is an easy walk that leads through forest to a lake with great fishing. A rougher trail continues past the lake to the deserted mine. Take caution of collapsing mine shafts. (Easy.) Two **cabins** on the lake can be reserved. (☎877-444-6777.) **The Saddlebag Glacier Trail** (3 mi. one-way, 2-3hr., 100ft. gain) begins at the end of the 1 mi. firewood-cutting road at Mile 25 of the Copper River Highway. The trail is an easy walk through forest and field to Saddlebag Lake, riddled with icebergs from Saddlebag Glacier and reflecting the large cirque with its many mountain goats. (Easy.)

🜍 OTHER OUTDOOR ACTIVITES

Fishing along **Orca Inlet Rd.,** on the **Eyak River,** or at **Hartney Bay** is outstanding for most of the summer. Kings return May-June, coho Aug.-Sept., and sockeye in late May-June. Contact Fish and Game for details. (☎424-7535.) In **Prince William Sound**

and **Orca Inlet, kayaking** is spectacular. The weather is often nicer out at sea, away from the mountains behind Cordova. Except for mountain peaks, everything Cordova has to offer, from bears to otters to birds to glaciers, is accessible by kayak. **Cordova Coastal Outfitters** (see **Practical Information,** above) offers guided tours, drop-offs, gear rental, and advice. ($65 for 4hr., $95 for 8hr.) The water in Cordova is warmer than in nearby Yakutat, making **surfing** appealing, although the waves are less than spectacular. The best breaks can be found off **Hinchinbrook Island, Hook Point,** and **Strawberry Beach.** You'll need to find a boat ride there, but you can stay at the **Hook Point** Forest Service cabin. Call local surfing guru Rick for advice. (☎424-7196.) At the end of 6th St., the oldest chairlift in Alaska swings over three runs at **Mt. Eyak Ski Area.** (☎424-7766. Open Dec. 25-snow melt. Lift tickets $15.) Excellent **cross-country skiing** is free along the Mt. Tripod Trail and at Mile 18.6 on the Copper River Hwy. at the Muskeg Meander Shi (3.1 mi. one-way, 300 ft. gain), which is marked by orange diamonds and ends at a point overlooking the Delta. (Moderate.) In the dark months, the adventurous go to **ice skating** on Lake Eyak.

▓ DAYTRIP FROM CORDOVA: CHILDS GLACIER

One of the most stupendous road-accessible sights in Alaska, Childs Glacier stands 300 ft. tall and calves actively throughout the summer months as the Copper River's level rises, sending 20-story chunks of ice plunging thunderously into the silty waters. The largest calvings can send 20 ft. waves over the observation area on the opposite bank of the river a quarter-mile away. Splintered trees and boulders strewn throughout the woods are testament to the power of these inland tsunamis. Although falls of this size are uncommon (occurring perhaps once per season), they are unpredictable and viewers should be prepared to run. It is also prohibited to harvest salmon flung into the woods by the waves (called "glacier fishing"). Visitors have a hard time tearing themselves away from the sight, always afraid to miss "the big one" as they head towards the parking lot and hear the thunder from afar. The **Million Dollar Bridge,** only a few hundred yards from the viewing area, was the key to the Copper River and Northwestern Railroad, and was once considered an engineering marvel in 1910 because of its placement between two active glaciers. **Miles Glacier** has retreated, but Childs is now less than half a mile away. The bridge was heavily damaged in the 1964 earthquake (8.4 on the Richter Scale), but a creative patch job has kept it standing. Daredevils drive across at their own risk. The combined splendor of the delta and the glacier makes the trip a virtual necessity. Although expensive, car rental gives you the most freedom to hit some teaser trails on the way (see *Take a Hike!* from the Forest Service) and linger at the glacier. If you can, pack a lunch (there's no food anywhere on the highway) and make a glorious day of it. The especially hardy choose to bike the stunning 100 mi. round-trip each way. **Copper River and North West Tours,** run by the folks at Northern Nights Inn (see **Accommodations and Camping,** above), offers several all-day bus trips every week when the rare cruise or ferry is in. The tour has a long stop at Childs. (☎424-5356. $35 per person, $40 with lunch. Call for schedule.) They'll also drop off and pick up hikers anywhere along the highway for $1 per mi.

KENAI PENINSULA

Many visitors spend their whole trip to Alaska in the Kenai Peninsula due to its endless wildlife, heart-stopping scenery, and fantastic fishing. South of Anchorage, the Seward Hwy. (Rte. 9) runs to Seward and the Sterling Hwy. (Rte. 1) branches off to Homer, skirting Chugach National Forest, Kenai Fjords National Park, and

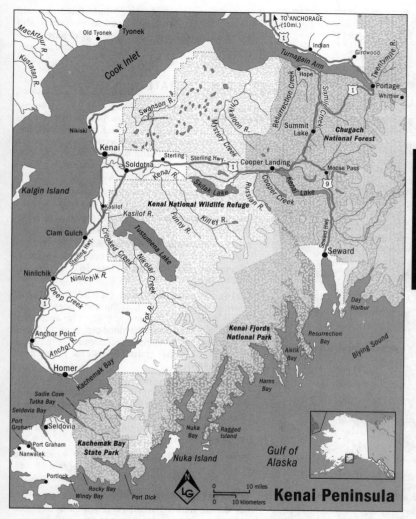

Kenai Peninsula

the Kenai National Wildlife Refuge. To the west, across the Cook Inlet, snow-capped volcanoes can be seen on a clear day; on the southern coast, glaciers reach out like enormous icy tongues from the **Harding Ice Field** to the sea.

SEWARD ☎907

Named for the Secretary of State who oversaw the purchase of Alaska from Russia in 1867, Seward was chosen as the terminus of the Alaska railroad for its ice-free, deep-water port. The lush alpine trails of Chugach National Forest and hulking tide-water glaciers of Kenai Fjords National Park see a massive wave of summer tourists

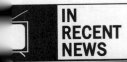

IN RECENT NEWS

ALIBUT OVERFISHING IN SEWARD

Sportfishing for Pacific Halibut has apidly gained popularity in Seward, but as more of the fish are caught off he shores of Alaska's ports, a subsequent decline in the fish population has been noted. The most striking evidence? Halibut charters that once ook customers on an hour-long boat ride out of Seward must now travel 2 or even 3 hours to find decent fishing waters. But where have these bottom-dwelling flat fish gone?

Halibut are famous for their size; he world record catch weighed in at ust over 450 lb. What people don't ealize is that these "barn doors," or arge halibut, play a role in determining the future survival of the species. Any halibut over 80 lb. is usually emale, and the amount of eggs emales lay is directly proportionate to heir size. A 50 lb. female will produce about 500,000 eggs, but a 250 lb. emale will produce 4,000,000! Keeping the big fish when they're caught can quickly lead to a decline n eggs, and a subsequent decline in halibut that survive to maturity.

While there hasn't been much official action to address the decreasing number of halibut in the waters surrounding the Kenai Peninsula, many charter companies now encourage customers to release any halibut over 00 lb. Some will even give you a discount for releasing the big ones. Most knowledgeable fishers agree that the meat from smaller "chickens," (20-60 b. fish) tastes better, anyway.

that locals proudly welcome. Whale-filled emerald waters and abundant halibut and salmon draw still more visitors, and bald-eagles share the skies with exotic seabirds. Hikers, kayakers, sailors, and anglers: rejoice!

⬚ TRANSPORTATION

Seward is 127 mi. south of Anchorage on the scenic **Seward Hwy.** (Rte. 9), which turns into 3rd Ave. in town. Most services and outdoor outfits cluster in the small-boat harbor on **Resurrection Bay.** The more charming **downtown** is nine blocks farther south on the Seward Hwy. and one block east on 4th Ave., between Railroad and Madison Ave.

Flights: The airport is 2 mi. north of town on the Seward Hwy. **FS Air Service** (☎248-9595) flies M-Sa and once on Su to **Anchorage** (30min., 2 per day, one-way $69). **Scenic Mountain Air** (☎224-9152) offers charters.

Ferries: Alaska Marine Highway (☎224-5485 or 800-526-6731). Follow Port Ave. to train tracks. To **Homer** (25hr., $115) via **Kodiak** (13hr., $61) and **Valdez** (11hr., $60).

Trains: Alaska Railroad (☎800-544-0552; www.alaskarailroad.com), at the north edge of town. Trains leave daily in summer at 6:45pm for **Anchorage** (4½hr.; $55 one-way; $90 round-trip, ages 2-11 half-price). The train is generally accommodating to visitors taking in the glacier cruises (see **Kenai Fjords Nat'l Park**, p. 506).

Buses: Park Connection (☎800-266-8625; www.alaskacoach.com) has two trips daily from Anchorage at 7am and 3pm ($41 one-way). **Seward Bus Line** (☎224-3608) runs daily to Anchorage (9am). The bus from Anchorage arrives in Seward at 5:30pm ($35 one-way, $68 round-trip).

Public Transportation: Seward's trolley has designated stops throughout town. $2, all day $5, ages 6-15 half-price. Runs daily 10am-7pm. Group tours available.

Taxis: Glacier Taxi (☎224-5678).

Car Rental: Harbor Rentals (☎224-8801 or 877-533-8801) rents compacts $65 per day, 100 free mi., $0.30 each additional mi. Must be 21. Required under-25 insurance $5 per day. Major credit card or $250 deposit required. Also rents vans and motor scooters. Group rates for shuttle services to Anchorage and towns on the Kenai.

Bike rentals available from **Seward Mtn. Bike Shop** (☎224-2448) by the Harbor Train Station, in a railroad car. Half-day $15-18, full-day $27-32. Open daily 9am-7pm.

⚡ PRACTICAL INFORMATION

Tourist Information: Seward Chamber of Commerce (☎224-8051), at Mile 2 on the Seward Hwy. Pictures and prices of local accommodations. Open M-F 8am-6pm, Sa 9am-5pm, Su 9am-4pm. There is also an annex at the small boat harbor, behind the Kenai Fjords National Park Visitor Center, with some info on tours and fishing derbies.

Outdoor Information: Kenai Fjords National Park Visitor Center, (☎224-3175 or 224-2132; www.nps.gov/kefj), at the small-boat harbor. A 12min. slideshow on the park is shown upon request and a film about a ranger's crossing of the Harding Icefield is shown every 2hr. 10am-6pm. Open in summer daily 8am-7pm; winter M-F 8am-5pm. The **Seward Ranger Station,** 334 4th Ave. (☎224-3374, reservations 877-444-6777; www.reserveusa.com), at Jefferson St., has info on cabins. Open M-F 8am-5pm.

Work Opportunities: Seward Employment Center, (☎224-5276) 5th Ave. and Adams St. in the City Building. Lots of seasonal work available. Open M-F 9am-noon and 1-4:30pm.

Equipment Rental: The Fish House, (☎224-3674) opposite the harbormaster, rents rods for $10. $50 cash or credit card deposit required. Tips and instructions free. They also offer a **Fishing Charter Reservation** service. Open daily 6am-9pm.

Laundromat and Public Showers: Seward Laundry (☎224-5727), at 4th Ave. and C St., is the only laundromat in town and can get crowded. Wash $2.50, dry $0.25 per 4min. Showers $5 per 15min. with towel and soap. Open M-Sa 8am-8pm, Su noon-6pm. Showers are also available 24hr. at the **harbormaster,** down by the small boat harbor. $2 per 7min. Change available in the harbormaster's office, but only until 5pm.

Road Conditions: ☎800-478-7675.

Emergency: ☎911.

Police: (☎224-3338), at 4th and Adams. Provides a 24hr. refuge.

Crisis Line: Seward Life Action Council (☎224-3027 or 888-224-5257).

Pharmacy: Seward Drug, 224 4th Ave. (☎224-8989) Open M-Sa 9am-6pm.

Hospital: Providence Seward Hospital (☎224-5205), at 1st Ave. and Jefferson St.

Internet Access: Seward Community Library (☎224-3646), at 5th and Adams. Free 30min.; call ahead. Open M-F noon-8pm, Sa noon-6pm.

Post Office: (☎224-3001), at 5th Ave. and Madison St. Open M-F 9:30am-4:30pm, Sa 10am-2pm. **Postal Code:** 99664.

🏠 ACCOMMODATIONS AND CAMPING

Seward has a host of reasonable housing and camping options that contribute to its popularity as a destination. **Connections** (☎224-5695, infoline 800-844-2424; www.alaskasview.com) is a general reservation number for accommodations. **Moose Pass ❶,** at Mile 29.5, has 4 campgrounds. (Call to reserve ☎877-444-6777; www.reserveusa.com. $10-13.) At the end of the road to Exit Glacier is the tents-only **Exit Glacier Campground ❶,** complete with food storage, pit toilets, and a cooking shelter. (Max. stay 14-days. **Free.**) There are plenty of pull-off spots along **Exit Glacier Rd.** Most are on the riverside, with excellent views of the valley.

▨ **Kate's Roadhouse** (☎224-5888), 5½ mi. outside town on the Seward Hwy. Huge, home-baked continental breakfast. Free shuttle service, bikes, car-cleaning station, and local calls included. Shared baths include Alaska's only outhouse with heat and a flush toilet. Dorms with breakfast are the best deal in town. Dorms $17; private rooms $59. ❶

Moby Dick Hostel (☎224-7072; www.mobydickhostel.com), at 3rd Ave. between Jefferson and Madison St. Conveniently located between downtown and the small boat harbor. Single-sex rooms, and a view of Mt. Marathon. Kitchen. Linen $2. Office open 9-11am and 5-10pm. $17; private room $45. Showers included. ❶

Fjords RV Park, down Exit Glacier Rd. a ½ mi., on the right. Clean, wooded sites in an open, old-growth forest. Tents $10 plus $5 per extra person; RVs $12-17. ❶

Municipal Waterfront Campground, along Ballaine Rd. between Railway Ave. and D St. Fish from your front door. 2-week max. stay. Check-out 4pm. Open May 15-Sept. 30. Sites $6; RV sites $10, RV sites $15. Week-long rate available. Showers included. ❶

◖ FOOD

Seward's fish is fantastic when it's fresh. Stock up on groceries at the **Eagle Quality Center,** 1907 Seward Hwy., at Mile 1.5. (☎224-3698. Open 24hr.)

Railway Cantina, 1401 4th St. (☎224-8226), on the corner of 4th St. and N Harbor. Fill up for $8 and under. Don't miss the halibut tacos ($7), complete with chips and mexican slaw. Veggie options. Open Jan.-Oct. daily 11am-8pm. ❷

Bakery at the Harbor (☎224-6091), across from the harbormaster. Slide in for a breakfast burrito ($3.50) or loaf of homemade bread ($4). ❶

Resurrect Art Coffee House Gallery, 320 3rd Ave. (☎224-7161). Sip Italian soda ($1.50) or play a board game in the balcony-turned-loft. Try a bagel with cream cheese ($1.50) with a latte ($2.50). Open M-Th 7am-10pm, F-Sa 7am-midnight, Su 7am-6pm. ❶

Red's (☎224-5995), at 3rd and Van Buren St. The best burgers in town, cooked in a white school bus fronted by picnic tables. Try the halibut burger ($7.50)—it doesn't get any fresher than here. Open M-Sa 11am-8pm. ❷

◪ NIGHTLIFE

With long daylight hours in the summer, outdoor activities can continue into the wee hours of the morning. Night owls head downtown to the local watering holes, concentrated in the blocks between Railway Ave. and Jefferson St.

New Seward Saloon (☎224-3095), on 5th Ave. The hot spot for Seward's younger set. Try one of their collection of martinis ($7), a tiny tini ($5.25), or a 32 oz. Long Island Iced tea ($12.50). Microbrews $3.75. Open daily May-Oct. noon-2am; Nov.-Apr. 5pm-2am.

Yukon Bar (☎224-3063), at 4th Ave. and Washington St., draws a young crowd with its frequent live music (Th-M). The Mt. Marathon race originated with a drunken bet here (see **Sights,** below). Micro-brew pints $3.75. Open-mic M. Open daily noon-2am.

The Pit (☎224-3006), Mile 3.5 on the Seward Hwy. After downtown closes at 2am, head out of town to The Pit to hang with the late, late crowd. Take advantage of 5am drinks with shuffleboard and a great deck to enjoy the midnight sun.

◉ ♫ SIGHTS AND ENTERTAINMENT

ALASKA SEALIFE CENTER. The $56 million Sealife Center has become one of Seward's prized attractions, giving visitors a glimpse of underwater Alaska. Touch starfish and watch tufted puffins, sea lions, and harbor seals play in large outdoor habitats. Visiting professors and resident biologists discuss current research, and kid-friendly programs include tours, films, and sleep-overs in front of the tanks. (*At the end of downtown on Railroad Ave. between 3rd and 4th Ave.* ☎224-6300 or 800-224-2525;

www.alaskasealife.org. Open May-Sept. daily 8am-8pm; Oct.-Mar. 10am-5pm; Apr. 9am-6pm. $12.50, ages 7-12 $10, children under 6 free. Family and group discounts available.)

POLAR BEAR JUMP-OFF. Seward's coldest test of physical endurance, the 3-day **Seward Polar Bear Jump,** raises money for the American Cancer Society by plunging participants into the frigid waters of Resurrection Bay. *(3rd weekend in January.)*

RACES. The principal insanity-inducing annual event in Seward is **Mount Marathon.** Alaska's oldest footrace (only the Boston Marathon is older in the US) began after a tipsy sourdough challenged a barmate to get up and down Mt. Marathon (3022 ft.) in under an hour: the modern men's record is 43min., the women's 50min. Every year on July 4th, hundreds of competitors run, slide, fall, and bleed up and down the mountainside. Bib numbers are drawn lottery-style in March, but a handful are auctioned off on July 3rd. In its 10th year, the annual **Lost Lake Breath of Life Run** covers 16 mi. over the course of what may be the most beautiful trail race around. Benefits go to cystic fibrosis research (☎ 224-3537). The **Exit Glacier 5K and 10K Run** begins in mid-May (☎ 224-4054).

🏔 OUTDOOR ACTIVITIES

The trails between Seward and its northern neighbor, **Portage,** are some of the most spectacular in the entire state. You really can't go wrong anywhere in Alaska, and the **Chugach National Forest** is no exception (see p. 482). Although many of these routes take days, portions of some can be turned into easily accessible day-hikes. Be advised that snow may exist at higher elevations well into July, and weather in the area can change rapidly. Bring rain gear and extra layers. **Public cabins ❷,** located throughout the forests and on several islands, sleep 4 to 8; they also have tables and wood stoves, but no water, electricity, or mattresses. (Reserve at ☎ 877-444-6777; www.reserveusa.com. $25-45.) The **Ranger Stations** in the area are your best bet for info on trail conditions and public cabins (see **Visitor Information,** p. 503).

HIKING

The **Exit Glacier** area of **Kenai Fjords National Park** (see p. 506) provides several hikes of varying degrees of difficulty. Lost Lake, Resurrection Pass and Johnson Pass may all be snowed in on their upper stretches well into July. Be sure to check the conditions and pack accordingly before heading out. For detailed topos of these and other shorter hikes, the **Kenai National Wildlife Refuge Topo** is an excellent, waterproof guide ($10 at the Portage Glacier Visitor Center; see p. 482).

Caines Head Trail (5 mi., several hours with an optional overnight). Turn right at the end of 3rd. Ave. and follow the gravel road for 3 mi. to Lowell Point. This popular trail weaves its way along the coastal beaches of Resurrection Bay for 5 mi., ending at the mouth of Seward's bay. 2½ mi. past Caine's Head's north beach, trailheads lead to the abandoned Fort McGilvary. After 1½ mi., there is a 2½ mi. stretch negotiable only at low tide. Most hikers stay overnight before returning in order to catch the next low tide. Several attractions lie on side trails; check your map carefully. Moderate.

Mt. Marathon (4-5hr.). From 1st Ave. and Jefferson St., take Lowell St. to reach the trail, which begins with a steep ascent up a stream bed. You don't need to be half-crazy (see **Races,** above) to get to the top. There is a more pedestrian, although still strenuous, route that leads to a glorious view of the sea and surrounding mountains. Strenuous.

Lost Lake Trail (16 mi., 1-2 days). The north trailhead is at Mile 17 of the Seward Hwy. Follow signs to Primrose Campground. An extremely pretty dayhike or overnight trip, leading the hiker through dense forest and alpine meadows before heading back down to Seward. It's best to stretch the views out with an overnight stay in the hills. The trail is open to mountain bikers in the summer and cross-country skiers in the winter. Strenuous.

Resurrection Pass Trail (39 mi., 3-5 days). North trailhead: turn south at Mile 16.2 of the Hope Hwy. on Palmer Cr. Rd. Take the right fork onto Resurrection Cr. Rd. and continue 4 mi. to trailhead. South Trailhead: head to Sterling Hwy. Mile 52. A local favorite—expect to see an eighth of Anchorage's population along this trail on any given Saturday. Leads to several public-use cabins and designated campsites. Easy.

Johnson Pass Trail (23 mi., 2-3 days). The north trailhead starts at Seward Hwy. Mile 64; go south on a gravel road ¼ mi. to the trailhead. The south trailhead lies at Seward Hwy. Mile 32.5. The trail, which starts steeply and then levels off, provides an ideal way to view different Kenai Peninsula ecosystems as it passes through a spruce forest, rises into shrubby subalpine regions, and finally extends into alpine tundra. Moderate.

FISHING AND MUSHING

Silver and King salmon can be caught before they hit their freshwater streams, while the deep ocean supports halibut, ling cod, black bass, red snapper, and other bottom dwellers. Pricey charters are the best way to go after these fish, although salmon can be caught from the shore. For fishing information, call the **Fish House** (see **Equipment Rental**); they have the skinny on salmon runs, gear rental, charter outfits and prices. (☎224-3674. $130 for a half-day salmon charter, $170 full-day halibut or salmon charters, $225 for a combined salmon/halibut day.) The annual **Silver Salmon Derby** creates a splash for nine days starting on the 2nd Saturday in August. The elusive tagged fish is worth $100,000; no one has caught it since 1980, when Japanese tourist Katsumi Takaku nabbed it from the city docks (☎224-8051). You can also try your luck at the longer **Seward Jackpot Halibut Tournament,** which runs from mid-May to August with weekly prizes for the largest fish (☎224-8051).

To reach **IdidaRide Sled Dog Tours,** turn left on Exit Glacier Rd. at Seward Hwy. Mile 3.7, continue 3½ mi., take a right on Old Exit Glacier Rd., and follow the signs for the next half-mile. IdidaRide's owner competes in the Iditarod every year—you can provide deadweight to help train his dogs in the summer. (☎224-8607 or 800-478-3139. Full tour 1¼hr.; 5 daily; $39, under 12 $19. Kennel tour $20, children $10.)

KENAI FJORDS NATIONAL PARK ☎907

Kenai Fjords National Park is dominated by the Harding Icefield, which covers over half of its 607,805 acres and spills 32 frozen rivers out into the Gulf of Alaska along one of the most stunning stretches of coast in the world. This icefield, thousands of feet thick, has engulfed over 60 mi. of mountain range in its slow recession, calving massive blocks of ice into waters teeming with otters, porpoises, whales, and hundreds of bird species. The wildlife alone is enough to warrant an extended stay among these icy waters, which are sadly not navigable to the novice kayaker. The lay traveler can revel in the park's glory by foot, tour boat, or plane.

HIKING

Hikes begin at **Exit Glacier,** the only road-accessible route into the park, 9 mi. west of Mile 3.7 of the Seward Hwy. A **shuttle** runs here four times per day from downtown Seward (☎224-5770; $20 round-trip), and the park entrance fee is good for a week ($5 per car, $2 on foot). From the **Ranger Station** at the end of the road, a leisurely half-mile stroll leads to the outlandishly blue glacier. The first quarter-mile is wheelchair-accessible. Rangers lead free, leisurely 45 min. **guided glacier walks.**

The **Harding Ice Field Trail** begins at the parking lot on a paved trail, and climbs 3000 ft. over 4 mi. to a storm shelter, and just a bit farther to an astonishing view of the **Harding Ice Field.** The glimmering 300 sq. mi. of ice is 3000-5000 ft. deep in some places and the source for dozens of glaciers. The trail is steep and often muddy or snow-covered, depending on conditions. Good boots with gaiters and a walking stick are recommended. If you still want to touch the ice, but can do without the incredible incline, try the more moderate quarter-mile **Overlook Trail,** which starts where the paved trail ends and provides direct access to the glacier.

TOURS

Boat cruises are the easiest way to see the park. All companies run basically the same trips, the difference being the size of the boat and the quality of food included. The longest and most expensive cruises access either **Aialik Bay** or the **Northwestern Fjord.** Both routes pass forested islands full of seabirds, and coastal mountains striped with waterfalls and streams. The half-day cruises seek wildlife inside Resurrection Bay. **Kenai Fjords Tours** are informative. (☎224-8068 or 800-478-8068; www.kenaifjords.com. To **Holgate Glacier,** 6hr.; $109, children $54. **Northwestern Fjord,** 9½hr.; $149, children $69.) **Major Marine Tours** brings along a ranger and serves the best all-you-can-eat salmon and prime rib buffet on the water for $12. (☎224-8030 or 800-764-7300. To **Holgate Glacier** $109, children $54.) Both companies also offer a variety of tours within Resurrection Bay, including overnights, and it pays to shop around for just the right type of trip (the cheapest start at $54.) Pick up a list of charters at the Chamber of Commerce or **The Fish House** (see **Fishing and Mushing,** p. 506). **Scenic Mountain Air** skims over the crevasses of the glaciers and soars high above the ice field. (☎288-3646 or 224-9152. 45min. tours from $79, 1hr. tours from $129 per person. Air taxi and drop-off service also available.)

KAYAKING

Experienced kayakers can water taxi to islands and cabins. Contact the rangers in Seward for advice and resources. **Sunny Cove Sea Kayaking** offers a joint trip with **Kenai Fjords Tours,** including the wildlife cruise, a salmon bake, kayaking instruction, and a 2½hr. wilderness paddle. (☎224-8810 or 800-770-9119; www.sunnycove.com. 8hr. $149-169.) **Kayak and Custom Adventures Worldwide** leads trips that include paddling instruction, and rents kayaks to the experienced. (☎258-3866 or 800-288-3134; www.KayakAK.com. Singles $35 per day, doubles $45.)

HOMER ☎907

Oh, how we all long to live among the unfettered and unemployed, a combination which suits the amiable population of this smoky little town quite well. If you descend upon Homer from the Sterling Hwy., glimpses of misty mountains and crackling glaciers give way to the Gulf of Alaska, which draws a large portion of Homer's population out each day for commercial and sport fishing. With more halibut charters than you can shake a stick at, and one of most active fishing ports in Alaska, you'd expect a salty, calloused folk. Quite the contrary, the other half lives in suspended 1960s animation, feeding a thriving community in a strange union of counterculture and working folk. So stay for the fish, or stay for the feel; either way, Homer may keep you longer than you expect.

✳ ⊏ ORIENTATION AND TRANSPORTATION

Surrounded by 400 million tons of coal, Homer rests on **Kachemak "Smokey" Bay,** named for the mysteriously burning deposits that first greeted settlers. The town is on the southwestern coast of **Kenai Peninsula,** on the north shore of the bay, and extends into the bay along an improbable 5 mi. tendril of sand, gravel, and RVs known as **the Spit.** The rugged, beautiful wilds and hiking trails of **Kachemak Bay State Park** lie across the bay, where the southern end of the **Kenai Mountains** reaches the sea. Also on the south side of the bay is the artist/fishing colony of **Halibut Cove,** the sparsely populated **Yukon Island,** the **Gull Island** bird rookery, and the Russian-founded town of **Seldovia** (see p. 532).

Across the Kenai peninsula, 226 mi. from Anchorage, the **Sterling Hwy.** (Hwy. 1) becomes the **Homer Bypass** as it enters downtown Homer. The Sterling changes names again to become **Ocean Dr.** and then veers right in its final transformation into the **Homer Spit Rd.** as it moves out into the bay. The walk from downtown to the Spit takes more than an hour. Reports say hitching is easy, but *Let's Go* doesn't recommend it. Biking is also an option; paths run parallel to most roads.

Homer

🏠🏠 ACCOMMODATIONS
Intl. Backpackers Hostel, 6
Karen Hornaday Park, 1
Seaside Farm, 2
Spit Municipal Camping, 13
The Sport Shed, 11
Sunspin Guest House, 3

🍴 FOOD
Finn's Pizza, 10
Don Jose's, 5
Sourdough Bakery, 8
Two Sisters Bakery, 7
Homer Brewing Co., 9

🍺 NIGHTLIFE
Alice's Champagne Palace, 4
The Salty Dawg, 12

Flights: Era Aviation (☎800-866-8394) flies to **Anchorage** (6 per day, one-way $95-120). **Homer Air** (☎235-8591) flies to **Seldovia** (15min., many per day, round-trip $55). **Smokey Bay Air,** 2100 Kachemak Dr. (☎235-1511), flies to Seldovia just about hourly (round-trip $55). Both **Homer** and **Smokey Bay Air** are located ½ mi. down Kachemak Dr., the 1st left at the beginning of the Spit Rd.

Buses: Homer Stage Line, 1242 Ocean Dr. (☎235-2252), next to Quicky Mart. To **Anchorage** (5½hr.; 1 per day M-Sa; $48, round-trip $85), **Seward** (4hr.; M, W, and F; $40, round-trip $75), and **Soldotna** (1½hr.; 1 per day M-Sa; $28, round-trip $45). $5 extra for drop-off at Anchorage Airport. Runs regularly Memorial Day to Labor Day with decreased service continuing in the off season.

Ferries: Alaska Marine Highway (☎235-8449 or 800-642-0066). Office and terminal just before the end of the Spit. To **Kodiak** 9½hr.; Su, M, Tu; round-trip $108); **Seldovia** (1½hr., Tu, round-trip $42); and once per month to **Dutch Harbor** in the Aleutian Islands (1 week, round-trip $542). Open M-Sa 7am-5pm and when ferry is in port.

Taxis: Chux Taxi (☎235-2489). To downtown from the airport ($5) or ferry ($10).

Car Rental: Polar, at the airport (☎235-5998 or 800-876-6417 until 9pm). Economy size $56 per day, $0.33 per mi. after 100 mi., 7th day free. Must be 21+ with credit card and insurance. Open daily 7:15am-9:30pm.

🔁 PRACTICAL INFORMATION

Tourist Information: (☎235-7740; www.homeralaska.org), near Main St. Local and long-distance courtesy phone. Be sure to pick up the Chamber of Commerce's exceptionally useful visitor's guide. Open June-Labor Day M-F 9am-8pm, Sa-Su 10am-6pm; Labor Day-May M-F 9am-5pm.

Outdoor Information: Alaska Maritime National Wildlife Refuge Visitor Center, 509 Sterling Hwy. (☎235-6961), next to the Best Western Bidarka Inn. Leads 1hr. bird and tide pool walks twice per week and shows videos upon request. Open May-Sept. daily 9am-5pm. **Southern District Ranger Station** (☎235-7024), 4 mi. out of town on the Sterling Hwy. has info on the park across the bay. Catch 'em when they're open F-Su 1-6pm. Call first in winter. **Fishing licenses** ($10 for 1 day, $20 for 3 days) available from many local stores. **Alaska Department of Fish and Game,** 3298 Douglas St. (☎235-8191), near Owen Marine, behind Peninsula Tire. Open M-F 8am-5pm.

Equipment Rental:

Chain Reaction (☎235-0750), in the Lakeside Mall. Bikes $15 per half-day, $25 per full-day. Open M-Sa 9am-6pm.

Sportsman's Supplies (☎235-2617), past the Fishing Hole. Rents salmon and halibut rods ($10 per 24hr.) and clamming gear ($5 a day). Open M-F 7am-9pm, Sa-Su 7-10pm.

The Sport Shed (☎235-5562), on the Spit, also rents bikes ($5 per half-day, $10 per full-day), salmon rods ($10 per day), and halibut rods ($15 per day), all free to those staying overnight (see **Accommodations,** below). Open in summer daily 5:30am-10pm.

Work Opportunities: Alaska State Employment Service, 270 W Pioneer Ave. (☎235-7791; www.jobs.state.ak.us/jobseeker). Open M-F 8:30am-noon and 1-5pm.

ATM: Eagle Quality Center (24hr.; see **Food,** below). **Salty Dawg Saloon,** on the Spit, and several banks around town.

Laundromat and Public Showers: East End Laundry, near Seaside Farm on East End Rd., just before the Tesoro. Wash $3.25, dry $0.25 for 7min. Showers $4 for 7min. Open May-Oct. daily 8am-9pm; Nov.-Apr. 8am-8pm. **The Washboard,** 1204 Ocean Dr., before the Spit. (☎235-6781). Wash $2.75, dry $0.25 for 7min. Their cozy, private shower rooms are $4.50, including towel. Open daily 7am-10pm.

Weather: ☎235-5600.

Emergency: ☎911.

Police: 4060 Heath St. (☎235-3150), off Pioneer Ave.

Women's Crisis Line: 3776 Lake St. (☎235-7712 or 235-8101 after hours). Open M-F 8:30am-5pm.

Hospital: South Peninsula Hospital, 4300 Bartlett (☎235-8101), off Pioneer St.

Internet Access: Free 30min. per day at the **Library,** 141 Pioneer Ave. (☎235-3180), near Main St. Open M, W, and F-Sa 10am-6pm, Tu and Th 10am-8pm.

Post Office: (☎235-6129), off Homer Bypass. Open M-F 8:30am-5pm, Sa noon-2pm. General delivery only held for 10 days. **Postal Code:** 99603.

ACCOMMODATIONS AND CAMPING

Affordable accommodations are not hard to come by in Homer. **The Bookie** (☎888-335-1581) and the **Homer's Finest B&B Network** (☎800-764-3211) can aid you in your search, as there is an endless supply of **B&Bs ④** in the $70-90 range. A few of the stores on the Spit have rooms for rent. At about $75, these tiny havens afford great views of the harbor, ocean, and surrounding mountains, not to mention a stellar location. Call the Chamber of Commerce for listings (☎235-7740).

Seaside Farm, 58335 E End Rd. (☎235-7850 or 235-2670), 4½ mi. (a $9 cab ride) out of town. Enjoy a covered outdoor common area, kitchen, hammock, and international visitors around the campfire. Sometimes you can trade work for lodging (1hr. of work, tent space; 2hr., bunk). Open May-Labor Day. Bunks $15. Tent sites $6. Private cabins $55. Discounts available for extended stays. ①

The Sport Shed (☎235-5562), on the Spit, across from the Fishing Hole. Large oceanfront studio apartments sleep 6. A great deal for larger groups or extended stays. Free bike and fishing rod guest loans. $100 per day, $85 for multi-days, $470 per week. ⑤

International Backpacker's Hostel/Inn (☎235-1463), on Pioneer near Pratt Museum. Attractive bunks and a common area with a stupendous view of the Spit and mountains. Internet and laundry facilities available. Bunks $18; private doubles $50. ②

Sunspin Guest House, 358 Lee Dr. (☎235-6677 or 800-391-6677). From Pioneer Ave., take Kachemak Way toward the bluff to Lee Dr. on the left. Convenient to downtown. Clean and warm decor. Beds with linens $30, private room with breakfast $75. ③

Karen Hornaday Park, within 1 mi. of downtown. From Pioneer St., go uphill on Bartlett St., left on Fairview, right on Campground Rd. Most sites grassy, secluded, and spacious. Water, pit toilets, and a great playground. Tents $6, RVs $10. ①

Spit Municipal Camping, 3735 Homer Spit Rd. (☎235-1583). Registration is at the booth across the road. Terrific views and tent-shaking winds make this a unique spot. Water, toilets. Tents $6, $36 per week; RVs $10, $60 per week. ①

FOOD

Homer provides ample opportunity to escape the hamburger and fries or fish and chips doldrums of the rest of the peninsula. Both the variety and the quality provide welcome refreshment. For groceries, try the huge **Eagle Quality Center,** 90 Sterling Hwy. (☎235-2408. 24hr.) **Smoky Bay Natural Foods,** 248 W Pioneer Ave., has outstanding produce. (☎235-7252. Open daily 10am-7pm.) Fresh seafood can be purchased retail or directly from fishing boats; check around for prices. A good deal is about $7 per lb. for salmon and halibut. After a long day of fishing, head to the **Homer Brewing Company,** 1411 Lakeshore Dr., for free samples of local brews like Broken Birch Bitter. (☎235-3626. Open M-Sa 11am-8pm, Su noon-6pm.)

UPS AND DOWNS OF LIFE ON THE SPIT

On July 1st, 1998, the Homer Spit suffered one of the worst disasters since it sank 30 ft. in the '64 Good Friday quake. At Icicle Seafood's processing plant, an ammonia leak and a pilot flame combined to blow the roof 30 ft. in the air—momentarily restoring it to its former height. Luckily, there were no casualties, but the Spit was closed down for three days. Hundreds of cannery workers lost jobs they'd only had since the day before. The result was a massive party the night of the disaster. The plant has yet to be rebuilt, and the question of whether or not to do so will affect Homer in the coming years. Will a steady stream of young college students hard-up for cash still flock here? Time will tell, and in the meantime, Homer's salmon and halibut will breathe that much easier.

■ **Two Sisters Bakery,** 106 W Bunnell St. (☎235-2280), off Main St. near the water. A meeting place for artists, the wayward, and locals. A cinnamon bun and coffee ($3.50) will get you going in the morning. Steaming bowls of soup ($5.50) warm the body on damp, cool days. Open M-F 7am-4pm, Sa 7am-2pm. ❶

■ **Sourdough Bakery,** 1301 Ocean Dr. (☎235-7571). You may think you're full after a tasty meal here, but one look at the baked goods will start you salivating for more. Sandwiches from $7.50, sweet rolls $4. Open daily 7am-9pm. ❷

Don Jose's Restaurant and Cantina, 127 Pioneer Rd. (☎235-7963). Spice up your life with the huge portions offered here. With an array of Mexican, Italian and American dishes, Don Jose's satisfies even the pickiest eater. Seafood lovers should try the crab enchiladas ($13). Lunches from $7, dinners from $10. Open daily 11am-10:30pm. ❹

Finn's Pizza (☎235-2840), on the Spit across from the Harborview Boardwalk. This small restaurant nestled among the charters offers gourmet wood-fired pizza by the slice ($3) or whole (12 in., $9). Open in summer daily noon-10pm. ❷

👁 SIGHTS AND EVENTS

SIGHTS. The ■**Pratt Museum** has been called one of the best museums of its size in the country and holds an impressive display of local art and artifacts, with displays on homesteader cabins, the oil spill, arts of the Inuit and Denali peoples, and marine mammals. Check out the live video feed of the McNeal bears during salmon season. (3779 Bartlett St. ☎235-8635. Open Mar.-Sept. daily 10am-6pm; Oct.-Dec. and Feb.-Apr. Tu-Su noon-5pm. $6, seniors $5.50, under 18 $3.) The **Center for Alaskan Coastal Studies,** 708 Smokey Bay Way, off Lake St. across from Lakeside Mall, has a small exhibit on marine life and offers natural history and seabird tours across Kachemak Bay in conjunction with the **Carl E. Wynn Nature Center** on East Skyline Drive. The Nature Center also offers a free **Thursday Evening Lecture Series** from late June to August at 7pm. (☎235-6667. Open M-F 10am-5pm.)

EVENTS. Homer is often billed as the Halibut Capital of the World, and the **Homer Jackpot Halibut Derby** is responsible for a lot of that hoopla. The competition runs from May 1 to Labor Day, and offers over $150,000 in prize money. Pull up a tagged fish and you can win from $500 to $10,000. Tickets ($10) are available in local charter offices on the Spit. Homer is blessed each year with an enormous seabird migration, and even more fortunate to bring all those bird-watchers together for the **Homer Shorebird Festival** (☎235-7337), during the second week in May, for educational workshops and other exciting events. On the last Sunday in July, KBBI (☎235-7721) stages the fabulous all-day **Homer Folk Festival** at the town commons, featuring blues, rock, and bluegrass.

CENTRAL ALASKA

⚑ OUTDOOR ACTIVITIES

FISHING. As many as 90 halibut charter boats leave the Spit each day. Choosing one, like fishing itself, can be a crap shoot; still, most charter companies are reputable businesses. Expect to pay around $170 for a full-day charter with all tackle and bait included. Half-day charters run about $85. You can book a boat through **Central Charters** (☎235-7847), near the middle of the Spit, but your best bet is to ask around. **The Bookie** can take care of charters, too, but keep in mind that booking outfits only advertise for companies that are in contract with them. They also book kayak trips, flightseeing, and lodgings at no charge. (☎235-1581 or 888-335-1581. Open in summer daily 6am-9pm; phone service in winter.) If you're without cash and want to chase the big ones, check the **fishing hole** near the start of the Spit for salmon. Ask around to see what lure to use and observe people who've bagged a fish for technique. Salmon can also be hooked at the end of the Spit, off the beach beyond the Land's End Hotel; ask if they're running when renting gear.

HIKING. The best **hiking** is across the bay at **Kachemak Bay State Park** (see below). In and around Homer, take the moderate 6½ mi. **Homestead Trail,** which features jaw-dropping views of the Bay. Pick up a trail guide from the visitors center or the maritime center to better identify the arctic star flowers, marsh violets, green rein orchids, and other wildflowers that bloom along the way. The trail is accessible from any of three points: take Roger's Loop Rd. off the Sterling across from the Bayview Inn, to the marked trailhead sign; take Diamond Ridge Rd. off West Hill Rd. to the trail sign; or drive past the reservoir on Skyline Dr. off West Hill to a parking lot and trail sign. Another trail near town is the **Calvin and Coyle Nature Trail,** a part of the Kachemak Heritage Land Trust that winds through the Beluga wetlands. Take East End Rd. a mile out of town and turn right on Mariner Dr. to reach the trailhead. With miles of coastline to explore, **beach walks** are a great way to get around and enjoy the view. Walking west from **Bishop's Beach Park,** you can stroll by a sea otter rookery at Mile 3. Head downhill on Main, turn left at Bunnell, and then turn right on Beluga to get to the parking lot.

OTHER ADVENTURES. **Midnight Sun Ultralight** gives an open-air, eagle's eye view of Homer and surroundings while flying their "trike," or Ultralight aircraft. (☎399-4253. 30min flight $60, 60min. flight $90; both include instruction and warm gear.) For a horse of a different color, take a ride of the four-legged kind. **Trails End Horse Adventures,** at 53435 East End Rd., offers trail rides ($20 per hr.), half-day ($65) and full-day trips ($110) and pack trips around the hills and beaches of Homer. (☎235-6393. Call for a quote on the pack trips.)

♫ ▥ ENTERTAINMENT AND NIGHTLIFE

Check the *Homer News* for live theater and other performance schedules. With a healthy mixture of young wanderers and salty fishermen, Homer nightlife can range from the late to the absurdly late and absurd as there is no enforced curfew. The ⬛**Salty Dawg Saloon,** under the log lighthouse near the end of the Spit, is something of an Alaskan landmark with sawdust-covered floors and long communal tables that breed tall tales and encourage arm wrestling. (☎235-9990. Open 11am-whenever.) **Alice's Champagne Palace,** 196 Pioneer Ave., is a wooden barn that hosts live music W-Sa. See Alaska's pride, **Hobo Jim,** rock the house every Wednesday night as old and young dance like fools and yell along to down-home Alaskan tunes. (☎235-7650. Pints $4, pool $0.75. No cover. Open M-Sa 2pm-5am.)

NEAR HOMER: KACHEMAK BAY STATE PARK

Kachemak Bay State Park, Alaska's first, is one of the largest coastal parks in the country. It contains 375,000 acres of beaches, 90 mi. of trails, tide pools, mountains, glaciers, and one of the northernmost temperate rainforests in the world. The **Grewink Glacier Trail,** one of the easiest hikes in the park, winds through tall stands of spruce and cottonwood up to the glacier's lake and outwash. With the right winds, you might even be able to snag a passing iceberg. The trail begins north of Glacier Spit at the east end of Kachemak Bay, and the 6½ mi. round-trip can easily be hiked in 2-3hr. If you're up for outstanding views of Kachemak Bay, the **China Poot Peak Trail** offers a stout outing, climbing over 2000 ft. from shore to skyline. Only experienced and equipped climbers should continue up the 500 ft. summit spur from the rocky bench at the "Lower Summit." The trail begins at China Poot Lake. Allow for 3-5hr. of strenuous hiking on its 4½ mi. round-trip. Public use **cabins ❸** are available in **Halibut Cove Lagoon, China Poot Bay,** and **Tutka Bay** for $50 per night. All cabins sleep six and have water, pit toilets, and woodburning stoves. The Halibut Cove Lagoon East cabin is also wheelchair-accessible. More information about the park and cabin reservations can be obtained by calling the Division of Parks office at ☎262-5581. The only way to access the park is via water or air taxi. **Inlet Charters** (☎235-6126 or 800-770-6126), on the Spit across from the harbormaster, books trips with several water taxi companies. **Mako's Water Taxi** (☎235-9055; www.makoswatertaxi.com) charges around $50 per person for the round-trip. The park's trail system winds around indefinitely, so pick up the **hiking trails** pamphlet ($1) at the visitors center for more options.

Rainbow Tours offers **whale watching** tours through Kachemak Bay, past **Gull Island,** home to murres, cormorants, guillemots, puffins, and a zillion gulls, and down to Lower Cook Inlet. (☎235-7272. Tours 10am-5pm, $75; 9am-6pm, $125, lunch included.) **Mako's** also rents kayaks only for use on the non-Homer side of the bay; for experienced sea kayakers only. (Single, $85 per day; double $150. Prices include round-trip taxi from the spit.) Guided **sea kayak** tours are available to many destinations in the Park from a few companies, including **Mako's** (☎235-9055), **St. Augustine's Kayak and Tours** (☎235-7568), and **True North Kayak Adventures** (☎235-0708. For all businesses, half-day tours $75-$120; full-day tours $135-$180.)

KATMAI NATIONAL PARK

AT A GLANCE

AREA: 3,674,529 acres.	**HIGHLIGHTS:** Seeing the Novarupta Volcano (p. 515), watching brown bears fish for salmon (p. 515).
CLIMATE: Maritime, continental, transitional; in short, variable.	
FEATURES: Valley of Ten Thousand Smokes, a large and active brown bear population.	**GATEWAYS:** Brooks Camp (p. 514), King Salmon (p. 514).
	FEES: $10 if you want to see the bears.

Words cannot adequately explain the haunting emptiness left in the wake of the Novarupta Volcano's 1912 eruption. On June 6, the 20th century's largest volcanic upheaval began, and it didn't stop for 60hr. A 25 mi. column of ash shot violently out of the earth, and a wave of semi-molten rock, gas, and steam charged down the valley at 100 mph. Dr. Robert Griggs visited the valley four years later on a National Geographic expedition, only to be stunned by the sight of a river of ash, in some places hundreds of feet deep and "full of hundreds, no thousands— literally tens of thousands—of smokes curling up from its fissured floor." So the

Valley of Ten Thousand Smokes was christened, and Griggs successfully convinced President Woodrow Wilson to declare Katmai a national monument in 1918.

As amazing as the Valley of Ten Thousand Smokes is, many people come to Katmai without seeing it. They come, instead, to **Brooks Camp**, 23 mi. from the valley, to see the region's chief draw: brown bears. Katmai's bears are drawn to her shores and streams for the same reason commercial fishers crowd Bristol Bay each season—sockeye salmon. The largest sockeye (red) salmon run in the world charges up the bay's six rivers each year, providing an abundant food source for the bears who comb the banks of the Brooks River. The bear-viewing platform (☎486-8380. Open M-Sa 11am-6pm.) allows visitors to watch up to 20 bears at a time. The facilities are open June 1-September 17. Use of the backcountry is free, although a $10 **day-use fee** is required for visitors taking advantage of Brooks Camp bear-watching and camping facilities (see below). To find out more, stop at the **Alaska Public Lands Info Center** in Anchorage (☎271-2737; see p. 473), or contact the park for a free info packet. (☎246-3305; www.nps.gov/katm.) The visitors center in King Salmon is helpful, as are the rangers at Brooks Camp. Jean Bodeau's *Katmai* ($15), available at Cook Inlet Book Co. in Anchorage (see p. 473) and at the King Salmon visitors center, is a comprehensive guide to the park's trails.

KING SALMON   ☎907

Though King Salmon, 300 mi. from Anchorage and 20 mi. from Brooks Camp, is the gateway to Katmai National Park, many travelers going to Katmai spend little time here. Both King Salmon and nearby Naknek (12 mi. west) are home to the world's largest sockeye (red) salmon fishery out of Bristol Bay. Every year, the six rivers flowing into the bay are flooded by the run and the accompanying commercial boats. The **King Salmon Visitors Center,** by the airport, is a great source of info for Katmai and the King Salmon area, with a rich library and 60 wildlife videos. (☎246-4250. Open May-Sept. daily 8am-5pm; Nov.-Apr. M-F 9am-5pm.) The **King Salmon Mall** opposite the airport has a **24hr. ATM** in the **Wells Fargo Bank.** The **King Ko Inn** runs a **laundromat** and **public showers** across from its trailer annex. (☎246-3377. Wash $2.50, dry $0.25 per 4min. Untimed showers $5 with soap and towel. Open Mar.-Oct. 24hr.) **Camai Medical Center** (☎246-6155), in Naknek, is just before the Naknek post office. **Internet access** can be had for $0.20 per minute at the **King Salmon Cafe** (see below). The **post office** is 2 mi. west of the airport. (☎246-3396. Open M-F 8am-4:30pm, Sa 9:30-11am.) **Postal Code:** 99613.

If you need a place to crash, 160-acre **Dave's World ❶** will do the trick. (☎246-3353. Sites $8, plus a $5 round-trip ferry ride across the river.) Another **camping ❶** option is to pitch a tent where the seasonal fishermen camp while waiting for outbound flights, in the wooded area just across the road from the airport. Cheap beds are almost nonexistent in King Salmon, but Dave has a few **cabins ❷** for rent. ($25 per person.) The **A C Value Center** is a small grocery with the basics (☎246-6109). **King Salmon Cafe ❷** (☎246-2233), in the Mall, is a hidden treasure with reasonably priced, incredibly satisfying fare.

BROOKS CAMP   ☎907

Brooks Camp provides direct access to Katmai National Park. Upon arriving, visitors need to check in at the **Park Service Visitor Center.** (Open daily 7am-6:30pm.) Several flight companies have packages to get you to Brooks, and all operators charge about the same amount for King Salmon-Brooks Camp flights ($140 round-trip). **Alaska Airlines** (☎800-426-0333) and **Pen Air** (☎800-448-4226) operate in a partnership here and fly five or six times a day to King Salmon from Anchorage (1hr.; fares vary from $360 to 500, so advance purchase is recommended). **Katmai Air** (☎800-544-0551) offers packages from Anchorage to Brooks, via King Salmon

($490 round-trip). **C-Air** (☎246-6318), **Katmai Air,** and **Branch River Air** make the run from King Salmon to Brooks Camp ($140 round-trip).

Katmailand ❺ rents pricey cabins that are almost always full. (☎243-5448 or 800-544-0551. $116 per person for 4 people.) **Brooks Campground ❶** technically holds 60 people, but this may entail sharing a tent site with another group. The campground is enclosed by an electric fence; it also has potable water, outhouses, food caches, and shelters for cooking in the rain. Call for advance reservations and to secure **day use permits.** (☎800-365-2267. Permits $10. Sites $6. Showers $5.) The antler-adorned **Brooks Lodge ❺** has a large stone fireplace and serves buffet-style breakfast ($12), lunch ($14), and dinner ($22). The bar serves Alaskan Amber (pints $4.75). Hot beverages cost $1.50. (Open 4pm-1am.)

◢ OUTDOOR ACTIVITIES IN THE PARK

THE VALLEY OF TEN THOUSAND SMOKES. Currently, the Katmailand **bus tour** is the only way to get to the valley. Trips fill up and should be booked ahead. (Bus leaves daily at 9am and returns at 4:30pm. $79 with bagged lunch, $72 without, $42 one-way.) A 23 mi. scenic dirt road into the park, ending at the **Three Forks Overlook Cabin,** offers an amazing view of the valley including **Baked Mt.** and **Mt. Katmai.** Upon arrival, a park service ranger gives talks on area ecology and geology and leads a 2hr. hike down the 1½ mi. Ukak Falls trail. If you plan on biking, let the bus service know ahead of time and they'll work out a way to give you a ride out and back. The unlocked ranger cabin at the end of the road has emergency supplies, a bunk, and a scrapbook with great pictures and articles about the valley.

From the end of the bus ride, Katmai really needs several days to be fully appreciated. One trail leading into the Valley begins from the right side of the road a half-mile before the ranger cabin. It begins on a relatively steep descent through alders and willows and then opens up into the great ashen valley. The trail crosses **Windy River,** which is luckily a shallow stream. The flat trail through soft ash and pumice along the hauntingly beautiful **River Lethe** leads to a perfect camping spot. The trail disappears in the valley, but orientation isn't a problem because of peaks on either side. A ranger cabin on **Baked Mt.** can offer shelter from high winds and blowing ash, but you'll be kicked around quite a bit, so make sure your tent can handle it. **Novarupta Volcano** (site of the 1912 explosion) is 13 mi. back and within range of **Mt. Katmai,** which sunk in the eruption, creating **Crater Lake** in its caldera.

If you only have a day in the valley, try the **Ukak Falls Trail,** a 3 mi. round-trip with 700 ft. of elevation loss and gain. The only established trail from the cabin, it leads down to the falls and views of the gorge. A short, flat, quarter-mile side trail offers an eerie view of the Windy River, **Snake River,** and River Lethe confluence. The tour bus allows plenty of time for hikers to check out both routes; for an extended stay in the valley, bring eye protection and a handkerchief. Winds can be fierce and ash can kick up into black-outs, making hiking and set-up very difficult.

BEAR VIEWING. You could spend days at the bear-viewing platforms. Visitors must head to the **Brooks Camp Visitor Center** run by the Park Service for the mandatory video on how to behave in a bear-abundant environment. A trail leads from the Trading Post across a gated wooden bridge to the **Lower Platform;** check in with a ranger who will radio ahead to the falls platform before you set out.

The road goes a quarter-mile to a flat half-mile trail heading off on the right and turning into a raised, bear-safe walkway to the **Upper Falls Platform.** Let the viewing begin—nowhere else in the world can you see so many bears from so close and still be safe. There are ethical issues involved in erecting permanent structures along the banks of such a feeding ground, but the park service has chosen to localize the destruction of the area as much as possible.

HIKING. The only established trail from Brooks Camp, the moderate 4 mi. **Mt. Dumpling Trail,** leaves from the campground and encounters a steep initial 1½ mi. rise through a poplar forest. In late August, high brush cranberries frame a panoramic view of **Brooks Lake, Naknek Lake,** and **Iliuk Arm.** On a clear day, the route through alders and willows into the open tundra will reward you with a killer view of all the volcanic peaks in the valley. A round-trip to the first overlook at 1½ mi. takes 1½hr.; going to the trail's end at 2400 ft. takes 5-6hr. The quick and easy **cultural walk** covers about a half-mile before coming to a reconstructed *inna* ("dwelling" in Sugpiak-Alutiiq), housed in an unlocked cabin. Placards tell of the Dena'ina and Yupik peoples, who historically called this area home.

KODIAK ISLAND

In the 20th century alone, Kodiak Island was rocked by earthquakes, engulfed by *tsunamis,* coated in crude oil from the Exxon *Valdez,* and blanketed in nearly 2 ft. of volcanic ash. Despite this, much of the island is still covered in thick spruce forests dripping with moss, and Kodiak's peaks open up into wild, geranium-speckled meadows. Tiny islands and rock outcroppings jut from the whale-filled waters. As the site of the Kodiak National Wildlife Refuge, the island is home to more than 3000 Kodiak brown bears, the world's largest carnivorous land mammal. The refuge's 800 mi. of coastline encircle the island's sharp inland peaks, pushing Kodiak's human population onto the eastern shore. Rich surrounding waters have historically made the island's fishing fleet one of the most productive in the state, drawing young people each summer to work in its canneries.

KODIAK   ☎907

Pressing out on the eastern edge of the island, the town of Kodiak lives and dies by the sea. The island's lifeblood is and always will be the waters that surround it. The last 10 years have seen politics and regulations tie the hands of the fishing industry and cripple an economy that is vital to the survival of all coastal towns, Kodiak in particular. It has survived nonetheless, a testament to the strength and tenacity of its people. Cruise ships have begun to venture into port, and sports fishermen and adventure seekers are starting to discover the fish and wilderness.

�⬛ TRANSPORTATION

The city of Kodiak is on the eastern tip of Kodiak Island, 250 mi. south of Anchorage. Paved and rutted gravel roads run 100 mi. along scenic coastlines north and south of the city. **Chiniak Rd.,** which heads south for 42 mi., makes for an especially impressive trip. In town, the main drag is **Center St.,** which starts at the ferry terminal and heads inland, ending at the intersection with **Rezanof Dr.** to the left and **Lower Mill Bay Rd.** to the right. The cluster of downtown shops and most of the good restaurants are within a 5min. walk from the ferry.

Flights: The **airport** is 5 mi. southwest of town on Rezanof Dr. **Alaska Airlines** (☎800-252-7522) offers commuter service. **Era Aviation** (☎800-866-8394) flies to Anchorage (1hr.; 7 per day; $130-175, round-trip $250-350, check for web specials running F-M, posted weekly). **Island Air** (☎486-6196 or 800-478-6196) offers 4 flights per day to such Kodiak destinations as **Old Harbor** ($61) and **Larsen Bay** ($68).

Ferries: Alaska Marine Highway (☎486-3800 or 800-526-6731) ferries depart Kodiak May-Sept. 1-3 times per week, less often in winter. The terminal is next to the visitors bureau, on the waterfront. Open M-F 8am-5pm, Sa 8am-4pm, Su 8am-4pm, and when ferries are in. To **Homer** (9½hr., one-way $54), **Seward** (13hr., $59), and **Valdez** (29hr., $108). 5-day round-trip to the **Aleutian Islands** (1 per month, $222).

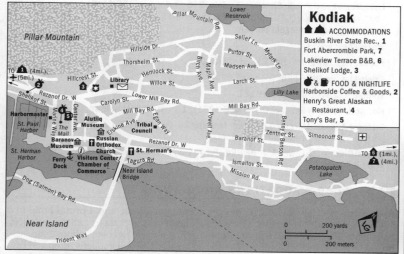

Kodiak

▲▲ ACCOMMODATIONS
Buskin River State Rec., 1
Fort Abercrombie Park, 7
Lakeview Terrace B&B, 6
Shelikof Lodge, 3

🍎&🍴 FOOD & NIGHTLIFE
Harborside Coffee & Goods, 2
Henry's Great Alaskan
    Restaurant, 4
Tony's Bar, 5

Taxis: A&B Taxi (☎486-4343). $3 base, $2 per mi.

Car Rental: Rent-a-Heap, at the airport (☎486-5220; open daily 6:30am-11pm) and downtown on the Mall (☎486-8550; open daily 9am-7pm). Rents cars for $38 per day, $0.35 per mi. 25+. **Avis** (☎487-2264) rents to those 21-25 for $64 per day.

🛈 PRACTICAL INFORMATION

Tourist Information: Kodiak Island Convention and Visitors Bureau, 100 Marine Way (☎486-4782; www.kodiak.org), in front of the ferry dock. Ask for their restaurant and lodging printouts or their guides on mountain biking ($4) and hiking ($5). Open summer M-F 8am-5pm, Sa-Su 10am-4pm; winter M-F 8am-noon and 1-5pm.

Outdoor Information: Fish and Wildlife Service and **National Wildlife Refuge Visitor Center,** 1390 Buskin River Rd. (☎487-2600), just outside Buskin State Recreation Site, 4 mi. southwest of town on Rezanof Dr. Wildlife displays, films, and info on Kodiak National Wildlife Refuge and its cabins. Excellent, free hiking guide. Open summer M-F 8am-7pm, Sa-Su noon-4:30; winter 8am-4:30pm. **State Department of Parks,** 1200 Abercrombie Dr. (☎486-6339), at Fort Abercrombie. Info on state parks, campgrounds, and public-use cabins on Shuyak Island and Afognak Island. Open M-F 8am-4:30pm.

Fishing Information: Alaska Department of Fish and Game, 211 Mission Rd. (☎486-1880). Open M-F 8am-4:30pm, closed noon-1pm. **Licenses** are available at local sporting goods stores.

Equipment Rental: 58° North, 1231 Mill Bay Rd. (☎486-6249), about 2 mi. from the ferry. Take Upper Mill Bay until it turns into Mill Bay. Rents bikes ($25 per 24hr.) and gear; great resource for hiking and biking trail info. Open M-Sa 11am-6pm. **Mack's Sports Shop,** 117 Lower Mill Bay Rd. (☎486-4276). Rods, guns, and advice. Rent rods for $15 a day plus $130 deposit. Open M-Sa 7am-7pm, Su 9am-5pm.

Banks: First National Bank on the corner of Center and Mill Bay has a **24hr. ATM,** as does the **First Union** at the inland end of Center Ave.

Work Opportunities: Alaska State Employment Service, 309 Center St. (☎486-3105), in Kodiak Plaza. First stop for fish-canners. Open M-F 8am-5pm.

Laundromat and Public Showers: Ernie's, 218 Shelikof (☎486-4119) opposite the harbor. Wash $3.25, dry $0.25 per 5min. Showers $5, towel $1.25. Open Su-Th 24hr., F until 9:30pm, open again Su 6am.

Emergency: ☎911.

Police: 217 Lower Mill Bay Rd. (☎486-8000).

Crisis Line: ☎486-3625.

Women's Crisis Line: ☎486-6171.

Hospital: 1915 W Rezanof Dr. (☎486-3281), 1 mi. northeast of town. On call 24hr.

Internet Access: Library, 319 Lower Mill Bay Rd. (☎486-8686). Free for 1hr. Open M-F 10am-9pm, Sa 10am-5pm, Su 1-5pm.

Post Office: 419 Lower Mill Bay Rd. (☎486-4721). Open M-F 9am-5:30pm. **Postal Code:** 99615.

🖪🖪 ACCOMMODATIONS AND CAMPING

Kodiak has no hostels, no true budget accommodations, and a brutal hotel tax (11% in town and 6% outside). There some cheap motels close by and several nice, somewhat affordable B&Bs farther out. Finding a room becomes almost impossible when the airport shuts down due to bad weather, which happens often and can make camping an unpleasantly wet experience. Some law-defiers pitch up on Near Island, but there is no free camping in town. The state runs two nice **campgrounds** (see below), but camping is perfectly silent and free on any trail outside of town.

🖪 **Lakeview Terrace B&B,** 2426 Spruce Cape Rd. (☎486-5135). Travel 2 mi. northeast of town at the bottom of Benny Benson Dr., on Mission Lake. Cable TV, shared bath, breakfast, and a playful dog. Singles $60; doubles $80. ❹

🖪 **Fort Abercrombie State Park** (☎486-6339), 4 mi. northeast of town on Rezanof-Monashka Rd. Built around the site of WWII cannon emplacements. The carpeted forest, dripping moss, ocean cliffs, and trout-stocked lake are worth the extra trek into town. Water, toilets, no RV sites. 7-night max. Open to motor traffic in summer only; walk-ins year-round. 13 sites, $10. ❶

Shelikof Lodge, 211 Thorsheim Ave. (☎486-4141), up the street to the right of McDonald's and 3 blocks from the ferry. Remodeled motel; green rooms with cable TV. Courtesy airport shuttle until 8pm. Singles $70; doubles $75. ❹

Buskin River State Recreation Site (☎486-6339), 4½ mi. southwest of town off Rezanof Dr. Water, pit toilets, RV dump station. Closer to the airport and the Buskin River, where over 50% of Kodiak's sport fish are caught. 14-night max. stay. 15 sites, $10. ❶

🖪🖪 FOOD AND NIGHTLIFE

Food is not Kodiak's strong suit. In fact, the several fast food options in town may appear especially tempting for lack of anything else. Groceries can be purchased 2 mi. from town at **Safeway,** 2685 Mill Bay Rd. (☎486-6811. Open daily 6am-midnight.) In the heart of town, **AC Value Center** also sells groceries. (☎486-5761. Open M-Sa 7am-10pm, Su 8am-8pm.) The bar scene in town is rowdy, between those out to escape the weather and Coast Guard troops from the nearby station; if action is your thing, Kodiak nights can dish it out.

🖪 **Martha's Place** (☎654-0752), could be anywhere, but always close to town. Ask any local where it is, and you'll soon be gorging yourself on a spicy steak burrito ($8.50) and wondering how you'll down that extra taco (from $3). Herbivores welcome, too. ❷

Harborside Coffee and Goods, 216 Shelikof (☎486-5862). Proximity to the harbor draws the summer fishing crowd. Tea comes in a big earthenware mug ($1). Soup and bread $4.50. Open M-Th 6:30am-9pm, F and Sa 6:30am-10pm, Su 7am-8pm. ❶

Henry's Great Alaskan Restaurant (☎486-8844), in the mall on Marine Way. The all-you-can-eat pork ribs dinner and pint of Alaskan Amber for $15 is a big winner. Lunch may be the best deal, with hot sandwiches and burgers from $8. Order up when the bell rings: someone just bought the house a round. Open M-Th 11:30am-9:30pm, F-Sa 11:30am-10:30pm, Su noon-9pm. Bar open until 11pm. ❷

Tony's Bar (☎486-9489), in the alley beside AC Center. Claims to be Kodiak's biggest navigational hazard with over a million drinks spilled in a friendly, laid-back atmosphere. Bottled beer $3-4, cocktails $4. Pool, darts, and a super bowling game. Live rock music F-Sa. Open daily 11am-2:30am. ❶

🆔 SIGHTS AND ENTERTAINMENT

▧ALUTIIQ MUSEUM AND ARCHAEOLOGICAL REPOSITORY. Artifacts dating to 4600 BC document the culture of the Alutiiq. The museum was built with restoration funds from the Exxon *Valdez* oil spill, and is supported by Alaska's native corporations. The Alutiiq building also doubles as the home-base for more than 800 archaeological expeditions on the island, attempting to piece together a rich heritage historically decimated by Russian fur traders, European explorers, and the American fishing industry. Visitors can volunteer to help on extensive archeological digs on Kodiak and neighboring islands during June and July. (*215 Mission Rd.* ☎*486–7004; www.alutiiqmuseum.com. Open M-F 9am-5pm, Sa 10am-5pm. $2, under 12 free.*)

BARANOV MUSEUM. Inside a building constructed in 1808 to store sea otter pelts, the museum is the oldest Russian structure standing in Alaska and the oldest wooden structure on the US West Coast. It displays a collection of Russian and Native Alaskan artifacts and a walrus skull complete with tusks. (*101 Marine Way, across from the visitors center.* ☎*486-5920. Open May to Sept. M-F 10am-4pm, Sa-Su noon-4pm; Oct. to April M-F 11am-3pm, Sa noon-3pm. $2; under 12 free.*)

FESTIVALS AND EVENTS. The five-day **Kodiak Crab Festival** celebrates a bygone industry with parades, fishing derbies, and kayak, bike, foot, crab, and survival-suit races. The festivities culminate with the **Chad Ogden Ultramarathon,** a superhuman race along 43 mi. of hilly roads from Chiniak to Kodiak. (☎*486-5557. May 25-29, 2003.*) The absurd **Pillar Mountain Golf Classic** is Alaska's answer to the Masters: one par-70 hole. The tee is at the base of Pillar Mountain; the snowy green is at the 1400 ft. summit. (*www.chiniak.net/pillar. March 29-31, 2003. $50 entry fee.*) The **Bear Country Music Festival** brings 100 rock, blues, jazz, Cajun, Russian, and world musicians together at the Kodiak Fairgrounds, from noon to 1:30am. (☎*486-6117. July 18-21, 2003. Tickets F $10, Sa $15; camping $10 for the weekend.*)

🏔 OUTDOOR ACTIVITIES

Largely due to a growing community of local enthusiasts, more varied and exciting outdoor options are sprouting up throughout the island. Where else in Alaska can you surf and ski in the same day, kayak among whales and otters along pristine coastal waters, or punish your body on miles of challenging mountain bike trails?

HIKING. Hikes around Kodiak generally come in one flavor: slog straight up though the pain of burning legs, and try not to injure yourself on the downhill flail. **Termination Point** (6 mi.) begins at the end of Monashka Bay Rd. and ends in the parking lot. There's no defined trailhead, but it would be difficult to get lost.

Easy, flat hiking offers a welcome respite to the legs. Cross the creek and head to the **beach**, where hikers can either stroll in the sand or on one of several paths that parallel the water. To hike **Barometer Mountain** (2 mi., 2hr.), head west out of town on Rezanof Dr., and take the first right past the end of the airport runway. The trail climbs steadily along a steep grassy ridge before arriving at the summit. On the rare clear day, the view at the top stretches from the Kenai Peninsula to the Alaska Peninsula. 2500 ft. gain. Strenuous.

FISHING. The island's 100 mi. road system gives access to several good **salmon streams.** In Kodiak, surfcasting into Mill Bay at high tide often yields a pink or silver from August to September. The **Buskin River,** just outside town, receives a good run of reds and silvers each year, and the fortunate baiter might pull a dolly varden or steelhead out. On the way to Pasagshak, the **American** has pinks, chum, and a late run of silvers. The **Pasagshak River** itself is a popular joint in that the rare king salmon gets lifted, along with a healthy supply of silvers and reds. For guided river fishing, check out the bargain that is **David's Family Guide Service,** with daytrips starting at $25 per person. Other options include the steeper-priced **Flyfish Kodiak** and **Salty Fly Safaris** ($125 for 8hr., all-inclusive trips). If you have waders, bring them or you may find yourself scrambling to **Mack's Sport Shop** (see **Practical Info,** above) for a pair. If the rivers beat you down, cast your flies into any of the lakes off the road system, all of which are stocked with trout by **Fish and Game** (many people do not know this, so keep quiet). The visitors center has brochures for **charter trips,** and the sporting goods stores give good advice.

KAYAKING AND ROCK CLIMBING. Guided **sea kayaking** trips will bring you eye-to-eye with sea otters, puffins, and bald eagles; on lucky days, you'll see giant Kodiak bears from a comfortable distance. **Kodiak Kayak Tours** explore Near Island and Mill Bay. Trips typically start at 9am and 2pm. No experience is necessary. (☎486-2722. 3hr. tours, 9am and 2pm. 2-person min. Call ahead. $45.) **Mythos Expeditions** runs similar trips, and more expensive trips to Shuyak and Afognak Islands. They also rent kayaks and provide water taxi service. (☎486-5536, www.mythos-expeditions.com.) The expert kayaker and rock climber can drive north to the end of the road to put in at Anton/Larsen Bay and kayak across to **Larsen Island.** One can also climb **Crown Mountain,** with either a hike-in or helicopter drop-off.

MOUNTAIN BIKING. A love-hate relationship exists between ATVers and bikers on "the rock." Digging deep ruts, clearing fragile flora, and many times reducing trail to a boggy mess, four-wheelers simultaneously create new trails and destroy established ones. Rentals, gear, and great advice are available from the staff at **58° North** (see **Practical Info,** above). Definitely pick up the *Kodiak Mountain Bike Guide: The Joys of Riding on "The Rock"* ($4) before you head out, because it has detailed info on 14 trails. There really are no easy rides in Kodiak, so be sure to inquire about specific trail features from experienced riders before heading out. For **Russian Ridge Trail** (8 mi.), head straight up Maple St. as it becomes Pillar Mountain Rd. and turns to gravel; take a right just after the quarry. The trail is a popular route due largely to its proximity to town. After a steady climb, you drop into dense, mossy forest on a somewhat technical trail. After spitting out onto Monashka Bay Rd., choose between a leisurely ride along the pavement, or a more challenging adventure through a rolling footpath in and out of Kodiak's neighborhoods. **Burma Road Trail** (12 mi.) is 4½ mi. out of town on Rezanof Dr. West to Anton Larson Bay Rd. Turn right and go a half-mile to Buskin Bridge No. 6. Take the second left, where you'll either park or find the trail. A less technical trail, Burma is a classic ride along an old WWII road. Watch out for nasty puddles.

BACKCOUNTRY SKIING. Having no ski lifts has forced the locals to venture into untouched areas, and their expeditions have yielded great rewards. The town itself may stay mired in rain and slush year-round, but this makes for perfect ski conditions in the island's high country. April through July is recognized as the most able season, but many areas retain snow through August. Still, you've got to "earn your turns" on Kodiak, so expect an average approach of 2hr. for most runs outside of town, unless you opt for the more expensive helicopter drop-off option. **Pyramid Mountain,** right off Anton Larson Bay Rd., has the most highly traveled slope; the backside of the **Three Sisters** (falsely labeled Devil's Prong on USGS maps) opens wide for bowl-skiing and touring. Make **Orion's** (see above) your one-stop shop for the latest conditions, directions, gear, and knowledgeable advice. Trails to most of the areas are not clearly marked, and snow conditions change, so make sure to inquire locally, and **bring your own gear** as there are no ski rental outfits on the island.

DRIVING AND SURFING. The 42 mi. coastal drive to **Chiniak** presents beautiful seascapes of small offshore islets bathed in fog, and dozens of mufflers lying along the rough road. Pick up Kodiak's visitor guide for mile-by-mile descriptions of several longer drives on the island, as well as a walking tour of downtown Kodiak. Take the turn-off for Pasagshak Bay Road at Mile 30 of the Chiniak for great hiking, fishing, camping, and, at the end of the road, one of the prettiest bays on Kodiak. Mile 12.5 on Pasagshak Bay Rd. is the **surfing** spot with the best breaks in Kodiak during the winter. Orion's (see above) sells surfboards.

KODIAK NATIONAL WILDLIFE REFUGE

Kodiak National Wildlife Refuge encompasses the western two-thirds of Kodiak Island. Since this is a refuge rather than a park, human recreational use is of secondary concern; no trails or roads lead into the region, and there are no official campgrounds. **Hiking** into the refuge demands a trek of 20 mi. or more across several mountains, while a flight to Larsen Bay (round-trip $110) will put you in range of the backcountry. Although the refuge contains seven public use **cabins,** only three can be reached by boat; the others require an expensive float plane ride (around $450). The cabins with a kerosene heater and an adjacent pit toilet rent for $20 a night and sleep four to five. Two cabins, **Blue Fox Bay ❷** and **Uganik Bay ❷,** are wheelchair accessible. Call the visitors center for more information. Any cabin can be booked by mail through the visitors center. Applications are processed in the first week of Jan. for dates in Apr.-June, the first week in Apr. for July-Sept., and the first week in July for Oct.-Dec. Not all dates get booked, but it is wise to plan ahead; call the refuge visitors center for an application. With so many bears around, it is important to store food properly and to be noisy when hiking.

Most visitors come to Kodiak to see the enormous bears. The numerous "guaranteed" brown-bear-viewing packages run $350-400 for a 3-4hr. float plane tour. Some of the prime viewing areas have visitor quotas, and reservations are made months ahead of time. Call the refuge visitors center or ask at the visitors center in town for permits and suggestions on the cheapest way to get close to the animals. A worthwhile alternative is a similarly priced plane trip to Katmai (see p. 513), where bears can be seen at closer range in as remarkable a setting.

ALEUTIAN ISLANDS

At the northern edge of the "Ring of Fire," the snow-capped volcanoes of the Alaska Peninsula and the Aleutian Islands stretch more than 1000 miles into the desolate North Pacific toward the coastal waters of Kamchatka, Russia. The Aleutians are one of the most remote locations on earth, and the lava-scarred cones on

WHEN WWII CAME TO ALASKA. On June 3rd, 1942, the Japanese began to bomb the Aleutian Islands and occupied Attu and Kiska in an attempt to divert American forces from the southern Pacific. The US responded by constructing the Alaska Hwy. and stationing nearly 60,000 soldiers on Unalaska. The remains of their occupation still mark the landscape—the last base is only now being gradually decommissioned. With as little as 24 hours notice, the US Army evacuated Aleut residents from many of the islands, ostensibly in the interest of safety, although Caucasians were allowed to remain. In the inhumane conditions of their exile, approximately 25% of the displaced Aleuts perished. Roughly 70% returned to find their property destroyed by American soldiers, and whole villages were abandoned. This is a little-known and shameful piece of American history, officially silenced until the passage of the Civil Liberties Act of 1988, when the Aleuts were offered an official apology and granted financial compensation. For information on the history of the Aleutian people, visit the Museum of the Aleutians in Unalaska (see **Sights**, p. 524).

these green but treeless isles are abused by some of the world's most vicious storms. Recent findings on Hog Island support a hypothesis that the ancestors of today's Aleuts migrated here from Asia by moving from island to island, rather than across the later-forming Bering Land Bridge.

Southeasterly weather patterns drive in from the brutally cold waters of the Bering Sea, numbing the senses and outbound flights for days. The waters also support an abundance of life; nutrients kick up from the depths of the Pacific onto the Bering's shallow shelf, creating a feeding ground for all species. Seafood has been a source of sustenance and commerce for over 8000 years of human habitants.

✈ TRANSPORTATION

The only two ways of reaching the Aleutian Islands are alarmingly expensive. A one-way **flight** from Anchorage to Dutch Harbor, the largest town on the Aleutians, costs about $450 and is only serviced by **Alaska Airlines** (☎800-252-7522). A one-way fare on the **Alaska Marine Highway** from Homer takes four days and costs $542 round-trip (children 2-11 $271, bikes/kayaks $42 extra). This route is serviced only six times per year between April and September. Clear days promise unique panoramas, and an on-board naturalist gives regular presentations on the plants and wildlife visible from the ship. The boat has showers, water, and a **dining room ❷** with limited hours and food (breakfast $5-7, lunch $6-10, dinner $9-13); bringing provisions from Homer is a good idea. Stock up on Dramamine before leaving; even in July, when the weather is mildest, the *M.V. Tustumena* still weathers 5- to 15-foot seas—it is not called the "Vomit Comet" for nothing.

UNALASKA AND DUTCH HARBOR ☎907

At the western limit of the Alaska Marine Highway's ferry service, Dutch Harbor and Unalaska (un-uh-LAS-ka) are as remote a community of 4100 as you'll find in North America. The name Unalaska comes from the original Aleut name for the area, "Agunalaksh." When the Russians came to the island, this evolved into "Ounalashka," and since 1890, the current name has persisted. Unalaska resides on a large island of the same name. A suburb has been built on the smaller Amaknak Island, about 2 mi. from downtown. The **Port of Dutch Harbor** gives this island its colloquial name. The **Bridge to the Other Side** connects the two islands.

The king crab boom of the late 1970s brought hordes of wide-eyed and hungry young men to the Bering Sea's cruel waters. Skyrocketing crab prices led to what many Alaskans call the "second gold rush," with some pocketing $20,000 in a week's work. This boom-time mentality, along with weeks of sea-time, fostered a hard-drinking, hard-living population. Overfishing led to quotas on the catch, but Unalaska and Dutch Harbor still hold the last of the cowboys, men who work and live in the most dangerous conditions imaginable. Unalaska has been the nation's top port for pounds of seafood caught and value of fish and crab delivered since 1988, and over 90% of the community depends on the fishing industry. Still, during the peak crab season, which takes place in the thick of an inhospitable winter, an average of one fisherman dies every week.

Unalaska is not a haven for the budget traveler, due to its remoteness and the unusually high incomes of the fisherfolk who are the port's most frequent visitors—over $130 million in seafood passes through here annually. But for those seeking what some tout as the best halibut fishing in the world, rare-bird sighting opportunities, or the view of treeless, snow-capped mountains soaring thousands of feet from the bay's chilly blue waters, the trip may be a worthwhile investment.

■■ ■ **ORIENTATION AND PRACTICAL INFORMATION.** Unalaska lies about 300 mi. from the tip of the Alaska Peninsula and 800 air miles from Anchorage. It is in the same time zone as the rest of the state. The **airport** is about a quarter-mile from City Dock on the main road into town, and is served by **Pen Air** (☎581-1383 or 800-478-2295) and **Alaska Airlines** (☎581-1380 or 800-225-2752). Planes sometimes don't fly in or out for a week at a time due to fog or wind. The **Alaska Marine Highway** departs City Dock, 1½ mi. from Dutch Harbor and 2½ mi. from Unalaska, for **Homer** (☎800-526-6731. 4 days, about once a month, round-trip $532). **Taxi service** is available from eight, yes, eight, companies (**Aleutian Taxi** ☎581-1866). The ride to town costs $12-14. Car rental is available from **North Port Rentals** (☎581-3880) and **B.C. Vehicle Rental** (☎581-6777), starting at $55 per day for compacts.

Visitor Information is available upstairs in the grey building next to the Parks Culture and Recreation Community Center on the corner of 5th and Broadway. (☎581-2612; www.arctic.net/~updhcvb. Open M-F 9am-5pm.) The **Ounalashka Corporation,** 400 Salmon Way in a low, orange-roofed building nearby, sells required **hiking and camping permits** and has a free trail map. Pick up the visitor's guide, a map of town, and an Aleutian *WWII National Historic Area Map and Guide* here. (☎581-1276. Open M-F 8am-noon and 1-5pm.) **Key Bank,** next to the Dutch Harbor post office, has a **24hr. ATM.** Jeff at **Aleutian Adventure Sports** (☎581-4489), at 4th and Broadway, rents mountain bikes ($25 per half-day, $35 per day, $125 weekly) and cross-country skis ($20 per day). He can also give great advice and directions for any outdoor adventures on or around the island. The **Parks Culture and Recreation Community Center,** on 5th St. across the Lliuliuk River from the Unalaska post office, provides untimed showers, free local calls, indoor swimming and track, a weight room, pool tables, video games, and parlor games. (☎581-1297. Open M-F 7am-10pm, Sa 8am-10pm, Su noon-7pm. $5.) **Lliuliuk Family and Health Services** is in a big gray building just down the street from the police station. (☎581-1202; after-hours 581-1233. Open M-F 8:30am-6pm, Sa 8:30am-6pm.) Call ☎911 in an **emergency.** The **police** are located at 29 Safety Way, just off Airport Beach Rd. on the Unalaska side (☎581-1233). Unalaska's **crisis line** can be reached at ☎581-1500. Get free **Internet access** on Elanor Dr., past the Unalaska post office. (☎581-5060. Open M-F 10am-9pm, Sa-Su noon-6pm.) There are **post offices** in Unalaska, 99685 (☎581-1232) and Dutch Harbor, 99692 (☎581-16570). Both are open M-F 9am-5pm and Sa 1-5pm.

ⅢⅢ ACCOMMODATIONS AND FOOD. The visitors center keeps a list of accommodations. Ninety percent of the land is owned by native corporations, and a fee is required for access. (Land-use $6 per day; camping $11 per night.) If the **Corporation** (see above) is closed, purchase land-use permits from patrol trucks. For those willing to brave the winds and drizzly weather, **Summer Bay ❶**, a 7 mi. hike from the ferry, is a popular unserviced camping spot. To camp closer to the town, walk up a hill directly behind the Unalaska **post office** and camp at the top. The prevailing winds are strong, so be sure your tent is sturdy; gusts have been recorded at up to 170 mph here, strong enough (as local legend has it) to blow the car door off a VW Bug and deposit it on a hillside where it has sat for over a decade. **Bunkhouse by the Sea ❸**, down Airport Rd. past the Dutch Harbor post office and about a half-mile down the left road, is nicer than the name suggests, with sparkling private rooms, shared baths, and a lounge with TV, fridge, and microwave. (☎581-4357. Meals are sometimes available for $10. Wash $2, dry $2. Free bike delivery when renting from **Aleutian Adventure Sports.** Singles $55, doubles $75.) The Bunkhouse is next to the Peking restaurant. **Unisea Inn ❺** has private rooms with baths, its own **Sports Bar,** and a location near the small boat harbor. (☎581-1425. Check in at the Grand Aleutian Hotel. $99.)

Eagle Quality Center ❶, in Dutch Harbor next to Grand Aleutian, sells overpriced groceries, but their huge deli sandwiches ($5) and salad bar ($4 per lb.) are some of the cheapest food in town. (☎581-4040. Open daily 7am-11pm.) The **A C Value Center,** the first right off Salmon Way, offers a selection of groceries as well as other odds and ends. (☎581-1245. Open daily 8am-10pm.) Fresh or frozen crab and fish can be bought straight from any seafood company: **Alyeska** (☎581-1211); **Royal Aleutian** (☎581-1671), **Westward** (☎581-1660), or **Unisea** (☎581-1258). Prices fluctuate season to season depending on availability. If you'd rather be served, check out 🖾**Amelia's ❷**, on Airport Beach Rd. next to the Eagle grocery, a 15min. walk from the airport. With a menu the size of mainland Alaska, Amelia serves up burgers ($9), piled-high nachos ($9), Mexican and Greek omelettes ($9), and burritos ($10). (☎581-2800. Open daily 6am-11pm.) In town on a Wednesday night? Get your fill of crab, halibut, salmon, and more at the pricey ($27) but worthwhile seafood buffet, at the Grand Aleutian Hotel's **Chart Room ❺** restaurant. (☎581-3844)

Looking for some nightlife on the island? Ask anyone to steer you to their favorite bar, but be sure to grab a drink at **The Elbow Room,** famous for its 1970s dubbing as the "most notorious bar on the North American continent" by Playboy Magazine. Inside you'll meet your fare share of Gibbers, Fishbones, and Coasties. (☎581-1271. Open M-F 11am-3am, Sa 11am-5am, yes, 5am.)

◧ SIGHTS. If it's sunny and clear when you arrive, hastily see **Outdoor Activities,** below. Otherwise, the **Museum of the Aleutians,** just past the Ounalashka Corporation building on Salmon Way, provides a colorful history of the entire Aleutian chain. (☎581-5150. Open June-Sept. M-Sa 10am-5pm, Su noon-5pm; Oct.-May W-Su 11am-4pm. $4.) Archeological digs are ongoing and visitors can frequently visit sites, some within 200 yards of the museum. The **Unalaska Cemetery and Memorial Park,** a mile past the church or 4 mi. from the City Dock on the eastern edge of Unalaska, presents a description of the Japanese air attacks of June 1942. If you haven't seen enough bald eagles, head to the landfill on Sommer Bay Rd. or the Westmark Cannery at Captains Bay.

◪ OUTDOOR ACTIVITIES. A **land-use pass** is required for venturing off the main roads. Purchase one at the visitors center or the **Ounalashka Corporation** ($6 per day, see **Practical Info,** p. 523). It's wise to rent a bike from **Aleutian Adventure Sports** ($35 per day, see **Practical Info**), which often greets the ferry. If you have the luxury of time, explore the extensive backcountry opportunities; you may run into wild horses and feral cows, but don't worry about large predators—there are no bears on the island. Even on local treks, prepare for sudden weather changes.

HIKING. If you have the good fortune to be in Unalaska on a sunny day, make haste to hike to the top of **Mt. Ballyhoo,** just behind the airport and christened by one-time resident Jack London. The trail starts behind the airport hangars and is clearly visible from the base. Allow 45min. to reach the summit, and another hour or more to climb down the backside. Ferry passengers can walk along the ridge for another 20-30min. past the summit, and still easily return to catch the boat. The summit affords beautiful sights with amazing gold, red, and black rock formations jutting out of a sheer cliff that drops 1634 ft. to the translucent green water of the ocean below; the 6880 ft. **Mt. Makushin Volcano** can be seen steaming on clear days. Following the ridge off Ballyhoo's backside leads to **Ulakta Head National Historic Area** and WWII bunkers on the cliffs. Just before the bridge to Unalaska (30min. walk from the ferry) sits **Bunker Hill,** which was heavily fortified during WWII. Following either the construction road clockwise from behind the hill or the beach counter-clockwise to reach the old trail, a quick but steep 420 ft. climb leads to a large concrete bunker and a great view of the bays and mountains.

If you happen to miss your ferry back and have a month to play with, the **Ugadaga Bay Trail** is an easy-to-moderate, extremely scenic trail passing waterfalls and steep-walled valleys along what was an ancient portage route for the Unangan people between Unalaska and the small outer islands. In colder weather, it may require crossing a snowfield. The marked trailhead begins on the right side of a small pond at the top of Overland Dr. (a continuation of Broadway), 2½ mi. from downtown. A perfect overnight hike would involve the **Agamgik Bay Trail,** which starts at Humpy Cove, past Summer Bay on Summer Bay Rd. This flat 4½ mi. trail follows a river bed for the first half and then drops into gorgeous Agamgik Bay, which offers sheltered camping and a great view of Eagle Rock. The trailhead begins at the pull-off on the right. Allow 2hr. one-way on this relatively flat trail.

BIKING. With no trees and old WWII access roads criss-crossing the island, Unalaska is a perfect town to explore on a bike. Expect steep hills and creek crossings; virtually every flat spot on the island is taken up by the village itself. The **Overland Trail** to **Summer Bay** is a good introduction, climbing switchbacks along the Ugadaga Bay trail to Summer Bay Lake before hooking back around and down to the road system leading to town. Climb Overland Rd., passing the Ugadaga Bay trailhead on top. Follow the road down to Summer Bay Lake, where it leads to Summer Bay Rd. and back to town. All 13½ mi. are on good road, so expect 3-4hr. of moderately challenging riding. You do not need a permit for the trail. If that isn't enough, true masochists can jump on the **Pyramid Peak Trail,** which combines a difficult climb with a challenging downhill over its 7 mi. route. Expect some bike-toting time on this trail, or else you might be nursing some war wounds. Access Pyramid Peak from Captain's Bay Rd. by turning left and onto the trail at Westwood Seafoods. Stay left at the two trail splits and pass through a gated trailhead. Be sure to stop off at **Aleutian Adventure Sports** and talk to Jeff before heading out. A fount of information, he'll be happy to give directions and advice.

BY WATER. World-record halibut are pulled out of the waters around Unalaska, attracting truly hardcore fishermen. **Charter** companies all have comparable rates (half-day $90, full-day $165), and can be booked through the visitors center or the Grand Aleutian gift shop. Trips are almost always full, so book well in advance. The kayaking from Unalaska is some of the finest you'll find in the Bering Sea. Unfortunately, there is no place to rent kayaks on the island, but **Aleutian Adventure Sports**

offers all sorts of trips; these range from 4-5hr. paddles to a tour of bird- and history-rich Hog Island and multi-day surveys of the Akutan Volcano and hot springs. They also offer mountaineering and hiking adventures.

ALONG RTE. 1: STERLING HWY. ☎907

The Sterling Hwy. begins 90 mi. south of Anchorage at the **Tern Lake Junction.** From here, the highway runs 66 mi. west to the Twin Cities of **Soldotna** and **Kenai.** On the way, it passes wonderful hiking, camping, and fishing in **Chugach National Forest** and the **Kenai National Wildlife Refuge.** From Soldotna, the highway runs south on the western side of the peninsula along **Cook Inlet** (see p. 531), ending after 75 mi. at the town of **Homer** (see p. 508). The Sterling passes through moose country, so drivers should be cautious. Mile markers measure the distance from Seward.

COOPER LANDING ☎907

Shortly after its intersection with the Seward Hwy., the Sterling passes the aquamarine **Kenai Lake**, which stretches in a giant Z through the Chugach Range. The next 120 mi. of highway, from Cooper Landing to Anchor Point, parallels some of the most spectacular **salmon fishing** grounds anywhere. The king in this town has fins and swims in streams. **Laundry, showers,** and an **ATM** are available at **WildWash** at Mile 47.5. (☎495-1888. Wash $2.25, dry $1.75 per 35min. Showers $3. Open daily 8am-midnight.) For dolly varden and **free camping ❶,** turn left onto Snug Harbor Rd. after the Kenai River Bridge and drive 3½ mi. on the dirt road. Park in the gravel lot adjacent to the large orange-and-white powerlines and scramble down to the lake. Another 10 mi. along Snug Harbor Rd. is trout-teeming **Cooper Lake,** with more remote **free camping ❶.** During the summer runs, it's not unusual to see anglers "combat fishing," standing shoulder-to-shoulder while filling their baskets. At Mile 52 of the Sterling Hwy. sits the log-cabin that is **Gwin's Roadhouse ❷,** a perfect place to eat on the drive to or from the peninsula. Burgers are $8, any time, day or night. (☎595-1266. Open May-Sept. 24hr.)

Fishing charters in the $90-200 range abound. A cheaper option for salmon is the **ferry trip** to the opposite bank of the Kenai River, which yields comparable views and access to good fishing. Parking is $7, so take advantage of the gravel pull-outs just before and after the entrance. (Ferry runs 6am-11pm. $6, ages 3-11 $3.) Be forewarned that restrictions on fishing (bag limit, type of tackle, etc.) vary often within very small areas. Licenses are available at most grocery and fishing stores. **Kenai Lake Tackle,** at Mile 47.1, sells licenses, guides trips, and rents gear. (☎595-2248. Spinning-rods and waders $10, fly-rods $15, all-day canoe $35.) The Kenai River offers several places to **whitewater raft** without substantially risking life and limb. Some of these floats are as scenic as Class III river-running gets. Outdoor outfitters generally supply lunch and gear on full-day trips, but anglers should buy their own licenses beforehand. **Alaska Wildland Adventures** at Mile 50.1 offers half-and full-day rafting trips. (☎595-1279 or 800-478-4100. $45-195, children $29-69.) The **Alaska Rivers Company** (☎595-1226; www.alaskariverscompany.com) has rafting, fishing, and hiking tours starting at $42.

KENAI NATIONAL WILDLIFE REFUGE ☎907

From Cooper Landing, the Sterling Hwy. stretches 50 mi. to **Soldotna,** with services at Cooper and Sterling. It runs alongside the chock-full-o'-fish Kenai River and through the Kenai National Wildlife Refuge's two million acres. The peninsula is prime moose territory—the area was originally designated the Kenai National Moose Refuge in 1941. Hiking trails within the refuge have become some of the most popular in the state, as droves of adventurers shuttle from Anchorage every weekend to walk, bike, run, and ski over 200 mi. of highly accessible and well-maintained paths. Let's not forget the famous fishing areas, spectacular canoe routes, and free camping everywhere.

▰ ▰ ORIENTATION AND PRACTICAL INFORMATION

For fishing regulations, trail conditions, and information, it is wise to check out one of the visitors centers. The **Kenai National Wildlife Refuge Visitor Contact Station,** at Sterling Mile 58, is close to many of the campgrounds and trailheads. This log cabin station sells maps ($3-5) and other outdoor literature. (Open May-Sept. Su-Th 10am-4pm, F-Sa 10am-6pm.) The **Kenai National Wildlife Refuge Visitor Center** is located just South of Soldotna; turn left at the light just south of the Kenai River bridge and follow the signs. (☎262-7021. Open M-F 8am-5pm, Sa-Su 9am-6pm.) The **State Park Headquarters,** located in Sterling off the Sterling Hwy. at Mile 85, has info on cabins, campsites, and trails. (☎262-5581. Open summer M-F 8am-5pm, winter M-F 8am-4pm. Closed holidays.) The **Kenai National Wildlife Refuge Headquarters** is in Soldotna off the Sterling Hwy. between Miles 96 and 97; turn left on Funny River Rd., then take an immediate right and follow the signs. *Refuge Reflections,* their free publication, gives detailed info on fishing, hiking, and canoeing. The center shows nature films daily (on the hour, noon-4pm) and leads a host of hikes, talks, and kid-friendly exhibits. A 10min., wheelchair-accessible, self-guided nature walk also leaves from the center. (☎262-7021. Open summer M-F 8am-5pm, Sa-Su 9am-6pm; winter M-F 8am-4pm, Sa-Su 10am-5pm.)

▰ CAMPING

Free **campgrounds ❶** with boat launch, water, and toilets are located on the lakes for which they are named. Look along Swanson River Rd. for **Dolly Varden Lake, Rainbow Lake, Swanson River,** along the Skilak Loop Rd. for **Engineer Lake, Lower Ohmer Lake,** and **Lower Skilak Lake,** or for **Watson Lake,** directly off the Sterling at Mile 71. Other free camping options, though less developed, abound along the loop and on lakes throughout the system. For info on other camping options, call the visitors center (☎262-7021) or check out the park paper, *Refuge Reflections.*

Alaska Canoe and Campground ❶, Mile 84 in Sterling, rents canoes (day use $24, overnight use $40, 3 or more days $30 per day), bikes ($35 per day) and fishing gear. To protect those precious canoes, they'll shuttle renters to their area of choice for $0.60 per mi.; this is a fair rate considering their proximity to Swan Lake Rd. (1½ mi.), the primary trailhead for canoe trips in the vicinity (☎262-2331; www.alaskacanoetrips.com. Tent sites $10, RV sites $16.)

▰ OUTDOOR ACTIVITIES

The southern reaches of the refuge are primarily flat and boggy. No worries for the adaptable adventurer, though; these waterways are teeming with many species of fish and are reachable by motorboat, foot, or even canoe. Winter recreation includes snowshoeing, snowmachining, backcountry ice-fishing, and cross-country skiing at the Kenai Golf Course. Call the visitors center for resources.

PADDLING

The refuge, lying north of the Sterling Hwy., boasts some of the best **canoeing** networks in Alaska. The **Swan Lake System** contains 30 lakes interconnected by waterways and portages, forming a possible 60 mi. of canoeing, though many less demanding routes exist. Find it at Mile 16.4 of the Swanson River Rd., turn right onto Swan Lake Rd. and continue 3½ mi. to the West Entrance, or an additional 6 mi. to the East Entrance. The more challenging **Swanson River System** connects 40 lakes with 46 mi. of the Swanson River for a trail system of over 80 mi. through marshy wetlands. This system is recommended for more experienced paddlers. Pick up *The Kenai Canoe Trails* ($19) or the Kenai National Wildlife Refuge topo map for a guide to these areas, and stop at the **Alaska Canoe and Campground** for advice. The **Swanson River** trailhead is at Mile 12 of the Swan Lake Rd.

HIKING

🏔 **Fuller Lakes Trail** (6 mi. round-trip, 4-7hr.). At Mile 57, a dirt pull-out points directly to the trailhead. After a challenging 1st mi. of steady ascent through dense forests, striking views highlight the glimmering Lower Fuller Lakes and the lush Kenai Mountains and precede slightly easier hiking above treeline. 1400 ft. gain. Moderately strenuous.

Kenai River Trails provide an alternative and access to the river. Both the upper and lower trails are accessible from Skilak Lake Rd. at Mile 58. The **upper trail** (5½ mi. round-trip) starts at Mile 0.6 of Skilak Lake Rd. The **lower trail** (5mi. round-trip) begins at Mile 2.3 of Skilak Lake Rd. Plenty of bears keep the moose company. Moderate.

FISHING

No boat? Fish can still be caught from the shoreline of many lakes and rivers along the Kenai Peninsula. Try your hand (or pole) at catching Arctic char from the banks of Silver Lake and the Finger Lakes. There are rainbow trout along the shores of Paddle, Forest, Eugumen, and Upper and Lower Ohmer Lakes. Red salmon, silver salmon and rainbows ply the ever popular Kenai River.

SOLDOTNA   ☎ 907

Soldotna spreads its strip mall tentacles for several miles along the northern stretch of the Sterling Hwy. and the branching Kenai Spur Hwy. This town revolves around fishing and supplies groceries, camping gear, and guides to those intent on catching the Big One. The location on the Sterling Hwy. makes it a prime stop for travelers en route to elsewhere.

ORIENTATION AND PRACTICAL INFORMATION. Soldotna's **visitors center,** just over the Kenai River on the way south to Homer (turn west at the light), has pamphlets on fishing and recreation possibilities in the area, a phone for local use, and free canoe route maps. (☎ 262-9814. Open daily 9am-7pm.) **Wilderness Way,** 2 mi. east of town, is well stocked with high-quality backpacking, biking, kayaking, and canoeing gear. (☎ 262-3880. Open M-Th 10am-6pm, F-Sa 10am-7pm, Su noon-5pm.) The **Sports Den,** located in a cabin at 44176 Sterling Hwy., sells gear and licenses and rents everything you need to fish. They also run guided fishing and trophy hunting trips and are a stellar source of outdoor info. (☎ 262-7491. Canoes $35 per day. Rod and reel $10 per day. Open daily mid-May to Aug. 8am-7pm; Sept. to mid-May M-Sa 10am-6pm.) Call ☎ 262-9228 for **road conditions. Central Peninsula General Hospital** is at 250 Hospital Pl. (☎ 262-4404), and the **post office** is located at 175 N Binkley St. (☎ 262-4760. Open M-F 8:30am-5pm, Sa 10am-2pm.) **Postal Code:** 99669.

▐▐ ACCOMMODATIONS AND FOOD. Camping is available pretty much everywhere along the Sterling Hwy., especially by **Skilak Lake Rd.** (see **Kenai Wildlife Refuge,** p. 526). With the exception of the **Kenai-Russian River, Upper Skilak Lake,** and **Hidden Lake Campgrounds ❶** (all $5-10), camping within the refuge is free.

The **Hogg Heaven Cafe ❷,** right before the Kenai bridge, serves up tasty omelettes (from $7) and greasy burgers starting at $5. Give the Kalif avocado burgers ($8) a shot.

The most comfortable and affordable lodging in the Twin City area is actually in **Sterling,** which is a short drive from Soldotna, and a bit farther from Kenai (worth the drive). To get to ▨**Jana House ❷,** turn down Swanson River Rd. at Mile 83.5 of the Sterling Hwy. and follow it a quarter-mile. The cavernous bunk rooms have a kitchen and bathrooms so fancy you'll wish you had them at home. (☎260-1451. Shuttle picks up in Soldotna and Kenai. Open June-Oct. 24hr. Full RV sites $12; tents $8; bunks $22; private rooms $50, $10 per additional person.)

KENAI ☎907

The Kenai River, by many accounts the best place to go for king salmon fishing in the world, lures unending swarms of tourists, weekenders, and die-hards to its jade green waters every summer to try their luck at the yearly runs of salmon flowing in from the waters of Cook Inlet. Perched on a bluff overlooking the place where the Kenai River empties into Cook Inlet, Kenai has a magical view of the Aleutian-Alaska Range and its prominent volcanoes, Mt. Redoubt and Mt. Augustine. Kenai culture bears the signs of its varied past; it was first inhabited by the Dena'ina Indians, then colonized by Russian fur traders and missionaries at the end of the 19th century, only to be fortified by the American military in the 1940s.

▐▘ TRANSPORTATION

Kenai, on the western Kenai Peninsula, is 158 mi. from Anchorage and 96 mi. north of Homer. The town can be reached via **Kalifornsky Beach Rd.,** which joins the **Sterling Hwy.** (Rte. 1) just south of Soldotna, or via the **Kenai Spur Rd.,** which runs north from Soldotna and west to Kenai. Kalifornsky mile markers measure distance from Kenai, while the Kenai Spur mile markers measure from Soldotna.

Flights: Airport 1 mi. north of downtown. Take Kenai Spur Rd. to Willow St. and follow signs. **Alaska Airlines** commuter service, **Era Aviation** (☎800-426-0333), has near hourly service to **Anchorage** (30min., $62-70).

Buses: Homer Stage Line (☎262-4585). 1 per day June-Aug. M-Sa. Service decreases in the offseason. To **Anchorage** (4hr., $35) and **Homer** (1½hr., $25). **Kachemak Bay Transit** (☎235-3795) runs between **Kenai** and **Homer** ($30), **Anchorage** and **Soldotna** ($35), and **Soldotna** and **Homer** ($25).

Taxis: Inlet Cab: Kenai (☎283-4711); Soldotna (☎262-4770). $1.60 base, $2 per mi.

Car Rental: Great Alaska Car Company (☎283-3469). Prices vary by month peaking in July when they start from $45 per day, $270 per week. Unlimited mileage for multiple day rentals. Must be 21+ with credit card.

▟ PRACTICAL INFORMATION

Tourist Information: Visitor and Cultural Center, 11471 Kenai Spur Hwy. (☎283-1991; www.visitkenai.com), just past the corner of the Spur Rd. and Main St. Hiking trail guide ($1), *Free and Inexpensive Things to Do in Kenai* (free), and a traditional artifacts museum. (Museum $3, students free.) Open summer M-F 9am-8pm, Sa 10am-7pm, Su 11am-7pm; winter M-F 9am-5pm, Sa-Su 10am-4pm.

Outdoor Information: For info on **Lake Clark National Park and Preserve,** across Cook Inlet from Kenai, call the superintendent in Anchorage (☎271-3751) or the park ranger (☎781-2218; both 8am-5pm). For information on local fishing charters, tours and gear, visit the **Kenai Vistors and Cultural Center,** (☎283-2230, see above) or check online at www.visitkenai.com to compare prices and options. A typical 6hr. salmon charter runs $120-160 per person. The **Kenai National Wildlife Refuge Headquarters** is 15min. away in Soldotna (see **Practical Information,** p. 528).

Work Opportunities: Alaska Employment Service ☎283-2900. **Dial-a-Job** ☎283-2924.

Laundromat and Public Showers: Wash-n-Dry (☎283-8473), at Lake St. and Spur. Wash $1.75, dry $0.25 per 7min. Untimed showers $4. Open daily 8am-10pm.

Emergency: ☎911.

Police: 107 S Willow St. (☎283-7879).

Crisis Line: ☎283-7257. 24hr.

Women's Services: Resource Center, 325 S Spruce St. (☎283-9479) Hotline, shelter. Open M-F 9am-5pm.

Hospital: Central Peninsula General Hospital, 250 Hospital Pl. (☎262-4404).

Internet: At the **library,** 163 Main St. Loop (☎283-4378). Free 1 hr. access. Open M-Th 10am-8pm, F-Sa 10am-5pm, Su noon-5pm.

Post Office: 140 Bidarka St. (☎283-7771). Open M-F 8:45am-5:15pm, Sa 9:30am-1pm. **Postal Code:** 99611.

⌂ ACCOMMODATIONS

There are few inexpensive lodgings in Kenai; the numerous B&Bs begin at $70. **The B&B Association** (☎888-266-9091) has all listings and rates. **Camping ❶** is available at the city campsite, located at Mile 10 of the Spur Rd. (Tents $8.) **Katmai Hotel ❹,** 10800 Kenai Spur Hwy., is part of the Katmai Pines Lodge and lies one block from downtown. Features small rooms with nice decor and cable. (☎283-6101 or 800-275-6101. Singles $79; doubles $89.) To reach **Beluga Lookout RV Park and Lodge ❷,** 929 Mission St., take Main St. toward the water and go right on Mission St. Has a great location on the bluff; scan the sea for belugas or gaze at volcanoes across the inlet from the lounge. (☎283-5999. Laundry $1.50. Full RV sites $25. Showers $2.)

◖ FOOD

There are fast food options aplenty on the Spur Rd. just before town. **Carr's Quality Center,** in the Kenai Plaza next to K-Mart on the Kenai Spur Rd., has a bakery and a pharmacy, and sells fruit, natural foods, and fast food. (☎283-6300. 24hr. grocery.)

Veronica's Coffee House (☎283-2725), at the end of Mission Rd. opposite the Russian church. Friendly service in a historically homey building decorated with paintings and overlooking the inlet. Half sandwich and cup of soup $6. Live folk Sa. Open M-Sa 9am-7pm, Su 10am-5pm. ❶

Old Town Village Restaurant, 1000 Mission Ave. (☎283-4515). Housed in a restored 1918 cannery building that was moved from Sitka. Old Town is known for its seafood dinners (from $15), salad bar ($6), and hearty Su brunch ($10; 10am-2pm). Open M-Sa 11am-9pm, Su 10am-8pm. ❸

New Peking, 145 S Willow St. (☎283-4662) off Kenai Spur Rd. Savor the all-you-can-eat lunch buffet ($9; M-Sa 11:30am-2pm) in a lush Far Eastern setting. Mongolian BBQ summer evenings ($12). Open daily 11:30am-10pm. ❸

◷ ☾ SIGHTS AND OUTDOOR ACTIVITIES

COOK INLET. Breathtaking **Cook Inlet** is framed by smooth sand, two mountain ranges, and volcanic **Mt. Augustine** and **Mt. Redoubt.** The best places to admire the view are at the state recreation area or at the beach at the end of Spruce Dr. The beach is also a great place to watch beluga, salmon, and eagles. *(The best time to see whales is 2hr. before or after high tide.)*

CAPTAIN COOK STATE RECREATION AREA. Premier views of the inlet and the Alaska-Aleutian Range make for a lovely picnic on a bluff or beach. You can swim or wet your line for trout and arctic char at **Stormy Lake,** and the downstream end of the **Swanson River Canoe Trail** begins nearby. *(At the northern end of the Kenai Spur Rd., 25 mi. from town. Campsites ❶, $10, feature water and pit toilets.)*

NIKISKI. The **North Peninsula Recreation Center** in Nikiski houses an indoor pool for rainy days (expect many), a hockey rink, a ski trail, outdoor volleyball and tennis courts, and a picnic area. You can also grab a shower and sauna here for $3. *(12½ mi. north of Kenai at Mile 23.4 of the Spur Rd. ☎ 776–8472 or 776-8800. Open 7am-5pm and 6-9pm. $3, seniors $2. Alaska's largest waterslides $6.)*

FISHING. Check at the visitors center for **charter** info (prices are comparable to those in Soldotna). Most are located along Beaver Loop Rd., off the Spur or Angler Dr. Anglers can get their lines wet on any public land along the **Kenai River,** where the majority of fishing takes place. Beginners should ask at fishing shops (most of which are in neighboring Soldotna on the Sterling Hwy.; see **Soldotna, Orientation and Practical Info,** p. 528) for recommended locations to avoid accidentally damaging the banks of the river and jeopardizing fish habitat. **Licenses** are available at gas stations, groceries, or outfitters.

NINILCHIK ☎907

From Kenai, the Sterling Hwy. (Rte. 1) winds through shoreline forest on a bluff overlooking the Cook Inlet. Across the inlet, the peaks of Mt. Redoubt and Mt. Iliamna are visible. Both volcanoes rise over 10,000 ft., and both have erupted in the last 50 years. The highway winds into the Russian-influenced town of Ninilchik, a stop on the highway best known for its combat-fishing king run. Although nearby **Clam Gulch** (Mile 117.4) is a clammer's paradise during low tides; *do not* eat shellfish harvested in the area without assurances from health authorities that they are toxin-free. Take Mission St. off the Sterling and drive through the old part of town for a step back in time.

The **General Store,** at Sterling Mile 137, sells fishing and clamming supplies, and has the town's only **ATM.** (☎ 567-3378. Open summer M-Th 7am-11pm, F 7am-midnight, Sa 6am-midnight, Su 6am-11pm; winter daily 9am-5pm.) The **Alaskan Angler RV Park,** on Kingsley at Mile 135 of the Sterling, rents clamming gear for $3 per day. (☎ 567-3393 or 800-347-4114. Office open Apr.-Sept. daily 9am-9pm. Tent sites $10; electric RV sites $15; full RV sites $24.) Their **showers** ($2 for 10min., with towel) and **laundromat** (wash and dry each $1.50) are open **24hr.**

For scenic dining, take Mission St. off the Sterling and follow signs for the beach and cannery to the **Boardwalk Cafe ❶.** This joint couldn't get much closer to the water—it literally hangs over the beach. Menu highlights include $2.75 homemade pie and great $2.50 seafood soup. (☎ 567-3388. Open daily May-Sept. M-Th 9am-9pm, F-Sa 9am-10:30pm, Su 8am-8pm.) The **Inlet View ❷** bar, at Mile 134.5, is a laid-back local hangout that stays open really late. (☎ 567-3337. Pints $3.50. Open daily 10am-5am.) **Deep Creek Packing ❶** (☎ 567-3396), at Mile 137, sells and gives bite-sized **free samples** of different kinds of smoked fish.

The supremely pleasant ▓**Eagle Watch Hostel (HI) ❶** is 3 mi. east of town on Oil Well Rd., which starts just before the Tesoro gas station. The building is spacious and clean; rooms feature views of the Ninilchik River. Eagles can always be seen (as advertised) and moose and bears can occasionally be seen from the deck. A BBQ, showers, fishing rods, new mattresses, and a playful dog seal the deal. (☎ 567-3905. Linen $2, towels $0.50. Lockout 10am-5pm. 11pm curfew enforced. $10; nonmembers $13. Private rooms $5 surcharge. Cash or traveler's checks.)

The several **state campgrounds** ❶ near Ninilchik have water and toilets. Sites along the river or beach are $10. Superb spots in the **Ninilchik State Recreation Area** overlook the inlet less than a mile north of town. The nearby beach-level **Deep Creek Recreation Area** ❶ (not the Deep Creek Campground) is one of the most popular campgrounds on the peninsula; turn west about a quarter-mile south of Deep Creek. ($10, day-use parking $5).

SELDOVIA ☎907

It would seem that Seldovia was founded by a small **Homer** (p. 508) migration. Talking with residents and walking its streets, the attitude and ambience seem much the same. Nonetheless, this sleepy, isolated sea-side town has carved itself out as a proud stepping stone to the Alaskan waters, and retains a charm that is not lost on daily tourists from Homer who descend upon Seldovia's kitschy shops and espresso machines. Unmatched views, a secluded feel, and halibut fishing "an hour closer than Homer" serve to bring its visitors back for more, time and again.

🚹 **PRACTICAL INFORMATION.** All you could ever want to know about Seldovia can be found on their award-winning web site, www.seldovia.com. The **airport** is less than 1 mi. out of town on Airport Ave. **Homer Air** (☎235-8591) and **Smokey Bay Air** (☎235-8591) both fly frequently to Homer for $55 round-trip. The **Alaska Marine Highway** chugs from Homer to Seldovia once per week, lingering for only 4hr. before heading back (☎235-8449 or 800-382-9229; 1½hr., Tu 10:30pm, one-way $20). Two **tour boats** also cruise daily to Homer. **Rainbow Tours** offers the least expensive service and gives you 5hr. to see the town before pushing off. (☎235-7272. One-way $20, round-trip $35.) **Jakolof Bay Express** provides a friendly ferry to the Jakolof dock, a 9 mi. bike ride from "downtown" Seldovia. Bringing a bike costs $5, a kayak $10. (☎235-6384. Round-trip $45.)

Bikes rent for a steep price in Seldovia; rent bikes in Homer and bring them across on the water taxi or ferry for about $10 (see Homer, **Equipment Rentals**). **Kayak'atak**, which can be called from Herring Bay Mercantile on Main St., rents kayaks for single or multiple day trips. (☎234-7425. Call between 8am-10pm. Single kayaks $50 per day, each additional day $35; doubles $75, $55.) Bring money to Seldovia; there are no banks, and not all establishments accept credit cards. **Sweet 'n Clean Laundromat** is on Main St. (☎234-7420. Showers $4 per 10min., towel and soap included. Wash $2.50-5, dry $0.25 per 5min. Open M-Sa 7am-9pm, Su 1pm-9pm.) In an **emergency**, call ☎911. The **police** can be reached at ☎234-7640, and a **clinic** is also available (☎234-7821; open M, W, F 9am-4pm). The **post office** is at Main and Seldovia St. (☎234-7831; open M-F 9am-5pm.) **Postal Code:** 99663.

🏠🍴 **ACCOMMODATIONS AND FOOD.** Try www.seldovia.com for full listings with pictures. **Across the Bay Tent and Breakfast** ❹, located 9 mi. out of town on Kasitsna Bay via Jacolof Bay Rd., offers 2- to 5-person canvas tents, plus kayaking, mountain biking, volleyball, horseshoe, showers, and a sauna. (☎235-3633 or 345-2571, www.tentandbreakfastalaska.com. Tent and breakfast $58 per person, tent and all meals $85 per person. Bikes $25 per day. Guided sea kayaking $75-95.) At the end of Main St. by the boardwalk, **Dancing Eagles Lodge** ❹ offers some tiny rooms and a beautiful private cabin, along with a private extension of the town boardwalk, a hot tub, and a terrific view of the bay. (☎234-7627. Rooms from $65, doubles $110. Cabin with full kitchen and bath $175 for 2, $50 per additional person.) The best deals for groups are the pleasant, newly furnished, multi-room, converted apartments with TV and kitchenette at the **Bayview Suites** ❺, above the Main St. Market. (☎234-7631 or 800-478-7898. Sleeps 4-6 all for the same rate. Street view $110; water view $140.) **Outside Beach** ❶ and **Wilderness**

Park ❶, both 1 mi. from town and adjacent, offer camping and close encounters with sea otters. Turn left off Jakolof Bay Rd. at the "Narrow Road" sign.

The Main St. Market stocks a modest supply of groceries, hardware, tackle, liquor, and pharmaceuticals. (☎234-7633. Open M-Sa 9am-8pm, Su 10am-6pm.) Frozen dairy treats and laundry services mingle in bizarre but happy harmony at the sparkling **Sweet 'N Clean Laundromat** (see **Practical Information,** above). **The Buzz ❶,** 231 Main St., serves coffee, espresso, and great food in a nice rainy-day loitering space. Cinnamon rolls ($2.75), local art, and friendly company abound. (☎234-7479. Open Mar.-Sept. daily 6:30am-4:30pm. The **Tidepool Cafe ❷,** on Main St. next to Herring Bay Mercantile, is the place to grab a meal and a book. Omelettes for breakfast ($8) will surely hit the spot, as will the view overlooking the water. (☎234-7502. Open Su-Tu 6am-3pm, W-Sa 6am-3pm and 5pm-8pm.) **Mad Fish Restaurant ❹,** 221 Main St., gives a unique twist to old favorites. Try the Asian seafood salad, complete with scallops, halibut, and shrimp ($15), or stick with an old standby, the $7 burger. (☎234-7676. Open Su-Th noon-3pm and 5:30pm-8pm F-Sa noon-3pm and 5:30pm-9pm.)

◨ ⚑ SIGHTS AND OUTDOOR ACTIVITIES. Seldovia's quiet, colorful homes, friendly locals, and beautiful harbor make for lovely strolls. Pick up a copy of the **Seldovia Summer Gazette,** either in town or at the Homer visitor center for info on activities in and around town. The Seldovia Native Association runs the **Alaska Tribal Cache Berry Kitchen/Museum,** which has a small case of native artifacts. Watch through the display window as they whip up and package their famous preserves, throwing together everything from fireweed jelly to a strangely enticing kelp concoction. (Open M-Sa 10am-6pm, Su 11am-5pm.)

The **Otterbahn Hiking Trail,** starting at the Susan B. English School near Winifred Ave., a half-mile from town, winds a moderate 1 mi. to the cliffs and tidal pools of Outside Beach, passing through old-growth and floral meadows. It grants a spectacular view of the volcanoes on clear days. The ride to **Jakolof Bay** can be a great bike trip on a good day as it winds through tall spruce and over a rolling dirt road. Shoreline Dr. terminates at Jakolof Bay Rd., which will take you the 9 mi. to the bay. The **Seldovia Native Corporation,** 328 Main St., owns much of the land above the reservoir and between the Jakolof dock and town, so secure a hiking and camping permit before exploring. (☎234-7625. Open M-F 8am-5pm. $1 per day.)

INTERIOR ALASKA

Banked by the Brooks Range to the north and the Alaska Range to the south, Alaska's expansive interior covers over 166,000 sq. mi. of the wildest and most untouched land in the world. While Fairbanks remains the second most populated city in the state (with 83,000 people), the majority of settlements throughout the interior are "bush" towns. These remote communities are populated primarily by Athabascan Indians and are often only accessible by boat, dogsled, snowmobile, or small plane. The Alaskan Natives have built their lifestyle and culture around Alaska's rugged interior in all its beauty, expanse, and unforgiving conditions. Though gold rushes, a Cold War, and oil booms have come and gone, the nature of the interior has remained largely unchanged. Even the undertaking of the Alaska Pipeline in the 1970s could not fluster the local culture.

"Big" describes almost everything in the interior; locals joke that should Alaska be split in two, Texas would become the third largest state. Everything from the unofficial state bird (mosquito) to Denali and the Alaska Pipeline is huge. Today, true adventurers will find untamed and majestic expanses of nature in the sparsely populated interior. The only accessible roads are the Parks Hwy.

from Anchorage to Fairbanks, the Glenn Hwy. from Anchorage east to Glenallen and the Yukon, and the Alaska Hwy. from the Yukon northwest to Fairbanks. The dirt road Denali Hwy. cuts east-west from the Richardson Hwy. to the Parks Hwy. and is a scenic route for the adventurous.

DENALI NAT'L PARK AND PRESERVE ☎907

AT A GLANCE	
AREA: 4,740,911 acres.	**GATEWAYS:** Cantwell (p. 541), Paxson. Easily reachable from Anchorage and Fairbanks.
CLIMATE: It's cold.	
FEATURES: Denali (Mt. McKinley), rampant wildlife.	**CAMPING:** Bountiful. See p. 537.
HIGHLIGHTS: Hiking in the backcountry, camping under the stars.	**FEES:** $5 per person for 7 days.

Denali's six million acres of snowcapped peaks, braided streams, and glacier-carved valleys are interrupted only by a lone gravel road less than 100 mi. long. Visitors to the park are guests of the countless grizzly bears, moose, caribou, wolves, Dall sheep, raptors, and wildflowers that thrive here. Over one million people come to the park every year, but there is little that crowds can do to take away from the glory of the vast and pristine wilderness. The park's centerpiece, Denali, only adds to the splendor. With 18,000 of its 20,320 ft. above the surrounding lands, it is the world's tallest mountain from base to peak. Although the US Geological Survey named the peak "Mt. McKinley," most Alaskans know it as Denali. Denali is so big that it makes its own weather: moist air from the Pacific Ocean collides with the cold mountaintop and storms encircle the summit. Since Denali's face is only visible about 10% of the time in summer, many visitors to the park will never see the peak.

Denali National Park

🏠 ACCOMMODATIONS
Mountain Morning Hostel, **7**

⛺ CAMPING
Carlo Creek, **8**   Sanctuary River, **2**
Grizzly Bear, **6**   Savage River, **3**
Morino Creek, **5**   Teklanika River, **4**
Riley Creek, **1**   Wonder Lake, **9**

In summer, especially from mid-June to mid-August, crowds and lines at the entrance are a frequent presence. Shuttle buses into the park only run from late May until mid-September, so the window of relatively crowd-free access is small. Mid- to late August is an excellent time to visit—fall colors peak, berries ripen, mosquito season has virtually ended, and September's snows have not yet arrived. Be sure to check out the park's newspaper, the *Alpenglow*, as soon as you get there. It has all the vital information that will help you avoid the lines at the visitors desk. Making advance reservations for campsites and shuttle buses will spare you a day or two of waiting for permits and tickets upon arrival at the park.

▐ TRANSPORTATION

The park is easily reached by road or rail. Anchorage lies 237 mi. south and Fairbanks 120 mi. north along the **George Parks Hwy.** (Rte. 3; see p. 542). The rough **Denali Hwy.** (Rte. 8; see p. 541) meets the Parks Hwy. 27 mi. south of the park entrance at Cantwell, and extends 136 mi. east to Paxson. **Camper buses** go into the Park at scheduled times for day or overnight trips (see **In The Park**).

Buses: Many of the buses that traverse the Parks Hwy. will drop off and pick up at trailheads along the park's edge with advance notice. **Parks Highway Express** (☎ 888-600-6001; www.alaskashuttle.com) runs daily to **Anchorage** (5hr., $39, round-trip $69) and **Fairbanks** (3½hr., $54, round-trip $99).

Trains: Alaska Railroad (☎ 265-2494 or 800-544-0552, www.alaskarailroad.com) stops at Denali Station, 1½ mi. from park entrance. Peak season June 8-Sept. 1; value season May 15-June 7, Sept. 2-16. Scenic rides to **Anchorage** (8hr.; $125 peak, $100 value) and **Fairbanks** (4½hr.; $50 peak, $40 value). Ages 2-11 50% off; under 2 free. Mid-Sept. to mid-May the train runs weekly at reduced rates. Open daily 10am-5pm.

AT THE ENTRANCE

The free **Riley Creek Loop Bus** (30min., 6am-9pm) runs between the visitors center, the Alaska Railroad station, the Horseshoe Lake trailhead, and the Riley Creek campground. Schedules are posted at each stop. Chalet-owned **courtesy buses** run from what was once the Denali Park Hotel to the McKinley Chalet (1 mi. north of the park entrance) and to McKinley Village (6 mi. south of the park) from 5am to midnight. **Caribou Cab,** complete with antlers on the roof, is at ☎ 683-5000.

MCKINLEY OR NOT MCKINLEY—THAT IS THE QUESTION

History has not been kind to William McKinley, 25th president of the United States. Washington, D.C. has no McKinley Memorial. Few have celebrated McKinley's birthday since he last marked the occasion himself in 1901.

In Alaska, however, an attempt was once made to memorialize McKinley in a form that would dwarf Mt. Rushmore. In 1896, William A. Dickey, a Princeton-educated prospector, named the highest mountain in North America "Mt. McKinley" to honor the then-new presidential candidate and his support of the gold standard. Of course, the mountain had a name long before any Ivy-League Republicans laid eyes on it. Athabascans of the interior had long called the 20,320 ft. giant Denali ("the Great One").

At 18,000 ft. from base to summit, Denali has the greatest total altitude gain of any mountain in the world. Mt. Everest—originally Sagarmatha or Jomolungma—is higher above sea level but rises only 11,000 ft. from its base on the Plateau of Tibet. In 1980, an official effort to rename Mt. McKinley failed, but the land on which it stands was designated Denali National Park as a compromise. Today, almost everyone ignores the US Geological Survey and uses the original name.

IN THE PARK

In order to limit human influence on the land and wildlife, only the first 15mi. of the park road are accessible by private vehicle (no special permit necessary). The remaining 75 mi. are open only to bicycles and park-run buses. In the summer, two services travel the park's interior in refurbished school buses.

Shuttle buses carrying talkative tour guides leave from the visitors center, stop when any passenger spots a bear or other large mammal, and turn back at various points along the road. (Tours daily 5am-6pm; $18.25, ages 13-16 50% off, under 13 free.) All travel times are round-trip: **Savage River,** Mile 15 (2hr., $2); **Polychorome Overlook,** Mile 47 (5½hr., $17); **Toklat,** Mile 53 (6hr., $17); **Eielson,** Mile 66 (8hr., $23); **Wonder Lake,** Mile 85 (11hr., $30); and **Kantishna,** Mile 89 (13hr., $33). For those who don't make it into the backcountry, taking a bus tour is a great way to see the park, and wildlife sightings are all but guaranteed. **Camper buses** ($18.50) transport only those visitors with campground or backcountry permits (available at the visitors center), have extra room for gear and **bikes,** and move faster than the shuttle buses without the narration. Ask at the visitors center for complete bus schedules. Both camper and shuttle buses stop to pick up pedestrians anywhere along the road back. **Bicyclists** must keep to the road and only the road. Backcountry travelers must leave bikes locked up on racks provided at the campgrounds.

Most shuttle tickets and campground spots are reserved in advance by phone (☎800-622-7175 or 272-7275). Nevertheless, those willing to wait in line can purchase their tickets up to the day of, if available. A set of **binoculars** (bring a pair or purchase at the visitors center for $25+) is recommended for up-close views of wildlife from the road.

ⓘ PRACTICAL INFORMATION

Tourist Information: Denali Visitor Center (☎683-2294; www.nps.gov/dena/home), ½ mi. from the Parks Hwy. The essential info and permit shop. Their free publication, the *Alpenglow,* contains park regulations, rates and history, and schedules of ranger-led events, including interpretive walks, discovery hikes, and sled dog demonstrations. A worthwhile 15min. **slide program** presents the history of Denali (repeats every 30min). Most park privileges are distributed on a first-come, first-served basis. Lockers $0.50 per day. Open Memorial Day-Labor Day 7am-8pm; late Apr. to Memorial Day and Labor Day-late Sept. 10am-4pm. Shuttle ticket lines form by 6:30am. All visitor center references refer to this location. **Eielson Visitor Center,** 66 mi. into the park, is accessible only by shuttle bus. Friendly rangers lead informative 1hr. **tundra walks** daily at 1pm. No food available. Running water, flush toilets. Open daily mid-June to Sept. 9am-7pm. Ranger Stations are located at **Kantishna, Toklat River,** and **Sanctuary River.** The **Park Headquarters** (☎683-2294; Open M-F 8am-4:30pm) is located near **Riley Creek.**

Bank: An **ATM** is available in the **Chalet Inn** gift shop, 1 mi. north of the park. Open mid-May to mid-Sept. 5am-10:30pm. **Healy,** 11 mi. north of the park entrance, has a few ATMs; locations include the gas station by **McKinley RV and Campground, Wally's Service Station,** and the **Totem Inn.** Most park services accept credit cards.

Entrance Fee: Payable at the time of reservation. $5 per person for 7 days.

Mountaineering Information: Talkeetna Ranger Station, in Talkeetna (see p. 543).

Equipment Rental: Denali Outdoor Center (☎683-1925 or 888-303-1925; www.denalioutdoorcenter.com), at Parks Hwy. Mile 238.5, just north of the park entrance. Bikes half-day $25, full-day $40, 5 or more days $35 per day.

Laundromat: McKinley Campground (☎683-2379 or 800-478-2562), in Healy, 11 mi. north of the park entrance. Wash $2.50, dry $1.75. Tokens sold June-Aug. daily 8am-10pm; winter 8am-8pm. Machines available 24hr.

Emergency: ☎911.

Medical Services: Healy Clinic (☎683-2211), 13 mi. north and ½ mi. east of Healy Spur Rd. park. Open May-Sept. M-F 9am-5pm; Oct.-Apr. M-F 10am-3pm. On call 24hr.

Internet Access: At the **Black Bear Coffee House.** $3 first 15min. $2.50 per each additional 15min. Open daily May-Sept. 6am-10pm.

Post Office: (☎683-2291) ¼ mi. from the park entrance, on the left. Open May-Sept. M-F 8:30am-5pm, Sa 10am-1pm; Oct.-Apr. M-Sa 10am-1pm. **Postal Code:** 99755.

🄿 🄲 CAMPING AND ACCOMMODATIONS

Travelers planning on staying at the established campgrounds must obtain a **permit** from the visitors center and may then stay for up to 14 nights on park campgrounds. Free permits are available on a first-come, first-served basis one day in advance. Sites at five of the seven campgrounds can be reserved in advance. Reservations are strongly recommended; without one, prepare to camp or stay outside the park for at least one night. Sixty-five percent of shuttle tickets and all of the campsites at **Riley Creek, Savage River, Teklanika,** and **Wonder Lake** can be reserved from February up until the day before travel. (☎800-622-7275 or 272-7275. Open daily 7am-5pm.) Permits for remaining sites are available two days in advance at the visitors center on a first-come, first-served basis. The visitors center opens at 7am; the early bird gets the permit. There is a $4 non-refundable fee for campground reservations, and there is a $6 fee per site or bus ticket to change your reservations. RV amenities are sparse in Denali: there are no RV sites and only one dump station, at Riley Creek. RV drivers can pay $12 per night to park at Riley Creek, Savage River, or Teklanika River, or they can head to any of the RV parks near the park entrance. Backcountry travelers must obtain a free backcountry permit; for info, see **Exploring the Backcountry,** p. 539. All campgrounds within the park, except Sanctuary River, are wheelchair accessible. Unless otherwise noted, all campgrounds are open from May to September. Options farther from the park include several motels in Healy (just over 11 mi. north of the park entrance) and a series of bed and breakfasts located off the Healy Spur Rd.

🏕 **Denali Mountain Morning Hostel** (☎683-7503 or in Alaska 866-346-7835). 13 mi. south of the Park entrance. Rustic, hand-crafted cabins. Clean rooms, full kitchen, Internet, groceries. **$3 park shuttles** (call for schedules), outdoor gear rentals and sales (backpacker kit $30 1st day, $7 additional days). Reservations strongly recommended. Bunks $23, ages 5-13 $17. More private rooms start at $50. Tent sites $15. ❷

Carlo Creek (☎683-2576). Also 13 mi. south of the Park entrance, this private campground offers covered picnic tables and fire pit grilles at every site. Tent sites $11 plus $3 per person. Showers $4, free with stay. ❶

Denali Grizzly Bear (☎683-2696, www.alaskaone.com/dengrzly). Mile 231 of the Parks Hwy. This campground offers riverside or mountain vista tent sites in close proximity to the Park. 89 sites $17.50; tent cabins $22-24; sleeping cabins from $49. Open mid-May to mid-Sept. Laundry wash and dry $2.50 each. Showers $1.50 per 4min. ❷

Riley Creek, Mile 0.25 Denali Park Rd. The only year-round campground in Denali. All sites assigned at the visitors center. Close to the highway and the visitors center, Riley Creek is louder and more congested than the other campgrounds. Piped water, flush toilets, and sewage dump. No water in winter. 100 sites, $16. ❶

Morino Creek, Mile 1.9 Denali Park Rd., next to the train tracks. 60 2-person sites for backpackers without vehicles. Register at Morino. Water, chemical toilets. No open fires (stoves only). Nearest showers at the Mercantile. Many backpackers stay here while they wait for permits and check out the park on the buses. Sites, $6. ❶

Savage River, Mile 13 Denali Park Rd. High, dry country with easy access to popular Primrose Ridge. Complimentary shuttle to and from visitors center. Flush toilets and water. Last area accessible by car without a permit. 33 sites for RVs and tents, $12. ❶

Sanctuary River, Mile 23 Denali Park Rd. Quiet, wooded campsite with river access. Chemical toilets, no fires (stoves only). Accessible only by bus. 7 tent sites, $6. ❶

Teklanika River, Mile 29 Denali Park Rd. Popular with members of the Winnebago tribe. Piped water and flush toilets. Accessible by shuttle bus or by vehicle with permit. 3-night min. for vehicle campers. Vehicles are permitted only to drive in and drive out and must remain parked for the duration of the stay. 53 tent and RV sites, $12. ❶

▐ FOOD

Denali is expensive, and local grocery options are limited. Wise is the traveler who stocks up in Fairbanks or Wasilla. **McKinley Mercantile** is at the Riley Creek Campground. (☎ 683-9246. Open daily 5am-11pm.) The **Denali General Store,** 1 mi. north of the park entrance, also stocks groceries, but be prepared to pay $4 for a loaf of bread. (☎ 683-2920. Open daily May-Sept. 6am-10pm.) Once you board the park bus, there is no food available anywhere past the Mercantile.

▧ **Black Bear Coffee House** (☎ 683-1656). 1 mi. north of the park entrance in the center of a long row of log cabin storefronts. The most affordable food stop near Denali as well as the only place to find Internet access (see **Practical Information,** p. 536). Hot and strong coffee is served up with fresh baked goods. Try the chunky homemade soup ($3.50) or half-sandwich with chips ($6). Open May-Sept. daily, approx. 6am-10pm. ❶

McKinley Creekside (☎ 683-2277), 13 mi. south of the park entrance and across the highway from the hostel (see **Accommodations and Camping**). The Creekside offers slightly more reasonable rates than places nearer to the entrance along with highly edible fare. Chow on a hot sandwich ($8-9), try a salad ($9), chug a brew or espresso and take the waiter up on one of the many desserts. Open May-Sept. daily 6am-10pm. ❷

▌ HIKING

The shuttle bus affords excellent views and wildlife-sighting opportunities, but the real Denali lies beyond the road. Past Mile 14 there are **no trails.** The park's backcountry philosophy rests on the idea that independent wandering creates more rewards and less impact than would a network of trails or routes. In an effort to disperse hikers as widely as possible, rangers will not recommend specific routes, although they will suggest areas that meet hikers' desires and abilities. Topographical maps ($4) are available at the visitors center.

DAYHIKING

Denali is full of wide open spaces, and this is a great way to explore them. You can begin dayhiking from anywhere along the park road by riding the shuttle bus to a suitable starting point and asking the driver to let you off. Don't feel obligated to get off at one of the designated rest stops (found every hour or so along the way); drivers will be happy to drop you off anywhere that isn't wildlife restricted. Once you've wandered to your heart's content, head back to the road and flag down a shuttle bus heading in your direction. The first couple of buses may be full (it's recommended to plan on waiting an hour), but it's rare to wait more than 30min. for a ride. Be sure to check when the last buses will be passing your area in order to guarantee a ride back. Stream crossings and bushwhacking are inevitable if you plan to get far from the road: good boots, long pants, and gaiters are all advisable.

For those waiting on permits, great dayhiking is accessible from many shuttle stops. **Polychrome Overlook** at Mile 47 offers a spectacular 360° view of the park and grants easy ridge access for those looking to gain some altitude. From the **Toklat River** stop at Mile 53 the wanderer can choose between a hike north up the river valley, or south into the larger drainage. Hikes following the many river systems are generally easier to negotiate and cover ground more quickly than bushwhacking. The visitors center is a great resource for planning dayhikes; if you come with an idea of what you'd like to do (ridges, glaciers, peaks, etc.), they are likely to point you in a good direction. A few easy-to-moderate trails are maintained around the park entrance. **Horseshoe Lake Trail** is 3 mi. round-trip with lovely mountain views, and the lake is popular with moose. **Roadside Trail** runs 2 mi. from the hotel toward Park Headquarters, where the sled-dog demonstrations are held. **Mt. Healy Overlook Trail** is more challenging and starts from the hotel parking lot. The 4½ mi. round-trip climbs 1700 ft. to an impressive view of the valley at 3400 ft. and takes 3-4hr. The particularly ambitious can continue up the ridge to the 5700 ft. summit. More information on entrance area trail hikes is available in the *Alpenglow*.

Discovery hikes are guided 3-5hr. hikes, departing on special buses from the visitors center. Topics vary; a ranger might lead you on a cross-country scramble or a moose-trail excursion, providing a comprehensive introduction to local wildlife, flowers, and geological formations. The hikes are free but require reservations and a bus ticket. More sedate 45min. **tundra walks** leave from the Eielson visitors center daily at 1:30pm, but many other talks and naturalist programs are posted.

EXPLORING THE BACKCOUNTRY

The road barely scratches the surface of Denali's wilderness, and the wildlife doesn't seem quite so wild through a bus window. With no major cities for 300 mi. in any direction, camping in Denali's backcountry is an experience like no other. Only 2-12 backpackers can camp at a time in each of the park's 41 units. Overnight stays in the backcountry require a **free permit**, available no earlier or later than one day in advance at the **backcountry desk** in the visitors center. The **quota board** there reports which units are still available. Eager hikers line up outside as early as 6:30am to grab permits for popular units. Some units may be temporarily closed after a fresh wildlife kill or bear encounter. The **Sable Pass** area has been off-limits to hikers since 1955 due to bear activity. There are several steps to obtaining a permit: among other things, one must have a planned itinerary, watch a video, and listen to a safety talk. For more info, check out the backcountry web site: www.nps.gov/dena/home/hiking/index/html.

The park covers a variety of terrain, with varying implications for hiking. **River bars** are level and rocky, offering very good footing for hikers but potentially difficult stream crossings. **Low tundra,** in brushy, soggy areas above the tree line, is not easily navigable and makes for exasperating hiking under insect-infested conditions. **Alpine tundra** (or **dry tundra**) is higher and drier which means fewer mosquitoes. Generally, the southern reaches of the park contain dry tundra and river bars. The northern reaches are brushier but include high points with incredible views of the mountain. Some of the most enjoyable hiking and wildlife-viewing awaits in the middle of the park near the Toklat River and Polychrome Pass.

Backcountry campers must stay within their registered unit, pitching tents at least half a mile from the road and out of sight. A compass (available at the visitors center for around $6) and **topographical maps** ($4) are essential. Before they head out, campers receive a short introduction to bear management, and are required to spend some quality time with the center's interactive **backcountry simulator.** This allows virtual hikers to learn about a number of potentially dangerous wilderness situations. Most zones require that food be carried in a 3 lb. plastic **bear-resistant food container (BRFC),** available for free loan at the backcountry desk. Be sure to leave space in your backpack. Backcountry hikers *will* cross streams, whack bushes, and battle mosquitoes: gaiters and head nets are luxuries to consider. Denali's backcountry provides ideal conditions for **hypothermia.** With the park's many rivers, streams, and pools, your feet *will* get wet. Under these conditions, hypothermia sets in quickly; talk with rangers about prevention and warning signs. **Mosquito repellent** is a necessity for anyone going into Denali's backcountry. These annoying insects have the ability to turn a pleasant bushwhack into a fly-swatting, arm-swinging itch-fest.

OTHER OUTDOOR ACTIVITIES

BIKING

Unlike private motor vehicles, **bicycles** are permitted on the entire length of the park road, making them a perfect way to escape the shuttle-bus ticket blues. Park at Savage River and ride into the heart of Denali. The park road is 90 mi. long, crossing four mountain passes, so if you're not up to the 180 mi. round-trip, feel free to turn back at any time. Most of the road is unpaved, so thicker tires work best. Off-road biking is not permitted anywhere in the park, but wild encounters can still occur; one *Let's Go* researcher found herself in a furious bicycle race against a persistent caribou. For bike rental info, see **Practical Information,** p. 536.

RAFTING

Several **rafting** companies run the Class III rapids of Denali's Nenana River; the stretch is swift, splashy, and scenic. Most companies provide dry suits—something you'll need if you fall into the 2°C water. The **Denali Outdoor Center** (**DOC**; see **Practical Information,** p. 536) and **Nenana Raft Adventures** boast the most experienced river guides. (2hr. whitewater runs $55-65 per person; 4hr. combined (float and paddle) $80-90. The DOC also runs guided **kayak** tours ($75), which don't require experience; they include a free shuttle. Open May-Sept. daily 8am-9pm.)

FLIGHTSEEING

Flightseeing tours are a wonderful way to see the Mountain, especially on a clear day. **Denali Air** (☎683-2261) is one option near the park. **ERA Helicopters Flightseeing Tours** (☎683-2574; www.eraaviation.com) offers mountain viewing as well as guided heli-hiking ($300), but the town of Talkeetna is closer to the Mountain and has companies that offer cheaper trips.

HORSEBACK RIDING

For horse-lovers and aspiring cowboys, trail rides are the way to go. **Denali Saddle Safaris** offers rides that wind through the taiga and tundra with spectacular views of surrounding mountains. (☎683-1200; 1hr. ride $65, 2hr. ride $85, 4hr. ride $125.)

WINTER SPORTS

Cross-country skiing, snowshoeing, and **dog sledding** allow visitors to see the park during the winter. Despite 20hr. nights and temperatures below -40°C, many perfectly sane individuals consider winter the most beautiful time of year in Denali. Call the Park Headquarters for information on winter camping (☎274-8440). If you plan to travel through Denali in the winter, you are strongly encouraged to stop by the visitors center to tell them your route. For the safety of rangers and travelers alike, rangers request route info and expected completion dates.

DENALI HWY. (RTE. 8)   ☎907

The breathtaking Denali Hwy. runs west from **Paxson,** 80 mi. (1¼hr.) south of Delta Junction on the Richardson Hwy. (Rte. 4), to **Cantwell,** 27 mi. (30min.) south of the Denali National Park entrance. Along the way, it skirts the foothills of the Alaska Range to the north and Talkeetna Mountains to the south, amid countless lakes and streams teeming with trout, Arctic char, burbot, and grayling. Pristine, free campgrounds and unique geological formations along the way make the road a destination in itself. The highway and many of the trails that branch off it, particularly in the Tangle Lakes district (see below), are ideal for mountain biking. The Denali Hwy. is **closed** from October to mid-May. Except for the 21 mi. west of Paxson, it is entirely gravel. Due to budget cuts, as of July 1, 2002 the road won't be maintained, so expect extra bumpy conditions. Most vehicles can expect to keep a pace of 30 mph. **Mile markers,** where they exist, measure the distance from Paxson. **Gas and services** are available at Mile 20 and Mile 82. Call ☎911 or a **state trooper** (☎768-2202) in an **emergency.**

TANGLE LAKES

The **Tangle Lakes National Register District,** between Mile 17 and 37, serves as a base for mountain bikers, ATVers, and birders. Pick up the Bureau of Land Management's free "Trail Map and Guide to the Tangle Lakes" at the **Tangle River Inn** (see below) for details. Archaeological sites in the area contain evidence of some of the first human settlements in North America, some of which are at least 10,000 years old. For more info, contact the **Bureau of Land Management** (☎822-3217).

Three established campgrounds exist along the highway, but anxious campers could feasibly set up shop almost anywhere. At Mile 21, the scenic **Tangle Lakes Campground** (free; toilets, water pump) provides easy access to the 30 mi., 2-3 day **Delta River Canoe Route,** with one difficult stretch of Class III rapids and one portage. Put in at Mile 212.5 of the Richardson Hwy. The **Upper Tangle Lakes Canoe Route** is an easier 9 mi. paddle beginning at **Tangle River** and ending at **Dickey Lake,** also the starting point for the extended middle fork of the **Gulkana Canoe Route.** The helpful "Delta" and "Gulkana" brochures are available free from the BLM and most highway establishments. The **Tangle River Campground** (Mile 21.7) and **Brushkana Campground** (Mile 104) offer similar services, in spite of a $6 fee at the latter.

The **Tangle River Inn ❸,** at Mile 20 across the highway from the boat launch, was homesteaded by the current owner's father via dog sled before the highway was built. Private rooms and beds all share a common area. The pool table, TV, and VCR are popular; book ahead. The inn offers a cafe, bar, gas, and canoe rental. (☎822-3970, winter 895-4022. Cafe open 7:30am-10pm., bar until midnight.

CENTRAL ALASKA

Canoe $4 per hr., $24 per day. Showers $5, free with stay. Dorms $27.50; private rooms $60; cabins with full bath $99.)

Fishers as well as lovers of flora and fauna flock to the **Tangle Lakes Lodge ❹**, at Mile 22. The owners have the lowdown on the area's wildlife and canoe routes. (☎ 822-4202. Canoes $3 per hr. and $30 per day. Rooms up to 4 $75, $10 extra with canoe for night.) The area hosts 140 different species of birds, including the arctic warbler and Smith's longspur (see www.alaskan.com/tanglelakes/cklist.htm for a **birding checklist**), and some of the best car-accessible arctic fishing in the state.

ALONG RTE. 3: GEORGE PARKS HWY. ☎907

Thirty-five miles out of Anchorage, the George Parks Hwy. splits from the Glenn Hwy. (Rte. 1) and runs 322 mi. north to Fairbanks, linking Alaska's two largest cities. A drive on "The Parks" is a visual feast, often featuring moose sightings, wolf crossings, and spectacular views on the approach to Denali. Its two lanes are paved and in good condition, except for a few frostheaves. Drivers heading north from Anchorage can stop in at the **Mat-Su Visitor Center,** on the Parks Hwy. just after it splits from the Glenn Hwy., for some friendly advice on where to stop along the way. (☎ 746-5000. Open mid-May to mid-Sept. daily 8:30am-7pm.)

TO TALKEETNA ☎907

Wasilla, at Mile 39.5, is home to the **Iditarod race headquarters and museum,** 2¼ mi. off the Parks on Knik Goose Bay Rd. Visitors can learn all about the famous dogsled race, watch a video, admire the trophies, and take a short ride on a dog-drawn wheeled buggy. (☎376-5155; www.iditarod.com. Open Memorial Day to mid-Sept. daily 8am-7pm; Sept.-May M-F 8am-5pm. Free. Sled rides, weather permitting June-Aug. $5 for about 5min.)

The ◪**Wasilla Backpackers Hostel ❷**, 3950 Carefree Dr., off Campbell St. at Parks Hwy. Mile 39, is equipped with a spacious guest kitchen for its diverse crowd. Other features include flowers and a hammock in the yard, horseshoes on the porch, and a basketball court. The owners have plenty of enthusiastic advice on nearby hiking, biking, and canoeing opportunities as well as a free local map. Mountain bikes available for $20 per day. (☎357-3699. Laundry $1, drying $1. Internet $3 per 30min., $5 per hr. 14 singles. $22.) **Nancy Lake campground ❶** is located just South of Willow at Mile 67.3 down Buckingham Place Rd. This is the avid canoeist's entry point to the many lakes in the Nancy Lake Recreation area, with over 30 first-come, first-served sites. (Pit toilets, water well. $10.) For canoeing, put in at one of the many trailheads along the 6 mi. Nancy Lake Parkway. Check it out at Alaska State Parks, (☎745-0938, www.alaskastateparks.org).

TALKEETNA ☎907

Talkeetna (tah-KEET-nah) is a Tanaina word meaning "rivers of plenty" and an apt name for this eclectic settlement—there's plenty to do here. Because of its proximity to Denali—only 60 mi. by air to the north—Talkeetna is the flight departure point for would-be climbers of the challenging peak. Every year between April and June, about 1300 mountaineers from around the globe converge on Talkeetna, giving the town an international flavor and creating a run on accommodations. The combination of climbers, tourists, and hardy year-round residents, coupled with amazing outdoor opportunities, makes this town a worthwhile stop.

⌨ TRANSPORTATION

Talkeetna lies at the end of the **Talkeetna Spur Rd.,** which runs 14 mi. northeast off the Parks Hwy. from Mile 98.5. The town is 113 mi. north of Anchorage, 124 mi. south of the Denali National Park entrance, and 273 mi. south of Fairbanks.

Trains: The **Alaska Railroad** station (☎800-544-0552; www.alaskarailroad.com) is a covered platform half a mile south of town. Trains run mid-May to mid-Sept. Peak season is June 4-Sept. 1. Value season May 15-June 7 and Sept 2-16. To: **Anchorage** (3½hr.; 1 per day; $75 peak, $60 value); **Denali** (4½hr.; 1 per day; $70 peak, $56 value); and **Fairbanks** (9hr.; 1 per day; $100 peak, $80 value).

Buses: Parks Highway Express (☎888-600-6001; www.alaskashuttle.com) stops at the Talkeetna junction, and if you call ahead they'll take you the remaining 14 mi. ($18 cab ride, $8 each additional person). Runs once per day mid-May to late Sept. to **Anchorage** (2hr.; $39, round-trip $69) and **Fairbanks** (7hr., $64, round-trip $119) via **Denali** (4hr., $44, round-trip $79). Call for winter info. **Talkeetna Shuttle Service** (☎888-288-6008) has daily service to Anchorage from town. Runs mid-Apr. to July. Added trips during climbing season. ($50, round-trip $90.) **The Park Connection,** run by Alaska Tour and Travel (☎800-266-8625) drops off in town during climbing season. Once per day to **Anchorage** (11am, $41) and **Denali** (6pm, $41).

ℹ PRACTICAL INFORMATION

Visitor Information: Talkeetna/Denali Visitors Center (☎733-2688), off Parks Hwy. Info on everything to do and see in Talkeetna and Denali. Open mid-May to mid-Sept. daily 9am-6pm. **Talkeetna Mountain Shop,** (☎733-1686) at Main St. and Spur Rd. Info on air charters and walking tours. Open Apr. to mid-Sept. daily 8am-6pm.

Outdoor Information: Talkeetna Ranger Station (☎733-2231; fax 733-1465; www.nps.gov/dena/home). Turn left at the terminus of Main St. With plenty of information and weather reports, the station is a required stop for those planning on climbing Denali. Climbers must be registered 60 days in advance. Registration fee $150. Open mid-May to Aug. daily 8am-6pm; Sept. to mid-May M-F 8am-4:30pm.

Equipment Rental: The **Talkeetna Outdoor Center** (☎733-4444), toward the end of town on Main St., sells mountaineering gear and some camping gear, rents mountain bikes, and provides outdoor information. Open mid-Apr. to mid-Oct. daily 9am-6pm; open based on demand during the off season. **Busy Bikes** (☎733-2675 or 232-5334), in a tin shed on the airport corner, rents multi-speed and cruiser bikes. Half-day $15 and $14 respectively, full-day $25 and $20.

Banks: There are **no banks**, but there are 2 **ATMs** ($1.50 surcharge): one at **Nagley's Store** on Main St. (see **Food and Nightlife**), the other at **Three Rivers Tesoro** gas station on Main St. Open daily 8am-9pm.

Laundromat: At the **Three Rivers Tesoro** gas station (☎733-6212), on Main St. Wash $2, dry $0.25 per 6min. Showers $2 per 8min. Open daily 8am-9pm. If you're too busy for laundry, drop it off at **Washi-Washi** to have it done for you. Wash and dry, $2 each.

Emergency: ☎911.

State Police: Just past the Talkeetna Alaska Lodge (☎733-2256), Mile 13, Spur Rd.

24hr. Crisis Line: ☎746-4080.

Medical Services: Sunshine Community Health Clinic (☎733-2273 or 24hr. emergency 733-2348), 9 mi. from town on Spur Rd. Open M-Tu and Th-F 9am-6pm, W 1-6pm, Sa 9am-5pm.

Internet Access: Free at the **library** (☎ 733-2359), 1 mi. from town on Spur Rd. Open Tu, W, F 11am-6pm, Th 11am-7pm, Sa 10am-5pm.

Post Office: (☎ 733-2275), in town on Spur Rd. Open M-F 9am-5pm, Sa 10am-2pm. **Postal Code:** 99676.

◤ ACCOMMODATIONS AND CAMPING

Indoor accommodations can fill up quickly during climbing season (Apr.-June). Memorial Day (the 4th weekend in May) and the 2nd weekend in May (Moosedropping Festival, see **Sights and Events**) are also particularly busy times for the campgrounds, so plan ahead.

Talkeetna Hostel International (☎ 733-4678). Turn off Spur Rd. by the airport onto 2nd St. Turn left on "I" street; it's the 3rd house on the right. A short walk from town, airport and rail, rates include a kitchen and a common area with TV and wood stove. 1 shared bath. 5-night max. stay. Closed Oct.-May. Comfy bunks $25; doubles $60. ❷

Talkeetna Roadhouse (☎ 733-1351). Centrally located at Main and C St. Built in 1917, it is the oldest building in town still in use. The living room of this cozy establishment features soft couches, old books, a guitar, and a piano. 3 shared bathrooms. During climbing season, reservations should be made well in advance. Bunks $21; singles $48; doubles downstairs $63 or upstairs $90. ❸

Talkeetna River Adventures (☎ 733-2604). Turn right off Spur Rd. at the airport, then turn left. Clean and quiet, located in a wooded area. Water, outhouses, and easy river access. Open May-Sept. 60 sites, $12. Showers $3 for 11min. ❶

River Park Campground, at the end of Main St. Because of its close proximity to town, River Park may not always be serene. Outhouses. First come, first served. $12. ❶

◖◗ FOOD AND NIGHTLIFE

Nagley's Store on Main St. stocks groceries, but also sells lattes for little more than $1 and footlong hotdogs for $2.50. (☎ 733-3663. Open Su-Th 8am-10pm, F-Sa 8am-11pm; in winter closes 1hr. earlier.) The **Three Rivers Tesoro** gas station (see **Practical Information,** above) also sells groceries.

▨ **Talkeetna Roadhouse Cafe,** (see **Accommodations and Camping,** above) offers famous Denali-sized breakfasts for around $7 and cinnamon rolls for $3. Other hearty options include sandwiches ($6) and homemade soup ($5 per bowl). Open Apr.-Sept. daily 6:30am-4pm; Dec.-Mar. Sa-Su 8am-2pm. ❶

West Rib, on Main St., proudly serves tasty musk-ox and caribou burgers ($8), plus veggie burgers ($7) for the faint of heart. Play a game of pool or darts as you enjoy an Alaskan beer ($4) in their outdoor beer garden. Open daily in summer noon-close (food until midnight); in winter noon-midnight. ❷

Fairview Inn offers bands on weekends and live music almost nightly. Party with the locals if the caribou, musk-ox, and bearskin trophy mounts don't scare you off. BBQ in summer. Burgers $5.50, beer $2. Open daily noon to "late." ❶

Main Street Cafe (☎ 733-1275). A quick option for any meal. Sit inside or on the deck. Either way, try breakfast ($3-6, served 8-11:30am). Features Talkeetna Cheese Steak ($5) and Oriental Chicken Salad ($9). Open daily 8am-10pm; closed M in winter. ❶

SIGHTS AND EVENTS

The **Talkeetna Historical Society Museum,** off Main St. between C and D St., includes the town's oldest cabin, a dramatic scale model of the Mountain, and daily ranger talks at 1pm. (☎733-2487. Open May-Sept. daily 9:30am-5:30pm; Oct.-Apr. Sa-Su 11am-5pm. $2.50.) Alaska's annual answer to Woodstock takes place at Parks Hwy. 102 during the ◧**Talkeetna Bluegrass Festival,** held on the first weekend in August. Alaska's rowdiest campout features a talented lineup of state bands and promises a wacky good time, rain or shine. The 2nd weekend in July brings Talkeetna's increasingly famous **Moose Dropping Festival** (www.moosedrop.com), sponsored by the Historical Society. Thousands flock to enjoy the two-day festival, complete with a parade, live bagpipes, and a moose dropping toss. Early December brings the **Bachelor Auction and Ball,** where eligible locals go to the highest bidder. Around the same time is the **Wilderness Women Contest,** with such events as wood-chopping, salmon-fishing, and sandwich making; a lighthearted competition involving skills "vital" to life on the frontier.

OUTDOOR ACTIVITIES

FLIGHTSEEING

Because of Talkeetna's proximity to Denali, flights from here are cheaper than those found directly outside the park. If the weather cooperates, these flights are worth every penny and will leave you itching for more. Flights come in two standard types: a 1hr. flight approaching the Mountain from the south, and a 1½hr. tour that circumnavigates the peak. Landing on a remote glacier at the base of Denali ups the cost but can be added to almost all flights. One-hour trips cost $115-$125 per person. The 15-30min. glacier stop-off (often at a climbing base camp) costs an extra $50-55 per person but is definitely worthwhile. All flights are weather-dependent, with most companies offering flights over the rugged Talkeetna Mountains to the south if Denali weather is uncooperative. Many companies, including **Doug Geeting Aviation,** offer discounts to groups of four or five. (☎733-2366 or 800-770-2366.) **Talkeetna Air Taxi** (☎733-2218 or 800-533-2219), **McKinley Air Service** (☎733-1765 or 800-564-1765), and **K2 Aviation** (☎733-2291 or 800-764-2291) offer standard services, plus a variety of other specialized trips. All flight services suspend glacier landings in mid-July due to unsafe and unpredictable snow conditions. To show tourists the top of the Mountain, **Talkeetna Air Taxi, K2 Aviation,** and **Talkeetna Aero Services** (☎733-2899 or 800-660-2688) offer oxygen-equipped twin engine planes that can reach the 20,000 ft. altitude needed to fly over the summit. If you come to Talkeetna hell-bent on flightseeing, be prepared to wait a few days for the clouds to break. Call the flight outfits regardless of the weather in town; the mountains can bask in sun even while clouds smother Talkeetna.

FISHING AND RIVER TOURS

Fishing and touring outfits abound in the waterways around town. **Talkeetna River Guides,** on Main St., offers fishing and float trips that grant views of Denali and its wildlife with the help of eagle-eyed guides. (☎733-2677 or 800-353-2677; www.talkeetnariverguides.com. Fishing half-day $129, full-day $175; float trip $54-$84.) **Mahay's Riverboat Service** (☎733-2223 or 800-736-2210; www.mahaysriverboat.com), on Main St. just before downtown, also offers fishing charters and leads tours geared more toward wildlife education. ($50, ages 2-12 $25.) **Tri-River Charters,** (☎733-2400; www.tririvercharters.com) next to the post office, runs fishing charters ($135, half-day; $185, full-day) and scenic tours ($55) along the Talkeetna River. Also offers drop-off services ($45) and equipment rentals ($40).

BIKING

Opportunities for mountain biking in the general vicinity of Talkeetna are abundant, and the **Talkeetna River Trail** is a gem among them. This trail leads the biker through a wide and easy-to-follow wooded path, intersecting with the Talkeetna River and Larson Creek for excellent fishing. This trail may lead to some bushwhacking and river crossings, which are negotiated easily by carrying your bike. Traveling north, turn right onto Comsat Rd. (unmarked) at Mile 12 of the Talkeetna Spur Rd. Drive to its end and park out of the way. Enter ski trails and follow to the right. Stay on the established trail until Mile 7.6 at "Y," then continue right to Larson Creek. For bike rental info, see **Equipment Rental,** p. 543.

HIKING

Trek around the backcountry through trails that offer striking views of Denali on a clear day. For specific trail information, check with the **Talkeetna/Denali Visitors Center** (see **Practical Information,** p. 543). For 5-10 mile guided hiking tours that provide info on local flora and fauna, try **Talkeetna Hiking Adventures** (☎ 733-8735, hiketalkeetna@yahoo.com) at the Talkeetna Outdoor Center.

TALKEETNA TO NENANA ☎ 907

From Talkeetna, the Parks Hwy. begins a gradual ascent into the Alaska Range and offers some of the finest views of Mt. McKinley available without bushwhacking into the backcountry. The road winds northward from here across the Alaska Range, passing over steep canyons and through **Denali National Park** (Mile 132-168) and **Broad Pass** (Mile 201), the scenic high points of the drive. Denali National Park is about 30min. past the turn-off for the **Denali Hwy.** (Rte. 8; see p. 541). North of the National Park, the highway follows the **Nenana River** for about 70 mi. to Nenana.

OUTDOOR EXCURSIONS

The **South Denali Viewpoint,** Mile 135, near the entrance to Denali State Park, offers a spectacular profile of the 20,320 ft. peak and keeps drivers from running off the road. The turn-off to the viewpoint is just a few miles from the **Ruth Glacier,** but may not be worth the trip when it's cloudy. **Denali National Park** (☎ 745-3975) offers plenty of hiking trails and solitude. Two pleasant **campgrounds,** both with toilets and drinking water, are accessible from the highway: **Troublesome Creek ❶** at Mile 137.2 (10 tent sites; $5) and **Byers Lake ❶** at Mile 147. A few short hikes put this site a cut above the rest. (☎ 745-3975 or 269-8000 for PUC reservations. 68 sites for tents and RVs, $10.) The **Denali Viewpoint North ❶,** Mile 162.5, provides a breathtaking evening for those looking for a place to camp or simply look at the Mountain (sites $10, RVs free). Canoe and kayak rentals are available from **Susitna Expeditions.** (☎ 800-891-6916 or 892-6916; Open Su-Th, 7am-6pm; F-Sa 7am-8pm.) The weary traveler looking for a bed should try the **Byers Creek General Store ❷,** at Mile 144. 8 bunks. (☎ 733-2990; $25; private cabins with great views of the Alaska Range, $75. Showers $4, free with stay. Wash $2, dry $1.)

Just past Byers lake, visit the **Alaska Veterans' Memorial** and the **Denali State Park Visitor Information Center** for the mountain view, the Alaskan history, and local outdoor lore. (Open daily Memorial Day-Labor Day 9am-6pm.) For a more stomach-churning view, peek down the 260-ft. ravine at **Hurricane Gulch,** Mile 174. If you're in dire need of gas, showers, a phone, or just a snack, you can't miss the 4-story igloo at **Igloo City,** Mile 188. (Open May-Oct. daily 8am-8pm, Nov.-Apr. F-M. Gas available 24hrs. with credit card. Showers $5.)

NENANA

Nenana (neh-NAH-na), 53 mi. south of Fairbanks, has played host to the **Nenana Ice Pool** since 1917. Bored out of their skulls during the long winter, residents of Alaska and the Yukon bet on the precise minute when the Nenana River will thaw in the spring. The 2002 pot climbed to $304,000. Stop by the **Visitors Center** off the Parks, or check out their web site, www.nenanaakiceclassic.com, to place a $2.50 bet. If waiting for the ice to break doesn't hold your interest, you may want to just move on to the **Two Choice Cafe ❷**, located on A St., which has burgers ($6) and more. (☎832-1010. Open May-Oct. daily 7:30am-3pm.) For a bed and "family-style" dining, the **Rough Woods Inn and Cafe ❹** at the corner of 2nd and A St. will serve up breakfast and lunch at reasonable prices ($6-9) to compensate for dinner ($11-28). (☎832-5299; open 8am-8pm daily. Rooms start at $68.)

FAIRBANKS ☎907

Had E.T. Barnette not run aground near the junction of the Tanana and Chena Rivers and decided on the spur of the moment to set up a trading post, and had Felix Pedro, an Italian immigrant-turned-prospector, not unearthed a golden fortune nearby, Fairbanks might never have been born. But both did happen, and today, Fairbanks stands unchallenged as North American civilization's northernmost hub. In this rough-and-tumble town, men noticeably outnumber women, the streets are filled with four-wheel-drive steeds, and the beer flows as freely as the Chena's muddy waters. The University of Alaska has brought "northern scholarship" and a coffee shop culture to the northwest corner of the city's large suburban area. Still, this is just about as Alaskan as a *city* can get.

▪ TRANSPORTATION

Fairbanks lies at the junction of three major routes: Prudhoe Bay lies 500 mi. north along the gravelly **Dalton Hwy.** (Rte. 11, see p. 567), Anchorage lies 358 mi. south along the **George Parks Hwy.** (Rte. 3, see p. 542), and Delta Junction lies 98 mi. southeast of Fairbanks along the **Richardson/Alaska Hwy.** (see p. 557). The highest concentration of services lies within a square formed by four thoroughfares: **Airport Way** to the south, **College Rd.** to the north, **Steese Expwy.** to the east, and **University Ave.** to the west. The city center lies along **Cushman St.**, north of Airport Way. Fairbanks is a **bicycle-friendly** city with wide shoulders, multi-use paths, and sidewalks. Indeed, a pair of wheels is downright necessary here and a car might make you even happier than a bike.

Flights: The airport is 5 mi. southwest of downtown on Airport Way. **Alaska Air** (☎452-1661) goes to **Anchorage** ($257.50) and **Juneau** ($468.50). Booking well ahead results in much lower fares. Other carriers include **Delta, Northwest,** and **United. Frontier Flyer Service** (☎474-0014) and **Larry's Flying Service** (☎474-9169) fly large prop planes into the Bush. Fares change frequently. To get to town from the airport, take **Airlink Shuttle** (☎452-3337). Airport to downtown $7 for 1 person; 2 people or more $3.50 per person.

Trains: Alaska Railroad, 280 N Cushman (☎458-6025 or 800-544-0552), behind the Daily News-Miner building. An excellent way to see the wilderness rather than the Alaskan highways. Depot open daily 6:30am-3pm and for evening arrivals. Winter hours generally 7am-noon; call in advance. From mid-May to mid-Sept., 1 train per day to **Anchorage** (12hr., $175) via **Denali National Park** (4hr., $50). From mid-Sept. to mid-Oct. and from early Feb. to mid-May, a train leaves for **Anchorage** once per week ($105).

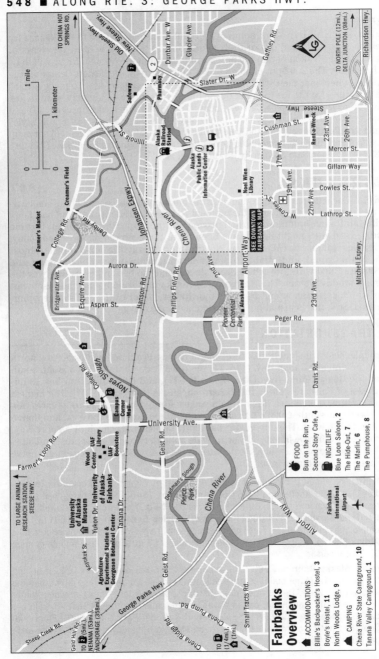

CENTRAL ALASKA

TO CHENA HOT SPRINGS RD.

Old Steese Hwy.

New Steese Hwy.

Dunbar Ave. W

Glacier Ave.

Gaffney Rd.

Richardson Hwy.

Slater Dr. W

TO NORTH POLE (12mi.),
DELTA JUNCTION (98mi.)

N

1 mile

1 kilometer

Safeway

Pharmacy

Cushman St.

Steese Hwy.

Rent-a-Wreck

23rd Ave.

26th Ave.

Illinois St.

Alaska
Railroad
Station

Alaska
Public Lands
Information Center

Mercer St.

Gillam Way

17th Ave.

Noel Wien
Library

19th Ave.

Cowles St.

W Cowles St.

22nd Ave.

Lathrop St.

Farmer's Market

College Rd.

Creamer's Field

Danby Rd.

Johansen Expwy.

Chena River

SEE DOWNTOWN
FAIRBANKS MAP

Airport Way

Aurora Dr.

Wilbur St.

Bridgewater Ave.

Esquire Ave.

Aspen St.

Hanson Rd.

Phillips Field Rd.

2nd Ave.

Alaskaland

Pioneer
Centennial
Park

23rd Ave.

Peger Rd.

Davis Rd.

Mitchell Expwy.

College Rd.

Noyes Slough

University Ave.

Campus
Corner
Mall

Geist Rd.

TO LARGE ANIMAL
RESEARCH STATION,
STEESE HWY.

Farmer's Loop Rd.

University of Alaska
Museum

Yukon Dr.

University of Alaska–
Fairbanks

Wood
Center

UAF
Library

UAF
Bookstore

Koyukuk St.

Agriculture
Experimental Station &
Georgeson Botanical Center

Tanana Dr.

Deadman's Slough

Pierce
Park

Chena River

Fairbanks
International
Airport

Airport Way

Gold Hill Rd.

TO
NENANA (53mi.),
ANCHORAGE (358mi.)

Sheep Creek Rd.

George Parks Hwy.

Geist Rd.

Chena Ridge Rd.

Chena Pump Rd.

Small Tracts Rd.

FOOD
Bun on the Run, **5**
Second Story Cafe, **4**
NIGHTLIFE
Blue Loon Saloon, **2**
The Hide-Out, **7**
The Marlin, **6**
The Pumphouse, **8**

Fairbanks
Overview

▲ ACCOMMODATIONS
Billie's Backpacker's Hostel, **3**
Boyle's Hostel, **11**
North Woods Lodge, **9**
▲ CAMPING
Chena River State Campground, **10**
Tanana Valley Campground, **1**

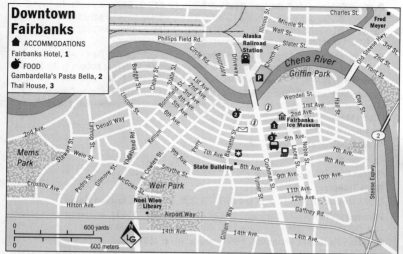

Downtown Fairbanks

🏠 ACCOMMODATIONS
Fairbanks Hotel, **1**

🍎 FOOD
Gambardella's Pasta Bella, **2**
Thai House, **3**

Buses: Alaska Trails Parks Highway Express (☎479-3065 or 888-600-6001; www.alaskashuttles.com) departs each day at 9am to **Anchorage** (9hr.; $54, round-trip $99) and **Denali** (3½hr.; $39, round-trip $69). Tickets are good for the entire season and people can get on and off the bus as their schedules permit. Pickup at the visitors center (9am), Billie's Backpackers Hostel (9:30am; see **Accommodations,** below), and elsewhere upon request. **Alaska Direct** (☎800-770-6652) runs 3 buses per week from the downtown bus terminal at 5th and Cushman to **Anchorage** (12½hr., $70), **Tok** (6hr., $45), and **Whitehorse, BC** (15hr., $140).

Public Transportation: Municipal Area Commuter Service, MACS (☎459-1011), at 5th Ave. and Cushman St. $1.50; under 18, over 60, and disabled $0.75; under 5 free. Day pass $3. Service M-F 7am-8pm, more limited on Sa. Schedules available at the visitors center, transit park at 6th Ave. and Cushman St., and post office.

Taxis: King Diamond Taxi (☎455-7777). $1 base, $2.50 per mi.

Car Rental: National companies offer free mileage, but won't allow driving on dirt roads; small companies generally charge hefty mileage fees. Call ahead. **Rent-a-Wreck,** 2105 Cushman St. (☎452-1606). Compact car $39 per day, four-wheel-drive $59, minivan $68. Must be 21+ with credit card. No gravel highways.

🛈 PRACTICAL INFORMATION

Tourist Information: Convention and Visitors Bureau, 550 1st Ave. (☎456-5774 or 800-327-5774), at Cushman. Free local calls and pamphlets, pamphlets, pamphlets. Open in summer daily 8am-7pm; winter M-F 9am-5pm. **Fairbanks Events Hotline:** ☎456-4636.

Outdoor Information: Alaska Public Lands Information Center, 250 Cushman #1A (☎456-0527), in the basement of the Old Federal building. Entrance under the awning around the corner on 3rd Ave. Invaluable resource for use of all public lands throughout the state. Maps of all kinds; maps of public campgrounds $0.25. Open in summer daily 9am-6pm; winter Tu-Sa 10am-6pm. **The Wood Center** at University of Alaska, Fairbanks has resources for trails throughout Alaska and the staff loves to help visitors plan trips.

Outdoor Equipment: 7 Bridges Boats & Bikes (☎479-0751) rents both. Canoes $30 per day, $100 per week. Bikes $10-15 per day, weekly rates negotiable. **Rocket Surplus,** 1401 Cushman St. (☎456-7078), vends military surplus camping supplies. Open M-F 9am-6pm, Sa 10am-6pm, Su 10am-5pm.

Bookstore: Gulliver's New and Used Books, 3525 College Rd. (☎474-9574), in the Campus Corner Mall. A huge selection of reading and free Internet access in the Second Story Cafe, known for its wraps. Open M-F 9am-9pm, Sa 9am-8pm, Su 11am-6pm.

Laundromat and Showers: B&C (☎479-2696), at University Ave. and College Rd., in Campus Corner Mall. Wash $2.25, dry $0.25 per 8min. Showers $3, towels $0.50. Open M-Sa 7:30am-9:30pm, Su 8am-9:30pm.

Weather: ☎452-3553.

Road Conditions: ☎456-7623.

Emergency: ☎911.

Police: 656 7th Ave. (☎459-6500), at the intersection with Cushman.

State Troopers: ☎451-5100.

Crisis Line: ☎452-4357 or 800-478-7273. Info on gay and lesbian groups.

Pharmacy: Fred Myer Pharmacy, 19 College Rd. (☎456-2151), at Steese, across from the Bentley Mall. Open M-F 9am-9pm, Sa 10am-7pm, Su 10am-6pm.

Hospital: Fairbanks Memorial, 1650 Cowles St. (☎452-8181), south of airport.

Internet Access: The enormous and pristine **Noel Wien Library,** 1215 Cowles St. (☎459-1020) at Airport Way, has free 15min. walk-in slots; 1hr. blocks should be reserved in advance by phone (reservations accepted day-of only, starting at 10am). Open M-Th 10am-9pm, F 10am-6pm, Sa 10am-5pm; open Su in winter 1-5pm.

Post Office: 315 Barnette St. (☎452-3223). Open M-F 9am-6pm, Sa 10am-2pm. **Postal Code:** 99707. **General Delivery:** 99701.

🏠🏠 ACCOMMODATIONS AND CAMPING

Hostels and campgrounds abound in Fairbanks. As might be expected in a town with no concentrated downtown, none of the hostels are near anything in particular and will be enjoyed more by those with bikes or cars.

■ **Boyle's Hostel,** 310 18th Ave. (☎456-4944). A 15 min. walk from downtown. Mr. Boyle acts as a grandfather to the travelers staying in his spacious, tidy rooms. Cabins outside are really beds-in-a-shed, but are surprisingly suitable. 2 large eat-in kitchens and TVs in every room. Laundry ($1.50). Dorms $17; private doubles $30, private triples $35; outside cabins $15 per person. Monthly rates available. ❶

■ **Billie's Backpackers Hostel,** 2895 Mack Blvd. (☎479-2034). Red bus to Westwood Way and College Rd. and follow Westwood 1 block to Mack Rd. A veritable hodgepodge of humanity, drawing a rugged, outdoorsy set. It has a bit of everything: 2 kitchens, files of traveling info, an outdoor garden, a deck, and 2 songbirds in a cage. 10 bunks in co-ed rooms; 4 of them near the kitchen are only for the immodest, $20. Tent space $15. Private double with jacuzzi $50. ❶

■ **North Woods Lodge** (☎479-5300 or 800-478-5305). From town, take Chena Pump Rd. out 2 mi. past the Parks Hwy. overpass, turn right onto Roland Rd., and take another right onto Chena Hill Dr. The lodge is ¼ mi. up on the right. This wooded hideaway provides a secluded feeling. Every building was built by Tom, the owner, starting in 1975. Private cabins $50-55; sleeping space on the floor of a loft $15; tent sites $15. ❶

■ **Fairbanks Hotel,** 517 Third Ave. (☎456-6411), two blocks from the visitors center in downtown. Clean, spacious, Art Deco rooms, all with cable TV and a slough of services. Complimentary airport/train shuttle. Singles $55-89, doubles $65-110. ❸

UM, HONEY, IS IT...COLD IN HERE? The thick blanket of snow that envelops Alaska in the winter months shields the state from the flood of tourism that washes over it in the summer. Those who brave the Alaskan winter come for the intense skiing and snowboarding opportunities. And for the luck. Japanese tradition has it that good luck will follow the couple whose marriage is consummated under the northern lights. The dead of winter thus finds Fairbanks deserted except for the locals and a few blushing Japanese newlyweds.

Chena River State Campground, north of Airport Way on University Ave. Landscaped, popular recreation site with a boat launch and a nature trail. Campsites are along the river. 5-night max. stay per vehicle. 56 walk-in sites, $10-15. ●

Tanana Valley Campground, 1800 College Rd. (☎456-7956). Near Aurora Ave. on the red bus route. Noisy but grassy, secluded, and in town. Laundry $2 wash, $2 dry. Tent sites $8; RV sites $12; RV sites $15. Showers $3. ●

🍴 FOOD

On Airport Way and College Rd., the northernmost franchises of almost every fast-food chain in existence lure burger lovers to their artery-blocked doom 24hr. a day. **Carr's,** 526 Gaffney (☎452-1121), and **Safeway** (☎479-4231), at University Ave. and Airport Way, supply groceries until 10pm. The **Farmers Market,** at the fairgrounds at Aurora and College, sells abnormally large local vegetables in mid- to late summer and early fall. (☎456-3276. Open W 11am-6pm, Sa 9am-4pm.)

🍴 **Bun on the Run,** a trailer in the parking lot between Beaver Sports and the Marlin on College Rd. Few, if any, are disappointed with the scones, meringues, and, of course, the buns this whimsical pink trailer produces. Open M-F 7am-6pm, Sa 9am-4pm. ●

🍴 **Second Story Cafe,** 3525 College Rd. above Gulliver's New and Used Books, has the best and freshest wraps in town, not to mention salads, sandwiches, and veggie-friendly soups. All wraps and sandwiches $6.50. Combinations $4.75-$9.50. Open M-F 9am-8pm, Sa 9am-7pm, Su 11am-5pm. ●

Gambardella's Pasta Bella, 706 2nd Ave. (☎456-3417). Italian music, authentic dishes, and flowers on the patio. Subs and small pizzas $6-9; dinner prices higher. Outdoor seating available. Open M-Sa 11am-10pm. Reservations recommended. ●

Thai House, 526 5th Ave. (☎452-6123), just east of Cushman in the heart of downtown. The spiciest and most authentic Thai joint in town—The Kao Khew Wan Neur seasoned with green curry and basil ($7) for lunch and ginger dishes like Pad-ped Samsahai ($12) for dinner are the chef's favorites. Open M-Sa 11am-10pm. ●

👁 SIGHTS

🏛 **UNIVERSITY OF ALASKA MUSEUM.** Fairbanks' proudest institution holds one of the top ten visitor attractions in the state. The museum is at the top of a hill overlooking the flat cityscape and distant mountains (even Denali on a clear day). Exhibits include displays on the Aurora Borealis, the pipeline, biographies of outstanding Alaskan women, and indigenous crafts and culture, and a thorough look at the little-known Aleut/Japanese evacuation during WWII. You would be truly foolish to miss Blue Babe, a 36,000-year-old steppe bison recovered from the permafrost. (*Museum ☎474-7505. A 10min. walk up Yukon Dr. from the bus stop at Wood Campus Center, or take a shuttle from the visitor parking lot. Audio tour $3. Free walking tours June-Aug. M-F at 10am. Open June-Aug. daily 9am-7pm; daily May and Sept. 9am-5pm; Oct.-Apr. M-F 9am-5pm. $5, seniors $4.50, ages 7-17 $3; videos $12 extra.*)

FAIRBANKS ICE MUSEUM. These ice sculptures are far more impressive than your average cornucopia or swan, but only a taste of what the masters carve. The exhibit begins with a 15 min. video of ice cultivation and harvesting and last year's artists at work, then a 15 min. slide show of the finished products. View the sculptures through the glass, or walk inside exhibits (15°F) to experience a Fairbanks winter. *(Around the corner from the visitors center on 2nd Ave. ☎451-8222. Open daily 10am-6pm. Video starts as people arrive. $8, seniors $7, ages 6-12 $5, under 6 free.)*

LARGE ANIMAL RESEARCH STATION. The University research station offers a rare chance to see baby musk oxen and other Arctic animals up close. If you miss the tour, grab some binoculars and ogle the musk ox and reindeer from the viewing stand on the road, but be sure to sit upwind. *(Take Farmer's Loop to Ballaine Rd. and turn left on Yankovich; farm is 1 mi. up on the right. ☎474-7207. Tours June-Aug. Tu, Th, and Sa at 11am and 1:30pm; Sept. Sa at 1:30pm. $5, students $2, seniors $4.)*

 EVENTS

GOLDEN DAYS. In mid-July Fairbanks citizens don old-time duds and whoop it up for Golden Days, a celebration of Felix Pedro's 1902 discovery that sparked the Fairbanks gold rush. The celebration is full of vendors and special daily events. Watch out for the traveling jail; without a silly-looking pin commemorating the event (sold at most stores), an unknowing tourist may be imprisoned and forced to pay a steep price to spring free. *(For more details, contact the visitors bureau.)*

SHAKESPEARE THEATER. During the first three weeks of July, the **Fairbanks Shakespeare Theater** puts on a play from the Bard's portfolio. Call to find 2003's location. *(North of town off Steese Hwy. ☎457-7638. $18, students $14, under 10 free.)*

TANANA VALLEY STATE FAIR. A traditional country fair with rides, lots of food, and competitions for biggest cabbage and cutest baby. If you're lucky, you'll be chosen to compete in the **kiss the cow contest,** although the cow is unfairly prohibited from judging. *(Fairground at intersection of College Rd. and Aurora. ☎452-3750. The first 2 weeks in August. $7; seniors and ages 6-17 $3.)*

WORLD ICE ART CHAMPIONSHIPS. Competitors from all over the world come to use the specially harvested and unusually clear ice that Fairbanks provides. Each contestant gets two days to make their masterpiece, but these remarkable sculptures remain on display until April 1. Now an Olympic event, the artists long familiar to Fairbanks will jump into international recognition during the Winter 2003 games. *(☎451-8250. March 5-16, 2003.)*

MIDNIGHT SUN INTERTRIBAL POWWOW. The third annual powwow of Alaskan, American and Canadian Indians will take place from July 3-6, 2003. The goal of the powwow is to honor elders and educate the general public about the many North American native cultures. *(☎456-2245.)*

SPORTING EVENTS. In the winter, February's **Yukon Quest Sled Dog Race** runs for 7 to 10 days between Fairbanks and Whitehorse, ending in Fairbanks on odd years. The Quest is considered more extreme than the famous Iditarod. There are fewer dogs and fewer stops, not to mention less concern for human welfare. For info, contact the Yukon Quest Business Office. *(558 2nd Ave. ☎452-7954. Race will start in Whitehorse Feb. 9, 2003.)* The **Limited North American Championship Sled Dog Race,** the second week in March, draws almost 80 teams annually and runs through Fairbanks. *(☎457-6874. Race will run Mar. 14-16, 2003.)*

The summer solstice inspires some wild activity in Fairbanks. The **Fairbanks Goldpanners** play their annual **Midnight Sun Baseball Game** on the solstice itself *(June 21, 2003)*. The game begins as the sun dips at 10:30pm, features a short pause near midnight for the celebration of the midnight sun, and ends at about 2am, in full daylight. Games are played at **Growden Memorial Park,** (☎451-0095), near Alaskaland. The high horsepower **Yukon 800 Marathon Riverboat Race** sends competitors in low-slung powerboats on an 800 mi. quest up the Tanana and Yukon Rivers to the town of Galena and back. (☎459-2023). On June 21st, thousands will join in the 10km **Midnight Sun Run** to run, walk, or compete in the costume division. (☎452-1976 outside of Alaska or 452-6046 in Alaska.) Fairbanks will host the annual **World Eskimo-Indian Olympics,** from July 17-20, 2003. A true sports spectacular, Native Alaskans from all over the state compete for three days in traditional tests of strength, balance, and survival. Witness the ear pull, traditionally played to prepare for frostbite. Sinew is wrapped around the ears of contestants, who then tug to see who can endure the most pain. Ears have been pulled off in this event. (☎452-6646. *Daily pass $6, season pass $20.)* The **Equinox Marathon** is one of the five most rigorous in the nation. About 300 hearty competitors run 26.2 mi. up Ester Dome, sometimes in frigid conditions, gaining 3500 ft. in elevation. (☎452-8531. *Sept. 20, 2003.)*

🎫 NIGHTLIFE

This is a good town to get pined in—there is lots of cheap beer and plenty of time to kill. The military presence and the general Alaskan stats give Fairbanks a downright boisterous bar scene that heartily welcomes female visitors.

- **The Marlin,** 3412 College Rd. (☎479-4646). This non-smoking bar burned down last year but recently reopened. A refreshingly mellow outlet amidst the rowdy norm of Fairbanks bars. Hosts frequent live music. Pints $3.50, pitchers $1. Open nightly until 2am.

- **Blue Loon Saloon,** 2999 Parks Hwy. (☎457-5666). Nights here range from gyrating with go-go dancers in cages to lounging on the couches and watching a movie. The grille serves a bar menu ($2.50-15.75) throughout the night. Cover $3. Movie $4 M and Tu, $5 W and Th, $6 F and Sa. Open M-Th 5pm-1am, F-Sa 5pm-3am.

- **The Pumphouse** (☎479-8452), at Mile 1.3 on Chena Pump Road. A calmer, older clientele sips their drinks on the deck to enjoy the view of the Chena River. Beer $2.50-5. Karaoke night on W gets rowdier. Open M-Sa 11:30am-2pm and 5pm-1am.

- **The Hide-Out** (☎457-1830), behind Dillinger's restaurant on Old Steese Hwy. between Trainer Gate Rd. and College Rd. Mix $6 pitchers (all draft beers including Newcastle and Sam Adams) with $1.50 shots and you get a full batch of the young and drunk. Foosball and pool tables ensure inebriated fun for everyone. Open daily until 2am.

🥾 OUTDOOR ACTIVITIES

Fairbanks is geared towards biking and running. Most of the best paths run through the university campus. Maps for **multi-use trails** are available at the Wood Center, in the UAF Student Activities Office, and at the Alaska Public Lands Information Center. **Cross-country skiing trails** cross near the UAF campus, and several begin and end at the University museum. Trip planning advice is available at the Wood Center or the Alaska Public Lands Information Center (see **Practical Information,** above). **Moose Mountain,** 20min. northeast from Fairbanks, grooms over 30 ski trails. Take Sheep Creek Rd. to Murphy Dome Rd. Make a right onto Moose Mt. Rd. (☎479-4732. $23, ages 7-12 $18, free in Moose Meadow only. Rentals $20, under 12 $15. Open Th-Su 10am-5pm, or dusk.)

Another option, 30min. north of Fairbanks and holding over 20 trails, is **Mt. Aurora Ski Land,** 2315 Skiland Rd. Take a right onto Fairbanks Creek Rd. off the Steese Hwy. (Rte. 6) at Mile 20.5 and then turn left. (☎389-2314. Lift tickets $24, students and military $20, ages 13-17 and seniors $17, ages 7-12 $10, under 6 or over 70 $5. Rentals $20, students, military, and seniors $15. Open Nov.-April. 10am-dusk.)

Awl Alaskan Mushing Adventures (☎389-6957) offers dogsled rides in winter for $75 an hour. Arctic outerwear is provided. **Sno-RV** rents all kinds of snowmobiles. (☎389-7669. Starts at $100 per day on weekdays, up to $155 per day for larger models on weekends. Deposit required. Must be 21+ with valid ID and demonstration of skill. Also offers guided tours for $65 per hr.)

NEAR FAIRBANKS ☎907

A short drive in any direction from Fairbanks plunges travelers into genuine Alaskan wilderness. Fish or look for wildlife in a river basin, hike up a ridge to view the Brooks or Alaska Ranges, and, after a long day, soak your sore muscles in hot-spring-fed pools. Maps and detailed info on hikes are available at the Alaska Public Lands Info Center in Fairbanks and the UAF Woods Center (see p. 547).

CHENA HOT SPRINGS RD. Chena Hot Springs Rd. branches off the Steese Hwy. (Rte. 3) at Mile 5 and ends 57 mi. later at the Chena Hot Springs Resort. The **Chena River State Recreation Area** (☎451-2695) spills across Chena Rd. between Miles 26 and 51. It encompasses almost 400 sq. mi. of wilderness and offers outstanding fishing, hiking, and canoeing. Graylings are common in the **Chena River,** and king salmon run in late July and early August. Moose abound in this area.

CAMPING. Campgrounds along the Chena River are more secluded than most established sites. **Rosehip ❶,** at Mile 27, has sites right on the water ($10). Although the water here has passed inspection, it is not treated and boiling is recommended. **Red Squirrel ❶,** at Mile 43, has two sheltered picnic tables and three firepits. No established sites, but plenty of open grassy space around the small pond. ($5).

HIKING. **Maps** and info on all these trails are available at the Public Lands Office in Fairbanks (see p. 549), **Tacks' General Store,** at Mile 23 of Chena Hot Springs Rd. (open daily 8am-8pm; also a post office), and at the Chena Hot Springs Resort. A fire during the summer of 2002 has made this region even more striking than usual: charcoal and burnt trees contrast with the red of dried needles and white and green of aspen and subalpine pine.

Granite Tors Trail (15 mi. round-trip, 2500 ft. gain, 6-10hr.). At Mile 39 of Chena Rd., across from Tors Trail campground. The trail climbs through birch, aspen, spruce, and eventually past the treeline to a peak covered with giant granite pillars ("Tors"). Blessed with fantastic views of Chena Dome and Flat Top Mountain. Moderate to difficult.

Chena Dome Trail (29 mi., 3421 ft. gain, 3-4 days). Lower Chena Dome Trailhead is at Mile 49.1 Chena Hot Springs Rd.; the Upper Chena Dome Trailhead is at Mile 50.5. Follow rock cairns above treeline. Open to mountain bikers and equestrians, this is the most spectacular trail in the park, following the high, rocky rim of the Angel Creek Valley. The climb from either trailhead is a steep one, and park rangers advise backpackers planning on covering the entire loop to begin at the northern trailhead. Those out for just the day can reach good views within 3 mi. of either trailhead. Difficult.

CHENA HOT SPRINGS. Fifty-seven miles northeast of Fairbanks steam the bubbling pools of **Chena Hot Springs Resort.** In winter, scores shiver their way to the resort for prime northern lights viewing from the "Aurorium," and soaking on a summer day is popular as well. A pool, 2 indoor hot tubs, and one outdoor hot tub are chlorinated and at a slightly lowered temperature. A "pond" nestled among boulders keeps the water au-naturel: 147 degrees and untreated. (Open 9am-midnight. $10, under 18 $7, free if staying in a room. 18+.)

Rooms ❺ at the Chena Hot Springs Resort are unkind to the pocketbook, but campsites ❶ are available by the river. (☎451-8104; Fairbanks office 452-7867. In summer doubles $105; suites $170. Small heated cabins with no running water $65, up to $200 for 6 people. Sites $20; dry RV sites $20. Showers $3.) The resort's restaurant ❸ serves standard expensive restaurant fare. Dinner costs $8.75-35.95. (Open daily 8am-10pm). The activity center has information on nearby hiking/biking trails, over 30 mi. of cross-country skiing trails, and fine fishing (after the spring thaw). They rent bikes ($6 per hr., $18 per half-day) and have a long list of activities including horseback riding ($50), outdoor survival class ($25), full swing indoor virtual golf ($30 per hr.), dog sled rides in winter ($80 for a 6 mi. run), and flightseeing ($75-265 per person). The resort is a good place to amass info, but it's not the only option for spending the night in a bed within the park. The Angel Creek Lodge ❸, at Mile 50 on the Chena Hot Springs Rd., provides more affordable accommodations. Its six rustic cabins sleep 3-5 people and have electricity and access to free showers and a sauna (☎369-4128. Call far in advance. $45-100.) A cafe, liquor store, and bar are open to any and everyone. The place bustles in February as a checkpoint on the Yukon Quest Sled Dog Race (see p. 403).

FROM FAIRBANKS: STEESE HWY. (RTE. 6)

☎907

The Steese Hwy. heads northeast out of Fairbanks and runs 162 mi. to the town of Circle on the Yukon River. Just 5 mi. outside Fairbanks, the Steese meets Chena Hot Springs Rd. (see p. 554). The Elliott Hwy. (Rte. 2) comes hard on the heels of the Chena Rd. at Mile 11 in Fox. Make a right turn at the intersection to stay on the Steese. Fox is the last place to fuel up for the next 117 mi. of the Steese until the town of Central (and gas is far from cheap in Central, $2.50 per gallon). For the next 20 mi. past Fox, the Steese winds through boreal forest, past two ski resorts, and into a region of stunted spruce and fir trees known as taiga. At Mile 16.5 is the Felix Pedro Monument, a plaque honoring Pedro's 1902 discovery of gold in the creek across the highway. At Mile 28, the Fairbanks Expeditions Gold Camp Mining Quarters have been turned into an immaculate and historic hotel ❸ and restaurant ❷. Lunch costs $6.75-10.95; dinner is slightly more expensive. (Singles $55; doubles $60. Restaurant open year-round M-Sa 11am-10pm, Su 11am-9pm.) The White Mountain National Recreation Area and the Steese National Conservation Area lie side-by-side to the north. At Mile 107, the highway passes over Eagle Summit, one of the most challenging points on the Yukon Quest International Sled Dog Race. The panoramic view of peaks and fragile tundra is well worth a stop.

📷 CAMPING. In the summer of 2002, many of the campgrounds along the Steese were closed for maintenance or because of budget cuts. You can still camp in them, but there are no toilet facilities and no water. Check with the Bureau of Public Lands for campsite closings before heading out. The Upper Chatanika River Campground ❶, at Mile 39, provides secluded, woodsy campsites ($10). At Mile 45.4, soon after the road turns to gravel, the Long Creek Trading Post ❶ offers tent sites ($5). They also have a small general store and liquor store, laundry and an RV park with dump station. (☎389-5287. Open daily 10am-6 or 8 pm. Sometimes closed Tu.) Cripple Creek Campground ❶, at Mile 60, offers good fishing and recreational goldpanning. (Sites $6; walk-ins $3.)

CENTRAL ALASKA

◪ OUTDOOR ACTIVITIES. The **Chatanika River,** which runs along the Steese Hwy. (Rte. 6) between Miles 29 and 39, teems with shellfish and northern pike. Call Fish and Game (☎459-7200) for more info. **Chatanika River Canoe Trail** parallels the Steese for nearly 30 mi. The easygoing stream is a clear Class II; its only treacherous obstacles are low water and overhanging trees. Both campgrounds (see above) have access to the river. Traveling from a headwater stream to a twisting river, **Birch Creek** (126 mi., 7-10 days) creates Class I, II, and III rapids. The ends are by Steese Hwy. at Mile 94.5 and 140.4. **Long Creek Trading Post** (see above) runs a shuttle service ($15 per trip) for paddlers and their canoes and rents canoes ($30 per day) and fishing gear ($5 per day).

Pinnell Mountain Trail is the most spectacular and popular hike in the vicinity of Fairbanks. The 27 mi. trail is rugged and exposed, and while it gains little elevation, it remains entirely above treeline and passes among alpine tundra flora, occasionally getting downright muddy. With proper timing, you can bask in the midnight sun (mid to late June, 2003), witness an explosion of wildflowers (late June), or watch caribou migration in the valleys below (Aug.-Sept.). Although it can be hiked either way, starting at Mile 107 eliminates some of the grueling uphill sections. Most hikers hitch back to their cars. Even if you don't have time to schlep 27 mi., a scramble up either end of the trail is worthwhile. Get to the trail at Mile 86 and 107 on Steese Hwy. The trail is marked with green posts and large granite slabs. Two small 4-walled shelters are available between Mileposts 10 and 11 and between Mileposts 17 and 18 of the trail. Allow three days for the entire trip. Topo maps are recommended. For more info on this and other trails, call the **Bureau of Land Management** in Fairbanks. (☎474-2200.)

CENTRAL, CIRCLE, AND CIRCLE HOT SPRINGS   ☎907

At Mile 127 of a gravel road, **Central** has an ironic name. Its 4100 residents prefer it that way. **Gas** is available at **Crabb's Corner ❸,** down the street, which also serves as barber shop, basic grocery store, motel, laundry stop, cafe, and local meeting area. Their rooms are clean and spacious. (Laundry $2 wash, $2 dry. Rooms $55. Store open 11am-7:30pm. Cafe open 8:30am-7:30pm.)

From Central, the road gets considerably worse, winding its way past the bodies of dead cars down towards the **Yukon River Flats Basin.** Unless you are planning to float the mighty **Yukon River,** there is little reason to drive the highway's final 34 mi. to **Circle.** Before the Klondike rush, Circle was the "Paris of the North," the largest log-cabin city in the world. Now Circle is a native village, population around 50, trying to find a way to bring the tourists back. If you do make it here, the **Yukon Trading Post ❶** has a small store and a cafe. (Meals $3.50-9.50. Open M-F 8am-6pm, Sa 9am-7pm, Su 10am-6pm.) **H.C. Co** has expensive gas, tire repair, an extensive store, and the town's **public phone.**

Instead of continuing on to Circle, most people turn right at Crabb's Corner in Central, and follow the signs to **Circle Hot Springs.** The outdoor springs are just 8 mi. from Central, and provide a pleasant and uncrowded reward for those who make the long drive. A day pass for non-guests at the **Arctic Circle Hot Springs Lodge ❶** is $5. The pool is open all hours, but is "clothing optional" after midnight. Rooms at the lodge are costly, but the hostel on the fourth floor provides cheaper beds, and campsites are available. (Singles $80; doubles $100. Cabins with electricity $85; with water, bathrooms and kitchens $110-125. Dorms first person $20; each extra adult $15; under 9 $7.50. Sites $5; RV sites $10; electrical $15.) The **dining room ❷** serves tasty sandwiches for $4-7 and dinner entrees for $10-18. (Open 9am-8pm.) **Cold Rush ❶** offers an abundance of ice cream in a homemade waffle cone for $3.50. (Open M-F 2-4pm and 6-9pm.)

ALONG RTE. 2: THE ALASKA HWY.

DELTA JUNCTION   ☎907

Aptly named the Crossroads of Alaska, Delta Junction is located at the intersection of the **Alaska Hwy. (Rte. 2)**, which leads 108 mi. southeast to **Tok**, and the **Richardson Hwy. (Rte. 4)**, which runs 95 mi. northwest to Fairbanks and 127 mi. south to Valdez (see p. 491). A 1920s buffalo importation scheme is responsible for Delta Junction's free-ranging buffalo herd, the largest in the US. Glimpse the domesticated version of the mighty bison from across the fence at the buffalo ranch 4 mi. up Clearwater Rd. (7 mi. toward Tok on the Alaska Hwy., on the left).

This year, Fort Greely Military Base has gotten a new lease on life, giving Delta Junction a new lease on life as well. A huge crew of military personnel is arriving to build, maintain, and man silos that will hold missiles that could be directed at enemy nations' warheads zooming overhead. Bison herds, high-powered missiles, and highways aside, there is not much to see or do in Delta Junction. Get your gas, eat some caribou or buffalo in patty form, and move on.

The huge post in front of the **visitors center** declares this site in Delta Junction the terminus of the Alaska Hwy., although Fairbanks argues otherwise. (☎895-5063 for office on the highway in summer, ☎895-5068 year-round. Open early May to mid-Sept. daily 8am-8pm.)

Services here are the last for miles: **Hendrick's Auto Parts** is 3 mi. north of the junction. (☎895-4221. Open M-Th 9am-6pm, F 9am-5pm, Sa 9am-3pm.) **Wells Fargo**, half a mile north of the visitors center, has a **24hr. ATM.** (☎895-4691. Open M-Th 10am-5pm, F 10am-6pm.) Other services include: **emergency,** ☎911 or 424-4800; **state police,** ☎895-4344; and a **Health Clinic,** (☎895-5100), off Richardson Highway 1½ mi. north of junction. **Internet access** is free at the **library,** located on the right past post office (☎895-4102. Open M-Th 10am-6pm, F-Sa 10am-4pm.) The **post office** is across the highway. (☎895-4601. Open M-F 9:30am-5pm, Sa 10:30am-noon.) **Postal Code:** 99737.

Nearby state park areas have **camping ❶** ($10, water and pit toilets), in addition to minimal hiking, biking, canoeing, and fishing. **Delta State Recreation Site ❶**, half a mile north, with 25 grassy sites near the road, and **Big Delta Historical Park ❶** (23 sites quite literally in a parking lot, $5), 8 mi. north, are nearest to the town center. **Clearwater Lake ❶**, at the end of Clearwater Rd. off the Alaska Hwy. toward Tok, offers 17 sites and bird-watching during migrations of waterfowl. **Quartz Lake ❶**, 12 mi. north on the Richardson, is known for sport fishing (16 sites, $10). **Lost Lake ❶**, adjacent to Quartz Lake, has more secluded sites for tent camping ($10) and a series of short, buggy, less than thrilling trails. A map of these is available at the visitors center. Two miles north, **Smith's Green Acres RV Park and Campground ❶** has shaded sites, vehicle washing, and a playground. (☎895-4369. Tents $10; dry RV $13; electric RV sites $17; full RV sites $21. Free showers.) The **Alaska Steakhouse and Motel ❸,** just south of the crossroads, is an option for small, reasonably priced rooms. (☎895-5175. Singles with shared bath $60; doubles $80. Meals run $6-10.) Pay a bit more for bigger rooms, more satellite TV channels, coffee, minifridges, and tidiness at **Alaska 7 Motel ❹.** (☎895-4848. Singles $70; doubles $80.)

The cheap **IGA Food Cache** is north on Richardson Hwy. (☎895-4653. Open M-F 6:30am-10pm, Sa 8am-6pm, Su 8am-10pm.) The speciality of **Buffalo Center Drive-in ❷**, south of the visitors center, is buffalo, in burger form ($7.25), or viewed for free in wildlife form out back. (☎895-4055. Open M-Sa 11am-10pm, Su noon-10pm.)

TOK   ☎ 907

There isn't much appeal to Tok, other than that you can pick up US Armed Forces Radio from nearby military installations. Originally a base camp for the construction of the Alaska Hwy. (Rte. 2) and Glenn Hwy./Tok Cutoff (Rte. 1), Tok (TOKE) calls itself "Main Street Alaska." Like most small towns along the highway, Tok is summer tourist-oriented and no place for the RV-shy. Tok, named in honor of a WWII US Army battalion's pet husky, revives its affection for sled dogs every winter in late March with the **Race of Champions** (☎ 883-6874), the last major dog race on the Alaska circuit. In summer, the **Burnt Paw Shop** offers free dog team demonstrations. (☎ 883-4121. Open M-Sa 7am-10pm.) Tok is 12 mi. east of the Alaska Hwy.'s intersection with the Taylor Hwy. (Rte. 5) at Tetlin Junction (see p. 559). Tok is 206 mi. southeast of Fairbanks on the Alaska Hwy., and is the halfway point on the 600 mi. drive from Whitehorse, YT, to Anchorage. **Alaska Direct** (☎ 800-770-6652) buses leave from the Texaco station W, F, and Su to **Anchorage** (7hr., $70); **Fairbanks** (4hr., $45); and **Whitehorse, YT** (9½hr., $90).

The large Alaskan log building houses the **visitors center** and its overwhelming collection of area brochures at the junction. (☎ 883-5775. Open M-Sa 8am-7pm, Su 10am-5pm.) Across the highway, the **Tetlin National Wildlife Refuge Headquarters** provides info on the preserve. (☎ 883-5312. Open M-F 8am-4:30pm.) **Bike rental and repair** are at **Alaska Biking Adventures,** at Cleft of Rock B&B west on Alaska Hwy. (☎ 883-4219. $5 per hr., $15 per day.) Other services include: **24hr. ATM, Young's Chevron** at the junction, ☎ 883-2821; **emergency,** ☎ 911; **police,** ☎ 883-5111; **ambulance,** ☎ 883-2301; **health Clinic,** half a mile down Tok Cut-off. (☎ 883-5855. Open M-Th 8am-5pm, F 8am-noon.) **Internet access** is at **Alaska Cyber Hub,** near the junction. (☎ 883-2665. May-Sept. $10 per hr., $3 min. Less in winter. Open in summer daily 7am-10pm; winter M-F 11am-6pm.) the **post office** is at the junction. (☎ 883-2025. Open M-F 8:15am-5:45pm, Sa 10am-3pm.) **Postal Code:** 99780.

An alternative to the pricey motels are the state campgrounds outside of town and the abundance of RV parks in town or the quiet, tent cabin **Tok International Youth Hostel ❶**, 8 mi. towards Delta Junction in a pine forest. Bring your own bedding. (☎ 883-3745. $10 YHA members, $13 nonmembers.) The **Tok River State Recreation Site ❶** offers 43 wooded sites 4 mi. east of town. Boil the water. (Sites $10.) **Young's Motel ❹**, at the east end of town, offers some of the lowest rates in Tok, although that isn't saying much. (☎ 883-4411. Singles $74; doubles $79.)

Earn a free RV or tent site after gorging on an all-you-can-eat grilled dinner at ▓**Gateway Salmon Bake ❶**, on the Alaska Hwy. at the east end of town. (☎ 883-5555. Open mid-May to mid-Sept. M-Sa 11am-9pm, Su 4-9pm. Sites $10; free with $18 salmon or halibut dinner, or $12 chicken dinner. Showers $2.) Plate-sized sourdough pancakes ($2.50) await at **Sourdough Campground ❶**, 1½ mi. down Tok Cut-off. (☎ 883-5543. Cafe open daily 7-11am.) Locals and tourists converge at **Fast Eddy's ❶** for heaping portions and good times. Specialty burgers are $6 and a trip to the well-stocked fresh fruit and veggie salad bar is $6. (☎ 883-4411. Open daily 6am-midnight.) **Fruit Cache** at Golden Bear RV Park has an unusually large selection of produce that traveled 44hr. by truck from Seattle (open M-Sa 8am-8pm, Su 1pm-8pm). **Three Bears Food Center** doubles as a hardware store with food available in giant-sized packages. (☎ 883-5195. Open in summer daily 7am-11pm; winter M-Sa 8am-9pm, Su 8am-7pm.)

Don't rush off to the Canadian border. East of Tok before the border, the **Tetlin National Wildlife Refuge** offers **hiking, boating, fishing,** and **hunting.** Hunting regulations are far more relaxed in Alaska than in any part of Canada—consult the Visitor's Center (below) for tag prices and area rules. Fishing conditions are updated daily and posted outside for after-hours reading. Visitors are regularly able to bag trophy moose, elk, and caribou in season. Free camping at two campgrounds on serene lakes around 50 mi. into the refuge at the **Lakeview Campground ❶** and **Dead-man Lake Campground ❶**. A sod-roofed visitors center near the border has an observation deck for an expansive view of the refuge (☎ 778-5312. Open Memorial Day to Labor Day M-F 8am-4:30pm.)

ALONG RTE. 5: TAYLOR HWY. ☎907

The Taylor Hwy. courses into the mountain and river valley wildlands of Eastern Alaska, plunging and climbing back and forth between ridge and lowland. With dirt or gravel roadbeds and countless hairpin turns, the Taylor Hwy. is definitely not for the timid. The road will, however, lead you to the remains and modern incarnations of the gold mining towns of Forty Mile, Wade Creek, and Chicken Creek, as well as historic dredges, some beautiful camping, good hunting, and scenic rivers jammed with grayling and trout.

TETLIN JUNCTION TO EAGLE

Beginning at **Tetlin Junction,** 12 mi. east of **Tok** (see p. 558), the highway is initially pleasant, with wide, smooth lanes. At Mile 96, the highway intersects another gold route, the **Top of the World Hwy.** (Hwy. 9; see p. 410), which continues 79 mi. east to **Dawson City, YT** (see p. 410). The Taylor continues north 64 mi. through narrowing roadbeds to the tiny town of **Eagle** (see below). The drive from Tetlin Junction to Eagle takes about 4½hr. Camping overnight along the way or in Eagle makes for a comfortable two-day round-trip.

THE BORDER. If you decide to cut off towards Dawson City, be prepared to cross the US/Canada border. (Open daily May-Sept. 8am-8pm Alaska time.) Make sure to have proof of citizenship. No scheduled passenger service buses run the Taylor, although there is boat service between Eagle and Dawson City (see p. 560). Some car-less travelers hitchhike, but sparse RV traffic makes this difficult. *Let's Go* does not recommend hitchhiking. Gas and food are available only at the **Boundary Cafe ❷**, just west of the border, and in **Chicken,** at Mile 66. From **Mile 0,** the Taylor Hwy. gradually climbs to over 3500 ft. as it rolls toward 5541 ft. Mt. Fairplay. The woodsy **West Fork Campground ❶** lies at Mile 49. (Pit toilets, water. 25 sites, $8.)

CHICKEN. The megalopolis of **Chicken,** rumored to have received the named after local miners couldn't spell their first choice, "Ptarmigan," lies at Mile 66. Without a landline phone or a flushing toilet, Chicken has little to offer the weary traveler. Each summer, Chicken's population explodes with an influx of gold miners from its usual 15 to upwards of 50. The **Chicken Creek Saloon** is a great stop to cool off your engine. The walls are decorated with hats and random pieces of clothing left by many passers-by. (Open daily 8am-close.) RV parking ($10), pricey gas ($2 per gallon) and tire repair (about $20) can be found at the **Goldpanner,** on the Taylor directly north of the "downtown" turn-off. (Open May-Oct. daily 8am-8pm.) In good weather, half-hour walking tours of old ghost-town Chicken leave three times per day from in front of the store; they are the only way to see the original mining cabins (For groups of four or more only. Donations encouraged.) The Goldpanner loans out pans for free gold-panning at one well-panned stretch of water. Tenters and RVs can set up on the lot next to the Chicken Creek Cafe for free, although the site is less than ideal. Next to the Saloon, the **Chicken Creek Cafe ❷** serves up burgers and sandwiches from $7. Two weighty flapjacks ($5) or a wiener with potato salad ($6) are more reasonable deals. (Open daily 8am-6pm; cold food served in the bar until midnight.) The cafe also hosts a nightly **Salmon Bake ❹**. (In summer 4-8pm. $15.) The **Chicken Mercantile Emporium** pushes souvenirs aplenty and also sells gas. (Open daily in summer 8am-8pm.)

MY CAR'S STUCK 5 MILES UP THE ROAD. DO YOU HAVE AN ATM? In the winter of 1905, the Norwegian explorer Roald Amundsen hiked several hundred miles across northern Canada into Eagle when his ship became locked in the ice floes of the Arctic Ocean. Amundsen used Eagle's new telegraph to cable his government for money, then mushed back to his ship and successfully completed the first journey from the Atlantic to the Pacific through the hitherto unthinkable Northwest Passage. Amundsen Park, on 1st St. at Amundsen, commemorates his voyage with a glistening silver globe etched in relief.

HIKING. Just past Chicken, at Mile 68, is a Bureau of Land Management **ranger station,** and an easy to moderate 3 mi., 2hr. round-trip **hike** along Mosquito Fork River towards an old dredge. The hike takes you through a patch of lowland spruce forest along the gurgling riverside, which cools the whole trail down—interior Alaska can get shockingly hot in summer. Take the mosquitoes seriously. Another 8 mi. north on the highway (Mile 82) will land you at **Walker Fork Campground ❶.** (Water, pit toilets, fishing. 20 riverside sites, $8.) Though there are no marked trails, the sparse vegetation makes it easy to pull the car over and scurry up to the top of several of the mountains skirted by the road. The views are haltingly attractive, but beware of clouds—lighting storms are not infrequent, even in summer, and the lack of trees makes YOU the tallest pole.

MINING RELICS. The **Jack Wade Dredge,** a huge machine used for placer mining, lies rusting away next to the highway at Mile 86. Safety around the deteriorated dredge's is dubious, but that doesn't stop travelers from wandering near its eerie skeleton. From this point until Eagle, evidence of mining abounds. At Jack Wade Junction, the road forks north for Eagle and east for Dawson via the Top of the World Hwy. For the last 64 mi. from the Eagle Junction, the road snakes along the mountainsides and canyons surrounding **Forty Mile River,** another popular, although difficult, spot for rafters to put in (see **Eagle,** below, for outfitters).

EAGLE ☎907

Before the Taylor Hwy. opens in the summer, this unpretentious wilderness town is connected to the outside world only by sled dog or air. Eagle is no tourist mecca, lacking a town water and sewage system and a police department. The town peaked in 1899—the Army even put up a base to keep the boomtime golddiggers from running roughshod. Today, eager Eagle-ites have quick grins and plenty of tales about pioneer great-grandmothers to share with travelers passing through.

🛈 PRACTICAL INFORMATION. The Taylor Hwy. closes from mid-October until at least mid-May. **Tatonduk Air** (☎547-2249) flies twice daily except Su to **Fairbanks** (1¼hr., $98). There is **no bank, no ATM,** and **only Bo takes credit cards.** Bo Fay, the proprietor of **Telegraph Hill Services,** on the Taylor Hwy., is an unofficial visitors center. He readily provides coffee, conversation, gas, car repairs, and an indispensable map. (☎547-2261. Open in summer daily 8am-6pm; winter 9am-5pm). The real **visitors center** and the **Yukon-Charley Rivers National Preserve Headquarters,** at the end of 1st St. toward the old airstrip, provide the lowdown on canoe trips to Circle and beyond. (☎547-2233. Open daily in summer 8am-5pm.) The **Eagle Trading Co.,** on Front St. by the river, carries hardware, groceries, and supplies. (☎547-2220. Open in summer daily 8am-8pm; winter 10am-6pm.) In an **emergency,** call the **Village Public Safety Officer** at ☎547-2300. The **post office** is on 2nd St. at Jefferson. (☎547-2211. Open M-F 8:30am-4:30pm.) **Postal Code:** 99738.

⌂⌂ ACCOMMODATIONS AND FOOD. The **Eagle Trading Co. ❸**, on Front St., also has hot showers, laundry, RV sites, and clean rooms with porches overlooking the river. (☎547-2220. Open in summer daily 8am-8pm; winter 10am-6pm. Laundry: wash $4 per load, dry $0.25. Singles $50; doubles $60. RV sites $15. Showers $4.) Campers will rejoice upon finding the **Eagle BLM Campground ❶**, a one-mile hike past Fort Egbert, or the first left after Telegraph Hill Services. Several short hiking trails start here. Ask Bo—he knows. (No water, pit toilets. Sites $8; seniors $4.) The **Riverside Cafe ❶** serves the usual but with a view of the Yukon River. Lunch $6-7. (☎547-2250. Breakfast all day. Open daily May-Oct. 7am-8pm.)

◪ FLOATING FROM EAGLE. The 1979 mi. Yukon River is one of the world's longest. No other American river is as undeveloped, and navigating the Yukon's entire length has become a cult experience. The trip takes 3-4 months and ends 1200 mi. from Eagle near Nome at the Bering Sea. If 4 months sounds too daunting, the 154 mi. trip between Eagle and Circle (see p. p. 556) takes only 4-6 days. The river runs through the **Yukon-Charley Rivers National Preserve** and some of Alaska's wildest country, but stays relatively calm the whole way (get ready to be battered if you start paddling from any of the Yukon's tributaries, though). **Eagle Canoe Rentals** will set you afloat for the five-day trip to Circle. (☎547-2203. $165; equipment return included.) Getting back is up to you, but flights to Fairbanks are available from Eagle and Circle, as is the daily river trip from Eagle to Dawson City on the *M/V Yukon Queen* (5hr., $US122; canoe or kayak $20). Eagle Canoe also provides a $160 route down the protected **Fortymile River** for experienced canoeists.

ARCTIC ALASKA ☎907

The farthest northern reaches of Alaska are home to some of the most unique and precious ecosystems in the world. They scrape out an existence in some of the world's harshest weather. Months pass in the winter without the sun peaking above the horizon, yet in the dead months the barren sky is lit by one of the world's most magical natural phenomena, the aurora borealis. Polar bears ride ice floes and hundreds of thousands of caribou roam freely. The Alaskan communities are few and far between, accessible only by plane, boat, or snowmobile. Life changes very little in the North: many Inupiat communities rely on the same subsistence methods their distant ancestors did. On the flip side, the difficulty of the Arctic lifestyle means that not much remains constant. Companies come and go, schedules are erratic, and consistency and reliability have a whole new meaning north of the Arctic Circle. Hours we list below are somewhat consistent, but there is little guarantee that things will be the same a year from now.

Any travel in this remote landscape will be expensive, but worth it. All supplies must be shipped in from Fairbanks, Kotzebue, or Nome; a general store does not cater to the backcountry hiker. While some communities are open and friendly, others are close-mouthed and less welcoming. Contact the **Nome Convention and Visitors Center**, p. 563 for more detailed information on which villages to visit, and which to leave respectfully private. There are more than 14,000 sq. mi. of protected wilderness in Northwest Alaska, comprising 11% of the land administered by the National Park Service. This is wilderness at its wildest, accessible to only the most experienced outdoors people. Daunting as the Arctic sounds, a venture into its complete solitude is unforgettable.

CENTRAL ALASKA

⚡ ORIENTATION

Arctic Alaska is separated from the Interior by the **Brooks Mountain Range**, which stretches from the Canadian border to the Chukchi Sea. Peaking at 10,000 ft., the Brooks are considered one of the most remote and inhospitable areas in the world, mountains of scree through which only the equipped and experienced should travel. Waters from the Brooks drain to the north, south, and west. The greatest river is the **Noatak**, flowing from the heart of the mountains, and then arcing a full 90° before spilling into **Kotzebue Sound**.

Beyond the Brooks lies the Arctic Slope. Continuously ensconced by permafrost (up to 2000 ft. underground in places), the Slope's terrain is markedly different from its mountainous border. The lay of the land is relatively flat, criss-crossed by braided streams and occasional lakes. Many lakes are oriented northwest, reflecting the prevailing winds. This frozen land thaws in the summer, becoming a tufted soggy vastness that challenges the hiker. Receiving less than eight inches of precipitation annually, the parched Arctic Slope is a desert. Yet while the combination of cold and dryness makes the land sound particularly inhospitable, it has in fact been inhabited on and off for the past 27,000 years.

Along Alaska's westernmost coast (not including the Aleutians) the towns of **Nome** and **Kotzebue** perch precariously. They are nestled among a trove of protected lands: **Bering Land Bridge National Park, Kobuk Valley National Park, Gates of the Arctic National Park and Preserve, Noatak National Preserve**, and **Cape Krusenstern National Monument**. On the eastern side of the plethora of parks and preserves, sit the small town of **Bettles** and the Nunamiut Eskimo village, **Anaktuvuk Pass**. More remote and desolate communities lie along the northernmost coast of Alaska. **Prudhoe Bay** and **Deadhorse** are the terminus of the **Dalton Hwy.** (p. 567) and the origin of the Alaska Pipeline. Their connection to a roadway makes them much less expensive, but they are merely functional and not towns at all. To the east lies the most controversial tract of land in Alaska, the oil-rich **Arctic National Wildlife Refuge.** West of Prudhoe Bay, inaccessible by any overland route, lies **Barrow**, the northernmost community in the US. Contacting the National Parks office and local towns you intend to visit will facilitate your travels.

◼ TRANSPORTATION

Bush planes are to the Arctic as cars are to the Lower 48. What few roads there are do not connect to the Interior and are often in poor repair. The exception is the **Dalton Hwy.** (p. 567), running from Fairbanks up to Prudhoe Bay. From **Anchorage, Alaska Airlines** (☎800-252-7522; www.alaskaairlines.com) services **Kotzebue** (3hr., $310.50 one-way) and **Nome** (2½hr., $310.50 one-way). The web site www.alaskaflight.com can get you price estimates for routes in the Arctic including the price of transporting your gear. Since 1979 **Bering Air** (☎443-5464; www.beringair.com) has offered comprehensive flights from both Kotzebue and Nome. They offer return tickets, triangle tickets, and flagstops at villages on unscheduled days. They also offer occasional flights to the Russian Far East. Besides Bering Air, flight options from Nome include **Baker Aviation** (☎443-3081) and **Grant Aviation** (☎443-4650). **Arctic Wilderness Lodge** (☎376-7955) offers fly-in services in the **Brooks Range, Gates of the Arctic,** and the **Alaska National Wildlife Reserve** from Prudhoe Bay. **Bettles Lodge** operates **Bettles Air Service** (☎692-5111 or 800-770-5111; www.bettleslodge.com) which offers fly-ins to the **Brooks Range** and **Gates of the Arctic National Park**. Prices start at $350 per hr., and are dependent on distance and the weight of you and your gear. Most backcountry dropoff locations are between 45 and 90min. from Bettles.

⚠ NATIONAL PARK OFFICES

Arctic National Wildlife Refuge (☎456-0250, fax: 456-0428), P.O. Box 20, 101 12th Ave., Rm. 236, Fairbanks, AK 99701. Open 8am-4:30pm.

West Arctic National Park Lands covers **Bering Land Bridge National Preserve, Cape Krusenstern National Monument** and **Noatak National Preserve.** In Nome: (☎443-2522), P.O. Box 220, Nome, AK 99762. In Kotzebue: (☎442-8300), P.O. Box 1029, Kotzebue, AK 99752. In Bettles: (652-9454). Open M-F 8am-noon and 1-5pm.

Gates of the Arctic National Park and Preserve (☎457-5752), P.O. Box 74680, Fairbanks, AK 99707. Open M-F 8am-4:30pm.

Kobuk Valley National Park (☎442-8300), P.O. Box 1029, Kotzebue, AK 99752.Open M-F 8am-4:30pm

BETTLES   ☎907

The region in which Bettles is located has been occupied by several Native groups in the course of time, including the Koyukon Athabascans and Kobuk, Selawik, and Nunamiut Eskimos. Today the village is primarily white and has a 90% employment rate, both uncharacteristic traits for rural villages. The town is accessible by road during the winter, meaning that goods and services are much cheaper than in other Bush towns. The **Hickel Trail,** a 30 mi. road, links residents to the Dalton Hwy. but is only accessible by snowmachine in winter (see p. 567). The Koyukuk River is the other main transportation route in the summer (although there is no barge service). The Park Service also operates the helpful **Gates of the Arctic Field Station.** (☎692-5494. Open June-Aug. M-F 8am-5pm; call for hours Sept.-May.) The **post office** is sometimes closes for lunch. (☎692-5236. Open M 8am-5pm, Tu-W 8am-3pm, Th-F 8am-2pm, Sa 1-4pm.) **Postal Code:** 99726.

Bettles Lodge ❺, which runs **Bettles Air Service** (see p. 562), has been declared a National Historic Site, but still rents rooms and acts as a trip planner. (☎800-770-5111; www.bettleslodge.com. Main lodge singles $115; doubles $135; triples $165. Aurora Lodge singles $135; doubles $160; triples $195.) At the lodge, the **Bettles Trading Post/Sourdough Outfitters** (see above) sells expensive groceries.

NOME   ☎907

Nome owes its existence to the "three lucky Swedes" who discovered gold on nearby Anvil Creek in 1898. Nome is now home to a population of 4000, over half of which is Native Alaskan. Those who can afford to

$$$ **THE BIG SPLURGE**

BARROW: HOW COLD CAN YOU GO?

Huddled on flat brown tundra next to the icy waters of the Chukchi Sea, Barrow endures some of the harshest conditions in the world: months without a hint of sunlight, temperatures below zero (-60°F), and windchills even lower. 50°F makes for a balmy summer day and the tundra wind always blows. Barrow represents Arctic Alaska in all its frigid beauty; it's the **northernmost point** on the North American mainland, almost 330 mi. north of the Arctic Circle. Travelers to Barrow come here because they want to visit the "top of the world." It's quite an experience, but one that doesn't come without a price.

As with all true bush communities, Barrow is only accessibly by plane. **Alaska Airlines** (☎852-8822 or 800-462-0333) flies in summer three times per day Monday-Friday and twice per day Saturday-Sunday and in winter twice per day Saturday-Sunday from **Fairbanks** ($376 round-trip) and **Anchorage** ($437 round-trip). A package tour can actually be the cheapest way to see Barrow. Call the **Northern Alaska Tours Company** for info. (☎800-474-1986. Day tours from **Fairbanks** $395, **Anchorage** $565. Overnight tours are also available.)

Accommodations in Barrow are outrageously expensive. **The Airport Inn,** P.O. Box 933, is one block from the airport on Momegana St. At $115 per night, they have the cheapest rooms in town. (☎852-2525.)

Yes, it's pricey. But if you have the money, it's an unforgettable trip.

get here will find untamed wilderness accessible by road, refreshingly non-commercialized relics of mining history, and a culture centered around the Iditarod dog sled race, the Midnight Sun Festival, and generally being hard-core.

7 PRACTICAL INFORMATION. Nome's **airport** is 2 mi. west of town. **Bering Air** (☎443-5464) is the only small airline company in the U.S. allowed to fly to Russia. They also do backcountry drop off and flightseeing, as does **Cape Smythe Air** (☎443-5334). Both have similar prices (around $350 per flight hr.) **Checker Cab** (☎443-5211), **Nome Cab** (☎443-3030), and **Village Taxi** (☎443-2333) all have the same rates ($3 point to point in town, $5 to the airport, $2 per mile outside of town). The **Alaska Cab Garage** (☎443-2939) rents 2WD trucks for around $75 per day. **Aurora/Stampede Vehicle** (☎443-3838) also rents trucks suited to the rocky rumbling roads outside of Nome for $90 per day. The **visitors center** on Front St. across from city hall has more information than you can handle. (☎443-6624; www.nomealaska.org. Open June-Sept. 15 daily 9am-9pm; in winter M-F 9am-6pm.) The **National Park Service** (☎443-2522), on Front St. in the Sitnasuak Native Corporation Building, can provide info on the Bering Land Bridge National Park and Preserve, other Western Alaska national parks, and local hiking. Since credit cards are not widely accepted, you may need to visit **Wells Fargo**, at 250 Front St. (☎443-2223. Open M-Th 9am-5pm, F 9am-6pm. **24hr. ATM.**) The **Nome Job Center** is at 306 Front St., or check the classifieds in the *Nome Nugget*, Alaska's oldest paper. Take **showers** at the **Recreation Center** (☎443-5431), at the northern edge of town on 6th Ave. (Open daily 5:30am-10pm. Longer hours in winter. $4 all-day admission.) To check the **weather** call ☎443-2321 or press the button on the magic box outside the visitors center. Other services include: **emergency,** ☎911; **police,** ☎443-5262; **hospital,** Norton **Sound Health Corporation** (☎443-3311), at the corner of 5th and Bering St. The **Kegoayah Kozga Library,** above the museum on Front St., has free **Internet access.** (☎443-6628. Open M-Th noon-8pm, F and Sa noon-6pm). The **post office** is at 240 E Front St. (☎443-2401). **Postal Code:** 99762.

⌂⌂ ACCOMMODATIONS AND FOOD. Beds in Nome are generally costly and are hard to come by in peak seasons (summer and during the Iditarod). **Weeks Apartments ❸,** 697 3rd. Ave. at G St., offers clean rooms with TV, kitchen, private bath, and private washer and dryer. (☎443-3194 or 800-448-3194. Singles $60; doubles $80; $10 per extra person. Call ahead.) **There's No Place Like Nome B&B ❹,** 605 Steadman St. between 5th and 6th. Smiling Jean has sunny, immaculate rooms off a greenhouse at the edge of town. Two common areas, coffee, and snacks are always available, and breakfast is made to your liking. (☎443-5869. Singles and doubles $75). The **Ponderosa Hotel ❹** (☎443-5737), on the corner of 3rd St. and Spokane, offers rooms with communal microwave and fridge for $75. Slightly larger rooms with kitchenette are $85. All have full bath. Although the land is privately owned, gold-panning and **free camping** are permitted on the flat, sandy beaches 2 mi. east of town on Front St., past the sea wall. Enjoy the company and hope to fall asleep despite the drone of the sluices. If you have a car, try **Salmon Lake State Campground ❶,** at Mile 38 of the Taylor Hwy. (see **Outdoor Activities,** below).

When it comes to food, Nome's reputation is mediocre. Front St. has a series of restaurants, all serving a burger or fish and chip lunch for around $10-12. Stock up on groceries at **Hanson's Safeway,** on Bering St. (☎443-5454. Open M-Sa 9am-9pm, Su 9am-5pm.) **Corner Market** (☎443-5940), at 4th and K St., also carries groceries. **Twin Dragon ❸** (☎443-5552), at the corner of Front St. and Steadman, has a bright, well-decorated interior. Extremely fresh vegetables—how'd they do that? Meals are $10-14, but look for cheaper lunch specials.

◉ 🔼 SIGHTS AND EVENTS. Isolation from the rest of the world makes people do strange things. The **Midnight Sun Festival,** on the weekend closest to the summer solstice, includes a parade, BBQ, simulated bank robbery, and a homemade raft race on Sunday, among other silliness. On Labor Day, the **Great Bathtub Race** sends wheeled bathtubs, filled with water, soap, and bather, hurtling down Front St. At the same time, **rubber duckies** meander their way down the Nome River, as those who placed bets on them cheer extravagantly for their particular ducks.

The biggest event of the year is the **Iditarod,** the world's foremost dog sled race. It begins each year in Anchorage on the first Saturday in March and finishes in Nome beneath the log arch by City Hall about two weeks later. The Iditarod is accompanied by a month of festivals from late February to late March, when the town comes under a near-constant attack of events celebrating the race, and thousands of out-of-town spectators journey in for the finish. Local accommodations are booked nearly a year in advance. (☎ 800-545-6874; www.iditarod.com.) The **Bering Sea Ice Golf Classic** is held two weeks after the race start in March on the frozen ocean. Contestants use bright orange balls and face a number of unique hazards: ice crevasses, bottomless snow holes, and frosted greens. Course rules dictate: "If you hit a polar bear (Endangered Species List) with your golf ball, you will have three strokes added to your score. If you recover said ball, we will subtract five strokes." Two of the holes are in **Nome National Forest** (a "seasonal forest" consisting of donated Christmas trees frozen into holes drilled in the treeless tundra).

🔼 OUTDOOR ACTIVITIES Branching out into the surrounding wilderness, Nome's three highways are a godsend for the adventurous traveler. The area around Nome is largely untouched tundra, home to a herd of 2000 musk oxen (generally found 10 mi. outside of Teller or around Pilgrim Hot Springs), and 160 species of birds, many of them Russian and rarely seen in America. The sound of two musk oxen butting heads when competing during mating season can be heard a mile away. There are excellent **fishing** rivers along the highways, including the **Nome** and **Pilgrim Rivers,** not to mention hiking opportunities. Although entirely gravel, all roads are generally navigable. According to the visitors bureau, hitchers can usually find rides fairly easily on weekends up the Taylor or Council Hwy., when many Nome residents head in that direction. *Let's Go* does not recommend hitchhiking. There are no gas stations or restaurants on these roads so make sure you have a full tank of gas and bring food and warm clothing. Most importantly, bring mosquito repellent or curse the day you heard of Nome.

Nome's outskirts house abandoned **gold dredges.** The closest, **Swanberg's Dredge,** is about 1½ mi. from downtown on Front St., en route to **Kougarok Rd.** (a.k.a. Taylor Hwy.), which heads north from Nome for 85 mi., then peters out without reaching any particular destination. Along the way is **Salmon Lake,** near Mile 38. Popular with locals, the lake offers fantastic fishing and primitive **campsites ❶**.

BERING LAND BRIDGE NATIONAL PRESERVE

Nome is also one of two departure points to the **Bering Land Bridge National Park and Preserve,** a testament to the once thousand-mile-wide land bridge now sunk beneath the shallow waters of the Bering Sea. The park is only accessible by plane in summer, making it the least visited National Park in the United States. For those who do make the trip, however, there is the most untouched wilderness in the Unites States as well. The **Serpentine Hot Springs,** just inside the southern border of the park and about 30 mi. from the end of the Taylor Hwy., is the most popular destination. A primitive bathhouse contains the 140-170°F water and is open year-round. The most common way to get there is by snowmobile in the winter. In summer, a charter flight can be taken to **Taylor;** from there,

Serpentine lies 8 mi. over the tundra. Contact the Park Service office in Nome (☎443-2522) for topographic maps and more info. If you are not going to the hot springs, fly to Bering Land Bridge from Kotzebue, which is cheaper. Contact the Park Service office there for more information. (☎442-3760.)

KOTZEBUE   ☎907

On the tip of the **Baldwin Peninsula**, 160 mi. northeast of Nome and 25 mi. north of the Arctic Circle, Kotzebue (KOTZ-ih-boo) is principally a transportation and commercial hub for the 11 native villages and other small communities in Alaska's Arctic Northwest. The wind-buffeted village has little to offer independent travelers except the kindness of its inhabitants and access to four remote and wild national park lands, three of which are above the Arctic Circle.

The **airport** is on the west end of town, a 10min. walk from Kotzebue's modest downtown. Locals will give directions more by landmark than street name, and you'll be hard pressed to find a street sign. The **Visitors Center and National Park Service** is two blocks from the airport on 2nd Ave. (☎442-3760 or 442-3890. Open daily 9am-6pm.) The center has maps and info about charters, along with a 15min. video about the parks and preserves that are serviced from Kotzebue (see below). The **Wells Fargo Bank** is at 2nd St. and Lagoon. (☎442-3258. Open M-Th 10am-5pm, F 10am-6pm.) **Internet access** is free at the **Chukchi Community College Library** on 3rd Ave., after Bison St. (Open M-Sa noon-8pm.) Free **camping** is allowed on the pebble beaches around town as long as it is just for one or two nights. Some visitors befriend locals and pitch tents in their backyards. The **Bayside Restaurant and Inn** ❺ (☎442-3600), on Shore Ave., rents modest rooms for $115. **LaVonne's Fish Camp** ❹ lies 2 mi. out of town. Lavonne, the owner of this elder hostel and culture camp, will let backpackers stay for $90 a night. Be prepared to harvest and cut fish. Call the visitors center for B&B options.

Hanson's, on Shore Ave., stocks the usual groceries, but be warned: all groceries are flown or barged in and a gallon of milk costs $6.50. (Open M-Sa 8am-9pm, Su 10am-7pm.) **Bayside Restaurant** ❸, on Shore Ave., serves American and Chinese for around $12 a meal. (☎442-3600. Open daily 7am-midnight.) **Empress Chinese** ❸ sits right next door to Bayside and serves the same food at the same prices.

OUTDOOR ACTIVITIES NEAR KOTZEBUE. Kotzebue is the jumping-off point for some of the most untouched wilderness in the world. All hiking in the Kotzebue area is wilderness hiking; the few trails are animal trails—don't follow them. Backcountry drop-offs are provided by boat and floatplane from different companies depending on the national park of destination. The visitors center and park service in Kotzebue (☎442-3760) has a complete list of outfitters, tour guides and transportation services. **Cape Kruzenstern National Monument** lies 10 mi. to the north of Kotzebue, across the Chukchi Sea. Treeless and riddled with lagoons, Kruzenstern explodes with wildflowers in summer and is home to one of the largest populations of musk-oxen in the world. Bush flights tend to run about $200 per hr., so Kruzenstern's proximity (half an hour from Kotzebue) makes it the least expensive destination. **Noatak National Preserve**, northeast of Kotzebue, cradles the Noatak River between the Brooks Range to the north and the Baird Range to the south. The **Noatak** is the largest untouched river in the world and is not technically challenging. It begins at **Gates of the Arctic National Park,** the northernmost range of the Rockies, and travels 400 mi. to the Chukchi Sea. Kayakers and rafters can put in anywhere along the river and make their way to the village of Noatak or paddle right into Kotzebue itself (12-17 days). The dry, cold climate of the **Kobuk Valley National Park,** south of Noatak and east of Kotzebue, approximates the ice age and the flora and fauna of the Bering Land Bridge 10,000 years ago. The Kobuk River's wild rapids should only be attempted by experienced rafters. South of the park, the **Kobuk Sand Dunes** form a

25 sq. km desert in arctic Alaska, a desert that can reach 100 degrees Fahrenheit in the summer. The Dunes' northern tip is accessible by an easy hike from the Kobuk River, but you'll have to float the river to get there.

DALTON HWY. (RTE. 11) ☎907

The Dalton Hwy. was constructed after the discovery of oil in Prudhoe Bay in 1968 as an access road for development of the oil-field and construction of the pipeline. The highway parallels the Alaska Pipeline from Fairbanks to Prudhoe Bay on the Arctic Ocean, crossing the Arctic Circle and three mountain ranges, and passing some of the most untouched frontier towns and vast expanses of land that are possible to encounter by road. The 1000 mi. round-trip is well worth it. That said, the Dalton is famous for breaking windshields and destroying tires. Consider the wear and tear on your car before heading out, and be prepared for anything to happen.

The entire Dalton Hwy. was opened to the public on January 1, 1995. Truckers and Alyeska vehicles predominate; a tiny number of RVs, a handful of 4WD vehicles and motorcyclists, and the occasional dedicated cyclist constitute the tourist traffic. The road is paved when it begins in Fairbanks, and does have extensive sections of pavement along the way (the DOT hopes to have it all paved by 2007 or 2010), but is still largely gravel and dirt with potholes, soft shoulders, blind curves and steep grades. The road is passable in a standard passenger car at speeds under 45mph, but it is unwise to try it—go with 4WD if at all possible. Most rental packages won't cover cars north of the Arctic Circle, and some won't even allow you to go north of Livengood where the Elliott Hwy. cedes its name to the Dalton. The drive *is* breathtaking, although almost entirely without services. There are four places to get **gas,** three of which are clustered together at the beginning, and two repair stops: one at the Yukon River and one at Prudhoe Bay.

If you would prefer not to risk dinging your car or your nerves, tours are available. Although the highway is the best it has been in years, the expensive tour may be far less of a financial drain than being towed to Fairbanks (which costs around $7 *per mile*) and fixing a pebble-puncture in your gas tank. The **Northern Alaska Tour Company** (☎474-8600; www.northernalaska.com) offers a daytrip from Fairbanks to the Arctic Circle (departs 6:30am, returns 11pm; $175), and a three-day trip to Prudhoe Bay including everything but meals. ($745. If traveling alone there is an additional $60 fee. Additional leg to Barrow an extra $450.) The tour starts in Fairbanks and spends 3 days driving the highway. They provide accommodations for 2 nights and a tour through the oilfields, and then fly you back.

FAIRBANKS TO THE ARCTIC CIRCLE ☎907

A drive up the Dalton Hwy. begins with an 84 mi. jaunt from Fairbanks along the **Elliott Hwy.** to Mile 0 of the Dalton. **Joy,** at mile 49.5 of the Elliott Hwy., consists entirely of the **Arctic Circle Trading Post ❶** (☎474-4565), the classiest giftshop/general store you will ever encounter. They have free coffee, inexpensive sandwiches ($5), and a barrage of arts and crafts. An updated, hand-scrawled map on the wipeboard by the door details the road conditions and construction you can expect for the next 450 mi. The Dalton begins 30 mi. later and crosses the **Yukon River** at Mile 56, 140 mi. from Fairbanks. On the north side of the river is **Yukon Ventures ❹**, one of the highway's two service stations, which sells gas, rents rooms, and has a cafe. The rooms are warm and functional. (☎655-9001. Open daily Apr.-Nov. 1st. Cafe open 7am-9pm. Shared bath. Singles $65; doubles $100. V/MC. Cash preferred.) The ◼**Hot Spot Cafe ❹**, at Mile 60.5, serves what many consider the best burgers in Alaska ($7.50-9.50). They also rent **rooms ❺** ($100), sell gas, and have a gift shop. **Camping ❶** is free on surrounding BLM land.

As it gains elevation, the road winds through its first alpine region: at Mile 97.5, it passes **Finger Rock** to the east and **Caribou Mountain** to the west. The **rest area** just past Finger Rock is an ideal place to learn a bit about the tundra and its inhabitants, and enjoy views of the Brooks Range. Next comes the **Arctic Circle** (Mile 115), the southernmost point at which the sun does not set on the longest day of the year. A recently constructed and surprisingly tasteful pull-off has several picnic tables and presents four displays on the Arctic seasons (summer, winter, winter, and winter). Most folks are satisfied with merely reaching the Arctic Circle, and quickly retreat to Fairbanks. Those who go farther north, however, can benefit from the **free camping ❶** in the labyrinthine roads above the sign. Follow the tent sign from the Arctic Circle sign. (No water.)

ARCTIC CIRCLE TO DEADHORSE   ☎ 907

Gobblers Knob (1500 ft.), at Mile 132, marks the beginning of long, steep grades. The Dalton rattles past Prospect Camp and Pump Station No. 5, before heading over Jim River and the South Fork of the Koyukuk River. A popular **rafting trip** is the middle fork of the Koyukuk River; many put in at **Coldfoot**, leaving their cars by the airstrip and arranging to be picked up 90 mi. down-river in Bettles and flown back (contact the Coldfoot Visitors Center, below, for more info; for Bettles charters and outfitters, see p. 563). Coldfoot has the **last services** before Prudhoe Bay, 240 mi. away. A mining town that once boasted a gambling hall, two roadhouses, seven saloons, and ten prostitutes, Coldfoot was named for the group of prospectors who briefly considered wintering above the Arctic Circle and then headed south again. The **Coldfoot Visitors Center,** just north of town, is a resource for travelers eyeing the Brooks Range. (☎ 678-5209. Open daily 10am-10pm; slide presentations 8pm.) Gas flows 24hr. in Coldfoot. The tire shop is on call until midnight, and the **Slate Creek Inn ❺** has 81 expensive rooms. They also rent RV **sites ❶,** tent sites, and have **showers.** (☎ 678-5224. Singles $135; doubles $145. Tent sites $15. RV sites $30, dump fee $25. Showers $10.) If you are willing to forego a shower, seek out the **Marion Creek Campground ❶,** 8 mi. north at Mile 180. The sites are quiet and set near muskeg forest (water and pit toilets, free firewood stacked by fee station. $8.) Away from Alaska access roads, **camping** is free. The **Coldfoot Cafe ❸** serves hot food around the clock in summer. The dinner buffet costs $17.95, but a soup and salad option is just $7.95. (☎ 678-5201. Buffet only from 5am-9am and 5pm-9pm.) Send news of your journey from the **post office.** (☎ 678-5204. Open M, W, F 1:30-6pm.) **Postal Code:** 99701.

Heidi, the owner of **Boreal Lodge ❸,** rents rooms with shared bath and can tell you anything about the area. (☎ 678-4566. Singles $55; doubles $75. Cash or traveler's checks only.) Across the street, **Arctic Getaway Igloo #8 Cabin and Breakfast ❺** offers two spacious, family-style half-cabins and a hearty breakfast. (☎ 678-4456. 3 person room $90; 5 person room $150.)

From Wiseman, the highway continues into the heart of the **Brooks Range,** a region frequented by moose, bear, caribou, Dall's sheep, and hawks. At Mile 235, the last tree along the highway—a majestic, surprisingly tall spruce—marks the beginning of the steep and awe-inspiring ascent toward **Atigun Pass** (4752 ft.), where the earth is upside down. When the mountains here were formed, the crust was flipped in the tectonic shifting, so the bedrock is above the sedimentary rock. Over the mountains lies the long descent toward the Arctic Ocean.

The mountains gradually flatten into tundra, a sea of brown and green that flourishes in July and August and takes fall colors as brilliant as New England's changing of the leaves. Its surface of bumps and moss lumps, called tussocks, covers water trapped beneath the frozen ground. The terrain makes for spongy and occasionally difficult walking, and supports wildlife not found below the Brooks

Range: musk oxen, arctic fox, snow owls, and tundra swans. Even during summer, the temperature on the coastal plain rarely breaks 50 degrees Fahrenheit.

Ten miles from the highway's end, coastal fog enshrouds the sun and the temperature plummets. After you pass a series of lakes named for worker's girlfriends (Prudhoe Bay's workforce is 75% male), Deadhorse appears on the horizon. Three miles later, you spot Prudhoe Bay (see below). You're there. The Arctic Ocean. The northernmost point accessible by road in North America.

DEADHORSE AND PRUDHOE BAY ☎ 907

Deadhorse, on the southern perimeter of Lake Colleen, got its name from the motto of the company that shipped the road-building materials north: "We'll haul anything, even a dead horse." Deadhorse was built as a staging area for the oilfield at Prudhoe Bay, and has never grown into anything else. The town is built entirely of prefabricated housing transported from the lower forty-eight on barges. The employees here work two weeks on, two weeks off, and are some of the most jovial people you'll meet, a pleasant surprise in the midst of the industrial charmlessness. The airstrip here is serviced by **Alaska Airlines** (☎ 800-252-7522; $300.50

INTO THE WILD Alaska has the highest per capita ownership of small planes, the greatest number of pilots, the highest number of float planes, and one of the nation's busiest airports (in Anchorage). Throughout much of the interior, small planes aren't simply the best way to get there; they're the only way. Some of the state's most colorful lore is steeped in aviation—like the story of Alaska's third governor, who broke both ankles crash-landing his small plane to avoid endangering the children playing on the airstrip. Tales of unusual landings are as common as tales of unusual cargo: bush pilots have been known to transport canoes, beer, furniture, pizza, and even moose to the farthest reaches of the state.

each way from Fairbanks). Staples are sold in the **general store** that shares a parking lot with the **Arctic Caribou Inn ❺**. (☎ 659-2368. Open daily 10:30am-9pm. Rooms from $120.) The only way to actually get to the Arctic Ocean is to take one of the Inn's underwhelming tours of the **Prudhoe Bay** oil fields. The tour begins with a video introduction to the oil fields and their history. Visitors pile into a school bus to cross the fields to the Arctic Ocean, where towels are ready for the lunatics who go skinny-dipping in the frigid waters. (2hr.; 5 times per day 9:30am-5:30pm. For security reasons, you must reserve 24hr. in advance and bring a photo ID. $37.)

The **Tesoro** has much needed **gas**. You can **park** in the lot here overnight, but tent camping is not recommended, for bear-shaped reasons. Kate, the local brown bear, has been known to wait for workers as they leave their houses in the morning. She charges until they drop their lunches, dines, and then waits for the next person to come out. Be aware that this is a dry community—no drinking. In an **emergency,** call the BP operator at ☎ 659-5634; there are no public emergency services. The **post office** is by the Arctic Caribou Inn. (☎ 659-2669. Open daily 1-3:30pm and 6:30-9pm.) **Postal Code:** 99734.

ARCTIC NATIONAL WILDLIFE REFUGE. Covering a vast swath of the northeast, the isolated 31,100 sq. mi. of the Arctic National Wildlife Refuge (ANWR) encompass the calving grounds of the teeming Porcupine caribou herd and the Brooks Range's highest mountains. Controversy surrounding oil-drilling has thrust this remote land into the political limelight in the lower forty-eight. Drilling would likely produce 2 million barrels of oil, significantly less than was available at Prudhoe Bay when drilling began, but would reduce US dependence on foreign oil, generate jobs, and create income for the Inupiat Natives. Environmentalists who fear a negative impact, however, are opposed to the drilling. Those in favor of drilling point to the already-successful arctic drilling at Prudhoe Bay that has had relatively little impact on the surrounding environment. US President George W. Bush supports recovering the oil, and it seems likely that drilling will occur eventually.

MILEAGE (DISTANCES)

	Anchorage	Calgary	Dawson City	Edmonton	Fairbanks	Portland	Prince George	Prince Rupert	Prudhoe Bay	Seattle	Spokane	Vancouver	Whitehorse	San Fran.
Anchorage		2160 mi.	515 mi.	1975 mi.	358 mi.	2610 mi.	1678 mi.	1605 mi.	847 mi.	2435 mi.	2578 mi.	2145 mi.	724 mi.	3153 mi.
Calgary	3478km		1747 mi.	184 mi.	2038 mi.	859 mi.	493 mi.	950 mi.	2527 mi.	738 mi.	443 mi.	609 mi.	1436 mi.	1514 mi.
Dawson City	829km	2812km		1562 mi.	393 mi.	2197 mi.	1390 mi.	1192 mi.	882 mi.	2022 mi.	2200 mi.	1764 mi.	327 mi.	2830 mi.
Edmonton	3180km	296km	2515km		1853 mi.	1043 mi.	461 mi.	906 mi.	2342 mi.	790 mi.	628 mi.	722 mi.	1251 mi.	1698 mi.
Fairbanks	576km	3281km	633km	2983km		2455 mi.	1668 mi.	1483 mi.	489 mi.	2313 mi.	2456 mi.	2137 mi.	602 mi.	3121 mi.
Portland	4202km	1383km	3537km	1679km	3953km		733 mi.	1208 mi.	2977 mi.	175 mi.	400 mi.	318 mi.	1886 mi.	655 mi.
Prince George	2701km	794km	2238km	742km	2686km	1180km		434 mi.	2074 mi.	558 mi.	663 mi.	486 mi.	983 mi.	1437 mi.
Prince Rupert	2584km	1529km	1919km	1459km	2388km	1945km	699km		1972 mi.	1033 mi.	1230 mi.	901 mi.	881 mi.	1880 mi.
Prudhoe Bay	1363km	4068km	1420km	3771km	787km	4793km	3339km	3175km		2802 mi.	2975 mi.	2541 mi.	1091 mi.	3610 mi.
Seattle	3920km	1188km	3255km	1271km	3724km	282km	898km	1663km	4511km		282 mi.	143 mi.	1711 mi.	808 mi.
Spokane	4151km	713km	3542km	1011km	3954km	644km	1067km	1980km	4790km	454km		400 mi.	1987 mi.	1055 mi.
Vancouver	3453km	981km	2840km	1162km	3440km	512km	782km	1451km	4091km	230km	644km		1450 mi.	973 mi.
Whitehorse	1166km	2312km	527km	2014km	969km	3036km	1583km	1418km	1756km	2755km	3199km	2334km		2519 mi.
San Fran.	5076km	2438km	4556km	2734km	5025km	1055km	2314km	3027km	5812km	1301km	1699km	1567km	4056km	

APPENDIX

INDEX

A

INDEX

INDEX

S

INDEX